Essentials of Marketing

SECOND EDITION

Charles W. Lamb, Jr.

M.J. Neeley Professor of Marketing
M.J. Neeley School of Business
Texas Christian University

Joseph F. Hair, Jr.

Alvin C. Copeland Endowed Chair of Franchising
and Director, Entrepreneurship Institute
Louisiana State University

Carl McDaniel

Chairman, Department of Marketing
College of Business Administration
University of Texas at Arlington

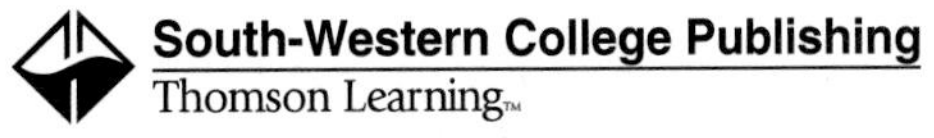
South-Western College Publishing
Thomson Learning™

Australia • Canada • Mexico • Singapore • Spain • United Kingdom • United States

Essentials of Marketing, 2e, by Charles W. Lamb, Jr., Joseph F. Hair, Jr. & Carl McDaniel

Publisher and Acquisitions Editor: Dave Shaut
Executive Marketing Director: Steve Scoble
Developmental Editor: Bryant Editorial Development
Production Editor: Elizabeth A. Shipp
Media Production Editor: Robin K. Browning
Media and Technology Editor: Kevin von Gillern
Manufacturing Coordinator: Sandee Milewski
Internal Design: Michael H. Stratton
Cover Design: Michael H. Stratton
Cover Illustrator: Michael H. Stratton
Photography Manager: Cary Benbow
Photo Researcher: Charlotte Goldman
Opener Photographs: © Randy Hoover Photography
Production House: Pre-Press Company, Inc.
Printer: R. R. Donnelley & Sons Company–Willard Manufacturing Division

Printed in the United States of America
1 2 3 4 5 03 02 01 00

For more information contact South-Western College Publishing, 5101 Madison Road, Cincinnati, Ohio, 45227 or find us on the Internet at http://www.swcollege.com

For permission to use material from this text or product, contact us by
• telephone: 1-800-730-2214
• fax: 1-800-730-2215
• web: http://www.thomsonrights.com

Library of Congress Cataloging-in-Publication Data
Lamb, Charles W.
Essentials of marketing / Charles W. Lamb, Jr., Joseph F. Hair, Jr., Carl McDaniel.—2nd ed.
p. cm.
Includes bibliographical references and index.
ISBN 0-324-04376-7 (alk. paper)
1. Marketing. 2. Marketing—Management. I. Hair, Joseph F. II. McDaniel, Carl D. III. Title.

HF5415 .L2623 2000
658.8—dc21

99-087757

This book is printed on acid-free paper.

To our children:
Christine Stock,
Jennifer Lamb,
Frank Baker, and
Kara Baker
—Charles W. Lamb, Jr.

To my wife Dale
and son Joe, III
—Joseph F. Hair, Jr.

To the kids: Raphaël,
Michèle, Sébastien,
Chelley, and Mark
—Carl McDaniel

BRIEF CONTENTS

CONTENTS

PART 1

The World of Marketing 1

PART 2

Analyzing Marketing Opportunities 105

Coca-Cola
CLASSIC

a special features sampler for students

A SPECIAL FEATURES SAMPLER FOR STUDENTS

The Subject is

Marketing

The Experience is Real

We've worked hard to produce the most practical, relevant marketing text available. This edition, like the one that preceded it, offers more windows into the real challenges, tools, and decisions of today's marketing professionals. From the Internet to small business issues to global marketing, the text is rich with insights into the real world of marketing. Here are some of the features that keep this text at the forefront of the field:

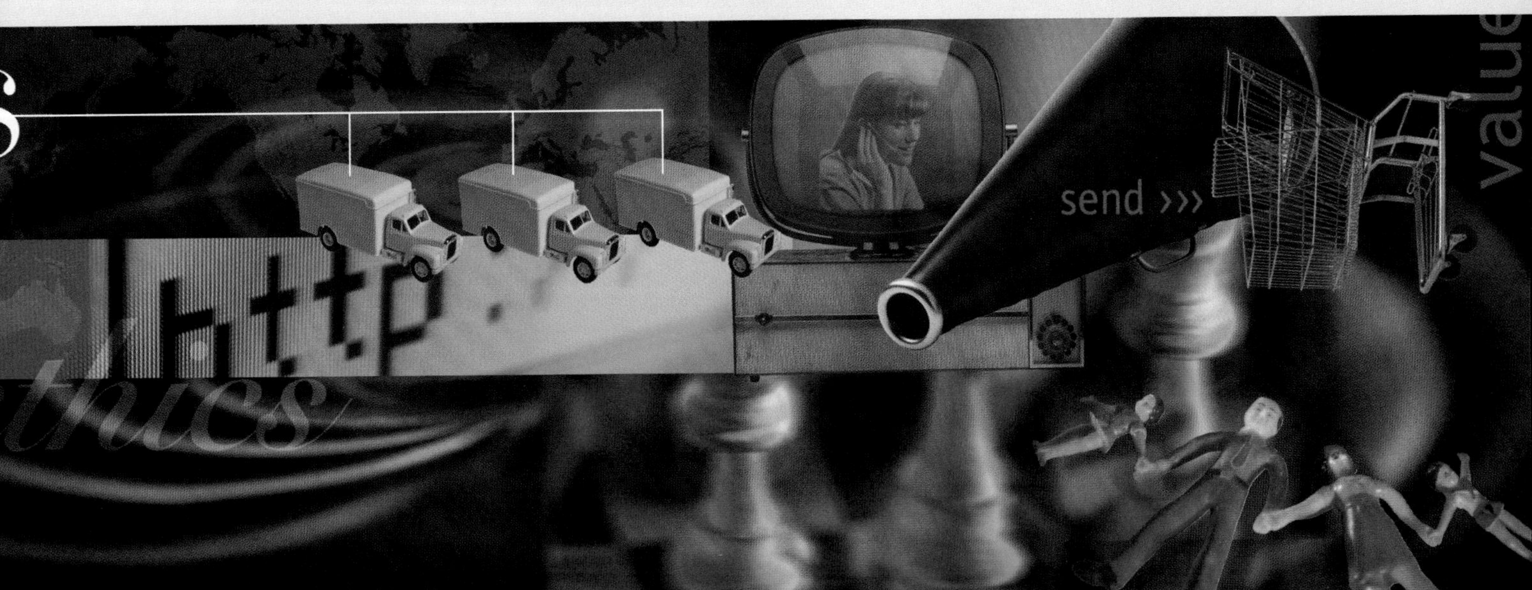

the internet chapter, ch 19

THE INTERNET CHAPTER

Many texts include Internet features, but we've taken it a giant leap farther. Chapter 14, Internet Marketing, goes beyond basic Internet marketing and takes you straight to the center of the e-action. We discuss how the Internet affects the business model, marketing strategy, marketing research, and business functions and relationships inside and outside the firm, as well as the financial implications of e-marketing. We also provide links to companies that are setting the pace in Web marketing, plus numerous tools and resources for online marketers. This chapter is truly one-of-a-kind. Find it only at **http://lamb.swcollege.com**

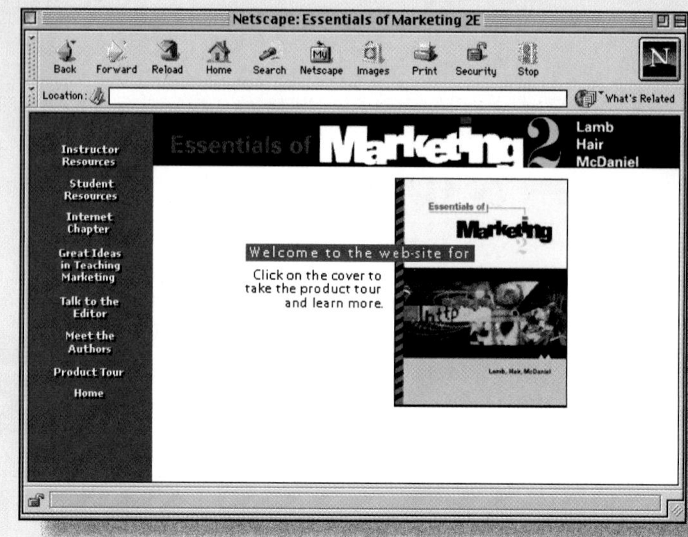

http://lamb.swcollege.com

internet examples, activities and references

INTERNET EXAMPLES, ACTIVITIES AND REFERENCES

Every chapter is enhanced with compelling examples and activities that expose you to state-of-the-Web marketing. You'll evaluate the Internet marketing efforts of famous and not-so-famous companies. There's no better way to see what works and what doesn't. You'll also find a wealth of marketing resources you might not have known even existed.

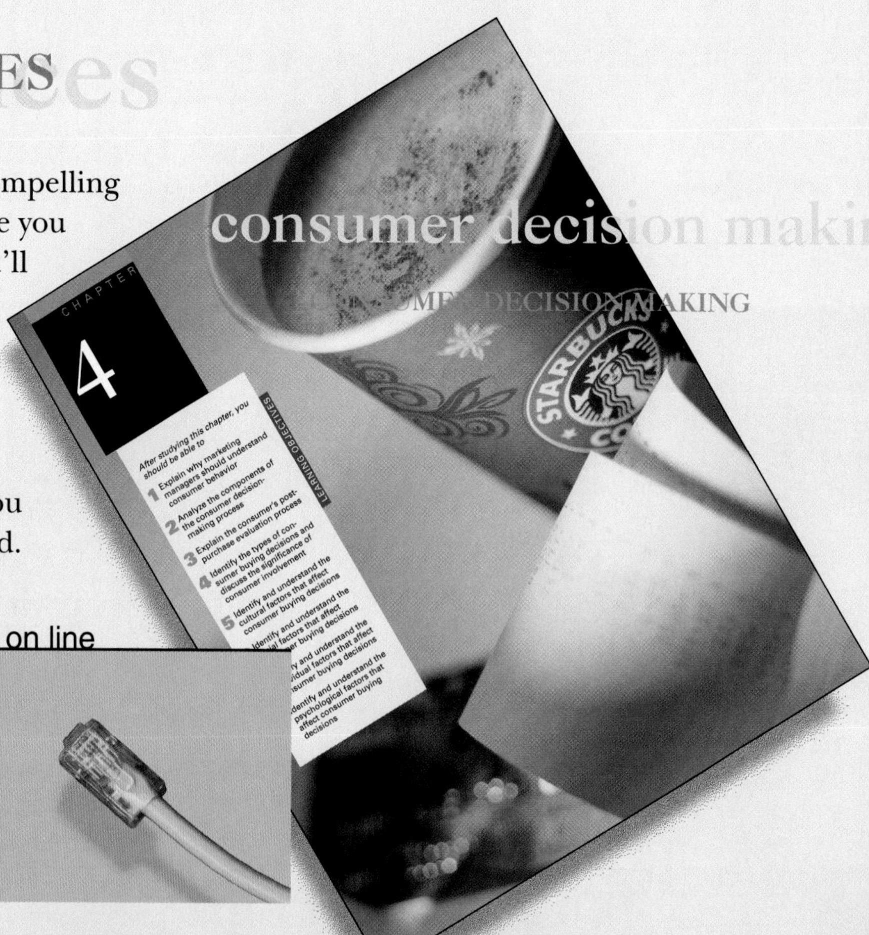

on line

Rossignol

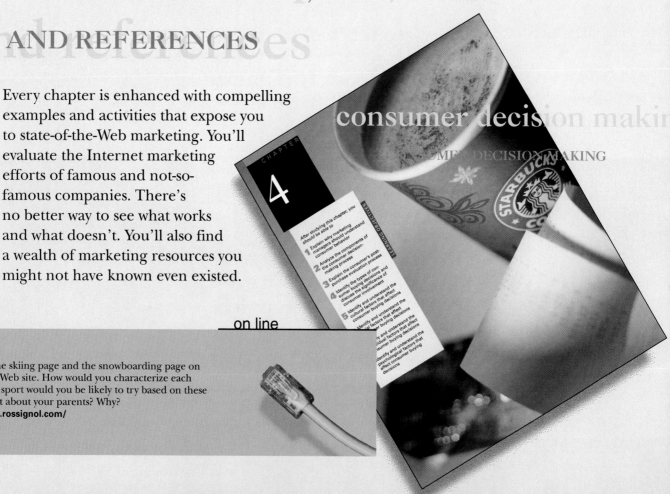

Compare the skiing page and the snowboarding page on Rossignol's Web site. How would you characterize each site? Which sport would you be likely to try based on these pages? What about your parents? Why?
http://www.rossignol.com/

MARKETING CASES ON VIDEO

VIDEO CASE

Lord of the Boards

gano, Japan.
ympics go to his
any on a clear
opment, R&D,
company pro-
to Stowe ski area
lessons for *new-*
ses for not riding
ort draws mainly
with 88 percent
rcent male and
Newbie snow-
e basics on the
g with the idea
thing can make
comes the choice

women, men, ar
abilities, and sty
more kids aged
Burton is steppi
products that m
these mini-snow
kids ride first an
suit. In the proc
becomes a famil
The Burton st
nual sales figure
well over $150 n
pany has 500 em
and around the
snowboarding n
the snowboardi

New end-of-chapter cases for all chapters come to life in interesting videos. The cases present the very real world experiences and challenges of innovative marketing organizations like Ben & Jerry's and Burton Snowboards.

NEW END-OF-CHAPTER QUIZZES

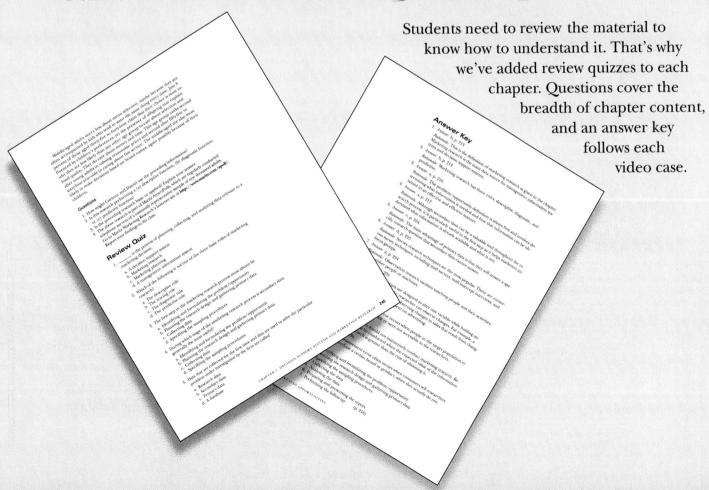

Students need to review the material to know how to understand it. That's why we've added review quizzes to each chapter. Questions cover the breadth of chapter content, and an answer key follows each video case.

CROSS-FUNCTIONAL CONNECTIONS

No marketer is an island. Marketing professionals work closely with almost every functional area in a company. Cross-Functional Connections explore the give-and-take between marketing and other business functions. Solutions to the topical questions appear at the end of each part so you can check your understanding of these important issues.

1 THE WORLD OF MARKETING
1 An Overview of Marketing
2 The Marketing Environment and Marketing Ethics
3 Developing a Global Vision

PART 1

CROSS-FUNCTIONAL CONNECTIONS

How Cross-Functional Coordination Will Lead to a Market-Oriented Firm

Three levels of strategy form a "hierarchy of strategy" within a company. At the highest level is the corporate strategy. Areas of interest at this level

Likewise, a marketing manager in a company has a greater interest in marketing-related issues than in finance- or operations-related issues.

Such vertical activities have resulted in departments composed of functional specialists who have tended to talk only with each other. For

REAL WORLD MARKETING MISCUES

Mistakes can have tough consequences, but they also offer great lessons. This is especially true in marketing.

New to this edition, end-of-part cases offer examples of good and bad ideas that flopped.

Often amusing and always interesting, these cases help you avoid making the same mistakes.

PART 3 CLOSING

3 Closing

still shak

Try making up your own test questions and then qu yourself. What seem to be the major topics in the Try explaining them to friends who are not in When you can clearly explain the concep way to mastery!

marketing miscues

McDonald's

Rarely has a dominant brand gone so wrong, seldom has a potent market leader wandered so far astray. McDonald's, the world's largest restaurant chain, has for decades set the standard for everything that matters in the fast-food business

ing thousands of new restaurants (approximately 850 in 1994, and 1,100 in 1995, 1,000 in 1996, and 1,100 in 1997), which proceeded to steal away customers and profits from existing franchises. Relations between McDonald's and its operators got so bad that Gary Dodd, who chairs the U.S. franchisee board,

tomers feel the chain has the best food for kids, but just 18 percent say it offers the best fare for adults.

Chairman and CEO of McDonald's U.S. operations Jack Greenberg is also moving to solve one of McDonald's worst pickles, falling customer satisfaction, by rolling out the "made for you" cooking system

CRITICAL THINKING CASES

Making smart decisions is at the heart of successful marketing. Critical Thinking Cases at the end of each part put you in the role of decision maker. You'll evaluate the marketing direction of well known firms including Streamline, Inc. and Home Depot and decide whether their strategies made sense in light of what you've learned.

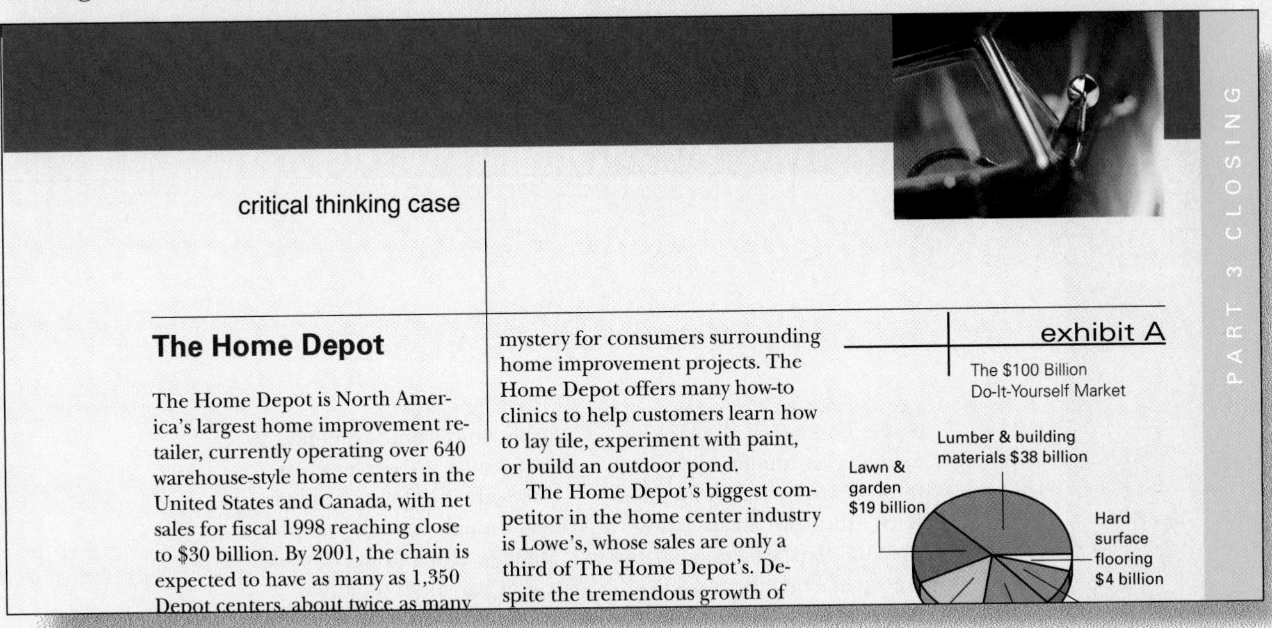

PART 3 CLOSING

critical thinking case

The Home Depot

The Home Depot is North America's largest home improvement retailer, currently operating over 640 warehouse-style home centers in the United States and Canada, with net sales for fiscal 1998 reaching close to $30 billion. By 2001, the chain is expected to have as many as 1,350 Depot centers, about twice as many

mystery for consumers surrounding home improvement projects. The Home Depot offers many how-to clinics to help customers learn how to lay tile, experiment with paint, or build an outdoor pond.

The Home Depot's biggest competitor in the home center industry is Lowe's, whose sales are only a third of The Home Depot's. Despite the tremendous growth of

exhibit A

The $100 Billion Do-It-Yourself Market

MarketingBuilder Express

The development of a sound and detailed marketing plan is one of the fundamental tasks in marketing. You'll learn to develop a successful plan using the text's comprehensive model, or using MarketingBuilder Express software from JIAN. It's an easy-to-use version of the same software used by today's top marketing professionals.

PART 1 CLOSING

Marketing Planning Activities

The World of Marketing

In the world of marketing, there are many different types of goods and services offered to many different markets. Throughout this text, you will construct a marketing plan for your chosen company. Writing a marketing plan will give you a full depth of understanding for your company, its customers, and its marketing mix elements. The company you choose should be one that interests you, such as the manufacturer of your favorite product, a local business where you would like to work, or even a business you would like to start yourself to satisfy an unmet need or want. Also refer

Marketing*Builder* Exercises

- **Industry Analysis** portion of the Market Analysis template
- **Competitive Analysis Matrix** spreadsheet
- **Competition** portion of the **Market Analysis** template
- **Competitive Roundup** portion of the **Market Analysis** template
- **Strengths, Weaknesses, Opportunities,** and **Threats** sections of the **Market Analysis** template

5. Does your chosen business have a differential or competitive advantage? If there is not one, there is no point in marketing the product. Can you create a sustainable advantage with skills, resources, or elements of the marketing mix?

OPENING EXAMPLES

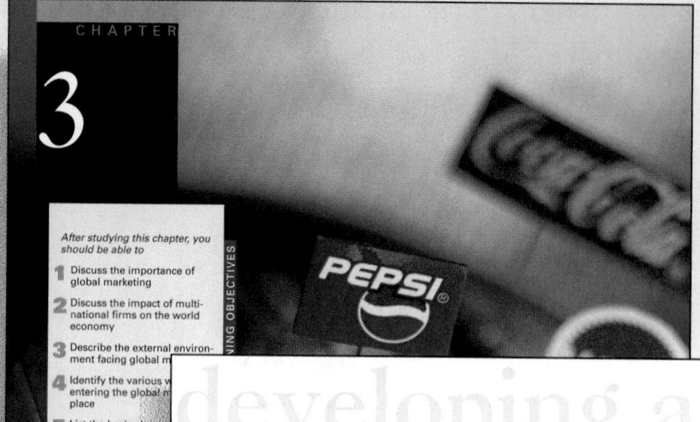

The best lessons come through true experiences. Real situations facing real companies are explored in chapter openers, designed to provide context for the material you are about to read. Each situation concludes with a series of questions that anticipate key issues in the chapter.

DEVELOPING A GLOBAL VISION

Market builders of all stripes—including an Iranian company whose detergent bears the name "Barf" (the word means "snow" in Persian)—are struggling for the same goal along the old Silk Road to China: building a brand-

Barbie dolls from Mattel Inc., for instance, are perceived as American and therefore have been thought fakes if stamped "Made in Hong Kong." Uzbeks peer at bar codes on Philip Morris Co.'s Marlboro cigarettes

LOOKING BACK AT OPENING EXAMPLES

How well can you apply what you've learned?
Can you answer the questions posed in the Opening Examples?

The Looking Back section at the end of each chapter re-examines these questions in light of what you have just read.

It's a great review, and the perfect way to see if you're ready to tackle the chapter cases.

LOOKING BACK

ɔk back at the story about marketing in the south of ssia. Besides cultural factors, other uncontrollable ables in the global external environment include nomic and technological, political, and nographic variables, as well as natural resources. Most products cannot be marketed exactly the same all over the world. Different cultures, languages, levels of economic development, and distribution channels in global markets usually require either new products or modified products. Pricing, promotion, and distribution strategies must often be altered as well. There is no doubt that international markets will become even more important in the future.

GLOBAL PERSPECTIVES

global perspectives

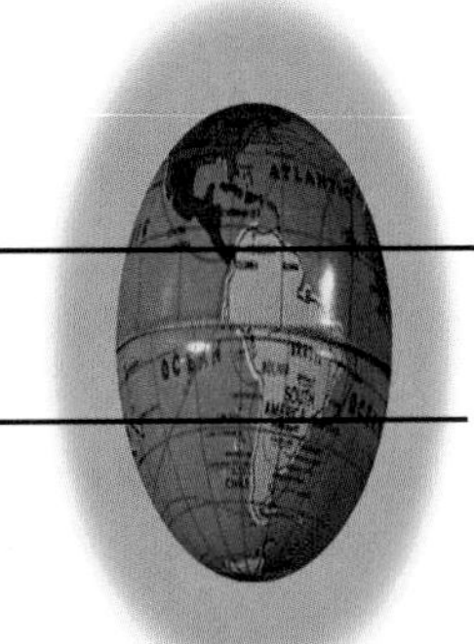

Where are the high potential markets? Where are your competitors? For more and more companies, the answers to these questions include faraway developing economies. This text takes a very global view of marketing, with international examples throughout. "Global Perspectives" features describe the experiences of real companies as they try to make the most of international opportunities.

SMALL BUSINESS ISSUES

entrepreneurial insights

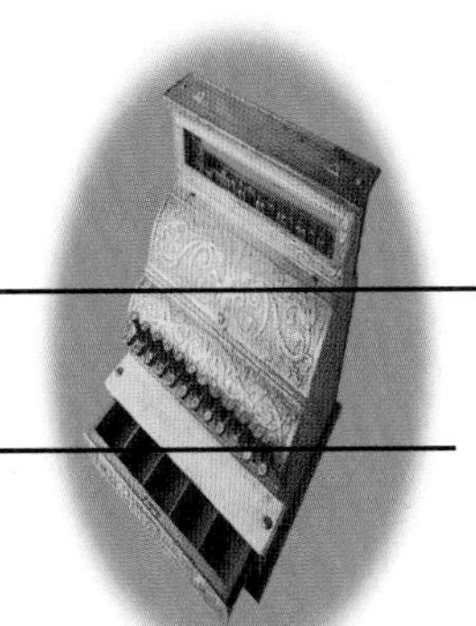

The fastest growing segment of the economy is small business. It's very likely that you will work for or run a small business during your career, and effective marketing will be key to its survival and success. "Entrepreneurial Insights" boxes examine issues of special importance to smaller firms. Also, an "Application of Small Business" exercise at the end of each chapter lets you apply chapter content to small business challenges.

ETHICS IN MARKETING

ethics in marketing

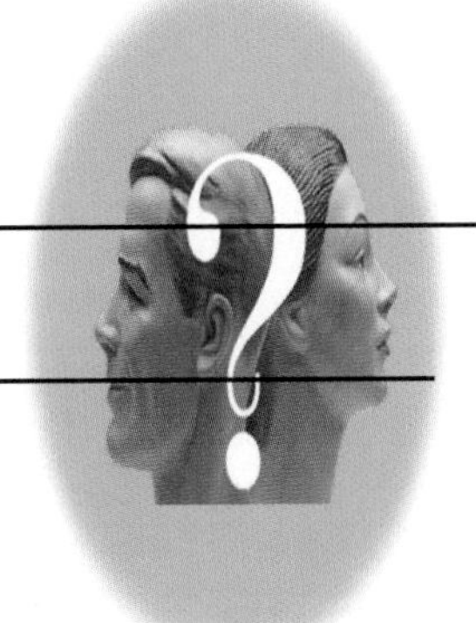

Is there such a thing as right and wrong in marketing? Or are ethical questions always defined in shades of gray? These provocative examples let you see how ethics come into play in many marketing and advertising decisions. Is marketing to children ethical? What about using fear as a selling tool? Consider these and many other hotly debated questions.

PREFACE

In the few short years since we wrote the first edition of *Essentials of Marketing*, the world has become more competitive, specialized, global, and Internet-reliant. To succeed in today's changing environment, successful marketing requires—now more than ever—a balance of creativity and knowledge. With its steadily growing market share, our *Marketing*, Fifth Edition, has demonstrated that it is the premier source for new and essential marketing knowledge.

Some of you, our customers, have told us that because you are teaching on the quarter system there was simply not enough time to cover 20 chapters. Some professors like to emphasize a major case or class project. In these situations, the text becomes a reference tool. Other professors, including the authors, are concerned about the increasing price of textbooks. *Essentials of Marketing*, Second Edition, has been created to meet your needs in every way. It delivers the needed and basic knowledge found in *Marketing*, Fifth Edition, delivered in an up-to-date, exciting, and highly readable format. Of course, it is economical, too!

Customer-Driven Innovations for the Second Edition

The guiding principle of this and past editions of all our marketing textbooks is that of building relationships. Relationship marketing is discussed from the beginning in Chapter 1, and we believe in it completely. We seek to build long-term relationships with our customers (both professors and students) that result in trust and confidence in our product. Our success is proven as the number of "new relationships" dramatically increases with each edition.

We feel a strong sense of responsibility to provide you and your students with the most exciting and up-to-date text and useful supplement package possible. To accomplish this, we have listened to your desires and comments and incorporated your feedback into *Essentials of Marketing*, Second Edition.

New Part Opening Cross-Functional Feature

Marketing is not an isolated activity. It relates to every aspect of doing business, from research and development to manufacturing and production and beyond. To help your students better understand how marketing affects and is affected by other business functions, we have created Cross-Functional Connections to open each part. Following each discussion are questions that are answered for the student at the end of the part.

New End-of-Chapter Review Quizzes

To help students check their progress, we have added a review quiz to the end of each chapter. Answers can be found at the end of each chapter and a rationale for the right answer is given. Page references help students find the material they need to review further.

All-New Internet Activities and Real-Time Examples

Each chapter contains several Internet activities tied to organizations mentioned in the text. For example, as students read about how McDonald's segments and targets markets, they're directed to real-time examples on McDonald's Web page. Because each activity calls for student production, you can use these miniexercises as additional homework or quizzing opportunities. In addition, we conclude each chapter with additional Internet activities that relate to chapter content. Students find valuable on-line resources and learn to analyze current Internet marketing strategies. Links to all URLs in the book are located on the text's Internet site at

http://lamb.swcollege.com. Should a URL listed in the book become obsolete, it will be replaced with a new one that still fits the particular context of the activity.

New Marketing Miscues Cases

To help your students recognize some of the obstacles that can surface in the creation and execution of a marketing plan, we have added a new Marketing Miscues case to the end of each part. These cases illustrate what happens when successful companies' marketing efforts fall short. Students can learn from the challenges faced by companies like Intel and General Motors.

New End-of Part Activities Help Students Build a Marketing Plan

To help you incorporate marketing strategy into your course, we have added exercises at each end-of-part that lead students step by step through the development of a marketing plan. As chapter topics such as market segmentation and consumer behavior are discussed, the corresponding end-of-part exercises direct students to create the related portions of their marketing plan. By the end of the semester, your class will have developed a complete marketing plan.

Classic Value-Based Features Have Been Updated and Enhanced

Internet Coverage

ON LINE

The hottest technology feature of the Second Edition is the all-new Internet chapter that goes beyond the Internet's impact on marketing strategy and the marketing mix and discusses the impact e-commerce has on finance, strategy, business relationships, and internal business functions. The chapter from the first edition is still available on-line, and it is titled "Fundamentals of Internet Marketing." Additionally, Internet coverage is integrated throughout the text and identified for you by a special icon.

The Popular Internet Site Connects You to Our Marketing Virtual Community: http://lamb.swcollege.com

A dedicated Internet site supports the text, featuring updates to URLs in the text, additional real-time marketing cases, Chapter 14 on "Internet Marketing," updates and articles, links to companies discussed in the text, plus a variety of materials to supplement your course.

All-New BusinessLink Video Cases

All new videos have been created for the Second Edition of *Essentials of Marketing*. Each video is enhanced by text material at the end of appropriate chapters. The companies we feature are ones that both you and your students will recognize: Burton Snowboards, Ben and Jerry's, World Gym, and many more. A detailed Video Guide previews each clip and keys it to the chapter content for easy integration. Previewing, viewing, and follow-up activities are included to help you present the content through the video, making the marketing experience real for your students.

Marketing*Builder* Express

JIAN®

An "express" version of JIAN's popular Marketing*Builder* software, this tool contains everything students need to develop a marketing plan. Students can complete the new end-of-part marketing plan activities using the shorter Marketing*Builder* Express software templates or using the original Academic Version of Marketing*Builder*.

Small Business and Entrepreneurship Are Emphasized in Every Chapter

Many students will either work for a small business or strike out on their own to form an organization. For this reason, each chapter contains a feature box called "Entrepreneurial Insights" and an "Application for Small Business" appears at the end of each chapter. The "Entrepreneurial Insights" boxes apply general marketing concepts to the world of small business. The "Applications" are minicases designed to illustrate how small businesses can create strategies and tactics using the material in the chapter. Anyone with an entrepreneurial flair will enjoy these features.

Customer Value and Quality Are Emphasized in Every Chapter

Delivering superior customer value is now key to success in an increasingly competitive marketplace. We have integrated examples throughout the text that show how issues of value and quality affect marketing decisions at every level. The new icon in the margin identifies the placement of these examples.

Careers in Marketing

The Appendix has been greatly expanded and placed on the Second Edition Web site. It presents information on a variety of marketing careers, with job descriptions and career paths, to familiarize students with employment opportunities in marketing. This appendix also indicates what people in various marketing positions typically earn and how students should go about marketing themselves to prospective employers. A self-assessment questionnaire, a sample résumé and cover letter, and interviewing checklists are only some of the tools we have provided to help your students enter the marketing field. A series of custom-produced video vignettes features recent graduates who explain how principles from the text apply to the real world of marketing.

Global Marketing Concepts Throughout the Text

Today most businesses compete not only locally and nationally, but globally as well. Companies that have never given a thought to exporting now face competition from abroad. "Thinking globally" should be a part of every manager's tactical and strategic planning. Accordingly, we address this topic in detail early in Chapter 3. We have also integrated numerous global examples within the body of the text and identified them with the new icon shown in the margin.

Global marketing is fully integrated throughout the book, cases, and videos as well. Our "Global Perspectives" boxes, which appear in most chapters, provide expanded global examples and concepts. Each box concludes with thought-provoking questions carefully prepared to stimulate class discussion. For example, the box in Chapter 5 describes how Whirlpool embarked on a joint venture with a Chinese company that made inferior products. Students are asked to evaluate the soundness of Whirlpool's decision.

Focus on Ethics

In this edition we continue our emphasis on ethics. "Ethics and Social Responsibility" has been incorporated into the chapter on the marketing environment and appears early in Chapter 2 to demonstrate its importance in management decision making. The "Ethics in Marketing" boxes, complete with questions focusing on ethical decision making, have been revised and added to every chapter. Questions and cases designed to highlight ethical issues, such as the Ben and Jerry's case appearing at the end of Chapter 2, give students a sense of the complexity of ethics issues as the cases lead them to look at the issues from all sides.

Value-Driven Pedagogy Puts You in the Know

Our pedagogy has been developed in response to what you told us delivers value to you and your students. You told us that current examples are important to you, so we have included all-new opening vignettes, new examples throughout the text, and new boxed material in every chapter. You told us that cases that students find relevant are important to you, so we have added a new Cross-Functional feature and replaced all of the video cases with new, current videos. You said that many of your students planned a career in small business, so we have numerous new small business examples, "Entrepreneurial Insights" boxes, and new small business exercises at the end of each chapter. Finally, you told us that the Integrated Learning System helped you organize your lectures and helped your students study more effectively, so we have retained that important feature.

3 **Fully Integrated Learning System**

The text and all major supplements are organized around the learning objectives that appear at the beginning of each chapter to provide you and your students with an easy-to-use Integrated Learning System. A numbered icon like the one shown in the margin identifies each objective in each chapter and appears next to its related material throughout the text, Instructor's Manual, Test Bank, and Study Guide. In other words, every learning objective links the text, Study Guide, Test Bank, and all components of the Instructor's Manual. The system is illustrated on the inside front cover of the text.

Chapter learning objectives are the linchpin of the Integrated Learning System. They provide a structure for your lesson plans—everything you need to assure complete coverage of each objective icon. Do you want to stress more on learning objective 4, Chapter 9, "Explain the diffusion process through which new products are adopted"? No problem. Go to the Instructor's Manual, objective 4, Chapter 9, and you'll find supplemental material. Do you want to emphasize the same objective on an exam? Go to the correlation table at the beginning of every chapter in the Test Bank. Here you will find under Chapter 9, learning objective 4, a matrix that lists question types (Definitions, Conceptual, or Applications) and level of difficulty. Now you can test on objective 4 by type of question and degree of difficulty. This value-driven system for you, the instructor, delivers what it promises—full integration.

The integrated system also delivers value for students as they prepare for exams. The learning objective icons identify all the material in the text and Study Guide that relate to each specific learning objective. Students can easily check their grasp of each objective by reading the text sections, reviewing the corresponding summary section, answering the Study Guide questions for that objective, and returning to the appropriate text sections for further review when they have difficulty with any of the questions. Students can quickly identify all material relating to an objective by simply looking for the learning objective icon.

Text Pedagogy That Adds Value, Excites Students, and Reinforces Learning

Pedagogical features are meant to reinforce learning, but they need not be boring. We have created teaching tools within the text that will excite student interest as well as teach.

- **Opening Vignettes, Revisited at Chapter Conclusions:** Each chapter begins with a new, current, real-world story about a marketing decision or situation facing a company. A special section before the chapter summary called "Looking Back" answers the teaser questions posed in the opening vignette and helps illustrate how the chapter material relates to the real world of marketing.
- **Key Terms:** Key terms appear in boldface in the text, with definitions in the margins, making it easy for students to check their understanding of key definitions. A complete alphabetical list of key terms appears at the end of each chapter as a study checklist, with page citations for easy reference.
- **Chapter Summaries:** Each chapter ends with a summary that distills the main points of the chapter. Chapter summaries are organized around the learning objectives so that students can use them as a quick check on their achievement of learning goals.
- WRITING **Discussion and Writing Questions:** To help students improve their writing skills, we have included writing exercises with the discussion questions at the end of each chapter. These exercises are marked with the icon shown here. The writing questions are designed to be brief so that students can accomplish writing assignments in a short time and grading time is minimized.
- TEAM **Team Activities:** The ability to work collaboratively is key to success in today's business world. End-of-chapter team activities, identified by the new icon shown here, give students opportunities to learn to work together.
- ENTREPRENEUR **Application for Small Business:** These short scenarios prompt students to apply marketing concepts to small business settings. Each scenario ends with provocative questions to aid student analysis.
- **Critical Thinking Part Cases:** Our society has an enormous capacity for generating data, but our ability to use the data to make good decisions has lagged behind. In the hope of better preparing the next generation of business leaders, many educators are beginning to place greater emphasis on developing critical thinking skills.

  Essentials of Marketing, Second Edition, contributes to this effort with a more challenging, comprehensive case at the end of each of the four major parts—all of them new for this edition. Critical Thinking Cases feature nationally known companies like The Gap, The Home Depot, and Amazon.com.
- **Video Cases:** All video cases in this edition are new. Nineteen video segments add a visual dimension to case analysis by demonstrating the marketing concepts presented in the chapter. Companies featured in the videos include Burton Snowboards, Ben and Jerry's, Vermont Teddy Bear, Red Roof Inns, Hudson's department stores, and many more.

Innovative Student Supplements

Essentials of Marketing, Second Edition, provides an excellent vehicle for students to learn the fundamentals. However, to truly understand the subject, students need to apply the principles to real-life situations. We have provided a variety of supplements that give students the opportunity to apply concepts through hands-on activities.

- ***Comprehensive GradeMaker Study Guide*** (ISBN 0-324-04378-3): All questions in the Study Guide are keyed to the learning objectives by numbered icons. In addition to true/false, multiple choice, and essay questions, every chapter includes application questions, many in the form of short scenarios, and agree/

disagree questions to help students articulate the concepts they are trying to master. Study Guide questions were designed to be similar in type and difficulty level to the Test Bank questions, so that review using the Study Guide will help students improve their test scores. Every chapter opens with a pre-test to help students assess their level of understanding before beginning to review. Other review tools in the chapter include chapter outlines with definitions of key terms, a synopsis of key points under the learning objectives, and vocabulary practice.

- JIAN® ***MarketingBuilder Express Software*** (ISBN 0-538-87574-7): We are pleased to make available to users of *Essentials of Marketing*, Second Edition, software by JIAN, specifically designed for creating a marketing plan.
- ***Fancy Footwork*** (ISBN 0-538-82642-8) ***Computer Simulation:*** This computer simulation enables students to make real-world product decisions. *Fancy Footwork* guides students through the development of strategies for the four Ps in marketing a new line of athletic footwear.

Innovative Instructor's Supplements

All components of our comprehensive support package have been developed to help you prepare lectures and tests as quickly and easily as possible. We provide a wealth of information and activities beyond the text to supplement your lectures, as well as teaching aids in a variety of formats to fit your own teaching style.

Instructor Resource CD-ROM

Managing your classroom resources is now easier than ever. The new Instructor Resource CD-ROM (ISBN 0-324-04381-3) contains all key instructor supplements—Instructor's Manual, Test Bank, and PowerPoint.

A Value-Based Instructor's Manual, the Core of Our Integrated Learning System

Each chapter of the Instructor's Manual (ISBN 0-324-04380-5) begins with the learning objectives and a brief summary of the key points covered by each objective. The Integrated Learning System then comes together in the detailed outlines of each chapter. Each outline, integrated with the textbook and with other supplements through the learning objectives, refers you to the support materials at the appropriate points in the lecture: transparencies with discussion suggestions, additional examples not included in the text, exhibits, supplemental articles, additional activities, boxed material, and discussion questions. These outlines assist you in organizing lectures, choosing support materials, bringing in outside examples not mentioned in the book, and taking full advantage of text discussion.

In addition to complete solutions to text questions and cases, the manual supplies ethical scenarios, summaries of current articles, and class activities. Our manual is truly "one-stop shopping" for everything you need for your complete teaching system.

Also included in the Instructor's Manual are detailed teaching notes for the video program. Each video lesson describes the segment(s) and provides outlines for previewing assignments, viewing tips, and follow-up activities.

Comprehensive Test Bank and Windows Testing Software

To complete the integrated system, our enhanced Test Bank (ISBN 0-324-04374-0), like the other supplements, is organized around the learning objectives. It is available in print and new Windows software formats (Thomson Learning Testing Tools™) (ISBN 0-324-04375-9).

A correlation table at the beginning of each Test Bank chapter classifies each question according to Bloom's taxonomy and to question type, complexity, and learning objective covered. Using this table, you can create exams with the appropriate mix of question types and level of difficulty for your class. You can choose to prepare tests that cover all learning objectives or emphasize those you feel are most important. The Test Bank is one of the most comprehensive on the market, with over 2,500 true/false, multiple-choice, and essay questions.

Complete Video Package and Instructor's Manual

This video package (ISBNs 0-324-04368-6, 0-324-04369-4, 0-324-04370-8) adds visual impact and current, real-world examples to your lecture presentation. The package includes 19 Video Cases and 7 Career Videos.

Other Outstanding Supplements

- ***PowerPoint Slides*** (ISBN 0-324-04372-4): More than 300 full-color images are provided with *Essentials of Marketing,* Second Edition. Most are creatively prepared visuals that do not repeat the text. Only images that highlight concepts central to the chapter are from the textbook. All you need is Windows to run the PowerPoint viewer and an LCD panel for classroom display.
- ***Transparency Acetates*** (ISBN 0-324-01444-9): To supplement the PowerPoint presentation, 196 transparency acetates are available. They include figures and ads from the text. Images are tied to the Integrated Learning System through the Instructor's Manual lecture outlines. Transparencies and their discussion prompts appear within the learning objective content where they apply.
- ***New Instructor's Handbook*** (ISBN 0-324-01698-0): This helpful booklet was specifically designed for instructors preparing to teach their first course in principles of marketing. It provides helpful hints on developing a course outline, lecturing, testing, giving feedback, and assigning projects.
- ***New Edition of Great Ideas for Teaching Marketing*** (ISBN 0-324-01441-4): Edited by the authors of the textbook, *Great Ideas for Teaching Marketing,* Fifth Edition, is a collection of suggestions for improving marketing education by enhancing teaching excellence. The publication includes teaching tips and ideas submitted by marketing educators across the United States and Canada.

Acknowledgments

This book could not have been written and published without the generous expert assistance of many people. First, we wish to thank Julie Baker, The University of Texas at Arlington, for her contributions to several chapters. J. D. Mosley-Matchett did an excellent job in updating the Internet chapter. Amelie Storment, once again, provided valuable assistance in the development of several chapters. We would also like to recognize and thank Vicki Crittenden, Boston College, and Bill Crittenden, Northeastern University, for contributing the Cross-Functional Connections that open each part. We must also thank John Weiss, Colorado State University, for creating the end-of-chapter quizzes; and Susan Leshnower, Midland College, for producing the end-of-chapter cases.

We also wish to thank each of the following persons for their work on the best supplement package for *Essentials of Marketing,* Second Edition, that is available today: Kathryn Dobie, University of Arkansas, for revising the Instructor's Manual; Theresa Williams, Indiana University, for revising the comprehensive Test Bank and including wonderful information on developing classroom achievement tests and writing good test questions; Susan Peterson, Scottsdale Community

College, for refreshing the questions of the GradeMaker Study Guide and creating some new features; Jack Gifford, Miami University (OH), for developing an extensive PowerPoint presentation that is vivid and goes beyond the basic treatment of key issues; and Susan Leshnower, Midland College, for writing the Video Instructor's Manual to accompany her end-of-chapter cases.

Our secretaries and administrative assistants, Fran Eller at TCU, RoseAnn Reddick at UTA, and Susan Sartwell at LSU, typed the manuscript, provided important quality control, and helped keep the project (and us) on schedule. Their dedication, hard work, and support were exemplary.

Our deepest gratitude goes to the team at Thomson Learning that has made this text a market leader. Jamie Gleich Bryant, our developmental editor, made this text a reality. A special thanks goes to Steve Scoble, our acquisitions editor, and Dave Shaut, our Publisher, for their suggestions and support.

Finally, we are particularly indebted to our reviewers:

Barry Ashmen
Bucks County Community College

Thomas S. Bennett
Gaston Community College

P. J. Forrest
Mississippi College

Daniel J. Goebel
University of Southern Mississippi

Mark Green
Simpson College

Richard A. Halberg
Houghton College

Thomas J. Lang
University of Miami

Ronald E. Michaels
University of Central Florida

Monica Perry
University of North Carolina, Charlotte

Dick Rose
University of Phoenix (deceased during the development of the text)

James V. Spiers
Arizona State University

We would also like to thank everyone who reviewed earlier editions of *Marketing. Essentials of Marketing,* Second Edition has benefited from your comments and suggestions.

Wayne Alexander
Moorhead State University

Linda Anglin
Mankato State University

Thomas S. Bennett
Gaston Community College

James C. Boespflug
Arapahoe Community College

Victoria Bush
University of Mississippi

Joseph E. Cantrell
DeAnza College

G. L. Carr
University of Alaska Anchorage

Deborah Chiviges Calhoun
College of Notre Dame of Maryland

John Alan Davis
Mohave Community College

William M. Diamond
SUNY–Albany

Jacqueline K. Eastman
Valdosta State University

Kevin M. Elliott
Mankato State University

Karen A. Evans
Herkimer County Community College

Randall S. Hansen
Stetson University

Hari S. Hariharan
University of Wisconsin–Madison

Dorothy R. Harpool
Wichita State University

Timothy S. Hatten
Black Hills State University

James E. Hazeltine
Northeastern Illinois University

Patricia M. Hopkins
California State Polytechnic

Kenneth R. Laird
Southern Connecticut State University

Kenneth D. Lawrence
New Jersey Institute of Technology

J. Gordon Long
Georgia College

Karl Mann
Tennessee Tech University

Cathy L. Martin
Northeast Louisiana University

Irving Mason
Herkimer County Community College

Anil M. Pandya
Northeastern Illinois University

Michael M. Pearson
Loyola University, New Orleans

Constantine G. Petrides
Borough of Manhattan Community College

Peter A. Schneider
Seton Hall University

Donald R. Self
Auburn University at Montgomery

Mark T. Spence
Southern Connecticut State College

James E. Stoddard
University of New Hampshire

Albert J. Taylor
Austin Peay State University

Janice E. Taylor
Miami University of Ohio

Ronald D. Taylor
Mississippi State University

Sandra T. Vernon
Fayetteville Technical Community College

Charles R. Vitaska
Metro State College, Denver

James F. Wenthe
Georgia College

Linda Berns Wright
Mississippi State University

William R. Wynd
Eastern Washington University

Meet the Authors

Charles W. Lamb, Jr.—Texas Christian University

Charles W. Lamb, Jr., is the M. J. Neeley Professor of Marketing, M. J. Neeley School of Business, Texas Christian University. He served as chair of the department of marketing from 1982 to 1988 and again from 1997 to the present. He is currently serving as chairman of the board of governors of the Academy of Marketing Science.

Lamb has authored or co-authored more than a dozen books and anthologies on marketing topics and over 150 articles that have appeared in academic journals and conference proceedings.

In 1997, he was awarded the prestigious Chancellor's Award for Distinguished Research and Creative Activity at TCU. This is the highest honor that the university bestows on its faculty. Other key honors he has received include the M. J. Neeley School of Business Research Award, selection as a Distinguished Fellow of the Academy of Marketing Science and a Fellow of the Southwestern Marketing Association.

Lamb earned an associate degree in business administration from Sinclair Community College, a bachelor's degree from Miami University, an MBA from Wright State University, and a doctorate from Kent State University. He previously served as assistant and associate professor of marketing at Texas A & M University.

Joseph F. Hair, Jr.—Louisiana State University

Joseph Hair is Alvin C. Copeland Endowed Chair of Franchising and Director, Entrepreneurship Institute, Louisiana State University. Previously, Hair held the Phil B. Hardin Chair of Marketing at the University of Mississippi. He has taught graduate and undergraduate marketing and marketing research courses.

Hair has authored 27 books, monographs, and cases and over 60 articles in scholarly journals. He also has participated on many university committees and has chaired numerous departmental task forces. He serves on the editorial review boards of several journals.

He is a member of the American Marketing Association, Academy of Marketing Science, Southern Marketing Association, and Southwestern Marketing Association.

Hair holds a bachelor's degree in economics, a master's degree in marketing, and a doctorate in marketing, all from the University of Florida. He also serves as a marketing consultant to businesses in a variety of industries, ranging from food and retailing to financial services, health care, electronics, and the U.S. Departments of Agriculture and Interior.

Carl McDaniel—University of Texas–Arlington

Carl McDaniel is a professor of marketing at the University of Texas–Arlington, where he has been chairman of the marketing department since 1976. He has been an instructor for more than 20 years and is the recipient of several awards for outstanding teaching. McDaniel has also been a district sales manager for Southwestern Bell Telephone Company. Currently, he serves as a board member of the North Texas Higher Education Authority.

In addition to *Marketing* and *Essentials of Marketing*, McDaniel also has co-authored numerous textbooks in marketing and business. McDaniel's research has appeared in such publications as the *Journal of Marketing Research*, *Journal of Marketing*, *Journal of Business Research*, *Journal of the Academy of Marketing Science*, and *California Management Review*.

McDaniel is a member of the American Marketing Association, Academy of Marketing Science, Southern Marketing Association, Southwestern Marketing Association, and Western Marketing Association.

Besides his academic experience, McDaniel has business experience as the co-owner of a marketing research firm. Recently, McDaniel served as senior consultant to the International Trade Centre (ITC), Geneva, Switzerland. The ITC's mission is to help developing nations increase their exports. He has a bachelor's degree from the University of Arkansas and his master's degree and doctorate from Arizona State University.

1 THE WORLD OF MARKETING

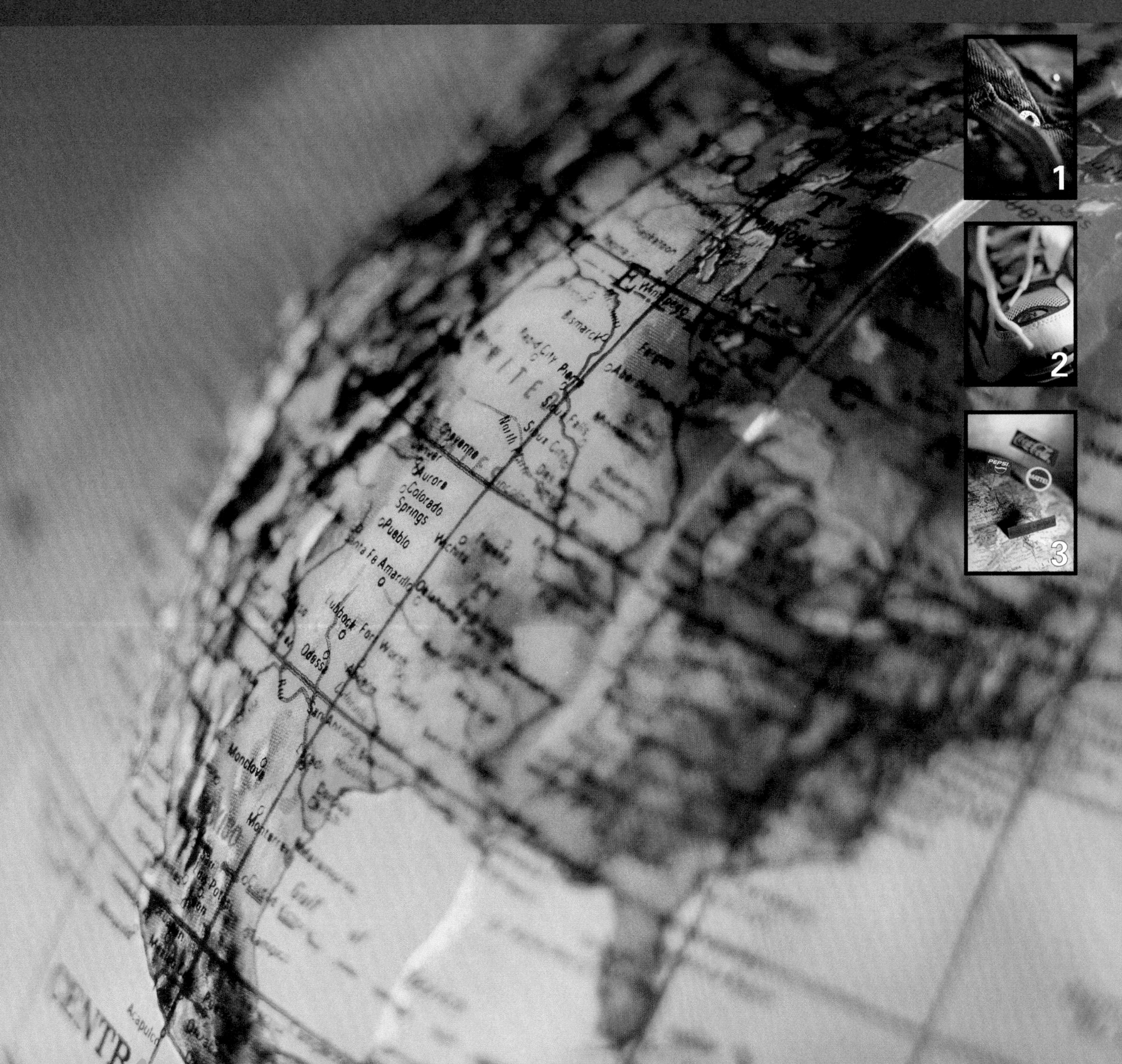

CROSS-FUNCTIONAL CONNECTIONS

How Cross-Functional Coordination Will Lead to a Market-Oriented Firm

Three levels of strategy form a "hierarchy of strategy" within a company. At the highest level is the corporate strategy. Areas of interest at this level include decisions about the types of business the firm will be in and the allocation of key company resources to different divisions. For example, ConAgra operates in three major business areas: Food Inputs & Ingredients (crop protection chemicals, fertilizers, seeds), Refrigerated Foods (beef and pork products, deli meats, chicken and turkey products, cheese products), and Grocery/Diversified Products (tomato-based products, oils, popcorn, beans, frozen foods).

The second level of strategy, business strategy, is associated with a strategic business unit (SBU). An SBU comprises related products that satisfy the needs of a particular market. For example, General Mills separates its food-related products into the following units: Big G cereals (includes Cheerios, Lucky Charms, Wheaties, Kix, Basic 4), Betty Crocker products (includes SuperMoist cake mixes, Creamy Deluxe frosting, Supreme brownie mixes, Hamburger Helper, Fruit Roll-Ups, Recipe Sauces, Pop Secret, FundaMiddles, Squeezits), Gorton's (seafood), and Yoplait yogurt.

The next level of strategy, functional strategy, supports the corporate- and business-level strategies by pulling together various activities necessary to gain the desired competitive advantage. Traditionally, each functional area performs specialized portions of the organization's tasks. The functional-level marketing strategy resolves questions concerning what products deliver customer satisfaction and value, what price to charge, how to distribute, and what type of marketing communication activities to engage in; whereas the functional-level manufacturing strategy decides what products manufacturing can make, at what rate to produce, and how to make the products (e.g., labor or capital intensive). Since such activities require expertise in only one functional area, managers have traditionally been trained to manage *vertically*. This functional training has also been the dominant framework in colleges and universities; a marketing major takes many more marketing courses than finance courses and vice versa. Likewise, a marketing manager in a company has a greater interest in marketing-related issues than in finance- or operations-related issues.

Such vertical activities have resulted in departments composed of functional specialists who have tended to talk only with each other. For example, marketers talk to other marketing people, manufacturing engineers have operational discussions on the shop floor, development team members talk within their R&D groups, and financial analysts and accountants talk to each other.

Individual functional-level strategies resulting from such departmentalization are the center of much intraorganizational conflict. Conflict between the marketing group and the production schedule is common. Marketing tends to want output increased or decreased immediately; but the production schedule, once made, is often seen as inflexible.

The effective formulation and implementation of corporate- and business-level strategies, however, depend on functional groups working in partnership with one another. Crossing functional boundaries is referred to as managing *horizontally* and requires a significant level of coordination among business functions. Horizontal management requires that marketing managers take a keen interest in financial issues and that operational managers have a better understanding of the firm's customers.

Today's business environment has put considerable pressure on functional groups to work together more harmoniously. As we move into the twenty-first century, there is a dramatic rush to get products into the marketplace at a much faster pace than ever before. At the same time, customers are much more demanding about what they want in these products. The end result is that we can expect customers to want customized products delivered immediately. The key to developing a truly market-oriented firm that achieves high levels of customer satisfaction is *cross-functional integration* (also referred to as *internal partnering*). Companies such as Hewlett-Packard, Deere & Co., and General Electric have dedicated considerable attention to the importance of cross-functional integration.

The marketing function is one of three departments that has a direct effect on product management. The other two departments are research and development (R&D) and manufacturing. Unfortu-

1 THE WORLD OF MARKETING

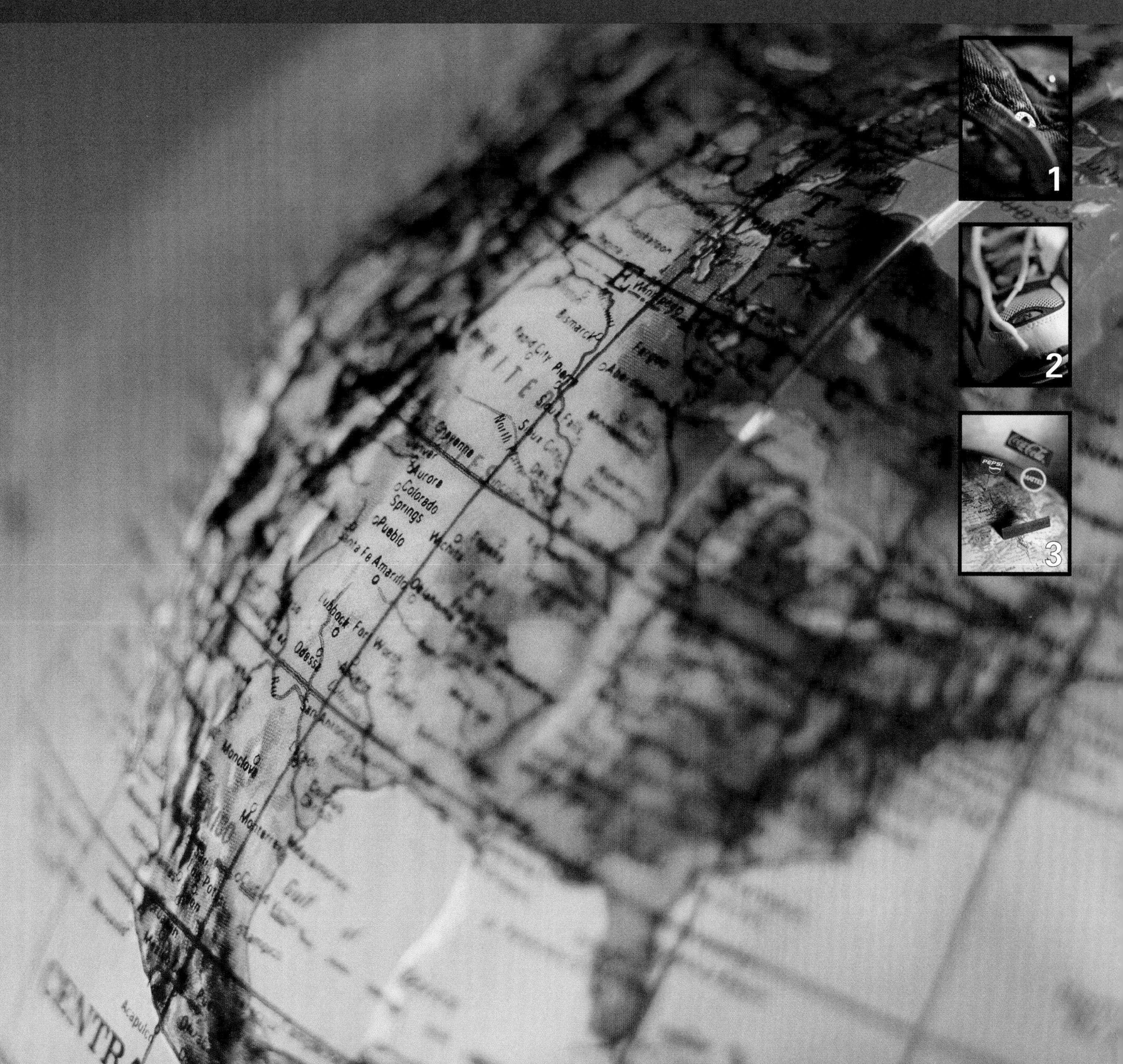

CROSS-FUNCTIONAL CONNECTIONS

How Cross-Functional Coordination Will Lead to a Market-Oriented Firm

Three levels of strategy form a "hierarchy of strategy" within a company. At the highest level is the corporate strategy. Areas of interest at this level include decisions about the types of business the firm will be in and the allocation of key company resources to different divisions. For example, ConAgra operates in three major business areas: Food Inputs & Ingredients (crop protection chemicals, fertilizers, seeds), Refrigerated Foods (beef and pork products, deli meats, chicken and turkey products, cheese products), and Grocery/Diversified Products (tomato-based products, oils, popcorn, beans, frozen foods).

The second level of strategy, business strategy, is associated with a strategic business unit (SBU). An SBU comprises related products that satisfy the needs of a particular market. For example, General Mills separates its food-related products into the following units: Big G cereals (includes Cheerios, Lucky Charms, Wheaties, Kix, Basic 4), Betty Crocker products (includes SuperMoist cake mixes, Creamy Deluxe frosting, Supreme brownie mixes, Hamburger Helper, Fruit Roll-Ups, Recipe Sauces, Pop Secret, FundaMiddles, Squeezits), Gorton's (seafood), and Yoplait yogurt.

The next level of strategy, functional strategy, supports the corporate- and business-level strategies by pulling together various activities necessary to gain the desired competitive advantage. Traditionally, each functional area performs specialized portions of the organization's tasks. The functional-level marketing strategy resolves questions concerning what products deliver customer satisfaction and value, what price to charge, how to distribute, and what type of marketing communication activities to engage in; whereas the functional-level manufacturing strategy decides what products manufacturing can make, at what rate to produce, and how to make the products (e.g., labor or capital intensive). Since such activities require expertise in only one functional area, managers have traditionally been trained to manage *vertically*. This functional training has also been the dominant framework in colleges and universities; a marketing major takes many more marketing courses than finance courses and vice versa. Likewise, a marketing manager in a company has a greater interest in marketing-related issues than in finance- or operations-related issues.

Such vertical activities have resulted in departments composed of functional specialists who have tended to talk only with each other. For example, marketers talk to other marketing people, manufacturing engineers have operational discussions on the shop floor, development team members talk within their R&D groups, and financial analysts and accountants talk to each other.

Individual functional-level strategies resulting from such departmentalization are the center of much intraorganizational conflict. Conflict between the marketing group and the production schedule is common. Marketing tends to want output increased or decreased immediately; but the production schedule, once made, is often seen as inflexible.

The effective formulation and implementation of corporate- and business-level strategies, however, depend on functional groups working in partnership with one another. Crossing functional boundaries is referred to as managing *horizontally* and requires a significant level of coordination among business functions. Horizontal management requires that marketing managers take a keen interest in financial issues and that operational managers have a better understanding of the firm's customers.

Today's business environment has put considerable pressure on functional groups to work together more harmoniously. As we move into the twenty-first century, there is a dramatic rush to get products into the marketplace at a much faster pace than ever before. At the same time, customers are much more demanding about what they want in these products. The end result is that we can expect customers to want customized products delivered immediately. The key to developing a truly market-oriented firm that achieves high levels of customer satisfaction is *cross-functional integration* (also referred to as *internal partnering*). Companies such as Hewlett-Packard, Deere & Co., and General Electric have dedicated considerable attention to the importance of cross-functional integration.

The marketing function is one of three departments that has a direct effect on product management. The other two departments are research and development (R&D) and manufacturing. Unfortunately, marketing's interface with these business functions is often mired in conflict. Reasons for this conflict include divergent personalities, physical separation, data differences, and suboptimal reward systems.

Marketing people tend to be extroverted and interact easily with others, whereas R&D and manufacturing people are frequently introverted and known to work well with individual work processes and output. In addition to being distinguished by their personalities, marketers and their product management colleagues in R&D and manufacturing often share the distinction of being housed in different locations. This is surprising when one thinks about the overlap in function the three groups have on a company's product.

The marketing department is typically located in the company's headquarters—which may be in the heart of a major business district, with sales located strategically close to customers. The company's manufacturing group is often located in low-wage areas, low-rent districts, or close to suppliers. The manufacturing group may even be located in a different country. This physical separation encourages each department to work independently instead of as a cohesive unit, particularly if the groups are separated by language differences as well as time zones.

Another major source of conflict between marketing and its R&D and manufacturing counterparts surrounds the type of data collected and used in decision making. Technical specialists in R&D and manufacturing have a difficult time understanding the lack of hard data that marketers work with. It is difficult to mesh marketing's attitudinal data with data on cycle times or tensile strength. Marketing's forecasts are rarely 100 percent accurate, but manufacturing can determine the precise costs associated with production processes.

Not surprisingly, marketing's reward system based on increased sales is often in direct conflict with manufacturing and R&D's reward systems that are driven by cost reduction. Marketing's ability to increase sales may be driven by offering consumers depth in the product line. Unfortunately, increased depth of the line leads to more changeover in the production lines, which, in turn, drives up the cost of production.

A major challenge for marketers has been the development of mechanisms for reducing conflict between the marketing department and other business functions. Working closely with human resources and information technology professionals, two major facilitating mechanisms have emerged: cross-functional teams and an information technology infrastructure.

To illustrate this functional integration, we can take a look at Hewlett-Packard's team approach to all of its product development. From concept to market entry, teams of engineers, marketers, manufacturers, financiers, and accountants bring together traditionally functional-level information into a cohesive program for product introduction. All information is shared across functional groups, and reports are prepared regularly that include details regarding interactions among functions.

The retailing industry has also made great strides to improve the interactions of various groups. For example, retailers, via the electronic highway, are now able to transmit orders directly to a supplier's computer. The supplier's computer will automatically send the order to the shop floor, while simultaneously reconciling the order with the retail store's credit history. This reduction in the need for human intervention not only speeds up the transaction process but also reduces the chance for error and conflict across functional groups. Teamwork and shared information will result in better communication between marketing and other business functions—ultimately resulting in a more satisfied customer.

Questions for Discussion:

1. Explain the differences between marketing and manufacturing's goals and marketing and R&D's goals.
2. What is the overlap among marketing, manufacturing, and R&D? What does each of these functions do that results in this overlap?
3. Why is cross-functional coordination necessary to have a market-oriented firm?

check it out

For articles and exercises on the material in this part, and for other great study aids, visit the *Marketing* Web site at **http://lamb.swcollege.com**

CHAPTER 1

LEARNING OBJECTIVES

After studying this chapter, you should be able to:

1 Define the term *marketing*

2 Describe four marketing management philosophies

3 Explain how firms implement the marketing concept

4 Describe the marketing process and identify the variables that make up the marketing mix

5 Describe several reasons for studying marketing

AN OVERVIEW OF MARKETING

To avoid being surprised by shifts in customer behavior, you must understand your customers better than they understand themselves. This understanding goes far beyond reviewing customer satisfaction surveys. It means appreciating your customers' unstated and unmet needs and knowing their businesses or lifestyles in ways that extend beyond their use of your current product or service.

When Tom Kasten, a vice president at Levi Strauss & Co., was a merchandiser responsible for developing Levi's Jeans products for the teenagers of America, he used to drive down weekly to the Fillmore Auditorium in San Francisco, where every Saturday kids would line up early in the morning to buy tickets for that night's rock concert. Tom would get out of his car, talk to the kids in line to determine what they were looking for in a pair of jeans, and observe what they were doing to their own jeans to customize them. Even now Tom takes more than his share of carpool turns each week driving his son and his friends to high school. This extra duty affords him additional opportunities to study the latest in teenage thinking and fashion. "The kids love to talk about where they shop, what they like, and what they hate," he says. "This is where it all begins, so this is what I do to learn, by watching consumers in their natural habitat."[1]

Describe Tom Kasten's philosophy of business and how this philosophy translates into sales and profits for Levi Strauss & Co. These issues are explored in Chapter 1.

on line

Levi Strauss

How does Levi Strauss use its U.S. Web page to connect with its market? What indications do you have that this is a youth-oriented company?
http://www.levi.com/

What Is Marketing?

1
Define the term *marketing*

marketing
The process of planning and executing the conception, pricing, promotion, and distribution of ideas, goods, and services to create exchanges that satisfy individual and organizational goals.

What does the term *marketing* mean to you? Many people think it means the same as personal selling. Others think marketing is the same as personal selling and advertising. Still others believe marketing has something to do with making products available in stores, arranging displays, and maintaining inventories of products for future sales. Actually, marketing includes all of these activities and more.

Marketing has two facets. First, it is a philosophy, an attitude, a perspective, or a management orientation that stresses customer satisfaction. Second, marketing is a set of activities used to implement this philosophy. The American Marketing Association's definition encompasses both perspectives: "**Marketing** is the process of planning and executing the conception, pricing, promotion, and distribution of ideas, goods, and services to create exchanges that satisfy individual and organizational goals."[2]

The Concept of Exchange

exchange
The idea that people give up something to receive something they would rather have.

Exchange is the key term in the definition of marketing. The concept of **exchange** is quite simple. It means that people give up something to receive something they would rather have. Normally we think of money as the medium of exchange. We "give up" money to "get" the goods and services we want. Exchange does not require money, however. Two persons may barter or trade such items as baseball cards or oil paintings.

Five conditions must be satisfied for any kind of exchange to take place:

- There must be at least two parties.
- Each party must have something the other party values.
- Each party must be able to communicate with the other party and deliver the goods or services sought by the other trading party.
- Each party must be free to accept or reject the other's offer.
- Each party must want to deal with the other party.[3]

Exchange will not necessarily take place even if all these conditions exist. They are, however, necessary for exchange to be possible. For example, you may place an advertisement in your local newspaper stating that your used automobile is for sale at a certain price. Several people may call you to ask about the car, some may test-drive it, and one or more may even make you an offer. All five conditions are necessary for an exchange to exist. But unless you reach an agreement with a buyer and actually sell the car, an exchange will not take place. Notice that marketing can occur even if an exchange does not occur. In the example just discussed, you would have engaged in marketing even if no one bought your used automobile.

Marketing Management Philosophies

2
Describe four marketing management philosophies

Four competing philosophies strongly influence an organization's marketing activities. These philosophies are commonly referred to as production, sales, market, and societal marketing orientations.

Production Orientation

A **production orientation** is a philosophy that focuses on the internal capabilities of the firm rather than on the desires and needs of the marketplace. A production orientation means that management assesses its resources and asks these questions: "What can we do best?" "What can our engineers design?" "What is easy to produce, given our equipment?" In the case of a service organization, managers ask, "What services are most convenient for the firm to offer?" and "Where do our talents lie?" Some have referred to this orientation as a *Field of Dreams* orientation, referring to the movie line, "If we build it, they will come."

production orientation
A philosophy that focuses on the internal capabilities of the firm rather than on the desires and needs of the marketplace.

There is nothing wrong with assessing a firm's capabilities; in fact, such assessments are major considerations in strategic marketing planning (see Chapter 2). A production orientation falls short because it does not consider whether the goods and services that the firm produces most efficiently also meet the needs of the marketplace. PPG Industries provides an interesting example. Throughout the 1980s researchers at PPG spent considerable time, effort, and money developing a bluish windshield that would let in filtered sunlight but block out the heat. Scientists were convinced that this new product would be significantly better than existing windshields. However, when the new windshield was introduced in 1991, the automobile manufacturers refused to buy it. They didn't like the color or the price. "We developed a great mousetrap, but there were no mice," reported Gary Weber, vice president for science and technology.[4]

A production orientation does not necessarily doom a company to failure, particularly not in the short run. Sometimes what a firm can best produce is exactly what the market wants. For example, the research and development department of 3M's commercial tape division developed and patented the adhesive component of Post-it™ Notes a year before a commercial application was identified. In other situations, as when competition is weak or demand exceeds supply, a production-oriented firm can survive and even prosper. More often, however, firms that succeed in competitive markets have a clear understanding that they must first determine what customers want and then produce it, rather than focus on what company management thinks should be produced.

Sales Orientation

A **sales orientation** is based on the ideas that people will buy more goods and services if aggressive sales techniques are used and that high sales result in high profits. Not only are sales to the final buyer emphasized but intermediaries are also encouraged to push manufacturers' products more aggressively. To sales-oriented firms, marketing means selling things and collecting money.

sales orientation
The idea that people will buy more goods and services if aggressive sales techniques are used and that high sales result in high profits.

The fundamental problem with a sales orientation, as with a production orientation, is a lack of understanding of the needs and wants of the marketplace. Sales-oriented companies often find that, despite the quality of their sales force, they cannot convince people to buy goods or services that are neither wanted nor needed.

Market Orientation

VALUE

The **marketing concept** is a simple and intuitively appealing philosophy. It states that the social and economic justification for an organization's existence is the satisfaction of customer wants and needs while meeting organizational objectives. It is based on an understanding that a sale does not depend on an aggressive sales force, but rather on a customer's decision to purchase a product. What a business thinks it produces is not of primary importance to its success. Instead, what customers think they are buying—the perceived value—defines a business. The marketing concept includes the following:

marketing concept
The idea that the social and economic justification for an organization's existence is the satisfaction of customer wants and needs while meeting organizational objectives.

- Focusing on customer wants and needs so the organization can distinguish its product(s) from competitors' offerings
- Integrating all the organization's activities, including production, to satisfy these wants
- Achieving long-term goals for the organization by satisfying customer wants and needs legally and responsibly

The marketing concept recognizes that there is no reason why customers should buy one organization's offerings unless they are in some way better at serving the customers' wants and needs than those offered by competing organizations.[5]

Firms that adopt and implement the marketing concept are said to be market oriented. **Market orientation** requires top-management leadership, a customer focus, competitor intelligence, and interfunctional coordination to meet customer wants and needs and deliver superior value. It also entails establishing and maintaining mutually rewarding relationships with customers.

market orientation
Philosophy that assumes that a sale does not depend on an aggressive sales force but rather on a customer's decision to purchase a product.

VALUE

Today, companies of all types are adopting a market orientation. Marriott International's CEO logs an average of 150,000 travel miles each year visiting the company's hotels, inspecting them, and talking to employees at all levels in the organization. According to Bill Marriott, "I want our associates to know that there really is a guy named Marriott who cares about them . . . . I also want to show our team in the field that I value their work enough to take time to check it."[6] Wal-Mart has become the leading discount retailer in the United States by focusing on what its customers want: everyday low prices, items always in stock, and cashiers always available. While Wal-Mart was growing rapidly throughout the 1980s and 1990s, Sears Roebuck and Company was losing business to newer specialty stores, superstores, and discounters. What happened? Sears lost out to competitors that were doing a better job of satisfying customers' wants and needs. "We didn't know who we wanted to serve," concedes CEO Arthur C. Martinez. "That was a huge hole in our strategy. It was also not clear on what basis we thought we could win against the competition."[7]

Understanding your competitive arena and competitors' strengths and weaknesses is a critical component of market orientation. This includes assessing what existing or potential competitors might be intending to do tomorrow as well as what they are doing today.[8] Western Union failed to define its competitive arena as telecommunications, concentrating instead on telegraph services, and was eventually outflanked by fax technology. Had Western Union been a market-oriented company, its management might have better understood the changes taking place, seen the competitive threat, and developed strategies to counter the threat.[9]

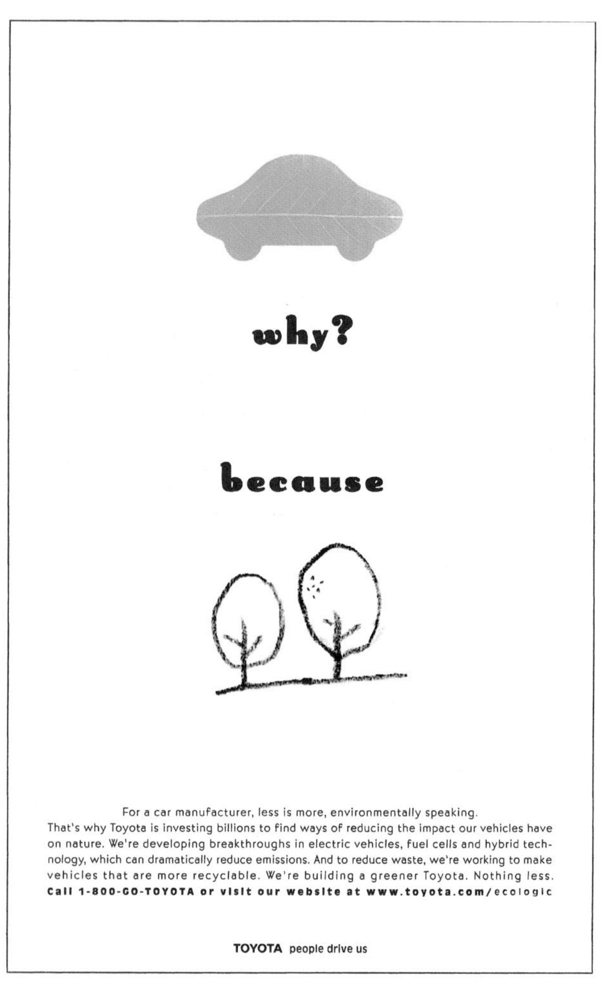

why?
because
For a car manufacturer, less is more, environmentally speaking.
That's why Toyota is investing billions to find ways of reducing the impact our vehicles have on nature. We're developing breakthroughs in electric vehicles, fuel cells and hybrid technology, which can dramatically reduce emissions. And to reduce waste, we're working to make vehicles that are more recyclable. We're building a greener Toyota. Nothing less.
Call 1-800-GO-TOYOTA or visit our website at www.toyota.com/ecologic
TOYOTA people drive us

Societal orientation, as seen in this Toyota ad, seeks to preserve or enhance society's long-term best interest. To see how large a role environmentally conscious issues play in Toyota's overall marketing philosophy, visit http://www.toyota.com/ecologic
Toyota Motor Corporate Services of North America, Inc.

Market-oriented companies are successful in getting all business functions working together to deliver customer value. Rubbermaid has developed "cross-functional entrepreneurial teams" to overcome the difficulty of getting people from different functional areas to work together in developing new houseware products. These teams are empowered to make decisions and are responsible for results.

Societal Orientation

societal orientation
The idea that an organization exists not only to satisfy customer wants and needs and to meet organizational objectives but also to preserve or enhance individuals' and society's long-term best interests.

One reason a market-oriented organization may choose not to deliver the benefits sought by customers is that these benefits may not be good for individuals or society. This philosophy, called a **societal orientation,** states that an organization exists not only to satisfy customer wants and needs and to meet organizational objectives but also to preserve or enhance individuals' and society's long-term best interests. Marketing products and containers that are less toxic than normal, are more durable,

Sears Roebuck

Wal-Mart

Has Sears identified its customers? Based on the organization of its Web page, how would you describe Sears' marketing management orientation? Compare the Sears site to Wal-Mart's site. How do these competitors stack up against each other?

http://www.sears.com/

http://www.wal-mart.com/

on line

ethics in marketing

Healthy Versus Healthy Looking

Sun-care products represent a $400 million industry. The trend throughout most of the 1990s was in favor of higher sun protection factor (SPF) sunscreens because of consumer concerns about skin cancer, wrinkles, premature aging, and other negative outcomes associated with sun exposure. That seems to be changing now.

Teenagers are apparently ignoring the warnings about the sun's potential harm. According to a survey conducted by *Seventeen* magazine, 17 percent of responding teenagers say they never use a sunscreen. Two-thirds don't know what an SPF label is. Spring breakers on Florida beaches have been reported using baby oil, Crisco, and even motor oil to enhance the tanning effects of the sun's rays.

How has the suntan industry responded? Coppertone has introduced a new low ultraviolet ray (UV) protection product called Coppertone Gold, Banana Boat has followed with Tan Express, and Hawaiian Tropic has launched an oil called Total Exposure.

The new low SPF products now represent 15 to 20 percent of industry sales. "The extreme segment of suncare is growing and it's going to grow more because of the new products," said Jack Surette, Hawaiian Tropic's vice-president for marketing.[10]

Industry executives defend the new lines, saying they're just giving consumers a choice. What do you think?

contain reusable materials, or are made of recyclable materials is consistent with a societal orientation. Duracell and Eveready battery companies have reduced the levels of mercury in their batteries and will eventually market mercury-free products. Turtle Wax car wash products and detergents are biodegradable and can be "digested" by waste treatment plants. The company's plastic containers are made of recyclable plastic, and its spray products do not use propellants that damage the ozone layer in the earth's upper atmosphere. The "Ethics in Marketing" story below illustrates a potential conflict between a market orientation and a societal orientation.

Implementation of the Marketing Concept

3

Explain how firms implement the marketing concept

In an established organization, changing to a customer-driven corporate culture must occur gradually. Furthermore, middle managers alone cannot effect a change in corporate culture; they must have the total support of the CEO and other top executives. According to Thomas J. Pritzker, president of Hyatt Hotels, the notion that a customer orientation can just be turned on is a fallacy: "Management has to set a tone and then constantly push, push, push."[11]

The success of Nordstrom, the Seattle-based retailer, illustrates the results of strong management support for customer-oriented service. Employees can do almost anything to satisfy shoppers. One story, which the company doesn't deny, tells of a customer who got his money back on a tire, even though Nordstrom doesn't sell tires. In 1993, Nordstrom received the highest overall customer satisfaction rating from 2,000 shoppers who participated in a study ranking 70 U.S. retail and department store chains on attributes such as price, convenience, and quality of

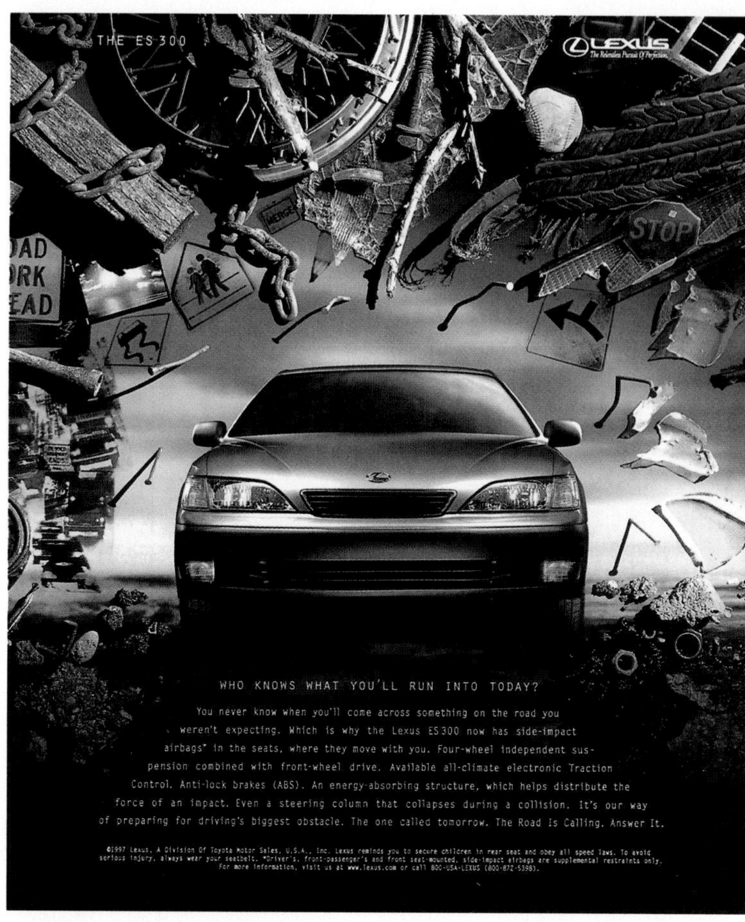

THE ES 300
LEXUS
The Relentless Pursuit Of Perfection.
STOP
WHO KNOWS WHAT YOU'LL RUN INTO TODAY?
You never know when you'll come across something on the road you weren't expecting. Which is why the Lexus ES300 now has side-impact airbags* in the seats, where they move with you. Four-wheel independent suspension combined with front-wheel drive. Available all-climate electronic Traction Control. Anti-lock brakes (ABS). An energy-absorbing structure, which helps distribute the force of an impact. Even a steering column that collapses during a collision. It's our way of preparing for driving's biggest obstacle. The one called tomorrow. The Road Is Calling. Answer It.
©1997 Lexus, A Division Of Toyota Motor Sales, U.S.A., Inc. Lexus reminds you to secure children in rear seat and obey all speed laws. To avoid serious injury, always wear your seatbelt. *Driver's, front-passenger's and front seat-mounted, side-impact airbags are supplemental restraints only. For more information, visit us at www.lexus.com or call 800-USA-LEXUS (800-872-5398).

Creating customer value is the linchpin to successful marketing, but because value is determined by the customer's perception alone, it can be difficult to quantify. Do you think this Lexus ad captures the quality image that the luxury car manufacturer wants to convey? Courtesy Lexus. Photography by Hans Neleman.

offerings.[12] Nordstrom, like many other successful marketers, understands that key issues in developing competitive advantage today include creating customer value, maintaining customer satisfaction, and building long-term relationships.

Customer Value **Customer value** is the ratio of benefits to the sacrifice necessary to obtain those benefits. As the "Global Perspectives" box in this section illustrates, the customer determines the value of both the benefits and the sacrifices.

customer value
The ratio of benefits to the sacrifice necessary to obtain those benefits.

The automobile industry also illustrates the importance of creating customer value. To penetrate the fiercely competitive luxury automobile market, Lexus adopted a customer-driven approach, with particular emphasis on service. Lexus stresses product quality with a standard of zero defects in manufacturing. The service quality goal is to treat each customer as one would treat a guest in one's home, to pursue the perfect person-to-person relationship, and to strive to improve continually. This pursuit has enabled Lexus to establish a clear quality image and capture a significant share of the luxury car market.

Customer value is not simply a matter of high quality. A high-quality product that is available only at a high price will not be perceived as a good value, nor will bare-bones service or low-quality goods selling for a low price. Instead, customers value goods and services of the quality they expect and that are sold at prices they are willing to pay. Value can be used to sell a $44,000 Nissan Infiniti Q45 as well as a $3 Tyson frozen chicken dinner.

Marketers interested in customer value

- *Offer products that perform:* This is the bare minimum requirement. Consumers have lost patience with shoddy merchandise.
- *Give consumers more than they expect:* Soon after Toyota launched Lexus, the company had to order a recall. The weekend before the recall, dealers telephoned all the Lexus owners in the United States, personally making arrangements to pick up their cars and offering replacement vehicles.
- *Avoid unrealistic pricing:* Consumers couldn't understand why Kellogg's cereals commanded a premium over other brands, so Kellogg's market share fell 5 percent in the late 1980s.
- *Give the buyer facts:* Today's sophisticated consumer wants informative advertising and knowledgeable salespeople.
- *Offer organizationwide commitment in service and after-sales support:* People fly Southwest Airlines because the airline offers superior value. Although passengers do not get assigned seats or meals (just peanuts or crackers) when they use the airline, its service is reliable and friendly and costs less than most major airlines. All Southwest employees are involved in the effort to satisfy customers. Pilots tend to the boarding gate when their help is needed and ticket agents help move luggage. One reservation agent flew from Dallas to Tulsa with a frail, elderly woman whose son was afraid she couldn't handle the change of planes by herself on her way to St. Louis.

global perspectives

The Customer, Not the Seller, Defines Value

Unlike some American industries that have trouble breaking into Japan's market, the mail-order catalog industry has been quite successful. Japanese shoppers are buying everything from L.L. Bean sportswear to Saks Fifth Avenue women's fashions.

These retailers are succeeding while other American businesses are still struggling because the merchants have found a market where Japanese companies are not fulfilling customer needs. Many middle- and upper-class consumers, especially the younger generation and city dwellers, have avoided Japanese catalogs for decades because of their hodgepodge mix of everything from cheap dresses and necklaces to diapers and dog food. By contrast, American catalogs offer high-quality merchandise carefully aimed at specific groups. And they often contain two other items unusual in Japan: a lifetime, no-questions-asked guarantee and pictures of top models. Clothing with recognized U.S. labels also sells for much less in the catalogs than do well-known Japanese fashions in Japan's expensive department stores. In addition, more and more of the catalogs are being translated into Japanese to make their use easier.

Miho Takauji, an upper-middle-class working woman who has been hooked on such foreign catalogs for a few years, is representative of the new wave of Japanese consumers. She often looks through them at her home in Tokyo and orders clothing for herself and her husband. " 'In Japan, it's almost impossible to find anything good quality at a reasonable price,' Takariji said. 'What I find in Japanese catalogs is cheap, but it looks cheap, too.' "[13]

Explain how American mail-order catalog firms are creating customer value in Japan.

Customer Satisfaction **Customer satisfaction** is the feeling that a product has met or exceeded the customer's expectations. Keeping current customers satisfied is just as important as attracting new ones and a lot less expensive. Firms that have a reputation for delivering high levels of customer satisfaction do things differently from their competitors. Top management is obsessed with customer satisfaction and employees throughout the organization understand the link between their job and satisfied customers. The culture of the organization is to focus on delighting customers rather than on selling products.

Staples, the office supply retailer, offers great prices on its paper, pens, fax machines, and other office supplies, but its main strategy is to grow by providing customers with the best solutions to their problems. Their approach is to emulate customer-intimate companies like Home Depot and Airborne Express. These companies do not pursue one-time transactions: They cultivate relationships.

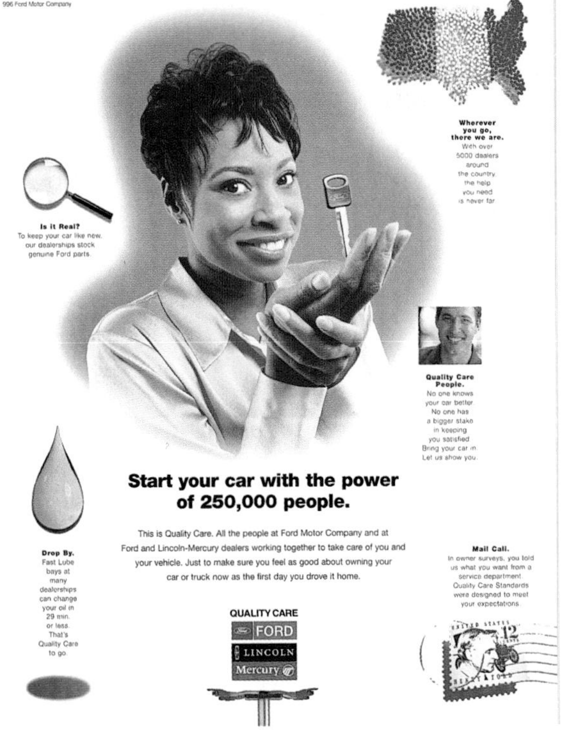

Ford Motor Company, through its "Quality Care" advertising, focuses on customer needs. Technical superiority cannot guarantee success unless customers are satisfied.
Courtesy Ford Motor Company

Building Relationships **Relationship marketing** is the name of a strategy that entails forging long-term partnerships with customers. Companies build relationships with customers by offering value and providing customer satisfaction. Companies benefit from repeat sales and referrals that lead to increases in sales, market share, and profits. Costs fall because serving existing customers is less expensive than attracting new ones. Keeping a customer costs about one-fourth of what it costs to attract a new customer; and the probability of retaining a customer is over 60 percent, whereas the probability of landing a new customer is less than 30 percent.[14]

Volvo

How does Volvo use its Web site to maintain customer relations? Do you think Volvo has a sales or a market orientation? What evidence do you have to support your conclusion?
http://www.volvocars.com/

customer satisfaction
The feeling that a product has met or exceeded the customer's expectations.

relationship marketing
The name of a strategy that entails forging long-term partnerships with customers.

Cable and Wireless Communications, a long-distance carrier, has generated loyal business clients by providing the best customer support in the telecommunications industry. Cable and Wireless also provides direct sales consultation that gives salespeople intimate knowledge of what makes its customers successful, allowing product customization.[15]

ON LINE The Internet is an effective tool for generating relationships with customers because of its ability to interact with the customer. With the Internet, companies can use e-mail for fast customer service, discussion groups for building a sense of community, and database tracking of buying habits for customizing products.[16]

Customers also benefit from stable relationships with suppliers. Business buyers have found that partnerships with their suppliers are essential to producing high-quality products while cutting costs.[17] Customers remain loyal to firms that provide them greater value and satisfaction than they expect from competing firms. This value and satisfaction can come in a variety of forms ranging from financial benefits to a sense of well-being or confidence in a supplier to structural bonds.[18]

Frequent flyer programs encourage customers to become loyal to specific airlines and rewards them for their continuing patronage.
© Terry Vine/Tony Stone Images

Frequent flyer programs are an example of financial incentives to customers in exchange for their continuing patronage. After flying a certain number of miles or flying a specified number of times, the frequent flyer program participant earns a free flight or some other award such as free lodging. Frequent flyer programs encourage customers to become loyal to specific airlines and reward them for this behavior.

A sense of well-being occurs when a customer establishes an ongoing relationship with a provider such as a physician, a bank, a hairdresser, or an accountant. The social bonding that takes place between provider and customer involves personalization and customization of the relationship. Firms can enhance these bonds by referring to customers by name and providing continuity of service through the same representative.

The FedEx Powership program, which installs computer terminals in the offices of its customers, is an example of structural bonding. FedEx Powership comprises a series of automated shipping, tracking, and invoicing systems that save customers time and money while solidifying their loyalty to FedEx. The systems are scaled to customers' usage. Customers receive a free microcomputer terminal with fully functional software, modem, bar-code scanner, and report printer. FedEx Powership rates packages with the correct freight charges, combines package weights by destination to provide volume discounts for intra-U.S. shipments, and prints address labels from the customer's own database. Users can automatically prepare their own invoices, analyze their shipping expenses, and track their packages through the FedEx® system.[19]

Most successful relationship marketing strategies depend on customer-oriented personnel, effective training programs, employees with authority to make decisions and solve problems, and teamwork. The "Entrepreneurial Insights" box in this section offers several relationship tips for small local firms to use in competing with large national or international marketers.

Customer-Oriented Personnel For an organization to be focused on building relationships with customers, employees' attitudes and actions must be customer oriented. An employee may be the only contact a particular customer has with the firm. In that customer's eyes, the employee is the firm. Any person, department, or division that is not customer oriented weakens the positive image of the entire organization. For example, a potential customer who is greeted discourteously may well assume that the employee's attitude represents the whole firm.

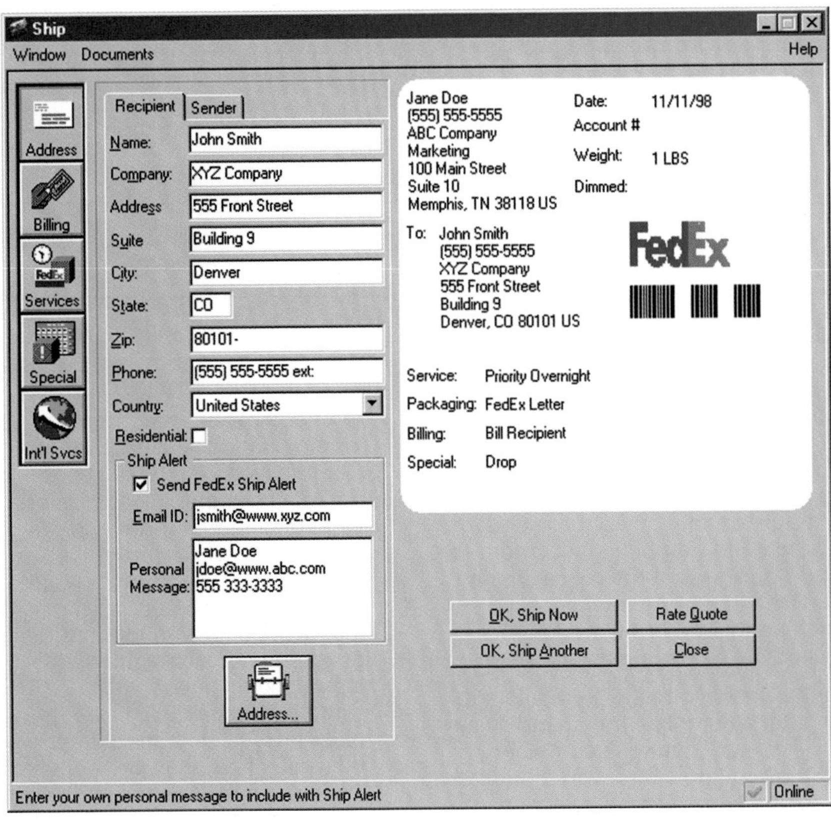

Through its Powership program, FedEx installs computer terminals in its customers' offices. This relationship marketing strategy is an example of structural bonding.

The Role of Training Leading marketers recognize the role of employee training in customer service and relationship building. For example, all new employees at Disneyland and Walt Disney World must attend Disney University, a special training program for Disney employees. They must first pass Traditions 1, a day-long course focusing on the Disney philosophy and operational procedures. Then they go on to specialized training. Similarly, McDonald's has Hamburger University. At American Express's Quality University, line employees and managers learn how to treat customers. There is an extra payoff for companies such as Disney and McDonald's that train their employees to be customer oriented. When employees make their customers happy, the employees are more likely to derive satisfaction from their jobs. Having contented workers who are committed to their jobs leads to better customer service and greater employee retention.

Empowerment In addition to training, many marketing-oriented firms are giving employees more authority to solve customer problems on the spot. The term used to describe this delegation of authority is **empowerment**. Federal Express's customer service representatives are trained and empowered to resolve customer problems. Although the average Federal Express transaction costs only $16, the customer service representatives are empowered to spend up to $100 to resolve a customer problem.

empowerment
Delegation of authority to solve customers' problems quickly—usually by the first person that the customer notifies regarding a problem.

Employees of Satisfaction Guaranteed Eateries, Inc., a highly successful restaurant chain whose motto is synonymous with its name, have wide authority to please customers. Founder and CEO Timothy Firnstal states: "I instituted the idea that employees could and should do anything to keep the customer happy. In the event of an error or delay, any employee, right down to the busboy, could provide complimentary wine or desserts, or pick up the entire tab, if necessary."[20]

Empowerment gives customers the feeling that their concerns are being addressed and gives employees the feeling that their expertise matters. The result is greater satisfaction for both customers and employees.

Teamwork Many organizations, such as Southwest Airlines and Walt Disney World, that are frequently noted for delivering superior customer value and providing high levels of customer satisfaction assign employees to teams and teach them team-building skills. **Teamwork** entails collaborative efforts of people to accomplish common objectives. Job performance, company performance, product value, and customer satisfaction all improve when people in the same department or work group begin supporting and assisting each other and emphasize cooperation instead of competition. Performance is also enhanced when people in different areas of responsibility such as production and sales or sales and service practice teamwork, with the ultimate goal of delivering superior customer value and satisfaction.

teamwork
Collaborative efforts of people to accomplish common objectives.

Disney

Disney training stretches beyond the bounds of its own organizational structures. Visit the Disney site listed below. Click on "Disney Difference." What are the major themes of these programs? View a sample agenda to find out. What does this tell you about Disney's business philosophy?
http://www.disney.com/DisneyWorld/DisneyInstitute/ProfessionalPrograms/

entrepreneurial insights

David Versus Goliath

The scenario is familiar, and much lamented this last quarter century: The big, heartless Wal-Mart or Target megastore moves in just outside of town, offering everything under the sun and trampling local mom-and-pop shops in the process. How can mom-and-pop retailers save their stores? A recent study produced the following seven tips:

1. Work with other local retailers to offer a complete merchandise selection. Consumers complained they couldn't find everything they needed on "Main Street," so they had to travel to shop.
2. Build strong customer relationships. Local retailers should think back to the days when salesclerks knew the name of every customer who walked in the door and try to build that kind of personal bond to offer a benefit that the large, impersonal store can't provide.
3. Get involved with local events and government. Local retailers should identify strongly and overtly with the communities they serve. This might include sponsoring local sports teams and breakfasts with industry and government leaders and helping local schools raise funds.
4. Update merchandise more frequently. If local retailers improve their selection, they can convince consumers the best products can be found close to home. They can even charge higher prices because consumers will be willing to pay them for the convenience.
5. Train your sales force so they understand their importance in delivering customer satisfaction.
6. Conduct formal customer research. Distribute customer satisfaction cards in stores with questions regarding service, merchandise selection, and store appearance. This may help spot problems before they drive customers away.
7. On the other hand, don't be afraid to send customers away. Use the *Miracle on 34th Street* approach if your business does not carry an item requested by a customer: Suggesting another local store will build trust and keep customers shopping in town.[21]

The Marketing Process

4

Describe the marketing process and identify the variables that make up the marketing mix

Earlier in this chapter, *marketing* was defined as the process of planning and executing the conception, pricing, promotion, and distribution of ideas, goods, and services to create exchanges that satisfy individual and organizational objectives. Marketing, therefore, includes the following activities:

- Gathering, analyzing, and interpreting information about the environment (environmental scanning).
- Understanding the organization's mission and the role marketing plays in fulfilling this vision.
- Finding out what benefits people want the organization to deliver and what wants they want the organization to satisfy (market opportunity analysis).
- Developing a marketing strategy by deciding exactly which wants, and whose wants, the organization will try to satisfy (target market strategy); by setting marketing objectives; and by developing appropriate marketing activities (the marketing mix) to satisfy the desires of selected target markets.
- Implementing the strategy.
- Periodically evaluating marketing efforts and making changes if needed.

These activities and their relationships, shown in Exhibit 1.1, form the foundation on which most of the rest of this book is based.

Environmental Scanning

Environmental scanning is the collection and interpretation of information about forces, events, and relationships that may affect the organization. It helps identify market opportunities and threats and provides guidelines for the marketing strategy.

environmental scanning
The collection and interpretation of information about forces, events, and relationships that may affect the future of an organization.

Chapter 2 examines the following six categories of uncontrollable environmental influences that affect marketing decisions:

- *Social forces* such as the values of potential customers and the changing roles of families and women working outside the home.
- *Demographic forces* such as the ages, birth and death rates, and locations of various groups of people.
- *Economic forces* such as changing incomes, inflation, and recession.
- *Technological forces* such as advanced communications and data retrieval capabilities.
- *Political and legal forces* such as changes in laws and regulatory agency activities.
- *Competitive forces* from domestic and foreign-based firms.

exhibit 1.1

The Marketing Process

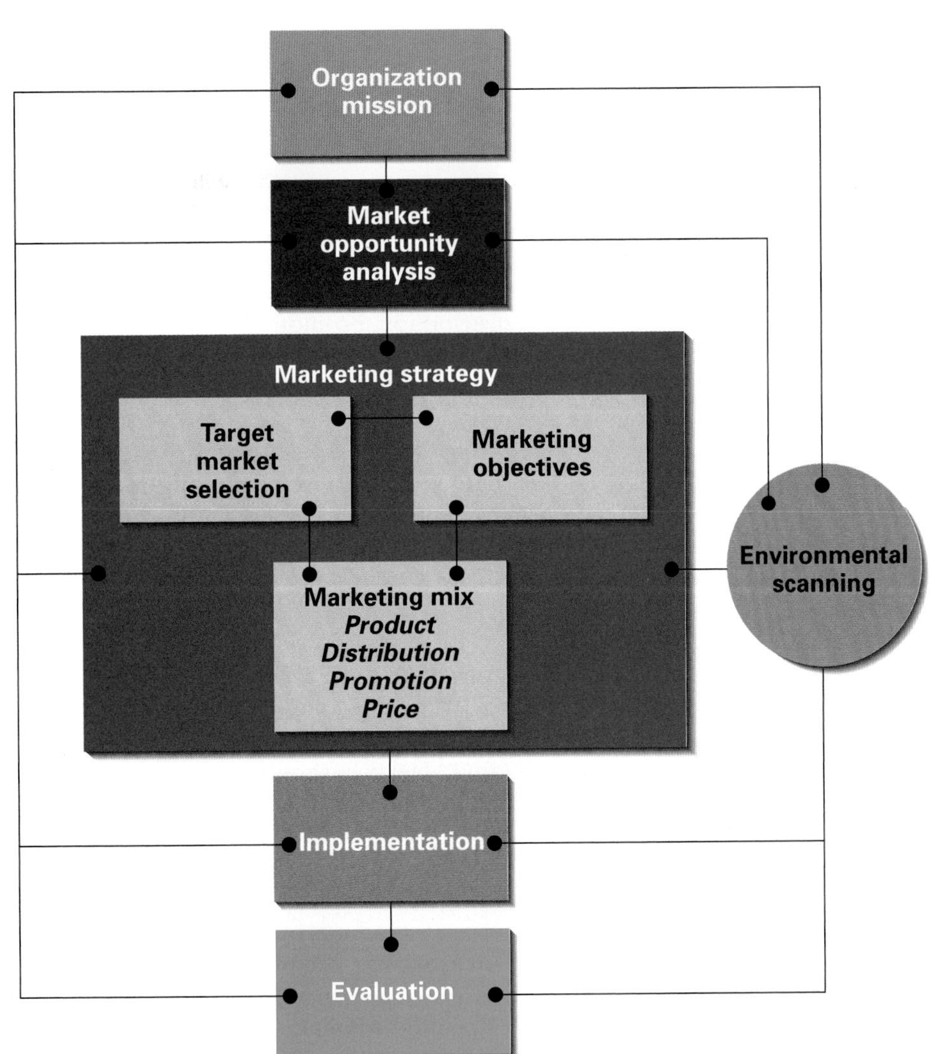

on line

Cincinnati Milacron

Cincinnati Milacron is a market leader in the machine tool industry. Evaluate its mission ("Vision and Values") as it is posted on its Web site. Based on what you learn "About Milacron," how well do you think this mission focuses on its markets? Why?

http://www.milacron.com/

Organization Mission

One of top management's most important responsibilities is to formulate the organization's basic statements of purpose and mission. An organization's mission statement answers the question, "What is this firm's business?" Mission statements are based on a careful analysis of the benefits sought by present and potential customers, as well as existing and anticipated environmental conditions. This long-term vision of what the organization is or is striving to become establishes the boundaries within which objectives, strategies, and actions must be developed.

Market Opportunity Analysis

market opportunity analysis
Description and estimation of the size and sales potential of market segments of interest to a firm and assessment of key competitors in these market segments.

A market segment is a group of individuals or organizations that shares one or more characteristics. It therefore has relatively similar product needs. A **market opportunity analysis** describes market segments of interest to the firm, estimates their size and sales potential, and assesses key competitors in these market segments.

Marketing Strategy

marketing strategy
Plan that involves selecting one or more target markets, setting marketing objectives, and developing and maintaining a marketing mix that will produce mutually satisfying exchanges with target markets.

marketing mix
Unique blend of product, distribution, promotion, and pricing strategies designed to produce mutually satisfying exchanges with a target market.

As Exhibit 1.1 illustrates, **marketing strategy** involves three activities: selecting one or more target markets, setting marketing objectives, and developing and maintaining a **marketing mix** (product, distribution, promotion, and pricing) that will produce mutually satisfying exchanges with target markets.

Target Market Strategy

The three general strategies for selecting target markets are to try to appeal to the entire market with a single marketing mix, to concentrate on only one segment of the market, or to attempt to appeal to multiple market segments using multiple marketing mixes. The characteristics, advantages, and disadvantages of each strategic option are examined in Chapter 6.

Marketing Objectives

marketing objective
Statement of what is to be accomplished through marketing activities.

A **marketing objective** is a statement of what is to be accomplished through marketing activities—for example, getting 100 people to test-drive a new car during the month of November or getting 2,000 passengers to fly on a new commuter airline during the first week in June. Marketing objectives should be consistent with organizational objectives, should be measurable, and should specify the timeframe during which they are to be achieved.

Carefully specifying marketing objectives offers two major benefits. First, when the objectives are attainable and challenging, they motivate those charged with achieving the objectives. They also serve as standards by which everyone in the organization can gauge their performance. Second, the process of writing specific marketing objectives forces executives to sharpen and clarify their thinking. Written objectives also allow marketing efforts to be integrated and pointed in a consistent direction.

Marketing Mix

As noted earlier, the term *marketing mix* refers to a unique blend of product, distribution (place), promotion, and pricing strategies (the **four Ps**) designed to produce mutually satisfying exchanges with a target market. The marketing manager can control each component of the marketing mix, but the strategies for all four components must be blended to achieve optimal results. Any mix is only as good as its weakest component. For example, an excellent product with a poor distribution system will likely fail.

four Ps
Product decisions, distribution (or place) decisions, promotion decisions, and pricing decisions, which together make up the marketing mix.

Successful marketing mixes have been carefully tailored to satisfy target markets. At first glance, McDonald's and Wendy's may appear to have roughly identical marketing mixes. After all, they are both in the fast-food business. However, McDonald's targets parents with young children. It has Ronald McDonald, special children's Happy Meals, and playgrounds. Wendy's generally targets the adult crowd. Wendy's doesn't have a playground, but it does have carpeting (for a more adult atmosphere), and it pioneered fast-food salad bars.

Variations in marketing mixes do not occur by chance. They represent fundamental marketing strategies devised by astute marketing managers attempting to gain advantages over competitors and to achieve competitive success.

Product Strategies

Typically, the marketing mix begins with the product offering. It is hard to devise a distribution system or set a price without knowing the product to be marketed. Thus, the heart of the marketing mix is a firm's product offerings.

Marketers view products in a much larger context than you might imagine. A product includes not only the physical unit but also many other factors, including the package, warranty, service subsequent to sale, and brand and company image. The names Yves St. Laurent and Gucci, for example, create additional value for everything from cosmetics to bath towels. We buy things not only for what they do but also for what they mean to us.

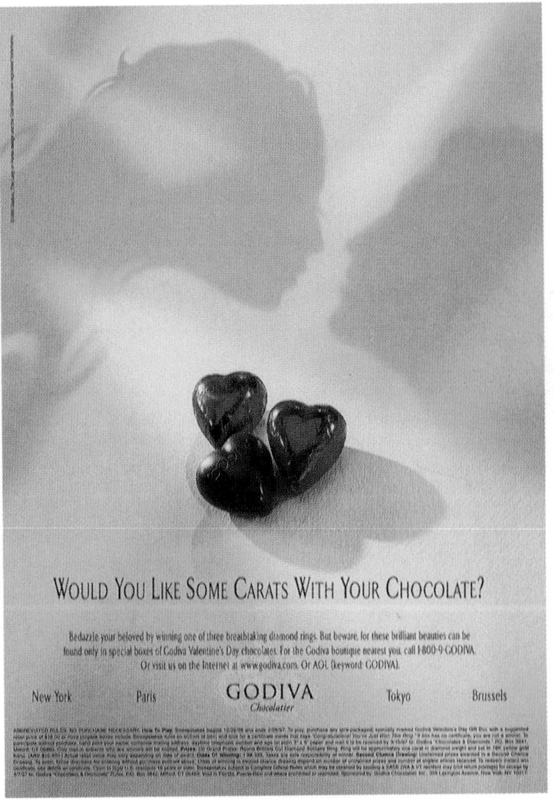

A Godiva chocolate has many product elements; the chocolate itself, a fancy gold wrapper, a customer satisfaction guarantee, and a prestigious brand name.
Courtesy Godiva Chocolatier, Inc.

Distribution (Place) Strategies

Distribution strategies are concerned with making products available when and where customers want them. Wholesalers and retailers assist manufacturers in distributing products to end users. Physical distribution consists of all business activities concerned with storing and transporting products so that they arrive in usable condition at designated places when needed. Physical distribution is also part of distribution strategy.

Promotion Strategies

Promotion includes personal selling, advertising, sales promotion, and public relations. Its role is to help bring about mutually satisfying exchanges with target markets by informing, educating, persuading, and reminding them about the benefits of an organization or a product. A good promotion strategy can sometimes dramatically increase a firm's sales. Each element of promotion is coordinated and managed with the others to create a promotional blend or mix.

Pricing Strategies

Price, what a buyer must give up to obtain a product, is the most flexible of the four components of the marketing mix. Marketers can raise or lower prices more

on line

Godiva

How does Godiva's Web site communicate its product strategy? What features are you surprised to see on this site?

http://www.godiva.com/

frequently than they can change any other marketing mix variable. Thus price is an important competitive weapon.

Implementation

implementation
Phase of the marketing process in which marketers turn their plans into action assignments and ensure that these assignments are executed in a way that will accomplish the marketing plans' objectives.

Implementation is the process that turns marketing plans into action assignments and ensures that these assignments are executed in a way that accomplishes the plans' objectives. Although implementation is essentially "doing what you said you were going to do," many organizations repeatedly experience failures in strategy implementation. Brilliant marketing strategies are doomed to fail if they are not properly implemented.

Evaluation

evaluation
Phase of the marketing process in which marketers gauge the extent to which objectives have been acheived during a specified time period.

Evaluation entails gauging the extent to which marketing objectives have been achieved during a specified time period. Four common reasons for failing to achieve a marketing objective are unrealistic marketing objectives, inappropriate marketing strategy, poor implementation, and changes in the environment after the objective was specified and the strategy was implemented.

Why Study Marketing?

5
Describe several reasons for studying marketing

Now that you understand the meaning of the term *marketing,* why it is important to adopt a marketing orientation, and how organizations implement this philosophy, you may be asking, "What's in it for me?" or "Why should I study marketing?" These are important questions, whether you are majoring in a business field other than marketing (such as accounting, finance, or management information systems) or a nonbusiness field (such as journalism, economics, or agriculture). There are several important reasons to study marketing: Marketing plays an important role in society, marketing is important to businesses, marketing offers outstanding career opportunities, and marketing affects your life every day.

Marketing Plays an Important Role in Society

The U.S. Bureau of the Census predicts that the total population of the United States will reach 268 million by the end of the 1990s. Think about how many transactions are needed each day to feed, clothe, and shelter a population of this size. The number is huge. And yet it all works quite well, partly because the well-developed U.S. economic system efficiently distributes the output of farms and factories. A typical U.S. family, for example, consumes 2.5 tons of food a year. Marketing makes food available when we want it, in desired quantities, at accessible locations, and in sanitary and convenient packages and forms (such as instant and frozen foods).

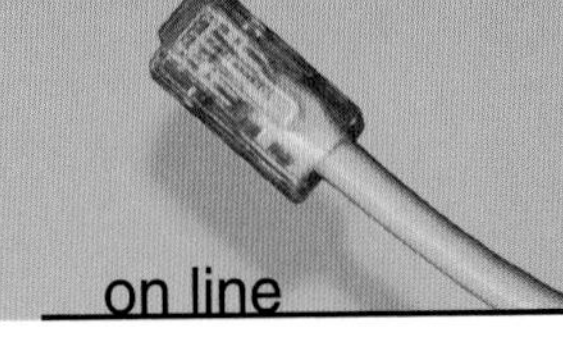

U.S. Census Bureau
How might you use the Census Bureau's WWW site to analyze a specific market segment?
http://www.census.gov/
on line

Marketing Is Important to Businesses

The fundamental objectives of most businesses are survival, profits, and growth. Marketing contributes directly to achieving these objectives. Marketing includes the following activities, which are vital to business organizations: assessing the wants and satisfactions of present and potential customers, designing and managing product offerings, determining prices and pricing policies, developing distribution strategies, and communicating with present and potential customers.

All businesspeople, regardless of specialization or area of responsibility, need to be familiar with the terminology and fundamentals of accounting, finance, management, and marketing. People in all business areas need to be able to communicate with specialists in other areas. Furthermore, marketing is not just a job done by people in a marketing department. Marketing is a part of the job of everyone in the organization. As David Packard of Hewlett-Packard put it: "Marketing is too important to be left to the marketing department."[22] Therefore, a basic understanding of marketing is important to all businesspeople.

THE HADLEY SCHOOL FOR THE BLIND

Celebrating Lifelong Learning

For more than 75 years, Hadley has been helping blind and visually impaired people reach for the future with confidence. Hadley opens a world of opportunity to over 11,000 students in the United States and 70 foreign countries each year by offering home-study courses completely free of charge.

Founded in 1920, Hadley is the single largest worldwide educator of blind and visually impaired people. Hadley's commitment to lifelong learning is evident by its broad range of courses, available in braille, large print, and on audiocassette.

The curriculum gives students the tools they need to be confident and independent at every stage of life. Students can select from more than 90 courses in six core course areas.

Since Hadley operates without state or federal funding and does not charge tuition, it relies on support from individuals. For more information on making a contribution, bequest, or other planned gift, please call the Development Department, The Hadley School for the Blind, toll free, 800-323-4238. In Illinois, call 847-446-8111.

THE HADLEY SCHOOL FOR THE BLIND
700 Elm Street, Winnetka, IL 60093

Not-for-profit organizations also perform marketing activities and so provide career opportunities in marketing. The Hadley School for the Blind used this ad to solicit donations to support its extensive curriculum.
Courtesy The Hadley School for the Blind

Marketing Offers Outstanding Career Opportunities

Between a fourth and a third of the entire civilian workforce in the United States performs marketing activities. Marketing offers great career opportunities in such areas as professional selling, marketing research, advertising, retail buying, distribution management, product management, product development, and wholesaling. Marketing career opportunities also exist in a variety of nonbusiness organizations, including hospitals, museums, universities, the armed forces, and various government and social service agencies.

As the world marketplace becomes more challenging, U.S. companies of all sizes are going to have to become better marketers. A recent survey of 160 companies by the search firm Korn Ferry International revealed that the fastest route up the corporate ladder is through marketing.[23]

The Careers in Marketing appendix at the end of this book provides additional information regarding career opportunities. Also, visit our Web site at **lamb.swcollege.com** for more career information and tools.

Marketing Affects Your Life Every Day

Marketing plays a major role in your everyday life. You participate in the marketing process as a consumer of goods and services. About half of every dollar you spend pays for marketing costs, such as marketing research, product development, packaging, transportation, storage, advertising, and sales expenses. By developing a better understanding of marketing, you will become a better-informed consumer. You will better understand the buying process and be able to negotiate more effectively with sellers. Moreover, you will be better prepared to demand satisfaction when the goods and services you buy do not meet the standards promised by the manufacturer or the marketer.

LOOKING BACK

Look back at the story at the beginning of this chapter about Tom Kasten. You should now find the questions at the end of the story to be simple and straightforward. Tom Kasten is clearly market oriented. His informal research focuses on identifying customer wants and, it's to be hoped, converting this information into want-satisfying new products before his competitors identify emerging trends.

If Levi Strauss is able to create more customer value than its competitors, customers will be satisfied with its product and remain loyal customers. As noted in the chapter, there is no reason why customers should buy one organization's offerings unless they in some way serve the customers' wants and needs better than those offered by competing organizations. Loyal customers who repeat purchase increase sales and profits for the seller.

SUMMARY

1 Define the term *marketing*. The ultimate goal of all marketing activity is to facilitate mutually satisfying exchanges between parties. The activities of marketing include the conception, pricing, promotion, and distribution of ideas, goods, and services.

2 Describe four marketing management philosophies. The role of marketing and the character of marketing activities within an organization are strongly influenced by its philosophy and orientation. A production-oriented organization focuses on the internal capabilities of the firm rather than on the desires and needs of the marketplace. A sales orientation is based on the beliefs that people will buy more products if aggressive sales techniques are used and that high sales volumes produce high profits. A market-oriented organization focuses on satisfying customer wants and needs while meeting organizational objectives. A societal market orientation goes beyond a market orientation to include the preservation or enhancement of individuals' and society's long-term best interests.

3 Explain how firms implement the marketing concept. To implement the marketing concept successfully, management must enthusiastically embrace and endorse the concept and encourage its spread throughout the organization. Changing from a production or sales orientation to a marketing orientation often requires changes in authority and responsibility as well as front-line experience for management.

4 Describe the marketing process and identify the variables that make up the marketing mix. The marketing process includes scanning the environment, analyzing market oppprtunities, setting marketing objectives, selecting a target market strategy, developing and implementing a marketing mix, implementing the strategy, and evaluating marketing efforts and making changes if needed. The marketing mix combines product, distribution (place), promotion, and pricing strategies (the four Ps) in a way that creates exchanges satisfying to individual and organizational objectives.

5 Describe several reasons for studying marketing. First, marketing affects the allocation of goods and services that influence a nation's economy and standard of living. Second, an understanding of marketing is crucial to understanding most businesses. Third, career opportunities in marketing are diverse and profitable and are expected to increase significantly during the next decades. Fourth, understanding marketing makes consumers more informed.

Key Terms

Discussion and Writing Questions

1. WRITING Your company president has decided to restructure the firm and become more market oriented. She is going to announce the changes at an upcoming meeting. She has asked you to prepare a short speech outlining the general reasons for the new company orientation.

2. Donald E. Petersen, chairman of the board of Ford Motor Company, remarked, "If we aren't customer driven, our cars won't be either." Explain how this statement reflects the marketing concept.
3. WRITING A friend of yours agrees with the adage "People don't know what they want—they only want what they know." Write your friend a letter expressing the extent to which you think marketers shape consumer wants.
4. WRITING Your local supermarket's slogan is "It's your store." However, when you asked one of the stock people to help you find a bag of chips, he told you it was not his job and that you should look a little harder. On your way out, you noticed a sign with an address for complaints. Draft a letter explaining why the supermarket's slogan will never be credible unless their employees carry it out.
5. Give an example of a company that might be successfully following a production orientation. Why might a firm in this industry be successful following such an orientation?
6. WRITING Write a letter to a friend or family member explaining why you think that a course in marketing will help you in your career in some field other than marketing.
7. ON LINE TEAM Form a small group of three or four members. Suppose you and your colleagues all work for an up-and-coming gourmet coffee company that has several stores, mostly in large cities across the United States. Your team has been assigned the task of assessing whether or not the company should begin marketing on the Internet.

   Each member has been assigned to visit three or four Internet sites for ideas. Some possibilities are

   Toys 'R' Us at **http://www.toysrus.com**
   Wal-Mart at **http://www.wal-mart.com**
   Godiva chocolates at **http://www.godiva.com**
   Levi Strauss at **http://www.levi.com**

   Use your imagination and look up others. As you can see, many companies are easy to find, as long as you can spell their names. Typically, you would use the following: **http://www.companyname.com**

   Has Internet marketing helped the companies whose sites you visited? If so, how? What factors should your company consider before committing to Internet activity? Prepare a three- to five-minute presentation to give to your class.
8. ON LINE What is the AMA? What does it do? How do its services benefit marketers? **http://www.ama.org/**
9. ON LINE What is an ExciteSeeing Tour? What kind of business tours does this site offer? **http://tours.excite.com/**

Application for Small Business

ENTREPRENEUR Lisa King enjoyed working as a camp counselor during the summer. She started about the time she entered high school and continued through college. She even took a job at a camp the summer after graduating from college. She rationalized that this "internship," developing the camp yearbook, would help prepare her for a job in advertising.

As the summer passed by, Lisa spent more time thinking about "what she was going to do when she grew up," as she liked to put it. Her thoughts always seemed to return to camping.

Lisa finally decided that she would like to open a small retail store specializing in camping supplies. The more she thought about it, the better she liked the idea.

She finally got up enough nerve to call her father, Tom, to discuss the idea. Tom's first response was, "Have you prepared a written plan?"

Lisa remembered preparing a marketing plan in her first class in marketing at the University of Miami. She asked her father to FedEx the text to her.

With financial backing from Tom, Lisa and her sister Jill opened Santorini Camping Supply the following fall. They picked the name Santorini because it was their favorite place in the Greek Isles and, as Jill put it, "We just like the name."

On the first day the store was open, a customer asked Lisa if Santorini's guaranteed the products it sold. Lisa proudly replied, "Every product that is purchased from Santorini Camping Supply has a lifetime guarantee. If at any time you are not satisfied with one of our products, you can return it to the store for a full refund or exchange."

Questions

1. What marketing management philosophy is Santorini's expressing? Why have you reached this conclusion?
2. Do you think a lifetime guarantee for this kind of product is too generous? Why or why not?
3. Do you think this policy will contribute to success or to bankruptcy?
4. Suggest other customer service policies that might be appropriate for Santorini Camping Supply.

Review Quiz

1. _______ is the process of planning and executing the conception, pricing, promotion, and distribution of ideas, goods, and services to create exchanges that satisfy individual and organizational goals.
   a. Exchange
   b. Marketing
   c. Selling
   d. Organizational focus

2. The marketing management philosophy in which the firm's focus is on its own internal capabilities rather than on the desires of the marketplace is called a
   a. Production orientation
   b. Sales orientation
   c. Market orientation
   d. Societal orientation

3. A sales orientation
   a. Helps firms to understand the needs and wants of the marketplace
   b. Focuses on customer wants and needs so the organization can distinguish its products from competitors' offerings
   c. Is based on the idea that people will buy more goods and services if aggressive sales techniques are used
   d. Proves that companies can convince people to buy goods and services that they neither want nor need

4. A manager states to the firm's shareholders: "We are in the business of maximizing perceived value for our customers." What marketing management philosophy is this firm practicing?
   a. A production orientation
   b. A sales orientation
   c. A market orientation
   d. A societal orientation

5. Which of the following marketing management philosophies is described by phrases such as "interfunctional coordination," "delivery of superior value," and "competitor intelligence"?
   a. A production orientation
   b. A sales orientation
   c. A market orientation
   d. A societal orientation
6. Customer value is
   a. The ratio of benefits to the sacrifice needed to obtain those benefits
   b. The outcome of most transactions for firms using a sales orientation
   c. The number of items sold that are of high quality and high cost
   d. The outcome of most transactions for firms using a production orientation
7. The key issues facing a manager whose firm is practicing a _______ are creating customer value, maintaining customer satisfaction, and building long-term relationships.
   a. Production orientation
   b. Sales orientation
   c. Simple trade orientation
   d. Market orientation
8. Many market-oriented firms are giving employees more authority to solve customer problems on the spot. This approach is called
   a. Employee-related marketing
   b. Delegation
   c. Empowerment
   d. Teamwork
9. In a sales orientation, the customer, not the seller, defines value.
   a. True
   b. False
10. The study of marketing is important in that it is something that affects most everyone's life each and every day.
    a. True
    b. False
11. To whom are products and services directed in a sales orientation versus a market orientation?

Check the Answer Key, which follows the Video Case, to see how well you understood the material.

VIDEO CASE

Lord of the Boards

Burton Snowboards, the industry leader, is the brainchild of Jake Burton, an avid rider. Jake's recipe for success is simple: "We always focused on the sport and everything else took care of itself." Burton practically invented the sport in 1977 when he first made crude snowboards in a Vermont workshop. By 1978, he had hit upon a successful formula (horizontally laminated wood) and made 300 boards with an $88 price tag. The next decade saw Jake spending time and money lobbying ski areas to open their slopes to snowboarders.

Now they are free to ride just about everywhere. Competitors noted that while they pegged snowboarding as a regional sport, Jake kept his eye on the big picture. He always had a vision. Campaigning tirelessly for snowboarding at resorts led to the creation of the U.S. Open snowboard competition. By 1994, the *Wall Street Journal* spotted the trend and called snowboarding the fastest-growing sport. And finally, the ultimate. Snowboarding made its debut in the 1998 Winter Olympics in Nagano, Japan.

Jake didn't let the Olympics go to his head. He kept his company on a clear course of product development, R&D, and lots of riding. The company provides a free season pass to Stowe ski area in Vermont and private lessons for *newbies,* new riders, so excuses for not riding are hard to find. The sport draws mainly the under-thirty crowd, with 88 percent 12 to 24 years old, 83 percent male and 17 percent female. The *Newbie* snowboarding guide gives the basics on the Burton Web site, starting with the idea that equipment and clothing can make or break the ride. First comes the choice of ride (Freestyle, Freeride, or Carving), then three riding options. Next is the choice of board produced in different lengths with different graphics. Boots and bindings are picked next, followed by clothing with the right fit. An on-snow demonstration is considered a must, so Burton posts its travel schedule on the Internet and offers free, local demonstrations and a chance to try on boots, bindings, and the whole setup on the snow. Burton also suggests taking a lesson for maximum fun and safety.

Staying close to the customer is a company hallmark. Burton Snowboards builds on a group of people to get feedback to improve both the company and the sport. Talking to pro riders, sales reps, designers, testers, and Internet users helps the company find out what the riders want. For example, when the company needs new ideas for graphics, designers fly all over the world, sit face to face, and look at what has been developed. The idea is to provide snowboard equipment to *all* people.

To do this, Burton keeps on adding to its product line. Snowboarding performance may be gender blind, but fit is not. That is why Burton manufactures gender-specific clothing and boots that are completely different for men and women in fit but are matched in performance. Years of refining the cut of women's clothing have yielded a line of fully featured gear that really works for snowboarding. Women are the fastest growing segment of riders, and while there are no specific women's boards or bindings, Burton works with their team riders to create board dimensions, flexes, and bindings that work well for smaller, lighter riders. Burton plans to offer functional gear for women, men, and riders of all sizes, abilities, and styles. And as more and more kids aged 6 to 14 get into riding, Burton is stepping up and delivering products that meet the demands of these mini-snowboarders. Sometimes kids ride first and the parents follow suit. In the process, snowboarding becomes a family passion.

The Burton strategy has paid off. Annual sales figures are now estimated at well over $150 million, and the company has 500 employees in Vermont and around the world. As the sport of snowboarding matures, many people in the snowboarding community are using the sport to make valuable social contributions that enrich lives. In 1994, Jake Burton started the Chill Program to share snowboarding with poor and at-risk kids. While it is true that heavy industry competition is out there, innovation and love of the sport still make Jake Burton Lord of the Boards.

Questions

1. Describe the exchange process at Burton.
2. How has Jake Burton's entrepreneurial philosophy made his company successful?
3. Does Burton use a sales orientation or a market orientation? Explain.
4. How does Burton Snowboards achieve customer satisfaction?

Bibliography

Reade Bailey, "Jake Burton, King of the Hill," *Ski,* February 1998, pp. 60–67.

Eric Blehm, "The Day of the Locusts," *GQ,* December 1997, pp. 186–187.

Burton Snowboards 1998 Press Kit

Burton Snowboards Web site: **http://www.burton.com/**

Answer Key

1. *Answer:* b, p. 6

   Rationale: This is the definition of marketing as given by the American Marketing Association.

2. *Answer:* a, p. 7

   Rationale: In production orientation the firm's management assesses its resources and abilities rather than the needs of the marketplace.

3. *Answer:* c, p. 7

   Rationale: The fundamental problem with the sales orientation is the lack of understanding of the needs and wants of the marketplace.

4. *Answer:* c, pp. 7–8

   Rationale: Remember what business the firm is in when practicing the marketing concept—that is, satisfaction of customer needs and wants.

5. *Answer:* c, pp. 7–8

   Rationale: Firms that adopt the market orientation focus on making the customer satisfied through delivering value. This goal is often achieved by carefully examining the internal and external environment facing the firm.

6. *Answer:* a, p. 10

   Rationale: A market orientation is based on the premise of customer value; offering benefits to the customer that are superior to those of competing goods or services.

7. *Answer:* d, pp. 10–12

   Rationale: Notice that these issues are "outward looking," which is a key attribute distinguishing a market orientation from a sales orientation.

8. *Answer:* c, p. 13

   Rationale: Empowerment is a form of delegation of authority that encourages employees to please customers in any way possible.

9. *Answer:* b, p. 7

   Rationale: This situation is true in a market orientation, not a sales orientation.

10. *Answer:* a, p. 18

    Rationale: About half of every dollar spent on goods and services goes toward marketing costs, such as marketing research, distribution, and promotion.

11. *Answer:* The product is directed toward everyone in the marketplace with a sales orientation versus specific groups of people in a market orientation. (pp. 9–10)

CHAPTER

2

LEARNING OBJECTIVES

After studying this chapter, you should be able to

1. Discuss the external environment of marketing, and explain how it affects a firm
2. Describe the social factors that affect marketing
3. Explain the importance to marketing managers of current demographic trends
4. Explain the importance to marketing managers of multiculturalism and growing ethnic markets
5. Identify consumer and marketer reactions to the state of the economy
6. Identify the impact of technology on a firm
7. Discuss the political and legal environment of marketing
8. Explain the basics of foreign and domestic competition
9. Describe the role of ethics and ethical decisions in business
10. Discuss corporate social responsibility

THE MARKETING ENVIRONMENT AND MARKETING ETHICS

New Balance, Inc., has been spending a scant $4 million a year to advertise its athletic shoes. Its best-known endorser is a marathoner named Mark Coogan, who placed forty-first in the last Olympics. Its logo is a prosaic NB, and its shoes are jumping off retailers' shelves.

While Nike, Inc., and other sneaker makers struggle to eke out gains in shoe sales, New Balance is riding a boom—specifically, the baby boom. Using an unflashy formula that includes moderate prices, links to podiatrists, and an expansive range of widths tailored to an aging population's expanding heft, the company gobbled up market share with sales of more than $560 million annually.

New Balance "is becoming the Nike of the baby-boom generation," says Mike Kormas, president of Footwear Market Insights, a research firm based in Nashville, Tennessee. Kormas, whose firm polls twenty-five thousand households every four months on footwear-purchasing preferences, states that "the average age of a Nike consumer is 25, the average age of a Reebok consumer is 33, and the average age of a New Balance consumer is 42." It's a triumph of demographics over razzle-dazzle. While industry leaders like Nike, Reebok International Ltd., and Fila Holdings SpA jump through expensive hoops to court youngsters, New Balance is quietly tracking America's changing population.

Although a youngster tends to buy more sneakers than a middle-ager, New Balance's older-age niche has some potent marketing virtues. Customers are less fickle, so the company doesn't worry as much about fashion swings. Thus, whereas competitors come out with new models about every six weeks, New Balance introduces one about every seventeen weeks. That schedule allows retailers to hold onto inventory longer without needing to discount it to free up space. With fewer models and fewer expensive updates, the company believes it can risk skimping on marketing and big-name endorsers. "You won't find a poster of Michael Jordan hanging in the bedroom of a New Balance customer," says Jim Davis, New Balance's president and chief executive. The $4 million the company spends on advertising and promotions is less than 1 percent

on line

New Balance

How does New Balance utilize its Web site to build brand identity? What clues do you see on the site that New Balance appeals to an older target market? Compare New Balance's Web site to Nike's. Which is more youth oriented? How did you reach this conclusion?

http://www.newbalanceus.com/ http://www.nike.com/

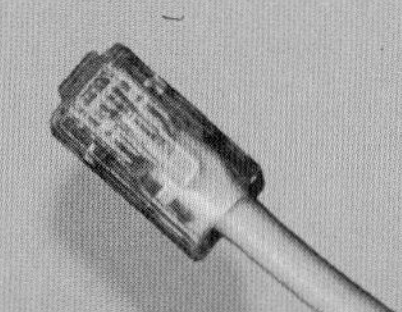

of Nike's $750 million or Reebok's $425 million.[1]

Changing demographics can pose both threats and opportunities to companies. Demographics is only one of a number of factors in the external environment that can impact a firm. Does the external environment affect the marketing mix of most companies? What other uncontrollable factors in the external environment might impact New Balance?

The External Marketing Environment

1

Discuss the external environment of marketing, and explain how it affects a firm

target market
A defined group most likely to buy a firm's product.

As you learned in Chapter 1, managers create a marketing mix by uniquely combining product, distribution, promotion, and price strategies. The marketing mix is, of course, under the firm's control and is designed to appeal to a specific group of potential buyers. A **target market** is a defined group that managers feel is most likely to buy a firm's product.

Over time, managers must alter the marketing mix because of changes in the environment in which consumers live, work, and make purchasing decisions. Also, as markets mature, some new consumers become part of the target market; others drop out. Those who remain may have different tastes, needs, incomes, lifestyles, and buying habits than the original target consumers.

Although managers can control the marketing mix, they cannot control elements in the external environment that continually mold and reshape the target market. Exhibit 2.1 shows the controllable and uncontrollable variables that affect the target market, whether it consists of consumers or business purchasers. The uncontrollable elements in the center of the diagram continually evolve and create changes in the target market. In contrast, managers can shape and reshape the marketing mix, depicted on the left side of the exhibit, to influence the target market.

Understanding the External Environment

Unless marketing managers understand the external environment, the firm cannot intelligently plan for the future. Thus, many organizations assemble a team of specialists to continually collect and evaluate environmental information, a process called environmental scanning. The goal in gathering the environmental data is to identify future market opportunities and threats.

For example, as technology continues to blur the line between personal computers, television, and compact disc players, a company like Sony may find itself competing against a company like Compaq. Research shows that children would like to find more games bundled with computer software, while adults are more likely to mention desiring various word-processing and business-related software.[2] Is this information an opportunity or a threat to Compaq marketing managers?

Environmental Management

GLOBAL

No one business is large or powerful enough to create major change in the external environment. Thus, marketing managers are basically adapters rather than agents of change. For example, despite the huge size of General Motors and Ford, these companies have only recently been able to stem the competitive push by the Japanese for an ever-growing share of the U.S.

exhibit 2.1

Effect of Uncontrollable Factors in the External Environment on the Marketing Mix

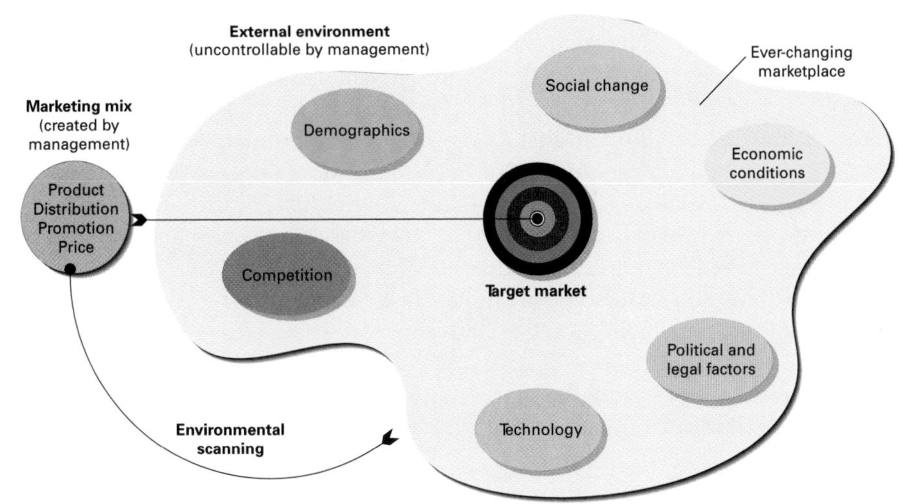

automobile market. Competition is basically an uncontrollable element in the external environment.

GLOBAL

However, a firm is not always completely at the mercy of the external environment. Sometimes a firm can influence external events. For example, extensive lobbying by Federal Express enabled it to recently acquire virtually all of the Japanese routes that it has sought. Japan had originally opposed new cargo routes for Federal Express. The favorable decision was based on months of lobbying by Federal Express at the White House, at several agencies, and in Congress for help in overcoming Japanese resistance. When a company implements strategies that attempt to shape the external environment within which it operates, it is engaging in **environmental management**.

environmental management
When a company implements strategies that attempt to shape the external environment within which it operates.

The factors within the external environment that are important to marketing managers can be classified as social, demographic, economic, technological, political and legal, and competitive.

Social Factors

2
Describe the social factors that affect marketing

Social change is perhaps the most difficult external variable for marketing managers to forecast, influence, or integrate into marketing plans. Social factors include our attitudes, values, and lifestyles. Social factors influence the products people buy, the prices paid for products, the effectiveness of specific promotions, and how, where, and when people expect to purchase products.

Marketing-Oriented Values of Today

A major change has been taking place in American culture. It is a comprehensive shift in values, world views, and ways of life. It appeals to nearly one-fourth of American adults, or forty-four million people. People who follow this new path are on the leading edge of several kinds of cultural change. They are interested in new kinds of products and services, and they often respond to advertising and marketing in unexpected ways. These people have been labeled *cultural creatives.* Cultural creatives are good at synthesizing this information into a "big picture." Their style is to scan an information source efficiently, seize on something they are interested in, and explore that topic in depth.

A second world view is that of traditionalism. It is the belief system for about 29 percent of Americans (fifty-six million adults), who might also be called *heartlanders.* In America, traditionalism often takes the form of country folks rebelling against big-city slickers. Heartlanders believe in a nostalgic image of small towns and strong churches that defines the Good Old American Ways.[3]

The third world view is modernism. It is the value set of 47 percent of Americans, or eighty-eight million adults. *Modernists* include politicians, military leaders, scientists, and intellectuals. Modernists place high value on personal success, consumerism, materialism, and technological rationality. It's valid to say that modernists see the world through the same filters as does *Time* magazine. The values of these three American subcultures are shown in Exhibit 2.2.

Today's shoppers are also environmentalists. Eight in ten U.S. consumers regard themselves as environmentalists, and half of those say they are strong ones.[4] Four out of five shoppers are willing to pay 5 percent more for products packaged with recyclable or biodegradable materials. Many marketers predict that soon it will be very hard to sell a product that isn't environmentally friendly.

In the 1990s, fewer consumers said that expensive cars, designer clothes, pleasure trips, and "gold" credit cards are necessary components of a happy life. Instead, they put value on nonmaterial accomplishments, such as having control of their lives and being able to take a day off when they want.[5] Dual-career families have a **poverty of time**, with few hours to do anything but work and commute to work, handle family situations, do housework, shop, sleep, and eat. Of the people who say they don't have enough time, only 33 percent said that they were very happy with their lives.[6]

poverty of time
Lack of time to do anything but work, commute to work, handle family situations, do housework, shop, sleep, and eat.

There's a sense that the daily slack of earlier eras—the weekday golf foursome, the bridge games and vegetable gardens, the three-martini lunches, chats across the fence, and pure, uncontrollable laughter—is fast disappearing. Work consumes a huge portion of Americans' days. Their productivity pressure is exacerbated by the explosion in two-income households: No chief operating officer manages the family—even though, with aging parents and growing children, it is an increasingly complex unit. Also, in the age of the "virtual office" (working at home with a computer and modem), it has become increasingly difficult for many professionals to separate or measure the time they spend on work or leisure. Perhaps, however, the 7 percent annual growth in home-based self-employment is a backlash against the lack of quality family time.[7]

The Growth of Component Lifestyles

People in the United States today are piecing together **component lifestyles**. A lifestyle is a mode of living; it is the way people decide to live their lives. In other words, they are choosing products and services that meet diverse needs and interests rather than conforming to traditional stereotypes.

component lifestyles
Practice of choosing goods and services that meet one's diverse needs and interests rather than conforming to a single, traditional lifestyle.

In the past, a person's profession—for instance, banker—defined his or her lifestyle. Today a person can be a banker and also a gourmet, fitness enthusiast, dedicated single parent, and Internet guru. Each of these lifestyles is associated with different goods and services and represents a target audience. For example, for the gourmet, marketers offer cooking utensils, wines, and exotic foods through magazines like *Bon Appetit* and *Gourmet.* The fitness enthusiast buys Adidas equipment and special jogging outfits and reads *Runner* magazine. Component lifestyles increase the complexity of consumers' buying habits. The banker may own a BMW but change the oil himself or herself. He or she may buy fast food for lunch but French wine for dinner, own sophisticated photographic equipment and a low-priced home stereo, and shop for socks at Kmart or Wal-Mart and suits or dresses at Brooks Brothers.

ON LINE

The unique lifestyles of every consumer can require a different marketing mix. Sometimes blending products for a single target market can result in failure. To the bright young founders of WebTV, it looked

exhibit 2.2

Values of the Three American Subcultures

	Heartlanders (%)	Modernists (%)	Cultural Creatives (%)	Total Sample (%)
Heartland Values				
Religious Right	70	26	31	40
Traditional relationships	55	25	26	34
Conservative religious beliefs	53	21	30	33
Conventional religious beliefs	47	36	15	34
Against feminism in work	46	35	20	35
Modernist Values				
Financial materialism	61	82	51	68
Not Religious Right	14	55	46	41
Not self-actualizing	43	51	26	43
Not altruistic	21	49	16	33
Cynicism about politics	29	48	19	35
Not idealistic	33	44	18	35
Secular/nature is sacred	15	42	29	31
Orthodox religion and beliefs	29	40	17	31
Success is high priority	11	36	12	23
Not relationship-oriented	14	32	8	21
Hedonism	5	12	4	48
Cultural Creative Values				
Want to rebuild neighborhoods/ communities	86	84	92	86
Fear violence	84	75	87	80
Like foreign places and the exotic	69	63	85	70
Nature as sacred	65	72	85	73
General green values	58	59	83	64
Ecological sustainability	52	56	83	61
Voluntary simplicity	65	53	79	63
Relationships important	65	49	76	60
Success is not high priority	61	39	70	53
Pro-feminism in work	45	56	69	56
Not concerned about job	41	50	62	50
Altruism	55	32	58	45
Idealsim	36	32	55	39
Religious mysteries exist	19	25	53	30
Self-actualization	29	32	52	36
Not financial materialism	34	17	48	29
Want to be activist	34	29	45	34
Not financial problems	33	31	44	34
Spiritual psychology	36	24	40	31
Not cynical on politics	24	21	40	27
Optimism about future	26	24	35	27
Want creative time	19	31	33	28

SOURCE: From "The Emerging Culture" by Paul H. Ray, *American Demographics*, February 1997, p. 31. Reprinted with permission from American Demographics Magazine. © 1997 PRIMEDIA Intertec, Stamford, CT.

like a home run: hook televisions up to the Net and tap into the vast market of couch potatoes curious about this new phenomenon called the World Wide Web. After burning through an estimated $50 million to advertise the new service, however, WebTV and partners Sony and Philips Electronics counted a disappointing fifty thousand subscribers.

The problem, WebTV now acknowledges, was the wrong marketing message. Couch potatoes want to be better entertained, whereas computer users are content to explore the Internet using small PC screens. A revamped campaign now emphasizes entertainment over education.[8]

The Changing Role of Families and Working Women

Component lifestyles have evolved because consumers can choose from a growing number of goods and services, and most have the money to exercise more options. Rising purchasing power has resulted from the growth of dual-income families. Approximately 58 percent of all females between sixteen and sixty-five years old are now in the workforce, and female participation in the labor force is expected to grow to 63 percent by 2005.[9] By the mid-1990s, more than 7.7 million women-owned businesses in the United States generated $1.4 trillion in revenues.[10] The phenomenon of working women has probably had a greater effect on marketing than has any other social change.

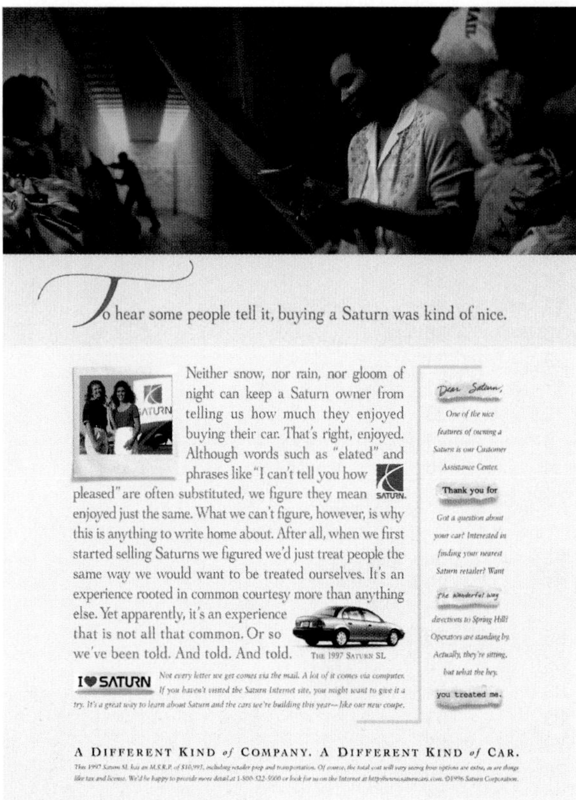

Saturn's advertising is designed to attract women not only as buyers but also as employees in its sales force. Women comprise 16% of Saturn's sales staff, and 64 percent of its cars are purchased by women.

As women's earnings grow, so do their levels of expertise, experience, and authority. Working-age women are not the same group businesses targeted thirty years ago. They expect different things in life—from their jobs, from their spouses, and from the products and services they buy.

The automotive industry has finally begun to realize the power of women in vehicle purchase decisions. Women are the principal buyers for 45 percent of all cars and trucks sold in the United States.[11] Saturn's advertising not only aims to attract women as customers, but also to woo them into the business. In an industry with a woefully small representation of women in sales, 16 percent of Saturn's sales staff are women, compared with 7 percent industry-wide. This has had a visible impact on sales to women. Even though about half of all automotive purchases are made by women, Saturn claims that women buy 64 percent of its cars.[12]

ENTREPRENEUR

The growth in the number of working women has meant an increase in dual-career families. Although dual-career families typically have greater household incomes, they have less time for family activities (poverty of time). Their purchasing roles (which define the items traditionally bought by the man or the woman) are changing, as are their purchasing patterns. Consequently, new opportunities are being created. For example, small businesses are opening daily that cater to dual-career households by offering specialized goods and services. Ice cream and yogurt parlors, cafes, and sports footwear shops have proliferated. With more women than ever working full time, there is a special demand for new household services. San Francisco Grocery Express, a warehouse operation, uses computers to take customers' telephone orders. Customers refer to a catalog listing grocery items and prices. Later, vans deliver the food to the purchasers' front doors.

Demographic Factors

3

Explain the importance to marketing managers of current demographic trends

demography
The study of people's vital statistics, such as their age, race and ethnicity, and location.

Demographic factors—another uncontrollable variable in the external environment—are also extremely important to marketing managers. **Demography** is the study of people's vital statistics, such as their age, race and ethnicity, and location. Demographics are significant because the basis for any market is people. Demographic characteristics are strongly related to consumer buyer behavior in the marketplace and are good predictors of how the target market will respond to a specific marketing mix. This section describes some marketing trends related to age and location. We will begin by taking a closer look at key age groups.

Generation Y: Born to Shop

Today, there are about fifty-eight million Americans age sixteen and under. These are the people of "Generation Y." Although Generation Y is much smaller than the baby boom, which lasted nearly twenty years and produced seventy-eight million children, its members are plentiful enough to put their own footprints on society.

The marketing impact of Generation Y has been immense. Companies that sell toys, videos, software, and clothing to kids have boomed in recent years. Nine of the ten best-selling videos of all time are animated films from Walt Disney Company. Club Med, the French vacation company, now earns half its U.S. revenues from family resorts. Generation Y was born into a world so different from the one their parents entered that they could be on different planets. The changes in families, the workforce, technology, and demographics in recent decades will no doubt affect their attitudes, but in unpredictable ways. Among those changes:

- Nearly 60 percent of children under the age of six have mothers who work outside the home, compared with just 18 percent in 1960.
- Some 61 percent of U.S. children aged three to five are attending preschool, compared with 38 percent in 1970.
- Nearly 60 percent of households with children aged seven or younger have personal computers, according to IDC/LINK Resources Corp., a market-research firm in New York.
- More than one-third of elementary school students nationwide are black or Hispanic, compared with 22 percent in 1974. If current trends continue, "minorities" will make up the majority of the U.S. population by 2050, according to the Census Bureau.
- Approximately 15 percent of U.S. births in recent years were to foreign-born mothers, with origins so diverse that more than one hundred different languages are spoken in the school systems of New York City, Chicago, Los Angeles, and Fairfax County, Virginia.
- Nearly one of three births in the early 1990s was to an unmarried woman. With approximately one in three marriages ending in divorce, a significant portion of this generation will spend at least part of childhood in a single-parent home.
- One-quarter of children under age six are living in poverty—that is, with cash income of less than $15,141 for a family of four.[13]

Although smaller in numbers than the baby boom generation, Generation Y has already had a significant impact on how companies market to families and to children and teens. Changes in demographics, workforce, and technology pose particular challenges as marketers attempt to identify the needs and wants of this group.
© Tom and DeeAnn McCarthy/The Stock Market

Generation Y is also driving the educational-software industry, which has grown to a $600 million business from practically nothing in 1990. Titles like Baby-ROM from Byron Preiss Multimedia Co. are designed to help infants as young as six months learn to identify numbers, shapes, colors, and body parts.

Apparel manufacturers from Ralph Lauren to Gap Inc. are also targeting the Generation Y crowd, which prefers jeans, sports jerseys, and baseball caps to dress-up clothes. Automakers are courting their parents with minivans and sport utility vehicles, many with built-in child seats. Hotels and cruise lines are offering kids programs. Some malls, furniture stores, and even supermarkets provide on-site baby-sitting. Restaurants are setting out crayons, putting changing tables in restrooms, and offering more take-out services, all to serve families with children.

Generation X: Savvy and Cynical

Generation X
People who are currently between the ages of 18 and 29 years of age.

Today, approximately forty-eight million consumers are between the ages of eighteen and twenty-nine. This group has been labeled **Generation X**. It is the first generation of latchkey children—products of dual-career households or, in roughly half of the cases, of divorced or separated parents. Generation X began entering the workforce in the era of downsizing and downturn, so its members are likelier than the previous generation to be unemployed, underemployed, and living at home with Mom and Dad. On the other hand, ten million are full-time college students, and fifteen million are married and not living at home.[14] Yet, as a generation that's been bombarded by multiple media since their cradle days, they're savvy and cynical consumers.

Generation Xers are savvy and cynical consumers who are more materialistic but less hopeful than previous generations. This combination of high aspirations and low expectations makes Generation X a challenge for marketers.
© Susan Werner/Tony Stone Images

The members of Generation X don't mind indulging themselves. Among the young women of Generation X, 38 percent go to the movies in a given month, compared with 19 percent of the women who are now in their thirties and forties. The members of Generation X devote a larger-than-average share of their spending dollars to restaurant meals, alcoholic beverages, clothing, and electronic items such as televisions and stereos.[15] One survey found that the members of Generation X aspire to having a home of their own (87 percent), a lot of money (42 percent), a swimming pool (42 percent), and a vacation home (41 percent).[16] They are more materialistic than past generations, but have less hope of achieving their goals.

Perhaps it is this combination of high aspirations and low expectations that makes Generation X such a challenge for marketers. "This is a generation that hates to be marketed to," says Scott Kauffman, vice president of broadcast and news media at *Entertainment Weekly*. "You have the youth of America reading novels in which chapters are titled, 'I am not a target market.'"[17]

For decades, Ford has marketed its light-duty pickups by showing roughness and toughness. Advertisements featured trucks climbing rugged mountains or four-wheeling through mud. But Ford quickly realized that this was not going to work with Generation Xers.

VALUE

Ford chose to lead with a new product. The company created a new version of its popular Ranger pickup, giving it flares on the fenders, jazzy graphics, and a youthful new name: Splash. The promotion campaign attempted to infuse the vehicle with personality by combining adventuresome sports with the truck. For example, one ad features a young surfer shooting the curl in the bed of a Splash parked in the middle of a wheat field. There is minimal copy—just one line listing five features and a new logo.[18]

Baby Boomers: America's Mass Market

baby boomers
People born between 1946 and 1964.

Almost seventy-eight million babies were born in the United States between 1946 and 1964, which created a huge market. The oldest **baby boomers** are now over fifty, but they cling to their youth. One study found that baby boomers see themselves as continuing to be very active after they turn fifty. They won't even think of themselves as being senior citizens until after they turn sixty (39 percent) or seventy (42 percent).[19]

This group cherishes convenience, which has resulted in a growing demand for home delivery of items like large appliances, furniture, and groceries. In addition, the spreading culture of convenience explains the tremendous appeal of prepared take-out foods and the necessity of VCRs and portable telephones.

Baby boomers' parents raised their children to think for and of themselves. Studies of child-rearing practices show that parents of the 1950s and 1960s consistently ranked "to think for themselves" as the number-one trait they wanted to instill in their children.[20] Postwar affluence also allowed parents to indulge their children as never before. They invested in their children's skills by sending them to college. They encouraged their children to succeed in a job market that rewarded competitive drive more than cooperative spirit and individual skills more than teamwork.

Arts and Entertainment Television Network

As its name indicates, A & E is a specialized television channel that broadcasts shows in arts and entertainment only, but it has even further customized programming. How? What audience(s) do you think it is targeting? Visiting its satellite pages may help you answer.

http://www.aande.com/ **http://www.biography.com/** **http://www.mysteries.com/** **http://www.historychannel.com/** **http://www.historytravel.com/**

In turn, the sheer size of the generation encouraged businesses to promote to the emerging individuality of baby boomers. Even before the oldest baby boomers started earning their own living more than two decades ago, astute businesspeople saw the profits that come from giving millions of young people what they want. Businesses offered individualistic baby boomers a growing array of customized products and services—houses, cars, furniture, appliances, clothes, vacations, jobs, leisure time, and even beliefs.

The importance of individualism among baby boomers led to a **personalized economy**. A personalized economy delivers goods and services at a good value on demand. Successful businesses in a personalized economy give customers what they want when they want it. To do this, they must know their customers extremely well. In fact, the intimacy between producer and consumer is exactly what makes an economy personalized.

personalized economy
Delivering goods and services at a good value on demand.

In the personalized economy, successful products share three characteristics:

- *Customization:* Products are custom designed and marketed to ever-smaller target markets. Today, for example, there are hundreds of cable TV channels from which to choose. In 1950, the average grocery store carried about four thousand items; today, that number is closer to sixteen thousand, as manufacturers target increasingly specific needs.[21]
- *Immediacy:* Successful businesses deliver products and services at the convenience of the consumer rather than the producer. Banc One, with locations in the eastern and southern states, for example, opens some of its branches on Saturdays and Sundays. Its twenty-four-hour hot line, staffed by real people, solves problems at the customer's convenience. The immediacy of the personalized economy explains the booming business in one-hour film processing, walk-in medical clinics, and thirty-minute pizzas.
- VALUE *Value:* Businesses must price competitively or create innovative products that can command premium prices. Even the most innovative products quickly become commodities in the fast-paced personalized economy, however. Apple fell prey to this danger: Its once-innovative Macintosh computers must now compete against less expensive machines that offer similar functions.

As the age of today's average consumer moves toward forty, average consumption patterns are also changing. People in their early forties tend to focus on their families and finances. As this group grows in number, its members will buy more furniture from manufacturers like Lazy Boy, American Martindale, Baker, and Drexel-Heritage to replace the furniture they bought early in their marriages. The demand for family counselors and wellness programs should also increase. Additionally, discount investment brokers like Charles Schwab and mutual funds like Fidelity and Dreyfus should profit. However, baby boomers are more likely than any other age group to have negative opinions about financial services such as banking and stockbrokers.[22] This may reflect the boomers' mistrust of authority. Because middle-aged consumers buy more reading materials than any other age group, the market for books and magazines should remain strong throughout the early 2000s. People who buy magazines on the newsstand tend to be younger, so newsstand sales may falter whereas subscription sales take off.

Right now, baby boomers are concerned with their children and their jobs. These worries will fade as the kids move out of the house and boomers retire. But some things will never change. Baby boomers may always be a little selfish about their leisure time. They may always be a little careless about the way they

on line

Grand Circle Travel
Maupintour

How does Grand Circle Travel dispel the stereotypes about seniors on its Web page? Compare it to Maupintour's site. Given that both companies target seniors, which company does this more effectively? Why do you think this is so?
http://www.gct.com/ **http://www.maupintour.com/**

spend their money. They will probably remain suspicious of the status quo. And they will always love rock and roll.

Older Consumers: Not Just Grandparents

As mentioned above, the oldest baby boomers have already crossed the fifty-plus threshold that many demographers use to define the "mature market." Yet, today's mature consumers are wealthier, healthier, and better educated than those of earlier generations.[23] Although they make up only 26 percent of the population, fifty-plus consumers buy half of all domestic cars, half of all silverware, and nearly half of all home remodeling.[24] Smart marketers are already targeting this growing segment. By 2020, over a third of the population will be fifty years old or older.

Many marketers have yet to tap the full potential of the huge and lucrative senior market because of enduring misconceptions about mature adults, all based on stereotypes. Here are a few:

- *Stereotype:* Older consumers are sick or ailing. *Fact:* A full 85 percent of mature citizens report themselves to be in good or excellent health. Over two-thirds of the elderly have no chronic health problems.[25] People like Mick Jagger are approaching fifty-five.[26] These people are fit and healthy.
- *Stereotype:* Older consumers are sedentary. *Fact:* Of all travel dollars spent in the United States, 80 percent are spent by people over fifty years old.
- *Stereotype:* Older consumers have a poor retention rate. *Fact:* Senior citizens are readers and much less influenced by TV than are younger consumers.[27] Not only do they retain what they read, but they are willing to read far more copy than younger people are.
- *Stereotype:* Older consumers are interested only in price and are intolerant of change. *Fact:* Although senior citizens are as interested in price as anyone else, they are more interested in value. And a generation that has survived the better part of a century characterized by more technological change than any other in history can hardly be considered resistant to change.[28]

Acceptance of change, however, doesn't mean a lack of brand loyalty. For example, the most critical factor in determining car-owner loyalty is age. The oldest consumers (ages sixty-five and up) are twice as loyal to the make of car as the youngest customers are.[29] The cars most popular with older Americans are Lincoln, Cadillac, and Buick.

Marketers who want to actively pursue the mature market must understand it. Aging consumers create some obvious opportunities. JCPenney's Easy Dressing clothes feature Velcro-fastened clothing for women with arthritis or other ailments who may have difficulty with zippers or buttons. Sales from the first Easy Dressing catalog were three times higher than expected.[30] Chicago-based Cadaco offers a line of games with easy-to-read big print and larger game pieces. The series focuses on nostalgia by including Michigan rummy, hearts, poker, and bingo. Trivia buffs more familiar with Mitch Miller than Guns 'n' Roses can play Parker Brothers' "The Vintage Years" edition of Trivial Pursuit. The game, aimed at the fifty-plus crowd, poses questions covering the era from Charles Lindbergh to Dwight D. Eisenhower. Consider these other examples, as well, of savvy marketers targeting the mature market:

- To counter sliding grip strength associated with advancing age, Procter & Gamble offers its Tide laundry detergent with snap-on lids rather than the usual perforated flap.
- Wheaton Medical Technologies markets a pill bottle that has a tiny battery-operated clock that registers the time the container was last opened to take out a pill.

- Knowing that grandparents purchase 25 percent of all toys (about $819 per year spent on their grandkids), F.A.O. Schwarz has added a Grandma's Shop to its two largest stores, complete with older-adult salespeople.
- Mattel, Inc., invited readers of *Modern Maturity* to join its Grandparents Club. For a $10 fee, readers could receive a book of discount coupons; meanwhile, Mattel acquired an invaluable mailing list of potential customers.[31]

Americans on the Move

The average U.S. citizen moves every six years.[32] This trend has implications for marketers. A large influx of new people into an area creates many new marketing opportunities for all types of businesses. Remember, the primary basis of all consumer marketing is people. Conversely, significant out-migration from a city or town may force many of its businesses to move or close down. The cities with the greatest projected population growth from 1995 to 2005 are Houston, Washington, D.C., Atlanta, San Diego, Phoenix, Orlando, and Dallas.[33]

The most populous metro area is Los Angeles–Long Beach with 9,605,904 by 2001. New York follows with 8,723,921 for the same year. New York also has the greatest population density at 7,464 persons per square mile. The lowest population density of the top twenty-four metro areas is Riverside–San Bernardino, California, at 123 people per square mile.[34]

The United States experiences both immigration from other countries and migration within U.S. borders. In the past decade, the six states with the highest levels of immigration from abroad were California, New York, New Jersey, Illinois, Texas, and Massachusetts. The six states with the greatest population increases due to interstate migration were Florida, Georgia, North Carolina, Virginia, Washington, and Arizona.[35]

Immigration raises the cost of public services in areas with large numbers of immigrants, but the influx also benefits the U.S. economy overall. Immigrants add approximately $10 billion to the economy each year with little negative impact on job opportunities for most other residents.[36]

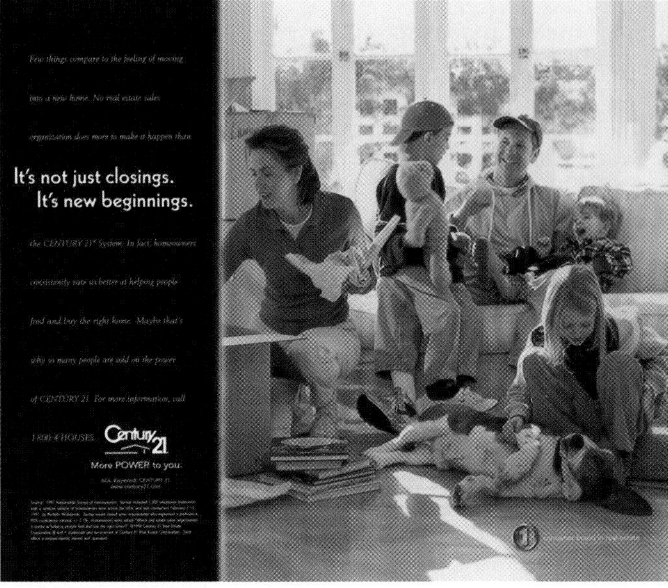

With Americans moving more often than ever before, marketers are feeling the impact of shifting populations. This Century 21 ad taps into the affective side of relocation and downplays the dread often associated with moving.
Courtesy Century 21 Real Estate Corporation

Growing Ethnic Markets

4
Explain the importance to marketing managers of multiculturalism and growing ethnic markets

The United States is undergoing a new demographic transition: It is becoming a multicultural society. The 1990 census found that eight in ten people in the United States are white, down from nine in ten in 1960. During the next decade, the United States will shift further from a society dominated by whites and rooted in Western culture to a society characterized by three large racial and ethnic minorities: African-Americans, U.S. Hispanics, and Asian-Americans. All three minorities will grow in size and in share of the population, while the white majority declines as a percentage of the total. Native Americans and people with roots in Australia, the Middle East, the former Soviet Union, and other parts of the world will further enrich the fabric of U.S. society.

The labor force of the past was dominated by white men who are now retiring. Today's senior workers are equal parts women and men, and still overwhelmingly white. But in the entry-level jobs of 1998, a multicultural labor force emerged. The proportion of workers who are non-Hispanic whites should decrease from 77 percent in 1998 to 74 percent in 2005.

Because so many white men are retiring, the non-Hispanic white labor force will grow only 8 percent between 1994 and 2005. The number of Hispanic workers should grow 36 percent, due to the continued immigration of young adults, higher birth rates, and relatively few retirees. These forces will also boost the number of Asian workers by 39 percent. The number of black workers will increase by 15 percent, a rate slightly slower than the rate of growth of black adults in general (16.5 percent).[37]

Ethnic and Cultural Diversity

multiculturalism
When all major ethnic groups in an area—such as a city, county, or census tract—are roughly equally represented.

Multiculturalism occurs when all major ethnic groups in an area—such as a city, county, or census tract—are roughly equally represented. Because of its current demographic transition, the trend in the United States is toward greater multiculturalism.

San Francisco County is the most diverse county in the nation. The proportions of major ethnic groups are closer to being equal there than anywhere else. People of many ancestries have long been attracted to the area. The least multicultural region is a broad swath stretching from northern New England through the Midwest and into Montana. These counties have few people other than whites. The counties with the very lowest level of diversity are found in the agricultural heartland: Nebraska and Iowa.

Marketing Implications of Multiculturalism The demographic shift and growing multiculturalism create new challenges and opportunities for marketers. The U.S. population grew from 226 million in 1980 to 274 million in 2000, much of that growth taking place in minority markets. Asians are the nation's fastest growing minority group, increasing 108 percent in the 1980s, to 7.3 million. The Hispanic population grew 53 percent, to 22.3 million; with 7.7 million new members, it had the biggest numerical gain of any minority group. African-Americans, who remain the largest minority, saw their numbers increase during the past decade by 13 percent, to 30 million. In contrast, the number of non-Hispanic whites grew by 4.4 percent. By 1994, about a quarter of the U.S. population were members of minority groups. The last census identified 110 different ethnic groups in the United States.[38]

Demographic shifts will be even more pronounced in the future. Exhibit 2.3 compares the 1999 population mix and the forecasted population mix for 2023. Note that Hispanics will be the fastest growing segment of the population. The diversity of the U.S. population is projected to stabilize around 2023, as the birthrate among minorities levels off.

VALUE

The marketer's task in a diverse society is more challenging because of differences in educational level and demand for goods and services. What's more, ethnic markets are not homogeneous. There is not an African-American market or a Hispanic market, any more than there is a white market. Instead, there are many niches within ethnic markets that require micromarketing strategies. For example, African Eye, which offers women's designer fashions from Africa, attracted a thousand women to a fashion show at Prince Georges Plaza near Washington, D.C. The show featured the latest creations by Alfadi, a high-fashion Nigerian designer, who also hosted the show. African Eye's dresses and outfits blend African and Western influences and are priced at $50 to $600. Says Mozella Perry Ademiluyi, the president and cofounder of African Eye: "Our customer is professional, 30 to 65, has an income level of $30,000-plus and often is well-traveled. They don't just want to wear something that is African. They want something that is well-tailored, unique, and creative as well."[39]

An alternative to the niche strategy is to maintain a brand's core identity while straddling different languages, cultures, ages, and incomes. Executives with BellSouth Corp. had a message for both Spanish-speaking Hispanic and English-speaking customers throughout the Southeast. Instead of going with two distinct campaigns, they chose Daisy Fuentes, a former MTV personality well known

exhibit 2.3

Multicultural Makeup of the United States

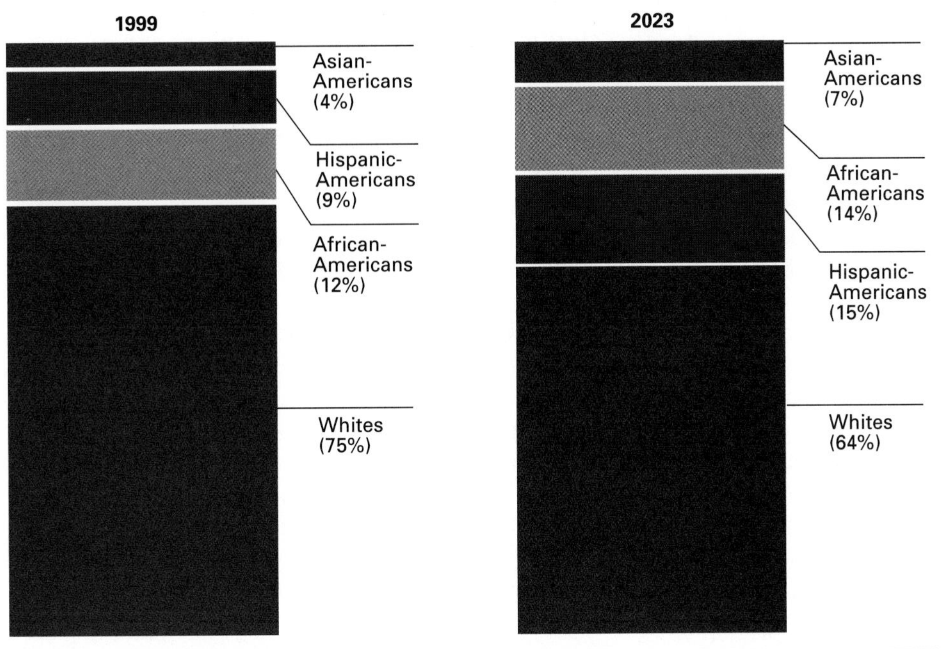

SOURCE: U.S. Department of Labor, Bureau of the Census projections.

among both audiences. More importantly, she spoke to a third audience: acculturated, bilingual Hispanics. The potential audience included more than 1.422 million Hispanics in 491,000 Hispanic households in Miami-Dade, Broward, and Monroe Counties plus an additional 1 million-plus general market households in the area, according to Strategy Research Corp.[40]

A third strategy for multicultural marketing is to seek common interests, motivations, or needs across ethnic groups. This strategy is sometimes called **stitching niches**, which means combining ethnic, age, income, and lifestyle markets, on some common basis, to form a large market. The result may be a cross-cultural product, such as a frozen pizza-flavored egg roll. Or it may be a product that serves several ethnic markets simultaneously. Ringling Brothers and Barnum and Bailey Circus showcases acts that appeal to many ethnic groups. It broadened its appeal to Asian-Americans by adding the "Mysterious Oriental Art of Hair Hanging." Marguerite Michelle, known as the "ravishing Rapunzel," is suspended in the air on a wire attached to her waist-length hair. When the circus comes to town, the Mexican-born Michelle also goes on Spanish-language radio shows to build recognition for Ringling in the Hispanic market. The circus is promoted as "*El Espectáculo Más Grande del Mundo.*"[41]

stitching niches
Strategy for multicultural marketing that combines ethnic, age, income, and lifestyle markets, on some common basis, to form a large market.

Economic Factors

5
Identify consumer and marketer reactions to the state of the economy

In addition to social and demographic factors, marketing managers must understand and react to the economic environment. The three economic areas of greatest concern to most marketers are the distribution of consumer income, inflation, and recession.

Rising Incomes

As disposable (or after-tax) incomes rise, more families and individuals can afford the "good life." Fortunately, U.S. incomes have continued to rise. After adjustment for inflation, median incomes in the United States rose less than 4 percent between 1980 and 2000.

Today about two-thirds of all U.S. households earn a "middle-class" income. The rough boundaries for a middle-class income are $18,000, above poverty, to about $75,000, just short of wealth. In 1999, almost half the households were in the upper end of the $18,000 to $75,000 range, as opposed to only a quarter in 1980. The percentage of households earning above $75,000 is now over 8 percent.[42] As a result, Americans are buying more goods and services than ever before. For example, in raising a child to age seventeen, a middle-class family will spend about $124,000 in 1999 dollars. This new level of affluence is not limited to professionals or even individuals within specific age or education brackets. Rather, it cuts across all household types, well beyond what businesses traditionally consider to be markets for high-priced goods and services. This rising affluence stems primarily from the increasing number of dual-income families.

During the 2000s, many marketing managers will focus on families with incomes over $35,000, because this group will have the most discretionary income. The average American household has over $12,000 in discretionary income each year. Some marketers will concentrate their efforts on higher quality, higher priced goods and services. The Lexus automobile and American Airlines' "international class" service for business-class seats on transcontinental flights are examples of this trend.

Inflation

inflation
A general rise in prices without a corresponding increase in wages, which results in decreased purchasing power.

Inflation is a general rise in prices without a corresponding increase in wages, which results in decreased purchasing power. Fortunately, the United States has had a low rate of inflation for over a decade. The late 1990s have been marked by an inflation rate under 4 percent. The low rate of inflation is due to the tremendous productivity of the high-tech sector of the economy and the stability of the price of services.[43] Both education and healthcare costs are rising much more slowly than in the past. The other good news is that the American economy has grown at an annual rate of 2.6 percent from 1992 to 1999.[44] This may not seem high, but it is twice the rate of Europe and Japan.[45] These economic conditions benefit marketers, because real wages, and hence purchasing power, go up when inflation stays down. A significant increase in inflation almost always depresses real wages and the ability to buy more goods and services.

In times of low inflation, businesses seeking to increase their profit margins can do so only by increasing their efficiency. If they significantly increase prices, no one will purchase their goods or services.

In more inflationary times, marketers use a number of pricing strategies to cope. (See Chapter 15 for more on these strategies.) But in general, marketers must be aware that inflation causes consumers to either build up or diminish their brand loyalty. In one research session, a consumer panelist noted, "I used to use just Betty Crocker mixes, but now I think of either Betty Crocker or Duncan Hines, depending on which is on sale." Another participant said, "Pennies count now, and so I look at the whole shelf, and I read the ingredients. I don't really understand, but I can tell if it's exactly the same. So now I use this cheaper brand, and honestly, it works just as well." Inflation pressures consumers to make more economical purchases. However, most consumers try hard to maintain their standard of living.

VALUE

In creating marketing strategies to cope with inflation, managers must realize that, despite what happens to the seller's cost, the buyer is not going to pay more for a product than the subjective value he or she places on it. No matter how compelling the justification might be for a 10 percent price increase, marketers must always examine its impact on demand. Many marketers try to hold prices level as long as is practical.

Recession

A **recession** is a period of economic activity when income, production, and employment tend to fall—all of which reduce demand for goods and services. The problems of inflation and recession go hand in hand, yet recession requires different marketing strategies:

recession
A period of economic activity when income, production, and employment tend to fall—all of which reduce demand for goods and services.

- *Improve existing products and introduce new ones:* The goal is to reduce production hours, waste, and the cost of materials. Recessions increase the demand for goods and services that are economical and efficient, offer value, help organizations streamline practices and procedures, and improve customer service.
- *Maintain and expand customer services:* In a recession, many organizations postpone the purchase of new equipment and materials. Sales of replacement parts and other services may become an important source of income.
- *Emphasize top-of-the-line products and promote product value:* Customers with less to spend will seek demonstrated quality, durability, satisfaction, and capacity to save time and money. High-priced, high-value items consistently fare well during recessions.

Technological and Resource Factors

6
Identify the impact of technology on a firm

Sometimes new technology is an effective weapon against inflation and recession. New machines that reduce production costs can be one of a firm's most valuable assets. The power of a personal-computer microchip doubles about every eighteen months. The Pentium Pro, for example, introduced in 1995, contains 5.3 million transistors and performs three hundred million instructions per second (MIPS). The 886 chip, due in 2000, will have fifteen million transistors and perform one thousand MIPS.[46] Our ability, as a nation, to maintain and build wealth depends in large part on the speed and effectiveness with which we invent and adopt machines that lift productivity. For example, coal mining is typically thought of as unskilled, backbreaking labor. But visit Cyprus Amax Mineral Company's Twenty-mile Mine near Oak Creek, Colorado, and you will find workers with push-button controls who walk along massive machines that shear thirty-inch slices from an 850-foot coal wall. Laptop computers help miners track equipment breakdowns and water quality.

GLOBAL

U.S. companies often have difficulty translating the results of R&D into goods and services. The Japanese are masters at making this transformation. For example, VCRs, flat-panel displays, and compact disc players are based on U.S. research that wasn't exploited at home. The United States excels at **basic research** (or pure research), which attempts to expand the frontiers of knowledge but is not aimed at a specific, pragmatic problem. Basic research aims to confirm an existing theory or to learn more about a concept or phenomenon. For example, basic research might focus on high-energy physics. **Applied research**, in contrast, attempts to develop new or improved products. It is where the United States sometimes falls short, although many U.S. companies do conduct applied research. For example, Motorola is using applied research to create Iridium, a constellation of sixty-six satellites that will offer telephone service anywhere on the globe.[47]

basic research
Pure research which aims to confirm an existing theory or to learn more about a concept or phenomenon.

applied research
Attempts to develop new or improved products.

The U.S. government spends about $75 billion a year on R&D; private industry spends another $120 billion.[48] In the 1990s, the United States has thus far spent 16 percent more on R&D than Japan, Germany, France, and the United Kingdom combined. Yet these four countries together spend 12 percent more than the United States on R&D not related to defense.[49]

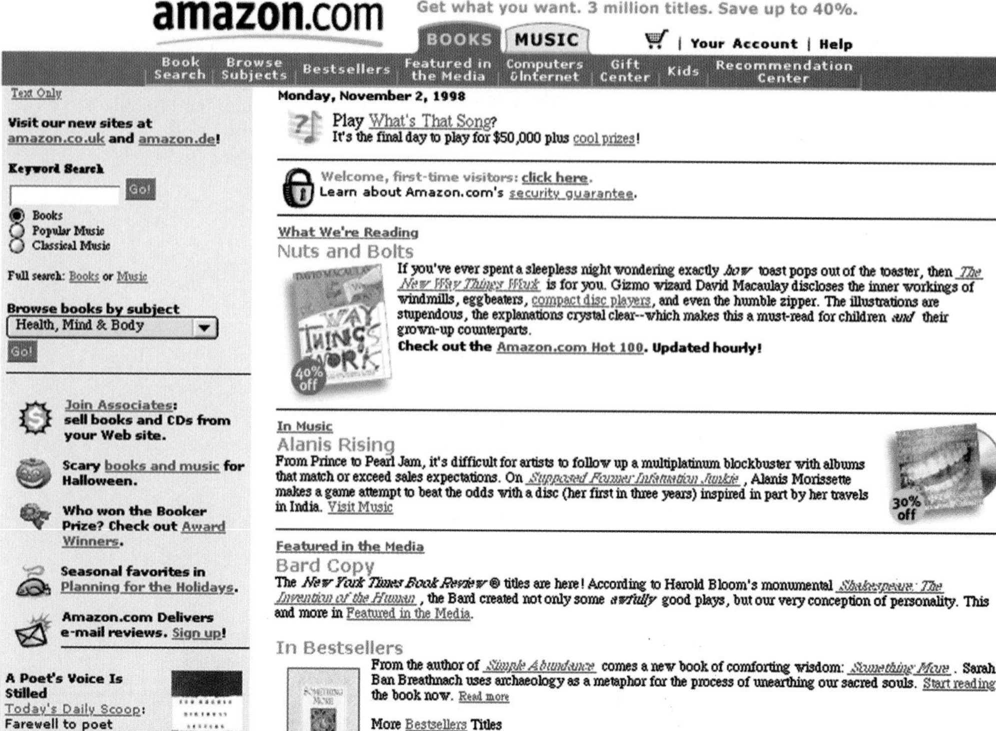

amazon.com
Get what you want. 3 million titles. Save up to 40%.
BOOKS
MUSIC
Your Account | Help
Book Search
Browse Subjects
Bestsellers
Featured in the Media
Computers &Internet
Gift Center
Kids
Recommendation Center
Text Only
Visit our new sites at amazon.co.uk and amazon.de!
Keyword Search
Go!
Books
Popular Music
Classical Music
Full search: Books or Music
Browse books by subject
Health, Mind & Body
Go!
Join Associates: sell books and CDs from your Web site.
Scary books and music for Halloween.
Who won the Booker Prize? Check out Award Winners.
Seasonal favorites in Planning for the Holidays.
Amazon.com Delivers e-mail reviews. Sign up!
A Poet's Voice Is Stilled
Today's Daily Scoop: Farewell to poet laureate Ted Hughes, John Glenn returns to orbit, and other books behind the
40% off
Monday, November 2, 1998
Play What's That Song?
It's the final day to play for $50,000 plus cool prizes!
Welcome, first-time visitors: click here.
Learn about Amazon.com's security guarantee.
What We're Reading
Nuts and Bolts
If you've ever spent a sleepless night wondering exactly how toast pops out of the toaster, then The New Way Things Work is for you. Gizmo wizard David Macaulay discloses the inner workings of windmills, eggbeaters, compact disc players, and even the humble zipper. The illustrations are stupendous, the explanations crystal clear--which makes this a must-read for children and their grown-up counterparts.
Check out the Amazon.com Hot 100. Updated hourly!
40% off
In Music
Alanis Rising
From Prince to Pearl Jam, it's difficult for artists to follow up a multiplatinum blockbuster with albums that match or exceed sales expectations. On Supposed Former Infatuation Junkie, Alanis Morissette makes a game attempt to beat the odds with a disc (her first in three years) inspired in part by her travels in India. Visit Music
30% off
Featured in the Media
Bard Copy
The New York Times Book Review ® titles are here! According to Harold Bloom's monumental Shakespeare: The Invention of the Human, the Bard created not only some awfully good plays, but our very conception of personality. This and more in Featured in the Media.
In Bestsellers
From the author of Simple Abundance comes a new book of comforting wisdom: Something More. Sarah Ban Breathnach uses archaeology as a metaphor for the process of unearthing our sacred souls. Start reading the book now. Read more
More Bestsellers Titles

The growth of the Internet has created new challenges and great opportunities for marketing managers in nearly all industries. Amazon.com has leveraged the technology of the Internet and created the most successful Web-based retail operation to date.
Courtesy amazon.com

R&D expenditures are only a rough measure of where the United States stands in terms of innovation. A look at management of the R&D process can be even more revealing. U.S. managers tend to be obsessed with short-term profits (one to three years) and minimal risk taking. The result is an infatuation with slight variations of existing products, which are often very profitable, instead of true innovations. Developing new products like Honey Nut Cheerios and Diet Cherry Coke is probably not the path to world economic leadership.

Companies must also learn how to innovate, and large R&D budgets aren't the sole answer. One of the biggest R&D spenders in the United States is General Motors, which by most standards is not a leading innovator. On the other hand, Corning has relatively low R&D budgets but is arguably one of the five most innovative companies in the world. The difference is in management and corporate culture.

GLOBAL

Again, we might take a cue from the Japanese. In Japan, a team composed of engineers, scientists, marketers, and manufacturers works simultaneously at three levels of innovation. At the lowest level, they seek small improvements in an existing product. At the second, they try for a significant jump, such as Sony's move from the microcassette tape recorder to the Walkman. The third is true innovation, an entirely new product. The idea is to produce three new products to replace each current product, with the same investment of time and money. One of the three may then become the new market leader and produce the innovator's profit.

ON LINE

Innovation and new products can create vast new challenges for marketing managers. One of the greatest opportunities of this decade is the tremendous growth of the Internet. In 1996, advertising on the Web was just $267 million. In 1998, advertising spending on the Internet topped $1 billion.[50] In addition to advertising, many retailers are finding the Web an excellent way to build direct sales. The most successful retail operation to date is Amazon.com: Books, Music & More at **http://www.amazon.com.**

The Net has also helped marketing operate more efficiently through better communications. The use of e-mail has exploded in the past several years. E-mail, for example, enables companies like Ford Motor and Nestlé to communicate quickly with employees in far-flung operations throughout the world. The convenience of e-mail results in many of us using it for personal messages as well as business matters. The notion of e-mail privacy is discussed in the "Ethics in Marketing" box.

Political and Legal Factors

7 Discuss the political and legal environment of marketing

Business needs government regulation to protect innovators of new technology, the interests of society in general, one business from another, and consumers. In turn, government needs business, because the marketplace generates taxes that support public efforts to educate our youth, protect our shores, and so on. The private sector also serves as a counterweight to government. The decentralization of power inherent in a private-enterprise system supplies the limitation on government essential for the survival of a democracy.

ETHICS

Every aspect of the marketing mix is subject to laws and restrictions. It is the duty of marketing managers or their legal assistants to understand these laws and conform to them, because failure to comply with regulations can have major consequences for a firm. Sometimes just sensing trends and taking corrective action before a government agency acts can help avoid regulation. This didn't happen in the case of the tobacco industry. As a result, Joe Camel and the Marlboro Man are fading into the sunset along with other strategies used to promote tobacco products.

However, the challenge is not simply to keep the marketing department out of trouble, but to help it implement creative new programs to accomplish

ethics in marketing

The Myth of E-Mail Privacy

. . . Michael Smyth, a regional manager at Pillsbury in Pennsylvania, fired an e-mail to his supervisor, blasting company managers and threatening to "kill the backstabbing ———." Backstabbing may have been the right word. Though Pillsbury had assured employees that e-mail was private, it intercepted the message and fired Smyth. When he sued for wrongful discharge, the court threw out the case. He learned the hard way: Never expect privacy for e-mail sent through a company system.

. . . Typically the company asserts ownership of e-mail messages. To boost morale and encourage communication among employees, the company may also promise a degree of privacy. But as the Pillsbury episode shows, such promises aren't binding. It will take time for practices to become more coherent.

Employees who are adept with computers occasionally take privacy into their own hands. Using software they buy or download from the Internet, they encrypt, or scramble, mail they don't want the boss to see. Before you try this, beware. Encryption is still somewhat cumbersome—penpals must have the same software, for one thing. And if you're working for a paranoid boss, scrambling may afford less protection than you think. Says a computer designer in an office where the boss's e-mail snooping preceded a savage firing spree: "I was afraid that if I merely sent an encrypted letter, they'd think I was up to something bad."

Bottom line: If you write love notes on a company PC, you're wearing your heart on your screen. The only truly safe ways to send? Be subtle when you flirt or lampoon the boss. Or pay for your own America Online account and use it at night on your home machine.[51]

Unless it is a customer service call, companies rarely monitor employees' telephone calls. Should they monitor an employee's e-mail? Did Michael Smyth deserve to be fired? What would you do if you were told to monitor another employee's e-mail and report your findings to your boss?

marketing objectives. It is all too easy for a marketing manager or sometimes a lawyer to say no to a marketing innovation that actually entails little risk. For example, an overly cautious lawyer could hold up sales of a desirable new product by warning that the package design could prompt a copyright infringement suit. Thus, it is important to understand thoroughly the laws established by the federal government, state governments, and regulatory agencies to control marketing-related issues.

Federal Legislation

Federal laws that affect marketing fall into several categories. First, the Sherman Act, the Clayton Act, the Federal Trade Commission Act, the Celler-Kefauver Antimerger Act, and the Hart-Scott-Rodino Act were passed to regulate the competitive environment. Second, the Robinson-Patman Act was designed to regulate pricing practices. Third, the Wheeler-Lea Act was created to control false advertising. These key pieces of legislation are summarized in Exhibit 2.4.

exhibit 2.4

Primary U.S. Laws That Affect Marketing

Legislation	Impact on Marketing
Sherman Act of 1890	Makes trusts and conspiracies in restraint of trade illegal; makes monopolies and attempts to monopolize a misdemeanor.
Clayton Act of 1914	Outlaws discrimination in prices to different buyers; prohibits tying contracts (which require the buyer of one product to also buy another item in the line); makes illegal the combining of two or more competing corporations by pooling ownership of stock.
Federal Trade Commission Act of 1914	Creates the Federal Trade Commission to deal with antitrust matters; outlaws unfair methods of competition.
Robinson-Patman Act of 1936	Prohibits charging different prices to different buyers of merchandise of like grade and quantity; requires sellers to make any supplementary services or allowances available to all purchasers on a proportionately equal basis.
Wheeler-Lea Amendments to the FTC Act of 1938	Broadens the Federal Trade Commission's power to prohibit practices that might injure the public without affecting competition; outlaws false and deceptive advertising.
Lanham Act of 1946	Establishes protection for trademarks.
Celler-Kefauver Antimerger Act of 1950	Strengthens the Clayton Act to prevent corporate acquisitions that reduce competition.
Hart-Scott-Rodino Act of 1976	Requires large companies to notify the government of their intent to merge.

State Laws

State legislation that affects marketing varies. Oregon, for example, limits utility advertising to 0.5 percent of the company's net income. California has forced industry to improve consumer products and has also enacted legislation to lower the energy consumption of refrigerators, freezers, and air conditioners. Several states, including New Mexico and Kansas, are considering levying a tax on all in-state commercial advertising.

Regulatory Agencies

Although some state regulatory bodies more actively pursue violations of their marketing statutes, federal regulators generally have the greatest clout. The Consumer Product Safety Commission, the Federal Trade Commission, and the Food and Drug Administration are the three federal agencies most directly and actively involved in marketing affairs. These agencies, plus others, are discussed throughout the book, but a brief introduction is in order at this point.

The sole purpose of the **Consumer Product Safety Commission (CPSC)** is to protect the health and safety of consumers in and around their homes. The CPSC has the power to set mandatory safety standards for almost all products that consumers use (about fifteen thousand items). The CPSC consists of a five-member committee and about eleven hundred staff members, including technicians, lawyers, and administrative help. The commission can fine offending firms up to $500,000 and sentence their officers to up to a year in prison. It can also ban dangerous products from the marketplace.

The **Federal Trade Commission (FTC)** also consists of five members, each holding office for seven years. The Federal Trade Commission is empowered to

Consumer Product Safety Commission (CPSC)
Federal agency established to protect the health and safety of consumers in and around their homes.

Federal Trade Commission (FTC)
Federal agency empowered to prevent persons or corporations from using unfair methods of competition in commerce.

exhibit 2.5

Powers of the Federal Trade Commission

Remedy	Procedure
Cease-and-Desist Order	A final order is issued to cease an illegal practice—and is often challenged in the courts.
Consent Decree	A business consents to stop the questionable practice without admitting its illegality.
Affirmative Disclosure	An advertiser is required to provide additional information about products in advertisements.
Corrective Advertising	An advertiser is required to correct the past effects of misleading advertising. (For example, 25% of a firm's media budget must be spent on FTC-approved advertisements or FTC-specified advertising.)
Restitution	Refunds are required to be given to consumers misled by deceptive advertising. According to a 1975 court-of-appeals decision, this remedy cannot be used except for practices carried out after the issuance of a cease-and-desist order (still on appeal).
Counteradvertising	The FTC proposed that the Federal Communications Commission permit advertisements in broadcast media to counteract advertising claims (also that free time be provided under certain conditions).

Federal Trade Commission

As a marketing manager, how would you use the FTC Web site in designing a new marketing campaign?

http://www.ftc.gov/index.html

Food and Drug Administration

What topics are currently receiving attention in FDA News? What effect has the attention had on marketers?

http://www.fda.gov/hometext.html

prevent persons or corporations from using unfair methods of competition in commerce. It is authorized to investigate the practices of business combinations and to conduct hearings on antitrust matters and deceptive advertising. The FTC has a vast array of regulatory powers. (See Exhibit 2.5.) Nevertheless, it is not invincible. For example, the FTC had proposed to ban all advertising to children under age eight, to ban all advertising of the sugared products that are most likely to cause tooth decay to children under age twelve, and to require dental health and nutritional advertisements to be paid for by industry. Business reacted by lobbying to reduce the FTC's power. The two-year lobbying effort resulted in passage of the FTC Improvement Act of 1980. The major provisions of the act are as follows:

- It bans the use of unfairness as a standard for industrywide rules against advertising. All the proposals concerning children's advertising were therefore suspended, because they were based almost entirely on the unfairness standard.
- It requires oversight hearings on the FTC every six months. This congressional review is designed to keep the commission accountable. Moreover, it keeps Congress aware of one of the many regulatory agencies it has created and is responsible for monitoring.

Food and Drug Administration (FDA)
Federal agency charged with enforcing regulations against selling and distributing adulterated, misbranded, or hazardous food and drug products.

Businesses rarely band together to create change in the legal environment as they did to pass the FTC Improvement Act. Generally, marketing managers only react to legislation, regulation, and edicts. It is usually less costly to stay attuned to the regulatory environment than to fight the government. If marketers had toned down their hard-hitting advertisements to children, they might have avoided an FTC inquiry altogether. The **Food and Drug Administration (FDA)**, another powerful agency, is charged with enforcing regulations against selling and distributing adulterated, misbranded, or hazardous food and drug products. It has recently taken a very aggressive stance against tobacco products.

Competitive Factors

8
Explain the basics of foreign and domestic competition

The competitive environment encompasses the number of competitors a firm must face, the relative size of the competitors, and the degree of interdependence within the industry. Management has little control over the competitive environment confronting a firm.

Even when faced with a highly competitive environment, innovative smaller firms can survive and even prosper. An excellent example of holding your own against the giants is offered by Wild Rumpus bookstore in the "Entrepreneurial Insights" story on the next page.

Competition for Market Share

As U.S. population growth slows, costs rise, and available resources tighten, firms find that they must work harder to maintain their profits and market share regardless of the form of the competitive market. Take, for example, the salty snacks market. Recently, Anheuser-Bush announced that it was selling its Eagle snacks business because it couldn't compete against Frito-Lay. One consultant noted, "Frito's is a fortress—I would tell anyone trying to get into the salty snack business not to impinge on Frito's territory or you'll get crushed."[52] Eagle is only the latest example. Borden, Inc., sold off many of its regional snack companies as part of a huge restructuring. Industry executives say dozens of regional companies have collapsed in the past year or two under Frito-Lay's weight.

The FDA is taking an aggressive stance against tobacco products. Here the heads of the largest U.S. tobacco companies are sworn in before a congressional committee meeting.
© John Duricka/AP Wide World Photos

Frito-Lay is feeding much of its growth with new products. The company's approach has been two-pronged—expanding its core line of Fritos, Doritos, Rold Gold Pretzels, and Lays potato chips, while branching out into new "better for you" products like Baked Lays, Baked Tostitos, and Rold Gold Fat Free Pretzels. Its cheesier Doritos have turned the previously sleepy chip into a billion-dollar brand, and spicier flavors have made Lays the No. 1 potato chip.

entrepreneurial insights

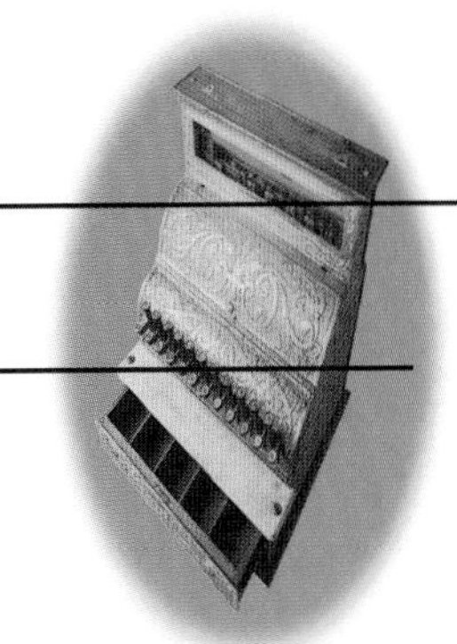

Wild Rumpus Sells Books and Fun

Minneapolis is home to the nation's largest mall and some of the first big Barnes & Noble and Borders bookstores. So you'd have to be crazy to open a small, neighborhood bookshop in that sort of retail environment, right? Well, maybe not—if you work hard at finding a market niche and learning all there is to know about your particular brand of customers. That's how husband-and-wife team Tom Braun and Collette Morgan, proprietors of a children's bookstore called Wild Rumpus, have managed to thrive in the land of giant retailers.

When the couple opened the store in 1992, Morgan had just finished a two-year stint at Odegard Books, an independent bookstore that had closed. She and Braun knew that they too would fail unless they understood their market better than anyone else. "Most children's bookstores are completely sterile," Morgan says. "There are walls painted in primary colors, but rarely does anyone stop and think about what actually excites children."

Depending on your size, you can enter Wild Rumpus through the standard-size front door or the purple four-foot children's aperture that's built into it. Immediately you encounter a kind of unruly menagerie. Two cats roam free, as does Flicka the rooster. There are songbirds, lizards, and a tarantula in cages. The scary-books section has a floor that's made partially of glass, so kids can see the family of rats that lives in a cage underneath.

Just for fun, try calling the store sometime to experience the cacophony of cackling roosters, shrieking children, and zydeco music. You could make a fortune selling Advil at this place. But kids aren't the only customers. One crucial part of running a children's bookstore is establishing strong links with educators, who can use the store to run school book fairs and bring classes in for field trips. Before Wild Rumpus even opened, Morgan and Braun invited teachers to visit, and they eventually returned with students in tow. "Very quickly we began to see weekend traffic," says Braun. "Kids who had been here with school groups were coming back with their parents to show them the store."

Early on, the staff also began scheduling regular Saturday events. "We wanted parents to bring their kids each week, knowing that we would have something creative planned," Morgan says. The staff has brought in a rock band that uses power tools for instruments and an archaeology professor who taught the assembled mass of little girls how to mummify their Barbies. One Mother's Day the staff even had llamas out back for a mama versus llama spitting contest. While these events don't have much to do with books, their sheer uniqueness draws tons of traffic.[53]

Who is the true customer for Wild Rumpus? Can the giant bookstore chains easily duplicate Wild Rumpus's tactics? What can the chains do to fight back?

Frito-Lay also kills the competition with its distribution. Over its thirty-five-year history, the company has built a network of forty-two plants, 12,800 delivery people, and more than nine hundred tractor trailers into a retail delivery powerhouse. The company was one of the first to give its drivers handheld computers to transmit sales back to headquarters. Frito-Lay is working on another overhaul of its distribution operation to better serve its expanding range of retail customers—everything from drugstores and discount giants to grocery stores and convenience marts.

Global Competition

Both Kraft General Foods and Procter & Gamble are savvy international competitors. They each conduct business in over a hundred different nations. Many foreign competitors also consider the United States to be a ripe target market. Thus, a U.S. marketing manager can no longer worry about only domestic competitors. In automobiles, textiles, watches, televisions, steel, and many other areas, foreign competition has been strong. Global competition is discussed in much more detail in Chapter 3.

In the past, foreign firms penetrated U.S. markets by concentrating on price, but today the emphasis has switched to product quality. Nestlé, Sony, Rolls Royce, and Sandoz Pharmaceuticals are noted for quality, not cheap prices.

With the expansion of global marketing, U.S. companies often battle each other in international markets just as intensively as in the domestic market, using very different marketing strategies. Consider the case of Coca-Cola Co. and PepsiCo, Inc., in the following "Global Perspectives" box.

global perspectives

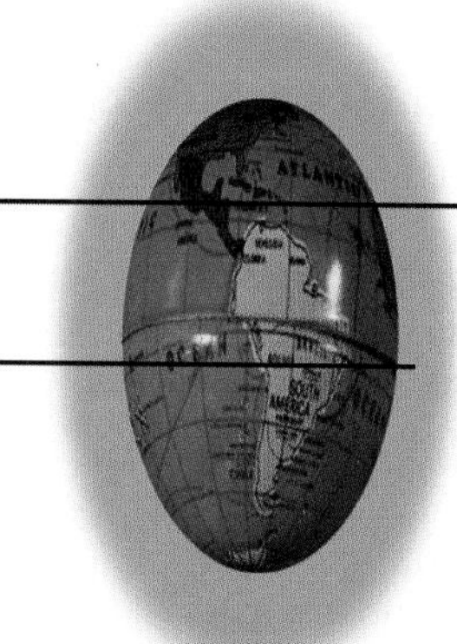

The French Government Steps into the Coke Versus Pepsi Turf Wars

The French government rejected Coca-Cola Co.'s proposed $880 million purchase of Orangina from Pernod Ricard, SA on antitrust grounds. The move shows how Coke is coming under greater scrutiny as rival PepsiCo, Inc., is drawing attention to Coke's dominance in the global soft-drink business.

When Coke reached its agreement to buy Orangina, Pepsi cried foul; it relies on Orangina to distribute Pepsi products in cafes, hotels, and other "on-premise" locations. Furthermore, Pepsi argued that coke's purchase of Orangina would give its archrival a near monopoly in France, because Coke already controls about 50 percent of the French carbonated soft-drink market.

Despite those complaints, Coke officials and industry analysts seemed confident that the French government would approve the deal, although only after Coke agreed to certain conditions to satisfy competition and labor concerns. Coke, based in Atlanta, addressed the latter concern by signing an accord with Orangina employees, guaranteeing jobs and salaries through the year 2000 and maintaining a thirty-five-hour workweek.

But the government, in its decision, said the French antitrust authorities' recommendation "substantiated the serious risks" to competition being impeded in the on-premise market. "Intensive discussion with the Coca-Cola Co. did not result in sufficient commitments to prevent the risks" to competition, the French government said.

Pepsi wouldn't speculate on whether it would make an offer for Orangina. "We're obviously pleased" by the government's decision, the spokesperson said. "This sends an important signal that France has solid and well-defined rules regarding open competition and is prepared to enforce those rules."[54]

Do you think that the French government should get involved in the Coke versus Pepsi battle for market share? If you were Pepsi management, what factors should you consider before making an offer to buy Orangina? Do you think Pepsi could market Orangina, which is a lightly carbonated drink that contains orange juice and pulp, in the United States?

Ethical Behavior in Business

Describe the role of ethics and ethical decisions in business

ethics
The standard of behavior by which conduct is judged.

Regardless of the intensity of the competition, firms must compete in an ethical manner. **Ethics** refers to the moral principles or values that generally govern the conduct of an individual or a group. Ethics also can be viewed as the standard of behavior by which conduct is judged. Standards that are legal may not always be ethical, and vice versa. Laws are the values and standards enforceable by the courts. Ethics consists of personal moral principles and values rather than societal prescriptions.

Defining the boundaries of ethicality and legality can be difficult. Often, judgment is needed to determine whether an action that may be legal is indeed ethical. For example, advertising liquor, tobacco, and X-rated movies in college newspapers is not illegal in many states, but is it ethical?

morals
The rules people develop as a result of cultural values and norms.

Morals are the rules people develop as a result of cultural values and norms. Culture is a socializing force that dictates what is right and wrong. Moral standards may also reflect the laws and regulations that affect social and economic behavior. Thus, morals can be considered a foundation of ethical behavior.

Morals are usually characterized as good or bad. "Good" and "bad" have different connotations, including "effective" and "ineffective." A good salesperson makes or exceeds the assigned quota. If the salesperson sells a new stereo or television set to a disadvantaged consumer—knowing full well that the person can't keep up the monthly payments—is the salesperson still a good one? What if the sale enables the salesperson to exceed his or her quota?

Another set of connotations for "good" and "bad" are "conforming" and "deviant" behaviors. A doctor who runs large ads for discounts on open-heart surgery would be considered bad, or unprofessional, in the sense of not conforming to the norms of the medical profession. "Bad" and "good" are also used to express the distinction between criminal and law-abiding behavior. And finally, the terms "good" and "bad" as defined by different religions differ markedly. A Moslem who eats pork would be considered bad, as would a fundamentalist Christian who drinks whiskey.

Morality and Business Ethics

Today's business ethics actually consists of a subset of major life values learned since birth. The values businesspeople use to make decisions have been acquired through family, educational, and religious institutions.

Ethical values are situation specific and time oriented. Nevertheless, everyone must have an ethical base that applies to conduct in the business world and in personal life. One approach to developing a personal set of ethics is to examine the consequences of a particular act. Who is helped or hurt? How long lasting are the consequences? What actions produce the greatest good for the greatest number of people? A second approach stresses the importance of rules. Rules come in the form of customs, laws, professional standards, and common sense. Consider these examples of rules:

- Always treat others as you would like to be treated.
- Copying copyrighted computer software is against the law.
- It is wrong to lie, bribe, or exploit.

The last approach emphasizes the development of moral character within individuals. Ethical development can be thought of as having three levels:[55]

- *Preconventional morality,* the most basic level, is childlike. It is calculating, self-centered, and even selfish, based on what will be immediately punished or rewarded. Fortunately, most businesspeople have progressed beyond the self-centered and manipulative actions of preconventional morality.

- *Conventional morality* moves from an egocentric viewpoint toward the expectations of society. Loyalty and obedience to the organization (or society) become paramount. At the level of conventional morality, an ethical marketing decision would be concerned only with whether or not it is legal and how it will be viewed by others. This type of morality could be likened to the adage "When in Rome, do as the Romans do."
- *Postconventional morality* represents the morality of the mature adult. At this level, people are less concerned about how others might see them and more concerned about how they see and judge themselves over the long run. A marketing decision maker who has attained a postconventional level of morality might ask, "Even though it is legal and will increase company profits, is it right in the long run? Might it do more harm than good in the end?"

Ethical Decision Making

ETHICS

How do businesspeople make ethical decisions? There is no cut-and-dried answer. Some of the ethical issues managers face are shown in Exhibit 2.6. Studies show that the following factors tend to influence ethical decision making and judgments:[56]

- *Extent of ethical problems within the organization:* Marketing professionals who perceive fewer ethical problems in their organizations tend to disapprove more strongly of "unethical" or questionable practices than those who perceive more ethical problems. Apparently, the healthier the ethical environment, the greater is the likelihood that marketers will take a strong stand against questionable practices.
- *Top-management actions on ethics:* Top managers can influence the behavior of marketing professionals by encouraging ethical behavior and discouraging unethical behavior.
- *Potential magnitude of the consequences:* The greater the harm done to victims, the more likely it is that marketing professionals will recognize a problem as unethical.

exhibit 2.6

Unethical Practices Marketing Managers May Have to Deal With

- Entertainment and gift giving
- False or misleading advertising
- Misrepresentation of goods, services, and company capabilities
- Lies told customers in order to get the sale
- Manipulation of data (falsifying or misusing statistics or information)
- Misleading product or service warranties
- Unfair manipulation of customers
- Exploitation of children and/or disadvantaged groups
- Invasion of customer privacy
- Sex-oriented advertising appeals
- Product or service deception
- Unsafe products or services
- Price deception
- Price discrimination
- Unfair remarks and inaccurate statements about competitors
- Smaller amounts of product in the same-size packages
- Stereotypical portrayals of women, minority groups, and senior citizens

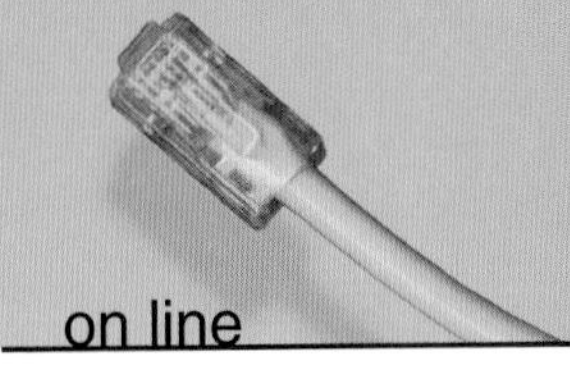

University of British Columbia Centre for Applied Ethics

Research corporate codes of ethics through the Applied Ethics Resources. Compare the codes of three companies. What common themes do you find?
http://www.ethics.ubc.ca/

- *Social consensus:* The greater the degree of agreement among managerial peers that an action is harmful, the more likely it is that marketers will recognize a problem as ethical.
- *Probability of a harmful outcome:* The greater the likelihood that an action will result in a harmful outcome, the more likely it is that marketers will recognize a problem as unethical.
- *Length of time between the decision and the onset of consequences:* The shorter the length of time between the action and the onset of negative consequences, the more likely it is that marketers will perceive a problem as unethical.
- *Number of people to be affected:* The greater the number of persons affected by a negative outcome, the more likely it is that marketers will recognize a problem as unethical.

Ethical Guidelines

ETHICS

Many organizations have become more interested in ethical issues. One sign of this interest is the increase in the number of large companies that appoint ethics officers—from virtually none five years ago to almost 25 percent of large corporations now. In addition, many companies of various sizes have developed a **code of ethics** as a guideline to help marketing managers and other employees make better decisions. In fact, in a recent national study, it was found that 60 percent of the companies maintained a code of ethics, 33 percent offered ethics training, and 33 percent employed an ethics officer.[57] Some of the most highly praised codes of ethics are those of Boeing, GTE, Hewlett-Packard, Johnson & Johnson, and Norton Company.

code of ethics
A guideline to help marketing managers and other employees make better decisions.

Creating ethics guidelines has several advantages:

- It helps employees identify what their firm recognizes as acceptable business practices.
- A code of ethics can be an effective internal control on behavior, which is more desirable than external controls like government regulation.
- A written code helps employees avoid confusion when determining whether their decisions are ethical.
- The process of formulating the code of ethics facilitates discussion among employees about what is right and wrong and ultimately creates better decisions.

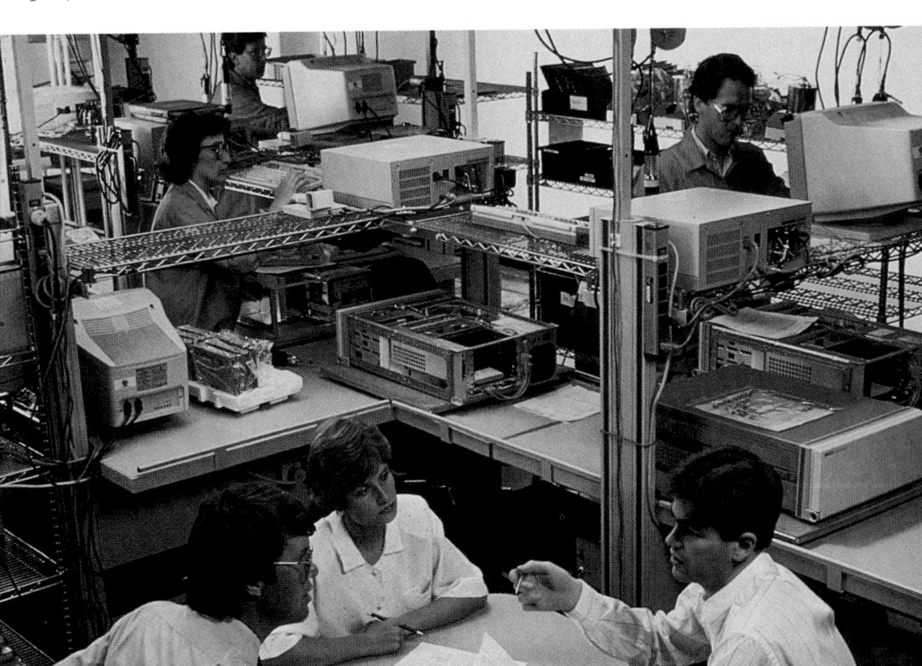

Hewlett-Packard's code of ethics for employees at all levels has been highly praised. This code helps marketing managers and other employees recognize acceptable business practices and make better decisions.
Courtesy Hewlett-Packard Company

Businesses, however, must be careful not to make their code of ethics too vague or too detailed. Codes that are too vague give little or no guidance to employees in their day-to-day activities. Codes that are too detailed encourage employees to substitute rules for judgment. For instance, if employees are involved in questionable behavior, they may use the absence of a written rule as a reason to

exhibit 2.7

Ethics Checklist

- Does the decision benefit one person or group but hurt or not benefit other individuals or groups? In other words, is my decision fair to all concerned?
- Would individuals or groups, particularly customers, be upset if they knew about my decision?
- Has important information been overlooked because my decision was made without input from other knowledgeable individuals or groups?
- Does my decision presume that my company is an exception to a common practice in this industry and that I therefore have the authority to break a rule?
- Would my decision offend or upset qualified job applicants?
- Will my decision create conflict between individuals or groups within the company?
- Will I have to pull rank or use coercion to implement my decision?
- Would I prefer to avoid the consequences of my decision?
- Did I avoid truthfully answering any of the above questions by telling myself that the risks of getting caught are low or that I could get away with the potentially unethical behavior?

continue behaving that way, even though their conscience may be saying no. The checklist in Exhibit 2.7 is an example of a simple but helpful set of ethical guidelines. Following the checklist will not guarantee the "rightness" of a decision, but it will improve the chances of the decision's being ethical.

Although many companies have issued policies on ethical behavior, marketing managers must still put the policies into effect. They must address the classic "matter of degree" issue. For example, marketing researchers must often resort to deception to obtain unbiased answers to their research questions. Asking for a few minutes of a respondent's time is dishonest if the researcher knows the interview will last forty-five minutes. Should researchers conducting focus groups inform the respondents that there are observers behind a one-way mirror? When respondents know they're being watched, they sometimes are less likely to talk and interact freely. Does a client have an ethical right to obtain questionnaires with the names and addresses of respondents from a market research firm? Many of these concerns have been addressed by the Professional Standards Committee of the American Marketing Association. The American Marketing Association's code of ethics is included on its Web site at **www.ama.org**.

Corporate Social Responsibility

10
Discuss corporate social responsibility

corporate social responsibility
Business's concern for society's welfare.

Ethics and social responsibility are closely intertwined. Besides questioning tobacco companies' ethics, one might ask whether they are acting in a socially responsible manner when they promote tobacco. Are companies that produce low-cost handguns socially responsible in light of the fact that these guns are used in the majority of inner-city crimes? **Corporate social responsibility** is business's concern for society's welfare. This concern is demonstrated by managers who consider both the long-range best interests of the company and the company's relationship to the society within which it operates.

One theorist suggests that total corporate social responsibility has four components: economic, legal, ethical, and philanthropic.[58] The **pyramid of corporate social responsibility**, shown in Exhibit 2.8, portrays economic performance as the foundation for the other three responsibilities. At the same time that it pursues profits (economic responsibility), however, business is expected to obey the law

Wm. Wrigley & Jr. Company
Apple Computer, Inc.
Ben & Jerry's

How are these companies publicizing their community involvement via the Web? Describe the community activities of each. Does the marketing of community involvement enhance the images of the companies?

http://www.wrigley.com/ **http://www.apple.com/** **http://www.benjerry.com/**

on line

(legal responsibility); to do what is right, just, and fair (ethical responsibility); and to be a good corporate citizen (philanthropic responsibility). These four components are distinct but together constitute the whole. Still, if the company doesn't make a profit, then the other three responsibilities are moot.

pyramid of corporate social responsibility
Model that suggests corporate social responsibility is composed of economic, legal, ethical, and philanthropic responsibilities and that the firm's economic performance supports the entire structure.

Many companies are already working to make the world a better place to live. Consider these examples:

- Colby Care Nurses, Inc., a home health care service located in Los Angeles County, is offering much needed health care to predominantly black and Hispanic communities that are not often covered by other providers. The company prides itself on giving back to the community by employing its residents and providing role models for its young people.[59]
- Wrigley, the Chicago gum maker, is producing a $10 million commercial campaign aimed at getting African-Americans, Asian-Americans, and Hispanic-Americans to use doctors for regular health maintenance instead of as a last resort.[60]
- Ben & Jerry's, the premium ice cream maker, sent seven workers to live with Cree Indians in Canada to see how they've been displaced by a new hydroelectric power complex.[61]
- Jantzen, the world's leading swimsuit manufacturer, makes direct grants through its clean water campaign to organizations that preserve and clean up beaches and waterways.[62]
- Apple Computer donates almost $10 million in computer equipment and advice to U.S. schools annually.

exhibit 2.8

Pyramid of Corporate Social Responsibility

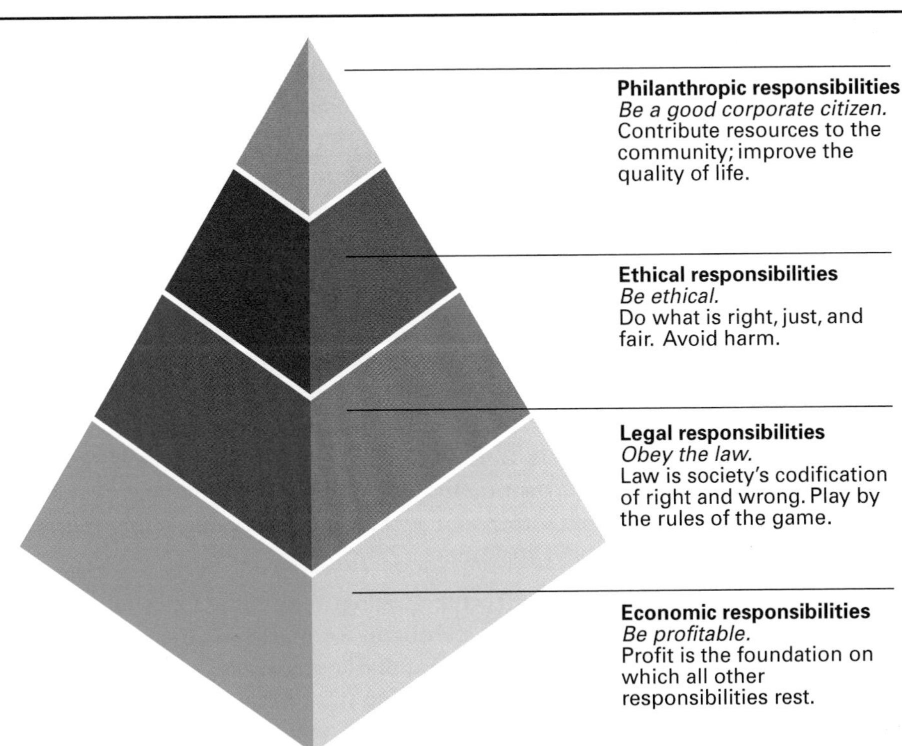
Philanthropic responsibilities
Be a good corporate citizen.
Contribute resources to the community; improve the quality of life.
Ethical responsibilities
Be ethical.
Do what is right, just, and fair. Avoid harm.
Legal responsibilities
Obey the law.
Law is society's codification of right and wrong. Play by the rules of the game.
Economic responsibilities
Be profitable.
Profit is the foundation on which all other responsibilities rest.

SOURCE: Adapted from Archie B. Carroll, "The Pyramid of Corporate Social Responsibility: Toward the Moral Management of Organizational Stakeholders," *Business Horizons*, July–August 1991, pp. 39–48.

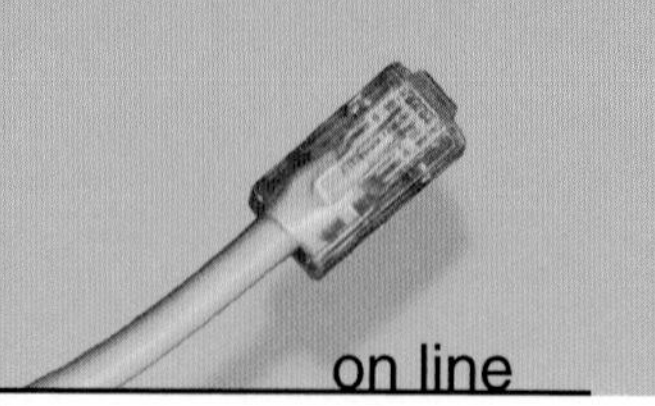

New Balance

Nike

Revisit the New Balance and Nike Web pages at the URLs below. How are these companies using the Internet to advance a social cause? What can you tell about these companies' markets based on the causes they promote and support?

http://www.newbalance.com/

http://www.nikebiz.com/

- G.D. Searle began a program in which its representatives regularly call hypertension (high blood pressure) patients, reminding them to take their medicine.[63]
- Ricoh, a Japanese office equipment maker, has developed a reverse copier that strips away the toner and allows the copy paper to be used again.[64]

GLOBAL Multinational companies also have important social responsibilities. In many cases a corporation can be a dynamic force for social change in host countries. For example, multinational corporations played a major role in breaking down apartheid (separation of the races) in South Africa, through their economic pressure on the South African government. Over three hundred apartheid laws were compiled over the years, based purely on the pigmentation of people's skin. Among other things, these laws forced blacks to live in the most arid regions of South Africa, banned mixed marriages, and segregated the schools. To protest apartheid, many multinational corporations closed their South African operations altogether. Other companies refused to trade with South Africa. These actions seriously impeded South Africa's economy, and by the early 1990s the government began making major social reforms. Once apartheid officially ended in the early 1990s, many of the companies that had participated in the boycott resumed their operations in South Africa.

LOOKING BACK

Looking back at the story on New Balance you should now understand that the external environment affects all firms and their marketing mixes. The opening vignette illustrated how changing demographics can present marketing opportunities. It enabled New Balance to serve a large, middle-aged target market effectively. All of the other uncontrollable variables could affect New Balance adversely. Changing cultural values could shift away from exercise and fitness for middle-aged consumers, thereby reducing demand for New Balance products. New shoe technology could render New Balance shoes obsolete. A general economic turndown might substantially decrease demand for all types of athletic goods.

Summary

1 Discuss the external environment of marketing and explain how it affects a firm. The external marketing environment consists of social, demographic, economic, technological, political and legal, and competitive variables. Marketers generally cannot control the elements of the external environment. Instead, they must understand how the external environment is changing and the impact of change on the target market. Then marketing managers can create a marketing mix to effectively meet the needs of target customers.

2 Describe the social factors that affect marketing. Within the external environment, social factors are perhaps the most difficult for marketers to anticipate. Several major social trends are currently shaping marketing strategies. First, people of all ages have a broader range of interests, defying traditional consumer profiles. Second, changing gender roles are bringing more women into the workforce and increasing the number of men who shop. Third, a greater number of dual-career families has led to a poverty of time, creating a demand for timesaving goods and services.

3 Explain the importance to marketing managers of current demographic trends. Today, several basic demographic patterns are influencing marketing mixes. Because the U.S. population is growing at a slower rate, marketers can no longer rely on profits from generally expanding markets. Marketers are also faced with increasingly experienced consumers among the younger generations, many of whom are "turned off" by traditional marketing mixes. And because the population is also growing older, marketers are offering more products that appeal to middle-aged and elderly markets.

4 Explain the importance to marketing managers of multiculturalism and growing ethnic markets. Multiculturalism occurs when all major ethnic groups in an area are roughly equally represented. Growing multiculturalism makes the marketer's task more challenging. Niches within ethnic markets may require micromarketing strategies. An alternative to a niche strategy is maintaining a core brand identity while straddling different languages, cultures, ages, and incomes with different promotional campaigns. A third strategy is to seek common interests, motivations, or needs across ethnic groups.

5 Identify consumer and marketer reactions to the state of the economy. Marketers are currently targeting the increasing number of consumers with higher discretionary income by offering higher-quality, higher-priced goods and services. During a time of inflation, marketers generally attempt to maintain level pricing in order to avoid losing customer brand loyalty. During times of recession, many marketers maintain or reduce prices to counter the effects of decreased demand; they also concentrate on increasing production efficiency and improving customer service.

6 Identify the impact of technology on a firm. Monitoring new technology is essential to keeping up with competitors in today's marketing environment. For example, in the technologically advanced United States, many companies are losing business to Japanese competitors, who are prospering by concentrating their efforts on developing marketable applications for the latest technological innovations. In the United States, many R&D expenditures go into developing refinements of existing products. U.S. companies must learn to foster and encourage innovation. Without innovation, U.S. companies can't compete in global markets.

7 Discuss the political and legal environment of marketing. All marketing activities are subject to state and federal laws and the rulings of regulatory agencies. Marketers are responsible for remaining aware of and abiding by such regulations. Some key federal laws that affect marketing are the Sherman Act, Clayton Act, Federal Trade Commission Act, Robinson-Patman Act, Wheeler-Lea Amendments to the FTC Act, Lanham Act, Celler-Kefauver Antimerger Act, and Hart-Scott-Rodino Act. The Consumer Product Safety Commission, the Federal Trade Commission, and the Food and Drug Administration are the three federal agencies most involved in regulating marketing activities.

8 Explain the basics of foreign and domestic competition. The competitive environment encompasses the number of competitors a firm must face, the relative size of the competitors, and the degree of interdependence within the industry. Declining population growth, rising costs, and shortages of resources have heightened domestic competition. Yet with an effective marketing mix, small firms continue to be able to compete with the giants. Meanwhile, dwindling international barriers are bringing in more foreign competitors and offering expanding opportunities for U.S. companies abroad.

9 Describe the role of ethics and ethical decisions in business. Business ethics may be viewed as a subset of the values of society as a whole. The ethical conduct of business-people is shaped by societal elements, including family, education, religion, and social movements. As members of society, businesspeople are morally obligated to consider the ethical implications of their decisions.

Ethical decision making is approached in three basic ways. The first approach examines the consequences of decisions. The second approach relies on rules and laws to guide decision making. The third approach is based on a theory of moral development that places individuals or groups in one of three developmental stages: preconventional morality, conventional morality, or postconventional morality.

Many companies develop a code of ethics to help their employees make ethical decisions. A code of ethics can help employees identify acceptable business practices, can be an effective internal control on behavior, can help employees avoid confusion when determining the ethicality of decisions, and can facilitate discussion about what is right and wrong.

10 Discuss corporate social responsibility. Responsibility in business refers to a firm's concern for the way its decisions affect society. There are several arguments in support of social responsibility. First, many consumers feel business should take responsibility for the social costs of economic growth. A second argument contends that firms act in their own best interest when they help improve the environment within which they operate. Third, firms can avoid restrictive government regulation by responding willingly to societal concerns. Finally, some people argue that because firms have the resources to solve social problems, they are morally obligated to do so.

In contrast, there are critics who argue against corporate social responsibility. According to one argument, the free enterprise system has no way to decide which social programs should have priority. A second argument contends that firms involved in social programs do not generate the profits needed to support the business's activities and earn a fair return for stockholders.

In spite of the arguments against corporate social responsibility, most businesspeople believe they should do more than pursue only profits. Although a company must consider its economic needs first, it must also operate within the law, do what is ethical and fair, and be a good corporate citizen.

Key Terms

applied research 41
baby boomers 34
basic research 41
code of ethics 51
component lifestyles 30
Consumer Product Safety Commission (CPSC) 45
corporate social responsibility 52
demography 32
environmental management 29
ethics 49
Federal Trade Commission (FTC) 45
Food and Drug Administration (FDA) 46
Generation X 34
inflation 40
morals 49
multiculturalism 38
personalized economy 35
poverty of time 30
pyramid of corporate social responsibility 53
recession 41
stitching niches 39
target market 28

Discussion and Writing Questions

1. What is the purpose of environmental scanning? Give an example.
2. Every country has a set of core values and beliefs. These values may vary somewhat from region to region of the nation. Identify five core values for your area of the country. Clip magazine advertisements that reflect these values and bring them to class.
3. Baby boomers in America are aging. Describe how this might affect the marketing mix for the following:
   a. Bally's Health Clubs
   b. McDonald's
   c. Whirlpool Corporation
   d. the State of Florida
   e. JCPenney
4. WRITING You have been asked to address a local chamber of commerce on the subject of the growing singles market. Prepare an outline for your talk.
5. WRITING Periods of inflation require firms to alter their marketing mix. A recent economic forecast expects inflation to be almost 10 percent during the next 18 months. Your company manufactures hand tools for the home gardener. Write a memo to the company president explaining how the firm may have to alter its marketing mix.
6. Give three examples in which technology has benefited marketers. Also, give several examples in which firms have been hurt by not keeping up with technological change.

7. TEAM Form six teams. Each team is responsible for one of the uncontrollable elements in the marketing environment. Your boss, the company president, has asked each team to provide a one-year and a five-year forecast of what major trends the firm will face. The firm is in the telecommunications equipment industry. It has no plans to become a telecommunications service provider, for example, like MCI and AT&T. Each team should use the library, the Internet, and other data sources to make its forecasts. Each team member should examine a minimum of one data source. The team should then pool its data and prepare its recommendation. A spokesperson for each team should present the findings to the class.
8. WRITING Write a paragraph discussing the ethical dilemma in the following situation and identifying possible solutions: An insurance agent forgets to get the required signature from one of her clients who is buying an automobile insurance policy. The client acknowledges the purchase by giving the agent a signed personal check for the full amount. To avoid embarrassment and inconvenience, the agent forges the client's signature on the insurance application and sends it to the insurance company for processing.
9. ON LINE What's the latest news at the following Web site? How can marketers benefit from such information?
http://www.ipo.org/
10. ON LINE What social responsibility concerns could be raised about the following Web site? For which issues does the Web site seem to exhibit social responsibility?
http://www.netcasino.com/

Application for Small Business

ENTREPRENEUR Eight years ago Betty Beal earned a bachelor's degree in business administration with a major in marketing. She has been very successful as a sales representative for a major pharmaceutical firm. Three months later Betty decided to give something back to the community by volunteering at the Judy Freemont Shelter for Battered Women. Judy founded the shelter two years ago. It has served as a safe haven for almost sixty women and numerous children. Other than a small grant from the city, the only other significant source of funds is donated clothes, which are then resold in the shelter's second-hand clothing shop.

Betty noticed very quickly that there was no organized way to obtain donated clothing. She quickly put her marketing skills to work and set up a phone bank to solicit clothes and a collection route to pick them up. Clothing donations quadrupled in two months.

Betty observed two things that disturbed her greatly. First, Judy would sort through all the donated items as they came in from the route truck and take anything that she wanted. Betty had seen Judy take two dresses, several sweaters, and a number of blouses. Second, as revenue grew from the second-hand shop sales, Betty couldn't see that additional monies were being spent on food, clients, or the shelter itself, yet Judy kept insisting that the operation was just breaking even.

Questions

1. Should Betty report Judy to the police, confront Judy, say nothing but continue to work at the shelter, or simply quit?
2. There is no doubt that the shelter is providing a useful service to many needy women. If word gets out to the general public about the alleged irregularities, the shelter may be forced to close. Should this influence Betty's course of action?
3. What would you do?

Review Quiz

1. Which of the following is *not* one of the uncontrollable factors for marketing managers?
   a. Social change
   b. Economic conditions
   c. The marketing mix
   d. Political and legal factors

2. The fact that many consumers are choosing products that meet diverse needs and interests rather than conforming to traditional stereotypes means they are likely piecing together
   a. The management of their environment
   b. Component lifestyles
   c. Changing roles
   d. The poverty of time

3. A viewpoint in American culture that places high value on personal success and technological rationality is known as
   a. Cultural creativity
   b. Traditionalism
   c. Heartlandering
   d. Modernism

4. This group of consumers is often known as "America's mass market" and yet today has the earning power to prefer many customized products and services.
   a. The baby boomers
   b. The seniors
   c. Generation X
   d. Generation Y

5. Which of the following represents a common stereotype of older consumers that is *not* an accurate reflection of that market?
   a. Older consumers are generally in good health
   b. Older consumers are typically sedentary in their lifestyle
   c. Older consumers are more price sensitive than other consumers
   d. Older consumers read and retain copy in advertisements as well or better than other consumers

6. ______ occur(s) when all major ethnic groups in an area, such as a city, are roughly equally represented.
   a. Poverty of time
   b. Modernist values
   c. Multiculturalism
   d. Stitching niches

7. Which of the following pieces of federal legislation was designed to control false advertising?
   a. The Sherman Act
   b. The Lanham Act
   c. The Wheeler-Lea Amendments to the FTC Act
   d. The Robinson-Patman Act

8. A power of the Federal Trade Commission (FTC) to have a business stop a questionable practice without admitting illegal behavior is called
   a. A consent decree
   b. A cease-and-desist order

c. Affirmative disclosure
d. Restitution

9. Marketers that have attained a _______ level of morality might ask, "Even though it is legal, is it right to do this in the long run?"
   a. Unconventional
   b. Preconventional
   c. Conventional
   d. Postconventional

10. According to the pyramid of corporate social responsibility, the foundation of such social responsibility comes from
    a. Philanthropic responsibilities
    b. Ethical responsibilities
    c. Legal responsibilities
    d. Economic responsibilities

11. Corporations that are multinational rarely have important social responsibilities.
    a. True
    b. False

12. Identify the six basic factors of the external environment facing marketers today.

Check the Answer Key, which follows the Video Case, to see how well you understood the material.

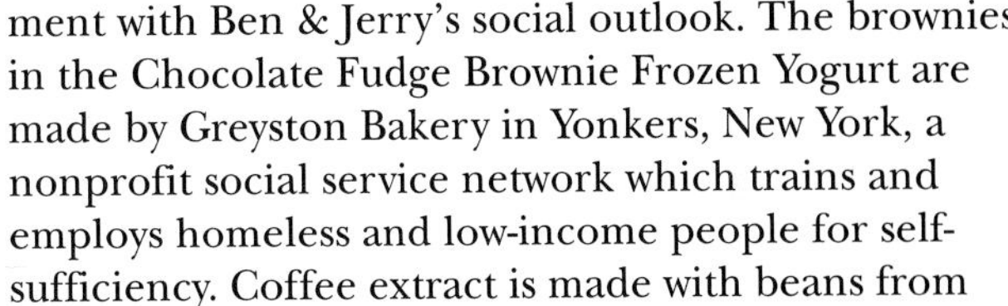

Ben & Jerry's: "We Do Good by Doing Good."

Ben & Jerry's tries to make the world a sweeter place. The Vermont manufacturer makes premium ice cream with catchy names like Cherry Garcia—after the Grateful Dead icon—and uses only top quality ingredients. We're all in this together, say the company founders, so let's find innovative ways to show concern for people—locally, nationally, and around the world. This philosophy is called "caring capitalism." How does it work?

The concept of linked prosperity goes beyond writing a check for charity. Ben & Jerry's actually links itself to others who also wish to improve the quality of life for themselves and others. There are many ways to forge alliances. One way is the PartnerShop, a Ben & Jerry franchise owned and operated by a nonprofit organization. A PartnerShop called Youth Scoops in Ithaca, New York, provides employment and training for youths at risk.

Another way to tie business to values is to buy products from "socially aligned" suppliers, those in agreement with Ben & Jerry's social outlook. The brownies in the Chocolate Fudge Brownie Frozen Yogurt are made by Greyston Bakery in Yonkers, New York, a nonprofit social service network which trains and employs homeless and low-income people for self-sufficiency. Coffee extract is made with beans from Aztec Harvests, a farming company owned by Mexican cooperatives. As part of the minority supplier program, Ben & Jerry's encourages its pecan processor to use the Federation of Southern Co-operatives, a co-op dedicated to supporting African-American family farms. About one third of 1997 purchases reflects this social mission.

Caring for our planet is still another part of the Ben & Jerry's business philosophy. The company is serious about using and producing environment-friendly products even if it means paying top dollar. The only milk and cream that go into the ice cream come from St. Alban's, a co-op of Vermont family farmers. These dairies do not use rBGH, a growth hormone believed to be bad for cows and bad for the future of small-scale dairy farms. In fact, Ben & Jerry's has started a food fight. The company is challenging laws against national rBGH labeling so consumers can make informed choices when buying dairy products. In 1997, the company won a court case against the state of Illinois, which had taken the position that no rBGH labeling was allowed.

Another bold step was the elimination of bleach in packaging. The pint container, the industry standard, was tested and found to be environmentally poor, so the company invested hundreds of staff hours to analyze chlorine-free packaging sources. Most of the technical problems are now solved, and new packaging material is on the way. One dimension of Ben & Jerry's social mission is to create models for change. The company hopes that its use of unbleached paper will stimulate similar demand by others.

Still, everything at Ben & Jerry's is not peachy. The decision to discontinue purchases of organic fruit and cancel the organic ice cream line caused quite a stir in-house. The high prices paid to dairy farmers were also paid to organic fruit farmers. Once again, the idea was not to create a fully organic line, but to support organic farming and create a model to stimulate demand for organic products. These initiatives would hopefully develop into fully organic products down the line. But organic ingredients proved to be too expensive, and the demand for them too weak. Market research showed that organic ingredient costs exceeded consumer price expectations. And suppliers could only produce 29 percent of Ben & Jerry's total fruit needs. So the project was shelved, but not without some soul searching. Were social mission values being sacrificed for short-term economic considerations? Was Ben & Jerry's selling out?

Maybe yes, maybe no. After all, growing competition and consumer concerns about eating too much fat have caused financial struggles in recent years. Returns to shareholders improved in 1998, with a 16 percent sales hike, yet share prices are still lower than in 1992. The company stakes its identity on the belief that the social mission enhances the economic mission. Yet, some feel that's a bit idealistic. Perhaps, Ben & Jerry's should ask, "Are we really doing good by doing good?"

Questions

1. What does values-led mean in tough, competitive times? How can Ben & Jerry's lead with its social mission if there is always an economic argument that can be made to act otherwise?
2. Do you think it's in the shareholders' best interest to select minority and disadvantaged suppliers?
3. Given Ben & Jerry's stance on environmental issues, do you feel that the company has an ethical responsibility (i.e., to do what is right, just, and fair and avoid harm) to use organic fruit and produce an organic ice cream despite the high cost? See Exhibit 2.8.
4. What do you think Ben & Jerry's should do to remain competitive?

Bibliography

Ben & Jerry's 1997 Annual Report.

Laura Johannes, "Ben & Jerry's to End Long Relationship with Dreyer's after Takeover Attempt," *Wall Street Journal*, 1 September 1998, p. A3.

Answer Key

1. *Answer:* c, p. 29

   Rationale: The marketing mix represents the group of factors in marketing planning that is under the control of the firm and its managers.

2. *Answer:* b, p. 30

   Rationale: In the past, lifestyles were often associated only with one's profession. Today, many consumers have component lifestyles—that is, they have many different lifestyles based on personal preferences. Thus they require many goods and services to meet their widely diverse lifestyles.

3. *Answer:* d, p. 30

   Rationale: Modernism is a value set, held by 47 percent of Americans, that places high value on consumerism and materialism.

4. *Answer:* a, pp. 34–35

   Rationale: At approximately seventy-eight million strong, this generation represents the largest subcultural group in the United States and has a sense of individualism that has led to preferences for customized products. The term personalized economy has been used to describe how products succeed by offering customization, immediacy, and value.

5. *Answer:* b, p. 36

   Rationale: There are many misconceptions about older adults in the marketplace. Seniors are not commonly sedentary. In fact, over 80 percent of consumer travel dollars are spent by consumers over fifty years old.

6. *Answer:* c, p. 38

   Rationale: Equal representation of ethnic groups defines multiculturalism. Growing multiculturalism is creating new challenges and opportunities for marketers. Diversity of the U.S. population is not expected to stabilize until around 2023.

7. *Answer:* c, p. 44

   Rationale: The Wheeler-Lea Act, passed in 1938, was created to broaden the power of the FTC to outlaw false and deceptive advertising practices.

8. *Answer:* a, pp. 45–46

   Rationale: Because FTC cease-and-desist orders, which demanded a firm stop a practice deemed illegal, were often challenged in the courts, the FTC has offered an alternative remedy called the *consent decree.* With this decree the firm agrees to stop a questionable business practice and settle with the FTC without admitting to behavior that is illegal and subject to further prosecution.

9. *Answer:* d, pp. 49–50

   Rationale: At the level of postconventional morality, marketing managers are less concerned about how some others might see them and are more concerned about how they judge themselves over the long run.

10. *Answer:* d, pp. 52–53

    Rationale: Unless the firm can make a profit and maintain good economic performance, the other three responsibilities are moot.

11. *Answer:* b, p. 54

    Rationale: In many cases, a corporation can have economic impacts on the host country that give it the opportunity to be a dynamic force for social change.

12. *Answer:* Demographics, social change, economic conditions, political and legal factors, technology, and competition. (p. 29)

CHAPTER

3

LEARNING OBJECTIVES

After studying this chapter, you should be able to

1. Discuss the importance of global marketing
2. Discuss the impact of multinational firms on the world economy
3. Describe the external environment facing global marketers
4. Identify the various ways of entering the global marketplace
5. List the basic elements involved in developing a global marketing mix

DEVELOPING A GLOBAL VISION

Market builders of all stripes—including an Iranian company whose detergent bears the name "Barf" (the word means "snow" in Persian)—are struggling for the same goal along the old Silk Road to China: building a brand-name presence in the republics south of Russia that until 1991 were domains of the Soviet Union.

Led by the likes of The Coca-Cola Company, The Procter & Gamble Co., and Colgate-Palmolive Co., these marketers brave bureaucracies and novice consumers to gain a beachhead in a region of fifty-five million people, where huge oil and gas reserves are fueling a rapidly growing consumer market. In an area where big global brands were unknown until a few years ago, these marketers struggle to dispel customers' quirky beliefs.

Two years ago, at the ceremonial opening of a Coca-Cola plant in Kazakstan's capital of Almaty, a young Kazak journalist sprang this question on Coca-Cola executives: "In Soviet times, they told us that if you put a tooth into a cup of cola in the evening, it would have disappeared by the morning. Is that true?"

Other brands are laboring to undo consumer misperceptions. Barbie dolls from Mattel Inc., for instance, are perceived as American and therefore have been thought fakes if stamped "Made in Hong Kong." Uzbeks peer at bar codes on Philip Morris Co.'s Marlboro cigarettes to learn where the pack was made; they will pay a premium for smokes made in the United States. Germany's Hoechst AG found that Central Asians thought non-German packaging meant a standard antibiotic was weaker. Some old-fashioned consumers still shun Western packaged foods in favor of Russian brands: The U.S. and European brands carry much shorter sell-by dates than Russian products, so people figure the Russian goods are superior.

PepsiCo, Inc. has had a particularly tough time. It is still struggling to shake off the stigma of having been the main cola of the drab old Soviet Union. Assorted other difficulties have cropped up as well, such as the brief house arrest of a delegation of Pepsi executives who journeyed to Azerbaijan and an explosion in Pepsi's Tashkent office. A Pepsi representative there says it was the heating system that blew up and that the widespread story that a grenade caused the blast is embroidery typical of the area's cutthroat business climate.[1]

on line

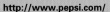

Pepsi Russia

Evaluate how well Pepsi's Web site supports its global initiatives.

http://www.pepsi.com/

Global marketers often face unique problems in the external environment compared to domestic marketers. Vastly different cultural values and ideas, for example, can present unique challenges as shown above. What are some other variables in the international external environment that can impact global marketers? Is it possible to market products the same way all over the world? Is globalization the wave of the future in international marketing?

Rewards of Global Marketing

1

Discuss the importance of global marketing

global marketing
Marketing to target markets throughout the world.

global vision
Recognizing and reacting to international marketing opportunities, being aware of threats from foreign competitors in all markets, and effectively using international distribution networks.

Today, global revolutions are under way in many areas of our lives: management, politics, communications, technology. The word *global* has assumed a new meaning, referring to a boundless mobility and competition in social, business, and intellectual arenas. No longer just an option, **global marketing** (marketing to target markets throughout the world) has become an imperative for business.

U.S. managers must develop a global vision not only to recognize and react to international marketing opportunities but also to remain competitive at home. Often a U.S. firm's toughest domestic competition comes from foreign companies. Moreover, a global vision enables a manager to understand that customer and distribution networks operate worldwide, blurring geographic and political barriers and making them increasingly irrelevant to business decisions. In summary, having a **global vision** means recognizing and reacting to international marketing opportunities, being aware of threats from foreign competitors in all markets, and effectively using international distribution networks.

Over the past two decades, world trade has climbed from $200 billion a year to $7 trillion. Countries and companies that were never considered major players in global marketing are now important, some of them showing great skill.

This display in a Shanghai department store is one of many global marketing efforts made by Gillette, whose international division generates two-thirds of the company's revenue.
© Adrian Bradshaw/SABA

Today, marketers face many challenges to their customary practices. Product development costs are rising, the life of products is getting shorter, and new technology is spreading around the world faster than ever. But marketing winners relish the pace of change instead of fearing it.

A young company with a global vision that has capitalized on new technology is Ashtech in Sunnyvale, California. Ashtech makes equipment to capture and convert satellite signals from the U.S. government's Global Positioning System. Ashtech's chief engineer and his team of ten torture and test everything built by Ashtech—expensive black boxes of chips and circuits that use satellite signals to tell surveyors, farmers, mining machine operators, and others where they are with great accuracy. Over half of Ashtech's output is exported. Its biggest customer is Japan.[2]

Adopting a global vision can be very lucrative for a company. Gillette, for example, gets about two-thirds of its revenue from its international division. About 70 percent of General Motors' profits come from operations outside the United States. While Cheetos and Ruffles haven't done very well in Japan, the potato chip has been quite successful. PepsiCo's (owner of Frito-Lay) overseas snack business brings in more than $3.25 billion annually.[3]

Global marketing is not a one-way street, whereby only U.S. companies sell their wares and services throughout the world. Foreign competition in the domestic market used to be relatively rare but now is found in almost every industry. In fact, in many industries the United States has lost significant market share to imported products. In electronics, cameras, automobiles, fine china, tractors, leather goods, and a host of other consumer and industrial products, U.S. companies have struggled at home to maintain their market shares against foreign competitors.

For the past two decades, U.S. companies often appeared not to be competitive with foreign rivals. Today, however, America has embarked on a new productivity boom. In the 1990s, nonfarm productivity rose at a 2.6 percent rate annually, more than twice the rate of the previous two decades.[4] The United States has the highest productivity among all industrialized countries. The United States, for example, has sixty-three personal computers per one hundred employed workers, to Japan's seventeen.[5] The United States is the low-cost producer among industrialized nations, with unit labor costs rising more slowly than in either Japan or Germany. American manufacturers are 10 to 20 percent more productive than German or Japanese manufacturers, and the U.S. service sector is 30 to 50 percent more productive. American business is fully prepared to compete in the global marketplace.

Importance of Global Marketing to the United States

Many countries depend more on international commerce than the United States does. For example, France, Great Britain, and Germany all derive more than 19 percent of their gross domestic product from world trade, compared to about 12 percent for the United States.[6] Nevertheless, the impact of international business on the U.S. economy is still impressive:

- The United States exports about a fifth of its industrial production and a third of its farm products.[7]
- One of every sixteen jobs in the United States is directly or indirectly supported by exports.
- U.S. businesses export over $500 billion in goods to foreign countries every year, and almost a third of U.S. corporate profits is derived from our international trade and foreign investment.[8]
- In 1999, exports accounted for 20 percent of America's growth in economic activity.[9]
- The United States is the world's leading exporter of grain, selling more than $12 billion of this product a year to foreign countries, or about one-third of all agricultural exports.[10]
- Chemicals, office machinery and computers, automobiles, aircraft, and electrical and industrial machinery make up almost half of all nonagricultural exports.

These statistics might seem to imply that practically every business in the United States is selling its wares throughout the world, but nothing could be further from the truth. About 85 percent of all U.S. exports of manufactured goods are shipped by 250 companies; less than 10 percent of all manufacturing businesses, or around twenty-five thousand companies, export their goods on a regular basis.[11] Most small and medium-size firms are essentially nonparticipants in global trade and marketing. Only the very large multinational companies have seriously attempted to compete worldwide. Fortunately, more of the smaller companies are now aggressively pursuing international markets.

A slight plurality of American men think that globalization has been good for the United States because it has opened up new markets for American products and resulted in more jobs. But a clear majority of women think it has been bad

exhibit 3.1

American Attitudes Toward Globalization

Is the fact that the American economy has become increasingly global good or bad?

All Adults	Good	Bad
Men	42%	48%
Women	46	44
Whites	43	46
Blacks	29	63
Urban	43	44
Suburbs/towns	45	46
Rural	32	57
Under $30,000	34	55
$30,000–$50,000	42	49
Over $50,000	52	40
Professional/managers	55	35
White-collar workers	40	49
Blue-collar workers	36	57
High school or less	33	59
College graduates	58	30

SOURCE: From "Opinions Diverge on Globalization" by Albert Hunt, *The Wall Street Journal,* June 27 1997. Reprinted by permission of The Wall Street Journal.

because it has subjected American companies and employees to unfair competition and cheap labor. Typically, more economically pressured groups have the most negative reactions to globalization (see Exhibit 3.1).

Multinational Firms

2

Discuss the impact of multinational firms on the world economy

multinational corporation
A company that is heavily engaged in international trade, beyond exporting and importing.

The United States has a number of large companies that are global marketers. Many of them have been very successful. A company that is heavily engaged in international trade, beyond exporting and importing, is called a **multinational corporation**. Multinational corporations move resources, goods, services, and skills across national boundaries without regard to the country in which the headquarters is located. The leading multinational firms in the world are listed in Exhibit 3.2.

A multinational corporation is more than a business entity, as the following paragraph explains:

> The multinational corporation is, among other things, a private "government," often richer in assets and more populous in stockholders and employees than are some of the nation-states in which it carries on business. It is simultaneously a "citizen" of several nation-states, owing obedience to their laws and paying them taxes, yet having its own objectives and being responsive to a management located in a foreign nation. Small wonder that some critics see in it an irresponsible instrument of private economic power or of economic "imperialism" by its home country. Others view it as an international carrier of advanced management science and technology, an agent for the global transmission of cultures bringing closer the day when a common set of ideals will unite mankind.[12]

Many multinational corporations are enormous. For example, the sales of both Exxon and General Motors are larger than the gross domestic product of all but twenty-two nations in the world. A multinational company may have several

exhibit 3.2

The World's Largest Multinational Corporations

Rank	Company	Country	Revenues ($ Millions)	Employees
1	General Motors	U.S.	178,174.0	608,000
2	Ford Motor	U.S.	153,627.0	363,892
3	Mitsui	Japan	142,688.3	40,000
4	Mitsubishi	Japan	128,922.3	36,000
5	Royal Dutch/Shell Group	Brit./Neth.	128,141.7	105,000
6	Itochu	Japan	126,631.9	6,675
7	Exxon	U.S.	122,379.0	80,000
8	Wal-Mart Stores	U.S	119,299.0	825,000
9	Marubeni	Japan	111,121.2	64,000
10	Sumitomo	Japan	102,395.2	29,500
11	Toyota Motor	Japan	95,137.0	159,035
12	General Electric	U.S.	90,840.0	276,000
13	Nissho Iwai	Japan	81,893.8	18,158
14	Intl. Business Machines	U.S.	78,508.0	269,465
15	Nippon Telegraph & Telephone	Japan	76,983.7	226,000
16	AXA	France	76,874.4	80,613
17	Daimler-Benz	Germany	71,561.4	300,068
18	Daewoo	South Korea	71,525.8	265,044
19	Nippon Life Insurance	Japan	71,388.2	75,851
20	British Petroleum	Britain	71,193.5	56,450
21	Hitachi	Japan	68,567.0	331,494
22	Volkswagen	Germany	65,328.2	279,892
23	Matsushita Electric Industrial	Japan	64,280.6	275,962
24	Siemens	Germany	63,754.6	386,000
25	Chrysler	U.S.	61,147.0	121,000

SOURCE: "The Fortune Global 500," *Fortune*, 3 August 1998, p. F1.

worldwide headquarters, depending on where certain markets or technologies are. Britain's APV, a maker of food-processing equipment, has a different headquarters for each of its worldwide businesses. Hewlett-Packard moved the headquarters of its personal computer business from the United States to Grenoble, France. ABB Asea Brown Boveri, the European electrical engineering giant based in Zurich, Switzerland, groups its thousands of products and services into fifty or so business areas. Each is run by a leadership team that crafts global business strategy, sets product development priorities, and decides where to make its products. None of the teams work out of Zurich headquarters; they are scattered around the world. Leadership for power transformers is based in Germany, electric drives in Finland, and process automation in the United States.

Multinational Advantage

Large multinationals have several advantages over other companies. For instance, multinationals can often overcome trade problems. Taiwan and South Korea have long had an embargo against Japanese cars for political reasons and to help domestic carmakers. Yet Honda USA, a Japanese-owned company based in the United States, sends Accords to Taiwan and Korea. Another example is Germany's BASF, a major chemical and drug manufacturer. Its biotechnology research at home is challenged by the environmentally conscious Green movement. So BASF moved its cancer and immune-system research to Cambridge, Massachusetts.

Another advantage for multinationals is their ability to sidestep regulatory problems. U.S. drugmaker SmithKline and Britain's Beecham decided to merge in part so they could avoid licensing and regulatory hassles in their largest markets. The merged company can say it's an insider in both Europe and the United States. "When we go to Brussels, we're a member state [of the European Union]," one executive explains. "And when we go to Washington, we're an American company."[13]

At Procter & Gamble's international research center, P&G laundry detergents are tested using water and washing machines from different countries. The multinational advantage means that products developed for one country can easily be tested and marketed in another.
© 1993 Louis Psihoyos/Matrix International, Inc.

Multinationals can also shift production from one plant to another as market conditions change. When European demand for a certain solvent declined, Dow Chemical instructed its German plant to switch to manufacturing a chemical that had been imported from Louisiana and Texas. Computer models help Dow make decisions like these so it can run its plants more efficiently and keep costs down.

Multinationals can also tap new technology from around the world. Xerox has introduced some eighty different office copiers in the United States that were designed and built by Fuji Xerox, its joint venture with a Japanese company. Versions of the superconcentrated detergent that Procter & Gamble first formulated in Japan in response to a rival's product are now being sold under the Ariel brand name in Europe and being tested under the Cheer and Tide labels in the United States. Also, consider Otis Elevator's development of the Elevonic 411, an elevator that is programmed to send more cars to floors where demand is high. It was developed by six research centers in five countries. Otis's group in Farmington, Connecticut, handled the systems integration, a Japanese group designed the special motor drives that make the elevators ride smoothly, a French group perfected the door systems, a German group handled the electronics, and a Spanish group took care of the small-geared components. Otis says the international effort saved more than $10 million in design costs and cut the process from four years to two.

Finally, multinationals can often save a lot in labor costs, even in highly unionized countries. For example, Xerox started moving copier-rebuilding work to Mexico, where wages are much lower. Its union in Rochester, New York, objected because it saw that members' jobs were at risk. Eventually the union agreed to change work styles and to improve productivity to keep the jobs at home.

Global Marketing Standardization

Traditionally, marketing-oriented multinational corporations have operated somewhat differently in each country. They use a strategy of providing different product features, packaging, advertising, and so on. However, Ted Levitt, a Harvard professor, described a trend toward what he referred to as "global marketing," with a slightly different meaning.[14] He contended that communication and technology have made the world smaller so that almost everyone everywhere wants all the things they have heard about, seen, or experienced. Thus, he saw the emergence of global markets for standardized consumer products on a huge scale, as opposed

Coca-Cola Company
How does Coca-Cola's mission statement reflect its commitment to global markets? Does the site as a whole reflect this commitment?
http://www.cocacola.com/

Colgate-Palmolive
Compare the Colgate-Palmolive site with the Coca-Cola site. Which more strongly conveys a global image?
http://www.colgate.com/

Procter & Gamble
Visit P&G's World Telescope to learn more about the company's global community. What countries do you find there?
http://www.pg.com/

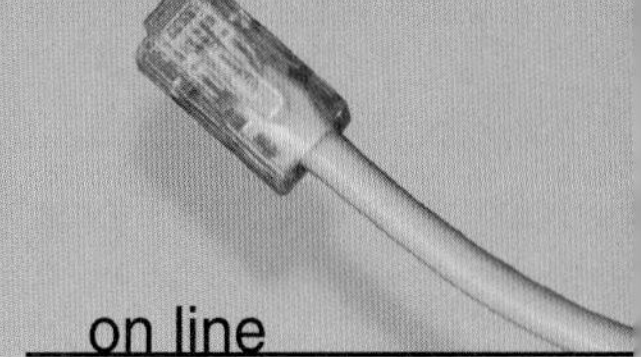
on line

to segmented foreign markets with different products. In this book, global marketing is defined as individuals and organizations using a global vision to effectively market goods and services across national boundaries. To make the distinction, we can refer to Levitt's notion as **global marketing standardization**.

global marketing standardization
Production of uniform products that can be sold the same way all over the world.

Global marketing standardization presumes that the markets throughout the world are becoming more alike. Firms practicing global marketing standardization produce "globally standardized products" to be sold the same way all over the world. Uniform production should enable companies to lower production and marketing costs and increase profits. However, research indicates that superior sales and profits do not necessarily follow from global standardization.[15]

Levitt cited Coca-Cola, Colgate-Palmolive, and McDonald's as successful global marketers. However, Levitt's critics point out that the success of these three companies is really based on variation, not on offering the same product everywhere. McDonald's, for example, changes its salad dressings for French tastes and sells beer and mineral water in its restaurants there. It also offers different products to suit tastes in Germany (where it offers beer) as well as in Japan (where it offers sake). Further, the fact that Coca-Cola and Colgate-Palmolive sell some of their products in more than 160 countries does not signify that they have adopted a high degree of standardization for all their products globally. Only three Coca-Cola brands are standardized, and one of them, Sprite, has a different formulation in Japan. Some Colgate-Palmolive products are marketed in just a few countries. Axion paste dishwashing detergent, for example, was formulated for developing countries, and La Croix Plus detergent was custom made for the French market. Colgate toothpaste is marketed the same way globally, although its advanced Gum Protection Formula is used in only twenty-seven nations.

Nevertheless, some multinational corporations are moving toward a degree of global marketing standardization. Eastman Kodak has launched a world brand of blank tapes for videocassette recorders. Procter & Gamble (P&G) calls its new philosophy "global planning." The idea is to determine which product modifications are necessary from country to country while trying to minimize those modifications. P&G has at least four products that are marketed similarly in most parts of the world: Camay soap, Crest toothpaste, Head and Shoulders shampoo, and Pampers diapers. However, the smell of Camay, the flavor of Crest, and the formula of Head and Shoulders, as well as the advertising, vary from country to country.

External Environment Facing Global Marketers

3
Describe the external environment facing global marketers

A global marketer or a firm considering global marketing faces problems, often due to the external environment, as many of the same environmental factors that operate in the domestic market also exist internationally. These factors include culture, economic and technological development, political structure, demographic makeup, and natural resources.

Culture

Central to any society is the common set of values shared by its citizens that determine what is socially acceptable. Culture underlies the family, the educational system, religion, and the social class system. The network of social organizations generates overlapping roles and status positions. These values and roles have a tremendous effect on people's preferences and thus on marketers' options. Inca

Coca-Cola uses superior distribution channels to gain a competitive advantage in U.S. and international markets.
© Paul Chesley/Tony Stone Images

Kola, a fruity, greenish-yellow carbonated drink, is the largest-selling soft drink in Peru. Despite being compared to "liquid bubble gum," the drink has become a symbol of national pride and heritage. The drink was invented in Peru and contains only fruit indigenous to the country. A local consumer of about a six-pack per day says, "I drink Inca Kola because it makes me feel like a Peruvian." He tells his young daughter, "This is our drink, not something invented overseas. It is named for your ancestors, the great Inca warriors."[16]

As new generations come along, old preconceptions about cultural values may no longer hold. For example, we think of the French as heavy wine drinkers. Yet, Pascal Guiard does not drink wine. "Wine is not as much a part of our culture anymore," says the twenty-eight-year-old Paris accountant, confessing his scandalous nondrinking habit over a cup of espresso. "We are a different generation from our parents, a generation that consumes more than any other, but wine is not part of it."[17] In 1965, each adult citizen consumed an average of forty-two gallons of wine per year. By 1995, average consumption had fallen by half, to twenty gallons. Frederick Fischler, a French sociologist who studies nutritional trends, believes the decline has to do with France's transformation into a postindustrial society. "The two social classes that traditionally consumed vast amounts of low-quality wine as an energy source—farmers and factory workers—have seen their numbers decline sharply in recent years," Fischler says.[18] The main substitutes for wine seem to be bottled water and soft drinks, particularly Coca-Cola.

Tampering with a product that has strong cultural connections for a country can often raise an emotional outcry. Consider the "Ethics in Marketing" box regarding Ricetec, Inc., an Alvin, Texas rice grower.

Language is another important aspect of culture. Marketers must take care in translating product names, slogans, and promotional messages so as not to convey the wrong meaning. For example, Mitsubishi Motors had to rename its Pajero model in Spanish-speaking countries because the term describes a sexual activity. Toyota Motor's MR2 model dropped the number 2 in France because the combination sounds like a French swearword.[19] The literal translation of Coca-Cola in Chinese characters means "bite the wax tadpole." Marketers must be careful in translating promotions, product instructions, and other materials from one language to another.

Each country has its own customs and traditions that determine business practices and influence negotiations with foreign customers. In many countries, personal relationships are more important than financial considerations. For instance, skipping social engagements in Mexico may lead to lost sales. Negotiations in Japan often include long evenings of dining, drinking, and entertaining, and only after a close personal relationship has been formed do business negotiations begin. The Japanese go through a very elaborate ritual when exchanging business cards. An American businesswoman had no idea about this important cultural tradition. She came into a meeting and tossed some of her business cards across the table at a group of stunned Japanese executives. One of them turned his back on her and walked out. The deal never went through.[20]

An area in which businesspeople often find it difficult to know what is right in different cultures is the notion of time. There are no overriding rights or wrongs to a particular pace of life. They are simply different. Not understanding a culture's notion of time can sometimes lead to situations that are awkward and embarrassing or, in extreme cases, to a loss of business. Exhibit 3.3 offers six lessons for global marketers about cultural differences on the concept of time.

Fortunately, some habits and customs seem to be the same throughout much of the world. A recent study of 37,743 consumers from forty different countries

Research Foundation for Science, Technology, and Ecology

Rice is only one crop of concern in the landscape of biotechnology. To read more about the dispute surrounding patenting plants native to India and other Asian countries, visit the Web site of the Research Foundation for Science, Technology, and Ecology at
http://www.indiaserver.com/betas/vshiva/

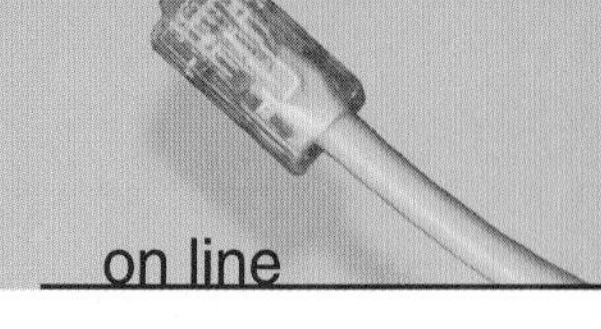

on line

ethics in marketing

Basmati Rice with a Texas Twist

Supermarkets across the country are selling purple boxes of rice that appear to be from India. Labels feature a scrawl of the Taj Mahal and the words: "Kasmati, Indian-style Basmati." But the rice is grown in Texas; and that goes against the grain of purists. In India, everyone—from politicians and editorialists to chefs, shippers, and rice farmers—is angry about this "imposter." Recently, hundreds of farmers gathered in New Delhi to protest against the American product, despite the fact that Kasmati's maker, Ricetec, Inc., has only 1 percent of the U.S. rice market.

Basmati is the gold standard of Indian rice. "How dare they call it basmati?" says Madhur Jaffrey, the Julia Child of Indian cooking. "It's our plant and has meaning and history." Adds Anil Adlakha, executive director of the All India Rice Exporters' Association, "People are ruthless."

As the American appetite grows for ethnic and exotic foods, more and more of it is being produced in the United States and packaged to look and sound foreign. Although American dairies have been making "Swiss" cheese for decades, there is much growth in products ranging from feta cheese to olive oil, ale, and couscous. To the cultures that developed these products over centuries, it can be shocking to see their appellations stolen. In rare cases, countries have done something about reserving the name; for example, scotch for the whisky of Scotland and Roquefort for the blue cheese from the town of the same name in southern France.

Basmati isn't a place but merely a word that means "fragrant and flavorful" in Hindi. The rice is distinctively shaped (slender and softly pointed at the ends); it provides a fluffy bed of long, separate grains with a mouthwatering aroma, thanks—Indians and Pakistanis say—to the water of Himalayan streams. Indeed, says G. L. Soni, a native Indian in Flushing, New York, who imports basmati to the United States, "You cannot grow basmati rice in the United States because the climate, soil, and water are different. There's no comparison."

India and Pakistan are contending that basmati could come only from a certain region in the two countries near the Himalayas. They also argue that consumers associate basmati with India and Pakistan. Certainly Britons do. The British government, which takes basmati to mean Indian rice, refused entry to Ricetec's Kasmati on the grounds that the company was passing it off as something it wasn't. Ricetec's Kasmati "has hijacked our history, geography and culture," wrote one man in a letter to the *Hindu*, a national daily newspaper, urging the Ministry of Commerce to fight Ricetec.[21]

Do you think Ricetec is simply engaged in "smart marketing?" Note that the package doesn't say "grown in India." Does this make it valid to sell as "Indian-style basmati?" The Indian government had failed to trademark the name *basmati*. The company says, "If you don't protect what you have, you don't have the right to keep it." Do you agree?

found that 95 percent brushed their teeth daily.[22] Other activities that majorities worldwide engage in include reading a newspaper, listening to the radio, taking a shower, and washing their hair.

Economic and Technological Development

A second major factor in the external environment facing the global marketer is the level of economic development in the countries where it operates. In general, complex and sophisticated industries are found in developed countries, and more basic industries are found in less developed nations. Higher average family incomes are common in the more developed countries compared to the less developed markets. Larger incomes mean greater purchasing power and demand not only for consumer goods and services but also for the machinery and workers required to produce consumer goods.

exhibit 3.3

Six Lessons About the Cultural Notion of Time

Lesson 1: Be punctual. Learn to translate appointment times. What is the appropriate time to arrive for an appointment with a professor? With a government official? For a party? When should you expect others to show up, if at all? Should we expect our hosts to be upset if we arrive late—or promptly? Are people expected to assume responsibility for their lateness?

Lesson 2: Understand the line between work time and social time. What is the relationship between work time and down time? Some questions have easy answers: How many hours are there in the workday? Other questions are more difficult to answer. For example, how much of the workday is spent on-task and how much time is spent socializing, chatting, and being pleasant? For Americans in a big city, the typical ratio is in the neighborhood of about 80:20; about 80 percent of work time is spent on-task and about 20 percent is used for fraternizing, chitchatting, and the like. But many countries deviate sharply from this formula. In countries like India and Nepal, for example, be prepared for a balance closer to 50:50. When you are in Japan, the distinction between work and social time can often be meaningless.

Lesson 3: Study the rules of the waiting game. When you arrive in a foreign culture, be sure to inquire about the specifics of their version of the waiting game. Are their rules based on the principle that time is money? Who is expected to wait for whom, under what circumstances, and for how long? Are some players exempt from waiting?

Lesson 4: Learn to reinterpret "doing nothing." How do your hosts treat pauses, silences, or doing nothing at all? Is appearing chronically busy a quality to be admired or pitied? Is doing nothing a waste of time? Is constant activity seen as an even bigger waste of time? What must it be like to live in a country like Brunei, where people begin their day by asking: "What isn't going to happen today?"

Lesson 5: Ask about accepted sequences. Be prepared for what time frames to expect. Each culture sets rules about the sequence of events. Is it work before play or vice versa? Do people take all of their sleep at night or is there a siesta in the mid-afternoon?

Lesson 6: Are people on clock time or event time? This may be the most slippery lesson of all. A move from clock time to event time requires a complete shift of consciousness. It entails the suspension of industrialized society's temporal golden rule: "Time is money."

SOURCE: From "Re-learning to Tell Time" by Robert Levine, *American Demographics,* January 1998. Reprinted with permission from American Demographics magazine.

One way to get an idea of price levels around the world is to compare the price of a Big Mac in various countries. In 1997, the average price of a Big Mac around the world was $2.42. The cheapest Big Mac was found in Beijing for $1.16, whereas the most expensive was in Geneva at $4.02. Big Macs are also expensive in Denmark ($3.95), Israel ($3.40), Sweden ($3.37), and Belgium ($3.09). They're a bargain in Poland ($1.39), Hungary ($1.52), Malaysia ($1.55), and South Africa ($1.76). The theory is that if all dollars were equal, they would buy the same in each country (after converting local currencies to dollars). If this theory holds, the Chinese Yuan is the most undervalued in the world (by 52%) and the Swiss franc the most overvalued (by 66%).[23]

To appreciate marketing opportunities (or lack of them), it is helpful to examine the five stages of economic growth and technological development: traditional society, preindustrial society, takeoff economy, industrializing society, and fully industrialized society.

traditional society
A society in the earliest stages of economic development, largely agricultural, with a social structure and value system that provide little opportunity for upward mobility.

The Traditional Society Countries in the traditional stage are in the earliest phase of development. A **traditional society** is largely agricultural, with a social structure and value system that provide little opportunity for upward mobility. The culture may be highly stable, and economic growth may not get started without a powerful disruptive force. Therefore, to introduce single units of technology into such a country is probably wasted effort. In Ghana, for instance, a tollway sixteen miles long and six lanes wide, intended to modernize distribution, does not connect to any city or village or other road.

The Preindustrial Society The second stage of economic development, the **preindustrial society**, involves economic and social change and the emergence of a middle class with an entrepreneurial spirit. Nationalism may begin to rise, along with restrictions on multinational organizations. Countries like Madagascar and Uganda are in this stage. Effective marketing in these countries is very difficult because they lack the modern distribution and communication systems that U.S. marketers often take for granted. Peru, for example, did not establish a television network until 1975.

preindustrial society
A society in the second stage of economic development, involving economic and social change and the emergence of a middle class with an entrepreneurial spirit.

The Takeoff Economy The **takeoff economy** is the period of transition from a developing to a developed nation. New industries arise and a generally healthy social and political climate emerges. Kenya and Vietnam have entered the takeoff stage. Although politics in Kenya are not considered particularly healthy, there are significant areas of economic growth. Oil exploration is increasing and Kenya is set to become the world's largest exporter of tea.[24] In an effort to develop its economy, Vietnam now offers large tax breaks to foreign investors who promise jobs. Gold Medal Footware, headquartered in Taiwan, now employs five hundred young workers in Danang and hopes to increase the number to twenty-five hundred.

takeoff economy
The third stage of economic development involves a period of transition from a developing to a developed nation.

The Industrializing Society The fourth phase of economic development is the **industrializing society**. During this era, technology spreads from sectors of the economy that powered the takeoff to the rest of the nation. Mexico, China, India, and Brazil are among the nations in this phase of development.

industrializing society
The fourth stage of economic development, when technology spreads from sectors of the economy that powered the takeoff to the rest of the nation.

Countries in the industrializing stage begin to produce capital goods and consumer durable products. These industries also foster economic growth. As a result, a large middle class begins to emerge, and the demand for luxuries and services grows.

One of the fastest growing economies in the world today (about 10 percent per year) is China. This has resulted in per capita incomes quadrupling in only the last decade and a half.[25] A population of 1.2 billion is producing a gross domestic product of over $1.2 trillion a year. This new industrial giant will be the world's largest manufacturing zone, the largest market for such key industries as telecommunications and aerospace, and one of the largest users of capital.

Rapidly growing large markets like China create enormous opportunities for American global marketers. One tempting market, for example, is the twenty-one million babies born in China each year. One-child families are the rule, so parents spare few expenses bringing up the baby. The Walt Disney Company is in department stores in a dozen or so Chinese cities with the Disney Babies line of T-shirts, rattles, and crib linens—all emblazoned with likenesses of baby Mickey Mouses and other characters.

Marmon Group Inc., a closely held Chicago manufacturer, was in China marketing heavy industrial equipment when executives saw an opportunity in baby food. The company went into business with a local manufacturer to produce a line of pureed meat, vegetables, and fruit for tiny diners, called Huiliduo, a mellifluous but meaningless word. Jeffrey Li, Marmon's director of China projects, says the venture is aiming to churn out three hundred thousand jars of baby food in 1999, its first year, and achieve an annual growth rate of 50 percent.[26]

The Fully Industrialized Society The **fully industrialized society**, the fifth stage of economic development, is an exporter of manufactured products, many of which are based on advanced technology. Examples include automobiles, computers, airplanes, oil exploration equipment, and telecommunications gear. Great Britain, Japan, Germany, France, Canada, and the United States fall into this category.

fully industrialized society
The fifth stage of economic development, a society that is an exporter of manufactured products, many of which are based on advanced technology.

The wealth of the industrialized nations creates tremendous market potential. Therefore, industrialized countries trade extensively. Also, industrialized nations usually ship manufactured goods to developing countries in exchange for raw materials like petroleum, precious metals, and bauxite.

Political Structure

Political structure is a third important variable facing global marketers. Government policies run the gamut from no private ownership and minimal individual freedom to little central government and maximum personal freedom. As rights of private property increase, government-owned industries and centralized planning tend to decrease. But rarely will a political environment be at one extreme or the other. India, for instance, is a republic with elements of socialism, monopoly capitalism, and competitive capitalism in its political ideology.

Many countries are changing from a centrally planned economy to a market-oriented one. Eastern European nations like Hungary and Poland have also been moving quickly with market reforms. Many of the reforms have increased foreign trade and investment. For example, in Poland, foreigners are now allowed to invest in all areas of industry, including agriculture, manufacturing, and trade. Poland even gives companies that invest in certain sectors some tax advantages.

Russia is progressing more slowly than many Eastern European countries, but it is still headed in the direction of a market-oriented economy. More than five thousand Russian managers are studying abroad, and many more are studying market-oriented principles within Russia. Moreover, growing Russian companies realize that installing professional management teams is the next step in legitimizing the empires built from speculative profits or cheap state assets.

An excellent example is ZAO Soyuzcontract. The $1 billion trading giant made U.S. chicken legs a hit on Russian dinner tables. It also took Herschi cola, a brand almost unknown outside of the Netherlands, and made it the number four soft drink in Russia. Yet costs were badly managed and operations were disorganized. Recently, a new management team has gradually emerged and it is tackling the partners' dream of becoming one of Russia's first true multinationals. A new vice president for marketing—a Russian lured from a major Western food company operating there—is planning branding and pricing strategies with the aim of raising Herschi from fourth to third place in the soft-drink market, behind Pepsi and Coca-Cola. A Swiss vice president for logistics is streamlining procedures for shipping from the United States. A French chief financial officer is consolidating international operations, overhauling accounting and securing trade financing from Western banks, partly to save the $5 million to $8 million a year that the company now pays in fines when it lacks the cash to pay for cargoes that have arrived.[27]

Changes leading to market-oriented economies are not restricted to Eastern Europe and Russia. Many countries within Latin America are also attempting market reforms. Countries like Brazil, Argentina, and Mexico are reducing government control over many sectors of the economy. They are also selling state-owned companies to foreign and domestic investors and removing trade barriers that have protected their markets against foreign competition. Brazil has now overtaken Italy and Mexico to become the tenth largest automobile manufacturer in the world. India has recently opened up its market of nine hundred million consumers. While India's per capita average income is quite low ($330), an estimated 250 million+ Indians have enough income to be considered middle class.[28]

Another trend in the political environment is the growth of nationalist sentiments among citizens who have strong loyalties and devotion to their country. Failure to appreciate emerging nationalist feelings can create major problems for multinational firms. In 1995, Hindus in India smashed Pepsi bottles and burned Pepsi posters. And the country's first Kentucky Fried Chicken, in Bangalore, was targeted by protesters claiming to defend Indian culture against Western encroachment.

Another potential cloud on the horizon for some types of companies doing business abroad is the threat of nationalization. Some countries have nationalized (taken ownership of) certain industries or companies, such as airlines in Italy and Bull Computer in France, to infuse more capital into their development. Industries are also nationalized to allow domestic corporations to sell vital goods below cost. For example, for many years France has been supplying coal to users at a loss.

Legal Considerations Closely related to and often intertwined with the political environment are legal considerations. Nationalistic sentiments of the French led to a 1996 law that requires pop music stations to play at least 40 percent of their songs in French. (French teenagers love American and English rock and roll.)[29] Christian Bellanger, president of a popular Paris station called "Skyrock," said the law was "totalitarian and useless. The major (French) recording companies do not produce enough good French music to fill the schedule."[30] The measure is being policed by the government's watchdog audiovisual committee, the Conseil Superieur de l'Audovisuel. With the help of computers, the official ear will be tuned to about thirteen hundred radio stations, which risk losing their broadcast licenses if they break the law.

Despite the protective stance taken by Beijing, China represents huge opportunities for direct sellers. These women are attending a training seminar held by Mary Kay Cosmetics for its new beauty consultants.
© Fritz Hoffman/The Image Works

In April 1998, the Chinese State Council ordered all direct-sales operations to cease immediately. Alarmed by a rise in pyramid schemes by some direct sellers and uneasy about the big sales meetings that direct sellers hold, Beijing gave all companies that hold direct-selling licenses until Oct. 31, 1998, to convert to retail outlets or shut down altogether. The move threatens Avon's China sales, now about $75 million a year, and puts Avon, Amway, and Mary Kay's combined China investment of roughly $180 million at risk. It also creates problems for Sara Lee Corp. and Tupperware Company, which recently launched direct-sales efforts in China.[31]

Many legal structures are designed to either encourage or limit trade. Some examples follow:

- *Tariff:* tax levied on the goods entering a country. For example, trucks imported into the United States face a 25 percent tariff. Since the 1930s, tariffs have tended to decrease as a barrier to trade. But they have often been replaced by nontariff barriers, such as quotas, boycotts, and other restrictions.
- *Quota:* limit on the amount of a specific product that can enter a country. The United States has strict quotas for imported textiles, sugar, and many dairy products. Several U.S. companies have sought quotas as a means of protection from foreign competition. For example, Harley-Davidson convinced the U.S. government to place quotas on large motorcycles imported to the United States. These quotas gave the company the opportunity to improve its quality and compete with Japanese motorcycles.
- *Boycott:* exclusion of all products from certain countries or companies. Governments use boycotts to exclude companies from countries with whom they have a political dispute. Several Arab nations boycotted Coca-Cola because it maintained distributors in Israel.

- *Exchange control:* law compelling a company earning foreign exchange from its exports to sell it to a control agency, usually a central bank. A company wishing to buy goods abroad must first obtain foreign exchange from the control agency. Generally, exchange controls limit the importation of luxuries. For instance, Avon Products drastically cut back new production lines and products in the Philippines because exchange controls prevented the conversion of pesos to dollars to ship back to the home office. The pesos had to be used in the Philippines. China restricts the amount of foreign currency each Chinese company is allowed to keep from its exports. Therefore, Chinese companies must usually get the government's approval to release funds before they can buy products from foreign companies.
- *Market grouping:* also known as a common trade alliance; occurs when several countries agree to work together to form a common trade area that enhances trade opportunities. The best-known market grouping is the European Community (EC), whose members are Belgium, France, Germany, Italy, Luxembourg, the Netherlands, Denmark, Ireland, Spain, the United Kingdom, Portugal, and Greece. The EC has been evolving for nearly four decades, yet until recently, many trade barriers existed among member nations.
- *Trade agreement:* agreement to stimulate international trade. Not all government efforts are meant to stifle imports or investment by foreign corporations. The **Uruguay Round** of trade negotiations, which created the World Trade Organization, is an agreement to dramatically lower trade barriers worldwide. Adopted in 1994, the agreement was signed by 117 nations in Marrakesh, Morocco. It is the most ambitious global trade agreement ever negotiated. The agreement reduces tariffs by one-third worldwide. This, in turn, should raise global income by $235 billion annually by 2005. Perhaps most notable is the recognition of the new global realities. For the first time there is an agreement covering services, intellectual property rights, and trade-related investment measures such as exchange controls.

Uruguay Round
An agreement to dramatically lower trade barriers worldwide.

World Trade Organization (WTO)
A new trade organization that replaces the old General Agreement on Tariffs and Trade (GATT).

General Agreement on Tariffs and Trade (GATT)
Provided loopholes that enabled countries to avoid trade-barrier reduction agreements.

The Uruguay Round makes several major changes in world trading practices:

- *Entertainment, pharmaceuticals, integrated circuits, and software:* New rules will protect patents, copyrights, and trademarks for twenty years. Computer programs receive fifty years' protection and semiconductor chips receive ten years'. But many developing nations will have a decade to phase in patent protection for drugs. France, which limits the number of U.S. movies and TV shows that can be shown, refused to liberalize market access for the U.S. entertainment industry.
- *Financial, legal, and accounting services:* Services come under international trading rules for the first time, potentially creating a vast opportunity for these competitive U.S. industries. Now it will be easier to admit managers and key personnel into a country. Licensing standards for professionals, such as doctors, cannot discriminate against foreign applicants. That is, foreign applicants cannot be held to higher standards than domestic practitioners.
- *Agriculture:* Europe will gradually reduce farm subsidies, opening new opportunities for such U.S. farm exports as wheat and corn. Japan and Korea will begin to import rice. But growers of U.S. sugar, citrus fruit, and peanuts will have their subsidies trimmed.
- *Textiles and apparel:* Strict quotas limiting imports from developing countries will be phased out over ten years, causing further job loss in the U.S. clothing trade. But retailers and consumers will be the big winners, because quotas now add $15 billion a year to clothing prices.
- *A new trade organization:* The new **World Trade Organization (WTO)** replaces the old **General Agreement on Tariffs and Trade (GATT)**, which was created in 1948. The old GATT agreements provided extensive loopholes that enabled

The movies showing at this cinema in Aix-en-Provence, France, represent a regulated mix of foreign and domestic films. France and more recently Canada have refused to liberalize market access to the U.S. entertainment and publishing industries, respectively.
© Stuart Cohen/The Image Works

countries to avoid the trade-barrier reduction agreements. It was like obeying the law if you wanted to! Today, all WTO members must fully comply with all agreements under the Uruguay Round. The WTO also has an effective dispute settlement procedure with strict time limits to resolve disputes.

The new service agreement under the Uruguay Round requires member countries to create adequate penalties against counterfeiting and piracy. China, which wants to join the WTO, has done little to control its rampant piracy problem. U.S. producers of records, books, motion pictures, and software lose about $2.5 billion a year to Chinese piracy.[32] Chinese authorities have destroyed eight hundred thousand pirated audio and videocassettes and more than forty thousand software programs. Some $3 million worth of fines have been levied in connection with nine thousand cases of trademark violation. Yet, the government has failed to close twenty-nine known plants pirating music and computer CDs. These production facilities have politically connected backers.[33]

The trend toward globalization has brought to the fore several specific examples of the influence of political structures and legal considerations: Japanese keiretsu, the North American Free Trade Agreement, and the European Union.

Japanese Keiretsu Japanese nationalism produced the **keiretsu,** or societies of business, which take two main forms. Bank-centered keiretsu are massive industrial combines of twenty to forty-five core companies centered on a bank (see Exhibit 3.4).

keiretsu
Japanese societies of business, which take one of two main forms: a bank-centered keiretsu, or a massive industrial combine centered around a bank; and a supply keiretsu, or a group of companies dominated by the major manufacturer they provide with supplies.

exhibit 3.4

A Japanese Keiretsu

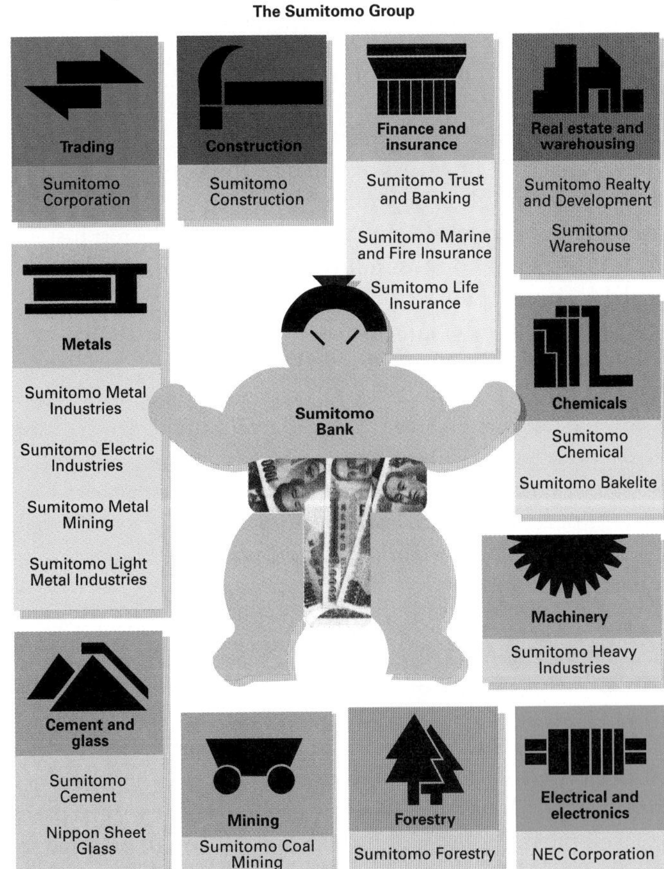

SOURCE: Adapted and reprinted by permission of *Harvard Business Review* from "A Brief History of Japan's Keiretsu" in *Computers and the Coming of the U.S. Keiretsu*, by Charles H. Ferguson, *Harvard Business Review* (July–August 1990).

They enable companies to share business risk and provide a way to allocate investment to strategic industries. Supply keiretsu are groups of companies dominated by the major manufacturer they provide with supplies. Keiretsu exist with the blessing of the Japanese government. After World War II, Japan wanted to help reestablish industry by encouraging cooperation. The Japanese government was also hoping the strong networks would help keep out foreign companies.[34]

Keiretsu have indeed blocked U.S. companies, and others, from the Japanese market. Consider the Matsushita keiretsu. Matsushita, one of the world's top twenty manufacturers, makes Panasonic, National, Technics, and Quasar brands. Matsushita also controls a chain of about twenty-five thousand National retail stores in Japan, which together generate more than half of Matsushita's domestic sales. From batteries to refrigerators, these shops agree to sell no other brands or just a few others. And the dealers agree to sell at manufacturers' recommended prices. In return, Matsushita essentially guarantees the livelihoods of the stores' owners. The Japan Fair Trade Commission has estimated that almost 90 percent of all domestic business transactions are "among parties involved in a long-standing relationship of some sort."[35]

Trade talks between Japan and the United States in the early 1990s centered on keiretsu, with little success. The U.S. government demanded that the keiretsu be opened to U.S. companies. But Japanese officials were reluctant to acknowledge the need to reform the keiretsu, arguing that they make the Japanese economy more efficient.[36]

North American Free Trade Agreement (NAFTA)
An agreement between Canada, the United States, and Mexico that created the world's largest free-trade zone.

The North American Free Trade Agreement The **North American Free Trade Agreement (NAFTA)** created the world's largest free-trade zone. The agreement was ratified by the U.S. Congress in 1993. It includes Canada, the United States, and Mexico, with a combined population of 360 million and economy of $6 trillion.[37]

Canada, the largest U.S. trading partner, entered a free-trade agreement with the United States in 1988. Most of the new long-run opportunities for U.S. business under NAFTA are thus in Mexico, America's third largest trading partner. Tariffs on Mexican exports to the United States averaged just 4 percent before the treaty was signed, and most goods entered the United States duty-free. Therefore, NAFTA opened the Mexican market primarily to U.S. companies. When the treaty went into effect, tariffs on about half the items traded across the Rio Grande disappeared. The pact removed a web of Mexican licensing requirements, quotas, and tariffs that limited transactions in U.S. goods and services. For instance, the pact allows U.S. and Canadian financial-services companies to own subsidiaries in Mexico for the first time in fifty years. However, a nagging recession in Mexico has, to date, limited American opportunities in the country. In a recent survey, 70 percent of U.S. corporations said that NAFTA had no effect on their businesses, while 24 percent reported positive results, and 6 percent described negative results.[38]

The real test of NAFTA will be whether it delivers rising prosperity on both sides of the Rio Grande. For Mexicans, NAFTA must provide rising wages, better benefits, and an expanding middle class with enough purchasing power to keep buying goods from the United States and Canada. That scenario is plausible in the long run, but not guaranteed. As for the United States, its gross domestic product will grow about $30 billion a year once NAFTA is fully implemented.[39] But for Americans, the trade agreement will need to prove that it can produce more well-paying jobs than it destroys. Although estimates of the employment effects of NAFTA vary widely, almost every study agrees that there will be gains. The Labor Department has certified—under a program that gives displaced workers retraining and unemployment relief—that 128,303 U.S. workers have lost their jobs so far because of increased competition from Mexico and

Canada. That compares with 2.2 million jobs created each year since NAFTA took effect.[40]

The intent of U.S. politicians is to ultimately expand NAFTA to South American and, indeed, all Latin American countries. Chile was to be the first new entrant into the organization. Wrangling within the U.S. Congress has blocked NAFTA expansion so far. The lack of American prosperity and job growth attributable to NAFTA has stalled congressional expansion of the agreement. As a result, countries south of the U.S. border have been forming their own trade agreements. Latin and South American nations are creating a maze of trading arrangements.

The largest new trade agreement is **Mercosur,** which includes Brazil, Argentina, Chile, Bolivia, Uruguay, and Paraguay. The elimination of most tariffs among the trading partners has resulted in trade revenues currently over $16 billion annually.[41] The economic boom created by Mercosur will undoubtedly cause other nations to seek trade agreements on their own or enter Mercosur. The European Union, discussed next, hopes to have a free-trade pact with Mercosur by 2005.

Mercosur
The largest new trade agreement, which includes Brazil, Argentina, Uruguay, and Paraguay.

The European Union In 1993, all twelve member countries of the European Community ratified the **Maastricht Treaty**. The treaty, named after the Dutch town where it was developed, proposes to take the EC further toward economic, monetary, and political union. Officially called the Treaty on European Union, the document outlines plans for tightening bonds among the member states and creating a single market. The European Commission, which drafted the treaty, predicts that Maastricht will create 1.8 million new jobs by 1999. Also, retail prices in the European Union are expected to fall by a minimum of 6 percent.[42]

Maastricht Treaty
Agreement among twelve countries of the European Community to pursue economic, monetary, and political union.

Although the heart of the treaty deals with developing a unified European market, Maastricht is also intended to increase integration among the European Union members in areas much closer to the core of national sovereignty. The treaty calls for economic and monetary coordination, including a common currency and an independent central bank by 1999. The new Economic Monetary Union (EMU) was launched January 1, 1999, with Germany, France, Spain, Portugal, Austria, The Netherlands, Luxembourg, Ireland, and Finland. Britain, Sweden, and Denmark chose not to join at the outset. Greece was too far from EMU's stringent fiscal requirement to join at the start. A new European Central Bank was also created along with an EMU currency called the *euro*. The EMU creates a $6.4 trillion economy, the second largest in the world.[43]

The move toward an increasingly global business environment is wonderfully illustrated by the euro. The first economic union to create a common currency, the EMU represents a $6.4 trillion economy.
© Peter Weber/Tony Stone Images

Common foreign, security, and defense policies are also goals, as well as European citizenship—whereby any European Union citizen can live, work, vote, and run for office anywhere in the member countries. The treaty standardizes trade rules and coordinates health and safety standards. Duties, customs procedures, and taxes are also standardized. A driver hauling cargo from Amsterdam to Lisbon can now clear four border crossings by showing a single piece of paper. Before the Maastricht Treaty, the same driver would have carried two pounds of paper to cross the same borders. The overall goal is to end the need for a special product for each country—for example, a different Braun electric razor for Italy, Germany, France, and so forth. Goods marked GEC (goods for EC) can be traded freely, without being retested at each border.

Some economists have called the European Union the "United States of Europe." It is an attractive market, with 320 million consumers and purchasing power almost equal to that of the United States. But the European Union will probably never be a United States of Europe. For one thing, even in a united Europe, marketers will not be able to produce a single Europroduct for a generic Euroconsumer.

With nine different languages and individual national customs, Europe will always be far more diverse than the United States. Thus, product differences will continue. It will be a long time, for instance, before the French begin drinking the instant coffee that Britons enjoy. Preferences for washing machines also differ: British homemakers want front-loaders, and the French want top-loaders; Germans like lots of settings and high spin speeds; Italians like lower speeds. Even European companies that think they understand Euroconsumers often have difficulties producing "the right product":

> Atag Holdings NV, a diversified Dutch company whose main business is kitchen appliances, reckoned it was well-placed to expand abroad. Its plant is a mile from the Dutch/German border and near Europe's geographic and population center. And Lidwien Jacobs, a product manager, says she was confident Atag could cater to both the "potato" and "spaghetti" belts—marketers' terms for consumer preferences in northern and southern Europe. But, as Atag quickly discovered, preferences vary much more than that. "To sell in America, you need one or two types of ceramic stove top," Ms. Jacobs says. "In Europe, you need 11."
>
> Belgians, who cook in huge pots, require extra-large burners. Germans like oval pots, and burners to fit. Italians boil large pots of water quickly, for pasta. The French need small burners and very low temperatures for simmering sauces and broths. Such quirks affect every detail. Germans like oven knobs on the front, the French on top. Even clock placement differs. And Atag has had to test market 28 colors. While Continentals prefer black and white, the British demand a vast range, including peach, pigeon blue and mint green.
>
> "Whatever the product, the British are always different," Ms. Jacobs says with a sigh. Another snag: "Domestic," the name of Atag's basic oven, turns off buyers in Britain, where "domestic" is a synonym for "servant."
>
> Atag's kitchenware unit has lifted foreign sales to 25 percent of its total from 4 percent in the mid-1980s. But it now believes that its range of designs and speed in delivering them, rather than the magic bullet of a Euro-product, will keep it competitive. "People would fight another war, I think, to keep their own cooking habits," Ms. Jacobs jokes.[44]

An entirely different type of problem facing global marketers is the possibility of a protectionist movement by the European Union against outsiders. For example, European automakers have proposed holding Japanese imports at roughly their current 10 percent market share. The Irish, Danes, and Dutch don't make cars and have unrestricted home markets; they would be unhappy about limited imports of Toyotas and Datsuns. But France has a strict quota on Japanese cars to protect Renault and Peugeot. These local carmakers could be hurt if the quota is raised at all.

Interestingly, a number of big U.S. companies are already considered more "European" than many European companies. Coca-Cola and Kellogg's are considered classic European brand names. Ford and General Motors compete for the largest share of auto sales on the continent. IBM and Dell Computer dominate their markets. General Electric, AT&T, and Westinghouse are already strong all over Europe and have invested heavily in new manufacturing facilities throughout the continent.

Although many U.S. firms are well prepared to contend with European competition, the rivalry is perhaps more intense there than anywhere else in the world. In the long run, it is questionable whether Europe has room for eight mass-market automakers, including Ford and GM, when the United States sustains just three. Similarly, an integrated Europe probably doesn't need twelve national airlines.

Demographic Makeup

The three most densely populated nations in the world are China, India, and Indonesia. But that fact alone is not particularly useful to marketers. They also need

Kellogg's

How has Kellogg's tailored its Planet K Web pages to attract its various global markets? Visit the main Kellogg's page at "Cereal City USA," then compare it to the Canadian, British, German, and Korean versions. Can you find a unifying theme?

http://www.kelloggs.com/ **http://www.kelloggs.ca/**
http://www.kelloggs.co.uk/ **http://www.kelloggs.de/**
http://www.kelloggs.co.kr/

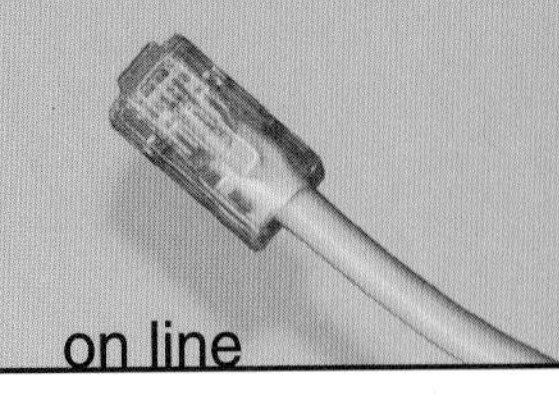

to know whether the population is mostly urban or rural, because marketers may not have easy access to rural consumers. In Belgium about 90 percent of the population lives in an urban setting, whereas in Kenya almost 80 percent of the population lives in a rural setting. Belgium is thus the more attractive market.

Just as important as population is personal income within a country. The wealthiest countries in the world include Japan, the United States, Switzerland, Sweden, Canada, Germany, and several of the Arab oil-producing nations. At the other extreme are countries like Mali and Bangladesh, with a fraction of the per capita purchasing power of the United States. However, a low per capita income is not in itself enough reason to avoid a country. In countries with low per capita incomes, wealth is not evenly distributed. There are pockets of upper- and middle-class consumers in just about every country of the world. In some cases, such as India, the number of consumers is surprisingly large.

The most significant global economic news of the past decade is the rise of a global middle class. From Shekou, China, to Mexico City and countless cities in between, there are traffic jams, bustling bulldozers, and people hawking tickets to various events. These are all symptoms of a growing middle class. In China, per capita incomes are rising rapidly.[45] Developing countries, excluding Eastern Europe and the former Soviet Union, should grow about 5 percent annually over the next decade.

Growing economies demand professionals. In Asia, accountants, stock analysts, bankers, and even middle managers are in short supply. Rising affluence also creates demand for consumer durables such as refrigerators, VCRs, and automobiles. As Central Europe's middle class grows, Whirlpool expects its sales to grow over 6 percent annually.[46] Companies like Procter & Gamble and Gillette offer an array of products at different price points to attract and keep customers as they move up the income scale. The percentage of the world's population that lives in industrialized nations has been declining since 1960, because industrialized nations have grown slowly and developing nations have grown rapidly. In this decade, more than 90 percent of the world's population growth will occur in developing countries and only 10 percent in the industrialized nations. The United Nations reports that in the year 2000, 79 percent of the world's population will reside in developing countries—for example, Guinea, Bolivia, and Pakistan.

Natural Resources

A final factor in the external environment that has become more evident in the past decade is the shortage of natural resources. For example, petroleum shortages have created huge amounts of wealth for oil-producing countries such as Norway, Saudi Arabia, and the United Arab Emirates. Both consumer and industrial markets have blossomed in these countries. Other countries—such as Indonesia, Mexico, and Venezuela—were able to borrow heavily against oil reserves in order to develop more rapidly. On the other hand, industrial countries like Japan, the United States, and much of Western Europe experienced rampant inflation in the 1970s and an enormous transfer of wealth to the petroleum-rich nations. But during much of the 1980s and 1990s, when the price of oil fell, the petroleum-rich nations suffered. Many were not able to service their foreign debts when their oil revenues were sharply reduced. However, Iraq's invasion of Kuwait in 1990 led to a rapid increase in the price of oil and focused attention on the dependence of industrialized countries on oil imports. The price of oil once again declined following the defeat of Iraq, but the U.S. dependence on foreign oil will likely remain high.

Petroleum is not the only natural resource that affects international marketing. Warm climate and lack of water mean that many of Africa's countries will remain importers of foodstuffs. The United States, on the other hand, must rely on Africa for many precious metals. Japan depends heavily on the United States for timber and logs. A Minnesota company manufactures and sells a million pairs of disposable chopsticks to Japan each year. The list could go on, but the point is clear. Vast differences in natural resources create international dependencies, huge shifts of wealth, inflation and recession, export opportunities for countries with abundant resources, and even a stimulus for military intervention.

Global Marketing by the Individual Firm

4
Identify the various ways of entering the global marketplace

A company should consider entering the global marketplace only after its management has a solid grasp of the global environment. Some relevant questions are "What are our options in selling abroad?" "How difficult is global marketing?" and "What are the potential risks and returns?" Concrete answers to these questions would probably encourage the many U.S. firms not selling overseas to venture into the international arena. Foreign sales could be an important source of profits.

Companies decide to "go global" for a number of reasons. Perhaps the most stimulating reason is to earn additional profits. Managers may feel that international sales will result in higher profit margins or more added-on profits. A second stimulus is that a firm may have a unique product or technological advantage not available to other international competitors. Such advantages should result in major business successes abroad. In other situations, management may have exclusive market information about foreign customers, marketplaces, or market situations not known to others. While exclusivity can provide an initial motivation for international marketing, managers must realize that competitors can be expected to catch up with the information advantage of the firm. Finally, saturated domestic markets, excess capacity, and potential for economies of scale can also be motivators to "go global." Economies of scale mean that average per-unit production costs fall as output is increased.

Many firms form multinational partnerships—called strategic alliances—to assist them in penetrating global markets; strategic alliances are examined in Chapter 5. Five other methods of entering the global marketplace are, in order of risk, export, licensing, contract manufacturing, the joint venture, and direct investment. (See Exhibit 3.5.)

exhibit 3.5

Risk Levels for Five Methods of Entering the Global Marketplace

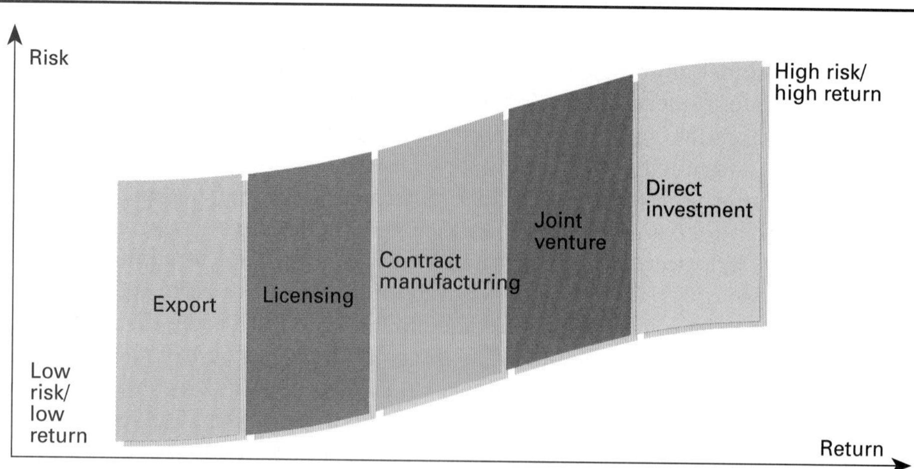

Export

When a company decides to enter the global market, exporting is usually the least complicated and least risky alternative. **Exporting** is selling domestically produced products to buyers in another country. A company, for example, can sell directly to foreign importers or buyers. Exporting is not limited to huge corporations such as General Motors or Westinghouse. Indeed, small companies account for 96 percent of all U.S. exporters, but only 30 percent of the export volume. The United States is the world's largest exporter.[47] Many small businesses claim that they lack the money, time, or knowledge of foreign markets that exporting requires. The U.S. Department of Commerce is trying to make it increasingly easy for small businesses to enter exporting. The department has created a pilot program in which it has hired a private company to represent up to fifty small businesses at specific international trade fairs. For example, FTS, Incorporated, was hired to represent small firms at a trade show in Italy in late 1996. The company handed out company brochures and other sales information to interested prospective Italian clients. Also, after the show was over, FTS gave each participating American company a list of potential Italian distributors for their products. Each American firm paid only $2,500 to be represented at the trade fair. For companies interested in exporting, the U.S. government stands ready to help in a variety of ways. Some of the federal resources available to companies wanting to enter exporting are shown in Exhibit 3.6.

exporting
Selling domestically produced products to buyers in another country.

Instead of selling directly to foreign buyers, a company may decide to sell to intermediaries located in its domestic market. The most common intermediary is the export merchant, also known as a **buyer for export**, who is usually treated like a domestic customer by the domestic manufacturer. The buyer for export assumes all risks and sells internationally for its own account. The domestic firm is involved only to the extent that its products are bought in foreign markets.

buyer for export
Intermediary in the global market that assumes all ownership risks and sells globally for its own account.

A second type of intermediary is the **export broker**, who plays the traditional broker's role by bringing buyer and seller together. The manufacturer still retains title and assumes all the risks. Export brokers operate primarily in agriculture and raw materials.

export broker
Intermediary who plays the traditional broker's role by bringing buyer and seller together.

Export agents, a third type of intermediary, are foreign sales agents–distributors who live in the foreign country and perform the same functions as domestic manufacturers' agents, helping with international financing, shipping, and so on. The U.S. Department of Commerce has an agent–distributor service that helps about five thousand U.S. companies a year find an agent or distributor in virtually any country of the world. A second category of agents resides in the manufacturer's country but represents foreign buyers. This type of agent acts as a hired purchasing agent for foreign customers operating in the exporter's home market.

export agent
Intermediary that acts like a manufacturer's agent for the exporter. The export agent lives in the foreign market.

Licensing

Another effective way for a firm to move into the global arena with relatively little risk is to sell a license to manufacture its product to someone in a foreign country. **Licensing** is the legal process whereby a licensor allows another firm to use its manufacturing process, trademarks, patents, trade secrets, or other proprietary knowledge. The licensee, in turn, pays the licensor a royalty or fee agreed on by both parties.

licensing
The legal process whereby a licensor agrees to let another firm use its manufacturing process, trademarks, patents, trade secrets, or other proprietary knowledge.

Because it has many advantages, U.S. companies have eagerly embraced the licensing concept. For instance, Philip Morris licensed Labatt Brewing Company to produce Miller High Life in Canada. The Spalding Company receives more than $2 million annually from licensing agreements on its sporting goods. Fruit-of-the-Loom manufactures nothing itself abroad but lends its name through licensing to forty-five consumer items in Japan alone, for at least 1 percent of the licensee's gross sales.

A licensor must make sure it can exercise the control over the licensee's activities needed to ensure proper quality, pricing, distribution, and so on. Licensing may also create a new competitor in the long run, if the licensee decides to void the license

exhibit 3.6 | Resources to Aid Companies Interested in Exporting

General Trade Information

The U.S. Department of Commerce (DOC) operates a multitude of programs and services designed for people and companies with interest in conducting business abroad:

- **The Trade Information Center Fax Retrieval Hotline** is a 24-hour fax information service. Dial (800) USA-TRADE from your Touch-Tone™ phone, follow the instructions, and the information you request will be automatically faxed to you.
- **Flash Facts** is another 24-hour DOC fax retrieval service for information on specific countries. Here are some of the main numbers to call:

  Eastern Europe Business Information Center:
  (202) 482-5749
  Offices of the Americas (Mexico, Canada, Latin America, and the Caribbean):
  (800) 872-8723
  Asia Business Center (Southeast Asia, Korea, Vietnam, China, Taiwan, Hong Kong, Australia, and New Zealand):
  (202) 482-3875
  Business Information Service for the Newly Independent (former USSR) States:
  (202) 482-3145
  Uruguay Round of the General Agreement on Tariffs and Trade (GATT):
  (800) USA-TRADE
  Business Information Center for Northern Ireland:
  (202) 501-7488

- **The National Trade Data Bank (NTDB)** is a one-stop source for export promotion and international trade data, collected by 17 U.S. government agencies.

  The NTDB is available on CD-ROM and by subscription via fax-on-demand and the Internet as part of STAT-USA (http://www.stat-usa.gov). For information on all of NTDB's services and costs, call (202) 482-1986.

Trade & Project Financing

- **The Export–Import Bank of the United States (Eximbank)** facilitates the export of U.S. goods and services by providing loans, guarantees, and insurance coverage. Call (800) 565-3946.
- **The Overseas Private Investment Corporation (OPIC)** provides investment services, financing, and political risk insurance in more than 130 developing countries. Call (202) 336-8799.
- **The Export Credit Guarantee** program of the Foreign Agriculture Service of the Department of Agriculture offers risk protection for U.S. exporters against nonpayment by foreign banks. Call (202) 720-3224.
- **The U.S. Small Business Administration** offers a 24-hour electronic bulletin board with professional marketing services and information on trade shows and other promotions overseas. Call (800) 827-5722.
- **The World Trade Centers Association**, with a total membership of 400,000 companies worldwide, provides international trade information, including freight forwarders, customs brokers, and international companies. Call (212) 432-2626.
- **The United States Council for International Business** is the official U.S. affiliate of the International Chamber of Commerce. Call (212) 354-4480.

Trade Fairs & Exhibitions

- **Certified Trade Fairs**, endorsed by the U.S. Department of Commerce, provide good opportunities to promote exports. For information, call Trade Fair Certification, (202) 482-1609.
- **Matchmaker Trade Delegations** are DOC-recruited and -planned missions designed to introduce businesses to representatives and distributors overseas. For further information, call (202) 482-3119.
- **The Certified Trade Missions Program**, sponsored by the International Trade Administration (ITA), provides a flexible format in which to conduct country-specific business overseas. Call (202) 482-4908.

Government Publications

- **The Export Yellow Pages** is a free directory of U.S. manufacturers, banks, service organizations, and export trading companies seeking to do business abroad. Contact your local DOC district office.
- **Eastern Europe Looks for Partners**, published bimonthly by the Central and Eastern Europe Business Information Center, highlights new markets and business opportunities for U.S. firms. Call (202) 482-2645.
- **Destination Japan: A Business Guide for the 90s**, published by the Japan Export Information Center, is a basic guide to doing business with Japan. Call (703) 487-4650 and ask for stock no. PB94164787.
- **Commercial News USA**, published by the ITA, is a 10-time-yearly catalog–magazine to promote U.S. products and services to overseas markets. It is disseminated to 125,000 business readers via U.S. embassies and consulates in 155 countries. For paid listings and advertising rates, call (202) 482-4918.
- **Business America**, published by the ITA, is a monthly compendium of U.S. trade policies and features a calendar of trade shows, exhibitions, fairs, and seminars. Call (202) 512-1800.

Internet Opportunities

- **Country Information**

  Yahoo Index to Countries & Regions
  http://www.yahoo.com/Regional/Countries/
  Internet Business Library
  http://www.bschool.ukans.edu/intbuslib/virtual.htm
  Stat-USA
  http://www.stat-usa.gov
  Worldbank
  http://www.worldbank.org/
  World Factbook
  http://www.odci.gov/cia/publications
  Japan Information Network
  http://jin.jcic.or.jp/statistics

- **International Commercial Web Sites**

  Malls of Canada International
  http://www.canadamalls.com/

MexPlaza
http://mexplaza.udg.mx

Virtual Business Plaza (Czech Republic)
http://www.inet.cz/

Asia Manufacturing Online
http://asia-mfg.com/

Yello Pages of Israel
http://gauss.technion.ac.il

- **Web Sites Fostering International Commerce**

Koblas Currency Converter
http://bin.gnn.com/cgi-bin/gnn/

World Index of Chambers of Commerce & Industry
http://www1.usa1.com/

U.S. Small Business Administration
http://www.sbaonline.sba.gov/OIT

Open Market
http://www.openmarket.com/

U.S. International Trade Administration
http://www.ita.doc.gov/

Trade Point Internet Incubator
http://www.wnicc.org/untpdc/training/
http://www.unicc.org/untpdc/eto/abouteto.html

Multilingual International Business Directory
http://m-link.com/menu.html

U.S. Council for International Business
http://www.uscib.org

Russian and East European Studies Business and Economic Resources
http://www.pitt.edu/~cjp/rsecon.html

Berkeley Roundtable on International Economy
http://server.berkeley.edu/BRIE

Pacific Region Forum on Business and Management Communication
gopher://hoshi.cic.sfu.ca/11/dlam/business/forum

- **Successful Global Marketing on the WWW**

Virtual Vineyards
http://www.virtualvin.com

International Sony Music Webs
http://www.sonymusic.be/

- **Search Engines**

Infoseek Ultra
http://www.ultra.infoseek.com/

Metacrawler
http://www.metacrawler.com/

There are also country-specific search engines. A few examples are

French
Recherche en français

Italian
Ricerca in italiano

German
Suchen Sie deutschsprachigen Webseiten

Spanish
Buscar en español

SOURCE: U.S. Department of Commerce.

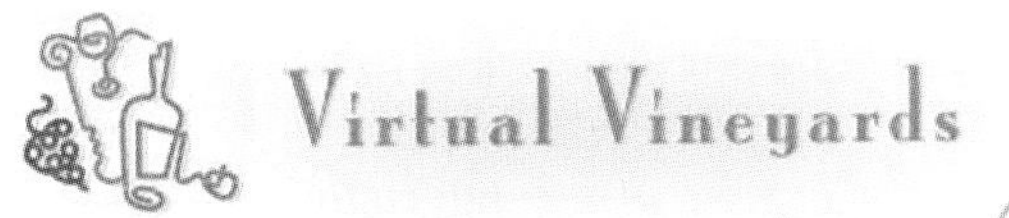

WELCOME

Hi! I'm Peter Granoff, head Cork Dork, and I'd like to welcome you to Virtual Vineyards. My goals are simple: to offer interesting and delicious wine, food, and gift selections for both everyday consumption and special occasions; to make shopping easy and enjoyable, and to make sure you're happy with everything you buy from us!

Begin shopping by using the menus to the right, or:

- Sign In
- Create a new account
- Security and Privacy

- Learn more about our site
- See how to order
- 日本語

Happy Shopping!

PETER GRANOFF, *Proprietor*

A successful global marketer, Virtual Vineyards has leveraged the technology of the Internet to sell its products around the world. http://www.virtualvin.com
Courtesy Virtual Vineyards

agreement. International law is often ineffective in stopping such actions. Two common ways of maintaining effective control over licensees are shipping one or more critical components from the United States or locally registering patents and trademarks to the U.S. firm, not to the licensee.

Franchising is one form of licensing that has grown rapidly in recent years. More than 350 U.S. franchisors operate more than thirty-two thousand outlets in foreign countries, bringing in sales of $6 billion.[48] Over half the international franchises are for fast-food restaurants and business services. As with other forms of licensing, maintaining control over the franchisees is important. For instance, McDonald's was forced to take legal action to buy back its Paris outlets because the franchisee failed to maintain quality standards. McDonald's claimed the Paris franchise was dirty and provided poor service and food. Investigators found dog droppings inside one outlet, and the franchise charged extra for catsup and hid the straws from customers. Because of the damage to McDonald's reputation, the chain was able to develop only 67 outlets in all of France, compared to 270 in Great Britain and 270 in Germany. To reestablish itself, McDonald's decided to project French style and class. The first outlet to appear after McDonald's repurchased its franchise was in a handsome turn-of-the-century building on one of Paris's grand boulevards.

Contract Manufacturing

contract manufacturing
Private-label manufacturing by a foreign company.

Firms that do not want to become involved in licensing or to become heavily involved in global marketing may engage in **contract manufacturing**, which is private-label manufacturing by a foreign company. The foreign company produces a certain volume of products to specification, with the domestic firm's brand name on the goods. The domestic company usually handles the marketing. Thus, the domestic firm can broaden its global marketing base without investing in overseas plant and equipment. After establishing a solid base, the domestic firm may switch to a joint venture or direct investment.

Joint Venture

joint venture
When a domestic firm buys part of a foreign company or joins with a foreign company to create a new entity.

Joint ventures are similar to licensing agreements. In a **joint venture**, the domestic firm buys part of a foreign company or joins with a foreign company to create a new entity. A joint venture is a quick and relatively inexpensive way to go global. After a three-year struggle to wire Europe on its own, America Online, Inc. entered into a series of joint ventures to build a less expensive system more easily.[49]

Joint ventures can be very risky. Many fail; others fall victim to a takeover, in which one partner buys out the other. In a survey of 150 companies involved in joint ventures that ended, three-quarters were found to have been taken over by Japanese partners. Gary Hamel, a professor at the London Business School, regards joint ventures as a race to learn: The partner that learns fastest comes to dominate the relationship and can then rewrite its terms.[50] Thus, a joint venture becomes a new form of competition.

Sometimes joint venture partners simply can't agree on management strategies and policies. For example, Procter & Gamble and its Vietnamese partner can't agree on what to do next in their unprofitable joint venture. Consumer-products giant P&G wants to inject more cash into the business; but because Phuong Dong Soap & Detergent, its state-owned partner, has said it's unable to provide the cash to match it, P&G has offered to buy out the Vietnamese stake. So far Phuong Dong has flatly refused to sell, and Ministry of Planning and Investment officials have described such an option as "impossible."[51]

In a successful joint venture, both parties gain valuable skills from the alliance. In the General Motors–Suzuki joint venture in Canada, for example, both parties have contributed and gained. The alliance, CAMI Automotive, was formed to manufacture low-end cars for the U.S. market. The plant, run by Suzuki management, produces the Geo Metro/Suzuki Swift—the smallest, highest-gas-mileage GM car

CAMI Automotive

Find out more about the joint venture between GM and Suzuki at the CAMI Web page. What parts of the page seem to be more Japanese? More American?
http://www.cami.ca/

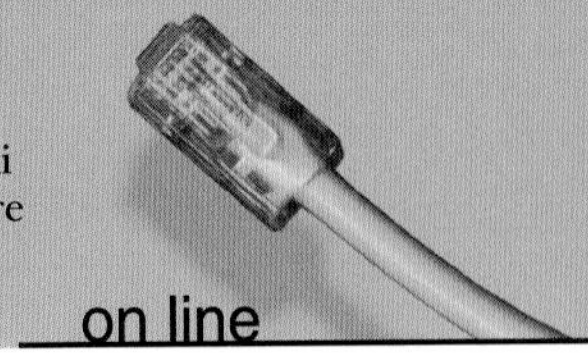

on line

sold in North America—as well as the Geo Tracker/Suzuki Sidekick sport utility vehicle. Through CAMI, Suzuki has gained access to GM's dealer network and an expanded market for parts and components. GM avoided the cost of developing low-end cars and obtained models it needed to revitalize the lower end of its product line and its average fuel-economy rating. The CAMI factory may be one of the most productive plants in North America. There GM has learned how Japanese carmakers use work teams, run flexible assembly lines, and manage quality control.

Direct Investment

Active ownership of a foreign company or of overseas manufacturing or marketing facilities is **direct foreign investment**. Worldwide foreign direct investment was about $360 billion in 1998. Direct investors have either a controlling interest or a large minority interest in the firm. Thus, they have the greatest potential reward and the greatest potential risk. Federal Express lost $1.2 billion in its attempt to build a hub in Europe. It created a huge infrastructure but couldn't generate the package volume to support it. To control losses, the company fired sixty-six hundred international employees and closed offices in over one hundred European cities. Federal Express, however, hasn't given up on expansion. It recently invested $400 million to create an Asian hub.[52] Direct investment can often lead to rapid success. MTV has been in the European market only since 1988, yet since 1994 it has had more viewers in Europe than in the United States.[53]

direct foreign investment
Active ownership of a foreign company or of overseas manufacturing or marketing facilities.

Sometimes firms make direct investments because they can find no suitable local partners. Also, direct investments avoid the communication problems and conflicts of interest that can arise with joint ventures. Other firms simply don't want to share their technology, which they fear may be stolen or ultimately used

entrepreneurial insights

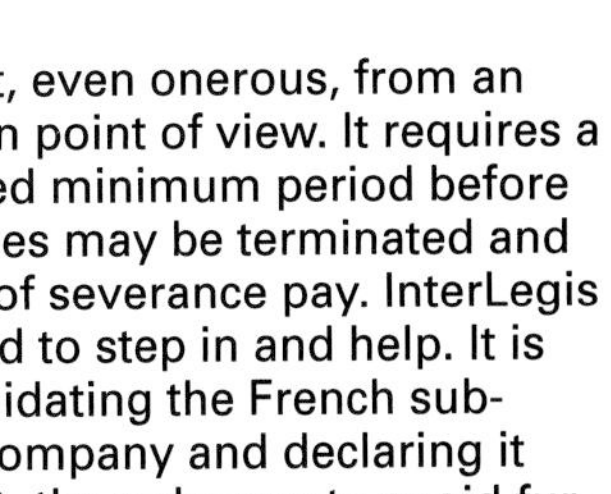

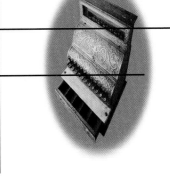

Consultants Can Make "Going Global" Easier

Often companies leap before they look at the business and legal issues in setting up operations abroad, says Steve Meier, principal with Dallas-based InterLegis Consulting Inc., a firm that provides business consulting and support services to companies in their international dealings. "American companies making a first foray abroad, or who want to expand their international operations, should seek out assistance with the business, legal, and cultural issues involved," he said. "Not doing so is a decision that may come back to haunt you."

Meier tells the cautionary tale of one Dallas-based high-tech firm that recently decided to market its products in Western Europe. The company's products were good but its implementation strategy bordered on the disastrous. The company had sent an international sales manager to sign contracts and set up subsidiaries in several countries. The initial response was promising. The company's hastily developed business plan, however, didn't account for issues such as how the foreign entities would mesh with the American business.

In France, for example, the company immediately hired full-time employees. This action turned out to be an expensive error when the company determined that it had hired the wrong people for the job, Meier says. The company didn't realize that French employment law is stringent, even onerous, from an American point of view. It requires a protracted minimum period before employees may be terminated and months of severance pay. InterLegis was hired to step in and help. It is now liquidating the French subsidiary company and declaring it bankrupt, the only way to avoid further financial penalties.[54]

Do you think that a global marketing consultant is necessary for an American firm that will only export merchandise? What about other strategies of going global?

against them by creating a new competitor. Texas Instruments (TI) has historically been one of the latter companies. "TI was a technology company that hated to share anything," said Akira Ishikawa, senior vice president of TI's semiconductor group. "It wasn't in the culture to share or teach the most advanced semiconductor technologies. It was taboo. If you talked about that, you might be fired immediately."[55] Now TI has changed its attitude and entered into five Asian joint ventures. The reason was primarily to spread its financial risk.

A firm may make a direct foreign investment by acquiring an interest in an existing company or by building new facilities. It might do so because it has trouble transferring some resource to a foreign operation or getting that resource locally. One important resource is personnel, especially managers. If the local labor market is tight, the firm may buy an entire foreign firm and retain all its employees instead of paying higher salaries than competitors.

The United States is a popular place for direct investment by foreign companies. In 1999, the value of foreign-owned businesses in the United States was more than $450 billion.

Regardless of how an organization decides to launch its global marketing effort, it may pay to hire a global marketing consultant. This is particularly true for a smaller firm that cannot afford the financial consequences of not getting it right the first time. The preceding "Entrepreneurial Insights" box describes the experiences of one such consultant.

The Global Marketing Mix

5

List the basic elements involved in developing a global marketing mix

To succeed, firms seeking to enter into foreign trade must still adhere to the principles of the marketing mix. Information gathered on foreign markets through research is the basis for the four Ps of global marketing strategy: product, place (distribution), promotion, and price. Marketing managers who understand the advantages and disadvantages of different ways to enter the global market and the effect of the external environment on the firm's marketing mix have a better chance of reaching their goals.

The first step in creating a marketing mix is developing a thorough understanding of the global target market. Often this knowledge can be obtained through the same types of marketing research used in the domestic market (see Chapter 7). However, global marketing research is conducted in vastly different environments. Conducting a survey can be difficult in developing countries, where telephone ownership is rare and mail delivery slow or sporadic. Drawing samples based on known population parameters is often difficult because of the lack of data. In some cities in South America, Mexico, and Asia, street maps are unavailable, streets are unidentified, and houses are unnumbered. Moreover, the questions a marketer can ask may differ in other cultures. In some cultures, people tend to be more private than in the United States and do not like to respond to personal questions on surveys. For instance, in France, questions about one's age and income are considered especially rude.

Product and Promotion

With the proper information, a good marketing mix can be developed. One important decision is whether to alter the product or the promotion for the global marketplace. Other options are to radically change the product or to adjust either the promotional message or the product to suit local conditions.

One Product, One Message The strategy of global marketing standardization, which was discussed earlier, means developing a single product for all markets

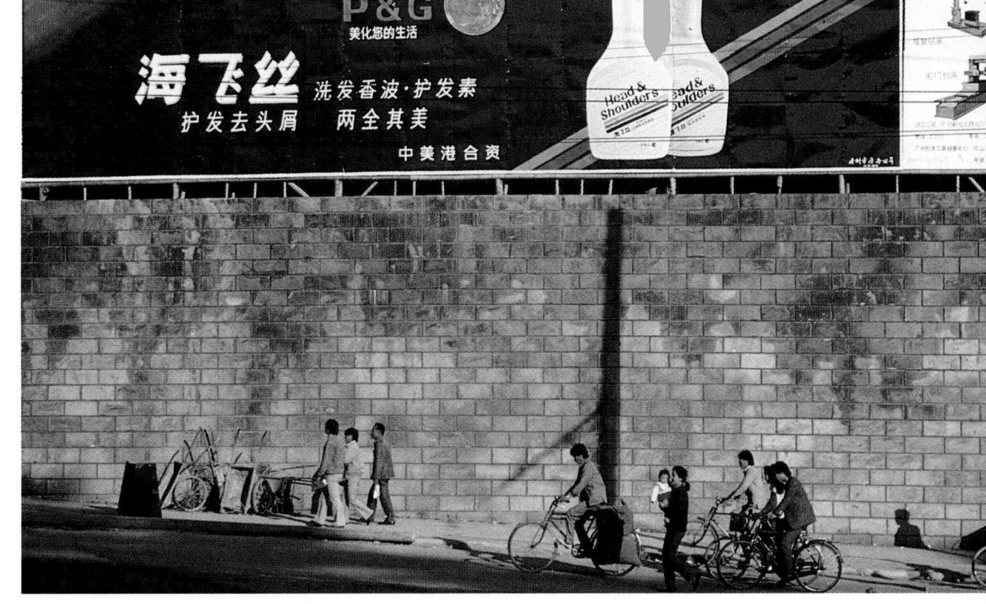

Using a strategy of global marketing standardization, Procter & Gamble uses the same product and promotional themes for Head and Shoulders in China as it does in the United States.
© 1993 Mary Beth Camp/Matrix International, Inc.

and promoting it the same way all over the world. For instance, Procter & Gamble uses the same product and promotional themes for Head and Shoulders in China as it does in the United States. The advertising draws attention to a person's dandruff problem, which stands out in a nation of black-haired people. Head and Shoulders is now the best-selling shampoo in China despite costing over 300 percent more than local brands. Buoyed by its success with Head and Shoulders, Procter & Gamble is using the same product and same promotion strategy with Tide detergent in China. It also used another common promotion tactic that it has found to be successful in the United States The company spent half a million dollars to reach agreements with local washing machine manufacturers, which now include a free box of Tide with every new washer.

Kodak is enjoying success in China with film sales up 50 percent since 1996. It uses the "Kodak moments" campaign theme to build brand awareness. One unique promotional tool is the use of scratch cards with the purchase of film. These cards are very popular with Chinese consumers but only if the card gives a guaranteed instant win.[56]

Global media—especially satellite and cable TV networks like Cable News Network International, MTV Networks, and British Sky Broadcasting—make it possible to beam advertising to audiences unreachable a few years ago. "Eighteen-year-olds in Paris have more in common with eighteen-year-olds in New York than with their own parents," says William Roedy, director of MTV Europe. Almost all of MTV's advertisers run unified, English-language campaigns in the twenty-eight nations the firm reaches. The audiences "buy the same products, go to the same movies, listen to the same music, sip the same colas. Global advertising merely works on that premise."[57] Although teens throughout the world prefer movies above all other forms of television programming, they are closely followed by music videos, stand-up comedy, and then sports.

The Council on American Islamic Relations called for Nike, Inc. to apologize for using this stylized "Air" logo on shoe samples because it resembles the word "Allah" in Arabic. To avoid critical marketing blunders, cultural implications must be considered before applying successful American marketing campaigns in other countries.
© Dennis Cook/AP Wide World Photos

Both Nike and Reebok spend over $100 million a year in promotion outside the United States. Each company practices global marketing standardization to keep its messages clear and its products desirable. Both companies have exploited basketball's surging popularity around the world. Nike sends Charles Barkley of the Houston Rockets to Europe and Asia touting its products. Reebok counters by sending basketball superstar Shaquille O'Neal overseas as its ambassador. One of the main appeals of sneakers is their American style; therefore, the more American an advertising commercial, the better it is. The tag lines—whether in Italy, Germany, Japan, or France—all read the same way in English: "Just do it" and "Planet Reebok." Nike has found, however, that its brashness doesn't always go over well in other countries. A TV commercial of Satan and his demons playing soccer against a team of Nike endorsers was a hit in America. It was deemed as too offensive to be shown in prime

Mattel, Scrabble

Hasbro, Monopoly

Visit Mattel's Scrabble site and Hasbro's Monopoly site. Which game has more of an international presence on the Internet? Does this surprise you? Why or why not?

http://www.mattelscrabble.com/

http://www.monopoly.com/

time in Europe. Nike's marketing buyout of the Brazilian national soccer foundation for $200 million also made the world's soccer officials extremely upset. Nike, with no tradition in *futbol,* was infecting the sport with American money.[58]

Even a one-product, one-message strategy may call for some changes to suit local needs, such as variations in the product's measurement units, package sizes, and labeling. Pillsbury, for example, changed the measurement unit for its cake mixes because adding "cups of" has no meaning in many developing countries. Also, in developing countries, packages are often smaller so that consumers with limited incomes can buy them. For instance, cigarettes, chewing gum, and razor blades may be sold individually instead of in packages.

Unchanged products may fail simply because of cultural factors. The game *Trivial Pursuit* failed in Japan. It seems that getting the answers wrong can be seen as a loss of face. Any type of war game tends to do very poorly in Germany, despite the fact that Germany is by far the world's biggest game-playing nation. A successful game in Germany has plenty of details and thick rulebooks. *Monopoly* remains the world's favorite board game; it seems to overcome all cultural barriers. The game is available in twenty-five languages, including Russian, Croatian, and Hebrew.[59]

Product Invention In the context of global marketing, product invention can be taken to mean either creating a new product for a market or drastically changing an existing product. For the Japanese market, Nabisco had to remove the cream filling from its Oreo cookies because Japanese children thought they were too sweet. Ford thinks it can save billions on its product development costs by developing a single small-car chassis and then altering its styling to suit different countries. Campbell Soup invented a watercress and duck gizzard soup that is now selling well in China. It is also considering a cream of snake soup. Frito-Lay's most popular potato chip in Thailand is shrimp flavored. Dormont Manufacturing Company makes a simple gas hose that hooks up to deep-fat fryers and similar appliances. Sounds like something that could be sold globally, right? Wrong—in Europe differing national standards means that a different hose is required for each country.[60] Minutiae such as the color of the plastic coating or how the end pieces should be attached to the rest of the hose and the couplings themselves create a myriad of design problems for Dormont Manufacturing.

Rather than creating a new product, Coca-Cola simply bought a small but growing soft drink company in India. Now its acquisition, Thums Up cola, outsells Coke by a four-to-one margin in most Indian markets. Donald Short, chief executive at Coca-Cola in India, says in Bombay his business card needs to read CEO of the Thums Up Company, not CEO of Coca-Cola.[61]

Consumers in different countries use products differently. For example, in many countries, clothing is worn much longer between washings than in the United States, so a more durable fabric must be produced and marketed. For Peru, Goodyear developed a tire that contains a higher percentage of natural rubber and has better treads than tires manufactured elsewhere in order to handle the tough Peruvian driving conditions. Rubbermaid has sold millions of open-top wastebaskets in America; Europeans, picky about garbage peeking out of bins, wanted bins with tight lids that snap into place.

Message Adaptation Another global marketing strategy is to maintain the same basic product but alter the promotional strategy. Bicycles are mainly pleasure vehicles in the United States. In many parts of the world, however, they are a family's main mode of transportation. Thus, promotion in these countries should stress durability and efficiency. In contrast, U.S. advertising may emphasize escaping and having fun.

Harley-Davidson decided that its American promotion theme, "One steady constant in an increasingly screwed-up world," wouldn't appeal to the Japanese market. The Japanese ads combine American images with traditional Japanese ones: American riders passing a geisha in a rickshaw, Japanese ponies nibbling at a Harley motorcycle. Waiting lists for Harleys in Japan are now six months long.

In a new effort to increase its international presence, Anheuser-Busch Companies is targeting the fast-growing markets of Argentina, Brazil, and Chile. But breaking with its promotion strategy at home, the brewer is positioning Bud as a trendy drink for affluent youth, peppering the hottest night clubs and bars with giant banners, neon signs, and other promotions. The result: Some rivals jokingly refer to Bud as a North-of-the-Border Corona. The company is handing out red neon signs to upscale discos and restaurants. They're also dispatching young women in tight Bud minidresses to offer free beer at the beach. And they're plastering cities with signs trumpeting Bud as "the most popular beer in the world."[62]

Global marketers find that promotion is a daunting task in some countries. For example, commercial television time is readily available in Canada but severely restricted in Germany. Until recently, marketers in Indonesia had only one subscription TV channel with few viewers (120,000 out of a nation of 180 million people). Because of this limited television audience, several marketers, such as the country's main Toyota dealer, had to develop direct-mail campaigns to reach their target markets.

Some cultures view a product as having less value if it has to be advertised. In other nations, claims that seem exaggerated by U.S. standards are commonplace. On the other hand, Germany does not permit advertisers to state that their products are "best" or "better" than those of competitors, a description commonly used in U.S. advertising. The hard-sell tactics and sexual themes so common in U.S. advertising are taboo in many countries. Procter & Gamble's advertisements for Cheer detergents were voted least popular in Japan because they used hard-sell testimonials. The negative reaction forced P&G to withdraw Cheer from the Japanese market. In the Middle East, pictures of women in print advertisements have been covered with censor's ink.

Language barriers, translation problems, and cultural differences have generated numerous headaches for international marketing managers. Consider these examples:

- A toothpaste claiming to give users white teeth was especially inappropriate in many areas of Southeast Asia, where the well-to-do chew betel nuts and black teeth are a sign of higher social status.
- Procter & Gamble's Japanese advertising for Camay soap nearly devastated the product. In one commercial, a man meeting a woman for the first time immediately compared her skin to that of a fine porcelain doll. Although the ad had worked in other Asian countries, the man came across as rude and disrespectful in Japan.

ENTREPRENEUR

Product Adaptation Another alternative for global marketers is to slightly alter a basic product to meet local conditions. Additional pizza toppings offered by Domino's in Japan include corn, curry, squid, and spinach. Japanese housewives couldn't fit American-size bottles of Joy dish soap on their shelves. Procter & Gamble changed the bottle to a compact cylinder that took less space.[63] When Lewis Woolf Griptight, a British manufacturer of infant accessories such as pacifiers, came to the United States, it found subtle differences between United Kingdom and American parents. Elizabeth Lee, marketing manager, noted, "There are subtle differences, but many problems are the same. Whether a cup spills in America or in Madagascar or in the U.K., moms aren't going to like it," she said. "We didn't need to redo all the research to find out that people didn't want cups that spill, but we still had to do research on things like color and packaging."[64] The brand name "Kiddiwinks" is a British word for children. In the United States, the name was changed to "Binky" because of positive parental reactions in marketing research tests.

Pricing Once marketing managers have determined a global product and promotion strategy, they can select the remainder of the marketing mix. Pricing presents some unique problems in the global sphere. Exporters must not only cover their production costs but also consider transportation costs, insurance, taxes, and tariffs. When deciding on a final price, marketers must also determine what customers are willing to spend on a particular product. Marketers also need to ensure that their foreign buyers will pay them. Because developing nations lack mass purchasing power, selling to them often poses special pricing problems. Sometimes a product can be simplified in order to lower the price. However, the firm must not assume that low-income countries are willing to accept lower quality. Although the nomads of the Sahara are very poor, they still buy expensive fabrics to make their clothing. Their survival in harsh conditions and extreme temperatures requires this expense. Additionally, certain expensive luxury items can be sold almost anywhere.

Companies must also be careful not to be so enthusiastic about entering a market that they extend credit haphazardly. Compaq Computers' sales have been growing very rapidly in China, but partially because it has been giving away computers against its will. Recently a Chinese distributor failed to repay $32 million for computers that Compaq had extended on credit. Analysts say Compaq is now owed over $100 million by delinquent dealers and distributors in China.

dumping
The sale of an exported product at a price lower than that charged for the same or a like product in the "home" market of the exporter.

Dumping **Dumping** is generally considered to be the sale of an exported product at a price lower than that charged for the same or a like product in the "home" market of the exporter. This practice is thought of as a form of price discrimination that can potentially harm the importing nation's competing industries. Dumping may occur as a result of exporter business strategies that include (1) trying to increase an overseas market share, (2) temporarily distributing products in overseas markets to offset slack demand in the home market, (3) lowering unit costs by exploiting large-scale production, and (4) attempting to maintain stable prices during periods of exchange rate fluctuations.

Historically, the dumping of goods has presented serious problems in international trade. As a result, dumping has led to significant disagreements among countries and diverse views about its harmfulness. Some trade economists view dumping as harmful only when it involves the use of "predatory" practices that intentionally try to eliminate competition and gain monopoly power in a market. They believe that predatory dumping rarely occurs and that antidumping enforcement is a protectionist tool whose cost to consumers and import-using industries exceeds the benefits to the industries receiving protection.

The Uruguay Round rewrites the international law on dumping. The agreement states:

1. Dumping disputes will be resolved by the World Trade Organization.
2. Dumping terms are specifically defined. For example, the "dumped price" must be at least five percent below the home market price before it is considered dumping.
3. At least 25 percent of the members of an industry must support its government filing a dumping complaint with the World Trade Organization. In other words, a government can't file a complaint if only one or two firms complain (unless they make up 25 percent of the industry).

Countertrade Global trade does not always involve cash. Countertrade is a fast-growing way to conduct global business. In **countertrade**, all or part of the payment for goods or services is in the form of other goods or services. Countertrade is thus a form of barter (swapping goods for goods), an age-old practice whose origins have been traced back to cave dwellers. The U.S. Department of Commerce says that roughly 30 percent of all global trade is countertrade.[65] In fact, both India and China have made billion-dollar government purchasing lists, with most of the goods to be paid for by countertrade.

countertrade
Form of trade in which all or part of the payment for goods or services is in the form of other goods or services.

One common type of countertrade is straight barter. For example, PepsiCo sends Pepsi syrup to Russian bottling plants and in payment gets Stolichnaya vodka, which is then marketed in the West. Another form of countertrade is the compensation agreement. Typically, a company provides technology and equipment for a plant in a developing nation and agrees to take full or partial payment in goods produced by that plant. For example, General Tire Company supplied equipment and know-how for a Romanian truck tire plant. In turn, General Tire sold the tires it received from the plant in the United States under the Victoria brand name. Pierre Cardin gives technical advice to China in exchange for silk and cashmere. In these cases, both sides benefit even though they don't use cash.

Distribution

Solving promotional, price, and product problems does not guarantee global marketing success. The product still has to get adequate distribution. For example, Europeans don't play sports as much as Americans do, so they don't visit sporting-goods stores as often. Realizing this, Reebok started selling its shoes in about eight hundred traditional shoe stores in France. In one year, the company doubled its French sales. Harley-Davidson had to open two company-owned stores in Japan to get distribution for its Harley clothing and clothing accessories.

VALUE

The Japanese distribution system is considered the most complicated in the world. Imported goods wind their way through layers of agents, wholesalers, and retailers. For example, a bottle of ninety-six aspirins costs about $20 because the bottle passes through at least six wholesalers, each of whom increases the selling price. The result is that the Japanese consumer pays the world's most exorbitant prices. These distribution channels seem to be based on historical and traditional patterns of socially arranged trade-offs, which Japanese officials claim are very hard for the government to change. Today, however, the system seems to be changing because of pressure from the Japanese consumer. Japanese shoppers are now placing low prices ahead of quality in their purchasing decisions. The retailer who can cut distribution costs and therefore the retail price gets the sale. For example, Kojima, a Japanese electronics superstore chain like the U.S. chains Circuit City or Best Buy, had to bypass GE's Japanese distribution partner Toshiba to import its merchandise at a good price. Toshiba's distribution system required refrigerators to pass through too many hands before they reached the retailer. Kojima went directly to GE headquarters in the U.S. and persuaded the company to sell it refrigerators, which were then shipped directly to Kojima. It is now selling GE refrigerators for about $800, which is half the price of a typical Japanese model.

Retail institutions in other countries also may differ from what a company is used to in its domestic market. The terms *department store* and *supermarket* may refer to types of retail outlets that are very different from those found in the United States. Japanese supermarkets, for example, are large multistory buildings that sell not only food but also clothing, furniture, and home appliances. Department stores are even larger outlets, but unlike their U.S. counterparts, they emphasize foodstuffs and operate a restaurant on the premises. For a variety of reasons, U.S.-type retail outlets do not exist or are impractical in developing countries. For instance, consumers may not have the storage space to keep food for several days. Refrigerators, when available, are usually small and do not allow for bulk storage. Attempting to build new retail outlets can be a frustrating battle. In Germany's Ruhr Valley, the discounter All Kauf SB-Warenhaus GmbH has struggled to build a store for fifteen years on land that it owns. Local authorities are blocking construction, however, because they are afraid the store will hurt local retailers.[66]

Channels of distribution and the physical infrastructure are also inadequate in many developing nations. In China, for example, most goods are carried on poles or human backs, in wheelbarrows and handcarts, or, increasingly (and this is an important advance), on bicycles. Procter & Gamble has resorted to taking traffic maps of the 228 Chinese cities with at least two hundred thousand citizens and marking them up with locations of small mom-and-pop shops and the big department stores. Divisions of its "ground troops," often wearing white sports shirts with "Winning Team" written on the back, "blitz" each locale and sell and distribute P&G products. Even street-stall owners get a personal pitch.

LOOKING BACK

Look back at the story about marketing in the south of Russia. Besides cultural factors, other uncontrollable variables in the global external environment include economic and technological, political, and demographic variables, as well as natural resources.

Most products cannot be marketed exactly the same way all over the world. Different cultures, languages, levels of economic development, and distribution channels in global markets usually require either new products or modified products. Pricing, promotion, and distribution strategies must often be altered as well. There is no doubt that international markets will become even more important in the future.

Summary

1 Discuss the importance of global marketing. Businesspeople who adopt a global vision are better able to identify global marketing opportunities, understand the nature of global networks, and engage foreign competition in domestic markets.

2 Discuss the impact of multinational firms on the world economy. Multinational corporations are international traders that regularly operate across national borders. Because of their vast size and financial, technological, and material resources, multinational corporations have a great influence on the world economy. They have the ability to overcome trade problems, save on labor costs, and tap new technology.

3 Describe the external environment facing global marketers. Global marketers face the same environmental factors as they do domestically: culture, economic and technological development, political structures, demography, and natural resources. Cultural considerations include societal values, attitudes and beliefs, language, and customary business practices. A country's economic and technological status depends on its stage of industrial development: traditional society, preindustrial society, takeoff economy, industrializing society, or fully industrialized society. The political structure is shaped by political ideology and such policies as tariffs, quotas, boycotts, exchange controls, trade agreements, and market groupings. Demographic variables include population, income distribution, and growth rate.

4 Identify the various ways of entering the global marketplace. Firms use the following strategies to enter global markets, in descending order of risk and profit: direct investment, joint venture, contract manufacturing, licensing, and export.

5 List the basic elements involved in developing a global marketing mix. A firm's major consideration is how much it will adjust the four Ps—product, promotion, place (distribution), and price—within each country. One strategy is to use one product and one promotion message worldwide. A second strategy is to create new products for global markets. A third strategy is to keep the product basically the same but alter the promotional message. A fourth strategy is to slightly alter the product to meet local conditions.

Discussion and Writing Questions

1. Many marketers now believe that teenagers in the developed countries are becoming "global consumers." That is, they all want and buy the same goods and services. Do you think this is true? If so, what has caused the phenomenon?
2. The sale of cigarettes in many developed countries either has peaked out or is declining. However, the developing markets represent major growth markets. Should U.S. tobacco companies capitalize on this opportunity?
3. Renault and Peugeot dominate the French market but have no presence in the U.S. market. Why do you think that this is true?
4. Candartel, an upscale manufacturer of lamps and lampshades in America, has decided to "go global." Top management is having trouble deciding how to develop the market. What are some market entry options for the firm?
5. Rubbermaid, the U.S. manufacturer of kitchen products and other household items, is considering moving to global marketing standardization. What are the pros and cons of this strategy?
6. WRITING Suppose you are marketing manager for a consumer products firm that is about to undertake its first expansion abroad. Write a memo for your staff reminding them of the role culture will play in the new venture. Give examples.
7. What is meant by "having a global vision"? Why is it important?
8. WRITING Suppose your state senator has asked you to contribute a brief article to her constituents' newsletter that answers the question, "Will there ever be a 'United States of Europe'?" Write a draft of your article, and include reasons why or why not.
9. TEAM Divide into six teams. Each team will be responsible for one of the following industries: entertainment; pharmaceuticals; computers and software; financial, legal, or accounting services; agriculture; and textiles and apparel. Interview one or more executives in each of these industries to determine how the Uruguay Round and NAFTA have affected and will affect their organizations. If a local firm cannot be contacted in your industry, use the library and the Internet to prepare your report.
10. What are the major barriers to international trade? Explain how government policies may be used to either restrict or stimulate global marketing.
11. Explain the impact of the Uruguay Round.
12. ON LINE How does the Web site called "The Paris Pages" handle language and translation issues? **http://www.paris.org/**
13. ON LINE What locations does ProNet serve? Obtain information about at least one arts-and-entertainment venture for three different regions. How does ProNet handle language and translation issues? **http://www.pronett.com/**
14. ON LINE What services does the Netzmarkt cyber-mall offer American businesses interested in marketing to Germans? **http://www.netzmarkt.de/neu/hinweise.htm**

Key Terms

buyer for export 83
contract manufacturing 86
countertrade 93
direct foreign investment 87
dumping 92
export agent 83
export broker 83
exporting 83
fully industrialized society 73
General Agreement on Tariffs and Trade (GATT) 76
global marketing 64
global marketing standardization 69
global vision 64
industrializing society 73
joint venture 86
keiretsu 77
licensing 83
Maastricht Treaty 79
Mercosur 79
multinational corporation 66
North American Free Trade Agreement (NAFTA) 78
preindustrial society 73
takeoff economy 73
traditional society 72
Uruguay Round 76
World Trade Organization (WTO) 76

Application for Small Business

Mark and Joe Belcher own a small but thriving nursery in Fenton, North Carolina, that caters to organic gardeners. They sell not only organically grown seeds but natural pest removers, such as ladybugs and praying mantises. The firm also does a good business in compost.

The brothers are considering going global now that they have a growing mail order business in the United States. Joe Belcher ran across an article from the Dentsu Institute that said the following:

> There is a new awareness of environmental issues in Japan. Laws were passed recently there that require for the first time the recycling of cans, bottles and newspapers, and for household waste to be separated into burnable and non-burnable trash in special clear plastic bags.
>
> And Japanese consumers, who continue to be interested in paying more for high-quality goods and favorite labels, also will pay more for environmentally friendly products. Advertising with an environmental theme has come to enjoy a high consumer recognition rate of 60% and has contributed greatly to improving corporate images.[67]

Joe thinks this is enough information to start marketing in Japan. Mark believes that a lot more information is needed before a decision is made.

Questions

1. What additional data should the brothers gather?
2. What are the brothers' options for going global?

Review Quiz

1. Global marketing is important to the United States. In fact, the U.S. exports about ______ of its industrial production and about ______ of its farm products.
   a. One-half; one-half
   b. One-third; one-half
   c. One-fifth; one-third
   d. One-half; one-third
2. The emergence of consumer markets on a huge scale throughout the world, with similar needs and wants, has been called
   a. Multinational marketing
   b. Global marketing standardization
   c. Global consumer culture
   d. International marketing
3. The common set of values shared by citizens of a society that tend to impact people's consumption preferences is
   a. Culture
   b. Standardization
   c. Demographics
   d. Ethics
4. Which of the following stages of economic growth and technological development is characterized by technology spreading from the sectors of the economy that powered the takeoff to the rest of the nation?
   a. Preindustrial society
   b. Takeoff economy
   c. Industrializing society
   d. Fully industrialized society

5. In the ______, manufactured products are produced for export.
   a. Preindustrial society
   b. Takeoff economy
   c. Industrializing society
   d. Fully industrialized society
6. A limit on the amount of a specific product that can enter a country is a
   a. Tariff
   b. Quota
   c. Boycott
   d. Trade agreement
7. Which of the following methods of entering the global marketplace is typically considered the most risky?
   a. Exporting
   b. Licensing
   c. Contract manufacturing
   d. Direct investment
8. Instead of selling directly to foreign buyers, some companies use intermediaries that assume all ownership risks. Such intermediaries are known as a(n)
   a. Exporter
   b. Buyer for export
   c. Export broker
   d. Export agent
9. Understanding the line between work time and social time is an important lesson for marketing managers selling their products in global markets.
   a. True
   b. False
10. Tariffs are a tax that is levied on goods by the country where they are produced.
    a. True
    b. False
11. The General Agreement on Tariffs and Trade (GATT) has been replaced by the International Exchange Control Organization (IECO).
    a. True
    b. False
12. Identify the five methods for entering the global marketplace in order of risk or return.

Check the Answer Key, which follows the Video Case, to see how well you understood the material.

VIDEO CASE

Autocite: The Ticket to Going Global

"It was a lot easier to sell AutoCite in Australia than in my hometown of Flint, Michigan," says Nick George, Chairman and Chief Financial Officer of Enforcement Technology (ETEC). As one of the pioneers of the handheld computer industry, ETEC produces AutoCite, a portable, light-weight, hand-held computer used to write traffic tickets in a streamlined, user-friendly manner. "American technology is highly respected in other countries, and when you are considered an authority in the field, a leader in parking technology, doors start to open," explains Mr. George.

Because developed countries everywhere have the same parking problems as the United States, they also have the same needs. A multitude of drivers hunting down prime parking places is a familiar scene around the world. ETEC saw this dilemma as a global business opportunity. The company understood that the benefits that appealed to Americans in over 350 agencies in fifty states would also appeal to law enforcement agencies in Australia, New Zealand, Canada, Mexico, and Argentina.

Countries such as Canada and Australia welcomed a product that could do away with ticket books, carbon copies, illegible scribbling, and writer's cramp—the byproducts of the tedious handwritten ticketing process. At the same time, AutoCite promised "payback factors" because the system pays for itself within a year. A city saves money because manually written tickets must be key-punched into data processing equipment and transferred to the main computer. Significant clerical and staff time is then required for shuffling, batching, and tracking citations. Both at home and abroad, the manual process means errors, job dissatisfaction, and unnecessary costs. And mistakes cost money. Foreign buyers saw how automated citations could reduce these errors and fill their city's coffers. They liked the time saved to improved efficiency, which in turn translated into better morale for police and parking departments.

When selling AutoCite in the global marketplace, ETEC relies on two strategies: product standardization and product customization. The hardware for AutoCite is the same everywhere with no modifications—a unique, single-unit construction with a built-in printer for creating parking citations and traffic tickets. There are different models, but they all produce machine-readable characters to issue tickets. Processing parking tickets and collection services are also part and parcel of ETEC's features. Even training is standardized, especially for English-speaking countries like Australia, New Zealand, and Canada.

Rather than design, manufacture, and install hardware and leave the software to somebody else à la Compaq and Microsoft, ETEC produces and maintains both. The company touts its status as a single-source vendor. This gives customers at home and abroad the convenience of one-stop shopping and one company to contact for customer service. Total product support is one of the ETEC's strongest selling points.

This leads to the second part of the global strategy—product customization. AutoCite's software is fully customized to meet each country's needs. For example, in 1994, Australia adopted AutoCite because it had a distinct technological advantage not available in domestic markets. ETEC's engineering division designed and developed a system specifically for the Australian Federal Police, allowing officers to issue traffic tickets, warnings for traffic violations, and parking citations. The codes are different than those used in the United States, and the sequence of information entered into the machine is different (e.g., the Australian AutoCite software prints the ticket number first). In Hispanic countries like Mexico and Argentina, AutoCite is programmed to print the tickets in Spanish.

The adoption of AutoCite by the Australian Federal Police was a world first because ETEC's computers had the capability of performing multiple law enforcement functions. The Australian government was so impressed with this innovation that it awarded its police department the technology and productivity prize. Positive results with the Australian Federal Police pushed ETEC to add more innovations to make its products useful to other Australian and New Zealand agencies, and this has led to increased international sales overall.

Although ETEC and other exporters face currency fluctuations and long-distance transportation issues, Mr. George adds quite readily that he spent far less time selling in Canada and other foreign countries than in Michigan. "It was easy to have an appointment with the mayor of Melbourne, Australia, but it took four police chiefs and ten years of effort to write my first order in Flint!"

Questions

1. How does ETEC's product uniqueness and technological advantage help the company do business abroad?
2. Discuss ETEC's global strategies.
3. Harvard professor Ted Levitt sees the emergence of global markets for standardized products as opposed to segmented foreign markets with different products. Do you agree? Explain.
4. What environmental factors might affect ETEC's success abroad?

Bibliography

1. Press Kit for Enforcement Technology, Inc.
2. Telephone interview with Nick George, Chairman and Chief Financial Officer of Enforcement Technology, Inc., September, 1998.

Answer Key

1. *Answer:* c, p. 65

   Rationale: Although some other industrialized nations derive more of their gross domestic product from world trade, the impact of international business on the U.S. economy is still significant.

2. *Answer:* b, p. 68

   Rationale: Global marketing standardization presumes that markets all over the world are becoming much more alike.

3. *Answer:* a, p. 69

   Rationale: Culture is an underlying factor that has a tremendous impact on consumption preferences and, thus, marketer's options.

4. *Answer:* c, p. 73

   Rationale: Countries in the industrializing stage begin to produce capital goods and consumer durables, which typically fosters economic growth for many other industries.

5. *Answer:* d, p. 73

   Rationale: Exports are a viable form of marketing since the technology used by fully industrialized societies is superior to those nations that are not yet in this final stage of development.

6. *Answer:* b, p. 75

   Rationale: A quota is a tool used by a government to limit the amount of imports in a specific industry or sector in an effort to help domestic producers.

7. *Answer:* d, p. 82

   Rationale: Active ownership of a foreign company or of overseas manufacturing and marketing facilities is direct investment. This option carries the greatest risk but also has the greatest potential for return.

8. *Answer:* b, p. 83

   Rationale: The buyer for export buys from the domestic manufacturer and assumes all risks; it then sells products internationally for its own account.

9. *Answer:* a, p. 72

   Rationale: For example, in the United States the ratio of work time to social time on the job is near 80:20, in other countries it may be closer to 50:50, and in still others it is not even a relevant distinction.

10. *Answer:* b, p. 75

    Rationale: Tariffs are a tax that is levied on goods entering a country to help control import levels.

11. *Answer:* b, p. 76

    Rationale: The World Trade Organization (WTO) was created in 1994 to replace GATT to help lower trade barriers worldwide.

12. *Answer:* From lowest risk/return to highest:

    Export

    Licensing

    Contract manufacturing

    Joint venture

    Direct investment (p. 82)

1 Closing

still shaky?

Use your *Grademaker Study Guide* to help you master the concepts in Part 1. Then redo the Review Quiz at the end of each chapter to check your progress.

marketing miscues

Intel Corp.

For the first time in many years, Intel Corp. is an underdog. The chip giant has reaped a long-running bonanza from its near monopoly in providing the microprocessors that are the brains of personal computers. Intel has raced ahead of competitors and made huge bets on future computer demand to become one of the richest and most powerful companies in the world, driven by Chief Executive Andrew Grove's twin mantras: "Only the paranoid survive!" and "Make the PC it!"

However, Intel wasn't paranoid enough—ironically, because it focused so much on the PC. It has missed, or is at least very tardy in recognizing, a fundamental change in the market, one driven by advances in the chip industry it dominates: the ability of Intel's competitors to create much cheaper microprocessors and place more of the functions of a machine on a single chip that is igniting a boom in consumer electronics.

Markets for non-PC devices such as smart identification cards, Internet-ready telephones, handheld computers, digital cameras, advanced video-game players and the like are already burgeoning, and new applications such as digital television and computers in car dashboards are on the horizon. The "convergence" of computing and consumer gadgets is the talk of both industries' trade shows.

Not only is Intel late to this party; also no one wants to dance with it. Most makers of hand-held computers or digital telephones have shunned Intel processors because they are at least several times more expensive than competitors' comparable chips.

In his recent book, "Only the Paranoid Survive," Dr. Grove wrote at length about the dangers of being caught flat-footed by a major technological change, or "strategic inflection point." In an interview, he said the shift to digital consumer electronics is such a change. Dr. Grove acknowledged that Intel isn't a leader in this market, but added that it will have to become one.

In a sense, Intel is trapped in a gilded cage. The vast $160 billion PC market is expected to continue to grow at 15 percent a year or more, a trend that could by itself make Intel the most profitable company in the world within a few years. However, if it can't retool its strategy to build low-cost, high-performance chips, Intel will miss out on a second stage of enormous growth, from digitizing the even more vast worldwide consumer electronics market. International Data Corp. predicts that, in the United States, unit shipments of non-PC devices for accessing the Internet will exceed consumer-PC shipments by 2002.

Dr. Grove says it made little sense for Intel to mount a big effort in consumer electronics until now. Many major manufacturers relied on their own in-house chips, and most of the products were analog, not digital. He predicts the industry will shift entirely to digital electronics, Intel's specialty, in five to ten years, but currently, "this is at a very early stage."

Competitors nonetheless assert that Intel was late in spotting the change. In his book, Dr. Grove notes the first sign of a strategic inflection point: "Competitors that you wrote off or hardly knew existed are stealing business from you," he wrote. "The trade shows seem weird."

It's understandable, however, that Intel could be late spotting the growing market for inexpensive consumer devices. Since 1986, when it was driven out of the dynamic random-access-memory chip market by price-cutting Japanese rivals, Intel has been focused fanatically on one strategy: building ever more powerful microprocessors in huge volumes that competitors couldn't match.

Questions

1. Place Intel chips for PCs and for non-PC devices on a portfolio matrix. Suggest strategies for Intel to adopt over the next five years.
2. What major external environmental forces should Intel monitor over the next five years? Why?
3. How important is a global vision to Intel?

SOURCE: "How the Competition Got Ahead of Intel" by Dean Takahashi, *The Wall Street Journal*, February 12, 1998.

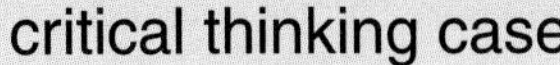
critical thinking case

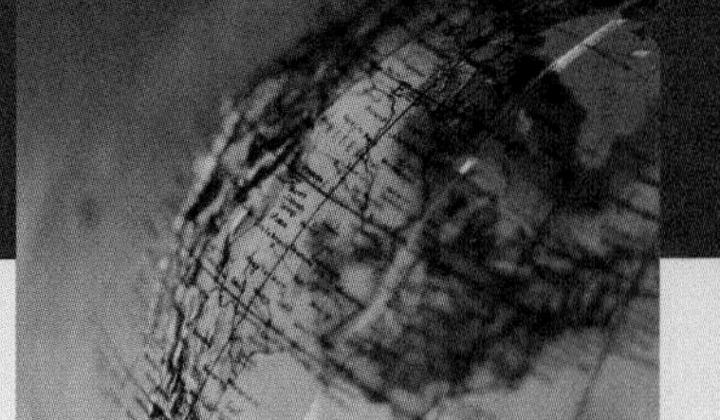

Streamline, Inc. (www.streamline.com)

About once an hour, a bell rings inside the headquarters of Streamline, Inc., a Web company based in Westwood, Massachusetts. It signals that yet another family has subscribed to the company's ever more popular home-delivery service. Every time that bell rings, Streamline's employees stand and applaud—not just because the company got a little bigger, but because one more family got a little saner.

"I want to simplify people's lives," says Tim DeMello, 39, Streamline's exuberant founder and CEO. "That's what I'm passionate about. That's what I believe in."

Most outsiders who try to understand DeMello's company *misunderstand* it—at least at first. Here's how the service works: Customers pay a $30-per-month subscription fee. In return, the company installs a Streamline Box in the customer's garage. The box has three parts: a refrigerator, a freezer, and a set of dry-storage shelves. Next a Streamline field agent, equipped with a bar-code scanner, visits the home and records what the customer already has in the fridge, the pantry, the medicine chest. The agent then creates a first draft of the customer's "personal shopping list."

Streamline posts the list to its Web site, where the customer can edit the list and place orders as often as once a week. Customers select from more than ten thousand grocery items—everything from diapers and cereal to fresh seafood and custom-sliced pastrami. They can also order prepared meals, rent videos, arrange for dry cleaning, and ship UPS packages. As the standard list gets more and more refined, the ordering process gets more and more simple. Eventually, Streamline estimates, the process requires only twenty to thirty minutes per week.

The obvious conclusion: Streamline is an on-line grocer that competes with rivals such as Peapod and NetGrocer. Right? *Wrong!* "We are not in the grocery business," DeMello insists. "We are in the lifestyle-solutions business. We're not a product business, and we're not a service business. We're a relationship business."

It's a distinction with a profound difference. Plenty of Web companies operate on the cutting edge of technology. Streamline operates on the cutting edge of service. It makes a stark promise to its customers: In return for $30 per month, it will save them three to five hours per week—hours that they now spend on routine chores. In addition, it will perform those chores with such attention to detail that customers will never consider going back. "We have taken the characteristics of the grocery product—necessity, frequency, reliability—and leveraged them into a home-based relationship with customers," says DeMello. "That's the asset we're creating."

Like most Web entrepreneurs, DeMello and his colleagues have huge ambitions. In five years, they plan to have eight operating regions, to be in the top twelve metropolitan areas, and to serve more than one million homes. (At which point, given current revenues per customer, Streamline would boast sales of more than $5 billion per year.) Unlike many Web entrepreneurs, however, the leaders at Streamline are patient and persistent. Forget "Get Big Fast," the current mantra of the on-line world. Streamline wants to Get It Right First—and *then* to grow like gangbusters.

"You have to get your business model absolutely perfect before you do a full-scale launch into the market," DeMello says. "Because if you succeed on the Web, you succeed big. And you can't change a tire on a car that's moving at 80 miles per hour."

Yes, the Web is global—but Streamline, for now, is unapologetically local. The company opened its first distribution center in October 1996. The fifty-six-thousand-square-foot facility, attached to Streamline headquarters in Westwood, is a high-tech marvel, but it services only the western suburbs of Boston (forty-four of them, at last count). DeMello vows that Streamline will limit its business to this market until it has improved enough to make the service work according to its ideal. Only then will its expansion campaign begin. Its next two markets: Washington, D.C., and Atlanta.

"The way you grow a company is to make it work for one customer," says DeMello. "Then you make it work for ten customers. Then for 100, and then for 1,000. Today we understand our customers. We understand their needs. Now we're ready for a national rollout."

Streamline's CEO has followed this less-is-more course from the beginning. When he founded the company in April 1993, he called it SkyRock. "That's my philosophy," he explains. "Head in the clouds, feet on the ground. Great companies try to make quantum leaps—and to get a little better every day."

Streamline is ruthlessly clear about who is in its target market: the BSF, or "busy suburban family."

BSFs are young and middle-age couples with high incomes and at least one child. Today more than 90 percent of Streamline's customer base lies within the BSF bull's-eye. A roughly equal percentage of its customers have household incomes of $75,000 or greater.

"We have a laserlike focus on BSFs," says Gina Wilcox, director of strategic relations. "Everything we do involves them." DeMello agrees: "Just because you can do business with someone doesn't mean that you should. It's easy to get customers. It's harder to get the right customers."

The right customers tend to do the right thing: they buy, and they buy often. On average, Streamline customers place orders forty-seven weeks out of fifty-two. The average order, which consists of about seventy-five items, totals more than $110—which means that the average customer buys nearly $5,000 worth of products and services per year. Streamline's annual customer-retention rate hovers at 90 percent.

DeMello understands the value of selectivity. He also understands the cost. Choosing to acquire the right customers means choosing to acquire *fewer* customers than the company would otherwise. "Everybody asks me the same question," DeMello sighs. "'How many customers do you have?' That's the wrong question! The right questions are: How much business is each customer doing? and How many customers are referring new people to you? In the categories we serve, we get 85 percent of the money that our customers spend each year. And our referral rate is out of sight."

Moreover, acquiring the right customers doesn't just let you do more business with them. It lets you get closer to them as well. Here's the real power of Streamline's business model: the company is leveraging the Web to build a physical channel into the home. There's nothing "virtual" about Streamline's relationship with customers. Delivery reps have permission to enter a customer's garage even when no one is home. How many companies have that kind of access?

What happens when customers depend on you—and you deliver? They decide to depend on you even more. One of Streamline's most popular services is called Don't Run Out. Families identify their must-have items—milk, toilet paper, diapers, pet food—and authorize the company to replenish their stock of each item automatically. Today, almost every Streamline household uses Don't Run Out. The average household has standing orders for more than ten items.

The company is fanatic about measuring customer satisfaction. Its Web site has a tool that lets customers use Java-enabled smiley faces to rate each interaction. DeMello keeps looking for ways to innovate. "We're not perfect," he says. "I want to get as much feedback as I can. We've even considered setting up a 'Streamline Screamline.' It would be a place where people could vent when we disappoint them. We've done a good job with customer service. But until we're perfect, it's not good enough."

Questions

1. What marketing management philosophy do you think Streamline is following?
2. Discuss Tim DeMello's statements that "We are not in the grocery business. We are in the lifestyle-solutions business."
3. Explain his comments that "We're not a product business, and we're not a service business. We're a relationship business."
4. Discuss DeMello's remarks that "Just because you can do business with someone doesn't mean you should. It's easy to get customers. It's harder to get the right customers."
5. WRITING Write an appropriate mission statement for Streamline, Inc.
6. Identify external marketing environment opportunities and potential threats Streamline should monitor.
7. Identify some problems Streamline might encounter if it tries to introduce its service in other countries.

SOURCE: "Streamline Delivers the Goods" by Eric Ramsdell, *Fast Company*, August 1998, pp. 154–156. Reprinted by permission.

Cross-Functional Connections Solutions

Questions

1. Explain the differences between marketing's and manufacturing's goals and marketing's and research and development's goals.

   Marketing and Manufacturing: Marketing's goals center on customer satisfaction in terms of providing the customer with what he/she wants and needs. Achieving this goal is generally measured in terms of sales revenue. Manufacturing's goals tend to focus internally and address such issues as capacity utilization, inventory reduction, and workforce leveling. These goals are measured in terms of keeping costs down. Unfortunately, providing the customer with what he or she wants is not always consistent with keeping costs down.

   Marketing and Research and Development: Marketing's goals center on customer satisfaction with sales revenue as the measure of this satisfaction. The nature of the R&D function naturally results in goals that involve cutting-edge research. Unfortunately, this cutting-edge research may take a long time, which results in products that are slow to reach the market. Because R&D is measured on bringing cost-saving products to the marketplace, the development cycle may be extended as R&D addresses cost-reduction issues. The inconsistency between marketing wanting to speed products to market and R&D wanting to develop cost-saving products can lead to conflict.

2. What is the overlap among marketing, manufacturing, and R&D? What does each of these functions do that results in this overlap?

   All three of these functions overlap specifically on the "product." It is these three functions that actually come into direct contact with a firm's product. Functional areas such as human resources, finance/accounting, and information technology work on the periphery and probably never come into contact with the physical aspects of the product. Every action of each of these functions leads to product-related overlap. Marketing addresses such issues as price, distribution, integrated marketing communications, and customer satisfaction. Manufacturing addresses how to produce and at what rate to produce. Research and development focuses on issues such as core architecture and product components.

3. Why is cross-functional coordination necessary to have a market-oriented firm?

   Historically, everyone assumed that the customer belonged to the marketing department. We know now that this is not true. Everyone in the organization must understand the customer's wants and needs in order to satisfy these needs. Without the customer, there would be no need for an organization. For example, no customers would mean no products to develop or manufacture, no accounts receivable, and no need for employees. From the customer's perspective, good or bad products belong to the entire company—not just one particular function. Customers will not keep coming back if the company produces only low-quality merchandise—even if the marketing group has some of the best marketers in the world. Likewise, a high-quality product will not be successful in the marketplace if the product is positioned inaccurately, advertised inappropriately, priced too high or too low, or not available in the right outlets. Therefore, it is imperative that the business functions work together to send the same message to the marketplace.

Suggested Readings

Glenn M. Parker, *Cross Functional Teams: Working with Allies, Enemies and Other Strangers* (San Francisco, CA: Jossey-Bass Publishers, 1994).

Richard J. Schonberger, *Building a Chain of Customers: Linking Business Functions to Create a World Class Company* (New York, NY: The Free Press, 1990).

Marketing Planning Activities

The World of Marketing

In the world of marketing, there are many different types of goods and services offered to many different markets. Throughout this text, you will construct a marketing plan for your chosen company. Writing a marketing plan will give you a full depth of understanding for your company, its customers, and its marketing mix elements. The company you choose should be one that interests you, such as the manufacturer of your favorite product, a local business where you would like to work, or even a business you would like to start yourself to satisfy an unmet need or want.

1. Describe your chosen company. How long has it been in business, or when will it start business? Who are the key players? Is the company small or large? Does it offer a good or service? What are the strengths and weaknesses of this company? What is the orientation and organizational culture?

Marketing*Builder* Exercise:

- **Top 20 Questions** template

2. Define the business mission statement for your chosen company (or evaluate and modify an existing mission statement).
3. Set marketing objectives for your chosen company. Make sure the objectives fit the criteria for good objectives.
4. Scan the marketing environment. Identify opportunities and threats to your chosen company in areas such as technology, the economy, the political and legal environment, and competition. Is your competition foreign, domestic, or both? Also identify opportunities and threats based on possible market targets, including social factors, demographic factors, and multicultural issues.

Marketing*Builder* Exercises

- **Industry Analysis** portion of the Market Analysis template
- **Competitive Analysis Matrix** spreadsheet
- **Competition** portion of the **Market Analysis** template
- **Competitive Roundup** portion of the **Market Analysis** template
- **Strengths, Weaknesses, Opportunities,** and **Threats** sections of the **Market Analysis** template

5. Does your chosen business have a differential or competitive advantage? If there is not one, there is no point in marketing the product. Can you create a sustainable advantage with skills, resources, or elements of the marketing mix?
6. Assume your company is or will be marketing globally. How should your company enter the global marketplace? How will international issues affect your firm?
7. Identify any ethical issues that could impact your chosen firm. What steps should be taken to handle these issues?
8. Is there a key factor or assumption that you are using when performing your SWOT analysis? What would happen if this key factor or assumption did not exist?

Marketing*Builder* Exercises

- **Business Risk** portion of the **Market Analysis** template
- **Environmental Risk** portion of the **Market Analysis** template
- **Elements of Risk** table in the **Market Analysis** template

ANALYZING MARKETING OPPORTUNITIES

4

5

6

7

cross-functional connections

CROSS-FUNCTIONAL CONNECTIONS

Information Gathering as an Interactive Process

Understanding customers is at the heart of the information-gathering process. Whether it is determining individual buying behavior, sharpening the company's target marketing skills, or understanding competitive actions, market research is the key to attaining company-wide success. The traditional perception of market research is that it is "owned" by the marketing department. However, many companies have come to realize that the market belongs to the entire company—making it everyone's responsibility to understand the marketplace.

Xerox has concentrated extensively on improving the focus of the company's research efforts. The company's strategy involves better acquisition and dissemination of market research information. The ultimate goal is to utilize such information to move new and improved products into the marketplace much more quickly.

The historical information debate between marketing and other business functions centers on the qualitative versus quantitative format of functional data. The data collected by marketers are perceived to be qualitative, "touchy-feely" data when compared to the quantitative, "hard" data utilized by other functional areas. It has been difficult to get engineers and accountants to understand that marketing data are statistically valid data to use in making company-wide decisions.

Aside from the need for a general cross-functional sharing of data, there are four major areas in which marketing's information-gathering and dissemination processes need to be formally integrated with its functional counterparts:

1. Benchmarking studies
2. Customer visits
3. Customer satisfaction studies
4. Forecasting

Benchmarking is the process of comparing a firm's performance in various activities against a competitor's performance in the same activities. Some benchmarking studies also incorporate information from noncompeting companies. A hotelier organization in Ireland might benchmark its practices against a world-class food distributor because both companies are involved in serving food to customers.

A benchmarking study may focus on cross-company comparisons of purchasing processes, inventory management, product development cycles, hiring practices, payroll processes, and order fulfillment. Gathering information on a firm's competitors during a benchmarking study clearly falls within the expertise of the marketing research department and involves an extensive amount of secondary research.

Additionally, the type of information collected during a benchmarking study crosses functional boundaries. Thus, it is imperative that marketing researchers understand the functional-level processes in all business areas. These marketing researchers will be communicating with managers in manufacturing (for inventory management and order fulfillment activities), research and development (for product development cycles), human resources (for hiring practices), and finance/accounting (for payroll processes). The marketing researcher needs input from all functional areas to collect the information that will allow his or her company to understand best practices.

The Ford Motor Co. was an early pioneer of the use of benchmarking. In the early 1980s, the company found itself at a competitive disadvantage when compared to many foreign automobile manufacturers. Ford executives recognized that remaining competitive would demand a steep reduction in costs. One benchmarking study focused on reducing the number of employees in the accounts payable department. Using information gained in benchmarking of competitors, Ford was able to decrease its accounts payable staff by more than one-half. The study involved both primary and secondary research—areas in which marketers have extensive training.

Many companies now thrive on sending members of the product development team for *customer visits.* It is not unusual to hear about research and development engineers making site visits to (1) better understand customers' needs or (2) watch how a finished product is utilized in the business process. When customer visits first became popular, engineers were accompanied by marketing people to the customer site. Companies felt that engineers were too focused on functional needs and would not be able to interact personally with the customer.

Companies and engineers have begun to realize that engineering is no longer a functional area that works internally, and site visits are now being completed by engineers alone. Intuit Corp. uses customer site visits in the ongoing development and refinement of the company's software products. It is not unusual for software developers to visit small business owners at their home offices to observe the company's software products in use. The software developers watch the customer's movements when using the computer program. The goal is to gain a better understanding of the way users "think" regarding logical next moves in the program and to incorporate these moves in later versions of the product or in new products.

Additionally, Kodak attempts to gain a better understanding of how customers use its film by sending manufacturing employees to visit with professional users of its film products. Kodak depends on accurate marketplace information in understanding both the customers' buying processes and actual usage of Kodak products.

Customer satisfaction is driven by issues related to the firm's operational functions (inventory management, capital budgeting) and the firm's operational capabilities (technology, procedures), as well as the firm's product mix. Therefore, a valid *customer satisfaction study* should gather information that can be shared with manufacturing (regarding satisfaction with speed of delivery), research and development (regarding satisfaction with product quality), human resources (regarding satisfaction with complaint handling), and finance/accounting (regarding satisfaction with credit policies). All of these functional areas need to have input into the design of such studies. Retailers have long included personnel as one element of a retailer's marketing mix. Bon-Ton Department Stores and Stew Leonard's have found that their personnel are critical in maintaining customer satisfaction.

Forecasting crosses the boundaries of multiple business functions. For example, marketing may offer a discount on a particular price. The impact of this price discount is felt simultaneously in many functional areas. A key functional partner in a price discount is manufacturing. The production plan will have to accommodate the expected increase in product sales and the oftentimes below-average product sales immediately after the discount period. Although it is easy for marketers to change price, manufacturing's plans cannot be changed overnight. The impact of a price change may be felt in the company's production schedule, the level of finished goods inventory, and the availability of raw materials. Unfortunately, marketing's ability to make price changes quickly has been the cause of much conflict between marketing and manufacturing.

Much of a firm's financial planning is driven by the company's sales forecast. Marketing has historically had a reputation of being too optimistic in its projections. Thus, financial planners have been known to take the sales forecast with "a grain of salt," and planning has often evolved around a lower-than-predicted level of sales. Marketing, then, looks at financial planners as too conservative and as basing their plans on internal data that are not driven by the marketplace.

Marketplace information is a key driver in all decisions made by a company. Therefore, it is imperative that all functional areas participate in the gathering and dissemination of information. Navistar International Transportation Corp. has attempted to bring its customer-oriented marketing research to the forefront in its production processes. Navistar has been an innovator in linking marketplace information to the shop floor—allowing manufacturing to quickly and efficiently customize products to meet specific customer demands. Through the use of electronic data interchange (EDI), the company has been able to integrate the company's marketing research results into its production processes. This strategy has enabled the company to adapt a true customer focus, while simultaneously cutting costs.

Success in today's global environment depends on all functional areas understanding the firm's customers and competitors. Thorough analysis of marketplace opportunities requires an interactive process between marketing and other business functions.

Questions for Discussion

1. Why is marketing research perceived as "owned" by the marketing department?
2. Where should marketing research be formally integrated across functional departments?
3. What data differences exist across functions?

check it out

For articles and exercises on the material in this part, and for other great study aids, visit the *Marketing* Web site at **http://lamb.swcollege.com**

CHAPTER 4

LEARNING OBJECTIVES

After studying this chapter, you should be able to

1 Explain why marketing managers should understand consumer behavior

2 Analyze the components of the consumer decision-making process

3 Explain the consumer's post-purchase evaluation process

4 Identify the types of consumer buying decisions and discuss the significance of consumer involvement

5 Identify and understand the cultural factors that affect consumer buying decisions

6 Identify and understand the social factors that affect consumer buying decisions

7 Identify and understand the individual factors that affect consumer buying decisions

8 Identify and understand the psychological factors that affect consumer buying decisions

CONSUMER DECISION MAKING

Marketers have always been interested in how consumers spend their money. How they spend defines who they are. Totaling cash-register receipts and interviewing consumers have produced volumes of spending data that reveal an evolving national portrait of consumption trends: concrete evidence of changing buying patterns as well as shifts in consumers' beliefs and attitudes. Consider the following trends found in America today.

Sales of sport utility vehicles and minivans, which boomed in the 1990s, have showed signs of cooling, whereas luxury cars and station wagons, once the ubiquitous family car, are making strong comebacks. Baby boomers, who fueled the surge in sport utility vehicles and minivans as a way to cart their kids around, are now growing older and their children are leaving home. Tired of driving trucks and large minivans, these consumers are now ready to step into cars with better performance and handling.[1]

Americans are no longer as enamored of fat-free or fat-reduced foods, as typified by the sluggish sales of Frito-Lay's new Wow! fat-free line of Doritos, Ruffles, Lay's, and Tostitos products made with the fat-substitute olestra. Instead, foods with protein are the hot thing. With more snacking among baby boomers and fewer regular meals, manufacturers of protein-rich foods are pitching their products as a quick and nutritious energy boost for a stressed-out society. Diet books are increasingly recommending protein-loaded meals as a way to shed pounds and the labels of cottage cheese and yogurt now draw more attention to their protein content. Even jerky, long a pariah among health-conscious consumers, is enjoying increased sales thanks to an abundance of protein.[2]

Recent evidence at a rural Arkansas gas station shows that Americans are becoming more cultured and sophisticated. A sign not only pitches hot dogs and propane gas but cappuccino as well. Across the country, historic levels of wealth, educational attainment, and cultural exposure have converged over the past decade so that the lowest common denominator of American culture is rising, transforming the middle class into sophisticated consumers. Americans are seeing regional theaters and opera companies popping up; more Americans are attending the

on line

Rossignol

Compare the skiing page and the snowboarding page on Rossignol's Web site. How would you characterize each site? Which sport would you be likely to try based on these pages? What about your parents? Why?
http://www.rossignol.com/

performing arts; and cinemagoers are turning movies based on classic dramas, such as Shakespeare's *Romeo and Juliet* and Jane Austen's *Sense and Sensibility*, into modest hits. This explosive change in Americans' taste is exemplified by the growth of specialized beers, better wine, and good coffee, not to mention the popularity of the History Channel and books with serious themes.[3]

Although America's teens have traditionally been characterized as rebellious, today's teenagers are epitomized by their love of anything that rings of antiestablishment and risk taking. Extreme sports, including skateboarding, stunt biking, and wakeboarding, have caught on like wildfire with today's youth, sports that their parents view as dangerous. Among winter sports, downhill skiing is considered wimpy and snowboarding is cool. In concert with their antiestablishment attitudes, they have thumbed their noses at "big-money" established brands like Nike, Coca-Cola, and Levi's, in favor of Vans sneakers, Mountain Dew, and wide-leg jeans made by JNCO.[4]

What factors are influencing these trends in American consumer decision making? What effect do you think consumers' cultural values, stage in the family life cycle, attitudes, and lifestyles have on the consumer decision-making process? How do marketers respond to the constantly changing values, demographics, attitudes, and corresponding spending habits of U.S. consumers? What other factors affect what consumers buy? Questions like these will be answered as you read this chapter on the consumer decision-making process and its influences.

The Importance of Understanding Consumer Behavior

1

Explain why marketing managers should understand consumer behavior

consumer behavior
Processes a consumer uses to make purchase decisions, as well as to use and dispose of purchased goods or services; also includes factors that influence purchase decisions and the use of products.

Consumers' product and service preferences are constantly changing. In order to address this constant state of flux and to create a proper marketing mix for a well-defined market, marketing managers must have a thorough knowledge of consumer behavior. **Consumer behavior** describes how consumers make purchase decisions and how they use and dispose of the purchased goods or services. The study of consumer behavior also includes the analysis of factors that influence purchase decisions and product use.

Understanding how consumers make purchase decisions can help marketing managers in several ways. For example, if a manager knows through research that gas mileage is the most important attribute for a certain target market, the manufacturer can redesign the product to meet that criterion. If the firm cannot change the design in the short run, it can use promotion in an effort to change consumers' decision-making criteria. For example, an automobile manufacturer can advertise a car's maintenance-free features and sporty European style while downplaying gas mileage.

The Consumer Decision-Making Process

When buying products, consumers generally follow the **consumer decision-making process** shown in Exhibit 4.1: (1) need recognition, (2) information search, (3) evaluation of alternatives, (4) purchase, and (5) postpurchase behavior. These five steps represent a general process that moves the consumer from recognition of a product or service need to the evaluation of a purchase. This process is a guideline for studying how consumers make decisions. It is important to note that this guideline does not assume that consumers' decisions will proceed in order through all of the steps of the process. In fact, the consumer may end the process at any time; he or she may not even make a purchase. Explanations as to why a consumer's progression through these steps may vary are offered at the end of the chapter in the section on the types of consumer buying decisions. Before addressing this issue, we will describe each step in the process in greater detail.

2
Analyze the components of the consumer decision-making process

consumer decision-making process
Step-by-step process used by consumers when buying goods or services.

Need Recognition

The first stage in the consumer decision-making process is need recognition. **Need recognition** occurs when consumers are faced with an imbalance between actual and desired states. For example, do you often feel thirsty after strenuous exercise? Has a television commercial for a new sports car ever made you wish you could buy it? Need recognition is triggered when a consumer is exposed to either an internal or an external **stimulus**. Hunger and thirst are *internal stimuli;* the color of an automobile, the design of a package, a brand name mentioned by a friend, an advertisement on television, or cologne worn by a stranger are considered *external stimuli.*

need recognition
Result of an imbalance between actual and desired states.

stimulus
Any unit of input affecting one or more of the five senses: sight, smell, taste, touch, hearing.

exhibit 4.1

Consumer Decision-Making Process

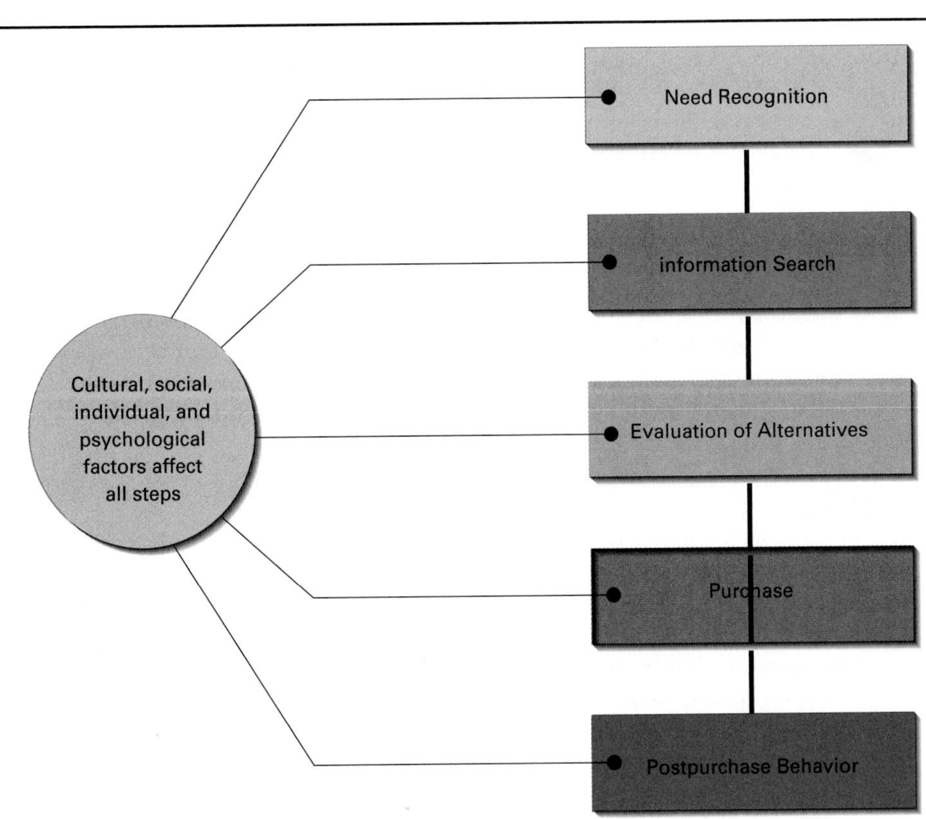

A marketing manager's objective is to get consumers to recognize an imbalance between their present status and their preferred state. Advertising and sales promotion often provide this stimulus. Surveying buyer preferences provides marketers with consumer wants and needs with which to tailor products and services. Home builder Kaufman & Broad (K&B) Home Corporation in Denver, for instance, annually surveys home buyers to determine which features they actually want in a home. It found that home buyers in Denver could do without fireplaces and basements; buyers in San Francisco wanted fireplaces; buyers everywhere preferred more square footage to vaulted ceilings, and large master bedrooms to formal dining rooms. Now, K&B offers home buyers more custom options instead of building homes first and then hoping for the best.[5]

want
Recognition of an unfulfilled need and a product that will satisfy it.

Marketing managers can create wants on the part of the consumer. A **want** exists when someone has an unfulfilled need and has determined that a particular good or service will satisfy it. Young children might want toys, video games, and baseball equipment to meet their innate need to play and learn new skills. Teenagers may want compact discs, fashionable sneakers, and wide-leg jeans to fulfill their need of belonging. A want can be for a specific product or it can be for a certain attribute or feature of a product. For instance, adults may want ready-to-eat meals, drive-through dry cleaning service, and catalog shopping to fulfill their need for convenience. Older consumers may want goods and services that offer convenience, comfort, and security. Remote-controlled appliances, home deliveries, speaker phones, and motorized carts are all designed for comfort and convenience. A personal transmitter that can signal an ambulance or the police in an emergency offers security for older consumers.

Consumers recognize unfulfilled wants in various ways. The two most common occur when a current product isn't performing properly and when the consumer is about to run out of something that is generally kept on hand. Consumers may also recognize unfulfilled wants if they become aware of a product whose features make it seem superior to the one currently used. Such wants are usually created by advertising and other promotional activities. For example, a young teenager may develop a strong desire for a new Sega video game set after seeing it on display in a store.

GLOBAL

Marketers selling their products in global markets must carefully observe the needs and wants of consumers in various regions. For example, Procter & Gamble hit on an unrecognized need of Japanese consumers when it introduced a highly concentrated liquid dishwashing soap. To determine what Japanese consumers wanted, P&G sent out researchers to study Japanese dishwashing rituals. What they discovered was that Japanese homemakers were frustrated by having to use a lot of soap to get the cleaning power to clean greasy dishes, and, as a result, they squirted out more detergent than needed. With its simple pitch "A little bit of Joy cleans better, yet is easier on the hands," its product flew off Japanese store shelves. Less than three years after its introduction, Joy commanded a 20 percent market share and Japanese competitors were busy launching their own concentrated versions.[6]

Information Search

internal information search
Process of recalling past information stored in the memory.

external information search
Process of seeking information in the outside environment.

nonmarketing-controlled information source
Product information source that is not associated with advertising or promotion.

After recognizing a need or want, consumers search for information about the various alternatives available to satisfy it. An information search can occur internally, externally, or both. **Internal information search** is the process of recalling information stored in the memory. This stored information stems largely from previous experience with a product. For instance, perhaps while shopping you encounter a brand of cake mix that you tried some time ago. By searching your memory, you can probably remember whether it tasted good, pleased guests, and was easy to prepare.

In contrast, an **external information search** seeks information in the outside environment. There are two basic types of external information sources: nonmarketing-controlled and marketing-controlled. A **nonmarketing-controlled information source** is not associated with marketers promoting a product. A friend

Nonmarketing-controlled information is often a key resource for consumers facing even the smallest of buying decisions. *Consumer Reports* is a highly recognized ratings organization that performs extensive tests on a wide variety of consumer goods and services.

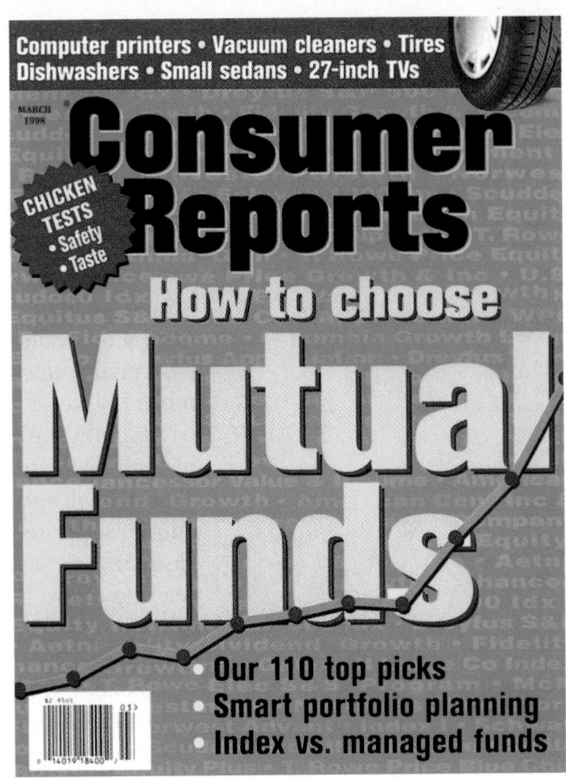

might recommend an IBM personal computer because he or she bought one and likes it. Nonmarketing-controlled information sources include personal experience (trying or observing a new product); personal sources (family, friends, acquaintances, and coworkers); and public sources, such as Underwriters Laboratories, *Consumer Reports*, and other rating organizations. For instance, consumers rely heavily on doctor and pharmacist recommendations when buying over-the-counter medications. In a recent survey that studied how consumers choose medicine, more than half started using an OTC drug because a pharmacist recommended it.[7]

A **marketing-controlled information source**, on the other hand, is biased toward a specific product, because it originates with marketers promoting that product. Marketing-controlled information sources include mass-media advertising (radio, newspaper, television, and magazine advertising), sales promotion (contests, displays, premiums, and so forth), salespeople, and product labels and packaging. For example, in the same survey on consumers and medicine, 56 percent of those interviewed said information on the label was very important in deciding whether or not to purchase an OTC medication for the first time.[8] Yet, many consumers are wary about the information they receive from marketing-controlled sources, arguing that most marketing campaigns stress the attributes of the product and don't mention the faults. These sentiments tend to be stronger among better-educated and higher-income consumers. For instance, only 13 percent of the consumers interviewed in the medicine study said that advertising is very important in their decision to purchase OTC medications.[9]

marketing-controlled information source
Product information source that originates with marketers promoting the product.

The extent to which an individual conducts an external search depends on his or her perceived risk, knowledge, prior experience, and level of interest in the good or service. Generally, as the perceived risk of the purchase increases, the consumer enlarges the search and considers more alternative brands. For instance, assume you want to buy a new car. The decision is a relatively risky one, mainly because of cost, so you are motivated to search for information about models, options, gas mileage, durability, and passenger capacity. You may also decide to gather information about more models, because the time expended in finding the data is less than the cost of buying the wrong car. In contrast, you are less likely to expend great effort in searching for the right kind of bath soap. If you make the wrong selection, the cost is minimal and you will have the opportunity to make another selection in a short period of time. A study on the effect of consumers' level of perceived risk found that those who perceive higher risk with a mail-order purchase expend more effort in an external information search and consult a greater number of information sources than do those who perceive lower levels of risk.[10]

A consumer's knowledge about the product or service will also affect the extent of an external information search. If the consumer is knowledgeable and well informed about a potential purchase, he or she is less likely to search for additional information. In addition, the more knowledgeable the consumer is, the more efficiently he or she will conduct the search process, thereby requiring less time to search. Another closely related factor that affects the extent of a consumer's external search is confidence in one's decision-making ability. A confident consumer not only has sufficient stored information about the product but also feels self-assured about making the right decision. People lacking this confidence will continue an information search even when they know a great deal about the product. Consumers with prior experience in buying a certain product will have less perceived risk than inexperienced consumers. Therefore, they will spend less time searching and limit the number of products that they consider.

A third factor influencing the external information search is product experience. Consumers who have had a positive prior experience with a product are more likely to limit their search to only those items related to the positive experience. For example, many consumers are loyal to Honda automobiles, which enjoy low repair rates and consequently high customer satisfaction, and they often own more than one.

Finally, the extent of the search undertaken is positively related to the amount of interest a consumer has in a product. A consumer who is more interested in a product will spend more time searching for information and alternatives. For example, suppose you are a dedicated runner who reads jogging and fitness magazines and catalogs. In searching for a new pair of running shoes, you may enjoy reading about the new brands available and spend more time and effort than other buyers in deciding on the right shoe.

evoked set (consideration set)
Group of brands, resulting from an information search, from which a buyer can choose.

The consumer's information search should yield a group of brands, sometimes called the buyer's **evoked set** (or **consideration set**), which are the consumer's most preferred alternatives. From this set, the buyer will further evaluate the alternatives and make a choice. Consumers do not consider all the brands available in a product category, but they do seriously consider a much smaller set. For example, there are dozens of brands of shampoos and close to two hundred types of automobiles available in the United States, yet most consumers seriously contemplate only about four shampoos and no more than five automobiles when faced with a purchase decision.

Evaluation of Alternatives and Purchase

After getting information and constructing an evoked set of alternative products, the consumer is ready to make a decision. A consumer will use the information stored in memory and obtained from outside sources to develop a set of criteria. These standards help the consumer evaluate and compare alternatives. One way to begin narrowing the number of choices in the evoked set is to pick a product attribute and then exclude all products in the set that don't have that attribute. For instance, assume that John is thinking about buying a new notebook computer to replace his current desktop machine. He is interested in one with a large color active-matrix display, CD-ROM drive, and with a processor speed of at least 300 megahertz, so he excludes all notebooks without these features.

Another way to narrow the number of choices is to use cutoffs, or minimum or maximum levels of an attribute that an alternative must pass to be considered. Suppose John still must choose from a wide array of notebook computers that have active-matrix screens, CD-ROM drives, and 300-plus processor speeds. He then names another product attribute: price. Given the amount of money he has set aside for a new computer, John decides he cannot spend more than $2,500. Therefore, he can exclude all notebook computers priced above $2,500. A final way to narrow the choices is to rank the attributes under consideration in order of importance and evaluate the products based on how well they perform on the most important attributes. To reach a final decision, John would pick the most important attributes, such as processor speed and active display, weigh the merits of each, and then evaluate alternative notebook computers on those criteria.

If new brands are added to an evoked set, the consumer's evaluation of the existing brands in that set changes. As a result, certain brands in the original set may become more desirable. Suppose John sees two notebook computers priced at $1,999 and $2,199. At the time, he may judge the $2,199 notebook computer as too expensive and choose not to purchase it. However, if he then adds to his list of alternatives another notebook computer that is priced at $2,499, he may view the $2,199 one as less expensive and decide to purchase it.

The goal of the marketing manager is to determine which attributes are most important in influencing a consumer's choice. Several factors may collectively affect a consumer's evaluation of products. A single attribute, such as price, may not adequately explain how consumers form their evoked set.[11] Moreover, attributes thought to be important to the marketer may not be very important to the consumer. For example, much to the surprise of car sellers, one study found that automobile warranty coverage was the least important factor in a consumer's purchase of a car.[12]

A brand name can also have a significant impact on a consumer's ultimate choice. Sears, Roebuck & Company is leveraging its well-known brand name to expand its service business. Since consumers are typically ill-prepared for the dishwasher overflowing or the refrigerator giving out, they frantically look for repair alternatives. Many turn to trusted sources, such as Sears, which markets itself as a logical alternative for harried consumers. In its advertising, it portrays itself as a reliable retail chain. By providing consumers with a certain set of promises, brands, in essence, simplify the consumer decision-making process so consumers do not have to rethink their options every time they need something.[13]

Following the evaluation of alternatives, the consumer decides which product to buy or decides not to buy a product at all. If he or she decides to make a purchase, the next step in the process is an evaluation of the product after the purchase.

Postpurchase Behavior

3
Explain the consumer's postpurchase evaluation process

When buying products, consumers expect certain outcomes from the purchase. How well these expectations are met determines whether the consumer is satisfied or dissatisfied with the purchase. For example, a person buys a used car with somewhat low expectations for the car's actual performance. Surprisingly, the car turns out to be one of the best cars she has ever owned. Thus the buyer's satisfaction is high, because her fairly low expectations were exceeded. On the other hand, a consumer who buys a brand-new car would expect it to perform especially well. But if the car turns out to be a lemon, she will be very dissatisfied because her high expectations have not been met. Price often creates high expectations. One study found that higher monthly cable TV bills were associated with greater expectations for cable service. Over time, cable subscribers tended to drop the premium-priced cable channels because their high expectations were not met.[14]

For the marketing manager, one important element of any postpurchase evaluation is reducing any lingering doubts that the decision was sound. When people recognize inconsistency between their values or opinions and their behavior, they tend to feel an inner tension called **cognitive dissonance**. For example, suppose a consumer spends half his monthly salary on a new high-tech stereo system. If he stops to think how much he has spent, he will probably feel dissonance. Dissonance occurs because the person knows the purchased product has some disadvantages as well as some advantages. In the case of the stereo, the disadvantage of cost battles the advantage of technological superiority.

cognitive dissonance
Inner tension that a consumer experiences after recognizing an inconsistency between behavior and values or opinions.

Consumers try to reduce dissonance by justifying their decision. They might seek new information that reinforces positive ideas about the purchase, avoid information that contradicts their decision, or revoke the original decision by returning the product. People who have just bought a new car often read more advertisements for the newly purchased car than for other cars in order to reduce dissonance. In some instances, people deliberately seek contrary information in order to refute it and reduce dissonance. Dissatisfied customers sometimes rely on word of mouth to reduce cognitive dissonance, by letting friends and family know they are displeased.

VALUE

Marketing managers can help reduce dissonance through effective communication with purchasers. For example, a customer service manager may slip a note inside the package congratulating the buyer on making a wise decision. Postpurchase letters sent by manufacturers and

Put your kids in
Lands' End® sleepwear, and
you'll sleep better, too.
It's cozy and warm as a lullaby–but our Sleepwear is practical, too.
For unlike some fleece that "pills" in washing, Polartec™100 stubbornly resists pilling. So, our PJ's, Blanket Sleeper and Robes won't turn threadbare before your little one outgrows them.
The fit's generous–we cut our patterns on real boys and girls, not the usual stiff mannequins.
And while your youngster sleeps, you can leisurely shop the rest of our Lands' End Kids' catalog.
That is, if you're not grabbing a little nap yourself.
Soft, cozy Polartec™ 100–holds in heat, yet breathes
Rib-knit cuff keeps its shape
Generous, "comfy" fit
Clean finished seams, no rough edges
Cotton feet (not sweaty plastic), with long-wearing rubber treads
LANDS' END
Guaranteed. Period.
For our free catalog of clothing for kids–from tots to teens–call anytime
1-800-990-5421
Name
Address
Apt.
City
State
Zip
Phone
Mail to: 1 Lands' End Lane, Dodgeville, WI 53595
http://www.landsend.com/catalogs

This Lands' End ad tells consumers the benefits and advantages of its product, children's sleepwear, to help consumers make the purchase decision.
Courtesy Lands' End Inc.

dissonance-reducing statements in instruction booklets may help customers feel at ease with their purchase. Advertising that displays the product's superiority over competing brands or guarantees can also help relieve the possible dissonance of someone who has already bought the product. Catalog merchant Lands' End, for example, offers consumers a no-questions-asked guarantee: If a product purchased through a Lands' End catalog does not work out, no matter what the reason, the company will provide a prompt, no-hassle refund or exchange. Infiniti car dealers recently offered refunds to new car buyers within three days of their purchase if they decided they were unsatisfied. Dealers also offered a price protection plan: If prices go down on a new Infiniti, anyone who paid more than the lower price in the previous thirty days was entitled to a refund of the difference.[15]

Types of Consumer Buying Decisions and Consumer Involvement

4

Identify the types of consumer buying decisions and discuss the significance of consumer involvement

involvement
Amount of time and effort a buyer invests in the search, evaluation, and decision processes of consumer behavior.

All consumer buying decisions generally fall along a continuum of three broad categories: routine response behavior, limited decision making, and extensive decision making (see Exhibit 4.2). Goods and services in these three categories can best be described in terms of five factors: level of consumer involvement, length of time to make a decision, cost of the good or service, degree of information search, and the number of alternatives considered. The level of consumer involvement is perhaps the most significant determinant in classifying buying decisions. **Involvement** is the amount of time and effort a buyer invests in the search, evaluation, and decision processes of consumer behavior.

exhibit 4.2

Continuum of Consumer Buying Decisions

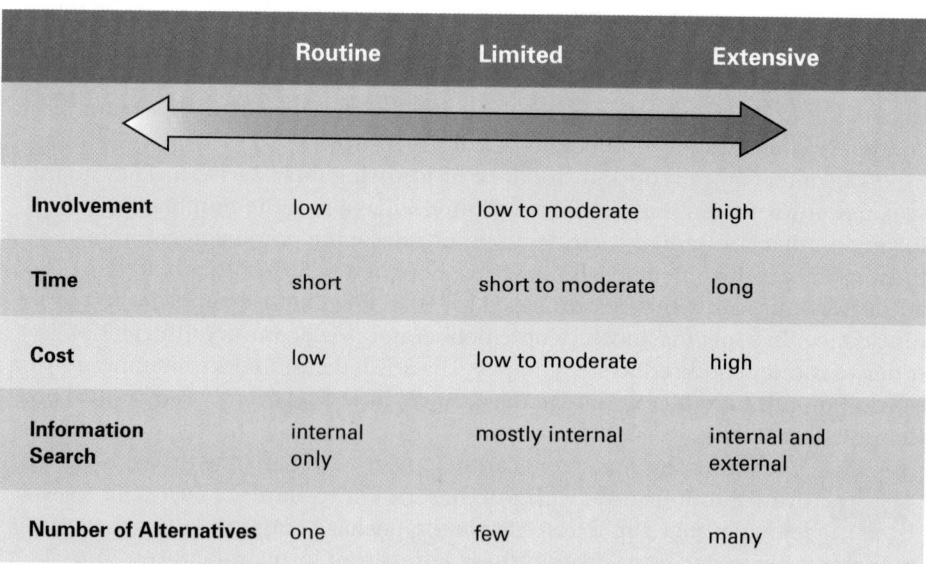

	Routine	Limited	Extensive
Involvement	low	low to moderate	high
Time	short	short to moderate	long
Cost	low	low to moderate	high
Information Search	internal only	mostly internal	internal and external
Number of Alternatives	one	few	many

Frequently purchased, low-cost goods and services are generally associated with **routine response behavior**. These goods and services can also be called low-involvement products, because consumers spend little time on search and decision before making the purchase. Usually, buyers are familiar with several different brands in the product category but stick with one brand. Consumers engaged in routine response behavior normally don't experience need recognition until they are exposed to advertising or see the product displayed on a store shelf. Consumers buy first and evaluate later, whereas the reverse is true for extensive decision making. A parent, for example, will not stand at the cereal shelf in the grocery store for twenty minutes thinking about which brand of cereal to buy for the children. Instead, he or she will walk by the shelf, find the family's usual brand, and put it into the cart.

routine response behavior
Type of decision making exhibited by consumers buying frequently purchased, low-cost goods and services; requires little search and decision time.

Limited decision making typically occurs when a consumer has previous product experience but is unfamiliar with the current brands available. Limited decision making is also associated with lower levels of involvement (although higher than routine decisions) because consumers do expend moderate effort in searching for information or in considering various alternatives. Suppose the children's usual brand of cereal, Kellogg's Corn Flakes, is unavailable in the grocery store. Completely out of cereal at home, the parent now must select another brand. Before making a final selection, he or she may pull from the shelf several brands similar to Kellogg's Corn Flakes, such as Corn Chex and Cheerios, to compare their nutritional value and calories and to decide whether the children will like the new cereal.

limited decision making
Type of decision making that requires a moderate amount of time for gathering information and deliberating about an unfamiliar brand in a familiar product category.

Consumers practice **extensive decision making** when buying an unfamiliar, expensive product or an infrequently bought item. This process is the most complex type of consumer buying decision and is associated with high involvement on the part of the consumer. This process resembles the model outlined in Exhibit 4.1. These consumers want to make the right decision, so they want to know as much as they can about the product category and available brands. People usually experience cognitive dissonance only when buying high-involvement products. Buyers use several criteria for evaluating their options and spend much time seeking information. Buying a home or a car, for example, requires extensive decision making.

extensive decision making
Most complex type of consumer decision making, used when buying an unfamiliar, expensive product or an infrequently bought item; requires use of several criteria for evaluating options and much time for seeking information.

The type of decision making that consumers use to purchase a product does not necessarily remain constant. For instance, if a routinely purchased product no longer satisfies, consumers may practice limited or extensive decision making to switch to another brand. And people who first use extensive decision making may then use limited or routine decision making for future purchases. For example, a new mother may first extensively evaluate several brands of disposable diapers before selecting one. Subsequent purchases of diapers will then become routine.

Factors Determining the Level of Consumer Involvement

The level of involvement in the purchase depends on five factors: previous experience, interest, perceived risk, situation, and social visibility.

- *Previous experience:* When consumers have had previous experience with a good or service, the level of involvement typically decreases. After repeated product trials, consumers learn to make quick choices. Because consumers are familiar with the product and know whether it will satisfy their needs, they become less involved in the purchase. For example, consumers with pollen allergies typically buy the sinus medicine that has relieved their symptoms in the past.
- *Interest:* Involvement is directly related to consumer interests, as in cars, music, movies, bicycling, or electronics. Naturally, these areas of interest vary from one individual to another. Although some people have little interest in nursing homes, a person with elderly parents in poor health may be highly interested.
- *Perceived risk of negative consequences:* As the perceived risk in purchasing a product increases, so does a consumer's level of involvement. The types of risks that concern consumers include financial risk, social risk, and psychological

risk. First, financial risk is exposure to loss of wealth or purchasing power. Because high risk is associated with high-priced purchases, consumers tend to become extremely involved. Therefore, price and involvement are usually directly related: As price increases, so does the level of involvement. For example, someone who is thinking of buying a home will normally spend much time and effort to find the right one. Second, consumers take social risks when they buy products that can affect people's social opinions of them (for example, driving an old, beat-up car or wearing unstylish clothes). Third, buyers undergo psychological risk if they feel that making the wrong decision might cause some concern or anxiety. For example, should a working parent hire a baby-sitter or enroll the child in a day-care center?

- *Situation:* The circumstances of a purchase may temporarily transform a low-involvement decision into a high-involvement one. High involvement comes into play when the consumer perceives risk in a specific situation. For example, an individual might routinely buy low-priced brands of liquor and wine. However, when the boss visits, the consumer might make a high-involvement decision and buy more prestigious brands.
- *Social visibility:* Involvement also increases as the social visibility of a product increases. Products often on social display include clothing (especially designer labels), jewelry, cars, and furniture. All these items make a statement about the purchaser and, therefore, carry a social risk.

Marketing Implications of Involvement

GLOBAL

Marketing strategy varies depending on the level of involvement associated with the product. For high-involvement product purchases, marketing managers have several responsibilities. First, promotion to the target market should be extensive and informative. A good ad gives consumers the information they need for making the purchase decision, as well as specifying the benefits and unique advantages of owning the product. For example, manufacturers of high-tech computers and peripheral equipment like scanners, printers, and modems run lengthy ads that detail technical information about such attributes as performance, resolution, and speed. Germany's Daimler-Benz AG, maker of Mercedes-Benz automobiles, is developing Virtual Vehicle, which uses virtual reality to let customers test different combinations of colors, fabrics, and hubcaps to make the purchase decision easier. A touch screen hung from the ceiling allows customers to walk around a computer-generated image of a car, changing color, fabric, hubcaps, or headlights with a click. Customers can even alter the speaker configuration and hear the result immediately in Dolby stereo sound.[16]

For low-involvement product purchases, consumers may not recognize their wants until they are in the store. Therefore, in-store promotion is an important tool when promoting low-involvement products. Marketing managers have to focus on package design so the product will be eye-catching and easily recognized on the shelf. Examples of products that take this approach are Campbell's soups, Tide detergent, Velveeta cheese, and Heinz ketchup. In-store displays also stimulate sales of low-involvement products. A good display can explain the product's purpose and prompt recognition of a want. Displays of health and beauty aid items in supermarkets have been known to increase sales many times above normal. Coupons, cents-off deals, and two-for-one offers also effectively promote low-involvement items.

Linking a product to a higher-involvement issue is another tactic that marketing managers can use to increase the sales of a low-involvement product. For example, many food products are no longer just nutritious but also low in fat or cholesterol. Although packaged food may normally be a low-involvement product, reference to health issues raises the involvement level. Oatmeal has been around for hundreds of years. To take advantage of today's interest in healthier foods, Quaker Oats used health appeals in its advertising, claiming that soluble fiber from oatmeal, as part of a low-fat, low-cholesterol diet, may reduce the risk of heart disease. Using the slogan "Oh, what those oats can do," Quaker's advertising of that claim helped reverse an oatmeal sales slump.[17] Many entrepreneurs are linking their product or service to the year 2000 and the coming of a new millennium. Read about this phenomenon in the "Entrepreneurial Insights" box.

entrepreneurial insights

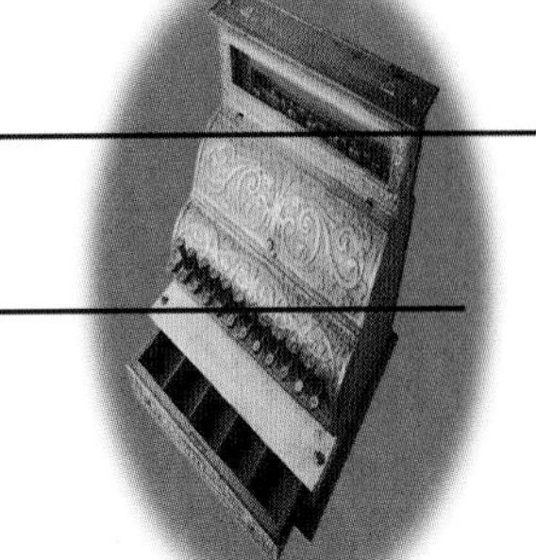

Millennium Fever Seizes the Nation's Marketers

The turn of the century in the year 2000 is driving consumer behavior in all sorts of interesting ways. The new millennium brings to mind images of death and rebirth, things ending and beginning, a time of celebration and a time of repentance. Turn-of-the-century fever characterizes every end-of-century period. But the phenomenon has special intensity this time around, for several reasons.

First, it's the turn of a millennium, not just a century. Today's consumers are the privileged few to usher in a new millennium. Second, the omnipresent and influential media are amplifying the importance of the year 2000. Already there are dozens of Web sites that provide a countdown to January 1, 2000. Scientists at the Center for Millennial Studies are busy recording and analyzing the prophecies and the events leading up to and following the year 2000. Third, the seventy-plus million baby boomers, already the most commercially influential population in history, have turned or will turn fifty between 1996 and 2014, more or less coinciding with the new millennium. Through their sheer size and penchant for glorifying the past and fantasizing about the future, baby boomers' attitudes will pervade society. Finally, the information age will help increase the fever because individuals are exposed to much more hype. Spurts of religious apocalyptic prophecies of the end of the world and an interest in spiritualism have figured in other end-of-century periods and will be prevalent this time as well.

In the wake of millennial fever, companies large and small are figuring that an event capable of inspiring apocalyptic novels, doomsday prophecies, shortages of vintage champagne, and plans for twenty-four-hour blowouts in the world's twenty-four time zones to ring in the year 2000 has to have some commercial potential. Associating a product or service with the millennium makes it seem forward looking and innovative. Already companies are changing their names, designing new logos, and introducing new products with millennial themes.

Companies are elbowing each other to cash in on the year 2000. The U.S. Patent and Trademark Office in Washington has been swamped with millennium-related trademark applications to trademark phrases and products with the word "millennium" and "Y2K," shorthand for the year 2000. A sampling of products and services seeking approval include millennium herbs, bells, health care, fishing tackle, biotherapeutics, bottled water, Internet-solutions providers, and pet food.

Already there are countless millennium products and services available. Batesville Casket Company of Batesville, Indiana, markets a stainless steel model called the Millennium. Iron Horse Vineyards in California has released a special vintage especially for the millennial celebration. There is also a "toothbrush for the millennium" designed with twin heads heralding "a new age in what a toothbrush can do"; a Third Millennium Bible; a millennium semiautomatic nine-millimeter gun; a "Third Millennium Cigar"; and a "personal injury firm of the new millennium" to call next time you're whiplashed in a car accident.

Even the major marketers are considering capitalizing on millennium fever. M&M/Mars has already launched an advertising campaign with a millennial theme, featuring the Roman-numeral equation MM = 2000. General Mills trademarked a Millennium Crunch cereal. Philip Morris's Miller Brewing Company has trademarked the word "Millerennium." Bell Atlantic has tagged its new electronic billing system "Billing Into the Next Millennium." Playboy Enterprises has trademarked "The Magazine of the Millennium." And News Corp.'s 20th Century Fox has trademarked the name "21st Century Fox."

The champagne industry, whose sales have been flat for years, is urging consumers to purchase their bubbly for the millennium celebration now. Rumors of champagne shortages in anticipation of the millennium have caused people to invest hundreds of thousands of dollars into vintage champagne, particularly Dom Perignon 1990.

Advertising experts, meanwhile, predict that the millennium might be a massive marketing bust. New York advertising agency Saatchi & Saatchi has been surveying consumers about the impending century since 1994 and has been amazed to learn that most people simply don't care and those with an opinion are filled with dread. Marketers, on the other hand, are betting that New Year's Eve 1999 will be a very special occasion, but just how special isn't yet clear.[18]

on line

M&M/Mars

Does the millennial theme advertising campaign launched by M&M/Mars in 1998 carry over into its Internet marketing? Explain what you find.

http://www.m-ms.com/millennium/

Factors Influencing Consumer Buying Decisions

The consumer decision-making process does not occur in a vacuum. On the contrary, underlying cultural, social, individual, and psychological factors strongly influence the decision process. They have an effect from the time a consumer perceives a stimulus through postpurchase behavior. Cultural factors, which include culture and values, subculture, and social class, exert the broadest influence over consumer decision making. Social factors sum up the social interactions between a consumer and influential groups of people, such as reference groups, opinion leaders, and family members. Individual factors, which include gender, age, family life cycle stage, personality, self-concept, and lifestyle, are unique to each individual and play a major role in the type of products and services consumers want. Psychological factors determine how consumers perceive and interact with their environments and influ-

exhibit 4.3

Factors That Affect the Consumer Decision-Making Process

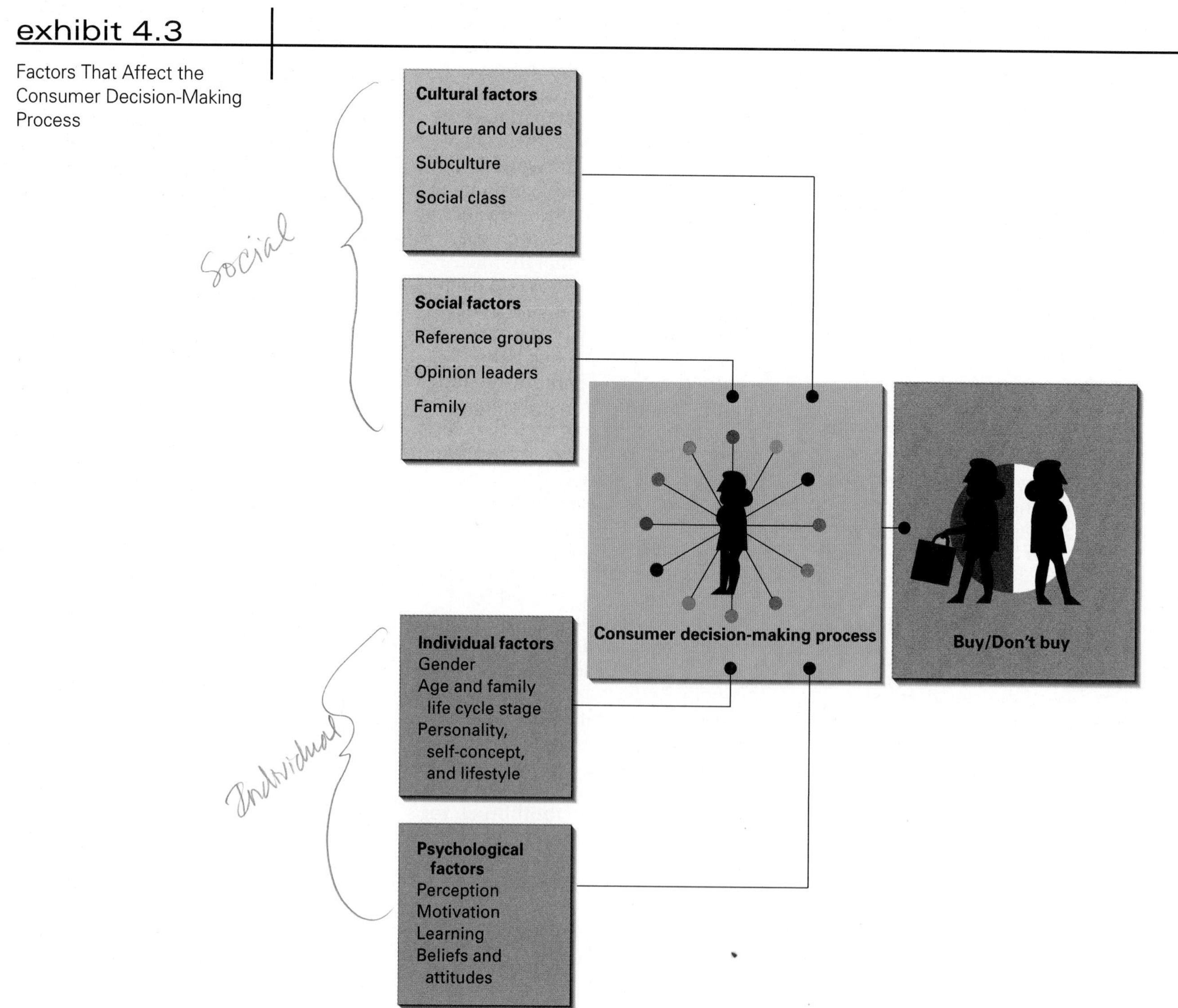

ence the ultimate decisions consumers make. They include perception, motivation, learning, beliefs, and attitudes. Exhibit 4.3 summarizes these influences.

Cultural Influences on Consumer Buying Decisions

The first major group of factors that influence consumer decision making are cultural factors. Cultural factors exert the broadest and deepest influence over a person's consumer behavior and decision making. Marketers must understand the way a person's culture and its accompanying values, as well as a person's subculture and social class, influence their buying behavior.

5
Identify and understand the cultural factors that affect consumer buying decisions

Culture and Values

Culture is the essential character of a society that distinguishes it from other cultural groups. The underlying elements of every culture are the values, language, myths, customs, rituals, and laws that shape the behavior of the culture, as well as the artifacts, or products, of that behavior as they are transmitted from one generation to the next. Exhibit 4.4 lists some defining components of American culture.

Culture is pervasive. Cultural values and influences are the ocean in which individuals swim, and of which most are completely unaware. What people eat, how

culture
Set of values, norms, attitudes, and other meaningful symbols that shape human behavior and the artifacts, or products, of that behavior as they are transmitted from one generation to the next.

exhibit 4.4

Components of American Culture

Component	Examples
Values	Success through hard work Emphasis on personal freedom
Language	English as the official language
Myths	Santa Claus delivers presents to good boys and girls on Christmas Eve. Abraham Lincoln walked a mile to return a penny.
Customs	Bathing daily Shaking hands when greeting new people Standard gratuity of 15 percent at restaurants
Rituals	Thanksgiving Day dinner Singing the "Star Spangled Banner" before baseball games Going to church on Sundays
Laws	Child labor laws Sherman Anti-Trust Act guarantees competition.
Material artifacts	Diamond engagement rings Beanie Babies

SOURCE: Adapted from *Consumer Behavior* by William D. Wells and David Prensky. Copyright © 1996 by John Wiley & Sons, Inc. Reprinted by permission of John Wiley & Sons, Inc. All Rights Reserved.

they dress, what they think and feel, what language they speak are all dimensions of culture. It encompasses all the things consumers do without conscious choice because their culture's values, customs, and rituals are ingrained in their daily habits.

Culture is functional. Human interaction creates values and prescribes acceptable behavior for each culture. By establishing common expectations, culture gives order to society. Sometimes these expectations are coded into laws. For example, drivers in our culture must stop at a red light. Other times these expectations are taken for granted. For example, grocery stores and hospitals are open twenty-four hours whereas bank lobbies are open only during banker's hours.

Culture is learned. Consumers are not born knowing the values and norms of their society. Instead, they must learn what is acceptable from family and friends. Children learn the values that will govern their behavior from parents, teachers, and peers. As members of our society, they learn to shake hands when they greet someone, to drive on the right-hand side of the road, and to eat pizza and drink Coca-Cola.

Culture is dynamic. It adapts to changing needs and an evolving environment. The rapid growth of technology at the end of the twentieth century has accelerated the rate of cultural change. Television has changed entertainment patterns and family communication and has heightened public awareness of political and other news events. Automation has increased the amount of leisure time we have and, in some ways, has changed the traditional work ethic. Cultural norms will continue to evolve because of our need for social patterns that solve problems.

value
Enduring belief that a specific mode of conduct is personally or socially preferable to another mode of conduct.

The most defining element of a culture is its **values**—the enduring beliefs shared by a society that a specific mode of conduct is personally or socially preferable to another mode of conduct. People's value systems have a great effect on their consumer behavior. Consumers with similar value systems tend to react alike to prices and other marketing-related inducements. Values also correspond to consumption patterns. People who want to protect the environment try to buy only products that don't harm it. Values can also influence consumers' TV viewing habits or the magazines they read. For instance, people who strongly object to violence avoid crime shows and those who oppose pornography do not buy *Hustler.* Core American values, or those values that are considered central to the American way of life, are presented in Exhibit 4.5.

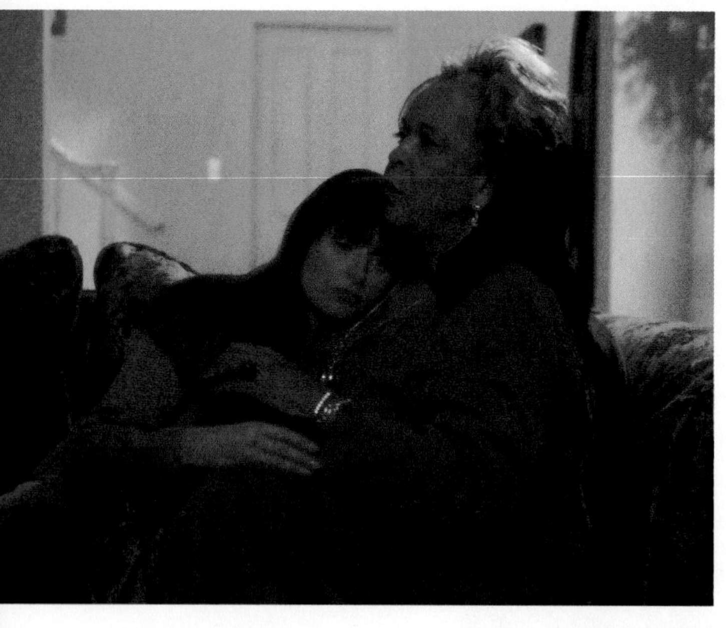

America's renewed passion for spirituality, as evidenced by the popularity of CBS's "Touched by an Angel" television show, has created new possibilities for marketers.
© Westenberger/Liaison

The personal values of target consumers have important implications for marketing managers. When marketers understand the core values that underlie the attitudes that shape the buying patterns of America's consumers and how these values were molded by experiences, they can then target their message more effectively. For example, the personal value systems of matures, baby boomers, and baby busters are quite different. The key to understanding *matures,* or everyone born before 1945, is recognizing the impact of the Great Depression and World War II on their lives. Facing these two immense challenges shaped a generation characterized by discipline, self-denial, financial and social conservatism, and a sense of obligation. Boomers, those individuals nurtured in the bountiful postwar period between 1945 and 1964, believe they are entitled to the wealth and opportunity that seemed endless in their youth. Baby busters, or Generation X as they are frequently referred to, are very accepting of diversity and individuality. They are also a very entrepreneurial-driven generation, ready to tackle life's challenges for themselves rather than as part of a crowd.[19]

Values represent what is most important in people's lives. Therefore, marketers watch carefully for shifts in consumers' values over time. For example, millions of

exhibit 4.5

Core American Values

Success	Americans admire hard work, entrepreneurship, achievement, and success. Those achieving success in American society are rewarded with money, status, and prestige. For example, Bill Gates, once a nerdy computer buff, built Microsoft Computers into an internationally known giant. Gates is now one of the richest people in the world today.
Materialism	Americans value owning tangible goods. American society encourages consumption, ownership, and possession. Americans judge others based on their material possessions; for example, the type of car they own, where they live, and what type of clothes they wear.
Freedom	The American culture was founded on the principle of religious and political freedom. The American Constitution and the Bill of Rights assure American citizens the right to life, liberty, and the pursuit of happiness. These freedoms are fundamental to the legal system and the moral fiber of the American culture. The Internet, for example, is built on the principle of the right to free speech. Lawmakers who have attempted to limit the material available on the Internet have met with tough free-speech opponents.
Progress	Technological advancements, as well as advances in medicine, science, health, and the quality of products and services, are important to Americans. Each year, for example, more than 25,000 new or improved consumer products are introduced on America's supermarket shelves.[20]
Youth	Americans are obsessed with youth and spend a good deal of time on products and procedures that make them feel and look younger. Americans spend millions each year on health and beauty aids, health clubs, and healthy foods. Media and advertising encourage the quest for youth by using young, attractive, slim models, such as those ads from fashion designer Calvin Klein.
Capitalism	Americans believe in a free enterprise system characterized by competition and the chance for monetary success. Capitalism creates choices, quality, and value for Americans. Laws prohibit monopolistic control of a market and regulate free trade. Americans encourage small business success, such as that found by Apple Computer, Wal-Mart, and McDonald's, all of which started as small enterprises with a better idea that toppled the competition.

SOURCE: From *Consumer Behavior* by William D. Wells and David Prensky. Copyright © 1996 John Wiley & Sons, Inc. Reprinted by permission of John Wiley & Sons, Inc. All Rights Reserved.

Americans have acquired a passion for spirituality, as evidenced by the soaring sales of books with religious or spiritual themes and the popularity of CBS's "Touched by an Angel" television show.[21] Many marketers are zeroing in on this spirituality phenomenon among Americans. For instance, after the San Diego Padres baseball team went through a losing streak, lost several key players, and changed ownership, the team needed to rebuild and regain the support of its demoralized fans. So it developed a campaign asking fans to "keep the faith" and resurrected the team's old

on line

Oprah Winfrey

What kind of role does spirituality play in Oprah Winfrey's show and her other ventures? Visit her Web page and find out.

http://www.oprah.com

mascot, a friar, as its new logo. Television ads introduced the "Gospel of Baseball" according to different players to the tunes of gospel music with the refrain "Support the Padres and keep the faith." As a result, attendance doubled and the fans were happy once again.[22]

Understanding Culture Differences

GLOBAL

Underlying core values can vary across cultures. For example, Asians tend to place a high value on social harmony; Americans put greater emphasis on individuals' rights and responsibilities. In a survey of Asian and American business executives, Asian businesspeople place hard work, respect for learning, and honesty among their top values. By contrast, honesty and accountability do not appear among American business executives' top-rated values. Instead, American executives rank freedom of expression as highly important, a value that did not even make the grade with Asian executives.[23]

Without understanding a culture, a firm has little chance of selling products in it. Like people, products have cultural values and rules that influence their perception and use. Culture, therefore, must be understood before the behavior of individuals within the cultural context can be understood.[24] Colors, for example, may have different meanings in global markets than they do at home. In China, white is the color of mourning, and brides wear red; in the United States, black is for mourning, and brides wear white. Pepsi had a dominant market share in Southeast Asia until it changed the color of its coolers and vending equipment from deep regal blue to light ice blue. In that part of the world, light blue is associated with death and mourning. Whirlpool Corporation had not counted on the huge cultural differences in European countries when it first entered the European market. Clothes washers sold in northern countries like Denmark must spin-dry clothes much better than in southern Italy, where consumers often line-dry clothes in warmer weather. As a result, Whirlpool recently redesigned more than half of its products sold in Europe.[25]

Language is another important aspect of culture that global marketers must deal with. They must take care in translating product names, slogans, and promotional messages into foreign languages so as not to convey the wrong message. Consider the following examples of blunders made by marketers when delivering their message to Spanish-speaking consumers: General Motors discovered too late that Nova (the name of an economical car) literally means "doesn't go" in Spanish; Coors encouraged its English-speaking customers to "Turn it loose," but the phrase in Spanish means "Suffer from diarrhea"; and when Frank Perdue said, "It takes a tough man to make a tender chicken," Spanish speakers heard "It takes a sexually stimulated man to make a chicken affectionate."

As more companies expand their operations globally, the need to understand the cultures of foreign countries becomes more important. Marketers should become familiar with the culture and adapt to it. What's all the rage in Boston could be a bust in Bombay if marketers are not sensitive to the nuances of the local culture. Read about the differences in how cultures around the world view and use time in the "Global Perspectives" box.

Subculture

subculture
Homogeneous group of people who share elements of the overall culture as well as unique elements of their own group.

A culture can be divided into subcultures on the basis of demographic characteristics, geographic regions, national and ethnic background, political beliefs, and religious beliefs. A **subculture** is a homogeneous group of people who share elements of the overall culture as well as cultural elements unique to their own group. Within subcultures, people's attitudes, values, and purchase decisions are even more similar than they are within the broader culture. Subcultural

global perspectives

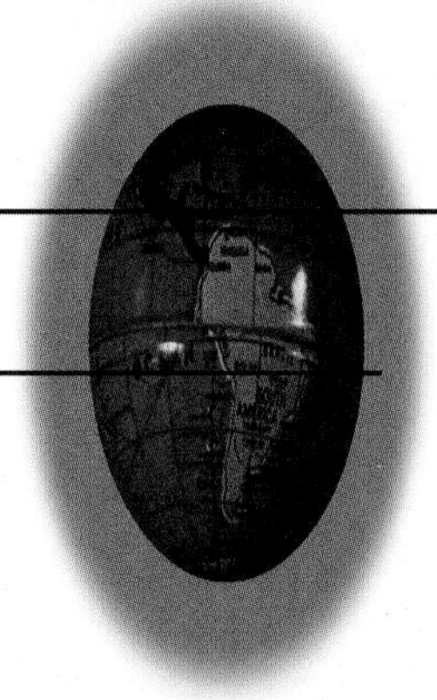

The Pace of Life and Use of Time Around the World

How consumers view and use time varies greatly across cultures. These measures relate to the deeply rooted values that each culture shares.

Several researchers have been studying the tempo of life in other cultures as well as how people spend their time. Robert Levine, professor of psychology at California State University, Fresno, has been studying the tempo of life in other cultures for over a decade. John Robinson, a sociology professor from the University of Maryland at College Park, has been involved in Americans' Use of Time Project since its beginnings in 1965. Here is what these two researchers have found on how Americans and other cultures view and use time.

From his research, Levine developed three measures of the pace of life: 1. walking speed—the speed with which pedestrians in downtown areas walk a distance of sixty feet; 2. work speed—how quickly postal clerks complete a standard request to purchase a stamp; and 3. accuracy of public clocks. Data were collected in at least one large city in each of thirty-one nations around the world to measure each country's pace of life.

Japan and Western European countries scored fastest overall, with Switzerland achieving the distinction of first place. Bank clocks in Switzerland, for example, were off by an average of only nineteen seconds. Following Switzerland were Ireland, Germany, Japan, Italy, England, Sweden, Austria, and the Netherlands. The United States, represented in the survey by New York City, scored a respectable sixth place on walking speed, but ranked twenty-third on postal times and twentieth on clock accuracy, for an overall rank of sixteenth place.

There were few surprises at the slow end of the list, where the last eight ranks were occupied by nonindustrialized countries from Africa, Asia, the Middle East, and Latin America. Slowness in countries such as Brazil, Indonesia, and Mexico, all of which fell to the bottom of the pace-of-life scale, seeps into the fabric of daily life. Brazilians not only expect a casual approach to time but seem to have abandoned any semblance of fidelity to the clock. When asked how long they would wait for a late arriver to show up at a nephew's birthday party, for example, Brazilians said they would hold on for an average of 129 minutes—over two hours! Few Brazilians wear watches and the watches they do wear are often inaccurate.

How people spend their time also varies from culture to culture. For example, time-use specialists often refer to France, Germany, and other Western European countries as "eating and sleeping cultures" because Europeans spend much more time than Americans or Asians on these two activities. Europeans also work fewer hours per week and enjoy more vacation time, up to six weeks mandatory vacation in some European countries. In Sweden, vacation time goes as high as eight weeks out of the year. In contrast, people in Japan and the United States spend more time working and take less vacation than their European counterparts. Workers in Japan, for instance, put in an annual average of 202 hours more than workers in the United States and 511 hours more than workers in West Germany. In a study comparing people living in the Netherlands to people in California, the Dutch spend much less time than Californians do working, traveling, shopping, and watching television. Instead, the Dutch spend their time on entertainment and social activities, education, child care, sports, hobbies, and housework.

How Americans spend their time also varies among ethnic subcultures. Over the decades that John Robinson has been studying how Americans use time, he has found distinct differences in how African-American, Asian, Hispanic, and non-Hispanic white subcultures in the United States spend their time. This phenomenon reflects in part on their value systems. African-Americans, for instance, tend to spend more time on religious activities, spending almost twice as much time going to church as whites do. Whites spend the most time on housework, Asians spend the most time on education, and Hispanics spend the most time on child care.

All cultures have something to learn from others' conceptions of time. Without fully understanding a cultural context, consumers are likely to misinterpret its people's motives. The result, inevitably, is conflict. Marketers who use sales personnel to sell in other countries where the pace of life and the use of time vary greatly must consider the customs of each culture. For instance, marketers from a relatively fast-paced culture like the United States can blunder badly when selling to slower-paced Mexican neighbors.

Marketers can adjust to another culture's sense of time by learning to translate appointment times. For instance, is it appropriate to arrive a little late or is punctuality important? In Mexico it is understood that you should arrive late when invited to a social function. Additionally, marketers should understand the line between work time and social time. Recall that in the United States, the typical ratio of time spent on-task and time spent socializing on the job is about 80:20. But in countries like India and Nepal, the balance is closer to 50:50.

One of the hardest aspects of time for people of fast cultures to assimilate is the move from "clock time" to "event time." Clock time uses the hour on the clock to schedule activities, and event time allows activities to transpire according to their own spontaneous schedule. A move from clock time to event time, however, requires a complete shift of consciousness and entails the suspension of industrialized society's golden rule: "Time is money." Middle Easterns, for example, resist fixed schedules, viewing them as rude and insulting. Americans, Japanese, and Europeans, on the other hand, are very tied to clock time in their daily life.[26]

Grateful Dead

What kind of marketing program could you design to attract the subculture of Grateful Dead followers? Visit the GD On-line Store to see how marketers are currently doing this. What other elements of the site could help you design a successful program?

http://www.dead.net

on line

differences may result in considerable variation within a culture in what, how, when, and where people buy goods and services.

In the United States alone, countless subcultures can be identified. Many are concentrated geographically. People belonging to the Mormon religion, for example, are clustered mainly in Utah; Cajuns are located in the bayou regions of southern Louisiana. Hispanics are more predominant in those states that border Mexico; whereas the majority of Chinese, Japanese, and Koreans are found in the Pacific region of the United States.

Other subcultures are geographically dispersed. For example, a recent study has identified Harley-Davidson bikers as a distinct subculture.[27] In addition, computer hackers, military families, and university professors may be found throughout the country. Yet they have identifiable attitudes and values that distinguish them from the larger culture.

If marketers can identify subcultures, they can then design special marketing programs to serve their needs. According to the U.S. Census Bureau, the Hispanic population is the largest and fastest-growing subculture, increasing at a rate of seven times that of the general population. To tap into this large and growing segment, Time Inc. recently launched *People en Espanol*, a Spanish-language version of its popular *People* magazine, to reach U.S. Hispanic readers and Anheuser-Busch created a Spanish-language television campaign that builds on core Latino values, like family and friendship.[28] Similarly, Bank of America recently attempted to raise its profile in California's large Asian-American community with new television ads that air in Cantonese, Mandarin, Korean and Vietnamese on several Asian-language stations throughout the state. The ads tout different products and services Bank of America offers Asian-Americans, such as small-business accounts and an Asian-language customer phone service.[29]

Identifying subcultures can be a difficult task for a marketing manager. If they can be identified, marketers can design products and services to meet the needs and wants of these specific market segments. The Spanish-language version of *People* magazine is an example of such a product.
PEOPLE en Espanol is a registered trademark of Time Inc., used with permission.

Social Class

The United States, like other societies, does have a social class system. A **social class** is a group of people who are considered nearly equal in status or community esteem, who regularly socialize among themselves both formally and informally, and who share behavioral norms.

social class
Group of people in a society who are considered nearly equal in status or community esteem, who regularly socialize among themselves both formally and informally, and who share behavioral norms.

A number of techniques have been used to measure social class, and a number of criteria have been used to define it. One view of contemporary U.S. status structure is shown in Exhibit 4.6.

As you can see from Exhibit 4.6, the upper and upper middle classes comprise the small segment of affluent and wealthy Americans. The upper social classes are more likely than other classes to contribute something to society—for example, by volunteer work or active participation in civic affairs. In terms of consumer buying patterns, the affluent are more likely to own their own home and purchase new cars and trucks and are less likely to smoke. The very rich flex their financial muscles by spending more on owned vacation homes, vacations and cruises, and housekeeping and gardening services. The most affluent consumers are more likely to attend art auctions and galleries, dance performances, operas, the theater, museums, concerts, and sporting events.[30]

The majority of Americans today define themselves as middle class, regardless of their actual income or educational attainment. This phenomenon is most likely due to the fact that working-class Americans tend to aspire to the middle-class lifestyle while some of those who do achieve affluence may downwardly aspire to

exhibit 4.6

U.S. Social Class

Upper Classes		
Capitalist Class	1%	People whose investment decisions shape the national economy; income mostly from assets, earned or inherited; university connections
Upper Middle Class	14%	Upper-level managers, professionals, owners of medium-sized businesses; college-educated; family income nearly twice national average
Middle Classes		
Middle Class	33%	Middle-level white-collar, top-level blue-collar; education past high school typical; income somewhat above national average
Working Class	32%	Middle-level blue-collar, lower-level white-collar; income slightly below national average
Lower Classes		
Working Poor	11–12%	Low-paid service workers and operatives; some high school education; below mainstream in living standard but above poverty line
Underclass	8–9%	People who are not regularly employed and who depend primarily on the welfare system for sustenance; little schooling; living standard below poverty line

SOURCE: Adapted from Richard P. Coleman, "The Continuing Significance of Social Class to Marketing," *Journal of Consumer Research*, December 1983, p. 267; Dennis Gilbert and Joseph A. Kahl, *The American Class Structure: A Synthesis* (Homewood, IL: Dorsey Press, 1982), ch. 11.

respectable middle-class status as a matter of principle.[31] Attaining goals and achieving status and prestige are important to middle-class consumers. People falling into the middle class live in the gap between the haves and the have-nots. They aspire to the lifestyle of the more affluent but are constrained by the economic realities and cautious attitudes they share with the working class.

The working class is a distinct subset of the middle class. Interest in organized labor is one of the attributes most common among the working class. This group is more likely to rate job security as the most important reason for taking a job.[32] The working-class person depends heavily on relatives and the community for economic and emotional support. The emphasis on family ties is one sign of the group's intensely local view of the world. They like the local news far more than do middle-class audiences who favor national and world coverage. They are also more likely to vacation closer to home.

Lifestyle distinctions between the social classes are greater than the distinctions within a given class. The most significant separation between the classes is the one between the middle and lower classes. It is here that the major shift in lifestyles appears. Members of the lower class typically fall at or below the poverty level in terms of income. This social class has the highest unemployment rate, and many individuals or families are subsidized through the welfare system. Many are illiterate, with little formal education. Compared to more affluent consumers, lower-class consumers have poorer diets and typically purchase much different types of foods when they shop.

Social class is typically measured as a combination of occupation, income, education, wealth, and other variables. For instance, affluent upper-class consumers are more likely to be executives or self-employed professionals with incomes over $70,000 and at least an undergraduate degree.[33] Working-class and middle-class consumers,

exhibit 4.7

Social Class and Education

Percentage of adults in self-identified social classes who have a bachelor's degree or higher, 1994

	Percent
Lower	8
Working	12
Middle	34
Upper	61

SOURCES: General Social Survey, National Opinion Research Center, Chicago, Illinois; Rebecca Piirto Heath, and "The New Working Class," *American Demographics*, January 1998, pp. 51–55.

on the other hand, are more likely to be service or blue-collar workers, have incomes below $70,000, and have attained only a high school education. Educational attainment, however, seems to be the most reliable indicator of a person's social and economic status (see Exhibit 4.7). Those with college degrees or graduate degrees are more likely to fall into the upper classes, while those people with some college experience but no degree fall closest to traditional concepts of the middle class.

Marketers are interested in social class for two main reasons. First, social class often indicates which medium to use for advertising. Suppose an insurance company seeks to sell its policies to middle-class families. It might advertise during the local evening news because middle-class families tend to watch more television than other classes do. If the company wants to sell more policies to upscale individuals, it might place a print ad in a business publication like the *Wall Street Journal*, which is read by more educated and affluent people.

Second, knowing what products appeal to which social classes can help marketers determine where to best distribute their products. For example, a recent survey of consumer spending in the Washington, D.C., area reveals a stark contrast between Brie-eaters and Velveeta-eaters. The buyers of Brie, the soft and savory French cheese, are concentrated in the upscale neighborhoods of Northwest D.C. and the western suburbs of Montgomery County, Maryland, and Fairfax County, Virginia, where most residents are executives, white-collar professionals or politicians. Brie fans tend to be college-educated professionals with six-figure incomes and an activist spirit. In contrast, aficionados of Velveeta, processed cheese marketed by Kraft, are concentrated in the middle-class, family-filled suburbs of Prince George's County and the predominantly black D.C. neighborhoods. Velveeta buyers tend to be married with children, high school educated, and employed at modestly paying service and blue-collar jobs.[34]

Social Influences on Consumer Buying Decisions

6
Identify and understand the social factors that affect consumer buying decisions

Most consumers are likely to seek out others' opinions to reduce their search and evaluation effort or uncertainty, especially as the perceived risk of the decision increases. Consumers may also seek out others' opinions for guidance on new products or services, products with image-related attributes, or because attribute information is lacking or uninformative.[35] Specifically, consumers interact socially with reference groups, opinion leaders, and family members to obtain product information and decision approval.

Reference Groups

All the formal and informal groups that influence the buying behavior of an individual are that person's **reference groups**. Consumers may use products or brands to identify with or become a member of a group. They learn from observing how members of their reference groups consume, and they use the same criteria to make their own consumer decisions.

reference group
Group in society that influences an individual's purchasing behavior.

Reference groups can be categorized very broadly as either direct or indirect (see Exhibit 4.8). Direct reference groups are face-to-face membership groups that touch people's lives directly. They can be either primary or secondary. **Primary membership groups** include all groups with which people interact regularly in an informal, face-to-face manner, such as family, friends, and coworkers. In contrast, people associate with **secondary membership groups** less consistently and more formally. These groups might include clubs, professional groups, and religious groups.

primary membership group
Reference group with which people interact regularly in an informal, face-to-face manner, such as family, friends, or fellow employees.

secondary membership group
Reference group with which people associate less consistently and more formally than a primary membership group, such as a club, professional group, or religious group.

Consumers also are influenced by many indirect, nonmembership reference groups that they do not belong to. **Aspirational reference groups** are those that a person would like to join. To join an aspirational group, a person must at least conform to the norms of that group. (**Norms** are the values and attitudes deemed acceptable by the group.) Thus a person who wants to be elected to public office may begin to dress more conservatively, as other politicians do. He or she may go to many of the restaurants and social engagements that city and business leaders attend and try to play a role that is acceptable to voters and other influential people. Similarly, a teenager may dye his hair, experiment with body piercing and tattoos, and listen to alternative music to fit in with the "in" group.

aspirational reference group
Group that someone would like to join.

norm
Value or attitude deemed acceptable by a group.

Nonaspirational reference groups, or dissociative groups, influence our behavior when we try to maintain distance from them. A consumer may avoid buying some types of clothing or car, going to certain restaurants or stores, or even buying a home in a certain neighborhood in order to avoid being associated with a particular group.

nonaspirational reference group
Group with which an individual does not want to associate.

The activities, values, and goals of reference groups directly influence consumer behavior. For marketers, reference groups have three important implications: They serve as information sources and influence perceptions; they affect an individual's aspiration levels; and their norms either constrain or stimulate consumer behavior.

exhibit 4.8

Types of Reference Groups

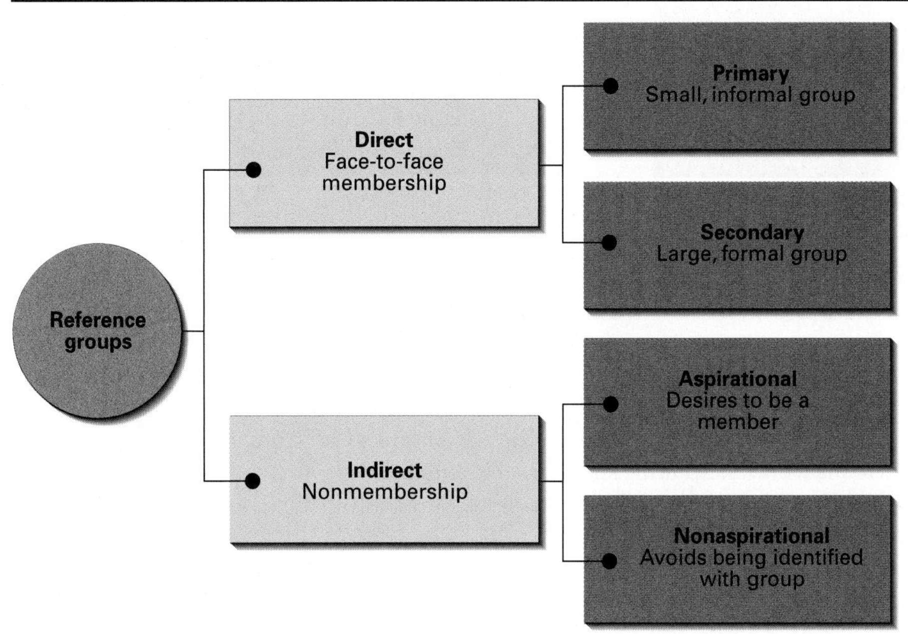

For example, over 40 percent of Americans seek the advice of family and friends when shopping for doctors, lawyers, or auto mechanics. Individuals also are likely to seek others' advice in selecting a restaurant for a special occasion or deciding which movie to see.[36]

GLOBAL In Japan, companies have long relied on the nation's high school girls to give them advice during product testing. Fads that catch on among teenage girls often become big trends throughout the country and among Japanese consumers in general. Food manufacturers frequently recruit Tokyo schoolgirls to sample potato chip recipes or chocolate bars. Television networks survey high school girls to fine-tune story lines for higher ratings on prime-time shows. Other companies pay girls to keep diaries of what they buy. Warner-Lambert hired high school girls in 1995 to help choose a new gum flavor. After extensive chewing and comparing, the girls settled on a flavor that became Trickle, now Japan's best-selling bubble gum.[37]

Opinion Leaders

opinion leader
Individual who influences the opinions of others.

Reference groups frequently include individuals known as group leaders, or **opinion leaders**—those who influence others. Obviously, it is important for marketing managers to persuade such people to purchase their goods or services. Many products and services that are integral parts of Americans' lives today got their initial boost from these influential opinion leaders. For example, VCRs and sport utility vehicles were embraced by opinion leaders well ahead of the general public.

The makers of JNCO jeans give free clothing to people who they believe will be opinion leaders: DJs, band members from new, hip rock groups, and so on. Can you identify the opinion leaders in your social group? Name some products or services that they seem to promote.
JNCO is a registered trademark of Revatex, Inc. All images are © Revatex and provided courtesy of Revatex.

Opinion leaders are often the first to try new products and services out of pure curiosity. They are typically activists in their communities, on the job, and in the marketplace. Opinion leaders tend to be self-indulgent, making them more likely to explore unproven but intriguing products and services. This combination of curiosity, activism, and self-indulgence makes opinion leaders trendsetters in the consumer marketplace.[38] Exhibit 4.9 lists some products and services for which individuals often seek the advice of an opinion leader before purchasing.

Opinion leadership is a casual, face-to-face phenomenon and usually inconspicuous, so locating opinion leaders can be a challenge. Thus marketers often try to create opinion leaders. They may use high school cheerleaders to model new fall fashions or civic leaders to promote insurance, new cars, and other merchandise. Revatex, the makers of JNCO wide-leg jeans, gives free clothes to trendsetters among teens in the hopes that they will influence the purchase of their brand. Big-name DJs in the rave scene are outfitted by JNCO, as are members of hip, alternative bands favored by the teen crowd. Revatex also sponsors extreme-sports athletes who appeal to the teen market.[39] Eastman Kodak relies on the country's one hundred thousand or so professional photographers to influence the millions of Americans who take pictures as a hobby. Amateur photographers tend to rely on film recommendations from retailers, who often follow recommendations from professional photographers.[40]

On a national level, companies sometimes use movie stars, sports figures, and other celebrities to promote products, hoping they are appropriate opinion leaders. American Express, for example, recently signed golf superstar Tiger Woods as a spokesperson for its financial products. The company is hoping that consumers

exhibit 4.9

Words of Wisdom: Opinion Leaders' Consumer Clout Extends Far Beyond Their Own Purchases

Average number of people to whom opinion leaders recommended products* in the past year, and millions of recommendations made, 1995

	Average Number of Recommendations	Millions of Recommendations Made
Restaurant	5.0	70
Vacation destination	5.1	44
TV Show	4.9	45
Car	4.1	29
Retail store	4.7	29
Clothing	4.5	24
Consumer electronics	4.5	16
Office equipment	5.8	12
Stock, mutual fund, CD, etc.	3.4	12

*Among those who recommended the product at all

SOURCE: Roper Starch Worldwide, Inc., New York, NY. Adapted from "Maximizing the Market with Influentials," *American Demographics*, July 1995, p. 42.

will see an affinity between the values that Woods represents and the values that American Express represents—earned success, discipline, hard work, achievement, and integrity.[41]

The effectiveness of celebrity endorsements depends largely on how credible and attractive the spokesperson is and how familiar people are with him or her. Endorsements are most likely to succeed if an association between the spokesperson and the product can be reasonably established. For example, comedian Bill Cosby failed as an endorser for financial products but succeeded with such products as Kodak cameras and Jell-O gelatin. Consumers could not mentally link Bill Cosby with serious investment decisions but could associate him with leisure activities and everyday consumption. Additionally, in the selection of a celebrity endorser, marketers must consider the broader meanings associated with the endorser. Although the endorser may have certain attributes that are desirable for endorsing the product, he or she may also have other attributes that are inappropriate.

A marketing manager can also try to use opinion leaders through group sanctioning or referrals. For example, some companies sell products endorsed by the American Heart Association or the American Cancer Society. McNeil Consumer Products joined forces with the Arthritis Foundation to launch the Arthritis Foundation line of pain relievers that quickly jumped to the number one selling position in the over-the-counter arthritis segment. McNeil and the Arthritis

Foundation both saw a unique opportunity to reach the millions of Americans living with the disease.[42] Marketers also seek endorsements from schools, churches, cities, the military, and fraternal organizations as a form of group opinion leadership. Salespeople often ask to use opinion leaders' names as a means of achieving greater personal influence in a sales presentation.

Family

The family is the most important social institution for many consumers, strongly influencing values, attitudes, self-concept—and buying behavior. For example, a family that strongly values good health will have a grocery list distinctly different from that of a family that views every dinner as a gourmet event. Moreover, the family is responsible for the **socialization process**, the passing down of cultural values and norms to children. Children learn by observing their parents' consumption patterns, and so they will tend to shop in a similar pattern.

socialization process
How cultural values and norms are passed down to children.

Decision-making roles among family members tend to vary significantly, depending on the type of item purchased. Family members assume a variety of roles in the purchase process. *Initiators* are the ones who suggest, initiate, or plant the seed for the purchase process. The initiator can be any member of the family. For example, Sister might initiate the product search by asking for a new bicycle as a birthday present. *Influencers* are those members of the family whose opinions are valued. In our example, Mom might function as a price-range watchdog, an influencer whose main role is to veto or approve price ranges. Brother may give his opinion on certain makes of bicycles. The *decision maker* is the member of the family who actually makes the decision to buy or not to buy. For example, Dad or Mom is likely to choose the final brand and model of bicycle to buy after seeking further information from Sister about cosmetic features such as color and imposing additional criteria of his or her own, such as durability and safety. The *purchaser* (probably Dad or Mom) is the one who actually exchanges money for the product. Finally, the *consumer* is the actual user—Sister, in the case of the bicycle.

Marketers should consider family purchase situations along with the distribution of consumer and decision-maker roles among family members. Ordinary marketing views the individual as both decision maker and consumer. Family marketing adds several other possibilities: Sometimes more than one family member or all family members are involved in the decision; sometimes only

exhibit 4.10

Relationships Among Purchasers and Consumers in the Family

		Purchase Decision Maker		
		Parent(s) Only	Child/Children Only	Some or All Family Members
Consumer	Parent(s)	golf clubs cosmetics wine	Mother's Day card	Christmas gifts minivan
	Child/ Children	diapers breakfast cereal	candy small toys	bicycle
	Some Family Members	videos long-distance phone service	children's movies	computers sports events
	All Family Members	clothing life insurance	fast-food restaurant	swim club membership vacations

SOURCE: From "Pulling The Family's Strings" by Robert Boutillier, *American Demographics*, August 1993. ©1993 PRIMEDIA Intertec, Stamford, CT. Reprinted with permission.

exhibit 4.11

Children's Influence on Household Purchases

Aggregate spending in millions of dollars influenced by children aged 4 to 12 on selected items, and per-child spending, 1997

	Aggregate Spending	Per-Child Spending
Food and beverages	$110,320	$3,131
Entertainment	$25,620	$727
Apparel	$17,540	$498
Automobiles	$17,740	$503
Electronics	$6,400	$182
Health and beauty	$3,550	$101

SOURCE: From "Tapping the Three Kids' Markets" by James U. McNeal, *American Demographics*, April 1998.

children are involved in the decision; sometimes more than one consumer is involved; and sometimes the decision maker and the consumer are different people. Exhibit 4.10 represents the patterns of family purchasing relationships that are possible.

Children today can have great influence over the purchase decisions of their parents. In many families, with both parents working and short on time, children may be encouraged to participate. In addition, children in single-parent households become more involved in family decision making at an earlier age than children in two-parent households. Children are especially influential in decisions about food, as shown in Exhibit 4.11. Children often help decide where the family goes for fast food and many influence the choice of a full-service restaurant. Kids have input into the kinds of food the family eats at home as well and often influence even the specific brands their parents buy. Finally, children influence purchase decisions for toys, clothes, vacations, recreation, and automobiles, even though they are usually not the actual purchasers of such items. Marketers are aware of the consumer power of children: It is estimated that children twelve and under directly spend $24 billion a year and influence another $300 billion in household spending.[43]

Individual Influences on Consumer Buying Decisions

7

Identify and understand the individual factors that affect consumer buying decisions

A person's buying decisions are also influenced by personal characteristics that are unique to each individual, such as gender; age and life cycle stage; and personality, self-concept, and lifestyle. Individual characteristics are generally stable over the course of one's life. For instance, most people do not change their gender, and the act of changing personality or lifestyle requires a complete reorientation of one's life. In the case of age and life cycle stage, these changes occur gradually over time.

Gender

Physiological differences between men and women result in different needs, such as health and beauty products. Just as important are the distinct cultural, social, and economic roles played by men and women and the effects that these have on their decision-making processes. Women, for example, look for different features when purchasing a car than do men. Since women in America assume the majority of child-rearing activities—shuttling the children to and from school, playdates, and sports, for instance—they often look for vehicles that are large enough and versatile enough for their daily activities. Minivan manufacturers, as a result, have implemented strategies to accommodate female drivers, such as resizing door handles and controls for women's smaller hands and repositioning seats and pedals.

Men and women also shop differently. Studies show that men and women share similar motivations in terms of where to shop—that is, seeking reasonable prices, merchandise quality, and a friendly, low-pressure environment—but they don't necessarily feel the same about shopping in general. Most women enjoy shopping; their male counterparts claim to dislike the experience and shop only out of necessity. Further, men desire simple shopping experiences, stores with less variety, and convenience. Stores that are easy to shop in, that are near home or office, or that have knowledgeable personnel appeal more to men than to women.[44]

Age and Family Life Cycle Stage

The age and family life cycle stage of a consumer can have a significant impact on consumer behavior. How old a consumer is generally indicates what products he or she may be interested in purchasing. Consumer tastes in food, clothing, cars, furniture, and recreation are often age related; for example, the favorite magazines for preteens aged eight to twelve include *Sports Illustrated for Kids*, *Nickelodeon*, and *Ranger Rick*. But as these consumers become teenagers their tastes in magazines diverge in favor of sports titles for boys and fashion/lifestyle titles for girls.[45]

Related to a person's age is his or her place in the family life cycle. As Chapter 6 explains in more detail, the *family life cycle* is an orderly series of stages through which consumers' attitudes and behavioral tendencies evolve through maturity, experience, and changing income and status. Marketers often define their target markets in terms of family life cycle, such as "young singles," "young married with children," and "middle-aged married without children." For instance, young singles spend more than average on alcoholic beverages, education, and entertainment. New parents typically increase their spending on health care, clothing, housing, and food and decrease their spending on alcohol, education, and transportation. Households with older children spend more on food, entertainment, personal care products, and education, as well as cars and gasoline. After their children leave home, spending by older couples on vehicles, women's clothing, health care, and long-distance calls typically increases. For instance, families with children aged six to seventeen years are the biggest ready-to-eat cereal consumers, spending 75 percent more than the average family. In contrast, young singles under age thirty-five spend 54 percent less than expected on ready-to-eat cereals.[46]

Marketers should also be aware of the many nontraditional life cycle paths that are common today that provide insights into the needs and wants of such consumers as divorced parents, lifelong singles, and childless couples. Since the 1950s, the influx of women into the labor force has transformed family structure so much that in 1997, only 17 percent of households conformed to the traditional model of a wage-earning dad, a stay-at-home mom, and one or more children.[47] Further, according to the U.S. Census Bureau, single-father families in which a single father has custody of his children are growing at an annual rate of 10 percent. The shift toward custodial fathers is part of a broader societal change that has put more women on the career track and given men more options at home.[48]

Personality, Self-Concept, and Lifestyle

Each consumer has a unique personality. **Personality** is a broad concept that can be thought of as a way of organizing and grouping how an individual typically reacts to situations. Thus personality combines psychological makeup and environmental forces. It includes people's underlying dispositions, especially their most dominant characteristics. Although personality is one of the least useful concepts in the study of consumer behavior, some marketers believe that personality influences the types and brands of products purchased. For instance, the type of car, clothes, or jewelry a consumer buys may reflect one or more personality traits. Personality traits like those listed in Exhibit 4.12 may be used to describe a consumer's personality.

personality
Way of organizing and grouping the consistencies of an individual's reactions to situations.

Self-concept, or self-perception, is how consumers perceive themselves. Self-concept includes attitudes, perceptions, beliefs, and self-evaluations. Although self-concept may change, the change is often gradual. Through self-concept, people define their identity, which in turn provides for consistent and coherent behavior.

self-concept
How a consumer perceives himself or herself in terms of attitudes, perceptions, beliefs, and self-evaluations.

Self-concept combines the **ideal self-image** (the way an individual would like to be) and the **real self-image** (how an individual actually perceives himself or herself). Generally, we try to raise our real self-image toward our ideal (or at least narrow the gap). Consumers seldom buy products that jeopardize their self-image. For example, someone who sees herself as a trend-setter wouldn't buy clothing that doesn't project a contemporary image.

ideal self-image
The way an individual would like to be.

real self-image
The way an individual actually perceives himself or herself.

Human behavior depends largely on self-concept. Because consumers want to protect their identity as individuals, the products they buy, the stores they patronize, and the credit cards they carry support their self-image. Men's and women's fragrances, for example, tend to reflect the self-images of their wearers. Chanel's Egoïste is for the man who has everything, and knows it; likewise, Elizabeth Taylor's White Diamonds perfume is "the fragrance dreams are made of," for all those women who strive for legendary beauty.[49] Lingerie retailer Victoria's Secret recently launched a line of cosmetics for women who want to show and enjoy their sexuality and sensuality.[50]

By influencing the degree to which consumers perceive a good or service to be self-relevant, marketers can affect consumers' motivation to learn about, shop for, and buy a certain brand. Marketers also consider self-concept important because it helps explain the relationship between individuals' perceptions of themselves and their consumer behavior.

An important component of self-concept is *body image*, the perception of the attractiveness of one's own physical features. For example, individuals who have cosmetic

exhibit 4.12
Some Common Personality Traits

- Adaptability
- Need for affiliation
- Aggressiveness
- Need for achievement
- Ascendancy
- Autonomy
- Dominance
- Deference
- Defensiveness
- Emotionalism
- Orderliness
- Sociability
- Stability
- Self-confidence

on line

Bally Total Fitness

Does Bally Total Fitness use its Web site as a means to connect with consumers via their body image? Does the content and design of the site surprise you? Why or why not?
http://www.ballyfitness.com/

surgery often experience significant improvement in their overall body image and self-concept. Moreover, a person's perception of body image can be a stronger reason for weight loss than either good health or other social factors.[51] With the median age of Americans rising, many companies are introducing products aimed at this group of aging baby boomers who are concerned about their physical appearance. Procter & Gamble recently extended its Oil of Olay line with a new ProVital sub-brand aimed at women over fifty. P&G's research showed that many women fifty and older feel more confident, wiser, and freer than ever before. Their primary spokesmodels for the ProVital line are older women who have been successful and visible in their professional careers. Similarly, oral-care marketer Den-Mat Corporation has introduced Rembrandt Age Defying, the first age-defined mouthwash and toothpaste. Advertising for the Rembrandt products claims to "help restore teeth and gums to a healthier, whiter and younger look."[52]

Body image is an important element in understanding consumer behavior. With the median age of Americans on the rise, products that promote youthfulness, such as Rembrandt's Age Defying dental products, may be more successful in influencing purchasing decisions in the supermarket.
Courtesy Den-Mat Corporation

lifestyle
Mode of living as identified by a person's activities, interests, and opinions.

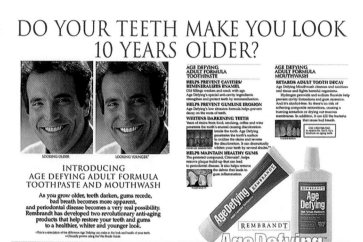

Personality and self-concept are reflected in lifestyle. A **lifestyle** is a mode of living, as identified by a person's activities, interests, and opinions. *Psychographics* is the analytical technique used to examine consumer lifestyles and to categorize consumers. Unlike personality characteristics, which are hard to describe and measure, lifestyle characteristics are useful in segmenting and targeting consumers. Lifestyle and psychographic analysis explicitly addresses the way consumers outwardly express their inner selves in their social and cultural environment.

Many industries now use psychographics to better understand their market segments. For example, the auto industry has a psychographic segmentation scheme for classifying car buyers into one of six groups according to their attitudes toward cars and the driving experience. At the two extremes are "gearheads," true car enthusiasts who enjoy driving and working on their cars themselves, and "negatives," who view cars as a necessary evil that they would just as soon do without. One interior/exterior design company uses lifestyle analysis to find colors that appeal to different lifestyle segments. When remodeling two bowling alleys in a Kansas City, Kansas, suburb, the company found that the clientele for the two facilities was different. The customers of one alley were primarily working-class people who were serious league bowlers. Customers at the other facility were more upscale and bowled primarily for relaxation and exercise. The first alley was decorated with energetic triangles and a folksy outdoors southwestern theme, featuring peach and green. The other was remodeled in soothing Art Deco curves, using a more complex color scheme favored by upper socioeconomic groups.[53] Psychographics and lifestyle segmentation schemes are discussed in more detail in Chapter 6.

Psychological Influences on Consumer Buying Decisions

8
Identify and understand the psychological factors that affect consumer buying decisions

An individual's buying decisions are further influenced by psychological factors: perception, motivation, learning, and beliefs and attitudes. These factors are what consumers use to interact with their world. They are the tools consumers use to recognize their feelings, gather and analyze information, formulate thoughts and opinions, and take action. Unlike the other three influences on consumer behavior, psychological influences can be affected by a person's environment because they are applied on specific occasions.[54] For example, you will perceive different stimuli and process these stimuli in different ways depending on whether you are sitting in class concentrating on the instructor, sitting outside of class talking to friends, or sitting in your dorm room watching television.

Perception

The world is full of stimuli. A stimulus is any unit of input affecting one or more of the five senses: sight, smell, taste, touch, hearing. The process by which we select, organize, and interpret these stimuli into a meaningful and coherent picture is called **perception**. In essence, perception is how we see the world around us and how we recognize that we need some help in making a purchasing decision.

perception
Process by which people select, organize, and interpret stimuli into a meaningful and coherent picture.

People cannot perceive every stimulus in their environment. Therefore, they use **selective exposure** to decide which stimuli to notice and which to ignore. A typical consumer is exposed to more than 250 advertising messages a day but notices only between 11 and 20.

selective exposure
Process whereby a consumer notices certain stimuli and ignores other stimuli.

The familiarity of an object, contrast, movement, intensity (such as increased volume), and smell are cues that influence perception. Consumers use these cues to identify and define products and brands. The shape of a product's packaging, such as Coca-Cola's signature contour bottle, for instance, can influence perception. Color is another cue, and it plays a key role in consumers' perceptions. Several years ago, Procter & Gamble added bleach to its laundry detergent Oxydol. But people didn't believe it was different because it looked the same. So P&G added blue beads to the normally white detergent. Although the blue beads had nothing to do with the bleaching action, consumers could "see" the difference. Oxydol with Bleach became a successful product because consumers perceived a difference from other detergents.[55]

What is perceived by consumers may also depend on the stimuli's vividness or shock value. Graphic warnings of the hazards associated with a product's use are perceived more readily and remembered more accurately than less vivid warnings or warnings that are written in text. "Sexier" ads excel at attracting the attention of younger consumers. Companies like Calvin Klein and Guess use sensuous ads to "cut through the clutter" of competing ads and other stimuli to capture the attention of the target audience. Similarly, Benetton ads use shock value by portraying taboo social issues, from racism to homosexuality.

Two other concepts closely related to selective exposure are selective distortion and selective retention. **Selective distortion** occurs when consumers change or distort information that conflicts with their feelings or beliefs. For example, suppose a consumer buys a Chrysler. After the purchase, if the consumer receives new information about a close alternative brand, such as a Ford, he or she may distort the information to make it more consistent with the prior view that the Chrysler is better than the Ford. Business travelers who fly often may distort or discount information about airline crashes because they must use air travel constantly in their jobs. People who smoke and have no plans to quit may distort information from medical reports and the Surgeon General about the link between cigarettes and lung cancer.

selective distortion
Process whereby a consumer changes or distorts information that conflicts with his or her feelings or beliefs.

Selective retention is remembering only information that supports personal feelings or beliefs. The consumer forgets all information that may be inconsistent. After reading a pamphlet that contradicts one's political beliefs, for instance, a person may forget many of the points outlined in it.

selective retention
Process whereby a consumer remembers only that information that supports his or her personal beliefs.

Which stimuli will be perceived often depends on the individual. People can be exposed to the same stimuli under identical conditions but perceive them very differently. For example, two people viewing a TV commercial may have different interpretations of the advertising message. One person may be thoroughly engrossed by the message and become highly motivated to buy the product. Thirty seconds after the ad ends, the second person may not be able to recall the content of the message or even the product advertised.

Marketing Implications of Perception Marketers must recognize the importance of cues, or signals, in consumers' perception of products. Marketing managers first identify the important attributes, such as price or quality, that the targeted consumers want in a product and then design signals to communicate these attributes. For example, consumers will pay more for candy wrapped in expensive-looking foil packages. But shiny labels on wine bottles signify less expensive wines; dull labels indicate more expensive wines. Marketers also often use price as a signal to consumers that the product is of higher quality than competing products. Gibson Guitar Corporation briefly cut prices on many of its guitars to compete with Japanese rivals Yamaha and Ibanez but found instead that it sold more guitars when it charged more for them. Consumers perceived the higher price indicated a better quality instrument.[56]

Of course, brand names send signals to consumers. The brand names of Close-Up toothpaste, DieHard batteries, and Caress moisturizing soap, for example, identify important product qualities. Names chosen for search engines and sites on the Internet, such as Yahoo!, Excite, and Jumbo!, are intended to convey excitement and intensity.[57] Companies might even change their names to send a message to consumers. Today's electric utility companies, faced with the looming prospect of fierce competition in the wake of deregulation, are increasingly changing their names to project a bright new image to customers. The traditional, stodgy "Power & Light & Electric" variety of electric utility names that consumers have often learned to dislike has given way to names such as Entergy, UtiliCorp, and Cinergy.[58]

VALUE

Consumers also perceive quality and reliability with certain brand names. Companies watch their brand identity closely, in large part because a strong link has been established between perceived brand value and customer loyalty. Brand names that consistently enjoy high perceived value from consumers include Kodak, Disney, National Geographic, Mercedes-Benz, and Fisher-Price. Naming a product after a place can also add perceived value by association. Brand names using the words Santa Fe, Dakota, or Texas convey a sense of openness, freedom, and youth, but products named after other locations might conjure up images of pollution and crime.

Marketing managers are also interested in the threshold level of perception: the minimum difference in a stimulus that the consumer will notice. This concept is sometimes referred to as the "just-noticeable difference." For example, how much would Sony have to drop the price of a VCR before consumers recognized it as a bargain—$25? $50? or more? One study found that the just-noticeable difference in a stimulus is about a 20 percent change. For example, consumers will likely notice a 20 percent price decrease more quickly than a 15 percent decrease. This marketing principle can be applied to other marketing variables as well, such as package size or loudness of a broadcast advertisement.[59]

Another study showed that the bargain-price threshold for a name brand is lower than that for a store brand. In other words, consumers perceive a bargain more readily when stores offer a small discount on a name-brand item than when they offer the same discount on a store brand; a larger discount is needed to achieve a similar effect for a store brand.[60] Researchers also found that for low-cost grocery items, consumers typically do not see past the second digit in the price. For instance, consumers do not perceive any real difference between two comparable cans of tuna, one priced at $1.52 and the other at $1.59 because they ignore the last digit.[61]

Besides changing such stimuli as price, package size, and volume, marketers can change the product. How many sporty features will General Motors have to add to a basic two-door sedan before consumers begin to perceive the model as a sports car? How many new services will a discount store like Kmart need to add before consumers perceive it as a full-service department store?

Marketing managers who intend to do business in global markets should be aware of how foreign consumers perceive their products. For instance, in Japan, product labels are often written in English or French, even though they may not translate into anything meaningful. But many Japanese associate foreign words on product labels with the exotic, the expensive, and high quality.

Marketers have often been suspected of sending advertising messages subconsciously to consumers in what is known as subliminal perception. The controversy began in 1957 when a researcher claimed to have increased popcorn and Coca-Cola sales at a movie theater after flashing "Eat popcorn" and "Drink Coca-Cola" on the screen every five seconds for 1/300th of a second, although the audience did not consciously recognize the messages. Almost immediately consumer protection groups became concerned that advertisers were brainwashing consumers and this practice was pronounced illegal in California and Canada. Although the researcher later admitted to making up the data and scientists have been unable to replicate the study since, consumers are still wary of hidden messages that advertisers may be sending.

Motivation

By studying motivation, marketers can analyze the major forces influencing consumers to buy or not buy products. When you buy a product, you usually do so to fulfill some kind of need. These needs become motives when aroused sufficiently. For instance, suppose this morning you were so hungry before class that you needed to eat something. In response to that need, you stopped at McDonald's for an Egg McMuffin. In other words, you were motivated by hunger to stop at McDonald's. **Motives** are the driving forces that cause a person to take action to satisfy specific needs.

motive
Driving force that causes a person to take action to satisfy specific needs.

Why are people driven by particular needs at particular times? One popular theory is **Maslow's hierarchy of needs**, shown in Exhibit 4.13, which arranges needs in ascending order of importance: physiological, safety, social, esteem, and self-actualization. As a person fulfills one need, a higher-level need becomes more important.

Maslow's hierarchy of needs
Method of classifying human needs and motivations into five categories in ascending order of importance: physiological, safety, social, esteem, and self-actualization.

The most basic human needs are *physiological*—that is, needs for food, water, and shelter. Because they are essential to survival, these needs must be satisfied first. Ads showing a juicy hamburger or a runner gulping down Gatorade after a marathon are examples of appeals to satisfy the physiological needs of hunger and thirst.

exhibit 4.13
Maslow's Hierarchy of Needs

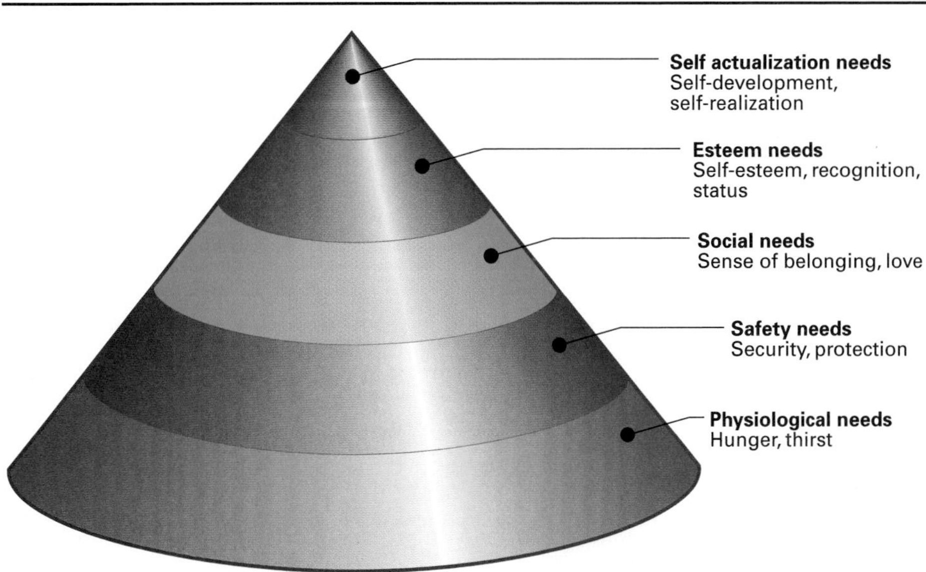

on line

Center for Science in the Public Interest

Does the Center for Science in the Public Interest use fear to influence public opinion? Read some of their on-line reports and make a decision.
http://www.cspinet.org/

Safety needs include security and freedom from pain and discomfort. Marketers often exploit consumers' fears and anxieties about safety to sell their products. For example, after the Environmental Protection Agency reported that perchloroethylene, a chemical used in dry cleaning, may be a probable human carcinogen, consumers became worried about toxic substances on their dry-cleaned clothes. Dry cleaners using alternative cleaning methods, such as petroleum-based or water-based methods, sprang up to take advantage of these fears, pitching themselves as a safe alternative to traditional dry cleaners using perchloroethylene.[62] The "Ethics in Marketing" box discusses how marketers often play on consumers' fears to sell their products.

After physiological and safety needs have been fulfilled, *social* needs—especially love and a sense of belonging—become the focus. Love includes acceptance by one's peers, as well as sex and romantic love. Marketing managers probably appeal more to this need than to any other. Ads for clothes, cosmetics, and vacation pack-

ethics in marketing

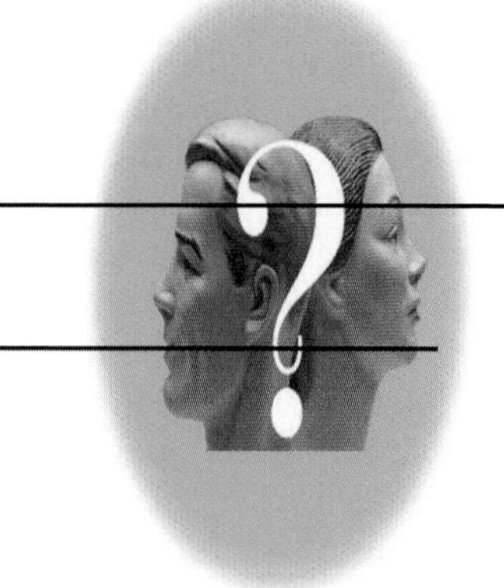

Fear as a Marketing Tool: Does It Sell?

Public-health advocates often use fear in their public service advertising to influence public opinion. For example, a recent magazine ad from the American Cancer Society featured a fancy tortoise-shell cigar cutter resting on green velvet. Nearby, a fat cigar burns in a crystal ashtray. It looks like another glamorous image promoting the cigar industry, except for the pointed tag line: "You can also use it to cut the tumor off your lip." Other related ads from California health authorities depict a woman tossing a cigar on the sidewalk. A man walking his dog uses a pooper scooper to clean it up. The tag line: "Cigars, they look like what they smell like. Don't put them in your mouth."

Like public-health advocate groups, mainstream marketers also use fear to persuade consumers to purchase their products. One popular advertising tactic is to claim that the other guy's products don't work. Recently, a splashy new ad campaign claimed the other guy's product may kill you. "A government panel has determined that some laxatives may cause cancer," blared the full-page ad that ran in forty newspapers, pointing the finger at the popular Ex-Lax brand. Looming behind the ad's headline was a giant American eagle, suggesting an official government pronouncement. The copy gave a toll-free number and raised the possibility of regulatory action that "may even include a recall." The ad was from Schering-Plough, maker of a rival laxative, Correctol, and a prime example of the use of fear to persuade consumers' purchase decisions. Although the Food and Drug Administration had not made a final determination on the safety of phenolphthalein, a key ingredient in Ex-Lax, Schering-Plough used the FDA report to instill fear in consumers using the competitor's brand.

Similarly, the use of alarming disease statistics is common among health-advocacy groups and marketers alike. Projections of the incidence of disease are rampant these days as advertisers compete for people's limited attention and money. For example, "twelve million Americans have asthma," "one in three Americans is obese," and "at least sixty million Americans have high blood pressure" are just a few of the statistics used in advertising today. Since big numbers get more attention than small ones, the estimates are often alarmingly high. Unfortunately, most of the numbers are extrapolations or estimates at best, because the government keeps only a few statistics—on birth, death, cancer, and infectious diseases. Most conditions for which people consult a doctor are not recorded in a national database. Yet the media report the numbers and marketers exploit them as quantifiable fact.[63]

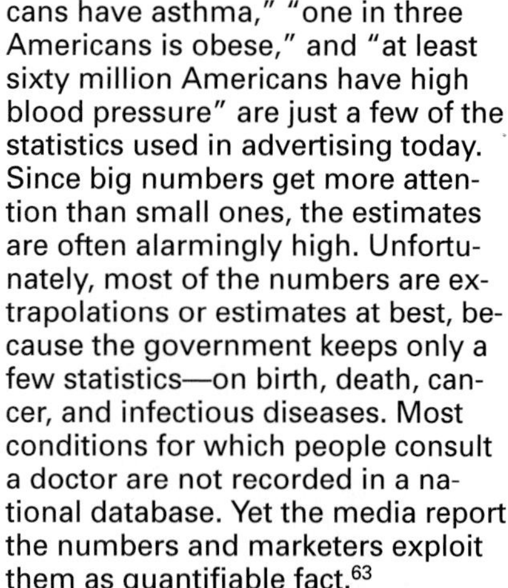

What current marketing or advertising examples can you think of that use fear or alarming statistics to sell their products? Would the use of such fear tactics cause you to distrust a marketer or vice versa? Explain your answer.

ages suggest that buying the product can bring love. The need to belong is also a favorite of marketers. Nike promotes its Air Jordan athletic shoes, for instance, as not just plain, old sneakers; they're part fashion statement, part athletic statement. Lace them up, and the wearer looks cool and plays cool—just like Michael Jordan, the shoe's spokesperson and namesake.[64]

GLOBAL

Love is acceptance without regard to one's contribution. Esteem is acceptance based on one's contribution to the group. *Self-esteem* needs include self-respect and a sense of accomplishment. Esteem needs also include prestige, fame, and recognition of one's accomplishments. Mont Blanc pens, Mercedes-Benz automobiles, and Neiman-Marcus stores all appeal to esteem needs. Asian consumers, in particular, are strongly motivated by status and prestige. Asian individuals are always conscious of their place in a group, institution, or society as a whole. The importance of gaining social recognition turns Asians into probably the most image-conscious consumers in the world. Status-conscious Asians will not hesitate to spend freely on premium brands, such as BMW, Mercedes-Benz, and the best Scotch whiskey and French cognac.[65] This may explain why jewelry sales at Tiffany's in Japan continue to rise even in the face of one of Japan's worst economic recessions.[66]

The highest human need is *self-actualization.* It refers to finding self-fulfillment and self-expression, reaching the point in life at which "people are what they feel they should be." Maslow felt that very few people ever attain this level. Even so, advertisements may focus on this type of need. For example, American Express ads convey the message that acquiring its card is one of the highest attainments in life. The U.S. Armed Forces' slogan urges young people to "Be all that you can be."

Even children must satisfy more than just the basic physiological and safety needs. Mattel's Barbie doll, for instance, fulfills a fundamental need that all girls share by playing out what it might be like in the grown-up world. Through Barbie, girls dream of achievement, glamour, romance, adventure, and nurturing. These dreams touch on many timeless needs, ranging from pride and success to belonging and love. Mattel zeros in on these core needs and addresses them with different Barbie products. Over the years, Barbie has been a teacher, a fashion model, a girlfriend, a dentist, an astronaut, a sister, and a veterinarian, to name a few.[67]

Learning

Almost all consumer behavior results from **learning**, which is the process that creates changes in behavior through experience and practice. It is not possible to observe learning directly, but we can infer when it has occurred by a person's actions. For example, suppose you see an advertisement for a new and improved cold medicine. If you go to the store that day and buy that remedy, we infer that you have learned something about the cold medicine.

learning
Process that creates changes in behavior, immediate or expected, through experience and practice.

There are two types of learning: experiential and conceptual. *Experiential learning* occurs when an experience changes your behavior. For example, if you try the new cold medicine when you get home and it does not relieve your symptoms, you may not buy that brand again. *Conceptual learning*, which is not learned through direct experience, is the second type of learning. Assume, for example, that you are standing at a soft-drink machine and notice a new diet flavor with an artificial sweetener. Because someone has told you that diet beverages leave an aftertaste, you choose a different drink. You have learned that you would not like this new diet drink without ever trying it.

Reinforcement and repetition boost learning. Reinforcement can be positive or negative. If you see a vendor selling frozen yogurt (stimulus), buy it (response), and find the yogurt to be quite refreshing (reward), your behavior has been positively reinforced. On the other hand, if you buy a new flavor of yogurt and it does not taste good (negative reinforcement), you will not buy that flavor of yogurt again (response). Without positive or negative reinforcement, a person will not be motivated to repeat the behavior pattern or to avoid it. Thus if a new brand evokes neutral feelings, some marketing activity, such as a price change or an increase in promotion, may be required to induce further consumption. Learning theory is helpful in reminding marketers that concrete and timely actions are what reinforce desired consumer behavior.

Repetition is a key strategy in promotional campaigns because it can lead to increased learning. Most marketers use repetitious advertising so consumers will learn what their unique advantage is over the competition. Generally, to heighten learning, advertising messages should be spread over time rather than clustered together.

stimulus generalization
Form of learning that occurs when one response is extended to a second stimulus similar to the first.

A related learning concept useful to marketing managers is stimulus generalization. In theory, **stimulus generalization** occurs when one response is extended to a second stimulus similar to the first. Marketers often use a successful, well-known brand name for a family of products because it gives consumers familiarity with and knowledge about each product in the family. Such brand-name families spur the introduction of new products and facilitate the sale of existing items. Jell-O frozen pudding pops rely on the familiarity of Jell-O gelatin; Clorox laundry detergent relies on familiarity with Clorox bleach; and Ivory shampoo relies on familiarity with Ivory soap. Starbucks Coffee Company recently introduced four premium flavors of Starbucks ice cream hoping that consumers would transfer their love of Starbucks coffee to ice cream. With only a little publicity and a one-time limited outdoor campaign, quarts of Starbucks coffee ice cream flew off the shelves. The company attributes much of its success with its ice cream brand extension to the strong brand power of Starbucks' fifteen hundred retail coffee stores nationwide.[68] Branding is examined in more detail in Chapter 8.

Imitation or counterfeit products are designed to confuse consumers, who buy the items thinking they are originals. This probelm is common in foreign markets where there is often little brand protection.
© Mark Richards/CONTACT Press Images

Another form of stimulus generalization occurs when retailers or wholesalers design their packages to resemble well-known manufacturers' brands. Such imitation often confuses consumers, who buy the imitator thinking it's the original. U.S. manufacturers in foreign markets have sometimes found little, if any, brand protection. In South Korea, Procter & Gamble's Ivory soap competes head-on with the Korean brand Bory, which has an almost identical logo on the package. Consumers dissatisfied with Bory may attribute their dissatisfaction to Ivory, never realizing that Bory is an imitator. Counterfeit products are also produced to look exactly like the original. For example, counterfeit Levi's jeans made in China are hot items in Europe, where Levi Strauss has had trouble keeping up with demand. The knockoffs look so much like the real thing that unsuspecting consumers don't know the difference—until after a few washes, when the belt loops fall off and the rivets begin to rust.

stimulus discrimination
Learned ability to differentiate among stimuli.

The opposite of stimulus generalization is **stimulus discrimination**, which means learning to differentiate among similar products. Consumers usually prefer one product as more rewarding or stimulating. For example, some consumers prefer Coca-Cola and others prefer Pepsi; many insist they can taste a difference between the two brands.

With some types of products—such as aspirin, gasoline, bleach, paper towels—marketers rely on promotion to point out brand differences that consumers would otherwise not recognize. This process, called *product differentiation*, is discussed in more detail in Chapter 6. Usually product differentiation is based on superficial differences. For example, Bayer tells consumers that it's the aspirin "doctors recommend most."

belief
Organized pattern of knowledge that an individual holds as true about his or her world.

Beliefs and Attitudes

Beliefs and attitudes are closely linked to values. A **belief** is an organized pattern of knowledge that an individual holds as true about his or her world. A consumer may believe that Sony's camcorder makes the best home videos, tolerates hard use, and is reasonably priced. These beliefs may be based on knowledge, faith, or hearsay. Consumers tend to develop a set of beliefs about a product's attributes and then, through these beliefs, form a *brand image*—a set of beliefs about a particular brand. In turn, the brand image shapes consumers' attitudes toward the product.

An **attitude** is a learned tendency to respond consistently toward a given object, such as a brand. Attitudes rest on an individual's value system, which represents personal standards of good and bad, right and wrong, and so forth; therefore, attitudes tend to be more enduring and complex than beliefs.

attitude
Learned tendency to respond consistently toward a given object.

GLOBAL

For an example of the nature of attitudes, consider the differing attitudes of consumers around the world toward the habit of purchasing on credit. Americans have long been enthusiastic about charging goods and services and are willing to pay high interest rates for the privilege of postponing payment. To many European consumers, doing what amounts to taking out a loan—even a small one—to pay for anything seems absurd. Germans especially are reluctant to buy on credit. Italy has a sophisticated credit and banking system well suited to handling credit cards, but Italians prefer to carry cash, often huge wads of it. Although most Japanese consumers have credit cards, card purchases amount to less than 1 percent of all consumer transactions. The Japanese have long looked down on credit purchases but acquire cards to use while traveling abroad.[69]

If a good or service is meeting its profit goals, positive attitudes toward the product merely need to be reinforced. However, if the brand is not succeeding, the marketing manager must strive to change target consumers' attitudes toward it. Changes in attitude tend to grow out of an individual's attempt to reconcile long-held values with a constant stream of new information. This change can be accomplished in three ways: changing beliefs about the brand's attributes, changing the relative importance of these beliefs, and adding new beliefs.

Changing Beliefs About Attributes The first technique is to turn neutral or negative beliefs about product attributes into positive ones. For example, the consumption of eggs has steadily decreased over the years because of consumer belief that eggs contribute to high cholesterol. To counter this belief, the American Egg Board launched a new advertising campaign with "If it ain't eggs, it ain't breakfast" and "the incredible edible egg" theme lines. Accompanying the board's advertising is an extensive public relations campaign that endeavors to give consumers "permission" to eat eggs again with proof of extensive research that shows eggs can be a part of a well-balanced diet.[70] Similarly, Procter & Gamble began a series of television ads to downplay the health worries surrounding the fat substitute olestra, which it manufactures and markets under the brand name Olean, used in Frito-Lay's line of Wow! fat-free chips and salty snacks. The campaign attempts to counter the fact that Olean is made in a laboratory by showing wholesome scenes from an American farm to remind consumers that olestra is made with soybeans.[71]

Changing beliefs about a service can be more difficult because service attributes are intangible. Convincing consumers to switch hairstylists or lawyers or to go to a mall dental clinic can be much more difficult than getting them to change brands of razor blades. Image, which is also largely intangible, significantly determines service patronage. For example, research by the American Bankers Association found that young adults do not have a good understanding of what banks are, and some feel that they don't need banks to invest their money. To counter this image, America's banking industry began a national advertising effort to dispel the belief that banks are just for checking and savings accounts. The association aired several television ads that were based on the stereotype of banks as old-fashioned in the hopes that consumers would see banks as a good place for their investments.[72] Service marketing is explored in detail in Chapter 8.

National Pork Producers Council

How is the NPPC trying to change the perception of pork as a fatty, marginally nutritional source of protein? Visit their Web site and determine if their information successfully counters this perception.
http://www.nppc.org

Changing the Importance of Beliefs The second approach to modifying attitudes is to change the relative importance of beliefs about an attribute. For years, consumers have known that bran cereals are high in natural fiber. The primary belief associated with this attribute is that the fiber tends to act as a mild, natural laxative. Today, however, cereal marketers promote the high fiber content of bran cereals as a possible factor in preventing certain types of cancer, vastly increasing the importance of this attribute in the minds of consumers.

Marketers can also downplay the importance of some beliefs in favor of others. For example, Chrysler Corporation's Jeep unit strives to maintain the Jeep Grand Cherokee's ruggedness while playing up its luxury features. The newest Grand Cherokees have even more off-road capability, but only 15 percent of owners ever take them off-road. So, its engineers made more room in the back to carry as many as eight bags of golf clubs, developed a climate-control system with infrared beams to track drivers' and passengers' skin temperature to adjust air-conditioning and heating, and designed his-and-her key fobs with buttons that remember settings for the power seats and mirrors and that reprogram the radio stations for different drivers.[73]

Adding New Beliefs The third approach to transforming attitudes is to add new beliefs. Although changes in consumption patterns often come slowly, cereal marketers are betting that consumers will eventually warm up to the idea of cereal as a snack. A print ad for Ralston Purina's Cookie-Crisp cereal features a boy popping the sugary nuggets into his mouth while he does his homework. Boxes of Kellogg's Cracklin' Oat Bran boast that the cereal tastes like oatmeal cookies and makes "a great snack . . . anytime." Similarly, commercials for Quaker Oats 100% Natural cereal promote eating it straight from the box. James River Corporation, the manufacturer of Dixie paper products, is also attempting to add new beliefs about the uses of its paper plates and cups with an advertising campaign aimed at positioning its product as a "home cleanup replacement." New commercials pitch Dixie paper plates as an alternative to washing dishes after everyday meals.[74]

Adding new beliefs is not easy. For example, when Anheuser-Busch first introduced Bud Dry beer, consumers were confused, because the word "dry" is commonly used to describe wines. Nevertheless, many consumers have since added the new belief that beer too can be described as dry. Volvo faced a similar problem in introducing its sporty C70 convertible and S80 luxury sedan models. For over a quarter of a century, Volvo has successfully crafted an image as the safest car on the road. Yet, with its core target market of baby boomers aging and their children moving out, Volvo also wanted to appeal emotionally to their desire for a fun, powerful, and sexy car while still being safe. Volvo had done such a good job driving home its safety message, however, that consumers had a hard time imagining a Volvo as anything other than a boxy, steel-reinforced tank.[75]

GLOBAL

U.S. companies attempting to market their goods overseas may need to help consumers add new beliefs about a product in general. After years of aggressive marketing campaigns and health awareness programs in Italy by the American cereal industry, promoting the benefits of cereal, most Italians continue to eat breakfast Italian-style: espresso or cappuccino and biscotti dipped into the coffee. Although a growing number of Italian parents are giving their children cereal for breakfast, Italy's per capita cereal consumption of 1.1 pounds annually is still only a spoonful compared with 14.5 pounds in Britain and 11.7 pounds in the United States, two of the world's biggest cereal-eating nations. American cereals like Corn Flakes have been available in Italy since the 1950s but are largely considered a niche product and sold mostly through the nation's pharmacies and health food stores.[76]

LOOKING BACK

Returning to the discussion that opened the chapter, you should now be able to see how cultural, social, individual, and psychological factors affect the consumer decision-making process. The age and family life cycle stage of consumers is driving a resurgence of station wagons; beliefs and attitudes about fat and protein in food products are causing sales of foods with more protein to surge while sales of those that tout less fat are flat. Increased wealth, higher education, and exposure to other cultures—all cultural factors—are making ordinary Americans more sophisticated, and the antiestablishment attitudes of America's youth are making lesser-known brands into marketing successes. Consumer behavior is a fascinating and often intricate process. An appreciation of consumer behavior and the factors that influence it will help you identify target markets and design effective marketing mixes.

Summary

1 Explain why marketing managers should understand consumer behavior. Consumer behavior describes how consumers make purchase decisions and how they use and dispose of the products they buy. An understanding of consumer behavior reduces marketing managers' uncertainty when they are defining a target market and designing a marketing mix.

2 Analyze the components of the consumer decision-making process. The consumer decision-making process begins with need recognition, when stimuli trigger awareness of an unfulfilled want. If additional information is required to make a purchase decision, the consumer may engage in an internal or external information search. The consumer then evaluates the additional information and establishes purchase guidelines. Finally, a purchase decision is made.

3 Explain the consumer's postpurchase evaluation process. Consumer postpurchase evaluation is influenced by prepurchase expectations, the prepurchase information search, and the consumer's general level of self-confidence. Cognitive dissonance is the inner tension that a consumer experiences after recognizing a purchased product's disadvantages. When a purchase creates cognitive dissonance, consumers tend to react by seeking positive reinforcement for the purchase decision, avoiding negative information about the purchase decision, or revoking the purchase decision by returning the product.

4 Identify the types of consumer buying decisions and discuss the significance of consumer involvement. Consumer decision making falls into three broad categories. First, consumers exhibit routine response behavior for frequently purchased, low-cost items that require very little decision effort; routine response behavior is typically characterized by brand loyalty. Second, consumers engage in limited decision making for occasional purchases or for unfamiliar brands in familiar product categories. Third, consumers practice extensive decision making when making unfamiliar, expensive, or infrequent purchases. High-involvement decisions usually include an extensive information search and a thorough evaluation of alternatives. In contrast, low-involvement decisions are characterized by brand loyalty and a lack of personal identification with the product. The main factors affecting the level of consumer involvement are price, interest, perceived risk of negative consequences, situation, and social visibility.

5 Identify and understand the cultural factors that affect consumer buying decisions. Cultural influences on consumer buying decisions include culture and values, subculture, and social class. Culture is the essential character of a society that distinguishes it from other cultural groups. The underlying elements of every culture are the values, language, myths, customs, rituals, laws, and the artifacts, or products, that are transmitted from one generation to the next. The most defining element of a culture is its values—the enduring beliefs shared by a society that a specific mode of conduct is personally or socially preferable to another mode of conduct. A culture can be divided into subcultures on the basis of demographic characteristics, geographic regions, national and ethnic background, political beliefs, and religious beliefs. Subcultures share elements of the overall culture as well as cultural elements unique to their own group. A social class is a group of people who are considered nearly equal in status or community esteem, who regularly socialize among themselves both formally and informally, and who share behavioral norms.

6 Identify and understand the social factors that affect consumer buying decisions. Social factors include such external influences as reference groups, opinion leaders, and family. Consumers seek out others' opinions for guidance on new products or services and products with image-related attributes or because attribute information is lacking or uninformative. Consumers may use products or brands to identify with or become a member of a reference group. Opinion leaders are members of reference groups who influence others' purchase decisions. Family members also influence purchase decisions; children tend to shop in similar patterns as their parents.

7 Identify and understand the individual factors that affect consumer buying decisions. Individual factors that affect consumer buying decisions include gender; age and family life cycle stage; and personality, self-concept, and lifestyle. Beyond obvious physiological differences, men and women differ in their social and economic roles that affect consumer buying decisions. How old a consumer is generally indicates what products he or she may be interested in purchasing. Marketers often define their target markets in terms of consumers' life cycle stage, following changes in consumers' attitudes and behavioral tendencies as they mature. Finally, certain products and brands reflect consumers' personality, self-concept, and lifestyle.

8 Identify and understand the psychological factors that affect consumer buying decisions. Psychological factors include perception, motivation, learning, values, beliefs, and attitudes. These factors allow consumers to interact with the world around them, recognize their feelings, gather and analyze information, formulate thoughts and opinions, and take action. Perception allows consumers to recognize their consumption problems. Motivation is what drives consumers to take action to satisfy specific consumption needs. Almost all consumer behavior results from learning, which is the process that creates changes in behavior through experience. Consumers with similar beliefs and attitudes tend to react alike to marketing-related inducements.

Discussion and Writing Questions

1. Describe the three categories of consumer decision-making behavior. Name typical products for which each type of consumer behavior is used.
2. The type of decision making a consumer uses for a product does not necessarily remain constant. Why? Support your answer with an example from your own experience.
3. How do beliefs and attitudes influence consumer behavior? How can negative attitudes toward a product be changed? How can marketers alter beliefs about a product? Give some examples of how marketers have changed negative attitudes about a product or added or altered beliefs about a product.
4. WRITING Recall an occasion when you experienced cognitive dissonance about a purchase. In a letter to a friend, describe the event and explain what you did about it.
5. Family members play many different roles in the buying process: initiator, influencer, decision maker, purchaser, and consumer. In your family, name who

might play each of these roles in the purchase of a personal computer system, Froot Loops breakfast cereal, Calvin Klein Obsession cologne for men, and dinner at McDonald's.

6. WRITING You are a new marketing manager for a firm that produces a line of athletic shoes to be targeted to the college student subculture. In a memo to your boss, list some product attributes that might appeal to this subculture and the steps in your customers' purchase processes, and recommend some marketing strategies that can influence their decision.
7. Assume you are involved in the following consumer decision situations: (a) renting a video to watch with your roommates, (b) choosing a fast-food restaurant to go to with a new friend, (c) buying a popular music compact disc, (d) buying jeans to wear to class. List the factors that would influence your decision in each situation and explain your responses.
8. ON LINE Visit Land Rover's "Authoritative Guide to SUVs" Web site at **www.best4x4.landrover.com/?authority/authority.html.** How does Land Rover assist consumers in the evaluation stage of choosing a new sport utility vehicle? Develop your own hypothetical evoked set of three or four SUV models and present your comparisons. Which vehicle attributes would be most important in your purchase decision?

Application for Small Business

ENTREPRENEUR Deli Depot is a new franchise opportunity offering cold and hot sandwiches, soup, chili, yogurt, pies, and cookies. It is positioned to compete with Subway and similar sandwich restaurants. Its unique advantages include special sauces on sandwiches, supplementary menu items like soup and pies, and quick delivery within specified zones.

The franchise package offered to franchisees includes information on the factors that typically influence consumers' selection of casual restaurants. These selection factors, in order from most important to least important, include food taste, food variety, value for the money, restaurant reputation, friendliness of employees, and convenience of location.

Robert Powell and a group of investors purchased the right to all franchise locations in the Atlanta metropolitan area. His group estimates that five units can be opened successfully in the first year and that a total of thirty can be opened in the first five years.

Because this is a new franchise, potential customers must first be made aware of Deli Depot and then convinced to try it. Over the long run a loyal customer base must be established to make each Deli Depot a success.

Questions:

1. Are Deli Depot's unique advantages strong enough to attract customers from Subway and other sandwich competitors? Why or why not?
2. Are all the important customer selection factors for sandwich restaurants included in the list? Do you agree with the importance rankings? Explain your answers.
3. How can Robert and his group make potential customers aware of the new Deli Depot locations and menu selections?
4. How can Robert and his group convince individuals who try Deli Depot to become regular customers?

Review Quiz

1. The first stage of consumer decision making when consumers are faced with an imbalance between desired and actual states is

Key Terms

aspirational reference group 129
attitude 143
belief 142
cognitive dissonance 115
consumer behavior 110
consumer decision-making process 111
culture 121
evoked set (consideration set) 114
extensive decision making 117
external information search 112
ideal self-image 135
internal information search 112
involvement 116
learning 141
lifestyle 136
limited decision making 117
marketing-controlled information source 113
Maslow's hierarchy of needs 139
motive 139
need recognition 111
nonaspirational reference group 129
nonmarketing-controlled information source 112
norm 129
opinion leader 130
perception 137
personality 135
primary membership group 129
real self-image 135
reference group 129
routine response behavior 117
secondary membership group 129
selective distortion 137
selective exposure 137
selective retention 137
self-concept 135
social class 126
socialization process 132
stimulus 111
stimulus discrimination 142
stimulus generalization 142
subculture 124
value 122
want 112

a. Need recognition
b. Information search
c. Evaluation of alternatives
d. Purchase

2. Information that a consumer receives that is biased toward a particular product is usually

   a. Internal information
   b. Internal stimuli
   c. Nonmarketing-controlled information
   d. Marketing-controlled information

3. A consumer's information search yields a group of brands that are the consumer's most preferred alternatives. This group is called

   a. The consumer wants
   b. The evoked set
   c. The external stimuli
   d. The set of possible alternatives

4. Frequently purchased, low-cost goods and services are usually associated with ______ consumer decision making.

   a. Constant
   b. Routine
   c. Limited
   d. Extensive

5. Which of the following is *not* a factor that determines the level of consumer involvement when making a purchase decision?

   a. Interest
   b. Perceived risk
   c. Price
   d. Social visibility

6. The most defining element of a culture is its

   a. Values
   b. Traditions
   c. Beliefs
   d. Religion

7. Attitudes, motivation, and learning influence consumer decision making. These factors are best classified as

   a. Cultural
   b. Social
   c. Individual
   d. Psychological

8. Since consumers cannot perceive every stimulus in their environment, they often use selective ______ to decide which stimuli to notice and which to ignore.

   a. Exposure
   b. Distortion
   c. Retention
   d. Attention

9. To get a consumer to buy a firm's product or service, it must often change the consumer's attitude toward it. Which of the following is not one of the three ways in which this attitude change can be accomplished?

a. Changing learning processes
b. Changing beliefs about product attributes
c. Changing the importance of beliefs
d. Adding new beliefs

10. Conceptual learning, which changes the consumer's marketplace behavior, is accomplished through direct product experience.

    a. True
    b. False

11. Social factors exert the broadest and deepest influence over a person's consumer behavior.

    a. True
    b. False

12. Limited decision making typically occurs when a consumer is buying an unfamiliar, expensive product or an infrequently bought item.

    a. True
    b. False

13. Identify, in order, the five steps of the consumer decision-making process.

Check the Answer Key, which follows the Video Case, to see how well you understood the material.

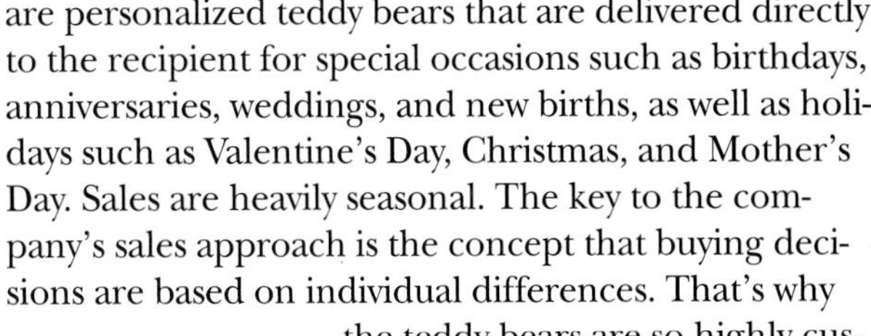

Vermont Teddy Bear Co.: Workin' Hard for the Honey

In the tradition of Teddy Roosevelt and the 1902 "Great American Teddy Bear," the Vermont Teddy Bear brand carries on a rich heritage based on the best American values of compassion, generosity, friendship, and a zesty sense of whimsy and fun. Founded in 1981, The Vermont Teddy Bear Co., Inc., is a designer, manufacturer, and marketer of teddy bears and related products that appeal to customers' core values. Because the Vermont Teddy Bear Co. believes that people's value systems have a great effect on what they buy, it has designed bears around popular American themes. Americans admire hard work, entrepreneurship, achievement, and success, so the company has a line of occupational bears. There's Businessman Bear, Doctor Bear, Webster the Computer Bear, and Teacher Bear. Americans also value youth and health, hence the appeal for Fitness Bear. And in this sports-crazed country, official NFL Bears score big points.

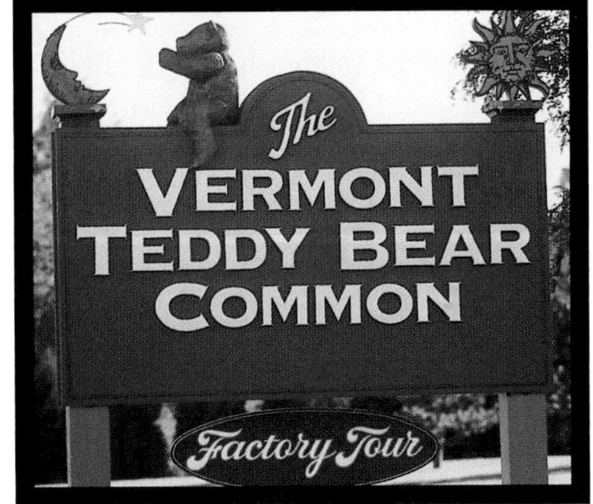

The backbone of the Vermont Teddy Bear Co. is the patented and trademarked Bear-Gram. Bear-Grams are personalized teddy bears that are delivered directly to the recipient for special occasions such as birthdays, anniversaries, weddings, and new births, as well as holidays such as Valentine's Day, Christmas, and Mother's Day. Sales are heavily seasonal. The key to the company's sales approach is the concept that buying decisions are based on individual differences. That's why the teddy bears are so highly customized. The company realizes that men and women shop differently, and their cultural, social, and economic roles affect their buying decisions. It has therefore identified its customer profile as being primarily the urban professional male who waits until the last minute to buy a gift but who still wants something special.

With individual differences in mind, the company created bears to fit different ages—Grandmother Bear, Baby Bears, and Classic Birthday Bears. Different lifestyles—Golf Bears, Cowboy and Cowgirl Bears. Different life cycle stages—Bride and Groom Bears, Pregnancy Bears, Anniversary Bears. Different personality traits—Cheerleader Bear. These irresistible furry creatures come in a variety of sizes with different colored fur dressed in nearly one hundred different personalized outfits.

Throughout the 1980s, the company wholesaled teddy bears to specialty stores and retailed them through its own outlets. Then in 1990, it introduced radio advertising for the Bear-Gram, positioning it as a novel gift for Valentine's Day and offering listeners a toll-free number to call to order from sales reps, known as Bear Counselors. This test proved so successful that the concept was expanded to other major radio markets. Now, advertising for Valentine's Day has grown to 105 radio stations in eleven different markets, as well as on one syndicated network. Radio ads are frequently tagged with a reference to the company Web site, which in turn provides visual support for the radio advertising. This advertising works well for impulse buyers who hear the radio spot and make the decision to buy.

It is not surprising that annual sales peak at Valentine's Day because the strongest and most endearing message of the teddy bears is the message of love. Even the company catalog is titled "Red Hot . . . Catalog of Love." Strong psychological influences affect consumer buying decisions, and teddy bears satisfy the important social needs of love and a sense of belonging. Whether it's the Sweetheart Bear or Cupid Bear, these romantic classics deliver the perfect bear hug. Family tours of the teddy bear factory and store in Shelburne, Vermont, drew over 129,000 visitors in 1997. And to make the factory visit more entertaining and draw additional traffic, the company implemented the Make-A-Friend-For-Life bear assembly area, where visitors can participate in the creation of their own teddy bear. Customers are not only buying a customized and personalized product, but they are also emotionally investing themselves in its design.

Unlike flowers, which only last for a short time, a Vermont Teddy Bear is steadfast and comes with a lifetime guarantee. Designed, cut, and sewn by hand, each bear can be a future heirloom, and if it becomes injured, it can be sent to the Teddy Bear Hospital to be repaired at no charge. All Vermont Teddy Bears arrive at their destinations smiling in a fun gift box with candy and a personalized message.

This complete understanding of its customers and what motivates their buying decisions has paid off. Total company revenues for 1997 reached $16,489,000, showing that these bears are workin' hard for the honey.

Questions

1. Describe the cultural effects on the consumer buying decision for a teddy bear. See Exhibit 4.5.
2. Describe the individual factors that affect the consumer buying decision for a teddy bear.
3. Describe the psychological factors that affect the consumer buying decision for a teddy bear. See Exhibit 4.13.
4. Describe the level of involvement for purchasing a teddy bear. See Exhibit 4.2.

Bibliography

Vermont Teddy Bear Co. catalog
Web site: **http://www.vtbear.com/**

Answer Key

1. *Answer:* a, p. 111

   Rationale: Need recognition is the first stage of consumer decision making and is triggered when the consumer is exposed to either an internal or external stimulus.

2. *Answer:* d, p. 113

   Rationale: Marketing controlled information sources provide information on specific products through advertising, sales promotion, and personal sales people.

3. *Answer:* b, p. 114

   Rationale: Sometimes known as the consideration set, the evoked set represents the group of products, within a particular category, that the buyer will further evaluate and make a choice from.

4. *Answer:* b, p. 117

   Rationale: These type of goods and services are also commonly called low-involvement products because consumers spend little time on search and decision making prior to purchase.

5. *Answer:* c, p. 118

   Rationale: While concern with price can be an element of perceived risk (financial risk), it is not automatically a factor that influences consumer involvement.

6. *Answer:* a, p. 122

   Rationale: Values are those enduring beliefs shared by a society that specify modes of conduct that are preferable over others.

7. *Answer:* d, p. 136

   Rationale: These factors are what consumers use to interact with their world, recognize feelings, and gather and analyze information.

8. *Answer:* a, p. 137

   Rationale: Selective exposure means that consumers will use certain cues such as packaging or brand names to identify what information about products they should process further and what should be ignored.

9. *Answer:* a, pp. 143–144

   Rationale: Changes in attitude can only be accomplished by a change in the way in which the individual attempts to reconcile old values with new information. This is done by changing beliefs about the product's attributes, changing the importance of certain beliefs, or adding new consumer beliefs.

10. *Answer:* b, p. 141

    Rationale: There are two types of learning: experiential and conceptual. Experiential learning occurs when a specific product experience changes the consumer's behavior.

11. *Answer:* b, p. 121

    Rationale: Cultural factors tend to exert the greatest influence over consumer behavior. Marketers must strive to understand how cultural and subcultural values and social class influence their customers' buying behavior.

12. *Answer:* b, p. 117

    Rationale: Limited decision making typically occurs when a consumer has previous product experience but is unfamiliar with current brands available.

13. *Answer:* Need recognition, information search, evaluation of alternatives, purchase, postpurchase behavior. (p. 111)

CHAPTER 5

LEARNING OBJECTIVES

After studying this chapter, you should be able to

1. Describe business marketing
2. Describe the role of the Internet in business marketing
3. Discuss the role of relationship marketing and strategic alliances in business marketing
4. Identify the four major categories of business market customers
5. Explain the North American Industry Classification System
6. Explain the major differences between business and consumer markets
7. Describe the seven types of business goods and services
8. Discuss the unique aspects of business buying behavior

BUSINESS MARKETING

The success of many corporations today is directly related not only to their relationships with customers but also to the number and quality of their business relationships with other companies. The reason is simple. Most companies can no longer operate by themselves to fulfill their needs. Alliances are a key to the future for businesses of all sizes and in every industry worldwide.

Nowhere is this statement truer than in the international airline business, where competition for passenger dollars has become cutthroat. The challenge has been to create alliances that offer passengers a seamless travel experience while preserving the unique cultures and products of the individual partners. Recently, a group of five carriers—United Airlines, Thai Airways, SAS, Lufthansa, and Air Canada—moved alliance building into a new era with the formation of the Star Alliance, which presents travelers with a more uniform product while retaining individual brands. Varig has subsequently joined the alliance as well. The alliance integrates the airlines' frequent flyer programs and offers seamless booking and travel capabilities across all six airlines.

"We believe our alliance helps each of us to secure our place among the successful competitors in a deregulated, liberalized, and highly competitive global air transport market," says Jan Stenberg, president and CEO of SAS, one of the partners. "But it is not our intention to merge our airlines or develop identical product offerings. Our research tells us categorically that our customers enjoy and appreciate our varied cultures. Our strength is in our diversity."

The six carriers combined now serve 600 cities in 108 countries—including 16 major hubs—with 6,233 daily departures and 1,334 aircraft. In 1996, their combined revenue was $42.3 billion and combined traffic was 229.3 billion revenue passenger miles, exclusive of Varig.

The airlines have been working closely together for some time to develop their relationship with each other. Dubbed the "Airline Network for Earth" by United Airlines chairman and CEO Gerald Greenwald and hailed by Thai Airways International president Thamnoon Wanglee as an engine of growth that will create world-class opportunities for employees, the new

on line

Star Alliance

How is the Star Alliance marketing itself on the Internet? How are the benefits of using Star Alliance carriers presented on its Web site? Based on what you see, would you choose Star Alliance carriers over other airlines? Why do you think as you do?
http://www.star-alliance.com/

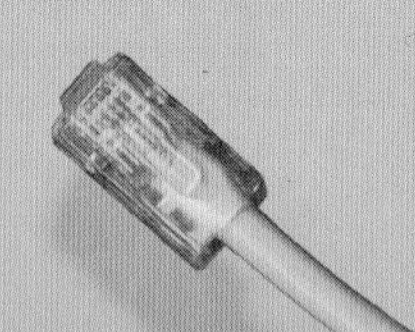

initiative will not only provide better customer recognition worldwide but will also create a powerful framework for future development. In addition, it enables each airline to benefit from considerable synergies, ranging from common utilization of facilities to joint purchasing. The Star Alliance logo will appear as an additional feature on the fuselage of all aircraft in each airline's fleet and on a wide range of information materials. It will also become a familiar sight at airports, ticket offices, and other locations around the world.

The alliance is committed to the introduction of further benefits for customers, including access to more flights and destinations, simplified ticketing and reservations, more convenient connections, and better baggage and ground services—all of which combine to create a hassle-free, seamless travel experience.

"We want to add more flights, more destinations, simplified ticketing and reservations procedures, easier connections, better baggage and ground services, and more schedule choices, just to name a few of the projects already in progress," says R. Lamar Durrett, president and CEO of Air Canada. "In short, our global alliance will stand apart from all others as a mark of quality, innovation, and service recognized by customers around the world."[1]

Identify several benefits members receive from participating in the Star Alliance. In what ways do customers benefit? Does the alliance threaten competition? These issues are addressed in this chapter.

What Is Business Marketing?

1

Describe business marketing

business marketing
The marketing of goods and services to individuals and organizations for purposes other than personal consumption.

Business marketing is the marketing of goods and services to individuals and organizations for purposes other than personal consumption. The sale of an overhead projector to your college or university is an example of business marketing. Business products include those that are used to manufacture other products, become part of another product, aid the normal operations of an organization, or are acquired for resale without any substantial change in form. The key characteristic distinguishing business products from consumer products is intended use, not physical characteristics. A product that is purchased for personal or family consumption or as a gift is a consumer good. If that same product, such as a microcomputer or a cellular telephone, is bought for use in a business, it is a business product.

Business Marketing on the Internet

2

Describe the role of the Internet in business marketing

In the twenty-first century, information technology industries will drive economic wealth. The innovations developed by the computing, telecommunications, and electronic media industries will affect every

With information technology developments affecting businesses everywhere, Internet presence is becoming extremely common in business marketing. Smaller businesses without Web page creation capabilities in-house can contract with an outside provider, such as WebCom, to develop and maintain their Web sites. Courtesy Web Communications LLC

business, large and small.[2] According to some sources, Internet presence is already becoming as common as business cards and fax machines in business marketing.[3] Over 95 percent of *Fortune* 1,000 companies use the Internet in one way or another.[4] Dell Computer sells $1 million worth of computers per day on the Internet; and Cisco Systems, a network-equipment maker, is selling products from its Web site at the rate of $1 billion per year.[5]

General Electric purchases $1 billion worth of goods and services per year from its Trading Process Network (TPN). This substantially exceeds all consumer Internet transactions, which totaled between $500 and $600 million in 1996.[6] Businesses are expected to buy over $200 billion worth of goods and services on-line in 2001—eight times more than consumers.[7]

GE has software that lets its purchasing agents specify to whom they want their requests for bids to go and what sort of information, such as drawings, potential vendors should submit. The software then manages the bids as they come back, ultimately notifying bidders of the outcome.[8]

Since the TPN was opened in 1996, the length of the bidding process in GE's lighting division has been reduced from twenty-one days to ten. Since requesting the bids is so easy, purchasing agents approach more potential vendors, which has lowered the cost of goods by 5 to 15 percent. TPN has also made it easier to solicit bids from foreign suppliers. One bid was awarded to a Hungarian firm at a savings of 20 percent.[9] GE expects to purchase 50 percent of its requirements through the Internet within a few years.[10]

The emergence of the Internet has made business markets more competitive than ever before. With the Internet, every business in the world is potentially a local competitor. Many business marketers now realize that the Internet is a valuable tool for expanding markets and better serving customers. Exhibit 5.1 identifies eight Internet sites that contain important information for firms interested in competing in foreign markets.

Cisco Systems, a network-equipment maker, is selling products from its Web site at the rate of $1 billion per year, demonstrating how lucrative business marketing on the Internet can be. Courtesy Cisco Systems

Relationship Marketing and Strategic Alliances

3
Discuss the role of relationship marketing and strategic alliances in business marketing

As Chapter 1 explained, relationship marketing is the strategy that entails seeking and establishing ongoing partnerships with customers. Relationship marketing is redefining the fundamental roles of business buyers and sellers. Suppliers are making major adjustments in their thinking, management styles, and methods of

exhibit 5.1

An Internet Guide to Small-Business Exporting

One of the easiest ways to delve into exporting is to utilize the Internet. Visit these sites, which offer valuable resources as well as links to additional information.

http://www.embpage.org Embassy Web.com is a valuable on-line resource for diplomatic information. This site is a window to hundreds of embassies and consulates around the world.

http://www.exim.gov The Export-Import Bank of the United States was established to aid in financing and to facilitate U.S. exports.

http://www.exporthotline.com Export Hotline® contains thousands of market research reports, a trade library, and a variety of other resources focused on all aspects of global trade and investment.

http://www.fita.org Trade associations are invaluable resources on exporting. Visit the Federation of International Trade Associations Web site to take advantage of all of its resources, including a network of three hundred thousand companies belonging to three hundred international trade associations in North America.

http://www.ita.doc.gov The International Trade Administration of the U.S. Department of Commerce is "dedicated to helping U.S. businesses compete in the global marketplace." It offers many resources to encourage, assist, and advocate U.S. exports.

http://www.sba.gov The U.S. Small Business Administration offers a wealth of basic information and resources, including various export support programs. It provides financial, technical, and management assistance to help Americans start, run, and help their businesses grow.

http://www.tradecompass.com Trade Compass® offers news, information, and sophisticated database products that help companies and individuals navigate the far reaches of trade, importing, exporting, sales, marketing, logistics, research, and e-business in today's global marketplace.

http://www.tscentral.com TSCentral is an Internet-based provider of information, products, and services for global events. It has global directories offering information on trade shows, seminars, and conferences as well as extensive directories of suppliers, venues, and facilities around the world.

SOURCE: Based on information from Christopher Farrell and Edith Updike, "So You Think the World Is Your Oyster," *Business Week*, 9 June 1997, p. ENT8.

responding to purchasers' standards and operational requirements. A satisfied customer is one of the best sources of new business. When the customer knows that the supplier can meet expectations and deliver on what the supplier has promised, trust is created; and trust is the foundation of most successful relationship marketing efforts.[11] According to Louis V. Gerstner, Jr., chairman and chief executive of IBM, the most basic notion of how to succeed in business is talking to customers, learning their needs, and figuring out how to satisfy them.[12]

strategic alliance (strategic partnership)
A cooperative agreement between business firms.

A **strategic alliance**, sometimes called a **strategic partnership**, is a cooperative agreement between business firms. Strategic alliances can take the form of licensing or distribution agreements, joint ventures, research and development consortia, and partnerships. They may be between manufacturers, manufacturers and customers, manufacturers and suppliers, and manufacturers and channel interme-

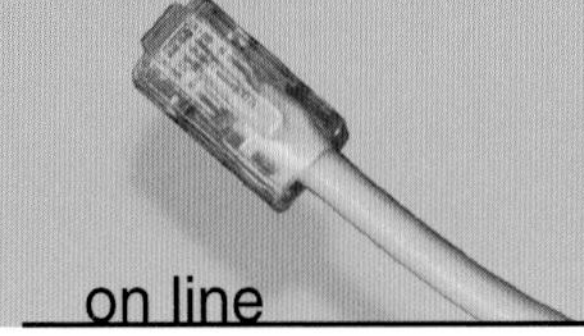

Xerox

What can you find out about Xerox's partnerships from its Web site?

http://www.xerox.com/

on line

diaries. Recall the story at the beginning of this chapter about the Star Alliance of airlines, developed to benefit the six partners as well as their customers. This is an example of a strategic alliance among manufacturers.

The trend toward forming strategic alliances is accelerating rapidly. The consulting firm Booz, Allen & Hamilton reports that some thirty-two thousand alliances were formed around the world between 1995 and 1998, and 75 percent of them were international alliances.[13] In Japan, IBM has a strategic alliance with Ricoh to distribute low-end computers and one with Fuji Bank to market financial systems. IBM has similar links with other Japanese firms. Ford and Mazda have collaborated on at least ten models. The "Global Perspectives" box in this chapter provides an example of strategic alliances between a U.S. manufacturer and six Asian producers of home appliances.

Alliances now account for 18 percent of the revenues of America's largest companies compared to about 7 percent in 1990.[14] These companies have realized that strategic partnerships are more than just important—they are critical. Xerox management, for example, has decided that in order to maintain its leadership position in the reprographics industry, the company must "include suppliers as part of the Xerox family." This strategy often means reducing the number of suppliers, treating those that remain as allies, sharing strategic information freely, and drawing on supplier expertise in developing new products that can meet the quality, cost, and delivery standards of the marketplace.

In a Volkswagen truck assembly plant in Brazil, seven main suppliers make components in the plant using their own equipment. These supplier workers then fasten the components to a chassis moving down an assembly line through the suppliers' spaces.[15]

Business marketers form strategic alliances to leverage what they do well by partnering with others who have complementary expertise to achieve the following[16]

global perspectives

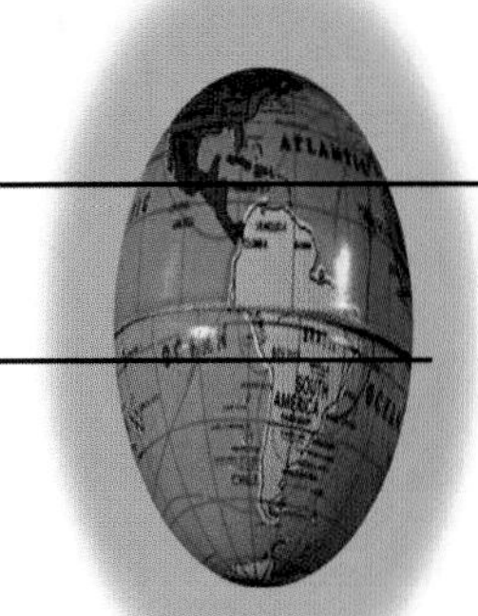

Whirlpool Ventures into a New Frontier

Between 1994 and 1996, Whirlpool Corp. spent $265 million to buy controlling interest in four competitors in China and two in India. Eventually, Whirlpool hopes to become one of Asia's top suppliers of washers, dryers, dishwashers, refrigerators, and household air conditioners.

According to the *Wall Street Journal*, Whirlpool management believes that the combination of Asia's fast growth and low proportion of households with modern appliances provides very promising market opportunities. For example, China has a population of over one billion people, but less than 10 percent of all households in China have air conditioners, microwave ovens, and clothes washers.

Whirlpool also hopes to export appliances manufactured in China to other Asian countries. In order to successfully implement this strategy, Whirlpool must substantially upgrade the quality of its joint venture partners' products. According to Whirlpool executives, the Chinese brands are not as reliable and durable as available Japanese brands. Typical air conditioners manufactured by Chinese partner firms last only five to eight years, which is half the life expectancy of a Whirlpool unit made in the United States. Whirlpool president and CEO William Marohn was quoted in the *Wall Street Journal* as saying, "Until we have a product that we can feel represents a modern, upscale product, we're not going to put the Whirlpool name on it."[17]

Why would Whirlpool invest $265 million to buy partial ownership in Chinese companies that produce inferior products? Why not just export products made in the United States to Asia or build Whirlpool manufacturing facilities in China and elsewhere? Assess the Whirlpool joint ventures in terms of the general strategic alliance goals, factors that contribute to successful alliances, and the three general problems that commonly plague strategic alliances.

- Access to markets or to technology
- Economies of scale that might be gained by combining manufacturing, R&D, or marketing activities
- Faster entry of new products to markets
- Sharing of risk

Some alliances are extremely successful and some are dismal failures. Exhibit 5.2 identifies six tips for making an alliance successful.

Major Categories of Business Customers

4

Identify the four major categories of business market customers

The business market consists of four major categories of customers: producers, resellers, governments, and institutions.

Producers

The producer segment of the business market includes profit-oriented individuals and organizations that use purchased goods and services to produce other products, to incorporate into other products, or to facilitate the daily operations of the organization. Examples of producers include construction, manufacturing, transportation, finance, real estate, and food service firms. In the United States there are over thirteen million firms in the producer segment of the business market. Some of these firms are small and others are among the world's largest businesses.

Individual producers often buy large quantities of goods and services. Companies like General Motors spend more than $70 billion annually—more than the gross domestic product of Ireland, Portugal, Turkey, or Greece—on such business products as steel, metal components, and tires. Companies like General Electric, Du Pont, and IBM spend over $60 million daily for business goods and services.[18]

The producer segment of the business market includes manufacturing, like this globe production line, as well as construction, finance, transportation, real estate, and others.
© Andy Sacks/Tony Stone Images

Resellers

The reseller market includes retail and wholesale businesses that buy finished goods and resell them for a profit. A retailer sells mainly to final consumers; wholesalers sell mostly to retailers and other organizational customers. There are

exhibit 5.2

Tips for Making Strategic Alliances Successful

- Trust one another (alliances break down when one partner becomes greedy).
- Share a common interest in meeting customer needs.
- Bring different skills to the table.
- Share gains (and have a built-in system for ongoing change).
- Understand which party will have direct contact with the customer.
- Understand that success and profitability are tied to customer satisfaction.

SOURCE: From "Alliance Highlights," *Fortune*, Best Practices Symposium, March 30, 1998. Reprinted by permission.

approximately 1.5 million retailers and five hundred thousand wholesalers operating in the United States. Consumer product firms like Procter & Gamble, Kraft General Foods, and Coca-Cola sell directly to large retailers and retail chains and through wholesalers to smaller retail units. Retailing and wholesaling are explored in detail in Chapter 11.

Business product distributors are wholesalers that buy business products and resell them to business customers. They often carry thousands of items in stock and employ sales forces to call on business customers. Businesses that wish to buy a gross of pencils or one hundred pounds of fertilizer typically purchase these items from local distributors rather than directly from manufacturers such as Empire Pencil or Dow Chemical.

Governments

A third major segment of the business market is government. Government organizations include thousands of federal, state, and local buying units. They make up what may be the largest single market for goods and services in the world.

Contracts for government purchases are often put out for bid. Interested vendors submit bids (usually sealed) to provide specified products during a particular time. Sometimes the lowest bidder is awarded the contract. When the lowest bidder is not awarded the contract, strong evidence must be presented to justify the decision. Grounds for rejecting the lowest bid include lack of experience, inadequate financing, or poor past performance. Bidding allows all potential suppliers a fair chance at winning government contracts and helps ensure that public funds are spent wisely. For more information about bidding, see the "Entrepreneurial Insights" box in this chapter.

Federal Government Name just about any good or service and chances are that someone in the federal government uses it. The U.S. federal government is the world's largest customer.

Although much of the federal government's buying is centralized, no single federal agency contracts for all the government's requirements, and no single buyer in any agency purchases all that the agency needs. We can view the federal government as a combination of several large companies with overlapping responsibilities and thousands of small independent units.

ON LINE

One popular source of information about government procurement is *Commerce Business Daily*. Until recently, businesses hoping to sell to the federal government found the document unorganized, and it often arrived too late to be useful. The new on-line version **(http://www.govcon.com/)** is more timely and lets contractors find leads using keyword searches. *Doing Business with the General Services Administration, Selling to the Military,* and *Selling to the U.S. Air Force* are other examples of publications designed to explain how to do business with the federal government.

State, County, and City Government Selling to states, counties, and cities can be less frustrating for both small and large vendors than selling to the federal government. Paperwork is typically simpler and more manageable than it is at the federal level. On the other hand, vendors must decide which of the over eighty-two thousand government units are likely to buy their wares. State and local buying agencies include school districts, highway departments, government-operated hospitals, and housing agencies.

Institutions

The fourth major segment of the business market is institutions that seek to achieve goals other than the standard business goals of profit, market share, and return on investment. This segment includes schools, hospitals, colleges and universities, churches, labor unions, fraternal organizations, civic clubs, foundations, and other so-called nonbusiness organizations.

Keebler
What special offers does Keebler have for its business customers? What sectors is it trying to service? Go to the Hollow Tree Web page to find out.
http://www.keebler.com/

The North American Industry Classification System (NAICS)

5
Explain the North American Industry Classification System

North American Industry Classification System (NAICS)
A detailed numbering system developed by the United States, Canada, and Mexico to classify North American business establishments by their main production processes.

The **North American Industry Classification System (NAICS)** is an industry classification system introduced in 1997 to replace the standard industrial classification system (SIC). NAICS (pronounced *nakes*) is an all-new system for classifying North American business establishments. The system, developed jointly by the United States, Canada, and Mexico, provides a common industry classification system for the North American Free Trade Association (NAFTA) partners. Goods- or service-producing firms that use identical or similar production processes are grouped together.

NAICS promises to be an extremely valuable tool for business marketers in analyzing, segmenting, and targeting markets. Each classification group should be relatively homogeneous in terms of raw materials required, components used, manufacturing processes employed, and problems faced.[19] The more digits in a code, the more homogenous the group will be. If a supplier understands the needs and requirements of a few firms within a classification, requirements can be projected for all firms in that category. The number, size, and geographic dispersion of firms can also be identified. This information can be converted to market potential estimates, market share estimates, and sales forecasts. It can also be used for identifying potential new customers. NAICS codes can help identify firms that may be prospective users of a supplier's goods and services.

Exhibit 5.3 provides an overview of NAICS. Exhibit 5.4 illustrates the six-digit classification system for two of the twenty NAICS economic sectors: manufacturing and information. The hierarchical structure of NAICS allows industry data to be summarized at several levels of detail.

Business Versus Consumer Markets

6
Explain the major differences between business and consumer markets

The basic philosophy and practice of marketing is the same whether the customer is a business organization or a consumer. Business markets do, however, have characteristics different from consumer markets. Exhibit 5.5 summarizes the main differences between business and consumer markets.

Demand

Consumer demand for products is quite different from demand in the business market. Unlike consumer demand, business demand is derived, inelastic, joint, and fluctuating.

derived demand
The demand for business products.

Derived Demand The demand for business products is called **derived demand** because organizations buy products to be used in producing consumer products. In other words, the demand for business products is derived from the demand for consumer products. For example, two-thirds of the components Chrysler Corporation uses in manufacturing automobiles come from outside sources. This includes sixty thousand different items purchased from 1,140 suppliers.[20]

Because demand is derived, business marketers must carefully monitor demand patterns and changing preferences in final consumer markets, even though their customers are not in those markets. Moreover, business marketers must carefully monitor their customers' forecasts, because derived demand is based on expectations of future demand for those customers' products.

exhibit 5.3

NAICS Two-Digit Codes and Corresponding Economic Sectors

NAICS Codes with Corresponding Economic Sectors	
NAICS Code	**Economic Sector**
11	Agriculture, forestry, and fishing
21	Mining
22	Utilities
23	Construction
31–33	Manufacturing
43	Wholesale trade
44–45	Retail trade
47–48	Transportation
51	Information
52	Finance and insurance
53	Real estate and rental and leasing
56	Professional and technical services
57	Management and support services
61	Education services
62	Health and social assistance
71	Arts, entertainment, and recreation
72	Food services, drinking places, and accommodations
81	Other services, except public administration
93	Public administration
98	Estates and trusts
99	Nonclassifiable

exhibit 5.4

Examples of NAICS Hierarchy

NAICS Level	NAICS Code	Example #1 Description	NAICS Code	Example #2 Description
Sector	31–33	Manufacturing	51	Information
Subsector	334	Computer and electronic product manufacturing	513	Broadcasting and telecommunications
Industry Group	3346	Manufacturing and reproduction of magnetic and optical media	5133	Telecommunications
Industry	33461	Manufacturing and reproduction of magnetic and optical media	51332	Wireless telecommunications carriers, except satellite
U.S. Industry	334611	Reproduction of software	513321	Paging

SOURCE: U.S. Census Bureau, "New Code System in NAICS," **http://www.census.gov/pub/epcd/www/naiscod.htm**, 6 March 1998.

exhibit 5.5

Major Characteristics of Business Markets Compared to Consumer Markets

Characteristic	Business Market	Consumer Market
Demand	Organizational	Individual
Purchase volume	Larger	Smaller
Number of customers	Fewer	Many
Location of buyers	Geographically concentrated	Dispersed
Distribution structure	More direct	More indirect
Nature of buying	More professional	More personal
Nature of buying influence	Multiple	Single
Type of negotiations	More complex	Simpler
Use of reciprocity	Yes	No
Use of leasing	Greater	Lesser
Primary promotional method	Personal selling	Advertising

Recent marketing campaigns highlight the convenience and recycling benefits of aluminum cans and products. By also mentioning the positive environmental impact of using aluminum, producers hope to influence consumer demand.

Some business marketers not only monitor final consumer demand and customer forecasts but also try to influence final consumer demand. Aluminum producers use television and magazine advertisements to point out the convenience and recycling opportunities that aluminum offers to consumers who can choose to purchase soft drinks in either aluminum or plastic containers.

Inelastic Demand The demand for many business products is inelastic with regard to price. *Inelastic demand* means that an increase or decrease in the price of the product will not significantly affect demand for the product.

The price of a product used in the production of or as part of a final product is often a minor portion of the final product's total price. Therefore, demand for the final consumer product is not affected. If the price of automobile paint or spark plugs rose significantly, say 200 percent in one year, do you think the number of new automobiles sold that year would be affected? Probably not.

Joint Demand **Joint demand** occurs when two or more items are used together in a final product. For example, a decline in the availability of memory chips will slow production of microcomputers, which will in turn reduce the demand for disk drives. Many business products, such as hammer heads and hammer handles, also exemplify joint demand.

joint demand
The demand for two or more items used together in a final product.

Fluctuating Demand The demand for business products—particularly new plants and equipment—tends to be more unstable than the demand for consumer products. A small increase or decrease in consumer demand can produce a much larger change in demand for the facilities and equipment needed to make the consumer product. Economists refer to this phenomenon as the **multiplier effect** (or **accelerator principle**).

multiplier effect (accelerator principle)
Phenomenon in which a small increase or decrease in consumer demand can produce a much larger change in demand for the facilities and equipment needed to make the consumer product.

Cummins Engine Company, a producer of heavy-duty diesel engines, uses sophisticated surface grinders to make parts. Suppose Cummins is using twenty surface grinders. Each machine lasts about ten years. Purchases have been timed so two machines will wear out and be replaced annually. If the demand for engine parts does not change, two grinders will be bought this year. If the demand for parts declines slightly, only eighteen grinders may be needed and Cummins won't replace the worn ones. However, suppose in the next year demand returns to previous levels plus a little more. To meet the new level of demand, Cummins will need to replace the two machines that wore out in the first year, the two that wore out in the second year, plus one or more additional machines. The multiplier effect works this way in many industries, producing highly fluctuating demand for business products.

Purchase Volume

Business customers buy in much larger quantities than consumers. Just think how large an order Kellogg typically places for the wheat bran and raisins used to manufacture Raisin Bran. Imagine the number of tires that Ford buys at one time.

Number of Customers

Business marketers usually have far fewer customers than consumer marketers. The advantage is that it is a lot easier to identify prospective buyers, monitor current customers' needs and levels of satisfaction, and personally attend to existing customers. The main disadvantage is that each customer becomes crucial—especially for those manufacturers that have only one customer. In many cases, this customer is the U.S. government.

Location of Buyers

Business customers tend to be much more geographically concentrated than consumers. For instance, more than half the nation's business buyers are located in New York, California, Pennsylvania, Illinois, Ohio, Michigan, and New Jersey. The aircraft and microelectronics industries are concentrated on the West Coast, and many of the firms that supply the automobile manufacturing industry are located in and around Detroit.

Distribution Structure

Many consumer products pass through a distribution system that includes the producer, one or more wholesalers, and a retailer. However, because of many of the characteristics already mentioned, channels of distribution are typically shorter in business marketing. Direct channels, where manufacturers market directly to users, are much more common.

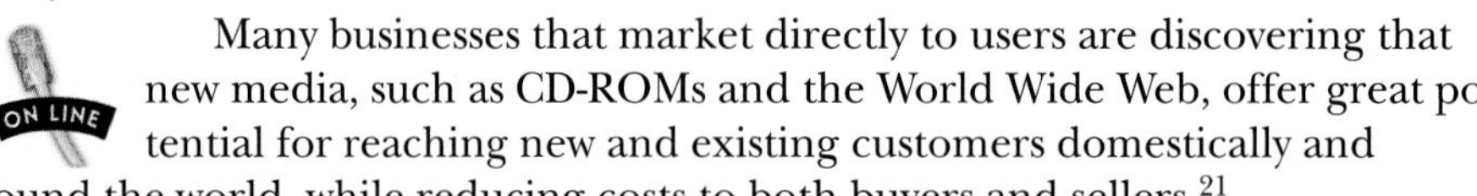

Many businesses that market directly to users are discovering that new media, such as CD-ROMs and the World Wide Web, offer great potential for reaching new and existing customers domestically and around the world, while reducing costs to both buyers and sellers.[21]

Nature of Buying

Unlike consumers, business buyers usually approach purchasing rather formally. Businesses use professionally trained purchasing agents or buyers who spend their entire career purchasing a limited number of items. They get to know the items and the sellers well. Some professional purchasers earn the designation of Certified Purchasing Manager (CPM) after participating in a rigorous certification program.

Nature of Buying Influence

Typically, more people are involved in a single business purchase decision than in a consumer purchase. Experts from fields as varied as quality control, marketing, and finance, as well as professional buyers and users, may be grouped in a buying center (discussed later in this chapter).

Type of Negotiations

Consumers are used to negotiating price on automobiles and real estate. In most cases, however, American consumers expect sellers to set the price and other conditions of sale, such as time of delivery and credit terms. In contrast, negotiating is common in business marketing. Buyers and sellers negotiate product specifications, delivery dates, payment terms, and other pricing matters. Sometimes these negotiations occur during many meetings over several months. Final contracts are often very long and detailed.

Use of Reciprocity

reciprocity
A practice where business purchasers choose to buy from their own customers.

Business purchasers often choose to buy from their own customers, a practice known as **reciprocity**. For example, General Motors buys engines for use in its automobiles and trucks from Borg Warner, which, in turn, buys many of the automobiles and trucks it needs from GM. This practice is neither unethical nor illegal unless one party coerces the other and the result is unfair competition. Reciprocity

Businesses commonly lease expensive equipment such as automobiles because it reduces capital outflow, allows them to acquire the latest models, gives them better services, and gains them tax advantages.

Say hello to Buick payments that are up to 30% lower than a bank loan.

Call 1-800-32-SMART.

BUICK RIVIERA

It's your call. But when you lease a new GM vehicle with SMARTLEASE® by GMAC, you can get monthly payments that are typically 30% lower than if you buy it with a bank auto loan. You can also afford more GM car or truck for the money. For more information about SMARTLEASE, see your GM dealer or call **1-800-32-SMART**. And say hello to lower monthly payments.

by GMAC

Chevrolet • Geo • Pontiac • Oldsmobile • Buick • Cadillac • GMC

http://www.gmacfs.com

is generally considered a reasonable business practice. If all possible suppliers sell a similar product for about the same price, doesn't it make sense to buy from those firms that buy from you?

Use of Leasing

Consumers normally buy products rather than lease them. But businesses commonly lease expensive equipment such as computers, construction equipment and vehicles, and automobiles. Leasing allows firms to reduce capital outflow, acquire a seller's latest products, receive better services, and gain tax advantages.

The lessor, the firm providing the product, may be either the manufacturer or an independent firm. The benefits to the lessor include greater total revenue from leasing compared to selling and an opportunity to do business with customers who cannot afford to buy.

Primary Promotional Method

Business marketers tend to emphasize personal selling in their promotion efforts, especially for expensive items, custom-designed products, large-volume purchases, and situations requiring negotiations. The sale of many business products requires a great deal of personal contact. Personal selling is discussed in more detail in Chapter 12.

Types of Business Products

7
Describe the seven types of business goods and services

Business products generally fall into one of the following seven categories, depending on their use: major equipment, accessory equipment, raw materials, component parts, processed materials, supplies, and business services.

Major Equipment

major equipment (installations)
Capital goods such as large or expensive machines, mainframe computers, blast furnaces, generators, airplanes, and buildings.

Major equipment includes such capital goods as large or expensive machines, mainframe computers, blast furnaces, generators, airplanes, and buildings. (These items are also commonly called **installations**.) Major equipment is depreciated over time rather than charged as an expense in the year it is purchased. In addition, major equipment is often custom-designed for each customer. Personal selling is an important part of the marketing strategy for major equipment because distribution channels are almost always direct from the producer to the business user.

Accessory Equipment

accessory equipment
Goods, such as portable tools and office equipment, that are less expensive and shorter-lived than major equipment.

Accessory equipment is generally less expensive and shorter-lived than major equipment. Examples include portable drills, power tools, microcomputers, and fax machines. Accessory equipment is often charged as an expense in the year it is bought rather than depreciated over its useful life. In contrast to major equipment, accessories are more often standardized and are usually bought by more customers. These customers tend to be widely dispersed. For example, all types of businesses buy microcomputers.

Local industrial distributors (wholesalers) play an important role in the marketing of accessory equipment because business buyers often purchase accessories

Senco Products, Inc.

What kind of business products does Senco make? Justify your decision. Is it only a business marketer? How do you know?

http://www.senco.com/

on line

from them. Regardless of where accessories are bought, advertising is a more vital promotional tool for accessory equipment than for major equipment.

Raw materials, such as logs, become part of finished products and are generally purchased in huge quantities.

Raw Materials

Raw materials are unprocessed extractive or agricultural products—for example, mineral ore, lumber, wheat, corn, fruits, vegetables, and fish. Raw materials become part of finished products. Extensive users, such as steel or lumber mills and food canners, generally buy huge quantities of raw materials. Because there is often a large number of relatively small sellers of raw materials, none can greatly influence price or supply. Thus, the market tends to set the price of raw materials, and individual producers have little pricing flexibility. Promotion is almost always via personal selling, and distribution channels are usually direct from producer to business user.

raw materials
Unprocessed extractive or agricultural products, such as mineral ore, lumber, wheat, corn, fruits, vegetables, and fish.

component parts
Either finished items ready for assembly or products that need very little processing before becoming part of some other product.

Component Parts

Component parts are either finished items ready for assembly or products that need very little processing before becoming part of some other product. Examples include spark plugs, tires, and electric motors for automobiles. A special feature of component parts is that they often retain their identity after becoming part of the final product. For example, automobile tires are clearly recognizable as part of a car. Moreover, because component parts often wear out, they may need to be replaced several times during the life of the final product. Thus, there are two important markets for many component parts: the original equipment manufacturer (OEM) market and the replacement market.

Many of the business features listed earlier in Exhibit 5.5 characterize the OEM market. The difference between unit costs and selling prices in the OEM market is often small, but profits can be substantial because of volume buying.

The replacement market is composed of organizations and individuals buying component parts to replace worn-out parts. Because components often retain their identity in final products, users may choose to replace a component part with the same brand used by the manufacturer—for example, the same brand of automobile tires or battery. The replacement market operates differently from the OEM market, however. Whether replacement buyers are organizations or individuals, they tend to demonstrate the characteristics of consumer markets that were shown in Exhibit 5.5. Consider, for example, an automobile replacement part. Purchase volume is usually small and there are many customers, geographically dispersed, who typically buy from car dealers or parts stores. Negotiations do not occur, and neither reciprocity nor leasing is usually an issue.

Manufacturers of component parts often direct their advertising toward replacement buyers. Cooper Tire & Rubber, for example, makes and markets component parts—automobile and truck tires—for the replacement market only. Ford and other car makers compete with independent firms in the market for replacement automobile parts.

Processed Materials

Processed materials are used directly in manufacturing other products. Unlike raw materials, they have had some processing. Examples include sheet metal, chemicals, specialty steel, lumber, corn syrup, and plastics. Unlike component parts, processed materials do not retain their identity in final products.

processed materials
Products used directly in manufacturing other products.

supplies
Consumable items that do not become part of the final product.

Most processed materials are marketed to OEMs or to distributors servicing the OEM market. Processed materials are generally bought according to customer specifications or to some industry standard, as is the case with steel and lumber. Price and service are important factors in choosing a vendor.

Supplies

Supplies are consumable items that do not become part of the final product—for example, lubricants, detergents, paper towels, pencils, and paper. Supplies are normally standardized items that purchasing agents routinely buy. Supplies typically have relatively short lives and are inexpensive compared to other business goods. Because supplies generally fall into one of three categories—maintenance, repair, or operating supplies—this category is often referred to as MRO items.

The digital age hasn't created a paperless society. Just a revolution in paper.

It's been suggested since the dawn of the computer age. A future in which everything worth knowing is accessible on screen.
But as it turns out, people don't just want information at their fingertips. They want it on their fingertips. They want to be able to touch, fold and dog-ear; to fax, copy and refer to; scribble in the margins or post proudly on the refrigerator door. And, above all, they want to print out – quickly, flawlessly and in vibrant color.
So today, as people require more (and more types of) paper than ever, our research centers are responding with new papers for home and business.
Printing papers such as our Hammermill® brand Jet Print Ultra® are one example. They enable anyone with an ink jet printer to print with the sort of brightness and smoothness you'd expect from fine magazines.
The introduction of a lightweight paper called Accolade® is another example. It results in superior printing quality for catalogs, magazines, brochures and the like, at less cost for paper and postage.
From printing paper to fine art paper to digital photography paper, we're committed to providing the "Paperless Society" with all the paper it needs.

INTERNATIONAL PAPER
We answer to the world.
www.ipaper.com

Supplies like staples, pens, and paper typically have short lives and are inexpensive. In light of—or perhaps because of—these qualities, competition in the MRO market is intense.
Courtesy International Paper

Competition in the MRO market is intense. Bic and PaperMate, for example, battle for business purchases of inexpensive ballpoint pens.

Business Services

Business services are expense items that do not become part of a final product. Businesses often retain outside providers to perform janitorial, advertising, legal, management consulting, marketing research, maintenance, and other services. Hiring an outside provider makes sense when it costs less than hiring or assigning an employee to perform the task and when an outside provider is needed for particular expertise.

business services
Expense items that do not become part of a final product.

Business Buying Behavior

As you probably have already concluded, business buyers behave differently from consumers. Understanding how purchase decisions are made in organizations is a first step in developing a business selling strategy. Five important aspects of business buying behavior are buying centers, evaluative criteria, buying situations, purchasing ethics, and customer service.

Discuss the unique aspects of business buying behavior

Buying Centers

A **buying center** includes all those persons in an organization who become involved in the purchase decision. Membership and influence vary from company to

buying center
All those persons who become involved in the purchase decision.

company. For instance, in engineering-dominated firms like Bell Helicopter, the buying center may consist almost entirely of engineers. In marketing-oriented firms like Toyota and IBM, marketing and engineering have almost equal authority. In consumer goods firms like Procter & Gamble, product managers and other marketing decision makers may dominate the buying center. In a small manufacturing company, almost everyone may be a member.

The number of people involved in a buying center varies with the complexity and importance of a purchase decision. The composition of the buying group will usually change from one purchase to another and sometimes even during various stages of the buying process. To make matters more complicated, buying centers do not appear on formal organization charts. Noting the change in buying center membership over time, an IBM executive remarked, "I started out (in the 1980s) selling to the corner office [CEO], then we got moved to the CFO, and then to the data processing manager, and finally to the data center manager."[22]

For example, even though a formal committee may have been set up to choose a new plant site, it is only part of the buying center. Other people, like the company president, often play informal yet powerful roles. In a lengthy decision-making process, such as finding a new plant location, some members may drop out of the buying center when they can no longer play a useful role. Others whose talents are needed then become part of the center. No formal announcement of "who is in" and "who is out" is ever made.

Roles in the Buying Center As in family purchasing decisions, several people may play a role in the business purchase process:

- *Initiator:* the person who first suggests making a purchase.
- *Influencers/evaluators:* people who influence the buying decision. They often help define specifications and provide information for evaluating options. Technical personnel are especially important as influencers.
- *Gatekeepers:* group members who regulate the flow of information. Frequently, the purchasing agent views the gatekeeping role as a source of his or her power. A secretary may also act as a gatekeeper by determining which vendors get an appointment with a buyer.
- *Decider:* the person who has the formal or informal power to choose or approve the selection of the supplier or brand. In complex situations, it is often difficult to determine who makes the final decision.
- *Purchaser:* the person who actually negotiates the purchase. It could be anyone from the president of the company to the purchasing agent, depending on the importance of the decision.
- *Users:* members of the organization who will actually use the product. Users often initiate the buying process and help define product specifications.

An example illustrating these basic roles is shown in Exhibit 5.6.

Implications of Buying Centers for the Marketing Manager Successful vendors realize the importance of identifying who is in the decision-making unit, each member's relative influence in the buying decision, and each member's evaluative criteria. Successful selling strategies often focus on determining the most important buying influences and tailoring sales presentations to the evaluative criteria most important to these buying-center members.

For example, Loctite Corporation, the manufacturer of Super Glue and industrial adhesives and sealants, found that engineers were the most important influencers and deciders in adhesive and sealant purchase decisions. As a result, Loctite focused its marketing efforts on production and maintenance engineers.

Evaluative Criteria

Business buyers evaluate products and suppliers against three important criteria: quality, service, and price—in that order.

Buying Center

exhibit 5.6

Buying Center Roles for Computer Purchases

Role	Illustration
Initiator	Division general manager proposes to replace company's computer network.
Influencers/evaluators	Corporate controller's office and vice president of data processing have an important say about which system and vendor the company will deal with.
Gatekeepers	Corporate departments for purchasing and data processing analyze company's needs and recommend likely matches with potential vendors.
Decider	Vice president of administration, with advice from others, selects vendor the company will deal with and system it will buy.
Purchaser	Purchasing agent negotiates terms of sale.
Users	All division employees use the computers.

VALUE

- *Quality:* In this case, quality refers to technical suitability. A superior tool can do a better job in the production process, and superior packaging can increase dealer and consumer acceptance of a brand. Evaluation of quality also applies to the salesperson and the salesperson's firm. Business buyers want to deal with reputable salespeople and companies that are financially responsible. Quality improvement should be part of every organization's marketing strategy.
- *Service:* Almost as much as they want satisfactory products, business buyers want satisfactory service. A purchase offers several opportunities for service. Suppose a vendor is selling heavy equipment. Prepurchase service could include a survey of the buyer's needs. After thorough analysis of the survey findings, the vendor could prepare a report and recommendations in the form of a purchasing proposal. If a purchase results, postpurchase service might consist of installing the equipment and training those who will be using it. Postsale services may also include maintenance and repairs. Another service that business buyers seek is dependability of supply. They must be able to count on delivery of what was ordered when it is scheduled to be delivered. Buyers also welcome services that help them sell their finished products. Services of this sort are especially appropriate when the seller's product is an identifiable part of the buyer's end product.
- *Price:* Business buyers want to buy at low prices—at the lowest prices, under most circumstances. However, a buyer who pressures a supplier to cut prices to a point where the supplier loses money on the sale almost forces shortcuts on quality. The buyer also may, in effect, force the supplier to quit selling to him or her. Then a new source of supply will have to be found.

Businesses require satisfactory postsales service. This may mean installing the equipment or training employees in its use.
© Bob Daemmrich/The Image Works

Loctite Corporation

What evidence do you see on Loctite's Web site that its marketing efforts focus on engineers? Read some of their on-line literature.
http://www.loctite.com/

on line

GLOBAL

Many international business buyers use similar evaluative criteria. One study of South African buyers of high-tech laboratory instruments found that they use the following evaluative criteria, in descending order: technical service, perceived product reliability, after-sales support, supplier's reputation, ease of maintenance, ease of operation, price, confidence in the sales representative, and product flexibility.[23]

Buying Situations

Often business firms, especially manufacturers, must decide whether to make something or buy it from an outside supplier. The decision is essentially one of economics. Can an item of similar quality be bought at a lower price elsewhere? If not, is manufacturing it in-house the best use of limited company resources? For example, Briggs & Stratton Corp., a major manufacturer of four-cycle engines, might be able to save $150,000 annually on outside purchases by spending $500,000 on the equipment needed to produce gas throttles internally. Yet Briggs & Stratton could also use that $500,000 to upgrade its carburetor assembly line, which would save $225,000 annually. If a firm does decide to buy a product instead of making it, the purchase will be a new buy, a modified rebuy, or a straight rebuy.

new buy
A situation requiring the purchase of a product for the first time.

New Buy A **new buy** is a situation requiring the purchase of a product for the first time. For example, suppose a law firm decides to replace word-processing machinery with microcomputers. This situation represents the greatest opportunity for new vendors. No long-term relationship has been established for this product, specifications may be somewhat fluid, and buyers are generally more open to new vendors.

If the new item is a raw material or a critical component part, the buyer cannot afford to run out of supply. The seller must be able to convince the buyer that the seller's firm can consistently deliver a high-quality product on time.

modified rebuy
Situation where the purchaser wants some change in the original good or service.

Modified Rebuy A **modified rebuy** is normally less critical and less time-consuming than a new buy. In a modified-rebuy situation, the purchaser wants some change in the original good or service. It may be a new color, greater tensile strength in a component part, more respondents in a marketing research study, or additional services in a janitorial contract.

Because the two parties are familiar with each other and credibility has been established, buyer and seller can concentrate on the specifics of the modification. But in some cases, modified rebuys are open to outside bidders. The purchaser uses this strategy to ensure that the new terms are competitive. An example would be a law firm deciding to buy more powerful microcomputers. The firm may open the bidding to examine the price/quality offerings of several suppliers.

straight rebuy
Buying situation in which the purchaser reorders the same goods or services without looking for new information or investigating other suppliers.

Straight Rebuy A **straight rebuy** is a situation vendors prefer. The purchaser is not looking for new information or other suppliers. An order is placed and the product is provided as in previous orders. Usually a straight rebuy is routine because the terms of the purchase have been agreed to in earlier negotiations. An example would be the law firm previously cited purchasing printer cartridges from the same supplier on a regular basis.

One common instrument used in straight-rebuy situations is the purchasing contract. Purchasing contracts are used with products that are bought often and in high volume. In essence, the purchasing contract makes the buyer's

ethics in marketing

Gifts from Suppliers: Ford Motor Company's Policy

What policies do firms set on accepting gifts from suppliers? Here's the policy at Ford. Although soliciting gifts and favors is never permissible, if there is a legitimate business purpose, it is permissable to accept gifts and favors that are freely offered by suppliers, dealers, and others with whom Ford does business, subject to these important limitations:

- The gift must be of nominal value and must involve no more than normal sales promotion or publicity.
- Social amenities must be appropriate and limited and must never give the appearance of impropriety.
- Any discounts on goods or services offered to you by a supplier must be made generally available and cannot be for your benefit only.
- You may never accept cash or gift certificates or gifts of food or alcohol.
- You may not borrow money, except from qualified financial institutions on generally available terms.

SOURCE: From Ford Motor Company's "Standards of Corporate Conduct," 1996, p. 6. Reprinted by permission.

decision making routine and promises the salesperson a sure sale. The advantage to the buyer is a quick, confident decision and, to the salesperson, reduced or eliminated competition.

Suppliers must remember not to take straight-rebuy relationships for granted. Retaining existing customers is much easier than attracting new ones.

Purchasing Ethics

The ethics of business buyer and seller relationships are often scrutinized and sometimes criticized by superiors, associates, other prospective suppliers, the general public, and the news media. Ford Motor Company, mindful of the key problems often faced by professional buyers, developed the guidelines shown in the "Ethics in Marketing" box.

Customer Service

VALUE

Business marketers are increasingly recognizing the benefits of developing a formal system to monitor customer opinions and perceptions of the quality of customer service. Companies like McDonald's, L.L. Bean, and Lexus build their strategies not only around products but also around a few highly developed service skills. Many firms are finding new ways to enhance customer service through technology. Business marketers are leading the way in adoption of new media technologies such as online services, CD-ROMs, and the World Wide Web.[24] Federal Express Corp., for example, began a service on the Web in November 1994 that gave customers a direct window into FedEx's package-tracking database. FedEx is now saving about $2 million per year and improving customer service by replacing humans with a Web site.[25]

L.L.Bean
For a wide variety of gear and clothing that looks good, feels great, and is always 100% guaranteed, there's only one place to turn. The new L.L. Bean Fall catalog.
Call for your FREE Fall catalog. 1-800-987-2326.
Or shop on-line at www.llbean.com

L.L. Bean has always been a leader in customer service with a complete satisfaction guarantee. New media technologies, such as on-line shopping, have only enhanced its ability to service its customers. Visit http://www.llbean.com to see how.
Courtesy L.L. Bean

on line

Federal Express

How has FedEx developed a Web site to address the service needs of its business customers? Check out the eBusiness Tools on its site.
http://www.fedex.com/

LOOKING BACK

Look back at the story about the Star Alliance of airlines at the beginning of this chapter. You now know that a strategic alliance is a cooperative agreement between business firms. General benefits to members identified in the chapter include access to markets or to technology, economies of scale, faster entry of new products to markets, and reduced risk. Specific benefits in the case include world-class opportunities for employees, better customer recognition worldwide, a framework for future development, and synergies such as common use of facilities and joint purchasing. Customers benefit from integrated frequent flyer programs, access to more flights and destinations, simplified ticketing and reservations, more convenient connections, and better baggage and ground services.

If the alliance is able to deliver the benefits to customers it claims it can, competition will definitely be threatened. Competitors will likely form alliances to maintain and enhance their market share. Other alliances such as the American Airlines–British Airways alliance are beginning to emerge.

Summary

1 Describe business marketing. Business marketing provides goods and services that are bought for use in business rather than for personal consumption. Intended use, not physical characteristics, distinguishes a business product from a consumer product.

2 Describe the role of the Internet in business marketing. The emergence of the Internet has made business markets more competitive than ever before. The number of business buyers and sellers using the Internet is rapidly increasing. Firms are seeking new and better ways to expand markets and sources of supply, increase sales and decrease costs, and better serve customers. With the Internet, every business in the world is potentially a local competitor.

3 Discuss the role of relationship marketing and strategic alliances in business marketing. Relationship marketing entails seeking and establishing long-term alliances or partnerships with customers. A strategic alliance is a cooperative agreement between business firms. Firms form alliances to leverage what they do well by partnering with others who have complementary skills.

4 Identify the four major categories of business market customers. Producer markets consist of for-profit organizations and individuals that buy products to use in producing other products, as components of other products, or in facilitating business operations. Reseller markets consist of wholesalers and retailers that buy finished products to resell for profit. Government markets include federal, state, county, and city governments that buy goods and services to support their own operations and serve the needs of citizens. Institutional markets consist of very diverse nonbusiness institutions whose main goals do not include profit.

5 Explain the North American Industry Classification System. The NAICS provides a way to identify, analyze, segment, and target business and government markets. Organizations can be identified and compared by a numeric code indicating business sector, subsector, industry group, industry, and country industry. NAICS is a valuable tool for analyzing, segmenting, and targeting business markets.

6 Explain the major differences between business and consumer markets. In business markets, demand is derived, price-inelastic, joint, and fluctuating. Purchase volume is much larger than in consumer markets, customers are fewer in number and more geographically concentrated, and distribution channels are more direct. Buying is approached more formally using professional purchasing agents, more people are involved in the buying process, negotiation is more complex, and reciprocity and leasing are more common. And, finally, selling strategy in business markets normally focuses on personal contact rather than on advertising.

7 Describe the seven types of business goods and services. Major equipment includes capital goods, such as heavy machinery. Accessory equipment is typically less expensive and shorter-lived than major equipment. Raw materials are extractive or agricultural products that have not been processed. Component parts are finished or near-finished items to be used as parts of other products. Processed materials are used to manufacture other products. Supplies are consumable and not used as part of a final product. Business services are intangible products that many companies use in their operations.

8 Discuss the unique aspects of business buying behavior. Business buying behavior is distinguished by five fundamental characteristics. First, buying is normally undertaken by a buying center consisting of many people who range widely in authority level. Second, business buyers typically evaluate alternative products and suppliers based on quality, service, and price—in that order. Third, business buying falls into three general categories: new buys, modified rebuys, and straight rebuys. Fourth, the ethics of business buyers and sellers are often scrutinized. Fifth, customer service before, during, and after the sale plays a big role in business purchase decisions.

Discussion and Writing Questions

1. How might derived demand affect the manufacturing of an automobile?
2. Why is relationship or personal selling the best way to promote in business marketing?
3. A colleague of yours has sent you an e-mail seeking your advice as he attempts to sell a new voice-mail system to a local business. Send him a return e-mail describing the various people who might influence the customer's buying decision. Be sure to include suggestions for dealing with the needs of each of these individuals.
4. Intel Corporation supplies microprocessors to Compaq for use in their computers. Describe the buying situation in this relationship, keeping in mind the rapid advancement of technology in this industry.
5. In small groups, brainstorm examples of companies that feature the products in the different business categories. (Avoid examples already listed in the chapter.) Compile a list of ten specific business products including at least one in each category. Then match up with another group. Have each group take turns naming a product and have the other group identify its appropriate category. Try to resolve all discrepancies by discussion. Some identified products might appropriately fit into more than one category.
6. 

The First American Group Purchasing Association (**http://www.first.gpa.com**) publishes a monthly list of the top ten Web sites it considers most useful to small businesses. Visit one or more of these sites and then write a memo to a colleague who is considering starting a new business. Describe why he or she should visit this Web site.
7. What business publications, search facilities, sources, and services does the following Web site offer? **http://www.demographics.com/**
8. How could you use the following site to help plan a business trip to Toronto? Name three articles featured in the latest issue of *Business To Business Magazine.* **http://www.business2business.on.ca/**

Key Terms

accessory equipment 165
business marketing 154
business services 167
buying center 167
component parts 166
derived demand 160
joint demand 163
major equipment (installations) 165
modified rebuy 170
multiplier effect (accelerator principle) 163
new buy 170
North American Industry Classification System (NAICS) 160
processed materials 167
raw materials 166
reciprocity 164
straight rebuy 170
strategic alliance (strategic partnership) 156
supplies 167

Application for Small Business

ENTREPRENEUR

Dan White is an independent video producer whose biggest client is the State of Illinois Agricultural Department. Although this account is big enough to support the entire business, Dan has developed other lines of business to eliminate the risks involved with having only one customer. Dan has also landed a sizable account through a high school friend who is the vice president of Good Hands Insurance. This also happens to be the company that underwrites Dan's life insurance. Additionally, Dan is hired to work on various projects for large production companies. Dan generated this business through long-term relationships built by working on projects for the State of Illinois.

As Dan prepares his business plan for the upcoming year, he is contemplating several strategic changes. Because of the increasing speed at which the video industry is evolving, Dan has observed two important trends. First, he is finding it increasingly difficult to own the latest video equipment that his customers are demanding. Second, Dan's clients are not able to keep up with the recent developments in the industry and would be willing to pay more for his expertise. Dan is looking into a lease for new equipment and he is contemplating an increase in price.

Questions

1. What two-digit NAICS code would you assign to Dan's business?
2. Is Dan's choice to use Good Hands Insurance ethical? Why or why not?
3. How can Dan use the inelasticity of demand to his advantage?
4. Would you advise Dan to lease or buy the new equipment? Why?

Review Quiz

1. Business products are those that
   a. Are used to manufacture other products
   b. Become part of another product
   c. Aid the normal operations of an organization
   d. Are all of the above

2. The Internet has
   a. Made business markets less competitive
   b. Made business markets more competitive
   c. Had little impact on the level of competitiveness in business markets
   d. Not significantly impacted the business marketplace

3. _______ marketing is the strategy that entails seeking and establishing ongoing partnerships with customers.
   a. Relationship
   b. Business
   c. Consumer
   d. Administered

4. The four major categories or segments of the business market are
   a. Schools, hospitals, factories, and warehouses
   b. Producers, consumers, retailers, and wholesalers
   c. Producers, resellers, governments, and institutions
   d. Institutions, agriculture, retailers, and wholesalers

5. What is NAICS?
   a. A system for classifying business establishments
   b. A free-trade agreement

c. A set of safety standards for business products
d. An organization of business marketers

6. If you market goods to producers, you must also research sales trends in related consumer markets because demand for your products is
   a. Relational
   b. Elastic
   c. Derived
   d. Institutional
7. The multiplier effect
   a. Is also known as the deceleration principle
   b. Indicates that a small increase or decrease in consumer demand can produce a much larger change in demand for the facilities that make the consumer product
   c. Requires that a large increase in consumer demand can produce a smaller change in demand for the facilities that make the consumer product
   d. Argues that demand for a consumer product is derived from demand for business goods
8. Which element of promotion is used most frequently with business products like major equipment, accessory equipment, or component parts?
   a. Personal selling
   b. Sales promotion
   c. Public relations
   d. Advertising
9. In a buying center, the gatekeeper
   a. First suggests making a purchase
   b. Influences the buying decision
   c. Regulates the flow of information
   d. Has the power to approve the selection of brand
10. In which criteria order do business buyers evaluate products?
    a. Quality, service, price
    b. Price, service, quality
    c. Service, price, quality
    d. Price, quality, service
11. In a straight rebuy situation, the purchaser typically wants at least some change in the original good or service to be purchased.
    a. True
    b. False
12. Identify the three types of buying situations that business marketers face.

Check the Answer Key, which follows the Video Case, to see how well you understood the material.

VIDEO CASE

Burke, Inc.: Business-to-Business Alliances

As one of the premier international business research and consulting firms in the world, Burke, Inc., provides services to other businesses to help them grow and remain competitive in the marketplace. The successful Cincinnati-based firm has offices and affiliates throughout the United States plus an international division, headquartered in London, which operates in eleven European countries and Japan. To offer solutions to businesses, Burke has four divisions: Burke Marketing Research, Burke Customer Satisfaction Associates, Burke Strategic

Consulting Group, and The Training and Development Center.

Burke, Inc., owes its success to the number and quality of its business relationships. Today's business environment is so complex that companies can no longer operate independently to fulfill their needs, and strategic alliances offer viable solutions. Burke brings more than 65 years of industry experience to each business alliance and has joined with companies in a wide variety of industries—agriculture, communications, financial services, entertainment, publishing, travel, insurance, communications, and health care.

According to Burke's business philosophy, a strategic alliance is particularly strong when both partners bring expertise and different skills to the table. These complementary assets might include access to markets or to technology, economies of scale gained by combining research and development or marketing activities, and sharing of risk. Recently, Burke teamed up with a publisher to produce a national consumer guide to non-prescription drugs. The publisher and author lacked the experience and sophisticated tools needed to gather immediate and accurate information from pharmacists, so they asked Burke Marketing Research to join them. Together, the writer, publisher, and researchers produced a very thorough national consumer's guide. Burke was able to provide the timely information that its partner needed to gain a competitive advantage. Strategic alliances can be particularly beneficial when companies face stiff competition in the marketplace.

Yet, Burke does not take a "cookie cutter" approach that gives different partners solutions cut from the same mold. Rather, working in teams, researchers customize methods for a specific industry and product or service category. Burke's strong belief in teamwork and specialized service influences every alliance and ultimately strengthens its relationships with its partners. Everyone at Burke understands that business clients operate in different marketing environments and have different business objectives, so each business client works with an account team to see that objectives are met efficiently, economically, and on time. The team analyzes each client's business needs and focuses Burke's broad resources on specific requirements.

Recently, the Burke Strategic Consulting Group formed a partnership with Armstrong Laing, a computer software company, to provide consulting support for businesses that purchase Armstrong Laing's management software. Burke will use the software to assist clients in understanding their true costs and in pinpointing the link between long-term strategies and day-to-day decisions. "This partnership allows us to provide innovative solutions to clients who want better financial results through cost management programs," said Diane Salamon, vice president of Burke, Inc. At the same time, Armstrong Laing describes the partnership as a marriage of management expertise and cutting-edge software that will help customers attain leadership positions in their industries. Teaming up with an outside provider of business services made sense for Armstrong Laing because the company did not have management consulting expertise in-house. And like most business-to-business marketers, Armstrong Laing was selling its products in very large quantities to established organizations like American Express and Blue Cross/Blue Shield and wanted to offer its clients a comprehensive approach of the highest quality.

Still another element of Burke's alliances is relationship marketing; that is, seeking and establishing *ongoing* partnerships. For example, one client was a multinational restaurant company that wished to define its strengths and determine the effect of a change in advertising. To provide this information, Burke built a model to show how market share might be affected by different advertising and made predictions based on this model. But the relationship did not end there. Burke continued to set clear priorities for future communication and operating strategies. This long-term relationship allowed the restaurant company to get maximum ROI (return on image) for its advertising dollars. Long-term relationships like this build trust among partners, especially when they share a common interest in meeting customer needs. In Burke's opinion, far greater customer satisfaction can be achieved through a strategic business alliance.

Questions

1. Why is Burke, Inc. considered a business marketer?
2. Review Exhibit 5.2. Does Burke follow the tips for making strategic alliances successful?
3. How did Burke's strategic business alliance with Armstrong Laing create a competitive advantage in the marketplace?
4. How does Burke use the principles of relationship marketing?

Bibliography

Burke Marketing Research Press Kit

Press Releases: *Burke Marketing Research Conducts Survey For National Consumer Guide; Burke Strategic Consulting Group, Armstrong Laing Form Partnership*

Burke, Inc., Web site is **http://www.burke.com**

Answer Key

1. *Answer:* d, p. 154

   Rationale: The key characteristic distinguishing business products from consumer products is intended use, not any physical characteristics.

2. *Answer:* b, p. 155

   Rationale: The emergence of the Internet has made business markets more competitive than ever because now every business in the world has the potential to become a local competitor.

3. *Answer:* a, p. 155

   Rationale: Relationship is a key term in marketing today. Marketers are learning that the best source of new business is from an existing relationship with a satisfied customer.

4. *Answer:* c, p. 158

   Rationale: Although these are the "major" categories of the business market, there are many different types of buyers under each category. For example, the reseller market includes all forms of distributors, wholesalers, and retailers who resell products for a profit.

5. *Answer:* a, p. 160

   Rationale: The North American Industry Classification System (NAICS) is a business establishment classification system introduced in 1997 to replace the standard industrial classification system (SIC).

6. *Answer:* c, p. 160

   Rationale: The demand for business products is called derived demand because organizations buy products to be used in producing products for consumers. Because demand is derived, business marketers must carefully monitor demand patterns and changing preferences in final consumer markets, even though their direct customers are not in those markets.

7. *Answer:* b, p. 163

   Rationale: Because the demand for business products is less stable than the demand for consumer goods, a small increase in consumer demand can produce a much larger increase in demand for facilities and equipment needed to make the consumer product. A small decrease in consumer demand may also lead to a large decline in demand for facilities and equipment.

8. *Answer:* a, pp. 165

   Rationale: Personal selling is often relied on to promote these products, in part, because they are often sold directly to the buyer from the producer without using any intermediaries in the distribution channel.

9. *Answer:* c, p. 168

   Rationale: Gatekeepers are often secretaries or administrative assistants to purchasing agents who control access to the buyer and information to and from that person.

10. *Answer:* a, p. 168

    Rationale: Although business buyers will shop for price and service, quality is usually the most important attribute they use in selection of a supplier.

11. *Answer:* b, p. 170

    Rationale: In a straight rebuy situation, an order is placed and the product is provided in the same way as it was in previous orders. This question describes a modified rebuy situation.

12. *Answer:* New buy, modified rebuy, straight rebuy. (p. 170)

CHAPTER 6

LEARNING OBJECTIVES

After studying this chapter, you should be able to

1 Describe the characteristics of markets and market segments

2 Explain the importance of market segmentation

3 Discuss criteria for successful market segmentation

4 Describe the bases commonly used to segment consumer markets

5 Describe the bases for segmenting business markets

6 List the steps involved in segmenting markets

7 Discuss alternative strategies for selecting target markets

8 Explain how and why firms implement positioning strategies and how product differentiation plays a role

9 Discuss global market segmentation and targeting issues

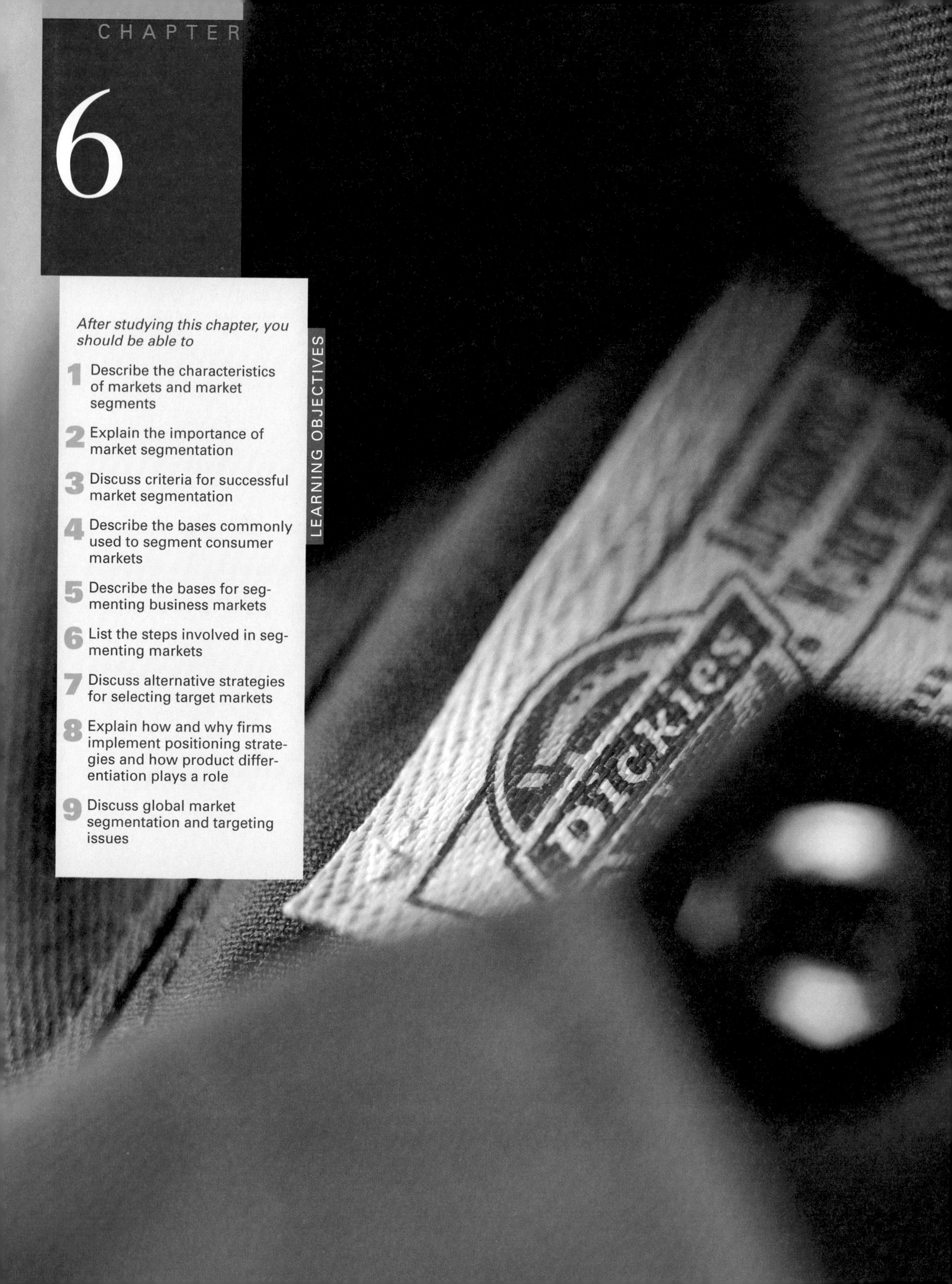

SEGMENTING AND TARGETING MARKETS

A few years ago, executives at work-apparel maker Williamson-Dickey noticed that its twill pants were becoming hugely popular with West Coast teens and young adults who are traditionally attracted to designer brands. They were buying Dickies clothes for everyday wear and buying items in slightly larger sizes to achieve a baggy look.

Company management, dubbing it an "antifashion fashion," did nothing about this trend; they predicted it was a fad that would be gone in a year. Instead, the trend expanded nationwide and onto the streets of Europe.

At the same time of the grassroots fashion movement, Dickies was in the midst of rolling out a new line of women's work wear, which was a significant departure and undertaking for a company that had been making men's work wear for more than seventy-five years. Through marketing research, the company learned that about one million women were buying and wearing its men's work pants. The company took three years to develop and test the women's work wear and it was not about to abandon these efforts. The women's line has earned the Good Housekeeping Seal, recognized as a mark of consumer product excellence.

A marketing team was called in to address the two markets. To reach the new customers, Dickies has shifted from advertising only in men's trade journals. Dickies uses *Parade*, which reaches more households than any medium except television, as its primary national advertising vehicle. Since it began using *Parade* to create brand awareness, the marketing director says sales have increased. Dickies has added magazines such as *Spin* and *Transworld Skateboarding* to reach the youth market and *Good Housekeeping* and *First for Women* to reach the female market.

Dickies is also getting back into boys' wear, a line it abandoned in the early 1980s because sales were sluggish. The new line will include twill pants, jeans, shorts, and oxford cloth and polo shirts. The line is being marketed as a choice in the growing public school uniform market, an estimated $11 billion segment. It is being advertised in trade publications such as *Principal, School Administrator,* and *School Uniforms.* The company has also started a Uniform Curriculum Program as an incentive

on line

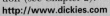

Dickies

How has Dickies' segmentation and targeting strategy influenced its Internet site? Are the Web pages for its diverse lines very differentiated? Does this shift in targeting strategy seem to represent a new business definition (see Chapter 2)?

http://www.dickies.com

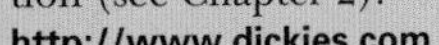

to get its clothing on children. Schools earn points redeemable for such things as computers, playground equipment, and school supplies when parents turn in Dickies labels.[1]

Based on this story, how would you define market segmentation and targeting? What type of targeting strategy is Dickies using? Do you think the company will be successful in its new efforts?

Market Segmentation

1
Describe the characteristics of markets and market segments

market
People or organizations with needs or wants and the ability and willingness to buy.

market segment
A subgroup of people or organizations sharing one or more characteristics that cause them to have similar product needs.

market segmentation
The process of dividing a market into meaningful, relatively similar, and identifiable segments or groups.

The term market means different things to different people. We are all familiar with terms like supermarket, stock market, labor market, fish market, and flea market. All these types of markets share several characteristics. First, they are composed of people (consumer markets) or organizations (business markets). Second, these people or organizations have wants and needs that can be satisfied by particular product categories. Third, they have the ability to buy the products they seek. Fourth, they are willing to exchange their resources, usually money or credit, for desired products. In sum, a **market** is (1) people or organizations with (2) needs or wants and with (3) the ability and (4) the willingness to buy. A group of people or an organization that lacks any one of these characteristics is not a market.

Within a market, a **market segment** is a subgroup of people or organizations sharing one or more characteristics that cause them to have similar product needs. At one extreme, we can define every person and every organization in the world as a market segment because each is unique. At the other extreme, we can define the entire consumer market as one large market segment and the business market as another large segment. All people have some similar characteristics and needs, as do all organizations.

From a marketing perspective, market segments can be described as somewhere between the two extremes. The process of dividing a market into meaningful, relatively similar, and identifiable segments or groups is called **market segmentation**. The purpose of market segmentation is to enable the marketer to tailor marketing mixes to meet the needs of one or more specific segments.

Exhibit 6.1 illustrates the concept of market segmentation. Each box represents a market consisting of seven persons. This market might vary as follows: one homogeneous market of seven people, a market consisting of seven individual segments, a market composed of two segments based on gender, a market composed of three age segments, or a market composed of five age and gender market segments. Age and gender and many other bases for segmenting markets are examined later in this chapter.

The Importance of Market Segmentation

2
Explain the importance of market segmentation

Until the 1960s, few firms practiced market segmentation. When they did, it was more likely a haphazard effort than a formal marketing strategy. Before 1960, for example, the Coca-Cola Company produced only one beverage and aimed it at the entire soft-drink market. Today, Coca-Cola offers over a dozen different products to market segments based on diverse consumer preferences for flavors and calorie and caffeine content. Coca-Cola offers traditional soft drinks, energy drinks (such as Power Ade), flavored teas, and fruit drinks (Fruitopia).

exhibit 6.1

Concept of Market Segmentation

No market segmentation

Fully segmented market

Market segmentation by gender: M,F

Market segmentation by age group: 1,2,3

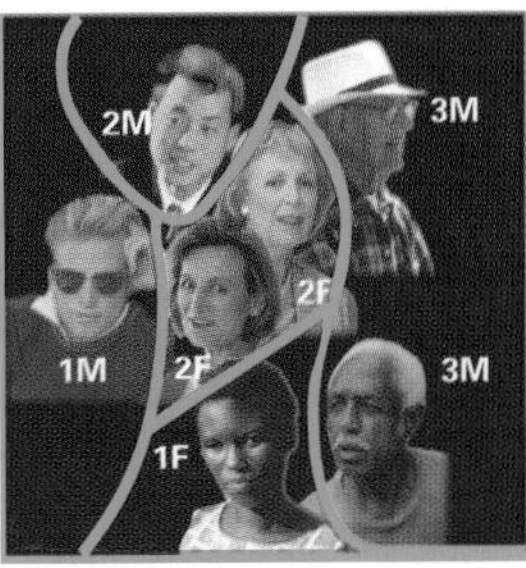

Market segmentation by gender and age group

Market segmentation plays a key role in the marketing strategy of almost all successful organizations and is a powerful marketing tool for several reasons. Most importantly, nearly all markets include groups of people or organizations with different product needs and preferences. Market segmentation helps marketers define customer needs and wants more precisely. Because market segments differ in size and potential, segmentation helps decision makers more accurately define marketing objectives and better allocate resources. In turn, performance can be better evaluated when objectives are more precise.

ENTREPRENEUR

The high-fashion furniture chain Domain offers an interesting example of how market segmentation can boost sales. Domain learned that its baby boomer clientele was as concerned about self-improvement as it was about decorating. To reach this segment, the store offered a series of in-store seminars that addressed topics such as women's issues and interior design. Repeat business of this group has increased 35 percent since the programs began. Another target segment was retired World War II and postwar clients, for whom the store offered narrower sofas with more back support that makes getting out of them easier. This segmentation approach allowed Domain to replace newspaper advertising with direct mail, bringing ad spending down 3 percent. Sales increased nearly 40 percent, to over $40 million.[2]

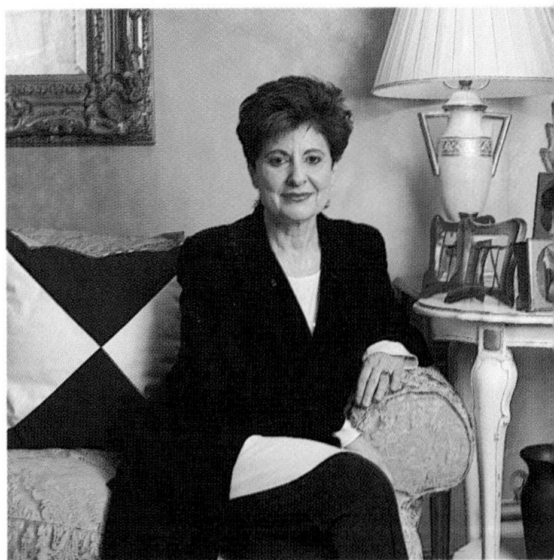

Judy George, owner of the Domain furniture chain, uses a segmentation approach to target baby boomers and retirees as purchasers of its high-fashion furniture.
© Steven L. Lewis

Criteria for Successful Segmentation

3

Discuss criteria for successful market segmentation

Marketers segment markets for three important reasons. First, segmentation enables marketers to identify groups of customers with similar needs and to analyze the characteristics and buying behavior of these groups. Second, segmentation provides marketers with information to help them design marketing mixes specifically matched with the characteristics and desires of one or more segments. Third, segmentation is consistent with the marketing concept of satisfying customer wants and needs while meeting the organization's objectives.

To be useful, a segmentation scheme must produce segments that meet four basic criteria:

- *Substantiality:* A segment must be large enough to warrant developing and maintaining a special marketing mix. This criterion does not necessarily mean that a segment must have many potential customers. Marketers of custom-designed homes and business buildings, commercial airplanes, and large computer systems typically develop marketing programs tailored to each potential customer's needs. In most cases, however, a market segment needs many potential customers to make commercial sense. IBM and fifteen of the largest U.S. banks started a company called Integrion Financial Network to offer a number of on-line banking services to its customers. However, only 1 percent of all banking transactions are conducted on-line, making this segment risky in terms of substantiality.[3] Undoubtedly, Integrion hopes that this segment will grow in the future.
- *Identifiability and measurability:* Segments must be identifiable and their size measurable. Data about the population within geographic boundaries, the number of people in various age categories, and other social and demographic characteristics are often easy to get, and they provide fairly concrete measures of segment size. Suppose that a social service agency wants to identify segments by their readiness to participate in a drug and alcohol program or in prenatal care. Unless the agency can measure how many people are willing, indifferent, or unwilling to participate, it will have trouble gauging whether there are enough people to justify setting up the service.
- *Accessibility:* The firm must be able to reach members of targeted segments with customized marketing mixes. Some market segments are hard to reach—for example, senior citizens (especially those with reading or hearing disabilities), individuals who don't speak English, and the illiterate.
- *Responsiveness:* As Exhibit 6.1 illustrates, markets can be segmented using any criteria that seem logical. However, unless one market segment responds to a marketing mix differently from other segments, that segment need not be treated separately. For instance, if all customers are equally price-conscious about a product, there is no need to offer high-, medium-, and low-priced versions to different segments.

Bases for Segmenting Consumer Markets

4
Describe the bases commonly used to segment consumer markets

segmentation bases (variables)
Characteristics of individuals, groups, or organizations.

Marketers use **segmentation bases,** or **variables,** which are characteristics of individuals, groups, or organizations, to divide a total market into segments. The choice of segmentation bases is crucial because an inappropriate segmentation strategy may lead to lost sales and missed profit opportunities. The key is to identify bases that will produce substantial, measurable, and accessible segments that exhibit different response patterns to marketing mixes.

Markets can be segmented using a single variable, such as age group, or several variables, such as age group, gender, and education. Although it is less precise, single-variable segmentation has the advantage of being simpler and easier to use than multiple-variable segmentation. The disadvantages of multiple-variable segmentation are that it is often harder to use than single-variable segmentation; usable secondary data are less likely to be available; and as the

Too Faced Cosmetics

Go to the Press Room at the Too Faced Web site. What age segment do you think this new cosmetic company is targeting? Defend your answer.
http://www.toofaced. com/

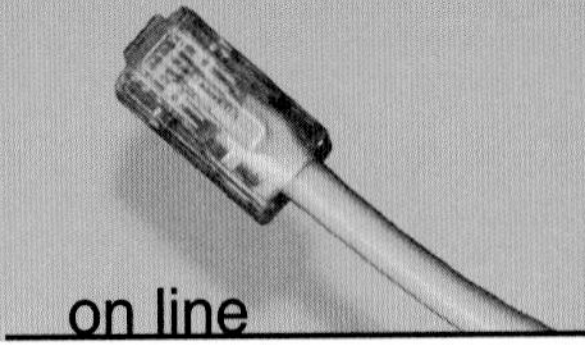

number of segmentation bases increases, the size of individual segments decreases. Nevertheless, the current trend is toward using more rather than fewer variables to segment most markets. Multiple-variable segmentation is clearly more precise than single-variable segmentation.

Consumer goods marketers commonly use one or more of the following characteristics to segment markets: geography, demographics, psychographics, benefits sought, and usage rate. A more detailed description of these characteristics follows.

Geographic Segmentation

Geographic segmentation refers to segmenting markets by region of the country or world, market size, market density, or climate. Market density means the number of people within a unit of land, such as a census tract. Climate is commonly used for geographic segmentation because of its dramatic impact on residents' needs and purchasing behavior. Snowblowers, water and snow skis, clothing, and air-conditioning and heating systems are products with varying appeal, depending on climate.

geographic segmentation
Segmenting markets by region of the country or world, market size, market density, or climate.

Consumer goods companies take a regional approach to marketing for four reasons. First, many firms need to find new ways to generate sales because of sluggish and intensely competitive markets. Second, computerized checkout stations with scanners enable retailers to assess accurately which brands sell best in their region. Third, many packaged-goods manufacturers are introducing new regional brands intended to appeal to local preferences. Fourth, a more regional approach allows consumer-goods companies to react more quickly to competition. For example, Cracker Barrel, a restaurant known in the South for home-style cooking, is altering its menu outside its core Southern market to reflect local tastes. Customers in upstate New York can order Reuben sandwiches, and those in Texas can get eggs with salsa.[4] Chrysler debuted its Sebring convertible ads in warm-weather markets during the winter, since few buyers in the North would have wanted a convertible in February.[5] The "Global Perspectives" box provides another example of geographic market segmentation.

Demographic Segmentation

Marketers often segment markets on the basis of demographic information because it is widely available and often related to consumers' buying and consuming behavior. Some common bases of **demographic segmentation** are age, gender, income, ethnic background, and family life cycle. The discussion here provides some important information about the main demographic segments.

demographic segmentation
Segmenting markets by age, gender, income, ethnic background, and family life cycle.

Age Segmentation Children influence a great deal of family consumption. Combining allowance, earnings, and gifts, children fourteen years old and younger spend an estimated $20 billion per year and influence how another $200 billion is spent.[6] The teenage population, already rising, will reach thirty million by 2006, the highest level since 1975.[7] Attracting children is a popular strategy for many companies because they hope to instill brand loyalty early. Finding that having to pester mom to take them to get their film processed inhibited kids from taking pictures, Kodak introduced a camera set that includes a single-use camera packaged with an envelope to mail the film back to Kodak for developing.[8] Cosmetics for children, once clearly marketed as make-believe to young girls, are starting to cross the line to real makeup. Children and teens now represent one-fifth of the cosmetic industry's sales.[9]

A relatively new and somewhat controversial development in marketing to children entails building children's databases on the Net. The "Ethics in Marketing" box in this chapter explains the practice and controversy.

global perspectives

Europe Is Deaf to Snap! Crackle! Pop!

Cereal companies view European countries such as Italy as an opportunity for growth at a time when the U.S. cereal market is in decline. However, after years of aggressive marketing campaigns and health-awareness programs in Italy, promoting the benefits of cereal, most Italians continue to eat breakfast Italian style: espresso or cappuccino and biscotti dipped into the coffee. American cereals like corn flakes have been available in Italy since the 1950s. But until this decade they were considered a niche product and relegated to the nation's pharmacies and health-food stores. Some progress has been made as a growing number of Italian parents are now giving their children cereal for breakfast.

In the early 1990s when U.S. companies started encountering problems at home, they began looking at markets abroad. Kellogg's, for example, started investing heavily in Europe, entering Italy full steam and opening manufacturing plants in Latvia and Denmark. For an American cereal company, Europe offered distinct advantages, including higher prices and profit margins, cheaper television time, and fewer competitors. But Kellogg's timing was unfortunate. The fall of European trade restrictions as the European Union moved toward the single market made so many plants unnecessary, especially when the number of people eating cereal was not multiplying that rapidly.

As they look for a turnaround, the cereal companies are trying to take advantage of some cultural shifts. The traditional long European lunch is giving way to the American habit of grabbing a quick bite, making a bigger breakfast essential. Also, large U.S.-style supermarkets with wide aisles are taking over from smaller mom-and-pop type stores, which are less inclined to switch to new, untried products.

At one modern Milanese supermarket, cereals occupy a prominent shelf position: The boxes are stacked on top of the fruit counter, and beneath them are multipacks of milk cartons. One mother in the store who is loading up on Kellogg's Corn Flakes and All-Bran says she buys the cereal for her kids—they see commercials on television and tell her what to buy.

Cereal ads in Italy feature hazy sunrises, fields of grain, and wholesome-looking families. They also emphasize the American nature of the product; one Kellogg's Corn Flakes ad uses a series of child Elvis impersonators and begins "the best things always come from America." Several newer ads have a more Italian look. For example, one ad shows an Italian farm family eating breakfast outside their old stone house while their child is talking on a mobile phone—an essential element of modern Italian life.

Kellogg's now dominates Italy's cereal market with an estimated 61 percent market share but has come under attack from store brands launched by domestic retail chains. Furthermore, U.S. cereal makers face new competition from an Italian food manufacturer, Banila SpA, which recently introduced a pressed cereal breakfast bar. Called Armonie, it is marketed as a nutritious breakfast food ideal for dipping in milk or coffee, just like biscotti. Ads for Armonie show a young woman flinging open the windows to let the sun shine in and then dipping the cereal bars in milk.[10]

Could cereal companies more effectively segment the Italian cereal market? What segments might be promising? How should they position their products?

Other age segments are also appealing targets for marketers. There are forty-seven million consumers born between 1966 and 1976, termed Generation X, and they have $125 billion in spending power. Lowe's, the giant home-improvement chain, is trying to attract Generation Xers by signing up as a sponsor for NASCAR, an auto-racing organization that has a large following of this segment.[11] The computer-literate Generation Xers also are a large and viable market for the Internet.

People between thirty-five and forty-four are likely to have school-age children at home and to outspend all other age groups on food at home, housing, clothing, and alcohol. Those between forty-five and fifty-four spend more than any other group on food away from home, transportation, entertainment, education, personal insurance, and pensions.[12] Research has shown that, contrary to popular opinion, 71 percent of those in the fifty-plus age group are willing to try new brands. Additionally, the over-fifty group controls 77 percent of total financial assets in this country and is healthier than most think.[13] In fact, consumers in this age group do not like to be

ethics in marketing

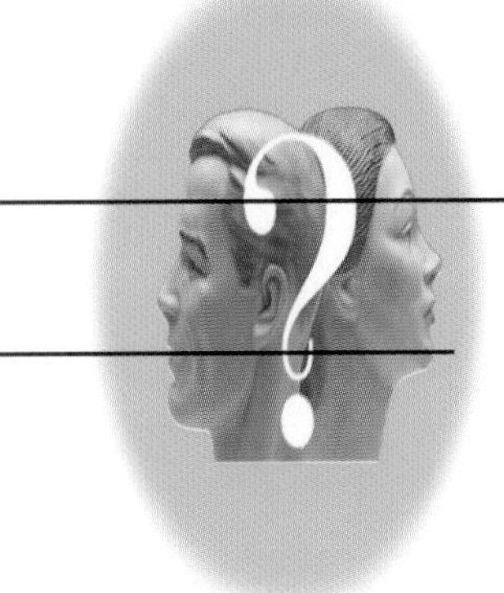

Building Children's Databases on the Net

Mr. Jelly Belly is awfully sweet to kids on-line. The rotund mascot at candy maker Herman Goelitz, Inc.'s World Wide Web site offers visitors free one-ounce samples of jelly beans—so long as they spill the beans about their name, address, gender, age, and where they shop. Only in the fine-print disclaimer does Mr. Jelly Belly reveal what might be done with this personal data: ". . . anything you disclose to us is ours. So we can do anything we want with the stuff you post. We can reproduce it, disclose it, transmit it, publish it, broadcast it, and post it someplace else."

As millions of kids go on-line, marketers are in hot pursuit. Eager to reach an enthusiastic audience more open to pitches than the typical adult buried in junk mail, companies often entertain tykes on-line with games and contests. But to play, these sites frequently require children to fill out questionnaires about themselves and their families and friends—valuable data to be sorted and stored in marketing databases.

"It's a huge problem. It's deceptive and fraudulent," says Marc Rotenberg, director of the Electronic Privacy Information Center, an on-line privacy-rights group. "Kids don't know how their personal information is being used." He adds that typical on-line questionnaires are "much more detailed than the traditional cereal-box promotion."

Marketers, however, have been gathering information about kids for decades, dating back to the first decoder ring and proof of purchase. Some experts question whether a raft of new legislation is the right answer, rather than simply extending current rules on fraudulent and deceptive practices to the on-line market.

Companies are chomping at the bit for details from on-line surfers, no matter how young. At Microsoft Corp.'s Kids pages, signing the guest book means offering up the name, e-mail address, whether the user is a boy or a girl, and the home address. Kids are encouraged to answer questions about what they like to do on-line but are also asked, ". . . can a Microsoft representative contact you?" If so, "Please include your telephone number including area code."

Isn't what Herman Goelitz, Inc. is doing with Mr. Jelly Belly just an extension of compiling a mailing list of who ordered decoder rings in the old days? Defend your answer. Do you agree with Marc Rotenberg or think that everyone should simply lighten up? Do you think new legislation is needed to address the building of Jelly Belly–type databases? Why or why not?

SOURCE: From "Ply and Pry: How Business Pumps Kids on Web," by Jared Sandberg, *The Wall Street Journal*, June 9, 1997. Reprinted by permission of the Wall Street Journal, © 1997 Dow Jones & Company, Inc. All Rights Reserved Worldwide.

stereotypically portrayed as "old." Fiskars was successful with its new spring-loaded scissors, which were developed for people with arthritis, because the company advertised them as being easier to use rather than as a product for old people.[14]

Seniors (aged sixty-five and over) are especially attracted to companies that build relationships by taking the time to get to know them and their preferences. As an example, older customers say they prefer catalog shopping to retail outlets because of dissatisfaction with customer service at retail stores. In comparison, a mailing done to target Medicare supplement prospects that included Valentine cards to seniors received a very positive response.[15]

Gender Segmentation Marketers of products such as clothing, cosmetics, personal care items, magazines, jewelry, and footwear commonly segment markets by gender. For example, 95 percent of users of Sports Zone, a Web site that offers a constant flow of sports news generated by ESPN (**http://espnet.sportszone.com/**), are men.[16] However, brands that have traditionally been marketed to men, such as Gillette razors and Rogaine baldness remedy, are increasing their efforts to attract women.[17] Even the National Football League has launched an aggressive effort to retain and add to its female viewership, which on an average football weekend accounts for 43 percent of the league's fan base.[18] "Women's" products such as cosmetics, household products, and furniture are also being marketed to men.

Barnes and Noble

How is Barnes and Noble targeting the African-American market via the Internet? Visit NetNoir's Black Book page and the Barnes and Noble home page to find out. Do you think their efforts are successful? Why or why not?
http://www.netnoir.com/
http://www.barnesandnoble.com/

Income Segmentation Income is a popular demographic variable for segmenting markets because income level influences consumers' wants and determines their buying power. Many markets are segmented by income, including the markets for housing, clothing, automobiles, and food. For example, value retailers such as Dollar General are drawing low- and fixed-income customers with easy access, small stores, and rock-bottom pricing.[19] Wal-Mart, on the other hand, is moving away from its traditional rural and middle-income markets by targeting higher-income consumers in upscale areas. The retailer is spending more money on its stores, introducing more high-end merchandise, and upgrading apparel lines.[20]

Ethnic Segmentation Many companies are segmenting their markets by ethnicity. The three largest ethnic markets are the African-American market, the Hispanic-American market, and the Asian-American market. In 1995, these three groups collectively made up 25.5 percent of the United States's population and are projected to make up one-third of the country's population by 2010.[21]

African-Americans African-Americans are the largest minority group in the United States. Total expenditures by this group top $400 billion a year.[22] Increasingly, marketers are finding this market segment very rewarding. Researchers have found some differences in consumption patterns between African-Americans and other groups; for example, blacks and whites often have different preferences in taste. Although blacks drink less coffee than average, they are much more likely than other Americans to flavor their coffee with large amounts of sugar, cream, or nondairy creamer. Recognizing this trend, Coffee-Mate began marketing its product to blacks. It advertised in national magazines like Ebony and Essence, broadcast its message on local black radio stations, and used outdoor advertising in black neighborhoods.

Many Fortune 500 companies have launched some ethnic marketing activities. Effectively penetrating the market, however, often requires a unique and distinctive marketing mix. Following are examples of how companies are targeting African-Americans:

- Coors Light sponsored "Roots of the Rhythm," a summer concert tour and sweepstakes in honor of Black Music Month. The promotion also partners the Coors brand with existing events, such as the Indianapolis Black Expo and Harlem Day in New York.[23]
- Schick introduced a new razor called the Schick Protector, which promises to offer a technological leap in shaving performance. Schick will target its advertising to African-American men, many of whom find shaving painful because of a condition that causes skin bumps.[24]
- African-Americans account for 15 percent of McDonald's business, so the group gets 15 percent of the marketing and advertising effort. Marketing professionals praise one McDonald's Breakfast Club campaign, which features "buppies" (black urban professionals) speaking Black English.

Hispanic-Americans By the year 2010, the Hispanic population is predicted to number nearly 39 million.[25] Hispanics are one of the fastest-growing minority groups in the United States. The total purchasing power of the Hispanic-American market is over $270 billion annually.[26]

The concept of diversity is nowhere more evident than in the Hispanic culture. This segment comprises twenty-one nationalities, each with different cultural, historic, and economic characteristics.[27] Therefore, marketing managers are carefully targeting major segments of this diverse market. One series of Campbell Soup ads, for instance, features a woman cooking, but the individual ads differ in such details as the character's age, the setting, and the music. In the version for Cuban-Americans, a grandmother cooks in a plant-filled kitchen to the sounds of salsa and merengue music. In contrast, the Mexican-American ad shows a young wife preparing food in a brightly colored Southwestern-style kitchen with pop music playing in the background.

Following are examples of companies targeting Hispanic-Americans:

- Based on research that showed Hispanics consume more than twice as many gelatin products as whites or African-Americans, Kraft's marketing of Jell-O to this group is aggressive, backed by heavy television advertising and sampling at events.[28]
- The number of Spanish-language media outlets in the United States has increased steadily during the past decade. There are now 42 major Spanish-language magazines, 31 English or bilingual Hispanic-oriented magazines, and 103 Hispanic newspapers.[29] TV and radio outlets have expanded as well.
- Shopping malls are trying to attract Hispanic-American customers. The Tucson Mall in Arizona advertises on three Spanish-language radio stations and hires a mariachi music group to help it celebrate the Mexican holiday Cinco de Mayo. Half the mall's staff is bilingual. A Florida mall that attracts about fifty thousand shoppers from Miami and Dade County appeals largely to Hispanic-Americans.[30]

Asian-Americans Like Hispanic-Americans, Asian-Americans are a diverse group with thirteen submarkets. The five largest are Chinese (1.6 million), Filipino (1.4 million), Japanese (848,000), Asian Indian (815,000), and Korean (799,000). Asian-American households are better educated and more affluent than those of any other racial or ethnic group, including whites. Their median household income was about $42,000 in 1996; 32 percent of Asian-American households have incomes of $50,000 or more, compared with only 29 percent of white households.[31]

Because Asian-Americans are better educated and have higher-than-average incomes, they are sometimes called a marketer's dream. The following are some examples of companies targeting Asian-Americans:

- Cadillac sponsored the Ameritech Senior Open Golf Tournament and ran Korean-language advertisements on a California television station.[32]
- Wrigley, the Chicago gum maker, is teaming up with Health Watch, a New York advocacy group, to produce a $10 million advertising campaign aimed at getting Asian-Americans and other minorities to use doctors for regular health maintenance instead of as a last resort.[33]
- Some entrepreneurs are building large enclosed malls that cater to Asian consumers. At the Aberdeen Centre near Vancouver, British Columbia, nearly 80 percent of the merchants are Chinese-Canadians, as are 80 percent of the customers. The mall offers fashions made in Hong Kong, a shop for traditional Chinese medicines, and a theater showing Chinese movies. Kung fu martial arts demonstrations and Chinese folk dances are held in the mall on weekends.

Family Life-Cycle Segmentation The demographic factors of gender, age, and income often do not sufficiently explain why consumer buying behavior varies. Frequently, differences in consumption patterns among people of the same age and gender result from their being in different stages of the family life cycle. The **family life cycle (FLC)** is a series of stages determined by a combination of age, marital status, and the presence or absence of children.

family life cycle (FLC)
A series of stages determined by a combination of age, marital status, and the presence or absence of children.

Exhibit 6.2 illustrates both traditional and contemporary FLC patterns and shows how families' needs, incomes, resources, and expenditures differ at each stage. The horizontal flow shows the traditional family life cycle. The lower part of the exhibit gives some of the characteristics and purchase patterns of families in each stage of the traditional life cycle. The exhibit also acknowledges that about half of all first marriages end in divorce. When young marrieds move into the young divorced stage, their consumption patterns often revert back to those of the young single stage of the cycle. About four out of five divorced persons remarry by middle age and reenter the traditional life cycle, as indicated by the "recycled flow" in the exhibit.

exhibit 6.2 | Family Life Cycle

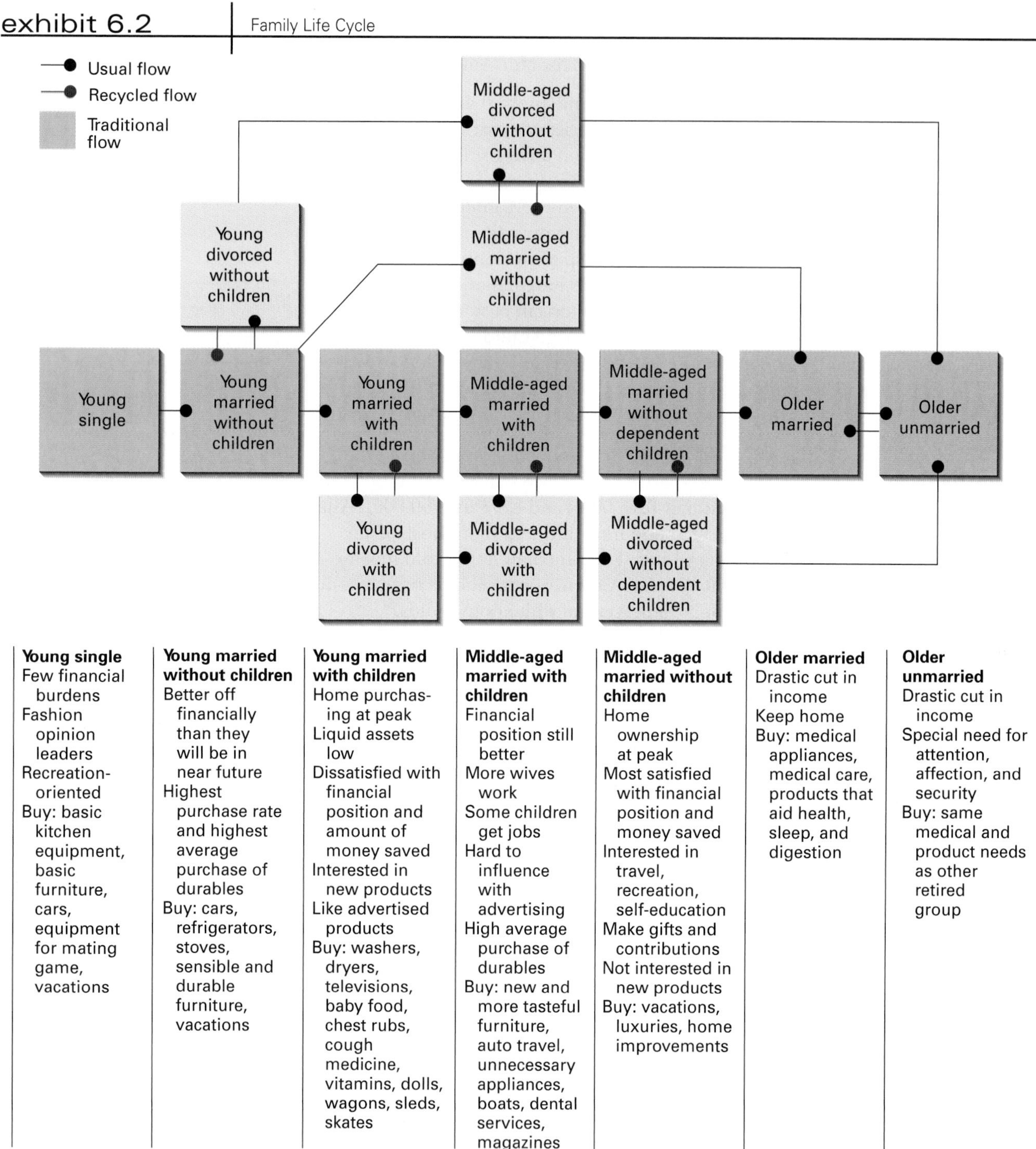

Young single	Young married without children	Young married with children	Middle-aged married with children	Middle-aged married without children	Older married	Older unmarried
Few financial burdens Fashion opinion leaders Recreation-oriented Buy: basic kitchen equipment, basic furniture, cars, equipment for mating game, vacations	Better off financially than they will be in near future Highest purchase rate and highest average purchase of durables Buy: cars, refrigerators, stoves, sensible and durable furniture, vacations	Home purchasing at peak Liquid assets low Dissatisfied with financial position and amount of money saved Interested in new products Like advertised products Buy: washers, dryers, televisions, baby food, chest rubs, cough medicine, vitamins, dolls, wagons, sleds, skates	Financial position still better More wives work Some children get jobs Hard to influence with advertising High average purchase of durables Buy: new and more tasteful furniture, auto travel, unnecessary appliances, boats, dental services, magazines	Home ownership at peak Most satisfied with financial position and money saved Interested in travel, recreation, self-education Make gifts and contributions Not interested in new products Buy: vacations, luxuries, home improvements	Drastic cut in income Keep home Buy: medical appliances, medical care, products that aid health, sleep, and digestion	Drastic cut in income Special need for attention, affection, and security Buy: same medical and product needs as other retired group

psychographic segmentation
Market segmentation on the basis of personality, motives, lifestyles, and geodemographics.

Psychographic Segmentation

Age, gender, income, ethnicity, family life-cycle stage, and other demographic variables are usually helpful in developing segmentation strategies, but often they don't paint the entire picture. Demographics provides the skeleton, but psychographics adds meat to the bones. **Psychographic segmentation** is market segmentation on the basis of the following variables:

- *Personality:* Personality reflects a person's traits, attitudes, and habits. Porsche Cars North America understood well the demographics of the Porsche owner: a forty-something male college graduate earning over $200,000 per year. However, research discovered that there were five personality types within this general demographic category that more effectively segmented Porsche buyers. Exhibit 6.3 describes the five segments. Porsche refined its marketing as a result of the study and, after a previous seven-year slump, the company's U.S. sales rose 48 percent.[34]

- *Motives:* Marketers of baby products and life insurance appeal to consumers' emotional motives—namely, to care for their loved ones. Using appeals to economy, reliability, and dependability, carmakers like Subaru and Suzuki target customers with rational motives. Carmakers like Mercedes-Benz, Jaguar, and Cadillac appeal to customers with status-related motives.
- *Lifestyles:* Lifestyle segmentation divides people into groups according to the way they spend their time, the importance of the things around them, their beliefs, and socioeconomic characteristics such as income and education. For example, Harley-Davidson divides its customers into seven lifestyle segments, from "cocky misfits" who are most likely to be arrogant troublemakers, to "laid-back camper types" committed to cycling and nature, to "classy capitalists" who have wealth and privilege.[35]
- *Geodemographics:* **Geodemographic segmentation** clusters potential customers into neighborhood lifestyle categories. It combines geographic, demographic, and lifestyle segmentations. Geodemographic segmentation helps marketers develop marketing programs tailored to prospective buyers who live in small geographic regions, such as neighborhoods, or who have very specific lifestyle and demographic characteristics. Kraft General Foods, Inc., plans to tailor different ads for different neighborhoods in the same region. For example, viewers watching a cable show in a Hispanic neighborhood in Chicago would see different ads during the same commercial breaks than would young, affluent professionals living in a different neighborhood.[36]

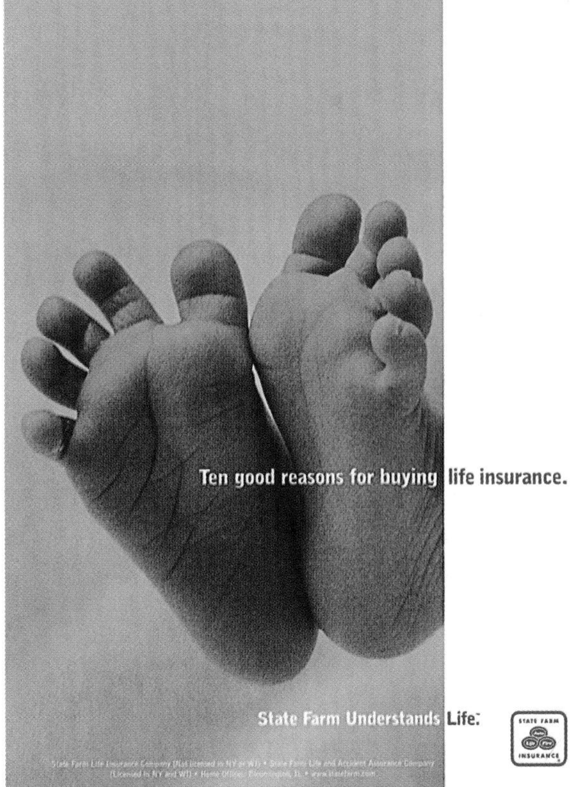

This ad for State Farm clearly appeals to consumers' emotional motives by associating the purchase of life insurance with the caring and responsibility of parenting.
Courtesy State Farm Insurance Companies

exhibit 6.3

Taxonomy of Porsche Buyers

Type	% of All Owners	Description
Top Guns	27%	Driven, ambitious types. Power and control matter. They expect to be noticed.
Elitists	24%	Old-money blue bloods. A car is just a car, no matter how expensive. It is not an extension of personality.
Proud Patrons	23%	Ownership is an end in itself. Their car is a trophy earned for hard work, and who cares if anyone sees them in it?
Bon Vivants	17%	Worldly jet setters and thrill seekers. Their car heightens the excitement in their already passionate lives.
Fantasists	9%	Walter Mitty types. Their car is an escape. Not only are they uninterested in impressing others with it, they also feel a little guilty about owning one.

geodemographic segmentation
Segmenting potential customers into neighborhood lifestyle categories.

Psychographic variables can be used individually to segment markets or can be combined with other variables to provide more detailed descriptions of market segments. One well-known combination approach, offered by SRI International, is called VALS 2 (version 2 of SRI's Values and Lifestyles program). VALS 2 categorizes U.S. consumers by their values, beliefs, and lifestyles rather than by traditional demographic segmentation variables. Many advertising agencies have used VALS segmentation to create effective promotion campaigns.

As Exhibit 6.4 shows, the segments in VALS 2 are classified on two dimensions: vertically by their resources and horizontally by their self-orientation. Resources include education, income, self-confidence, health, eagerness to buy, intelligence, and energy level. The resources dimension is a continuum ranging from minimal to abundant. Resources generally increase from adolescence through middle age and decrease with extreme age, depression, financial reverses, and physical or psychological impairment. In contrast, the self-orientation dimension classifies three different ways of buying:

- Beliefs or principles rather than feelings, events, or desire for approval guide principle-oriented consumers in their choices.
- Other people's actions, approval, and opinions strongly influence status-oriented consumers.
- Action-oriented consumers are prompted by a desire for social or physical activity, variety, and risk.

Exhibit 6.5 describes the eight VALS 2 psychographic segments. Using only the two key dimensions—resources and self-orientation—VALS 2 defines groups of adult consumers who have distinctive attitudes, behavior patterns, and decision-making styles.

exhibit 6.4

VALS 2 Dimensions

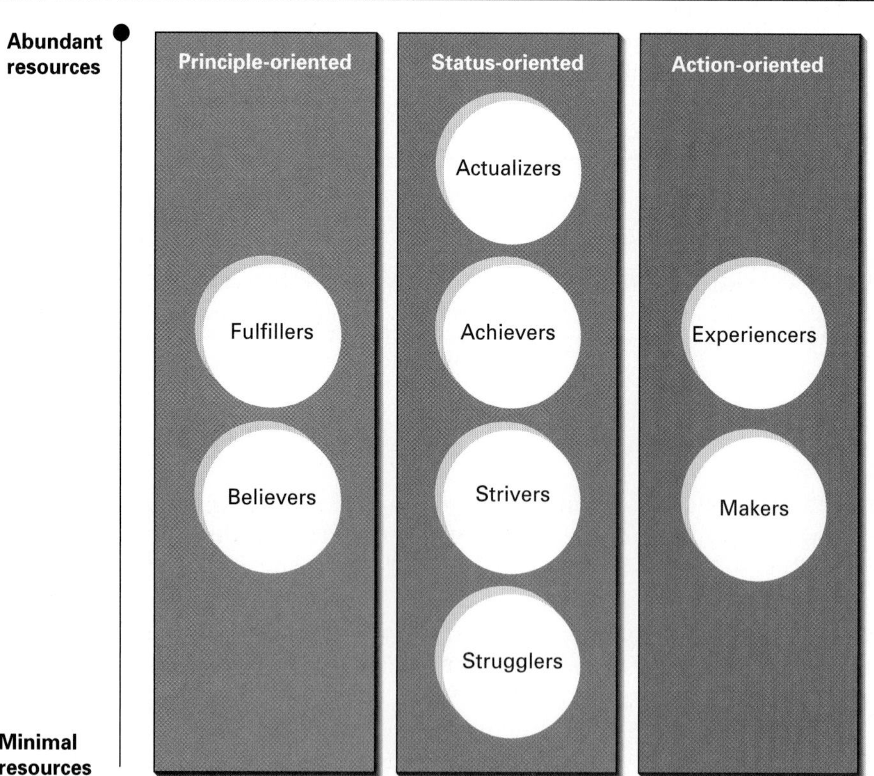

exhibit 6.5

VALS™ 2 Psychographic Segments

Actualizers are successful, sophisticated, active, "take-charge" people with high self-esteem and abundant resources. They are interested in growth and seek to develop, explore, and express themselves in a variety of ways. Their possessions and recreation choices reflect a cultivated taste for the finer things in life.

Fulfillers are mature, satisfied, comfortable, reflective people who value order, knowledge, and responsibility. Most are well educated, well informed about world events, and professionally employed. Fulfillers are conservative, practical consumers; they are concerned about value and durability in the products they buy.

Believers are conservative, conventional people with concrete beliefs and strong attachments to traditional institutions—family, church, community, and nation. As consumers they are conservative and predictable, favoring U.S. products and established brands.

Achievers are successful career- and work-oriented people who like to, and generally do, feel in control of their lives. Achievers live conventional lives, are politically conservative, and respect authority and the status quo. As consumers they favor established goods and services that demonstrate success to peers.

Strivers seek motivation, self-definition, and approval from the world around them. They are easily bored and impulsive. Money defines success for strivers, who lack enough of it. They emulate those who own more impressive possessions, but what they wish to obtain is generally beyond their reach.

Experiencers are young, vital, enthusiastic, and impulsive. They seek variety and excitement and combine an abstract disdain for conformity and authority with an outsider's awe of others' wealth, prestige, and power. Experiencers are avid consumers and spend much of their income on clothing, fast food, music, movies, and video.

Makers are practical people who value self-sufficiency. They live within a traditional context of family, practical work, and physical recreation and have little interest in what lies outside that context. They are unimpressed by material possessions other than those with a practical or functional purpose (for example, tools, pickup trucks, or fishing equipment).

Strugglers have lives that are constricted—chronically poor, ill educated, and low skilled. They lack strong social bonds; they are focused on meeting the urgent needs of the present moment. Aging strugglers are concerned about their health. Strugglers are cautious consumers who represent a very modest demand for most goods and services but are loyal to favorite brands.

Benefit Segmentation

Benefit segmentation is the process of grouping customers into market segments according to the benefits they seek from the product. Most types of market segmentation are based on the assumption that this variable and customers' needs are related. Benefit segmentation is different because it groups potential customers on the basis of their needs or wants rather than some other characteristic, such as age or gender. The snack-food market, for example, can be divided into six benefit segments, as shown in Exhibit 6.6.

benefit segmentation
The process of grouping customers into market segments according to the benefits they seek from the product.

Customer profiles can be developed by examining demographic information associated with people seeking certain benefits. This information can be used to match marketing strategies with selected target markets. For example, *Reader's Digest*

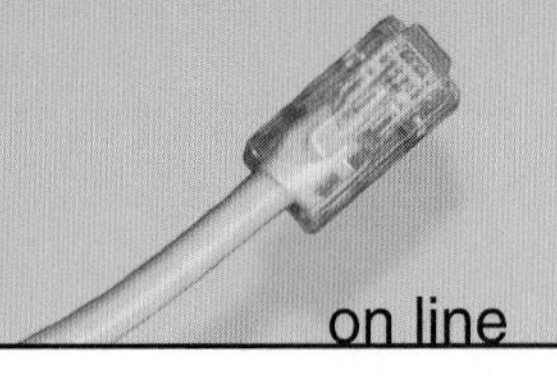

Mead Johnson Nutritionals
How does Mead Johnson, maker of the Boost line of nutritional products, use benefit segmentation on its Web site? What other types of segmentation are evident on the site?
http://www.meadjohnson.ca/

exhibit 6.6 | Lifestyle Segmentation of the Snack-Food Market

	Nutritional Snackers	Weight Watchers	Guilty Snackers	Party Snackers	Indiscriminate Snackers	Economical Snackers
% of Snackers	22%	14%	9%	15%	15%	18%
Lifestyle Characteristics	Self-assured, controlled	Outdoorsy, influential, venturesome	Highly anxious, isolated	Sociable	Hedonistic	Self-assured, price-oriented
Benefits Sought	Nutritious, without artificial ingredients, natural	Low in calories, quick energy	Low in calories, good tasting	Good to serve guests, served with pride, go well with beverages	Good tasting, satisfies hunger	Low in price, best value
Consumption Level of Snacks	Light	Light	Heavy	Average	Heavy	Average
Type of Snacks Usually Eaten	Fruits, vegetables, cheese	Yogurt, vegetables	Yogurt, cookies, crackers, candy	Nuts, potato chips, crackers, pretzels	Candy, ice cream, cookies, potato chips, pretzels, popcorn	No specific products
Demographics	Better educated, have younger children	Younger, single	Younger or older, female, lower socio-economic status	Middle-aged, nonurban	Teenager	Have large family, better educated

plans to send millions of people with different medical conditions, such as high blood pressure or high cholesterol, a booklet filled with articles and prescription-drug ads, all about the very condition each subscriber has.[37]

Usage-Rate Segmentation

usage-rate segmentation
Dividing a market by the amount of product bought or consumed.

Usage-rate segmentation divides a market by the amount of product bought or consumed. Categories vary with the product, but they are likely to include some combination of the following: former users, potential users, first-time users, light or irregular users, medium users, and heavy users. Segmenting by usage rate enables marketers to focus their efforts on heavy users or to develop multiple marketing mixes aimed at different segments. Because heavy users often account for a sizable portion of all product sales, some marketers focus on the heavy-user segment.

80/20 principle
Principle that holds that 20 percent of all customers generate 80 percent of the demand.

The **80/20 principle** holds that 20 percent of all customers generate 80 percent of the demand. Although the percentages are not usually exact, the general idea often holds true. For example, Sav-On Stores, which operates a number of Piggly Wiggly grocery stores, learned that 25 percent to 30 percent of its shopping base is responsible for 70 percent of its dollar business. Stores like Piggly Wiggly are developing loyalty programs that reward the heavy-user segment with deals available only to them, such as in-store coupon dispensing systems, loyalty card programs, and special price deals on selected merchandise.[38]

In a variant of usage-rate segmentation, some companies try to attract nonusers. Using a public database, Menly and James identified arthritis sufferers who did not use their pain reliever, Ecotrin. Three different direct-mail packages were sent to these nonusers: the first included a free sample with a 50¢ coupon, the second enclosed a $1 rebate coupon, and the third package had an invitation to send for a free sample. All three promotional offers resulted in at least a 50 percent redemption rate (compared to the usual nontargeted direct-mail response rate of 1 or 2 percent).[39]

Bases for Segmenting Business Markets

5
Describe the bases for segmenting business markets

The business market consists of four broad segments: producers, resellers, institutions, and government (for a detailed discussion of the characteristics of these segments, see Chapter 5). Whether marketers focus on only one or on all four of these segments, they are likely to find diversity among potential customers. Thus, further market segmentation offers just as many benefits to business marketers as it does to consumer product marketers. Business market segmentation variables can be classified into two major categories: macrosegmentation variables and microsegmentation variables.

Macrosegmentation

macrosegmentation
Method of dividing business markets into segments based on general characteristics such as geographic location, customer type, customer size, and product use.

Macrosegmentation variables are used to divide business markets into segments according to the following general characteristics:

- *Geographic location:* The demand for some business products varies considerably from one region to another. For instance, many computer hardware and software companies are located in the Silicon Valley region of California. Some markets tend to be regional because buyers prefer to purchase from local suppliers, and distant suppliers often have difficulty competing in terms of price and service. Therefore, firms that sell to geographically concentrated industries benefit by locating operations close to the market.
- *Customer type:* Segmenting by customer type allows business marketers to tailor their marketing mixes to the unique needs of particular types of organizations or industries. Many companies are finding this form of segmentation to be quite effective. For example, The Home Depot, the largest do-it-yourself retail business in the United States, has announced plans to begin targeting professional repair and remodeling contractors in addition to consumers.[40]
- *Customer size:* Volume of purchase (heavy, moderate, and light) is a commonly used business-to-business segmentation basis. Another is the buying organization's size, which may affect its purchasing procedures, the types and quantities of products it needs, and its responses to different marketing mixes. Banks frequently offer different services, lines of credit, and overall attention to commercial customers based on their size.
- *Product use:* Many products, especially raw materials like steel, wood, and petroleum, have diverse applications. How customers use a product may influence the amount they buy, their buying criteria, and their selection of vendors. For example, a producer of springs may have customers that use the product in applications as diverse as making machine tools, bicycles, surgical devices, office equipment, telephones, and missile systems.

Microsegmentation

Macrosegmentation often produces market segments that are too diverse for targeted marketing strategies. Thus, marketers often find it useful to divide macrosegments based on such variables as customer size or product use into

microsegmentation
The process of dividing business markets into segments based on the characteristics of decision-making units within a macrosegment.

smaller microsegments. **Microsegmentation** is the process of dividing business markets into segments based on the characteristics of decision-making units within a macrosegment. Microsegmentation enables the marketer to more clearly identify market segments and more precisely define target markets. These are some of the typical microsegmentation variables:[41]

- *Key purchasing criteria:* Marketers can segment some business markets by ranking purchasing criteria such as product quality, prompt and reliable delivery, supplier reputation, technical support, and price. For example, Atlas Corporation developed a commanding position in the industrial door market by providing customized products in just four weeks, which is much faster than the industry average of twelve to fifteen weeks. Atlas's primary market is companies with an immediate need for customized doors.
- *Purchasing strategies:* The purchasing strategies of buying organizations can shape microsegments. Two purchasing profiles that have been identified are satisficers and optimizers. **Satisficers** contact familiar suppliers and place the order with the first to satisfy product and delivery requirements. **Optimizers** consider numerous suppliers (both familiar and unfamiliar), solicit bids, and study all proposals carefully before selecting one. Recognizing satisficers and optimizers is quite easy. A few key questions during a sales call, such as "Why do you buy product X from vendor A?", usually produce answers that identify purchaser profiles.
- *Importance of purchase:* Classifying business customers according to the significance they attach to the purchase of a product is especially appropriate when customers use the product differently. This approach is also appropriate when the purchase is considered routine by some customers but very important by others. For instance, a small entrepreneur would consider a laser printer a major capital purchase, but a large office would find it a normal expense.
- *Personal characteristics:* The personal characteristics of purchase decision makers (their demographic characteristics, decision style, tolerance for risk, confidence level, job responsibilities, and so on) influence their buying behavior and thus offer a viable basis for segmenting some business markets. IBM computer buyers, for example, are sometimes characterized as being more risk averse than buyers of less expensive clones that perform essentially the same functions. In advertising, therefore, IBM stresses its reputation for high quality and reliability.

satisficers
Type of business customer that places an order with the first familiar supplier to satisfy product and delivery requirements.

optimizers
Type of business customer that considers numerous suppliers, both familiar and unfamiliar, solicits bids, and studies all proposals carefully before selecting one.

Steps in Segmenting a Market

6
List the steps involved in segmenting markets

The purpose of market segmentation, in both consumer and business markets, is to identify marketing opportunities. Exhibit 6.7 traces the steps in segmenting a market. Note that steps 5 and 6 are actually marketing activities that follow market segmentation (steps 1 through 4).

1. *Select a market or product category for study:* Define the overall market or product category to be studied. It may be a market in which the firm already competes, a new but related market or product category, or a totally new one. For instance, Anheuser-Busch closely examined the beer market before introducing Michelob Light and Bud Light. Anheuser-Busch also carefully studied the market for salty snacks before introducing the Eagle brand.
2. *Choose a basis or bases for segmenting the market:* This step requires managerial insight, creativity, and market knowledge. There are no scientific procedures for selecting segmentation variables. However, a successful segmentation scheme must produce segments that meet the four basic criteria discussed earlier in this chapter.

Steps in Segmenting a Market and Subsequent Activities

exhibit 6.7

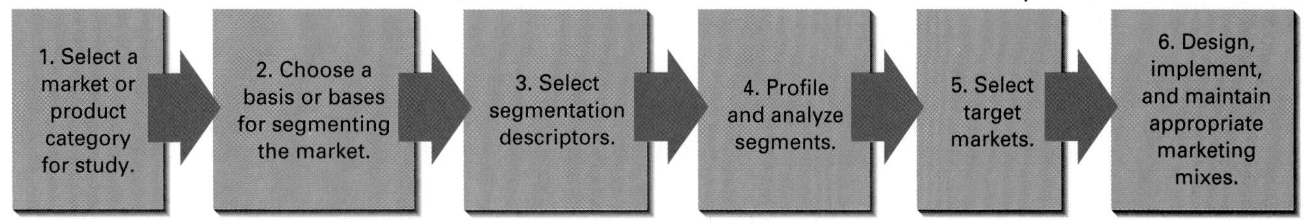

3. *Select segmentation descriptors:* After choosing one or more bases, the marketer must select the segmentation descriptors. Descriptors identify the specific segmentation variables to use. For example, if a company selects demographics as a basis of segmentation, it may use age, occupation, and income as descriptors. A company that selects usage segmentation needs to decide whether to go after heavy users, nonusers, or light users.
4. *Profile and evaluate segments:* The profile should include the segments' size, expected growth, purchase frequency, current brand usage, brand loyalty, and long-term sales and profit potential. This information can then be used to rank potential market segments by profit opportunity, risk, consistency with organizational mission and objectives, and other factors important to the firm.
5. *Select target markets:* Selecting target markets is not a part of but a natural outcome of the segmentation process. It is a major decision that influences and often directly determines the firm's marketing mix. This topic is examined in greater detail later in this chapter.
6. *Design, implement, and maintain appropriate marketing mixes:* The marketing mix has been described as product, distribution, promotion, and pricing strategies intended to bring about mutually satisfying exchange relationships with target markets. Chapters 8 through 15 explore these topics in detail.

Strategies for Selecting Target Markets

7

Discuss alternative strategies for selecting target markets

So far this chapter has focused on the market segmentation process, which is only the first step in deciding whom to approach about buying a product. The next task is to choose one or more target markets. A **target market** is a group of people or organizations for which an organization designs, implements, and maintains a marketing mix intended to meet the needs of that group, resulting in mutually satisfying exchanges. The three general strategies for selecting target markets—undifferentiated, concentrated, and multisegment targeting—are illustrated in Exhibit 6.8. Exhibit 6.9 illustrates the advantages and disadvantages of each targeting strategy.

target market
A group of people or organizations for which an organization designs, implements, and maintains a marketing mix intended to meet the needs of that group, resulting in mutually satisfying exchanges.

Undifferentiated Targeting

A firm using an **undifferentiated targeting strategy** essentially adopts a mass-market philosophy, viewing the market as one big market with no individual segments. The firm uses one marketing mix for the entire market. A firm that adopts an undifferentiated targeting strategy assumes that individual customers have similar needs that can be met with a common marketing mix.

undifferentiated targeting strategy
Marketing approach that views the market as one big market with no individual segments and thus requires a single marketing mix.

The first firm in an industry sometimes uses an undifferentiated targeting strategy. With no competition, the firm may not need to tailor marketing mixes to the preferences of market segments. Henry Ford's famous quote about the Model T is a classic example of an undifferentiated targeting strategy: "They

The Ford Model T is a classic example of undifferentiated targeting. Could you argue that by producing a single product for all markets, Henry Ford was positioning his car as a commodity? Why or why not?
© Corbis-Bettmann

can have their car in any color they want, as long as it's black." At one time, Coca-Cola used this strategy with a single product and a single size of its familiar green bottle. Marketers of commodity products, such as flour and sugar, are also likely to use an undifferentiated targeting strategy.

One advantage of undifferentiated marketing is the potential for saving on production and marketing. Because only one item is produced, the firm should be able to achieve economies of mass production. Also, marketing costs may be lower when there is only one product to promote and a single channel of distribution. Too often, however, an undifferentiated strategy emerges by default rather than by design, reflecting a failure to consider the advantages of a segmented approach. The result is often sterile, unimaginative product offerings that have little appeal to anyone.

Another problem associated with undifferentiated targeting is that it makes the company more susceptible to competitive inroads. Hershey lost a big share of the candy market to Mars and other candy companies before it changed to a multisegment targeting strategy. Coca-Cola forfeited its position as the leading seller of cola drinks in supermarkets to Pepsi-Cola in the late 1950s, when Pepsi began offering several sizes of containers.

You might think a firm producing a standard product like toilet tissue would adopt an undifferentiated strategy. However, this market has industrial segments and consumer segments. Industrial buyers want an economical, single-ply product sold in boxes of a hundred rolls. The consumer market demands a more versatile product in smaller quantities. Within the consumer market, the product is differentiated as colored or white, with designer print or no print, cushioned or noncushioned,

exhibit 6.8

Three Strategies for Selecting Target Markets

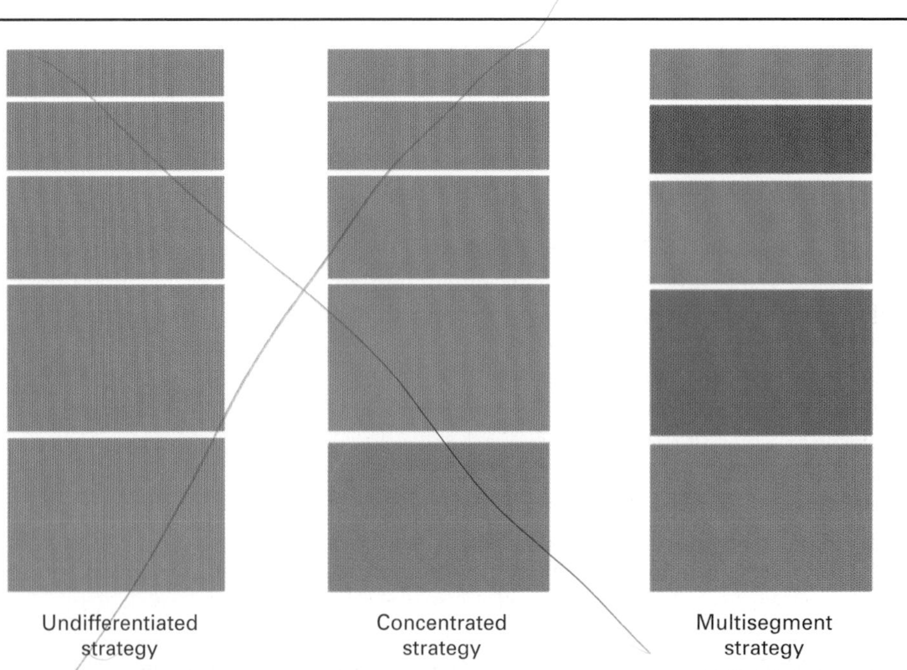

exhibit 6.9

Advantages and Disadvantages of Target Marketing Strategies

Targeting Strategy	Advantages	Disadvantages
Undifferentiated Targeting	• Potential savings on production/marketing costs	• Unimaginative product offerings • Company more susceptible to competition
Concentrated Targeting	• Concentration of resources • Can better meet the needs of a narrowly defined segment • Allows some small firms to better compete with larger firms • Strong positioning	• Segments too small, or changing • Large competitors may more effectively market to niche segment
Multisegment Targeting	• Greater financial success • Economies of scale in production/marketing	• High costs • Cannibalization

and economy priced or luxury priced. Fort Howard Corporation, the market share leader in industrial toilet paper, does not even sell to the consumer market.

Concentrated Targeting

With a **concentrated targeting strategy**, a firm selects a market **niche** (one segment of a market) for targeting its marketing efforts. Because the firm is appealing to a single segment, it can concentrate on understanding the needs, motives, and satisfactions of that segment's members and on developing and maintaining a highly specialized marketing mix. Some firms find that concentrating resources and meeting the needs of a narrowly defined market segment is more profitable than spreading resources over several different segments.

concentrated targeting strategy
A strategy used to select one segment of a market for targeting marketing efforts.

niche
One segment of a market.

For example, shopping center marketers have developed niche malls specifically to attract such groups as working women and African-Americans. The malls include a customized retail mix, easy parking, phone-in shopping, and targeted promotions.[42] Many travel agencies, facing tougher competition, are trying to stand apart from one another by appealing to niche groups. For instance, some agencies are targeting Japanese travelers by publicizing such cultural sites as Little Tokyo in Los Angeles.[43]

ENTREPRENEUR

Small firms often adopt a concentrated targeting strategy to compete effectively with much larger firms. For example, First Business Bank targets midsized companies with annual sales between $3 million and $10 million. The bank accepts only ten to fifteen new accounts each month, and these accounts are carefully screened before they are accepted. With this concentrated targeting strategy, the bank has been extremely profitable. In addition, the bank's customers believe they are the number one priority, instead of feeling neglected at a much larger bank. Niche markets often provide opportunities for the entrepreneur, as illustrated in the "Entrepreneurial Insights" box.

Some firms, on the other hand, use a concentrated strategy to establish a strong position in a desirable market segment. Porsche, for instance, targets an upscale automobile market through "class appeal, not mass appeal."

Concentrated targeting violates the old adage "Don't put all your eggs in one basket." If the chosen segment is too small or if it shrinks because of environmental changes, the firm may suffer negative consequences. For instance, OshKosh

The Baby Jogger Company

Which consumer segments do you think would be most attracted by The Baby Jogger Company's products? What kind of targeting strategy does the company seem to be following? Why do you think so?
http://www.babyjogger.com/

on line

entrepreneurial insights

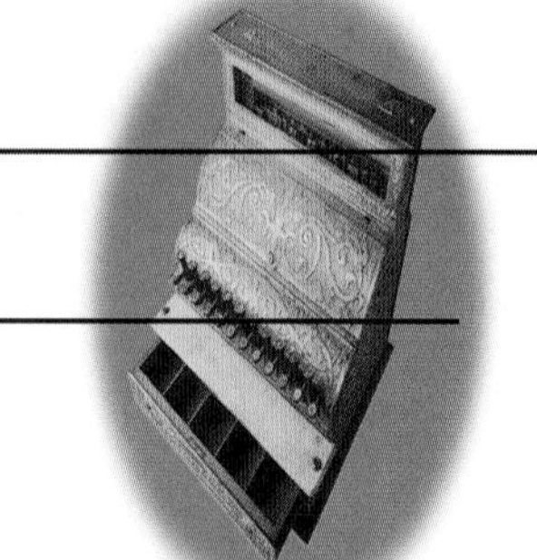

Businesses Gain a Foothold Through Niche Marketing

The estimated annual sales for retail franchising are expected to reach more than $1 trillion by the year 2000, accounting for more than 50 percent of all U.S. retail sales. According to analysts, niche marketing is the biggest source for this success, enabling small retailers to compete with big retailers like Wal-Mart.

Analysts say the key to a successful retail franchise is to identify and exploit a specialist product that satisfies consumer needs. A number of companies are doing this. For example, Battery Patrol, Inc., stocks more than five thousand different batteries, from hearing-aid batteries to 140-pound batteries for earth-moving equipment. Battery Patrol expects annual growth of at least 30 percent in 1998, the president of the company says. The company has five wholly owned stores and began franchising last year.

Another example is Honolulu-based Magneato, which sells refrigerator magnets—six hundred different types ranging in price from $5 to $10. Magneato's flagship five-hundred-square-foot store in the Waikiki Beachcomber Hotel is joined by one in Honolulu and another in a shopping mall in Guam. The Guam store did $17,600 in sales on New Year's Day alone. A new shop is scheduled to open in Oakland, Michigan, and the company is also discussing a franchise with a New York-based group.

Tried and tested retail concepts are frequently being franchised with an emphasis on extraordinary service to distinguish them from more traditional stores. Michael Charles Premier Wine Shops in Warren, Ohio, hopes to franchise the company's idea for unpretentious, low-key wine stores. The three existing stores try for a "Barnes and Noble" approach (which encourages customers to spend hours at the store mixing shopping with sociability) by offering wine tastings and classes to help overcome any embarrassment customers may feel about a limited knowledge of fine wines. The company has plans to open ten to twelve carefully chosen franchises throughout the Midwest.

Mark Siebert, president of a Chicago-based franchising consulting firm, emphasizes the tremendous amount of potential in sticking with a well-defined niche. "We're seeing more and more specialization," he says. "If you try to be too much, you're going to have a hard time. By focusing, you're going to be successful."[44]

B'Gosh, Inc., was highly successful selling children's wear in the 1980s. It was so successful, however, that the children's line came to define OshKosh's image to the extent that the company could not sell clothes to anyone else. Attempts at marketing older children's clothing, women's casual clothes, and maternity wear were all abandoned. Now, recognizing it is in the children's-wear business, the company is expanding into products such as kids' shoes, children's eyewear, and plush toys.[45]

A concentrated strategy can also be disastrous for a firm that is not successful in its narrowly defined target market. Before Procter & Gamble introduced Head and Shoulders shampoo several years ago, several small firms were already selling antidandruff shampoos. Head and Shoulders was introduced with a large promotional campaign, and the new brand captured over half the market immediately. Within a year, several of the firms that had been concentrating on this market segment went out of business.

Multisegment Targeting

multisegment targeting strategy
A strategy that chooses two or more well-defined market segments and develops a distinct marketing mix for each.

A firm that chooses to serve two or more well-defined market segments and develops a distinct marketing mix for each has a **multisegment targeting strategy**. Stouffer's, for example, offers gourmet entrees for one segment of the frozen dinner market and Lean Cuisine for another. Hershey offers premium candies like Golden Almond chocolate bars, packaged in gold foil, that are marketed to an adult audience. Another chocolate bar, called RSVP, is targeted toward consumers who crave the taste of Godiva chocolates at the price of a Hershey bar. Cosmetics companies seek to increase sales and market share by targeting multiple age and ethnic groups. May-

OshKosh B'Gosh, Inc., was so successful with its children's wear that it could not sell to anyone else. Faced with a concentrated market, the company is expanding into children's shoes, eyewear, and plush toys.
Courtesy OshKosh B'Gosh, Inc.

Rembrandt Displays The Style That Makes Him Such A Renaissance Boy.
Rembrandt Art Duran, age 8, New York, New York
Strong lines and bold strokes combine to make the OshKosh B'Gosh holiday collection a body of art anyone can appreciate. For the store nearest you, call

OshKosh
B'gosh
THE GENUINE ARTICLE
The Biggest Name In Kids' Clothes.

belline and Cover Girl, for example, market different lines to teenage women, young adult women, older women, and African-American women. JCPenney introduced the Diahann Carroll clothing line aimed at African-American women over thirty-five years old who work in suits and dress up for church.[46]

Sometimes organizations use different promotional appeals, rather than completely different marketing mixes, as the basis for a multisegment strategy. Beer marketers such as Adolph Coors Co. and Anheuser-Busch Companies advertise and promote special events targeted toward African-American, Hispanic-American, and Asian-American market segments. The beverages and containers, however, do not differ by ethnic market segment.[47]

Multisegment targeting offers many potential benefits to firms, including greater sales volume, higher profits, larger market share, and economies of scale in manufacturing and marketing. Yet it may also involve greater product design, production, promotion, inventory, marketing research, and management costs. Before deciding to use this strategy, firms should compare the benefits and costs of multisegment targeting to those of undifferentiated and concentrated targeting.

Another potential cost of multisegment targeting is **cannibalization**, which occurs when sales of a new product cut into sales of a firm's existing products. For example, pharmaceutical firms have been introducing new over-the-counter antacids that block the production of stomach acids (like Tagamet HB or Pepcid AC), rather than treat heartburn with traditional antacids that work by neutralizing stomach acids (like Tums or Mylanta). However, these firms are aware that the new heartburn drugs are likely to cannibalize their traditional antacid products. In advertising Tagamet HB, for instance, SmithKline has to avoid comparing it to Tums, the firm's antacid moneymaker.[48]

cannibalization
Situation that occurs when sales of a new product cut into sales of a firm's existing products.

Positioning

8
Explain how and why firms implement positioning strategies and how product differentiation plays a role

The term **positioning** refers to developing a specific marketing mix to influence potential customers' overall perception of a brand, product line, or organization in general. (**Position** is the place a product, brand, or group of products occupies in consumers' minds relative to competing offerings.) Consumer goods marketers are particularly concerned with positioning. Procter & Gamble, for example, markets eleven different laundry detergents, each with a unique position, as illustrated in Exhibit 6.10.

Positioning assumes that consumers compare products on the basis of important features. Marketing efforts that emphasize irrelevant features are therefore likely to misfire. For example, Crystal Pepsi and a clear version of Coca-Cola's Tab failed because consumers perceived the "clear" positioning as more of a marketing gimmick than a benefit.[49]

Effective positioning requires assessing the positions occupied by competing products, determining the important dimensions underlying these positions, and choosing a position in the market where the organization's marketing efforts will have the greatest impact. For example, General Motors Corp. recently adopted a strategy to position its Sierra trucks against its major competitors. The target market was defined as college-educated professionals in their forties with an annual income of $75,000 or more. The company hopes to establish a super-premium position for Sierra.[50]

positioning
Developing a specific marketing mix to influence potential customers' overall perception of a brand, product line, or organization in general.

position
The place a product, brand, or group of products occupies in consumers' minds relative to competing offerings.

exhibit 6.10

Positioning of Procter & Gamble Detergents

Brand	Positioning	Market Share
Tide	Tough, powerful cleaning	31.1%
Cheer	Tough cleaning and color protection	8.2%
Bold	Detergent plus fabric softener	2.9%
Gain	Sunshine scent and odor-removing formula	2.6%
Era	Stain treatment and stain removal	2.2%
Dash	Value brand	1.8%
Oxydol	Bleach-boosted formula, whitening	1.4%
Solo	Detergent and fabric softener in liquid form	1.2%
Dreft	Outstanding cleaning for baby clothes, safe for tender skin	1.0%
Ivory Snow	Fabric and skin safety on baby clothes and fine washables	0.7%
Ariel	Tough cleaner, aimed at Hispanics	0.1%

SOURCE: Reprinted with permission from the May 3, 1993, issue of *Advertising Age*. Copyright, Crain Communications Inc., 1993.

product differentiation
A positioning strategy that some firms use to distinguish their products from those of competitors.

As the previous example illustrates, **product differentiation** is a positioning strategy that many firms use to distinguish their products from those of competitors. The distinctions can be either real or perceived. Tandem Computer designed machines with two central processing units and two memories for computer systems that can never afford to be down or lose their databases (for example, an airline reservation system). In this case, Tandem used product differentiation to create a product with very real advantages for the target market. However, many everyday products, such as bleaches, aspirin, unleaded regular gasoline, and some soaps, are differentiated by such trivial means as brand names, packaging, color, smell, or "secret" additives. The marketer attempts to convince consumers that a particular brand is distinctive and that they should demand it over competing brands.

Some firms, instead of using product differentiation, position their products as being similar to competing products or brands. Artificial sweeteners advertised as tasting like sugar or margarine tasting like butter are two examples.

perceptual mapping
A means of displaying or graphing, in two or more dimensions, the location of products, brands, or groups of products in customers' minds.

Perceptual Mapping

Perceptual mapping is a means of displaying or graphing, in two or more dimensions, the location of products, brands, or groups of products in customers' minds.

Perceptual Maps and Positioning Strategies for General Motors Passenger Cars **exhibit 6.11**

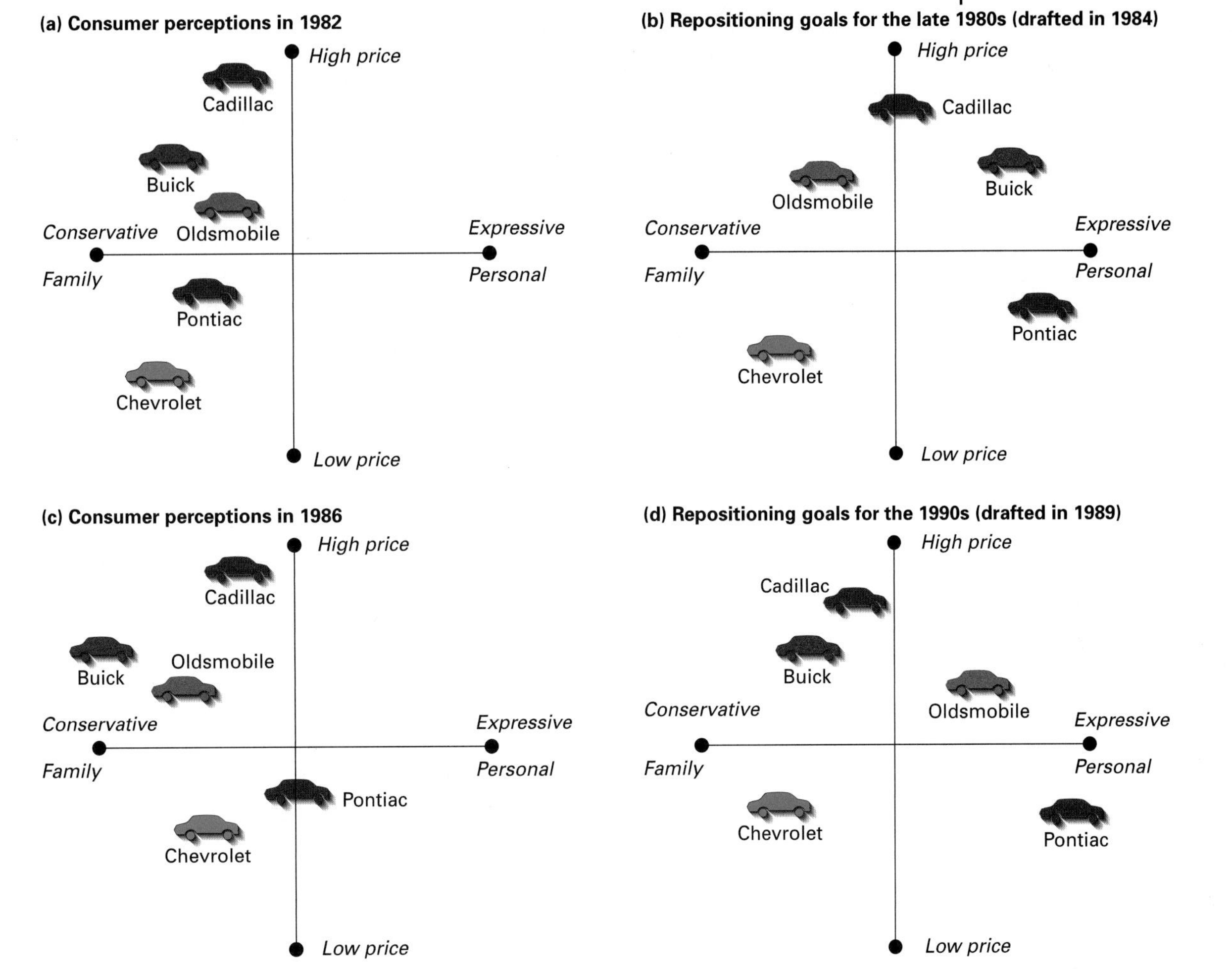

SOURCE: Reprinted with permission from the May 3, 1993, issue of *Advertising Age*. Copyright © 1993, Crain Communications Inc.

For example, the perceptual map in Exhibit 6.11a is the result of a 1982 study by General Motors of consumers' perceptions of the five GM automobile divisions: Buick, Cadillac, Chevrolet, Oldsmobile, and Pontiac. Consumer perceptions are plotted on two axes. The horizontal axis ranges from conservative and family oriented at one extreme to expressive and personal at the other. The vertical axis is used to rate price perceptions, and it ranges from high to low. Note that in 1982 the various GM divisions were not perceived as especially distinctive. Consumers didn't clearly distinguish one brand from another, especially on the conservative/family versus expressive/personal dimension.

In 1984, General Motors was reorganized to reduce overlap and duplication among divisions and to produce fewer, more distinctive models. The perceptual map in Exhibit 6.11b shows GM's plans for repositioning, or changing consumers' perceptions of the various models. As Exhibit 6.11c shows, however, consumer perceptions changed very little between 1982 and 1986.

Positioning Bases

Firms use a variety of bases for positioning, including the following:[51]

- *Attribute:* A product is associated with an attribute, product feature, or customer benefit. Rockport shoes are positioned as an always comfortable brand that is available in a range of styles from working shoes to dress shoes.[52]

Positioning against competitors is part of any positioning strategy, and Avis rental car's position as number two exemplifies using this base against specific competitors (for example, against Hertz). Why would it be to Avis's advantage to stay in the number two slot? Explain your answer.
© 1997 Mark Richards/CONTACT Press Images

- GLOBAL *Price and quality:* This positioning base may stress high price as a signal of quality or emphasize low price as an indication of value. Neiman Marcus uses the high-priced strategy; Kmart has successfully followed the low-price and value strategy. Cunard's, a London-based cruise-liner company that had fallen on hard times, was able to launch a turnaround by repositioning the brand to compete in the affluent consumer market. Changes included a new corporate identity, a series of elegant ad campaigns, and improved customer service.[53]
- *Use or application:* During the past few years, AT&T telephone service advertising has emphasized communicating with loved ones using the "Reach Out and Touch Someone" campaign. Stressing uses or applications can be an effective means of positioning a product with buyers. The advertising slogan "Orange juice isn't just for breakfast anymore" is an effort to reposition the product, in terms of time and place of use, as an all-occasion beverage.
- *Product user:* This positioning base focuses on a personality or type of user. Zale Corporation has several jewelry store concepts, each positioned to a different user. The Zale stores cater to middle-of-the-road consumers with traditional styles. Their Gordon's stores appeal to a slightly older clientele with a contemporary look. Guild is positioned for the more affluent fifty-plus consumer.[54]
- *Product class:* The objective here is to position the product as being associated with a particular category of products; for example, positioning a margarine brand with butter.
- *Competitor:* Positioning against competitors is part of any positioning strategy. The Avis rental car positioning as number two exemplifies positioning against specific competitors.

It is not unusual for a marketer to use more than one of these bases. The AT&T "Reach Out and Touch Someone" campaign that stressed use also emphasized the relatively low cost of long-distance calling. Mountain Dew positions its soft drink to the youth market as a thirst-quenching drink that is associated with teens having fun outdoors.[55]

Repositioning

repositioning
Changing consumers' perceptions of a brand in relation to competing brands.

Sometimes products or companies are repositioned in order to sustain growth in slow markets or to correct positioning mistakes. **Repositioning** is changing consumers' perceptions of a brand in relation to competing brands. To cope with a stagnant liquor industry, a number of companies are attempting to reposition vodka, a spirit without taste, color, or aroma, as a fashion icon with a complex taste. Part of the repositioning effort includes prestige packaging and higher prices.[56] Florsheim, known for its conservative styles tailored to the well-dressed man of about fifty, started to lose money as American shoes and dress turned more casual. The company is now aiming for the twenty-something customer, selling shoes other than its signature brands and renovating its 350 stores so that they look more contemporary.[57] Midas, an automobile muffler specialist chain, added brake repairs to its services in 1978. After spending millions of dollars promoting the added service, customer recall was less than 50 percent for brakes. Midas is now repositioning itself as the stop for all car care repair needs.[58]

By expanding its list of services, Midas has been able to reposition itself as a complete car repair shop rather than just a source for mufflers.
© Brent Jones/Tony Stone Images

Global Issues in Market Segmentation and Targeting

9 Discuss global market segmentation and targeting issues

Chapter 4 discussed the trend toward global market standardization, which enables firms like Coca-Cola, Colgate-Palmolive, McDonald's, and Nike to market similar products using similar marketing strategies in many different countries. This chapter has also discussed the trend toward targeting smaller, more precisely defined markets.

The tasks involved in segmenting markets, selecting target markets, and designing, implementing, and maintaining appropriate marketing mixes (described in Exhibit 6.7) are the same whether the marketer has a local perspective or a global vision. The main difference is the segmentation variables commonly used. Countries are commonly grouped using such variables as per capita gross domestic product, geography, religion, culture, or political system.

Some firms have tried to group countries or customer segments around the world using lifestyle or psychographic variables. So-called "Asian yuppies" in places like Singapore, Hong Kong, Japan, and South Korea have substantial spending power and exhibit purchase and consumption behavior similar to that of their better-known counterparts in the United States. In this case, firms may be able to use a global market standardization approach.

LOOKING BACK

In the story at the beginning of this chapter, market segmentation refers to the process of dividing a market into meaningful, relatively similar, and identifiable segments or groups. Targeting is selecting one or more market segments for which an organization designs, implements, and maintains distinctive marketing mixes. Dickies has changed from using a concentration targeting strategy (men's work apparel) to using a multisegment targeting strategy by trying to appeal to several different demographic segments: men, women, teens/young adults, and boys. The company is likely to be successful in its efforts to target multiple markets because women and teens/young adults were already buying the work apparel before Dickies had marketed to them specifically. The boys' market for school uniforms is a large ($11 billion) segment, and Dickies' brand name is known for its quality, so the company should do well in this market as well.

Summary

1 Describe the characteristics of markets and market segments. A market is composed of individuals or organizations with the ability and willingness to make purchases to fulfill their needs or wants. A market segment is a group of individuals or organizations with similar product needs as a result of one or more common characteristics.

2 Explain the importance of market segmentation. Before the 1960s, few businesses targeted specific market segments. Today, segmentation is a crucial marketing strategy for nearly all successful organizations. Market segmentation enables marketers to tailor marketing mixes to meet the needs of particular population segments. Segmentation helps marketers identify consumer needs and preferences, areas of declining demand, and new marketing opportunities.

3 **Discuss criteria for successful market segmentation.** Successful market segmentation depends on four basic criteria. First, a market segment must be substantial; it must have enough potential customers to be viable. Second, a market segment must be identifiable and measurable. Third, members of a market segment must be accessible to marketing efforts. Fourth, a market segment must respond to particular marketing efforts in a way that distinguishes it from other segments.

4 **Describe the bases commonly used to segment consumer markets.** There are five commonly used bases for segmenting consumer markets. Geographic segmentation is based on region, size, density, and climate characteristics. Demographic segmentation consists of age, gender, income level, ethnicity, and family life-cycle characteristics. Psychographic segmentation includes personality, motives, and lifestyle characteristics. Benefits sought is a type of segmentation that identifies customers according to the benefits they seek in a product. Finally, usage segmentation divides a market by the amount of product purchased or consumed.

5 **Describe the bases for segmenting business markets.** Business markets can be segmented on two bases. First, macrosegmentation divides markets according to general characteristics, such as location and customer type. Second, microsegmentation focuses on the decision-making units within macrosegments.

6 **List the steps involved in segmenting markets.** Six steps are involved when segmenting markets: (1) Selecting a market or product category for study; (2) choosing a basis or bases for segmenting the market; (3) selecting segmentation descriptors; (4) profiling and evaluating segments; (5) selecting target markets; and (6) designing, implementing, and maintaining appropriate marketing mixes.

7 **Discuss alternative strategies for selecting target markets.** Marketers select target markets using three different strategies: undifferentiated targeting, concentrated targeting, and multisegment targeting. An undifferentiated targeting strategy assumes that all members of a market have similar needs that can be met with a single marketing mix. A concentrated targeting strategy focuses all marketing efforts on a single market segment. Multisegment targeting is a strategy that uses two or more marketing mixes to target two or more market segments.

8 **Explain how and why firms implement positioning strategies and how product differentiation plays a role.** Positioning is used to influence consumer perceptions of a particular brand, product line, or organization in relation to competitors. The term *position* refers to the place that the offering occupies in consumers' minds. To establish a unique position, many firms use product differentiation, emphasizing the real or perceived differences between competing offerings. Products may be differentiated on the basis of attribute, price and quality, use or application, product user, product class, or competitor.

9 **Discuss global market segmentation and targeting issues.** The key tasks in market segmentation, targeting, and positioning are the same regardless of whether the target market is local, regional, national, or multinational. The main differences are the variables used by marketers in analyzing markets and assessing opportunities and the resources needed to implement strategies.

Discussion and Writing Questions

1. Describe market segmentation in terms of the historical evolution of marketing.
2. WRITING Choose magazine ads for five different products. For each ad, write a description of the demographic characteristics of the targeted market.

3. TEAM Form a team with two other students. Select a product category and brand that are familiar to your team. Using Exhibit 6.9, prepare a market segmentation report and describe a targeting plan.
4. Explain concentrated (niche) targeting. Describe a company not mentioned in the chapter that uses a concentrated targeting strategy.
5. TEAM Form a team with two or three other students. Create an idea for a new product. Describe the segment (or segments) you are going to target with the product and develop a positioning strategy for the product.
6. Choose a product category (e.g., blue jeans) and identify at least three different brands and their respective positioning strategies. How is each position communicated to the target audience?
7. Create a perceptual map for the different brands of one of the following products: diet and regular colas, Ford automobiles, fast-food hamburger restaurants, or a product of your choice.
8. ON LINE Investigate how Delta Airlines uses its Web site to cater to its market segments.
http://www.delta-air.com/
9. ON LINE How are visitors to the following Web site segmented when seeking relevant job openings? Try this search engine and report your results. **http://www.careermag.com/**
10. WRITING Write a letter to the president of your bank suggesting ideas for increasing profits and enhancing customer service by improving segmentation and targeting strategies. Make your suggestions specific.

Application for Small Business

ENTREPRENEUR Judy Brown has always loved working with animals. She has experience in pet grooming, boarding, and in-home pet sitting. Judy wants to open a full-service business utilizing her skills that is uniquely positioned in relation to the traditional pet grooming/boarding businesses that operate in the town where she lives. Customers that use these current pet services deliver their pets to the firms and later pick them up. Most are open between 9 A.M. and 6 P.M. from Monday through Friday.

Judy lives in a midsize city that is close to a major airport. Many high-tech industries are located in or near her city, so there are a large number of men and women in managerial and information technology positions, and travel is a frequent part of their jobs. A lot of families have pets, so Judy thinks there is a market for pet-related services, despite the current competition.

Questions

1. How should Judy segment the market for pet services?
2. What targeting strategy should Judy use to start her business? Should this strategy change as her business prospers and grows?
3. How should Judy position her pet services business against her competition?

Review Quiz

1. The process of dividing a market into meaningful, relatively similar, and identifiable groups is called
   a. Product positioning
   b. Market segmentation
   c. Product differentiation
   d. Market penetration

Key Terms

benefit segmentation 191
cannibalization 199
concentrated targeting strategy 197
demographic segmentation 183
80/20 principle 192
family life cycle (FLC) 187
geodemographic segmentation 190
geographic segmentation 183
macrosegmentation 193
market 180
market segment 180
market segmentation 180
microsegmentation 194
multisegment targeting strategy 198
niche 197
optimizers 194
perceptual mapping 200
position 199
positioning 199
product differentiation 200
psychographic segmentation 188
repositioning 202
satisficers 194
segmentation bases (variables) 182
target market 195
undifferentiated targeting strategy 195
usage-rate segmentation 192

2. Why is market segmentation a key to successful marketing strategy?
   a. Many groups of customers have different needs and preferences.
   b. It helps define customer needs and wants more precisely.
   c. It helps more accurately define marketing objectives and allocate resources.
   d. All of the above are reasons that segmentation is important to marketing strategy.

3. Which of the following are important criteria for successful market segmentation?
   a. Product differentiation, concentrated targeting, and perceptual mapping
   b. A clearly defined target market, highly educated marketers, and experienced management teams
   c. Substantiality, measurability, accessibility, and responsiveness
   d. Product positioning, product development, and product differentiation

4. Variables such as age, gender, and income represent common bases of ______ segmentation.
   a. Demographic
   b. Geographic
   c. Psychographic
   d. Benefit

5. Variables such as personality, motives, and lifestyles represent common bases of ______ segmentation.
   a. Demographic
   b. Geographic
   c. Psychographic
   d. Benefit

6. Macrosegmentation of businesses divides business markets according to which of the following general characteristics?
   a. Geographic location
   b. Customer type
   c. Product use
   d. All of the above

7. Once a firm selects a market or product category for study, what is the next step in the market segmentation process?
   a. Selecting segmentation descriptors
   b. Profiling market segments
   c. Designing appropriate marketing mixes for each segment
   d. Choosing the bases for segmenting the market

8. Which of the following does *not* describe undifferentiated targeting?
   a. Undifferentiated targeting views the market as one big market with no individual segments.
   b. Undifferentiated targeting is a strategy for the first firm to enter an industry.
   c. Undifferentiated targeting selects a specific niche within which to market.
   d. Undifferentiated targeting can save companies money on production and marketing.

9. Repositioning is
   a. A positioning strategy companies use to distinguish their products from those of their competitors
   b. Dividing a market by the amount of product bought or sold
   c. Changing consumers' perceptions of a brand in relation to competing brands
   d. Grouping customers into market segments according to the benefits they seek from the product

10. Positioning is a means of displaying or graphing, in two or more dimensions, the locations of products, brands, or groups of producers in customers' minds.
    a. True
    b. False
11. The tasks involved in segmenting markets; selecting target markets; and designing, implementing, and maintaining appropriate marketing mixes are the same whether the marketer is pursuing local or global marketing areas.
    a. True
    b. False
12. Identify commonly used bases for positioning.

Check the Answer Key, which follows the Video Case, to see how well you understood the material.

VIDEO CASE

Labelle Management: Something for Everyone

Sizzling burgers, shakes and fries, pizza, or a thick steak. What's your pleasure? Labelle Management, which owns and operates thirty-one restaurants and hotels, has them all. Headquartered in Mt. Pleasant, Michigan, Labelle has been in the restaurant business since 1948. When McDonald's came to town in the 1970s, Labelle's owners faced stiff competition and decided to add franchises to their holdings. They now own six restaurants located on the main street in town. The key to Labelle's success is its use of benefit segmentation. It groups its customers into market segments according to the benefits they seek from the various restaurant formats. Customers are mainly targeted on the basis of needs and wants. Although Labelle's restaurants compete with one another for customers, they can all coexist because the same people want different benefits at different times.

How does this concept work? Mt. Pleasant is a college town, home to Central Michigan University, an undergraduate campus with seventeen thousand students who choose different restaurants on different occasions. Late at night after studying, the students crave pizza delivered to their dorm, so they call Pixies. This original Labelle, 1950s style, drive-in restaurant offers fast food at low prices, plus rock & roll and lots of nostalgia. Labelle works with sororities, fraternities, athletic groups, and clubs on campus for special events. Students, however, aren't the only ones who are in a hurry. Pixies is the perfect dinner stop for moms on the go, driving the kids to soccer games, piano lessons, or swimming.

For those not interested in fast food but still interested in low prices, Labelle has other options. Ponderosa Steak House is a no-frills franchise offering very good value. For those who are really hungry—students or workers—there are big, juicy steaks, big helpings of potatoes, veggies, and desserts. Customers get a lot of food for the money, and Ponderosa is a natural for groups. The atmosphere is simple, and service is mainly buffet-style.

Labelle's Big Boy Restaurants appeal to families, blue-collar workers, and seniors because of the moderate prices ($3 to $8) for the famous double-decker hamburgers, sandwiches, salads, and dinners. Students also turn out in droves for the $4.99 all-you-can-eat breakfast buffet. Big Boy has been around for a long time, and customers can always count on getting the same good food at the same price. The familiar menu and friendly service account for the high customer loyalty at Big Boy, where managers are selected for their ability to get along with customers of all ages.

On the weekends, students, families, and friends in Mt. Pleasant like to relax and have fun, so ethnic food can be a nice change of pace from everyday meals. The family-priced Italian bistro, Italian Oven, features pasta, salads, and pizza cooked in wood-burning ovens. What makes Italian Oven even more attractive is that it offers entertainment in the form of wandering singers, musicians, and magicians.

It's hard to beat the old Irish pub atmosphere of Bennigan's. Out for a beer, the twenty-somethings like to hang out at this upbeat, upscale bar and grill, although the average tab is at least $10 per person. Part of creating a fun dining experience is creating a daring menu, and new items with trendy names and spicy tastes are standard fare at Bennigan's. Customers expect a high level of service at this Labelle restaurant, which means orders taken promptly and tasty food. College students, businesspeople, and the ladies' lunch crowd like to come to Bennigan's, so the managers and staff have to be attentive, laid-back, and fun in order to meet the needs of such a diverse customer base.

Although Labelle Management casts its nets to attract a wide variety of customers, it adds perks for frequent patrons. Based on the old 80/20 adage that 20 percent of all customers generate 80 percent of demand, Labelle Management tries hard to keep its steady customers happy so they will come back more often. Because 25 percent of Bennigan's sales comes from the bar, Bennigan's offers a beer card; those who drink a hundred or more imported beers get their names on the plaque over the bar. And those who eat six of Pixies' famous Coney Dogs or eight Bitty Burgers have their names written on the wall of fame. Labelle Management knows Mt. Pleasant backwards and forwards and works overtime through diversified restaurant concepts to give community members what they want.

Questions

1. How does LaBelle Management use benefit segmentation to target various market segments?
2. Describe the benefits provided by each restaurant format.
3. How does LaBelle Management use usage-rate segmentation?
4. Explain how service is a benefit that varies with restaurant format.

Bibliography

Labelle Management Web site:
http://www.labellemgt.com
Video by Learnet Inc.

Answer Key

1. *Answer:* b, p. 180

   Rationale: The idea of market segmentation is to enable marketers to tailor marketing mixes to better meet the needs of specific groups of customers.

2. *Answer:* d, p. 181

   Rationale: Segmentation is important for all of these reasons because they are consistent with the marketing concept: satisfying customer needs while meeting organizational objectives.

3. *Answer:* c, pp. 181–182

   Rationale: Segments that can meet these four criteria are useful to marketers because they assure that an organization can effectively market to members of the segment.

4. *Answer:* a, p. 183

   Rationale: Demographic segmentation uses characteristics of customers that are easily measured, such as age, income, gender, ethnic background, and family life cycle.

5. *Answer:* c, pp. 188–189

   Rationale: Psychographic segmentation uses characteristics of customers, in addition to traditional demographic variables, that help to add a further understanding of their marketplace behavior.

6. *Answer:* d, p. 193

   Rationale: These three sets of variables, as well as customer size, are all used as macrosegmentation variables in the segmentation of business markets.

7. *Answer:* d, p. 194

   Rationale: Once the firm defines the overall market or product category to be studied, it must select the segmentation bases or variables. Remember, these bases must meet the four basic criteria discussed in the chapter.

8. *Answer:* c, pp. 195–196

   Rationale: A firm using an undifferentiated targeting strategy adopts a mass-market philosophy, viewing the market as one big market with no individual segments.

9. *Answer:* c, p. 202

   Rationale: Sometimes products, services, or companies need to be repositioned in order to sustain growth in slow markets or to correct past positioning errors.

10. *Answer:* b, p. 199

    Rationale: The term positioning refers to the development of a specific marketing mix to influence potential customers' overall perception of a brand relative to competitive offerings.

11. *Answer:* a, p. 203

    Rationale: Although the tasks of segmenting markets remains the same between local or global markets, the segmentation variables are likely different.

12. *Answer:* There are six bases for positioning described in the chapter, including attributes, price and quality, use or application, product user, product class, and competitor. (pp. 201–202)

CHAPTER

7

LEARNING OBJECTIVES

After studying this chapter, you should be able to

1 Explain the concept and purpose of a marketing decision support system

2 Define marketing research and explain its importance to marketing decision making

3 Describe the steps involved in conducting a marketing research project

4 Discuss the growing importance of scanner-based research

5 Explain when marketing research should and should not be conducted

DECISION SUPPORT SYSTEMS AND MARKETING RESEARCH

NetSmart discovered there are no cohesive subgroups of the female on-line population; women have overlapping, multifaceted responsibilities and interests. They are overwhelmed with multiple demands and their focus is based on the current priority rather than on a single-minded pursuit. As a career woman and investor, she goes on-line for convenience and success.

Almost two-thirds of women on-line work full-time (64 percent) and make computers and the Internet a routine part of the way they work, play, interact, and shop. Instead of picking up a phone, women log on-line, with e-mail their preferred means of communication.

Perceived Benefits

- 88 percent feel the Internet saves them time
- 86 percent value the convenience
- 71 percent say it lets them bank and shop after retail hours

Role of the Internet as an Important Business Tool

These career women use the Internet to

- Send or respond to e-mail
- Do business research on-line
- Communicate with other employees
- Work from home (25 percent)

Along with career and family responsibilities, women have personal needs and interests, from finance to fitness to fashion. They go on-line to stay on top of current events, get stock tips and, of course, find out about the latest fashion trends. There are actually two aspects to this personal online usage: "Escape from Stress" and "Self-Indulgence."[1]

This type of marketing research can help companies better understand women who use the Web. Managers can better target specific women's markets. They can also build more effective Web sites. What are the various techniques for conducting marketing research? Should managers always do marketing research before they make a decision? How does marketing research relate to decision support systems?

on line

Want to know more about women on the Web?
Read the Executive Summary at
http://www.netsmart-research.com/main-sum.html

Quaker Oatmeal
Gatorade
How do these Quaker companies use e-mail to build their databases?
http://www.quakeroatmeal.com
http://www.gatorade.com/

Marketing Decision Support Systems

1
Explain the concept and purpose of a marketing decision support system

marketing intelligence
Everyday information about developments in the marketing environment that managers use to prepare and adjust marketing plans.

decision support system (DSS)
An interactive, flexible computerized information system that enables managers to obtain and manipulate information as they are making decisions.

Accurate and timely information is the lifeblood of marketing decision making. Good information can help maximize an organization's sales and efficiently use scarce company resources. To prepare and adjust marketing plans, managers need a system for gathering everyday information about developments in the marketing environment—that is, for gathering **marketing intelligence.** The system most commonly used these days for gathering marketing intelligence is called a *marketing decision support system.*

A marketing **decision support system (DSS)** is an interactive, flexible computerized information system that enables managers to obtain and manipulate information as they are making decisions. A DSS bypasses the information-processing specialist and gives managers access to useful data from their own desks.

These are the characteristics of a true DSS system:

- *Interactive:* Managers give simple instructions and see immediate results. The process is under their direct control; no computer programmer is needed. Managers don't have to wait for scheduled reports.
- *Flexible:* A DSS can sort, regroup, total, average, and manipulate the data in various ways. It will shift gears as the user changes topics, matching information to the problem at hand. For example, the CEO can see highly aggregated figures, and the marketing analyst can view very detailed breakouts.
- *Discovery-oriented:* Managers can probe for trends, isolate problems, and ask "what if" questions.
- *Accessible:* DSS is easy to learn and use by managers who aren't skilled with computers. Novice users should be able to choose a standard, or default, method of using the system. They can bypass optional features so they can work with the basic system right away while gradually learning to apply its advanced features.

A hypothetical example showing how DSS can be used is provided by Renee Smith, vice president and manager of new products for Central Corporation. To evaluate sales of a recently introduced product, Renee can "call up" sales by the week, then by the month, breaking them out at her option by, say, customer segments. As she works at her desktop computer, her inquiries can go in several directions, depending on the decision at hand. If her train of thought raises questions about monthly sales last quarter compared to forecasts, she can use her DSS to analyze problems immediately. Renee might see that her new product's sales were significantly below forecast. Were her forecasts too optimistic? She compares other products' sales to her forecasts and finds that the targets were very accurate. Was something wrong with the product? Is her sales department getting insufficient leads, or is it not putting leads to good use? Thinking a minute about how to examine that question, she checks ratios of leads converted to sales product by product. The results disturb her. Only 5 percent of the new product's leads generated orders, compared to the company's 12 percent all-product average. Why? Renee guesses that the sales force is not supporting the new product vigorously enough. Quantitative information from the DSS perhaps could provide more evidence to back that suspicion. But already having enough quantitative knowledge to satisfy herself, the VP acts on her intuition and experience and decides to have a chat with her sales manager.

database marketing
The creation of a large computerized file of customers' and potential customers' profiles and purchase patterns.

Perhaps the fastest-growing use of DSS is for **database marketing,** which is the creation of a large computerized file of customers' and potential customers' pro-

Coca-Cola

When you are asked for your "two cents' worth" on Coke's Web site, is Coca-Cola doing marketing research or DSS? Read the whole survey before deciding. Which did you pick and why?

http://www.cocacola.com

on line

files and purchase patterns. It is usually the key tool for successful micromarketing, which relies on very specific information about a market.

The Role of Marketing Research

2

Define marketing research and explain its importance to marketing decision making

marketing research
The process of planning, collecting, and analyzing data relevant to a marketing decision.

Marketing research is the process of planning, collecting, and analyzing data relevant to a marketing decision. The results of this analysis are then communicated to management. Marketing research plays a key role in the marketing system. It provides decision makers with data on the effectiveness of the current marketing mix and also insights for necessary changes. Furthermore, marketing research is a main data source for both management information systems and DSS.

Marketing research has three roles: descriptive, diagnostic, and predictive. Its *descriptive* role includes gathering and presenting factual statements. For example, what is the historic sales trend in the industry? What are consumers' attitudes toward a product and its advertising? Its *diagnostic* role includes explaining data. For instance, what was the impact on sales of a change in the design of the package? Its *predictive* function is to address "what if" questions. For example, how can the researcher use the descriptive and diagnostic research to predict the results of a planned marketing decision?

Differences Between Marketing Research and DSS

Because marketing research is problem oriented, managers use it when they need guidance to solve a specific problem. Marketing research, for example, has been used to find out what features consumers want in a new personal computer. It has also aided product development managers in deciding how much milk to add in a new cream sauce for frozen peas. The U.S. Army has used marketing research to develop a profile of the young person most likely to be positively influenced by recruiting ads.

In contrast, DSS continually channels information about environmental changes into the organization. This information is gathered from a variety of sources, both inside and outside the firm. One important information source is marketing research. For example, Mastic Corporation, a leading supplier of vinyl siding, asks its nationwide network of distributors and their dealers questions about product quality, Mastic's service to the distributor, the amount of vinyl the distributor sells, and the percentage used for new construction. This information then becomes part of Mastic's DSS. Other data in the system include new housing starts, national unemployment figures, age of housing, and changes in housing styles. Its marketing research is therefore a component or input source for its DSS.

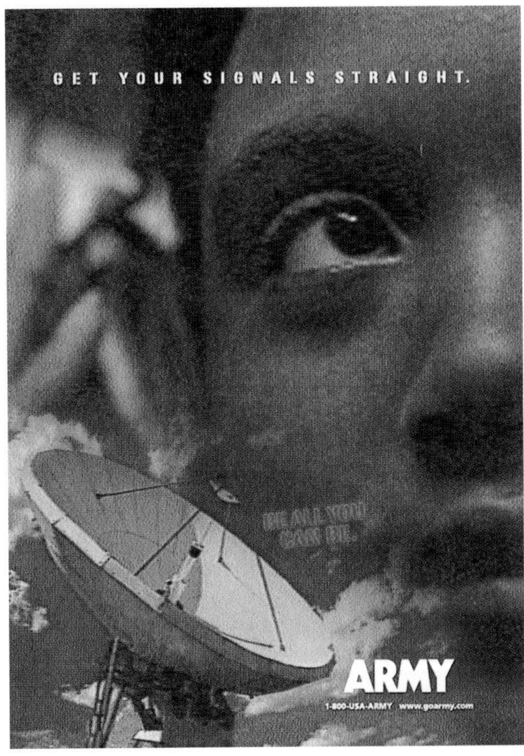

The U.S. Army used marketing research to develop a profile of the young person most likely to be positively influenced by its recruiting ads.
Army materials courtesy of the U.S. Government, as represented by the Secretary of the Army.

Management Uses of Marketing Research

Marketing research can help managers in several ways. It improves the quality of decision making and helps managers trace problems. Most important, sound marketing research helps managers focus on the paramount importance of keeping existing customers, aids them to better understand the marketplace, and alerts them to marketplace trends. Marketing research helps managers gauge the perceived value of their goods and services as well as the level of customer satisfaction.

Improving the Quality of Decision Making Managers can sharpen their decision making by using marketing research to explore the desirability of various marketing alternatives. For example, some years ago General Mills decided to expand into full-service restaurants. Marketing research indicated that the most popular ethnic food category in the United States was Italian and that interest in pasta and preference for Italian food would continue to increase. The company conducted many taste tests to find appropriate spice levels and to create a menu sure to please target customers. These marketing research studies led to the creation of The Olive Garden Italian restaurants, the fastest-growing and most popular full-service Italian restaurant chain in the nation.

Tracing Problems Another way managers use marketing research is to find out why a plan backfires. Was the initial decision incorrect? Did an unforeseen change in the external environment cause the plan to fail? How can the same mistake be avoided in the future?

Keebler introduced Sweet Spots, a shortbread cookie with a huge chocolate drop on it. It has had acceptable sales and is still on the market, but only after using marketing research to overcome several problems. Soon after the cookie's introduction, Keebler increased the box size from 10 ounces at $2.29 to 15 ounces at $3.19. Demand immediately fell. Market research showed that Sweet Spots were now considered more of a luxury than an everyday item. Keebler lowered the price and went back to the 10-ounce box. Even though Sweet Spots originally was aimed at upscale adult females, the company also tried to appeal to kids. In subsequent research, Keebler found that the package graphics appealed to mothers but not to children.[2]

Focusing on the Paramount Importance of Keeping Existing Customers An inextricable link exists between customer satisfaction and customer loyalty. Long-term relationships simply don't just happen but are grounded in the delivery of service and value by the firm. Customer retention pays big dividends for organizations. Powered by repeat sales and referrals, revenues and market share grow. Costs fall because firms spend less money and energy attempting to replace defectors. Steady customers are easy to serve because they understand the modus operandi and make fewer demands on employees' time. Increased customer retention also drives job satisfaction and pride, which leads to higher employee retention. In turn, the knowledge employees acquire as they stay longer increases productivity. A Bain & Company study estimates that a decrease in the customer defection rate by 5 percent can boost profits by 25 percent to 95 percent.[3]

The ability to retain customers is based on an intimate understanding of their needs. This knowledge comes primarily from marketing research. For example, British Airways recast its first-class transatlantic service based on detailed marketing research. Most airlines stress top-of-the-line service in their transatlantic first-class cabins. British Air research found that most first-class passengers simply wanted to sleep. British Air now gives premium flyers the option of dinner on the ground, before takeoff, in the first-class lounge. Once on board, they can slip into British Air pajamas, put their heads on comfortable pillows, slip under blankets, and enjoy an interruption-free flight. On arrival, first-class passengers can have breakfast, use comfortable dressing rooms and showers, and even have their clothes pressed before they set off for business. These changes in British Air's first-class service were driven strictly by marketing research.[4]

Understanding the Ever-Changing Marketplace Marketing research also helps managers understand what is going on in the marketplace and take advantage of opportunities. Historically, marketing research has been practiced for as long as marketing has existed. The early Phoenicians carried out market demand studies as they traded in the various ports of the Mediterranean Sea. Marco Polo's diary indicates he was performing a marketing research function as he traveled to China. There is even evidence that the Spanish systematically conducted market surveys as they ex-

exhibit 7.1

Demographics of Heavy Coupon Users

	Heavy (Top 20%)	Medium–Light	Nonuser
Average Household Size	3.6	3.2	3.4
Average Age Female Head	43.1	45.2	41.9
Household Income (in thousands)	$30.9	$29.1	$28.7
Female Head Attended College	51%	50%	52%
Average Monthly Grocery Bill	$334	$292	$303
Female Head Does Not Work Outside or Works Part-time	65%	61%	55%

SOURCE: From "Strategic Shift: Major U.S. Companies Expand Efforts To Sell To Consumers Abroad" by G. Pascal Zachary, *Wall Street Journal*, June 13, 1996. Reprinted by permission of The Wall Street Journal, ©1996 Dow Jones & Company, Inc. All Rights Reserved Worldwide.

plored the New World, and there are examples of marketing research conducted during the Renaissance. Today, a marketing manager might consider offering coupons with the introduction of a new frozen pastry. The coupon would be used along with network television advertising to induce trial of the new pastry. The question arises as to who should receive the coupons. The sales promotion expenditure would be more effective if coupons were to be mailed to those households most likely to redeem them. Previous experience with frozen pastry coupon redemptions suggests that heavy coupon users in general are most likely to redeem the new pastry coupons. The next logical question for the marketing manager would be, "Are there any identifiable demographic characteristics of heavy coupon users versus light users?" Market research revealed that the only statistically significant difference is that the female head of household is not employed full time (see Exhibit 7.1). The marketing manager would then specify this characteristic when purchasing the mailing list for the new frozen pastry coupons.

Understanding the marketplace is not just a United States or industrialized market phenomenon. It is important for managers all over the world to understand the ever-changing marketplace and their customers. See the following box.

global perspectives

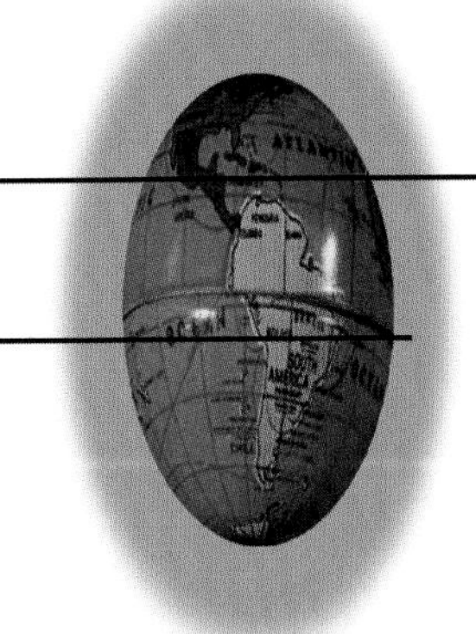

Marketing Research Examines Demand for a Prawn-Flavored Potato Chip

Janjaree Thanma flips through a fat folder of market research, thinking about a prawn-flavored potato chip. Janjaree, who directs marketing for Frito-Lay chips in Bangkok, Thailand, has found that prawn is the favorite flavor of Thais—based on marketing research. But that doesn't necessarily put it in the chips. The Thais said they thought an American snack with a native flavor such as *tom yam*, or prawn, is inappropriate—much as Frito-Lay people in China, after similar tests, ruled out the most popular flavor, dog.

Thais may "perceive a good snack as a Western snack," Thanma says. After testing five hundred flavors, her management team eschewed *tom yam* for now and stayed with American flavors such as barbecue.

Such painstaking research helps Frito-Lay's blitz of the market in Thailand. In 1995, the PepsiCo, Inc., unit bought out its Thai partner, took over a production plant, hired fifteen hundred farmers to grow potatoes according to its strict criteria, and unleashed a market campaign featuring television ads and a brigade of "promoter girls" who greeted shoppers in stores. Frito-Lay's sales in Thailand tripled in the first twelve months after the takeover and are forecast at seventy million bags a year.[5]

Do you think that marketing research can be effectively used in most countries of the world? What might be different about conducting marketing research abroad versus in the United States?

Steps in a Marketing Research Project

3
Describe the steps involved in conducting a marketing research project

Virtually all firms that have adopted the marketing concept engage in some marketing research because it offers decision makers many benefits. Some companies spend millions on marketing research; others, particularly smaller firms, conduct informal, limited-scale research studies. For example, when Eurasia restaurant, serving Eurasian cuisine, first opened along Chicago's ritzy Michigan Avenue, it drew novelty seekers. But it turned off the important business lunch crowd, and sales began to decline. The owner surveyed several hundred businesspeople working within a mile of the restaurant. He found that they were confused by Eurasia's concept and wanted more traditional Asian fare at lower prices. In response, the restaurant altered its concept; it hired a Thai chef, revamped the menu, and cut prices. The dining room was soon full again.

Whether a research project costs $200 or $2 million, the same general process should be followed. The marketing research process is a scientific approach to decision making that maximizes the chance of getting accurate and meaningful results. Exhibit 7.2 traces the steps: (1) defining the marketing problem, (2) planning the research design and gathering primary data, (3) specifying the sampling procedures, (4) collecting the data, (5) analyzing the data, (6) preparing and presenting the report, and (7) following up.

The research process begins with the recognition of a marketing problem or opportunity. As changes occur in the firm's external environment, marketing managers are faced with the questions, "Should we change the existing marketing mix?" and, if so, "How?" Marketing research may be used to evaluate product, promotion, distribution, or pricing alternatives. In addition, it is used to find and evaluate new market opportunities.

For example, there have been over thirty million babies born in the United States since 1990. It is the largest generation since the baby boomers. More

exhibit 7.2

The Marketing Research Process

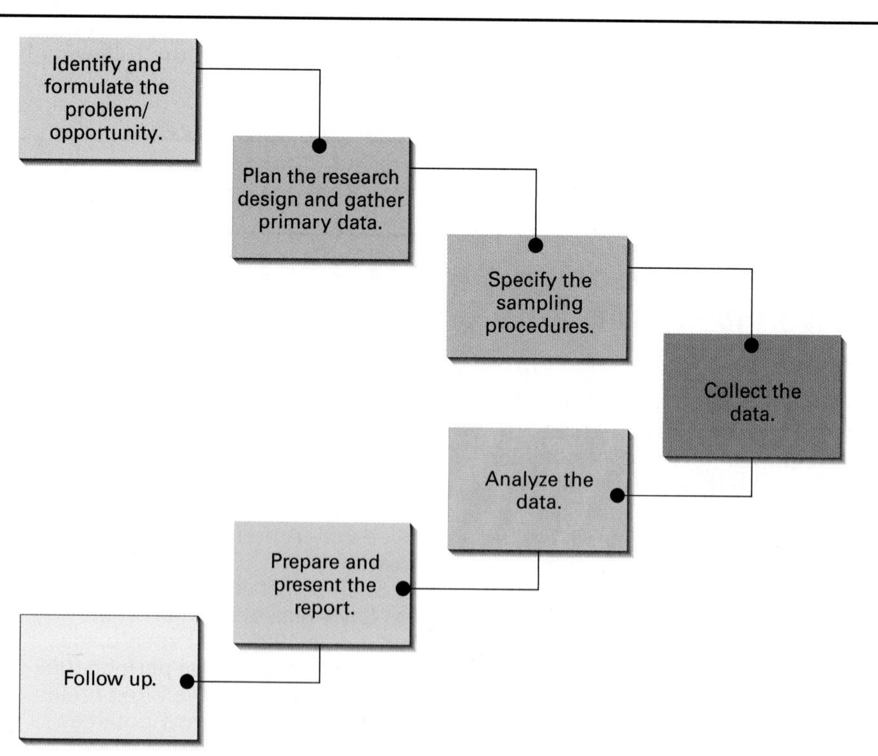

impressive than their numbers, though, is their wealth. The increase in single-parent and dual-earner households means kids are making shopping decisions once left to mom. Combining allowance, earnings, and gifts, kids fourteen and under will directly spend an estimated $20 billion this year, and they will influence the spending of another $200 billion.[6]

For savvy marketers, these statistics represent opportunity. Marketing research can hone in and clarify where the best opportunities lie. Walt Disney, for example, is launching a twenty-four-hour kids' radio network based on its marketing research. Sometimes research can lead to unexpected results requiring creative uses of the marketing mix. General Motors recently completed an analysis of "backseat consumers," that is, children between five and fifteen years of age. Marketing research discovered that parents often let their children play a tie-breaking role in deciding what car to purchase. Marketing managers, armed with this information, launched several programs. In late 1997, GM purchased the inside cover of *Sports Illustrated for Kids*, a magazine targeted to boys from eight to fourteen years old. The ad featured a brightly colored two-page spread for the Chevy Venture minivan, a vehicle targeted toward young families. GM also sent the minivan into malls and showed Disney movies on a VCR inside the van.

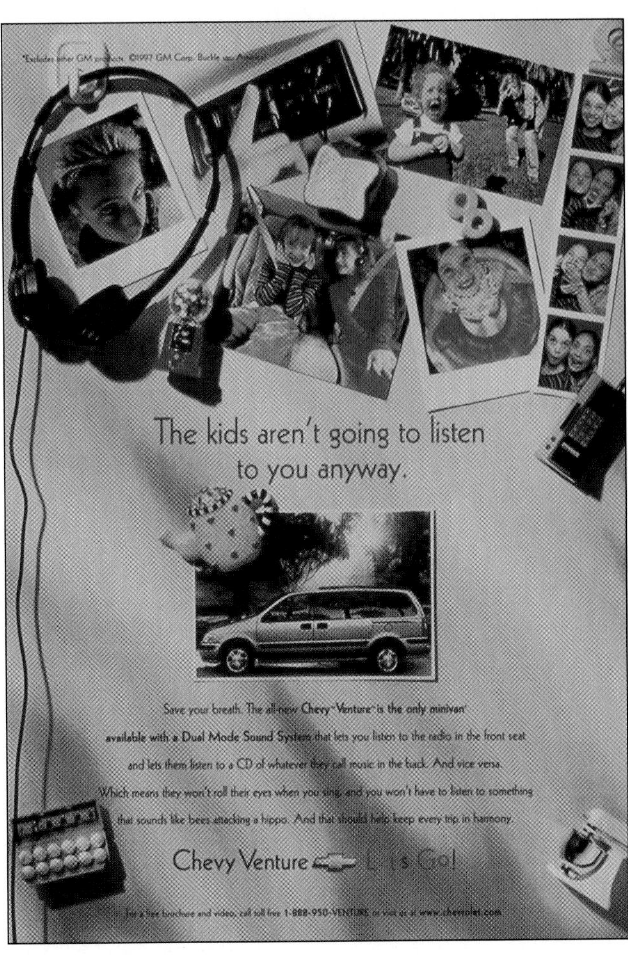

The kids aren't going to listen to you anyway.
Save your breath. The all-new Chevy Venture is the only minivan available with a Dual Mode Sound System that lets you listen to the radio in the front seat and lets them listen to a CD of whatever they call music in the back. And vice versa. Which means they won't roll their eyes when you sing, and you won't have to listen to something that sounds like bees attacking a hippo. And that should help keep every trip in harmony.
Chevy Venture
call toll free 1-888-950-VENTURE
www.chevrolet.com

Marketing research conducted by GM revealed that parents often let their children play a tie-breaking role in the selection of a new car. This information helped GM launch several programs, including brightly colored ads for the Chevy Venture minivan placed in *Sports Illustrated for Kids*.
Copyright 1997 GM Corp. Used with permission GM Media Archives.

The GM story illustrates an important point about problem/opportunity definition. The **marketing research problem** is information oriented. It involves determining what information is needed and how that information can be obtained efficiently and effectively. The **marketing research objective**, then, is to provide insightful decision-making information. This requires specific pieces of information needed to answer the marketing research problem. Managers must combine this information with their own experience and other information to make a proper decision. In the GM scenario, the marketing research objective was to determine what role, if any, backseat consumers play in a family's decision to purchase an automobile. In contrast, the **management decision problem** is action oriented. Management problems tend to be much broader in scope and far more general, whereas marketing research problems must be more narrowly defined and specific if the research effort is to be successful. Sometimes several research studies must be conducted to solve a broad management problem. Once GM determined that children within this target market played a tie-breaker role, the question became one of what should be done to influence the tie-breakers. GM used marketing research to determine that direct advertising to children in the target market and mall promotions would be the best form of promotion.

marketing research problem
Determining what information is needed and how that information can be obtained efficiently and effectively.

marketing research objective
Specific information needed to solve a marketing research problem; the objective should provide insightful decision-making information.

management decision problem
Broad-based problem that requires marketing research in order for managers to take proper actions.

Secondary Data A valuable tool throughout the research process but particularly in the problem/opportunity identification stage is secondary data. **Secondary data** are data previously collected for any purpose other than the one at hand. People both inside and outside the organization may have gathered secondary data to meet their needs. Exhibit 7.3 describes traditional sources of secondary data. Most research efforts rely at least partly on secondary data, which can usually be obtained quickly and inexpensively. The problem is locating relevant secondary data.

Secondary data save time and money if they help solve the researcher's problem. Even if the problem is not solved, secondary data have other advantages. They can aid in formulating the problem statement and suggest research methods and

exhibit 7.3

Traditional Sources of Secondary Data

Source	Description
Internal Information	Internal company information may be helpful in solving a particular marketing problem. Examples include sales invoices, other accounting records, data from previous marketing research studies, and historical sales data.
Market Research Firms	Companies such as A. C. Nielsen, Arbitron, and IMS International are major sources of secondary data regarding market share for consumer products and the characteristics of media audiences.
Trade Associations	Many trade associations, such as the National Industrial Conference Board and the National Retail Merchants Association, collect data of interest to members.
National Research Bureaus, Professional Associations, Foundations	A variety of nonprofit organizations collect and disseminate data of interest to marketing researchers.
Commercial Publications	*Advertising Age, Sales Management, Product Marketing, Merchandising Week,* and many other commercial publications provide useful research data.

secondary data
Data previously collected for any purpose other than the one at hand.

other types of data needed for solving the problem. In addition, secondary data can pinpoint the kinds of people to approach and their locations and serve as a basis of comparison for other data. The disadvantages of secondary data stem mainly from a mismatch between the researcher's unique problem and the purpose for which the secondary data were originally gathered, which are typically different. For example, a major consumer products manufacturer wanted to determine the market potential for a fireplace log made of coal rather than compressed wood byproducts. The researcher found plenty of secondary data about total wood consumed as fuel, quantities consumed in each state, and types of wood burned. Secondary data were also available about consumer attitudes and purchase patterns of wood byproduct fireplace logs. The wealth of secondary data provided the researcher with many insights into the artificial log market. Yet nowhere was there any information that would tell the firm whether consumers would buy artificial logs made of coal.

The quality of secondary data may also pose a problem. Often secondary data sources do not give detailed information that would enable a researcher to assess their quality or relevance. Whenever possible, a researcher needs to address these important questions: Who gathered the data? Why were the data obtained? What methodology was used? How were classifications (such as heavy users versus light users) developed and defined? When was the information gathered?

The New Age of Secondary Information—The Internet and World Wide Web

Gathering secondary data, although necessary in almost any research project, has traditionally been a tedious and boring job. The researcher often had to write to government agencies, trade associations, or other secondary data providers and then wait days or weeks for a reply that might never come. Often, one or more trips to the library were required and the researcher might find that needed reports were checked out or missing. In the last few years, the rapid development of the Internet and World Wide Web promises to eliminate the drudgery associated with the collection of secondary data.

ON LINE

The **Internet** is a worldwide telecommunications network that allows computers and the people who use them to access data, pictures, sound, and files throughout the world without regard to their physical location or the type of computer on which they reside. The **World Wide Web** (or **Web**) is one component of the Internet that was designed to simplify transmission of text and images. The Web is considered the most user-friendly portion of the Internet. Though not introduced until 1994, the Web leads all other Internet services in size and publicity, making the Web and the Internet synonymous to most users.

Internet
Worldwide telecommunications network allowing access to data, pictures, sound, and files throughout the world.

World Wide Web (Web)
Component of the Internet designed to simplify text and images.

Finding Secondary Data on the Internet

If you know the address of a particular Web site that contains the secondary data you need, you can type a description of what you are looking for directly into your Web browser (Netscape Navigator or Microsoft Internet Explorer are the dominant browsers). A Web address, or URL (**Uniform Reference Locator**), is similar to a street address in that it identifies a particular location (Web server and file on that server) on the Web. A typical Web address looks like the following:

http://www.microsoft.com/imagecomposer/download.htm

This Web address points to a document for downloading the free Image Composer software offered by Microsoft. "*http*" stands for Hypertext Transfer Protocol, which is the method by which information is exchanged between Web servers and browsers (Web clients). There are a few other protocols used (FTP, gopher, etc.), but *http* is synonymous with Web usage for most. The "*www*" is short for World Wide Web. This prefix is not required by all sites and is sometimes replaced with a different prefix such as *ww2* or no prefix at all. However, most Web addresses begin with *www.* The next item is called the domain name; in this case it is *microsoft.com.* This is a unique name registered for use on the Internet, much like a trademark is registered and used by a business. The extension (*.com*) tells you that the company is a for-profit company. Other extensions are *.edu* (educational institutions), *.org* (not-for-profit organizations), *.gov* (government sites), and *.net* (Internet service providers). After the domain name is the information that tells the Web server which document you are requesting. There can be multiple subdirectories that end with a specific file name (*download.htm*) or the path may end with a slash (/) indicating that you want the default document in that directory. (Some Web servers do not provide for default documents so you will get an error message in those instances.)

Uniform Reference Locator (URL)
Similar to a street address in that it identifies a unique location on the Web.

ON LINE

Search Engines Sites such as Yahoo!, AltaVista, Excite, and HotBot have become popular destinations for Web users looking for information on the Web. These organizations offer what are called *search engines.* Each of these search engines contains collections of links to documents throughout the world. Each uses its own indexing system to help you locate what you are looking for. All of them allow you to enter one or more keywords and search their databases of Web sites for all occurrences of those words. They then return listings that you can click on to go immediately to the site described. URLs and other information on some of the popular search engines are provided in Exhibit 7.4.

Finding the information that you need on the Web can be very easy or it can require some work and trial and error. Your Web connection provides access to approximately seventy-five million Web sites throughout the world, more information than any library can offer. It doesn't matter where you are—in New York City, Whitefish, Montana, or any other place on the globe—as long as you have an Internet connection, you have access to all this information. There are basically two ways to find the information you need. First, as already mentioned, if you

exhibit 7.4

Major Search Engines

Search Site	URL	Comments
AltaVista	http://www.alta-vista.com	Probably the biggest and fastest search engine available
DejaNews	http://www.dejanews.com	Most powerful Usenet search engine
Excite	http://www.excite.com	Cutting edge, fast, with site reviews and travel guides
HotBot	http://www.hotbot.com	Uses Inktomi search engine technology, which makes it very fast
Infoseek	http://www.infoseek.com	Easy-to-use search engine, plus Web directory with site reviews; good place to start for new user
Internet Public Library	http://www.ipl.org	Giant cyber library
Lycos	http://www.lycos.com	An old standard; dated in comparison to some of the new search engines
Magellan	http://www.mckinley.com	Family-oriented Web directory and search engine
SavvySearch	http://www.cs.colostate.edu/~dreiling/smartform.html	Search consolidator that submits your query to several search engines at the same time
World Wide Web Virtual Library	http://www.w3.org/vl	A volunteer effort to organize the World Wide Web by subject
Yahoo!	http://www.yahoo.com	Very organized and easy to use; another good place to start for the new user

know the URL (Uniform Resource Locator) of the site where the information you need is located, you can simply enter the URL for that site in the search window of your Web browser and go directly to that site. A list of some of the Web sites that have useful information for someone conducting marketing research is provided in Exhibit 7.5 on p. 222.

The second way of finding the information you need is to use a search engine. If, for example, you are looking for information on population estimates, you would go through the following steps:

- First, you would use your Web browser to go to one of the search engine sites on the Web (see Exhibit 7.4). You go to a search engine site by entering the URL for the search engine that you want in the search window of your Web browser. If you want to go to the Yahoo! site, you enter the URL for that site: **www.yahoo.com**.

Database America contains accurate, detailed marketing information and analytic services. This site and the others listed in Exhibit 7.5 have useful information for someone conducting marketing research.
Courtesy Info USA

Home | Go to SalesLeadsUSA | Index of Site | Help

DATABASE
AMERICA
COMPANIES

The Marketing Information Company

Sales Leads
Find new customers and increase sales!

Biz Finder
Need to know more about any particular business? We can help!

People Finder
Look up people by name, anywhere in the U.S., and get their addresses and phone numbers.

Free Stuff
Register NOW! and get the best Free Stuff!

Products & Services
We can help your business grow.

Site Map
A table of contents for Database America's web site.

Small Biz Forum
Get the information you need to make your small business reach new heights!

What is DBA?
Learn more about the company that gives you this site's hot information.

Press Releases/ Ads -- Job Opportunities -- Partner Pavilion

Legal Stuff

© 1996 Database America Companies, Inc.

- After you get to the search engine site, you enter a search request in the search window provided. Different search engines use slightly different rules for controlling the parameters of your search.
- You click on a "search" button, provided for all search engines, after you enter your search request. The search engine then searches the entire Web or a subset of the Web to locate sites that include information that meets the requirements you entered.
- Normally, in less than a minute (sometimes several minutes), the search engine returns a list of sites that have information that meets your requirements.
- The first thing you should do is look at the number of sites located. This number is typically printed at the top of a list of qualifying sites on the output returned by the engine. If your search is too broad, you may receive too much extraneous information; start over at this point and narrow your search with more specific criteria. For example, a search on the term "population" on the AltaVista search engine returned a list of over nine hundred thousand sites with some mention of "population." If you are actually looking for Texas population estimates, you should narrow your search. By changing the search request to "Texas population estimates," you will reduce the number of sites located to approximately two hundred.

Discussion Groups and Special Interest Groups on the Internet as Sources of Secondary Data

ON LINE

A primary means of communicating with other professionals and special interest groups on the Internet is through newsgroups. With an Internet connection and newsreader software, you can visit any newsgroup supported by your service provider. If your service provider does not offer newsgroups or does not carry the group in which you are interested, you can find one of the publicly available newsgroup servers that does carry the group in which you are interested.

Newsgroups function much like bulletin boards for a particular topic or interest. A newsgroup is established to focus on a particular topic. Readers stop by that newsgroup to read messages left by other people, post responses to others' questions and send rebuttals to comments with which they disagree. Generally, there is some management of the messages to keep discussions within the topic area and to remove offensive material. However, readers of a newsgroup are free to discuss any issue and communicate with anyone in the world that stops by that newsgroup. Images and data files can be exchanged in newsgroups, just as they can be exchanged via e-mail.

exhibit 7.5 | Some Sources of Secondary Data for Conducting Marketing Research on the Web

Organization	URL	Description
American Demographics/ Marketing Tools	http://www.marketingtools.com	Searches the full text of all of their publications (American Demographics and Marketing Tools)
American Marketing Association	http://www.ama.org	Lets you search all of the AMA's publications by using keywords
BLS Consumer Expenditure Surveys	http://stats.bls.gov/csxprod.htm	Provides information on the buying habits of American consumers, including data on their expenditures, income, and credit
Bureau of Economic Analysis	http://www.bea.doc.gov	Wide range of economic statistics
Bureau of Labor Statistics	http://stats.bls.gov	Allows you to obtain BLS time-series data based on a query you formulate and execute; has a table containing current data on various economic indicators produced by BLS along with other major statistical categories
Bureau of Transportation Statistics	http://www.bts.gov	Great source for all kinds of statistics on transportation
Census and Demographic Information	http://www.clark.net	A private, government-sponsored research organization dedicated to disseminating information on global environmental change and demographics
Database America	http://www.databaseamerica.com	Contains accurate, detailed marketing information and analytic services; can help strengthen your Internet site and also get more responses from your mailings
Economic Research Service, Department of Agriculture	http://www.econ.ag.gov	Wide range of agricultural statistics
Equifax National Decision Systems	http://www.ends.com	Includes many databases, reports, maps, graphs, industry-focused applications expertise and advanced computer technologies for data access, analysis, planning, and targeting
Find/SVP	http://www.findsvp.com	Offers consulting and research service; contains the country's largest private information center
Geographic Data Technology	http://www.geographic.com	Services include geocoding software, geocoding services, mapping services, nationwide street databases, and nationwide boundary products
National Management Services	http://www.dallas.net	Consumer household database system that measures exactly which household audiences buy, pay for, and take delivery of your products; select household audiences in the metro and suburban North Dallas area
Office of Research & Statistics, SSA	http://www.ssa.gov/statistics/ ors_home.html	Another source of a range of government statistics

exhibit 7.5 | *continued*

Organization	URL	Description
Pcensus for Windows	http://www.tetrad.com	Detailed information about the population of the New York metropolitan area
Population Reference Bureau	http://www.prb.org/prb/	Source of demographic information on population issues
Statistics of Income, Internal Revenue Service	http://www.irs.ustreas.gov/basic/tax_stats/index.html	Great source of income data
STAT-USA, Commerce	http://www.stat-usa.gov	Variety of statistical information
Strategic Mapping	http://www.stratmap.com	Offers extensive selection of geographic files including detailed geography for entire United States
U.S. Census Bureau	http://www.census.gov	Very useful source of virtually all census data
U.S. Demography	http://www.ciesin.org/datasets/us–demog/us–demog–home.html	Excellent source of U.S. demographic information
U.S. Department of Education	http://www.ed.gov	Contains information specifically for teachers and their current budget
USA Data	http://www.usadata.com	Provides access to consumer lifestyle measurements, integrated with product consumption, demographics, shopping habits, and medical information; information can be viewed on a local, regional, or national basis

With over two hundred fifty thousand newsgroups currently in existence and more being added every day, there is a newsgroup for nearly every hobby, profession, and lifestyle. Both Netscape Navigator and Microsoft Internet Explorer, as well as other browsers, come with newsgroup readers. If you do not already have a newsgroup reader, you can go to one of the search engines and search for one of the freeware or shareware newsgroup readers. These newsgroup readers function much like e-mail programs. To find a particular newsgroup:

- Connect to the Internet in your usual way.
- Open your newsreader program.
- Search for the topic of interest. Most newsreaders allow you to search for the names of the newsgroups using any keywords or topics you are interested in. Some newsreaders, like Microsoft Internet Explorer, also allow you to search the brief descriptions that accompany most newsgroups.
- Select the newsgroup in which you are interested.
- Begin scanning messages. The titles of each message generally give an indication as to what the message contains.

Newsgroup messages look like e-mail messages. They contain a subject title, author, and a message body. Unlike normal e-mail messages, newsgroup messages are threaded discussions. This means that any reply to a previous message will appear linked to that message. Therefore, you can follow a discussion between two or more people by starting at the original message and following the links (or threads) to each successive reply. You can send images, sound files, and video clips attached to your message for anyone to download and examine.

Databases on CD-ROM

A number of companies offer database packages on CD-ROM for personal computers. For example, the Claritas Corporation has created a package called Compass/Agency designed for advertising agencies and Compass/Newspapers for newspapers to do segmentation and demographic studies and mapping. Claritas recently added Arbitron ratings and data from Simmons Marketing Research Bureau and Mediamark on product usage to Compass/Agency. The Compass/Newspaper system contains more than two hundred preformatted reports and maps. Users can also import data on subscribers, readership, or advertisers and display them as reports and maps or export data into other standard software packages, such as spreadsheets, word processing, and graphics applications.

The Department of Commerce has also made 1990 census data available on CD-ROM for use on PCs. Information available includes thirteen hundred categories of population, education, marital status, number of children in the home, home value or monthly rent, and income. The bureau also offers TIGER files, which provide a digital street map of the entire United States. They include mapping files that identify the locations of streets, highways, railroads, pipelines, power lines, and airports. Boundary files identify counties, municipalities, census tracts, census block groups, congressional districts, voter precincts, rivers, and lakes.

Planning the Research Design and Gathering Primary Data

Good secondary data can help researchers conduct a thorough situation analysis. With that information, researchers can list their unanswered questions and rank them. Researchers must then decide the exact information required to answer the questions. The **research design** specifies which research questions must be answered, how and when the data will be gathered, and how the data will be analyzed. Typically, the project budget is finalized after the research design has been approved.

research design
Specifies which research questions must be answered, how and when the data will be gathered, and how the data will be analyzed.

primary data
Information collected for the first time. Can be used for solving the particular problem under investigation.

Sometimes research questions can be answered by gathering more secondary data; otherwise, primary data may be needed. **Primary data,** or information collected for the first time, can be used for solving the particular problem under investigation. The main advantage of primary data is that they will answer a specific research question that secondary data cannot answer. For example, suppose Pillsbury has two new recipes for refrigerated dough for sugar cookies. Which one will consumers like better? Secondary data will not help answer this question. Instead, targeted consumers must try each recipe and evaluate the tastes, textures, and appearances of each cookie. Moreover, primary data are current and researchers know the source. Sometimes researchers gather the data themselves rather than assign projects to outside companies. Researchers also specify the methodology of the research. Secrecy can be maintained because the information is proprietary. In contrast, secondary data are available to all interested parties for relatively small fees.

Gathering primary data is expensive; costs can range from a few thousand dollars for a limited survey to several million for a nationwide study. For instance, a nationwide, fifteen-minute telephone interview with one thousand adult males can cost $50,000 for everything, including a data analysis and report. Because primary data gathering is so expensive, firms commonly cut back on the number of interviews to save money. Larger companies that conduct many research projects use another cost-saving technique. They piggyback studies, or gather data on two different projects using one questionnaire. The drawback is that answering questions about, say, dog food and gourmet coffee may be confusing to respondents. Piggybacking also requires a longer interview (sometimes a half hour or longer), which tires respondents. The quality of the answers typically declines, with people giving curt replies and thinking, "When will this end!" A lengthy interview also makes people less likely to participate in other research surveys.[7]

However, the disadvantages of primary data gathering are usually offset by the advantages. It is often the only way of solving a research problem. And with a variety of techniques available for research—including surveys, observations, and experiments—primary research can address almost any marketing question.

Survey Research The most popular technique for gathering primary data is **survey research,** in which a researcher interacts with people to obtain facts, opinions, and attitudes. Exhibit 7.6 summarizes the characteristics of the most popular forms of survey research.

survey research
The most popular technique for gathering primary data in which a researcher interacts with people to obtain facts, opinions, and attitudes.

In-Home Interviews Although in-home, personal interviews often provide high-quality information, they tend to be very expensive because of the interviewers' travel time and mileage costs. Therefore, market researchers tend to conduct fewer in-home personal interviews today than they did in the past.

Nevertheless, this form of survey research has some important advantages. The respondent is interviewed at home, in a natural setting where many consumption decisions are actually made. Also, the interviewer can show the respondent items (for example, package designs) or invite the respondent to taste or use a test

exhibit 7.6 | Characteristics of Various Types of Survey Research

Characteristic	In-home Personal Interviews	Mall Intercept Interviews	Telephone Interviews from Interviewer's Home	Central-Location Telephone Interviews	Self-Administered and One-Time Mail Surveys	Mall Panel Surveys	Internet Interviews	Computer Disk by Mail	Focus Groups
Cost	High	Moderate	Moderate to low	Moderate	Low	Moderate	Moderate to low	Moderate	Low
Time span	Moderate	Moderate	Fast	Fast	Slow	Relatively slow	Moderate	Relatively slow	Fast
Use of interviewer probes	Yes	Yes	Yes	Yes	No	Yes	Yes, if interactive	No	Yes
Ability to show concepts to respondent	Yes (also taste tests)	Yes (also taste tests)	No	No	Yes	Yes	Yes	Yes	Yes
Management control over interviewer	Low	Moderate	Low	High	n/a	n/a	High, if interviewer used	n/a	High
General data quality	High	Moderate	Moderate to low	High to moderate	Moderate to low	Moderate	High to moderate	High to moderate	Moderate
Ability to collect large amounts of data	High	Moderate	Moderate to low	Moderate to low	Low to moderate	Moderate	High	High	Moderate
Ability to handle complex questionnaires	High	Moderate	Moderate	High if computer-aided	Low	Low	High	High	Low

product. An interviewer can also probe when necessary—a technique used to clarify a person's response. For example, an interviewer might ask, "What did you like best about the salad dressing you just tried?" The respondent might reply, "Taste." This answer doesn't provide a lot of information, so the interviewer could probe by saying, "Can you tell me a little bit more about taste?" The respondent then elaborates: "Yes, it's not too sweet, it has the right amount of pepper, and I love that hint of garlic."

mall intercept interview
Survey research method that involves interviewing people in the common areas of shopping malls.

Mall Intercept Interviews The **mall intercept interview** is conducted in the common areas of shopping malls or in a market research office within the mall. It is the economy version of the door-to-door interview with personal contact between interviewer and respondent, minus the interviewer's travel time and mileage costs. To conduct this type of interview, the research firm rents office space in the mall or pays a significant daily fee. One drawback is that it is hard to get a representative sample of the population.

Mall intercept interviews must be brief. Only the shortest ones are conducted while respondents are standing. Usually researchers invite respondents to their office for interviews, which are still rarely over fifteen minutes long. The researchers often show respondents concepts for new products or a test commercial or have them taste a new food product. The overall quality of mall intercept interviews is about the same as telephone interviews.

computer-assisted personal interviewing
Interviewing method in which the interviewer reads the questions from a computer screen and enters the respondent's data directly into the computer.

computer-assisted self-interviewing
Interviewing method in which a mall interviewer intercepts and directs willing respondents to nearby computers where the respondent reads questions off a computer screen and directly keys his or her answers into a computer.

Marketing researchers are applying new technology in mall interviewing. The first technique is **computer-assisted personal interviewing**. The researcher conducts in-person interviews, reads questions to the respondent off a computer screen, and directly keys the respondent's answers into the computer. A second approach is **computer-assisted self-interviewing**. A mall interviewer intercepts and directs willing respondents to nearby computers. Each respondent reads questions off a computer screen and directly keys his or her answers into a computer. The third use of technology is fully automated self-interviewing. Respondents are guided by interviewers or independently approach a centrally located computer station or kiosk, read questions off a screen, and directly key their answers into the station's computer.

Telephone Interviews Compared to the personal interview, the telephone interview costs less and may provide the best sample of any survey procedure. Although it is often criticized for providing poorer-quality data than the in-home personal interview, studies have shown that this criticism may not be deserved.[8]

central-location telephone (CLT) facility
A specially designed phone room used to conduct telephone interviewing.

Most telephone interviewing is conducted from a specially designed phone room called a **central-location telephone (CLT) facility**. A phone room has many phone lines, individual interviewing stations, sometimes monitoring equipment, and headsets. The use of Wide Area Telephone Service (WATS) lines permits the research firm to interview people nationwide from a single location.

Many CLT facilities offer computer-assisted interviewing. The interviewer reads the questions from a computer screen and enters the respondent's data directly into the computer. The researcher can stop the survey at any point and immediately print out the survey results. Thus, a researcher can get a sense of the project as it unfolds and fine-tune the research design as necessary. An on-line interviewing system can also save time and money because data entry occurs as the response is recorded rather than as a separate process after the interview. Hallmark Cards found that an interviewer administered a printed questionnaire for its Shoebox Greeting cards in twenty-eight minutes. The same questionnaire administered with computer assistance took only eighteen minutes.

in-bound telephone surveys
A new trend in telephone interviewing in which an information packet is sent to consumers, who are then asked to call a toll-free, interactive voice-mail system and answer questions.

A new trend in telephone interviewing is **in-bound telephone surveys.** M/A/R/C, one of America's largest marketing research firms, has developed what it calls Brand Quality Monitoring. The process is simple: M/A/R/C sends a consumer an information packet with coupons for free samples of a client's product and a competitor's product, such as peanut butter, instant soup or microwave popcorn. The consumer is asked to use both products, one after the other. After using each sample, the survey respondent is asked to call a toll-free number that uses an interactive voice-mail system that operates seven days a week, twenty-four hours a day. The system takes the consumer through a scripted menu of options. By pushing phone buttons, the consumer records his or her opinion about each product. M/A/R/C tabulates the results weekly and delivers them to clients in monthly, quarterly, or annual formats. By using database information, only consumers who use a particular product, such as cereal, are sent cereal coupons.[9]

Trish Shukers, director of survey center operations for Maritz Marketing Research, envisions in the near future a system she calls **integrated interviewing**. She describes it as follows:

integrated interviewing
A new interviewing method in which a respondent is interviewed on the Internet.

> A potential respondent sees our survey ad on the Internet and uses a modem to dial our 800 number and reach our telephone center. A telephone interviewer receives the in-bound call, screens to determine if the respondent is qualified, clicks an icon on the computer screen to send a fax about the survey to the respondent, and then transfers the respondent into an automated survey. If, at any time, the respondent has a question, he or she may return to the "live" interviewer.
>
> Imagine the possibilities of interviewing a respondent on-line and being able to display advertising copy or packaging prototypes (which we generally believe we have to do in person), and then administering a lengthy telephone interview (either live or automated) and e-mailing verbatim responses to the client at the end of the interview.[10]

Mail Surveys Mail surveys have several benefits: relatively low cost, elimination of interviewers and field supervisors, centralized control, and actual or promised anonymity for respondents (which may draw more candid responses). Some researchers feel that mail questionnaires give the respondent a chance to reply more thoughtfully and to check records, talk to family members, and so forth. Yet mail questionnaires usually produce low response rates.

Low response rates pose a problem because certain elements of the population tend to respond more than others. The resulting sample may therefore not represent the surveyed population. For example, the sample may have too many retired people and too few working people. In this instance, answers to a question about attitudes toward Social Security might indicate a much more favorable overall view of the system than is actually the case. Another serious problem with mail surveys is that no one probes respondents to clarify or elaborate on their answers.

Mail panels like those operated by Market Facts, National Family Opinion Research, and NPD Research offer an alternative to the one-shot mail survey. A mail panel consists of a sample of households recruited to participate by mail for a given period. Panel members often receive gifts in return for their participation. Essentially, the panel is a sample used several times. In contrast to one-time mail surveys, the response rates from mail panels are high. Rates of 70 percent (of those who agree to participate) are not uncommon.

Computer Disk by Mail The **computer disk by mail survey** medium basically has all the advantages and disadvantages of a typical mail survey. An additional advantage is that a disk survey can incorporate skip patterns into the survey. For example, a question might ask "Do you own a cat?" If the answer is "no" then you would skip all questions related to cat ownership. A disk survey will perform this function automatically. A disk survey can also use respondent-generated words in questions throughout the survey. It can easily display a variety of graphics and directly relate them to questions. Finally, a disk survey eliminates the need to encode data from paper surveys. The primary disadvantage is that the respondent must have access and be willing to use a computer.

computer disk by mail survey
Like a typical mail survey only the respondents receive and answer questions on a disk.

Internet Surveys

Advantages of Internet Surveys The popularity of Internet surveys surged in the late 1990s. There are several reasons for this trend.[11] First, there is the speed with which a questionnaire can be created, distributed to respondents, and the data returned. Since printing, mailing, and data keying delays are eliminated, you can have data in hand within hours of writing a questionnaire. Data are obtained in electronic form, so statistical analysis software can be programmed to process standard questionnaires and return statistical summaries and charts automatically.

A second reason to consider Internet surveys is cost. Printing, mailing, keying, and interviewer costs are eliminated, and the incremental costs of each respondent are typically low, so studies with large numbers of respondents can be done at substantial savings compared to mail or telephone surveys.

Another reason is that, with the creation of respondent panels on the Internet, the researcher can create longitudinal studies by tracking attitudes, behavior, and perceptions over time. Sophisticated panel tracking software can tailor follow-up questions in the next survey, based on responses from a previous survey; also, missing answers can be filled in.[12]

A fourth reason is that it typically isn't worthwhile to conduct a phone survey to ask two or three questions. On the Internet, however, a survey component could unobtrusively be included within a general site that is used for marketing or business transactions. For example, if a person accesses a banking home page and then goes to the "credit card" link, he or she could be asked a few questions about the features of a credit card they find most important before moving along to the information component.[13]

Yet another benefit of using the Internet for market research is the ability to reach large numbers of people. It is hard to imagine another medium that can provide so much potential while remaining economically feasible. The Internet is an international arena where many barriers to communication have been erased. The Graphics, Visualization and Usability Center (GVC) and the Georgia Institute of Technology, which report conducting "the oldest and largest public service Web-based surveys" (**http://www.cc.gatech.edu/gvu/user_surveys**), are currently experimenting with surveys in French, German, Spanish, and Japanese.

Finally, Internet questionnaires delivered using the Web have some unique advantages. They can be made visually pleasing with attractive fonts and graphics. The graphical and hypertext features of the Web can be used to present products for reaction or to explain service offerings. For respondents with current versions of Netscape Navigator or Internet Explorer, the two most popular Web browsers, audio and video can be added to the questionnaire. This multimedia ability of Web-delivered questionnaires is unique.

Disadvantages of Internet Surveys Despite the advantages of Internet surveys there are still many drawbacks. Perhaps the largest problem is that Internet users are not representative of the population as a whole. Fewer than 10 percent of U.S. households use the Internet regularly (although more are connected, many are infrequent users). Users tend to be male, well educated, technically oriented, and relatively young, and have above average incomes. This is changing, however, as more people access the Internet.

The CommerceNet/Nielsen Internet Demographics Study (**http://www.nielsenmedia.com**) is a World Wide Web survey done in conjunction with a phone survey to assess the bias inherent in the Web data. As the discrepancy between the two survey formats decreases, the Web becomes more of a mass market vehicle. This situation may be several years away, but in the age of rapid change and widespread adoption of new technologies, many are betting on its happening sooner rather than later.[14]

There are some populations, such as computer products purchasers and home users of Internet services, who are ideal for Internet surveys. Business and professional users of Internet services are also an excellent population to reach with Internet surveys. Over 80 percent of businesses are currently estimated to have Internet connections, with the number expected to reach 90 percent by 2000.[15]

A second problem is security on the Internet. Users today are understandably worried about privacy issues. This fear has been fueled by sensational media accounts of cyberstalkers and con artists who prey on Internet users. However, given the commercial incentives for ensuring that information such as credit card numbers can be transmitted safely, encryption methodology will be at the forefront of Internet developments. This will—it is hoped—resolve the security problem.

A third problem occurs when an **unrestricted Internet sample** is set up on the Internet. In such a sample, anyone who desires can complete the questionnaire. It is fully self-selecting and probably representative of nothing except Web surfers. The problem is exacerbated if the same Internet user can access the questionnaire repeatedly. For example, *InfoWorld*, a computer user magazine, decided to conduct its 1997 Readers Choice survey for the first time on the Internet. The results were so skewed by repeat voting for one product that the entire survey was publicly abandoned and the editor asked for readers' help to avoid the problem again.[16] A simple solution to repeat respondents is to lock respondents out of the site after they have filled out the questionnaire.

unrestricted Internet sample
Anyone with a computer and modem can fill out the questionnaire.

Internet Samples Internet samples may be classified as unrestricted, screened, and recruited.[17] Unrestricted samples were just discussed. **Screened Internet samples** adjust for the unrepresentativeness of the self-selected respondents by imposing quotas based on some desired sample characteristics. These are often demographic characteristics such as gender, income, and geographic region, or product-related criteria such as past purchase behavior, job responsibilities, or current product use. The applications for screened samples are generally similar to those for unrestricted samples.

screened Internet sample
Internet sample with quotas based on desired sample characteristics.

Screened sample questionnaires typically use a branching or skip pattern for asking screening questions to determine whether or not the full questionnaire should be presented to a respondent. Some Web survey systems can make immediate market segment calculations that assign a respondent to a particular segment based on screening questions, then select the appropriate questionnaire to match the respondent's segment.

Alternatively, some Internet research providers maintain a "panel house" that recruits respondents who fill out a preliminary classification questionnaire. This information is used to classify respondents into demographic segments. Clients specify the desired segments, and the respondents who match the desired demographics are permitted to fill out the questionnaires of all clients who specify that segment.

Recruited Internet samples are used for targeted populations in surveys that require more control over the makeup of the sample. Respondents are recruited by telephone, mail, e-mail, or in person. After qualification, they are sent the questionnaire by e-mail or are directed to a Web site that contains a link to the questionnaire. At Web sites, passwords are normally used to restrict access to the questionnaire to the recruited sample members. Since the makeup of the sample is known, completions can be monitored, and follow-up messages can be sent to those who do not complete the questionnaire, in order to improve the participation rate.

recruited Internet sample
Respondents are prerecruited. After qualifying to participate, they are sent a questionnaire by e-mail or directed to a secure Web site to fill out a questionnaire.

Recruited samples are ideal in applications that already have a database from which to recruit the sample. For example, a good application would be a survey that used a customer database to recruit respondents for a purchaser satisfaction study.

There is no doubt that the Internet is a boon to small businesses and entrepreneurs who wish to conduct marketing research. The reasons why are discussed in the following "Entrepreneurial Insights" box.

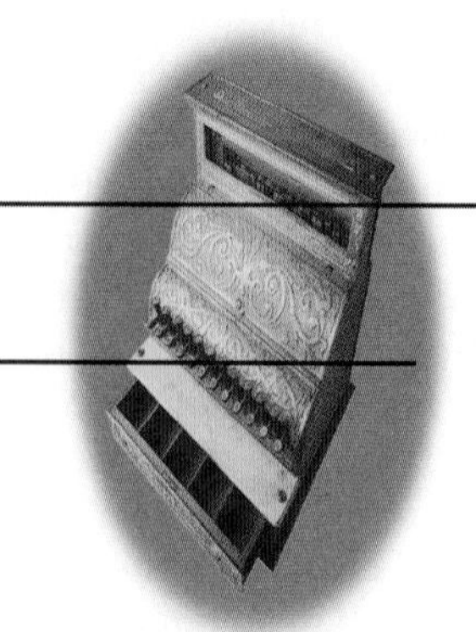

entrepreneurial insights

The Internet Is a Great Tool for Entrepreneurs Who Want to Conduct Marketing Research

The Internet is the "great equalizer" for small business owners wishing to conduct marketing research. Secondary research, for example, is at your fingertips simply through the use of a search engine. Do you want to know what people are saying about your industry and products? Go to a chat room.

Survey research was often too expensive for small businesses to hire a marketing research firm. Even without using a research company, hiring and training interviewers was expensive and many entrepreneurs simply didn't have the knowledge of how to conduct a survey.

On-line surveys offer a whole new approach for small businesses to inexpensively conduct survey research. Current versions of Microsoft Internet Explorer and Netscape Navigator fully support transparent interactivity for on-line surveys. This development allows the entrepreneur to create a much more sophisticated survey than is possible through mail surveys. For example, complicated skip patterns can be built into on-line surveys. A simple skip pattern would be, "Do you own a dog?" If the answer is no, all of the questions pertaining to dog ownership would be skipped.

What are several pitfalls that the entrepreneur should guard against when conducting on-line surveys? When should a small businessperson rely on the expertise of the marketing research firm?

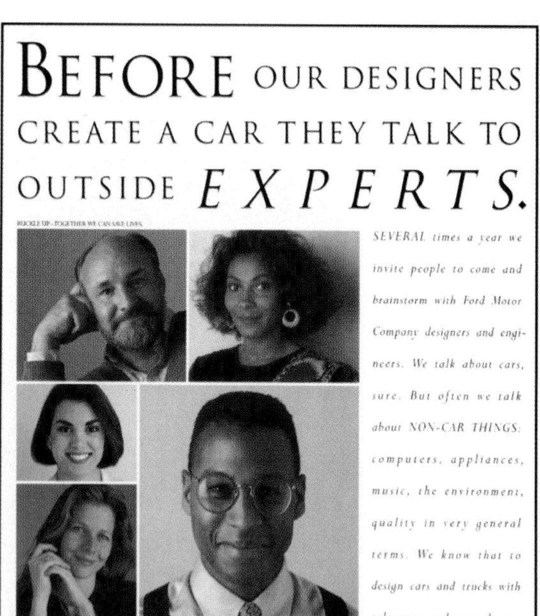

Ford Motor Company asks consumers to drive new automobiles and then brings them into a focus group to get their feedback.
Courtesy Ford Motor Company

Focus Groups A **focus group** is a type of personal interviewing. Often recruited by random telephone screening, seven to ten people with certain desired characteristics form a focus group. These qualified consumers are usually offered an incentive (typically $30 to $50) to participate in a group discussion. The meeting place (sometimes resembling a living room, sometimes featuring a conference table) has audiotaping and perhaps videotaping equipment. It also likely has a viewing room with a one-way mirror so that clients (manufacturers or retailers) may watch the session. During the session, a moderator, hired by the research company, leads the group discussion.

Focus groups are much more than question-and-answer interviews. The distinction is made between "group dynamics" and "group interviewing." The interaction provided in **group dynamics** is essential to the success of focus-group research; this interaction is the reason for conducting group rather than individual research. One of the essential postulates of group-session usage is the idea that a response from one person may become a stimulus for another, thereby generating an interplay of responses that may yield more than if the same number of people had contributed independently.

Focus groups are occasionally used to brainstorm new product ideas or to screen concepts for new products. Ford Motor Company, for example, asked consumers to drive several automobile prototypes. These "test drivers" were then brought together in focus groups. During the discussions, consumers complained that they were scuffing their shoes because the rear seats lacked foot room. In response, Ford sloped the floor underneath the front seats, widened the space between the seat adjustment tracks, and made the tracks in the Taurus and Sable models out of smooth plastic instead of metal.

A new system by Focus Vision Network allows client companies and advertising agencies to view live focus groups in Chicago, Dallas, Boston, and fifteen other major cities. For example, the private satellite network lets a General Motors researcher observing a San Diego focus group control two cameras in the viewing room. The researcher can get a full-group view or a close-up, zoom, or pan the participants. The researcher can also communicate directly with the moderator using an ear receiver. Ogilvy and Mather (a large New York advertising agency whose clients include StarKist Sea Foods, Seagrams, Mastercard, and Burger King) has installed the system.

focus group
Seven to ten people who participate in a group discussion led by a moderator.

group dynamics
Group interaction essential to the success of focus group research.

The newest development in qualitative research is the on-line or cyber focus group. A number of organizations are currently offering this new means of conducting focus groups. The process is fairly simple.

- The research firm builds a database of respondents via a screening questionnaire on its Web site.
- When a client comes to them with a need for a particular focus group, the firm goes to its database and identifies individuals who appear to qualify. It sends an e-mail message to these individuals, asking them to log on to a particular site at a particular time scheduled for the group. The firm pays them an incentive for their participation.
- The firm develops a discussion guide similar to one for a conventional focus group.
- A moderator runs the group by typing in questions on-line for all to see. The group operates in an environment similar to that of a chat room so that all participants see all questions and all responses.
- The firm captures the complete text of the focus group and makes it available for review after the group has finished.

Many advantages are claimed for cyber groups. Cyber Dialogue, a marketing research company specializing in cyber groups, lists the following benefits of on-line focus groups on its Web site:

- *Speed:* Typically, focus groups can be recruited and conducted, with delivery of results, within five days of client approval.
- *Cost effectiveness:* Off-line focus groups incur costs for facility rental, air fare, hotel, and food. None of these costs is incurred with on-line focus groups.
- *Broad geographic scope:* In a given focus group, you can speak to people in Boise, Idaho and Miami, Florida, at the same time.
- *Accessibility:* On-line focus groups give you access to individuals who otherwise might be difficult to recruit (e.g., business travelers, doctors, mothers with infants).
- *Honesty:* From behind their screen names, respondents are anonymous to other respondents and tend to talk more freely about issues that might create inhibitions in a face-to-face group.

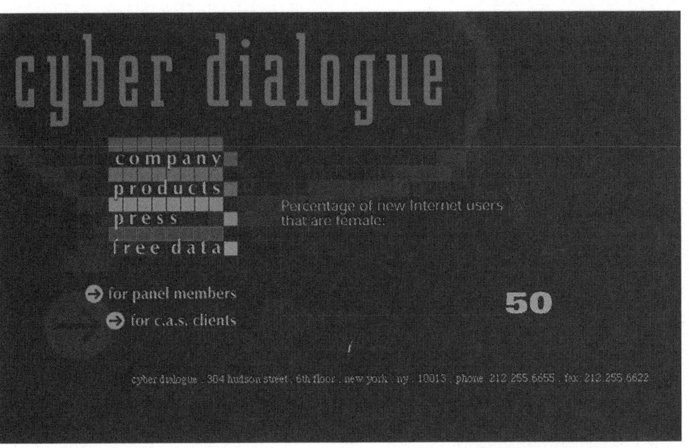

Cyber Dialogue specializes in conducting on-line focus groups in which discussion occurs in a forum similar to that of a chat room. This latest development in qualitative research can mean faster, more cost-effective results for the client. (http://www.cyberdialogue.com/)
Courtesy Cyber Dialogue

Cyber Dialogue prices their focus groups at $3,000. This compares very favorably to a cost in the range of $7,000 without travel costs for conventional focus groups.

Unfortunately, no systematic evaluation of on-line focus groups in comparison to conventional focus groups has been done at this time. There are some obvious and some not-so-obvious disadvantages of on-line focus groups. First, if the goal of the research is to quantitatively represent the sentiments of a broad segment of the population, cyber groups come up short. Only a minority of the population is on the Internet with any frequency, and a number of studies have demonstrated that

Greenfield On-line

Find out how on-line focus groups work by signing up to be a participant. Check out some of Greenfield's on-line surveys in the Survey Center. Go to **http://www.greenfieldonline.com/**

on line

the profile of on-line individuals is quite different from the profile of the broader population. This will become less of an issue as more and more people join the population of Internet users. However, at the current time it is a significant problem.

Second, no one has demonstrated whether the group dynamics process, so important to the success of conventional focus groups, works in cyber groups. Third, some have hypothesized that cyber group participants will be more honest about their behavior, opinions, and feelings than participants in conventional focus groups; others have hypothesized the opposite. No one knows which hypothesis is correct at this time. Finally, the ability to observe appearance and body language of the participants is absent in a cyber group. An informal study of moderators, conducted by the authors, indicates that most moderators consider this a negative factor.

Questionnaire Design All forms of survey research require a questionnaire. Questionnaires ensure that all respondents will be asked the same series of questions. Questionnaires include three basic types of questions: open-ended, closed-ended, and scaled-response (see Exhibit 7.7). An **open-ended question** encourages an answer phrased in the respondent's own words. Researchers get a rich array of information based on the respondent's frame of reference. In contrast, a **closed-ended question** asks the respondent to make a selection from a limited list of responses. Traditionally, marketing researchers separate the two-choice question (called *dichotomous*) from the many-item type (often called *multiple choice*). A **scaled-response question** is a closed-ended question designed to measure the intensity of a respondent's answer.

open-ended question
Interview question that encourages an answer phrased in the respondent's own words.

closed-ended question
Interview question that asks the respondent to make a selection from a limited list of responses.

scaled-response question
A closed-ended question designed to measure the intensity of a respondent's answer.

Closed-ended and scaled-response questions are easier to tabulate than open-ended questions because response choices are fixed. On the other hand, if the researcher is not careful in designing the closed-ended question, an important choice might be omitted. For example, suppose this question were asked on a food study: "What do you normally add to a taco, besides meat, that you have prepared at home?"

Avocado	1
Cheese (Monterey Jack/cheddar)	2
Guacamole	3
Lettuce	4
Mexican hot sauce	5
Olives (black/green)	6
Onions (red/white)	7
Peppers (red/green)	8
Pimento	9
Sour cream	0

The list seems complete, doesn't it? However, consider the following responses: "I usually add a green, avocado-tasting hot sauce"; "I cut up a mixture of lettuce and spinach"; "I'm a vegetarian; I don't use meat at all. My taco is filled only with guacamole." How would you code these replies? As you can see, the question needs an "other" category.

A good question must also be asked clearly and concisely, and ambiguous language must be avoided. Take, for example, the question "Do you live within ten minutes of here?" The answer depends on the mode of transportation (maybe the person walks), driving speed, perceived time, and other factors. Instead, respondents should see a map with certain areas highlighted and be asked whether they live within one of those areas.

Clarity also implies using reasonable terminology. A questionnaire is not a vocabulary test. Jargon should be avoided, and language should be geared to the target audience. A question such as "What is the level of efficacy of your preponderant dishwasher powder?" would probably be greeted by a lot of blank stares. It would be much simpler to say "Are you (1) very satisfied, (2) somewhat satisfied, or (3) not satisfied with your current brand of dishwasher powder?"

Retailer Urban Outfitters sends its marketing researchers to the streets to scout teen and young adult fashion trends.
© Guy Aroch

Types of Questions Found on Questionnaires for National Market Research **exhibit 7.7**

Open-Ended Questions	Closed-Ended Questions	Scaled-Response Question
1. What advantages, if any, do you think ordering from a mail-order catalog offers compared to shopping at a local retail outlet? (*Probe:* What else?) 2. Why do you have one or more of your rugs or carpets professionally cleaned rather than having you or someone else in the household clean them? 3. What is there about the color of the eye shadow that makes you like it the best?	**Dichotomous** 1. Did you heat the Danish product before serving it? Yes . . . . .1 No . . . . .2 2. The federal government doesn't care what people like me think. Agree . . . . .1 Disagree . . . . .2 **Multiple choice** 1. I'd like you to think back to the last footwear of any kind that you bought. I'll read you a list of descriptions and would like for you to tell me which category they fall into. (*Read list and check proper category.*) Dress and/or formal . . . . .1 Casual . . . . .2 Canvas/trainer/gym shoes . . . . . . .3 Specialized athletic shoes . . . . . . .4 Boots . . . . .5 2. In the last three months, have you used Noxzema skin cream . . . (*Check all that apply.*) As a facial wash . . . . .1 For moisturizing the skin . . . . .2 For treating blemishes . . . . .3 For cleansing the skin . . . . .4 For treating dry skin . . . . .5 For softening skin . . . . .6 For sunburn . . . . .7 For making the facial skin smooth 8	Now that you have used the rug cleaner, would you say that you . . . (*Check one*) ____Would definitely buy it ____Would probably buy it ____Might or might not buy it ____Probably would not buy it ____Definitely would not buy it

Stating the survey's purpose at the beginning of the interview also improves clarity. The respondents should understand the study's intentions and the interviewer's expectations. Sometimes, of course, to get an unbiased response, the interviewer must disguise the true purpose of the study. If an interviewer says, "We're conducting an image study for American National Bank" and then proceeds to ask a series of questions about the bank, chances are the responses will be biased. Many times respondents will try to provide answers that they believe are "correct" or that the interviewer wants to hear.

Finally, to ensure clarity, the interviewer should avoid asking two questions in one; for example, "How did you like the taste and texture of the Pepperidge Farm coffee cake?" This should be divided into two questions, one concerning taste and the other texture.

A question should not only be clear but also unbiased. A question such as "Have you purchased any quality Black & Decker tools in the past six months?" biases respondents to think of the topic in a certain way (in this case, to link quality and

Brand Marketing International

Learn more about mystery shopping by requesting a mystery shopper kit from BMI and reading their shopper application.
http://www.bmiltd.com/

on line

observation research
Research method that relies on three types of observation: people watching people, people watching activity, and machines watching people.

Black & Decker tools). Questions can also be leading: "Weren't you pleased with the good service you received last night at the Holiday Inn?" (The respondent is all but instructed to say yes.) These examples are quite obvious; unfortunately, bias is usually more subtle. Even an interviewer's clothing or gestures can create bias.

Observation Research In contrast to survey research, **observation research** does not rely on direct interaction with people. The three types of observation research are people watching people, people watching an activity, and machines watching people. There are two types of *people watching people* research:

Fisher-Price runs a play laboratory in which children are observed through a one-way mirror. Toy designers can see how children react to a variety of toys and get ideas for new creations.

- *Mystery shoppers:* Researchers posing as customers observe the quality of service offered by retailers. The largest mystery shopper company is Shop 'N Chek, an Atlanta company that employs over sixteen thousand anonymous shoppers nationwide. The firm evaluates salespeople's courtesy for General Motors, flight service for United Airlines, and the efficiency of hamburger ordering for Wendy's, among other clients. Texaco recently introduced a program entitled "Building Tomorrow Together" that uses mystery shoppers to evaluate each of its fourteen thousand U.S. locations. All station managers, truck-stop owner-operators, and employees are eligible to earn recognition awards based heavily on the evaluations of mystery shoppers.[18]
- *One-way mirror observations:* At the Fisher-Price Play Laboratory, children are invited to spend twelve sessions playing with toys. Toy designers watch through one-way mirrors to see how children react to Fisher-Price's and other makers' toys. Fisher-Price, for example, had difficulty designing a toy lawn mower that children would play with. A designer, observing behind the mirror, noticed the children's fascination with soap bubbles. He then created a lawn mower that spewed soap bubbles. It sold over a million units in the first year.

One form of observation research that features people watching an activity is known as an **audit**, the examination and verification of the sale of a product. Audits generally fall into two categories: retail audits, which measure sales to final consumers, and wholesale audits, which determine the amount of product moved from warehouses to retailers. Wholesalers and retailers allow auditors into their stores and stockrooms to examine the company's sales and order records in order to verify product flows. In turn, the retailers and wholesalers receive cash compensation and basic reports about their operations from the audit firms.

audit
Form of observation research that features people examining and verifying the sale of a product.

For *machines watching people*, the three common types are

- *Traffic counters:* The most popular form of machine-based observation research relies on machines that measure the flow of vehicles over a stretch of roadway. Outdoor advertisers rely on traffic counts to determine the number of exposures per day to a billboard. Retailers use the information to decide where to place a store. Convenience stores, for example, require a moderately high traffic volume to be profitable.
- *Passive people meter:* Soon a cameralike device will be available to measure the size of television audiences. The passive system, packaged to resemble a VCR and placed on top of the TV, will be programmed to recognize faces and record electronically when specific members of a family watch TV. It will note when viewers leave the room and even when they avert their eyes from the screen. Strangers would be listed simply as visitors. Passive people meters are eagerly anticipated

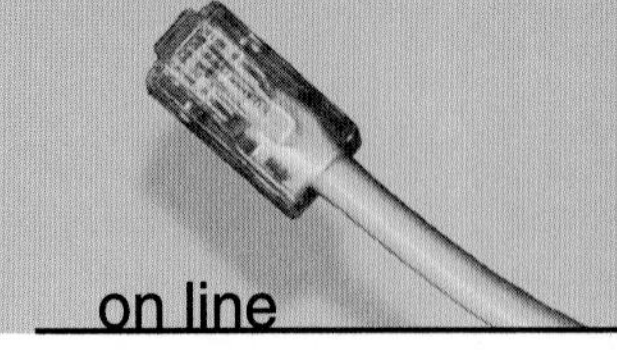

A.C. Nielsen Company, Inc.

How does A.C. Nielsen's 40,000-household Consumer Panel provide insights into consumer purchase behavior? What Internet resources are available through this site?

http://www.acnielsen.com/

because advertisers are demanding more proof of viewership and the networks are under pressure to show that advertising is reaching its intended targets. (Ratings are used to help set prices for commercial time.) An A.C. Nielsen executive has said that a passive system should yield "even higher quality, more accurate data because the respondents don't have to do anything" other than "be themselves." Already, however, the networks and advertisers are criticizing the passive people meter. One executive noted, "Who would want or allow one of those things in their bedroom?"[19] Others claim that the system requires bright light to operate properly. Also, the box has limited peripheral vision, so it might not sense all the people in a given room. Will the passive people meter work better than the present diary system? As of late 1999, the passive people meter had not been perfected. The four major networks are now working together to develop another mechanical device for measuring the size of television audiences.[20]

All observation techniques offer at least two advantages over survey research. First, bias from the interviewing process is eliminated. Second, observation doesn't rely on the respondent's willingness to provide data.

Conversely, observation techniques also have two important disadvantages. First, subjective information is limited because motivations, attitudes, and feelings are not measured. Second, data collection costs may run high unless the observed behavior patterns occur frequently, briefly, or somewhat predictably.

Experiments An **experiment** is another method a researcher can use to gather primary data. The researcher alters one or more variables—price, package design, shelf space, advertising theme, advertising expenditures—while observing the effects of those alterations on another variable (usually sales). The best experiments are those in which all factors are held constant except the ones being manipulated. The researcher can then observe that changes in sales, for example, result from changes in the amount of money spent on advertising.

experiment
Method a researcher uses to gather primary data.

Holding all other factors constant in the external environment is a monumental and costly, if not impossible, task. Such factors as competitors' actions, weather, and economic conditions are beyond the researcher's control. Yet market researchers have ways to account for the ever-changing external environment. Mars, the candy company, was losing sales to other candy companies. Traditional surveys showed that the shrinking candy bar was not perceived as a good value. Mars wondered whether a bigger bar sold at the same price would increase sales enough to offset the higher ingredient costs. The company designed an experiment in which the marketing mix stayed the same in different markets but the size of the candy bar varied. The substantial increase in sales of the bigger bar quickly proved that the additional costs would be more than covered by the additional revenue. Mars increased the bar size—and its market share and profits.

Specifying the Sampling Procedures

Once the researchers decide how they will collect primary data, their next step is to select the sampling procedures they will use. A firm can seldom take a census of all possible users of a new product, nor can they all be interviewed. Therefore, a firm must select a sample of the group to be interviewed. A **sample** is a subset from a larger population.

sample
A subset of a population.

Several questions must be answered before a sampling plan is chosen. First, the population, or **universe**, of interest must be defined. This is the group from which the sample will be drawn. It should include all the people whose opinions, behavior, preferences, attitudes, and so on are of interest to the marketer. For example, in a study whose purpose is to determine the market for a new canned dog food, the universe might be defined to include all current buyers of canned dog food.

universe
The population from which a sample will be drawn.

After the universe has been defined, the next question is whether the sample must be representative of the population. If the answer is yes, a probability sample is needed. Otherwise, a nonprobability sample might be considered.

probability sample
A sample in which every element in the population has a known statistical likelihood of being selected.

random sample
Sample arranged in such a way that every element of the population has an equal chance of being selected as part of the sample.

Probability Samples A **probability sample** is one in which every element in the population has a known statistical likelihood of being selected. Its most desirable feature is that scientific rules can be used to ensure that the sample represents the population.

One type of probability sample is a random sample. A **random sample** must be arranged in such a way that every element of the population has an equal chance of being selected as part of the sample. For example, suppose a university is interested in getting a cross section of student opinions on a proposed sports complex to be built using student activity fees. If the university can acquire an up-to-date list of all the enrolled students, it can draw a random sample by using random numbers from a table (found in most statistics books) to select students from the list. Common forms of probability and nonprobability samples are shown in Exhibit 7.8.

nonprobability sample
Any sample in which little or no attempt is made to get a representative cross section of the population.

convenience sample
A form of nonprobability sample using respondents who are convenient or readily accessible to the researcher, for example, employees, friends, or relatives.

Nonprobability Samples Any sample in which little or no attempt is made to get a representative cross section of the population can be considered a **nonprobability sample**. A common form of a nonprobability sample is the **convenience sample**, based on using respondents who are convenient or readily accessible to the researcher—for instance, employees, friends, or relatives.

Nonprobability samples are acceptable as long as the researcher understands their nonrepresentative nature. Because of their lower cost, nonprobability samples are the basis of much marketing research.

measurement error
Error that occurs when there is a difference between the information desired by the researcher and the information provided by the measurement process.

sampling error
Error that occurs when a sample somehow does not represent the target population.

Types of Errors Whenever a sample is used in marketing research, two major types of error occur: measurement error and sampling error. **Measurement error** occurs when there is a difference between the information desired by the researcher and the information provided by the measurement process. For example, people may tell an interviewer that they purchase Coors beer when they do not. Measurement error generally tends to be larger than sampling error.

Sampling error occurs when a sample somehow does not represent the target population. Sampling error can be one of several types. Nonresponse error occurs when the sample actually interviewed differs from the sample drawn. This error happens because the original people selected to be interviewed either refused to cooperate or were inaccessible. For example, people who feel embarrassed about their drinking habits may refuse to talk about them.

frame error
Error that occurs when a sample drawn from a population differs from the target population.

Frame error, another type of sampling error, arises if the sample drawn from a population differs from the target population. For instance, suppose a telephone survey is conducted to find out Chicago beer drinkers' attitudes toward Coors. If a Chicago telephone directory is used as the *frame* (the device or list from which the respondents are selected), the survey will contain a frame error. Not all Chicago beer drinkers have a phone, and many phone numbers are unlisted. An ideal sample (for example, a sample with no frame error) matches all important characteristics of the target population to be surveyed. Could you find a perfect frame for Chicago beer drinkers?

random error
Error that occurs because the selected sample is an imperfect representation of the overall population.

Random error occurs because the selected sample is an imperfect representation of the overall population. Random error represents how accurately the chosen sample's true average (mean) value reflects the population's true average (mean) value. For example, we might take a random sample of beer drinkers in Chicago and find that 16 percent regularly drink Coors beer. The next day we might repeat the same sampling procedure and discover that 14 percent regularly drink Coors beer. The difference is due to random error.

field service firm
Firm that specializes in interviewing respondents on a subcontracted basis.

Collecting the Data

Marketing research field service firms collect most primary data. A **field service firm** specializes in interviewing respondents on a subcontracted basis. Many have offices

exhibit 7.8

Types of Samples

Probability Samples	
Simple Random Sample	Every member of the population has a known and equal chance of selection.
Stratified Sample	Population is divided into mutually exclusive groups (such as gender or age), then random samples are drawn from *each* group.
Cluster Sample	Population is divided into mutually exclusive groups (such as geographic areas), then a random sample of clusters is selected. The researcher then collects data from all the elements in the selected clusters or from a probability sample of elements within each selected cluster.
Systematic Sample	A list of the population is obtained, i.e., all persons with a checking account at XYZ Bank, and a *skip interval* is obtained. The skip interval is obtained by dividing the sample size by the population size. If the sample size is 100 and the bank has 1,000 customers, then the skip interval is 10. The beginning number is randomly chosen within the skip interval. If the beginning number is 8, then the skip pattern would be 8, 18, 28, . . .
Nonprobability Samples	
Convenience Sample	The researcher selects the easiest population members from which to obtain information.
Judgment Sample	The researcher's selection criteria are based on personal judgment that the elements (persons) chosen will likely give accurate information.
Quota Sample	The researcher finds a prescribed number of people in several categories, i.e., owners of large dogs versus owners of small dogs. Respondents are not selected on probability sampling criteria.
Snowball Sample	The selection of additional respondents is made on the basis of referrals from the initial respondents. This is used when a desired type of respondent is hard to find, i.e., persons who have taken round-the-world cruises in the last three years. This technique employs the old adage "Birds of a feather flock together."

throughout the country. A typical marketing research study involves data collection in several cities, requiring the marketer to work with a comparable number of field service firms. To ensure uniformity among all subcontractors, detailed field instructions should be developed for every job. Nothing should be open to chance; no interpretations of procedures should be left to subcontractors.

Besides conducting interviews, field service firms provide focus group facilities, mall intercept locations, test product storage, and kitchen facilities to prepare test food products. They also conduct retail audits (counting the amount of a product sold off retail shelves). After an in-home interview is completed, field service supervisors validate the survey by recontacting about 15 percent of the respondents. The supervisors verify that certain responses were recorded properly and that the people were actually interviewed.

Analyzing the Data

After collecting the data, the marketing researcher proceeds to the next step in the research process: data analysis. The purpose of this analysis is to interpret and draw conclusions from the mass of collected data. The marketing researcher tries to organize and analyze those data by using one or more techniques common to marketing research: one-way frequency counts, cross-tabulations, and more sophisticated statistical analysis. Of these three techniques, one-way frequency counts are the simplest. One-way frequency tables record the responses to a question. For example, the answers to the question "What brand of microwave popcorn do you buy most often?" would provide a one-way frequency distribution. One-way frequency tables are always done in data analysis, at least as a first step, because they provide the researcher with a general picture of the study's results.

cross-tabulation
A method of analyzing data that lets the analyst look at the responses to one question in relation to the responses to one or more other questions.

A **cross-tabulation**, or "cross-tab," lets the analyst look at the responses to one question in relation to the responses to one or more other questions. For example, what is the association between gender and the brand of microwave popcorn bought most frequently? Hypothetical answers to this question are shown in Exhibit 7.9. Although the Orville Reddenbacher brand was popular with both males and females, it was more popular with females. Compared with women, men strongly preferred Pop Rite, whereas women were more likely than men to buy Weight Watchers popcorn.

Researchers can use many other more powerful and sophisticated statistical techniques, such as hypothesis testing, measures of association, and regression analysis. A description of these techniques goes beyond the scope of this book but can be found in any good marketing research textbook. The use of sophisticated statistical techniques depends on the researchers' objectives and the nature of the data gathered.

exhibit 7.9

Hypothetical Cross-Tabulation Between Gender and Brand of Microwave Popcorn Purchased Most Frequently

	Purchase by Gender	
Brand	Male	Female
Orville Reddenbacher	31%	48%
T.V. Time	12	6
Pop Rite	38	4
Act Two	7	23
Weight Watchers	4	18
Other	8	0

Preparing and Presenting the Report

After data analysis has been completed, the researcher must prepare the report and communicate the conclusions and recommendations to management. This is a key step in the process. If the marketing researcher wants managers to carry out the recommendations, he or she must convince them that the results are credible and justified by the data collected.

Researchers are usually required to present both written and oral reports on the project. These reports should be tailored to the audience. They should begin with a clear, concise statement of the research objectives, followed by a complete, but brief and simple, explanation of the research design or methodology employed. A summary of major findings should come next. The conclusion of the report should also present recommendations to management.

Most people who enter marketing will become research users rather than research suppliers. Thus, they must know what to notice in a report. As with many other items we purchase, quality is not always readily apparent. Nor does a high price guarantee superior quality. The basis for measuring the quality of a marketing research report is the research proposal. Did the report meet the objectives established in the proposal? Was the methodology outlined in the proposal followed? Are the conclusions based on logical deductions from the data analysis? Do the recommendations seem prudent, given the conclusions?

Another criterion is the quality of the writing. Is the style crisp and lucid? It has been said that if readers are offered the slightest opportunity to misunderstand, they probably will. The report should also be as concise as possible.

Although the vast majority of marketing researchers are highly ethical, this profession, like every other, sometimes faces unethical practices and practitioners. The "Ethics in Marketing" box provides such an example.

Following Up

The final step in the marketing research process is to follow up. The researcher should determine why management did or did not carry out the recommendations in the report. Was sufficient decision-making information included? What could have been done to make the report more useful to management? A good rapport between the product manager, or whoever authorized the project, and the market researcher is essential. Often they must work together on many studies throughout the year.

Scanner-Based Research

Discuss the growing importance of scanner-based research

scanner-based research
A system for gathering information from a single group of respondents by continuously monitoring the advertising, promotion, and pricing they are exposed to and the things they buy.

BehaviorScan
Scanner-based research program that tracks the purchases of 3,000 households through store scanners.

Scanner-based research is a system for gathering information from a single group of respondents by continuously monitoring the advertising, promotion, and pricing they are exposed to and the things they buy. The variables measured are advertising campaigns, coupons, displays, and product prices. The result is a huge database of marketing efforts and consumer behavior. Scanner-based research is bringing ever closer the Holy Grail of marketing research: an accurate, objective picture of the direct causal relationship between different kinds of marketing efforts and actual sales.

The two major scanner-based suppliers are Information Resources Incorporated (IRI) and the A.C. Nielsen Company. Each has about half the market. However, IRI is the founder of scanner-based research.

IRI's first product is called **BehaviorScan**. A household panel (a group of three thousand long-term participants in the research project) has been recruited and maintained in each BehaviorScan town. Panel members shop with an ID card, which is presented at the checkout in scanner-equipped grocery stores and drugstores, allowing IRI to track electronically each household's purchases, item by item, over time. It uses microcomputers to measure TV viewing in each panel

ethics in marketing

It Seems That I've Heard This Before

When Nissan Motor Co. U.S.A. decided to establish a workplace-diversity program, it turned for guidance to one of the nation's leading human resources specialists: Towers Perrin. The New York consulting firm had recently built a diversity practice to capitalize on companies' growing concerns about race and gender relations. Towers Perrin's pitch was that it would study a company in detail and then customize a program to fit the client's needs.

Towers Perrin launched its painstaking review of the giant Japanese automaker's U.S. unit. Charging up to $360 an hour, the consultants conducted one-on-one interviews with fifty-five executives, analyzed surveys of hundreds of additional workers, and reviewed company antidiscrimination policies and other internal documents. The project, which took four months to complete at a cost to the client of more than $105,000, appeared to reflect Towers Perrin's credo: "Prescription without diagnosis is malpractice." But when the prescription arrived, Nissan U.S.A. officials say they were far from impressed. "The recommendations were so broad, so generic, we didn't think it reflected what we thought we were going to get," says spokesman Kurt von Zumwalt. The 121-page report "did not seem to be particularly tailored to Nissan."

It wasn't. On the same day that Towers Perrin sent its written findings to Nissan, the consulting firm submitted a strikingly similar report to French-owned Thomson Consumer Electronics, Inc., half a continent away in Indianapolis. Except for the companies' names, all nine major recommendations made to Thomson matched Nissan's word for word, as did all fifty-four accompanying "tactics and objectives" and all thirteen elements of a proposed implementation plan.

In offering its services, Towers Perrin had said its recommendations would be based on the company's specific needs, as gleaned from the data Towers Perrin would collect. "No two organizations are identical," the firm wrote in its standard thirty-five-page proposal. "They are all as diverse as their workforces and the markets they serve." Later in the proposal, the firm added that "no textbook solutions exist."

Although each client's report contained a long section quoting from the interviews and other research, the recommendations didn't refer to any findings that were unique to either company. When Towers Perrin discussed employee polls, it described the results identically. In both instances, it said the polling showed that "women and minorities believe there is little or no understanding by supervisors and managers of how to tap their potential or how to mentor them effectively."

Nissan and Thomson weren't the only Towers Perrin clients that received nearly identical advice on workplace relations. The *Wall Street Journal* reviewed reports provided to eleven of the firm's diversity clients. The vast majority of the advice given to seven clients was identical. Three clients received more individualized suggestions. One client canceled its contract with the consultants before receiving a final report.

Privately held Towers Perrin, with revenue of just over $1 billion, doesn't dispute that many of its reports use the same language. Indeed, Towers Perrin asserts, it is standard practice for the firm and the industry to give clients with similar problems similar or identical advice. "There are only a finite number of things you can do to make diversity work," says Margaret Regan, current coleader of Towers Perrin's global diversity practice. All of Towers Perrin's diversity clients, a total of about sixty companies in recent years, received one of several "templates," she says. Clients "do not expect to get something very different from the next client in terms of recommendations." One reason, she says, is that most clients come to the firm precisely because they are at the same early stage of dealing with diversity issues.

Regan says the firm's consultants compose recommendations for clients using a shared word-processing file. The consultants go "into WordPerfect," she says, and select "the pieces that apply" to a particular client. In some situations, standard solutions provided by consultants have become widely accepted as appropriate and even necessary. In the highly technical world of actuarial, benefits, and compensation services, for example, where Towers Perrin built its expertise and reputation, consultants routinely use multicompany survey research to develop pay and pension systems that are then sold repeatedly. Similarly, law firms sometimes provide virtually identical memos to different clients facing similar problems, without disclosing that the work has been recycled.[21]

Were the actions of Towers Perrin unethical? Why or why not? Is there anything wrong with consultants using a shared word-processing file from other similar studies to prepare a report? Is this any different from a lawyer giving an identical opinion to different clients for the same problem? Why or why not?

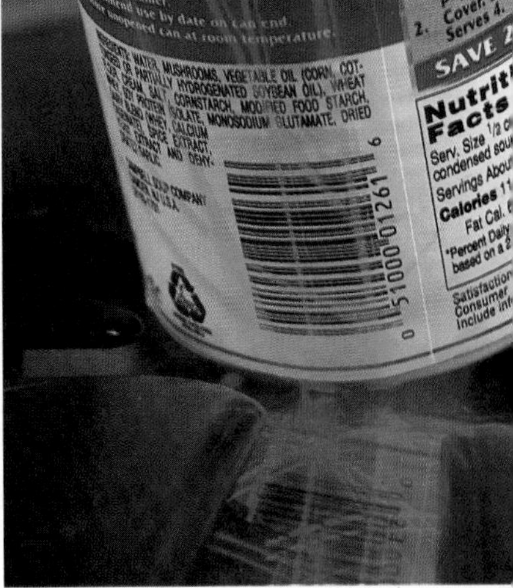

Scanner-based research helps marketers identify how successful their marketing efforts actually are. For example, by tracking sample households' purchases, researchers can measure the relationship between an advertising or promotional campaign and actual sales.

household and can send special commercials to panel member television sets. With such a measure of household purchasing, it is possible to manipulate marketing variables, such as TV advertising or consumer promotions, or to introduce a new product and analyze real changes in consumer buying behavior.

IRI's most successful product, with sales of over $130 million per year and 740 U.S. clients, is InfoScan. **InfoScan** is a scanner-based sales-tracking service for the consumer packaged-goods industry. Retail sales, detailed consumer purchasing information (including measurement of store loyalty and total grocery basket expenditures), and promotional activity by manufacturers and retailers are monitored and evaluated for all bar-coded products.

InfoScan
A scanner-based sales-tracking service for the consumer packaged-goods industry.

When Should Marketing Research Be Conducted?

5
Explain when marketing research should and should not be conducted

When managers have several possible solutions to a problem, they should not instinctively call for marketing research. In fact, the first decision to make is whether to conduct marketing research at all.

Some companies have been conducting research in certain markets for many years. Such firms understand the characteristics of target customers and their likes and dislikes about existing products. Under these circumstances, further research would be repetitive and waste money. Procter & Gamble, for example, has extensive knowledge of the coffee market. After it conducted initial taste tests with Folgers Instant Coffee, P&G went into national distribution without further research. Consolidated Foods Kitchen of Sara Lee followed the same strategy with its frozen croissants, as did Quaker Oats with Chewy Granola Bars. This tactic, however, does not always work. P&G marketers thought they understood the pain reliever market thoroughly, so they bypassed market research for Encaprin aspirin in capsules. Because it lacked a distinct competitive advantage over existing products, however, the product failed and was withdrawn from the market.

Managers rarely have such great trust in their judgment that they would refuse more information if it were available and free. But they might have enough confidence that they would be unwilling to pay very much for the information or to wait a long time to receive it. The willingness to acquire additional decision-making information depends on managers' perceptions of its quality, price, and timing. Of course, if perfect information were available—that is, the data conclusively showed which alternative to choose—decision makers would be willing to pay more for it than for information that still left uncertainty. In summary, research should only be undertaken when the expected value of the information is greater than the cost of obtaining it.

LOOKING BACK

Look back at the story about women on the Web at the beginning of the chapter. A company can use survey research, observations, or experiments to conduct marketing research.

Unless a company has extensive knowledge of the problem at hand, which is based on research, it should probably conduct marketing research. Yet, managers should also be reasonably sure that the cost of gathering the information will be less than the value of the data gathered.

Key marketing data often come from a company's own decision support system, which continually gathers data from a variety of sources and funnels it to decision makers. It then manipulates the data to make better decisions. DSS data are often supplemented by marketing research information.

Summary

1 Explain the concept and purpose of a marketing decision support system. Decision support systems make data instantly available to marketing managers and allow them to manipulate the data themselves to make marketing decisions. Four characteristics of decision support systems make them especially useful to marketing managers: They are interactive, flexible, discovery oriented, and accessible. Decision support systems give managers access to information immediately and without outside assistance. They allow users to manipulate data in a variety of ways and to answer "what if" questions. And, finally, they are accessible to novice computer users.

2 Define marketing research and explain its importance to marketing decision making. Marketing research is a process of collecting and analyzing data for the purpose of solving specific marketing problems. Marketers use marketing research to explore the profitability of marketing strategies. They can examine why particular strategies failed and analyze characteristics of specific market segments. Managers can use research findings to help keep current customers. Moreover, marketing research allows management to behave proactively rather than reactively by identifying newly emerging patterns in society and the economy.

3 Describe the steps involved in conducting a marketing research project. The marketing research process involves several basic steps. First, the researcher and the decision maker must agree on a problem statement or set of research objectives. The researcher then creates an overall research design to specify how primary data will be gathered and analyzed. Before collecting data, the researcher decides whether the group to be interviewed will be a probability or nonprobability sample. Field service firms are often hired to carry out data collection. Once data have been collected, the researcher analyzes them using statistical analysis. The researcher then prepares and presents oral and written reports, with conclusions and recommendations, to management. As a final step, the researcher determines whether the recommendations were implemented and what could have been done to make the project more successful.

4 Discuss the growing importance of scanner-based research. A scanner-based research system enables marketers to monitor a market panel's exposure and reaction to such variables as advertising, coupons, store displays, packaging, and price. By analyzing these variables in relation to the panel's subsequent buying behavior, marketers gain useful insight into sales and marketing strategies.

5 Explain when marketing research should and should not be conducted. Marketing research helps managers by providing data to make better marketing decisions. However, firms must consider whether the expected benefits of marketing research outweigh its costs. Before approving a research budget, management also should make sure adequate decision-making information doesn't already exist.

Discussion and Writing Questions

1. The task of marketing is to create exchanges. What role might marketing research play in the facilitation of the exchange process?
2. Marketing research has traditionally been associated with manufacturers of consumer goods. Today, we are experiencing an increasing number of organizations, both profit and nonprofit, using marketing research. Why do you think this trend exists? Give some examples.
3. WRITING Write a reply to the following statement: "I own a restaurant in the downtown area. I see customers every day whom I know on a first-name basis. I understand their likes and dislikes. If I put something on the menu and it doesn't sell, I know that they didn't like it. I also read the

magazine *Modern Restaurants,* so I know what the trends are in the industry. This is all of the marketing research I need to do."

4. Give an example of (a) the descriptive role of marketing research, (b) the diagnostic role, and (c) the predictive function of marketing research.
5. Critique the following methodologies and suggest more appropriate alternatives:
   a. A supermarket was interested in determining its image. It dropped a short questionnaire into the grocery bag of each customer before putting in the groceries.
   b. To assess the extent of its trade area, a shopping mall stationed interviewers in the parking lot every Monday and Friday evening. Interviewers walked up to persons after they had parked their cars and asked them for their zip codes.
   c. To assess the popularity of a new movie, a major studio invited people to call a 900 number and vote yes, they would see it again, or no, they would not. Each caller was billed a two-dollar charge.
6. You have been charged with determining how to attract more business majors to your school. Write an outline of the steps you would take, including the sampling procedures, to accomplish the task.
7. Why is secondary data sometimes preferred to primary data?
8. In the absence of company problems, is there any reason to develop a marketing decision support system?
9. Discuss when focus groups should and should not be used.
10. Divide the class into teams of eight persons. Each group will conduct a focus group on the quality and number of services that your college is providing to its students. One person from each group should be chosen to act as moderator. Remember, it is the moderator's job to facilitate discussion, not to lead the discussion. These groups should last approximately forty-five minutes. If possible, the groups should be videotaped or recorded. Upon completion, each group should write a brief report of its results. Consider offering to meet with the dean of students to share the results of your research.
11. Use the Internet and a Web browser, such as Lycos or Yahoo!, and type "marketing research." You will then have thousands of options. Pick a Web site that you find interesting and report on its content to the class.
12. Why has the Internet been of such great value to researchers seeking secondary data?
13. Go to **http://www.yankelovich.com**. Explain to the class the nature and scope of the Yankelovich MONITOR. How can marketing researchers use the data from this research?
14. Go to **http://www.icpsr.umich.edu/gss**. What is the General Social Survey? Compare and contrast its usefulness to marketing researchers with the Yankelovich MONITOR.
15. You are interested in home-building trends in the United States because your company (Whirlpool) is a major supplier of kitchen appliances. Go to **http://www.nahb.com** and describe what types of information at this site might be of interest to Whirlpool.
16. What are the advantages and disadvantages of conducting surveys on the Internet?
17. Explain the three types of Internet samples and discuss why a researcher might choose one over the other.

Key Terms

18. Go to **http://www.raosoft.com/raosoft** and explain how the company's software lets you distribute questionnaires over the Internet.

19. Go to **http://acop.com/** and tell the class about the site and what type of Internet sample is being drawn. Also, describe the types of surveys being taken.

20. Go to **http://www.autonomy.com/** and explain what type of marketing research resources are offered at the site.

21.  Go to **http://www.acnielsen.com** and **http://www.infores.com** and determine what A.C. Nielsen and IRI are saying on the Web about their latest scanner-based technology.

22.  Participate in a survey at one of the following URLs and report your experience to the class:

GVU Semi-annual Survey on Web Usage
http://www.cc.gatech.edu/gvu/user_surveys/
Personality test
http://www.users.interport.net/~zang/personality.html
Emotional intelligence test
http://www.utne.com/lens/bms/9bmseq.html
Values and Lifestyles (VALS) test
http://future.sri.com/vals/valshome.html
On-line transactions and privacy survey
http://www.hermes.bus.umich.edu/cgi-gin/spsurvey/questi.pl
Various on-line surveys on topics like politics and consumer trends
http://www.survey.net/
Prudential Securities Investment Personality Quiz
http://www.prusec.com/quiz.htm
Various surveys
http://www.dssresearch.com/mainsite/surveys.htm

Application for Small Business

Corinne and Daniel Orset are thinking about opening an independent fast-food restaurant specializing in deli-style sandwiches and quiches. Daniel recently ran across some marketing research information, as described here.

Consumers claim that fast service is less important than the convenience of getting to the restaurant in the first place. Twenty-six percent of adults surveyed by Maritz Marketing Research of Fenton, Missouri, say that a convenient location is the most influential factor in their choice of fast-food restaurants. Men are more likely than women to value convenience, at 31 percent versus 23 percent, and those aged sixty-five and older value it less than younger adults.

The thing average Americans value most highly after location is the fast food itself. Twenty-five percent of respondents say that quality of food is the deciding factor in their choice of restaurant. This may mean they consider the food superior, but it could also mean that they appreciate the consistency of knowing they'll get the same thing every time, every place. Women, young adults, and seniors are more likely than average to claim that quality is the key ingredient.

Only 12 percent of adults say they make fast-food choices based on speed of service, and just 8 percent say price is the key. Adults under age twenty-five have lower-than-average incomes, and they are more likely than those with average incomes to cite price as the most important reason for their restaurant choices.

Middle-aged adults worry less about menu selection, maybe because they are often accompanied by kids who tend to want the same thing every time. Just 3 percent of those aged thirty-five to forty-four claim that their choice is most influenced by children's preferences, yet the presence of offspring may explain why they are less likely than any other age group to care about selection and food quality. They do care about money and time. This age group ranks second after young adults in valuing reasonable prices and second after fifty-five to sixty-four-year-olds in caring about fast service. The middle-aged are also most likely to make decisions based on brand names, again possibly because of their children.

Questions

1. How might Corinne and Daniel use the preceding information?
2. Is this research performing a (a) descriptive function, (b) diagnostic function, or (c) predictive function?
3. Is the preceding research basic or applied? Explain your answer.
4. The above research is part of Maritz AmeriPolls, which are regularly conducted telephone surveys of a nationally representative sample of one thousand adults. Go to Maritz Marketing Research's Internet site at **http://www.maritz.com/apoll/**. Report your findings to the class.

Review Quiz

1. ______ is the process of planning, collecting, and analyzing data relevant to a marketing decision.
   a. A decision support system
   b. Marketing research
   c. Marketing planning
   d. A management information system
2. Which of the following is *not* one of the three basic roles of marketing research?
   a. The descriptive role
   b. The tracing role
   c. The diagnostic role
   d. The predictive role
3. The first step in the marketing research process must always be
   a. Identifying and formulating the problem/opportunity
   b. Planning the research design and gathering primary data
   c. Collecting data
   d. Specifying the sampling procedures
4. During which stage of the marketing research process is secondary data generally the most useful?
   a. Identifying and formulating the problem/opportunity
   b. Planning the research design and gathering primary data
   c. Collecting data
   d. Specifying the sampling procedures
5. Data that are collected for the first time and that are used to solve the particular problem under investigation by the firm are called
   a. Research data
   b. Secondary data
   c. Primary data
   d. A database

6. Which of the following primary data collection techniques is the most popular and useful for obtaining facts, opinions, and attitudes from people?
   a. Observation research
   b. Experiments
   c. On-line research
   d. Survey research
7. Which of the following methods of marketing research data collection does not rely on direct interaction with people?
   a. Observation research
   b. Experiments
   c. Reliability research
   d. Survey research
8. When marketing researchers alter variables such as price or package design and observe the effects of those alterations, they are likely using
   a. Observation research
   b. Experiments
   c. Validity research
   d. Survey research
9. A research error that occurs when a sample somehow does not represent the target population is called a
   a. Measurement error
   b. Frame error
   c. Sampling error
   d. Random error
10. When managers have several possible solutions to a problem, they should call for marketing research to help solve this dilemma.
    a. True
    b. False
11. Error that occurs when there is a difference between the information desired by the researcher and the information provided by the research process is known as measurement error.
    a. True
    b. False
12. Identify, in order, the steps in the marketing research process.

Check the Answer Key, which follows the Video Case, to see how well you understood the material.

VIDEO CASE

Burke Marketing Research: The Right Way to Make the Right Decision

Accurate and timely information is the lifeblood of marketing decision making. With good information, a company can increase sales and use its resources wisely. At Burke, Inc. Marketing Research, planning, collecting, and analyzing data is an integral part of helping clients make key decisions by answering important questions. What is the historic sales trend in the industry? What was the impact of a change in package design on sales? What if we change flavors? To answer questions like these, Burke has developed several research methods that examine and diagnose common marketing problems. The methods result from years of experience dealing with recurrent marketing problems across many industry and product categories. Some of these methods include PricePoint, STAGES, and ICE, or Integrated Concept Evaluation System.

PricePoint is a research method designed for use within the communications and technology industry. It is ideal for new products or services that are so original that buyers cannot compare them with other products on the market. As part of the PricePoint research, Burke interviews potential buyers and describes and demonstrates the new product or service idea. After that, researchers ask key questions to measure perceptions about price and willingness to pay. These results are used in a model that can estimate demand for the new product at various price levels. In the face of brutal competition, Burke's clients receive the edge they need to make decisions about a new product based on possible demand. With tools like this, companies can then set solid pricing strategies.

Another useful research method Burke offers its clients is STAGES. This model was developed to learn how attitudes affect each of the five stages of the buying process: awareness, consideration, trial, adoption, and customer loyalty. STAGES can answer important questions such as: How does awareness become a willingness to buy? Why do some buyers reject products? and Why do others become loyal customers? At Burke, researchers picture the purchase decision process as a funnel, where customers are lost at each stage. This loss occurs because customers lack awareness, have misperceptions, or do not have needs that match the product messages. The goal of STAGES is to help Burke's clients reduce the number of customers lost at each step in the buying process.

With STAGES, Burke can also respond to research findings that show that customers continuously evaluate products and services throughout the buying process but use different criteria at each stage. For example, a product must meet one set of requirements to get considered and another set for purchase on a trial basis. Once tried, there may be different requirements for a product to be adopted or bought repeatedly. Burke's customized STAGES model can identify the key attributes that drive each stage of a purchase, simulate these changes in attributes, and predict the overall effect on purchase decisions.

PricePoint and STAGES are not, however, always used alone. Burke researchers can combine them to produce a more detailed analysis for a client. An integrated approach helps a company understand the ever-changing dynamics of the market so it can seize the best business opportunity. One integrated approach employed by Burke is called ICE, or Integrated Concept Evaluation system. This model combines several research methods to help clients select which product idea would best meet the customer's need. One of Burke's clients was a major communications company that wanted to explore consumer interest in several new product ideas. These concepts were so innovative that there was no framework in place for comparing them to each other or to existing products, or for determining what price consumers would be willing to pay. The client needed information about the potential demand for each product concept under various pricing plans. In addition, the client wanted to be able to evaluate the specific benefits associated with each product. This information would be helpful in providing direction for future communications campaigns. The ICE research model used a combination of methods, including PricePoint and another method to evaluate benefits called Benefit Deficiency Analysis, to help the communications company map out a product development strategy.

To support all its customized models, Burke uses proven data collection methods such as focus groups, mail and telephone surveys, and mall intercepts. The completed research leads to results that, once interpreted, serve as the basis for the research analysis. This analysis is communicated clearly and concisely to the client in the research report, which in turn helps the company make better decisions and develop better products and services to satisfy customers. In every business relationship, Burke picks the right research method to help clients make the right decisions.

Questions

1. Does Burke, Inc. fulfill the roles of marketing research as described in the chapter? Explain.
2. What are the ways that Burke, Inc. benefits a client?
3. How does Burke improve the quality of decision making for its clients?
4. How does Burke keep its clients competitive?

Answer Key

1. *Answer:* b, p. 213

   Rationale: This is the definition of marketing research as given in the chapter. Marketing research is the main data source for management information systems and decision support systems.

2. *Answer:* b, p. 213

   Rationale: Marketing research has three roles: descriptive, diagnostic, and predictive.

3. *Answer:* a, p. 216

   Rationale: The problem/opportunity definition is always first and involves determining what information is needed and how that information can be obtained in an effective and efficient manner.

4. *Answer:* a, p. 217

   Rationale: Although secondary data can be a valuable tool throughout the research process, it is particularly useful in the first step as it helps marketers understand what information is already available and what is not.

5. *Answer:* c, p. 224

   Rationale: The main advantage of primary data is that they will answer a specific research question that secondary data cannot answer.

6. *Answer:* d, p. 225

   Rationale: Survey research techniques are the most popular. There are numerous survey techniques, including mail surveys, mall intercept interviews, and focus groups.

7. *Answer:* a, p. 234

   Rationale: Observation research involves watching people and their activities, using either people or machines.

8. *Answer:* b, p. 235

   Rationale: Experiments are designed to alter one variable while holding another constant so that the researcher can observe changes. For example, a firm might be interested in observing changes in sales that result from changing the amount of money spent on advertising.

9. *Answer:* c, p. 236

   Rationale: A sampling error occurs when people in the target population either refused to cooperate or were not accessible to the researchers.

10. *Answer:* b, p. 241

    Rationale: Managers should not instinctively conduct marketing research. Research should only be conducted when the expected value of the information gained from research is greater than the cost of obtaining it.

11. *Answer:* a, p. 236

    Rationale: Measurement error often occurs when consumers tell researchers that they purchase a certain brand or product, when they actually do not.

12. *Answer:*

    1. Identifying and formulating the problem/opportunity
    2. Planning the research design and gathering primary data
    3. Specifying the sampling procedures
    4. Collecting the data
    5. Analyzing the data
    6. Preparing and presenting the report
    7. Performing the follow-up (p. 216)

still shaky?

Visit the *Marketing* Web site at **http://lamb.swcollege.com** for review opportunities. Don't forget your *Grademaker Study Guide* can help you with difficult material in Part 2.

marketing miscues

General Motors Is Too General

General Motors' top management has gone through a number of shake-ups in the past decade, yet the problem remains the same: GM doesn't create cars that people want, build them effectively, or market them efficiently. To some observers, the company is in a slow-moving time warp that continually lags behind the competition.

GM has more than twice as many brands and 70 percent more U.S. dealerships than Ford, even though GM's unit sales are only 19 percent greater. Critics say GM should stop trying to resuscitate dying divisions and instead spend more on promising newcomers like Saturn Corp. "This is like watching a grade-B movie—you know exactly how it ends," says marketing analyst Mary Ann Keller. "Either Buick or Oldsmobile is going to have to disappear." Analysts also would like GM to add more high-profit trucks and new car–truck hybrids like Honda's CR-V and Lexus's RX300. John Zarrella, GM's vice president of marketing, acknowledges that "we have more cars than we need, and not enough trucks."

Ford, Chrysler, and other rivals long ago moved on—cutting costs, streamlining distribution, raising efficiency, and cranking out innovative models in record time. They have left GM behind, and in key areas it continues to slip: productivity, market-share growth, product development times, overhead expenses, and revenue per vehicle sold. GM's U.S. market share—near 50 percent three decades ago—dropped to a dismal 28.6 percent in early 1998. Its spanking-new midsize sedans—among the vaunted successes—weren't selling as well as their lackluster predecessors. It took the biggest rebates in Detroit to boost GM market share back above 30 percent. In addition, analysts say that without the rebates, share will drop back. "The dogs don't like the dog food," says Arthur D. Little Inc. auto consultant John Wolkonowicz. "GM has neither a golden gut (instinct) nor a way of understanding the needs of future customers." A perfect example: Although consumers clamor for four-door pickups such as those produced by Dodge and Ford, GM is introducing a three-door.

Even GM cars that are well conceived sink in the market because of the company's poor brand image, too much competing advertising, and botched manufacturing launches. The new Intrigue sedan is one of the finest cars in its class, but it's doubtful that many baby boomers will ever wander into an Oldsmobile showroom to check it out.

GM still has factory capacity, marketing structure, and distribution geared to owning 35 percent or more of the market—a share it may never see again. It still has seven marketing divisions with eighty car and truck models. Likewise, there aren't enough sales to support GM's sprawling network of eight-thousand-plus dealers profitably. This excess baggage is crippling. "GM can no longer afford to keep all those car lines current—they don't have the cash flow," explains consultant Wolkonowicz. "They fall further and further behind because the competition can change product more quickly."

Questions

1. Using the consumer behavior model in Chapter 5, explain what variables in the model GM might attack to influence people to buy GM cars.
2. Do you think GM has done a good job segmenting its markets? Defend your answer.
3. Which GM brand appeals the most to you as a consumer? The least? Explain your preferences. How can GM change the latter?
4. If you planned to recommend marketing research to GM, what would be the first four projects you would recommend? Why?
5. Explain how GM might use competitive intelligence to better its position in the marketplace.

SOURCES: "GM Goes on Ad-fensive with Campaign," *USA Today,* 23 July 1998, p. 3B. Jean Halliday, "GM Pondering Consolidation in Marketing," *Advertising Age,* 11 May 1998, p. 4. Kathleen Kerwin, "GM: It's Time to Face the Future," *Business Week,* 27 July 1998, pp. 25–28. Kathleen Kerwin, "The Shutdown GM Needs?" *Business Week,* 13 July 1998, pp. 34–36. David Kiley, "Optimum Target," *BrandWeek,* 18 May 1998, pp. 38–42.

critical thinking case

The Gap Gets It

Mickey Drexler, chief executive of Gap Inc., may have more influence on American style than anyone else. Yes, Ralph Lauren embodies a certain American look, but how many of us have the money or inclination to imitate the Kennedys? Drexler, by contrast, is a mass marketer. He intends to bring style to everyone, from Tupelo, Mississippi, to Fargo, North Dakota; from Humble, Texas, to Anchorage, Alaska.

"Think about it," Drexler says, over a ham and Swiss cheese sandwich with mustard and a bag of Lay's baked potato chips. "If you go into a supermarket, you would expect to find some fundamental items. You would expect to find milk: nonfat, 1%, 2%, whole milk. You'd expect the dates to be fresh. You want butter. You want certain types of bread. You have your list. I don't know why apparel stores should be any different. I mean, think about it."

What Drexler has done is to transform Gap from a national retail chain into a recognizable global brand. Above all, he is determined to make Gap ubiquitous. If Coke is available in every airport, in every grocery store, in every McDonald's, shouldn't Gap be everywhere too? Since Drexler arrived in 1983, Gap Inc. has grown from 566 stores to 2,237. Gap now operates in Japan, the United Kingdom, Canada, France, and Germany. One new store opens every day.

"I find clothing very complicated to buy," Drexler says. "It shouldn't be that complicated. It should be simple." Simplicity may be what defines Gap, but making Gap work is not so simple. Clothing companies usually depend on the vision and taste of just one person. As soon as that person's vision is tired, it's all over, and the line becomes a parody of itself, which is what happened at Laura Ashley, for example. That's why Paris design houses work so hard to bring in new, young talent. Everything at Gap depends on Drexler's eye; it isn't like making turbine engines.

Most clothing companies want their products to be a sign of something else—money, power, class, virility, sex, privilege, access. Beneath an unstructured Armani suit lurks a whiff of power, worldliness, competitiveness, *la dolce vita.* Ralph Lauren tries hard to suggest long weekends in the Hamptons, ease, trust funds, and other old things. However, Drexler knows instinctively that Americans aren't all that comfortable with class. Gap is democratic and familiar—ordinary, unpretentious, understated, almost lowbrow.

Drexler is famous for wandering around Gap headquarters repeating a sort of mantra: "Think negative five comp. Think negative five comp." Everyone knows he's talking about comparable store sales—that he doesn't want employees to celebrate the 15% increase this past June, but to pretend instead that the numbers were down. It's a sort of superstition. He worries constantly about becoming complacent—and he doesn't want to attract the evil eye. The mantra seems to work. "Even after a great quarter everyone in that company comes together and says, 'We didn't do well enough. How can we do better?'" says Rick Lyons, who left last year after thirteen years at Gap, most recently as an executive vice president. "There's always a gray feeling. I was always gray. Oh sure, we'd celebrate, briefly, after a great quarter, but it was always right back to, 'What did we do wrong?'"

Sometimes things have gone wrong. In 1983, Gap bought Banana Republic. The company sold jodhpurs, travel trunks, hunting jackets. It was very Indiana Jones, very *Out of Africa.* Which was great, until 1987, when the safari look went out of fashion. To restructure Banana Republic, Gap took a $6.8 million pretax writeoff. Then, in 1987, Drexler launched Hemispheres, a chain of shops selling expensive "European-inspired" clothes that never caught on.

By 1995, Gap found many competitors selling "basics." As competition increased, the Gap seemed old, tired, and out of ideas. Drexler responded to this crisis with a bold gamble, an approach to discount marketing that had never been tried before. Out of this experience grew the new business model that now has Wall Street thinking Gap might be the next Coke.

The gamble was Old Navy, a new division Drexler launched in 1994 to compete with stores like Sears and Target. Discount shopping was the hot growth area in retailing, but, Drexler asked, did it need to be so depressing? Big, loud, fun, and cheap, Old Navy stores are fitted out with exposed pipes and raw concrete floors. There are listening booths where customers can sample CDs and old grocery-store refrigerator cases stocked with T-shirts shrinkwrapped like packages of lean ground beef.

"When we started Old Navy, we sat around and we talked about what we didn't like about discount stores —poor quality, colors that are always just a hair off. We really thought, 'What do we not want to be?' and took it from there," explains Jenny Ming, executive vice president for merchandising at Old Navy.

The pitch was perfect, and Old Navy was an instant success. "There was a time, not so long ago, when people who shopped at department stores wouldn't shop at Wal-Mart—

that was déclassé," explains Kurt Barnard, of *Barnard's Retail Trend Report.* "Then it became chic to shop downscale, to shop for a bargain. People used to pay $10 and they said they paid $20. Now they pay $20 and say they paid $10." Old Navy captures this trend brilliantly. It's discount shopping with an edge, discount shopping that appeals even to people who can afford Gucci. "Old Navy is a concept for a decade. If you create an idea like that once every ten years, you're fine," remarks Baum, the Goldman analyst.

In less than three years, Gap opened 282 Old Navy stores; sales hit $1 billion. However, as if to confirm how badly this business depends on the vision of just one man, even as Drexler focused on building Old Navy, things at the Gap division went from bad to dreadful. It didn't help that his attention was further distracted by the search for a post-safari identity for Banana Republic.

One day in the summer of 1996, Drexler wandered slowly through a Gap store and was shocked. The clothes were ugly, the carpet was frayed, the fixtures looked cheap. Simplicity and cleanliness had been forgotten. However, what he really hated that summer was a series of new Gap print ads that included a young, androgynous-looking man with long blond hair (unclean?), a pierced lip, and an attitude. It was heroin chic. It was also Calvin Klein—it wasn't Gap. "It was so incompatible in my mind with what made Gap right," says Drexler. "I think this campaign said more and more, 'If you're a Gap customer, don't come into the Gap.'" The campaign lasted two months. Maggie Gross, Gap's longtime ad director, promptly took a leave of absence, then resigned. A handful of other Gap advertising people left with her. There were departures in the New York design department too.

Drexler didn't go on vacation that summer. Instead he spent two and a half months, from June to August, going through every item of clothing in the line—clothes that were to hit stores in the spring of 1997. He got rid of everything that wasn't pure Gap. Away went the skinny plaid pants and the zip-up men's shirts in '50s orange and brown. Away went the shiny green disco shirts. "It was a good kick," remarks Drexler. "I think the most important thing I learned was the importance of consistency when branding a business." (Did somebody say McDonald's?)

Around the same time, in late 1996, while he was reading a Coca-Cola annual report, Drexler realized that Gap as a concept wasn't "mature" after all. Coke didn't go out of style. It wasn't superannuated. His reasoning continued: Was a can of Coke any more basic, more fundamental to Americans than a white Gap men's shirt? "We started to think about our business in different terms," says Drexler. "We started to think about our brand in a more ubiquitous way. Before, for example, we would have had one store in a particular market. But if you think about great brands in America and the world, they usually dominate a much larger percent of market share than any apparel company does." Thinking big, thinking in terms of Coca-Cola, Drexler then became obsessed with Gap's comparatively small market share: "The average per capita expenditure on clothing in America is $700. We own about $23 of that. So I'm saying, 'Gee, we only have $23 of the $700? You would think Gap should own a lot more of the customer's wardrobe.'"

To multiply that $23, Gap has started opening stores at a quick pace and in towns that Drexler once would have considered too small. By the end of 1998, Gap and GapKids were in places like Falls Church, Virginia; Prairie Village, Kansas; and Joplin, Missouri. In cities where Gap already exists, stores continue to open. There have been Gap, GapKids, Banana Republic, and Old Navy stores in Wichita, for example. Recently, however, when Drexler visited Wichita, he recognized that the market was far from saturated. Now there are two GapKids and two Gap stores there, with a third Gap on its way. In June 1998, Gap launched Gap-to-go in Manhattan, on the theory that buying clothes should be as easy as ordering in Chinese food. Menus from Gap-to-go list twenty-one basic Gap items; fax your order in and it will be delivered to your office or home by the end of the day. If Gap-to-go works in Manhattan, it will be introduced in other cities. Of course there's also the Internet; Gap Online was introduced in November 1997. In September, Banana Republic will mail out a catalog. This fall, Gap plans to test GapBody stores that will sell boxer shorts, cotton panties and bras, pajamas, Gap fragrances, soaps, and candles.

Questions

1. Explain how the safari-look could have gone out of style and almost bankrupted Banana Republic. Use the consumer decision-making process in Chapter 5 as the basis for your explanation.
2. Describe the various market segments that each Gap company appeals to.
3. What is the primary form of segmentation used by Gap? Defend your answer.
4. How can Gap use marketing research to more effectively accomplish its goals?
5. What forms of competitive intelligence would be beneficial to Gap?
6. Comment on Drexler's management style.

SOURCE: From "Gap Gets It" by Nina Munk, *Fortune*, August 3, 1998.

Suggested Readings

Kelly Barron, "Grow Up Already," *Forbes,* 27 July 1998, pp. 58–60.

Becky Ebenkamp, "Extensions: Old Navy Continues to Push Brand Scope with Cosmetics," *Brandweek,* 27 April 1998, pp. 41–42.

Katherine Weisman, "Gap Getting the French Knack," *WWD,* 9 July 1998, pp. 16–17.

Cross-Functional Connections Solutions

Questions

1. Why is marketing research perceived as "owned" by the marketing department?

   There are probably a few general answers to this question. One, because the research is referred to as "marketing" rather than "market" or "marketplace," it automatically denotes that it is part of the marketing department. Also, the research has traditionally been conducted by the marketing department—reinforcing the notion that the marketing department owns it. Additionally, prior to the 1990s, the marketing department was the only formal link between the company and customer. Because a primary focus of marketing research is the customer, it was always owned by the marketing department.

2. Where should marketing research be formally integrated across functional departments?

   There are four major areas in which marketing research needs to be integrated formally within an organization: (1) benchmarking studies, (2) customer visits, (3) customer satisfaction studies, and (4) forecasting. (The "hows" and "whys" of each of these areas are described in detail in the reading.)

3. What data differences exist across functions?

   The historical data debate between marketing and other business functions centers on the qualitative versus quantitative format of the data. The data collected by marketers are perceived to be "touchy-feely" data when compared to the "hard" data utilized by other functional areas. In addition to unit sales and competitive offerings, marketing data looks at customers' perceptions—something very "soft" when compared to other functional data. For example, manufacturing can cite exact production output, cost, and cycle data; and R&D has precise specifications for tensile strength, electrical usage, and battery power. Add accounting data with its general accounting standards to the "hard" data side of the picture, and it's not surprising that data differences cause cross-functional conflict within a firm.

Suggested Readings

Gary S. LeVee, "The Key to Understanding the Forecasting Process," *The Journal of Business Forecasting,* Winter 1992–93, pp. 12–16.

Todd Vogel, "At Xerox, They're Shouting 'Once More into the Breach,'" *Business Week,* 28 July 1990, pp. 62–63.

Marketing Planning Activities

Analyzing Marketing Opportunities

The next step in preparing a marketing plan for the company you have already chosen is to get a thorough understanding of the marketing opportunities in terms of marketing to customers. The following activities will help you better understand the marketplace, which will increase your chances of success in developing an appropriate marketing mix.

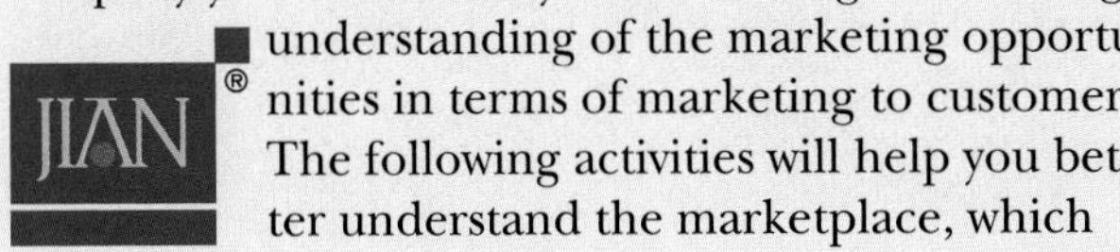

1. Identify the NAIC code for your chosen company's industry. Perform a brief industry analysis (from U.S. *Industrial Outlook,* for example) of your firm's industry, based on the NAIC code.
2. To whom does your company market (consumer, industrial, government, not-for-profit, or a combination of targets)? Within each market, are there specific segments or niches that your company can concentrate on? If so, which one(s) would you focus on and why? What are the factors used to create these segments?

Marketing*Builder* Exercise

- **Market Segment** portion of the **Market Analysis** template

3. Describe your company's target market segment(s). Use demographics, pyschographics, geographics, economic factors, size, growth rates, trends, SIC codes, and any other appropriate descriptors.

Marketing*Builder* Exercise

- **Customer Profile** portion of the **Market Analysis** template

4. Describe the decision-making process that customers go through when purchasing your company's product or service. What are the critical factors that influence this purchase-behavior process?
5. Choose four characteristics of your firm's product offering. Using these factors for axes, draw two positioning grids and fill in the quadrants with competitor's offerings as well as your own. Are there any "holes" of needs and wants that are not being filled?

Marketing*Builder* Exercise

- **Positioning** portion of the **Marketing Communications** template

6. Are there critical issues that must be explored with primary marketing research before you can implement your marketing plan? These might include items such as customer demand, purchase intentions, customer perceptions of product quality, price perceptions, and reaction to critical promotion.

Marketing*Builder* Exercises

- **Product Launch Chart** spreadsheet
- **Operating Budget** spreadsheet
- **Sales Forecast and Analysis** spreadsheet

PRODUCT AND DISTRIBUTION DECISIONS

cross-functional connections

CROSS-FUNCTIONAL CONNECTIONS

A High Quality Product at the Right Place, at the Right Time

Achieving customer satisfaction means that the company must have the right product at the right place at the right time (and at the right price). The giant retailer, Wal-Mart, has based much of its competitive success on its ability to get the right product in the right stores at the right time—products that are then sold to customers via the company's helpful, friendly sales people.

Marketing focuses on the company's products/services from a *demand-side* perspective. Via marketing research methods, marketers determine current and future wants and needs. Once these wants and needs are determined, marketing then expects the research & development group to develop a device that will satisfy customer demands. Once the device is developed, the expectation is that the manufacturing group will produce it. The device becomes a true product with the development of a marketing program that adds values for customers.

Typically, however, manufacturing and research and development view products from a *supply-side* perspective. In this supply-side framework, the marketing department focuses on me-too products, leaving new products to the research and development group for design and the manufacturing group for production. Marketers, then, are responsible for getting the marketplace to want the product. According to this framework, marketing is the functional group that tells the marketplace about the product's performance but has no input as to what actually goes into the product.

Many businesspeople have suggested that whether a company or product is driven by a demand-side focus or a supply-side focus depends on the nature of the product. For example, highly technological products such as component parts of a computer would be based more on supply-side thinking. Prior to the development of products such as Intel components (which make computers function better) or PCMCIA cards by SystemSoft Corp. (which allow computers to communicate via a modem), consumers probably did not have sufficient knowledge to ask for such component parts. Consumer products, however, appear to be better examples of demand-side product concepts.

Demand-side versus supply-side thinking has resulted in three major areas of conflict between marketing and research and development/manufacturing: managing variety, managing availability, and managing reliability. Generally, marketing wants a large variety of high-quality products for customers to choose from and will promise the shortest delivery time necessary to get the order. On the flip side, research and development and manufacturing prefer fewer models so that they can devote attention to a smaller number of projects—resulting in the highest possible quality as soon as possible, without holding too many products in inventory.

By the mid 1990s, the research and development and manufacturing functional groups had become quite efficient at working together, using processes referred to as *design-factory fit, concurrent engineering, design for manufacturability and assembly, and early manufacturing involvement.* Basically, all of these concepts refer to advance linkage between a product's design and its manufacturing needs so that the manufacturing group will be ready to make the product once it has been designed.

Today's marketplace is increasingly demanding that companies compete on both time and customization. Customers demand highly customized products that can be delivered immediately. Such expectations are in direct contrast to traditional thinking. Traditionally, companies made standardized products available immediately, with customers understanding that customization would result in delays in delivery.

The key to providing customized products quickly is a multidisciplinary approach to business. There are considerable costs associated with getting a high-quality, customized product out the door quickly, and manufacturing has been a key marketing partner in making the delivery process possible. *Advanced Manufacturing Systems* (AMS) have been developed that not only reduce costs (ultimately affecting the price charged to the customer) but also allow faster product delivery. Some of the more popular advanced manufacturing systems are just-in-time (JIT), manufacturing resources planning (MRP), and electronic data interchange (EDI).

A just-in-time (JIT) manufacturing system allows the production of a product as needed, instead of producing for stock. The effect that such a manufacturing system has on a channel intermediary is to ultimately change the channel structure. Customers may be able to receive a product directly from the manufacturer rather than receiving it via a longer distribution channel. The absence of a channel intermediary not only makes products available quickly, but fewer channel members may also mean decreased costs—the ultimate in efficiency of operations. However, marketing must make sure that the change in the channel structure is not only more efficient but also more effective—that is, marketing must determine whether the channel intermediary provides a service that will otherwise be unavailable if the product is shipped directly from the manufacturer.

The use of electronic data interchange (EDI) also can significantly increase the efficiency of operations between the shop floor and distribution of the product. EDI permits the exchange of information between computers—no human involvement is necessary. Data collected at the point-of-sale can be transmitted automatically, via an electronic network, to the manufacturing department. This system allows manufacturing to know the exact number of units on the retail floor at any point in time, allowing the manufacturing group to time its production and delivery to meet the retailer's specific needs.

Navistar International Transportation Corp., manufacturer and marketer of medium- and heavy-duty trucks, implemented electronic data interchange as one element of the company's cost-cutting strategy. Prior to EDI, the company's monthly needs were mailed to suppliers and daily production requirements were phoned in. With EDI, the company was able to instantaneously transmit and receive documents that had previously taken a week of processing time. Navistar experienced a 33 percent reduction in its inventory in the first eighteen months of EDI implementation. This inventory reduction took place at the same time that the company was focusing on the need to be more market-oriented.

The expectation is that the final product is high quality and has moved through the company's functional processes in at least half the time of the traditional linear process. The general idea is that a company can design a product that satisfies customers' demands and also is quicker and easier to assemble and deliver. This type of design, assembly, and delivery requires a high level of coordination among marketing, research and development, and manufacturing. Boeing refers to this type of coordination as *paperless design.* The design of the Boeing 777 utilized teams of research and development, manufacturing, marketing, customers, and finance—with all team members interacting to assemble an airplane on a computer system that allowed them to model the airplane and iron out bugs long before the major expense of building a prototype.

Making a company's product or service available to the customer is the joint effort of many different business functions. Operational efficiencies in linking marketing's product and distribution requirements to research and development's design and manufacturing's production processes are the result of well-thought-out cross-functional plans. Such plans have to be developed in conjunction with all major functional groups. Benefits to consumers appear in both dollar savings and improved customer service. Companies such as United Parcel Service and Federal Express that compete for the same customers have become experts at developing products and channel systems that utilize all functional components of the organization in getting the right product/service to the right customer at just the right time.

Questions for discussion:

1. What is the difference between the demand-side perspective and the supply-side perspective to doing business? Is either perspective more appropriate?
2. What are some of the popular business terms used to describe cross-functional integration?
3. What are some of the popular Advanced Manufacturing Systems and how do they interact with marketing?

check it out

For articles and exercises on the material in this part, and for other great study aids, visit the *Marketing* Web site at **http://lamb.swcollege.com**

CHAPTER

8

LEARNING OBJECTIVES

After studying this chapter, you should be able to

1 Define the term "product"

2 Classify consumer products

3 Discuss the importance of services to the economy

4 Identify the differences between services and goods

5 Explain why services marketing is important to manufacturers

6 Define the terms "product item," "product line," and "product mix"

7 Describe marketing uses of branding

8 Describe marketing uses of packaging and labeling

9 Describe how and why product warranties are important marketing tools

distribution channel. The absence of a channel intermediary not only makes products available quickly, but fewer channel members may also mean decreased costs—the ultimate in efficiency of operations. However, marketing must make sure that the change in the channel structure is not only more efficient but also more effective—that is, marketing must determine whether the channel intermediary provides a service that will otherwise be unavailable if the product is shipped directly from the manufacturer.

The use of electronic data interchange (EDI) also can significantly increase the efficiency of operations between the shop floor and distribution of the product. EDI permits the exchange of information between computers—no human involvement is necessary. Data collected at the point-of-sale can be transmitted automatically, via an electronic network, to the manufacturing department. This system allows manufacturing to know the exact number of units on the retail floor at any point in time, allowing the manufacturing group to time its production and delivery to meet the retailer's specific needs.

Navistar International Transportation Corp., manufacturer and marketer of medium- and heavy-duty trucks, implemented electronic data interchange as one element of the company's cost-cutting strategy. Prior to EDI, the company's monthly needs were mailed to suppliers and daily production requirements were phoned in. With EDI, the company was able to instantaneously transmit and receive documents that had previously taken a week of processing time. Navistar experienced a 33 percent reduction in its inventory in the first eighteen months of EDI implementation. This inventory reduction took place at the same time that the company was focusing on the need to be more market-oriented.

The expectation is that the final product is high quality and has moved through the company's functional processes in at least half the time of the traditional linear process. The general idea is that a company can design a product that satisfies customers' demands and also is quicker and easier to assemble and deliver. This type of design, assembly, and delivery requires a high level of coordination among marketing, research and development, and manufacturing. Boeing refers to this type of coordination as *paperless design.* The design of the Boeing 777 utilized teams of research and development, manufacturing, marketing, customers, and finance—with all team members interacting to assemble an airplane on a computer system that allowed them to model the airplane and iron out bugs long before the major expense of building a prototype.

Making a company's product or service available to the customer is the joint effort of many different business functions. Operational efficiencies in linking marketing's product and distribution requirements to research and development's design and manufacturing's production processes are the result of well-thought-out cross-functional plans. Such plans have to be developed in conjunction with all major functional groups. Benefits to consumers appear in both dollar savings and improved customer service. Companies such as United Parcel Service and Federal Express that compete for the same customers have become experts at developing products and channel systems that utilize all functional components of the organization in getting the right product/service to the right customer at just the right time.

Questions for discussion:

1. What is the difference between the demand-side perspective and the supply-side perspective to doing business? Is either perspective more appropriate?
2. What are some of the popular business terms used to describe cross-functional integration?
3. What are some of the popular Advanced Manufacturing Systems and how do they interact with marketing?

check it out

For articles and exercises on the material in this part, and for other great study aids, visit the *Marketing* Web site at **http://lamb.swcollege.com**

CHAPTER

8

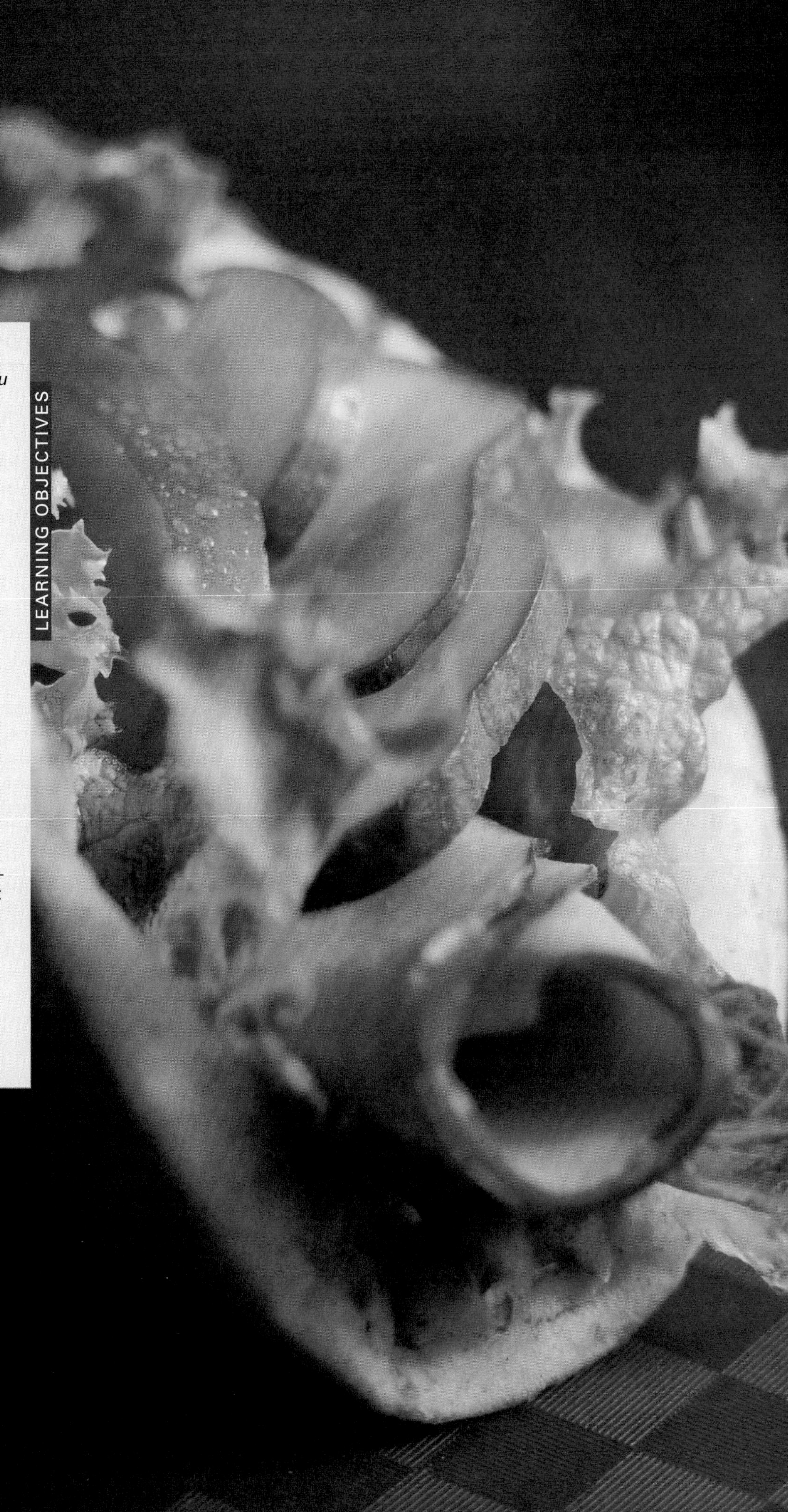

LEARNING OBJECTIVES

After studying this chapter, you should be able to

1 Define the term "product"

2 Classify consumer products

3 Discuss the importance of services to the economy

4 Identify the differences between services and goods

5 Explain why services marketing is important to manufacturers

6 Define the terms "product item," "product line," and "product mix"

7 Describe marketing uses of branding

8 Describe marketing uses of packaging and labeling

9 Describe how and why product warranties are important marketing tools

PRODUCT AND SERVICES CONCEPTS

McDonald's has teamed up with ConAgra to test a line of wrapped sandwiches made with Healthy Choice deli meats. The line, which has four varieties, puts McDonald's in the trendy wrap sandwich category and could provide a much needed food item that is low in fat, portable, and convenient. The sandwich is targeted to adult consumers, long a demographic sore spot with the restaurant chain.

For McDonald's, the Healthy Choice brand will provide a good-for-you image that is lacking in many of the restaurant's food items. McDonald's USA president Alan Feldman has noted that he is interested in borrowing brand equity from other brands as well. A source close to the company said, "I think you're going to see a lot more of this co-branding at McDonald's."

The McDeli test is part of McDonald's attempt to upgrade its overall food quality and to develop new products that will attract consumer groups other than kids. Its last adult-targeted Deluxe sandwich line proved to be an expensive disappointment. The Arch Deluxe burger has been dropped from many stores, and the Fish Deluxe is being redesigned.

The McDeli Wraps, developed by a franchisee in Michigan, have an average six to twelve grams of fat. The four varieties—Grilled Chicken Caesar, Turkey & Swiss, Turkey Club, and a no-meat Veggie Wrap—are intended to be a healthier product that mothers can have while the kids eat Happy Meals and that's easy to eat while driving. The wraps have been selling briskly in test markets, with one store manager reporting sales of two hundred wraps daily.

Wrap sandwiches have grown in popularity and are meant to address three large trends among time-pressed consumers: portability, a growing concern over fat content, and a desire for more freshly made, out-of-home dining solutions. However, wrap sandwiches have a mixed record among fast-food restaurants. Long John Silver's, KFC, and Wendy's have all introduced wrap-style offerings. KFC has since pulled its entry, whereas wraps at Long John's and Wendy's have not produced incremental sales.[1]

Why would a company like McDonald's—which already has a strong brand name and identity—choose to team up with another brand? What are the positives and negatives of such a strategy? Do you think that McDonald's strategy is sound?

on line

McDonald's
Healthy Choice

Are McDonald's and Healthy Choice promoting this partnership? Visit their Web sites to find out. How can you account for what you discover?

http://www.mcdonalds.com/ **http://www.healthychoice.com/**

What Is a Product?

1
Define the term "product"

product
Everything, both favorable and unfavorable, that a person receives in an exchange.

The product offering, the heart of an organization's marketing program, is usually the starting point in creating a marketing mix. A marketing manager cannot determine a price, design a promotion strategy, or create a distribution channel until the firm has a product to sell. Moreover, an excellent distribution channel, a persuasive promotion campaign, and a fair price have no value with a poor or inadequate product offering.

A **product** may be defined as everything, both favorable and unfavorable, that a person receives in an exchange. A product may be a tangible good like a pair of shoes, a service like a haircut, an idea like "don't litter," or any combination of these three. Packaging, style, color, options, and size are some typical product features. Just as important are intangibles such as service, the seller's image, the manufacturer's reputation, and the way consumers believe others will view the product.

To most people, the term "product" means a tangible good. However, services and ideas are also products. The marketing process identified in Chapter 1 is the same whether the product marketed is a good, a service, an idea, or some combination of these.

Types of Consumer Products

2
Classify consumer products

business product (industrial product)
Product used to manufacture other goods or services, to facilitate an organization's operations, or to resell to other customers.

consumer product
Product bought to satisfy an individual's personal wants.

Products can be classified as either business (industrial) or consumer products, depending on the buyer's intentions. The key distinction between the two types of products is their intended use. If the intended use is a business purpose, the product is classified as a business or industrial product. As explained in Chapter 5, a **business product** is used to manufacture other goods or services, to facilitate an organization's operations, or to resell to other customers. A **consumer product** is bought to satisfy an individual's personal wants. Sometimes the same item can be classified as either a business or a consumer product, depending on its intended use. Examples include lightbulbs, pencils and paper, and microcomputers.

We need to know about product classifications because business and consumer products are marketed differently. They are marketed to different target markets and tend to use different distribution, promotion, and pricing strategies.

Chapter 5 examined seven categories of business products: major equipment, accessory equipment, component parts, processed materials, raw materials, supplies, and services. The current chapter examines an effective way of categorizing consumer products. Although there are several ways to classify them, the most popular approach includes these four types: convenience products, shopping products, specialty products, and unsought products. (See Exhibit 8.1.) This approach classifies products according to how much effort is normally used to shop for them.

Convenience Products

convenience product
A relatively inexpensive item that merits little shopping effort.

A **convenience product** is a relatively inexpensive item that merits little shopping effort—that is, a consumer is unwilling to shop extensively for such an item. Candy, soft drinks, combs, aspirin, small hardware items, dry cleaning, and car washes fall into the convenience product category.

Consumers buy convenience products regularly, usually without much planning. Nevertheless, consumers do know the brand names of popular convenience products, such as Coca-Cola, Bayer aspirin, and Right Guard deodorant. Convenience products normally require wide distribution in order to sell sufficient quantities to meet profit goals.

exhibit 8.1

Classification of Consumer Products

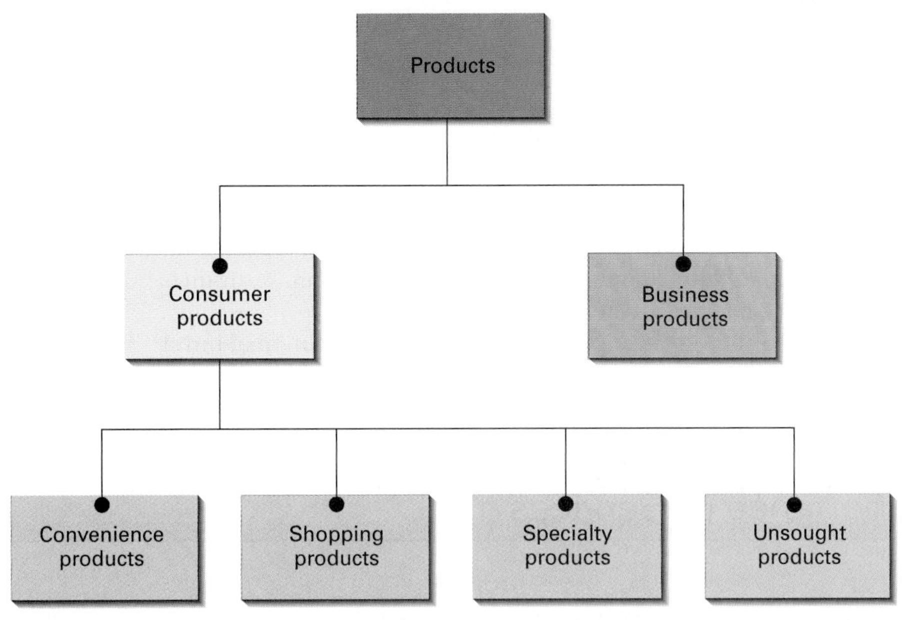

Shopping Products

A **shopping product** is usually more expensive than a convenience product and is found in fewer stores. Consumers usually buy a shopping product only after comparing several brands or stores on style, practicality, price, and lifestyle compatibility. They are willing to invest some effort into this process to get the desired benefits.

shopping product
Product that requires comparison shopping, because it is usually more expensive than a convenience product and found in fewer stores.

There are two types of shopping products: homogeneous and heterogeneous. Consumers perceive *homogeneous* shopping products as basically similar—for example, washers, dryers, refrigerators, and televisions. With homogeneous shopping products, consumers typically look for the lowest-priced brand that has the desired features.

In contrast, consumers perceive *heterogeneous* shopping products as essentially different—for example, furniture, clothing, housing, and universities. Consumers often have trouble comparing heterogeneous shopping products because the prices, quality, and features vary so much. The benefit of comparing heterogeneous shopping products is "finding the best product or brand for me"; this decision is often highly individual.

With homogenous products such as televisions, consumers typically buy the lowest-priced brand that has the desired features.
© Jeff Greenberg

Specialty Products

When consumers search extensively for a particular item and are very reluctant to accept substitutes, that item is a **specialty product**. Fine watches, Rolls Royce automobiles, expensive stereo equipment, gourmet restaurants, and highly specialized forms of medical care are generally considered specialty products.

specialty product
A particular item that consumers search extensively for and are very reluctant to accept substitutes.

Marketers of specialty products often use selective, status-conscious advertising to maintain their product's exclusive image. Distribution is often limited to one or a very few outlets in a geographic area. Brand names and quality of service are often very important.

Unsought Products

unsought product
A product unknown to the potential buyer or a known product that the buyer does not actively seek.

A product unknown to the potential buyer or a known product that the buyer does not actively seek is referred to as an **unsought product**. New products fall into this category until advertising and distribution increase consumer awareness of them.

Some goods are always marketed as unsought items, especially needed products we do not like to think about or care to spend money on. Insurance, burial plots, encyclopedias, and similar items require aggressive personal selling and highly persuasive advertising. Salespeople actively seek leads to potential buyers. Because consumers usually do not seek out this type of product, the company must go directly to them through a salesperson, direct mail, or direct-response advertising.

The Importance of Services

3
Discuss the importance of services to the economy

service
The result of applying human or mechanical efforts to people or objects.

A **service** is the result of applying human or mechanical efforts to people or objects. Services involve a deed, a performance, or an effort that cannot be physically possessed. Today, the service sector substantially influences the U.S. economy. More than eight in ten workers currently labor to produce services, such as transportation, retail trade, and finance.[2] The service sector accounts for 74 percent of the U.S. gross domestic product, and services produced a balance-of-trade surplus that reached $55.7 billion in 1993 (compared to a $132.4 billion deficit for goods), which significantly reduced this country's overall trade deficit.[3] The demand for services is expected to continue. According to the Bureau of Labor Statistics, service occupations will be responsible for all net job growth through the year 2005. Much of this demand results from demographics. An aging population will need nurses, home health care, physical therapists, and social workers. Two-earner families need child care, housecleaning, and lawn care services. Also increasing will be the demand for information managers, such as computer engineers and systems analysts.

Services are also important to the world economy. In Great Britain, 73 percent of jobs are in services; 57 percent of German workers and 62 percent of Japanese workers are in services.[4]

The marketing process described in Chapter 1 is the same for all types of products, whether they are goods or services. Many ideas and strategies discussed throughout this book have been illustrated with service examples. In many ways, marketing is marketing, regardless of the product's characteristics. However, services have some unique characteristics that distinguish them from goods, and marketing strategies need to be adjusted for these characteristics.

How Services Differ from Goods

Identify the differences between services and goods

Services have four unique characteristics that distinguish them from goods: intangibility, inseparability, heterogeneity, and perishability.

Intangibility

The basic difference between services and goods is that services are intangible. Because of their **intangibility**, they cannot be touched, seen, tasted, heard, or felt in the same manner in which goods can be sensed. Services cannot be stored and are often easy to duplicate.

VALUE

Evaluating the quality of services before or even after making a purchase is harder than evaluating the quality of goods because, compared to goods, services tend to exhibit fewer search qualities. A **search quality** is a characteristic that can be easily assessed before purchase—for instance, the color of an appliance or automobile. At the same time, services tend to exhibit more experience and credence qualities. An **experience quality** is a characteristic that can be assessed only after use, such as the quality of a meal in a restaurant or the actual experience of a vacation. A **credence quality** is a characteristic that consumers may have difficulty assessing even after purchase because they do not have the necessary knowledge or experience. Medical and consulting services are examples of services that exhibit credence qualities.

intangibility
Services that cannot be touched, seen, tasted, heard, or felt in the same manner in which goods can be sensed.

search quality
A characteristic that can be easily assessed before purchase.

experience quality
A characteristic that can be assessed only after use.

credence quality
A characteristic that consumers may have difficulty assessing even after purchase because they do not have the necessary knowledge or experience.

These characteristics also make it harder for marketers to communicate the benefits of an intangible service than to communicate the benefits of tangible goods. Thus, marketers often rely on tangible cues to communicate a service's nature and quality. For example, Traveler's Insurance Company's use of the umbrella symbol helps make tangible the benefit of protection that insurance provides.

The facilities that customers visit, or from which services are delivered, are a critical tangible part of the total service offering. Messages about the organization are communicated to customers through such elements as the decor, the clutter or neatness of service areas, and the staff's manners and dress. Conoco opened a gas station/convenience store outside Chattanooga, Tennessee, that was designed to be different from the traditional convenience store. The exterior of the store resembles a trendy restaurant, with red brick, a vaulted entryway, and green awnings. "Retro" pictures on the inside walls and corrugated metal on the coolers evoke a nostalgic yet contemporary feel. Large windows allow customers to see outside and ensure safety. Coffee is brewed fresh, and a coffee grinder is placed at the front door so customers smell fresh coffee as they walk in.[5] By designing its store to make shopping a pleasant experience, Conoco has communicated that it is a quality organization.

Inseparability

Goods are produced, sold, and then consumed. In contrast, services are often sold, produced, and consumed at the same time. In other words, their production and consumption are inseparable activities. **Inseparability** means that, because consumers must be present during the production of services like haircuts or surgery, they are actually involved in the production of the services they buy. For example, in many fast-food restaurants, touch-activated video screens that display words and/or pictures where customers order their own meals can speed up the ordering process.[6] That type of consumer involvement is rare in goods manufacturing.

inseparability
Characteristic of services that allows them to be produced and consumed simultaneously.

Inseparability also means that services cannot normally be produced in a centralized location and consumed in decentralized locations, as goods typically are. Services are also inseparable from the perspective of the service provider. Thus, the quality of service that firms are able to deliver depends on the quality of their employees.

Heterogeneity

One great strength of McDonald's is consistency. Whether customers order a Big Mac and french fries in Fort Worth, Tokyo, or Moscow, they know exactly what they are going to get. This is not the case with many service providers. **Heterogeneity** means that services tend to be less standardized and uniform than goods. For example, physicians in a group practice or barbers in a barber shop differ within each group in their technical and interpersonal skills. A given physician's or barber's

heterogeneity
Characteristic of services that makes them less standardized and uniform than goods.

Hilton

Find out about current values and specials that Hilton Hotels is offering in your state by visiting its Web site. Are the discounts what you would expect? Do they seem to be only available on certain days?
http://www.hilton.com/

on line

performance may even vary depending on time of day, physical health, or some other factor. Because services tend to be labor intensive and production and consumption are inseparable, consistency and quality control can be hard to achieve.

Standardization and training help increase consistency and reliability. Limited-menu restaurants like Pizza Hut and KFC offer customers high consistency from one visit to the next because of standardized preparation procedures. Another way to increase consistency is to mechanize the process. Banks have reduced the inconsistency of teller services by providing automated teller machines. Airport x-ray surveillance equipment has replaced manual searching of baggage. Automatic coin receptacles on toll roads have replaced human collectors.

Perishability

perishability
Characteristic of services that prevents them from being stored, warehoused, or inventoried.

Perishability means that services cannot be stored, warehoused, or inventoried. An empty hotel room or airplane seat produces no revenue that day. The revenue is lost. Yet service organizations are often forced to turn away full-price customers during peak periods.

One of the most important challenges in many service industries is finding ways to synchronize supply and demand. The philosophy that some revenue is better than none has prompted many hotels to offer deep discounts on weekends and during the off-season and has prompted airlines to adopt similar pricing strategies during off-peak hours. Car rental agencies, movie theaters, and restaurants also use discounts to encourage demand during nonpeak periods.

5
Explain why services marketing is important to manufacturers

Services Marketing in Manufacturing

By bundling computer hardware, software, maintenance, and Internet services, Gateway 2000 can better position itself as a full-service provider in the computer market. http://www.gateway.com/
Web Page courtesy Gateway 2000, Inc. © 1998.

A comparison of goods and services marketing is beneficial, but in reality it is hard to distinguish clearly between manufacturing and service firms. Indeed, many manufacturing firms can point to service as a major factor in their success. For example, maintenance and repair services are important to buyers of copy machines.

One reason that goods manufacturers stress service is that it might give them a strong competitive advantage, especially in industries in which products are perceived as similar. In the automobile industry, for example, few quality differences between car brands are perceived by consumers. Knowing that, General Motors has developed new guidelines for sales techniques and quality customer service and will link dealer incentive payments to how well the guidelines are followed. Gateway now bundles a number of different services into the sale of a personal computer to a consumer, including a wide range of software, maintenance, and troubleshooting, and even its own Internet service.[7]

Rubbermaid

Go to Rubbermaid's Web site and identify its product items, product lines, and product mix. Do any of these surprise you? Why or why not? How wide do you think Rubbermaid's lines are?

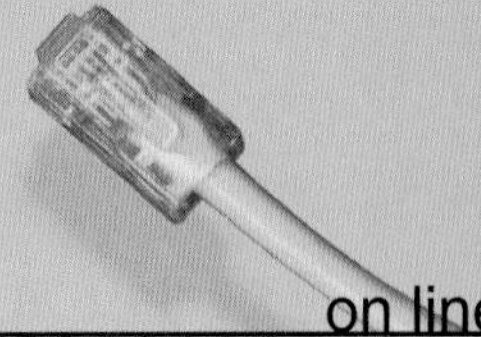

on line

Product Items, Lines, and Mixes

6

Define the terms "product item," "product line," and "product mix"

Rarely does a company sell a single product. More often, it sells a variety of things. A **product item** is a specific version of a product that can be designated as a distinct offering among an organization's products. Gillette's MACH 3 razor is an example of a product item. (See Exhibit 8.2.)

product item
A specific version of a product that can be designated as a distinct offering among an organization's products.

A group of closely related product items is a **product line**. For example, the column in Exhibit 8.2 titled "Blades and Razors" represents one of Gillette's product lines. Different container sizes and shapes also distinguish items in a product line. Diet Coke, for example, is available in cans and various plastic containers. Each size and each container are separate product items.

product line
A group of closely related product items.

An organization's **product mix** includes all the products it sells. All Gillette's products—blades and razors, toiletries, writing instruments, and lighters—constitute its product mix. Each product item in the product mix may require a separate marketing strategy. In some cases, however, product lines and even entire product mixes share some marketing strategy components. The Pontiac division of General Motors has promoted all Pontiac items and lines with its theme "We build excitement—Pontiac."

Organizations derive several benefits from organizing related items into product lines, including the following:

- *Advertising economies:* Product lines provide economies of scale in advertising. Several products can be advertised under the umbrella of the line. Campbell's can talk about its soup being "m-m-good" and promote the entire line.
- *Package uniformity:* A product line can benefit from package uniformity. All packages in the line may have a common look and still keep their individual identities. Again, Campbell's soup is a good example.
- *Standardized components:* Product lines allow firms to standardize components, thus reducing manufacturing and inventory costs. For example, many of the components Samsonite uses in its folding tables and chairs are also used in its patio furniture. General Motors uses the same parts on many automobile makes and models.
- *Efficient sales and distribution:* A product line enables sales personnel for companies like Procter & Gamble to provide a full range of choices to customers. Distributors and retailers are often more inclined to stock the company's products if it offers a full line. Transportation and warehousing costs are likely to be lower for a product line than for a collection of individual items.
- *Equivalent quality:* Purchasers usually expect and believe that all products in a line are about equal in quality. Consumers expect that all Campbell's soups and all Mary Kay cosmetics will be of similar quality.

Campbell's soup is an excellent example of advertising economies. Without singling out a specific flavor, Campbell's can promote its entire line of soup with the single phrase "m-m-good."
© Rich LaSalle/Tony Stone Images

Product mix width (or breadth) refers to the number of product lines an organization offers. In Exhibit 8.2, for example, the width of Gillette's product mix is four product lines. **Product line depth** is the number of product items in a product line. As shown in Exhibit 8.2, the blades and razors product line consists of ten product items; the toiletries product line includes ten product items.

product mix
All products an organization sells.

product mix width
The number of product lines an organization offers.

product line depth
The number of product items in a product line.

Firms increase the *width* of their product mix to diversify risk. To generate sales and boost profits, firms spread risk across many product lines rather than depend on only one or two. Firms also widen their product mix to capitalize on established reputations. By introducing new product lines, Kodak capitalized on its image as a leader in photographic products. Kodak's product lines now include film, processing, still cameras, movie cameras, paper, and chemicals. Limited Inc., a company that mostly comprises women's apparel stores (Limited, Limited Too,

exhibit 8.2

Gillette's Product Lines and Product Mix

	Width of the Product Mix			
	Blades and Razors	Toiletries	Writing Instruments	Lighters
Depth of the Product Lines	MACH 3	Series	Paper Mate	Cricket
	Sensor	Adorn	Flair	S.T. Dupont
	Trac II	Toni		
	Atra	Right Guard		
	Swivel	Silkience		
	Double-Edge	Soft and Dri		
	Lady Gillette	Foamy		
	Super Speed	Dry Look		
	Twin Injector	Dry Idea		
	Techmatic	Brush Plus		

Victoria's Secret) is experimenting in cosmetics lines—it is developing a line of make-up under the Victoria's Secret brand.[8]

Firms increase the *depth* of product lines to attract buyers with different preferences, to increase sales and profits by further segmenting the market, to capitalize on economies of scale in production and marketing, and to even out seasonal sales patterns. Between 1970 and 1993, Timex increased the depth of its wristwatch line from three hundred items to fifteen hundred items.[9]

Adjustments to Product Items, Lines, and Mixes

Over time, firms change product items, lines, and mixes to take advantage of new technical or product developments or to respond to changes in the environment. They may adjust by modifying products, repositioning products, or extending or contracting product lines.

Product Modifications

product modification
Changing one or more of a product's characteristics.

Marketing managers must decide if and when to modify existing products. **Product modification** changes one or more of a product's characteristics:

VALUE

- *Quality modification:* change in a product's dependability or durability. Reducing a product's quality may let the manufacturer lower the price and appeal to target markets unable to afford the original product. On the other hand, increasing quality can help the firm compete with rival firms. Increasing quality can also result in increased brand loyalty, greater ability to raise prices, or new opportunities for market segmentation. Eastman Kodak is considering launching a discount film, called Colorburst, that does not carry Kodak's well-recognized brand name in order to reach consumers who want to buy less-expensive, lower-quality film.[10] Conversely, in order to appeal to a more upscale market, Robert Mondavi Winery is introducing a high-end wine called Twin Oaks to prestige restaurants and hotels. The company is trying to differentiate this wine from the one they sell in supermarkets.[11]
- *Functional modification:* change in a product's versatility, effectiveness, convenience, or safety. Hostess is introducing a line of fruit and grain cereal bars to extend its equity in the snack market beyond the dessert-type products they have traditionally offered. These bars are targeted to higher-income females who want a tastier version of a low-fat, vitamin-fortified breakfast alternative.[12] Lea & Perrins is offering its steak sauce in a value-priced squeeze bottle with a "no mess, stay clean" cap.[13]

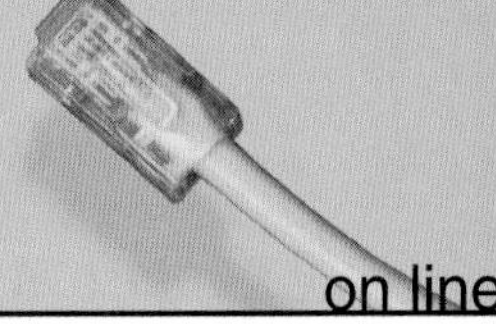

- *Style modification:* aesthetic product change, rather than a quality or functional change. Clothing manufacturers commonly use style modifications to motivate customers to replace products before they are worn out. **Planned obsolescence** is a term commonly used to describe the practice of modifying products so those that have already been sold become obsolete before they actually need replacement. Some argue that planned obsolescence is wasteful; some claim it is unethical. Marketers respond that consumers favor style modifications because they like changes in the appearance of goods like clothing and cars. Marketers also contend that consumers, not manufacturers and marketers, decide when styles are obsolete.

planned obsolescence
The practice of modifying products so those that have already been sold become obsolete before they actually need replacement.

Repositioning

Repositioning, as Chapter 6 explained, is changing consumers' perceptions of a brand. For example, "restaurant-style" has become a popular positioning for soup companies. Pillsbury has launched a line of herb-infused pasta soups for Progresso, and ConAgra will introduce two new Healthy Choice flavors—gumbo with chicken and sausage and a cheese-based potato soup.[14]

Changing demographics, declining sales, or changes in the social environment often motivate firms to reposition established brands. The changing demographics of snackers and eroding market share led Frito-Lay to reposition its top-selling brand, Fritos, after fifty-eight years of successfully targeting all ages. The repositioning effort included making major changes in the Fritos logo and packaging, focusing on those between the ages of nine and eighteen, and launching a major new radio and TV advertising campaign. Playboy, one of the world's most well-known brands, is being repositioned to better reflect contemporary values and lifestyles. "Our core customers have always been men, but we're trying now to extend the brand attributes to couples," said Christie Hefner. "Playboy is a classic American brand, a brand that is sexy, romantic, fun, and sophisticated. It should have a broader audience."[15]

Product Line Extensions

Product line extension occurs when a company's management decides to add products to an existing product line in order to compete more broadly in the industry. Mercedes-Benz AG plans to add eleven cars to its line of passenger vehicles between 1997 and 2000, including two "mini" city cars and a sports utility vehicle.[16] Procter & Gamble is extending its shampoo brand Pantene with its first anti-dandruff product—Pro V Anti-Dandruff—positioned distinctly for women.[17]

product line extension
Adding additional products to an existing product line in order to compete more broadly in the industry.

Product Line Contraction

Does the world really need thirty-one varieties of Head & Shoulders shampoo? Or fifty-two versions of Crest? Procter & Gamble Co. has decided the answer is no.[18] Procter & Gamble (P&G) is contracting product lines by eliminating unpopular sizes, flavors, and other variations to make it easier for customers to find what they are looking for. After decades of introducing new-and-improved this, lemon-flavored that, and extra-jumbo-size the other thing, P&G has decided that its product lines are overextended.[19] Likewise, Black & Decker has decided to delete a number of household products—Dustbusters, SnakeLight flashlights, and toaster ovens—and concentrate on power tools.[20] Symptoms of product line overextension include the following:

- Some products in the line do not contribute to profits because of low sales or cannibalize sales of other items in the line.
- Manufacturing or marketing resources are disproportionately allocated to slow-moving products.
- Some items in the line are obsolete because of new product entries in the line or new products offered by competitors.

Three major benefits are likely when a firm contracts overextended product lines. First, resources become concentrated on the most important products. Second, managers no longer waste resources trying to improve the sales and profits of poorly performing products. Third, new product items have a greater chance of being successful because more financial and human resources are available to manage them.

Branding

7

Describe marketing uses of branding

brand
A name, term, symbol, design, or combination thereof that identifies a seller's products and differentiates them from competitors' products.

brand name
That part of a brand that can be spoken, including letters, words, and numbers.

brand mark
The elements of a brand that cannot be spoken.

brand equity
The value of company and brand names.

master brand
A brand so dominant in consumers' minds that they think of it immediately when a product category, use situation, product attribute, or customer benefit is mentioned.

The success of any business or consumer product depends in part on the target market's ability to distinguish one product from another. Branding is the main tool marketers use to distinguish their products from the competition's.

A **brand** is a name, term, symbol, design, or combination thereof that identifies a seller's products and differentiates them from competitors' products. A **brand name** is that part of a brand that can be spoken, including letters (GM, YMCA), words (Chevrolet), and numbers (WD-40, 7-Eleven). The elements of a brand that cannot be spoken are called the **brand mark**—for example, the well-known Mercedes-Benz and Delta Airlines symbols.

Benefits of Branding

Branding has three main purposes: product identification, repeat sales, and new-product sales. The most important purpose is *product identification.* Branding allows marketers to distinguish their products from all others. Many brand names are familiar to consumers and indicate quality. Exhibit 8.3 lists, in order, the brand names that U.S. consumers believe are the best brands. The coolest brands, according to U.S. teenagers, are Nike, Levi's, Guess?, Gap, Coke, Pepsi, and Sega.[21]

The term **brand equity** refers to the value of company and brand names. A brand that has high awareness, perceived quality, and brand loyalty among customers has high brand equity. A brand with strong brand equity is a valuable asset.

The term **master brand** has been used to refer to a brand so dominant in consumers' minds that they think of it immediately when a product category, use, attribute, or customer benefit is mentioned.[22] Exhibit 8.4 lists the master brands in several product categories. How many other brands can you name in these eleven categories? Can you name any other product categories in which the master brands listed in Exhibit 8.4 compete? Probably not many. Campbell's means soup to consumers; it doesn't mean high-quality food products.

What constitutes a good brand name? Most effective brand names have several of the following features:

- Is easy to pronounce (by both domestic and foreign buyers)
- Is easy to recognize
- Is easy to remember
- Is short
- Is distinctive, unique
- Describes the product
- Describes product use
- Describes product benefits
- Has a positive connotation
- Reinforces the desired product image
- Is legally protectable in home and foreign markets of interest

Obviously no brand exhibits all of these characteristics. The most important issue is that the brand can be protected for exclusive use by its owner.

exhibit 8.3

What Are the Best Brands?

Ford's profit margins may be slumping, but to consumers, Ford comes out as the best U.S. brand. In a survey asking for spontaneous replies, the public gave some names that aren't even strictly brands. One example is General Motors (No. 2), which owns brands. However, the poll confirms the tenet that a strong corporate identity helps a brand.

1997	1996	1995
1. FORD	3	2
2. GENERAL MOTORS	4	4
3. SONY	1	3
4. PROCTER & GAMBLE	5	8
5. GENERAL ELECTRIC	2	1
6. CHEVROLET	6	8
7. COCA-COLA	8	23
8. KELLOGG	25	7
9. CAMPBELL'S SOUP	19	21
10. PEPSI-COLA, JOHNSON & JOHNSON, AT&T		

From a telephone poll of 1,005 adults
DATA: LOUIS HARRIS & ASSOCIATES INC.
SOURCE: "What Are the Best Brands?" *Business Week*, April 7, 1997, p. 6.

GLOBAL

U.S. brands command substantial premiums in many places around the world. For example, Gillette disposable razors sell for twice the price of local brands in India. However, companies need to make sure their brand names translate appropriately in other languages, as the "Global Perspectives" examples illustrate.

The best generator of *repeat sales* is satisfied customers. Branding helps consumers identify products they wish to buy again and avoid those they do not. **Brand loyalty**, a consistent preference for one brand over all others, is quite high in some product categories. Over half the users in product categories such as cigarettes, mayonnaise, toothpaste, coffee, headache remedies, photographic film, bath soap, and catsup are loyal to one brand. One annual Monitor poll conducted by Yankelovich Partners reported that 74 percent of respondents "find a brand they like, then resist efforts to get them to change." Once consumers are convinced of the quality and value of a particular brand, it takes a lot of money and effort to change their minds.[23] Brand identity is essential to developing brand loyalty.

brand loyalty
A consistent preference for one brand over all others.

The third main purpose of branding is to *facilitate new-product sales.* Company and brand names like those listed in Exhibit 8.3 and Exhibit 8.4 are extremely useful when introducing new products.

exhibit 8.4

Master Brands in Selected Product Categories

Product Category	Master Brand
Baking soda	Arm & Hammer
Adhesive bandages	Band-Aid
Rum	Bacardi
Antacids	Alka-Seltzer
Gelatin	Jell-O
Soup	Campbell's
Salt	Morton
Toy Trains	Lionel
Cream cheese	Philadelphia
Crayons	Crayola
Petroleum jelly	Vaseline

SOURCE: From "Strategies for Leveraging Master Brands" by Peter H. Farquhar et al., *Marketing Research,* September 1992, pp. 32–43. Reprinted by permission of the American Marketing Association.

global perspectives

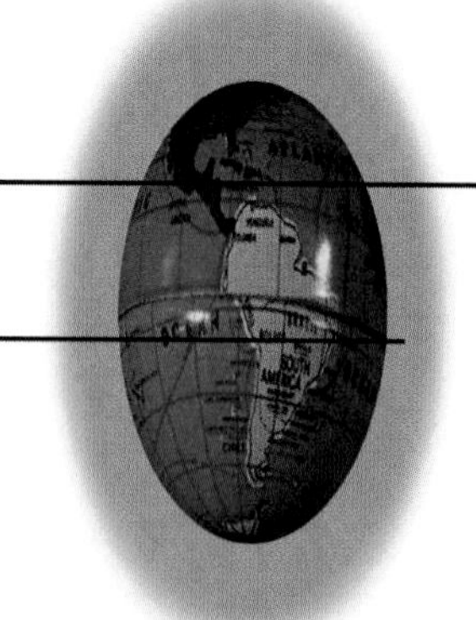

The Name Game Heats Up

As the world goes global, it is more important than ever that companies screen their brand names for multilingual suitability. Here are a few examples of U.S. companies that ran into brand-name problems overseas:

- General Motors named a new Chevrolet Beretta without getting permission from the Italian arms manufacturer. It cost GM $500,000 to settle the lawsuit.
- Estee Lauder was set to export its Country Mist makeup when German managers pointed out that "mist" in German is slang for "manure." The name became Country Moist in Germany.
- A food company advertised its giant burrito as Burrada. The colloquial meaning of that word is "big mistake."

Imported names can be just as embarrassing. Consider:

- Creap (Japanese coffee creamer)
- Bimbo (Mexican bread)
- Darkie (Asian toothpaste)[24]

What should companies do to avoid these kinds of mistakes? What would also be some important considerations for brand names used in other countries?

Fuji

Tylenol

What elements on Fuji film's **fujifilm.net** Web site seem to encourage brand loyalty? Be sure to check out the list of services. What about elements on Tylenol's site? Why do you think so?

http://www.fujifilm.net/ **http://www.tylenol.com/**

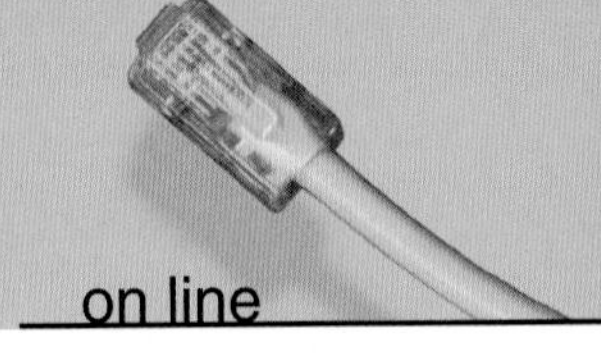

exhibit 8.5

Major Branding Decisions

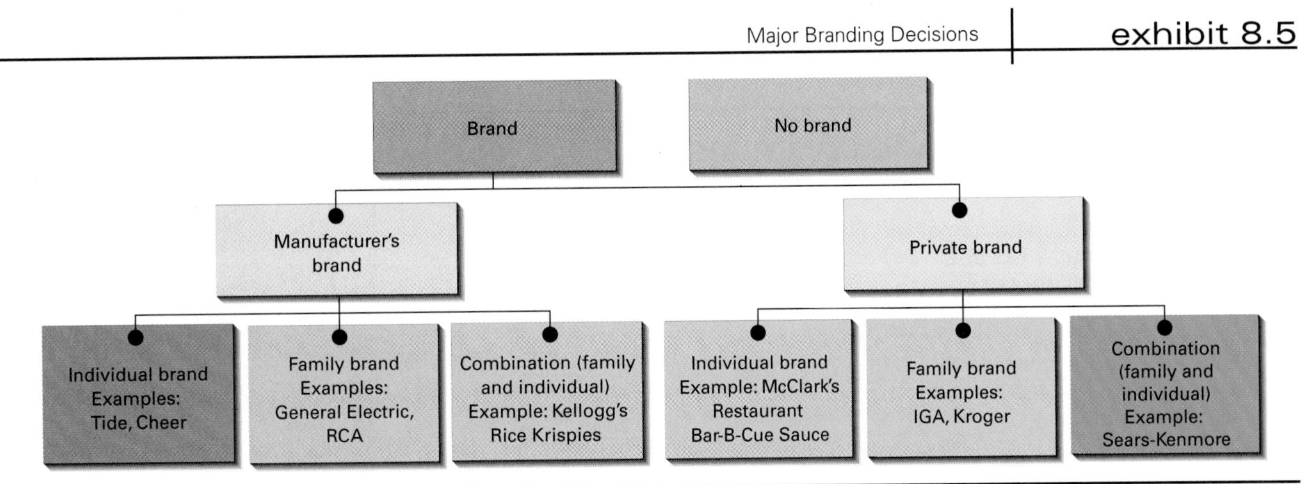

The Internet provides firms a new alternative for generating brand awareness, promoting a desired brand image, stimulating new and repeat brand sales, and enhancing brand loyalty and building brand equity. A number of packaged goods firms, such as Procter & Gamble, Campbell's Soup, and Gerber, have a presence on-line. Unilever's Lipton Recipe Secrets has launched a Web site that will be a part of an interactive test in which the company plans to measure brand awareness, attitudes, and product usage as a result of consumers' exposure to the site.[25]

Branding Strategies

Firms face complex branding decisions. As Exhibit 8.5 illustrates, the first decision is whether to brand at all. Some firms actually use the lack of a brand name as a selling point. These unbranded products are called generic products. Firms that decide to brand their products may choose to follow a policy of using manufacturers' brands, private (distributor) brands, or both. In either case, they must then decide among a policy of individual branding (different brands for different products), family branding (common names for different products), or a combination of individual branding and family branding.

Generic Products Versus Branded Products

A **generic product** is typically a no-frills, no-brand-name, low-cost product that is simply identified by its product category. (Note that a generic product and a brand name that becomes generic, such as cellophane, are not the same thing.) Generic products have captured significant market shares in some product categories, such as canned fruits, canned vegetables, and paper products. These unbranded products are frequently identified only by black stenciled lettering on white packages.

generic product
A no-frills, no-brand-name, low-cost product that is simply identified by its product category.

The main appeal of generics is their low price. Generic grocery products are usually 30 to 40 percent less expensive than manufacturers' brands in the same product category and 20 to 25 percent less expensive than retailer-owned brands.

Pharmaceuticals make up another product category where generics have made inroads. When patents on successful pharmaceutical products expire, low-cost generics rapidly appear on the market. For example, when the patent on Merck's popular antiarthritis drug Clinoril expired, sales declined by 50 percent almost immediately.

entrepreneurial insights

Staking Claim on Branded Diamonds

Consumers look for a brand name when they buy products like soda and soap. Why not diamonds?

A Boston entrepreneur is borrowing from the world of consumer products with an unusual plan to separate his diamonds from those of competitors. Retailers usually sell diamonds based on their own reputations and the "Four Cs": carat weight, color, clarity, and cut.

But Glen Rothman, owner of a diamond wholesaler, wants diamond shoppers to ask for his gems by name: Hearts on Fire. They are cut in a special way designed to give them perfect symmetry and extra sparkle. And he has a gimmick to help promote the diamonds: a "proportion scope" that is provided to retailers. It magnifies the stone while filtering out white light. When shoppers look in, they see the signature details of the Hearts of Fire cut: eight perfect hearts and eight arrows. The proportion scope gives consumers confidence that they are getting what they pay for.

The hearts-and-arrows cut was perfected in quality-conscious Japan during the mid-1980s and soon spread elsewhere. Mr. Rothman learned about it in 1996 from an Antwerp, Belgium, cutter and came up with the name Hearts on Fire. Early sales are promising, he says, with an anticipated $6 million his first full year, as consumers pay about a 20 percent premium per carat.

Other diamond marketers have played with brand names. Keepsake Diamonds were big in the 1960s, but the company that created them sold out and the brand died. Lazare Kaplan International, Inc. of New York says it has been selling diamonds under the Lazare label since 1986 and now sells to five hundred retailers.

The "ideal cut" market—diamonds sold for the way they are cut—encompasses less than 2 percent of the U.S. diamond market but is growing rapidly. Some people in the industry say that cut is too subjective a way to sell diamonds. They argue that there is no internationally accepted grading system for cut.

However, retailers and consumers alike are impressed with the Hearts on Fire diamonds. For example, one independent jeweler in Warner Robins, Georgia, says his store's diamond sales are up 10 percent to 15 percent since he introduced Hearts on Fire. Even if customers don't buy Hearts on Fire, the demonstration keeps people in the store and creates a positive aura for his other jewelry. Indeed, small independent retailers, battling chains like Zales and Kay, are flocking to Rothman's door. After a year, Hearts on Fire has expanded to more than two hundred stores in forty-two states. Mr. Rothman also says his profits are up from his days as a traditional wholesaler.[26]

Conversely, products in categories that traditionally have not been branded are now attempting to establish brand names that companies hope will build loyalty. For example, a Boston diamond distributor has developed the first branded diamond, called Hearts on Fire, which is described in the "Entrepreneurial Insights" box above.

Manufacturers' Brands Versus Private Brands

manufacturer's brand
The brand name of a manufacturer.

The brand name of a manufacturer—such as Kodak, Lazy Boy, and Fruit of the Loom—is called a **manufacturer's brand**. Sometimes the term "national brand" is used as a synonym for "manufacturer's brand." This term is not always accurate, however, because many manufacturers serve only regional markets. The term manufacturer's brand more precisely defines the brand's owner.

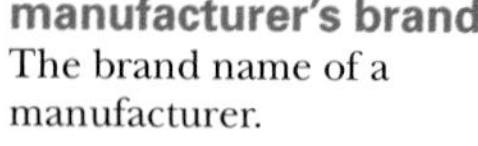

private brand
A brand name owned by a wholesaler or a retailer.

A **private brand** is a brand name owned by a wholesaler or a retailer. Hunt Club (a JCPenney brand), Sam's American Choice (Wal-Mart), and IGA (Independent Grocers' Association) are all private brands. A Gallup survey, conducted for the Private Label Manufacturers Association, revealed that 83 percent of consumers say they regularly buy less expensive retailer brands.[27] Private brands account for about 20 percent of supermarket sales, 8.6 percent of drugstore sales, and over 9 percent of mass merchandiser sales.[28]

Who buys private brands? According to one expert, "the young, discerning, educated shopper is the private label buyer." These individuals are willing to

exhibit 8.6

Comparing Manufacturers' and Private Brands from the Reseller's Perspective

Key Advantages of Carrying Manufacturers' Brands	Key Advantages of Carrying Private Brands
• Heavy advertising to the consumer by manufacturers like Procter & Gamble helps develop strong consumer loyalties.	• A wholesaler or retailer can usually earn higher profits on its own brand. In addition, because the private brand is exclusive, there is less pressure to mark the price down to meet competition.
• Well-known manufacturers' brands, such as Kodak and Fisher-Price, can attract new customers and enhance the dealer's (wholesaler's or retailer's) prestige.	• A manufacturer can decide to drop a brand or a reseller at any time or even to become a direct competitor to its dealers.
• Many manufacturers offer rapid delivery, enabling the dealer to carry less inventory.	• A private brand ties the customer to the wholesaler or retailer. A person who wants a Die-Hard battery must go to Sears.
• If a dealer happens to sell a manufacturer's brand of poor quality, the customer may simply switch brands but remain loyal to the dealer.	• Wholesalers and retailers have no control over the intensity of distribution of manufacturers' brands. Wal-Mart store managers don't have to worry about competing with other sellers of Sam's American Choice products or Ol' Roy dog food. They know that these are brands are sold only in Wal-Mart and Sam's Wholesale Club stores.

purchase private brands because they have confidence in their ability to assess quality and value.[29] Exhibit 8.6 illustrates key issues that wholesalers and retailers should consider in deciding whether to sell manufacturers' brands or private brands. Many firms, such as JCPenney, Kmart, and Safeway, offer a combination of both. In fact, JCPenney and Sears have turned their low-priced, private-label jeans into some of the most popular brands around, thanks to hip marketing campaigns that feature rock bands, Web sites and imagery targeted at teens.[30]

Individual Brands Versus Family Brands

Many companies use different brand names for different products; this practice is referred to as **individual branding**. Companies use individual brands when their products vary greatly in use or performance. For instance, it would not make sense to use the same brand name for a pair of dress socks and a baseball bat. Procter & Gamble targets different segments of the laundry detergent market with Bold, Cheer, Dash, Dreft, Era, Gain, Ivory Snow, Oxydol, Solo, and Tide. Marriott International, Inc., also targets different market segments with Courtyard by Marriott, Residence Inn, and Fairfield Inn.

individual branding
Using different brand names for different products.

On the other hand, a company that markets several different products under the same brand name is using a **family brand**. Sony's family brand includes radios, television sets, stereos, and other electronic products. A brand name can only be stretched so far, however. Do you know the differences among Holiday Inn, Holiday Inn Express, Holiday Inn Select, Holiday Inn Sunspree Resort, Holiday Inn

family brand
Marketing several different products under the same brand name.

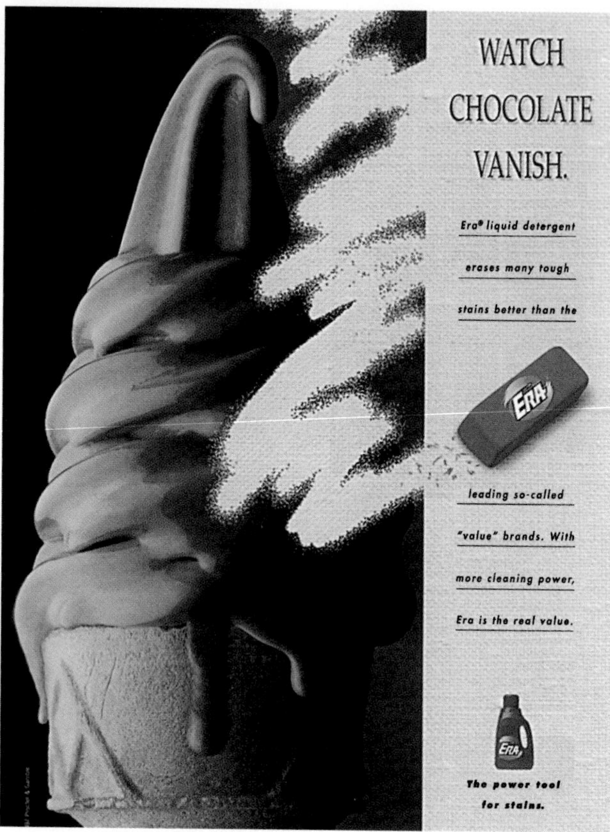

WATCH
CHOCOLATE
VANISH.
Era® liquid detergent
erases many tough
stains better than the
ERA
leading so-called
"value" brands. With
more cleaning power,
Era is the real value.
ERA
The power tool
for stains.

Procter & Gamble uses individual branding to target different segments of the laundry detergent market. How successful do you think the company would be if it shifted to a family branding strategy? Do you think Era would be able to compete as effectively? More effectively? Less effectively? Why or why not?

Garden Court, and Holiday Inn Hotel & Suites? Neither do most travelers.[31]

Cobranding

Cobranding entails placing two or more brand names on a product or its package. There are three types of cobranding. *Ingredient branding* identifies the brand of a part that makes up the product. Examples of ingredient branding are Intel (a microprocessor) in a personal computer, such as Compaq, or a premium leather interior (Coach) in an automobile (Lincoln). *Cooperative branding* is where two brands receiving equal treatment borrow on each other's brand equity, such as Citibank and American Airlines, or American Express and Sheraton. Finally, there is *complementary branding*, where products are advertised or marketed together to suggest usage, such as a spirits brand (Seagram's) and a compatible mixer (7-Up).[32]

cobranding
Placing two or more brand names on a product or its package.

Cobranding is a useful strategy when a combination of brand names enhances the prestige or perceived value of a product or when it benefits brand owners and users. Cobranded Six Flags Theme Parks/Master Cards allow cardholders to earn points toward season passes, free admissions, and in-park spending vouchers at Six Flags theme parks throughout the United States.[33]

Cobranding may also be used when two or more organizations wish to collaborate to offer a product. Frito-Lay and McIllhenny's have joined together to market The Original Tabasco Chips.[34] Nabisco and Kraft Foods' Post cereal have teamed up to offer Oreo O's cereal.[35]

GLOBAL

European firms have been slower to adopt cobranding than U.S. firms have. One reason is that European customers seem to be more skeptical than U.S. customers in trying new brands. European retailers also typically have less shelf space than their U.S. counterparts and are less willing to give new brands a try.[36]

Trademarks

trademark
The exclusive right to use a brand or part of a brand.

service mark
Trademark for a service.

A **trademark** is the exclusive right to use a brand or part of a brand. Others are prohibited from using the brand without permission. A **service mark** performs the same function for services, such as H&R Block and Weight Watchers. Parts of a brand or other product identification may qualify for trademark protection. Some examples are

- Shapes, such as the Jeep front grille and the Coca-Cola bottle
- Ornamental color or design, such as the decoration on Nike tennis shoes, the black-and-copper color combination of a Duracell battery, Levi's small tag on the left side of the rear pocket of its jeans, or the cutoff black cone on the top of Cross pens
- Catchy phrases, such as Prudential's "Own a piece of the rock," Merrill Lynch's "We're bullish on America," and Budweiser's "This Bud's for you"
- Abbreviations, such as Bud, Coke, or The Met

A New York property company that purchased the Chrysler Building in Manhattan has even sought trademark registration for the building's elaborate exterior, its lobby's ceiling, and even its elevator doors. Its distinctive pinnacle is already trademarked.[37] In 1977, General Electric Broadcasting Co. was one of the

ethics in marketing

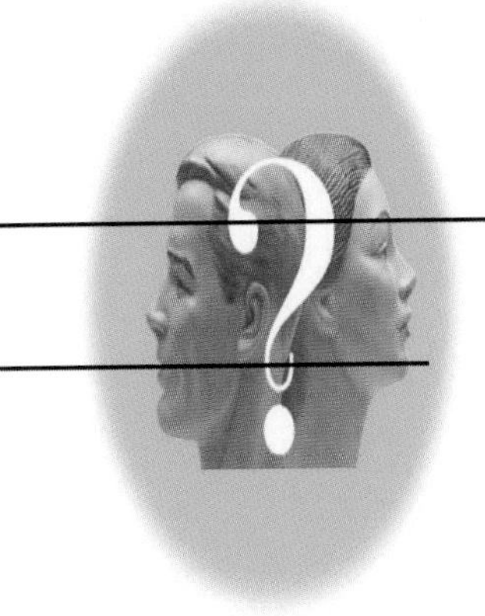

Ti-Gear: Owning Up to a Name

The name of GolfGear International Inc.'s new product offering, the "Ti-Gear" wood, is raising a few eyebrows. On the one hand, "They (GolfGear International) don't have Tiger (Woods') authorization, and we can't give further comment on the advice of our attorneys," says Bev Norwood, spokesperson for Cleveland-based International Management Group, the sports representative's agency working on behalf of Woods. On the other hand, the golf club is made with a patented "forged titanium insert" intended to help the ball travel farther.

GolfGear International's president and chairman, Don Anderson, noted in a written statement that his company has been using the name Titanium Gear since 1990 or 1991.

"(W)e shortened it to Ti-Gear: 'Ti' is the symbol of Titanium, and 'Gear' follows our family of products since we started in business nearly 10 years ago. The name . . . clearly has nothing to do with Tiger Woods," the statement read. He also noted that other GolfGear products use similar names that reflect their components, such as "Carbon Gear."

"Determining whether or not the use of a particular mark is likely to cause confusion with another mark is based on a number of factors. The fact that two marks may look or sound similar is important, but it's only one factor," said Bart Lazar, a partner specializing in the protection and enforcement of trademark rights with the Seyfarth, Shaw, Fairweather and Geraldson law firm in Chicago. Among the criteria that would factor into a trademark infringement case would be whether GolfGear knew of Tiger Woods at the time the company adopted the mark, and whether consumers are likely to be confused, Lazar said.[38]

Is the Ti-Gear brand a trademark violation? Is the branding strategy ethical? Discuss.

first companies to register a sound (the sound that a ship's bell clock makes) as a service mark.[39]

The Trademark Revision Act of 1988 allows organizations to register trademarks based on a bona fide intention to use them (normally, within six months following the issuance of the trademark) for ten years. To renew the trademark, the company must prove it is using it. Rights to a trademark last as long as the mark is used. Normally, if the firm does not use it for two years, the trademark is considered abandoned, and a new user can claim exclusive ownership of the mark. Businesses planning to introduce new brands, trademarks, or packages should consider the following suggestions:[40]

- Check carefully before adopting a trademark or packaging style to make sure you're not infringing on someone else's.
- After a thorough search, consider registering your trademark.
- Make your packaging as distinctive as possible.
- Police your trademark.

Sometimes it is difficult to determine whether a particular brand or package design infringes on another's trademark. GolfGear International's new product branding strategy described in the "Ethics in Marketing" example above illustrates this point.

Companies that fail to protect their trademarks face the problem of their product names becoming generic. A **generic product name** identifies a product by class or type and cannot be trademarked. Former brand names that were not sufficiently protected by their owners and were subsequently declared to be generic product names in U.S. courts include aspirin, cellophane, linoleum, thermos, kerosene, monopoly, cola, and shredded wheat.

generic product name Identifies a product by class or type and cannot be trademarked.

Companies like Rolls Royce, Cross, Xerox, Levi Strauss, Frigidaire, and McDonald's aggressively enforce their trademarks. Rolls Royce, Coca-Cola, and Xerox even run newspaper and magazine ads stating that their names are trademarks and should not be used as descriptive or generic terms. Some ads threaten lawsuits against competitors that violate trademarks.

Despite severe penalties for trademark violations, trademark infringement lawsuits are not uncommon. One of the major battles is over brand names that closely resemble another brand name. Donna Karan filed a lawsuit against Donnkenny Inc., whose Nasdaq trading symbol—DNKY—is too close to Karan's DKNY trademark.[41] Polo Ralph Lauren is concerned about the potential confusion with a magazine named *Polo,* a twenty-three-year-old publication aimed at equestrians. The company is worried that readers will mistake the magazine for something associated with the designer.[42]

Companies must also contend with fake or unauthorized brands, such as fake Levi's jeans, Microsoft software, Rolex watches, Reebok and Nike footwear, and Louis Vuitton handbags. Copycat golf clubs, such as Big Bursa, a knockoff of Callaway's popular Big Bertha, are growing in sales.[43]

GLOBAL

In Europe, you can sue counterfeiters only if your brand, logo, or trademark is formally registered. Until recently, formal registration was required in each country in which a company sought protection. A company can now register its trademark in all European Union (EU) member countries with one application.[44]

Packaging

8
Describe marketing uses of packaging and labeling

Packages have always served a practical function—that is, they hold contents together and protect goods as they move through the distribution channel. Today, however, packaging is also a container for promoting the product and making it easier and safer to use.

Packaging Functions

The three most important functions of packaging are to contain and protect products, promote products, and facilitate the storage, use, and convenience of products. A fourth function of packaging that is becoming increasingly important is to facilitate recycling and reduce environmental damage.

Containing and Protecting Products The most obvious function of packaging is to contain products that are liquid, granular, or otherwise divisible. Packaging also enables manufacturers, wholesalers, and retailers to market products in specific quantities, such as ounces.

Physical protection is another obvious function of packaging. Most products are handled several times between the time they are manufactured, harvested, or otherwise produced and the time they are consumed or used. Many products are shipped, stored, and inspected several times between production and consumption. Some, like milk, need to be refrigerated. Others, like beer, are sensitive to light. Still others, like medicines and bandages, need to be kept sterile. Packages protect products from breakage, evaporation, spillage, spoilage, light, heat, cold, infestation, and many other conditions. Mission Foods is using modified-atmosphere packaging for tortillas, which are usually refrigerated. Oxygen-collecting films now in development could improve shelf-life for refrigerated pastas.[45]

Promoting Products Packaging does more than identify the brand, list the ingredients, specify features, and give directions. A package differentiates a product from competing products and may associate a new product with a family of other products from the same manufacturer. Welch's spent over $1 million to repackage

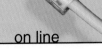

Hewlett-Packard

Find out about how Hewlett-Packard facilitates recycling and refurbishing of its products by visiting its Web site. What role do environmental concerns play in HP's packaging?
http://www.hp.com/abouthp/environment/

its line of grape juice-based jams, jellies, and juices to unify the line and get more impact on the shelf.[46]

Packages use designs, colors, shapes, and materials to try to influence consumers' perceptions and buying behavior. For example, marketing research shows that health-conscious consumers are likely to think that any food is probably good for them as long as it comes in green packaging. Two top brands of low-fat foods—Snackwell's and Healthy Choice—use green packaging.[47] Kimberly-Clark Corp. and Procter & Gamble Co. recently introduced a wide array of more appealing boxes for Kleenex and Puffs tissues. The idea is that if boxes are more attractive, people won't mind sticking them in every room of the house. So far, the strategy appears to be working. Almost 25 percent of the money spent on this $1.5 billion market goes for premium varieties.[48]

Packaging has a measurable effect on sales. Quaker Oats revised the package for Rice-a-Roni without making any other changes in marketing strategy and experienced a 44 percent increase in sales in one year.

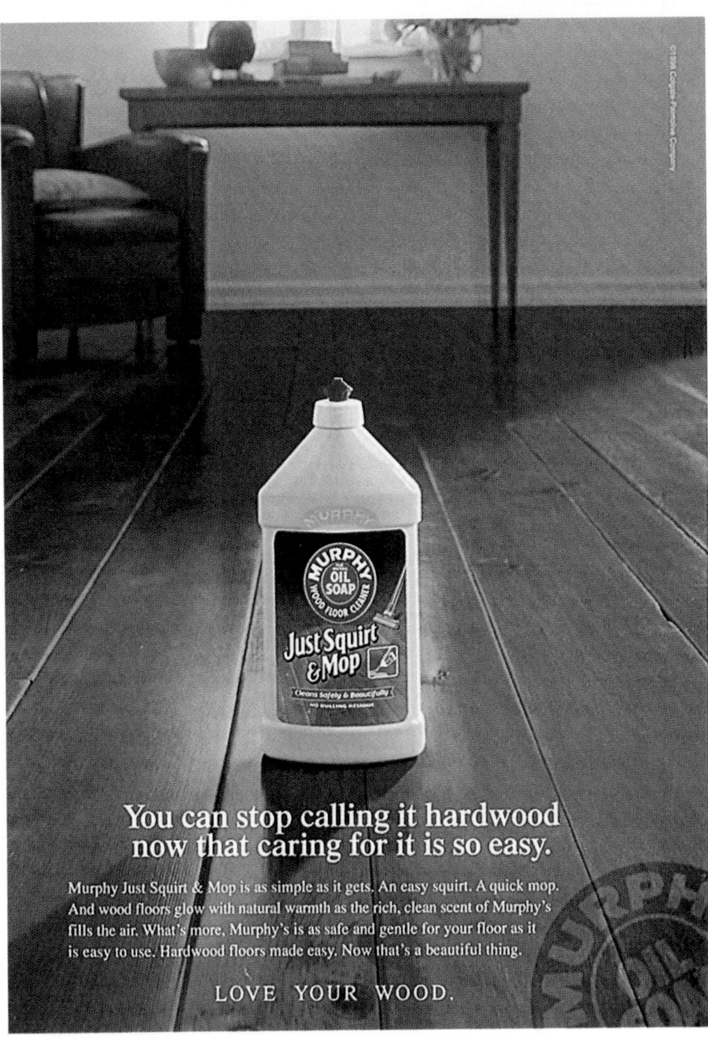

Murphy Oil Soap
Just Squirt & Mop
You can stop calling it hardwood now that caring for it is so easy.
Murphy Just Squirt & Mop is as simple as it gets. An easy squirt. A quick mop. And wood floors glow with natural warmth as the rich, clean scent of Murphy's fills the air. What's more, Murphy's is as safe and gentle for your floor as it is easy to use. Hardwood floors made easy. Now that's a beautiful thing.
LOVE YOUR WOOD.

The squirt bottle is a packaging innovation that has been successful in many contexts: from syrup to floor cleaner.
Courtesy Colgate-Palmolive Company

Facilitating Storage, Use, and Convenience
Wholesalers and retailers prefer packages that are easy to ship, store, and stock on shelves. They also like packages that protect products, prevent spoilage or breakage, and extend the product's shelf life.

Consumers' requirements for convenience cover many dimensions. Consumers are constantly seeking items that are easy to handle, open, and reclose, although some consumers want packages that are tamperproof or childproof. Consumers also want reusable and disposable packages. Surveys conducted by *Sales & Marketing Management* magazine revealed that consumers dislike—and avoid buying—leaky ice cream boxes, overly heavy or fat vinegar bottles, immovable pry-up lids on glass bottles, key-opener sardine cans, and hard-to-pour cereal boxes. Such packaging innovations as zipper tear strips, hinged lids, tab slots, screw-on tops, and pour spouts were introduced to solve these and other problems. C&H Sugar designed a new four-pound carton with an easy-to-pour, reclosable top.[49]

Some firms use packaging to segment markets. For example, the C&H carton is targeted to consumers who don't do a lot of baking and are willing to pay at least twenty cents more for the package. Different-size packages appeal to heavy, moderate, and light users. Salt is sold in package sizes ranging from single serving to picnic size to giant economy size. Campbell's soup is packaged in single-serving cans aimed at the elderly and singles market segments. Beer and soft drinks are similarly marketed in various package sizes and types. Packaging convenience can increase a product's utility and, therefore, its market share and profits.

Facilitating Recycling and Reducing Environmental Damage One of the most important packaging issues in the 1990s is compatibility with the environment.

Dietary Components

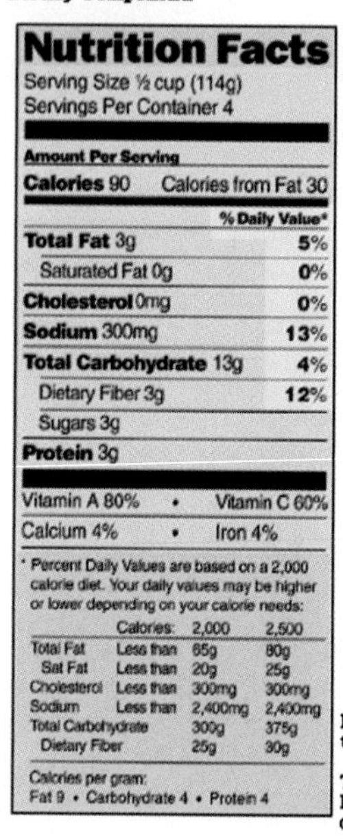

Nutrition Facts

Serving Size ½ cup (114g)
Servings Per Container 4

Amount Per Serving

Calories 90 Calories from Fat 30

	% Daily Value*
Total Fat 3g	5%
Saturated Fat 0g	0%
Cholesterol 0mg	0%
Sodium 300mg	13%
Total Carbohydrate 13g	4%
Dietary Fiber 3g	12%
Sugars 3g	
Protein 3g	

Vitamin A 80% • Vitamin C 60%
Calcium 4% • Iron 4%

* Percent Daily Values are based on a 2,000 calorie diet. Your daily values may be higher or lower depending on your calorie needs:

	Calories:	2,000	2,500
Total Fat	Less than	65g	80g
Sat Fat	Less than	20g	25g
Cholesterol	Less than	300mg	300mg
Sodium	Less than	2,400mg	2,400mg
Total Carbohydrate		300g	375g
Dietary Fiber		25g	30g

Calories per gram:
Fat 9 • Carbohydrate 4 • Protein 4

What can consumers expect? First, they will see a new name for the nutrition panel. It used to go by "Nutrition Information Per Serving." Now, it will be called "Nutrition Facts." That title will signal to consumers that the product is newly labeled according to FDA and FSIS' new regulations.

The new panel will be built around a new set of dietary components. The mandatory (boldfaced) and voluntary dietary components and order in which they must appear are:

- **total calories**
- **calories from fat**
- calories from saturated fat
- **total fat**
- **saturated fat**
- stearic acid (on meat and poultry products only)
- polyunsaturated fat
- monounsaturated fat
- **cholesterol**
- **sodium**
- potassium
- **total carbohydrate**
- **dietary fiber**
- soluble fiber
- insoluble fiber
- **sugars**
- sugar alcohol (for example, the sugar substitutes xylitol, mannitol and sorbitol)
- other carbohydrate (the difference between total carbohydrate and the sum of dietary fiber, sugars, and sugar alcohol, if declared)
- **protein**
- **vitamin A**
- percent of vitamin A present as beta-carotene
- **vitamin C**
- **calcium**
- **iron**
- other essential vitamins and minerals.

If a food is fortified or enriched with any of the optional components, or if a claim is made about any of them, the pertinent nutrition information then becomes mandatory.

These mandatory and voluntary components are the only ones allowed on the nutrition panel. The listing of single amino acids, maltodextrin, calories from polyunsaturated fat, and calories from carbohydrate, for example, may not appear on the label.

This screen shot from the Federal Food and Drug Administration shows exactly what information food manufacturers must include on their nutrition labels. Go to the site to find out more about the 1990 Nutritonal Labeling and Education Act. SOURCE: www.fda.gov

According to one study, 90 percent of surveyed consumers say no more packaging material should be used than is necessary. The ability to recycle is also important.[50]

Some firms use their packaging to target environmentally concerned market segments. Brocato International markets shampoo and hair conditioner in bottles that are biodegradable in landfills. Procter & Gamble markets Sure Pro and Old Spice in "eco-friendly" pump-spray packages that do not rely on aerosol propellants. Other firms that have introduced pump sprays include S.C. Johnson (Pledge furniture polish), Reckitt & Coleman Household Products (Woolite rug cleaner), Rollout L.P. (Take 5 cleanser), and Richardson-Vicks (Vidal Sassoon hair spray).[51]

Labeling

persuasive labeling
Focuses on a promotional theme or logo and consumer information is secondary.

An integral part of any package is its label. Labeling generally takes one of two forms: persuasive or informational. **Persuasive labeling** focuses on a promotional theme or logo, and consumer information is secondary. Price Pfister developed a new, persuasive label—featuring a picture of a faucet, the brand name, and the logo—with the goal of strengthening brand identity and becoming known as a brand instead of as a manufacturer.[52] Note that the standard promotional claims—such as "new," "improved," and "super"—are no longer very persuasive. Consumers have been saturated with "newness" and thus discount these claims.

informational labeling
Designed to help consumers make proper product selections and lower their cognitive dissonance after the purchase.

Informational labeling, in contrast, is designed to help consumers make proper product selections and lower their cognitive dissonance after the purchase. Sears attaches a "label of confidence" to all its floor coverings. This label gives such product information as durability, color, features, cleanability, care instructions, and construction standards. Most major furniture manufacturers affix labels to their wares that explain the products' construction features, such as type of frame, number of coils, and fabric characteristics. The Nutritional Labeling and Education Act of 1990 mandated detailed nutritional information on most food packages and standards for health claims on food packaging. An important outcome of this legislation is guidelines from the Food and Drug Administration for using terms like *low fat, light, reduced cholesterol, low sodium, low calorie,* and *fresh*.[53]

Universal Product Codes

universal product codes (UPCs)
Series of thick and thin vertical lines (bar codes), readable by computerized optical scanners, that represent numbers used to track products.

The **universal product codes (UPCs)** that appear on many items in supermarkets and other high-volume outlets were first introduced in 1974. Because the numerical codes appear as a series of thick and thin vertical lines, they are often called bar codes. The lines are read by computerized optical scanners that match codes with brand names, package sizes, and prices. They also print information on cash register tapes and help retailers rapidly and accurately prepare records of customer purchases, control inventories, and track sales. The UPC system and scanners are also used in single-source research. (See Chapter 7.)

Product Warranties

Just as a package is designed to protect the product, a **warranty** protects the buyer and gives essential information about the product. A warranty confirms the quality or performance of a good or service. An **express warranty** is a written guarantee. Express warranties range from simple statements—such as "100 percent cotton" (a guarantee of quality) and "complete satisfaction guaranteed" (a statement of performance)—to extensive documents written in technical language. In contrast, an **implied warranty** is an unwritten guarantee that the good or service is fit for the purpose for which it was sold. All sales have an implied warranty under the Uniform Commercial Code.

Congress passed the Magnuson-Moss Warranty–Federal Trade Commission Improvement Act in 1975 to help consumers understand warranties and get action from manufacturers and dealers. A manufacturer that promises a full warranty must meet certain minimum standards, including repair "within a reasonable time and without charge" of any defects and replacement of the merchandise or a full refund if the product does not work "after a reasonable number of attempts" at repair. Any warranty that does not live up to this tough prescription must be "conspicuously" promoted as a limited warranty.

9
Describe how and why product warranties are important marketing tools

warranty
Confirms the quality or performance of a good or service.

express warranty
A written guarantee.

implied warranty
An unwritten guarantee that the good or service is fit for the purpose for which it was sold.

LOOKING BACK

Look back at the story that opens the chapter about McDonald's introducing a new wrap sandwich to its product line. McDonald's has chosen to cobrand with Healthy Choice because of the latter's low fat content, which is important to the adult market McDonald's is trying to reach. McDonald's has been criticized in the past for its high-fat foods. With more and more adults wanting lower-fat, healthier foods, the Healthy Choice brand should be an attractive partner for McDonald's. A potential negative is that the emphasis on the Healthy Choice brand may serve to confirm adult consumers' perceptions that McDonald's traditional menu items are less healthy. The company hopes to boost overall sales by attracting adult consumers—a market segment that has been a challenge in the past. Healthy Choice has strong brand recognition as a low-fat product line, and given that more adults are health-conscious, the cobranding strategy seems to be sound.

Summary

1 Define the term "product." A product is anything, desired or not, that a person or organization receives in an exchange. The basic goal of purchasing decisions is to receive the tangible and intangible benefits associated with a product. Tangible aspects include packaging, style, color, size, and features. Intangible qualities include service, the retailer's image, the manufacturer's reputation, and the social status associated with a product. An organization's product offering is the crucial element in any marketing mix.

2 Classify consumer products. Consumer products are classified into four categories: convenience products, shopping products, specialty products, and unsought products. Convenience products are relatively inexpensive and require limited shopping effort. Shopping products are of two types: homogeneous and heterogeneous. Because of the similarity of homogeneous products, they are differentiated mainly by price and features. In contrast, heterogeneous products appeal to consumers because of their distinct characteristics. Specialty products possess unique benefits that are highly desirable to certain customers. Finally, unsought products are either new products or products that require aggressive selling because they are generally avoided or overlooked by consumers.

3 **Discuss the importance of services to the economy.** The service sector plays a crucial role in the U.S. economy, employing about three-quarters of the workforce and accounting for more than 60 percent of the gross domestic product.

4 **Discuss the differences between services and goods.** Services are distinguished by four characteristics: intangibility, inseparability, heterogeneity, and perishability. Services are intangible in that they lack clearly identifiable physical characteristics, making it difficult for marketers to communicate their specific benefits to potential customers. The production and consumption of services are typically inseparable. Services are heterogeneous because their quality depends on such variables as the service provider, individual consumer, location, and so on. Finally, services are perishable in the sense that they cannot be stored or saved. As a result, synchronizing supply with demand is particularly challenging in the service industry.

5 **Explain why services marketing is important to manufacturers.** Although manufacturers are marketing mainly goods, the related services they provide often give them a competitive advantage—especially when competing goods are quite similar.

6 **Define the terms "product item," "product line," and "product mix."** A product item is a specific version of a product that can be designated as a distinct offering among an organization's products. A product line is a group of closely related products offered by an organization. An organization's product mix includes all the products it sells. *Product mix width* refers to the number of product lines an organization offers. *Product line depth* is the number of product items in a product line. Firms modify existing products by changing their quality, functional characteristics, or style. *Product line extension* occurs when a firm adds new products to existing product lines.

7 **Describe marketing uses of branding.** A brand is a name, term, or symbol that identifies and differentiates a firm's products. Established brands encourage customer loyalty and help new products succeed. Branding strategies require decisions about individual, family, manufacturers', and private brands.

8 **Describe marketing uses of packaging and labeling.** Packaging has four functions: containing and protecting products; promoting products; facilitating product storage, use, and convenience; and facilitating recycling and reducing environmental damage. As a tool for promotion, packaging identifies the brand and its features. It also serves the critical function of differentiating a product from competing products and linking it with related products from the same manufacturer. The label is an integral part of the package, with persuasive and informational functions. In essence, the package is the marketer's last chance to influence buyers before they make a purchase decision.

9 **Describe how and why product warranties are important marketing tools.** Product warranties are important tools because they offer consumers protection and help them gauge product quality.

Discussion and Writing Questions

1. TEAM Break into groups of 4 or 5. From the following list of products, have the members of the group classify each product into the category (convenience, shopping, specialty, unsought) that they think fits best from their perspective as consumers (i.e., if they were buying the product):

Coca-Cola (brand), car stereo, winter coat, pair of shoes, life insurance, blue jeans, hamburgers.

2. A local civic organization has asked you to give a luncheon presentation about planned obsolescence. Rather than pursuing a negative approach by talking about how businesses exploit customers through planned obsolescence, you have decided to talk about the benefits of producing products that do not last forever. Prepare a one-page outline of your presentation.
3. A local supermarket would like to introduce their own brand of paper goods (e.g., paper towels, facial tissue, etc.) to sell alongside their current inventory. The company has hired you to generate a report outlining the advantages and disadvantages of doing so. Write the report.
4. Identify five outstanding brand names, and explain why each is included in your list.
5. Break into small groups, and discuss the packaging of a product familiar to all of your group members. Make a brief presentation to your class describing the pros and cons of this package.
6. How have several snack food companies modified their product to serve the emerging needs of their customers?
7. What is the product mix offered at the following Web site? **http://www.marriott.com**
8. 

List the countries to which Levi Strauss & Co. markets through the following Web site. How do the product offerings differ between the United States and European selections? **http://www.levi.com/**

Application for Small Business

The Baker family owns one of the largest catfish farms in central Texas, known for raising the sweetest catfish in the area. After graduating from college with a degree in marketing, Frank Baker returned to the farm with a mind full of new ways to cash in on the farm's reputation. At the time, the family allowed the butcher at the local supermarket to use the Baker name on their catfish. In central Texas, eating Baker Farms catfish was a sign of status. Frank, eager to put his degree to work, convinced his family that they could make money off their name by selling their catfish products already packaged to supermarkets. After hearing the idea, the family quickly met to formulate a plan to begin selling Baker Farms catfish.

Questions

1. What type of product is the Baker family selling? List your reasons.
2. What type of branding is the Baker family using? List your reasons.
3. How should Baker Farms catfish be packaged?
4. Assuming that the Baker family wishes to reposition their catfish products, what would be an optimal strategy?

Review Quiz

1. A relatively inexpensive item that merits little shopping effort is a(n)
   a. Convenience product
   b. Shopping product
   c. Specialty product
   d. Unsought product

Key Terms

brand 268
brand equity 268
brand loyalty 269
brand mark 268
brand name 268
business product (industrial product) 260
cobranding 274
consumer product 260
convenience product 260
credence quality 263
experience quality 263
express warranty 279
family brand 273
generic product 271
generic product name 275
heterogeneity 263
implied warranty 279
individual branding 273
informational labeling 278
inseparability 263
intangibility 263
manufacturer's brand 272
master brand 268
perishability 264
persuasive labeling 278
planned obsolescence 267
private brand 272
product 260
product item 265
product line 265
product line depth 265
product line extension 267
product mix 265
product mix width 265
product modification 266
search quality 263
service 262
service mark 274
shopping product 261
specialty product 261
trademark 274
universal product codes (UPCs) 278
unsought product 262
warranty 279

2. An item that consumers will search extensively for and are very reluctant to accept substitutes for is a(n)
   a. Convenience product
   b. Shopping product
   c. Specialty product
   d. Unsought product
3. A specific and distinct version of a product offered by an organization is defined as a
   a. Product item
   b. Product category
   c. Product line
   d. Product mix
4. A modification of an existing product in which there is a change in the product's versatility or effectiveness is a
   a. Line modification
   b. Quality modification
   c. Functional modification
   d. Style modification
5. A brand name that is owned by a wholesaler or a retailer is known as a
   a. Distributor's brand
   b. Private brand
   c. Manufacturer's brand
   d. Generic brand
6. When a firm places two or more brand names on a product, it is known as
   a. Individual branding
   b. Unique branding
   c. Cobranding
   d. Family branding
7. An exclusive right to use a brand is a
   a. Brand mark
   b. Copyright
   c. Trademark
   d. Private brand
8. ______ labeling focuses on a promotional theme or logo.
   a. Positioning
   b. Persuasive
   c. Informational
   b. Functional
9. Organizing related items into product lines often results in advertising efficiencies for the producer of these goods.
   a. True
   b. False
10. When a firm increases the width of a product line, it is generally also increasing risk in the marketplace.
   a. True
   b. False
11. Identify the three most important functions of product packaging.

Check the Answer Key, which follows the Video Case, to see how well you understood the material.

Ben & Jerry's: Taste and Innovation

What's in a name? Everything, at Ben & Jerry's, makers of mouth-watering ice cream in smooth and chunky flavors. Produced in Vermont from local dairy products and spring water, Ben & Jerry's strong brand image is one of high quality, innovative flavors, and barrel-of-laughs names. Products like Chunky Monkey, Vanilla Like It Oughta Be, Chubby Hubby, and Chocolate Chip Cookie Dough delight the palette and underscore the whimsical image of the company. To honor Grateful Dead icon, Jerry Garcia, and to appeal to youthful audiences, the company created Cherry Garcia ice cream in 1987. And today their newest flavor is Dilbert: Totally Nuts, named for the hapless comic strip hero of today's workaday world.

But the names aren't only funny. They carry a lot of weight supporting the company's brand equity. They have also created value based on customer recognition of the brand and loyalty among customers who like both the ice cream and the company mandate to improve society and the environment. Actually, Ben & Jerry's social philosophy plays a major role in making the company name well known. For example, Phish Food, chocolate ice cream with fish-shaped chocolate chunks, is named for the Vermont-based rock band Phish. On each pint container of Phish Food, the band pledges, "Our share of the proceeds from this pint goes to environmental efforts in the Lake Champlain Region of Vermont, so enjoy the good taste and karma." In 1997, sales of Phish Food generated royalties of $159,000.

Also in 1997, royalties in the amount of $55,000 were paid on the sale of Doonesberry Sorbet. Pints of Doonesberry include the following message, signed by the cartoon strip's character Mike Doonesbury: "P.S. All creator royalties go to charity, so your purchase represents an orderly transfer of wealth you can feel proud of." Royalty funds from Doonesberry Sorbet go to education, AIDS treatment and prevention, reducing poverty, and human rights.

Though premium ice cream is still the company favorite, Ben & Jerry's expanded the product mix because the original product was high in fat, and today's consumers wanted low-fat, healthier products with more nutritional value. So, product lines now include low-fat ice cream, low-fat and nonfat frozen yogurts, and fat-free sorbet. The idea is "to blend flavor that tastes very fattening into ice cream that isn't." All the product lines share the same marketing strategy, complete with offbeat humor and catchy names. For Ben & Jerry's twentieth birthday, new low-fat flavors were introduced—Coconut Cream Pie Low Fat, S'Mores, and Blackberry Cobbler. Within each product line, some flavors have become so well known that they constitute brands unto themselves. For example, Cherry Garcia is available in both the premium and frozen yogurt categories.

Catchy names and expanded product lines are not the only marketing strategies followed at Ben & Jerry's, where even the packaging is considered a promotional element. That's why all product lines are packaged in similarly designed and illustrated pint containers. Because consumers often believe that different product lines made by the same manufacturer are equal in quality, those who love the ice cream may try the yogurt, especially because their packaging looks alike.

To celebrate the company's twentieth birthday, the pint package was redesigned to be fun and colorful and to have an appetizing look. Packaging at Ben & Jerry's, however, also conveys important messages regarding the ingredients. In addition to the information on charitable contributions, the labels on pint cartons state, "We oppose rBGH, Recombinant Bovine Growth Hormone. The family farmers who supply our milk and cream pledge not to treat their cows with rBGH . . . ." The company's overarching belief in social responsibility—whether it be the consumers' right to know what they are eating or the corporate call to social giving—is reflected and advertised in its package designs.

Packaging materials themselves have become a test case of the company's pledge to improve the environment. One goal is to make the transition to totally chlorine-free paper for pint containers because the bleaching process releases pollutants into the air. Although these kinds of measures seem on the surface to be great marketing hooks, still the public does not always favor company initiatives. Packaging for Peace Pops ice cream bars was redesigned and this message added: "We package our Peace Pops in bags, not individual boxes, because it puts less trash in the landfill."

But sales declined as a result because customers wanted the packaging of their premium ice cream to reflect its high quality and high price. Reluctantly, the company changed packaging back to boxes. As a compromise, the new Peanut Butter & Jelly bar is in a plastic bag inside a chlorine-free box.

Questions

1. What are the tangible and intangible dimensions of Ben & Jerry's products?
2. Why did Ben & Jerry's develop several product lines?
3. Describe Ben & Jerry's brand equity.
4. What is the advantage of Ben & Jerry's using one marketing strategy for the entire product mix?

Bibliography

Ben & Jerry's annual report

Ben & Jerry's Web site: **http://www.benjerry.com/**

Answer Key

1. *Answer:* a, p. 260

   Rationale: Convenience products are those that the consumer is unwilling to shop extensively for. Consumers buy these products regularly and are aware of brand names of such goods.

2. *Answer:* c, p. 261

   Rationale: Specialty products are often expensive goods that try to maintain an exclusive image in the marketplace. Distribution is typically limited and brand names are very important.

3. *Answer:* a, p. 265

   Rationale: A product item is a single product that can be designated as a distinct offering among an organization's products.

4. *Answer:* c, p. 266

   Rationale: A functional modification occurs when the firm changes a product's versatility, effectiveness, convenience, or safety.

5. *Answer:* b, p. 272

   Rationale: Private brands are those that are owned by distribution channel members such as retailers and wholesalers.

6. *Answer:* c, p. 274

   Rationale: Cobranding is a strategy that is used when a combination of brand names enhances the prestige or perceived value of a product.

7. *Answer:* c, p. 274

   Rationale: A trademark is the exclusive right to use a brand or a part of a brand and prohibits others from using a brand without permission.

8. *Answer:* b, p. 278

   Rationale: The goal of persuasive labeling is to strengthen the brand identity of the product by focusing on the brand instead of the manufacturer with the label.

9. *Answer:* a, p. 266

   Rationale: Product lines do provide economies of scale in advertising since several products can be advertised under the umbrella of the line.

10. *Answer:* b, p. 265

    Rationale: Firms increase the width of the product mix to diversify risk by spreading it across many product lines rather than depending on only one or two.

11. *Answer:*

    Containing and protecting products

    Promoting products

    Facilitating the storage, use, and convenience of products

    (pp. 276–277)

CHAPTER

9

LEARNING OBJECTIVES

After studying this chapter, you should be able to

1. Explain the importance of developing new products and describe the six categories of new products
2. Explain the steps in the new-product development process
3. Explain the concept of product life cycles
4. Explain the diffusion process through which new products are adopted

DEVELOPING AND MANAGING PRODUCTS

The Advanced Photo System (APS) is a new 24mm photography system developed by Eastman Kodak Co. in conjunction with Japanese camera manufacturers Canon, Fuji, Minolta, and Nikon.[1] APS film is sold by Kodak under the brand name Advantix. The system, which requires an APS camera, APS film, and APS developing equipment, offers photographers the option of ordering photos in three different sizes from the same roll of film using the same lens. The options are 4 × 6, 4 × 7, and 4 × 11½. APS film comes in a cartridge that is easier to load than 35mm film and automatically adjusts for errors such as poor lighting. Developed photos are returned by processors accompanied by a proof set of numbered mini-snapshots and the developed film still in its original canister. These features make selecting reprints easier and protect negatives.

Kodak is reported to have spent $1 billion developing APS and another $100 million in first-year promotion. "It was a big flop at first (but) now it's gaining momentum and will continue to gain momentum," said the owner of a chain of photography stores.[2]

Following slow sales in 1996, Kodak estimates that APS accounted for nearly $36 million in U.S. camera sales and $21.6 million in film sales in 1997. Three times as many reprints are being made from APS film rolls compared to 35mm film rolls. This is attributed to the new film size options, better photos, and the ease of identifying negatives. APS sales are growing more rapidly in Europe than in the United States.[3]

Why do you think APS sales started slowly and what do you think may have led to increased momentum in the second year? What might Kodak management have done to avoid such a slow start?

on line

Kodak

How does Kodak's Web site support its new Advantix system? Find out at **http://www.kodak.com/**

The Importance of New Products

1
Explain the importance of developing new products and describe the six categories of new products

New products are important to sustain growth and profits and to replace obsolete items. 3M Corp. introduces about five hundred new products each year.[4] Colgate-Palmolive Company credits new products launched over the last five years (1993–1997) for bringing in $2.8 billion or almost one-third of total sales revenue.[5] Johnson & Johnson and Gillette Co. expect products launched in the past five years to account for 36 and 50 percent of annual revenue, respectively.[6] New brands account for 80 percent of the sales increase in cereals in the past ten years.[7]

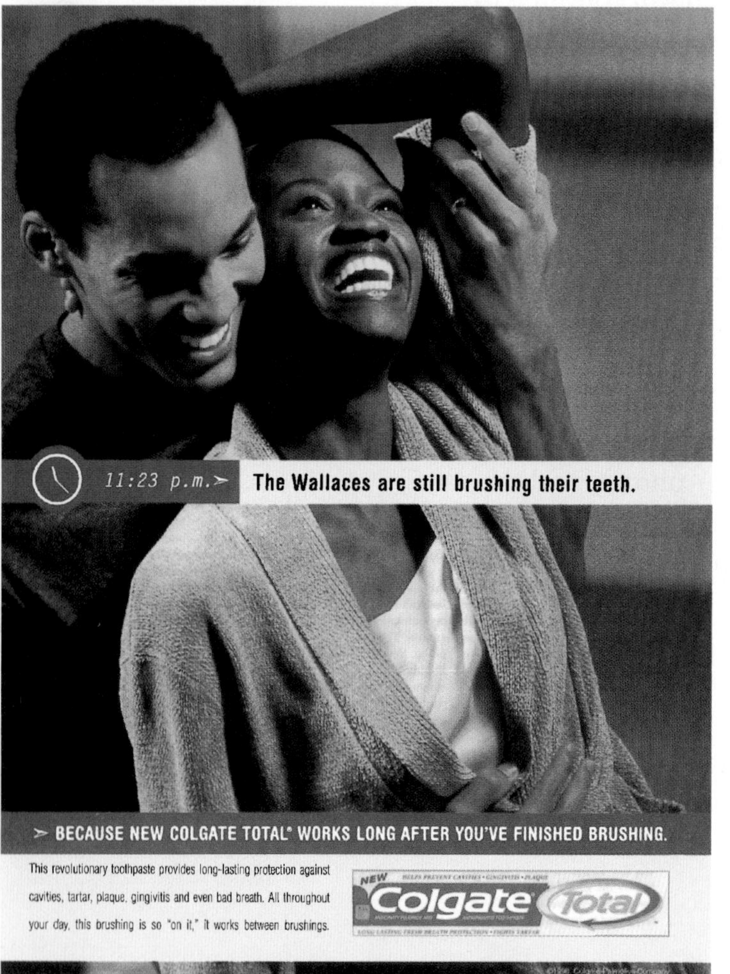

11:23 p.m.
The Wallaces are still brushing their teeth.
BECAUSE NEW COLGATE TOTAL® WORKS LONG AFTER YOU'VE FINISHED BRUSHING.
This revolutionary toothpaste provides long-lasting protection against cavities, tartar, plaque, gingivitis and even bad breath. All throughout your day, this brushing is so "on it," it works between brushings.
NEW
Colgate Total

Colgate Total fits into the new product category called improvements or revisions of existing products. This category represents 25 to 30 percent of all new products introduced each year.
Courtesy Colgate-Palmolive Company

Categories of New Products

The term **new product** is somewhat confusing, because its meaning varies widely. Actually, there are several "correct" definitions of the term. A product can be new to the world, to the market, to the producer or seller, or to some combination of these. There are six categories of new products:

- *New-to-the-world products* (also called *discontinuous innovations):* These products create an entirely new market. The telephone, television, computer, and facsimile machine are commonly cited examples of new-to-the-world products.
- *New product lines:* These products, which the firm has not previously offered, allow it to enter an established market. The Justin Boot Company, a leader in the western boot market, recently entered the work boot segment for the first time. Justin now offers thirteen styles of men's and women's work boots.[8]
- *Additions to existing product lines:* This category includes new products that supplement a firm's established line. Hallmark recently announced the addition of 117 new greeting cards—for pets. According to Hallmark's research, 75 percent of pet owners give Christmas presents to their pets, and 40 percent celebrate their pets' birthdays.[9] The "Ethics in Marketing" box in this chapter describes several new brands that fit into this category of new product.
- *Improvements or revisions of existing products:* The "new and improved" product may be significantly or slightly changed. For example, Breyers Soft 'n Creamy! ice cream "scoops right out without bending the spoon."[10] Anyone who has ever sat around for fifteen minutes waiting for a half-gallon of ice cream to thaw would certainly agree that this is a product improvement. The new film described in the story at the beginning of this chapter and the tooothpaste featured on this page also fit into this category.

Most new products fit into this category. According to one expert, "companies are making low-risk launches—a lot of line extensions, new colors and flavors."[11]

new product
Product new to the world, the market, the producer, the seller, or some combination of these.

- *Repositioned products:* These are existing products targeted at new markets or market segments. Quaker Oats Co. abandoned its fat-free positioning strategy for Rice Cakes following an 11 percent drop in sales over two years. The new strategy focuses on great taste and includes Chocolate Chip and Peanut Butter flavors.[12]

Keebler

Visit Keebler's on-line newsroom to read about new product offerings. What categories of new products are represented?

http://www.keebler.com/

on line

ethics in marketing

A New Breed of Smokes

The MTV generation likes its vices with a hint of rebellious posturing. Why drink a Pabst when you can have a Pete's Wicked (legally or not)? Now, cigarette makers are going after this high school- and college-age market with a new crop of "microsmokes," a dozen or so offbeat brands with attitude. Although the manufacturers say that all new brands are aimed at the over-twenty-one set, the cool packages, in-your-face ad copy, and quirky flavors have undeniable youth appeal. "These aren't something you see 40-year-olds walking around with," says Michael Cummings, an epidemiologist at the Roswell Park Cancer Institute in Buffalo. Black Death cigarettes, for example, scoff at cancer warnings by using a skull in a top hat as their mascot and, as their motto, "I like 'em and I'm going to smoke 'em."

Industry titan R. J. Reynolds got in on the act in late 1995 with its Moonlight Tobacco line. Available only in youth meccas like Seattle and New York, it boasts oddball tastes (including a smoke formulated to complement coffee), hip-sounding names like Planet and Icebox, and eye-catching packaging. Red Kamels, discontinued in 1936 and relaunched by RJR a year ago, are now a hit. Thanks to splashy Soviet-style graphics and wise-guy slogans like "Back for No Good Reason, Except They Taste Good," they've just expanded from four to fourteen markets.

Antismoking advocates are troubled by the sleek marketing, which they say is geared toward turning today's adolescents into tomorrow's pack-a-day smokers. Notes John Slade, an internist who deals with tobacco-related issues at New Jersey's St. Peter's Medical Center: "Those are the markets that the companies need."[13]

Are brands such as Black Death and Red Kamels new products? Explain your answer. Should tobacco companies be allowed to market these products?

SOURCE: "A New Breed of Smokes" by Brendan I. Koemer, *U.S. News & World Report.* Copyright, April 21, 1997, U.S. News & World Report. Reprinted by permission.

- *Lower-priced products:* This category refers to products that provide performance similar to competing brands at a lower price. Hewlett-Packard Co. introduced the Laser Jet 3100 in 1998. It is a scanner, copier, printer, and fax machine combined. This new product is priced lower than many conventional color copiers and much lower than the combined price of the four items purchased separately.[14]

The New-Product Development Process

2

Explain the steps in the new-product development process

The management and technology consulting firm Booz, Allen, and Hamilton has studied the new-product development process for over thirty years. Analyzing five major studies undertaken during this period, the firm has concluded that the companies most likely to succeed in developing and introducing new products are those that take the following actions:

- Make the long-term commitment needed to support innovation and new product development
- Use a company-specific approach, driven by corporate objectives and strategies, with a well-defined new-product strategy at its core
- Capitalize on experience to achieve and maintain competitive advantage

exhibit 9.1

New-Product Development Process

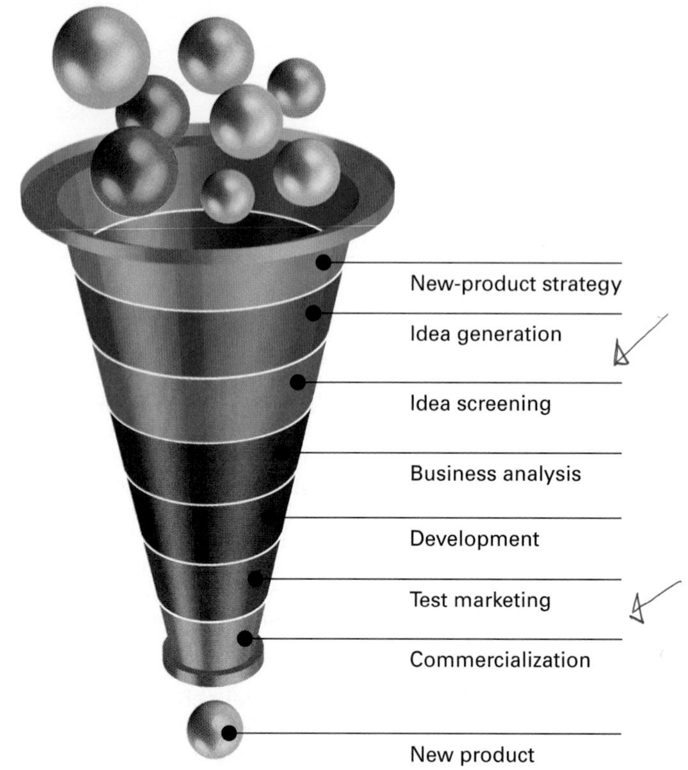

- Establish an environment—a management style, organizational structure, and degree of top-management support—conducive to achieving company-specific new-product and corporate objectives[15]

Most companies follow a formal new-product development process, usually starting with a new-product strategy. Exhibit 9.1 traces the seven-step process, which is discussed in detail in this section. The exhibit is funnel-shaped to highlight the fact that each stage acts as a screen. The purpose is to filter out unworkable ideas.

New-Product Strategy

new-product strategy
Linking the new-product development process with the objectives of the marketing department, the business unit, and the corporation.

A **new-product strategy** links the new-product development process with the objectives of the marketing department, the business unit, and the corporation. A new-product strategy must be compatible with these objectives, and in turn, all three objectives must be consistent with one another.

New-product strategy is part of the organization's overall marketing strategy. It sharpens the focus and provides general guidelines for generating, screening, and evaluating new-product ideas. The new-product strategy specifies the roles that new products must play in the organization's overall plan and describes the characteristics of products the organization wants to offer and the markets it wants to serve.

Idea Generation

New-product ideas come from many sources, such as customers, employees, distributors, competitors, research and development, and consultants.

- *Customers:* The marketing concept suggests that customers' wants and needs should be the springboard for developing new products. Thermos, the vacuum bottle manufacturer, provides an interesting example of how companies tap customers for ideas. The company's first step in developing an innovative home barbecue grill was to send ten members of its interdisciplinary new-product

Healthy Choice

How does Healthy Choice use its Web site to generate new product ideas? Go to "Table One" on its Web site to find out.

http://www.healthychoice.com/

on line

team into the field for about a month. Their assignment was to learn all about people's cookout needs and to invent a product to meet them. In cities that include Boston, Los Angeles, and Columbus, Ohio, the team conducted focus groups, visited people's homes, and even videotaped barbecues.

Going direct to the customer to learn about people's cookout needs is what helped the Thermos work team create a new type of outdoor grill. Tapping customers can be a very effective method of generating new product ideas.

© James Schnepf/Liaison International

- *Employees:* Marketing personnel—advertising and marketing research employees, as well as salespeople—often create new-product ideas, because they analyze and are involved in the marketplace. Firms should encourage their employees to submit new-product ideas and reward them if their ideas are adopted. The very successful introduction of Post-it® Notes started with an employee's idea. In 1974, the research and development department of 3M's commercial tape division developed and patented the adhesive component of Post-it® Notes. However, it was a year before an employee of the commercial tape division, who sang in a church choir, identified a use for the adhesive. He had been using paper clips and slips of paper to mark places in hymn books. But the paper clips damaged his books, and the slips of paper fell out. The solution, as we now all know, was to apply the adhesive to small pieces of paper and sell them in packages.
- *Distributors:* A well-trained sales force routinely asks distributors about needs that are not being met. Because they are closer to end users, distributors are often more aware of customer needs than are manufacturers. The inspiration for Rubbermaid's litter-free lunch box, named Sidekick, came from a distributor. The distributor suggested that Rubbermaid place some of its plastic containers inside a lunch box and sell the box as an alternative to plastic wrap and paper bags.
- *Competitors:* No firms rely solely on internally generated ideas for new products. A big part of any organization's marketing intelligence system should be monitoring the performance of competitors' products. One purpose of competitive monitoring is to determine which, if any, of the competitors' products should be copied. Competitive monitoring may include tracking products sold by a company's own customers. The "Global Perspectives" box on the next page illustrates how Coca-Cola has used this strategy successfully in Japan.

ON LINE

There is plenty of information about competitors on the World Wide Web.[16] For example, AltaVista (**http://www.altavista.digital.com**) is a powerful index tool that can be used to locate information about products and companies. Fuld & Co.'s competitive intelligence guide provides links to a variety of market intelligence sites.

- *Research and development (R&D):* R&D is carried out in four distinct ways. Basic research is scientific research aimed at discovering new technologies. Applied research takes these new technologies and tries to find useful applications for them. **Product development** goes one step further by converting applications into marketable products. *Product modification* makes cosmetic or functional changes in existing products. Many new-product breakthroughs come from R&D activities. Pert Plus, Procter & Gamble's combination shampoo and conditioner, was invented in the laboratory.

product development
Marketing strategy that entails the creation of marketable new products; process of converting applications for new technologies into marketable products.

- *Consultants:* Outside consultants are always available to examine a business and recommend product ideas. Examples include the Weston Group; Booz, Allen, and Hamilton; and Management Decisions. Traditionally, consultants determine whether a company has a balanced portfolio of products and, if not, what new-product ideas are needed to offset the imbalance. For instance, an outside consultant conceived Airwick's highly successful Carpet Fresh carpet cleaner.

brainstorming
Getting a group to think of unlimited ways to vary a product or solve a problem.

Creativity is the wellspring of new-product ideas, regardless of who comes up with them. A variety of approaches and techniques have been developed to stimulate creative thinking. The two considered most useful for generating new-product ideas are brainstorming and focus group exercises. The goal of **brainstorming** is to get a group to think of unlimited ways to vary a product or solve a problem. Group members avoid criticism of an idea, no matter how ridiculous it may seem. Objective evaluation is postponed. The sheer quantity of ideas is what matters. As noted in Chapter 7, an objective of focus group interviews is to stimulate insightful comments through group interaction. Focus groups usually consist of seven to ten people. Sometimes consumer focus groups generate excellent new-product ideas—for example, Cycle dog food, Stick-Up room deodorizers, Dustbuster vacuum cleaners, and Wendy's salad bar. In the industrial market, machine tools, keyboard designs, aircraft interiors, and backhoe accessories have evolved from focus groups.

A study recently conducted by the Product Development and Management Association found that it took seven ideas to generate a new commercial product in 1995, down from eleven ideas in 1990. In 1967, it took fifty-eight ideas for one new item. Today, companies do more work at the beginning of the development process (such as identifying final users) and can, in some cases, use computer-simulation tools to speed up the design stage.[17]

screening
The first filter in the product development process, which eliminates ideas that are inconsistent with the organization's new-product strategy or are obviously inappropriate for some other reason.

Idea Screening

After new ideas have been generated, they pass through the first filter in the product development process. This stage, called **screening,** eliminates ideas that are inconsistent with the organization's new-product strategy or are obviously inappropriate for some other reason. The new-product committee, the new-product department, or

global perspectives

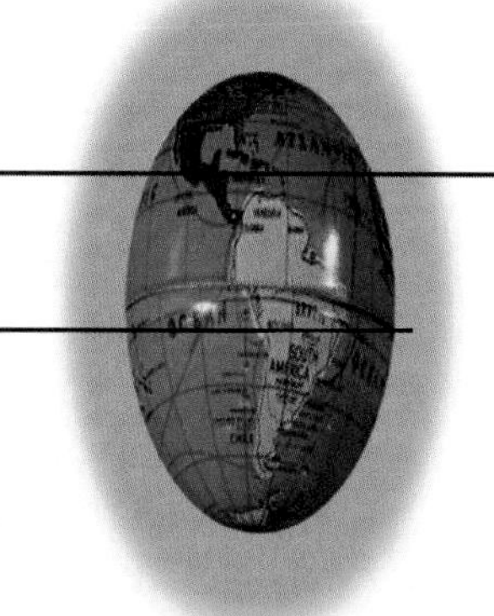

Monitoring Competition Pays Off

In 1990, the Coca-Cola Company dominated the soft-drink market in Japan. Coke controlled 90 percent of the carbonated drink market and over 30 percent of the entire soft-drink market, including noncarbonated drinks.

But consumer preferences began changing rapidly. Demand for less-sweet noncarbonated drinks rose quickly. Japanese companies such as Suntory, Ltd., Asahi Soft Drinks Co., and Calpis Food Industry Co. began attracting large numbers of purchasers with new products such as Asian teas, fruit-flavored sodas, teas, coffees, and fermented-milk drinks. Coke's market share began falling rapidly. According to one industry analyst, "Coke used to have trouble with product development—with its speed and coming up with new localized products—but they've gotten faster and smarter.[18]

Since 1994 Coke has reversed declining market share by introducing more than thirty new drinks, including an Asian tea called Sokenbicha, an English tea called Kochakaden, a coffee drink called Georgia, and a fermented-milk drink called Lactia.

"Coca-Cola is mean and scary," says one competitor. "They have deep pockets, and these days they study us closely and challenge us with all these me-toos. That's something they never did before."[19]

A Coca-Cola representative asked to respond to this charge said that the company does not follow a copy-cat strategy. Instead, it improves on competitors' product ideas and introduces superior products.

What category of new products is Coca-Cola Company introducing into Japan? Is their strategy of monitoring competitors' new products and introducing similar items ethical? Does it make good business sense?

some other formally appointed group performs the screening review. Most new-product ideas are rejected at the screening stage.

Concept tests are often used at the screening stage to rate concept (or product) alternatives. A **concept test** evaluates a new-product idea, usually before any prototype has been created. Typically, researchers get consumer reactions to descriptions and visual representations of a proposed product.

concept test
Test to evaluate a new-product idea, usually before any prototype has been created.

Concept tests are considered fairly good predictors of success for line extensions. They have also been relatively precise predictors of success for new products that are not copycat items, are not easily classified into existing product categories, and do not require major changes in consumer behavior—such as Betty Crocker Tuna Helper, Cycle dog food, and Libby Fruit Float. However, concept tests are usually inaccurate in predicting the success of new products that create new consumption patterns and require major changes in consumer behavior—such as microwave ovens, videocassette recorders, computers, and word processors.

Business Analysis

New-product ideas that survive the initial screening process move to the **business analysis** stage, where preliminary figures for demand, cost, sales, and profitability are calculated. For the first time, costs and revenues are estimated and compared. Depending on the nature of the product and the company, this process may be simple or complex.

business analysis
The second stage of the screening process where preliminary figures for demand, cost, sales, and profitability are calculated.

The newness of the product, the size of the market, and the nature of competition all affect the accuracy of revenue projections.[20] In an established market like soft drinks, industry estimates of total market size are available. Forecasting market share for a new entry is a bigger challenge.

Analyzing overall economic trends and their impact on estimated sales is especially important in product categories that are sensitive to fluctuations in the business cycle. If consumers view the economy as uncertain and risky, they will put off buying durable goods like major home appliances, automobiles, and homes. Likewise, business buyers postpone major equipment purchases if they expect a recession.

These questions are commonly asked during the business analysis stage:

- What is the likely demand for the product?
- What impact would the new product probably have on total sales, profits, market share, and return on investment?
- How would the introduction of the product affect existing products? Would the new product cannibalize existing products?
- Would current customers benefit from the product?
- Would the product enhance the image of the company's overall product mix?
- Would the new product affect current employees in any way? Would it lead to hiring more people or reducing the size of the workforce?
- What new facilities, if any, would be needed?
- How might competitors respond?
- What is the risk of failure? Is the company willing to take the risk?

Answering these and related questions may require studies of markets, competition, costs, and technical capabilities. But at the end of this stage, management should have a good understanding of the product's market potential. This full understanding is important, because costs increase dramatically once a product idea enters the development stage.

The "Entrepreneurial Insights" box that follows provides a checklist that small businesses might use for evaluating new-product ideas.

Development

In the early stage of **development**, the R&D department or engineering department may develop a prototype of the product. During this stage, the firm should start sketching a marketing strategy. The marketing department should decide on

development
Stage in the product development process in which a prototype is developed and a marketing strategy is outlined.

Checklist for Evaluating New-Product Concepts

If a small business is lucky enough to have stable or increasing sales, new-product additions can boost profits and market share. Small-business managers must be careful, however, not to expand beyond the firm's financial capacities. A new product requires shelf space, investment in inventory, perhaps spare parts, and maybe even a new salesperson—all of which require an extra financial commitment.

A new small business usually has only one chance to "do it right." A failure in introducing a new product means bankruptcy and perhaps the loss of a person's life savings. Conversely, for the owner of an established small business who suddenly finds that his or her source of livelihood has evaporated, the right new product can help offset declining demand.

The product development process is generally the same for both large and small firms. However, many entrepreneurs must do most steps in the process themselves rather than rely on specialists or outside consultants.

Here's a simple checklist for evaluating new-product concepts for a small business. By adding up the points, a small-business owner can more accurately estimate success.

1. Contribution to before-tax return on investment:

More than 35 percent	+2
25–35 percent	+1
20–25 percent	−1
Less than 20 percent	−2

2. Estimated annual sales:

More than $10 million	+2
$2 million–$10 million	+1
$1 million–$1.99 million	−1
Less than $1 million	−2

3. Estimated growth phase of product life cycle:

More than three years	+2
Two or three years	+1
One or two years	−1
Less than one year	−2

4. Capital investment payback:

Less than one year	+2
One to two years	+1
Two to three years	−1
More than three years	−2

5. Premium-price potential:

Weak or no competition, making entry easy	+2
Mildly competitive entry conditions	+1
Strongly competitive entry conditions	−1
Entrenched competition that makes entry difficult	−2

This checklist is by no means complete, but a neutral or negative total score should give an entrepreneur reason to consider dropping the product concept.

the product's packaging, branding, labeling, and so forth. In addition, it should map out preliminary promotion, price, and distribution strategies. The technical feasibility of manufacturing the product at an acceptable cost should also be thoroughly examined.

The development stage can last a long time and thus be very expensive. Crest toothpaste was in the development stage for 10 years. It took 18 years to develop Minute Rice, 15 years to develop the Polaroid Colorpack camera, 15 years to develop the Xerox copy machine, and 55 years to develop television. Gillette spent 6 years and more than $750 million developing the MACH 3 razor.[21] Preliminary efforts to develop a three-bladed razor began 28 years before the 1998 launch of MACH 3.[22]

ON LINE

The development process works best when all the involved areas (R&D, marketing, engineering, production, and even suppliers) work together rather than sequentially, a process called simultaneous product development (discussed later in this chapter). The Internet is a useful tool for improving communications between marketing personnel, advertising agencies, graphic designers, and others involved in developing products. On the Net, multiple parties from a number of different companies can meet regularly with new ideas and information at their fingertips, an inexpensive way to help get products to the shelf faster.[23]

Laboratory tests are often conducted on prototype models during the development stage. User safety is an important aspect of laboratory testing, which actually subjects products to much more severe treatment than is expected by end users. The Consumer Product Safety Act of 1972 requires manufacturers to conduct a "reasonable testing program" to ensure that their products conform to established safety standards.

Many products that test well in the laboratory are also tried out in homes or businesses. Examples of product categories well suited for such use tests include human and pet food products, household cleaning products, and industrial chemicals and supplies. These products are all relatively inexpensive, and their performance characteristics are apparent to users. For example, at a Boston factory that Gillette Co. calls "World Shaving Headquarters," about two hundred male and thirty female employee volunteers evaluate potential new razors and blades each weekday morning. They report their assessment of features such as sharpness, smoothness, and ease of handling.[24] In addition to employee feedback, research teams count razor strokes, clock the length of dewhiskerization, and observe split-face shaving, in which dueling products are tested on opposite sides of a subject's face.[25] Gillette also employs twenty-seven hundred off-site shavers who evaluate products at home.

Most products require some refinement based on the results of laboratory and use tests. A second stage of development often takes place before test marketing.

Test Marketing

After products and marketing programs have been developed, they are usually tested in the marketplace. **Test marketing** is the limited introduction of a product and a marketing program to determine the reactions of potential customers in a market situation. Test marketing allows management to evaluate alternative strategies and to assess how well the various aspects of the marketing mix fit together. Febreze, Procter & Gamble Co.'s new spray that permanently removes odors such as cigarette smoke or pet odors from garments, was test marketed in Phoenix, Salt Lake City, and Boise, Idaho, in 1996.[26]

test marketing
The limited introduction of a product and a marketing program to determine the reactions of potential customers in a market situation.

The cities chosen as test sites should reflect market conditions in the new product's projected market area. Yet no "magic city" exists that can universally represent market conditions, and a product's success in one city doesn't guarantee that it will be a nationwide hit. When selecting test market cities, researchers should therefore find locations where the demographics and purchasing habits mirror the overall market. The company should also have good distribution in test cities. Moreover, test locations should be isolated from the media. If the TV stations in a particular market reach a very large area outside that market, the advertising used for the test product may pull in many consumers from outside the market. The product may then appear more successful than it really is. Exhibit 9.2 provides a useful checklist of criteria for selecting test markets.

The High Costs of Test Marketing

Test marketing frequently takes one year or longer and costs can exceed $1 million. Some products remain in test markets even longer. McDonald's spent twelve years developing and testing salads before introducing them. Despite the cost, many firms believe it is a lot better to fail in a test market than in a national introduction.

Because test marketing is so expensive, some companies do not test line extensions of well-known brands. For example, because the Folger's brand is well known, Procter & Gamble faced little risk in distributing its instant decaffeinated version nationally. Consolidated Foods Kitchen of Sara Lee followed the same approach with its frozen croissants. Other products introduced without being test marketed include General Foods' International Coffees,

What can you find out on the Internet about current test marketing? Use AltaVista search engine and type in "Test Marketing."
http://www.altavista.com

exhibit 9.2

Checklist for Selecting Test Markets

In choosing a test market, many criteria need to be considered, especially the following:
Similarity to planned distribution outlets
Relative isolation from other cities
Availability of advertising media that will cooperate
Diversified cross section of ages, religions, cultural-societal preferences, etc.
No atypical purchasing habits
Representative population size
Typical per capita income
Good record as a test city, but not overly used
Not easily "jammed" by competitors
Stability of year-round sales
No dominant television station; multiple newspapers, magazines, and radio stations
Availability of retailers that will cooperate
Availability of research and audit services
Freedom from unusual influences, such as one industry's dominance or heavy tourism

Quaker Oats' Chewy Granola Bars and Granola Dipps, and Pillsbury's Milk Break Bars.

The high cost of test marketing is not purely financial. One unavoidable problem is that test marketing exposes the new product and its marketing mix to competitors before its introduction. Thus, the element of surprise is lost. Several years ago, for example, Procter & Gamble began testing a ready-to-spread Duncan Hines frosting. General Mills took note and rushed to market with its own Betty Crocker brand, which now is the best-selling brand of ready-to-spread frosting. Competitors can also sabotage or "jam" a testing program by introducing their own sales promotion, pricing, or advertising campaign. The purpose is to hide or distort the normal conditions that the testing firm might expect in the market. When Coca-Cola tested its contour can (a curvy can inspired by Coke's trademark bottle) in 1997 at a premium price, PepsiCo counterattacked furiously by offering discounts on its cola products.[27]

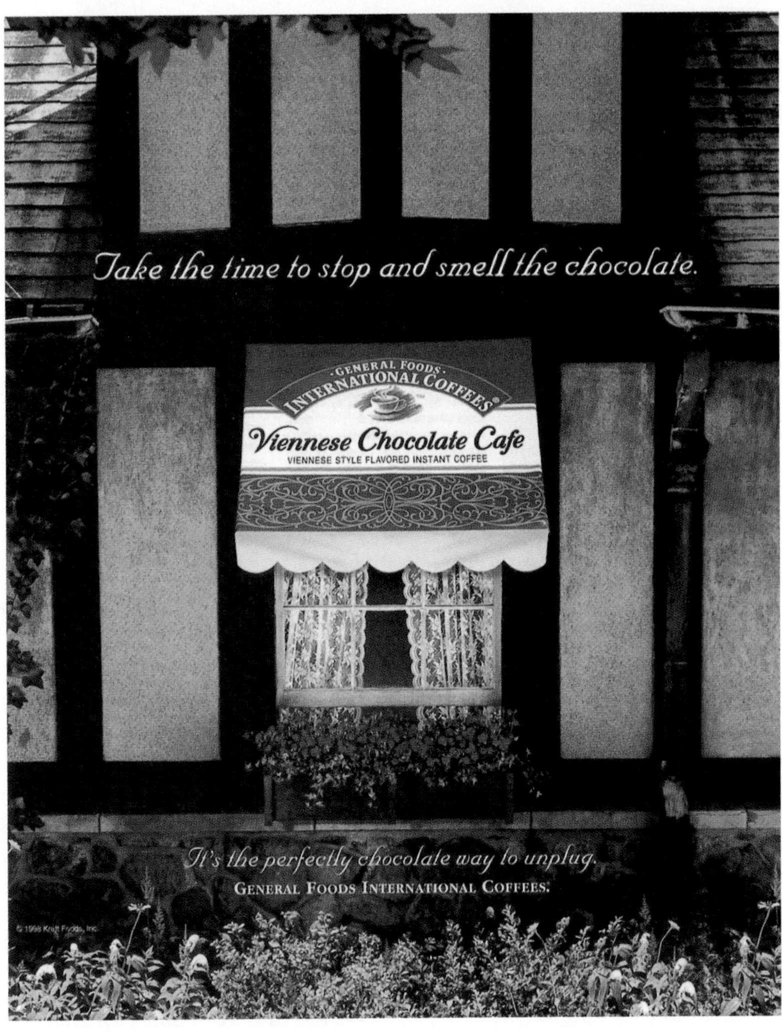

Because of the high costs associated with test marketing, companies may choose not to test line extensions of popular brands. General Foods International Coffees is one example of a product that went direct to market without being tested.
Courtesy Kraft Foods, Inc.

Alternatives to Test Marketing

Many firms are looking for cheaper, faster, safer alternatives to traditional test marketing. In the early 1980s, Information Resources Incorporated pioneered one alternative: single-source research using supermarket scanner data. A typical supermarket scanner test costs about $300,000. Another alternative to traditional test marketing is **simulated (laboratory) market testing**. Advertising and other promotional materials for several products, including the test product, are shown to members of the product's target market. These people are then taken to shop at a mock or real store, where their purchases are recorded. Shopper behavior, including repeat purchasing, is monitored to assess the product's likely performance under true market conditions. Research firms offer simulated market tests for $25,000 to $100,000, compared to $1 million or more for full-scale test marketing.

Despite these alternatives, most firms still consider test marketing essential for most new products. The high price of failure simply prohibits the widespread introduction of most new products without testing. Sometimes, however, when risks of failure are estimated to be low, it is better to skip test marketing and move directly from development to commercialization.

simulated (laboratory) market testing
Presentation of advertising and other promotion materials for several products, including a test product, to members of the product's target market.

Commercialization

The final stage in the new-product development process is **commercialization**, the decision to market a product. The decision to commercialize the product sets several tasks in motion: ordering production materials and equipment, starting production, building inventories, shipping the product to field distribution points, training the sales force, announcing the new product to the trade, and advertising to potential customers.

commercialization
The decision to market a product.

The time from the initial commercialization decision to the product's actual introduction varies. It can range from a few weeks for simple products that use existing equipment to several years for technical products that require custom manufacturing equipment.

The total cost of development and initial introduction can be staggering. Recall from the story at the beginning of this chapter that Kodak spent over $1 billion to develop APS and another $100 million for first-year promotion. Gillette spent $750 million developing MACH 3 and the first-year marketing budget for the new three-bladed razor was $300 million.[28]

ON LINE

For some products, a well-planned Internet campaign can provide new-product information for people who are looking for the solutions that a particular new product offers. Attempting to reach customers at the point in time when they need a product is much more cost-effective and efficient than communicating with a target market that may eventually have a need for the product.[29]

Product Life Cycles

3
Explain the concept of product life cycles

The product life cycle (PLC) is one of the most familiar concepts in marketing. Few other general concepts have been so widely discussed. Although some researchers have challenged the theoretical basis and managerial value of the PLC, most believe it has great potential as a marketing management tool.

product life cycle
A concept that provides a way to trace the stages of a product's acceptance, from its introduction (birth) to its decline (death).

product category
All brands that satisfy a particular type of need.

The **product life cycle** concept provides a way to trace the stages of a product's acceptance, from its introduction (birth) to its decline (death). As Exhibit 9.3 shows, a product progresses through four major stages: introduction, growth, maturity, and decline. Note that the product life cycle illustrated does not refer to any one brand; rather, it refers to the life cycle for a product category or product class. A **product category** includes all brands that satisfy a particular type of need. Product categories include passenger cars, cigarettes, soft drinks, and coffee.

The time a product spends in any one stage of the life cycle may vary dramatically. Some products, such as fad items, move through the entire cycle in weeks. Others, such as electric clothes washers and dryers, stay in the maturity stage for decades. Exhibit 9.3 illustrates the typical life cycle for a consumer durable good, such as a washer or dryer. In contrast, Exhibit 9.4 illustrates typical life cycles for styles (such as formal, business, or casual clothing), fashions (such as miniskirts or stirrup pants), and fads (such as leopard-print clothing). Changes in a product, its uses, its image, or its positioning can extend that product's life cycle.

The product life cycle concept does not tell managers the length of a product's life cycle or its duration in any stage. It does not dictate marketing strategy. It is simply a tool to help marketers forecast future events and suggest appropriate strategies.

Introductory Stage

introductory stage
The full-scale launch of a new product into the marketplace.

The **introductory stage** of the product life cycle represents the full-scale launch of a new product into the marketplace. Computer databases for personal use, room-deodorizing air-conditioning filters, and wind-powered home electric generators are all product categories that have recently entered the product life cycle. A high failure rate, little competition, frequent product modification, and limited distribution typify the introduction stage of the PLC.

exhibit 9.3

Four Stages of the Product Life Cycle

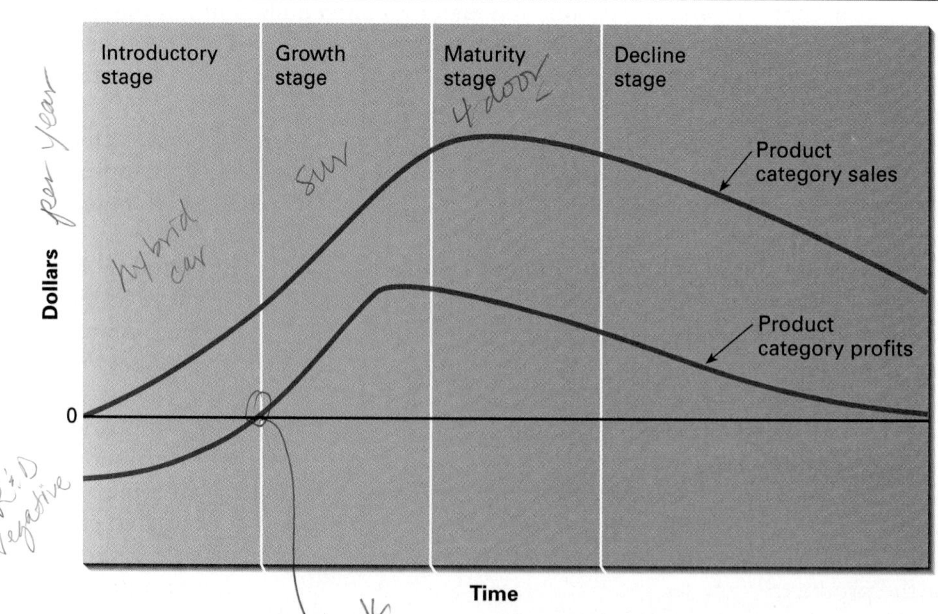

exhibit 9.4

Product Life Cycles for Styles, Fashions, and Fads

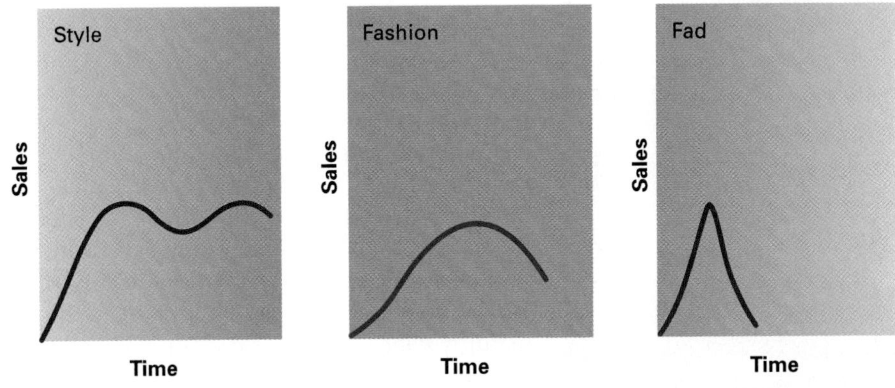

Marketing costs in the introductory stage are normally high for several reasons. High dealer margins are often needed to obtain adequate distribution, and incentives are needed to get consumers to try the new product. Advertising expenses are high because of the need to educate consumers about the new product's benefits. Production costs are also often high in this stage, as product and manufacturing flaws are identified and corrected and efforts are undertaken to develop mass-production economies.

As Exhibit 9.3 illustrates, sales normally increase slowly during the introductory stage. Moreover, profits are usually negative because of research and development costs, factory tooling, and high introduction costs. The length of the introductory phase is largely determined by product characteristics, such as the product's advantages over substitute products, the educational effort required to make the product known, and management's commitment of resources to the new item. A short introductory period is usually preferred to help reduce the impact of negative earnings and cash flows. As soon as the product gets off the ground, the financial burden should begin to diminish. Also, a short introduction helps dispel some of the uncertainty regarding whether or not the new product will be successful.

Promotion strategy in the introductory stage focuses on developing product awareness and informing consumers about the product category's potential benefits. At this stage, the communication challenge is to stimulate primary demand—demand for the product in general rather than for a specific brand. Intensive personal selling is often required to gain acceptance for the product among wholesalers and retailers. Promotion of convenience products often requires heavy consumer sampling and couponing. Shopping and specialty products demand educational advertising and personal selling to the final consumer.

Growth Stage

If a product category survives the introductory stage, it advances to the **growth stage** of the life cycle. In this stage, sales typically grow at an increasing rate, many competitors enter the market, and large companies may start to acquire small pioneering firms. Profits rise rapidly in the growth stage, reach their peak, and begin declining as competition intensifies. Emphasis switches from primary demand promotion (for example, promoting compact disc players) to aggressive brand advertising and communication of the differences between brands (for example, promoting Sony versus Panasonic and RCA).

growth stage
The second stage of the product life cycle when sales typically grow at an increasing rate, many competitors enter the market, large companies may start acquiring small pioneering firms, and profits are healthy.

Distribution becomes a major key to success during the growth stage, as well as in later stages. Manufacturers scramble to sign up dealers and distributors and to build long-term relationships. Without adequate distribution, it is impossible to establish a strong market position.

Coffee is an example of a product in the maturity stage where niche marketers have emerged. Starbucks, for example, targets its gourmet products at newer, younger, more affluent coffee drinkers.
© Vincent Dewitt/Stock Boston Inc./PNI

Maturity Stage

A period during which sales increase at a decreasing rate signals the beginning of the **maturity stage** of the life cycle. New users cannot be added indefinitely, and sooner or later the market approaches saturation. Normally, this is the longest stage of the product life cycle. Many major household appliances are in the maturity stage of their life cycles.

maturity stage
A period during which sales increase at a decreasing rate.

For shopping products and many specialty products, annual models begin to appear during the maturity stage. Product lines are lengthened to appeal to additional market segments. Service and repair assume more important roles as manufacturers strive to distinguish their products from others. Product design changes tend to become stylistic (How can the product be made different?) rather than functional (How can the product be made better?).

As prices and profits continue to fall, marginal competitors start dropping out of the market. Dealer margins also shrink, resulting in less shelf space for mature items, lower dealer inventories, and a general reluctance to promote the product. Thus promotion to dealers often intensifies during this stage, in order to retain loyalty.

Heavy consumer promotion by the manufacturer is also required to maintain market share. Consider these well-known examples of competition in the maturity stage: the so-called "cola war" featuring Coke and Pepsi, the "beer war" featuring Anheuser-Busch's Budweiser brands and Philip Morris's Miller brands, and the "burger wars" pitting leader McDonald's against challengers Burger King and Wendy's.

Another characteristic of the maturity stage is the emergence of so-called "niche marketers" that target narrow, well-defined, underserved segments of a market. Starbucks Coffee targets its gourmet line at the only segment of the coffee market that is growing: new, younger, more affluent coffee drinkers.

Decline Stage

decline stage
A long-run drop in sales.

A long-run drop in sales signals the beginning of the **decline stage**. The rate of decline is governed by how rapidly consumer tastes change or substitute products are adopted. Many convenience products and fad items lose their market overnight, leaving large inventories of unsold items, such as designer jeans. Others die more slowly, like citizen band (CB) radios, black-and-white console television sets, and nonelectronic wristwatches.

Music cassette tapes declined from 29 percent of all retail music sales in 1991 to 18 percent in 1997.[30] Retailers such as Tower and HMV reduced the space allocated to cassettes by 50 percent during this time period.

Is the music cassette dead? No! It is clearly in the decline stage but still represents $1.4 billion in annual sales.[31] Music cassettes are still quite profitable to some marketers that continue offering customers this option.

Some firms have developed successful strategies for marketing products in the decline stage of the product life cycle. They eliminate all nonessential marketing expenses and let sales decline as more and more customers discontinue purchasing the products. Eventually, the product is withdrawn from the market.

Implications for Marketing Management

The product life cycle concept encourages marketing managers to plan so they can take the initiative instead of reacting to past events. The product life cycle is espe-

Wendy's

Follow Wendy's advertisements from the first network commercials to present-day ads. How has Wendy's developed and promoted new products to successfully compete in the maturity stage?
http://www.wendys.com/the_ads/ads_frame.html

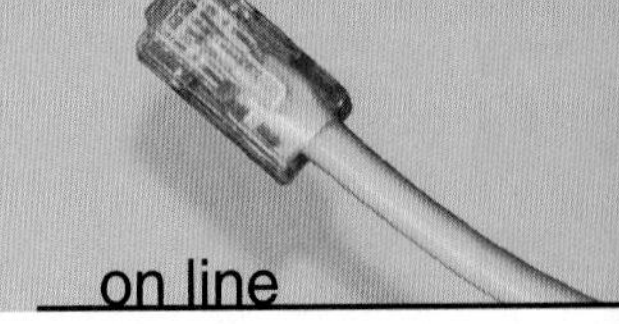

on line

Typical Marketing Strategies During the Product Life Cycle

exhibit 9.5

Marketing Mix Strategy	Product Life Cycle Stage			
	Introduction	Growth	Maturity	Decline
Product Strategy	Limited number of models; frequent product modifications	Expanded number of models; frequent product modifications	Large number of models	Elimination of unprofitable models and brands
Distribution Strategy	Distribution usually limited, depending on product; intensive efforts and high margins often needed to attract wholesalers and retailers	Expanded number of dealers; intensive efforts to establish long-term relationships with wholesalers and retailers	Extensive number of dealers; margins declining; intensive efforts to retain distributors and shelf space	Unprofitable outlets phased out
Promotion Strategy	Develop product awareness; stimulate primary demand; use intensive personal selling to distributors; use sampling and couponing for consumers	Stimulate selective demand; advertise brand aggressively	Stimulate selective demand; advertise brand aggressively; promote heavily to retain dealers and customers	Phase out all promotion
Pricing Strategy	Prices are usually high to recover development costs (see Chapter 20)	Prices begin to fall toward end of growth stage as result of competitive pressure	Prices continue to fall	Prices stabilize at relatively low level; small price rises are possible if competition is negligible

cially useful as a predicting or forecasting tool. Because products pass through distinctive stages, it is often possible to estimate a product's location on the curve using historical data. Profits, like sales, tend to follow a predictable path over a product's life cycle. Exhibit 9.5 briefly summarizes some typical marketing strategies during each stage of the product life cycle.

The Spread of New Products

Managers have a better chance of successfully marketing products if they understand how consumers learn about and adopt products. A person who buys a new product never before tried may ultimately become an **adopter**, a consumer who was happy enough with his or her trial experience with a product to use it again.

adopter
A consumer who was happy enough with his or her trial experience with a product to use it again.

Diffusion of Innovation

An **innovation** is a product perceived as new by a potential adopter. It really doesn't matter whether the product is "new to the world" or some other category of new product. If it is new to a potential adopter, it is an innovation in this context. **Diffusion** is the process by which the adoption of an innovation spreads.

4

Explain the diffusion process through which new products are adopted

3Com, Palm

Who do you think the adopters of PalmPilot organizers are? Read the "Customer Testimonials" on the 3Com Web site to help you decide who 3Com thinks are the innovators, the early majority, and the late majority. What other clues on the site can help you determine what kind of people are adopting PalmPilots?

http://www.palm.com/newspromo/index.html

on line

innovation
A product perceived as new by a potential adopter.

diffusion
The process by which the adoption of an innovation spreads.

Five categories of adopters participate in the diffusion process:

- *Innovators:* the first 2½ percent of all those who adopt the product. Innovators are eager to try new ideas and products, almost as an obsession. In addition to having higher incomes, they are more worldly and more active outside their community than noninnovators. They rely less on group norms and are more self-confident. Because they are well educated, they are more likely to get their information from scientific sources and experts. Innovators are characterized as being venturesome.
- *Early adopters:* the next 13½ percent to adopt the product. Although early adopters are not the very first, they do adopt early in the product's life cycle. Compared to innovators, they rely much more on group norms and values. They are also more oriented to the local community, in contrast to the innovator's worldly outlook. Early adopters are more likely than innovators to be opinion leaders because of their closer affiliation with groups. The respect of others is a dominant characteristic of early adopters.
- *Early majority:* the next 34 percent to adopt. The early majority weighs the pros and cons before adopting a new product. They are likely to collect more information and evaluate more brands than early adopters, therefore extending the adoption process. They rely on the group for information but are unlikely to be opinion leaders themselves. Instead, they tend to be opinion leaders' friends and neighbors. The early majority is an important link in the process of diffusing new ideas, because they are positioned between earlier and later adopters. A dominant characteristic of the early majority is deliberateness.
- *Late majority:* the next 34 percent to adopt. The late majority adopts a new product because most of their friends have already adopted it. Because they also rely on group norms, their adoption stems from pressure to conform. This group tends to be older and below average in income and education. They depend mainly on word-of-mouth communication rather than on the mass media. The dominant characteristic of the late majority is skepticism.
- *Laggards:* the final 16 percent to adopt. Like innovators, laggards do not rely on group norms. Their independence is rooted in their ties to tradition. Thus, the past heavily influences their decisions. By the time laggards adopt an innovation, it has probably been outmoded and replaced by something else. For example, they may have bought their first black-and-white TV set after color television was already widely diffused. Laggards have the longest adoption time and the lowest socioeconomic status. They tend to be suspicious of new products and alienated from a rapidly advancing society. The dominant value of laggards is tradition. Marketers typically ignore laggards, who do not seem to be motivated by advertising or personal selling.

Exhibit 9.6 illustrates the diffusion of several familiar products throughout the United States. Virtually every household is equipped with electricity, a range, a refrigerator, and a radio. Interestingly, a larger portion of U.S. households are now equipped with color televisions than with telephones. Note that some of these product categories may never be adopted by 100 percent of the population. The adopter categories refer to all of those who will eventually adopt a product, not the entire population.

Product Characteristics and the Rate of Adoption

Five product characteristics can be used to predict and explain the rate of acceptance and diffusion of a new product:

- *Complexity:* the degree of difficulty involved in understanding and using a new product. The more complex the product, the slower is its diffusion. For instance, before many of their functions were automated, 35mm cameras were

The Diffusion of Selected Products Within the United States **exhibit 9.6**

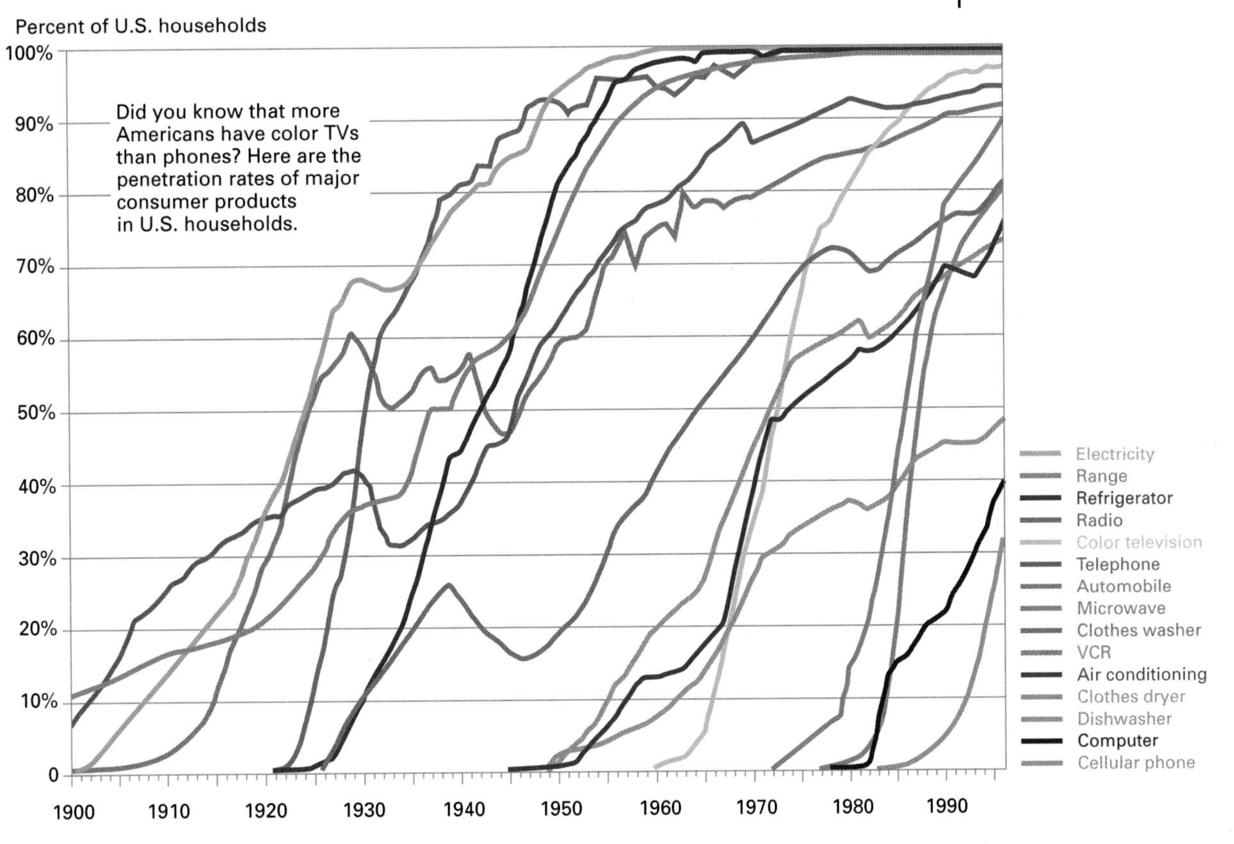

SOURCE: FORTUNE CHART/SOURCE: FEDERAL RESERVE BANK OF DALLAS. From *Fortune,* June 8, 1998, p. 64.

used primarily by hobbyists and professionals. They were just too complex for most people to learn to operate.

- *Compatibility:* the degree to which the new product is consistent with existing values and product knowledge, past experiences, and current needs. Incompatible products diffuse more slowly than compatible products. For example, the introduction of contraceptives is incompatible in countries where religious beliefs discourage the use of birth control techniques.
- *Relative advantage:* the degree to which a product is perceived as superior to existing substitutes. For example, because it reduces cooking time, the microwave oven has a clear relative advantage over a conventional oven.
- *Observability:* the degree to which the benefits or other results of using the product can be observed by others and communicated to target customers. For instance, fashion items and automobiles are highly visible and more observable than personal care items.
- *"Trialability":* the degree to which a product can be tried on a limited basis. It is much easier to try a new toothpaste or breakfast cereal than a new automobile or microcomputer. Demonstrations in showrooms and test drives are different from in-home trial use. To stimulate trials, marketers use free-sampling programs, tasting displays, and small package sizes.

Marketing Implications of the Adoption Process

Two types of communication aid the diffusion process: *word-of-mouth communication* among consumers and communication from marketers to consumers. Word-of-

exhibit 9.7

Relationship Between the Diffusion Process and the Product Life Cycle

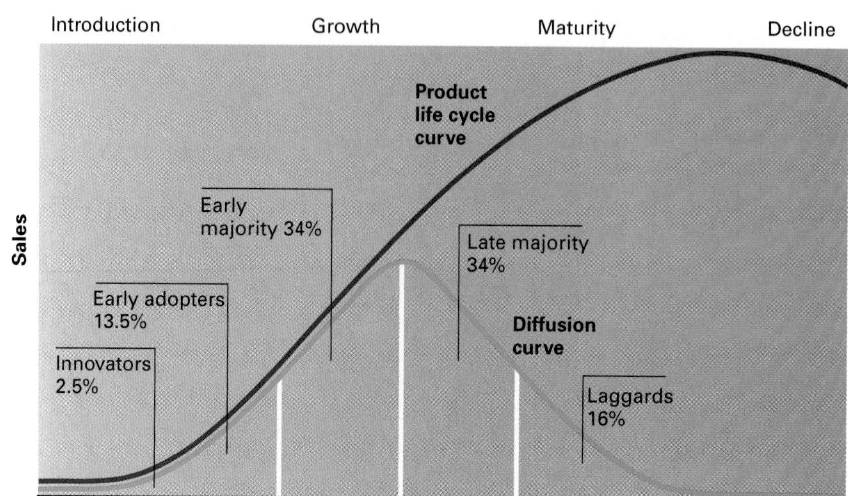

mouth communication within and across groups speeds diffusion. Opinion leaders discuss new products with their followers and with other opinion leaders. Marketers must therefore ensure that opinion leaders have the types of information desired in the media that they use. Suppliers of some products, such as professional and healthcare services, rely almost solely on word-of-mouth communication for new business.

The second type of communication aiding the diffusion process is *communication directly from the marketer to potential adopters.* Messages directed toward early adopters should normally use different appeals than messages directed toward the early majority, the late majority, or the laggards. Early adopters are more important than innovators because they make up a larger group, are more socially active, and are usually opinion leaders.

As the focus of a promotional campaign shifts from early adopters to the early majority and the late majority, marketers should study the dominant characteristics, buying behavior, and media characteristics of these target markets. Then they should revise messages and media strategy to fit. The diffusion model helps guide marketers in developing and implementing promotion strategy. Exhibit 9.7 shows the relationship between the adopter categories and stages of the product life cycle. Note that the various categories of adopters first buy products in different stages of the product life cycle. Almost all sales in the maturity and decline stages represent repeat purchasing.

LOOKING BACK

Look back at the story at the beginning of this chapter about the Advanced Photo System (APS). Sales of APS started slowly for several reasons. First, APS film cannot be used in 35mm cameras—a new 24mm camera is required. Demand for film was restricted by the lack of availability of cameras. Because manufacturers could not keep up with the demand for cameras, they did not advertise. Film processors also wanted to "wait-and-see" before investing the $200,000 necessary for equipment that develops APS film in one hour. The lack of convenient processing further deterred customers from buying the cameras. Second-year sales increased dramatically after a special team at Kodak was assigned the task of making APS a success. Armed with a $100 million marketing budget and pledges from Canon, Fuji, and Nikon to provide a sufficient supply of cameras, the team challenged retailers to support APS with advertising. Kodak also introduced APS training sessions for store clerks across the United States and began offering salespeople cash and prizes for selling

APS cameras. All of these efforts plus the effect of word-of-mouth among consumers have had a dramatic effect on sales.

Kodak hopes to profit mostly from the sales of Advantix film. It cannot be successful without cameras, film and camera retailers, and developers. Having the partner firms in place and prepared to aggressively market APS would have likely enhanced the first-year sales of film.

Summary

1 Explain the importance of developing new products and describe the six categories of new products. New products are important to sustain growth and profits and to replace obsolete items. New products can be classified as new-to-the-world products (discontinuous innovations), new product lines, additions to existing product lines, improvements or revisions of existing products, repositioned products, or lower-cost products. To sustain or increase profits, a firm must introduce at least one new successful product before a previous product advances to the maturity stage and profit levels begin to drop. Several factors make it more important than ever for firms to consistently introduce new products: shortened product life cycles, rapidly changing technology and consumer priorities, the high rate of new-product failures, and the length of time needed to implement new-product ideas.

2 Explain the steps in the new-product development process. First, a firm forms a new-product strategy by outlining the characteristics and roles of future products. Then new-product ideas are generated by customers, employees, distributors, competitors, and internal research and development personnel. Once a product idea has survived initial screening by an appointed screening group, it undergoes business analysis to determine its potential profitability. If a product concept seems viable, it progresses into the development phase, in which the technical and economic feasibility of the manufacturing process is evaluated. The development phase also includes laboratory and use testing of a product for performance and safety. Following initial testing and refinement, most products are introduced in a test market to evaluate consumer response and marketing strategies. Finally, test market successes are propelled into full commercialization. The commercialization process means starting up production, building inventories, shipping to distributors, training a sales force, announcing the product to the trade, and advertising to consumers.

3 Explain the concept of product life cycles. All product categories undergo a life cycle with four stages: introduction, growth, maturity, and decline. The rate at which products move through these stages varies dramatically. Marketing managers use the product life cycle concept as an analytical tool to forecast a product's future and devise effective marketing strategies.

4 Explain the diffusion process through which new products are adopted. The diffusion process is the spread of a new product from its producer to ultimate adopters. Adopters in the diffusion process belong to five categories: innovators, early adopters, the early majority, the late majority, and laggards. Product characteristics that affect the rate of adoption include product complexity, compatibility with existing social values, relative advantage over existing substitutes, visibility, and "trialability." The diffusion process is facilitated by word-of-mouth communication and communication from marketers to consumers.

Discussion and Writing Questions

1. Explain what the search, experience, and credence qualities are for medical services.

2. TEAM In small groups, brainstorm ideas for a new wet-weather clothing line. What type of product would potential customers want and need? Prepare and deliver a brief presentation to your class.

3. WRITING You are a marketing manager for Nike. Your department has come up with the idea of manufacturing a baseball bat for use in colleges around the nation. Assuming you are in the business analysis stage, write a brief analysis based on the questions in the "Business Analysis" section of the chapter.

4. What are the major disadvantages to test marketing and how might they be avoided?

5. Describe some products whose adoption rates have been affected by complexity, compatibility, relative advantage, observability, and/or "trialability."

6. What type of adopter behavior do you typically follow? Explain.

7. Place the personal computer on the product life cycle curve, and give reasons for placing it where you did.

8. ON LINE How could information from customer orders at the following site help the company's marketers plan new-product developments? **http://www.pizzahut.com**

9. ON LINE How is customer input affecting the development of Baked Lay's potato chips? **http://www.fritolay.com**

Application for Small Business

ENTREPRENEUR Joyce Strand went to the oven to remove the newest batch of beef jerky that she would later sell to the Frontenac Central Store. To her surprise, she had turned the oven up too high, and the beef jerky had dried to a crisp. Although the texture was much different, the jerky still had its unmistakable taste. Joyce decided to take it to the Central Store anyway and let the customers decide. The new snack became a huge success in the snack food section of the store. Because of her recent success, Joyce began experimenting with different tastes and textures of snack foods that she sells at the Central Store. Realizing that innovation can be very profitable, Joyce now actively looks for new ways to please her customers.

Questions

1. How might Joyce ensure that proper attention is paid to developing new products?
2. What factors should she be aware of that might lead to product failure?
3. Prepare a list of criteria similar to those in the "Entrepreneurial Insights" box in this chapter that might be used to evaluate Joyce's new-product ideas.

Review Quiz

1. Which of the following types of new products are best described as existing products targeted at new markets?
   a. Additions to existing product lines
   b. Improvements or revisions of existing products
   c. Repositioned products
   d. New product lines

Key Terms

adopter 301
brainstorming 292
business analysis 293
commercialization 297
concept test 293
decline stage 300
development 293
diffusion 302
growth stage 299
innovation 302
introductory stage 298
maturity stage 300
new product 288
new-product strategy 290
product category 298
product development 291
product life cycle 298
screening 292
simulated (laboratory) market testing 297
test marketing 295

2. Evaluation of a new-product idea before any prototype is created is known as

   a. Research and development
   b. A concept test
   c. Development
   d. Brainstorming

3. During which stage of the new-product development process are preliminary figures for costs, sales, and profits estimated?

   a. Idea screening
   b. Development
   c. Business analysis
   d. Test marketing

4. According to the diffusion process model, which of the following categories of adopters is the first group to accept a new product?

   a. Innovators
   b. Early adopters
   c. Early majority
   d. Laggards

5. Five characteristics affect the rate of acceptance of a new product. ________ is the degree to which a product is perceived as superior to existing substitutes.

   a. Compatability
   b. Relative advantage
   c. Complexity
   d. Trialability

6. In the ______ stage of the product life cycle, sales grow at an increasing rate, many competitors enter the market, and profits rise rapidly.

   a. Introduction
   b. Growth
   c. Maturity
   d. Decline

7. Primary demand promotion must occur during which of the following stages of the product life cycle?

   a. Introductory
   b. Growth
   c. Maturity
   d. Decline

8. The real purpose of using a formal new-product development process is to filter out unworkable product ideas.

   a. True
   b. False

9. The time a product spends in any one stage of the product life cycle does not typically vary from item to item.

   a. True
   b. False

10. Identify the six categories of new products.

Check the Answer Key, which follows the Video Case, to see how well you understood the material.

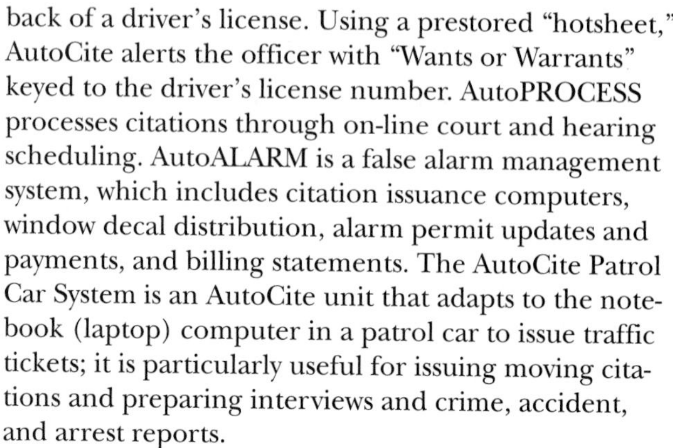

VIDEO CASE

AutoCite: Traffic Ticket and Parking Citation System

For decades, the writing of a ticket was only the first step in a long manual process. An officer dropped off the ticket at the station, and from there it went to the records department for sorting and batching. It was then transmitted to the judicial system and data processing. The handwritten information was keypunched into the mainframe and then returned for filing. At each step, tickets were flagged for errors, but mistakes regularly surfaced, resulting in an inefficient process.

This situation prompted companies such as Epson, Grid, Husky, Symbol, and Telxon to market general purpose, hand-held computers to police departments. But these devices required officers to wear a clumsy printer on their belts or strapped over their shoulders, and such computer configurations were not designed for citation management.

Enforcement Technology, Inc. (ETEC) recognized an unsatisfied need and set out to develop a new product that would deal the final blow to the bulky, inefficient computers. ETEC focused on developing a product so unique that once introduced, it would outdate the competition. The new product, called AutoCite, is a portable, lightweight, hand-held computer with a built-in printer, specialized for issuing traffic tickets and parking citations.

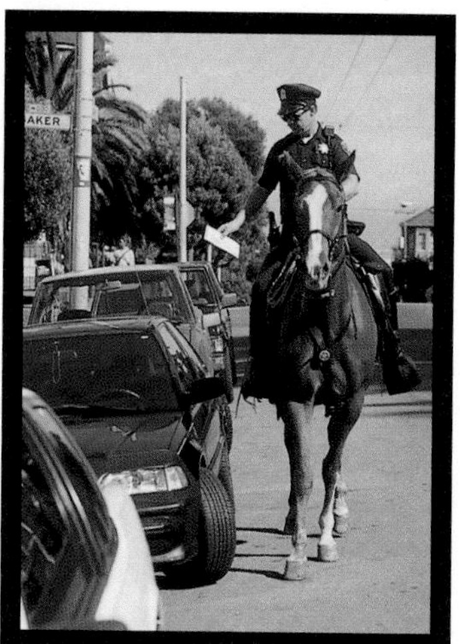

ETEC's new product strategy was to carve out a market niche through specialization. Competitors sold general purpose computers—hardware only, requiring customers to purchase obligatory software from other companies. To distinguish AutoCite from other brands, ETEC produced a complete package of hardware *and* software. In addition, ETEC provided product training and totally maintained AutoCite at every level. Customers found it highly convenient to look to a single supplier for both sales and service.

AutoCite's success encouraged ETEC to analyze other needs in the citation process and develop the technology to meet them. The result is a fully automated system of products that work in harmony. AutoCite is now updated to include a magnetic stripe and bar code reading capability so that information is entered automatically from the magnetic stripe on the back of a driver's license. Using a prestored "hotsheet," AutoCite alerts the officer with "Wants or Warrants" keyed to the driver's license number. AutoPROCESS processes citations through on-line court and hearing scheduling. AutoALARM is a false alarm management system, which includes citation issuance computers, window decal distribution, alarm permit updates and payments, and billing statements. The AutoCite Patrol Car System is an AutoCite unit that adapts to the notebook (laptop) computer in a patrol car to issue traffic tickets; it is particularly useful for issuing moving citations and preparing interviews and crime, accident, and arrest reports.

This product line is fully supported by ETEC's cash management and delinquent collection services. The company has parking enforcement centers to process in- and out-of-state tickets for their customers and has implemented a follow-up service to collect delinquent citations. But these services are only part of the benefits. Cities, universities, and agencies are saving money in processing costs and recovery of delinquent fines. In one year, ETEC collected $600,000 for the city of San Diego by taking a backlog of sixty thousand citations and going back as far as two years for collections. Now ETEC processes about three thousand delinquent out-of-state parking citations each month for roughly $50,000 in new revenue. With results like this, AutoCite can pay for itself within a year.

Revenue generation is complemented by an additional benefit: The use of AutoCite has been shown to reduce the indirect costs associated with low staff productivity. Data entry, which used to eat into staff and clerical time, is now a memory in departments and agencies. And the error rate is smaller. There's also an intangible benefit—better employee morale. In Long Beach, California, officers have been pleased with ETEC's reliable computers and high-quality customer service. Their increased efficiency has led to greater job satisfaction, which in turn has positively affected morale on the entire police force.

By creating a fully automated citation management process, ETEC has police departments and agencies in the United States and abroad singing its praises. Adopted by over three hundred agencies in the United States, over fifty colleges and universities, and agencies in eight foreign countries, the AutoCite full-service solution for citation management is well positioned to build on its resounding success.

Questions

1. Describe the product development process for AutoCite.
2. Why has AutoCite been successful?
3. How did ETEC develop the product line?
4. What strategy should ETEC follow in introducing new products for law enforcement?

Bibliography

Press Kit: Enforcement Technology, Inc.

Answer Key

1. *Answer:* c, p. 288

   Rationale: Repositioned products are those that are existing products targeted at new markets or market segments.

2. *Answer:* b, p. 293

   Rationale: A concept test evaluates a new-product idea before a prototype is created by gathering consumer reactions to descriptions and visual representations of a proposed product.

3. *Answer:* c, p. 293

   Rationale: Such figures are typically first calculated during business analysis. The newness of the product, the size of the market, and the nature of competition all affect the accuracy of these projections.

4. *Answer:* a, p. 302

   Rationale: Innovators are the most eager to try new products and are characterized as being venturesome.

5. *Answer:* b, p. 303

   Rationale: Relative advantage is the degree to which a new products is seen as having a clear advantage over existing products.

6. *Answer:* b, p. 299

   Rationale: Competition intensifies, sales grow rapidly, and profits grow to their peak during the growth stage of the product life cycle.

7. *Answer:* a, p. 298–299

   Rationale: Promotion expenses are often high in the introductory stage of the product life cycle because marketers must educate consumers about the new product's benefits.

8. *Answer:* a, p. 290

   Rationale: The new-product development process provides guidelines to the firm for generating, screening, and evaluating new-product ideas.

9. *Answer:* b, p. 298

   Rationale: The time a product spends in any single stage of the product life cycle may vary dramatically. Some products move through an entire cycle in weeks; others stay in a single stage for decades.

10. *Answer:*

    New-to-the-world products (discontinuous innovations)
    New product lines
    Additions to existing product lines
    Improvements of existing products
    Repositioned products
    Lower-priced products

    (pp. 288–289)

CHAPTER

10

LEARNING OBJECTIVES

After studying this chapter, you should be able to

1 Explain what a marketing channel is and why intermediaries are needed

2 Define the types of channel intermediaries and describe their functions and activities

3 Describe the channel structures for consumer and business-to-business products and discuss alternative channel arrangements

4 Discuss the issues that influence channel strategy

5 Explain channel leadership, conflict, and partnering

6 Discuss logistics and supply chain management and their evolution into distribution practice

7 Discuss the concept of balancing logistics service and cost

8 Describe the integrated functions of the supply chain

9 Discuss new technology and emerging trends in logistics

10 Identify the special problems and opportunities associated with distribution in service organizations

11 Discuss channel structure and logistics issues in global markets

MARKETING CHANNELS AND LOGISTICS DECISIONS

Shell Oil Products, a division of Shell Oil Company, used to buy all of its personal computers from Compaq Computers or IBM. In 1997, however, it switched its allegiance and its \$26 million in annual PC purchases to Austin-based Dell Computer. The reason had less to do with the computers than the way Dell sells them. Unlike Compaq and IBM, Dell sells directly to customers, eliminating distributors and resellers who bring up the price and lengthen the time it takes to get the hardware. On top of that, Dell only sells custom-made machines built to the customer's exact specifications. Its competitors build machines first and then wait for customers to order a particular model.

Dell Computer, which began as a mail-order company started out of founder Michael Dell's University of Texas dorm room, deploys a direct sales force to cut out the retailers, specialty stores, and distributors who can drive prices up. The success of Dell's marketing model—selling through direct sales channels, building custom-made PCs, and streamlining the distribution process—is well known and amply reflected in its stock price. Since 1990, Dell stock has increased by 29,600 percent! Today, the \$13 billion company is the world's biggest direct seller of computers.

To really understand Dell's eye-popping growth, you need only to look at how fully it exploits the model of selling custom-made machines directly to buyers. First, Dell has no finished inventory because PCs are built on demand. As soon as a computer is built it is immediately shipped off to the customer. The whole process from phone call to loading onto a delivery truck takes just thirty-six hours. Orders are instantly relayed to one of Dell's three plants in Austin, Malaysia, or Ireland. After the order is received, a Dell PC can be custom-built to the customer's exact specifications, software installed, tested, and packed in eight hours.

Second, Dell can ship machines with the latest high-margin components. Because it employs close relationships with component suppliers like Intel for chips and Maxtor for hard drives, these components arrive just in time to be installed in its machines, virtually eliminating any raw materials stockpiling that can quickly become obsolete in the fast-changing computer industry. This saves money, too, because component prices tend to fall many times throughout the year.

on line

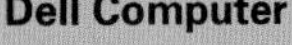

Dell Computer

Visit Dell Computer's Web site. How is the site set up to sell in marketing channels directly to the customer?
http://www.dell.com/

Third, unlike IBM and Compaq, who use resellers to sell their PCs, Dell has direct contact with its customers. If customers start requesting an 8.4-gigabyte drive, Dell knows immediately what consumers are asking for and can make split-second procurement decisions. Additionally, knowing their customers personally gives Dell considerable leverage the next time customers have hardware needs or want to upgrade their entire stock of computers. Fourth, selling directly means that Dell isn't getting paid by resellers but by large corporations such as Boeing, Ford, and Shell Oil. Not surprisingly, Dell receivables have a great credit rating—Dell typically has its money in the bank before the computer is even built.

ON LINE

Dell's latest drive is boosting sales over the Internet, the ultimate direct channel. The company is already the biggest on-line seller of computers, selling more than $6 million in computers a day from its Web site. Dell has also become one of the first personal computer suppliers in China to conduct electronic commerce through its virtual store on the Internet.

Compaq and IBM are dabbling in direct sales, but risk losing relationships with dealers if they go too far. Compaq and IBM depend on resellers for 90 percent of their sales, and resellers can easily retaliate if a supplier gets too aggressive with selling direct. Giving in to this reality, Compaq and IBM have been trying to make their three-step distribution process—manufacturer to distributor to reseller to customer—work as efficiently as the one-step model that Dell uses. Both have enlisted distributors to do part of the assembly of their computers as a way to lower costs. Distributors can also assemble customized PCs based on what customers want, as Dell does. However, because they must still pay dealers, they must either charge slightly more or accept lower profit margins.[1]

What advantages does Dell receive from selling in marketing channels directly to the customer? Could Compaq or IBM expand their use of direct channels as did Dell without alienating their current network of resellers? What areas of distribution, such as inventory, materials handling, or transportation, could be streamlined to help Dell's competitors compete more effectively? Similar questions will be addressed throughout the chapter discussion on marketing channels and logistics.

Marketing Channels

1
Explain what a marketing channel is and why intermediaries are needed

The term *channel* is derived from the Latin word *canalis,* which means canal. A marketing channel can be viewed as a large canal or pipeline through which products, their ownership, communication, financing and payment, and accompanying risk flow to the consumer. Formally, a **marketing channel** (also called a **channel of distribution**) is a business structure of interdependent organizations that reach from the point of product origin to the consumer with the purpose of moving products to their final consumption destination.

marketing channel (channel of distribution)
Set of interdependent organizations that ease the transfer of ownership as products move from producer to business user or consumer.

Many different types of organizations participate in marketing channels. **Channel members** (also called intermediaries, resellers, and middlemen) negotiate with one another, buy and sell products, and facilitate the change of ownership between buyer and seller in the course of moving the product from the manufacturer into the hands of the final consumer. As products move through the marketing channel, channel members provide economies to the distribution process in the form of specialization and division of labor, overcoming discrepancies, and contact efficiency.

channel members
All parties in the marketing channel that negotiate with one another, buy and sell products, and facilitate the change of ownership between buyer and seller in the course of moving the product from the manufacturer into the hands of the final consumer.

Providing Specialization and Division of Labor

According to the concept of specialization and division of labor, breaking down a complex task into smaller, simpler ones and allocating them to specialists will create greater efficiency and lower average production costs. Manufacturers achieve economies of scale through the use of efficient equipment capable of producing large quantities of a single product.

Marketing channels can also attain economies of scale through specialization and division of labor by aiding producers who lack the motivation, financing, or expertise to market directly to end users or consumers. In some cases, as with most consumer convenience goods such as soft drinks, the cost of marketing directly to millions of consumers—taking and shipping individual orders—is prohibitive. For this reason, producers hire channel members such as wholesalers and retailers to do what the producers are not equipped to do or what channel members are better prepared to do. Channel members can do some things more efficiently than producers because they have built good relationships with their customers. Therefore, their specialized expertise enhances the overall performance of the channel.

Overcoming Discrepancies

Marketing channels also aid in overcoming discrepancies of quantity, assortment, time, and space created by economies of scale in production. For example, assume that Pillsbury can efficiently produce its Hungry Jack instant pancake mix only at a rate of five thousand units in a typical day. Not even the most ardent pancake fan could consume that amount in a year, much less in a day. The quantity produced to achieve low unit costs has created a **discrepancy of quantity**, which is the difference between the amount of product produced and the amount an end user wants to buy. By storing the product and distributing it in the appropriate amounts, marketing channels overcome quantity discrepancies by making products available in the quantities that consumers desire.

discrepancy of quantity
Difference between the amount of product produced and the amount a customer wants to buy.

Mass production creates not only discrepancies of quantity but also discrepancies of assortment. A **discrepancy of assortment** occurs when a consumer does not have all of the items needed to receive full satisfaction from a product. For pancakes to have maximum satisfaction, several other products are required to complete the assortment. At the very least, most people want a knife, fork, plate, butter, and syrup. Others might add orange juice, coffee, cream, sugar, eggs, and bacon or sausage. Although Pillsbury is a large consumer products company, it does not come close to providing the optimal assortment to go with its Hungry Jack pancakes. To overcome discrepancies of assortment, marketing channels assemble in one place many of the products necessary to complete a consumer's needed assortment.

discrepancy of assortment
Lack of all the items a customer needs to receive full satisfaction from a product or products.

A **temporal discrepancy** is created when a product is produced but a consumer is not ready to buy it. Marketing channels overcome temporal discrepancies by maintaining inventories in anticipation of demand. For example, manufacturers of seasonal merchandise such as Christmas decorations are in operation all year, even though consumer demand is concentrated during certain months of the year.

temporal discrepancy
Difference between when a product is produced and when a customer is ready to buy it.

spatial discrepancy
Difference between the location of the producer and the location of widely scattered markets.

Furthermore, because mass production requires many potential buyers, markets are usually scattered over large geographic regions, creating a **spatial discrepancy**. Often, global or at least nationwide markets are needed to absorb the outputs of mass producers. Marketing channels overcome spatial discrepancies by making products available in locations convenient to consumers. For example, automobile manufacturers overcome spatial discrepancies by franchising dealerships close to consumers.

Providing Contact Efficiency

The third need fulfilled by marketing channels is a way to overcome contact inefficiency. Consider your extra costs if supermarkets, department stores, and shopping centers or malls did not exist. Suppose you had to buy your milk at a dairy and your meat at a stockyard. Imagine buying your eggs and chicken at a hatchery and your fruits and vegetables at various farms. You would spend a great deal of time, money, and energy just shopping for a few groceries. Channels simplify distribution by cutting the number of transactions required to get products from manufacturers to consumers and making an assortment of goods available in one location.

Consider another example, which is illustrated in Exhibit 10.1. Four students in your class each want to buy a television set. Without a retail intermediary like Circuit City, television manufacturers Magnavox, Zenith, Sony, Toshiba, and RCA would each have to make four contacts to reach the four buyers who are in the target market, totaling twenty transactions. However, each producer only has to make one contact when Circuit City acts as an intermediary between the producer and consumers, reducing the number of transactions to nine. Each producer sells to one retailer rather than to four consumers. In turn, your classmates buy from one retailer instead of from five producers.

exhibit 10.1 | How Marketing Channels Reduce the Number of Required Transactions

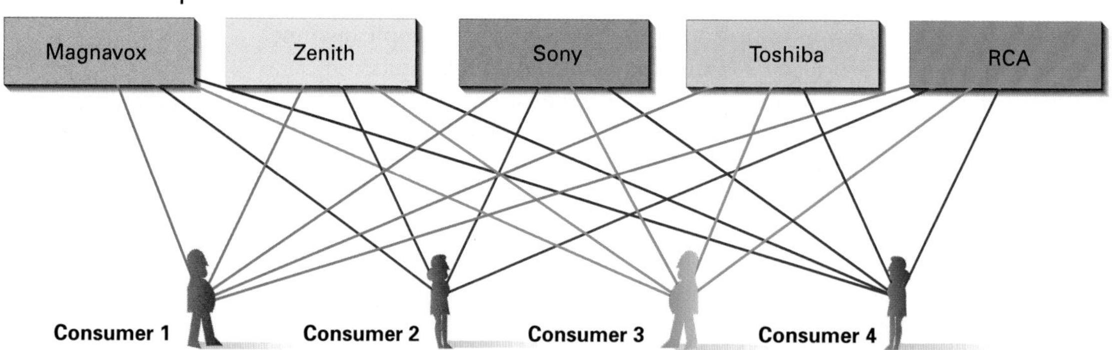

Without an intermediary: 5 producers x 4 consumers = 20 transactions

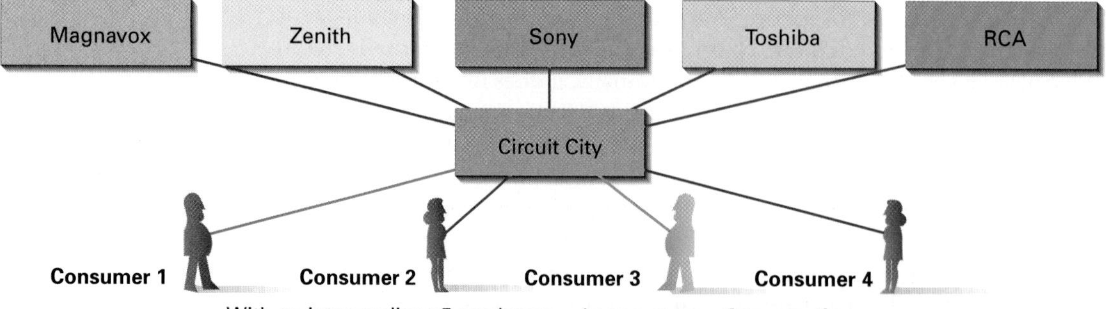

With an intermediary: 5 producers + 4 consumers = 9 transactions

This simple example illustrates the concept of contact efficiency. U.S. manufacturers sell to millions of individuals and families. Using channel intermediaries greatly reduces the number of required contacts. As a result, producers are able to offer their products cost effectively and efficiently to consumers all over the world.

Channel Intermediaries and Their Functions

As you have just learned, a marketing channel provides countless efficiencies in bringing a product to the consumer through the use of other channel members. Next, we will discuss who these channel intermediaries are and the specific functions they provide.

Types of Channel Intermediaries

2

Define the types of channel intermediaries and describe their functions and activities

Intermediaries in a channel negotiate with one another, facilitate the change of ownership between buyers and sellers, and physically move products from the manufacturer to the final consumer. The most prominent difference separating intermediaries is whether or not they take title to the product. Taking title means they own the merchandise and control the terms of the sale—for example, price and delivery date. Retailers and merchant wholesalers are examples of intermediaries who take title to products in the marketing channel and resell them. **Retailers** are firms that sell mainly to consumers. Retailers will be discussed in more detail in Chapter 11.

retailer
Channel intermediary that sells mainly to consumers.

Merchant wholesalers are organizations that facilitate the movement of products and services from the manufacturer to producers, resellers, governments, institutions, and retailers. All merchant wholesalers take title to the goods they sell. Most merchant wholesalers operate one or more warehouses in which they receive goods, store them, and later reship them. Customers are mostly small- or moderate-size retailers, but merchant wholesalers also market to manufacturers and institutional clients.

merchant wholesaler
Institution that buys goods from manufacturers and resells them to businesses, government agencies, and other wholesalers or retailers and that receives and takes title to goods, stores them in its own warehouses, and later ships them.

Other intermediaries do not take title to goods and services they market but do facilitate the exchange of ownership between sellers and buyers. **Agents and brokers** simply facilitate the sale of a product from producer to end user by representing retailers, wholesalers, or manufacturers. Title reflects ownership, and ownership usually implies control. Unlike wholesalers, agents or brokers only facilitate sales and generally have little input into the terms of the sale. They do, however, get a fee or commission based on sales volume.

agents and brokers
Wholesaling intermediaries who facilitate the sale of a product from producer to end user by representing retailers, wholesalers, or manufacturers and do not take title to the product.

Variations in channel structures are due in large part to variations in the numbers and types of wholesaling intermediaries. Generally, product characteristics, buyer considerations, and market conditions determine which type of intermediary the manufacturer should use. Product characteristics that may dictate a certain type of wholesaling intermediary include whether the product is standardized or customized, the complexity of the product, and the gross margin of the product. Buyer considerations affecting wholesaler choice include how often the product is purchased and how long the buyer is willing to wait to receive the product. Market characteristics determining wholesaler type include how many buyers are in the market and whether they are concentrated in a general location or are widely dispersed. Exhibit 10.2 shows these determining factors. A manufacturer that produces only a few engines a year for space rockets will probably use an agent or broker to sell its product. In addition, the handful of customers that need the product are most likely concentrated near rocket launching sites, again making an agent or broker more practical. On the other hand, a book publisher that prints thousands of books and has many widely dispersed customers with year-round demand for its product will probably use a merchant wholesaler.

exhibit 10.2

Factors Suggesting the Type of Wholesaling Intermediary to Use

Factor	Merchant Wholesalers	Agents or Brokers
Nature of Product	Standard	Nonstandard, custom
Technicality of Product	Complex	Simple
Product's Gross Margin	High	Low
Frequency of Ordering	Frequent	Infrequent
Time Between Order and Receipt of Shipment	Buyer desires shorter lead time	Buyer satisfied with long lead time
Number of Customers	Many	Few
Concentration of Customers	Dispersed	Concentrated

SOURCE: Reprinted from *Industrial Marketing Management*, February 1989, Donald M. Jackson and Michael F. D'Amico, "Products and Markets Served by Distributors and Agents," pp. 27–33. Copyright 1989, with permission from Elsevier Science.

Channel Functions Performed by Intermediaries

Retailing and wholesaling intermediaries in marketing channels perform several essential functions that make the flow of goods between producer and buyer possible. The three basic functions that intermediaries perform are summarized in Exhibit 10.3.

Transactional functions involve contacting and communicating with prospective buyers to make them aware of existing products and explain their features, advantages, and benefits. *Logistical* functions include transporting, storing, sorting out, accumulating, allocating, and assorting products into either homogeneous or heterogeneous collections. For example, grading agricultural products typifies the sorting-out process whereas consolidation of many lots of grade A eggs from different sources into one lot illustrates the accumulation process. Supermarkets or other retailers perform the assorting function by assembling thousands of different items that match their customers' desires.

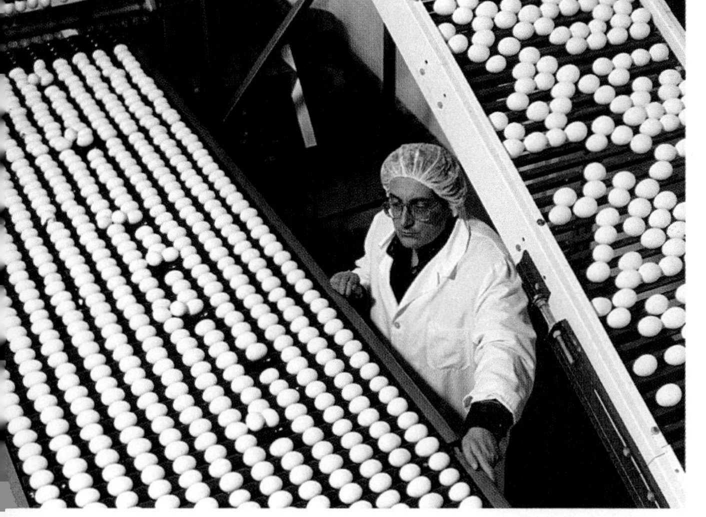

The agricultural process of grading is a logistical function. This heterogeneous collection of eggs is being sorted into separate homogeneous groupings that meet the different needs of supermarkets and other retailers.
© Corbis/Layne Kennedy

The third basic channel function, *facilitating*, includes research and financing. Research provides information about channel members and consumers by getting answers to questions such as Who are the buyers?, Where are they located?, and Why do they buy? Financing ensures that channel members have the money to keep products moving through the channel to the ultimate consumer.

A single company may provide one, two, or all three functions. Consider Kramer Beverage Company, a Coors beer distributor. As a beer distributor, it provides transactional, logistical, and facilitating channel functions. Kramer sales representatives contact local bars and restaurants to negotiate the terms of the sale, possibly giving the customer a discount for large purchases, and to make arrange-

exhibit 10.3

Marketing Channel Functions Performed by Intermediaries

Type of Function	Description
Transactional Functions	**Contacting and promoting:** Contacting potential customers, promoting products, and soliciting orders **Negotiating:** Determining how many goods or services to buy and sell, type of transportation to use, when to deliver, and method and timing of payment **Risk taking:** Assuming the risk of owning inventory
Logistical Functions	**Physically distributing:** Transporting and sorting goods to overcome temporal and spatial discrepancies **Storing:** Maintaining inventories and protecting goods **Sorting:** Overcoming discrepancies of quantity and assortment by *Sorting out:* Breaking down a heterogeneous supply into separate homogeneous stocks *Accumulation:* Combining similar stocks into a larger homogeneous supply *Allocation:* Breaking a homogeneous supply into smaller and smaller lots ("breaking bulk") *Assortment:* Combining products into collections or assortments that buyers want available at one place
Facilitating Function	**Researching:** Gathering information about other channel members and consumers **Financing:** Extending credit and other financial services to facilitate the flow of goods through the channel to the final consumer

ments for when the beer will be delivered. At the same time, Kramer also provides a facilitating function by extending credit to the customer. Meanwhile, Kramer merchandising representatives assist in promoting the beer on a local level by hanging Coors beer signs and posters. Kramer also provides logistical functions by accumulating the many types of Coors beer from the Coors manufacturing plant in Golden, Colorado, and storing them in its refrigerated warehouse. When an order needs to be filled, Kramer then sorts the beer into heterogeneous collections for each particular customer. For example, the local Chili's Grill & Bar may need two kegs of Coors, three kegs of Coors Light, and two cases of Killian's Red in bottles. The beer will be loaded onto a refrigerated truck and transported to the restaurant. The Kramer delivery person will transport the kegs and cases of beer into the restaurant's refrigerator and may also restock the coolers behind the bar.

Although individual members can be added to or deleted from a channel, someone must still perform these essential functions. They can be performed by producers, end users or consumers, channel intermediaries such as wholesalers and retailers, and sometimes nonmember channel participants. For example, if a manufacturer decides to eliminate its private fleet of trucks, it must still have a way to move the goods to the wholesaler. This task may be accomplished by the wholesaler, which may have its own fleet of trucks, or by a nonmember channel participant such as an independent trucking firm. Nonmembers also provide many other essential functions that may have at one time been provided by a channel member. Research firms may perform the research function; advertising agencies, the promotion function; transportation and storage firms, the physical distribution function; and banks, the financing function.

What kind of marketing channel functions can be performed over the Internet? Why do you think so?

Channel Structures

3
Describe the channel structures for consumer and business-to-business products and discuss alternative channel arrangements

A product can take many routes to reach its consumer. Marketers search for the most efficient channel from the many alternatives available. Marketing a consumer convenience good like gum or candy differs from marketing a specialty good like a Mercedes-Benz. The two products require much different distribution channels. Likewise, the appropriate channel for a major equipment supplier like Boeing Aircraft would be unsuitable for an accessory equipment producer like Black & Decker. To illustrate the differences in typical marketing channels for consumer and business-to-business products like these, the next sections discuss the structures of marketing channels for each product type. Alternative channel structures are also discussed.

Channels for Consumer Products

direct channel
Distribution channel in which producers sell directly to consumers.

Exhibit 10.4 illustrates the four ways manufacturers can route products to consumers. Producers use the **direct channel** to sell directly to consumers. Direct marketing activities—including telemarketing, mail-order and catalog shopping, and forms of electronic retailing like on-line shopping and shop-at-home television networks—are a good example of this type of channel structure. Home computer users can purchase Dell computers directly over the telephone or directly from Dell's Internet Web site. There are no intermediaries. Producer-owned stores and factory outlet stores—like Sherwin-Williams, Polo/Ralph Lauren, Oneida, and West Point Pepperel—are other examples of direct channels. Farmers' markets are also direct channels. Direct marketing and factory outlets are discussed in more detail in Chapter 11.

exhibit 10.4 | Marketing Channels for Consumer Products

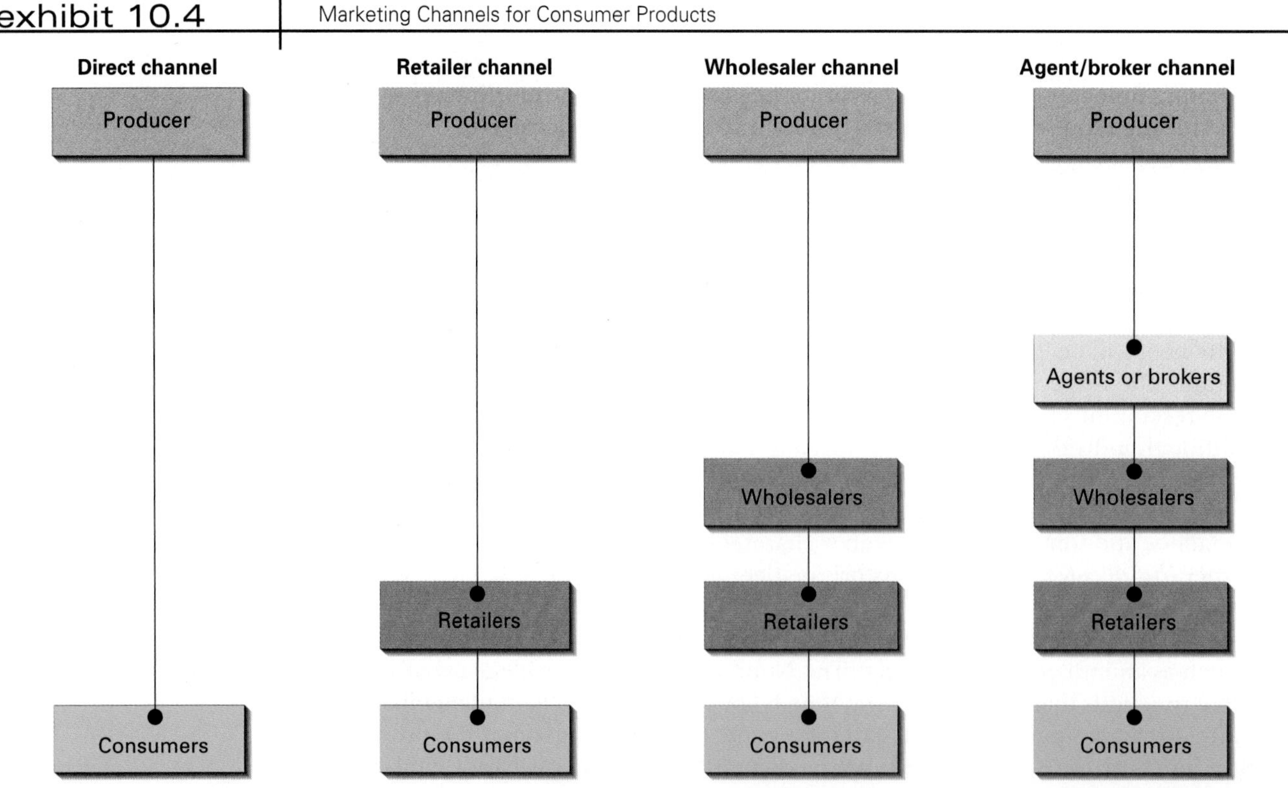

Oneida Limited

Visit Oneida's home page to see how and where it sells its products. Are there different channels for its consumer products and its business products?
http://www.oneida.com

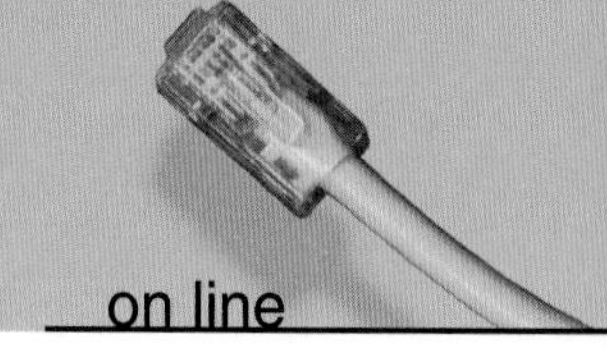

At the other end of the spectrum, *agent/broker channels* involve a fairly complicated process. Agent/broker channels are typically used in markets with many small manufacturers and many retailers that lack the resources to find each other. Agents or brokers bring manufacturers and wholesalers together for negotiations, but do not take title to merchandise. Ownership passes directly to one or more wholesalers and then to retailers. Finally, retailers sell to the ultimate consumer of the product. A food broker represents buyers and sellers of grocery products. The broker acts on behalf of many different producers and negotiates the sale of their products to wholesalers that specialize in foodstuffs. These wholesalers in turn sell to grocers and convenience stores.

Most consumer products are sold through distribution channels similar to the other two alternatives: the retailer channel and the wholesaler channel. A *retailer channel* is most common when the retailer is large and can buy in large quantities directly from the manufacturer. Wal-Mart, Sears, and car dealers are examples of retailers that often bypass a wholesaler. A *wholesaler channel* is often used for low-cost items that are purchased frequently, such as candy, cigarettes, and magazines. For example, M&M/Mars sells candies and chocolates to wholesalers in large quantities. The wholesalers then break these quantities into smaller quantities to satisfy individual retailer orders.

Channels for Business-to-Business and Industrial Products

As Exhibit 10.5 illustrates, five channel structures are common in business-to-business and industrial markets. First, direct channels are typical in business-to-business and industrial markets. Manufacturers buy large quantities of raw materials, major equipment, processed materials, and supplies directly from other manufacturers. Manufacturers that require suppliers to meet detailed technical specifications often prefer direct channels. The direct communication required between Chrysler and its suppliers, for example, along with the tremendous size of the orders, makes anything but a direct channel impractical. The channel from producer to government buyers is also a direct channel. Because much of government buying is done through bidding, a direct channel is attractive. Dell Computer Corporation, for example, is the top seller of desktop computers to federal, state, and local government agencies in the United States, to whom it sells through direct channels.[2]

Companies selling standardized items of moderate or low value often rely on *industrial distributors.* In many ways, an industrial distributor is like a supermarket for organizations. Industrial distributors are wholesalers and channel members that buy and take title to products. Moreover, they usually keep inventories of their products and sell and service them. Often small manufacturers cannot afford to employ their own sales force. Instead, they rely on manufacturers' representatives or selling agents to sell to either industrial distributors or users.

Alternative Channel Arrangements

Rarely does a producer use just one type of channel to move its product. It usually employs several different or alternative channels, which include multiple channels, nontraditional channels, adaptive channels, and strategic channel alliances.

Multiple Channels When a producer selects two or more channels to distribute the same product to target markets, this arrangement is called **dual distribution** (or **multiple distribution**). Whirlpool sells its washers, dryers, and refrigerators directly to home and apartment builders and contractors, but it also sells these same appliances to retail stores that sell to consumers. J. Crew, which has traditionally used direct-mail channels, has now opened retail and outlet stores. Multiple channels may also be employed by producers with unique second brands. For example, the Walt Disney Company routinely releases first-run animated films to movie

dual distribution (multiple distribution)
Use of two or more channels to distribute the same product to target markets.

exhibit 10.5 Channels for Business-to-Business and Industrial Products

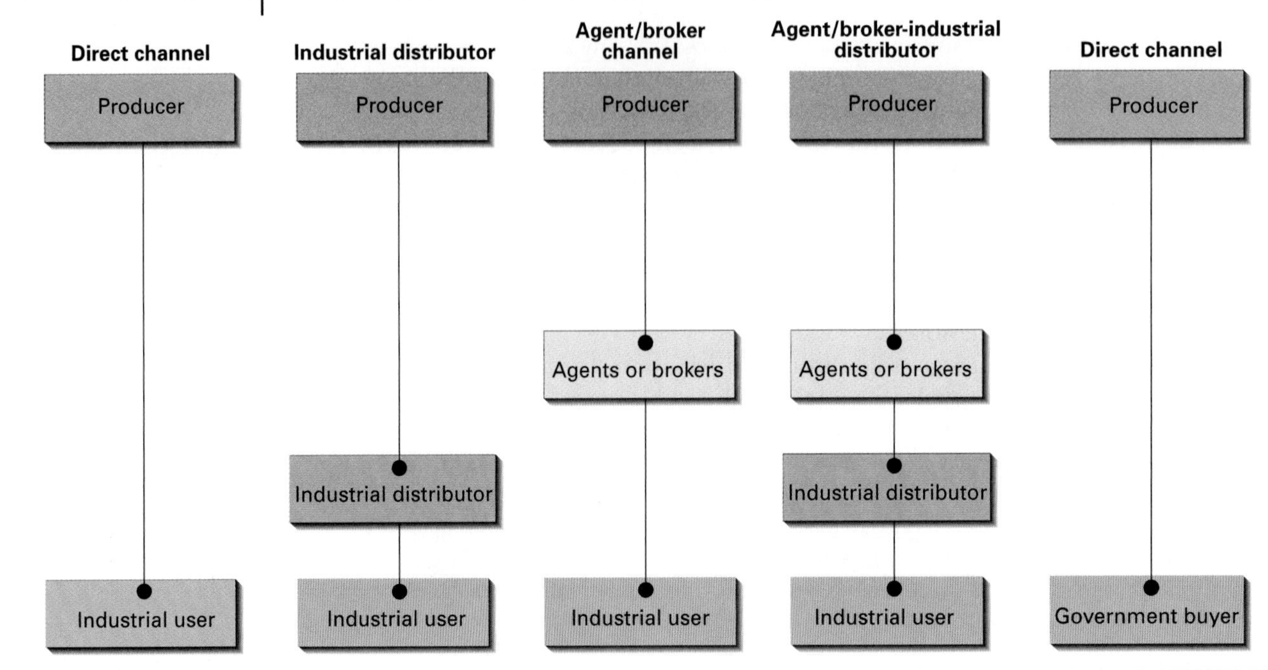

theaters and then releases a sequel directly to the home-video market. Such sequels as *Aladdin and the King of Thieves* and *Pocahontas: Journey to a New World* follow up its theater blockbusters. Similarly, computer maker Gateway, which has traditionally sold PCs to consumers who ordered them over the telephone and the Internet, has forged new dealer channels to reach the business market through a program called Gateway Partners. The company has also opened over forty retail stores across the United States in which customers can purchase custom-built systems.[3]

Nontraditional Channels Nontraditional channel arrangements often help differentiate a firm's product from the competition. Manufacturers may decide to use nontraditional channels such as the Internet, mail-order channels, or infomercials to sell its products instead of going through traditional retailer channels. Although nontraditional channels may limit a brand's coverage, they can give a producer serving a niche market a way to gain market access and customer attention without having to establish channel intermediaries. Nontraditional channels can also provide another avenue of sales for larger firms. For example, students can now purchase fast food from Taco Bell, Pizza Hut, and Subway Sandwiches & Salads in many public school cafeterias across the country. Fast-food giant Pizza Hut delivers pizzas ready-made to schools and also sells frozen pizza-making kits to school cafeterias, sending out trainers to teach cafeteria workers how to make the pizzas.[4] Similarly, many Wal-Mart stores now let customers order McDonald's burgers and fries as they check out. The order is sent from Wal-Mart's cash register to the McDonald's kitchen located within the store. The food is then whisked up to the departing customer. McDonald's is also expanding its partnership with Walt Disney to build kiosks to sell its famous french fries in Disney World's Frontierland.[5]

Consumers looking for a new car can now purchase one over the Internet. Read about how entrepreneurial companies are transforming the way cars are sold in the "Entrepreneurial Insights" box.

Adaptive Channels Many companies today are realizing that they do not have the capability to completely serve their customers in all situations. Innovative channel members have come to recognize that by sharing their resources with

Autobytel.com
CarPoint
Visit Autobytel.com and CarPoint to see what advantages they have over traditional car lots. If you were in the market for a new or used car, would you use an Internet broker? Why or why not?
http://www.autobytel.com/ **http://carpoint.msn.com/**

on line

others in their channel, they can take advantage of profit-making opportunities. This concept of a flexible and responsive channel of distribution is called an **adaptive channel**. Adaptive channels are initiated when a firm identifies critical but rare customer requirements that they do not have the capability to fulfill. Once these requirements are identified, the firm can make arrangements with other channel members to help satisfy these requests. One such firm utilizing the adaptive channel concept is Volvo GM. Volvo was having problems getting replacement parts where needed for emergency roadside repairs, even though its inventory levels were quite high. To overcome this problem, Volvo united with

adaptive channel
An alternative channel initiated when a firm identifies critical but rare customer requirements that they do not have the capability to fulfill.

entrepreneurial insights

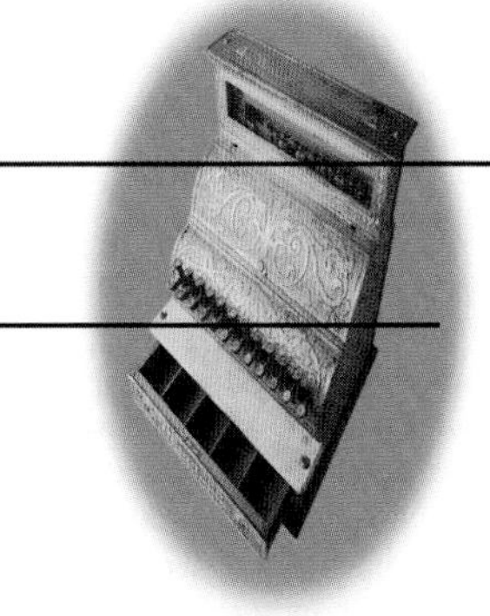

The Internet Shakes Up Traditional Car-Buying Channels

Is traditional car buying as we know it about to end? Savvy customers in the United States and Australia can now purchase a car over the Internet without ever haggling with a car salesperson and visit a dealership only to pick up the keys and the car. Some can even get the car delivered to their door without ever stepping foot inside a dealership.

Already, millions of American car buyers use the Internet for research. According to J.D. Power and Associates, 25 percent of all new vehicle buyers in the United States are using the Internet for vehicle product and pricing information. This number is expected to jump to 50 percent by 2000. Now, Internet car brokers like Autobytel.com and Microsoft's CarPoint allow car buyers to go the next step: securing financing and completing the purchase of a new car on-line. The highest volume car brokerage services estimate that their sites generate over seven hundred thousand new car sales annually, or about 4.6 percent of the total fifteen million+ new vehicles sold annually in the United States. Autobytel.com was recently ranked as one of the fastest growing small businesses in the United States by *Entrepreneur* magazine and Dun & Bradstreet.

Here's how the Internet sale works: Car buyers can browse Autobytel.com's site (**www.autobytel.com**) to find the precise make of car they desire, read on-line reviews, and compare models. Once a customer chooses a make and model, he or she fills out a form on the Autobytel.com Web site, including a postal code. Financing or leasing and insurance can also be arranged at the Web site. The information is automatically routed to the closest Autobytel.com-accredited dealer. After getting the purchase order, the dealer calls or e-mails the customer within forty-eight hours to confirm the exact features wanted. Later, the dealer calls back the customer with a price. The price quoted starts with the dealer's invoice rather than the sticker price used by showroom salespeople. After a price is finalized, the customer drops by the dealer to pick up the new car.

Internet brokers appeal to many consumers who are frustrated with the traditional horse-trading, time-wasting, and ritual haggling that have been part of the car industry since the Model T. The lure of buying a car over the Internet is convenience, along with low, fixed prices and a fast, pain-free transaction. Internet car purchasers also tend to be richer and better educated.

Although skeptical at first, dealers are also coming out winners through Internet brokering. Even with the monthly fees they pay to auto brokers like Autobytel.com and CarPoint, dealers get hot prospects at lower cost than through traditional advertising. For the monthly dues, a dealer is also guaranteed to be the exclusive dealer for the brand in a particular region.

The number of new cars being sold over the Internet has caught the attention of the big three U.S. automakers: General Motors, Ford, and Chrysler. Surveys show that most on-line car shoppers start with the manufacturers' sites before going on to other sites for more specific price and availability information. GM's new site, called GM BuyPower, offers consumers access to dealer inventory information. Customers who visit GM's main Web site can select options and then find a showroom in their area with the exact car they want. Then they can schedule a test drive on-line and even ask the dealer to hold the car until they can come in. Area dealers respond with best-price quotes. Similar Web site services are also in the works at Ford and Chrysler.[6]

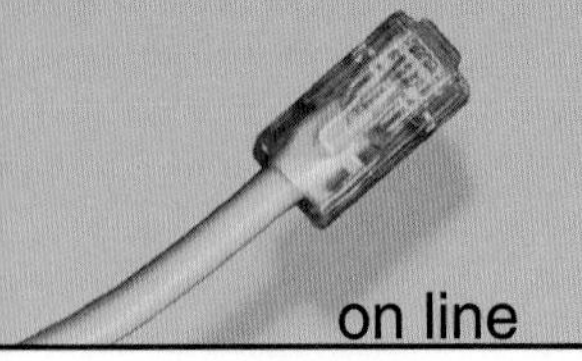

Kraft Foods
Starbucks Coffee

Visit Kraft's and Starbucks's Web sites to find out information on their strategic channel alliance. Does what you find (or don't find) surprise you? Why do you think they have decided not to publicize this alliance on their Web sites?
http://www.kraftfoods.com **http://www.starbucks.com**

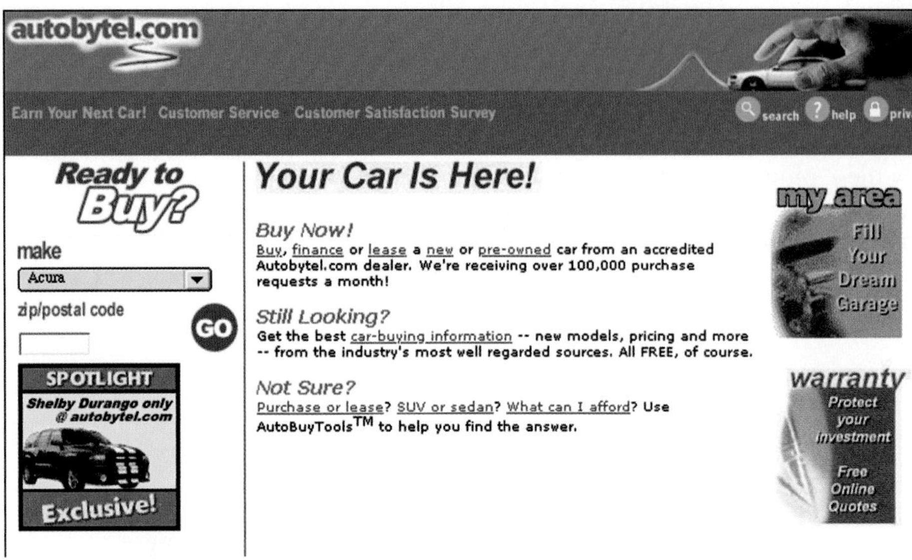

The Internet has had a drastic impact on retail channels in many industries, and now Internet purchasing is moving into the car industry. Would you buy a car over the Internet? Go to Autobytel.com to see what it is all about.
Courtesy Autobytel.com inc.

FedEx Logistics. Now, a dealer who needs a part calls a toll-free number for FedEx, and the parts are shipped and usually arrive the same evening. This arrangement helped Volvo eliminate three warehouses and decrease its inventory levels by 15 percent.[7]

Strategic Channel Alliances

Producers often form **strategic channel alliances**, which use another manufacturer's already established channel. Alliances are used most often when the creation of marketing channel relationships may be too expensive and time consuming. Starbucks Coffee Company and Kraft Foods recently announced a long-term licensing arrangement to begin stocking Starbucks coffee on supermarket shelves nationwide. Under the arrangement, Seattle-based Starbucks will roast and package the coffee, and Kraft will market and distribute it in supermarkets, first in the United States and eventually around the world. Through a strategic channel alliance with Kraft, Starbucks's brand of coffee will be sold by Kraft's thirty-five hundred salespeople, who make up one of the largest direct-selling teams in the food industry. The alliance will allow Starbucks to distribute its coffee through grocery stores nationwide much quicker than it would have been able to do alone.[8]

strategic channel alliance
Cooperative agreement between business firms to use the other's already established distribution channel.

Strategic channel alliances are also common for selling in global markets where cultural differences, distance, or other barriers can inhibit channel establishment. U.S. software giant Oracle recently formed a strategic alliance with Japanese computer giant Fujitsu in the Asia-Pacific region. Under the alliance, Fujitsu will distribute and market Oracle's information management software on Fujitsu servers in Australia, China, Hong Kong, Thailand, and Vietnam.[9]

Channel Strategy Decisions

Discuss the issues that influence channel strategy

Devising a marketing channel strategy requires several critical decisions. Marketing managers must decide what role distribution will play in the overall marketing strategy. In addition, they must be sure that the channel strategy chosen is consistent with product, promotion, and pricing strategies. In making these decisions, marketing managers must analyze what factors will influence the choice of channel and what level of distribution intensity will be appropriate.

Factors Affecting Channel Choice

Marketers must answer many questions before choosing a marketing channel. The final choice depends on analysis of several factors, which often interact. These factors can be grouped as market factors, product factors, and producer factors.

Market Factors Among the most important market factors affecting the choice of distribution channel are target customer considerations. Specifically, marketing managers should answer the following questions: Who are the potential customers? What do they buy? Where do they buy? When do they buy? How do they buy? Additionally, the choice of channel depends on whether the producer is selling to consumers or to industrial customers. Industrial customers' buying habits are very different from those of consumers. Industrial customers tend to buy in larger quantities and require more customer service. Consumers usually buy in very small quantities and sometimes do not mind if they get no service at all, as in a discount store.

Geographic location and size of the market are also important to channel selection. As a rule, if the target market is concentrated in one or more specific areas, then direct selling through a sales force is appropriate. When markets are more widely dispersed, intermediaries are less expensive. The size of the market also influences channel choice. Generally, a very large market requires more intermediaries. Procter & Gamble has to reach millions of consumers with its many brands of household goods. It needs many intermediaries, including wholesalers and retailers.

Product Factors Products that are more complex, customized, and expensive tend to benefit from shorter and more direct marketing channels. These types of products sell better through a direct sales force. Examples include pharmaceuticals, scientific instruments, airplanes, and mainframe computer systems. On the other hand, the more standardized a product is, the longer its distribution channel can be and the greater the number of intermediaries that can be involved. For example, the formula for chewing gum is about the same from producer to producer, with the exception of flavor and shape. Chewing gum is also very inexpensive. As a result, the distribution channel for gum tends to involve many wholesalers and retailers.

The product's life cycle is also an important factor in choosing a marketing channel. In fact, the choice of channel may change over the life of the product. When photocopiers were first available, they were typically sold by a direct sales force. Now, however, photocopiers can be found in several places, including warehouse clubs, electronics superstores, and mail-order catalogs. As products become more common and less intimidating to potential users, producers tend to look for alternative channels. Gatorade was originally sold to sports teams, gyms, and fitness clubs. As the drink became more popular, mainstream supermarket channels were added, followed by convenience stores and drugstores. Now Gatorade can be found in vending machines and even in some fast-food restaurants.

Another factor is the delicacy of the product. Perishable products like vegetables and milk have a relatively short life span. Fragile products like china and crystal require a minimum amount of handling. Therefore, both require fairly short marketing channels.

Producer Factors Several factors pertaining to the producer are important to the selection of a marketing channel. In general, producers with large financial, managerial, and marketing resources are better able to use more direct channels. These producers have the ability to hire and train their own sales force, warehouse their own goods, and extend credit to their customers. Smaller or weaker firms, on the other hand, must rely on intermediaries to provide these services for them. Compared to producers with only one or two product lines, producers that sell several products in a related area are able to choose channels that are more direct. Sales expenses then can be spread over more products.

A producer's desire to control pricing, positioning, brand image, and customer support also tends to influence channel selection. For instance, firms that sell products with exclusive brand images, such as designer perfumes and clothing, usually avoid channels in which discount retailers are present. Manufacturers of upscale products, such as Gucci (handbags) and Godiva (chocolates), may sell their wares only in expensive stores in order to maintain an image of exclusivity.

exhibit 10.6

Intensity of Distribution Levels

Intensity Level	Distribution Intensity Objective	Number of Intermediaries in Each Market	Examples
Intensive	Achieve mass market selling; popular with health and beauty aids and convenience goods that must be available everywhere	Many	Pepsi-Cola, Frito-Lay potato chips, Huggies diapers, Alpo dog food, Crayola crayons
Selective	Work closely with selected intermediaries who meet certain criteria; typically used for shopping goods and some specialty goods	Several	Donna Karan clothing, Hewlett-Packard printers, Burton snowboards, Aveda aromatherapy products
Exclusive	Work with a single intermediary for products that require special resources or positioning; typically used for specialty goods and major industrial equipment	One	BMW cars, Rolex watches, Subway franchise

Many producers have opted to risk their image, however, and test sales in discount channels. Levi Strauss expanded its distribution to include JCPenney and Sears. JCPenney is now Levi Strauss's biggest customer.

Levels of Distribution Intensity

Organizations have three options for intensity of distribution: intensive distribution, selective distribution, or exclusive distribution. (See Exhibit 10.6.)

intensive distribution
Form of distribution aimed at having a product available in every outlet at which target customers might want to buy it.

Intensive Distribution **Intensive distribution** is distribution aimed at maximum market coverage. The manufacturer tries to have the product available in every outlet from which potential customers might want to buy it. If buyers are unwilling to search for a product (as is true of convenience goods and operating supplies), the product must be very accessible to buyers. A low-value product that is purchased frequently may require a lengthy channel. For example, candy is found in almost every type of retail store imaginable. It is typically sold to retailers in small quantities by a food or candy wholesaler. The Wrigley Co. could not afford to sell its gum directly to every service station, drugstore, supermarket, and discount store. The cost would be too high.

Most manufacturers pursuing an intensive distribution strategy sell to a large percentage of the wholesalers willing to stock their products. Retailers' willingness (or unwillingness) to handle items tends to control the manufacturer's ability to achieve intensive distribution. A retailer already carrying ten brands of gum may show little enthusiasm for one more brand.

selective distribution
Form of distribution achieved by screening dealers to eliminate all but a few in any single area.

Selective Distribution **Selective distribution** is achieved by screening dealers to eliminate all but a few in any single area. Maytag uses a selective distribution

DKNY uses selective distribution for its clothing and accessories. Since the clothes are sold only in select retail outlets, customers must seek them out.
© Hugh Sitton/Tony Stone Images

system by choosing a select handful of appliance dealers in a geographic area to sell its line of washers and dryers and other appliances. Likewise, DKNY clothing is sold only in select retail outlets. Because only a few retailers are chosen, the consumer must seek out the product. Shopping goods and some specialty products are distributed selectively. Accessory equipment manufacturers in the business-to-business market also tend to follow a selective distribution strategy.

Several screening criteria are used to find the right dealers. An accessory equipment manufacturer like NEC may seek firms that are able to service its products properly. A television manufacturer like Zenith may look for service ability and a quality dealer image. If the manufacturer expects to move a large volume of merchandise through each dealer, it will choose only those dealers that seem able to handle such volume. As a result, many smaller retailers may not be considered.

Exclusive Distribution The most restrictive form of market coverage is **exclusive distribution,** which entails only one or a few dealers within a given area. Because buyers may have to search or travel extensively to buy the product, exclusive distribution is usually confined to consumer specialty goods, a few shopping goods, and major industrial equipment. Products such as Rolls Royce automobiles, Chris-Craft power boats, and Pettibone tower cranes are distributed under exclusive arrangements. Sometimes exclusive territories are granted by new companies (such as franchisers) to obtain market coverage in a particular area. Limited distribution may also serve to project an exclusive image for the product.

exclusive distribution
Form of distribution that establishes one or a few dealers within a given area.

Retailers and wholesalers may be unwilling to commit the time and money necessary to promote and service a product unless the manufacturer guarantees them an exclusive territory. This arrangement shields the dealer from direct competition and enables it to be the main beneficiary of the manufacturer's promotion efforts in that geographic area. With exclusive distribution, channels of communication are usually well established, because the manufacturer works with a limited number of dealers rather than many accounts.

Exclusive distribution has been part of retailing for years. In the toy industry, toy maker Hasbro makes Luke and Wampa Star Wars collector dolls only for Target stores. It makes other figures in the Star Wars series exclusively for other retailers, including Toys 'R' Us, Wal-Mart, JCPenney and KB Toys. Toy retailer F.A.O. Schwarz estimates that as much as 30 percent of all toys it sells are unavailable in other stores. In an era when a few big toy makers are making lots of similar-looking toys, exclusive help stores stand out from the crowd and draw more customers.[10]

Although exclusivity has its advantages, it also can have its pitfalls. An exclusive network may not be large enough, for instance, if demand is brisk. Manufacturers and retailers run the risk of angering customers who can't get the product. In addition, the producer's insistence on exclusivity might put the channel in financial jeopardy during times of weak demand. Honda's Acura division uses an exclusive distribution strategy to create a distinctive image for its high-priced cars. Acura dealers struggled initially because of the car's small niche market, low resale demand, and ironically, infrequent need for follow-up service and repair. After several years, however, Acura dealerships have become very strong competitors by promoting quality and service.

Channel Relationships

A marketing channel is more than a set of institutions linked by economic ties. Social relationships play an important role in building unity among channel members. The basic social dimensions of channels are power, control, leadership, conflict, and partnering.

5
Explain channel leadership, conflict, and partnering

channel power
The capacity of a particular marketing channel member to control or influence the behavior of other channel members.

channel control
A situation that occurs when one marketing channel member intentionally affects another member's behavior.

channel leader (channel captain)
Member of a marketing channel who exercises authority and power over the activities of other channel members.

Channel Power, Control, and Leadership

Channel power is a channel member's capacity to control or influence the behavior of other channel members. **Channel control** occurs when one channel member affects another member's behavior. To achieve control, a channel member assumes channel leadership and exercises authority and power. This member is termed the **channel leader**, or **channel captain**. In one marketing channel, a manufacturer may be the leader because it controls new product designs and product availability. In another, a retailer may be the channel leader because it wields power and control over the retail price, inventory levels, and postsale service. Read about how some retailers are wielding their power in the "Ethics in Marketing" box.

The exercise of channel power is a routine element of many business activities in which the outcome is often more efficient operations and cost savings. For years, distributing magazines was a simple, inefficient business. Most cities had one wholesaler who purchased magazine titles from publishers for 60 percent of the magazine's cover price. The wholesaler delivered new issues to retail stores, who purchased the magazines from the wholesaler at 80 percent of the magazine's cover price. The retailer, the wholesaler, and the publisher each got a cut from every magazine sold. The wholesalers sent unsold magazines back to the publisher. Then supermarket giant Safeway, in an effort to control costs, decided to reduce the number of single-city magazine wholesalers it traditionally dealt with by opening up several large regions to competitive bidding. Other big retailers, such as Wal-Mart, Albertson's, Kroger, and Walgreen, soon followed suit. In order to win contracts for larger regions, wholesalers were forced to offer better terms and expand their operations or go out of business. Now retailers typically pay just 70 to 75 percent of a magazine's cover price, and the number of wholesalers they deal with has been drastically reduced. Wal-Mart, for instance, now deals with just three distributors nationwide, down from over three hundred. In turn, many wholesalers are exerting their own power over magazine publishers in an effort to remain profitable. One wholesaler recently required that for new titles publishers must provide a "minimum discount" from the cover price of 44 percent (meaning it would pay no more than 56 percent, compared with the current 60 percent norm) in an effort to reduce returns, an expensive and unprofitable part of the business. Other wholesalers are demanding new fees from publishers for magazines deemed unprofitable.[11]

channel conflict
A clash of goals and methods between distribution channel members.

Channel Conflict

Inequitable channel relationships often lead to **channel conflict**, which is a clash of goals and methods among the members of a distribution channel. In a broad context, conflict may not be bad. Often it arises because staid, traditional channel members refuse to keep pace with the times. Removing an outdated intermediary may result in reduced costs for the entire supply chain.

Sources of conflicts among channel members can be due to many different situations and factors. Conflict often arises because channel members have conflicting goals. Athletic footwear retailers want to sell as many shoes as possible in order to maximize profits, regardless of whether the shoe is manufactured by Nike, Adidas, or Saucony, but the Nike manufacturer wants a certain sales volume and market share in each market.

ethics in marketing

Retailers Gain the Upper Hand

Marketing channels, by their nature, lend themselves to conflict among channel members. More often than not, the larger player in the channel dictates the rules of the game to the smaller players. Whereas in the past manufacturers were the typical big guys directing retailers from above like pieces in a chess game, today's channel leader is just as likely to be the retailer. Mega-retailers like Wal-Mart or large consolidated department store chains can make life for manufacturers and suppliers just as hard. Toys 'R' Us was recently charged by the Federal Trade Commission for pressuring manufacturers, in particular Mattel and Hasbro, to deny popular toys to warehouse clubs and other discounters. Because of the huge marketing clout that Toys 'R' Us wields within its marketing channels, the retailer was able to demand exclusive arrangements with manufacturers of hot toys, such as Mattel's Holiday Barbie doll, so that they could not be sold by discounters at a lower price than at Toys 'R' Us.[12]

Another example of retailers' channel power is slotting allowances. Many large retailers charge slotting allowances—payments that manufacturers must make to buy space for new products on retailers' shelves—to reduce their risk in stocking new products. In some markets, slotting fees can run into the thousands of dollars per store. Retailers say the fees are justified given the uncertain impact on profit of the ever-growing number of new products. Some retailers even demand slotting allowances to keep established products on the shelves.

Many manufacturers, particularly smaller ones, consider slotting allowances extortion. Zapp's Potato Chips, a cajun-flavored chip company in south Louisiana, found it was impossible to get their new flavored chips in major supermarkets in their early years because they could not afford the slotting fees. They were forced to sell in independent stores until they were successful enough to pay slotting fees. Their story is similar to thousands of small manufacturers with new and innovative products. Some products are never introduced to the market while other good products fail because they are prevented from getting good distribution to potential customers.

Aside from slotting fees, many large department stores are making greater-than-ever demands from their apparel suppliers to cover the costs of heavy discounts and markdowns on their own selling floors. They are increasingly demanding that suppliers guarantee their stores' profit margins and insisting on cash rebates if the guarantee isn't met. For example, May Department Store's Lord & Taylor chain has been known to set guaranteed profit margins as high as 48 percent. Suppliers' products that don't meet these margins are required to pay the large retailers' rebates on the markdowns. Some rebates paid by suppliers have exceeded $1 million. In addition to profit guarantees, large department store chains are increasingly levying fines for violations of ticketing, packing, and shipping rules. When apparel designer Pamela Dennis shipped its evening gowns in one box to Neiman Marcus, the retailer fined the company $225 because it wanted orders packed separately for each store. Department stores say that the rebates and fines are necessary and that suppliers in today's market have to bear their share of the risk of selling fashion. Hardest hit have been smaller apparel companies, where the payments to retailers often can outweigh profits. Some small and midsize suppliers are now banding together to study whether the stores' profit-margin guarantees violate antitrust statutes.[13]

How can power struggles among channel members affect the ultimate consumer? Should retailers be permitted to charge slotting fees, which prevent small manufacturers from using the best channels to reach their potential customers? Do you agree with retailers that apparel suppliers should bear some of the risk of fashion?

Conflict can also arise when channel members fail to fulfill expectations of other channel members, such as when a franchisee does not follow the rules set down by the franchiser or when communications channels break down between channel members. For example, if a manufacturer reduces the length of warranty coverage and fails to communicate this change to dealers, then conflict may occur when dealers make repairs with the expectation that they will be reimbursed by the manufacturer. Further, ideological differences and different perceptions of reality can also cause conflict among channel members. For example, retailers may believe "the customer is always right" and offer a very liberal return policy.

Wholesalers and manufacturers may feel that people "try to get something for nothing" or don't follow product instructions carefully. Their differing views of allowable returns will undoubtably conflict with the retailers'.

horizontal conflict
Channel conflict that occurs among channel members on the same level.

Conflict within a channel can be either horizontal or vertical. **Horizontal conflict** occurs among channel members on the same level—such as two or more different wholesalers or two or more different retailers—that handle the same manufacturer's brands. This type of channel conflict is found most often when manufacturers practice dual or multiple distribution strategies. There was considerable channel conflict after computer manufacturers began distributing their computers beyond the traditional computer resellers and to discount stores, department stores, warehouse clubs, and giant electronic superstores, such as Circuit City and CompUSA. Horizontal conflict can also occur when channel members on the same level feel they are being treated unfairly by the manufacturer. The American Booksellers Association, a group representing small independent booksellers, recently filed a lawsuit against bookstore giants Barnes & Noble and Borders, who they claimed violated antitrust laws by using their buying power to demand "illegal and secret" discounts from publishers. These deals, the association contended, put independent booksellers at a serious competitive disadvantage.[14]

vertical conflict
Channel conflict that occurs between different levels in a marketing channel, most typically between the manufacturer and wholesaler or between the manufacturer and retailer.

Many regard horizontal conflict as healthy competition. Vertical conflict is much more serious. **Vertical conflict** occurs between different levels in a marketing channel, most typically between the manufacturer and wholesaler and the manufacturer and retailer. Producer versus wholesaler conflict occurs when the producer chooses to bypass the wholesaler to deal directly with the consumer or retailer. For example, conflict arose when several producers agreed to Wal-Mart's request to deal with it directly, bypassing middlemen altogether.

Dual distribution strategies can also cause vertical conflict in the channel. For example, wireless telephone carriers, such as AT&T and Bell Atlantic, traditionally sold cellular phone service through local dealers, usually small electronics stores. Faced with increased competition from upstarts, carriers recently began opening their own stores and mall kiosks, as well as offering special prices and telemarketing to reach potential customers in their homes. Local dealers, who helped build the cell phone market in the early 1980s, say the carriers are trying to squeeze them out of business.[15] Similarly, manufacturers who are experimenting with selling to customers directly over the Internet are also creating conflict with their traditional retailing intermediaries. For example, experts predict that total on-line travel sales will increase to over $11 billion by 2002 and will threaten the livelihood of thousands of travel agents.[16]

Producers and retailers may also disagree over the terms of the sale or other aspects of the business relationship. When Procter & Gamble introduced "everyday low pricing" to its retail channel members—a strategy designed to standardize wholesale prices and eliminate most trade promotions—many retailers retaliated. Some cut the variety of P&G sizes they carried or eliminated marginal brands. Others moved P&G brands from prime shelf space to less visible shelves.

Channel Partnering

Regardless of the locus of power, channel members rely heavily on one another. Even the most powerful manufacturers depend on dealers to sell their products; even the most powerful retailers require the products provided by suppliers. In sharp contrast to the adversarial relationships of the past between buyers and sellers, contemporary management thought emphasizes the development of close working partnerships among channel members. **Channel partnering**, or **channel cooperation**, is the joint effort of all channel members to create a supply chain that serves customers and creates a competitive advantage. Channel partnering is vital if each member is to gain something from other members. By cooperating, retailers, wholesalers, manufacturers, and suppliers can speed up inventory replenishment, improve customer service, and reduce the total cost of the marketing channel.

channel partnering (channel cooperation)
The joint effort of all channel members to create a supply chain that serves customers and creates a competitive advantage.

Transaction- Versus Partnership-Based Firms | **exhibit 10.7**

Transaction-Based	Partnership-Based
Short-term relationships	Long-term relationships
Multiple suppliers	Fewer suppliers
Adversarial relationships	Cooperative partnerships
Price dominates	Value-added services dominate
Minimal investment from suppliers	High investment for both buyer and supplier
Minimal information sharing	Extensive product, marketing, and logistics information sharing
Firms are independent	Firms are interdependent with joint decision making.
Minimal interaction between respective functional areas	Extensive interaction between buyer and supplier functional areas

SOURCE: From *Competing Through Supply Chain Management: Creating Market-Winning Strategies Through Supply Chain Partnerships* by David Frederick Ross (New York: Chapman & Hall, 1998), p. 61. Reprinted by permission of the publisher.

Channel alliances and partnerships can be traced, in part, directly to attempts by firms to leverage the intellectual, material, and marketing resources of their business partners worldwide to make entry into far-flung markets easier and more cost effective. The growth of channel partnering is also due to the growth of an information infrastructure that fosters cooperation and sharing of information in national as well as global markets.[17] A comparison between companies that approach the marketplace unilaterally and those that engage in channel cooperation and form partnerships is detailed in Exhibit 10.7.

Collaborating channel partners meet the needs of consumers more effectively by ensuring the right products reach shelves at the right time and at a lower cost, boosting sales and profits. Forced to become more efficient in a highly competitive environment, retailers and their vendors have turned many formerly adversarial relationships into partnerships. Wal-Mart's Retail Link technology gives some thirty-two hundred vendors access to its point-of-sale data to replenish inventory at its more than two thousand stores. Based on sales data, vendors customized Wal-Mart's workwear clothing inventory at each store according to demographics, regional tastes, and weather patterns. As a result of vendor partnerships, Wal-Mart's overall inventory was reduced by 25 percent while sales rose 15 percent.[18]

Logistics Decisions and Supply Chain Management

Discuss logistics and supply chain management and their evolution into distribution practice

Now that you are familiar with the structure and strategy of marketing channels, it is important to also understand the physical means through which products move through a channel of distribution, or the supply chain. **Logistics** is a term borrowed from the military that describes the process of strategically managing the

logistics
The process of strategically managing the efficient flow and storage of raw materials, in-process inventory, and finished goods from point of origin to point of consumption.

efficient flow and storage of raw materials, in-process inventory, and finished goods from point of origin to point of consumption. An integral part of marketing strategy, logistics represents "place" in the marketing mix (product, price, promotion, and place) and encompasses the logistical processes involved in getting the right product to the right place at the right time.

WE'RE GENERATING $50,000,000,000
IN CUSTOMER VALUE.
Motorola
Philips
British Steel
Bristol-Myers Squibb
Toshiba Corporation
Healthtex
E & J Gallo Winery
3M
COMPAQ
Bridgestone
Johnson & Johnson Medical
i2 Technologies is committed to a singular vision: to add $50 billion in value through growth and savings for our customers by the year 2005.
ONE SUPPLY CHAIN AT A TIME.
Today our customers are gaining quantum improvements to their bottom line with i2's RHYTHM®—the leading solution in supply chain optimization.
Discover how your company can achieve world-class results by attending Planet '98: i2's Supply Chain Summit, September 20-23 at the Wyndham Anatole Hotel in Dallas.
909 E. Las Colinas Blvd.
Irving, TX 75039
Phone: 214-860-6000
Fax: 214-860-6060
E-mail: planet@i2.com
www.i2.com

The **supply chain** is the connected chain of all of the business entities, both internal and external to the company, that perform or support the logistics function. It incorporates all of the logistical activities associated with moving goods from the raw-materials stage through to the end user. These include sourcing and procurement of raw materials, production scheduling, order processing, inventory management, transportation, warehousing, customer service, the information systems necessary to monitor these activities, and the external partners, such as vendors, carriers, and third-party companies.[19]

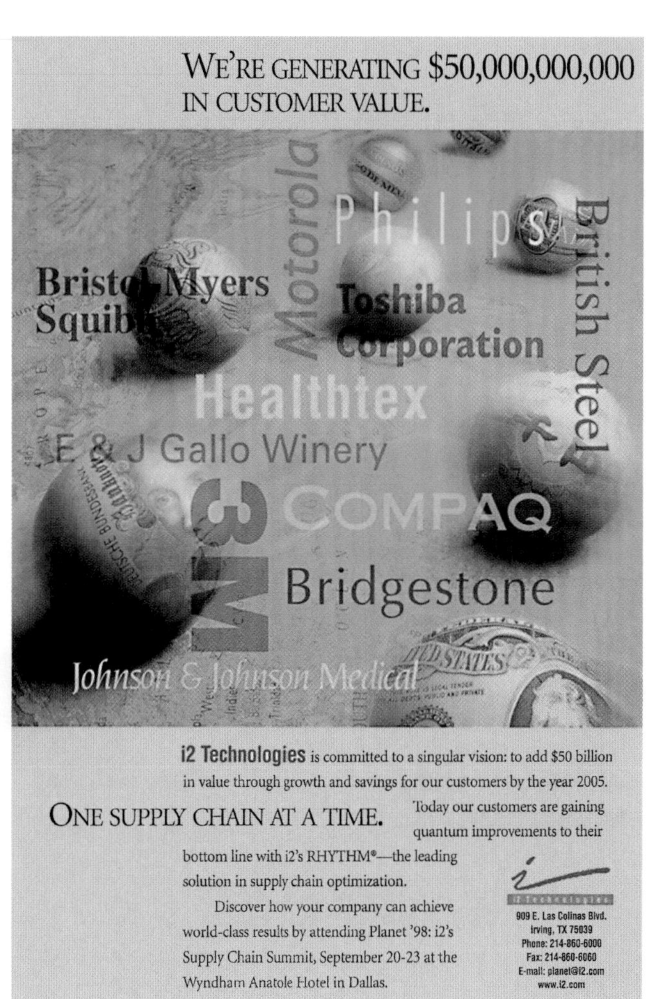

i2 Technologies is a supply chain management company that helps its clients coordinate and integrate all logistical functions into a seamless process. Visit *www.i2.com* to find out more about how it does this.
Courtesy i2 Technologies

Supply chain management or **integrated logistics**, then, coordinates and integrates all of these activities performed by supply chain members into a seamless process. This continuously evolving management philosophy seeks to unify the competencies and resources of business functions both within the firm and outside in the firm's allied channel partners. The result is a highly competitive, customer-satisfying supply system focused on developing innovative solutions and synchronizing the flow of goods, services, and information to create enhanced customer value.[20] Bernard J. LaLonde, professor emeritus of logistics at Ohio State University, defines supply chain management as "the delivery of enhanced customer and economic value through synchronized management of the flow of physical goods and associated information from sourcing to consumption."[21] Exhibit 10.8 depicts the supply chain process.

An important element of supply chain management is that it is completely customer driven. In the mass-production era, manufacturers produced standardized products that were "pushed" down through the supply channel to consumers. In contrast, in today's marketplace, products are being driven by the customers, who expect to receive product configurations and services matched to their unique needs.[22]

This reversal of the flow of demand from a "push" to a "pull" has resulted in a radical reformulation of market expectations and traditional marketing, production, and distribution functions. Through the channel partnership of suppliers, manufacturers, wholesalers, and retailers along the entire supply chain who work together toward the common goal of creating customer value, supply chain management allows companies to respond with the unique product configuration and mix of services demanded by the customer. Today, supply chain management plays a dual role: first, as a *communicator* of customer demand that extends from the point of sale all the way back to the supplier; and second, as a *physical flow process* that engineers the timely and cost-effective movement of goods through the entire supply pipeline.[23]

supply chain
The connected chain of all of the business entities, both internal and external to the company, that perform or support the logistics function.

Supply chain management includes these activities:

- Managing the movement of information and customer requirements up and down the supply chain

EXE Technologies

What tools can EXE provide a company to help with its supply chain management functions? Which of EXE's services and products do you think would be the most valuable to a company?
http://www.exe.com/

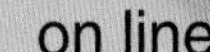

on line

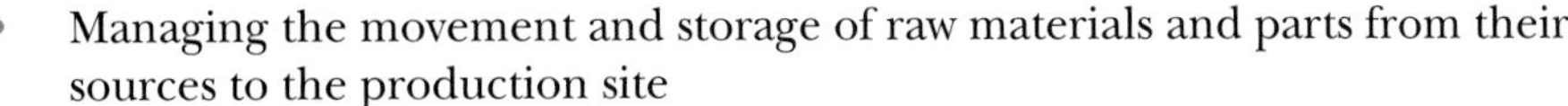

- Managing the movement and storage of raw materials and parts from their sources to the production site
- Managing the movement of raw materials, semimanufactured products, and finished products within and among plants, warehouses, and distribution centers
- Planning production in response to consumer demand
- Planning and coordinating the physical distribution of finished goods to intermediaries and final buyers
- Cultivating and coordinating strategic partnerships with supply chain members to meet the unique needs of the customer and create customer value

supply chain management (integrated logistics)
Management system that coordinates and integrates all of the activities performed by supply chain members from source to the point of consumption that results in enhanced customer and economic value.

In summary, supply chain management logisticians are responsible for directing raw materials and parts to the production department and the finished or semifinished product through warehouses and eventually

The Supply Chain | **exhibit 10.8**

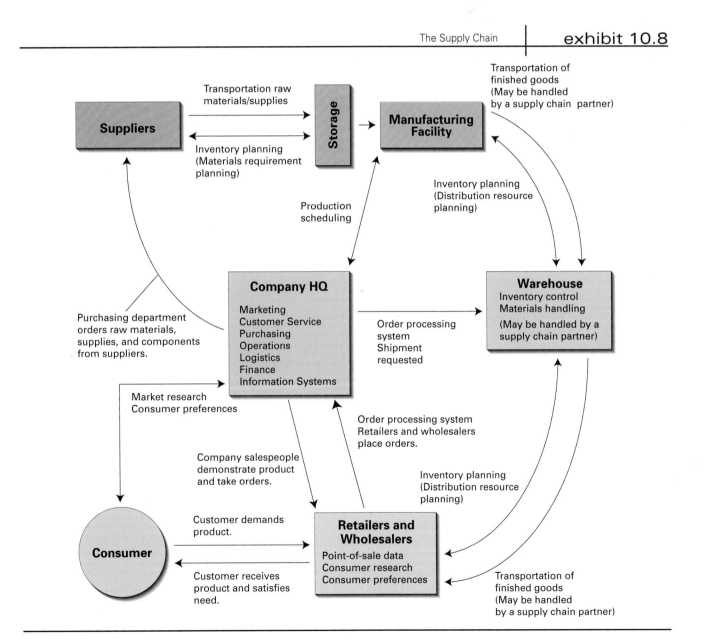

Suppliers

Transportation raw materials/supplies

Inventory planning (Materials requirement planning)

Storage

Manufacturing Facility

Transportation of finished goods (May be handled by a supply chain partner)

Inventory planning (Distribution resource planning)

Production scheduling

Company HQ
Marketing
Customer Service
Purchasing
Operations
Logistics
Finance
Information Systems

Purchasing department orders raw materials, supplies, and components from suppliers.

Order processing system
Shipment requested

Warehouse
Inventory control
Materials handling
(May be handled by a supply chain partner)

Market research
Consumer preferences

Order processing system
Retailers and wholesalers place orders.

Company salespeople demonstrate product and take orders.

Inventory planning (Distribution resource planning)

Consumer

Customer demands product.

Customer receives product and satisfies need.

Retailers and Wholesalers
Point-of-sale data
Consumer research
Consumer preferences

Transportation of finished goods (May be handled by a supply chain partner)

to the intermediary or end user. Above all, supply chain management begins and ends with the customer. Instead of forcing into the market products that may or may not sell quickly, supply chain management logisticians react to actual customer demand. By doing so, the flow of raw materials, finished products, and packaging materials are minimized at every point in the supply chain, resulting in lower costs and increased customer value.

The Evolution of Integrated Logistics and Supply Chain Management

Although the concept of an integrated supply chain has only recently been given top priority by corporate management, its roots go back to a process simply called *physical distribution*.[24] In the early 1900s, the focus was on moving agricultural products to market. For businesses, production output was cascaded, or pushed, down the channel with the focus on transporting and storing finished goods from the manufacturer to the next member in the channel. Until the late 1950s, business saw physical distribution as a subset of marketing and viewed it from a functional, compartmentalized perspective. Thus, warehousing, materials handling, wholesaling, transportation, and inventory control were distinct and independent parts of the distribution process. The process only concerned those activities directly related to physically moving the product. Distribution or "traffic" managers were solely responsible for knowing the tariff and regulatory mysteries of moving outbound freight.

Beginning in the early 1960s, there was a shift from physical distribution as the main focus to an entire system of activities working with and relying on one another. This era of *logistics management* was marked by a systems approach and a total cost perspective. Costs along the entire logistics system were analyzed and streamlined in an attempt to balance physical distribution service with cost. Management was consolidated for both inbound (raw materials for production) and outbound (finished goods to final consumers) transportation, warehousing, inventory control, and materials handling.

In the early 1970s, the concept of logistics management was broadened to include the customer as the primary focus of the firm. Customer service, of which physical distribution is a component, became a significant issue. Minimizing cost gave way to maximizing profits and using logistics as a way to create customer value and satisfy the customer. The more progressive companies began migrating from an inventory "push" to a customer "pull" channel as power began to move downstream to the customer.

As the 1980s drew to a close, logistics began to be considered as a key means of differentiation for a firm and a critical component in marketing and corporate strategy. Globalization of markets and advances in information technology had significant influences on supply chain partnering. During this phase, the concept of an integrated supply chain, sharing information, and working together to satisfy the customer emerged as the focus of distribution. Such concepts as integrated logistics, supply chain management, global logistics, and information technology became important to the success of a firm. Advocates of this distribution focus realize that significant productivity increases can only come from managing supply chain relationships, information, and material flow across enterprise borders—that is, becoming a truly integrated supply chain that shares information and works together for the common goal of increasing customer value.

The future of logistics lies in a deeper understanding of customers' behavioral processes and their perceptions of a firm's logistics systems. Specifically, what are the reactions of customers when aspects of logistics are changed? As the boundaries between supply chain partners partially disappear, an absolute need for understanding all components of the supply chain is inevitable. Firms that are able to bring about greater cooperation of supply chain partners and

Evolution of Integrated Logistics and Supply Chain Management **exhibit 10.9**

Distribution Phase	Time Period	Characteristics
Farm to Market	Up to the 1940s	Distribution attention centered on transporting products from the farm to point of sale
Segmented Functions	1940s to 1950s	Independent departments focused on moving finished goods to the next member of the channel; inventory "push" orientation
Integrated Functions	1960s to early 1970s	Recognized inbound transportation as part of the logistics system; focus on streamlining costs along entire logistics system
Customer Focus	1970s to mid-1980s	The customer regarded as the primary focus of the firm; movement toward inventory "pull" orientation
Logistics as Differentiator	Early 1980s to present	Logistics as a key means of competitive differentiation and a critical component of the strategy of the firm; integration of all members of the supply chain; the emergence of concepts such as integrated logistics and supply chain management and a heightened awareness of globalization; information technology important to success; marked inventory "pull" from the customer
Behavioral and Boundary Spanning	2000 and beyond	Search for deeper understanding of behavioral issues, specifically customer perceptions of a firm's logistics systems and their related behaviors; greater interfunctional cooperation and coordination across the boundaries of supply chain partners

SOURCE: From "Perspectives on the Evolution of Logistics Thought" by John L. Kent, Jr., and Daniel J. Flint, *Journal of Business Logistics*, Volume 18, Number 2, 1997. Reprinted by permission of the Council of Logistics Management.

span the boundaries to create a value-enhanced experience for customers will be successful.

Exhibit 10.9 provides a summary of the evolution of logistics thought from a management perspective.

Benefits of Supply Chain Management

Companies are increasingly recognizing the tremendous payoff potential of successful supply chain management, such as Wal-Mart's leveraging of the supply chain to achieve a dominant position in the retail marketplace, Dell Computer's reconfiguring the supply chain to respond almost immediately to customer orders, or the bold measures taken by M&M/Mars to virtually eliminate standing inventory in the supply chain.

VALUE

The benefits of an integrated supply chain are many.[25] A study by the Center for Transportation Studies at the Massachusetts Institute of Technology found that the most commonly reported bottom-line benefits center on reduced costs in inventory management, transportation, warehousing, and packaging; improved service through techniques like time-based delivery and make-to-order; and enhanced revenues, which result from such supply-chain-related achievements as higher product availability and more customized products. The companies studied by the Center recorded a number of impressive supply chain accomplishments:

- A 50 percent reduction in inventory
- A 40 percent increase in on-time deliveries
- A 27 percent decrease in cumulative cycle times (length of time from customer placing order to customer receiving order)
- A doubling of inventory turns coupled with a ninefold reduction in out-of-stock rates
- A 17 percent increase in revenues

Another study by A.T. Kearney looked at supply chain management from another angle—specifically, the costs of not paying careful attention to the supply chain process. The Kearney consultants found that supply chain inefficiencies, such as late deliveries, stagnant inventories, and the higher costs they produce, could waste as much as 25 percent of a company's operating costs. Assuming even a relatively low profit margin of 3 to 4 percent, a 5 percent reduction in supply chain waste could double a company's profitability. Another recent study found that best-practice supply chain management companies enjoyed a 45 percent total supply chain cost advantage over their median competitors. Specifically, their supply chain costs as a percentage of revenues were 3 to 7 percent less than the median, depending on the industry.

Balancing Logistics Service and Cost

7
Discuss the concept of balancing logistics service and cost

logistics service
Interrelated activities performed by a member of the supply chain to ensure that the right product is in the right place at the right time.

Logistics service is the package of activities performed by a supply chain member to ensure that the right product is in the right place at the right time. Customers are rarely interested in the activities themselves; instead, they are interested in the results or the benefits they receive from those activities—namely, efficient distribution. At the most basic level, customers demand availability, timeliness, and quality. Specifically, customers expect product availability at the time of order, minimal effort required to place the order, prompt and consistent delivery, and undamaged goods when they are finally received.

Most logistics managers try to set their service level at a point that maximizes service yet minimizes cost. To do so, they must examine the total cost of all parts of the supply chain—sourcing and procurement of raw materials, warehousing and materials handling, inventory control, order processing, and transportation—using the *total cost approach.* The basic idea of the total cost approach is to examine the relationship of factors such as cost of raw materials, number of warehouses, size of finished-goods inventory, and transportation expenses. Of course, the cost of any single element should also be examined in relation to the level of customer service. Thus, the supply chain is viewed as a whole, not as a series of unrelated activities.

Ideally, the logistics manager would like to optimize overall logistics performance so that overall logistics costs are minimized while the desired level of supply chain service is maintained. Consequently, implementing the total cost approach requires trade-offs. For example, a supplier that wants to provide next-day delivery to its customers and also to minimize transportation costs must make a trade-off between the desired level of service (expensive next-day delivery) and the transportation goal (minimal costs).

Often the high cost of air transportation can be justified under the total cost approach. Rapid delivery may drastically reduce the number of warehouses required at distant locations. Therefore, the higher cost of using air freight may be more than justified by the savings in inventory and warehouse expenses, as shown in Exhibit 10.10. The Limited uses a quick-response logistics infrastructure to respond to market information collected from actual point-of-sale data that tracks

exhibit 10.10

How Using Air Freight Lowers Logistics Cost Under the Total Cost Approach

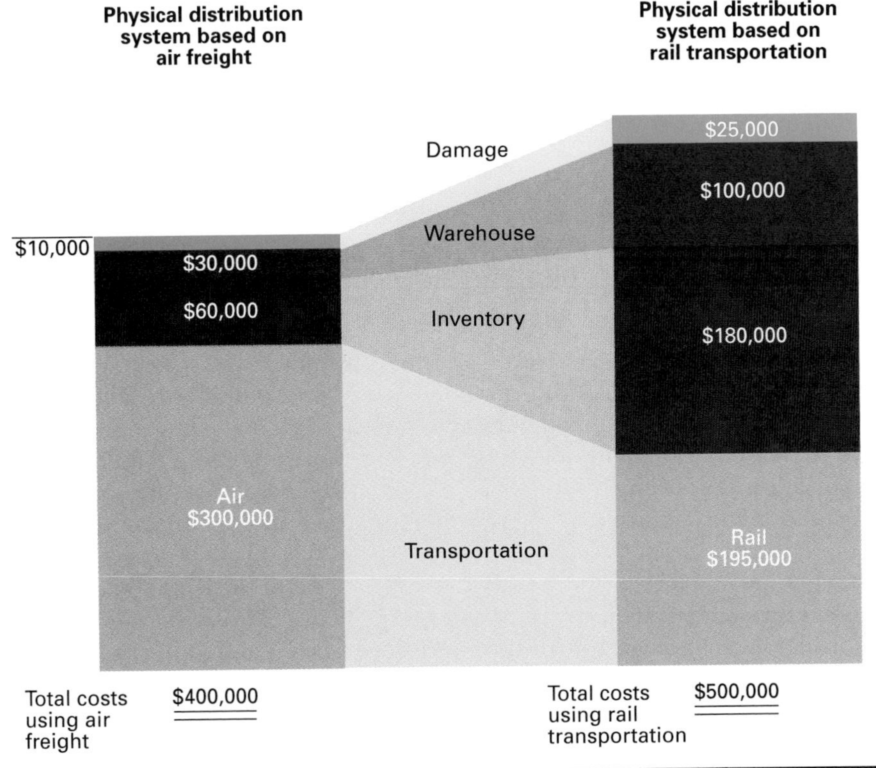

real-time consumer preferences. Premium air transportation is used for time-sensitive fashions to ensure immediate market availability, whereas basic articles of clothing are shipped by less costly means. The savings from reduced inventory levels make this a cost-effective solution.[26]

A new breed of logistics managers, however, are decreasing their emphasis on reducing logistics costs to the lowest possible level. Instead, they are favoring the exploitation of logistics capabilities to increase customer satisfaction and maintain customer demand. According to the Global Logistics Research Team at Michigan State University, many firms are using their logistics capabilities to achieve business success. These firms are developing competencies that are "superior to competition in terms of satisfying customer expectations and requirements." They define world-class logistical competencies to include

- Devising logistics service strategies to meet the specific requirements of customers as a way to position and differentiate themselves from the competition
- Integrating all members of the supply chain to achieve internal logistical operating excellence and development of external supply chain relationships
- Determining and responding quickly to changing logistical requirements
- Constant monitoring of all internal and external aspects of the supply chain to ensure that the right product is in the right place at the right time[27]

For example, warehousing facilities are increasingly providing value-added services that go well beyond mere storage. In the past, overnight delivery was considered an extra service for a warehouse to provide. Today, warehouses are more likely to engage in product-transformation services, such as custom palletization, kitting, repackaging, or even final assembly of a product.[28] A recent study by KPMG Management Consulting found that there is a growing belief among executives that the supply chain can contribute to corporate success as much as or more than branding. Specifically, these companies believe that an efficiently managed supply chain can result in service excellence and this, ultimately, may mean more to customers than branding.[29]

Integrated Functions of the Supply Chain

8
Describe the integrated functions of the supply chain

The logistics supply chain consists of several interrelated and integrated functions: (1) procuring supplies and raw materials, (2) scheduling production, (3) processing orders, (4) managing inventories of raw materials and finished goods, (5) warehousing and materials handling, and (6) selecting modes of transportation. These components are shown in Exhibit 10.11. Although these components are discussed here separately, they are, of course, highly interdependent.

logistics information system
Information technology that integrates and links all of the logistics functions of the supply chain.

Integrating and linking all of the logistics functions of the supply chain is the **logistics information system**. Today's supply chain logisticians are at the forefront of information technology. Information technology is not just a functional affiliate of supply chain management. Rather it is the enabler, the facilitator, the linkage that connects the various components and partners of the supply chain into an integrated whole. Electronic data interchange, on-board computers, satellite and cellular communications systems, materials-handling and warehouse-management software, enterprise-wide systems solutions, and the Internet are among the information enablers of successful supply chain management.[30]

supply chain team
Entire group of individuals who orchestrate the movement of goods, services, and information from the source to the consumer.

The **supply chain team**, in concert with the logistics information system, orchestrates the movement of goods, services, and information from the source to

exhibit 10.11

Integrated Components of the Logistics Supply Chain

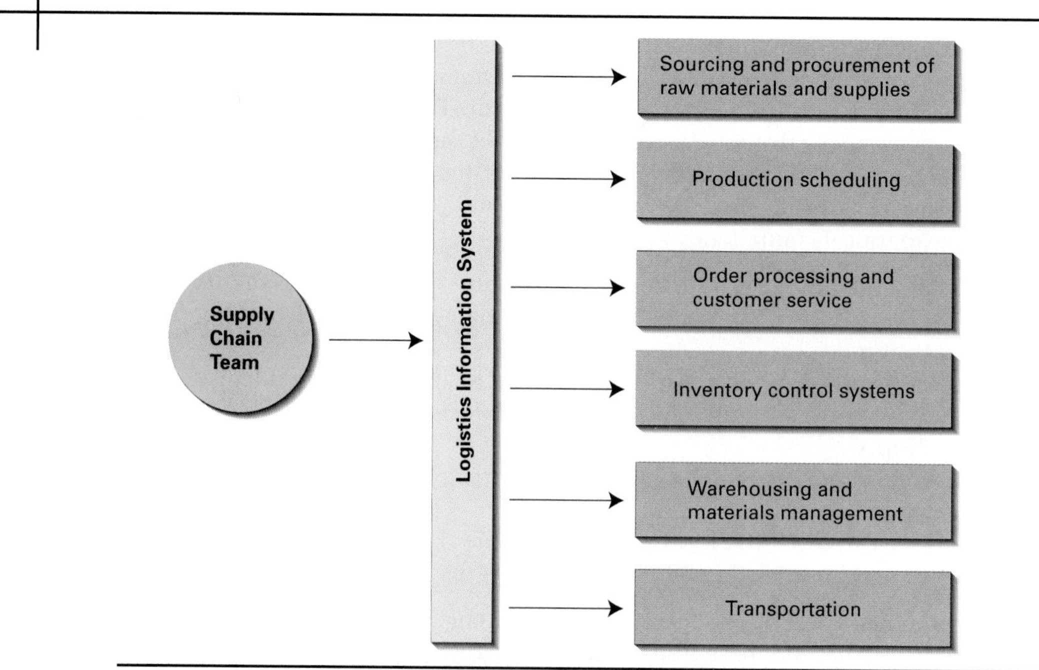

the consumer. Supply chain teams typically cut across organizational boundaries, embracing all parties who participate in moving product to market. The best supply chain teams also move beyond the organization to include the external participants in the chain, such as suppliers, transportation carriers, and third-party logistics suppliers. Members of the supply chain communicate, coordinate, and cooperate extensively.[31]

Sourcing and Procurement

One of the most important links in the supply chain is that between the manufacturer and the supplier. Purchasing professionals are on the front lines of supply chain management. Purchasing departments plan purchasing strategies, develop specifications, select suppliers, and negotiate price and service levels.

The goal of most sourcing and procurement activities is to reduce the cost of raw materials and supplies. Purchasing professionals traditionally rely on tough negotiations to get the lowest price possible from suppliers of raw materials, supplies, and components. However, the traditional approach of simply negotiating the lowest price doesn't always fit well with the philosophy of supply chain management. In its position at the top of the supply chain, purchasing is crucial to the success of the manufacturer's relationship with its customers down the line. Yet, purchasing efforts rarely look toward the bottom of the chain to the customers.[32]

Perhaps the biggest contribution purchasing can make to supply chain management is in the area of vendor relations. Companies can use the purchasing function to strategically manage suppliers in order to reduce the total cost of materials and services. Through enhanced vendor relations, buyers and sellers can develop cooperative relationships that reduce costs and improve efficiency with the aim of lowering prices and enhancing profits.[33] By integrating suppliers into their companies' businesses, purchasing managers have become better able to streamline purchasing processes, manage inventory levels, and reduce overall costs of the sourcing and procurement operations.[34]

Production Scheduling

In traditional mass-market manufacturing, production begins when forecasts call for additional products to be made or inventory control systems signal low inventory levels. The firm then makes product and transports it to their own warehouses or those of intermediaries, where it waits to be ordered from retailers or customers. Production scheduling based on pushing product down to the consumer obviously has its disadvantages, the most notable being that companies risk making products that may become obsolete or that consumers don't want in the first place.

In a customer "pull" manufacturing environment, which is growing in popularity, production of goods or services is not scheduled until an order is placed by the customer specifying the desired configuration. For instance, at Gateway Computers a personal computer is not built until a customer selects the desired configuration and places an order over the telephone or on the Internet. This process, known as **mass customization** or **build-to-order**, uniquely tailors mass-market goods and services to the needs of the individuals who buy them. Companies as diverse as BMW, Dell Computer, Levi Strauss & Co., Mattel, and a slew of Web-based businesses are adopting mass customization to maintain or obtain a competitive edge.

mass customization (build-to-order)
Production method whereby products are not made until an order is placed by the customer; products are made according to customer specifications.

As more companies move toward mass customization versus the mass marketing of goods, continuous dialogue with the customer becomes ever more important. For example, Levi Strauss & Co. has made measure-to-fit women's jeans for several years. With the help of a sales associate, customers create the jeans they want by picking from six colors, three basic models, five different leg openings, and two types of fly. Each customer is measured for a correct fit. Then their order is entered into a Web-based terminal linked to the stitching machines in the factory. Two to three weeks later the jeans arrive in the mail. A bar-code tag sealed to the pocket lining stores the measurements for simple reordering.[35]

just-in-time production (JIT) Redefining and simplifying manufacturing by reducing inventory levels and delivering raw materials just when they are needed on the production line.

Just-in-Time Manufacturing An important manufacturing process common today among manufacturers is just-in-time manufacturing. Borrowed from the Japanese, **just-in-time production (JIT)**, sometimes called *lean production*, requires manufacturers to work closely with suppliers and transportation providers to get required items to the assembly line or factory floor at the precise time they are needed for production. For the manufacturer, JIT means that raw materials arrive at the assembly line in guaranteed working order just in time to be installed, and finished products are generally shipped to the customer immediately after completion. For the supplier, JIT means supplying customers with products in just a few days, or even a few hours, rather than weeks. For the ultimate consumers, JIT means lower costs, shorter lead times, and products that more closely meet their needs.

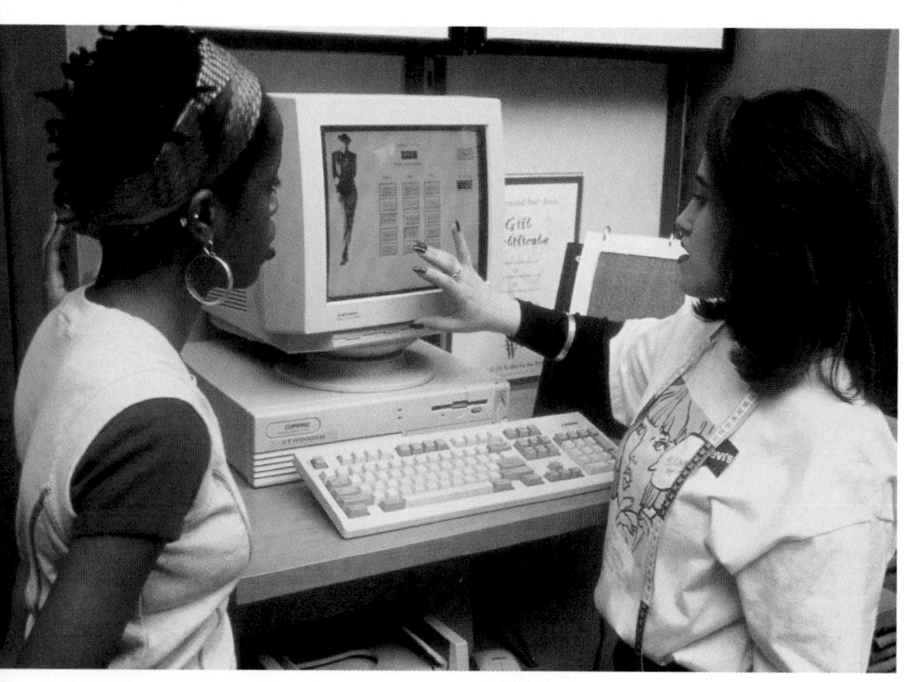

Mass customization is a way for companies to meet each individual customer's needs. Levi Strauss & Co. has been using this type of build-to-order strategy in the manufacture of women's jeans. The custom order is transmitted to production at the point of sale and the measured-to-fit jeans arrive two to three weeks later.
Photo courtesy of Levi Strauss & Co.

JIT benefits manufacturers most by reducing their raw materials inventories. For example, at Dell Computer Corp.'s Texas plant, computer components are often delivered just minutes before they are needed. Chips, boards, and drives are kept in trucks backed up into bays located fifty feet from the beginning of the production line. On average, the time it takes between when Dell buys parts and sells them as a finished product is only eight days.[36] Similarly, at Saturn's powertrain manufacturing and assembly plant in Spring Hill, Tennessee, the inventory of powertrains at any given time is barely two hours, in sharp contrast to the two weeks of inventory generally carried by other auto manufacturers.

Additionally, JIT creates shorter lead times, or the time it takes to get parts from a supplier after an order has been placed. Manufacturers also enjoy better relationships with suppliers and can decrease their production and storeroom costs. Because there is little safety stock and therefore no margin for error, the manufacturer cannot afford to make a mistake. As a result, a manufacturer using JIT must be sure it receives high-quality parts from all vendors and must be confident that the supplier will meet all delivery commitments. Finally, JIT tends to reduce the amount of paperwork.

Many companies have adopted JIT II, an updated form of just-in-time manufacturing. JIT II involves the sharing of up-to-the-minute internal, proprietary data such as sales forecasts with suppliers. In addition, agents of suppliers may be allowed to set up office in the manufacturer's facility and may be asked to replace purchasing agents and place orders for themselves.

Order Processing

order processing system System whereby orders are entered into the supply chain and filled.

The order is often the catalyst that brings the supply chain in motion, especially in the build-to-order environments of leading computer manufacturers such as Dell, Gateway, and now Compaq. The **order processing system** processes the re-

GE Information Systems

Find out more about EDI by visiting the Products and Services page of GE Information Systems' Web site. What are current new articles saying about EDI technology? Link to them through the GE IS page.

http://www.geis.com/

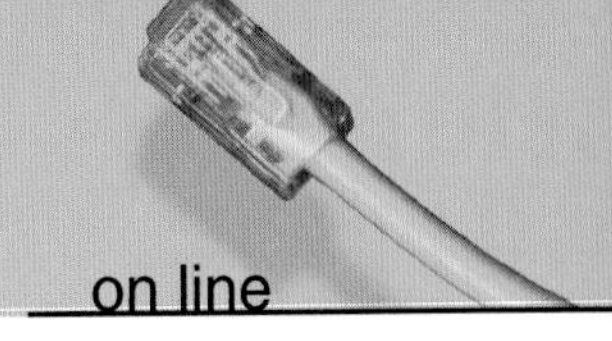

on line

quirements of the customer and sends the information into the supply chain via the logistics information system. The order goes to the manufacturer's warehouse, where it is checked whether the product is in stock. If the product is in stock, the order is fulfilled and arrangements are made to ship. If the product is not in stock, a replenishment request is triggered that finds its way to the factory floor.

The role of proper order processing in providing good service cannot be overemphasized. As an order enters the system, management must monitor two flows: the flow of goods and the flow of information. Often the best-laid plans of marketers can get entangled in the order processing system. Obviously, good communication among sales representatives, office personnel, and warehouse and shipping personnel is essential to correct order processing. Shipping incorrect merchandise or partially filled orders can create just as much dissatisfaction as stockouts or slow deliveries. The flow of goods and information must be continually monitored so mistakes can be corrected before an invoice is prepared and the merchandise shipped.

ON LINE

Order processing is becoming more automated through the use of computer technology known as **electronic data interchange (EDI).** The basic idea behind EDI is to replace the paper documents that usually accompany business transactions, such as purchase orders and invoices, with electronic transmission of the needed information. Companies that use EDI can reduce inventory levels, improve cash flow, streamline operations, and increase the speed and accuracy of information transmission. EDI is also believed to create a closer relationship between buyers and sellers.

electronic data interchange (EDI)
Information technology that replaces the paper documents that usually accompany business transactions, such as purchase orders and invoices, with electronic transmission of the needed information to reduce inventory levels, improve cash flow, streamline operations, and increase the speed and accuracy of information transmission.

It should not be surprising that retailers have become major users of EDI. For Wal-Mart, Target, Kmart, and the like, logistics speed and accuracy are crucial competitive tools in an overcrowded retail environment. Many big retailers are helping their suppliers acquire EDI technology so that they can be linked in the system. EDI works hand in hand with retailers' *efficient consumer response* programs, which are designed to have the right products on the shelf, in the right styles and colors, through improved inventory, ordering, and distribution techniques. (See Chapter 11 for more discussion of retailers' use of EDI techniques.)

Inventory Control

Closely interrelated to the procurement, manufacturing, and ordering processes is the inventory control system. An **inventory control system** develops and maintains an adequate assortment of materials or products to meet a manufacturer's or a customer's demands.

inventory control system
Method of developing and maintaining an adequate assortment of products to meet customer demand.

Inventory decisions, for both raw materials and finished goods, have a big impact on supply chain costs and the level of service provided. If too many products are kept in inventory, costs increase—as do risks of obsolescence, theft, and damage. If too few products are kept on hand, then the company risks product shortages and angry customers, and ultimately lost sales. A study by Procter & Gamble found that out-of-stock products reduced consumer purchases by more than 3 percent per shopping trip, and 48 percent of P&G's products were out of stock at least once a month, costing the company valuable sales and customer satisfaction.[37] The goal of inventory management, therefore, is to keep inventory levels as low as possible while maintaining an adequate supply of goods to meet customer demand.

Managing inventory from the supplier to the manufacturer is called **materials requirement planning (MRP)** or materials management. This system also encompasses the sourcing and procurement operations, signaling purchasing when

materials requirement planning (MRP)
Inventory control system that manages the replenishment of raw materials, supplies, and components from the supplier to the manufacturer.

exhibit 10.12

Inventory Replenishment Example

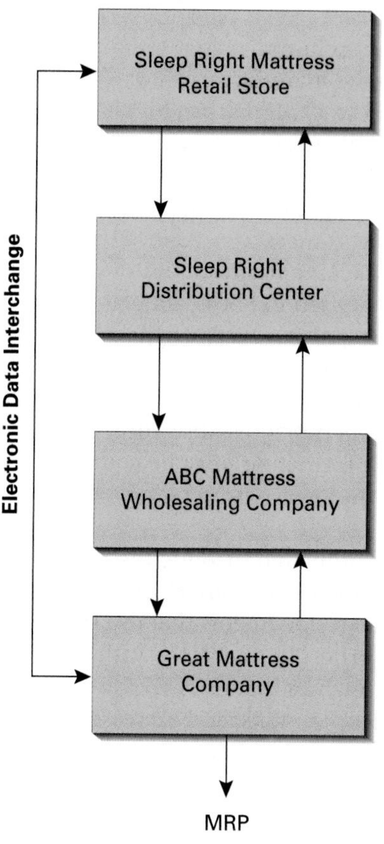

Sleep Right is planning a promotion on the Great Mattress Company's Gentle Rest mattress. Sales forecast is for fifty units to be sold. Sleep Right has ten open Gentle Rest orders with its distribution center. New mattresses must be delivered in two weeks in time for the promotion.

Sleep Right's Distribution Center is electronically notified of the order of fifty new Gentle Rest mattresses. It currently has twenty Gentle Rest mattresses in inventory and begins putting together the transportation plans to deliver these to the Sleep Right Store. Delivery takes one day. It orders forty new mattresses from its mattress wholesaler to make up the difference.

ABC Mattress Wholesaling Company is electronically notified of Sleep Right DC's order of forty new Gentle Rest mattresses. It currently does not have any of these in stock but electronically orders forty from the Great Mattress Company's factory. Once it receives the new mattresses, it can have them delivered to the Sleep Right DC in two days.

The Great Mattress Company electronically receives ABC's order and forwards it to the factory floor. Production of a new mattress takes twenty minutes. The total order of forty mattresses can be ready to be shipped to ABC in two days. Delivery takes one day. Raw material supplies for this order are electronically requested from Great Mattress's supply partners, who deliver the needed materials just-in-time to its stitching machines.

distribution resource planning (DRP)
Inventory control system that manages the replenishment of goods from the manufacturer to the final consumer.

more raw materials, supplies, or components will need to be replenished for the production of more goods. Systems that manage the finished goods inventory from the manufacturer to end user are commonly referred to as **distribution resource planning (DRP)**. Both inventory systems use various inputs—such as sales forecasts, available inventory, outstanding orders, lead times, and mode of transportation to be used—to determine what actions must be taken to replenish goods at all points in the supply chain. Demand in the system is collected at each level in the supply chain, from the retailer back up the chain to the manufacturer. With the use of electronic data interchange, the transmission speed of the information can be greatly accelerated, thereby enhancing the quick-response needs of today's competitive marketplace.[38] Exhibit 10.12 provides an example of inventory replenishment using distribution resource planning from the retailer to the manufacturer.

Enhanced versions of DRP have emerged, especially in the retailing and supermarket industries, under the names of *continuous replenishment* (CR), *efficient consumer response* (ECR), and *vendor managed inventory* (VMI). Although these systems are beyond the scope of this discussion, all are designed to increase the speed by which inventory needs can be communicated throughout the supply chain by utilizing information technology to migrate from pushing product down the supply chain to pulling inventory onto retailers' shelves, driven by actual customer demand. The mechanics of CR, ECR, and VMI focus on increasing the flow and sharing of sensitive information across the distribution pipeline, which, in turn, accelerates the flow of product from the manufacturer to the point of sale. Procter & Gamble estimates it has saved its retail partners, such as retail giant Wal-Mart, more than $65 million through more efficient logistics management resulting from such inventory control methods.[39]

Just-in-time manufacturing processes have had a significant impact on reducing inventory levels. Because JIT requires supplies to be delivered at the time they are needed on the factory floor, little inventory is needed. With JIT the purchasing firm can reduce the amount of raw materials and parts it keeps on hand by ordering more often and in smaller amounts. Lower inventory levels due to JIT also can give firms a competitive edge through the flexibility to halt production of existing products in favor of ones gaining popularity with consumers. Additional savings come from less capital tied up in inventory and from the reduced need for storage facilities.[40]

GLOBAL

In a true supply chain management environment where all members of the supply chain are working closely together, companies are substituting information for inventory. Cisco Systems recently partnered with UPS Worldwide Logistics to develop a more efficient process for sending its routers to Europe. Of the tons of routers it ships to European markets each week, Cisco needed to know where each box was at all times with the ability to reroute an order to fill an urgent request. Using its knowledge of international plane, train, and trucking schedules, UPS can send and track Cisco's routers from the company's manufacturing facility in California to European customers in under four days. When Cisco did the job, deliveries took up to three weeks. The partnership with UPS saves Cisco precious dollars once tied up in inventory.[41]

Warehousing and Materials Handling

Supply chain logisticians oversee the constant flow of raw materials from suppliers to manufacturer and finished goods from the manufacturer to the ultimate consumer. Although just-in-time manufacturing processes may eliminate the need to warehouse many raw materials, manufacturers may often keep some safety stock on hand in the event of an emergency, such as a strike at a supplier's plant or a catastrophic event that temporarily stops the flow of raw materials to the production line. Likewise, the final user may not need or want the goods at the same time the manufacturer produces and wants to sell them. Products like grain and corn are produced seasonally, but consumers demand them year-round. Other products such as Christmas ornaments and turkeys are produced year-round, but consumers do not want them until autumn or winter. Therefore, management must have a storage system to hold these products until they are shipped.

Storage is what helps manufacturers manage supply and demand, or production and consumption. It provides time utility to buyers and sellers, which means that the seller stores the product until the buyer wants or needs it. Even when products are used regularly, not seasonally, many manufacturers store excess products in case the demand surpasses the amount produced at a given time. Storing additional product does have disadvantages, however, including the costs of insurance on the stored product, taxes, obsolescence or spoilage, theft, and warehouse operating costs. Another drawback is opportunity costs—that is, the lost opportunities of using for something else the money that is tied up in stored product.

A **materials-handling system** moves inventory into, within, and out of the warehouse. Materials handling includes these functions:

materials-handling system
Method of moving inventory into, within, and out of the warehouse.

- Receiving goods into the warehouse or distribution center
- Identifying, sorting, and labeling the goods
- Dispatching the goods to a temporary storage area
- Recalling, selecting, or picking the goods for shipment (may include packaging the product in a protective container for shipping)

The goal of the materials-handling system is to move items quickly with minimal handling. With a manual, nonautomated materials-handling system, a product may be handled more than a dozen times. Each time it is handled, the cost and risk of damaging it increase; each lifting of a product stresses its package. Consequently, most manufacturers today have moved to automated systems. Scanners quickly identify goods entering and leaving a warehouse through bar-coded labels affixed to the packaging. Automatic storage and retrieval systems automatically store and pick goods in the warehouse or distribution center. Automated materials-handling systems decrease product handling and ensure accurate placement of product, as well as improve the accuracy of order picking and the rates of on-time shipment.

Baxter Health Care, a leading manufacturer and marketer of health-care products, uses a sophisticated materials-handling system to reduce product handling and keep costs to a minimum. As goods are received into the warehouse, bar-coded labels are affixed to the pallets of incoming product, which are then placed on a fully automated conveyor to be sent to the storage area. There, truck operators scan the labels while an on-board, radio-controlled computer tells the operator exactly where to drop off the load. When the items to fill an order are picked off the shelves and placed in a carton, another bar-coded label is applied, and the carton is placed on the conveyor system. Automatic scanners posted throughout the intricate conveyor system read each bar code and divert each carton to the proper shipping lane. This automated system gives Baxter a high degree of control over how orders are handled, placed, picked, and sequenced for shipping.

Transportation

Transportation typically accounts for between 5 and 10 percent of the price of goods.[42] Supply chain logisticians must decide which mode of transportation to use to move products from supplier to producer and from producer to buyer. These decisions are, of course, related to all other logistics decisions. The five major modes of transportation are railroads, motor carriers, pipelines, water transportation, and airways. Logistics managers generally choose a mode of transportation on the basis of several criteria:

- *Cost:* The total amount a specific carrier charges to move the product from the point of origin to the destination
- *Transit time:* The total time a carrier has possession of goods, including the time required for pickup and delivery, handling, and movement between the point of origin and the destination
- *Reliability:* The consistency with which the carrier delivers goods on time and in acceptable condition
- *Capability:* The ability of the carrier to provide the appropriate equipment and conditions for moving specific kinds of goods, such as those that must be transported in a controlled environment (for example, under refrigeration)
- *Accessibility:* The carrier's ability to move goods over a specific route or network
- *Traceability:* The relative ease with which a shipment can be located and transferred

The mode of transportation used depends on the needs of the shipper, as they relate to the six criteria described above. Exhibit 10.13 compares the advantages and problems of the basic modes of transportation on these criteria.

In many cases, especially in a just-in-time manufacturing environment, the transportation network replaces the warehouse or eliminates the expense of storing inventories because goods are timed to arrive the moment they're needed on the assembly line or for shipment to customers. Dell Computer has

exhibit 10.13

Criteria for Ranking Modes of Transportation

	Highest				Lowest
Relative Cost	Air	Truck	Rail	Pipe	Water
Transit Time	Water	Rail	Pipe	Truck	Air
Reliability	Pipe	Truck	Rail	Air	Water
Capability	Water	Rail	Truck	Air	Pipe
Accessibility	Truck	Rail	Air	Water	Pipe
Traceability	Air	Truck	Rail	Water	Pipe

gone even further to trim inventory of parts by, for instance, taking delivery of components just minutes before they are needed. Instead of going to a Dell distribution center, monitors are shipped from the supplier's factory in Mexico at the same time that a finished computer leaves Dell's factory in Texas. The two components meet for the first time in a delivery van just before reaching the customer.[43]

Trends in Logistics

9 Discuss new technology and emerging trends in logistics

Several technological advances and business trends affect the logistics industry today. Three of the most outstanding trends are increased automation, outsourcing of logistics functions, and electronic distribution.

Automation

Computer technology has boosted the efficiency of logistics dramatically. One of the major goals of automation is to bring up-to-date information to the logistics manager's desk. For instance, logisticians have long referred to the transportation system as the "black hole," where products and materials fall out of sight until they reappear some time later in a plant, store, or warehouse. Now carriers have systems that track freight, monitor the speed and location of carriers, and make routing decisions on the spur of the moment. Over three-fourths of the nation's major trucking companies now use computers to help plan routes and over half have computers aboard each truck to monitor location by satellite. Such systems help transportation firms compete in today's demanding economy. With retailers and manufacturers keeping less inventory, deliveries must often be made at exact times to avoid shutting down a plant or forcing a store to run out of a popular product.[44]

The rapid exchange of information that automation brings to the distribution process helps each supply chain partner plan more effectively. The links among suppliers, buyers, and carriers open up opportunities for joint decision making. As more companies compete in global markets, timely information becomes even more important. For example, some 17,500 UPS employees are now equipped with "ring scanners"—small, electronic devices worn on their index finger and wired to a small computer on their wrists. When a handler holds a package, the ring shoots a pattern of photons at a bar code on the package. Within moments, its location flashes to customers trolling the Internet. The Internet service can also zap the signature of whoever signs for a shipment anywhere in the world.[45]

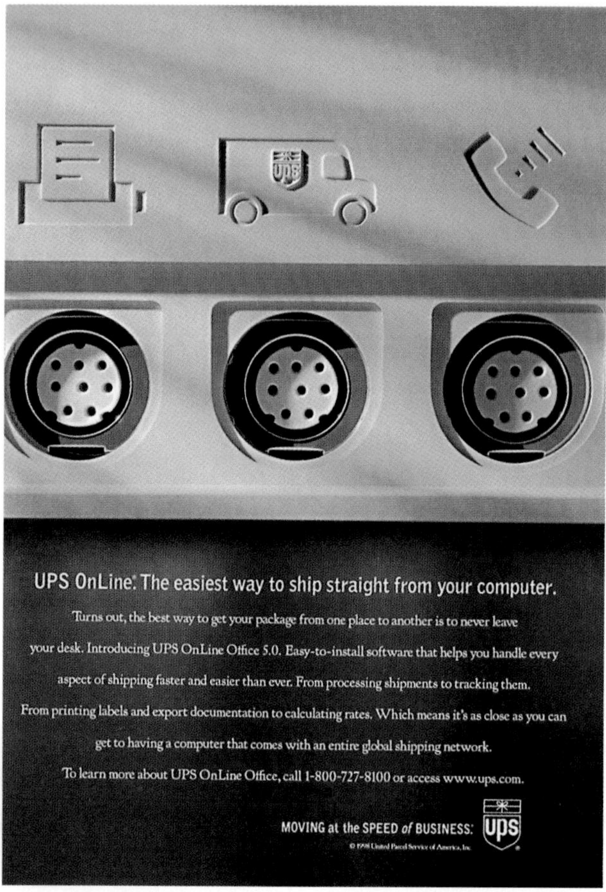

UPS
UPS OnLine: The easiest way to ship straight from your computer.
Turns out, the best way to get your package from one place to another is to never leave your desk. Introducing UPS OnLine Office 5.0. Easy-to-install software that helps you handle every aspect of shipping faster and easier than ever. From processing shipments to tracking them. From printing labels and export documentation to calculating rates. Which means it's as close as you can get to having a computer that comes with an entire global shipping network.
To learn more about UPS OnLine Office, call 1-800-727-8100 or access www.ups.com.
MOVING at the SPEED of BUSINESS.
UPS

UPS OnLine helps its clients to be more self-sufficient in processing and tracking shipments. UPS customers can take more ownership of their logistics functions without having to invest in customized logistics technology.
Courtesy United Parcel Service of America, Inc.

outsourcing (contract logistics)
Manufacturer's or supplier's use of an independent third party to manage an entire function of the logistics system, such as transportation, warehousing, or order processing.

Outsourcing Logistics Functions

External partners are becoming increasingly important in the efficient deployment of supply chain management. **Outsourcing** or **contract logistics** is a rapidly growing segment of the distribution industry in which a manufacturer or supplier turns over the entire function of buying and managing transportation or another function of the supply chain, such as warehousing, to an independent third party. Many manufacturers are turning to outside partners for their logistics expertise in an effort to focus on the core competencies that they do best. Partners create and manage entire solutions for getting products where they need to be, when it needs to be there. Logistics partners offer staff, an infrastructure, and services that reach consumers virtually anywhere in the world. Because a logistics provider is focused, clients receive service in a timely, efficient manner, thereby increasing customers' level of satisfaction and boosting their perception of added value to a company's offerings.[46] A recent study found that nearly 75 percent of U.S. manufacturers and suppliers are either using or considering using a third-party logistics service.[47]

Third-party contract logistics allows companies to cut inventories, locate stock at fewer plants and distribution centers, and still provide the same service level or even better. The companies then can refocus investment on their core business. Whirlpool decided to use a third-party logistics provider after realizing it was spending too much on moving products—costs that were cutting into profits. Each of Whirlpool's eleven U.S. plants handled its own logistics, resulting in a tangle of routes and inefficiencies that spiraled costs out of control. On a single day two or more Whirlpool trucks might make stops to pick up goods from a supplier when a single truck could have done the job. Whirlpool decided outsourcing was the best option, allowing the company to concentrate on what it does best: make appliances. The company selected Ryder Dedicated Logistics, which soon untangled and coordinated the transport routes. Ryder now runs warehouses for Whirlpool and collects data that let it analyze supplier performance and spot new cost-cutting opportunities.[48]

Many firms are taking outsourcing one step further by allowing business partners to take over the final assembly of their product or its packaging in an effort to reduce inventory costs, speed up delivery, or meet customer requirements better. Ryder assembles and packages twenty-two different combinations of shrink-wrapped boxes that contain the ice trays, drawers, shelves, doors, and other accessories for the various refrigerator models Whirlpool sells. Before, Whirlpool would install the accessories in the refrigerators at the plant—a source of considerable factory-floor confusion.[49] IBM allows some of its distributors to do more of the final product assembly. Today, about 31 percent of its U.S. desktop personal computers are assembled by eleven business partners, many of

Outpost

What kind of downloadable software can you purchase on the Outpost Web page? Are there any free programs available?

http://www.outpost.com/

on line

whom may install non-IBM components. One reseller actually assembles some of its IBM orders in a warehouse right next to IBM's factory in North Carolina, saving on distribution costs.[50] For Nike's new athletic-equipment division, contract logistics provider Menlo Logistics inflates basketballs, soccer balls, and footballs, which come in half-inflated because they take up less room. The logistics company also puts the balls in colorful packages and sticks on price tags for some sports retailers.[51]

Electronic Distribution

ON LINE

Electronic distribution is the most recent development in the logistics arena. Broadly defined, **electronic distribution** includes any kind of product or service that can be distributed electronically, whether over traditional forms such as fiber-optic cable or through satellite transmission of electronic signals. The Internet Shopping Network (**http://www.isn.com/**), the largest on-line seller of computer hardware and software, just added a Downloadable Software division. Customers access the ISN over the Internet, select the software program they wish to purchase, transfer their credit card information, and have the software available for use immediately. Using new technology that compresses data much more than in the past, movies and music CDs are now downloadable and playable on computerized home entertainment systems. This method will revolutionize physical distribution as we know it today for any product that can be transmitted through electronic means, including newspapers, books, magazines, and audio and video entertainment.

electronic distribution
Distribution technique that includes any kind of product or service that can be distributed electronically, whether over traditional forms such as fiber-optic cable or through satellite transmission of electronic signals.

Channels and Distribution Decisions for Services

The fastest-growing part of our economy is the service sector. Although distribution in the service sector is difficult to visualize, the same skills, techniques, and strategies used to manage inventory can also be used to manage service inventory—for instance, hospital beds, bank accounts, or airline seats. The quality of the planning and execution of distribution can have a major impact on costs and customer satisfaction.

10
Identify the special problems and opportunities associated with distribution in service organizations

One thing that sets service distribution apart from traditional manufacturing distribution is that, in a service environment, production and consumption are simultaneous. In manufacturing, a production setback can often be remedied by using safety stock or a faster mode of transportation. Such substitution is not possible with a service. The benefits of a service are also relatively intangible—that is, you can't normally see the benefits of a service, such as a doctor's physical exam. A consumer can, however, normally see the benefits provided by a product—for example, a vacuum cleaner removing dirt from the carpet.

Because service industries are so customer oriented, customer service is a priority. Service distribution focuses on three main areas:

- *Minimizing wait times:* Minimizing the amount of time customers wait in line to deposit a check, wait for their food at a restaurant, or wait in a doctor's office for an appointment is a key factor in maintaining the quality of service. People tend to overestimate the amount of time they spend waiting in line, researchers report, and unexplained waiting seems longer than explained waits. To reduce anxiety among waiting customers, some restaurants give patrons pagers that allow them to roam around or go to the bar. Banks sometimes

USAirways

Visit USAir's Web site to find out more about its on-line service delivery. Try to book a flight for your next trip over the Internet. Is it as convenient as you thought it would be?
http://www.usair.com/

install electronic boards displaying stock quotes or sports scores. Car rental companies reward repeat customers by eliminating their waits altogether.[52] Airports have designed comfortable sitting areas with televisions and children's play areas for those waiting to board planes.

- *Managing service capacity:* For a product manufacturer, inventory acts as a buffer, enabling it to provide the product during periods of peak demand without extraordinary effort. Service firms don't have this luxury. If they don't have the capacity to meet demand, they must either turn down some prospective customers, let service levels slip, or expand capacity. For instance, at tax time a tax preparation firm may have so many customers desiring its services that it has to either turn business away or add temporary offices or preparers. Popular restaurants risk losing business when seating is unavailable or the wait is too long.
- *Improving delivery through new distribution channels:* Like manufacturers, service firms are now experimenting with different distribution channels for their services. These new channels can increase the time that services are available (such as using the Internet to disseminate information and services twenty-four hours a day) or add to customer convenience (like pizza delivery, walk-in medical clinics, or a dry cleaner located in the supermarket). Many banks are experimenting with mobile bank branches. NationsBank sends a portable ATM machine to dispense cash at parades and provide banking services during emergencies such as hurricanes. First Chicago NBD drives its mobile bank into inner-city neighborhoods to reach poorer customers often given scant attention by other banks.[53] KeyCorp has replaced many of its full-service branches with mini-branches, called Key Centers, in high-traffic locations, such as supermarkets. It addition, telephone banking generates more than a hundred thousand inbound calls a day.[54]

ON LINE

The Internet is fast becoming an alternative channel through which to deliver services. Consumers can now purchase plane tickets, plan a vacation cruise, reserve a hotel room, pay bills, purchase mutual funds, and receive electronic newspapers in cyberspace. USAirways, for instance, sells 20 percent of its tickets over the Internet. Travelers visit USAirways' Web site, purchase a ticket, receive a reservation number, and present the number at the airport to board the plane.[55]

Channels and Distribution Decisions for Global Markets

11 Discuss channel structure and logistics issues in global markets

GLOBAL

The world is indeed becoming a friendlier place for marketers. The surging popularity of free-market economics, such as the European Community and the North American Free Trade Agreement, over the past decade or so has swept away many barriers. As a result, businesses are finding that the world market is more appealing than ever. Thus, global marketing channels and management of the supply chain are important to U.S. corporations that export their products or manufacture abroad.

Developing Global Marketing Channels

Executives should recognize the unique cultural, economic, institutional, and legal aspects of each market before trying to design marketing channels in foreign countries. Manufacturers introducing products in global markets face a tough decision: what type of channel structure to use. Specifically, should the product be marketed directly, mostly by company salespeople, or through independent foreign intermediaries such as agents and distributors? Using company salespeople generally provides more control and less risk than using foreign intermediaries. However, setting up a sales force in a foreign country also entails a greater commitment, both financially and organizationally.

Marketers should be aware that the channel structure abroad may not be very similar to channels in the United States. For instance, U.S. firms wishing to sell goods in Japan frequently must go through three layers of wholesalers and subwholesalers: the national or primary wholesalers, the secondary or regional wholesalers, and the local wholesalers. Amway succeeded in Japan by circumventing Japan's inefficient and expensive retail distribution system by offering alternative ways to shop via mail-order catalogs and home visits by Amway distributors. Through its savvy distribution system, Amway Japan is one of that country's most profitable companies.[56]

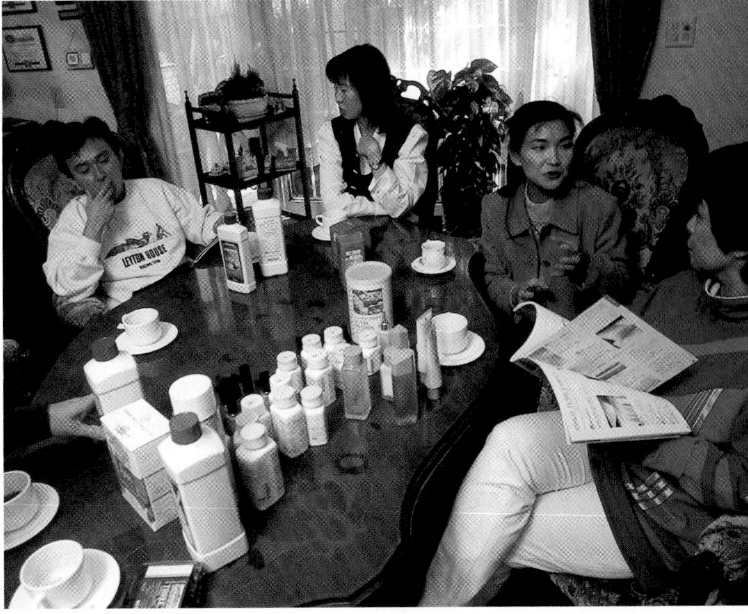

By creating a channel that circumvented Japan's inefficient and expensive retail distribution system, Amway has become one of the country's most profitable companies. As a result, Amway has many more distributors in Japan than it does in the United States.
© Tom Wagner/SABA

The channel types available in foreign countries usually differ as well. The more highly developed a nation is economically, the more specialized its channel types. Therefore, a marketer wishing to sell in Germany or Japan will have several channel types to choose from. Conversely, developing countries like India, Ethiopia, and Venezuela have limited channel types available; there are typically few mail-order channels, vending machines, or specialized retailers and wholesalers.

Marketers must also be aware of "gray" marketing channels in many foreign countries, in which products are distributed through unauthorized channel intermediaries. For example, GM imports only a handful of its Chevy Astro vans into Japan, but more than 80 percent of the van's sales are made through a shadowy network of independent gray-market importers, where prices are substantially cheaper. Astros sold in Japan through official channels start at $41,000. Because gray-market dealers keep inventories low and avoid costly overhead, prices start at about $35,000, and dickering can knock off another 5 to 10 percent. However, because the vehicles aren't sold through proper channels, gray-market cars aren't covered by factory warranties. Service and repairs can also be a hassle because gray-market dealers aren't equipped to handle them. Gray-market sales divert business from GM's official importers, and GM occasionally has to deal with angry gray-market customers who complain when they can't get service. In fact, GM is trying to limit gray-market sales by policing dealers in port cities on the East and West Coasts of the United States, where most of the vehicles originate. GM has also stopped allowing Japanese tourists to buy Astros in the United States and take them home.[57]

Global Logistics and Supply Chain Management

As global trade becomes a more decisive factor in success or failure for firms of all sizes, a well-thought-out global logistics strategy becomes ever more important. Uncertainty regarding shipping usually tops the list of reasons why companies, especially smaller ones, resist international markets. Even companies that have scored overseas successes often are vulnerable to logistical problems. Large companies have the capital to create global logistics systems, but smaller companies often must rely on the services of carriers and freight forwarders to get their products to overseas markets. Read about one company's successful strategy for global distribution in the "Global Perspectives" box.

global perspectives

How Rich Products Created a Global Supply Chain

When Rich Products began expanding overseas, it found that the secret of success was establishing the right mix of corporate control and local management.

A family-owned business, Rich Products, based in Buffalo, New York, reported more than $1.1 billion in revenue from sales in some fifty countries in 1997. The company is the largest U.S. supplier of frozen bread dough to in-store bakeries and food services. It also produces nondairy products like dessert toppings and creamers, and a Georgia-based subsidiary processes more frozen shrimp than any other U.S. concern.

Although it has operated north of the U.S. border in Canada since the early 1960s, Rich products didn't expand aggressively overseas until the early 1990s. Jack T. Ampuja, Rich's vice president of logistics, says Rich decided to go overseas as a way to grow business. "Like most food companies, we didn't see much growth opportunity in North America because consumption is directly related to population increases."

Foreign countries offered an untapped market with strong growth potential. Rich's discovered that, although dairy-product concerns were well-established abroad, its nondairy products were unheard of in many countries. On top of that, many cultures were interested in alternatives to traditional dairy products.

The company usually tries to gain a foothold in a foreign market by selling exported products before establishing a plant there. This tactic was used when it moved into Mexico and then into the European market. In Europe, for instance, it began shipping product made in the United States to develop a market in England. When it had built up sufficient sales volume, it turned over operations to two co-packers in the United Kingdom. These co-packers, one in England and the other in Scotland, piggybacked on Rich's existing arrangements with suppliers to obtain ingredients in an effort to duplicate the product's taste and appearance. They then packaged the goods for sale throughout Europe.

When it expanded to the Indian market in 1995, however, Rich Products tried a different tactic. The company struck a partnership with India's largest ice-cream vendor, Kwality Foods in Pune, India. Rich's provides the technology to Kwality Foods to make nondairy consumer goods. The Indian company, in turn, provides manufacturing plants and an established distribution system. "A joint venture allows a company to know the culture and work through its partner's infrastructure," says Ampuja. The company's move into South Africa two years later took a similar tactic. Rich entered into a joint venture with a Johannesburg company to make and distribute frozen dough.

When Rich Products began its expansion abroad, it established an international distribution group within the logistics department, in which many members speak a foreign language. Because each person in the group is assigned to a specific geographic region such as the Middle East or Southeast Asia, he or she gets to know the customers, carriers, and other supply chain members for that region. The international group selects the carriers and forwarders to handle the physical movement of the ingredients and products for the worldwide supply chain. The group also works closely with the various worldwide divisions, venture partners, and co-packers providing training and selecting managers.

Although the group encourages the local partners to take advantage of existing relationships with carriers and third-party logistics providers, it leaves the internal distribution decisions, such as warehousing and transportation, to the managers in each country. "It's impossible to manage the local distribution from some point in the United States," says Ampuja. "We're not aware of all the local nuances and service nuances."

Such nuances can take the form of a country's individual shipping regulations, transportation infrastructure, or cultural practices. For instance, when Rich Products moved into Mexico, it discovered that the warehouse operations normally ceased work at 2 P.M. It had to find a volunteer to come in and load a truck to move product from the plant to its market after 2 P.M. In India, the plant based in Pune was some 120 miles outside of Mumbai (formerly Bombay). It took trucks six or more hours to navigate that stretch of two-lane road from the factory to the port because when cattle crossed the road or a bus stopped to let off passengers, all vehicles would stop and wait. In addition, the warehouse in India had no power equipment because labor was so cheap and plentiful.

In establishing a global supply chain, the most difficult part is making the initial foray into a country's market. Because each country has its own transportation network, laws, and ways of doing business, establishing a distribution operation takes work each time. That's why Ampuja says it's critical to have local distribution personnel working in any given country. "It makes all the difference in the world to have contacts who speak the local language," he says. "To do it from the United States, you run into language and time barriers. You have to have someone looking out for your welfare on the other end."

SOURCE: From "Global Supply Chain: How Rich Products Went Global" by James Aaron Cooke, September 1998. Reproduced with permission from *Logistics Management & Distribution Report*.

One of the most critical global logistical issues for importers of any size is coping with the legalities of trade in other countries. Shippers and distributors must be aware of the permits, licenses, and registrations they may need to acquire and, depending on the type of product they are importing, the tariffs, quotas, and other regulations that apply in each country. Another important factor to consider is the transportation infrastructure in a country. For example, the Commonwealth of Independent States (the former Soviet Union) has little transportation infrastructure outside the major cities, such as roads that can withstand heavy freight trucks, and few reliable transportation companies of any type. In China, post offices aren't equipped for bulk mailings and they don't deliver parcels to residential addresses, so Germany's Bertelsmann Book Club created its own crew of seventy bicycle-riding deliverymen in Shanghai to deliver books to book club members.[58]

Other emerging countries have similar situations. In Nigeria, for example, a crumbling road system, aging trucks, and safety concerns forced Nestlé to rethink its traditional distribution methods. Instead of operating a central warehouse, the company built small warehouses across the country. For safety reasons, trucks carrying Nestlé goods are allowed to travel only during daylight hours, frequently under armed guard.[59] Similarly, a wave of coffee heists from trucks and warehouses in Brazil prompted coffee exporters to develop new safety systems in the supply chain. Most Brazilian coffee exporters now send their coffee on the road in convoys of at least three trucks, do not allow travel at night, and have equipped drivers with cellular phones. They are even prepared to send a security car with the convoy if necessary.[60]

LOOKING BACK

As you complete this chapter, you should be able to see how marketing channels operate and how physical distribution is necessary to move goods from the manufacturer to the final consumer. Companies can choose from several different marketing channels to sell their products or sell in several channels. For example, as the opening story discussed, computer manufacturers can use direct channels, like Dell has done, or indirect channels using one or more resellers. Computer manufacturers Compaq and IBM have been experimenting with direct channels. Dell and Gateway also utilize the Internet as a distribution channel for their products.

Summary

1 Explain what a marketing channel is and why intermediaries are needed. Marketing channels are composed of members that perform negotiating functions. Some intermediaries buy and resell products; other intermediaries aid the exchange of ownership between buyers and sellers without taking title. Nonmember channel participants do not engage in negotiating activities and function as an auxiliary part of the marketing channel structure. Intermediaries are often included in marketing channels for three important reasons. First, the specialized expertise of intermediaries may improve the overall efficiency of marketing channels. Second, intermediaries may help overcome discrepancies by making products available in quantities and assortments desired by consumers and business buyers and at locations convenient to them. Third, intermediaries reduce the number of transactions required to distribute goods from producers to consumers and end users.

2 Define the types of channel intermediaries and describe their functions and activities. The most prominent difference separating intermediaries is whether or not they take title to the product, such as retailers and merchant wholesalers. Retailers are firms that sell mainly to consumers. Merchant wholesalers are those organizations who facilitate the movement of products and services from the manufacturer to producers, resellers, governments, institutions, and retailers.

Agents and brokers, on the other hand, do not take title to goods and services they market but do facilitate the exchange of ownership between sellers and buyers. Channel intermediaries perform three basic types of functions. Transactional functions include contacting and promoting, negotiating, and risk taking. Logistical functions performed by channel members include physical distribution, storing, and sorting functions. Finally, channel members may perform facilitating functions such as researching and financing.

3 Describe the channel structures for consumer and business-to-business products and discuss alternative channel arrangements. Marketing channels for consumer and business-to-business products vary in degree of complexity. The simplest consumer product channel involves direct selling from producers to consumers. Businesses may sell directly to business or government buyers. Marketing channels grow more complex as intermediaries become involved. Consumer product channel intermediaries include agents, brokers, wholesalers, and retailers. Business product channel intermediaries include agents, brokers, and industrial distributors. Marketers often use alternative channel arrangements to move their products to the consumer. With dual distribution or multiple distribution, they choose two or more different channels to distribute the same product. Nontraditional channels help differentiate a firm's product from the competitor's or provide a manufacturer with another avenue for sales. Adaptive channels are flexible and responsive channels of distribution initiated when a firm identifies critical but rare customer requirements that they do not have the capability to fulfill. Once the requirements are identified, arrangements with other channel members are made to help satisfy these requests. Finally, strategic channel alliances are arrangements that use another manufacturer's already established channel.

4 Discuss the issues that influence channel strategy. When determining marketing channel strategy, the marketing manager must determine what market, product, and producer factors will influence the choice of channel. The manager must also determine the appropriate level of distribution intensity. Intensive distribution is distribution aimed at maximum market coverage. Selective distribution is achieved by screening dealers to eliminate all but a few in any single area. The most restrictive form of market coverage is exclusive distribution, which entails only one or a few dealers within a given area.

5 Explain channel leadership, conflict, and partnering. Power, control, leadership, conflict, and partnering are the main social dimensions of marketing channel relationships. Channel power refers to the capacity of one channel member to control or influence other channel members. Channel control occurs when one channel member intentionally affects another member's behavior. Channel leadership is the exercise of authority and power. Channel conflict occurs when there is a clash of goals and methods among the members of a distribution channel. Channel conflict can be either horizontal, among channel members at the same level, or vertical, among channel members at different levels of the channel. Channel partnering is the joint effort of all channel members to create a supply chain that serves customers and creates a competitive advantage. Collaborating channel partners meet the needs of consumers more effectively by ensuring that the right products reach shelves at the right time and at a lower cost, boosting sales and profits.

6 Discuss logistics and supply chain management and their evolution into distribution practice. Logistics is the process of strategically managing the efficient flow and storage of raw materials, in-process inventory, and finished goods from point of origin to point of consumption. The supply chain connects all of the business entities, both internal and external to the company, that perform or support the logistics function. Supply chain management, or integrated logistics, coordinates and integrates all of these activities performed by supply chain members into a seamless process that delivers enhanced customer and economic value through synchronized management of the flow of goods and information from sourcing to consumption. The concept of supply chain management evolved from the physical distribution of agricultural goods in the early 1900s, which focused on pushing products to market. Today, logistics and supply chain management are viewed as a key means of differentiation for a firm and a critical component in marketing and corporate strategy. The focus is on pulling products into the marketplace and partnering with members of the supply chain to work together and share information with the goal of enhancing customer value.

7 Discuss the concept of balancing logistics service and cost. Today, logistics service is recognized as an area in which a firm can distinguish itself from the competition. Many logisticians strive to achieve an optimal balance of customer service and total distribution cost. Important aspects of service are availability of product, timeliness of deliveries, and quality (accuracy and condition) of shipments. In evaluating costs, logistics managers examine all parts of the supply chain—sourcing and procurement of raw materials, warehousing and materials handling, inventory control, order processing, and transportation—using the total cost approach. Many logisticians are decreasing their emphasis on reducing logistics costs to the lowest possible level in favor of exploiting logistics capabilities to increase customer satisfaction and maintain customer demand.

8 Describe the integrated functions of the supply chain. The logistics supply chain consists of several interrelated and integrated functions: (1) procuring supplies and raw materials, (2) scheduling production, (3) processing orders, (4) managing inventories of raw materials and finished goods, (5) warehousing and materials handling, and (6) selecting modes of transportation. Integrating and linking all of the logistics functions of the supply chain is the logistics information system. Information technology connects the various components and partners of the supply chain to make an integrated whole. The supply chain team, in concert with the logistics information system, orchestrates the movement of goods, services, and information from the source to the consumer. Supply chain teams typically cut across organizational boundaries, embracing all parties who participate in moving product to market. Procurement deals with the purchase of raw materials, supplies, and components according to production scheduling. Order processing monitors the flow of goods and information (order entry and order handling). Inventory control systems regulate when and how much to buy (order timing and order quantity). Warehousing provides storage of goods until needed by the customer while the materials-handling system moves inventory into, within, and out of the warehouse. Finally, the major modes of transportation include railroads, motor carriers, pipelines, waterways, and airways.

9 Discuss new technology and emerging trends in logistics. Several trends are emerging in today's logistics industry. Technology and automation are bringing up-to-date distribution information to the decision maker's desk. Technology is also linking suppliers, buyers, and carriers for joint decision making and has created a new electronic distribution channel. Many companies are saving money and time by out- sourcing third-party carriers to handle some or all aspects of the distribution process.

10 Identify the special problems and opportunities associated with distribution in service organizations. Managers in service industries use the same skills, techniques, and strategies to manage logistics functions as managers in goods-producing industries. The distribution of services focuses on three main areas: minimizing wait times, managing service capacity, and improving delivery through new distribution channels.

11 Discuss channel structure and logistics issues in global markets. Global marketing channels are becoming more important to U.S. companies seeking growth

KeyTerms

adaptive channel 321
agents and brokers 315
channel conflict 326
channel control 326
channel leader (channel captain) 326
channel members 313
channel partnering (channel cooperation) 328
channel power 326
direct channel 318
discrepancy of assortment 313
discrepancy of quantity 313
distribution resource planning (DRP) 340
dual distribution (multiple distribution) 319
electronic data interchange (EDI) 339
electronic distribution 345
exclusive distribution 325
horizontal conflict 328
intensive distribution 324
inventory control system 339
just-in-time production (JIT) 338
logistics 330
logistics information system 336
logistics service 334
marketing channel (channel of distribution) 313
mass customization (build-to-order) 337
materials-handling system 341
materials requirement planning (MRP) 339
merchant wholesaler 315
order processing system 338
outsourcing (contract logistics) 344
retailer 315
selective distribution 324
spatial discrepancy 314
strategic channel alliance 322
supply chain 330
supply chain management (integrated logistics) 331
supply chain team 336
temporal discrepancy 313
vertical conflict 328

abroad. Manufacturers introducing products in foreign countries must decide what type of channel structure to use—in particular, whether the product should be marketed through direct channels or through foreign intermediaries. Marketers should be aware that channel structures in foreign markets may be very different from those they are accustomed to in the United States. Global distribution expertise is also emerging as an important skill for logistics managers as many countries are removing trade barriers.

Discussion and Writing Questions

1. Describe the most likely marketing channel structure for each of these consumer products: candy bars, Tupperware products, nonfiction books, new automobiles, farmers' market produce, and stereo equipment. Construct alternative channels for these same products.
2. Discuss the reasons intermediaries are important to the distribution of most goods. What important functions do they provide?
3. ON LINE Amazon.com successfully uses a direct channel to sell books and music to consumers over the Internet. How has Amazon affected traditional book retailers with brick and mortar buildings? How have giant booksellers Barnes & Noble and Borders countered Amazon's competitive advantage in its direct channel?
4. Decide which distribution intensity level—intensive, selective, or exclusive—is used for the following products and why: Rolex watches, Land Rover sport utility vehicles, M&Ms, special edition Barbie dolls, Crest toothpaste.
5. WRITING You have been hired to design an alternative marketing channel for a firm specializing in the manufacturing and marketing of novelties for college student organizations. In a memo to the president of the firm, describe how the channel operates.
6. Discuss the benefits of supply chain management. How does the implementation of supply chain management result in enhanced customer value?
7. Discuss the trade-offs between logistics service and cost. How can the high cost of expensive air transportation to enhance service be offset? How does logistics service impact customer satisfaction?
8. Discuss the impact of just-in-time production on the entire supply chain. Specifically, how does JIT affect suppliers, procurement planning, inventory levels, mode of transportation selected, and warehousing? What are the benefits of JIT to the end consumer?
9. Assume that you are the logistics manager for a producer of high-tech, expensive computer components. Identify the most suitable method(s) of transporting your product in terms of cost, transit time, reliability, capability, accessibility, and traceability. Now assume you are the logistics manager for a producer of milk. How does this change your choice of transportation?
10. WRITING Assume that you are the marketing manager of a hospital. Write a report indicating the distribution functions that concern you. Discuss the similarities and dissimilarities of distribution for services and for goods.
11. ON LINE Visit the Web site of Menlo Logistics at **http://www.menlolog.com**. What logistics functions can this third-party logistics supplier provide? How does their mission fit in with the supply chain management philosophy?

Application for Small Business

ENTREPRENEUR

Boudreaux has owned and operated a small spice-manufacturing business in south Louisiana for about ten years. Boudreaux has also experimented with preparing and selling several sauces, mostly for meats and salads. For the most part, his firm has sold its products locally. On occasion, however, distributors have signed contracts to sell Boudreaux's products regionally.

Boudreaux's most recent product—a spicy Cajun mayonnaise—has been a huge success locally, and several inquiries have come from large distributors about the possibilities of selling the mayonnaise regionally and perhaps nationally. No research has been conducted to determine the level or scope of demand for the mayonnaise. Also, it has been packaged and sold in only a twelve-ounce bottle. The red-and-white label just says "Boudreaux's Cajun Mayonnaise" and lists the major ingredients.

Questions

1. What should Boudreaux do to help the firm decide how best to market the new Cajun mayonnaise?
2. Should Boudreaux sign a contract with one of the distributors to sell the Cajun mayonnaise, or should his firm try to sell the product directly to one or more of the major supermarket chains?

Review Quiz

1. Which of the following is *not* another name for a channel member?
   a. Intermediary
   b. Reseller
   c. Middleman
   d. All of the above are names for channel members
2. Marketing channels overcome _______ by maintaining inventories in anticipation of future demand for products.
   a. Discrepancies of quantity
   b. Discrepancies of assortment
   c. Temporal discrepancies
   d. Spatial discrepancies
3. Channels can help simplify distribution by reducing the number of transactions required to get products from manufacturers to consumers. This need that is fulfilled by a distribution channel is
   a. Providing specialization of labor
   b. Providing division of labor
   c. Overcoming discrepancies
   d. Providing contact efficiency
4. Which of the following types of channels would most likely be used when there are many manufacturers and many retailers who often lack the resources to find each other?
   a. Direct channel
   b. Agent/broker channel
   c. Retailer channel
   d. Wholesaler channel

5. The concept of a flexible and responsive channel of distribution is called a(n):
   a. Multiple channel
   b. Nontraditional channel
   c. Adaptive channel
   d. Strategic channel alliance
6. ______ is distribution that is aimed to maximize marketplace coverage.
   a. Intensive distribution
   b. Selective distribution
   c. Strategic distribution
   d. Exclusive distribution
7. According to the evolution of integrated logistics, what distribution phase are marketers in today?
   a. The segmented functions phase
   b. The integrated functions phase
   c. The customer focus phase
   d. The logistics as differentiator phase
8. Some independent channel members can perform channel duties more efficiently than can the manufacturer of the product.
   a. True
   b. False
9. Merchant wholesalers always take title to the goods that they sell.
   a. True
   b. False
10. The product life cycle can have a significant impact on the producer's choice of a distribution channel.
    a. True
    b. False
11. The total cost approach to logistics suggests that the supply chain be analyzed as a set of individual and unrelated set of activities.
    a. True
    b. False
12. Identify the three basic channel functions performed by intermediaries and give an example of each.

Check the Answer Key, which follows the Video Case, to see how well you understood the material.

VIDEO CASE

Burton Snowboards: Going Global

Burton Snowboards is a designer and manufacturer of premier snowboarding equipment, and since its somewhat humble start in 1977, the company has grown from a single workshop in Vermont into an international retailer. Higher sales require a more involved distribution system, so in 1992, Burton relocated its offices to Burlington, Vermont. Because Burlington offered easy access to an international airport, a larger workforce, and more business services, Burton expected to achieve better distribution of its products from its new headquarters. In conjunction with smaller offices in Austria and Japan, the Burlington office links Burton to retailers and consumers in the United States and abroad. Although Burton does all its manufacturing in Vermont, it has warehouses in Vermont, New York, Europe, and Asia.

In order to reach the maximum number of customers, Burton uses dual distribution. This means that it sells the same products to snowboarders through direct and indirect marketing channels. One outlet in its direct marketing strategy is its headquarters in Burlington, where Burton sells to roughly one hundred customers a day. The headquarters houses the manufacturing facility, offices, and a factory showroom, whose retail store sells everything Burton makes, from hard goods to soft goods. The hard-good line includes snowboards, bindings, boots, board and travel bags, and back packs, and the soft goods are five categories of specially designed clothing made from highly breathable and highly waterproof insulated fabrics. Direct marketing of products is also handled through mail order, catalog shopping, and online Internet retailing. The latest addition to the company's direct marketing efforts, the Burton Web site gives a detailed description of all the products and explains the many different kinds of snowboards and gear available each season. Internet users can then order the catalog from the American, European, or Japanese offices.

The Internet and Burton's dual distribution strategy have made it easy for customers around the world to buy Burton products, but this has not always been so. Prior to 1985, Burton was sending snowboards to Europe based on individual requests, but the company finally realized that it could simplify distribution by cutting the number of transactions required to get products from the factory to the rider. In response to this need, the Burton Snowboard company decided to develop a marketing channel using intermediaries, dealers, and distributors who buy and resell the products.

Burton intermediaries provide the specialized expertise necessary for efficient product education and distribution. Distributors and dealers communicate with new and repeat customers to create awareness of Burton's product features, advantages, and benefits. Perhaps more importantly, however, intermediaries ensure that the right quantities, proportions, and assortments of products are available at one location so that riders have the right number and kind of items they need when they need them. After all, having a great snowboard doesn't mean much unless you have the bindings to go with it. Burton's supply chain connects all the business entities that move company products to the right place at the right time, and this chain allows Burton to avoid discrepancies that could reduce customer satisfaction, cost the company repeat business, or compromise its reputation. To support its extensive distribution network, Burton uses a supply chain information system to track every piece of inventory throughout the world and to monitor ordering, delivery, and bill payment.

When the company first decided to use intermediaries, Jake Burton, the company founder and owner, had to choose a marketing channel strategy that took the particulars of the market, his company, and its products into consideration. He had to ask the question, "Where are the potential snowboarders?" The answer to that primary question has been constantly evolving since it was first asked. When the company started, it advertised in major publications and filled orders as they came in directly to the Vermont office. As the popularity of snowboarding increased to the point of being accepted at most American ski resorts, national distribution began to make more sense. When Burton saw the untapped potential of the European market, he opened up shop in Austria. By the late 1990s, Burton Snowboards was doing business in twenty-seven countries.

Product factors also influenced the company channel decisions. Burton snowboards are highly customized, varying in length, type of ride (freestyle, freeride, or carving), and graphic design. For such specialized products, a shorter, more direct marketing channel is preferable. Channel selection is also influenced by the type of manufacturer. Jake Burton's investment in Burton Snowboards is reflected in the distribution strategy the company has pursued. Because he personally spent years developing the sport of snowboarding and the products that go with it, Burton wanted to control his company's pricing, positioning, brand image, and customer support initiatives.

Another issue affecting Burton's channel strategy was the level of distribution intensity—that is, the number of outlets available to customers for buying snowboards and other Burton products. Jake Burton chose selective distribution, screening dealers to eliminate all but a few retailers in any single area and having the company's outside sales force and internal distribution management staff work closely with this focused group of American retailers. In Europe, the challenge of screening prospective distributors was more difficult, so Jake Burton carefully selected only dealers who were dedicated to the sport of snowboarding.

Burton Snowboards has risen to be the industry leader in its market, and its multipronged distribution strategy that uses both direct and indirect channels is what allows the company to provide top-of-the-line snowboards, bindings, boots, and clothing to snowboarders worldwide.

Questions

1. Describe Burton Snowboards' dual distribution.
2. What advantages does Burton gain from using a channel of distribution?
3. How do marketing channels help Burton overcome discrepancies?
4. Using Exhibit 10.6, explain the intensity of distribution levels. Why did Burton choose selective distribution?

Bibliography

Reade Bailey, "Jake Burton, King of the Hill," *Ski*, February 1998, pp. 67–68.

Burton Snowboards Press Kit

Burton Web site: **http://www.burton.com**

Answer Key

1. *Answer:* d, p. 313

   Rationale: A channel member is any organization that helps producers move goods to their final consumers.

2. *Answer:* c, p. 313

   Rationale: A temporal discrepancy is created when a product is produced but a consumer is not yet ready to buy it.

3. *Answer:* d, p. 314

   Rationale: Increasing the number of channel members in a marketing system is a way to overcome contact inefficiency, making an assortment of goods possible at a single location.

4. *Answer:* b, p. 315

   Rationale: An agent/broker channel is often very complicated and the agents or brokers typically act on behalf of many producers at once.

5. *Answer:* c, pp. 320–322

   Rationale: Adaptive channels are flexible and typically involve close relationships between channel members so that customer requests can be more easily satisfied.

6. *Answer:* a, p. 324

   Rationale: With intensive distribution, the manufacturer tries to have the product available in every outlet in which a potential customer might look for it.

7. *Answer:* d, p. 332

   Rationale: As the 1980s drew to a close, logistics began to be viewed as a key way for a firm to differentiate itself from its competitors.

8. *Answer:* a, p. 313

   Rationale: Marketing channels can often perform functions more efficiently than producers by obtaining economies of scale through specialization and division of labor.

9. *Answer:* a, p. 315

   Rationale: Merchant wholesalers help facilitate exchange in a distribution channel and always take title to the goods they distribute.

10. *Answer:* a, p. 323

    Rationale: The product life cycle is an important factor in choosing a marketing channel and thus causes channels to change over the life of a product in the marketplace.

11. *Answer:* b, p. 334

    Rationale: When using the total cost approach, the supply chain must be viewed as a whole rather than as a series of unrelated functions and activities.

12. *Answer:*

    Transactional functions—contacting and promoting
    Logistical functions—storing
    Facilitating functions—financing
    (p. 316)

CHAPTER

11

LEARNING OBJECTIVES

After studying this chapter, you should be able to

1. Discuss the importance of retailing in the U.S. economy
2. Explain the dimensions by which retailers can be classified
3. Describe the major types of retail operations
4. Discuss nonstore retailing techniques
5. Define franchising and describe its two basic forms
6. List the major tasks involved in developing a retail marketing strategy
7. Discuss the challenges of expanding retailing operations into global markets
8. Describe future trends in retailing

RETAILING

Old Navy's sales are soaring and the bargain basement never looked so good. What started as The Gap's attempt to compete with discount stores like Sears and Target, which had been eating into its sales by selling their own brands of basics, has turned into retail's biggest success story.

Old Navy is The Gap's answer to the modern-day discount store. Although about 80 percent of its merchandise is priced under $30, Old Navy is anything but your plain vanilla discount store. Instead, it's part bargain hunter's paradise and way-cool hangout—and the combination is irresistible to shoppers, not only stealing sales away from the likes of Kmart but department store shoppers as well. "Very basic merchandise in a very sophisticated physical environment," says Ed Nardoza, editor of the fashion bible *Women's Wear Daily*, who thinks Old Navy is a brilliant example of shopping as entertainment.

In retrospect, the idea that makes Old Navy sail seems obvious enough: make the clothes inexpensive and the environment amusing. When The Gap CEO Mickey Drexler hatched the concept, however, no one catering to the bargain shopper paid much attention to atmosphere. As executives at The Gap started Old Navy in 1994, they talked about what they didn't like about discount stores—poor quality, colors that were always just a bit off. Discount shopping was the hot growth area in retailing, but, Drexler asked, did it need to be so depressing?

What emerged from their brainstorming is Old Navy—big, loud, fun, and cheap. Old Navy stores are fitted out with exposed pipes and raw concrete floors. Neon signs guide shoppers down wide aisles. Instead of shopping carts, there are the cool mesh shopping bags. There are listening booths where customers can sample CDs and old grocery-store refrigerator cases stocked with T-shirts shrink-wrapped like packages of ground beef. Customers are greeted with free lemonade, pretzels, and a fleet of golf carts to ease the long walk from the parking lot. Then there's Magic, Old Navy's irresistible mutt mascot.

The pitch was perfect and Old Navy was an instant success. Sales at Old Navy have already passed a billion dollars in annual sales—a feat no other retail clothier has managed so quickly. By 2000, there will likely be close to five hundred Old Navy stores around the country with

on line

The Gap

How would you like to buy your clothes on-line? Go to The Gap Web site and see what you think of the experience.
http://www.gap.com/onlinestore/gap/

sales approaching or surpassing $4 billion. Although profit margins are slimmer at Old Navy stores compared to its siblings The Gap and Banana Republic, the chain solves this problem by keeping the design of its clothing very basic—simple A-line dresses, drawstring pants, and T-shirts are standard items—and making them in attractive but less costly fabrics. To make its clothes more fashionable, the store often relies on clever packaging. Such common, disparate pieces as underwear, socks, and long-sleeved tees might be dyed the same color and showcased together in an eye-catching bundle or in a refurbished ice cream truck.

Old Navy will soon begin selling its clothing on the Web, like its older sibling The Gap, giving shoppers another avenue to experience the chain's "discount shopping with an edge." Visit The Gap's site at **http://www.gap.com.**[1]

Attracting consumers is a major concern for today's retailers. What factors do you see as being important to a store's retailing mix? This chapter seeks to answer this question and many more by discussing retailers and wholesalers as intermediaries in the channel of distribution. Each performs an important role in moving products and services to the ultimate consumer.

The chapter begins with a discussion of the role of retailing and the ways in which retail operations can be classified. Also included is a description of the decisions involved in developing a retail marketing strategy. The chapter concludes with a summary of the types of wholesalers.

The Role of Retailing

1

Discuss the importance of retailing in the U.S. economy

retailing
All the activities directly related to the sale of goods and services to the ultimate consumer for personal, nonbusiness use.

Retailing—all the activities directly related to the sale of goods and services to the ultimate consumer for personal, nonbusiness use—has enhanced the quality of our daily lives. When we shop for groceries, hair styling, clothes, books, and many other products and services, we are involved in retailing. The millions of goods and services provided by retailers mirror the needs and styles of U.S. society.

Retailing affects all of us directly or indirectly. The retailing industry is one of the largest employers; over 1.6 million U.S. retailers employ more than twenty million people, or nearly one out of every five workers. Retailers ring up over $2.2 trillion in sales annually, amounting to over a quarter of the U.S. gross domestic product (GDP).[2] Small retailers, including small restaurateurs, account for more than half of that sales volume.

Although most retailers are quite small, a few giant organizations dominate the industry. Fewer than 10 percent of all retail establishments account for over half of total retail sales and employ about 40 percent of all retail workers. Who are these giants? Exhibit 11.1 lists the ten largest U.S. retailers.

exhibit 11.1

Ten Largest U.S. Retailers

1997 Rank	Company	Retailing Formats	1997 Revenues ($ billions)	1997 Number of Stores
1	**Wal-Mart** Bentonville, AR	Discount stores, supercenters, and warehouse clubs	118.0	3,406
2	**Sears, Roebuck and Company** Hoffman Estates, IL	Department stores, catalogs, home centers, and specialty	41.2	3,530
3	**Kmart** Troy, MI	Discount stores and supercenters	32.2	2,136
4	**JCPenney** Plano, TX	Department stores, catalogs, and drug stores	29.6	3,981
5	**Dayton Hudson Corporation** Minneapolis, MN	Discount stores and department stores	27.8	1,130
6	**Kroger** Cincinnati, OH	Supermarkets and convenience stores	26.6	2,208
7	**Home Depot** Atlanta, GA	Home centers	24.2	624
8	**Safeway, Inc.** Pleasanton, CA	Supermarkets	22.4	1,368
9	**Costco** Issaquah, WA	Warehouse clubs	21.9	261
10	**American Stores Company** Salt Lake City, UT	Supermarkets and drug stores	19.1	1,557

SOURCE: From "State of the Industry Report: Top 100 Companies," *Chain Store Age*, August 1998. Reprinted by permission from Chain Store Age. Copyright (1998) Lebhar-Friedman, Inc. 425 Park Avenue, NY, NY 10022.

Classification of Retail Operations

2

Explain the dimensions by which retailers can be classified

A retail establishment can be classified according to its ownership, level of service, product assortment, and price. Specifically, retailers use the latter three variables to position themselves in the competitive marketplace. (As noted in Chapter 6,

exhibit 11.2

Types of Stores and Their Characteristics

Type of Retailer	Level of Service	Product Assortment	Price	Gross Margin
Department store	Moderately high to high	Broad	Moderate to high	Moderately high
Specialty store	High	Narrow	Moderate to high	High
Supermarket	Low	Broad	Moderate	Low
Convenience store	Low	Medium to narrow	Moderately high	Moderately high
Drugstore	Low to moderate	Medium	Moderate	Low
Full-line discount store	Moderate to low	Medium to broad	Moderately low	Moderately low
Discount specialty store	Moderate to low	Medium to broad	Moderately low to low	Moderately low
Warehouse clubs	Low	Broad	Low to very low	Low
Off-price retailer	Low	Medium to narrow	Low	Low
Restaurant	Low to high	Narrow	Low to high	Low to high

positioning is the strategy used to influence how consumers perceive one product in relation to all competing products.) These three variables can be combined in several ways to create distinctly different retail operations. Exhibit 11.2 lists the major types of retail stores discussed in this chapter and classifies them by level of service, product assortment, price, and gross margin.

Ownership

Retailers can be broadly classified by form of ownership: independent, part of a chain, or franchise outlet. Retailers owned by a single person or partnership and not operated as part of a larger retail institution are **independent retailers**. Around the world, most retailers are independent, operating one or a few stores in their community. Local florists, shoe stores, and ethnic food markets typically fit this classification.

independent retailers
Retailers owned by a single person or partnership and not operated as part of a larger retail institution.

Chain stores are owned and operated as a group by a single organization. Under this form of ownership, many administrative tasks are handled by the home office for the entire chain. The home office also buys most of the merchandise sold in the stores.

chain stores
Stores owned and operated as a group by a single organization.

Franchises are owned and operated by individuals but are licensed by a larger supporting organization. Franchising combines the advantages of independent

franchise
The right to operate a business or to sell a product.

ownership with those of the chain store organization. Franchising is discussed in more detail later in the chapter.

Level of Service

The level of service that retailers provide can be classified along a continuum, from full service to self-service. Some retailers, such as exclusive clothing stores, offer high levels of service. They provide alterations, credit, delivery, consulting, liberal return policies, layaway, gift wrapping, and personal shopping. Discount stores usually offer fewer services. Retailers like factory outlets and warehouse clubs offer virtually no services.

Product Assortment

The third basis for positioning or classifying stores is by the breadth and depth of their product line. Specialty stores—for example, Hallmark card stores, Lady Foot Locker, and TCBY yogurt shops—are the most concentrated in their product assortment, usually carrying single or narrow product lines but in considerable depth. On the other end of the spectrum, full-line discounters typically carry broad assortments of merchandise with limited depth. For example, Target carries automotive supplies, household cleaning products, and pet food. However, Target may carry only four or five brands of canned dog food; a supermarket may carry as many as twenty.

Other retailers, such as factory outlet stores, may carry only part of a single line. Liz Claiborne, a major manufacturer of women's clothing, sells only certain items of its own brand in its many outlet stores. Discount specialty stores like Home Depot or Toys 'R' Us carry a broad assortment in concentrated product lines, such as building and home supplies or toys.

Price

Price is a fourth way to position retail stores. Traditional department stores and specialty stores typically charge the full "suggested retail price." In contrast, discounters, factory outlets, and off-price retailers use low prices as a major lure for shoppers.

The last column in Exhibit 11.2 shows the typical gross margin for each type of store. **Gross margin** is how much the retailer makes as a percentage of sales after the cost of goods sold is subtracted. The level of gross margin and the price level generally match. For example, a traditional jewelry store has high prices and high gross margins. A factory outlet has low prices and low gross margins. Markdowns on merchandise during sale periods and price wars among competitors, in which stores lower prices on certain items in an effort to win customers, cause gross margins to decline. When Wal-Mart entered the grocery business in a small Arkansas community, a fierce price war ensued. By the time the price war was in full swing, the price of a quart of milk had plummeted by more than 50 percent (below the price of a pint) and a loaf of bread sold for only 9¢, prices at which no retailer could make a profit.

gross margin
Amount of money the retailer makes as a percentage of sales after the cost of goods sold is subtracted.

Major Types of Retail Operations

There are several types of retail stores. Each offers a different product assortment, type of service, and price level, according to its customers' shopping preferences.

3
Describe the major types of retail operations

Department Stores

Housing several departments under one roof, a **department store** carries a wide variety of shopping and specialty goods, including apparel, cosmetics, housewares, electronics, and sometimes furniture. Purchases are generally made within each department rather than at one central check-out area. Each department is treated as a

department store
A store housing several departments under one roof.

separate buying center to achieve economies in promotion, buying, service, and control. Each department is usually headed by a **buyer**, who not only selects the merchandise for his or her department but may also be responsible for promotion and for personnel. For a consistent, uniform store image, central management sets broad policies about the types of merchandise carried and price ranges. Central management is also responsible for the overall advertising program, credit policies, store expansion, customer service, and so on.

buyer
Department head who selects the merchandise for his or her department and may also be responsible for promotion and personnel.

Large independent department stores are rare today. Most are owned by national chains. Among the largest U.S. department store chains are Sears, Dayton Hudson, JCPenney, Federated Department Stores, and May Department Stores. All operate more than one chain of retail stores, from discount chains to upscale clothiers. Two up-and-coming department store chains are Dillard's, based in Little Rock, Arkansas, and Nordstrom, with corporate headquarters in Seattle. Dillard's is known for its distribution expertise; Nordstrom offers innovative customer service. In the past few years, much attention has been centered on these two growing chains, and both have a very promising future.

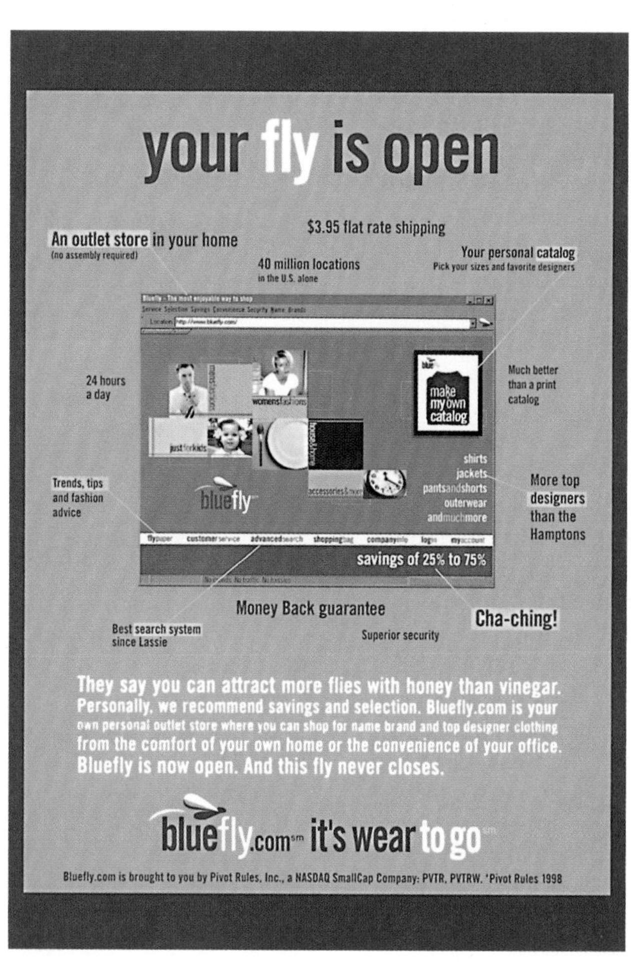

On-line Internet shopping has given consumers an alternative to the often high-priced, stale merchandise offered in department stores. Bluefly.com has capitalized on consumers' desire for high quality, low prices, and convenience.
Courtesy Bluefly.com

In recent years, consumers have become more cost conscious and value oriented. Specialty retailers like The Gap, discounters, catalog outlets, and even on-line Internet shopping alternatives are offering superior merchandise selection and presentation, sharper pricing, and greater convenience to take sales away from department stores. They have also been quicker to adopt new technology and invest in labor-saving strategies. In addition, their leaner cost structure translates into lower prices for the customer. Meanwhile, manufacturers like Liz Claiborne, Bass, Calvin Klein, and Polo/Ralph Lauren have opened outlet stores of their own and more discount stores such as Wal-Mart and Target have upgraded their apparel assortments, taking more sales away from department stores.

Department store managers are using several strategies to preserve their market share. One is to reposition department stores as specialty outlets. They are dividing departments into miniboutiques, each featuring a distinct fashion taste, as specialty stores do. For example, many upscale department stores feature Donna Karan and Liz Claiborne boutiques within their stores. Department stores are also enhancing customer service to shift the focus away from price. Services include complimentary alterations, longer store hours, personalized attention, after-sale follow-up, and personal wardrobe planning. Finally, department stores are expanding, remodeling, and revitalizing to show off new merchandising directions and to reflect the growth in their marketing areas.

Specialty Stores

specialty store
Retail store specializing in a given type of merchandise.

Specialty store formats allow retailers to refine their segmentation strategies and tailor their merchandise to specific target markets. A **specialty store** is not only a type of store but also a method of retail operations—namely, specializing in a given type of merchandise. Examples include children's clothing, men's clothing, candy, baked goods, gourmet coffee, sporting goods, and pet supplies. A typical specialty store carries a deeper but narrower assortment of specialty merchandise than does a department store. Generally, specialty stores' knowledgeable sales clerks offer more attentive customer service. The format has become very powerful in the apparel market and other areas. Benetton, Waldenbooks,

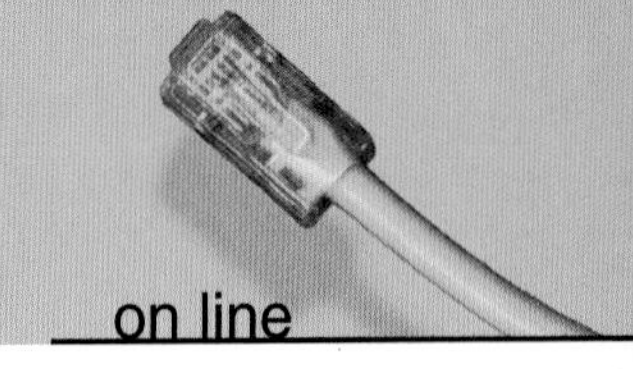

Foot Locker

What do the featured shoes on the Foot Locker Web site have in common? How do Foot Locker's prices on popular brands compare with the prices at your local sporting goods store? Why do you think this is so?
http://www.footlocker.com

Victoria's Secret, The Body Shop, Foot Locker, and Crate & Barrel are several successful chain specialty retailers.

Consumers in specialty outlets usually consider price to be secondary. Instead, the distinctive merchandise, the store's physical appearance, and the caliber of the staff determine its popularity. Independent specialty toys stores, for instance, often shun the mass-produced toys that typically sell in Kmart or Toys 'R' Us in favor of more educational toys or toys that are hard to find, such as Brio's wooden train sets. Because they cannot compete on price with the big toy stores, independent toy retailers offer enhanced service such as personal shopping and free gift wrapping.[3] Manufacturers often favor introducing new products in small specialty stores before moving on to larger retail and department stores. Foot Locker, for example, has been the top retailer of athletic footwear for years, and its full-price shopping mall stores are the major venue for expensive new shoe introductions from Nike and Reebok. Introducing new sport shoes through specialty retailers like Foot Locker creates an image of exclusivity for Nike and Reebok.[4] Small specialty stores also provide a low-risk testing ground for many new product concepts.

Supermarkets

U.S. consumers spend about a tenth of their disposable income in supermarkets. A **supermarket** is a large, departmentalized, self-service retailer that specializes in food and some nonfood items.

supermarket
A large, departmentalized, self-service retailer that specializes in food and some nonfood items.

A decade ago, industry experts predicted the decline of the supermarket industry, whose slim profit margins of just 1 to 2 percent of sales left it vulnerable. These experts originally felt that supermarkets would merely need an ever-growing customer base to sustain volume and compensate for low margins. Although the annual population growth averaged less than 1 percent a year, supermarkets still experienced declining sales. As a result, experts were forced to examine not only population trends but also demographic and lifestyle changes of consumers. They have discovered several trends affecting the supermarket industry.

For example, as dual-income and single-parent families increase, consumers are eating out more or are too busy to prepare meals at home. According to the U.S. Department of Agriculture, Americans spent only about two-thirds of their food money in retail grocery stores, compared with a third spent for food away from home. In comparison, Americans spent over three-fourths of their food money in grocery stores in 1950.[5] The growth in the away-from-home food market has been driven by the entry of more women into the workforce and their need for convenience and time-saving products. Working couples need one-stop shopping, and the increasing number of affluent customers are willing to pay for specialty and prepared foods.

As stores seek to meet consumer demand for one-stop shopping, conventional supermarkets are being replaced by bigger *superstores*, which are usually twice the size of supermarkets. Superstores meet the needs of today's customers for convenience, variety, and service. Superstores offer one-stop shopping for many food and nonfood needs, as well as many services—including pharmacies, flower shops, salad bars, in-store bakeries, take-out food sections, sit-down restaurants, health food sections, video rentals, dry-cleaning services, shoe repair, photo processing, and banking. Some even offer family dentistry or optical shops. This tendency to offer a wide variety of nontraditional goods and services under one roof is called **scrambled merchandising**. Hy-Vee, a supermarket chain based in West Des Moines, Iowa, for instance, sells gift items, such as Barbie and Elmo dolls, decorative clocks, and humidors, during the Christmas season and even offers a holiday decorating service.[6]

scrambled merchandising
The tendency to offer a wide variety of nontraditional goods and services under one roof.

Another demographic trend affecting supermarkets is expanding ethnicity. Over the next fifty years, nonwhite ethnic groups will constitute the fastest-growing segments of the American population. According to the U.S. Census Bureau, the most pronounced population growth will be seen among Hispanics, Asian-Americans, and African-Americans. If current trends in shopping patterns among ethnic groups continue, these demographic changes promise to have a vast impact on supermarket retailers. For example, both African-American and Hispanic households now outspend white American households on weekly grocery shopping. In terms of shopping habits, African-Americans and Hispanics tend to be conservative, looking for products and brands they know and trust and patronizing stores that reliably meet their needs. It will also be increasingly important for supermarkets to tailor their stores' product mix to reflect the demographics of the population they serve.[7]

Many supermarket chains are tailoring marketing strategies to appeal to specific consumer segments to help them stand out in an increasingly competitive marketplace. Most notably is the shift toward *loyalty marketing programs* that reward loyal customers carrying frequent-shopper cards with discounts or gifts. Once scanned at the checkout, frequent-shopper cards help supermarket retailers like American Stores, Food Lion, and Safeway electronically track shoppers' buying habits. The supermarkets then can use the information to "microtarget" customers through direct mail. Other supermarket chains such as Albertson's are attempting to attract customers with an "everyday-low-price" strategy.[8]

Drugstores

drugstore
A retail store that stocks pharmacy-related products and services as its main draw.

VALUE

Drugstores stock pharmacy-related products and services as their main draw. Consumers are most often attracted to a drugstore by its pharmacy or pharmacist, its convenience, or because it honors their third-party prescription drug plan. Drugstores also carry an extensive selection of over-the-counter (OTC) medications, cosmetics, health and beauty aids, seasonal merchandise, specialty items such as greeting cards and a limited selection of toys, and some nonrefrigerated convenience foods.[9] As competition has increased from mass merchandisers and supermarkets with their own pharmacies, as well as from direct-mail prescription services, drugstores have been adding value-added services such as twenty-four-hour operations and drive-through pharmacies. Even more competition could be expected as Wal-Mart develops its newest retailing concept, the Wal-Mart Neighborhood Market, a smaller store format featuring general grocery items, health and beauty aids, cosmetics, and a drive-through pharmacy.[10]

Demographic trends in the United States look favorable for the drugstore industry. As the baby boom population continues to age, they will spend an increasing percentage of their disposable income on health care and wellness. This is good news for the drugstore industry, as the average sixty-year-old purchases fifteen prescriptions per year, nearly twice as many as the average thirty-year-old. Because baby boomers are attentive to their health and keenly sensitive about their looks, the increased traffic at the pharmacy counter in the future should also spur sales in other traditionally strong drugstore merchandise categories, most notably over-the-counter drugs, vitamins, and health and beauty aids.[11]

Convenience Stores

convenience store
A miniature supermarket, carrying only a limited line of high-turnover convenience goods.

A **convenience store** can be defined as a miniature supermarket, carrying only a limited line of high-turnover convenience goods. These self-service stores are typically located near residential areas and are open twenty-four hours, seven days a week. Convenience stores offer exactly what their name implies: convenient location, long hours, fast service. However, prices are usually higher at a convenience store than at a supermarket. Thus the customer pays for the convenience.

From the mid-1970s to the mid-1980s, hundreds of new convenience stores opened, many with self-service gas pumps. Full-service gas stations fought back by closing service bays and opening miniature stores of their own, selling convenience items like cigarettes, sodas, and snacks. Supermarkets and discount stores also wooed customers with one-stop shopping and quick checkout. To combat the gas stations' and supermarkets' competition, convenience store operators have changed their strategy. They have expanded their offerings of nonfood items with video rentals, health and beauty aids, upscale sandwich and salad lines, and more fresh produce. Some convenience stores are even selling Pizza Hut and Taco Bell products prepared in the store.

Discount Stores

A **discount store** is a retailer that competes on the basis of low prices, high turnover, and high volume. Discounters can be classified into four major categories: full-line discount retailers, discount specialty retailers, warehouse clubs, and off-price retailers.

discount store
A retailer that competes on the basis of low prices, high turnover, and high volume.

Full-Line Discounters Compared to traditional department stores, **full-line discount stores** offer consumers very limited service and carry a much broader assortment of well-known, nationally branded "hard goods," including housewares, toys, automotive parts, hardware, sporting goods, and garden items, as well as clothing, bedding, and linens. Some even carry limited nonperishable food items, such as soft drinks, canned goods, and potato chips. As with department stores, national chains dominate the discounters. Full-line discounters are often called mass merchandisers. **Mass merchandising** is the retailing strategy whereby retailers use moderate to low prices on large quantities of merchandise and lower service to stimulate high turnover of products.

full-line discount stores
A retailer that offers consumers very limited service and carries a broad assortment of well-known, nationally branded "hard goods."

mass merchandising
Retailing strategy using moderate to low prices on large quantities of merchandise and lower service to stimulate high turnover of products.

GLOBAL

Wal-Mart is the largest full-line discount organization in terms of sales. With over thirty-four hundred stores, Wal-Mart has expanded rapidly by locating on the outskirts of small towns and absorbing business for miles around. Much of Wal-Mart's success has been attributed to its merchandising foresight, cost consciousness, efficient communication and distribution systems, and involved, motivated employees. Wal-Mart is credited with pioneering the retail strategy of "every-day low pricing," a strategy now widely copied by retailers the world over. Besides expanding throughout all fifty states, Wal-Mart has expanded globally into Mexico, Canada, Puerto Rico, Brazil, Argentina, China, Indonesia, and, most recently, Germany through its acquisition of the German hypermarket chain Wertkauf and Korea with its acquisition of the Korea Makro chain.[12] Retailing abroad has proved to be quite a challenge for the giant discounter.

Kmart, the number-two discounter, has about twenty-one hundred stores but has annual sales that are roughly a third of Wal-Mart's. Kmart has been modernizing stores and boosting its merchandising and advertising to improve its image, but is still finding competition very stiff. In fact, Kmart has had to close some stores and has experienced declining sales. Like Wal-Mart, Kmart also expanded internationally but experienced much less success. The discounter recently sold its entire 123-store Kmart Canada as well as its Builders Square home centers. The sale of its Canadian stores divested Kmart of essentially all foreign involvements, leaving it free to focus entirely on its U.S. operations.[13]

A hybrid of the full-line discounter is the hypermarket, a concept adapted from the Europeans. The flashy **hypermarket** format combines a supermarket and full-line discount store in a space ranging from 200,000 to 300,000 square feet. Although they have enjoyed widespread success in Europe, where consumers have fewer retailing choices, hypermarkets have been much less successful in the United States. Most Europeans still need to visit several small stores just for their food needs, which makes hypermarkets a good alternative. Americans, on the other hand, can easily pick among a host of stores that offer large selections of merchandise. According to retailing executives and analysts, American customers have found hypermarkets to

hypermarket
Retail store that combines a supermarket and full-line discount store in a space ranging from 200,000 to 300,000 square feet.

be too big. Both Wal-Mart's Hypermart USA and Kmart's American Fare hypermarket formats never got beyond the experimental stage.

supercenter
Retail store that combines groceries and general merchandise goods with a wide range of services.

Similar to a hypermarket, but only half the size, are **supercenters,** which combine groceries and general merchandise goods with a wide range of services including pharmacy, dry cleaning, portrait studios, photo finishing, hair salons, optical shops, and restaurants—all in one location. For supercenter operators like Wal-Mart, food is a customer magnet that sharply increases the store's overall volume, while taking customers away from traditional supermarkets.[14] Wal-Mart now operates over 480 SuperCenters and plans to replace many older Wal-Marts with this format. Along with Kmart, which is opening similar Big Kmart supercenters of its own, the two retailers pose a significant threat to traditional supermarkets and drugstores. Target is also opening supercenters, which include a more upscale general merchandise and apparel store combined with a grocery, bank branch, pharmacy, photo studio, and restaurant.

GLOBAL

Supercenters are also threatening to push Europe's traditional small and medium-size food stores into extinction. Old-fashioned corner stores and family businesses are giving way to larger chains that offer food, drugs, services, and general merchandise all in one place. Many European countries are passing legislation to make it more difficult for supercenters to open. In France, for example, laws were passed that banned authorizations for new supercenters over 1,000 square meters (10,800 square feet). Belgium and Portugal have passed similar bans. In Britain and the Netherlands, areas outside towns and cities are off limits to superstores. By imposing planning and building restrictions for large stores, these countries are trying to accommodate environmental concerns, movements to revive city centers, and the worries of small shopkeepers.

VALUE

An increasingly popular variation of the full-line discounter off-price retailing is *extreme-value retailing*, the most notable examples being Dollar General and Family Dollar. Extreme-value retailers have grown in popularity as major discounters continue to shift toward the supercenter format, broadening their customer base and increasing their offerings of higher-priced goods aimed at higher-income consumers. This has created an opening for extreme-value retailers to entice shoppers from the low-income segment. Low- and fixed-income customers are drawn to extreme-value retailers, which offer easy access, small stores (at an average 6,400 square feet, a Dollar General is about the size of one department in a Wal-Mart superstore), a narrow selection of basic merchandise, and rock-bottom prices.[15]

specialty discount store
Retail store that offers a nearly complete selection of single-line merchandise and uses self-service, discount prices, high volume, and high turnover.

category killers
Term often used to describe specialty discount stores because they so heavily dominate their narrow merchandise segment.

Discount Specialty Stores Another discount niche includes the single-line **specialty discount stores**—for example, sporting goods stores, electronics stores, auto parts stores, office supply stores, and toy stores. These stores offer a nearly complete selection of single-line merchandise and use self-service, discount prices, high volume, and high turnover to their advantage. Discount specialty stores are often termed **category killers** because they so heavily dominate their narrow merchandise segment. Examples include Toys 'R' Us in toys, Circuit City and BestBuy in electronics, Staples and Office Depot in office supplies, Home Depot in home improvement supplies, IKEA in home furnishings, and Lil' Things and Babies 'R' Us in baby supplies.

GLOBAL

Toys 'R' Us was the first category killer, offering a giant selection of toys, usually over fifteen thousand different items per store, at prices usually 10 to 15 percent less than competitors'. When Toys 'R' Us came on the retail scene, department stores were generally limiting their toy assortments to the Christmas season. Toys 'R' Us offered a broad assortment of inventory all year long. Additionally, the playing field was scattered with many small toy chains or mom-and-pop stores. With its bright warehouse-style stores, Toys 'R' Us gobbled up market share, and many small toy stores failed and department stores eliminated their toy departments. The Toys 'R' Us chain—currently a $10 billion com-

Toys 'R' Us

Who seems to be the marketing audience for the Toys 'R' Us Web site? Is the site as kid friendly as you expected it to be?

http://www.toysrus.com

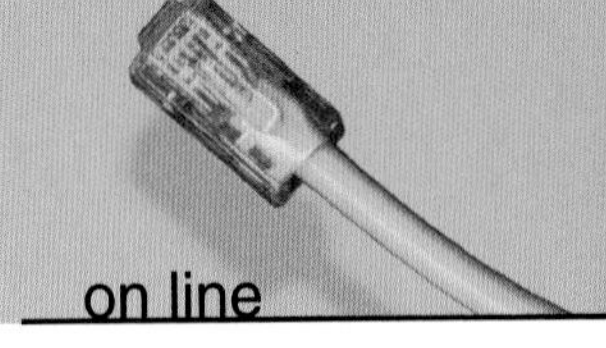

pany with about fourteen hundred stores worldwide—now commands about a quarter of the U.S. retail toy business. Toys 'R' Us first went international in 1984—initially in Canada, then in Europe, Hong Kong, and Singapore. Since then, the company has opened over 450 stores in over two dozen foreign countries. Toys 'R' Us expanded its category killer retailing concept to include the Kids 'R' Us childrens clothing chain and the Babies 'R' Us baby products stores. Most recently, the retailer has entered the mail-order business with its first catalog mailed to more than two million customers. Initial sales generated from the catalog were 40 percent more than expected, showing that customers enjoy the ease and convenience of shopping from their homes.[16] In addition, Toys 'R' Us has ventured into on-line retailing at its Web site. There, customers can choose toys, games, and play equipment to be shipped directly to their home, use the site's gift selection service, or search for a hard-to-find toy.[17]

Other specialty segments have followed the lead of Toys 'R' Us, hoping to build similar retailing empires in highly fragmented mom-and-pop markets. For instance, the home improvement industry was once dominated by professional builders and small hardware stores that offered a basic staple of products. Similarly, prior to the creation of PETsMart and Petco pet supplies chains, the pet industry was dominated by thousands of independent neighborhood pet stores. Another industry that was very fragmented was the office products industry. As more people began to work from home, replacing their typewriters with personal computers and purchasing fax machines, the local stationery store, with its limited selection of paper and writing materials, quickly became obsolete. The industry is now dominated by Office Depot, Staples, and Office Max, each stocking some five thousand to seven thousand different types of products. Category-dominant retailers like these serve their customers by offering an unequaled selection of merchandise, stores that make shopping easy, and low prices every day, which eliminates the need for time-consuming comparison shopping.[18]

Warehouse Clubs **Warehouse membership clubs** sell a limited selection of brand-name appliances, household items, and groceries. These are usually sold in bulk from warehouse outlets on a cash-and-carry basis to members only. Individual members of warehouse clubs are charged low or no membership fees.

warehouse membership clubs
Limited-service merchant wholesaler that sells a limited selection of brand-name appliances, household items, and groceries on a cash-and-carry basis to members, usually small businesses and groups.

Warehouse clubs have had a major impact on supermarkets. With 90,000 square feet or more, warehouse clubs offer 60 to 70 percent general merchandise and health and beauty care products, with grocery-related items making up the difference.[19] Warehouse club members tend to be more educated and more affluent and have a larger household than regular supermarket shoppers. These core customers use warehouse clubs to stock up on staples; then they go to specialty outlets or food stores for perishables.

Fierce competition is commonplace in the warehouse club industry. Common practices include price slashing, selling below cost, locating outlets to compete directly with each other, and sometimes hiring away rivals' employees to get an edge in local markets. Currently, the stores primarily comprising the warehouse club category are Wal-Mart, Sam's Club, Costco, and BJ's Wholesale Club.

Off-Price Discount Retailers An **off-price retailer** sells at prices 25 percent or more below traditional department store prices because it pays cash for its stock and usually doesn't ask for return privileges. Off-price retailers buy manufacturers' overruns at cost or even less. They also absorb goods from bankrupt stores, irregular merchandise, and unsold end-of-season output. Nevertheless, much off-price retailer merchandise is first-quality, current goods. Because buyers for off-price retailers purchase only what is available or what they can get a good deal on, merchandise styles and brands often change monthly. Today there are hundreds of

off-price retailer
Retailer that sells at prices 25% or more below traditional department store prices because it pays cash for its stock and usually doesn't ask for return privileges.

off-price retailers, the best known being T J Maxx, Ross Stores, Marshall's, and Tuesday Morning.

factory outlet
An off-price retailer that is owned and operated by a manufacturer.

Factory outlets are an interesting variation on the off-price concept. A **factory outlet** is an off-price retailer that is owned and operated by a manufacturer. Thus it carries one line of merchandise—its own. Each season, from 5 to 10 percent of a manufacturer's output does not sell through regular distribution channels because it consists of close-outs (merchandise being discontinued), factory seconds, and canceled orders. With factory outlets, manufacturers can regulate where their surplus is sold, and they can realize higher profit margins than they would by disposing of the goods through independent wholesalers and retailers. Factory outlet malls typically locate in out-of-the-way rural areas or near vacation destinations. Most are situated at least thirty miles from urban or suburban shopping areas so manufacturers don't alienate their department store accounts by selling the same goods virtually next door at a discount.

Several manufacturers reaping the benefits of outlet mall popularity include Liz Claiborne, J. Crew, and Calvin Klein clothiers; West Point Pepperel textiles; Oneida silversmiths; and Dansk kitchenwares. Top-drawer department stores—including Saks Fifth Avenue and Neiman Marcus—have also opened outlet stores to sell hard-to-move merchandise. Dillard Department Stores has opened a series of clearance centers to make final attempts to move merchandise that failed to sell in the department store. In order to move their clearance items, Nordstrom operates Nordstrom Rack and Boston's Filene's has Filene's Basement.

As outlet malls have gained in popularity, however, they are beginning to act less and less like traditional outlets in which manufacturers sold surplus or damaged goods. For instance, some manufacturers such as The Gap, Brooks Brothers, Ann Taylor, and Donna Karan now make lower-quality lines specifically for their outlet stores.[20] Further, outlet centers in many locations are competing head-on with regional malls by incorporating entertainment to draw customers. Sawgrass Mills located outside of Ft. Lauderdale, Florida, boasts an eighteen-screen theater, forty restaurants, and a Sega GameWorks, featuring high-tech games in a nightclub atmosphere. The center is now Florida's second-largest tourist attraction after Disney World.[21] Outlet store centers are also cropping up closer and closer to major metropolitan centers. Manufacturers are decreasing their sensitivity toward department stores that carry their brands at full retail price and choosing to locate closer to the customer to be more accessible. Prime Outlets Hagerstown (Maryland), for instance, is only a short distance away from two major urban centers, Baltimore and Washington, D.C., and it is loudly advertising some of the manufacturer names in the center.[22]

Restaurants

Restaurants straddle the line between a retailing establishment and a service establishment. Restaurants do sell tangible products, food and drink, but they also provide a valuable service for consumers in the form of food preparation and food service. Most restaurants could even fall into the definition of a specialty retailer given that most concentrate their menu offerings on a distinctive type of cuisine—for example, Olive Garden Italian restaurants, Starbucks coffeehouses, Popeye's Fried Chicken, and Pizza Hut pizza restaurants.

As a retailing institution, restaurants must deal with many of the same issues as a more traditional retailer, such as personnel, distribution, inventory management, promotion, pricing, and location. Restaurants and food service retailers run the spectrum from those offering limited service and inexpensive food, such as fast-food chains or the local snack bar or coffee house, to those that offer sit-down service and moderate to high prices, such as the likes of the Outback Steakhouse & Saloon chain or a local trendy Italian bistro.

Eating out is an important part of American's daily activities and is growing in strength. According to the National Restaurant Association, Americans consume an average of 4.1 commercially prepared meals per week. Moreover, food away

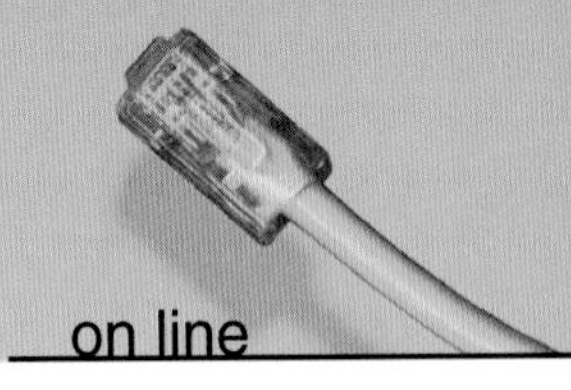

Eatzi's Market & Bakery

How easy do you think it would be for Eatzi's to add Internet ordering to its services? Visit its Web site and then write a short proposal discussing the pros and cons of ordering meals over the Internet.
http://www.eatzis.com

from home accounts for anywhere from 25 percent of the household food budget for low-income families to nearly 50 percent for those with high incomes. The trend in eating out has been fueled in large part by the increase in working mothers and dual-income families who have more money to eat out but less time to spend preparing meals at home.[23] Although consumers are eating out more, however, food service companies have generally overexpanded in terms of the number of retail locations. In the fast-food segment, for instance, the number of restaurants has increased from one outlet per 1,672 people in the United States to one for every 1,343 persons.[24]

ENTREPRENEUR Still, the restaurant industry remains one of the most entrepreneurial of businesses and one of the most competitive. Because barriers to entering the restaurant industry are low, the opportunity appeals to many people. The risks, however, are great. About 50 percent of all new restaurants fail within the first year of operation. Restaurants face competition not only from other restaurants but also from the consumer who can easily choose to cook at home. Competition has fostered innovation in the restaurant industry, such as Pizza Hut's introduction of The Edge pizza, to the ever-changing menus at fast-food restaurants. Seeking out and targeting underserved distribution niches is another way restaurants are competing with one another to reach consumers. Fast-food operators are increasingly looking to provide service at locations such as hospitals, airports, schools, and highway rest stops.[25] Some Mobil stations feature Dunkin' Donuts shops, and Church's Chicken shares space with some Texaco convenience store franchises. These pairings save money on property leases, lure more customers, and foster innovation.[26]

More restaurants are now competing directly with supermarkets by offering take-out and delivery in an effort to capture more of the home meal replacement market. Eatzi's Market & Bakery, for instance, is a cross between a gourmet grocery store and an upscale delicatessen where chefs behind counters cook, bake, and prepare meals. Eatzi's now has markets open in Dallas, Houston, Atlanta, and New York City where their chefs create over 100 ready-to-go entrees, 50 breads, and 125 desserts. Consumers can even purchase wine, flowers, and cigars to complement their prepared meal.[27]

Nonstore Retailing

4 Discuss nonstore retailing techniques

nonstore retailing Shopping without visiting a store.

The retailing methods discussed so far have been in-store methods, in which customers must physically shop at stores. In contrast, **nonstore retailing** is shopping without visiting a store. Because consumers demand convenience, nonstore retailing is currently growing faster than in-store retailing. The major forms of nonstore retailing are automatic vending, direct retailing, and direct marketing.

Automatic Vending

automatic vending The use of machines to offer goods for sale.

A low-profile yet important form of retailing is automatic vending. **Automatic vending** is the use of machines to offer goods for sale—for example, the cola, candy, or snack vending machines found in college cafeterias and office buildings. Vending is the most pervasive retail business, with about 1.5 million locations in the United States with vending equipment. The most frequent purchases from automatic vending machines are soft drinks, candy, and salty snacks.[28] Due to their convenience, consumers are willing to pay higher prices for products from a vending machine than for the same products in traditional retail settings.

Retailers are constantly seeking new opportunities to sell via vending. For example, in an attempt to expand its distribution beyond supermarkets, convenience stores, and delicatessens, Snapple has developed a glass-front vending machine capable of offering fifty-four different flavors simultaneously. Many vending machines today also sell nontraditional kinds of merchandise, such as videos, toys, stickers, and sports cards. Vending machines in college libraries sell computer diskettes, pens and highlighters, and other office-type supplies. Kodak cameras and film can now be purchased from vending machines in sports stadiums, on beaches, and on mountains. Vending machines in theater lobbies now sell T-shirts imprinted with movie themes. For a *Lost in Space* T-shirt, moviegoers can buy the T-shirt for $16.95 by inserting their credit card into the machine.[29] Marketers are also experimenting with fresh foods in vending machines. Canteen Vending Services, the largest vending operator in the United States, has been stocking fresh sandwiches in its food machines from nationally known restaurants such as Hardee's hamburgers, Rally's hamburgers, and Blimpie subs.[30]

Retailing through vending machines can be especially beneficial to small businesses hard-pressed to find sales help. This form of retailing has been extremely successful in Japan, where everything from jewelry to cubed beef to religious icons can be purchased from vending machines.
© Fujifotos/The Image Works

Direct Retailing

In **direct retailing**, representatives sell products door-to-door, office-to-office, or at home sales parties. Companies like Avon, Mary Kay Cosmetics, The Pampered Chef, Usbourne Books, and World Book Encyclopedia depend on these techniques. Even personal computers are now being sold through direct retailing methods, as you can read about in the "Entrepreneurial Insights" box.

direct retailing
Representatives selling products door-to-door, office-to-office, or at home parties.

Most direct retailers seem to favor party plans these days in lieu of door-to-door canvassing. Party plans call for one person, the host, to gather as many prospective buyers as possible. Most parties are a combination social affair and sales demonstration. For instance, d.terrell, an Atlanta-based direct-sales apparel manufacturer, sells its fashionable women's clothes through wardrobe consultants who several times a year transform their homes into makeshift boutiques. Friends and acquaintances can select a full season's wardrobe in a friendly environment while bypassing the inconveniences and unknowledgeable salespeople at the mall.[31]

The sales of direct retailers have suffered as women have entered the workforce. Working women are not home during the day and have little time to attend selling parties. Although most direct sellers like Avon and Tupperware still advocate the party plan method, the realities of the marketplace have forced them to be more creative in reaching their target customer. Direct sales representatives now hold parties in offices, parks, and even parking lots. Others hold informal gatherings in which shoppers can just drop in at their convenience or offer self-improvement classes. Many direct retailers are also turning to direct mail and telephone orders to find new avenues to their customers and increase sales. Others, like Avon, are turning to more traditional retailing venues. Avon is opening over one hundred retail cosmetics kiosk counters, called Avon Beauty Centers, in an attempt to serve the millions of consumers who say they would buy Avon products if they were available in malls and strip centers.[32]

In response to the decline in U.S. sales, many direct retailers are exploring opportunities in other countries. Amway, the direct seller of shampoo, detergent, toothpaste, and other household products, is one company that has benefited from overseas expansion. Bypassing the joint ventures and lavish advertising campaigns most consumer companies must use to expand overseas, Amway instead mobilized its ethnically diverse sales force to return to their home countries and spread the word, missionary-like, to friends and families. This strategy has helped turn the company into a multinational juggernaut with a sales force of 2.5 million and $68 billion in sales. Today, Amway peddles its products in forty-three countries from Hungary to Malaysia to Brazil. Amway's goal is to have overseas markets account for 80 percent of its sales during the next decade.[33]

entrepreneurial insights

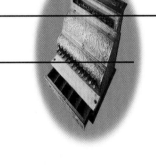

Hand Technologies Sells PCs Like Tupperware

Hand Technologies, an Austin, Texas, startup company, is hoping that what worked for cosmetics and plastic food storage bins in the 1960s will work again for computers today.

Founded by members of the management team that set up Dell Computers in the United Kingdom, Hand Technologies sells computers through a direct retailing method using a team of consultants to sell computer products via demonstrations in the home and local seminars for schools and families. The company now has over one thousand part-time computer buffs, mostly men, in the United States and United Kingdom to sell personal computers directly to the customer.

As many computer sellers try to follow Dell's and Gateway's direct approach of selling directly to customers over the telephone or Internet, Hand Technologies is betting on the personal approach. Chief executive Andrew Harris explains that whereas Dell caters to businesses and experienced users, Hand's mission is to provide a friendly face before people decide to buy a computer. Hand customers are generally not as computer literate as Dell buyers or they are first-time computer buyers.

Harris cofounded Hand on the premise that new users of technology are poorly served by traditional retail and mail-order suppliers. More than anything else, new users need time from a friendly, computer-knowledgeable person, not just during the buying process, but while setting up and learning about the computer and the Internet. In fact, the company's name has a double meaning: every sale begins with a *hand*shake, and the company provides *hand*-holding to get a customer started and supported down the line.

Hand supplies all the products and services that home or small business users need to set up and run a computer and gain access to the Internet. It has priced all its products and services to be a better value than superstores with no price premium, while still offering respected brands such as Compaq, Hewlett-Packard, IBM, Fujitsu, Apple, Microsoft, and Lexmark.

People becoming Hand technology consultants are able to use their technical knowledge to earn money in a flexible working environment. Using the company's Web page, prospective Hand salespeople take a hundred-question on-line quiz to test their computer skills. After passing the test, salespeople can set up a Web page of their own on the site and start making contacts to sell computers. For $95, each Hand sales consultant receives a starter pack that includes business cards, brochures, and a T-shirt. Commissions average about 10 percent of sales.

Hand's aim is to give people quality personal service while they are in the process of buying a computer. Technology consultants demonstrate and explain products and the Internet in a customer's home or office, at a level to suit their existing knowledge. If a customer decides to buy, technology consultants order electronically via Hand's Web site and the products are shipped directly to the customer. The technology consultant then visits the customer to set up the computer and help him or her learn how to use it.

The Hand personal approach to selling computers is expected to be quite successful. Because buyers are able to understand and assimilate the technology properly, they are more satisfied with their purchase. This encourages more sales, leads to fewer product returns, and helps alleviate the level of demand for customer support in the set-up and learning phase of owning a computer.[34]

What other product can you think of that would sell successfully using a direct retailing approach? Explain your choice.

direct marketing (direct-response marketing)
Techniques used to get consumers to make a purchase from their home, office, or other nonretail setting.

Direct Marketing

Direct marketing, sometimes called **direct-response marketing**, refers to the techniques used to get consumers to make a purchase from their home, office, or other nonretail setting. Those techniques include direct mail, catalogs and mail order, telemarketing, and electronic retailing. Shoppers using these methods are less bound by traditional shopping situations. Time-strapped consumers and those who live in rural or suburban areas are most likely to be direct-response shoppers, because they value the convenience and flexibility that direct marketing provides.

Direct Mail Direct mail can be the most efficient or the least efficient retailing method, depending on the quality of the mailing list and the effectiveness of the mailing piece. With direct mail, marketers can precisely target their customers according to demographics, geographics, and even psychographics. Good mailing lists come from an internal database or are available from list brokers for about $35 to $150 per thousand names. For example, a Los Angeles computer software manufacturer selling programs for managing medical records may buy a list of all the physicians in the area. The software manufacturer may then design a direct-mail piece explaining the benefits of its system and send the piece to each physician. Today, direct mailers are even using videocassettes in place of letters and brochures to deliver their sales message to consumers.

Direct mailers are becoming more sophisticated in their targeting of the "right" customers. Using statistical methods to analyze census data, lifestyle and financial information, and past-purchase and credit history, direct mailers can pick out those most likely to buy their products. For example, a direct marketer like Dell Computers might use this technique to target five hundred thousand people with the right spending patterns, demographics, and preferences. Without it, Dell could easily mail millions of solicitations annually. Some solicitations could be targeted to only ten thousand of the best prospects, however, saving the company millions in postage while still preserving sales.

Catalogs and Mail Order Consumers can now buy just about anything through the mail, from the mundane like books, music, and polo shirts to the outlandish, such as the $5 million diamond-and-ruby-studded bra available through the Victoria's Secret catalog. Although women make up the bulk of catalog shoppers, the percentage of male catalog shoppers has soared in recent years. As changing demographics has shifted more of the shopping responsibility onto men, shopping via catalog or mail order is seen as a more sensible solution to men than a trek to a mall.[35]

Successful catalogs are usually created and designed for highly segmented markets. Sears, whose catalog sales had dropped off, replaced its "big book" with a collection of more successful specialty catalogs targeted to specific market segments. Certain types of retailers are also using mail order to good effect. For example, computer manufacturers have discovered that mail order is a lucrative way to sell computers to home and small-business users, evidenced by the huge successes of Dell Computers and Gateway. A fifth of all personal computers sold in the U.S. market are sold through the mail. Consumers can save up to 20 percent off traditional dealer prices by buying their computers from a mail-order house.[36] Some mail-order computer firms also offer free in-home repairs for a year, thirty-day money-back guarantees, and toll-free phone lines for answers to questions.

Improved customer service and quick delivery policies have boosted consumer confidence in mail order. L.L. Bean and Lands' End are two catalog companies known for their excellent customer service. Shoppers may order twenty-four hours a day and can return any merchandise for any reason for a full refund. Other successful mail-order catalogs—including Spiegel, J. Crew, Victoria's Secret, and Lillian Vernon—target hard-working, home-oriented baby boomers who don't have time to visit or would rather not visit a retail store. To remain competitive and save time for customers, catalog companies are building computer databases contain-

Lillian Vernon

How does Lillian Vernon use its successful catalog and mail-order business as a springboard into on-line shopping? Would you prefer to order over the Internet or to call the toll-free number and order from the catalog?

http://www.lillianvernon.com

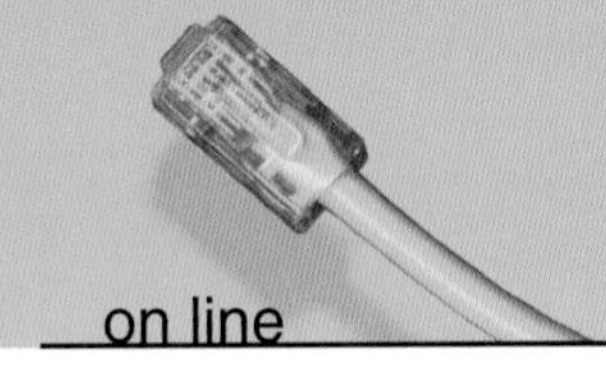

on line

ing customer information so they do not have to repeatedly give their addresses, credit card information, and so on. They also are working with overnight shippers such as UPS and FedEx to speed up deliveries. Indeed, some products can be ordered as late at 12:30 A.M. and still arrive the same day by 10:30 A.M.

Telemarketing **Telemarketing** is the use of the telephone to sell directly to consumers. It consists of outbound sales calls, usually unsolicited, and inbound calls—that is, orders through toll-free 800 numbers or fee-based 900 numbers.

telemarketing
The use of the telephone to sell directly to consumers.

Outbound telemarketing is an attractive direct-marketing technique because of rising postage rates and decreasing long-distance phone rates. Skyrocketing field sales costs also have put pressure on marketing managers to use outbound telemarketing. Searching for ways to keep costs under control, marketing managers are discovering how to pinpoint prospects quickly, zero in on serious buyers, and keep in close touch with regular customers. Meanwhile, they are reserving expensive, time-consuming, in-person calls for closing sales.

Inbound telemarketing programs, which use 800 and 900 numbers, are mainly used to take orders, generate leads, and provide customer service. Inbound 800 telemarketing has successfully supplemented direct-response TV, radio, and print advertising for more than twenty-five years. The more recently introduced 900 numbers, which customers pay to call, are gaining popularity as a cost-effective way for companies to target customers. One of the major benefits of 900 numbers is that they allow marketers to generate qualified responses. Although the charge may reduce the total volume of calls, the calls that do come through are from customers who have a true interest in the product.

Behind the scenes, on the set at QVC broadcasting: QVC moves goods at the rate of $39 per second by broadcasting product pitches around the clock from its television studios in West Chester, Pennsylvania.

Electronic Retailing

Electronic retailing includes the twenty-four-hour, shop-at-home television networks and on-line retailing.

Shop-at-Home Networks The shop-at-home television networks are specialized forms of direct-response marketing. These shows display merchandise, with the retail price, to home viewers. Viewers can phone in their orders directly on a toll-free line and shop with a credit card. The shop-at-home industry has quickly grown into a billion-dollar business with a loyal customer following. Shop-at-home networks have the capability of reaching nearly every home that has a television set.

The best-known shop-at-home networks are the Home Shopping Network and the QVC (Quality, Value, Convenience) Network. Home shopping networks are now branching out with new products to appeal to more affluent audiences—the age and income profile of a typical home-shopping viewer is 31+ with household earnings of more than $60,000. Food marketers like Hershey Foods, Campbell Soup, and Kellogg's are the latest companies to test the potential of shop-at-home networks, especially with new product introductions. Hershey introduced its Pot of Gold boxed candy line on QVC, selling sixteen hundred boxes of candy in four minutes. Campbell plans a full hour on the QVC network to sell reproductions of the first Campbell Kid dolls. Campbell will also showcase historical advertising and videos related to the merchandise being sold. Similarly, Kellogg's introduced Cocoa Frosted Flakes on home shopping channels rather than using traditional channels.[37]

On-line Retailing On-line retailing is a two-way, interactive service available to consumers with personal computers and access to the Internet. Large Internet service providers, like America Online and Microsoft

Network, typically provide shopping services or virtual shopping malls for subscribers. Retailers can also set up their own site on the World Wide Web for on-line shoppers to find. The Gap, for example, operates its own Web site **(http://www.gap.com)** where it sells its clothes and accessories on-line. The site has done considerably well since many Gap products, such as T-shirts and socks, don't require trying on for size.[38] By the year 2000, on-line consumer sales are expected to reach $20 billion, an increase of 233 percent from 1998's sales of about $6.1 billion.[39] Retail products expected to sell well over the Internet include books, computer hardware and software, music and videos, toys, consumer electronics, and even wines.[40] Online retailing also fits well with traditional catalog companies such as Lands' End and Eddie Bauer, who already have established distribution networks.

Despite its potential convenience, on-line shopping has had a slow start. Although the number of consumers purchasing goods on-line has increased dramatically, on-line shopping has not reached the masses. Only about half of all U.S. homes have computers and about thirty percent have on-line access. Further, Web shoppers worry about security and the privacy of their personal information on-line, where marketers can track far more about customer behavior than they can off-line.[41]

Another reason on-line shopping is lagging is that Internet users are overwhelmingly male, but most shopping dollars nationally are spent by women. Additionally, merchants are finding that in the vastness of cyberspace, it can be tough for a single Web site to get noticed. Even many virtual shopping malls (Web sites that feature several retailers at one location) have failed to offer the advantages of their brick-and-mortar counterparts. Whereas physical shopping malls let shoppers visit dozens of stores by traveling to a single location, *everything* is next door on the World Wide Web. Further, the role of anchor stores—department stores and other large retailers likely to draw customers to the mall—seems vastly reduced on the Internet. For example, IBM's World Avenue virtual shopping mall closed its Web site after only about a year in operation. Retailers at the now-defunct virtual mall complained that a lack of promotion or links from other sites attracted few shoppers. In contrast, Marketplace, one of the few successful virtual shopping malls, is accessible via America Online, which gives it a shot at attracting "foot traffic" from the more than eight million AOL subscribers.[42]

However, many on-line merchants are thriving. Selling books, music, and flowers on-line are a few bright spots in terms of sales and visits. 1-800-Flowers has become one of the nation's biggest florists via America Online. Floral wire service is a perfect match to on-line demographics, because men buy the most flowers. Similarly, Amazon.com has become one of the nation's biggest booksellers via the Internet. On-line shoppers can search Amazon's database of over one million titles, read on-line reviews, and receive e-mail alerts about their favorite subjects and authors. CDNow's Internet site offers more than 166,000 music CD titles and buyers can receive their orders within twenty-four hours. Egghead Computer recently closed all of its physical retail stores to become a Web-only retailer of computer software and components. Software purchased at the company's site, **www.egghead.com**, can be downloaded directly to the purchaser's computer.[43]

Franchising

5

Define franchising and describe its two basic forms

A *franchise* is a continuing relationship in which a franchiser grants to a franchisee the business rights to operate or to sell a product. The **franchiser** originates the trade name, product, methods of operation, and so on. The **franchisee**, in return, pays the franchiser for the right to use its name, product, or business methods. A franchise agreement between the two parties usually lasts for ten to twenty years, at which time the franchisee can renew the agreement with the franchiser if both parties are agreeable.

franchiser
Originator of a trade name, product, methods of operation, and so on, that grants operating rights to another party to sell its product.

franchisee
Individual or business that is granted the right to sell another party's product.

To be granted the rights to a franchise, a franchisee usually pays an initial, one-time franchise fee. The amount of this fee depends solely on the individual franchiser, but it generally ranges from \$5,000 to \$150,000. In addition to this initial franchise fee, the franchisee is expected to pay weekly, biweekly, or monthly royalty fees, usually in the range of 3 to 7 percent of gross revenues. The franchisee may also be expected to pay advertising fees, which usually cover the cost of promotional materials and, if the franchise organization is large enough, regional or national advertising. A McDonald's franchise, for example, costs an initial \$45,000 per store with an 8 percent-of-sales fee for royalties and advertising. Franchisee start-up costs include up to \$440,000 for equipment, seating, golden arches, and other signs; \$12,000 to \$22,000 for opening inventory; plus miscellaneous opening expenses that can run into the thousands of dollars.[44] Fees such as this are typical for all major franchisers, including Burger King, Wendy's, Applebee's, and TGI Fridays.

Franchising is not new. General Motors has used this approach since 1898, and Rexall drugstores, since 1901. Today there are over half a million franchised establishments in the United States, with combined sales approaching \$1 trillion by the year 2000. Most franchises are retail operations. There are about two thousand different kinds of franchises in seventy different industries. Of the \$2 trillion in total retail sales, franchising accounts for over 40 percent.[45] Exhibit 11.3 lists some facts about the largest U.S. companies in franchising. For more information, contact the International Franchise Association in Washington, D.C., or go to their Internet Web site at **www.franchise.org**.

There are two basic forms of franchises today: product and trade name franchising and business format franchising. In *product and trade name franchising*, a dealer agrees to sell certain products provided by a manufacturer or a wholesaler. This approach has been used most widely in the auto and truck, soft-drink bottling, tire, and gasoline service industries. For example, a local tire retailer may hold a franchise to sell Michelin tires. Likewise, the Coca-Cola bottler in a particular area is a product and trade name franchisee licensed to bottle and sell Coca-Cola's soft drinks.

Business format franchising is an ongoing business relationship between a franchiser and a franchisee. Typically, a franchiser "sells" a franchisee the rights to use the franchiser's format or approach to doing business. This form of franchising has rapidly expanded since the 1950s through retailing, restaurant, food-service, hotel and motel, printing, and real estate franchises. Fast-food restaurants like McDonald's, Wendy's, and Burger King use this kind of franchising, as well as other companies such as Hyatt Corporation, Unocal Corporation, and Mobil Corporation. Prospective McDonald's franchisees must be willing to train at least a year and work in restaurants without pay before they are granted a franchise to operate. Months of training teaches franchisees how to adhere to the detailed business system that made McDonald's famous for consistency around the world.[46]

GLOBAL

Like other retailers, franchisers are seeking new growth abroad. According to the International Franchise Association, about 450 U.S. franchisers have begun international expansion and a thousand more are preparing to enter the worldwide market soon.[47] Australia is one of the more popular expansion countries for U.S. franchisers. Emerging nations like Mexico, Turkey, Venezuela, and China also are appealing. In fact, the U.S. government is making it easier to open franchises in developing countries by guaranteeing 50 percent of loans obtained to open foreign franchise locations.

Franchisers sometimes allow franchisees to alter their business format slightly in foreign markets. For example, McDonald's franchisees in Japan offer food items that appeal to Japanese tastes, such as steamed dumplings, curry with rice, and

exhibit 11.3 | Largest U.S. Franchisers

Franchiser	Type of Business	Total Units	Initial Investment
McDonald's Corporation Oak Brook, Illinois	Fast food	Franchised units: 18,361 Company-owned units: 5,262	$408,600–$647,000
Southland Corporation (7-Eleven) Dallas	Convenience stores	Franchised units: 13,819 Company-owned units: 2,467	Not available
Subway Sandwiches & Salads Milford, Connecticut	Fast food	Franchised units: 13,300 Company-owned units: 1	$61,900–$291,000
Burger King Corporation Miami	Fast food	Franchised units: 7,495 Company-owned units: 758	$73,000–$511,000
KFC Corporation Louisville, Kentucky	Fast food	Franchised units: 3,255 Company-owned units: 1,759	Not available
Pizza Hut, Inc. Dallas	Pizza	Franchised units: 7,200 Company-owned units: 3,800	Not available
Tandy Corporation Fort Worth, Texas	Consumer electronics	Franchised units: 6,779 Company-owned units: 1,890	$60,000+
Jani-King International Dallas	Janitorial, cleaning services	Franchised units: 6,700 Company-owned units: 35	$6,500–$80,000
Taco Bell Corporation Dallas	Fast food	Franchised units: 4,600 Company-owned units: 3,044	$200,000+
International Dairy Queen Minneapolis	Ice cream, fast food	Franchised units: 5,347 Company-owned units: NA	Not available

SOURCE: Franchise Opportunities Guide Online, International Franchise Association, Washington, D.C., **http://www.franchise.org**.

roast pork cutlet burgers with melted cheese. McDonald's franchisees in India serve mutton instead of beef because most Indians are Hindu, a religion whose followers believe cows to be a sacred symbol of the source of life. The menu also features rice-based Vegetable Burgers made with peas, carrots, red pepper, beans, and Indian spices as well as Vegetable McNuggets.

Retail Marketing Strategy

List the major tasks involved in developing a retail marketing strategy

Retailers must develop marketing strategies based on overall goals and strategic plans. Retailing goals might include more traffic, higher sales of a specific item, a more upscale image, or heightened public awareness of the retail operation. The strategies that retailers use to obtain their goals might include a sale, an updated decor, or a new advertisement. The key tasks in strategic retailing are defining and selecting a target market and developing the "six Ps" of the retailing mix to successfully meet the needs of the chosen target market: the traditional four Ps plus personnel and presentation.

Defining a Target Market

The first and foremost task in developing a retail strategy is to define the target market. This process begins with market segmentation, the topic of Chapter 6. Successful retailing has always been based on knowing the customer. Sometimes retailing chains have floundered because management loses sight of the customers the stores should be serving. For example, The Limited experienced phenomenal growth in the 1980s selling trendy apparel to young women. As their customer base matured, however, The Limited missed the opportunity to provide them with fashion options that better reflected the sensibilities of an older consumer. Furthermore, The Limited moved into careerwear, an unsuccessful strategy that only confused its remaining customers and forced the company to close some units.

Target markets in retailing are often defined by demographics, geographics, and psychographics. Claire's Stores, for instance, targets twelve- to fourteen-year-old girls who may get most of their wardrobe at The Gap but spend their allowances accessorizing at Claire's. To keep up with the fashion trends of its target market, Claire's executives read teen magazines, watch teen-oriented shows like *Friends* and *Beverly Hills 90210*, and listen to a lot of music.[48]

Determining a target market is a prerequisite to creating the retailing mix. For example, Target's merchandising approach for sporting goods is to match its product assortment to the demographics of the local store and region. The amount of space devoted to sporting goods, as well as in-store promotions, also varies according to each store's target market. Similarly, Macy's West, with 101 stores located on the West Coast, 80 percent of which are in California, uses a customized approach for each of its stores according to store demographics. A large Latino community characterizes store customers in southern California, whereas northern California is a more upscale, high-tech, white-collar crowd. Macy's West store planners use customer demographics, their shopping preferences, sales history, and local weather conditions, among other things, to tailor their mix of store merchandise to each individual store.[49]

Choosing the Retailing Mix

Retailers combine the elements of the retailing mix to come up with a single retailing method to attract the target market. The **retailing mix** consists of six Ps: the four Ps of the marketing mix (product, place, promotion, and price) plus personnel and presentation. (See Exhibit 11.4.)

retailing mix
Combination of the six Ps—product, place, promotion, price, personnel, and presentation—to sell goods and services to the ultimate consumer.

The combination of the six Ps projects a store's image, which influences consumers' perceptions. Using these impressions of stores, shoppers position one store against another. A retail marketing manager must make sure that the store's positioning is compatible with the target customers' expectations. As discussed at the beginning of the chapter, retail stores can be positioned on three broad dimensions: service provided by store personnel, product assortment, and price. Management should use everything else—place, presentation, and promotion—to fine-tune the basic positioning of the store.

The Product Offering

The first element in the retailing mix is the **product offering**, also called the product assortment or merchandise mix. Retailers decide what to sell on the basis of what their target market wants to buy. They can base their decision on market research, past sales, fashion trends, customer requests, and other sources. After more companies began promoting office casual days, Brooks Brothers, the upscale retailer of men's and women's conservative business wear, updated its product line with khaki pants, casual shirts, and a selection of brightly colored shirts and ties.[50]

product offering
The mix of products offered to the consumer by the retailer, also called the product assortment or merchandise mix.

exhibit 11.4

The Retailing Mix

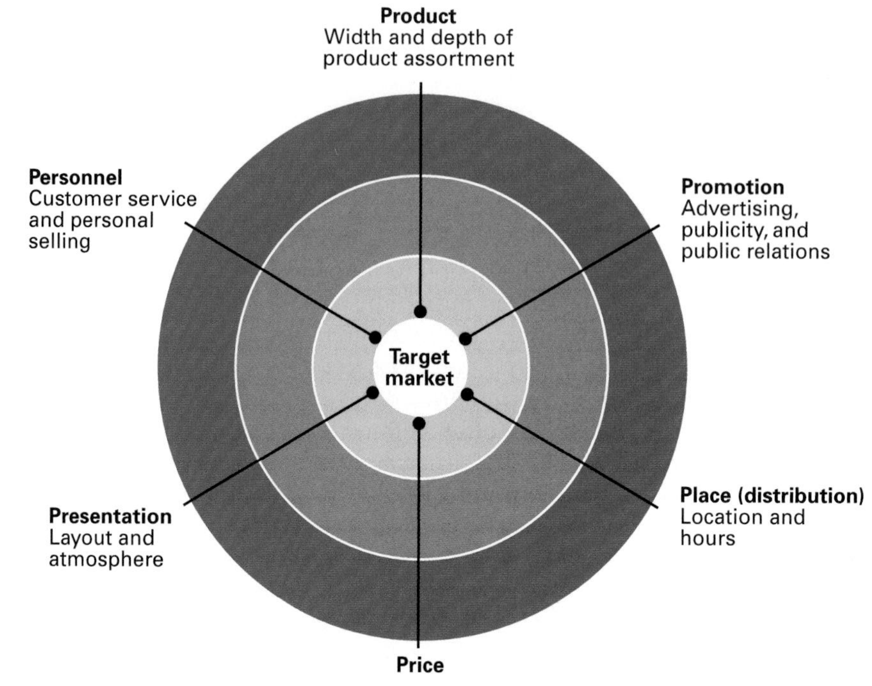

Developing a product offering is essentially a question of width and depth of the product assortment. *Width* refers to the assortment of products offered; *depth* refers to the number of different brands offered within each assortment. Price, store design, displays, and service are important to consumers in determining where to shop, but the most critical factor is merchandise selection. In an ambitious program to reposition itself into a competitive, moderate-priced department store, Sears has increased the amount of store space dedicated to clothes and home fashions and deemphasized tools and appliances. Sears's strategy has included a remodeling phase as well as a push to bring women in the store to shop for apparel and cosmetics. For instance, Sears now carries a line of apparel designed by Italy's Benetton Group, which it hopes will boost its women's apparel sales.[51]

After determining what products will satisfy target customers' desires, retailers must find sources of supply and evaluate the products. When the right products are found, the retail buyer negotiates a purchase contract. The buying function can either be performed in-house or be delegated to an outside firm. The goods must then be moved from the seller to the retailer, which means shipping, storing, and stocking the inventory. The trick is to manage the inventory by cutting prices to move slow goods and by keeping adequate supplies of hot-selling items in stock. As in all good systems, the final step is to evaluate the entire process to seek more efficient methods and eliminate problems and bottlenecks.

One of the more efficient new methods of managing inventory and streamlining the way products are moved from supplier to distributor to retailer is called *efficient consumer response*, or ECR. At the heart of ECR is *electronic data interchange*, or EDI, the computer-to-computer exchange of information, including automatic shipping notifications, invoices, inventory data, and forecasts. In a full implementation of ECR, products are scanned at the retail store when purchased, which updates the store's inventory lists. Headquarters then polls the stores to retrieve the data needed to produce an order. The vendor confirms the order, shipping date, and delivery time, then ships the order and transmits the invoice electronically.

EDI is a critical element of retail transactions. GEIS offers a line of EDI services to help retailers capture valuable information and better manage the complete sales transaction, from the purchase down to the ordering of goods.
Courtesy GE Information Systems

Outsourcing makes it simple.

Managing your EDI programs in-house is not easy. Especially with ERP and Y2K issues sapping your already scarce IT resources. But you can make it simple by outsourcing EDI to GE Information Services.

Just ask the global companies who already rely on us. They are leaders of the retail, manufacturing, transportation, high-tech and healthcare industries who outsourced their EDI efforts so they could focus on the business of doing business. Now, while we ensure their EDI efforts are done right, they spend their time managing results and expanding business opportunities.

By choosing GE as your EDI technology partner, you'll benefit from 30 years of expertise, a team of IT professionals, comprehensive project management and end-to-end support. You'll have access to the Electronic Commerce Service Center and advanced GE technologies. You'll be connected to the world's largest trading network of more than 90,000 trading partners.

It's that simple. In the world of electronic commerce . . . ***We bring good things to life.***

Rely on the experts: Attend a **free seminar** to learn how electronic commerce outsourcing can create a competitive advantage for your company. For dates and locations, check the GE Web site at **www.geis.com.**

GE Information Services

For more information call 800-560-GEIS, www.geis.com

The item is received at the warehouse, scanned into inventory, and then sent to the store. The invoice and receiving data are reconciled, and payment via an electronic transfer of funds completes the process.

Many retailers are experimenting with or have successfully implemented ECR and EDI. Calendar Club, a mall-based kiosk retailer of calendars, uses ECR and EDI to get the right products at each kiosk, which only operate about 120 days of the year, as quickly as possible. With virtually zero storage space in its kiosks, Calendar Club has to keep close tabs on what is selling in each kiosk. During the hectic holiday season, some kiosks sell more than one thousand calendars a day. Therefore, replenishment has to be fast enough to take advantage of the brief sales window. To do that, Calendar Club developed an ECR replenishment solution in which point-of-sale data from each kiosk are electronically communicated to company headquarters every night. Once received, the information is analyzed, and unique replenishment orders for each kiosk are generated and sent to the distribution center for picking, packing, and shipping.[52]

Advances in computer technology have also helped retailers spot new opportunities, such as the latest fashions. These styles can be recreated on a computer, and the designs can be transmitted electronically to manufacturers for production. New merchandise can be produced and put on store shelves in weeks rather than months. This speed gives retailers like Dillard's a competitive advantage over other fashion retailers.

As margins drop and competition intensifies, retailers are becoming ever more aware of the advantages of **private-label brands**, or those brands that are designed and developed using the retailer's name. Because the cost of goods typically makes up between 70 and 85 percent of a retailer's expenses, eliminating middlemen can shave costs. As a result, prices of private-label goods are typically lower than for national brands, giving customers greater value. Over the past decade, JCPenney has developed a host of private-label brands: Worthington® career apparel; the Original Arizona Jean Company® brand, which has blossomed into a leading jeanswear brand; and the JCPenney Home Collection®, whose bed, bath, and window coverings are the largest in volume in the home furnishings industry.[53] Many retailers have been gravitating toward premium private-label brands. Safeway, the country's second-largest supermarket chain, sells its Safeway Select brand aimed at competing directly with top national brands such as Tide detergent and Coca-Cola. Because the company does not have to spend the same amount of promotional money on its private-label brand as it does on national brands, Safeway enjoys higher profit margins. Customers save from the resulting lower prices, and the high quality of Safeway Select builds loyalty by giving shoppers more reason to buy at Safeway. The company now has over 850 Safeway Select items.[54]

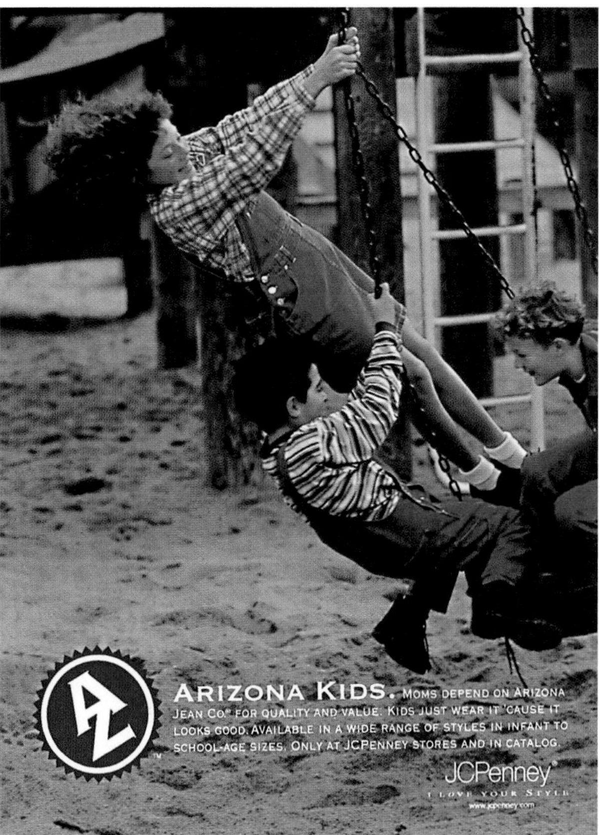

ARIZONA KIDS. MOMS DEPEND ON ARIZONA JEAN CO.® FOR QUALITY AND VALUE. KIDS JUST WEAR IT 'CAUSE IT LOOKS GOOD. AVAILABLE IN A WIDE RANGE OF STYLES IN INFANT TO SCHOOL-AGE SIZES. ONLY AT JCPENNEY STORES AND IN CATALOG.
JCPenney®
I LOVE YOUR STYLE

Private-label brands, such as JCPenney's Arizona Jean Company, can help retailers eliminate the middleman and offer lower-priced merchandise to their customers.
Courtesy JCPenney

Kroger Company

How extensive are Kroger's private-label brands? Visit its Web site to find out.
http://www.kroger.com

on line

private-label brands
Brands that are designed and developed using the retailer's name.

Promotion Strategy

Retail promotion strategy includes advertising, public relations and publicity, and sales promotion. The goal is to help position the store in consumers' minds. Retailers design intriguing ads, stage special events, and develop promotions aimed at their target markets. For example, today's grand openings are a carefully orchestrated blend of advertising, merchandising, goodwill, and glitter. All the elements of an opening—press coverage, special events, media advertising, and store displays—are carefully planned.

Retailers' advertising is carried out mostly at the local level, although retail giants like Sears and JCPenney can advertise nationally. Local advertising by retailers is more specific communication about their stores, such as location, merchandise, hours, prices, and special sales. On the other hand, national advertising by retailers generally focuses on image. The "Softer Side of Sears" national advertising campaign, for example, was used to help reposition Sears as a low-priced but fashion-conscious apparel retailer. An accompanying campaign, "Come See the Many Sides of Sears," was used to promote the retailer's nonapparel merchandise, such as tools, paint, and car parts.

Often large retailers and well-known clothing designers or manufacturers of exclusive specialty products share the spotlight in an advertisement. For example, ads linking Ralph Lauren and Foley's, a department store chain, let everyone know that Foley's sells the latest fashions. In turn, they enhance Ralph Lauren's prestige by associating it with a successful, distinguished fashion retailer. Although this type of arrangement, called *cooperative advertising,* is prevalent in the apparel industry, it has only recently become more common between packaged goods companies and retailers. Traditionally, marketers would just pay retailers to feature products in store mailers or a marketer would develop a TV campaign and simply tack on several retailers' names at the end of a product commercial or at the bottom of a print ad. However, now the spots have become more collaborative, with clear dual objectives. For example, a Kool-Aid commercial might invite viewers to "come on into Kroger" for ten packs of their favorite thirst quencher at a competitive price.[55]

Many retailers are forgoing media advertising these days in favor of direct mail or frequent shopper programs. Direct mail and catalog programs are luring many retailers in the hope they will prove a cost-effective means of increasing brand loyalty and spending by core customers. Nordstrom, for example, mails catalogs featuring brand-name and private-brand clothing, shoes, and accessories to target the shop-at-home crowd. Home repair outlets such as Lowe's and Home Depot have also used direct mail, often around holidays when people have time off to complete needed repairs. Restaurants and small retailers have successfully used frequent diner or frequent shopper programs for years. Now many big retailers, like mass merchandiser Sears and Neiman Marcus and Federated department store chains, are offering frequent shopper programs or loyalty programs that shower top shoppers with perks ranging from advance notice of sales and free gift wrapping to store discounts based on spending. Saks Fifth Avenue rewards its customers who charge more than $2,000 annually on their Saks credit cards with points convertible to Saks gift certificates. These customers also enjoy fashion newsletters and invitations to special events at Saks. Those who spend even more can become members of the Fifth Avenue Club, which offers a private shopping environment within Saks stores.[56]

The Proper Location

Another element in the retailing mix is place, or site location. Selecting a proper site is a critical decision. First, it is a large, long-term commitment of resources that can reduce a retailer's future flexibility. Whether the retailer leases or purchases, the location decision implies some degree of permanence. Second, the location will affect future growth. The chosen area should be growing economically so it can sustain the original store and any future stores. Last, the local environment may change over time. If the location's value deteriorates, the store may have to be relocated or closed.

Site location begins by choosing a community. This decision depends largely on economic growth potential and stability, the competition, political climate, and so on. Some of the savviest location experts in recent years have been T J Maxx and Toys 'R' Us. Both retailers put the majority of their new locations in rapidly growing areas where the population closely matches their customer base.

Sometimes it is not the economic profile or political climate that makes a community a good location but rather its geographic location. Locating its stores in over two hundred small towns and cities has made the Buckle, a retailer of designer apparel aimed at teens, quite a success. Big-name designer retailers have traditionally shunned rural America, harboring the illusion that rural youths don't know or care about fashion. However, the Buckle, which stocks such well-known fashion names as Tommy Hilfiger, Nautica, Polo by Ralph Lauren, and JNCO, is a hit with rural teens who possess the means and willingness to pay full price for fashion.[57] Office-supply superstores have also found small towns to be more attractive than larger cities. The Staples store located in Lebanon, New Hampshire, a town of 12,600 people, produces twice the annual sales of the average Staples store.[58]

After settling on a geographic region or community, retailers must choose a specific site. In addition to growth potential, the important factors are neighborhood socioeconomic characteristics, traffic flows, land costs, zoning regulations, and public transportation. Retailers should also consider where competitors are located as well as their own stores. A particular site's visibility, parking, entrance and exit locations, accessibility, and safety and security issues are other variables contributing to site selection success. Additionally, *retail synergy*, or how well a store's format meshes with the surrounding retail environment, is also important.[59] Retail decision makers probably would not locate a Dollar General store next door to a Neiman-Marcus department store.

"Location, location, location" has long been the retailing axiom emphasizing the importance of site selection in making a store profitable. Wal-Mart became the largest retailer in the country by locating in underserved small towns. Offering such services as hair salons, mail centers, optometrists, travel agencies, pharmacies, and food outlets, a discounter like Wal-Mart has every retail destination that the average small town has, translated to a single site. Similarly, Saks Fifth Avenue has been slowly branching out beyond malls by locating smaller Saks stores, called Saks Main Street, in the heart of affluent suburbia. At about forty-six thousand square feet, about a third of the size or less than the full-line Saks Fifth Avenue store, Main Street stores can locate where its core customers already live and shop: the main shopping streets of affluent suburbs and towns. Saks' research told them that more and more of their customers did not want to leave their communities to go shopping in huge regional malls, so Saks made it more convenient by opening Main Street stores where they live. Main Street stores are already proving to be more productive than its full-line versions, averaging $400 to $500 per square foot compared to $300 to $350 for full-line stores. Also, people who live close to a Main Street store shop as much as eight times a month; regional mall locations are more likely to be shopped only twice a month.[60]

One final decision about location faces retailers: whether to have a freestanding unit or to become a shopping center or mall tenant.

Freestanding Stores An isolated, freestanding location can be used by large retailers like Wal-Mart, Kmart, or Target and sellers of shopping goods like furniture and cars, because they are "destination" stores, or those stores consumers will purposely plan to visit. In other words, customers will seek them out. An isolated store location may have the advantages of low site cost or rent and no nearby competitors. On the other hand, it may be hard to attract customers to a freestanding location, and no other retailers are around to share costs.

Freestanding units are increasing in popularity by retailers as they strive to make their stores more convenient to access, more enticing to shop, and more profitable. Freestanding site location now accounts for more than half of the millions of square feet of retail construction starts in the United States as more and more retailers are deciding not to locate in pedestrian malls. Perhaps the greatest reason for developing a freestanding site is greater visibility. Retailers often feel they get lost in huge centers and malls, but freestanding units can help stores develop an identity with shoppers. The ability to grow at faster rates through freestanding buildings has also propelled the surge toward stand-alone units. Retailers like The Sports Authority, Linens & Things, and Bed Bath & Beyond choose to be freestanding in order to achieve their expansion objectives. Waiting for shopping centers to be built can be counterproductive to an aggressive expansion plan.[61] Drugstore giant Walgreens has been aggressively relocating its existing mall and shopping center stores to freestanding sites, especially street-corner sites, to help them gain dominance with twenty-four-hour drive-through locations.[62]

Shopping Centers The tremendous boom in shopping centers began after World War II, as the U.S. population started migrating to the suburbs. The first shopping centers were *strip centers*, typically located along a busy street. They usually included a supermarket, a variety store, and perhaps a few specialty stores. Essentially unplanned business districts, these strip centers remain popular.

Next, the small *community shopping centers* emerged, with one or two small department store branches, more specialty shops, one or two restaurants, and several apparel stores. These centers offer a broader variety of shopping, specialty, and convenience goods, provide large off-street parking lots, and usually span 75,000 to 300,000 square feet of retail space.

Finally, along came the huge *regional malls*. Regional malls are either entirely enclosed or roofed to allow shopping in any weather. Many are landscaped with trees, fountains, sculptures, and the like to enhance the shopping environment. They have acres of free parking. The *anchor stores* or *generator stores* (JCPenney, Sears, or major department stores) are usually located at opposite ends of the mall to create heavy foot traffic. The newly opened superregional Coral Ridge Mall located in Coralville, Iowa, for instance, occupies 1.2 million square feet of space and is conveniently located next to Iowa City, a state university campus, and major interstates and highways. An Iowa State University study found that Iowa City lacked a number of the retail facilities common to similar-sized metropolitan areas and that residents frequently traveled to Cedar Rapids, about thirty minutes away, for items they could not find at the local malls or the downtown shopping district. This lack of retail presence made Coral Ridge an immediate success in its market.[63]

Locating in a community shopping center or regional mall offers several advantages. First, the facilities are designed to attract shoppers. Second, the shopping environment, anchor stores, and "village square" activities draw customers. Third, ample parking is available. Fourth, the center or mall projects a unified image. Fifth, tenants also share the expenses of the mall's common area and promotions for the whole mall. Finally, malls can target different demographic groups. Some malls are considered upscale; others are aimed at people shopping for bargains.

Locating in a shopping center or mall does have disadvantages. These include expensive leases, the chance that common promotion efforts will not attract customers to a particular store, lease restrictions on merchandise carried and hours of operation, the anchor stores' domination of the tenants' association, and the possibility of having direct competitors within the same facility.

Strip centers and small community shopping centers account for about 85 percent of all retail centers and only about 50 percent of total shopping center retail sales. Retail analysts expect that by the year 2000, U.S. consumers will do even more of their shopping at neighborhood strip shopping centers. With increasing demands on their time, they will choose speed and convenience instead of the elegance and variety offered by large regional malls. In anticipation of this trend, many of the nation's shopping malls are reinventing themselves to resemble open strip malls. This move to redevelop malls is being termed *demalling*, reflecting the move away from enclosed malls.[64]

Retail Prices

Another important element in the retailing mix is price. It is important to understand that retailing's ultimate goal is to sell products to consumers and that the right price is critical in ensuring sales. Because retail prices are usually based on the cost of the merchandise, an essential part of pricing is efficient and timely buying.

Price is also a key element in a retail store's positioning strategy and classification. Higher prices often indicate a level of quality and help reinforce the prestigious image of retailers, as they do for Lord & Taylor, Saks Fifth Avenue, Gucci, Cartier, and Neiman Marcus. On the other hand, discounters and off-price retailers, such as Target and T J Maxx, offer a good value for the money. There are even stores, such as Dollar Tree, where everything costs shoppers one dollar. Dollar Tree's single-price-point strategy is aimed at getting higher-income customers to make impulse purchases through what analysts call the "wow factor"—the excitement of discovering an item costs only a dollar.[65]

A pricing trend among American retailers that seems to be here to stay is *everyday low pricing*, or EDLP. Introduced to the retail industry by Wal-Mart, EDLP offers consumers a low price all the time rather than holding periodic sales on merchandise. Even large retail giants, like Federated Department Stores, parent of Macy's and Bloomingdales, have phased out deep discounts and sales in favor of lower prices every day. Similarly, The Gap reduced prices on denim jeans, denim shirts, socks, and other items to protect and broaden the company's share of the casual clothes market. Supermarkets such as Albertson's and Winn Dixie have also found success in EDLP.

Rent-to-own retailers, those retail stores that offer ownership of merchandise after a customer fulfills their obligation under a rental agreement, have been under close scrutiny lately for their high ultimate retail prices and their target marketing practices. Read about the ethical dilemma facing the rent-to-own industry in the "Ethics in Marketing" box.

Presentation of the Retail Store

The presentation of a retail store helps determine the store's image and positions the retail store in consumers' minds. For instance, a retailer that wants to position itself as an upscale store would use a lavish or sophisticated presentation.

The main element of a store's presentation is its **atmosphere**, the overall impression conveyed by a store's physical layout, decor, and surroundings. The atmosphere might create a relaxed or busy feeling, a sense of luxury or of efficiency, a friendly or cold attitude, a sense of organization or of clutter, or a fun or serious mood. For example, the look at Express stores is designed to make suburban shoppers feel as though they have just strolled into a Parisian boutique. Signage is often in French, and the background music has a European flair. Likewise, retail stores based on the colorful, quirky world of Nickelodeon television feature cabinets covered with green slime, garbage cans at the end of aisles, tilted walls, purple ceilings, and bright hues and bold patterns. Nickelodeon stores include plenty of interactive features, making the space a fun place for children of all ages.[66]

atmosphere
The overall impression conveyed by a store's physical layout, decor, and surroundings.

More often these days retailers are adding an element of entertainment to their store atmosphere. The Nike Town store in Chicago looks more like a

How can a company create an atmosphere on its Web site? Visit the pages of some of your favorite retailers to see if they have been able to recreate the store atmosphere on the Internet.

ethics in marketing

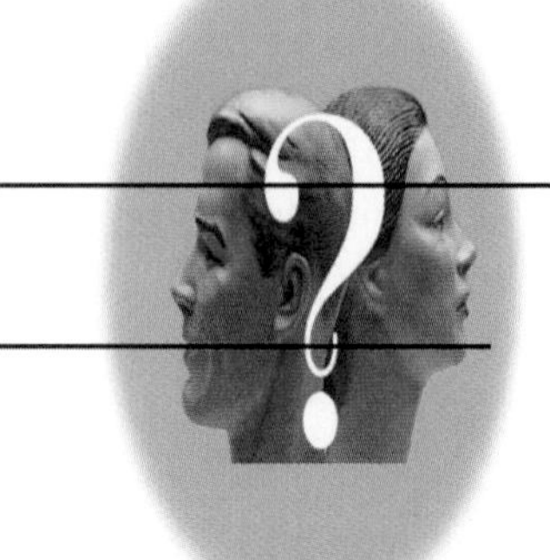

The Ethical Dilemma of Rent-to-Own Retailers

More than seventy-five hundred retail outlets nationwide operate in the rent-to-own (RTO) industry. RTO retail outlets provide a variety of products to their customers, including furniture, appliances, electronics, and jewelry. RTO contracts allow customers to take ownership of the merchandise at the end of a specified series of payments. However, the $4 billion RTO retailing industry has been under fire lately from critics who allege these stores charge exorbitant interest rates on consumer goods and unfairly target poor and minority consumers who don't have credit cards. Several lawsuits have already been decided in favor of customers who dealt with rent-to-own retailers. In Minnesota, a federal judge awarded about $30 million to consumers in a class-action suit that accused the former Rent-A-Center of charging them unlawful and excessive interest rates on rent-to-own sales contracts.

A report by the U.S. Public Interest Research Group found average annual interest rates charged by rent-to-own retailers of 100 percent, five times the typical rate on credit cards. Some were as high as 275 percent. The survey also found that the rates were not disclosed to the customer and that 37 percent of items in stores were not clearly marked to show whether they were new or used. RTO agreements generally only make explicit the cash price (the retail price of the merchandise if purchased in full immediately) and the weekly or monthly installment, but typically fail to disclose the interest associated with the difference in the two.

Depending on the company, the product, and the terms of the contract, renting-to-buy will cost one and a half to three times more than purchasing the item outright—even if the customer financed the purchase with a high-rate credit card. One source describes how a Rent-A-Center store in Roanoke, Virginia, profited by offering a 20-inch Zenith television for $14.99 a week for seventy-four weeks, totaling $1,109.26. The same set was on sale at a Sears store across town for $329.99. A 1995 *Consumer Reports* article narrates similar situations in which consumers are unaware that they are purchasing merchandise at effective annual interest rates that exceed 250 percent.

Most often, rent-to-own customers are consumers who can least afford the interest rates and fees charged—low-income individuals whose credit is not good or who have difficulty establishing credit. In some cases, these individuals believe they have nowhere else to turn to buy the goods they want, or they simply don't understand how much they are being charged in the long run. RTO outlets are generally located in or near communities of relative poverty. Promotions are targeted toward members of these communities, offering the opportunity to rent to own at weekly or monthly rental rates with no credit checks. Because of their lower socioeconomic status, these customers generally lack cash to purchase outright from ordinary retailers and are therefore particularly sensitive to no-credit-check policies.

At the heart of the RTO dispute is a single question: Are rent-to-own transactions installment sales at usurious interest rates, or are they, as the industry says, unique transactions with exceptionally high costs to justify the high prices? To decide, readers must first understand how RTO deals work. At the onset of the agreement, the customer signs a contract spelling out the cost of the weekly or monthly payments, the number of payments to be made, and the total that will be paid. If the consumer makes all payments as scheduled, he or she keeps the item at the end of the deal. If the consumer is late or misses a payment, the property can be repossessed and any equity that the consumer thought was built up in the item is gone. In some cases, if a payment is simply late, the contract allows the consumer to "reinstate" the existing contract for a fee.

Critics argue that the RTO industry legally gets around truth-in-lending laws that require uniform disclosure of annual interest rates and usury laws, which can cap the interest rates lenders charge, by calling their agreements rental contracts. Further, the industry's "reinstatement" charges are nothing more than a late fee on a consumer credit transaction. The rent-to-own industry counters that about 75 percent of customers cancel their contracts within four months. Rental companies must then go through the cost of collecting their merchandise, refurbishing it, and renting it out again. Only 25 percent of the industry's customers rent long enough to own.[67]

What solutions do you think are needed to resolve the ethical dilemmas in the rent-to-own industry? What consumer education programs could be developed to assist lower-income consumers purchase the goods they want without having to pay the higher prices charged by RTO retailers? Are there some programs that other retailers could develop that would provide low-income consumers with less costly retail options?

Nike has taken store atmosphere to new heights with its Nike Town stores. By creating a look that is more museum than retail, the company has added an element of entertainment and popular culture to its dedicated stores.
© James Leynse/SABA

museum than like a traditional retail store. The three-story space displays products amid life-size Michael Jordan statues and glassed-in relics like baseball legend Nolan Ryan's shoes. A History of Air exhibit explains the pockets of air on the bottom of some Nike shoes. A video theater plays Nike commercials and short films featuring Nike gear.

The layout of retail stores is a key factor in their success. Layout is planned so that all space in the store is used effectively, including aisles, fixtures, merchandise displays, and nonselling areas. Effective store layout ensures the customer's shopping ease and convenience, but it has a powerful influence on customer traffic patterns and purchasing behavior.

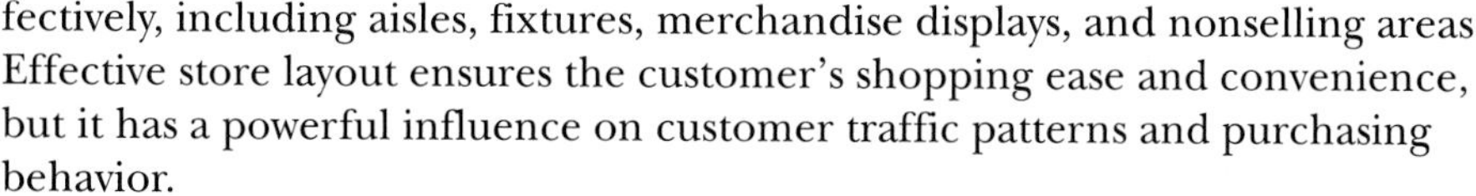

Layout also includes where products are placed in the store. Many technologically advanced retailers are using a technique called *market-basket analysis* to analyze the huge amounts of data collected through their point-of-purchase scanning equipment. The analysis looks for products that are commonly purchased together to help retailers remerchandise their stores to place products in the right places.[68] Wal-Mart uses market-basket analysis to determine where in the store to stock products for customer convenience. Bananas are placed not only in the produce section but also in the cereal aisle. Kleenex tissues are in the paper-goods aisle and also mixed in with the cold medicines. Measuring spoons are in the housewares and also hanging next to Crisco shortening. During October, flashlights are not only in the hardware aisle but also with the Halloween costumes.[69]

These are the most influential factors in creating a store's atmosphere:

- *Employee type and density:* Employee type refers to an employee's general characteristics—for instance, neat, friendly, knowledgeable, or service oriented. Density is the number of employees per thousand square feet of selling space. A discounter like Kmart has a low employee density that creates a "do-it-yourself," casual atmosphere. In contrast, Neiman Marcus's density is much higher, denoting readiness to serve the customer's every whim. Too many employees and not enough customers, however, can convey an air of desperation and intimidate customers.
- *Merchandise type and density:* The type of merchandise carried and how it is displayed add to the atmosphere the retailer is trying to create. A prestigious retailer like Saks or Marshall Field's carries the best brand names and displays them in a neat, uncluttered arrangement. Discounters and off-price retailers may sell some well-known brands, but many carry seconds or out-of-season goods. Their merchandise may be stacked so high that it falls into the aisles, helping create the impression that "We've got so much stuff, we're practically giving it away."
- *Fixture type and density:* Fixtures can be elegant (rich woods), trendy (chrome and smoked glass), or consist of old, beat-up tables, such as in an antique store. The fixtures should be consistent with the general atmosphere the store is trying to create. The Gap creates a relaxed and uncluttered atmosphere by displaying its merchandise on tables and shelves rather than on traditional pipe rack, allowing customers to see and touch the merchandise more easily. Adding technology as a fixture is a recent successful trend in coffee shops and

lounges. The most popular examples include adding PCs to provide Internet access to customers and ultimately get them to remain in the store longer.

- *Sound:* Sound can be pleasant or unpleasant for a customer. Classical music at a nice Italian restaurant helps create ambiance, just as country-and-western music does at a truck stop. Kmart recently installed wireless telephone service in all of its Super Kmarts to help create a more peaceful environment for customers who were irritated by overhead paging.[70] Music can also entice customers to stay in the store longer and buy more or eat quickly and leave a table for others. For instance, researchers have found that rapid music tends to make people eat more, chew less, and take bigger bites whereas slow music prompts people to dine more leisurely and eat less.[71] Retailers can tailor their musical atmosphere to their shoppers' demographics and the merchandise they're selling. Music can control the pace of the store traffic, create an image, and attract or direct the shopper's attention. For example, Harrods in London features music by live harpists, pianists, and marching bagpipers to create different atmospheres in different departments. Coffee shops are also getting into the music business as are theme restaurants like Hard Rock Cafe, Planet Hollywood, Harley Davidson Cafe, and Rainforest Cafe that turn eating a hamburger and fries into an experience. Au Bon Pain, Starbucks, and Victoria's Secret have all sold copies of their background music, hoping that the music will remind consumers of the feeling of being in their stores.
- *Odors:* Smell can either stimulate or detract from sales. The wonderful smell of pastries and breads entices bakery customers. Conversely, customers can be repulsed by bad odors such as cigarette smoke, musty smells, antiseptic odors, and overly powerful room deodorizers. If a grocery store pumps in the smell of baked goods, sales in that department increase threefold. Department stores have pumped in fragrances that are pleasing to their target market, and the response has been favorable. Not surprisingly, retailers are increasingly using fragrance as a key design element, as important as layout, lighting, and background music. Research suggests that people evaluate merchandise more positively, spend more time shopping, and are generally in a better mood when an agreeable odor is present. Retailers use fragrances as an extension of their retail strategy. The Rainforest Cafe, for instance, pumps fresh-flower extracts into its retail sections. Similarly, the Christmas Store at Disney World, which is open year-round, is infused with the scents of evergreen and spiced apple cider. Jordan's Furniture in Massachusetts and New Hampshire uses the scent of pine in its country-style sections to make the environment more interesting and make customers linger longer.[72]
- *Visual factors:* Colors can create a mood or focus attention and therefore are an important factor in atmosphere. Red, yellow, and orange are considered warm colors and are used when a feeling of warmth and closeness is desired. Cool colors like blue, green, and violet are used to open up closed-in places and create an air of elegance and cleanliness. Some colors are better for display. For instance, diamonds appear most striking against black or dark blue velvet. The lighting can also have an important effect on store atmosphere. Jewelry is best displayed under high-intensity spotlights and cosmetics under more natural lighting. Many retailers have found that natural lighting, either from windows or skylights, can lead to increased sales. Outdoor lighting can also impact consumer patronage. Consumers often are afraid to shop after dark in many areas and prefer strong lighting for safety. The outdoor facade of the store also adds to its ambiance and helps create favorable first impressions by shoppers. For example, on the top of the roof over the door at Cup o' Joe specialty coffee shop in Lennox Town Square, Columbus, Ohio, sits a twelve-foot wide by six-foot tall coffee mug. The coffee shop's designers used the exaggerated storefront to call attention to its site, which would have otherwise gotten lost amid its big-box neighbors Old Navy, Target, and an AMC Theater.[73]

Personnel and Customer Service

People are a unique aspect of retailing. Most retail sales involve a customer–salesperson relationship, if only briefly. When customers shop at a grocery store, the cashiers check and bag their groceries. When customers shop at a prestigious clothier, the sales clerks may help select the styles, sizes, and colors. They may also assist in the fitting process, offer alteration services, wrap purchases, and even offer a glass of champagne. Sales personnel provide their customers with the amount of service prescribed in the retail strategy of the store.

A recent study found that 35 percent of consumers have had negative shopping experiences, with nearly one in ten switching retailers afterwards.[74] Good service, therefore, is even more important in a slow-growth economy, when companies survive by keeping the customers they have. Studies show that customer retention results in above-average profits and superior growth. Home Depot is one company that has embraced that philosophy and provides its customers with excellent service. Home Depot salespeople, often recruited from the ranks of carpenters and electricians, are encouraged to spend all the time needed with customers, even if it's hours.

Retail salespeople serve another important selling function: They persuade shoppers to buy. They must therefore be able to persuade customers that what they are selling is what the customer needs. Salespeople are trained in two common selling techniques: trading up and suggestion selling. Trading up means persuading customers to buy a higher-priced item than they originally intended to buy. However, to avoid selling customers something they do not need or want, salespeople should take care when practicing trading-up techniques. Suggestion selling, a common practice among most retailers, seeks to broaden customers' original purchases with related items. For example, McDonald's cashiers may ask customers whether they would like a hot apple pie with their hamburger and fries. Suggestion selling and trading up should always help shoppers recognize true needs rather than sell them unwanted merchandise.

Global Retailing

GLOBAL

7

Discuss the challenges of expanding retailing operations into global markets

It is no accident that U.S. retailers are now testing their store concepts on a global basis. With the battle for market share among domestic retailers showing no sign of abating and growth prospects dismal, mature retailers are looking for growth opportunities in the growing consumer economies of other countries. American retailers have made quite an impact on the global market, as Exhibit 11.5 displays. Four of the top ten global retailers are from the United States, with Wal-Mart holding the top spot with sales about three times that of its nearest competitors.

Several events have made expansion across national borders more feasible. First, the spread of communication networks and mass media has homogenized tastes and product preferences to some extent around the world. As a result, the casual American lifestyle and the products that symbolize it, such as Levi's jeans and Nike sportswear, have become more appealing. Second, the lowering of trade barriers and tariffs, such as with the North American Free Trade Agreement (NAFTA) and the formation of the European Union (EU), has facilitated the expansion of American retailers to Mexico, Canada, and Europe.[75] Last, high growth potential in underserved markets is also luring U.S. retailers abroad into Latin America, South America, and Asia. China contains a quarter of the world's population and only recently opened its markets to outside concerns. Although the majority of China's population still lacks adequate consumer spending power, projections call for the country's economy to eclipse all others in the next twenty-five years.[76]

exhibit 11.5

The United States and Germany Dominate Global Retailing

Rank	Retailer	Country of Origin	Formats	1996 Sales ($ million)*
1	Wal-Mart Stores	United States	General merchandise, wholesale clubs	104,859
2	Sears Roebuck	United States	Department, general merchandise	38,236
3	Metro (including Kaufhof and Asko)	Germany	Diversified	36,567
4	Tengelmann	Germany	Supermarket	33,155
5	Kmart	United States	General merchandise, discount	31,437
6	Carrefour	France	Hypermarket	30,290
7	Rewe Zentrale	Germany	Supermarket	29,834
8	Edeka Zentrale (including AVA)	Germany	Supermarket, hypermarket	27,615
9	Auchan	France	Hypermarket, diversified	25,616
10	Dayton Hudson	United States	Discount, department store	25,371

* All amounts are in millions of U.S. dollars, using average 1996 exchange rates. All data are corporate level for retail-diversified companies, excluding VAT and nonretailing revenue when available.

SOURCE: From "Global Retailing '97," Ernst & Young special report for *Chain Store Age*, December 1997. Reprinted by permission from Chain Store Age. Copyright Lebhar-Friedman, Inc. 425 Park Avenue, NY, NY 10022.

Before taking the plunge into the international retailing arena, the soundest advice retailers can heed is to do their homework. (See Exhibit 11.6.) Analysts from consulting firm Ernst & Young count among the prerequisites for going global a secure and profitable position domestically, a long-term perspective as many foreign operations take longer to set up and longer to turn a profit, and a global strategy that meshes with the retailer's overall corporate strategy. Retailers should first determine what their core competency is, whether it be low prices, a distinctive fashion look, or excellent customer service, and determine whether this differentiation is what the local market wants. For instance, The Gap's international success is attributable to its allegiance to the "American casual" formula that made it so successful in its home market, including The Gap name. Similarly, wherever shoppers travel, they can reasonably expect to experience Wal-Mart's friendliness; the quality, service, and cleanliness of McDonald's; or the brand statements of Marks & Spencer, The Body Shop, and IKEA.[77]

However, in addition to keeping their core strengths when going global, retailers also need to skillfully make adjustments. Therefore, a major part of a retailer's advance "homework" is to understand what products will sell in foreign locales.

By implementing a uniform retail strategy across the globe, companies can assure their customers consistency and reliability. The Wal-Mart formula of friendliness and value is equally valid in China as it is in the United States.
© 1997 Greg Girard/CONTACT Press Images

Color preferences, taste preferences, service expectations, the preferred cut of a garment, and shoppers' physiques vary worldwide, as does customer acceptance of foreign brands or private-label merchandise. Differences also dictate the placement of goods within a retail store. In some cultures, for instance, men's and women's clothing should not be merchandised adjacent to each other. Latin Americans want fruits and vegetables located at the front of a store. In the United States it's standard practice to place lower-priced

exhibit 11.6

Factors Used to Analyze Global Retail Markets

- *Market size and economics:* Analyzing factors such as population and demographic trends, economics (including gross domestic product and consumer spending), and political trends that could make or break the success of a retailer in a foreign country. For instance, in China the central government has been urging middle-income Chinese to buy their own housing. For retailers, this means plenty of new apartments and homes to fill with more electronics, bigger refrigerators and kitchens for edibles, and roomier closets.
- *Infrastructure and distribution:* Building global supply chains and securing qualified labor can be particularly challenging in emerging markets. Expansion to Canada and Mexico is simpler logistically for U.S. retailers than transporting their stores across oceans. In many developing countries such as China, underdeveloped transportation infrastructures as well as few logistics providers pose daunting distribution challenges to retailers trying to stock products in stores.
- *Competition:* Assessing the current competitive landscape and how the retailer could bring innovations to the market. Compared to the United States, Mexico, for instance, is considered grossly understored; the country has less than 550 square feet of food and apparel stores per thousand people, compared to 20,000 square feet per thousand people in the United States. Similarly, Europe has a higher percentage of independent, mom-and-pop operations. The highly fragmented European market appears ripe for well-capitalized U.S. big-box retailers.
- *Operations:* Assessing how operational concerns, such as real estate, labor and inventory, will affect the success of an overseas unit. For instance, labor laws vary drastically from country to country. Cultural differences also affect holidays, number of vacation days for employees, and hours of operation. U.S. retail stores are open an average of seventy hours a week whereas retail stores in Greece are only open about forty-six hours a week.
- *Financial and tax reporting:* Addressing issues such as currency fluctuations, the hedging of risks, and how a region's tax regime and incentives would fit into a retailer's overall tax strategy. A lot of retailers are entering Argentina, Brazil, and Chile because their markets are open and their business economies and financial systems are more "Western-like."
- *Merchandise acceptability:* Conducting research to understand local consumer needs, preferences, and buying habits, and then reinventing the assortment to match the culture of the region. For instance, back-to-school sales occur in April in Japan, and August in Europe is a traditionally slow retailing month because most Europeans are on vacation. When IKEA came to the United States it learned that it needed to offer larger beds, furniture with larger drawers, and different assortments of kitchen utensils.
- *Partnering capability:* Considering the availability of suitable partners in a desired country or region. Starbucks Coffee typically picks distribution and supply partners before it decides on a country or region because poor strategic alliances or logistics partnering can make or break a retail operation.

SOURCE: From "Global Retailing '97," Ernst & Young special report for *Chain Store Age,* December 1997. Reprinted by permission from Chain Store Age. Copyright Lebhar-Friedman, Inc., 425 Park Avenue, NY, NY 10022.

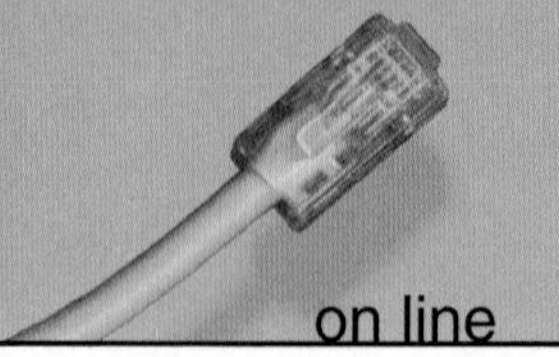

Auchan

Visit the Web site of one of France's largest retailers. How well is Auchan reaching global customers with its site? Click on "anglais" for the English version.

http://www.auchan.com/ **http://www.wal-mart.com/** **http://www.kmart.com/**

on line

private-label merchandise to the right of name brands because "natural" eye flow will cause a shopper to comparison shop to the right. That merchandising approach doesn't necessarily hold true, however, in countries where people read up and down or right to left.[78]

Read about Starbucks's adventures in breaking into the Japanese market in the "Global Perspectives" box.

global perspectives

Japan Wakes Up and Smells Starbucks

Starbucks is giving Japanese coffee-bar chains the jitters. When a billboard proclaiming "Opening Soon: Starbucks Coffee" appeared in Tokyo's fashionable Omotesando district, local coffee bars went into a flurry of activity. One nearby coffee bar enlisted real estate agents to help determine where the new Starbucks might open shop. Other Japanese coffee bars began offering "Seattle Coffee" or remodeled their shops to look like those of Starbucks. Still others went on intelligence missions to the United States to study Starbucks's secrets—all for good reason. Starbucks plans to open at least forty new stores in the Pacific Rim by mid-1998, including South Korea, Singapore, Taiwan, and the Philippines. Indeed, Starbucks is so committed to having a presence in every major market in the Pacific Rim and Asia that it's very possible that the coffee chain may one day have more stores there than it does in North America.

Such anxiety may seem odd for Japanese coffee retailers, given that Japan is already the world's number three coffee consumer, after the United States and Germany. With so many coffee shops and coffee vending machines already in place—Coca-Cola alone has more than eight hundred thousand vending machines that sell canned coffee—Japan's market looks saturated. Meanwhile, the Japanese haven't developed a taste for espresso drinks like caffe latte and caffe mocha; instead, they drink a lot of instant coffee or ready-to-drink coffee in cans, as well as American-style hot coffee.

Starbucks has a reputation for knowing how to create a thirst, though, and Japanese coffee purveyors fear the new Starbucks's coffee bars, the first of which opened in Tokyo's swank Ginza shopping district, may be able to create new coffee markets in Japan where Japanese efforts have failed. Starbucks's entrance in the Japanese market worries Japanese coffee executives because they don't know how to replicate its touch. The fact that the Japanese see big openings in Japan for a U.S. company like Starbucks suggests how far behind Japan is in fostering creative, consumer-oriented service companies.

Some Japanese coffee-chain operators admit they lack Starbucks's sophistication in what they call "packaging the store": meshing such elements as store design, package design, and other merchandising techniques into a compelling identity.

Japanese consumers might need a little hand-holding at first to guide them through the thicket of grandes and frappucinos. However, Yuji Tsunoda, president of Starbucks Coffee Japan, thinks they'll catch on fast. "Four years ago, how many Americans knew what a latte, doppio espresso, or cappucino were?" he said. "It's up to us to help our customers understand coffee better."

Indeed, at Tokyo's new Starbucks outlet, the wall menu is posted in both English and Japanese. Starbucks is even providing Japanese-language versions of pamphlets like "Espresso—What You Need to Know." Employees and customers alike can refer to blueprint-like diagrams detailing the exact specifications of a caffe latte, down to the quarter inch of foamed milk that goes on top. The Tokyo shop features the same colorful coffee paraphernalia featured in U.S. stores, including mugs, espresso makers, plunger coffee brewers, filters, and coasters.

Although the coffee is cheaper at the local coffee bar down the street—just 160 yen, or $1.50, versus 250 yen, about $2.30—the atmosphere with its low ceiling, somber interior, and cafeteria-style trays hardly evokes the ambiance of a gourmet coffee house. Neither does the food. Coffee-accompanying snacks include fried chicken with spaghetti on a hot dog bun and a salty fried noodle sandwich with seaweed on top. Starbucks, on the other hand, takes a more epicurean tack—cookies, muffins, croissants, and sandwiches made from pita bread and sesame seed bagels.[79]

What retailing strategies would you suggest local Japanese coffee retailers consider to compete with Starbucks? Do you think Starbucks's cookie-cutter approach to selling coffee and accompanying food in global markets will be successful? Why or why not?

Trends in Retailing

Predicting the future is always risky, but the use of entertainment to lure customers, a shift toward providing greater convenience to receive the patronage of today's precision shoppers, and the emergence of customer management programs to foster loyalty and enhance communications with a retailer's best customers are three of the more important trends for retailing's future.

8
Describe future trends in retailing

Entertainment

Adding entertainment to the retail environment is one of the most popular strategies in retailing in recent years. Small retailers as well as national chains are using entertainment to set themselves apart from the competition.

The weaving of entertainment into retailing has proved to be a sales stimulation for may small firms. At Elaine Petrocelli's Corete Madera, California, store, Book Passage, "entertaining" is crafted to generate customer loyalty.

Entertainment is not limited to music, videos, fashion shows, or guest appearances by soap opera stars or book authors. Entertainment includes anything that makes shoppers have a good time, that stimulates their senses or emotions, and that gets them into a store, keeps them there, and encourages them to buy and to keep coming back. The quiet, comfortable couches and cafes of bookstores and combination book and music retailers such as Barnes & Noble, Books-a-Million, Borders, and Media Play are entertaining just as are the Gershwin tunes coming from the piano in a Nordstrom's atrium. Catching the attention of many younger consumers, however, involves the flash and glitz of video screens on walls in clothing stores, hair salons, and theme restaurants. For example, the Virgin Megastore located in Lake Buena Vista, Florida, next door to Walt Disney World's Pleasure Island, features a platform over the entrance that can be lowered for live-music performances. Inside, the atmosphere is electrified by the ever-changing backdrop of music, video images, banners, and lighting. A live disc jockey spins tunes high above the crowd from a metal and glass booth. Customers can sample music at one of the more than three hundred listening stations that line the first floor perimeter. On the second floor, customers can sip coffee in the cafe, use demo games and software, view videos, or surf the Web.[80]

Convenience and Efficiency

Today's consumer is increasingly looking for ways to shop more quickly and efficiently. With 75 percent of women working full- or part-time, consumers no longer have the time to devote to shopping as they once did. A recent study found the number of trips that consumers take to the mall, for instance, has declined by more than 50 percent since the early 1990s. On top of that, the number of stores that they visit when they get there is down by two-thirds.[81] Consumers are also spending less time when they do visit a mall. Today, the average mall visit lasts just an hour, down from ninety minutes in 1982.[82]

The declines not only reflect the increase in working women but can also be attributed to all consumers being more stretched for time. As consumers have become more focused on entertainment and leisure activities, they have become "precision shoppers." Consumers are more purposeful in their shopping, reducing the number of stores they visit and the time they spend shopping. The precision shopper is also less likely to buy on impulse.[83]

As a result, retailers must learn to better manage the patronage experience. Consumers are no longer satisfied because a store merely met their expectations. They desire delightful experiences brought about by retailers who anticipate consumers' expectations and go the extra mile to exceed them on a regular basis. Dimensions in which retailers can far exceed expectations include shopping assistance, the buying process, delivery and installation of the product, service after the sale, and disposal and renewal of the product.

Examples of ways this can be done include offering services such as pick-up for shoppers who do not want to fight traffic, baby-sitting services, free drinks and refreshments during shopping, and preferred shopper parking spaces. For example, IGA supermarkets in Ohio offer parents a child-care center where they can leave their kids while buying groceries. The play area includes computers, puzzles and crayons, a two-level maze, and a thirty-two-inch television. Video monitors throughout the stores allow parents to check in on their kids.[84] Supermarkets and drugstores are adding conveniences such as drive-through windows to pick up prescriptions and are offering additional services such as flu shots, cholesterol screenings, and even in-store health clinics.[85] In addition, retailers who maintain records of consumers' preferences in product features will be able to offer individualized attention to consumers during product selection. Sales associates can preselect items that are most likely to be preferred by the customer. For example, the store's records may indicate that a consumer prefers a particular style of suit, leading the sales associate to show the consumer the new suits for the season in that style.[86]

Experts predict that in the future retailers, especially supermarkets, will become true marketers rather than marketers that act as distribution centers. For instance, packaged goods and staples won't be sold in supermarkets. Instead, they will be delivered directly to consumers at home, within fifteen minutes of an order's placement, freeing shoppers to visit stores for things they enjoy buying—fresh produce, meats, and the fixings for a dinner party. Consumers who need staples would use hand scanners to record products' bar codes and update electronic shopping lists. Magazine ads would also carry bar codes so consumers could scan pages to put new products on their lists. The Gap is already experimenting with this concept. The retail chain is testing a program, called Gap to Go, in Manhattan and the Hamptons, offering quick home or office delivery of apparel. After filling out a form listing items such as socks, caps, belts, and jeans and faxing it or submitting it on-line, customers can have orders delivered within an hour for a delivery fee.[87]

Customer Management

Today, prime locations and unique merchandise are not the primary indicators of success they once were in the retail environment.[88] Instead, retailers are recognizing that customer equity is one of the only ways to sustain true competitive advantage. Through customer management strategies, leading retailers are intensifying their efforts to identify, satisfy, retain, and maximize the value of their best customers. Enabled by database technology, these forward-focused retailers are employing strategies designed to capture customers' share of mind, wallet, and time.

Three emerging customer management strategies retailers are embracing include customer relationship marketing, loyalty programs, and clienteling. Regardless of the strategy used, the intent is the same—to foster loyalty and develop an ongoing dialogue with a retailer's best customers. *Customer relationship marketing* (CRM) originated out of the need to more accurately target a fragmented customer base that was becoming increasingly more difficult to reach with mass advertising vehicles like television and newspapers. True CRM links customer information to transaction data collected through point-of-sale scanning systems to glean knowledge about customer purchase histories, shopping preferences, motivations, and triggers and leverages that knowledge throughout the organization to make customer-centric business decisions. After Camelot Music analyzed the data it keeps on customers, it discovered that a large number of seniors were purchasing rap and alternative music as gifts for younger relatives. In response, Camelot targeted a mailing to those seniors identifying music selections and genres that would appeal to the youngsters on their holiday shopping lists. Camelot received a 17 percent response rate to the mailer, which accounted for a sales increase of 37 percent more than for a control group that did not receive the mailer. The seniors came in and bought merchandise, thanking Camelot for making their gift-buying decisions easy for them.[89]

Armed with richer customer databases and the technology to gather and analyze customer and sales data, retailers are now taking active measures to develop loyalty programs that identify and reward their best customers. Sears' KidVantage program, for example, provides savings to members with young children. Similarly, specialty retailer Loehmann's, which offers women's designer apparel at discounted prices, uses data from its Insider Club to understand what customers are purchasing, when they are purchasing, and the type of events they prefer. In addition to periodic coupon and members-only savings, Insider Club members, currently 1.6 million strong, are notified of items and sales events. Loehmann's also launched a cobranded Insider Club Platinum Visa Card that provides a rebate on purchases.

Another approach to managing and building long-term relationships with best customers is *clienteling.* Saks Fifth Avenue, for example, strongly emphasizes personal contact on the part of managers and sales associates with customers. Associates collect and maintain detailed electronic client profiles that can be used to provide enhanced service. Sales associates are also encouraged to service clients across all departments so that the associates, already familiar with size and style preferences, can address clients' complete wardrobe needs as opposed to merely selling merchandise from their assigned department.

LOOKING BACK

Think back now to the opening story about The Gap's newest retailing phenomenon, Old Navy. Retailers are no longer just competing with other retailers such as discounters, specialty stores, and department stores and other forms of retailing such as direct-mail retailers, but they are faced with having to identify ways to attract customer attention. Retailers are realizing that they must give consumers a good reason to shop in their stores. To do this, many stores are transforming their retailing strategies to reflect what the consumer wants: more for less. Old Navy accomplishes this by providing great prices on quality clothing in a fun atmosphere.

Summary

1 Discuss the importance of retailing in the U.S. economy. Retailing plays a vital role in the U.S. economy for two main reasons. First, retail businesses contribute to our high standard of living by providing a vast number and diversity of goods and services. Second, retailing employs a large part of the U.S. working population—over nineteen million people.

2 Explain the dimensions by which retailers can be classified. Many different kinds of retailers exist. A retail establishment can be classified according to its ownership, level of service, product assortment, and price. On the basis of ownership, retailers can be broadly differentiated as independent retailers, chain stores, or franchise outlets. The level of service retailers provide can be classified along a continuum of high to low. Retailers also classify themselves by the breadth and depth of their product assortment; some retailers have concentrated product assortments whereas others have extensive product assortments. Last, general price levels also classify a store, from discounters offering low prices to exclusive specialty stores where high prices are the norm. Retailers use these latter three variables to position themselves in the marketplace.

3 Describe the major types of retail operations. The major types of retail stores are department stores, specialty retailers, supermarkets, drugstores, convenience stores, discount stores, and restaurants. Department stores carry a wide assortment of shopping and specialty goods, are organized into relatively independent departments, and offset higher prices by emphasizing customer service and decor. Specialty retailers typically carry a narrower but deeper assortment of merchandise, emphasizing distinctive products and a high level of customer service. Supermarkets are large self-service retailers that offer a wide variety of food products and some nonfood items. Drugstores are retail formats that sell mostly prescription and over-the-counter medications, health and beauty aids, cosmetics, and specialty items. Convenience stores carry a limited line of high-turnover convenience goods. Discount stores offer low-priced general merchandise and consist of four types: full-line discounters, discount specialty retailers, warehouse clubs, and off-price retailers. Finally, restaurants straddle the line between the retailing and services industries; whereas restaurants sell a product, food and drink, to final consumers, they also can be considered service marketers because they provide consumers with the service of preparing food and providing table service.

4 Discuss nonstore retailing techniques. Nonstore retailing, which is shopping outside a store setting, has three major categories. Automatic vending uses machines to offer products for sale. In direct retailing, the sales transaction occurs in a home setting, typically through door-to-door sales or party plan selling. Direct marketing refers to the techniques used to get consumers to buy from their homes or place of business. Those techniques include direct mail, catalogs and mail order, telemarketing, and electronic retailing, such as home shopping channels and on-line shopping over the Internet.

5 Define franchising and describe its two basic forms. Franchising is a continuing relationship in which a franchiser grants to a franchisee the business rights to operate or to sell a product. Modern franchising takes two basic forms. In product and trade name franchising, a dealer agrees to buy or sell certain products or product lines from a particular manufacturer or wholesaler. Business format franchising is an ongoing business relationship in which a franchisee uses a franchiser's name, format, or method of business in return for several types of fees.

6 List the major tasks involved in developing a retail marketing strategy. Retail management begins with defining the target market, typically on the basis of demographic, geographic, or psychographic characteristics. After determining the target market, retail managers must develop the six variables of the retailing mix: product, promotion, place, price, presentation, and personnel.

7 Discuss the challenges of expanding retailing operations into global markets. With increased competition and slow domestic growth, mature retailers are looking for growth opportunities in the developing consumer economies of other countries. The homogenization of tastes and product preferences around the world, the lowering of trade barriers, and the emergence of underserved markets have made the prospects of expanding across national borders more feasible for many retailers. Retailers wanting to expand globally should first determine what their core competency is and determine whether this differentiation is what the local market wants. Retailers also need to skillfully make adjustments in product mix to meet local demands.

8 Describe future trends in retailing. Three major trends are evident in retailing today. First, adding entertainment to the retail environment is one of the most popular strategies in retailing in recent years. Small retailers as well as national chains are using entertainment to set themselves apart from the competition. Second, retailers of the future will offer more convenience and efficiency to consumers as consumers become more precise on their shopping trips. Staples won't be sold in stores but instead will be delivered directly to the consumer, freeing shoppers to visit stores for products they enjoy buying. Advances in technology will make it easier for consumers to obtain the products they want. Last, more and more retailers are using the information they collect about their customers at the point of sale to develop customer management programs, including customer relationship marketing, loyalty programs, and clienteling.

Discussion and Writing Questions

1. Discuss the possible marketing implications of the recent trend toward supercenters, which combine a supermarket and a full-line discount store.
2. Explain the function of warehouse clubs. Why are they classified as both wholesalers and retailers?
3. Identify a successful retail business in your community. What marketing strategies have led to its success?
4. WRITING You want to convince your boss, the owner of a retail store, of the importance of store atmosphere. Write a memo citing specific examples of how store atmosphere affects your own shopping behavior.
5. What advantages does franchising provide to franchisers as well as franchisees?
6. WRITING You have been asked to write a brief article about the way consumer demand for convenience and efficiency is influencing the future of retailing. Write the outline for your article.
7. Your retail clothing company is considering expanding into Mexico. What information about the country and its customs should you collect before opening a store in Mexico?
8. TEAM WRITING Form a team of three classmates to identify the different retail stores in your city where VCRs, CD players, and TVs are sold. Team members should divide up and visit all the different stores and describe the products and brands that are sold in each. Prepare a report describing the differences in brands and products sold at each of the stores and the differences in stores characteristics and service levels. For example, which brands are sold in Wal-Mart and Kmart versus Campo and Silo versus independent, specialty outlets. Suggest why different products and brands are distributed through different types of stores.
9. ON LINE Go to the food shop at the following Web site. How does the "Demonstration Kitchen" help retail sales of food and wine for this site?
   http://www.virtualvin.com/

KeyTerms

atmosphere 385
automatic vending 371
buyer 364
category killers 368
chain stores 362
convenience store 366
department store 363
direct marketing (direct-response marketing) 374
direct retailing 372
discount store 367
drugstore 366
factory outlet 370
franchise 362
franchisee 377
franchiser 377
full-line discount store 367
gross margin 363
hypermarket 367
independent retailers 362
mass merchandising 367
nonstore retailing 371
off-price retailer 369
private-label brands 382
product offering 379
retailing 360
retailing mix 379
scrambled merchandising 365
specialty discount store 368
specialty store 364
supercenter 368
supermarket 365
telemarketing 375
warehouse membership clubs 369

10. ON LINE How much does the most powerful computer with the fastest modem, most memory, largest monitor, biggest hard drive, and all the available peripherals cost at this Web site? Now configure a more affordable computer and compare the differences in features and prices. **http://www.dell.com/**

11. ON LINE Why should retailers market their printed catalogs on-line? **http://www.catalogsite.com/**

Application for Small Business

ENTREPRENEUR Ron Johnson is developing a retail strategy to open up his new athletic shoe and sports equipment store. He has decided to carry Nike and Converse as his two lines of athletic shoes. This will give him top-of-the-line merchandise (Nike) and a lower-priced, high-quality alternative (Converse). He obtained permission from one of his former professors to hold brainstorming sessions in a couple of his classes. From these sessions, he identified the following evaluative criteria customers might use in selecting a particular athletic shoe to purchase: (1) attractiveness/style/color, (2) brand name, (3) comfort, (4) price, (5) endorsement, and (6) quality. He also determined that location, friend's recommendation, brands carried, and store atmosphere are important in selecting a place to purchase athletic shoes.

Questions

1. What type of retailing strategy should Ron use?
2. Which elements of the retailing mix are relatively more important?

Review Quiz

1. Which of the following types of retailers is characterized by high levels of service and narrow product line assortments.
   a. Department stores
   b. Specialty stores
   c. Convenience stores
   d. Warehouse clubs
2. Which of the following is *not* an example of nonstore retailing?
   a. Direct mail
   b. Automatic vending
   c. Warehouse clubs
   d. Telemarketing
3. In ______ a dealer agrees to sell certain products provided by a manufacturer.
   a. Nonstore retailing
   b. Business format franchising
   c. Product and trade name franchising
   d. Off-price retailing
4. The first step in developing any retail strategy is to
   a. Define the target market
   b. Determine the product offering
   c. Determine promotion strategy
   d. Identify the proper location
5. Today, retailers often feel that the greatest reason for developing a ______ is the visibility afforded to customers.

a. Strip center
b. Community shopping center
c. Regional mall
d. Freestanding store

6. Which of the following is *not* an advantage of locating a retailer in a regional mall?
   a. Anchor stores draw many customers.
   b. Direct competitors are often nearby in the same facility.
   c. Ample parking is provided.
   d. Tenants share the mall's promotional expenses.

7. The single largest global retailer today is
   a. Wal-Mart Stores, United States
   b. Tengelmann, Germany
   c. Carrefour, France
   d. Dayton Hudson, United States

8. Scrambled merchandising means that a retailer is offering a wide variety of unrelated goods under one roof.
   a. True
   b. False

9. Category killers are a more modern form of department store retailing.
   a. True
   b. False

10. In retailing, as margins drop and competition intensifies, manufacturer's brands become more attractive to retailers.
    a. True
    b. False

11. Today's consumer is looking to shop more quickly and efficiently than consumers of the recent past.
    a. True
    b. False

12. Identify the four basic ways in which retail establishments are classified.

Check the Answer Key, which follows the Video Case, to see how well you understood the material.

VIDEO CASE

Hudson's: Shopping Euphoria at the Somerset Collection

The Somerset Collection is an upscale shopping mall outside of Detroit, complete with a glass dome that encloses the center and casts natural light throughout. Somerset features elegant specialty stores and department stores such as Neiman Marcus and Saks Fifth Avenue. In 1995, Somerset planned for major expansion, with two new anchor department stores—Nordstrom and Hudson's—to open in late 1996. The simultaneous opening of these stores would pit Hudson's against the legendary customer service of Nordstrom. The challenge for Hudson's was to build a store to compete head-to-head with Nordstrom on all levels, especially customer service.

In order to successfully meet this challenge, Hudson's had to develop a sound retailing strategy to carry them past the grand opening and into the future. The first task was to define the target market; this decision would influence all subsequent planning and was a prerequisite to creating the right retailing mix. Since Hudson's stores typically target middle-income shoppers, not the high-end buyers of Somerset, the management team had to completely rethink its target market. The new store would have to appeal to the upscale shopper, and the product assortment had to match the demographics of *this* local store and region—not those of Hudson's other locations.

Hudson's combined and built upon the elements of the retailing mix to arrive at a retailing method tailored to Somerset's target market. Hudson's retailing mix consisted of the four Ps of the marketing mix (product, place, promotion, and price) plus personnel and presentation. Managers realized that the right combination of the six Ps would project Hudson's image into the higher echelons of retailing and influence customer perception. Based on their general impression of the Somerset stores, shoppers would position Hudson's against Saks, Neiman's and the new Nordstrom on three broad dimensions: product assortment, price, and service by store personnel.

Managers at Hudson's saw Somerset as a golden opportunity to showcase their store's strengths: assortment and service. Unlike the other anchor stores at Somerset, Hudson's offered a broad assortment of products and services, including a spa and a home division. Hudson's merchandise provided *width,* the assortment of products offered, as well as *depth,* the number of different brands offered within each assortment. Hudson's had the full power of the Dayton Hudson Company behind it, giving it access to many sources of supply for the very best merchandise, from high fashion to upscale bed and bath items. Price was also a key element in Hudson's positioning strategy because higher prices indicate a certain level of quality and help reinforce the prestigious image of a retailer.

A critical piece of Hudson's new upscale strategy was creating the right atmosphere through the physical layout, decor, and surroundings. The presentation of the store needed to make a great first and lasting impression. Hudson's market research had shown that customers wanted an appealing shopping environment with wide aisles and fitting rooms with seats. The new Hudson's store fit the bill, conveying a sense of luxury. It was designed with elegant lighting, ten-foot-wide aisles, real wood flooring and paneling, and rugs designed by the firm that had carpeted the Oval Office. Elegant displays accented the decor and added visual appeal to the merchandise.

Entertainment was another element of Hudson's strategy. Rather than limit themselves to a pianist playing a baby grand piano, the Hudson's marketers wanted music that would mirror both their shoppers' demographics and the merchandise throughout the store. For these reasons, they elected to vary music selection by department: classical music for the evening wear department, pop music in sportswear. By playing with the music selection throughout the store, Hudson's managers felt they could control the pace of store traffic, create an image, and attract or direct a shopper's attention to specific merchandise and services. Pleasant odors, like the smell of fragrances, were incorporated to further enhance the store's atmosphere and to stimulate shoppers' senses or emotions. All of these elements, along with visual factors such as colors, were strategically combined to create the desired store presentation that would favorably influence buying decisions and win repeat customers.

Excellent customer service was another key part of Hudson's plan at the Somerset Collection. Always looking closely at service, Hudson's kept raising the benchmark. The managers added a dedicated trainer to hire and train employees at the Somerset store alone. Instead of making prior retail experience a requirement for employment, Hudson's managers preferred to build a staff of amiable individuals with good interpersonal skills. When customers come to Hudson's at Somerset, sales personnel perform the ritual tasks of helping them select styles, sizes, and colors, but the sales staff also assists in the fitting process, offers alteration services, wraps purchases, and offers refreshments.

Successfully implementing its detailed retail strategy has led Hudson's to adopt programs that foster more personal contact between managers, sales associates, and customers. Both their experience and research indicate that customer retention leads to above-average profits and superior growth. By identifying, satisfying, retaining, and maximizing the value of its best customers, the Hudson's store at Somerset has competed effectively against not only customer service giant Nordstrom but also the other anchor stores. A well-planned retail strategy, combined with strong assortment and service, has allowed Hudson's Somerset Collection store to prosper.

Questions

1. Why was target marketing so important to Hudson's retail strategy?
2. Why did Hudson's feel that its product assortment was a competitive strength?
3. Identify the elements of the store presentation. Why is presentation important?
4. How does Hudson's service make the store competitive?

Bibliography

Video by Learnet: A Case Study in Retail Strategy: Hudson's Somerset Collection

Answer Key

1. *Answer:* b, p. 364

   Rationale: Specialty stores allow retailers to use segmentation strategies to tailor their offerings to specific markets through narrow product line offerings and high levels of customer service.

2. *Answer:* c, pp. 371–376

   Rationale: Warehouse clubs are an example of traditional instore retailing.

3. *Answer:* c, p. 377

   Rationale: In this approach, which is common in the tire and gasoline service industries, a dealer agrees to sell certain specific products provided by manufacturers or wholesalers.

4. *Answer:* a, pp. 378–379

   Rationale: Successful retailing always begins with a thorough understanding of the customer.

5. *Answer:* d, pp. 383–384

   Rationale: The freestanding format is increasingly popular with today's retailers because it increases the store's visibility and helps customers identify the store more easily.

6. *Answer:* b, p. 384

   Rationale: Many times several direct competitors will be located in a large regional mall, creating a difficult marketing environment for the retailer.

7. *Answer:* a, pp. 389–390

   Rationale: Wal-Mart's global sales are almost three times as much as its nearest global rival at over $104 billion.

8. *Answer:* a, p. 365

   Rationale: The advent of superstores has led to more use of scrambled merchandising to appeal to the needs of today's customers for convenience and variety.

9. *Answer:* b, p. 368

   Rationale: Category killer is a term used to describe modern discount specialty stores because they so heavily dominate a narrow merchandise segment.

10. *Answer:* b, p. 381

    Rationale: Private-label brands often become more advantageous for retailers when competition is intense and margins are depressed. These brands can reduce retailers' costs and give consumers better value at the same time.

11. *Answer:* a, p. 393

    Rationale: With more consumers working than ever before, convenience and efficiency in shopping are more important to most customers than ever.

12. *Answer:*

    Ownership
    Level of service
    Product assortment
    Price
    (pp. 361–363)

still shaky?

Try making up your own test questions and then quizzing yourself. What seem to be the major topics in these chapters? Try explaining them to friends who are not in the class. When you can clearly explain the concepts, you're on the way to mastery!

marketing miscues

McDonald's

Rarely has a dominant brand gone so wrong, seldom has a potent market leader wandered so far astray. McDonald's, the world's largest restaurant chain, has for decades set the standard for everything that matters in the fast-food business—innovative marketing, superior products, impeccable operations, devoted franchisees. It has been, quite simply, a jewel of a company. Thus industry experts, along with Wall Street, have watched in stunned fascination as the giant continues to stumble.

The ailment has been mostly contained in the United States, where business has been flatter than an all-beef patty. In market-share terms, McDonald's has slipped slightly to 41.9 percent, while Burger King's share has inched up a full point to 19.2 percent. Even more telling, average store sales have been down for nine of the past ten quarters, causing anger and panic among franchisees. Despite record revenues of $10.7 billion, the company hasn't had a new product hit since the mid-1980s.

The company was pathetically slow to respond to the discounting craze in the late 1980s. A series of new product gaffes didn't help: the flaky McPizza, the ill-conceived McLean burger, and the "adult" Arch Deluxe. Failing at innovation, McDonald's went for market share the only way it knew how—by building thousands of new restaurants (approximately 850 in 1994, and 1,100 in 1995, 1,000 in 1996, and 1,100 in 1997), which proceeded to steal away customers and profits from existing franchises. Relations between McDonald's and its operators got so bad that Gary Dodd, who chairs the U.S. franchisee board, told management, "It's like you're flying the plane, and we operators are in the back of a smoke-filled cabin with no idea what's going on."

Now struggling in a slow-growth market, the chain is looking for baby boomers, the massive gang it grew up with, to rejuvenate its U.S. business. However, luring more baby-boomers, by far the meatiest segment of the grownup market, won't be easy. From 1989 to 1994, adults between the ages of forty-five and fifty-four trimmed their dining-out budgets by 19 percent; boomers of thirty-five to forty-four years sucked in even more, paring their expenditures by 24.5 percent. Although the cuts primarily affected white-table-cloth, or fine, dining, these folks have also curbed their takeout habits, becoming choosier about where to spend their fast-food dollars. "Huge numbers of baby-boomers now have sophisticated tastes," notes Cheryl Russell, a demographer and editor of *The Boomer Report.* "They want less of the cheap, fattening foods at places like McDonald's. As soon as their kids are old enough, they go elsewhere." Indeed, McDonald's own internal research shows that 78 percent of its customers feel the chain has the best food for kids, but just 18 percent say it offers the best fare for adults.

Chairman and CEO of McDonald's U.S. operations Jack Greenberg is also moving to solve one of McDonald's worst pickles, falling customer satisfaction, by rolling out the "made for you" cooking system. Five years in development, the "made for you" process is hardly revolutionary. Instead of the old predictable premade burger in a warmer, this burger will be assembled for you on the spot while you wait, fast as ever. You can now "have it your way" at McDonald's. Whatever the payoff, the new system is necessary just to give McDonald's a shot at catching up with Burger King and Wendy's in the taste game.

Questions

1. What do you see as the major problems facing McDonald's?
2. What are McDonald's historic strengths?
3. What are the strengths and weaknesses of the "made for you" cooking system?
4. Critique McDonald's apparent targeting strategy.
5. Critique McDonald's distribution strategy.
6. Critique McDonald's product strategy.

SOURCES: Shelly Branch, "McDonald's Strikes Out with Grownups," *Fortune,* 11 November 1997, on-line. Shelly Branch, "What's Eating McDonald's?" *Fortune,* 13 October 1997, pp. 122–125. Patricia Sellers, "McDonald's Starts Over," *Fortune,* 22 June 1998, pp. 34–36.

critical thinking case

The Home Depot

The Home Depot is North America's largest home improvement retailer, currently operating over 640 warehouse-style home centers in the United States and Canada, with net sales for fiscal 1998 reaching close to $30 billion. By 2001, the chain is expected to have as many as 1,350 Depot centers, about twice as many stores as at the end of 1998. Two new stores open every week. Since founders Arthur Blank and Bernie Marcus opened the first Depot store in Atlanta in 1978, they have watched their trademark orange aprons become just as much a part of Americana as the golden arches.

The Home Depot is synonymous with home improvement and has built its reputation on broad assortments, low prices, and quality customer service. Depot stores cater to do-it-yourselfers as well as to professionals in the home improvement, construction, and building maintenance trades. Each store stocks approximately forty thousand to fifty thousand different kinds of building materials, home improvement supplies, and lawn and garden products. Stores have a design center staffed by professional designers who offer free in-store consultation for home improvement projects ranging from lighting to computer-assisted design for kitchens and bathrooms.

The Home Depot is credited with being the leading innovator in the home improvement retail industry by combining the economies of scale inherent in a warehouse format with a level of customer service unprecedented among warehouse-style retailers. Its emphasis on customer service and education eliminates much of the mystery for consumers surrounding home improvement projects. The Home Depot offers many how-to clinics to help customers learn how to lay tile, experiment with paint, or build an outdoor pond.

The Home Depot's biggest competitor in the home center industry is Lowe's, whose sales are only a third of The Home Depot's. Despite the tremendous growth of both companies, however, the sales at both The Home Depot and Lowe's still account for only about a fifth of the home center market. The industry remains relatively fragmented, with ongoing opportunities for the strong to get stronger while the weaker chains and local hardware stores get acquired or go out of business.

exhibit A

The $100 Billion Do-It-Yourself Market

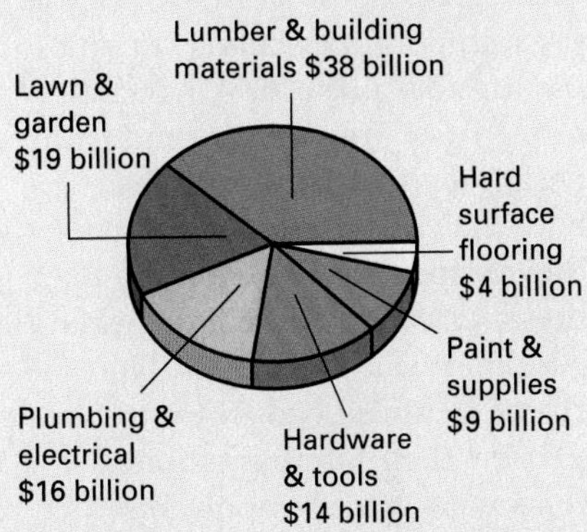

The Do-It-Yourself Market

The Home Improvement Research Institute estimates that the do-it-yourself home center market had sales of $100 billion in 1997, up 4 percent from the previous year. By the end of 2001, it estimates that this market will swell to over $121 billion, a 21 percent increase in just four years. Future growth of the home center market depends on many factors, including the number of homeowners, the age of the housing stock, interest rates, housing turnover, and housing prices. Home ownership rates, currently about 65 percent, continue to rise due to low interest rates, a robust economy, and a wave of empowered baby boomers who feel more comfortable doing home repairs and improvement projects.

Studies show that people are staying in their homes later in life, a trend that enhances The Home Depot's opportunities to add new stores across North America as well as increase sales in its existing stores. This trend, along with a strong housing market and low interest rates, seems to be working in The Home Depot's favor. Today, the typical Home Depot store generates $43 million in annual sales, up from $29 million in 1990. Between 1990 and 1998, annual average household spending in Depot stores jumped 141 percent, from $191 to $462. That dropped the number of households needed to support a single store from 154,000 to 93,000 in the same period.

Even in an economic turndown, in which home sales slow and interest rates rise, The Home Depot feels confident that it can grow. When people aren't buying houses, the thinking goes, they are more likely to fix up their old ones.

The Home Depot reaches more do-it-yourself customers every year by opening new stores at a steady rate. Growing the do-it-yourself customer base through store expansion is the company's primary growth vehicle. Research shows that do-it-yourself spending increases when a Home Depot store enters a market for the first time. As a result, the company continues to add stores to even its most mature markets to further penetrate and increase its presence in the marketplace.

Added services targeted to the do-it-yourselfer promise to expand The Home Depot's reach into everyone's home improvement project. How-to clinics teach customers to take on projects of varying degrees of difficulty, from closet organization to installing ceramic tile. In-store professional decorators provide free kitchen and bath design services. Customers can have their purchases delivered to their home seven days a week, or, if they can't wait to have it delivered, customers can rent one of The Home Depot's Load 'N Go trucks to bring their purchases home. Customers can also apply for a Home Depot charge card for an affordable way to finance their home improvement purchases. Several stores are also experimenting with twenty-four-hour operations as well as installation services for roofing, vinyl siding, and vinyl replacement windows. Some Depot stores are pushing even further into the remodeling business by offering various remodeling services such as complete kitchen and bath makeovers.

The Professional Market

The Home Depot also targets the professional market, which includes contractors, electricians, landscapers, plumbers, remodelers, and property maintenance managers. The professional market, currently estimated at $215 billion annually, provides the company with attractive growth opportunities because The Home Depot's share of this market is only about 4 percent. The typical Home Depot professional customer is a repair and remodeling professional who purchases up to $200,000 of products annually but buys less than 10 percent of this from the chain. The Home Depot's goal is to capture more of this customer's purchases by responding to his or her distinct product and service needs.

exhibit B

The $215 Billion Professional Business Customer Market

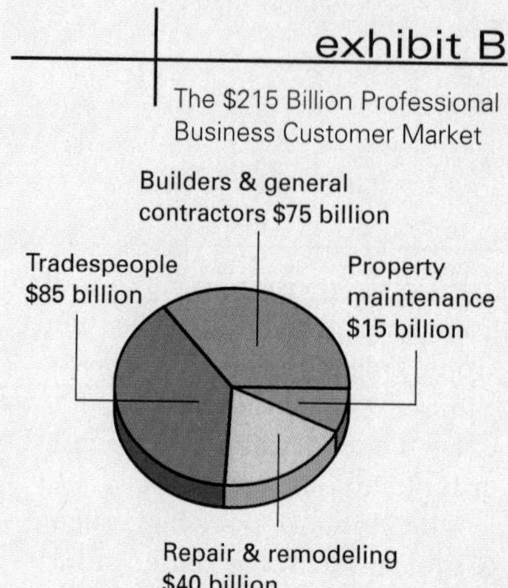

A study conducted by The Home Depot on the professional business market found that the professional buyer wants efficient, personalized service, convenient locations and hours, appropriate products and product quantities, competitive prices, customized delivery services, and flexible credit programs. The Home Depot has responded to these needs by offering such things as packaging in multiple quantities and the availability of "job lot quantities" for professional customers who need to buy in larger quantities than the do-it-yourselfers. Providing job lot quantities not only makes shopping easier for professionals but also increases The Home Depot's sales in these product areas.

A test in The Home Depot's Austin, Texas, market includes adding associates whose primary responsibility is serving and building relationships with professional business customers. An in-store Pro Service Desk assists professional customers to more quickly meet their product and service needs. Additionally, customized services such as enhanced ordering, credit programs, and delivery options are available to professional business customers.

The Home Depot also distributes its ProBook professional equipment and supply catalog to professional customers across North America as a way to further reach this market. The ProBook contains over fifteen thousand products from its stores chosen especially for facility maintenance managers and the building trades.

Future Expansion

With only a fraction of the home improvement market dominated by big-box retailers, The Home Depot is looking for more ways to expand its market share. Besides its aggressive goal of 1,350 stores by 2001 and its enhanced service tests in the do-it-yourself and professional business buyer markets, The Home Depot is experimenting with several alternative store formats, different distribution methods, and global expansion.

Smaller Stores Realizing that its warehouse-sized Depot stores (the typical new store is 108,000 square feet) turn off many customers who say it is difficult to get in and out quickly when all they need are a few specific items, The Home Depot is introducing new scaled-down versions (between 35,000 and 40,000 square feet) with the look and feel of a traditional hardware store. The company plans to open several stores in the Northeast and on the East coast to serve do-it-yourselfers who prefer the layout of a smaller shop. The smaller stores will have The Home Depot's trademark quality service and low prices. The test will help The Home Depot determine the best products, services, and methods of gaining home improvement sales it would not be able to get inside its traditional Home Depot stores.

Stores for the "Have-Someone-Do-It-For-You" Market As household income levels increase, baby boomers age, and the elderly stay in their homes longer, The Home Depot speculates that a number of today's do-it-yourselfers will become tomorrow's buy-it-yourselfers: customers who select and purchase the products they put in their homes, but who prefer to hire someone else to complete the project. In addition to the installation services that are currently available in Depot stores, the company introduced Expo Design Centers to cater to this growing market.

Through its Expo Design Centers, The Home Depot is pursuing a similar strategy to that of The Gap Inc., which operates its separate Banana Republic chain to sell more stylish and expensive apparel. Instead of gazing at sawdust and spackling paste in a Depot store, customers at Expo outlets stroll through romantically lit mazes of model kitchens and bathrooms. The Expo formula focuses on total solutions for customers undertaking renovation projects throughout their homes. Each store features more than twenty complete kitchen and bath vignettes to help customers visualize their dreams. The stores also offer a broad array of appliances, floor coverings, tiles, lighting products, and window and wall-coverings, such as $6,599 Sub-Zero refrigerators and $39,500 Schonbek chandeliers. Only about 10 percent of Expo's inventory is the same as that at Depot stores.

The first Expo Design Center opened in 1990. After several years of tinkering with the format and merchandise mix, The Home Depot is ready for mass expansion. The Expo division is expected to grow to approximately two hundred stores by 2005. Sears is opening up similar retail stores, called The Great Indoors, aimed at challenging Expo stores.

New Distribution Methods The Home Depot's recent acquisitions of National Blind & Wallpaper Factory, a $70 million Detroit-based catalog company specializing in window coverings and wallpaper, and Maintenance Warehouse/America Corporation, a private company that was the nation's top direct-mail marketer of maintenance and repair products to lodging and multifamily housing facilities managers, add direct distribution channels to the company's already strong retail channel.

The Home Depot is hoping the purchase of National Blind will improve customer service in its hundreds of Depot stores. Company executives admit that Depot employees, after helping customers pick out window and wall covering products in the stores, sometimes stumble in the fitting process, often omitting key questions that can lead to the wrong size being ordered. Because National Blind sells all its products by telephone, operators follow a strict script designed to ensure the customer gets the right product, size, and color. Depot stores are now experimenting with having customers order their blinds and wallpaper directly through National Blind after picking it out in the store.

The acquisition of Maintenance Warehouse provides The Home Depot with the means to add a high-growth direct mail distribution channel to its business and to reach a larger segment of customers for maintenance and repair products. Through the combination of Maintenance Warehouse's capabilities and The Home Depot's purchasing and marketing powers, the company plans to grow its position aggressively in this attractive segment of the professional business customer market.

The Internet also holds some promise for increasing sales through direct channels. An initial foray into on-line sales is expected in 1999 from the company's Web site at **http://www.homedepot.com**.

Global Expansion The Home Depot recently opened its first stores outside of North America in Santiago, Chile, through a joint venture agreement with S.A.C.I. Falabella, the largest department store retailer in Chile. The company plans to employ a focused, regional strategy in its global expansion. Given a successful entry into Chile, its plans are to expand into other areas of South America, most likely Argentina, Peru, and Brazil. Its experiments in Chile will serve as an interesting case study of whether a highly successful American corporation can take its winning culture abroad and make it work despite language barriers, long supply lines, and differing customer tastes.

Questions

1. How can The Home Depot maintain its high customer-service standards with a workforce approaching 150,000 associates, some now in countries abroad, over the next several years?
2. Do you feel the company can successfully penetrate and dominate new markets, like the $216 billion professional maintenance industry and the have-someone-do-it-for-you market, while keeping its core do-it-yourself customers from growing bored with existing stores?
3. Do you feel The Home Depot risks cannibalization at its traditional Depot store by opening smaller Depot hardware stores and specialized Expo stores?
4. Lowe's plans a similar strategy of opening up big-box retail stores to challenge The Home Depot's share of the home improvement market. How can Lowe's distinguish itself in the marketplace to obtain a competitive advantage over The Home Depot?

5. The Home Depot plans to continue its global expansion into other South American countries like Argentina and Brazil. What factors should the company analyze before building stores in these countries?

SOURCES: Jed Graham, "Home Depot Shrinks Format to Lure Hardware Store Fans," *Investor's Business Daily*, 14 July 1998, p. A29. James R. Hagerty, "Gilding the Drill Bit? Hardware Giants Go High-End," *Wall Street Journal*, 28 July 1998, pp. B1, B8. James R. Hagerty, "Home Depot Offering Home-Remodeling Services in Limited Test," *Dow Jones Online News*, 27 July 1998. James R. Hagerty, "Home Depot's New Advice for Do-It-Yourselfers: Don't," *Wall Street Journal*, 19 October 1998, p. B1, B4. Press releases and information at The Home Depot's Web site, **http://www.homedepot.com.** *The Home Depot 1995 Annual Report. The Home Depot 1996 Annual Report. The Home Depot 1997 Annual Report.* Robert J. Izmirlian, "Retailing: Specialty," *Standard & Poor's Industry Surveys*, Volume 166, Number 4, Section 2, 22 January 1998, pp. 7–8. Roy S. Johnson, "Home Depot Renovates," *Fortune*, 23 November 1998, pp. 200–212. Clifford Krauss, "Foreign Expansion: Well-Planned or Ill-Timed?" *The New York Times*, 6 September 1998, p. 1.

Cross-Functional Connections Solutions

Questions

1. What is the difference between the demand-side perspective and the supply-side perspective to doing business? Is either perspective more appropriate?

   The demand-side perspective focuses on determining, via marketing research, the customer's wants and needs. Products/services are then developed that satisfy these wants and needs. Once developed, marketing adds the finishing touches by positioning the products/services in such a manner that the customers recognize that the products/services will fulfill their demands. Demand-side starts with the customer and ends with the customer, with marketing and the other business functions working in the middle.

   The supply-side perspective takes the position that engineers should develop and manufacture leading-edge products. Once developed and manufactured, marketing then introduces the product to the customer by telling the customer about the product's performance. Supply-side tends to start with the research and development group, move to the manufacturing group, then move to marketing, and end with the customer.

   As marketers, we believe that the demand-side perspective is the best approach to doing business. However, some argue that the supply-side perspective is more appropriate for high-technology products—that if we waited for the customer, we would not yet have call-waiting, microwave ovens, or video games.

2. What are some of the popular business terms used to describe cross-functional integration?

   - design-factory fit
   - concurrent engineering
   - design for manufacturability and assembly
   - early manufacturing involvement
   - paperless design
   - modularization

3. What are some of the popular Advanced Manufacturing Systems and how do they interact with marketing?

   Advanced Manufacturing Systems include: Just-in-Time (JIT), Manufacturing Resources Planning (MRP), and Electronic Data Interchange (EDI).

   Advanced Manufacturing Systems allow a firm to compete on both time and quality. The systems allow for a quicker response to customers' demands as well as shortening the new product production cycle. The systems allow firms to produce a large variety of high quality products in a reduced cycle time. Such systems, then, result in more timely deliveries.

Suggested Readings

B. Joseph Pine II, *Mass Customization: The New Frontier in Business Competition* (Boston: Harvard Business School Press, 1993).

Steven P. Schnaars, *Marketing Strategy: A Customer-Driven Approach* (chapter 13) (New York: The Free Press, 1991).

Pete Engardio, "Souping Up the Supply Chain," *Business Week,* 31 August 1998, pp. 110–112.

Vaman Shenoy Kudpi and Niranjan Pati, "How Advanced Manufacturing Systems Affect Marketing Channels," *Business Forum,* Winter/Spring 1996, pp. 16–20.

Marketing Planning Activities

Product Decisions

The next part of the marketing plan is a description of the elements of the marketing mix, starting with the product or service offering. Be sure that your product plans match the needs and wants of the target market identified and described in the previous section.

1. What type(s) of consumer or business-to-business product is your chosen firm offering?
2. Place your company's offerings into a product portfolio. Consider the broader impact of marketing a product item within a line or mix. Factors to consider are those such as price, image, complementary products, distribution relationship, and so on.
3. Does your chosen company have a brand name and brand mark? If not, design both. If so, evaluate the ability of the brand name and mark to communicate effectively to the target market.
4. How is your firm's product packaged and labeled? Is the packaging strategy appropriate for the target market(s)? Does the package "fit" with distribution, promotion, and price elements?
5. Evaluate the warranties or guarantees offered by your firm, including product return policies.

Marketing*Builder* Exercise

- **Returns and Adjustments Policy** portion of the **Sales Plan** template

6. Place your company's product in the appropriate stage of the product life cycle. What are the implications of being in this stage? What should your firm prepare for in the future?

Marketing*Builder* Exercise

- **Product Life Cycles** portion of the **Market Analysis** template

7. What categories of adopters are likely to buy your company's products? Is the product diffusing slowly or quickly throughout the marketplace? Why?
8. What service aspects are provided with the product? How is customer service handled? What elements of service quality can your firm focus on?

Marketing*Builder* Exercise

- **Customer Service** portion of the **Sales Plan** template

9. With whom should your chosen company practice relationship marketing?
10. Does the product offer good customer value?

Marketing*Builder* Exercise

- **Product Launch Budget** in the **Marketing Budget** spreadsheet

Distribution Decisions

The next part of the marketing mix to be described for the marketing plan is the "place" portion, or distribution. Be sure that your distribution plans match the needs and wants of the target market identified and described earlier and are compatible with the product and service issues discussed in the previous section.

1. Discuss the implications of dual/multiple distribution. If your firm sells through a major department store and its own catalog and then decides to have an on-line World Wide Web site and open its own store in a factory outlet, what will happen to channel relationships? To the final price offered to consumers? To promotional vehicles?

Marketing*Builder* Exercise

- **Distribution Channels** portion of the **Sales Plan** template

2. Decide what channel(s) your chosen company should be using. Describe the intermediaries involved and their likely behavior. What are the implications of these channels?

Marketing*Builder* Exercise

- **Alliances** portion of the **Sales Source Analysis** spreadsheet

3. Which distribution intensity level would be best for your company's product? Justify your decision.
4. What type of physical distribution facilities will be necessary to distribute the product? Where should they be located? How should the product be distributed? Justify your selection of transportation mode(s).
5. What types of retail establishments might be used for your firm's product? Are they in locations convenient to the target customers? What is the atmosphere of the facility for each type?

4 INTEGRATED MARKETING COMMUNICATION AND PRICING CONCEPTS

CROSS-FUNCTIONAL CONNECTIONS

Will the Internet Facilitate Cross-Functionality in Communicating and Pricing Products?

It is the company's responsibility to make certain that the product or service received by the customer is consistent with the message the customer received via the firm's integrated marketing communications and that the quality of the product or service is worth the price paid by the customer. Product quality is an issue that touches the heart of a firm's operational processes. Marketers love to tout a product's superior quality when communicating and pricing products to potential customers. If the pricing and communications programs entice a consumer to try a product or service, the product or service must then be consistent with the consumer's expectations of quality. The only way to ensure this consistency is with a strong integration of business functions.

When a company's communications strategy focuses on promoting quality, high-priced features, pressure is placed on research and development, manufacturing, and human resources to deliver on quality. Unfortunately, issues that mean quality to a scientist or an engineer in a manufacturing or research and development department may not readily translate to perceptions of quality by the customer. Furthermore, research and development and manufacturing departments often have completed their product-related tasks by the time marketing develops the communications campaign and begins to price the product. This linear completion process can also cause some concerns between marketing and accounting since costs determine the floor on prices. Naturally, finance has a keen interest in the pricing process in relation to its targets for return on investment.

The relationship between price and demand has downstream effects on the manufacturing process. Research and development pays close attention to the introductory price of the product because this is considered to be the point at which development costs will begin to be recouped. If marketing identifies an initial price as too high to capture customer interest, research and development and manufacturing must be consulted to see whether product features, product materials, or assembly processes can be modified to decrease costs.

A company's Web site may be the customer's first and only contact with the company. Traditionally, the marketing group was in charge of developing the marketing communications that reached the potential customer. Now, one only has to access the Web to see that the nature of a firm's marketing communication has changed dramatically. The information that traditionally may have been in the form of a brochure or print ad is now on the consumer's computer screen. Traditional "hard-copy" of a company's product offering generally included the price of the product. These prices were basically set for the life of the marketing brochure or catalog. In today's computer age, product prices are set only for as long as the company wants them to remain constant. Prices can change many times a day on the company's retail Internet site.

Often, the responsibility for the actual development and functional capabilities of a company's Web site—a major element of the firm's marketing communications and pricing programs—is in the hands of information technology experts. These experts, through their technical control of the computer program manning the firm's marketing communications and pricing efforts, need to understand the importance of the display the customer views on the computer and the response time necessary to keep the company's products priced competitively.

Companies often refer to marketers as the site/content *strategists* and information technologists as the site/content *implementators.* Unfortunately, the separation into strategy and implementation has tended to exacerbate the conflict between marketing and information technology. The information technologists do not like "taking orders" from marketers about something that has always come under their purview (computers). Likewise, marketers fear that letting information technologists build the Web site will result in something too technologically advanced as well as something that will not appeal to a customer.

Despite the potential conflict between marketing and information technology regarding the design and maintenance of the company's web site, the Internet has worked wonders for customer service. Electronically fulfilling customer requests for technical support can dramatically improve customer satisfaction. Technicians are able to respond much more quickly to requests—bringing positive results to marketing in the form of satisfied customers and to engineering in that the number of engineers needed for product support is reduced. The decreased need for technical product support engineers means that these engineers can devote more time to new product development issues.

Marketing direct to the consumer pays off from manufacturing's viewpoint, too. Network capabilities can lead to little or no inventory requirements. Basically, when the consumer places an order, the firm's suppliers receive electronic messages indicating what raw materials will be needed to satisfy the customer's product demands. The raw materials can be shipped immediately to the manufacturing facility, which received the order transmission at the same time as the suppliers.

Internet marketing also allows customers to receive their orders more quickly. No longer does the customer's order have to work its way through various steps before finally reaching the production people. Instead, electronic order taking can transmit the customer's order directly to the company's order fulfillment center—drawing into focus the need for close relations with the logistics and transportation people.

Not surprisingly, marketing via the Internet calls for necessary interaction between marketing and research and development—particularly as it relates to what engineers can do and what customers desire. One area, in the late 1990s, in which research and development reached beyond the consumer's wants and needs is television via the Internet. Known as video datacasting, the technology used television airwaves to send Internet data. Additionally, the technology allowed consumers to watch television on their personal computers. However, development engineers failed to recognize that consumers were unwilling to pay for having the television data receiving cards installed in their computer systems. As the manufacturer of such a card, Compaq Computer Company has yet to experience anything but mediocre consumer receptiveness to the product.

Successful Internet marketing requires close interaction with the company's financial groups. A major concern about ordering products over the Internet is payment. If the customer is using a credit card, the company is responsible for making sure that the person placing the order is the rightful holder of the credit card. American Express is considering electronic commerce the next wave in its corporate purchasing card's product life cycle. The company hopes to build on its current strengths of company acceptance of the card and databases already in place that link suppliers and buyers as tools to overcome competitive corporate card expansion by MasterCard and VISA.

Purchasing over the Internet for most firms, however, will result in some initial costs. A firm's security expenses increase when involved in Internet marketing. Additionally, the initial financial investment for marketing on the Internet can be very high. Therefore, marketing has to work closely with the company's financial groups to make sure the investment will result in long-term positive gains. Keys to receiving a return on this investment are developing interactive marketing sites that (1) encourage and entice customers to repeat visits and (2) utilize marketplace information across all functional departments.

Technology is changing the way we communicate about companies and products. Additionally, technology is changing the pricing arena in that it allows companies to quickly change prices to meet marketplace demand. It is also expected to have long-term implications for a company's organization structure and management processes. Changes in the way consumers interact with companies will no doubt lead to even greater challenges regarding cross-functional coordination.

Questions for Discussion:

1. Why is the company's pricing strategy and marketing communications of particular concern to research & development, manufacturing, finance, accounting, and human resources?
2. How has today's technology altered the role of information technologists?
3. What are some the benefits of networking functional departments, customers, and suppliers?

check it out

For articles and exercises on the material in this part, and for their great study aids, visit the *Marketing* Web site at
http://lamb.swcollege.com

CHAPTER

12

LEARNING OBJECTIVES

After studying this chapter, you should be able to

1 Discuss the role of promotion in the marketing mix

2 Discuss the elements of the promotional mix

3 Describe the communication process

4 Explain the goals and tasks of promotion

5 Discuss the AIDA concept and its relationship to the promotional mix

6 Describe the factors that affect the promotional mix

7 Describe personal selling

8 Discuss the key differences between relationship selling and traditional selling

9 List the steps in the selling process

10 Describe the functions of sales management

MARKETING COMMUNICATION AND PERSONAL SELLING

Chips and dips are hardly big-ticket items. Most people don't think twice about the bag of chips or cheese snacks that they throw into their shopping carts. Consumers just know that the Frito-Lay name and its brands mean good-quality, good-tasting salty snacks. Revenues at Frito-Lay, a subsidiary of PepsiCo, grew by more than $600 million—6 percent—in one year alone. Annual worldwide sales of Frito-Lay snacks are over $10 billion. Imagine selling billions of dollars in chips a year!

Americans know Frito-Lay brands at sight: Doritos, Fritos, Lay's, Cheetos, Ruffles, Rold Gold, and Baked Lay's, to name its most popular. But how did Frito-Lay get where it is today? How has the company developed such astounding sales and loyalty among chip aficionados? Much of it has to do with Frito-Lay's promotional plan, encompassing advertising, sales promotion, public relations, and personal selling.

With a $30 million a year U.S. ad budget, Frito-Lay has plenty of opportunity to get its message of great-tasting snacks across to consumers. Frito-Lay has been a long-time repeat advertiser during the annual Super Bowl telecast, shelling out more than a million dollars for just one ad during the program. The vast audience provided by the Super Bowl telecast has proved to be an excellent launching pad for Frito-Lay's new brands, such as Baked Lay's Potato Crisps in 1995 and Lay's Deli Style Potato Chips in 1998. Baked Lay's went on to become the most successful new food product launch in the 1990s and the biggest-selling salty snack product ever.

Realizing the natural link between salty snacks and beer and soda, Frito-Lay continues its successful sales promotional strategy of offering supermarket-friendly promotions with Pepsi-Cola products, its sister company, and Anheuser-Busch beer brands. Its combined promotion with Pepsi included a "Halloween House Party" with joint Pepsi and Frito-Lay displays at retailers, special packaging, and coupons offering $1 off a purchase of Doritos with the purchase of Pepsi. In a combined sales promotion with Anheuser-Busch, Frito-Lay linked Ruffles and Lay's with Budweiser beer through joint in-store displays. The displays offered instantly redeemable $1 discounts with the purchase of both products.

Kids' lunches represent a sizable opportunity for Frito-Lay snacks. Research shows that kids

on line

Frito-Lay

To see more information on Frito-Lay's snack brands and its promotional strategies, learn more about olestra, or to peruse the company's annual report, visit Frito-Lay's Web site.
http://www.fritolay.com/

aged one to twelve brown-bag 2.5 billion meals a year, yet less than a quarter of those lunches include a salty snack. As a result, Frito-Lay developed the Planet Lunch program specifically targeted to kids and teens. Planet Lunch focuses on single-serving variety packs of its chips and snacks promoted through some fifteen thousand in-store displays, including a continuity program offering kids "Planet Points" redeemable for Frito-Lay merchandise like Chester Cheetah posters and mini radios.

The introduction of its Wow! fat-free snacks, made with the controversial fat substitute olestra, created a formidable public relations task for Frito-Lay. Fat calories from foods fried with olestra, developed by Procter & Gamble under the brand name Olean, are not digested by the human body because the additive's fat molecules are too large. Therefore, consumers get the taste of fat without the added baggage of unwanted calories. Although the Wow! brand was supported by a national advertising campaign and sales promotion activities such as free samples in grocery store aisles and through mass mailings, the brand had to overcome opposition from groups who insisted that olestra caused gastrointestinal problems and posed potentially serious health risks. Prior to its national release, P&G and Frito-Lay held several news conferences with the media and dispatched scientists to meet with dieticians and health professionals. P&G also offers a toll-free number and a Web site with links to medical groups like the American Dietetic Association, which describes olestra as "one of the many acceptable ways to reduce the amount of fat and calories in your diet." The companies have also released countless press releases that back up its research into the safety of olestra and detail the Food & Drug Administration's approval of the additive. To date, the public relations plan seems to be working. Since olestra's approval, tens of millions of people have eaten over a half-billion servings of the new snacks made with olestra with relatively few complaints.

Given all of Frito-Lay's advertising, promotional, and public relations activities that consumers are familiar with, its backbone lies in the behind-the-scenes work of its eighteen-thousand-strong sales force, voted one of the best sales forces by *Sales & Marketing Management* magazine in 1998. Senior executives at Frito-Lay understand that continued growth is not only the result of good advertising campaigns but also the culmination of thousands of five-minute, face-to-face conversations their individual sales reps have daily with store managers at supermarkets and convenience stores. Frito-Lay's route service reps (RSRs) use technology and selling skills to convince store managers to stock more Frito-Lay products and position them prominently on their shelves. With handheld computers, RSRs track how products are selling in each store. The company does a monthly analysis of which sizes and flavors sell well in each sales territory. It knows, for instance, that spicier snacks are popular in the South and Cheetos sell well in large cities. Frito-Lay then uses these data to optimize what they stock on shelves, as well as to plan promotions tied around certain brands. RSRs visit small accounts at least three times a week and visit large stores like Kroger and Wal-Mart daily. With this frequency, RSRs can closely monitor sales and assist store managers with promotional ideas.[1]

As you can see, Frito-Lay places considerable emphasis on promotion in its marketing mix. What is the role of promotion in the marketing mix? What types of promotional tools are available to companies and what factors influence the choice of tool? How is the promotion plan created? The rest of the chapter answers these questions.

The Role of Promotion in the Marketing Mix

1
Discuss the role of promotion in the marketing mix

Few goods or services, no matter how well developed, priced, or distributed, can survive in the marketplace without effective promotion. **Promotion** is communication by marketers that informs, persuades, and reminds potential buyers of a product in order to influence their opinion or elicit a response.

Promotional strategy is a plan for the optimal use of the elements of promotion: advertising, public relations, personal selling, and sales promotion. As Exhibit 12.1 shows, the marketing manager determines the goals of the company's promotional strategy in light of the firm's overall goals for the marketing mix—product, place (distribution), promotion, and price. Using these overall goals, marketers combine the elements of the promotional strategy (the promotional mix) into a coordinated plan. The promotion plan then becomes an integral part of the marketing strategy for reaching the target market.

The main function of a marketer's promotional strategy is to convince target customers that the goods and services offered provide a differential advantage over the competition. A **differential advantage** is the set of unique features of a company and its products that are perceived by the target market as significant and superior to the competition. Such features can include high product quality, rapid delivery, low prices, excellent service, or a feature not offered by the competition. For example, Revlon ColorStay Lipcolor promises unsmeared lipstick all day long. By effectively communicating this differential advantage through advertising featuring model Cindy Crawford, Revlon can stimulate demand for its smudge-free line of makeup. Promotion is therefore a vital part of the marketing mix, informing consumers of a product's benefits and thus positioning the product in the marketplace.

Revlon ColorStay Lipcolor promises unsmeared lipstick all day long. By effectively communicating this differential advantage through advertising, Revlon can stimulate demand for its smudge-free line of make-up.
Courtesy Revlon

exhibit 12.1

Role of Promotion in the Marketing Mix

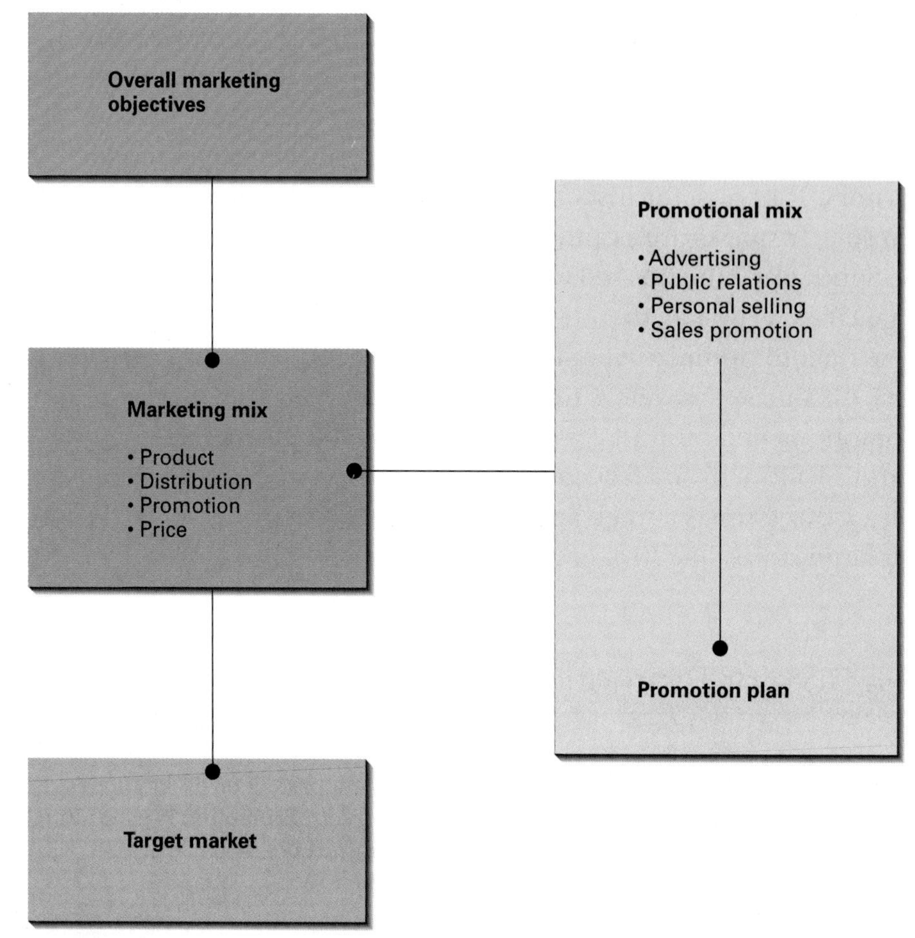

The Promotional Mix

2

Discuss the elements of the promotional mix

promotion
Communication by marketers that informs, persuades, and reminds potential buyers of a product in order to influence an opinion or elicit a response.

promotional strategy
Plan for the optimal use of the elements of promotion: advertising, public relations, personal selling, and sales promotion.

differential advantage
One or more unique aspects of an organization that cause target consumers to patronize that firm rather than competitors.

Most promotional strategies use several ingredients—which may include personal selling, advertising, sales promotion, and public relations—to reach the target market. That combination is called the **promotional mix**. The proper promotional mix is the one that management believes will meet the needs of the target market and fulfill the organization's overall goals. The more funds allocated to each promotional ingredient and the more managerial emphasis placed on each technique, the more important that element is thought to be in the overall mix.

Personal Selling

Personal selling is a purchase situation in which two people communicate in an attempt to influence each other. In this dyad, both the buyer and seller have specific objectives they wish to accomplish. The buyer may need to minimize cost or assure a quality product, for instance, while the salesperson may need to maximize revenue and profits.[2]

Traditional methods of personal selling include a planned presentation to one or more prospective buyers for the purpose of making a sale. Whether it takes place face-to-face or over the phone, personal selling attempts to persuade the buyer to accept a point of view or convince the buyer to take some action. For example, a car salesperson may try to persuade a car buyer that a particular model is superior to a competing model in certain features, such as gas mileage, roominess, and interior styling. Once the buyer is somewhat convinced, then the salesperson may attempt to elicit some action from the buyer, such as a test drive or a purchase. Frequently, in this traditional view of personal selling, the objectives of the salesperson are at the expense of the buyer, creating a win-lose outcome.

More current notions on the subject of personal selling emphasize the relationship that develops between a salesperson and a buyer. This concept is more typical with business- and industrial-type goods, such as heavy machinery or computer systems, than with consumer goods. Relationship selling emphasizes a win-win outcome and the accomplishment of mutual objectives that benefits both buyer and salesperson in the long term. Relationship selling does not seek either a quick sale or a temporary increase in sales—rather, it attempts to create involvement and loyalty by building a lasting bond with the customer.[3] Personal selling and relationship selling are discussed later in this chapter.

promotional mix
Combination of promotion tools—including advertising, public relations, personal selling, and sales promotion—used to reach the target market and fulfill the organization's overall goals.

personal selling
Planned presentation to one or more prospective buyers for the purpose of making a sale.

Advertising

Almost all companies selling a good or a service use some form of advertising, whether it be in the form of a multimillion-dollar campaign or a simple classified ad in a newspaper. **Advertising** is any form of paid communication in which the sponsor or company is identified. Traditional media—such as television, radio, newspapers, magazines, books, direct mail, billboards, and transit cards (advertisements on buses and taxis and at bus stops)—are most commonly used to transmit advertisements to consumers. Marketers, however, are finding many new ways to send their advertisements, most notably through such electronic means as the Internet, computer modems, and fax machines.

advertising
Impersonal, one-way mass communication about a product or organization that is paid for by a marketer.

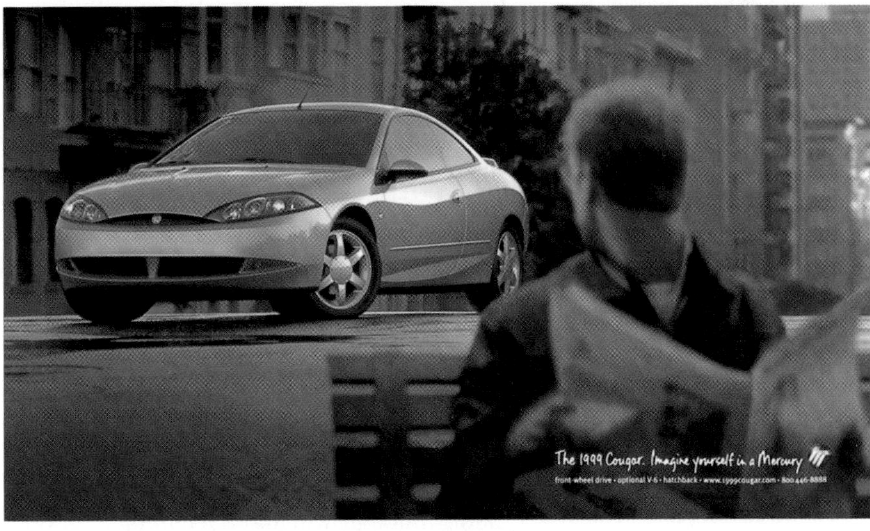

The 1999 Cougar. Imagine yourself in a Mercury
front-wheel drive • optional V-6 • hatchback • www.1999cougar.com • 800-446-8888

Advertising costs can sometimes be prohibitive for smaller companies. For example, few small companies can match the $40 million spent by Ford's Mercury division in the national rollout of the new Cougar.
Courtesy Ford Motor Company. Photograph by Robert Stevens ©

One of the primary benefits of advertising is its ability to communicate to a large number of people at one time. Cost per contact, therefore, is typically very low. Advertising has the advantage of being able to reach the masses (for instance, through national television networks), but it can also be microtargeted to small groups of potential customers, such as television ads on a targeted cable network or through print advertising in a trade magazine.

Although the cost per contact in advertising is very low, the total cost to advertise is typically very high. This hurdle tends to restrict advertising on a national basis to only those companies that are financially able to do so. For instance, to introduce its redesigned 1999 Cougar coupe, Ford Motor Company's Mercury brand spent about $40 million in media advertising such as network television and print advertisements.[4] Few small companies can match this level of spending for a national campaign. Chapter 13 examines advertising in greater detail.

Sales Promotion

Sales promotion consists of all marketing activities—other than personal selling, advertising, and public relations—that stimulate consumer purchasing and dealer effectiveness. Sales promotion is generally a short-run tool used to stimulate immediate increases in demand. Sales promotion can be aimed at end consumers, trade

sales promotion
Marketing activities—other than personal selling, advertising, and public relations—that stimulate consumer buying and dealer effectiveness.

on line

Nabisco

Nabisco lists its promotions on its Web site. What do think the advantages and disadvantages of this are? Visit the site to get more information.
http://www.nabisco.com/

customers, or a company's employees. Sales promotions include free samples, contests, premiums, trade shows, vacation giveaways, and coupons. A major promotional campaign might use several of these sales promotion tools. For example, Nabisco routinely issues coupons good for cents off of its Oreo brand sandwich cookies. To celebrate holidays and grab shoppers' attention, the company also uses red food dye at Christmas and blue at Easter, giving Oreos a holiday twist.[5]

Often marketers use sales promotion to improve the effectiveness of other ingredients in the promotional mix, especially advertising and personal selling. Research shows that sales promotion complements advertising by yielding faster sales responses. Pizza Hut handed out over 1 million reformulated pizzas at special events or offered a coupon for a complimentary pie. In markets where coupons were distributed, nearby restaurants saw an instant spike in traffic. The sampling and coupons were critical to Pizza Hut's goal of driving trials and getting people who may have migrated to another pizza chain to come back to Pizza Hut.[6] Sales promotion is discussed in more detail in Chapter 13.

Public Relations

public relations
Marketing function that evaluates public attitudes, identifies areas within the organization that the public may be interested in, and executes a program of action to earn public understanding and acceptance.

Concerned about how they are perceived by their target markets, organizations often spend large sums to build a positive public image. **Public relations** is the marketing function that evaluates public attitudes, identifies areas within the organization that the public may be interested in, and executes a program of action to earn public understanding and acceptance. Public relations helps an organization communicate with its customers, suppliers, stockholders, government officials, employees, and the community in which it operates. Marketers use public relations not only to maintain a positive image but also to educate the public about the company's goals and objectives, introduce new products, and help support the sales effort. Southwest Airlines has captured three-fourths of Florida's intrastate traffic due to a savvy public relations plan designed to enhance its image. To give itself a familiar local face, the airline recruited and trained Florida residents who, in return for free airline tickets, were dispatched to local airports to answer questions about Southwest and promote the airline's low fares. The airline also became the official airline of the Tampa Bay Buccaneers, the Miami Heat, and other professional sports teams. Southwest also gave employees special training in handling senior citizens with mobility problems, as well as families with small children who come to Florida to vacation.[7]

publicity
Public information about a company, good, or service appearing in the mass media as a news item.

A solid public relations program can generate favorable publicity. **Publicity** is public information about a company, good, or service appearing in the mass media as a news item. The organization is not generally identified as the source of the information. The wine industry received favorable publicity and an increase in sales after several medical studies found a link between good health and the consumption of red wine. This incident underscores a peculiar reality of marketing: No matter how many millions are spent on advertising, nothing sells a product better than free publicity.

Although an organization does not pay for this kind of mass media exposure, publicity should not be viewed as free. Preparing news releases, staging special events, and persuading media personnel to print or broadcast them costs money. To promote its Bisquick brand as more than a biscuit mix, General Mills sponsored a Bisquick pancake breakfast for New Hampshire senior citizens the day before the presidential primary. Presidential candidates were invited to compete in a pancake-flipping contest. That evening, two of the three national network news broadcasts showed candidates wearing Bisquick aprons and flipping pancakes. The breakfast cost General Mills about $25,000 compared with about $400,000 for one thirty-second television commercial.[8] Public relations and publicity are examined further in Chapter 13.

Marketing Communication

3

Describe the communication process

communication
Process by which we exchange or share meanings through a common set of symbols.

Promotional strategy is closely related to the process of communication. As humans, we assign meaning to feelings, ideas, facts, attitudes, and emotions. **Communication** is the process by which we exchange or share meanings through a common set of symbols. When a company develops a new product, changes an old one, or simply tries to increase sales of an existing good or service, it must communicate its selling message to potential customers. Marketers communicate information about the firm and its products to the target market and various publics through its promotion programs. Pepsi commercials, for example, send messages to their target audience of kids through the use of sports figures such as basketball star Shaquille O'Neal. Read Shaq's own words about the power of Pepsi's communication efforts below.

interpersonal communication
Direct, face-to-face communication between two or more people.

Communication can be divided into two major categories: interpersonal communication and mass communication. **Interpersonal communication** is direct, face-to-face communication between two or more people. When communicating face to face, people see the other person's reaction and can respond almost immediately. A salesperson speaking directly with a client is an example of marketing communication that is interpersonal.

mass communication
Communication to large audiences.

Mass communication refers to communicating to large audiences. A great deal of marketing communication is directed to consumers as a whole, usually through a mass medium such as television or newspapers. When a company advertises, it generally does not personally know the people with whom it is trying to communicate. Furthermore, the company is unable to respond immediately to consumers' reactions to its message. Instead, the marketing manager must wait to see whether people are reacting positively or negatively to the mass-communicated promotion. Any clutter from competitors' messages or other distractions in the environment can reduce the effectiveness of the mass communication effort.

Dreamful Attraction
Shaquille O'Neal's Thoughts on Marketing and Advertising

While on the outside looking in, I did not realize that marketing was so complicated. I never knew that a person, such as an athlete, could have such a powerful effect on peoples' thought processes and purchasing behavior. The use of a well-known athlete in marketing a product or service can have a great impact on the sales of that product or service. Look at Michael Jordan. Almost overnight most every kid either was wearing or wanted to wear Air Jordan shoes.

Why does this happen? Is it the appeal of a great athlete or is it great marketing? The answer is "none of the above." It's both. In my years as a professional basketball player, I have seen first-hand the dramatic appeal that athletes have for the fans and public in general. Top-name athletes are like E.F. Hutton—when they talk, people listen. But why do they listen? I believe they listen to us, the athletes, because we have credibility. The effectiveness of celebrity endorsements depends largely on how credible and attractive the spokesperson is and how familiar people are with him or her. Companies sometimes use sports figures and other celebrities to promote products hoping they are appropriate opinion leaders.

Because of an athlete's fame and fortune, or attraction, the athlete can often have the right credibility to be a successful spokesperson. The best definition of credibility that I could find was by James Gordon in his book, *Rhetoric of Western Thought*. He said that attraction "can come from a person's observable talents, achievements, occupational position or status, personality and appearance, and style."* That may be why a famous athlete's personality and position can help him or her communicate more effectively than a not-so-famous athlete.

Credibility is a positive force in the persuasive promotion used predominantly by cola marketers like Pepsi because of what I like to call "dreamful attraction." For example, when I was young, I dreamed that I was like Dr. J., the famous basketball player for the Philadelphia 76ers. I would take his head off a poster and put my head on it. I wanted to be Dr. J. That is dreamful attraction. The youth of today are no different. Just the other day a kid stopped me and told me that he wanted to be like me. He had a dreamful attraction. This dreamful attraction can help sell products. In my case, Pepsi, Spalding, Kenner, and

Reebok are hoping that they are able to package properly and market whatever dreamful attraction I might have for their target audience—kids.

There are many ways to communicate to my target audience. I find that the most effective way for me is through television commercials. This avenue gives me a chance to express myself and show my real feelings about a message we are trying to communicate—either visually or vocally. I feel that I have what Clint Eastwood has—"Sudden Impaq." My impact is revealed through my sense of humor and my non-verbal communication. Take a look at the videos that come with this text and you will hear more about my role in developing TV commercials.

Why does Shaq sell? Communication. Although the verbal communication in many of my commercials is slim, the impact is still there. This makes me believe even more in the quote that who you are can almost be as important as what you say. But if you can blend the two together—who you are and what you have to say—then imagine how much more successful the communication message can be in the marketing process. Andre Agassi's favorite quote from his Canon commercial is "Image is everything." If it is not everything, it is almost everything. If you have the right image, match it with the right product, and market it properly, then success should follow.

I have been involved in commercials and the marketing of products for only a short time, but I have learned a great deal. If there is one formula for success in selling products, it would be this: Marketing plus credibility and image plus effective communications equals increase in sales—hopefully.

Now, you can call me Dr. Shaq, M.E. (Marketing Expert).

Why has Shaq been such a success as an athlete-endorser?

*James Gordon, *Rhetoric of Western Thought*, Dubuque, Iowa: Kendall-Hunt Publishing Co., 1976, p. 207.

The Communication Process

Marketers are both senders and receivers of messages. As *senders*, marketers attempt to inform, persuade, and remind the target market to adopt courses of action compatible with the need to promote the purchase of goods and services. As *receivers*, marketers attune themselves to the target market in order to develop the appropriate messages, adapt existing messages, and spot new communication opportunities. In this way, marketing communication is a two-way, rather than one-way, process.[9] The two-way nature of the communication process is shown in Exhibit 12.2.

exhibit 12.2 | Communication Process

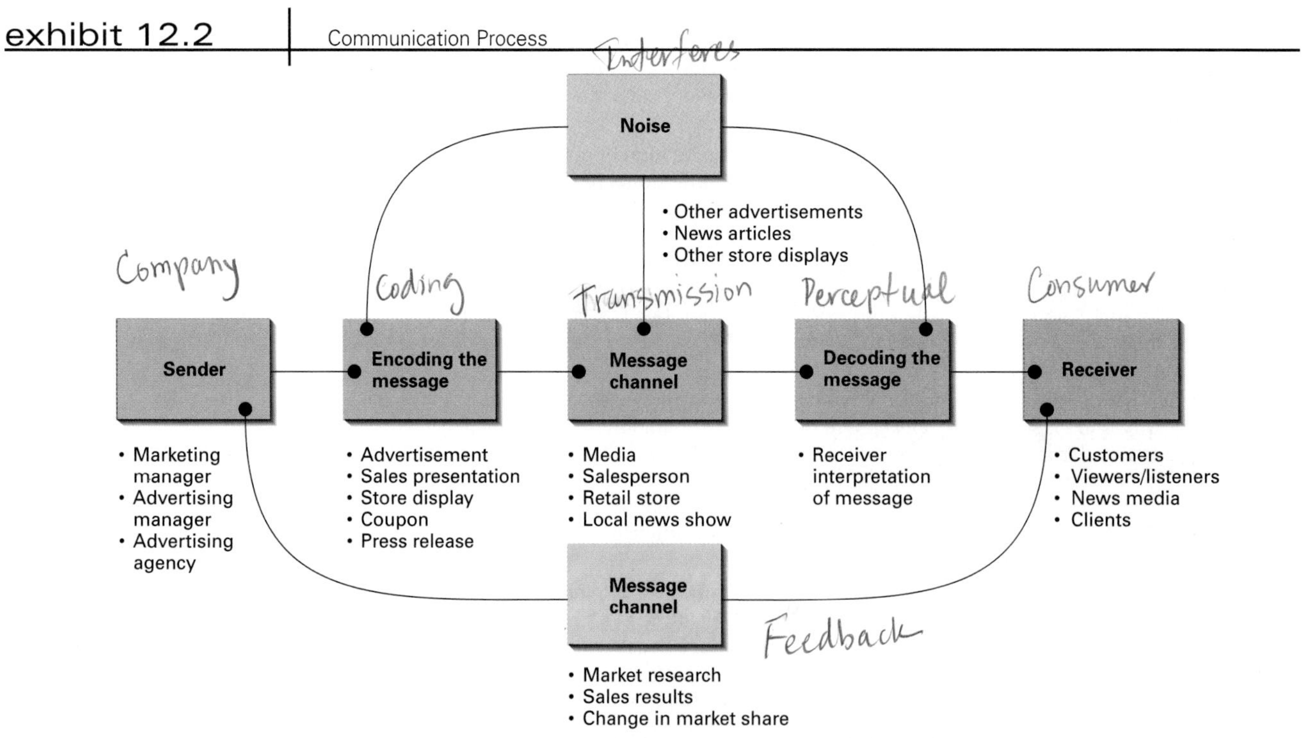

Every communication needs a sender and a receiver. The WNBA sends messages promoting its league to sports fans. Can its corporate sponsors also be senders along with the WNBA? Why or why not?
© Bebeto Matthews/AP Wide World Photos

The **sender** is the originator of the message in the communication process. In an interpersonal conversation, the sender may be a parent, a friend, or a salesperson. For an advertisement or press release, the sender is the company itself. The Women's National Basketball Association, for example, is the sender of a message introducing and promoting its women's basketball league to sports fans.

Encoding is the conversion of the sender's ideas and thoughts into a message, usually in the form of words or signs. Microsoft might encode its message into an advertisement, or a Microsoft salesperson might encode the promotional message as a sales presentation.

sender
Originator of the message in the communication process.

encoding
Conversion of the sender's ideas and thoughts into a message, usually in the form of words or signs.

A basic principle of encoding is that what matters is not what the source says but what the receiver hears. One way of conveying a message that the receiver will hear properly is to use concrete words and pictures. For example, television and print advertising announcing the inception of the WNBA gave detailed information about when the games would begin. Print advertising concentrated on detailed biographies of league players.

Message Transmission Transmission of a message requires a **channel**—a voice, radio, newspaper, or other communication medium. A facial expression or gesture can also serve as a channel.

channel
Medium of communication—such as a voice, radio, or newspaper—for transmitting a message.

Reception occurs when the message is detected by the receiver and enters his or her frame of reference. In a two-way conversation such as a sales pitch given by a sales representative to a potential client, reception is normally high. In contrast, the desired receivers may or may not detect the message when it is mass communicated, because most media are cluttered by "noise." **Noise** is anything that interferes with, distorts, or slows down the transmission of information. In some media overcrowded with advertisers, such as newspapers and television, the noise level is high and the reception level is low. For example, reception of the WNBA's ads may be hampered by competing sports-related ads or by other sports-related stories in a magazine or newspaper. Transmission can also be hindered by situational factors such as physical surroundings like light, sound, location, and weather; the presence of other people; or the temporary moods consumers might bring to the situation. Mass communication may not even reach all the right consumers. Some members of the target audience may be watching television when the WNBA is advertised, but others may not be.

noise
Anything that interferes with, distorts, or slows down the transmission of information.

The Receiver and Decoding Marketers communicate their message through a channel to customers, or **receivers**, who will decode the message. **Decoding** is the interpretation of the language and symbols sent by the source through a channel. Common understanding between two communicators, or a common frame of reference, is required for effective communication. Therefore, marketing managers must ensure a proper match between the message to be conveyed and the target market's attitudes and ideas.

receiver
Person who decodes a message.

decoding
Interpretation of the language and symbols sent by the source through a channel.

Even though a message has been received, it will not necessarily be properly decoded—or even seen, viewed, or heard—because of selective exposure, distortion, and retention (refer to Chapter 4).[10] Even when people receive a message, they tend to manipulate, alter, and modify it to reflect their own biases, needs, knowledge, and culture. Factors that can lead to miscommunication are differences in age, social class, education, culture, and ethnicity. Further, because people don't always listen or read carefully, they can easily misinterpret what is said or written. In fact, researchers have found that a large proportion of both printed and televised communications are misunderstood by consumers. Bright colors and bold graphics have been shown to increase consumers' comprehension of marketing communication. However, even these techniques are not foolproof. A classic example of miscommunication occurred when Lever Brothers mailed out samples of its new dishwashing liquid, Sunlight, which contains real lemon juice. The package clearly stated that Sunlight was a household cleaning product. However, many people saw the word sunlight, the large picture of lemons, and the phrase "with real lemon juice" and thought the product was lemon juice.

feedback
Receiver's response to a message.

Feedback In interpersonal communication, the receiver's response to a message is direct **feedback** to the source. Feedback may be verbal, as in saying "I agree," or nonverbal, as in nodding, smiling, frowning, or gesturing.

Because mass communicators like the WNBA are often cut off from direct feedback, they must rely on market research or analysis of sales trends, such as ticket sales, for indirect feedback. The WNBA might use such measurements as the percentage of television viewers or magazine readers who recognize, recall, or state that they have been exposed to the league's message. Indirect feedback enables mass communicators to decide whether to continue, modify, or drop a message.

The Communication Process and the Promotional Mix

The four elements of the promotional mix differ in their ability to affect the target audience. For instance, promotional mix elements may communicate with the consumer directly or indirectly. The message may flow one way or two ways. Feedback may be fast or slow, a little or a lot. Likewise, the communicator may have varying degrees of control over message delivery, content, and flexibility. Exhibit 12.3 outlines differences among the promotional mix elements with respect to mode of communication, marketer's control over the communication process, amount and speed of feedback, direction of message flow, marketer's control over the message, identification of the sender, speed in reaching large audiences, and message flexibility.

From Exhibit 12.3, you can see that most elements of the promotional mix are indirect and impersonal when used to communicate with a target market, providing only one direction of message flow. For example, advertising, public relations, and sales promotion are generally impersonal, one-way means of mass communication. Because they provide no opportunity for direct feedback, they cannot adapt easily to consumers' changing preferences, individual differences, and personal goals.

Personal selling, on the other hand, is personal, two-way communication. The salesperson is able to receive immediate feedback from the consumer and adjust the message in response. Personal selling, however, is very slow in dispersing the marketer's message to large audiences. Because a salesperson can only communicate to one person or a small group of persons at one time, it is a poor choice if the marketer wants to send a message to many potential buyers.

Integrated Marketing Communications

Ideally, marketing communications from each promotional mix element (personal selling, advertising, sales promotion, and public relations) should be integrated—that is, the message reaching the consumer should be the same regardless of whether it is from an advertisement, a salesperson in the field, a magazine article, or a coupon in a newspaper insert.

From the consumer's standpoint, a company's communications are already integrated. Consumers do not think in terms of the four elements of promotion: advertising, sales promotion, public relations, and personal selling. Instead, everything is an "ad." The only people who can disintegrate these communications elements are the marketers themselves. Unfortunately, many marketers neglect this

Characteristics of the Elements in the Promotional Mix **exhibit 12.3**

	Personal Selling	Advertising	Sales Promotion	Public Relations
Mode of Communication	Direct and face-to-face	Indirect and nonpersonal	Usually indirect and nonpersonal	Usually indirect and nonpersonal
Communicator Control over Situation	High	Low	Moderate to low	Moderate to low
Amount of Feedback	Much	Little	Little to moderate	Little
Speed of Feedback	Immediate	Delayed	Varies	Delayed
Direction of Message Flow	Two-way	One-way	Mostly one-way	One-way
Control over Message Content	Yes	Yes	Yes	No
Identification of Sponsor	Yes	Yes	Yes	No
Speed in Reaching Large Audience	Slow	Fast	Fast	Usually fast
Message Flexibility	Tailored to prospective buyer	Same message to all audiences	Same message to varied target audiences	Usually no direct control over message

fact when planning promotional messages and fail to integrate their communication efforts from one element to the next. The most common rift typically occurs between personal selling and the other elements of the promotional mix.

This unintegrated, disjointed approach to promotion has propelled more companies to adopt the concept of **integrated marketing communications (IMC)**. IMC is the method of carefully coordinating all promotional activities—media advertising, sales promotion, personal selling, public relations, as well as direct marketing, packaging, and other forms of communication—to produce a consistent, unified message that is customer focused.[11] Following the concept of IMC, marketing managers carefully work out the roles that various promotional elements will play in the marketing mix. Timing of promotional activities is coordinated and the results of each campaign are carefully monitored to improve future use of the promotional mix tools. Typically, a marketing communications director is appointed who has overall responsibility for integrating the company's marketing communications.

integrated marketing communications (IMC)
The method of carefully coordinating all promotional activities to produce a consistent, unified message that is customer focused.

Movie marketing campaigns benefit greatly from an integrated marketing communications approach. Those campaigns that are most integrated generally have more impact and make a deeper impression on potential moviegoers, leading to higher box-office sales. An integrated marketing approach, for instance, was used for the summer release of *Godzilla* by TriStar Pictures and Sony Pictures Entertainment. To heighten the anticipation for the film and its monster star, the movie's producers kept *Godzilla* under wraps until the day the film opened.

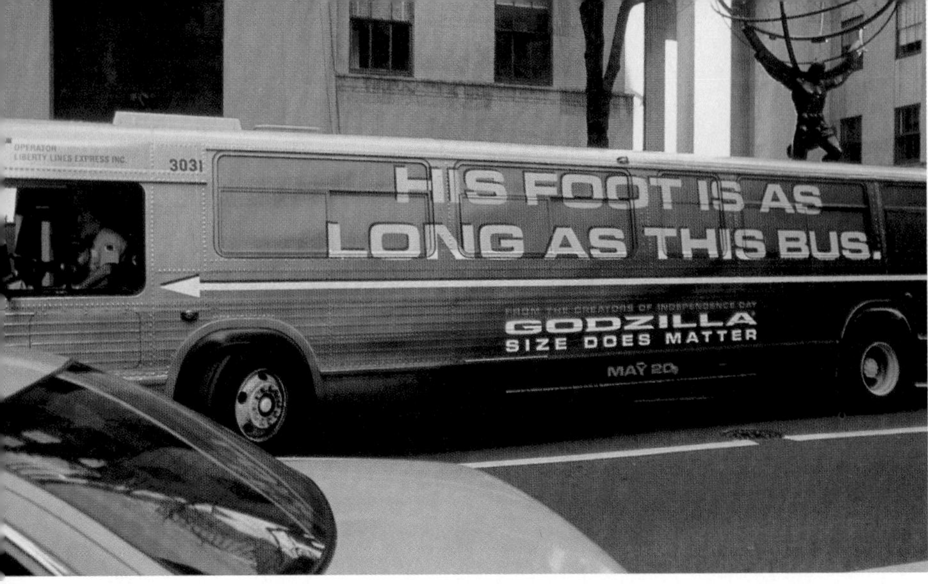

Outdoor advertising was a key part in the integrated marketing campaign Sony put together to promote its feature film *Godzilla*. Newspaper and magazine ads could not convey the monster's size, but buses worked just fine.
© Tobias Everke/Liaison International

Consumers only saw the film's signature green and the line "Size does matter." The first previews for the movie arrived a full year in advance, proclaiming Memorial Day 1998 as the day *Godzilla* would be revealed. Outdoor advertising compared the yet-to-be-seen monster's twenty-three-story size to famous urban landmarks such as Yankee Stadium in New York. Sales promotional support for the movie included Dreyer's Grand Ice Cream, which created a special flavor, Godzilla Vanilla, with vanilla chunks in the shape of the monster; a sweepstakes sponsored by Duracell that gave the winner a swimming pool shaped like Godzilla's foot; a Kodak television spot that blended movie footage to dramatize a young man's efforts to photograph Godzilla with a disposable camera; and Taco Bell, which paired Godzilla with its talking chihuahua. Commemorative tickets were also issued to those who bought seats at the first screening of the film on opening day, autographed by the film's makers and accompanied by Taco Bell coupons.[12]

The Goals and Tasks of Promotion

4
Explain the goals and tasks of promotion

People communicate with one another for many reasons. They seek amusement, ask for help, give assistance or instructions, provide information, and express ideas and thoughts. Promotion, on the other hand, seeks to modify behavior and thoughts in some way. For example, promoters may try to persuade consumers to eat at Burger King rather than at McDonald's. Promotion also strives to reinforce existing behavior—for instance, getting consumers to continue to dine at Burger King once they have switched. The source (the seller) hopes to project a favorable image or to motivate purchase of the company's goods and services.

Promotion can perform one or more of three tasks: *inform* the target audience, *persuade* the target audience, or *remind* the target audience. Often a marketer will try to accomplish two or more of these tasks at the same time. Exhibit 12.4 lists the three tasks of promotion and some examples of each.

Informing

Informative promotion may seek to convert an existing need into a want or to stimulate interest in a new product. It is generally more prevalent during the early stages of the product life cycle. People typically will not buy a product service or support a nonprofit organization until they know its purpose and its benefits to them. Informative messages are important for promoting complex and technical products such as automobiles, computers, and investment services. Informative promotion is also important for a "new" brand being introduced into an "old" product class—for example, a new brand of detergent entering the well-established laundry detergent product category dominated by well-known brands such as Tide and Cheer. The new product cannot establish itself against more mature products unless potential buyers are aware of it, understand its benefits, and understand its positioning in the marketplace.

Burger King

Do Burger King's "Burger Bucks" qualify as a promotion? Why or why not? Visit the Web site to make your determination.
http://www.burgerking.com/

on line

exhibit 12.4

Promotion Tasks and Examples

Informative promotion:
Increasing the awareness of a new brand, product class, or product attribute
Explaining how the product works
Suggesting new uses for a product
Building a company image

Persuasive promotion:
Encouraging brand switching
Changing customers' perceptions of product attributes
Influencing customers to buy now
Persuading customers to call

Reminder promotion:
Reminding consumers that the product may be needed in the near future
Reminding consumers where to buy the product
Maintaining consumer awareness

Persuading

Persuasive promotion is designed to stimulate a purchase or an action—for example, to drink more Coca-Cola or to use H&R Block tax services. Persuasion normally becomes the main promotion goal when the product enters the growth stage of its life cycle. By this time, the target market should have general product awareness and some knowledge of how the product can fulfill their wants. Therefore, the promotional task switches from informing consumers about the product category to persuading them to buy the company's brand rather than the competitor's. At this time, the promotional message emphasizes the product's real and perceived differential advantages, often appealing to emotional needs such as love, belonging, self-esteem, and ego satisfaction.

Persuasion can also be an important goal for very competitive mature product categories such as many household items, soft drinks, beer, and banking services. In a marketplace characterized by many competitors, the promotional message often encourages brand switching and aims to convert some buyers into loyal users. For example, to persuade new customers to switch their checking accounts, a bank's marketing manager may offer a year's worth of free checks with no fees.

Reminding

Reminder promotion is used to keep the product and brand name in the public's mind. This type of promotion prevails during the maturity stage of the life cycle. It assumes that the target market has already been persuaded of the good's or service's merits. Its purpose is simply to trigger a memory. Crest toothpaste, Tide laundry detergent, Miller beer, and many other consumer products often use reminder promotion.

Promotional Goals and the AIDA Concept

5
Discuss the AIDA concept and its relationship to the promotional mix

The ultimate goal of any promotion is to get someone to buy a good or service or, in the case of nonprofit organizations, to take some action (for instance, donate blood). A classic model for reaching promotional goals is called the

AIDA concept
Model that outlines the process for achieving promotional goals in terms of stages of consumer involvement with the message; the acronym stands for Attention, Interest, Desire, and Action.

AIDA concept.[13] The acronym stands for Attention, Interest, Desire, and Action—the stages of consumer involvement with a promotional message.

This model proposes that consumers respond to marketing messages in a cognitive (thinking), affective (feeling), and conative (doing) sequence. First, the promotion manager attracts a person's *attention* by (in personal selling) a greeting and approach or (in advertising and sales promotion) loud volume, unusual contrasts, bold headlines, movement, bright colors, and so on. Next, a good sales presentation, demonstration, or advertisement creates *interest* in the product and then, by illustrating how the product's features will satisfy the consumer's needs, *desire.* Finally, a special offer or a strong closing sales pitch may be used to obtain purchase *action.*

The AIDA concept assumes that promotion propels consumers along the following four steps in the purchase-decision process:

1. *Attention:* The advertiser must first gain the attention of the target market. A firm cannot sell something if the market does not know that the good or service exists. Imagine that Acme Company, a pet food manufacturer, is introducing a new brand of cat food called Stripes, specially formulated for finicky cats. To gain attention for its new brand, Acme heavily publicizes the introduction and places several ads on TV and in consumer magazines.
2. *Interest:* Simple awareness of a brand seldom leads to a sale. The next step is to create interest in the product. A print ad or TV commercial can't actually tell pet owners whether their cats will like Stripes. Thus, Acme might send samples of the new cat food to cat owners to create interest in the new brand.
3. *Desire:* Even though owners (and their cats) may like Stripes, they may not see any advantage over competing brands, especially if owners are brand loyal. Therefore, Acme must create brand preference by explaining the product's differential advantage over the competition. Specifically, Acme has to show that cats want to eat nothing else. Advertising at this stage claims that Stripes will satisfy "even the pickiest of the litter." Although pet owners may come to prefer Stripes to other brands, they still may not have developed the desire to buy the new brand. At this stage Acme might offer the consumer additional reasons to buy Stripes, such as easy-to-open, zip-lock packaging that keeps the product fresh; additional vitamins and minerals that healthy cats need; or feline taste-test results.
4. *Action:* Some members of the target market may now be convinced to buy Stripes but have yet to make the purchase. Displays in grocery stores, coupons, premiums, and trial-size packages can often push the complacent shopper into purchase.

Most buyers involved in high-involvement purchase situations pass through the four stages of the AIDA model on the way to making a purchase. The promoter's task is to determine where on the purchase ladder most of the target consumers are located and design a promotion plan to meet their needs. For instance, if Acme has determined that about half its buyers are in the preference or conviction stage but have not bought Stripes cat food for some reason, the company may mail cents-off coupons to cat owners to prompt them to buy.

The AIDA concept does not explain how all promotions influence purchase decisions. The model suggests that promotional effectiveness can be measured in terms of consumers progressing from one stage to the next. However, the order of stages in the model as well as whether consumers go through all steps has been much debated. For example, purchase can occur without interest or desire, perhaps when a low-involvement product is bought on impulse. Regardless of the order of the stages or consumers' progression through these stages, the AIDA concept helps marketers by suggesting which promotional strategy will be most effective.[14]

exhibit 12.5

When the Elements of Promotion Are Most Useful

	Attention	Interest	Desire	Action
Personal Selling	Somewhat effective	Very effective	Very effective	Somewhat effective
Advertising	Very effective	Very effective	Somewhat effective	Not effective
Sales Promotion	Somewhat effective	Somewhat effective	Very effective	Very effective
Public Relations	Very effective	Very effective	Very effective	Not effective

AIDA and the Promotional Mix

Exhibit 12.5 depicts the relationship between the promotional mix and the AIDA model. It shows that, although advertising does have an impact in the later stages, it is most useful in creating awareness about goods or services. In contrast, personal selling reaches fewer people at first. Salespeople are more effective at creating customer interest for merchandise or a service and at gaining desire. For example, advertising may help a potential computer purchaser gain knowledge and information about competing brands, but the salesperson in an electronics store may be the one who actually encourages the buyer to decide a particular brand is the best choice. The salesperson also has the advantage of having the computer physically there to demonstrate its capabilities to the buyer.

Sales promotion's greatest strength is in creating strong desire and purchase intent. Coupons and other price-off promotions are techniques used to persuade customers to buy new products. Frequent-buyer sales promotion programs, popular among retailers, allow consumers to accumulate points or dollars that can later be redeemed for goods. Frequent-buyer programs tend to increase purchase intent and loyalty and encourage repeat purchases. Randall's food stores in Texas, for example, annually reward loyal shoppers with "turkey bucks" during the weeks prior to Thanksgiving. Turkey bucks can then be redeemed for free turkeys.

Public relations has its greatest impact in gaining attention about a company, good, or service. Many companies can attract attention and build goodwill by sponsoring community events that benefit a worthy cause such as antidrug and antigang programs. Such sponsorships project a positive image of the firm and its products into the minds of consumers and potential consumers. Good publicity can also help develop consumer desire for a product. Book publishers push to get their titles listed on the best-seller lists of major publications, such as *Publishers Weekly* or the *New York Times*. Book authors also make appearances on talk-shows and at book stores to personally sign books and speak to fans. Similarly, movie marketers use prerelease publicity to raise the profile of their movies and to increase initial box office sales. For example, most major motion picture studios have their own Web sites with multimedia clips and publicity photos of their current movies to attract viewers. Furthermore, movie promoters will include publicity gained from reviewers' quotes and Academy Award nominations in their advertising.

Factors Affecting the Promotional Mix

6 Describe the factors that affect the promotional mix

Promotional mixes vary a great deal from one product and one industry to the next. Normally, advertising and personal selling are used to promote goods and services, supported and supplemented by sales promotion. Public relations helps develop a positive image for the organization and the product line. However, a firm may choose not to use all four promotional elements in its promotional mix, or it may choose to use them in varying degrees. The particular promotional mix chosen by a firm for a product or service depends on several factors: nature of the product, stage in the product life cycle, target market characteristics, type of buying decision, available funds for promotion, and use of either a push or a pull strategy.

Nature of the Product

Characteristics of the product itself can influence the promotional mix. For instance, a product can be classified as either a business product or a consumer product (refer to Chapters 5 and 8). As business products are often custom-tailored to the buyer's exact specifications, they are often not well suited to mass promotion. Therefore, producers of most business goods, such as computer systems or industrial machinery, rely more heavily on personal selling than on advertising. Informative personal selling is common for industrial installations, accessories, and component parts and materials. Advertising, however, still serves a purpose in promoting business goods. Advertisements in trade media may be used to create general buyer awareness and interest. Moreover, advertising can help locate potential customers for the sales force. For example, print media advertising often includes coupons soliciting the potential customer to "fill this out for more detailed information."

On the other hand, because consumer products generally are not custom-made, they do not require the selling efforts of a company representative who can tailor them to the user's needs. Thus consumer goods are promoted mainly through advertising to create brand familiarity. Broadcast advertising, newspapers, and consumer-oriented magazines are used extensively to promote consumer goods, especially nondurables. Sales promotion, the brand name, and the product's packaging are about twice as important for consumer goods as for business products. Persuasive personal selling is important at the retail level for shopping goods such as automobiles and appliances.

The costs and risks associated with a product also influence the promotional mix. As a general rule, when the costs or risks of using a product increase, personal selling becomes more important. Items that are a small part of a firm's budget (supply items) or of a consumer's budget (convenience products) do not require a salesperson to close the sale. In fact, inexpensive items cannot support the cost of a salesperson's time and effort unless the potential volume is high. On the other hand, expensive and complex machinery, new buildings, cars, and new homes represent a considerable investment. A salesperson must assure buyers that they are spending their money wisely and not taking an undue financial risk.

Social risk is an issue as well. Many consumer goods are not products of great social importance because they do not reflect social position. People do not experience much social risk in buying a loaf of bread or a candy bar. However, buying some shopping products and many specialty products such as jewelry and clothing does involve a social risk. Many consumers depend on sales personnel for guidance and advice in making the "proper" choice.

Stage in the Product Life Cycle

The product's stage in its life cycle is a big factor in designing a promotional mix. (See Exhibit 12.6.) During the *introduction stage,* the basic goal of promotion is to inform the target audience that the product is available. Initially, the emphasis is on the

Product Life Cycle and the Promotional Mix **exhibit 12.6**

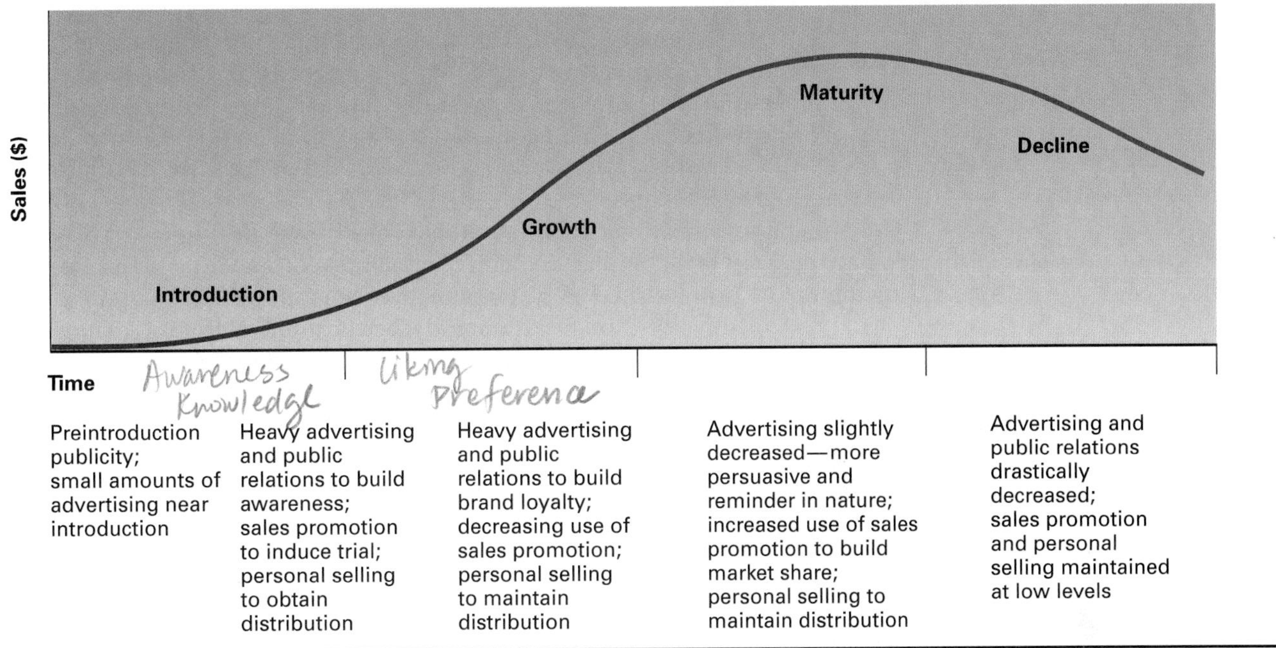
Sales ($)
Maturity
Decline
Growth
Introduction
Time
Preintroduction publicity; small amounts of advertising near introduction
Heavy advertising and public relations to build awareness; sales promotion to induce trial; personal selling to obtain distribution
Heavy advertising and public relations to build brand loyalty; decreasing use of sales promotion; personal selling to maintain distribution
Advertising slightly decreased—more persuasive and reminder in nature; increased use of sales promotion to build market share; personal selling to maintain distribution
Advertising and public relations drastically decreased; sales promotion and personal selling maintained at low levels

general product class—for example, personal computer systems. This emphasis gradually changes to awareness of specific brands, such as IBM, Apple, and Compaq. Typically, both extensive advertising and public relations inform the target audience of the product class or brand and heighten awareness levels. Sales promotion encourages early trial of the product, and personal selling gets retailers to carry the product.

When the product reaches the *growth stage* of the life cycle, the promotion blend may shift. Often a change is necessary because different types of potential buyers are targeted. Although advertising and public relations continue to be major elements of the promotional mix, sales promotion can be reduced, because consumers need fewer incentives to purchase. The promotional strategy is to emphasize the product's differential advantage over the competition. Persuasive promotion is used to build and maintain brand loyalty to support the product during the growth stage. By this stage, personal selling has usually succeeded in getting adequate distribution for the product.

As the product reaches the *maturity stage* of its life cycle, competition becomes fiercer, and thus persuasive and reminder advertising are more strongly emphasized. Sales promotion comes back into focus as product sellers try to increase their market share.

All promotion, especially advertising, is reduced as the product enters the *decline stage.* Nevertheless, personal selling and sales promotion efforts may be maintained, particularly at the retail level.

Target Market Characteristics

A target market characterized by widely scattered potential customers, highly informed buyers, and brand-loyal repeat purchasers generally requires a promotional mix with more advertising and sales promotion and less personal selling. Sometimes, however, personal selling is required even when buyers are well informed and geographically dispersed. Although industrial installations and component parts may be sold to extremely competent people with extensive education and work experience, salespeople must still be present to explain the product and work out the details of the purchase agreement.

New York Times
USA Today

What can you tell about the target market for the *New York Times* and *USA Today* from their respective Web sites? How will this information influence any promotions either paper would want to do?
http://www.nytimes.com/ **http://www.usatoday.com/**

Often firms sell goods and services in markets where potential customers are hard to locate. Print advertising can be used to find them. The reader is invited to call for more information or to mail in a reply card for a detailed brochure. As the calls or cards are received, salespeople are sent to visit the potential customers.

Type of Buying Decision

The promotional mix also depends on the type of buying decision—for example, a routine decision or a complex decision. For routine consumer decisions like buying toothpaste or soft drinks, the most effective promotion calls attention to the brand or reminds the consumer about the brand. Advertising and, especially, sales promotion are the most productive promotion tools to use for routine decisions.

Consumers making complex buying decisions often depend on the salesperson to provide important product information. Purchasing a car is one such example. Can you think of others?
© Christopher Bissell/Tony Stone Images

If the decision is neither routine nor complex, advertising and public relations help establish awareness for the good or service. Suppose a man is looking for a bottle of wine to serve to his dinner guests. As a beer drinker, he is not familiar with wines, yet he has seen advertising for Sutter Home wine and has also read an article in a popular magazine about the Sutter Home winery. He may be more likely to buy this brand because he is already aware of it.

In contrast, consumers making complex buying decisions are more extensively involved. They rely on large amounts of information to help them reach a purchase decision. Personal selling is most effective in helping these consumers decide. For example, consumers thinking about buying a car usually depend on a salesperson to provide the information they need to reach a decision. Print advertising may also be used for high-involvement purchase decisions because it can often provide a large amount of information to the consumer.

Available Funds

Money, or the lack of it, may easily be the most important factor in determining the promotional mix. A small, undercapitalized manufacturer may rely heavily on free publicity if its product is unique. If the situation warrants a sales force, a financially strained firm may turn to manufacturers' agents, who work on a commission basis with no advances or expense accounts. Even well-capitalized organizations may not be able to afford the advertising rates of publications like *Better Homes and Gardens, Reader's Digest,* and the *Wall Street Journal.* The price of a high-profile advertisement in these media could support a salesperson for a year.

When funds are available to permit a mix of promotional elements, a firm will generally try to optimize its return on promotion dollars while minimizing the *cost per contact,* or the cost of reaching one member of the target market. In general, the cost per contact is very high for personal selling, public relations, and sales promotions like sampling and demonstrations. On the other hand, for the number of people national advertising reaches, it has a very low cost per contact.

Usually there is a trade-off among the funds available, the number of people in the target market, the quality of communication needed, and the relative costs of the promotional elements. A company may have to forgo a full-page, color advertisement in *People* magazine in order to pay for a personal selling effort. Although the magazine ad will reach more people than personal selling, the high cost of the magazine space is a problem.

Push and Pull Strategies

GLOBAL

The last factor that affects the promotional mix is whether a push or a pull promotional strategy will be used. Manufacturers may use aggressive personal selling and trade advertising to convince a wholesaler or a retailer to carry and sell their merchandise. This approach is known as a **push strategy.** (See Exhibit 12.7.) The wholesaler, in turn, must often push the merchandise forward by persuading the retailer to handle the goods. The retailer then uses advertising, displays, and other forms of promotion to convince the consumer to buy the "pushed" products. This concept also applies to services. For example, the Jamaican Tourism Board targets promotions to travel agencies, which in turn tell their customers about the benefits of vacationing in Jamaica.

push strategy
Marketing strategy that uses aggressive personal selling and trade advertising to convince a wholesaler or a retailer to carry and sell particular merchandise.

At the other extreme is a **pull strategy**, which stimulates consumer demand to obtain product distribution. Rather than trying to sell to the wholesaler, the manufacturer using a pull strategy focuses its promotional efforts on end consumers or opinion leaders. For example, Colgate-Palmolive sent thirty million samples of its new Colgate Total toothpaste to dental practitioners nationwide to create demand.[15] As consumers begin demanding the product, the retailer orders the merchandise from the wholesaler. The wholesaler, confronted with rising demand, then places an order for the "pulled" merchandise from the manufacturer. Consumer demand pulls the product through the channel of distribution. (See Exhibit 12.7.) Heavy sampling, introductory consumer advertising, cents-off campaigns, and couponing are part of a pull strategy. Using a pull strategy, the Jamaican Tourism Board may entice travelers to visit by advertising heavily in consumer magazines or offering discounts on hotels or airfare.

pull strategy
Marketing strategy that stimulates consumer demand to obtain product distribution.

Rarely does a company use a pull or a push strategy exclusively. Instead, the mix will emphasize one of these strategies. For example, pharmaceutical companies generally use a push strategy, through personal selling and trade advertising, to promote their drugs and therapies to physicians. Sales presentations and advertisements in medical journals give physicians the detailed information they need to prescribe medication to their patients. Most pharmaceutical companies supplement their push promotional strategy with a pull strategy targeted directly

exhibit 12.7

Push Strategy Versus Pull Strategy

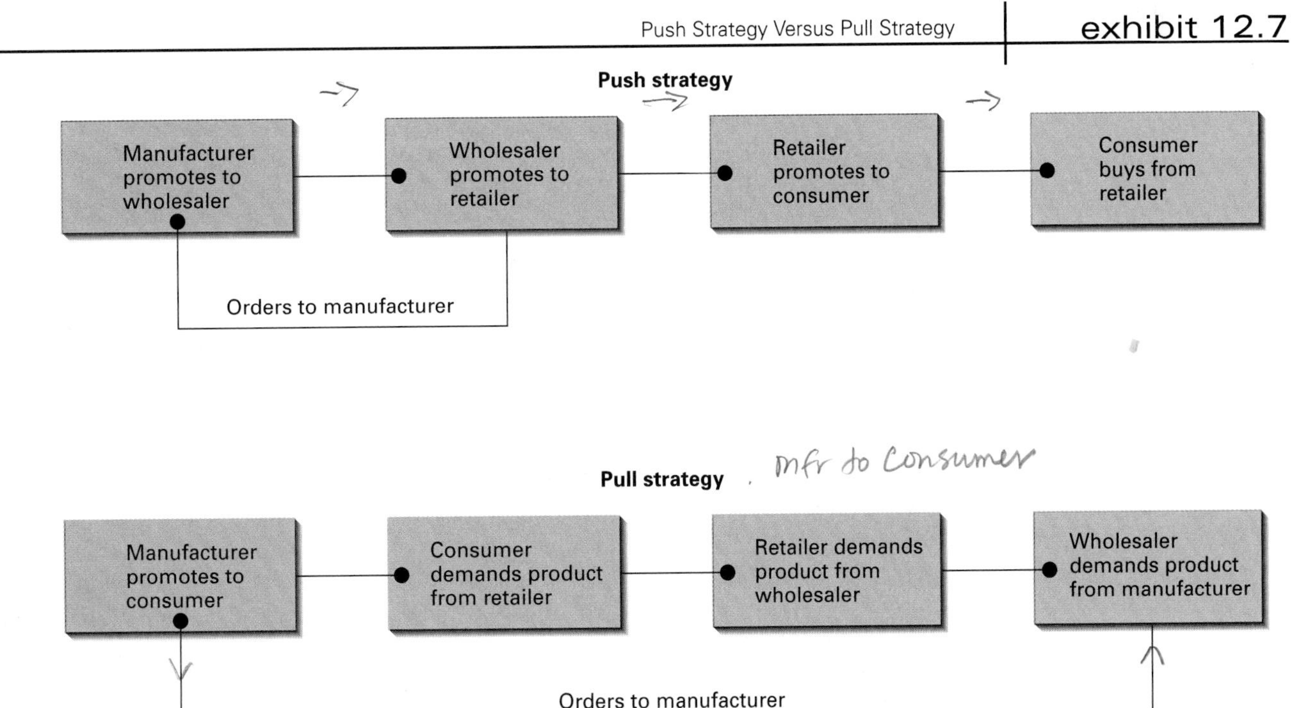
Push strategy
Manufacturer promotes to wholesaler
Wholesaler promotes to retailer
Retailer promotes to consumer
Consumer buys from retailer
Orders to manufacturer
Pull strategy
mfr to consumer
Manufacturer promotes to consumer
Consumer demands product from retailer
Retailer demands product from wholesaler
Wholesaler demands product from manufacturer
Orders to manufacturer

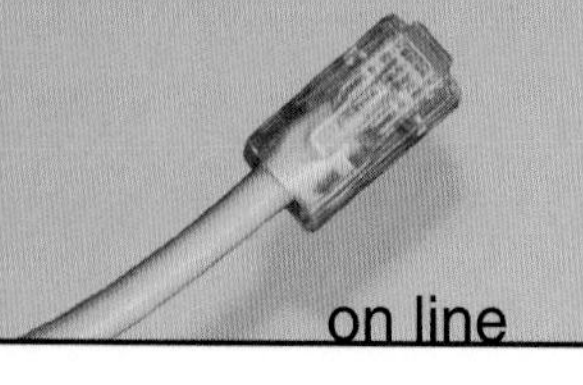

Upjohn

Is Upjohn using its Web site for direct-to-consumer advertising? What makes you think as you do? How is the company promoting its latest drugs on its Web site? What is your opinion of how Upjohn is informing or promoting its products?

http://www.upjohn.com/

to potential patients through advertisements in consumer magazines and on television. Many physicians, however, are concerned with the increasing amount of direct-to-consumer advertising that prompts many patients to demand drugs they either do not need or that may cause adverse reactions. Read the "Ethics in Marketing" article to learn more about this controversial promotional practice.

Personal Selling

7
Describe personal selling

As mentioned in the beginning of the chapter, *personal selling* is direct communication between a sales representative and one or more prospective buyers in an attempt to influence each other in a purchase situation.

In a sense, all businesspeople are salespeople. An individual may become a plant manager, a chemist, an engineer, or a member of any profession and yet still have to sell. During a job search, applicants must "sell" themselves to prospective employers in an interview. To reach the top in most organizations, individuals need to sell ideas to peers, superiors, and subordinates. Most important, people must sell themselves and their ideas to just about everyone with whom they have a continuing relationship and to many other people they see only once or twice. Chances are that students majoring in business or marketing will start their professional careers in sales. Even students in nonbusiness majors may pursue a sales career.

Personal selling offers several advantages over other forms of promotion:

- Personal selling provides a detailed explanation or demonstration of the product. This capability is especially needed for complex or new goods and services.
- The sales message can be varied according to the motivations and interests of each prospective customer. Moreover, when the prospect has questions or raises objections, the salesperson is there to provide explanations. In contrast, advertising and sales promotion can only respond to the objections the copywriter thinks are important to customers.
- Personal selling can be directed only to qualified prospects. Other forms of promotion include some unavoidable waste because many people in the audience are not prospective customers.
- Personal selling costs can be controlled by adjusting the size of the sales force (and resulting expenses) in one-person increments. On the other hand, advertising and sales promotion must often be purchased in fairly large amounts.
- Perhaps the most important advantage is that personal selling is considerably more effective than other forms of promotion in obtaining a sale and gaining a satisfied customer.

Personal selling might work better than other forms of promotion given certain customer and product characteristics. Generally speaking, personal selling becomes more important as the number of potential customers decreases, as the complexity of the product increases, and as the value of the product grows. (See Exhibit 12.8.) When there are relatively few potential customers and the value of the good or service is relatively sufficient, the time and travel costs of personally visiting each prospect are justifiable. For highly complex goods, such as business jets or private communication systems, a salesperson is needed to determine the prospective customer's needs, explain the product's basic advantages, and propose the exact features and accessories that will meet the client's needs.

ethics in marketing

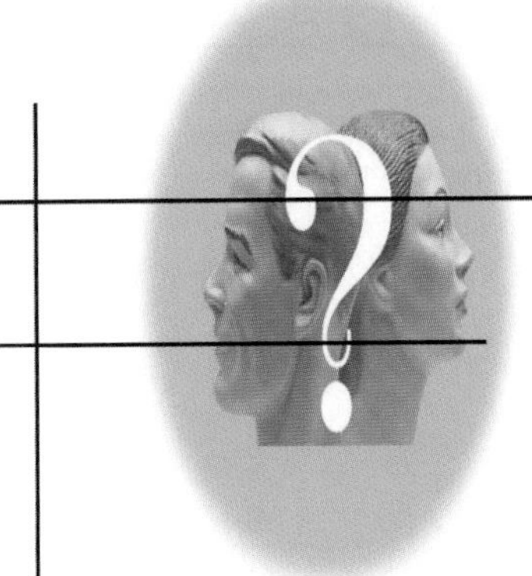

Pull Strategy for Prescription Drugs Puts Doctors in the Hot Seat

During the diet-drug debacle, doctors wrote millions of prescriptions for the fen-phen drug combination for patients wanting to lose weight, despite little hard scientific evidence. Doctors also prescribed Redux, a drug intended only for the dangerously obese patients, to many patients who wanted to trim ten or twenty pounds. And they wrote some fifteen thousand to twenty thousand prescriptions for the impotency drug Viagra when it first appeared on the market for many men who were not clinically impotent but wanted a boost. Fen-phen and Redux were eventually called off the market, whereas Viagra was found to be potentially dangerous for men with certain types of heart disease.

In the fallout, doctors are under attack for prescribing the drugs too much, too readily, and to the wrong patients. Doctors contend it isn't all their fault. Prodded by an explosion in direct-to-consumer advertising of prescription drugs, patients pressure their physicians for quick treatments. Prozac, the most widely prescribed drug in the world, is often prescribed to patients who are only mildly depressed. Likewise, many patients pressure their family physicians and pediatricians for antibiotics to treat flu symptoms, even though antibiotics are ineffective against viral-type infections.

Prescription drug advertising has become a billion-dollar consumer media tidal wave since the Food and Drug Administration loosened its rules on pharmaceutical advertising. The biggest boom came after the FDA allowed drug companies to advertise on television as long as the ad mentioned major side effects and directed viewers to a print ad and Web site for detailed disclosures. In the early 1990s, prescription drug marketers spent only about $160 million on direct-to-consumer advertising, mostly in consumer magazines. That figure jumped to $350 million in 1995 to match industry spending on advertising directed to physicians. By 1998, pharmaceutical companies' direct-to-consumer advertising spending was close to $1 billion due to fewer restrictions. As a result, direct-to-consumer advertising today confronts the public with such squeamish subjects as herpes, HIV, impotence, and toenail fungus, as well as more mainstream treatment information for allergies, high cholesterol, and migraines.

Many physicians dislike the increase in advertising directed at their patients, saying that the information is given to patients in limited form. Patients then diagnose themselves and come to their physicians with a particular therapy in mind without knowing its drawbacks or even if the drug is right for them. Drug advertising also tends to present the pharmaceutical products as wonder drugs. Ads for allergy medicine are particularly dramatic, offering allergy sufferers visions of happiness and serenity.

On the other hand, many believe the benefits of direct-to-consumer advertising of prescription drugs far outweigh its disadvantages. Drug advertising leads to more informed patients who are able to ask better questions while with their physicians. Further, consumers are presented with information concerning treatments they might have never known existed. Drug ads may also help consumers determine whether they have a medical problem. Many serious medical conditions remain undiagnosed because Americans don't know about the symptoms or don't regularly see a doctor. For instance, it is estimated that only half of the 16 million Americans with diabetes know they have the disease. In the end, proponents claim, the doctor makes the prescribing decision based on what is best for the patient.[16]

What is your opinion on direct-to-consumer advertising of prescription drugs? Do you believe there should be restrictions on what drug advertisers can do? How can doctors cope with the increased pressure from patients due to drug advertising?

Relationship Selling

8 Discuss the key differences between relationship selling and traditional selling

Until recently, marketing theory and practice concerning personal selling focused almost entirely on a planned presentation to prospective customers for the sole purpose of making the sale. Marketers were most concerned with making a one-time sale and then moving on to the next prospect. Whether it took place face-to-face during a personal sales call or by selling over the telephone (telemarketing), traditional personal selling methods attempted to persuade the buyer to accept a point of view or convince the buyer to take some action. Once the customer was somewhat convinced, then the salesperson used a variety of techniques in an

exhibit 12.8

Comparison of Personal Selling and Advertising/Sales Promotion

Personal selling is more important if . . .	Advertising and sales promotion are more important if . . .
The product has a high value. It is a custom-made product. There are few customers. The product is technically complex. Customers are concentrated.	The product has a low value. It is a standardized product. There are many customers. The product is simple to understand. Customers are geographically dispersed.
Examples: insurance policies, custom windows, airplane engines	Examples: soap, magazine subscriptions, cotton T-shirts

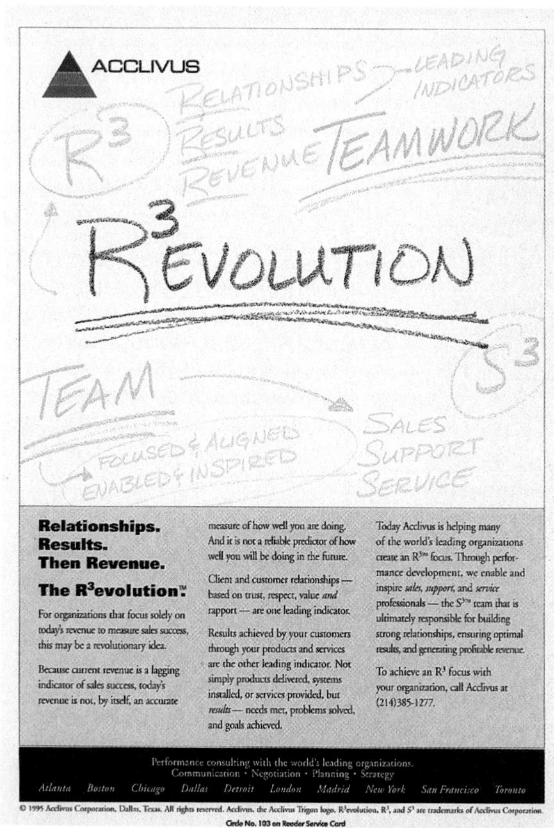

A multistage process focusing on developing trust over time, relationship selling emphasizes a win-win outcome.
Courtesy Acclivus

attempt to elicit a purchase. Frequently, the objectives of the salesperson were at the expense of the buyer, creating a win-lose outcome.[17] Although this type of sales approach has not disappeared entirely, it is being used less and less often by professional salespeople.

In contrast, modern views of personal selling emphasize the relationship that develops between a salesperson and a buyer. **Relationship selling**, or **consultative selling**, is a multistage process that emphasizes personalization and empathy as key ingredients in identifying prospects and developing them as long-term, satisfied customers. The focus is on building mutual trust between the buyer and seller with the delivery of anticipated, long-term, value-added benefits to the buyer.[18] Relationship or consultative salespeople, therefore, become consultants, partners, and problem solvers for their customers. They strive to build long-term relationships with key accounts by developing trust over time. The focus shifts from a one-time sale to a long-term relationship in which the salesperson works with the customer to develop solutions for enhancing the customer's bottom line. Thus, relationship selling emphasizes a win-win outcome.[19]

The end result of relationship selling tends to be loyal customers who purchase from the company time after time. A relationship selling strategy focused on retaining customers costs a company less than if it were constantly prospecting and selling to new customers. One consulting firm estimates that if a small to midsize company were to increase its customer retention rate by just 5 percent, its profits would double in about ten years. Further, the average Fortune 500 company could instantly double its revenue growth with that same 5 percent boost in retention.[20]

relationship selling (consultative selling)
Sales practice of building, maintaining, and enhancing interactions with customers in order to develop long-term satisfaction through mutually beneficial partnerships.

Relationship selling is more typical with selling situations for industrial-type goods, such as heavy machinery or computer systems, and services, such as airlines and insurance, than for consumer goods. For example, American Airlines recently entered into a long-term relationship with Perot Systems to become the company's exclusive airline. When Perot employees book flights, they are not required to wait for tickets. Instead, they simply present a card at the ticket counter or gate. Miles are automatically credited to the Perot Systems employees' American frequent

exhibit 12.9

Key Differences Between Traditional Selling and Relationship Selling

Traditional Personal Selling	Relationship Selling
Sell products (goods and services)	Sell advice, assistance, and counsel
Focus on closing sales	Focus on improving the customer's bottom line
Limited sales planning	Consider sales planning as top priority
Spend most contact time telling customers about product	Spend most contact time attempting to build a problem-solving environment with the customer
Conduct "product-specific" needs assessment	Conduct discovery in the full scope of the customer's operations
"Lone wolf" approach to the account	Team approach to the account
Proposals and presentations based on pricing and product features	Proposals and presentations based on profit-impact and strategic benefits to the customer
Sales follow-up is short term, focused on product delivery	Sales follow-up is long term, focused on long-term relationship enhancement

SOURCE: Robert M. Peterson, Patrick L. Schul, and George H. Lucas, Jr., "Consultative Selling: Walking the Walk in the New Selling Environment," National Conference on Sales Management, *Proceedings*, March 1996.

flyer accounts. Upgrades are readily available and, to complete the package, American allows all Perot employees to use its Ambassadors Clubs for business and leisure travel. For all of this, Perot Systems is charged a discounted travel rate against a corporate commitment for a specified number of travel miles.[21]

Exhibit 12.9 lists the key differences between traditional personal selling and relationship or consultative selling. These differences will become more apparent as we explore the personal selling process later in the chapter.

ON LINE

Advances in electronic commerce on the Internet, however, are threatening the buyer–seller relationship as more and more companies are choosing to conduct business and purchase supplies and materials through a computer screen rather than face-to-face with a salesperson. Read about one start-up company whose mission is to bring together buyers and sellers in bidding wars over the Internet in the "Entrepreneurial Insights" box.

sales process (sales cycle)
The set of steps a salesperson goes through in a particular organization to sell a particular product or service.

Steps in the Selling Process

List the steps in the selling process

Although personal selling may sound like a relatively simple task, completing a sale actually requires several steps. The **sales process**, or **sales cycle**, is simply the set of steps a salesperson goes through to sell a particular product or service. The sales process or cycle can be unique for each product or service, depending on the

entrepreneurial insights

Web Service Helps Buyers Get Right Price at the Expense of Relationships

A new type of commerce is emerging on the Internet that is endangering the traditional buyer–seller relationship in personal selling.

FreeMarkets Online (**www.freemarkets.com**), a Pittsburgh-based Internet bidding service, helps buyers of industrial products find the best possible suppliers. These suppliers then must bid to get the business. Founded in 1995 by two former McKinsey & Company consultants, Geln Meakem and Sam Kinney, the service aims to put more power in the hands of buyers.

Here's how it works: FreeMarkets Online consultants work with purchasing managers and agents to develop a comprehensive request for quotation (RFQ). Then potential suppliers respond to the RFQ in order to be considered in the bidding process. After being qualified, suppliers, usually between four and six, are invited by FreeMarkets to participate in an on-line bidding event that takes place during a specified four- to six-hour period on a secure extranet. Without identifying themselves, suppliers submit their bids for the business and watch as their rivals undercut their prices. Suppliers can respond with lower and lower bids. The result is usually 15 percent savings for purchasers.

Electronic bidding helps companies save millions on their supply purchases by cutting out the salesperson. For manufacturers that use FreeMarkets' RFQ and on-line bidding technology, the advantages include decreasing the cost of procuring parts and offering customers the best value on finished goods. Electronic bidding not only expands buyers' available universe of potential suppliers, but it also forces those suppliers to be more efficient so they can bid the lowest possible price. It also optimizes time by cutting out the hassles of lengthy and potentially acrimonious negotiations with suppliers.

United Technologies Corporation is one manufacturer that has embraced on-line bidding as a means to help cut supply costs. UTC, which spends more than $10 billion a year with suppliers, was one of the first buying organizations to use FreeMarkets Online. With a goal of cutting costs by $750 million by the year 2000, UTC's supply management group is meeting the challenge with a mix of traditional and nontraditional supply strategies, including heavy use of the Internet and related technologies.

However, the implications of electronic bidding can be especially frightening for companies that rely heavily on sales forces. In a recent electronic bidding event sponsored by FreeMarkets Online for 350 million pounds of a food ingredient, for instance, the incumbent supplier chose not to participate. Three weeks later the company was forced to close its plant as a result of having lost a relationship with one of its biggest customers. As this example illustrates, electronic bidding could easily jeopardize the success of salespeople who have long relied on the relationships they have painstakingly cultivated. While on-line bidding may actually help companies, especially smaller ones, in broadening their customer base, these same companies lose the opportunity to enhance the sale with a win-win relationship. Additionally, the buyer may give up the satisfaction of meeting with suppliers face-to-face.[22]

In this age of electronic commerce, has the salesperson become an endangered species? How can salespeople take advantage of this information technology that threatens their existence?

features of the product or service, characteristics of customer segments, and internal processes in place within the firm, such as how leads are gathered.

Some sales take only a few minutes, but others may take months or years to complete, especially when selling customized goods or services. The typical sale for Eastman Kodak's line of high-speed motion analysis cameras takes anywhere from nine to eighteen months to close.[23] On the other end of the spectrum, sales of its more basic cameras to retailers are generally more routine and may take only a few days. Whether a salesperson spends a few minutes or a few years on a sale, these are the seven basic steps in the personal selling process:

1. Generating leads
2. Qualifying leads
3. Approaching the customer and probing needs ★ Know customer
4. Developing and proposing solutions
5. Handling objections
6. Closing the sale
7. Following up

exhibit 12.10

Relative Amount of Time Spent in Key Steps of the Selling Process

Key Selling Steps	Traditional Selling	Relationship/Consultative Selling
Generating leads	High	Low
Qualifying leads	Low	High
Approaching the customer and probing needs	Low	High
Developing solutions	Low	High
Proposing solutions through a sales presentation	High	Low
Closing the sale	High	Low
Following up	Low	High

Like other forms of promotion, these steps of selling follow the AIDA concept discussed in the first half of the chapter. Once a salesperson has located a prospect with the authority to buy, he or she tries to get the prospect's attention. A thorough needs assessment turned into an effective sales proposal and presentation should generate interest. After developing the customer's initial desire (preferably during the presentation of the sales proposal), the salesperson seeks action in the close by trying to get an agreement to buy. Follow-up after the sale, the final step in the selling process, not only lowers cognitive dissonance (refer to Chapter 4) but also may open up opportunities to discuss future sales. Effective follow-up will also lead to repeat business in which the process may start all over again at the needs assessment step.

Traditional selling and relationship selling follow the same basic steps. What is different between the two selling methods is the relative importance placed on key steps in the process. (See Exhibit 12.10.) Traditional selling efforts are transaction oriented, focusing on generating as many leads as possible, making as many presentations as possible, and closing as many sales as possible. Minimal effort is placed on asking questions to identify customer needs and wants or matching these needs and wants to the benefits of the product or service. In contrast, the salesperson practicing relationship selling emphasizes an upfront investment in the time and effort needed to uncover each customer's specific needs and wants and matching to them, as closely as possible, the product or service offering. By doing the homework upfront, the salesperson creates the conditions necessary for a relatively straightforward close.[24] Let's look at each step of the selling process individually.

Generating Leads

Initial groundwork must precede communication between the potential buyer and the salesperson. **Lead generation**, or **prospecting**, is the identification of those firms and people most likely to buy the seller's offerings. These firms or people become "sales leads" or "prospects."

lead generation (prospecting)
Identification of those firms and people most likely to buy the seller's offerings.

ON LINE

Sales leads can be secured in several different ways, most notably through advertising, trade shows and conventions, or direct-mail and telemarketing programs. Favorable publicity also helps to create leads. Company records of past client purchases are another excellent source of leads. Many sales professionals are also securing valuable leads from their firm's Internet Web site. Today about 55 percent of all Web sites are used for some sort of lead generation.[25]

referral
Recommendation to a salesperson from a customer or business associate.

Another way to gather a lead is through a **referral**—a recommendation from a customer or business associate. The advantages of referrals over other forms of prospecting include highly qualified leads, higher closing rates, larger initial transactions, and shorter sales cycles. Simply put, the salesperson and the company can earn more money in less time when prospecting using referrals. To increase the number of referrals they receive, some companies even pay or send small gifts to customers or suppliers who provide referrals. Research has suggested that one referral is as valuable as up to twelve cold calls. However, although 80 percent of clients would be willing to give referrals, only 20 percent are ever asked.[26]

networking
Process of finding out about potential clients from friends, business contacts, coworkers, acquaintances, and fellow members in professional and civic organizations.

Networking is the related method of using friends, business contacts, coworkers, acquaintances, and fellow members in professional and civic organizations to find out about potential clients. Salespeople for BKM Total Office, an office furniture supplier in San Diego, regularly visit with local architects and designers who build new office space in the area. They also network with people in other industries, such as telecommunications. If a company is buying a new phone system for a facility, for example, it's likely they may need office furniture as well.[27]

cold calling
Form of lead generation in which the salesperson approaches potential buyers without any prior knowledge of the prospects' needs or financial status.

Before the advent of more sophisticated methods of lead generation, such as direct mail and telemarketing, most prospecting was done through cold calling. **Cold calling** is a form of lead generation in which the salesperson approaches potential buyers without any prior knowledge of the prospects' needs or financial status. Although this method is still used, many sales managers have realized the inefficiencies of having their top salespeople use their valuable selling time searching for the proverbial "needle in a haystack." Passing the job of cold calling to a lower-cost employee, such as a sales support person, allows salespeople to spend more of their time and use their relationship-building skills on prospects that have already been identified.[28]

Qualifying Leads

When a prospect shows interest in learning more about a product, the salesperson has the opportunity to follow up, or qualify, the lead. Personally visiting unqualified prospects wastes valuable salesperson time and company resources. Often many leads go unanswered because salespeople are given no indication as to how qualified the leads are in terms of interest and ability to purchase. One study that surveyed four hundred marketers whose companies advertise in trade publications found that almost 40 percent of the leads generated went completely unanswered, most likely due to the fact that they were unqualified.[29]

lead qualification
Determination of a sales prospect's authority to buy and ability to pay for the good or service.

Lead qualification consists of determining whether the prospect has three things:[30]

- *A recognized need:* The most basic criterion for determining whether or not someone is a prospect for a product is a need that is not being satisfied. The salesperson should first consider prospects who are aware of a need but should not discount prospects who have not yet recognized that they have one. With a little more information about the product, they may decide they do have a need for it. Preliminary interviews and questioning can often provide the salesperson with enough information to determine whether there is a need.
- *Buying power:* Buying power involves both authority to make the purchase decision and access to funds to pay for it. To avoid wasting time and money, the salesperson needs to identify the purchasing authority and the ability to pay

before making a presentation. Organizational charts and information about a firm's credit standing can provide valuable clues.
- *Receptivity and accessibility:* The prospect must be willing to see the salesperson and be accessible to the salesperson. Some prospects simply refuse to see salespeople. Others, because of their stature in their organization, will only see a salesperson or sales manager with similar stature.

Often the task of lead qualification is handled by a telemarketing group or a sales support person who *prequalifies* the lead for the salesperson. Prequalification systems free sales representatives from the time-consuming task of following up on leads to determine need, buying power, and receptiveness. Prequalification systems may even set up initial appointments with the prospect for the salesperson. The result is more time for the sales force to spend in front of interested customers. Macromedia, a San Francisco-based software company, recently implemented a comprehensive, automated lead-management system that allows it to track leads from inception to close. Leads gathered are qualified by phone, fax, or on the Internet. Based on this information, the system assigns each lead a grade and priority status and then directs it to the appropriate salesperson. The system continues to track the leads in order to create sales and manufacturing forecasts. And when a sale is closed it allows management to evaluate return on investment for its different lead-generation programs.[31]

ON LINE

With more and more companies setting up Web sites on the Internet, qualifying on-line leads has also received some attention. The object of a company's Web site should be to get visitors to register, indicate what products they are interested in, and offer up some information on their time frame and resources. Leads from the Internet can then be prioritized (those indicating a short time frame, for instance, given a higher priority) and then transferred to salespeople. Often Web site visitors can be enticed to answer questions with offers of free merchandise or information. Enticing visitors to register also allows companies to customize future electronic interactions—for example, by giving prospects who visit the Web site their choice from a menu of products tailored specifically to their needs.[32]

Approaching the Customer and Probing Needs

Prior to approaching the customer, the salesperson should learn as much as possible about the prospect's organization and its buyers. This process, called the **preapproach**, describes the "homework" that must be done by the salesperson before contacting the prospect. This may include consulting standard reference sources, such as Moody's, Standard & Poor's, or Dun & Bradstreet, or contacting acquaintances or others who may have information about the prospect. Another preapproach task is to determine whether the actual approach should be a personal visit, a phone call, a letter, or some other form of communication.

preapproach
A process that describes the "homework" that must be done by the salesperson before he or she contacts the prospect.

During the sales approach, the salesperson either talks to the prospect or secures an appointment for a future time in which to probe the prospect further as to his or her needs. Relationship selling theorists suggest that salespeople should begin developing mutual trust with their prospect during the approach. Salespeople should use the approach as a way of introducing themselves and their company and products. They must sell themselves before they can sell the product. Small talk that introduces sincerity and some suggestion of friendship is encouraged to build rapport with the prospect, but remarks that could be construed as insincere should be avoided.[33]

The salesperson's ultimate goal during the approach is to conduct a **needs assessment** to find out as much as possible about the prospect's situation. This involves interviewing the customer to determine his or her specific needs and wants and the range of options the customer has for satisfying them. The salesperson should be determining how to maximize the fit between what he or she can offer

needs assessment
Determination of the customer's specific needs and wants and the range of options a customer has for satisfying them.

Moody's Investors Services

How can you use Moody's Web site for preapproach work? Would Moody's be best used for certain companies and not others? Why do you think as you do?
http://www.moodys.com/

and what the prospective customer wants. As part of the needs assessment, the consultative salesperson must know everything there is to know about[34]

- *The product or service:* Product knowledge is the cornerstone for conducting a successful needs analysis. The consultative salesperson must be an expert on his or her product or service, including technical specifications, the product's features and benefits, pricing and billing procedures, warranty and service support, performance comparisons with the competition, other customers' experiences with the product, and current advertising and promotional campaign messages.
- *Customers and their needs:* The salesperson should know more about customers than they know about themselves. That's the secret to relationship and consultative selling, where the salesperson acts not only as a supplier of products and services but also as a trusted consultant and advisor. The professional salesperson doesn't just sell products. He or she brings to each client business-building ideas and solutions to problems. For the customer, consulting a professional salesperson is like having another vital person on the team at no cost.
- *The competition:* The salesperson must know as much about the competitor's company and products as he or she knows about his or her own company. *Competitive intelligence* includes who the competitors are and what is known about them, how their products and services compare, advantages and disadvantages, and strengths and weaknesses.
- *The industry:* Knowing the industry involves active research on the part of the salesperson. This means attending industry and trade association meetings, reading articles published in industry and trade journals, keeping track of legislation and regulation that affect the industry, awareness of product alternatives and innovations from domestic and foreign competition, and having a feel for economic and financial conditions that may impact the industry.

Creating a *customer profile* during the approach helps salespeople optimize their time and resources. This profile is then used to help develop an intelligent analysis of the prospect's needs in preparation for the next step, developing and proposing solutions. Customer profile information is typically stored and manipulated using sales force automation software packages designed for use on laptop computers. Sales force automation software provides sales reps with a computerized and efficient method of collecting customer information for use during the entire sales process. Further, customer and sales data stored in a computer database can be easily shared among sales team members. The information can also be appended with industry statistics, sales or meeting notes, billing data, and other information that may be pertinent to the prospect or the prospect's company. The more salespeople know about their prospects, the better they can meet their needs.

Salespeople should wrap up their sales approach and need-probing mission by summarizing the prospect's need, problem, and interest. The salesperson should also get a commitment from the customer to some kind of action, whether it's reading promotional material or agreeing to a demonstration. This commitment helps qualify the prospect further and justify further time invested by the salesperson. The salesperson should reiterate the action he or she promises to take, such as sending information or calling back to provide answers to questions. The date and time of the next call should be set at the conclusion of the sales approach as well as an agenda for the next call in terms of what the salesperson hopes to accomplish, such as providing a demonstration or presenting a solution.[35]

Developing and Proposing Solutions

Once the salesperson has gathered the appropriate information about the client's needs and wants, the next step is to determine whether his or her company's products or services match the needs of the prospective customer. The salesperson then develops a solution, or possibly several solutions, in which the salesperson's product or service solves the client's problems or meets a specific need.

These solutions are typically presented to the client in the form of a sales proposal presented at a sales presentation. A **sales proposal** is a written document or professional presentation that outlines how the company's product or service will meet or exceed the client's needs. The **sales presentation** is the formal meeting in which the salesperson has the opportunity to present the sales proposal. The presentation should be explicitly tied to the prospect's expressed needs. Further, the prospect should be involved in the presentation by being encouraged to participate in demonstrations or by exposure to computer exercises, slides, video or audio, flipcharts, photographs, and so on.[36]

sales proposal
A formal written document or professional presentation that outlines how the salesperson's product or service will meet or exceed the prospect's needs.

sales presentation
Face-to-face explanation of the sales proposal to a prospective buyer.

Technology has become an important part of presenting solutions for many salespeople. Salespeople for Dell Computer Corporation, for example, don't just tell potential clients how much money they will save if they buy Dell PCs, they prove it. Through a sophisticated software program called Product Expert, Dell's corporate account reps show clients how much it will cost to buy, deploy, and maintain a Dell PC over its lifetime. The software, which reps download onto their laptop PCs before going on a sales call, allows the client to plug in variables specific to their business, such as how many employees use PCs, how many desktop units are purchased annually, what their integration needs are, and how much technical support is required. After manipulating and tallying the data, clients can then print out an executive summary. Because the savings information is presented to clients in a tangible format, the software is now an integral part of Dell's sales proposals.[37]

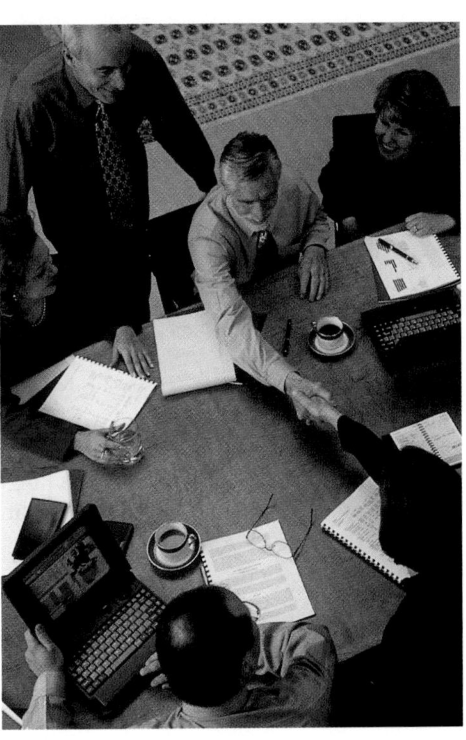

Closing the sale is the result of thorough preparation, a professional presentation, and skillful negotiation. It is, however, only the first step in building and maintaining a good customer relationship.
© Jon Feingersh/The Stock Market

Because the salesperson often has only one opportunity to present solutions, the quality of both the sales proposal and presentation can make or break the sale. Salespeople must be able to present the proposal and handle any customer objections confidently and professionally. For a powerful presentation, salespeople should be well prepared, rehearse what they are going to say, use direct eye contact, ask open-ended questions, and be poised. Nothing dies faster than a boring presentation. Salespeople should add energy to the presentation through gestures, voice inflection, and speaking forcefully.[38] If the salesperson doesn't have a convincing and confident manner, then the prospect will very often forget the information. Prospects take in body language, voice patterns, dress, and body type. Often customers are more likely to remember how salespeople present themselves than what salespeople say.

Handling Objections

Rarely does a prospect say "I'll buy it" right after a presentation. Often there are objections raised or perhaps questions about the proposal and the product. The potential buyer may insist that the price is too high, that he or she does not have enough information to make a decision, or that the good or service will not satisfy the present need. The buyer may also lack confidence in the seller's organization or product.

One of the first lessons that every salesperson learns is that objections to the product should not be taken personally as confrontations or insults. Rather, a salesperson should view objections as requests for information. A good salesperson considers objections a legitimate part of the purchase decision. To handle objections effectively, the salesperson should anticipate specific objections such as concerns about price, fully investigate the objection with the customer, be wary of what the competition is offering, and, above all, stay calm. Before a crucial sales presentation with an important prospect, for example, Dell Computer salespeople anticipated that the customer would have doubts that Dell's direct selling model would provide them with the same level of service and dedication they could get from a reseller. Being prepared helped Dell win the contract.[39]

Often, the salesperson can use the objection to close the sale. If the customer tries to pit suppliers against each other to drive down the price, the salesperson should be prepared to point out weaknesses in the competitor's offer and stand by the quality in his or her own proposal.[40]

Closing the Sale

At the end of the presentation, the salesperson should ask the customer how he or she would like to proceed. If the customer exhibits signs that he or she is ready to purchase and all questions have been answered and objections have been met, then the salesperson can try to close the sale. Customers often give signals during or after the presentation that they are ready to buy or are not interested. Examples include changes in facial expressions, gestures, and questions asked. The salesperson should look for these signals and respond appropriately.

Closing requires courage and skill. Naturally, the salesperson wants to avoid rejection, and asking for a sale carries with it the risk of a negative answer. A salesperson should keep an open mind when asking for the sale and be prepared for either a yes or a no. Rarely is a sale closed on the first call. In fact, the typical salesperson averages about 765 sales calls a year, many of which are repeat calls to the same client in an attempt to make the sale.[41] Some salespeople may negotiate with large accounts for several years before closing a sale. As you can see, building a good relationship with the customer is very important. Often, if the salesperson has developed a strong relationship with the customer, only minimal efforts are needed to close a sale.

negotiation
Process of both the salesperson and the prospect offering special concessions in an attempt to arrive at a sales agreement.

Negotiation often plays a key role in the closing of the sale. **Negotiation** is the process of both the salesperson and the prospect offering special concessions in an attempt to arrive at a sales agreement. For example, the salesperson may offer a price cut, free installation, free service, or a trial order. Effective negotiators, however, avoid using price as a negotiation tool because cutting price directly affects a company's profitability. Because companies spend millions on advertising and product development to create value, when salespeople give in to price negotiations too quickly, it decreases the value of the product. Instead, effective salespeople should emphasize value to the customer, rendering price a nonissue. Salespeople should also be prepared to ask for trade-offs and try to avoid giving unilateral concessions. If the customer asks for a five percent discount, the salesperson should be ready with what to ask for in return, such as more volume or flexibility with a delivery schedule.[42]

GLOBAL

More and more U.S. companies are expanding their marketing and selling efforts into global markets. Salespeople selling in foreign markets should tailor their presentation and closing styles to each market. Different personalities and skills will be successful in some countries and absolute failures in others. For instance, if a salesperson is an excellent closer and always focused on the next sale, doing business in Latin America might be difficult. The reason is that in Latin America people want to take a long time building a personal relationship with their suppliers.[43] Read about other global dos and don'ts of selling in the "Global Perspectives" box.

Following Up

Unfortunately, many salespeople hold the attitude that making the sale is all that's important. Once the sale is made, they can forget about their customers. They are wrong. Salespeople's responsibilities do not end with making the sales and placing

global perspectives

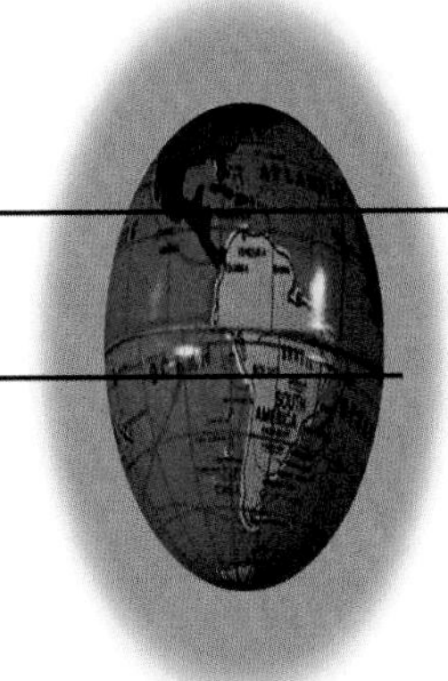

Global Dos and Don'ts in Selling

Most large companies with operations on foreign soil are employing locals to sell their products—international buyers are often cold to Americans trying to peddle their wares. So the American who finds him- or herself trying to sell internationally better be prepared.

Most selling skills that are successful in America also will work overseas. However, knowing how to act in certain cultures can be the difference between closing the deal and losing a customer. There are certain things Americans take for granted that could easily cost them a deal overseas. A simple thumbs-up sign that we give everyday could offend a customer in another country. Here, from many international business experts, are some things to watch out for in certain countries and regions around the world.

Arab Countries: Don't use your left hand to hold, offer, or receive materials because Arabs use their left hand to touch toilet paper. If you must use your left hand to write, apologize for doing so. Handshakes in Arab countries are a bit limp and last longer than typical American handshakes.

China: Never talk business on the first meeting—it's disrespectful. Don't refuse tea during a business discussion. Always drink it, even if you're offered a dozen cups a day. Never begin to eat or drink before your host does. Also, printed materials presented to Chinese business leaders should be in black and white, because colors have great significance for the Chinese. The Chinese tend to be extremely meticulous, looking to create long-term relationships with a supplier before agreeing to buy anything. Chinese are more intradependent and tend to include more people in on a deal. Most deals in China are finalized in a social setting, either over drinks or dinner. Additionally, getting to know the businessperson's family will personalize and strengthen the relationship.

European Countries: Western and Eastern Europeans reshake hands whenever they're apart for even a short period of time, for example, lunch.

France: Don't schedule a breakfast meeting—the French tend not to meet until after 10 A.M. Since the French knowledge of wine is far greater than that of most Americans, avoid giving wine or wine-related gifts to French clients. The French also prefer gifts that are of French origin.

Germany: Don't address a business associate by his or her first name, even if you've known each other for years. Always wait for an invitation to do so. Also, breakfast meetings are unheard of here, too. Salespeople should expect a sober, rigid business climate and negotiations that lack flexibility and compromise.

Central and South America: People here don't take the clock too seriously—scheduling more than two appointments in one day can prove disastrous. Latin Americans also tend to use a lighter, lingering handshake. Negotiations with Central and South American customers typically include a great deal of bargaining. Personal relationships are also important in Central and South America, so salespeople should make face-to-face contact with their clients during meetings and presentations.

Japan: Don't bring up business on the golf course—always wait for your host to take the initiative. Don't cross your legs in Japan—showing the bottom of the foot is insulting. Japanese businesspeople shake hands with one firm gesture combined with a slight bow, which should be returned. Japanese prefer gifts from well-known American stores, such as Tiffany's or Saks Fifth Avenue. Also, the higher the position of the recipient, the more elaborately wrapped the gift should be.

Mexico: Don't send a bouquet of red or yellow flowers as a gift—Mexicans associate those colors with evil spirits and death. Instead, send a box of premium chocolates. Including a small gift for the client's children creates a positive impression.

Vietnam: When meeting a Vietnamese woman, wait for her to extend a hand first—she may simply nod or bow slightly, the most common form of greeting in Vietnam. Vietnamese do not like to be touched or patted on the back or shoulders in social situations.

Miscellaneous: The thumbs-up gesture is considered offensive in the Middle East, rude in Australia, and a sign of "OK" in France. It's rude to cross your arms while facing someone in Turkey. In the Middle East don't ask, "How's the family?"—it's considered too personal. In most Asian countries, staring directly into a person's eyes is considered discourteous.[44]

the orders. One of the most important aspects of their jobs is **follow-up**. They must ensure that delivery schedules are met, that the goods or services perform as promised, and that the buyers' employees are properly trained to use the products.

follow-up
Final step of the selling process, in which the salesperson ensures that delivery schedules are met, that the goods or services perform as promised, and that the buyers' employees are properly trained to use the products.

Whereas the traditional sales approach's extent of follow-up with the customer is generally limited to successful product delivery and performance, a basic goal of relationship selling is to motivate customers to come back, again and again, by developing and nurturing long-term relationships. Most businesses depend on repeat sales, and repeat sales depend on thorough and continued follow-up by the salesperson. Finding a new customer is far more expensive than retaining an existing customer. When customers feel abandoned, cognitive dissonance arises and repeat sales decline. Today this issue is more pertinent than ever, because customers are far less loyal to brands and vendors. Buyers are more inclined to look for the best deal, especially in the case of poor after-the-sale follow-up. More and more buyers favor building a relationship with sellers.

ON LINE

Dell Computer Corporation is one company that is committed to enhancing its customers' satisfaction through effective follow-up and customer support. Dell developed an extensive extranet system, called Premier Pages, that is designed to give Dell's contract customers product, pricing, and service information at the touch of a mouse. Each Dell customer gets its own password-protected Premier Page found at an unlisted URL on the Web. Access includes product information, pricing structures, an employee-purchase plan (which gives customers' employees discounts on Dell products bought for personal use), on-line product ordering, and up-to-date purchase-history reports. The costs to Dell have been justified in customer satisfaction alone. One customer estimated saving $2 million on technical support costs thanks to Premier Pages. Another customer reported that it redeployed most of its procurement people and uses the remaining ones more efficiently.[45]

Sales Management

10
Describe the functions of sales management

There is an old adage in business that nothing happens until a sale is made. Without sales there is no need for accountants, production workers, or even a company president. Sales provide the fuel that keeps the corporate engines humming. Companies like West Point Pepperel, Dow Corning, Alcoa, and several thousand other industrial manufacturers would cease to exist without successful salespeople. Even companies like Procter & Gamble and Kraft General Foods that mainly sell consumer goods and use extensive advertising campaigns still rely on salespeople to move products through the channel of distribution. Thus sales management is one of marketing's most critical specialties. Effective sales management stems from a highly success oriented sales force that accomplishes its mission economically and efficiently. Poor sales management can lead to unmet profit objectives or even to the downfall of the corporation.

Just as selling is a personal relationship, so is sales management. Although the sales manager's basic job is to maximize sales at a reasonable cost while also maximizing profits, he or she also has many other important responsibilities and decisions. The tasks of sales management are to

1. Define sales goals and the sales process
2. Determine the sales force structure
3. Recruit and train the sales force
4. Compensate and motivate the sales force
5. Evaluate the sales force

Defining Sales Goals and the Sales Process

Effective sales management begins with a determination of sales goals. Without goals to achieve, salesperson performance would be mediocre at best, and the company would likely fail. Like any marketing objective, sales goals should be stated in clear, precise, and measurable terms and should always specify a time frame for their fulfillment. Overall sales force goals are usually stated in terms of desired dollar sales volume, market share, or profit level. For example, a life insurance company may have a goal to sell $50 million in life insurance policies annually, to attain a 12 percent market share, or to achieve $1 million in profits. Individual salespeople are also assigned goals in the form of quotas. A **quota** is simply a statement of the salesperson's sales goals, usually based on sales volume alone but sometimes including key accounts (those with greatest potential), new accounts, repeat sales, and specific products.

quota
Statement of the individual salesperson's sales objectives, usually based on sales volume alone but sometimes including key accounts (those with greatest potential), new accounts, and specific products.

Great sales managers focus not only on sales goals but also on the entire process that drives their sales organizations to reach those goals. Without a keen understanding of the sales process, a manager will never be successful—no matter how defined the sales goals or how great the sales reps. An important responsibility of the sales manager, therefore, is to determine the most effective and efficient sales process to follow in selling each different product and service. Although the basic steps of the sales process are the same as discussed earlier in the chapter (i.e., lead generation and qualification, approach and needs assessment, proposal creation and presentation, handling objections, closing, and follow-up), a manager must formally define the specific procedures salespeople go through to do their jobs—for example, where leads are generated, how they are qualified, what the best way is to approach potential clients, and what terms can be negotiated during closing.

Determining the Sales Force Structure

Because personal selling is so costly, no sales department can afford to be disorganized. Proper design helps the sales manager organize and delegate sales duties and provide direction for salespeople. Sales departments are most commonly organized by geographic regions, by product line, by marketing function performed (such as account development or account maintenance), by market or industry, or by individual client or account. The sales force for IBM could be organized into sales territories covering New England, the Midwest, the South, and the West Coast or could be organized into distinct groups selling personal computer systems and mainframe computer systems. IBM salespeople may also be assigned to a specific industry or market, for example, the telecommunications industry, or to key clients such as AT&T and MCI.

Market- or industry-based structures and key account structures are gaining popularity in today's competitive selling environment, especially with the emphasis on relationship selling. Being familiar with one industry or market allows sales reps to become experts in their fields and thereby offer better solutions and service. Further, by organizing the sales force around specific customers, many companies hope to improve customer service, encourage collaboration with other arms of the company, and unite salespeople in customer-focused sales teams. Hewlett-Packard is one such company that has realigned its sales force from a geographical focus to an industry focus. HP reps are now trained and deployed to be experts in key customer segments like manufacturing or financial services. HP has found that its customers prefer having access to all of HP's products and having to deal with only one salesperson.[46]

Recruiting and Training the Sales Force

Sales force recruitment should be based on an accurate, detailed description of the sales task as defined by the sales manager. Aside from the usual characteristics such as level of experience or education, what traits should sales managers look for in applicants? The most important quality of top performers is that they are driven by their own goal—that is, they usually set personal goals higher than those management sets for them. Moreover, they are achievement oriented, talk about

on line

Mary Kay Cosmetics

What can you find out about Mary Kay's sales network from the company Web site? What can you find out about the compensation of Mary Kay's sales force? How else does the company use the site to promote itself to future salespeople?

http://www.marykay.com/

their sales accomplishments, and are self-confident. Effective salespeople are also self-competitive; they keep close tabs on their own performance and compare it with their previous performance. They are optimistic, highly knowledgeable about the product, and assertive. They know how to listen to customers and are team players who support their coworkers. They are self-trainers who are continually engaged in upgrading their selling skills. The way sales candidates close the employment interview suggests how they will close a sale. Do they ask the manager how and when they are to follow up for the position or what the next step will be? Effective salespeople always plan the next step before they leave the client's office.

After the sales recruit has been hired and given a brief orientation, training begins. A new salesperson generally receives instruction in company policies and practices, selling techniques, product knowledge, industry and customer characteristics, and nonselling duties such as filling out sales and market information reports or using a sales automation computer program. Firms that sell complex products generally offer the most extensive training programs.

Most successful sales organizations have learned that training is not just for newly hired salespeople. Instead, training is offered to all salespeople in an ongoing effort to hone selling skills and relationship building. In pursuit of solid salesperson–client relationships, training programs now seek to improve salespeople's consultative selling and listening skills and to broaden their product and customer knowledge. In addition, training programs stress the interpersonal skills needed to become the contact person for customers. Because negotiation is increasingly important in closing a sale, salespeople are also trained to negotiate effectively without risking profits.

Compensating and Motivating the Sales Force

Compensation planning is one of the sales manager's toughest jobs. Only good planning will ensure that compensation attracts, motivates, and retains good salespeople. Generally, companies and industries with lower levels of compensation suffer higher turnover rates, which increases costs and decreases effectiveness. Therefore, compensation needs to be competitive enough to attract and motivate the best salespeople. Firms sometimes take profit into account when developing their compensation plans. Instead of paying salespeople on overall volume, they pay according to the profitability achieved from selling each product. Still other companies tie a part of the salesperson's total compensation to customer satisfaction assessed through periodic customer surveys.

straight commission
Method of compensation in which the salesperson is paid some percentage of sales.

straight salary
Method of compensation in which the salesperson receives a salary regardless of sales productivity.

The three basic compensation methods for salespeople are commission, salary, and combination plans. A typical commission plan gives salespeople a specified percentage of their sales revenue. A **straight commission** system compensates the salesperson only when a sale is made. On the other end of the spectrum, a **straight salary** system compensates a salesperson with a stated salary regardless of sales productivity. Most companies, however, offer a compromise between straight commission and straight salary plans. A *combination system* offers a base salary plus an incentive—usually a commission or a bonus. Combination systems have benefits for both the sales manager and the salesperson. The salary portion of the plan helps the manager control the sales force; the incentive provides motivation. For the salesperson, a combination plan offers an incentive to excel while minimizing the extremely wide swings in earnings that may occur when the economy surges or contracts too much.

As the emphasis on relationship selling increases, many sales managers feel that tying a portion of a salesperson's compensation to a client's satisfaction with the salesperson and the company encourages relationship building. To determine this sales managers can survey clients on a salesperson's ability to create realistic expectations and how responsive the person is to customer needs.[47] At GE Aircraft Engines, a portion of its salespeople's total compensation plan is tied to customer service and satisfaction measured through surveys. Therefore, making sure that the customer is satisfied leads to a bigger paycheck for the salesperson.[48]

Although the compensation plan motivates a salesperson to sell, sometimes it is not enough to produce the volume of sales or the profit margin required by sales management. Sales managers, therefore, often offer rewards or incentives, such as recognition at ceremonies, plaques, vacations, merchandise, and pay raises or cash bonuses. The most popular incentives are cash rewards, used by over 60 percent of sales organizations.[49] Rewards may help increase overall sales volume, add new accounts, improve morale and goodwill, move slow items, and bolster slow sales. They can be used to achieve long-term or short-term objectives, such as unloading overstocked inventory and meeting a monthly or quarterly sales goal.

Motivation also takes the form of effective sales leadership on the part of the sales manager. An effective sales manager is inspirational to his or her salespeople, encouraging them to achieve their goals through clear and enthusiastic communications. He or she has a clear vision and commitment to the mission of the organization and the ability to instill pride and earn the respect of employees. Effective sales leaders continuously increase their knowledge and skill base while also encouraging others to do so. In a recent study that assessed the attributes of sales leaders, the best sales leaders share a number of key personality traits (see Exhibit 12.11), such as a sense of urgency, openness to new ideas, and a desire to take risks. These traits separate motivational sales leaders from mere sales managers.

exhibit 12.11

Seven Key Leadership Traits of Effective Sales Leaders

Effective sales leaders . . .	
Are assertive	Assertive sales leaders know when and how to get tough and how to assert their authority.
Possess ego drive	Sales leaders with ego drive have the desire and ability to persuade their reps to take action.
Possess ego strength	Sales leaders with ego strength are able to not only make sure they bounce back from rejection but also make sure their reps rebound, too.
Take risks	Risk-taking sales leaders are willing to go out on a limb in an effort to make a sale or enhance a relationship.
Are innovative	Innovative sales leaders stay open to new ideas and new ways of conducting business.
Have a sense of urgency	Urgent sales leaders understand that getting things done now is critical to winning and keeping business.
Are empathetic	Empathetic sales leaders help their reps grow by listening and understanding.

SOURCE: Table adapted from "The 7 Traits of Great Sales Leaders" by Geoffrey Brewer, *Sales & Marketing Management*, July 1997, pp. 38–46. Reprinted with permission.

Evaluating the Sales Force

The final task of sales managers is evaluating the effectiveness and performance of the sales force. To evaluate the sales force, the sales manager needs feedback—that is, regular information from salespeople. Typical performance measures include sales volume, contribution to profit, calls per order, sales or profits per call, or percentage of calls achieving specific goals such as sales of products that the firm is heavily promoting.

Performance information helps the sales manager monitor a salesperson's progress through the sales cycle and pinpoint where breakdowns may be occurring. For example, by knowing the number of prospects an individual salesperson has in each step of the sales cycle process and determining where prospects are falling out of the sales cycle, a manager can determine how effective a salesperson may be at lead generation, needs assessment, proposal generation, presenting, closing, and follow-up stages. This information can then tell a manager what sales skills may need to be reassessed or retrained. For example, if a sales manager notices a sales rep seems to be letting too many prospects slip away after presenting proposals, it may mean he or she needs help with developing proposals, handling objections, or closing sales.

looking back LOOKING BACK

Snack-maker Frito-Lay does not use just one element of the promotional mix to promote its many brands of salty snacks. Rather, it uses a mix of promotional elements: advertising, public relations and publicity, and sales promotion. Promotion proved crucial to Frito-Lay's successful launch of brands such as Baked Lay's and Wow!. As you read the next chapter, keep in mind that marketers try to choose the mix of promotional elements that will best promote their good or service. Rarely will a marketer rely on just one method of promotion.

Summary

1 Discuss the role of promotion in the marketing mix. Promotion is communication by marketers that informs, persuades, and reminds potential buyers of a product in order to influence an opinion or elicit a response. Promotional strategy is the plan for using the elements of promotion—personal selling, advertising, sales promotion, and public relations—to meet the firm's overall objectives and marketing goals. Based on these objectives, the elements of the promotional strategy become a coordinated promotion plan. The promotion plan then becomes an integral part of the total marketing strategy for reaching the target market along with product, distribution, and price.

2 Discuss the elements of the promotional mix. The elements of the promotional mix include personal selling, advertising, sales promotion, and public relations. Personal selling typically involves direct communication, in person or by telephone; the seller tries to initiate a purchase by informing and persuading one or more potential buyers. More current notions of personal selling focus on the relationship developed between the seller and buyer. Advertising is a form of impersonal, one-way mass communication paid for by the source. Sales promotion is typically used to back up other components of the promotional mix by motivating employees and stimulating consumer and business-customer purchasing. Finally, public relations is the function of promotion concerned with a firm's public image. Firms can't buy good publicity, but they can take steps to create a positive company image.

3 Describe the communication process. The communication process has several steps. When an individual or organization has a message it wishes to convey to a target audience, it encodes that message using language and symbols familiar to the intended receiver and sends the message through a channel of communication. Noise in the transmission channel distorts the source's intended message. Reception occurs if the message falls within the receiver's frame of reference. The receiver decodes the message and usually provides feedback to the source. Normally, feedback is direct for interpersonal communication and indirect for mass communication.

4 Explain the goals and tasks of promotion. The fundamental goals of promotion are to induce, modify, or reinforce behavior by informing, persuading, and reminding. Informative promotion explains a good's or service's purpose and benefits. Promotion that informs the consumer is typically used to increase demand for a general product category or to introduce a new good or service. Persuasive promotion is designed to stimulate a purchase or an action. Promotion that persuades the consumer to buy is essential during the growth stage of the product life cycle, when competition becomes fierce. Reminder promotion is used to keep the product and brand name in the public's mind. Promotions that remind are generally used during the maturity stage of the product life cycle.

5 Discuss the AIDA concept and its relationship to the promotional mix. The AIDA model outlines the four basic stages in the purchase decision-making process, which are initiated and propelled by promotional activities: (1) attention, (2) interest, (3) desire, and (4) action. The components of the promotional mix have varying levels of influence at each stage of the AIDA model. Advertising is a good tool for gaining attention and knowledge of a good or service. Sales promotion is effective when consumers are at the purchase stage of the decision-making process. Personal selling is most effective in developing customer interest and desire.

6 Describe the factors that affect the promotional mix. Promotion managers consider many factors when creating promotional mixes. These factors include the nature of the product, product life cycle stage, target market characteristics, the type of buying decision involved, availability of funds, and feasibility of push or pull strategies. Because most business products tend to be custom-tailored to the buyer's exact specifications, the marketing manager may choose a promotional mix that relies more heavily on personal selling. On the other hand, consumer products are generally mass produced and lend themselves more to mass promotional efforts such as advertising and sales promotion. As products move through different stages of the product life cycle, marketers will choose to use different promotional elements. For example, advertising is emphasized more in the introductory stage of the product life cycle than in the decline stage. Characteristics of the target market, such as geographic location of potential buyers and brand loyalty, influence the promotional mix as does whether the buying decision is complex or routine. The amount of funds a firm has to allocate to promotion may also help determine the promotional mix. Small firms with limited funds may rely more heavily on public relations, whereas larger firms may be able to afford broadcast or print advertising. Last, if a firm uses a push strategy to promote the product or service, the marketing manager may choose to use aggressive advertising and personal selling to wholesalers and retailers. If a pull strategy is chosen, then the manager often relies on aggressive mass promotion, such as advertising and sales promotion, to stimulate consumer demand.

7 Describe personal selling. Personal selling is direct communication between a sales representative and one or more prospective buyers in an attempt to influence each other in a purchase situation. Broadly speaking, all businesspeople use personal selling to promote themselves and their ideas. Personal selling offers several advantages over other forms of promotion. Personal selling allows salespeople to thoroughly explain and demonstrate a product. Salespeople have the flexibility to tailor a sales proposal to the needs and preferences of individual customers. Personal selling is more efficient than other forms of promotion because salespeople target qualified prospects and avoid wasting efforts on unlikely buyers. Personal selling affords greater managerial control over promotion costs. Finally, personal selling is the most effective method of closing a sale and producing satisfied customers.

8 Discuss the key differences between relationship selling and traditional selling. Relationship selling is the practice of building, maintaining, and enhancing interactions with customers in order to develop long-term satisfaction through mutually beneficial partnerships. Traditional selling, on the other hand, is transaction focused. That is, the salesperson is most concerned with making one-time sales and moving on to the next prospect. Salespeople practicing relationship selling spend more time understanding a prospect's needs and developing solutions to meet those needs.

9 List the steps in the selling process. The selling process is composed of seven basic steps: (1) generating leads, (2) qualifying leads, (3) assessing approach and needs, (4) developing and proposing solutions, (5) handling objections, (6) closing the sale, and (7) following up.

10 Describe the functions of sales management. Sales management is a critical area of marketing that performs several important functions. Sales managers set overall company sales goals and define the sales process most effective for achieving those goals. They determine sales force structure based on geographic, product, functional, or customer variables. Managers develop the sales force through recruiting and training. Sales management motivates the sales force through compensation planning, motivational tools, and effective sales leadership. Finally, sales managers evaluate the sales force through salesperson feedback and other methods of determining their performance.

Key Terms

advertising 417
AIDA concept 426
channel 421
cold calling 438
communication 419
decoding 421
differential advantage 416
encoding 421
feedback 422
follow-up 444
integrated marketing communications (IMC) 423
interpersonal communication 419
lead generation (prospecting) 437
lead qualification 438
mass communication 419
needs assessment 439
negotiation 442
networking 438
noise 421
personal selling 417
preapproach 439
promotion 415
promotional mix 417
promotional strategy 415
publicity 418
public relations 418
pull strategy 431
push strategy 431
quota 445
receiver 421
referral 438
relationship selling (consultative selling) 434
sales presentation 441
sales process (sales cycle) 435
sales promotion 417
sales proposal 441
sender 421
straight commission 446
straight salary 446

Discussion and Writing Questions

1. What is a promotional strategy? Explain the concept of a differential advantage in relation to promotional strategy.
2. Why is understanding the target market a crucial aspect of the communication process?
3. Discuss the importance of integrated marketing communications. Give some current examples of companies that are and are not practicing integrated marketing communications.
4. Why might a marketing manager choose to promote his or her product using persuasion? Give some current examples of persuasive promotion.
5. Discuss the role of personal selling and advertising in promoting industrial products. How does their role differ in promoting consumer products?
6. What are the key differences between relationship selling and traditional methods of selling? What types of products or services do you think would be conducive to relationship selling?
7. WRITING You are a new salesperson for a well-known business computer system, and one of your customers is a large group of physicians. You have just arranged an initial meeting with the office manager. Develop a list of questions you will ask at this meeting to uncover the group's specific needs.

8. What does sales follow-up entail? Why is it an essential step in the selling process, particularly from the perspective of relationship selling? How does it relate to cognitive dissonance?

9. TEAM WRITING Choose a partner from class and go together to interview the owners or managers of several small businesses in your city. Ask them what their promotional objectives are and why. Are they trying to inform, persuade, or remind customers to do business with them? Also determine whether they believe they have an awareness problem or whether they need to persuade customers to come to them instead of to competitors. Ask them to list the characteristics of their primary market, the strengths and weaknesses of their direct competitors, and how they are positioning their store to compete. Prepare a report to present in class summarizing your findings.

10. ON LINE Visit **http://www.pm-a.com/**. What statements does this Web site make about the buying power, size, and growth of the Hispanic market in the United States? Why are these statistics important for marketing communication and promotion strategy in the United States?

11. ON LINE Visit **http://www.teamxrx.com**. In what ways does this Web site generate a sense of personal selling?

Application for Small Business

ENTREPRENEUR Morgan's is a retail clothing store offering high-quality, reasonably priced merchandise. Its target markets include students at the local university and working individuals, primarily in the age range eighteen to thirty-five. The location is about three miles from the campus in an upscale strip center next to a small, local mall. For several years the owner has been using several student interns as part-time salespersons and assistant managers. He has been able to find good workers, but turnover is high and training new employees takes a lot of time. Also, his sales training has consisted mostly of asking new student interns to review the internship reports of former student employees. To reduce these problems he has considered hiring a college graduate full-time and fewer part-time interns. The full-time employee should reduce turnover and the need for repeated training and be able to help him develop a better sales training approach. He pays the interns between $5.00 and $8.00 per hour, depending on their experience. College graduates would have to be paid between $22,000 and $27,000 per year plus benefits.

Questions

1. What factors must be considered in making this decision?
2. Should he hire a college graduate as a full-time employee? Why?

Review Quiz

1. Most promotional strategies use several ingredients. Which of the following is *not* one of the elements of the promotional mix?
   a. Personal selling
   b. Informative promotion
   c. Sales promotion
   d. Public relations

2. Any form of paid communications in which a sponsor or company is identified is the definition of

   a. Advertising
   b. The promotional mix
   c. Sales promotion
   d. Publicity

3. ______ communication is direct, face-to-face communication; ______ communication refers to communicating to large audiences.

   a. Interpersonal, mass
   b. Mass, interpersonal
   c. Encoded, decoded
   d. Decoded, encoded

4. With which element of the promotional mix does the communication sender receive the greatest amount of feedback?

   a. Advertising
   b. Personal selling
   c. Public relations
   d. Sales promotion

5. Influencing customers to buy a product now is accomplished with ______ promotion.

   a. Informative
   b. Advocacy
   c. Persuasive
   d. Reminder

6. The first step for the marketer following the AIDA concept for reaching promotional goals is

   a. Attention
   b. Action
   c. Desire
   d. Interest

7. Which of the elements of the promotional mix is most effective in stimulating action in the target market?

   a. Advertising
   b. Personal selling
   c. Sales promotion
   d. Public relations

8. Products with high value are usually best suited to using ______ as the primary element of the promotional mix.

   a. Advertising
   b. Personal selling
   c. Sales promotion
   d. Public relations

9. A positioning statement is the set of unique features of a company and its products that are perceived by the target market as significant and superior to the competition.

   a. True
   b. False

10. A promotion strategy designed to stimulate consumer demand to obtain product distribution is called a push strategy.

   a. True
   b. False

11. In personal selling, a qualified lead is one that has demonstrated a recognized need for the product or service being offered.
    a. True
    b. False
12. Identify the four stages of consumer involvement with a promotional message.

Check the Answer Key, which follows the Video Case, to see how well you understood the material.

VIDEO CASE

Boyne USA Resorts' *Lifestyles* Magazine: Promoting the Ultimate Playground

Boyne USA Resorts' *Lifestyles* magazine has a circulation of five hundred thousand. Through direct mail, newsstand distribution, and trade show exposure, the magazine reaches an audience from Montana to Michigan and from Washington to Utah. Boyne USA Resorts is the largest privately owned resort corporation in the country and has a very diverse audience. In many ways, *Lifestyles* epitomizes Boyne's integrated approach to communication about available services. All promotional activities—media advertising, sales promotion, personal selling, public relations, as well as direct marketing—have a consistent, unified message. This integrated approach to promotion can be seen in every issue of *Lifestyles,* which informs the target audience of skiers and golfers, persuades them to come to a Boyne resort, and reminds them of special events and sales promotions.

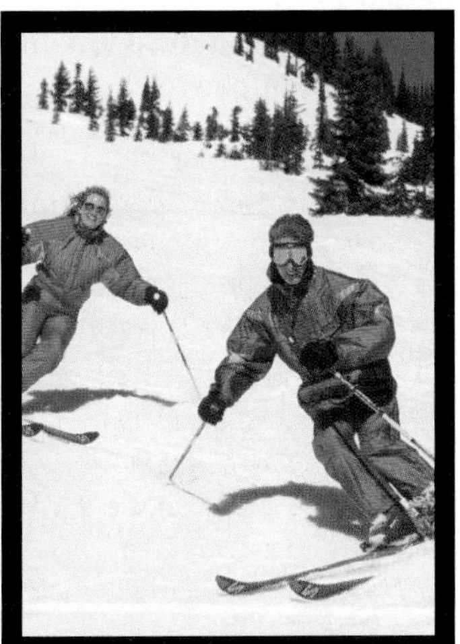

Lifestyles articles advertise all the amenities of the resorts: the inns, condominiums, and vacation homes; the superb quality of the slopes, cross-country skiing trails, and manicured golf courses; other activities such as hiking, biking, and fishing; and the gourmet restaurants. The section entitled "Distinctive Resort Properties for Sale" lists available real estate for sale and invites readers to contact a Boyne real estate professional who will work one-to-one with prospective buyers. Also highlighted in *Lifestyles* is the Boyne team of convention planners, who offer companies a wide choice of tastefully decorated facilities and conferences for six to six hundred people.

Lifestyles also describes Boyne's special events, which are carefully orchestrated to build good public relations nationwide. By identifying areas of public interest and offering programs to generate public awareness, Boyne USA maintains a positive image and educates the public about its goal to be a premier ski and golf resort. The company's special events calendar at the Michigan resorts is full. Ski with the Greats is a popular event with celebrities on hand to hold clinics, a challenge race, and award prizes at the après-ski party. At the Hawaiian Tropic, contestants from around the state come to Boyne Mountain to compete in an evening gown and swimsuit competition, a fashion show, a limbo dance, and a Mr. Boyne contest, all of which culminate in a party with live entertainment. Dannon Winterfest, put on in conjunction with the Dannon Company, has tents and inflatables set up around Boyne Mountain with product sampling, a dance contest, an après-ski party, and merchandise giveaways. And the World Pro Snowboard Tour features international racers who compete for $250,000 in prize money. These events give the resorts lots of publicity, and regardless of how much advertising is done, nothing generates more excitement about Boyne USA than extensive media coverage.

In addition to informing readers about the resorts, *Lifestyles* persuades them to visit. "Want your ten-year-olds to spend more time outside? Get them a FREE Gold Season Pass to Boyne USA Resorts!" This promotion offers a complimentary pass that entitles ten-year-olds to unlimited skiing and snowboarding at Boyne Mountain and Boyne Highlands. Another powerful way to draw skiers to the resorts is to make skiing affordable. As the *Lifestyles* article explains, "No longer will non-skiers be able to use the expense of skiing or snowboarding as an excuse to remain couch potatoes this winter. For just $29, beginners will get a 90-minute lesson, equipment, and a beginner area lift ticket." The promotions information in *Lifestyles* is regularly updated on the Boyne Web site to remind vacationers about special events, skiing and golfing packages, and clothing or equipment.

A key element in the promotional mix for Boyne USA resorts is *Lifestyles* magazine's pull strategy to stimulate consumer demand. The scenic photos of the slopes and golf courses, lovely inns, and sumptuous dining entice readers to learn more about the resorts, and such deep discounts on weekday packages encourage readers to call travel agencies, use the toll-free number, or e-mail for information. Once visitors arrive at the resorts, this pull strategy is supported by a push strategy through the personal selling of real estate, clothing and equipment, and conventions. At Boyne, the push strategy is more about relationships and trust, so sales people are viewed as consultants who help the resort connect with its guests. For example, meeting planners work diligently with key accounts to develop long-term relationships, and carefully planned family events, such as Take Your Daughter to the Slopes Day or Ski Free with Lodging, make skiing affordable and so build customer loyalty.

Lifestyles is just the beginning of Boyne USA's well-coordinated promotion strategy, a strategy that is customer focused to bring vacationers back to the ultimate playground year after year.

Questions

1. Using Exhibit 12.1, what is the role of promotion in Boyne USA's marketing mix?
2. How does *Lifestyle* magazine encompass all of Boyne's promotional activities?
3. Using Exhibit 12.4, explain the three tasks of promotion at Boyne USA resorts.
4. How do push and pull strategies affect Boyne's promotional mix?

Bibliography

Boyne USA Resorts, *Lifestyles* magazine: Winter 1997–98; Spring/Summer 1998.

Boyne USA Web site: **http://www.boyneusa.com**

Answer Key

1. *Answer:* b, p. 416

   Rationale: The promotional mix includes personal selling, sales promotion, advertising, and public relations.

2. *Answer:* a, p. 417

   Rationale: This is the proper definition of advertising.

3. *Answer:* a, p. 419

   Rationale: A salesperson speaking directly with a client is an example of interpersonal communication; advertising is an example of mass communication.

4. *Answer:* b, p. 422

   Rationale: Because of the two-way message flow in personal selling, feedback is the greatest and the quickest for any of the promotional mix elements.

5. *Answer:* c, p. 425

   Rationale: Persuasive promotion is designed to stimulate a purchase or action of the customer.

6. *Answer:* a, p. 426

   Rationale: A firm cannot sell anything until the target market knows that the good or service exists, through promotion to gain attention.

7. *Answer:* c, p. 427

   Rationale: Sales promotion's greatest strength is in creating desire and purchase intent.

8. *Answer:* b, p. 432

   Rationale: When a product has high value, the costs associated with personal selling become more justifiable.

9. *Answer:* b, p. 415

   Rationale: This statement defines the notion of a differential advantage.

10. *Answer:* b, p. 431

    Rationale: This statement describes a pull strategy.

11. *Answer:* a, pp. 438–439

    Rationale: Lead qualification requires that the prospect have a recognized need, buying power, and receptivity and accessibility.

12. *Answer:*

    Attention
    Interest
    Desire
    Action
    (p. 426)

CHAPTER

13

LEARNING OBJECTIVES

After studying this chapter, you should be able to

1. Discuss the effect advertising has on market share, consumers, brand loyalty, and perception of product attributes
2. Identify the major types of advertising
3. Describe the advertising campaign process
4. Describe media evaluation and selection techniques
5. Define and state the objectives of sales promotion
6. Discuss the most common forms of consumer sales promotion
7. List the most common forms of trade sales promotion
8. Discuss the role of public relations in the promotional mix

advertising, sales promotion, and public relations

ADVERTISING, SALES PROMOTION, AND PUBLIC RELATIONS

Watch out Coke. Pepsi-Cola's Mountain Dew is making a splash with teenagers and sending the brand's sales soaring.

Pepsi-Cola over the years has transformed Mountain Dew, its neon lemon-lime drink with a caffeine kick, from a soft-drink with a hillbilly theme to a cutting-edge brand that's grown faster than any other. In 1997, Mountain Dew's sales volume shot up 13 percent, far outpacing the overall sales growth of about 3 percent in the carbonated soft-drink segment.

Industry experts have contributed Mountain Dew's stellar growth to its far-sighted promotional strategy and a consistent promotional message that has changed with the times without radical shifts in positioning. The image that Mountain Dew has portrayed over the years in its advertising is a tight link between thirst quenching and teens having an outrageous time with the brand outdoors. Although Pepsi has made subtle changes to contemporize the brand over the last twenty years, it has not deviated far from its core market of fun-loving, high-energy teens.

Mountain Dew's advertising shows why the soft drink is the most popular brand among teenagers and college kids. Dedicating about $40 million a year in media advertising, Mountain Dew spots feature hip-looking youths watching or participating in daredevil stunts and extreme sports. Mountain Dew ads have been wildly popular with teenagers and young adults, with 31 percent giving the ads high popularity marks. One such television ad shows a teenage boy and a teenage girl skysurfing off opposite mountains, meeting in mid-air to share a Mountain Dew. The girl seductively whispers in the boy's ear, "Let's be friends," as she pulls the cord on his parachute while swiping his Mountain Dew. Two other popular spots feature Olympic Gold Medal track star Michael Johnson in a spoof on time travel and a boy and a girl snowboarding to a tune from the musical *West Side Story*. Both spots use the theme: "Do the Dew."

Mountain Dew's sales promotion activities are not to be overshadowed by its high-budget advertising counterpart. In one of the most innovative promotions ever, Mountain Dew gave out over 250,000 pagers to teenagers who sent in ten proofs of purchase plus $29.99. Besides the pagers, consumers

on line

PepsiCo
Coca-Cola

See the latest promotional efforts from Mountain Dew at Pepsi's Web site. Compare these efforts to those used by Coca-Cola to promote Surge. Based on what you see, which cola are you motivated to buy? Why?
http://www.pepsico.com/ http://www.surge.com/

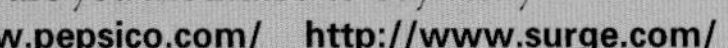

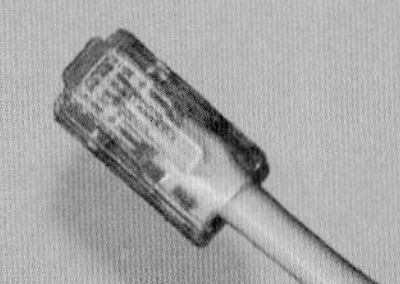

received six months of free airtime. In addition to normal paging functions, the pagers were programmed to receive Extreme Network announcements once a week alerting teens to special offers and giveaways worth $50 million in merchandise from Mountain Dew and twenty-six other "Extreme" partners including MTV, ESPN, Burton Snowboards, Killer Loop sunglasses, and Sony Music. Not only did the pagers tap into a teen trend, they also enabled Mountain Dew to create and wire its own teen network directly.

Complementing Mountain Dew's traditional media advertising and sales promotion is a savvy public relations plan designed to influence those free-spirited youths it targets. Mountain Dew's long-standing association with extreme sports, such as its sponsorship of the ESPN's X Games, has made it a favorite of the high-energy set. Mountain Dew also is the sponsor of an extreme mountain biking team that routinely competes in the X Games.

Although Mountain Dew now enjoys a prominent rank in the soft-drink market, it faces the enviable challenge of keeping momentum in the face of new competition from Coca-Cola's Surge, which was rolled out to most of the country in 1997 and 1998. Although Surge is still a long way from catching up with Mountain Dew's impressive growth and market share, the introduction of Surge has helped build the segment for caffeinated soft drinks. See the latest promotional efforts from Mountain Dew at Pepsi's Web site, **www.pepsi.com**.[1]

How do advertisers like Pepsi-Cola decide what type of message should be conveyed to promote Mountain Dew to teenagers? What types of appeals and executional styles are most effective? How does Pepsi-Cola decide which media to use for Mountain Dew to reach its target consumers? What are the benefits of sales promotion and public relations to advertisers such as Pepsi-Cola? Answers to these questions and many more will be found as you read through this chapter.

Effects of Advertising

1

Discuss the effect advertising has on market share, consumers, brand loyalty, and perception of product attributes

Advertising is defined in Chapter 10 as any form of nonpersonal, paid communication in which the sponsor or company is identified. It is a popular form of promotion, especially for consumer packaged goods and services. Advertising spending increases annually, with estimated U.S. advertising expenditures now exceeding $187 billion per year.[2]

Although total advertising expenditures seem large, the industry itself is very small. Only about 272,000 people are employed in the advertising departments of manufacturers, wholesalers, and retailers and in the five thousand or so U.S. advertising agencies.[3] This figure also includes people working in media services, such as radio and television, magazines and newspapers, and direct-mail firms.

The amount of money budgeted for advertising by some firms is staggering (see Exhibit 13.1.) General Motors, Procter & Gamble, and Philip Morris each spend over $2 billion annually on national advertising alone. That's over $6 million a day by each company. If sales promotion and public relations are included, this figure rises even higher. Over ninety additional companies spend over $200 million each.

Spending on advertising varies by industry. For example, the game and toy industry has one of the highest ratios of advertising dollars to sales. For every dollar of merchandise sold in the toy industry, about fifteen cents is spent on advertising the toy to consumers. Other consumer goods manufacturers that spend heavily on advertising in relation to total sales include book publishers, sugar and confectionary products manufacturers, watch makers, perfume and cosmetic manufacturers, detergent makers, and wine and liquor companies.[4]

Advertising and Market Share

Today's most successful brands of consumer goods, like Ivory soap and Coca-Cola, were built by heavy advertising and marketing investments long ago. Today's advertising dollars are spent on maintaining brand awareness and market share.

New brands with a small market share tend to spend proportionately more for advertising and sales promotion than those with a large market share, typically for two reasons. First, beyond a certain level of spending for advertising and sales

exhibit 13.1

Top Ten Leaders by U.S. Advertising Spending: 1997

Rank	Advertiser	Total U.S. Ad Spending in 1997 (in $ millions)	Average Ad Spending per Day in 1997 ($)
1	*General Motors,* Detroit	3,087.4	8,460,000
2	*Procter & Gamble,* Cincinnati	2,743.2	7,520,000
3	*Philip Morris,* New York	2,137.8	5,860,000
4	*Chrysler,* Highland Park, Michigan	1,532.4	4,200,000
5	*Ford Motor,* Dearborn, Michigan	1,281.8	3,510,000
6	*Sears, Roebuck,* Chicago	1,262.0	3,460,000
7	*Walt Disney,* Burbank, California	1,249.7	3,420,000
8	*PepsiCo,* Purchase, New York	1,244.7	3,410,000
9	*Diageo,* London	1,206.6	3,310,000
10	*McDonald's,* Oak Brook, Illinois	1,041.7	2,850,000

SOURCE: Computed from data obtained from "100 Leaders by U.S. Advertising Spending," *Advertising Age*, 28 September 1998, p. s4.

advertising response function
Phenomenon in which spending for advertising and sales promotion increases sales or market share up to a certain level but then produces diminishing returns.

promotion, diminishing returns set in. That is, sales or market share begins to decrease no matter how much is spent on advertising and sales promotion. This phenomenon is called the **advertising response function**. Understanding of the advertising response function helps marketers use budgets wisely. A market leader like Ruffles potato chips may spend proportionately less on advertising than newcomer Frito-Lay's Baked Lay's brand. Frito-Lay spends more on its brand in an attempt to increase awareness and market share. Ruffles, on the other hand, spends only as much as needed to maintain market share; anything more would reap diminishing benefits. Because Ruffles has already captured the attention of the majority of the target market, it needs only to remind customers of its product.

The second reason that new brands tend to require higher spending for advertising and sales promotion is that a certain minimum level of exposure is needed to measurably affect purchase habits. If Frito-Lay advertised Baked Lay's chips in only one or two publications and bought only one or two television spots, it certainly would not achieve the exposure needed to penetrate consumers' perceptual defenses, obtain awareness and comprehension, and ultimately affect their purchase intentions. Instead, Baked Lay's was introduced through advertising in many different media for a sustained period of time.

Advertising and the Consumer

Advertising affects everyone's daily life and influences many purchases. Consumers turn to advertising for its informativeness as well as its entertainment value. The average U.S. citizen is exposed to hundreds of advertisements a day from all types of advertising media. In just the television media alone, researchers estimate that the average person spends over four hours a day watching TV. With network television airing an average of eighteen minutes of commercials during each hour of daytime programming, consumers are surely affected in some way by advertising.[5] Advertising affects the TV programs people watch, the content of the newspapers they read, the politicians they elect, the medicines they take, and the toys their children play with. Consequently, the influence of advertising on the U.S. socioeconomic system has been the subject of extensive debate among economists, marketers, sociologists, psychologists, politicians, consumerists, and many others.

Although advertising cannot change consumers' deeply rooted values and attitudes, advertising may succeed in transforming a person's negative attitude toward a product into a positive one. When prior evaluation of the brand is negative, serious or dramatic advertisements are more effective at changing consumers' attitudes. Humorous ads, on the other hand, have been shown to be more effective at shaping attitudes when consumers already have a positive image of the advertised brand.[6]

Advertising and Brand Loyalty

Consumers with a high degree of brand loyalty are least susceptible to the influences of advertising for competing goods or services. For instance, new competitors found it hard to dislodge AT&T after deregulation of the long-distance telephone industry. After relying on "Ma Bell" for a lifetime of service, many loyal customers showed little response to advertising by competing companies.

Advertising also reinforces positive attitudes toward brands. When consumers have a neutral or favorable frame of reference toward a product or brand, they are often positively influenced by advertising for it. When consumers are already highly loyal to a brand, they may buy more of it when advertising and promotion for that brand increase.[7]

Advertising and Product Attributes

Advertising can affect the way consumers rank a brand's attributes, such as color, taste, smell, and texture. For example, in the past a shopper may have selected a brand of luncheon meat based on taste and variety of cuts available. However, advertising may influence that consumer to choose luncheon meat on the basis of other attributes, such as calories and fat content. Luncheon meat marketers like Louis Rich, Oscar Mayer, and Healthy Choice now stress the amount of calories and fat when advertising their products.

Automobile advertisers also understand the influence of advertising on consumers' rankings of brand attributes. Car ads have traditionally emphasized in years past such brand attributes as roominess, speed, and low maintenance. Today, however, car marketers have added safety to the list. Safety features like antilock brakes, power door locks, and air bags are now a standard part of the message in many carmakers' ads.

Major Types of Advertising

The firm's promotional objectives determine the type of advertising it uses. If the goal of the promotion plan is to build up the image of the company or the industry, **institutional advertising** may be used. In contrast, if the advertiser wants to enhance the sales of a specific good or service, **product advertising** is used.

2
Identify the major types of advertising

Institutional Advertising

Advertising in the United States has historically been product oriented. However, modern corporations market multiple products and need a different type of advertising. Institutional advertising, or corporate advertising, promotes the corporation as a whole and is designed to establish, change, or maintain the corporation's identity. It usually does not ask the audience to do anything but maintain a favorable attitude toward the advertiser and its goods and services. Ford Motor Company recently embarked on a corporate campaign to promote the Ford brand as a whole rather than one specific model. The $30 million campaign, which features Ford employees, is designed to tout the automaker's accomplishments in safety, security, and protecting the environment. The ultimate goal of the corporate campaign is to build a relationship with consumers based on trust.[8]

A form of institutional advertising called **advocacy advertising** is typically used to safeguard against negative consumer attitudes and to enhance the company's credibility among consumers who already favor its position.[9] Often, corporations use advocacy advertising to express their views on controversial issues. At other times, firms' advocacy campaigns react to criticism or blame, some in direct response to criticism by the media. Other advocacy campaigns may try to ward off increased regulation, damaging legislation, or the outcome of a lawsuit. Dow Chemical ran a series of ads in the New Orleans market that played up its corporate citizenship in the weeks preceding a silicone breast implant trial there. Other spots running at the same time, courtesy of a nonprofit group of which Dow is a member, highlighted the benefits of silicone products. The spot featured a little girl with a life-saving silicone device called a shunt in her brain, and her mother railing against greedy personal-injury lawyers.[10]

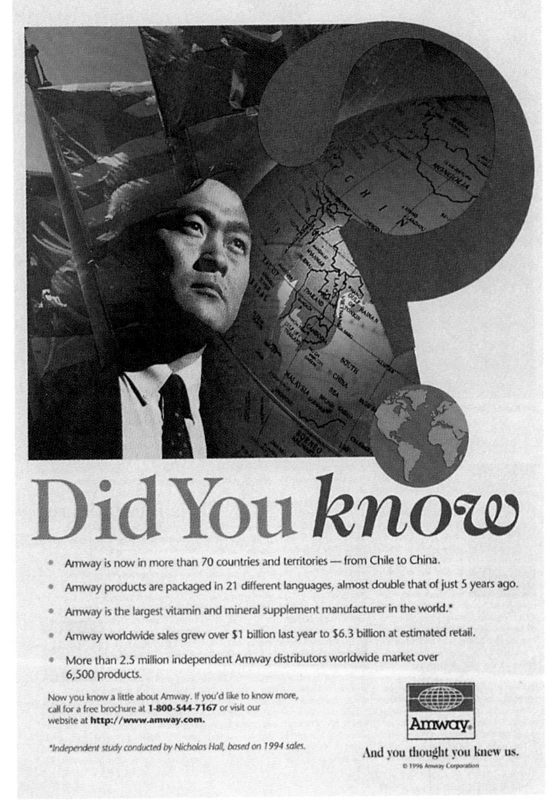

Did You know
Amway is now in more than 70 countries and territories — from Chile to China.
Amway products are packaged in 21 different languages, almost double that of just 5 years ago.
Amway is the largest vitamin and mineral supplement manufacturer in the world.*
Amway worldwide sales grew over $1 billion last year to $6.3 billion at estimated retail.
More than 2.5 million independent Amway distributors worldwide market over 6,500 products.
Now you know a little about Amway. If you'd like to know more, call for a free brochure at 1-800-544-7167 or visit our website at http://www.amway.com.
*Independent study conducted by Nicholas Hall, based on 1994 sales.
Amway
And you thought you knew us.
© 1996 Amway Corporation

This ad for Amway Corporation is a good example of institutional advertising. Notice how the ad focuses on the corporation as a whole rather than on any specific products marketed by the corporation.
Courtesy Amway Corporation

Product Advertising

Unlike institutional advertising, product advertising promotes the benefits of a specific good or service. The product's stage in its life cycle often determines which type of product advertising is used: pioneering advertising, competitive advertising, or comparative advertising.

Archer Daniels & Midland
BASF

ADM is a business marketer, but it has recently begun to pay for TV advertising. How does its Web site reflect this new consumer orientation? Compare ADM's site to that of BASF, another business marketer that in the past has also advertised in primarily consumer venues. Which company's site demonstrates an attempt to connect with the end user of its products? Why is this?

http://www.admworld.com/ **http://www.basf.com/**

on line

institutional advertising
Form of advertising designed to enhance a company's image rather than promote a particular product.

product advertising
Form of advertising that touts the benefits of a specific good or service.

advocacy advertising
Form of advertising in which an organization expresses its views on controversial issues or responds to media attacks.

pioneering advertising
Form of advertising designed to stimulate primary demand for a new product or product category.

competitive advertising
Form of advertising designed to influence demand for a specific brand.

comparative advertising
Form of advertising that compares two or more specifically named or shown competing brands on one or more specific attributes.

Pioneering Advertising **Pioneering advertising** is intended to stimulate primary demand for a new product or product category. Heavily used during the introductory stage of the product life cycle, pioneering advertising offers consumers in-depth information about the benefits of the product class. Pioneering advertising also seeks to create interest. Food companies, which introduce many new products, often use pioneering advertising. Gillette used pioneering advertising to introduce its revolutionary three-bladed MACH3 shaver to American consumers. The company embarked on a $300 million global ad campaign capitalizing on the high-tech theme of the product. The pioneering ad campaign's goal was to attract men seeking an even better shave than possible with premium razors on the market.[11]

Competitive Advertising Firms use competitive or brand advertising when a product enters the growth phase of the product life cycle and other companies begin to enter the marketplace. Instead of building demand for the product category, the goal of **competitive advertising** is to influence demand for a specific brand. Often promotion becomes less informative and appeals more to emotions during this phase. Advertisements may begin to stress subtle differences between brands, with heavy emphasis on building recall of a brand name and creating a favorable attitude toward the brand. Automobile advertising has long used very competitive messages, drawing distinctions based on such factors as quality, performance, and image.

Comparative Advertising **Comparative advertising** directly or indirectly compares two or more competing brands on one or more specific attributes. Some advertisers even use comparative advertising against their own brands. Products experiencing sluggish growth or those entering the marketplace against strong competitors are more likely to employ comparative claims in their advertising. For instance, comparative ads from pizza maker Papa Johns claims its pizza beat Pizza Hut pizza in a blind taste test. The comparative television spot contrasts its sauce—using a glamour shot of vine-ripened tomatoes—with Pizza Hut's, depicted as thick red goo scooped from a plastic bag.[12]

ETHICS

Before the 1970s, comparative advertising was allowed only if the competing brand was veiled and unidentified. In 1971, however, the Federal Trade Commission (FTC) fostered the growth of comparative advertising by saying that it provided information to the customer and that advertisers were more skillful than the government in communicating this information. Federal rulings prohibit advertisers from falsely describing competitors' products and allow competitors to sue if ads show their products or mention their brand names in an incorrect or false manner. These rules also apply to advertisers making false claims about their own products. The FTC recently brought charges against Gerber Products for making false and misleading advertising claims about its baby food. The company's ad campaign boasted that four of five pediatricians recommended Gerber baby food to parents, when in fact only 12 percent of those surveyed did. The FTC found that Gerber skewed the results by weeding out doctors who don't recommend baby food at all and those who don't recommend specific brands.[13]

GLOBAL

In some other nations, particularly newly capitalized countries in eastern Europe, claims that seem exaggerated by U.S. standards are commonplace. More often, however, the hard-sell tactics found in comparative ads in the United States are taboo. Until the 1980s, Japanese regulations all but prohibited comparative ads; ads that failed to compare objectively were considered slanderous. Nevertheless, although the Japanese have traditionally favored a soft-sell advertising approach, consumers are witnessing a trend toward comparative ads. Germany, Italy, Belgium, and France do not permit advertisers to claim that their products are best or better than competitors' products, which are common claims in U.S. advertising. In fact, the French are so adamant toward comparative ads that a Paris court banned a Philip Morris ad campaign comparing second-hand smoke to eating cookies for violating comparative advertising laws, even though no specific brands of cookies were mentioned in the ad.[14]

Steps in Creating an Advertising Campaign

An **advertising campaign** is a series of related advertisements focusing on a common theme, slogan, and set of advertising appeals. It is a specific advertising effort for a particular product that extends for a defined period of time. Management of advertising begins with understanding the steps in developing an advertising campaign and then making the important decisions relating to each step. Exhibit 13.2 traces the steps in this process.

3
Describe the advertising campaign process

advertising campaign
Series of related advertisements focusing on a common theme, slogan, and set of advertising appeals.

The advertising campaign process is set in motion by a promotion plan. The promotion planning process identifies the target market, determines the overall promotional objectives, sets the promotion budget, and selects the promotional mix. Advertising, which is usually part of the promotional mix, is used to encode a selling message to the target market. The advertisement is then conveyed to the target market, or receivers of the message, through such advertising vehicles as broadcast or print media.

Determine Campaign Objectives

The first step in the development of an advertising campaign is to determine the advertising objectives. An **advertising objective** identifies the specific communication task a campaign should accomplish for a specified target audience during a specified period of time. The objectives of a specific advertising campaign depend on the overall corporate objectives and the product being advertised.

advertising objective
Specific communication task a campaign should accomplish for a specified target audience during a specified period.

The DAGMAR approach (Defining Advertising Goals for Measured Advertising Results) is one method of setting objectives. According to this method, all advertising objectives should precisely define the target audience, the desired percentage change in some specified measure of effectiveness, and the time frame in which that change is to occur. For example, the objectives of an advertising campaign for

exhibit 13.2
Advertising Campaign Decision Process

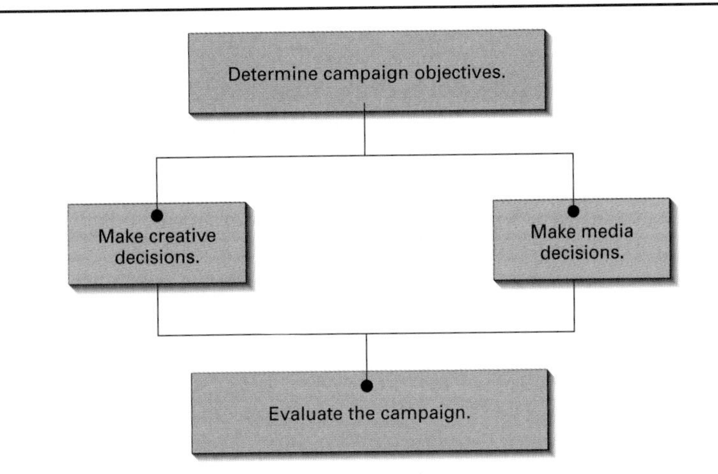

Gillette's MACH3 shaving system might be to achieve a 90 percent conversion rate within the first six months of introduction as a result of sending free shavers to a sample of the target audience.

Make Creative Decisions

The next step in developing an advertising campaign is to make the necessary creative and media decisions. Note in Exhibit 13.2 that both creative and media decisions are made at the same time. Creative work cannot be completed without knowing which **medium**, or message channel, will be used to convey the message to the target market. For instance, creative planning will likely differ for an ad to be displayed on an outdoor billboard versus that placed in a print medium, such as a newspaper or magazine. However, in this chapter media decisions are addressed after creative decisions.

medium
Channel used to convey a message to a target market.

In many cases, the advertising objectives dictate the medium and the creative approach to be used. For example, if the objective is to demonstrate how fast a product operates, then a TV commercial that shows this action may be the best choice. Creative decisions include identifying the product's benefits, developing possible advertising appeals, evaluating the advertising appeals and selecting one with a unique selling proposition, and executing the advertising message. An effective advertising campaign follows the AIDA model, which was discussed in Chapter 10.

Identifying Product Benefits A well-known rule of thumb in the advertising industry is "Sell the sizzle, not the steak"—that is, in advertising the goal is to sell the benefits of the product, not its attributes. An attribute is simply a feature of the product such as its easy-open package or special formulation. A benefit is what consumers will receive or achieve by using the product. A benefit should answer the consumer's question "What's in it for me?" Benefits might be such things as convenience, pleasure, savings, or relief. A quick test to determine whether you are offering attributes or benefits in your advertising is to ask "So?" Consider this example:

> *Attribute:* "The Gillette MACH3 shaving system has three blades aligned progressively nearer to the face, each coated with a microscopic layer of carbon, mounted on a forward-pivoting shaver to automatically adjust to the curves and contours of a man's face." "So . . . ?"
> *Benefit:* "So, you'll get a closer, smoother, and safer shave than ever before with fewer strokes and less irritation."[15]

Marketing research and intuition are usually used to unearth the perceived benefits of a product and to rank consumers' preferences for these benefits. Gillette's rival Schick is advertising its razors on the basis of safety. Schick's research shows that safety is among the top three attributes men look for in a razor. As a result, its advertising campaign touts the benefits of a safe shave rather than a close shave.[16]

Developing and Evaluating Advertising Appeals An **advertising appeal** identifies a reason for a person to buy a product. Developing advertising appeals, a challenging task, is typically the responsibility of the creative people in the advertising agency. Advertising appeals typically play off of consumers' emotions, such as fear or love, or address some need or want the consumer has, such as a need for convenience or the desire to save money.

advertising appeal
Reason for a person to buy a product.

Advertising campaigns can focus on one or more advertising appeals. Often the appeals are quite general, thus allowing the firm to develop a number of subthemes or minicampaigns using both advertising and sales promotion. Several possible advertising appeals are listed in Exhibit 13.3.

Choosing the best appeal from those developed normally requires market research. Criteria for evaluation include desirability, exclusiveness, and believability. The appeal first must make a positive impression on and be desirable to the target

exhibit 13.3

Common Advertising Appeals

Profit	Lets consumers know whether the product will save them money, make them money, or keep them from losing money
Health	Appeals to those who are body-conscious or who want to be healthy
Love or romance	Is used often in selling cosmetics and perfumes
Fear	Can center around social embarrassment, growing old, or losing one's health; because of its power, requires advertiser to exercise care in execution
Admiration	Is the reason that celebrity spokespeople are used so often in advertising
Convenience	Is often used for fast-food restaurants and microwave foods
Fun and pleasure	Are the key to advertising vacations, beer, amusement parks, and more
Vanity and egotism	Are used most often for expensive or conspicuous items such as cars and clothing
Environmental consciousness	Centers around protecting the environment and being considerate of others in the community

market. It must also be exclusive or unique; consumers must be able to distinguish the advertiser's message from competitors' messages. Most important, the appeal should be believable. An appeal that makes extravagant claims not only wastes promotional dollars but also creates ill will for the advertiser.

The advertising appeal selected for the campaign becomes what advertisers call its **unique selling proposition**. The unique selling proposition usually becomes the campaign's slogan. Gillette's MACH3 advertising campaign aimed at men carries the slogan "Three blades, fewer strokes, less irritation." This is also MACH3's unique selling proposition, implying that its razor's high-tech features are important and can help reduce discomfort caused by shaving.[17]

All advertising campaigns revolve around an advertising appeal. What do you think is the advertising appeal for this DiGiorno ad? The executional style? Consult Exhibits 13.3 and 13.4.
Courtesy Kraft Foods, Inc.

Effective slogans often become so ingrained that consumers can immediately conjure up images of the product just by hearing the slogan. For example, most consumers can easily name the companies and products behind these memorable slogans or even hum the jingle that goes along with some of them: "Have it your way," "Tastes great, less filling," "Ring around the collar," and "Tum te Tum Tum." Advertisers often revive old slogans or jingles in the hope that the nostalgia will create good feelings with consumers. Miller Brewing Company recently reintroduced advertising for its Miller High Life brand using the "Champagne of beers" slogan, not used since the early 1980s, in the hope of inspiring nostalgic baby boomers to boost sales.[18] Similarly, after a decade-long absence from national television, StarKist's Charlie the Tuna appeared in television ads with the famous "Sorry, Charlie," tag line.[19]

StarKist Foods

How does StarKist use Charlie to promote its tuna on the company's Web site? Do you think he is still an effective advertising tool? Why or why not?
http://www.starkist.com/

on line

unique selling proposition Desirable, exclusive, and believable advertising appeal selected as the theme for a campaign.

Executing the Message Message execution is the way the advertisement portrays its information. In general, the AIDA plan is a good blueprint for executing an advertising message. Any ad should immediately draw the reader's, viewer's, or listener's attention. The advertiser must then use the message to hold consumers' interest, create desire for the good or service, and ultimately motivate action: a purchase.

The style in which the message is executed is one of the most creative elements of an advertisement. Exhibit 13.4 lists some examples of executional styles

exhibit 13.4

Ten Common Executional Styles for Advertising

Slice-of-life	Is popular when advertising household and personal products; depicts people in normal settings, such as at the dinner table
Lifestyle	Shows how well the product will fit in with the consumer's lifestyle. Volkswagen ads showing two silent young men on an aimless Sunday drive in a VW Golf appeal to the lifestyle of Generation Xers.
Spokesperson/ testimonial	Can feature a celebrity, company official, or typical consumer making a testimonial or endorsing a product. Basketball star Grant Hill endorses Fila athletic shoes and Shaquille O'Neal drinks Pepsi.
Fantasy	Creates a fantasy for the viewer built around use of the product, such as Levi's spot of jean-clad strangers on an elevator, who eye each other, share the same daydream—falling in love, marriage, raising a family—and then silently go their separate ways.
Humorous	Advertisers often use humor in their ads, such as Snicker's "Not Going Anywhere for a While" campaign featuring hundreds of souls waiting, sometimes impatiently, to get into heaven.
Real/animated product symbols	Create a character that represents the product in advertisements, such as the Energizer bunny, the Budweiser frogs and lizards, or Old Navy's canine mascot, Magic
Mood or image	Builds a mood or image around the product, such as peace, love, or beauty. DeBeers ads depicting shadowy silhouettes wearing diamond engagement rings and diamond necklaces portray passion and intimacy while extolling that a "diamond is forever."
Demonstration	Shows consumers the expected benefit. Many consumer products use this technique. Laundry detergent spots are famous for demonstrating how their product will clean clothes whiter and brighter.
Musical	Conveys the message of the advertisement through song. Examples are Mercedes-Benz ads depicting historical car shots while strains of Marlene Dietrich's "Falling in Love Again" are heard in the background and the "Khakis Swing" spots by The Gap, which feature khakis-clad dancers swinging to a Louis Prima tune.
Scientific	Uses research or scientific evidence to give a brand superiority over competitors. Pain relievers like Advil, Bayer, and Excedrin use scientific evidence in their ads.

used by advertisers. Executional styles often dictate what type of media is to be employed to convey the message. Scientific executional styles lend themselves well to print advertising where more information can be conveyed. On the other hand, demonstration and musical styles are more likely found in broadcast advertising.

Injecting humor into an advertisement is a popular and effective executional style. Humorous executional styles are more often used in radio and television advertising than in print or magazine advertising where humor is less easily communicated. Humorous ads are typically used for lower risk, routine purchases such as candy, cigarettes and soft drinks than for higher risk purchases or those that are expensive, durable, or flamboyant.[20] Mars, for example, recently used humor in its television advertising using animated M&M characters. The ads led to a 3 percent increase in sales and better "likability" for the M&Ms brand.[21]

Executional styles for foreign advertising are often quite different from those we are accustomed to in the United States. Sometimes they are sexually oriented or aesthetically imaginative. For example, European advertising avoids the direct-sell approaches common in United States ads and instead is more indirect, more symbolic, and above all more visual. Nike, known in the United States for "in-your-face" advertising and irreverent slogans such as "Just Do It," discovered that its brash advertising did not appeal to Europeans. A television commercial of Satan and his demons playing soccer against a team of Nike endorsers was a hit in America. However, many European stations refused to run it, saying it was too scary and offensive to show in prime time, when kids were watching.[22]

GLOBAL

Japanese advertising is known for relying on fantasy and mood to sell products. Ads in Japan notoriously lack the emphatic selling demonstrations found in U.S. advertising, limit the exposure of unique product features, and avoid direct comparisons to competitors' products. Japanese ads often feature cartoon characters or place the actors in irrelevant situations. For example, one advertisement promotes an insect spray while showing the actor having teeth extracted at the dentist's office. One explanation of Japan's preference for soft-sell advertising is cultural: Japanese consumers are naturally suspicious of someone who needs to extol the virtues of a product. Additionally, unlike advertising agencies in the United States, which consider working for competing companies to be unethical, Japan's larger ad agencies customarily maintain business relationships with competing advertisers. Ads are less hard-hitting so as not to offend other clients.[23]

Advertising in Japan takes a soft-sell approach because Japanese consumers are naturally suspicious of companies that need to emphasize the virtues of a product.
© Tom Wagner/SABA

Global advertising managers are increasingly concerned with the issue of standardization versus customization of their advertising appeals and executional styles when delivering advertising messages around the world. Read about this dilemma in the "Global Perspectives" box.

Make Media Decisions

Describe media evaluation and selection techniques

As mentioned at the beginning of the chapter, U.S. advertisers spend over $187 billion annually on media advertising. Where does all this money go? About 45 percent, or $84 billion, is spent in media monitored by national reporting services—magazines, newspapers, outdoor, radio, television, Yellow Pages, and the Internet. The remaining 55 percent, or $103 billion, is spent in unmonitored media, such as direct mail, trade exhibits, cooperative advertising, brochures, couponing, catalogs, and special events. Exhibit 13.5 (see p. 469) breaks down the $84 billion spent in monitored advertising by media type. As you can see, nearly half of every dollar spent in measured media goes toward purchasing time for TV ads. The nation's largest advertisers, such as those listed in Exhibit 13.1 at the beginning of the chapter, spend even more on television advertising—about sixty-six cents of every dollar spent.[24]

global perspectives

Global Challenges for Advertisers

One of the hottest debates for global advertising professionals today is whether to customize or standardize advertising. On one side of the fence are those who believe the advertisement's appeals and execution style should be tailored to each country or region to be most effective. Because cultures perceive and react to advertising differently, this school of thought advocates that the advertiser must know something about the intended audiences' culture in order to communicate effectively.

Kodak, for instance, favors a customized approach to advertising in China because consumer tastes and values vary between mainland China and the more progressive Taiwan and Hong Kong. In Taiwan and Hong Kong, which are quickly catching up to the United States and Europe in film sales volume, Kodak targets a young, innovative audience. In mainland China, which is comparatively far behind technologically except in a few urban centers, the approach will be more lifestyle oriented.

Some would disagree with this distinction, however, and would advocate a single advertising campaign for all countries. Following this standardized approach, an advertiser would develop one advertising campaign, appeal, and execution style and deliver this same message, translated into the language of each country, to all target markets. Supporters of this approach insist that consumers everywhere have the same basic needs and desires and can therefore be persuaded by universal advertising appeals. Furthermore, they say, standardized advertising campaigns create unified brand images worldwide and the advertiser eliminates the inefficiencies of trying to reinvent the meaning of its brand in every country. Athletic shoemaker Reebok recently embarked on a $100 million global ad campaign in an attempt to make its message more cohesive throughout the world. In the past, Reebok sent out confusing messages—it was known as a running shoe in the United Kingdom and a fashion statement in the United States. Moreover, Reebok generally was seen as a women's fitness and aerobics sneaker, not an ideal image for winning over male consumers.

Possibly the best answer to this dilemma is to use a mixture of standardization and customization—that is, standardizing the message while paying attention to local differences in the execution of the message. For example, Unilever uses a standardized appeal when promoting its Dove soap but it uses models from Australia, France, Germany, and Italy to appeal to women in those places. Although this mixture of standardization and customization seems to be successful for many global marketers, it only works as long as the message truly plays to a worldwide audience. For example, because parents around the world are deeply concerned about the welfare of their children, advertising for childrens' products generally represents an area of universal concern or agreement. Fisher-Price, therefore, is effective using a standardized approach because no matter where they live, parents want the best for their kids. Similarly, IBM was successful with its "Solutions for a Small Planet" campaign because people all over the world have similar information and computing needs. The global imagery of the campaign is achieved through the use of the same footage in each country. The difference is the use of local subtitles to translate the "foreign" language of the commercial.

Although efficiencies can be achieved by producing a single advertising campaign and message for worldwide use, the approach only makes sense if it does not run counter to social mores, ethnic issues, or religious taboos. For example, a food commercial showing hungry kids licking their lips would be taboo in a country where exposing the tongue is considered obscene. Similarly, an ad portraying a young couple running barefoot, hand-in-hand down a beautiful, sandy beach would be offensive in a country in which naked feet are never to be seen by the public.[25]

Some of the marketers discussed here have been successful using a global approach to advertising, but not every product or service is suited for a unified advertising message. What types of products do you think would benefit from a standardized approach to advertising? What types would fare better using a tailored approach?

exhibit 13.5

National Ad Spending in Measured Media for 1997

Medium	Percent of Total Ad Spending
Magazines	16.2
Newspapers	20.6
Outdoor media	1.7
Television	45.0
Radio	3.0
Yellow Pages	12.8
Internet	0.01

SOURCE: "National Ad Spending by Media," *Advertising Age*, 28 September 1998, p. s50.

Media Types

Advertising media are channels that advertisers use in mass communication. The six major advertising media are newspapers, magazines, radio, television, outdoor media, and the Internet and World Wide Web. Exhibit 13.6 summarizes the advantages and disadvantages of these major channels. In recent years, however, alternative media vehicles have emerged that give advertisers innovative ways to reach their target audience and avoid advertising clutter.

Newspapers The advantages of newspaper advertising include geographic flexibility and timeliness. Because copywriters can usually prepare newspaper ads quickly and at a reasonable cost, local merchants can reach their target market almost daily. However, because newspapers are generally a mass-market medium, they may not be the best vehicle for marketers trying to reach a very narrow market. For example, local newspapers are not the best media vehicles for reaching purchasers of specialty steel products or even tropical fish. These target consumers make up very small, specialized markets. Newspaper advertising also encounters a lot of distractions from competing ads and news stories; thus one company's ad may not be particularly visible.

The largest source of newspaper ad revenue is local retailers, classified ads, and cooperative advertising. In **cooperative advertising**, the manufacturer and the retailer split the costs of advertising the manufacturer's brand. One reason manufacturers use cooperative advertising is the impracticality of listing all their dealers in national advertising. Also, co-op advertising encourages retailers to devote more effort to the manufacturer's lines.

cooperative advertising
Arrangement in which the manufacturer and the retailer split the costs of advertising the manufacturer's brand.

Magazines Compared to the cost of other media, the cost per contact in magazine advertising is usually high. However, the cost per potential customer may be much lower, because magazines are often targeted to specialized audiences and thus reach more potential customers. The most frequent types of products advertised in magazines include automobiles, apparel, computers, and cigarettes.

One of the main advantages of magazine advertising is its market selectivity. Magazines are published for virtually every market segment. For instance, *PC Week* is a leading computer magazine; *Working Mother* targets one of the fastest growing consumer segments; *Sports Illustrated* is a successful all-around sporting publication; *Marketing News* is a trade magazine for the marketing professional; *The Source* is a niche publication geared to young urbanites with a passion for hip-hop music.

Radio Radio has several strengths as an advertising medium: selectivity and audience segmentation, a large out-of-home audience, low unit and production costs, timeliness, and geographic flexibility. Local advertisers are the most frequent users of radio advertising contributing over three-quarters of all radio ad revenues. Like newspapers, radio also lends itself well to cooperative advertising.

exhibit 13.6

Advantages and Disadvantages of Major Advertising Media

Medium	Advantages	Disadvantages
Newspapers	Geographic selectivity and flexibility; short-term advertiser commitments; news value and immediacy; year-round readership; high individual market coverage; co-op and local tie-in availability; short lead time	Little demographic selectivity; limited color capabilities; low pass-along rate; may be expensive
Magazines	Good reproduction, especially for color; demographic selectivity; regional selectivity; local market selectivity; relatively long advertising life; high pass-along rate	Long-term advertiser commitments; slow audience buildup; limited demonstration capabilities; lack of urgency; long lead time
Radio	Low cost; immediacy of message; can be scheduled on short notice; relatively no seasonal change in audience; highly portable; short-term advertiser commitments; entertainment carryover	No visual treatment; short advertising life of message; high frequency required to generate comprehension and retention; distractions from background sound; commercial clutter
Television	Ability to reach a wide, diverse audience; low cost per thousand; creative opportunities for demonstration; immediacy of messages; entertainment carryover; demographic selectivity with cable stations	Short life of message; some consumer skepticism about claims; high campaign cost; little demographic selectivity with network stations; long-term advertiser commitments; long lead times required for production; commercial clutter
Outdoor media	Repetition; moderate cost; flexibility; geographic selectivity	Short message; lack of demographic selectivity; high "noise" level distracting audience
Internet and World Wide Web	Fastest growing medium; ability to reach a narrow target audience; relatively short lead time required for creating Web-based advertising; moderate cost	Difficult to measure ad effectiveness and return on investment; ad exposure relies on "click-through" from banner ads; not all consumers have access to the Internet

Long merely an afterthought to many advertisers, radio advertising is enjoying a resurgence in popularity. As Americans become more mobile and pressed for time, other media such as network television and newspapers struggle to retain viewers and readers. Radio listening, however, has grown in step with population increases mainly because its immediate, portable nature meshes so well with a fast-paced lifestyle. The ability to target specific demographic groups is also a major selling point for radio stations, attracting advertisers who are pursuing narrowly defined audiences that are more likely to respond to certain kinds of ads and products. Moreover, radio listeners tend to listen habitually and at predictable times, with the most popular radio listening hours during "drive time," when commuters form a vast captive audience.[26]

Fox Network
ABC
What kind of advertising is done on Fox Network's Web site? Compare this with the site for ABC. What differences do you notice? Why do you think a television network would choose not to sell ad space on its Web site?
http://www.fox.com/ **http://www.abc.com/**

on line

Television Because television is an audiovisual medium, it provides advertisers with many creative opportunities. Television broadcasters include network television, independent stations, cable television, and a relative newcomer, direct broadcast satellite television. ABC, CBS, NBC, and the Fox Network dominate network television, which reaches a wide and diverse market. Conversely, cable television and direct broadcast satellite systems, such as DirecTV and PrimeStar, offer consumers a multitude of channels devoted exclusively to particular audiences—for example, women, children, African-Americans, nature lovers, senior citizens, Christians, Hispanics, sports fans, fitness enthusiasts. Because of its targeted channels, cable television is often characterized as "narrowcasting" by media buyers.

Advertising time on television can be very expensive, especially for network stations and popular cable stations. A thirty-second spot during an ESPN regular season NFL football game goes for $105,000, whereas the same spot sells for $45,000 during Comedy Central's popular *South Park* comedy.[27] Rates are even more expensive during prime time or special television events. One thirty-second spot during 1999's Super Bowl telecast, for example, cost advertisers about $1.6 million, and advertisers forked over a record $1.7 million to $1.8 million for a thirty-second spot during the last episode of *Seinfeld*.[28]

A relatively new form of television advertising is the **infomercial**, a thirty-minute or longer advertisement. Infomercials are an attractive advertising vehicle for many marketers because of the cheap air time and the relatively small production cost. Advertisers say the infomercial is an ideal way to present complicated information to potential customers, which other advertising vehicles typically don't allow time to do. The Arthritis Foundation recently traded in its annual telethon for an infomercial for their fund-raising. The infomercial sold subscriptions for *Arthritis Today*, membership to the foundation, and various resources, including a guide called "101 Tips for Better Living" and a videotape on exercises for arthritis sufferers.[29]

infomercial
Thirty-minute or longer advertisement that looks more like a TV talk show than a sales pitch.

Outdoor Media Outdoor or out-of-home advertising is a flexible, low-cost medium that may take a variety of forms. Examples include billboards, skywriting, giant inflatables, minibillboards in malls and on bus stop shelters, signs in sports arenas, lighted moving signs in bus terminals and airports, and ads painted on the sides of cars, trucks, buses, or even water towers. Outdoor advertising reaches a broad and diverse market. Therefore, it is normally limited to promoting convenience products and selected shopping products such as cigarettes, business services, and automobiles.

The main advantage of outdoor advertising over other media is that its exposure frequency is very high, yet the amount of clutter from competing ads is very low. Outdoor advertising also has the ability to be customized to local marketing needs. For this reason, retail stores are the largest outdoor advertisers.

Outdoor advertising has been growing in recent years mainly due to the fragmentation of other media, more exposure as people spend more time commuting, and improved billboard quality through the use of computers.[30] Outdoor advertising is also becoming more innovative. For example, when Delta Air Lines wanted to make a big splash earlier this year to launch its new business class service, it kicked off the effort by creating a so-called living billboard overlooking Manhattan's Times Square. Live humans could be seen lounging in a replica of its redesigned airline seats high above the street below.[31]

ON LINE

The Internet and World Wide Web The World Wide Web and the Internet have undoubtedly shaken up the advertising world. With ad revenue approaching $1 billion, the Internet has established itself as a solid advertising medium.[32] Traditional marketers nearly tripled their Internet advertising spending to an average of three-quarters of a million dollars from 1997 to 1998. Additionally, whereas only 38 percent of companies were advertising on the

Internet in 1997, 68 percent were doing so in 1998. Although on-line advertising has made significant gains since the early 1990s, however, it still makes up only a small portion of companies' total advertising budgets. The two top barriers to Internet advertising, according to a survey conducted by the Association of National Advertisers, are the difficulty of tracking return on investment and the lack of reliable and accurate measurement information.[33]

Popular Internet sites and search engines such as Netscape and Yahoo!, as well as on-line service providers like America Online, generally sell advertising space, called "banners," to major consumer product and service companies to promote their goods and services. Internet surfers click on these banners, which link them to the advertiser's site. New forms of Web advertising are starting to transcend the static company logo and message in a banner ad. Using new technologies such as Shockwave and Java, advertisers are developing Web ads that incorporate interactivity, electronic commerce, sound, and animation. For example, a banner ad from John Hancock Mutual Life Insurance Company lets users input their children's ages to find out how much money they need to invest each month for a college education.[34]

A recent survey on the effectiveness of on-line banner ads concluded that they actually work as well at boosting brand and advertising awareness as their TV or magazine counterparts. On-line ads also boost the likelihood that a consumer will want to buy a product, just as traditional ads do. Best of all, on-line ads are even more memorable than commercials on TV, the survey data show. More people could recall seeing banner ads versus seeing a TV ad after one exposure.[35]

However, on-line media pose a daunting challenge for advertisers because consumers have more control over the marketing relationship than they have had with traditional advertising media. With traditional media, consumers passively view commercials during their favorite sitcom or avoid commercials by pushing a button on a remote-control device. Surfers on the Internet, however, generally have to find the marketer rather than vice versa. Some have likened the Internet to an electronic trade show and a virtual flea market—a trade show in that it can be thought of as a giant international exhibition hall where potential buyers can enter at will and visit prospective sellers; a flea market in the sense that it possesses the fundamental characteristics of openness, informality, and interactivity similar to a community marketplace.[36] One Web site actually pays consumers to view ads that have been automatically targeted to fit their interests. Users must peruse each Web ad to its last page, then click on a special symbol to receive credit. Ad viewers can choose to have their earnings transferred to an on-line bank account or applied toward frequent flyer miles, a product purchase, or a charitable donation. They can even use their earnings to credit their Visa card account.[37]

Another challenge for on-line and Internet advertisers is measuring the effectiveness of their electronic advertisement or site. Although there are methods already in use that can count the number of visitors to an advertiser's Web site, advertisers don't know how their site ranks compared to the competition. Also lacking are the kinds of in-depth demographic and psychographic information about Web page users that television, magazines, radio, and newspapers provide about their viewers and subscribers.[38]

The Internet and World Wide Web provide countless opportunities for entrepreneurs and small business startups. One entrepreneurial endeavor seeks to sell on-line advertising space targeted to the college crowd. Read more about on-line college newspaper broker Future Pages in the "Entrepreneurial Insights" box that follows. Advertising on the Internet and World Wide Web is discussed in more detail in Chapter 14, "Internet Marketing."

Alternative Media To cut through the clutter of traditional advertising media, advertisers are now looking for new ways to promote their products. Alternative vehicles include fax machines, video shopping carts in grocery stores, computer screen savers, CD-ROMs, interactive kiosks in department stores, and advertisements run before movies at the cinema and on rented videocassettes. In fact, just about anything can become a vehicle for displaying advertising. Walt Disney recently placed ads promoting *Mulan* and *Armageddon* on the rubbery dividers shoppers use to separate their groceries from another person's at the checkout aisle.[39]

Media Selection Considerations

Promotional objectives and the type of advertising a company plans to use strongly affect the selection of media. An important element in any advertising campaign is the

entrepreneurial insights

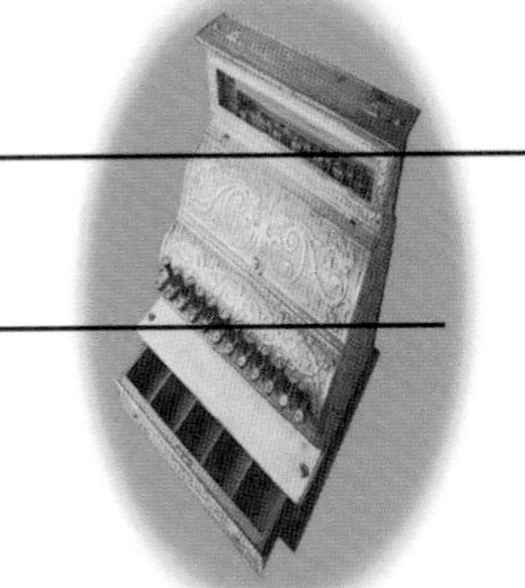

Web Ad Broker Start-up Helps Marketers Reach the College Crowd

Marketers who want to hit the college crowd in their on-line media buys but don't know where to start have an ally. Their link to the college market lies with Future Pages College Network, the Internet's leading collegiate advertising broker. Future Pages provides custom advertising solutions for marketers wanting to reach the 12.5 million college students age eighteen to twenty-four who access the Internet on a regular basis.

Future Pages' core business is brokering ads for over 110 on-line college publications across the country reaching a potential student body of about two million. The St. Paul, Minnesota-based start-up partners with on-line college publications to reach students at schools such as Boston University, Duke University, Harvard University, and Stanford University. Banner ads brokered through Future Pages cost marketers $35 per thousand impressions.

Since its launch in 1996, Future Pages College Network has attracted some heavy-duty marketers. Internet music site SonicNet, for instance, recently launched an end-of-school-year on-line effort to gain recognition among college students in its quest to top MTV's on-line music site. Computer software giant Microsoft recently advertised through the Future Pages College Network offering free copies of its Internet Explorer browser to students, as well as an introductory campaign for its new Windows 98 operating system. Future Pages has also completed successful campaigns for Paramount Pictures' Star Trek and Encyclopaedia Britannica.

Advertising through on-line college newspapers is complemented by Future Pages' partnerships with Internet sites frequented by college students and educators. Advertising placed on sites where students like to hang out helps marketers carry their message even further than on-line college newspapers alone. Some important sites in Future Pages' network include *theglobe.com*, a virtual community of 960,000 subscribers mostly in the eighteen to twenty-four age group; *TWEN*, The West Education Network, an on-line learning center for law students; *College-beat.com*; an on-line community of colleges and universities; and *Virtual Stock Exchange*, a destination site for college students participating in the Virtual Stock Exchange game.

Cross-promotional opportunities are also available to Future Pages' advertisers. With its off-line network, Future Pages provides advertisers access to alternative campus media such as campus billboards, inserts, and custom publishing, campus posters, and ads on newspaper distribution stands.

Future Pages got its start by helping small business owners create their own mini-Web sites in a small business directory. Feeling that they were not focused enough, founders and former fraternity brothers Lance Stendal, 28, and Tom Borgerding, 24, turned to Alan Fine, president of Strategic Management Solutions and professor at the Carlson School of Business, University of Minnesota. Fine encouraged Stendal and Borgerding to find a niche on the Internet in which they could excel. Knowing that almost all college students were on-line and that most college newspapers had an on-line presence, Stendal and Borgerding narrowed their focus by becoming the middleman between the advertiser and the college newspaper. Now the company brings together major marketers such as Microsoft and Sprint with on-line college newspapers such as Arizona State University's *State Press*, the *Harvard Crimson*, and the University of Texas's *Daily Texan*.

Borgerding, vice president of marketing and sales for Future Pages, feels that the benefit of their network partnership extends beyond advertisers alone. "Our mission focuses not only on providing advertisers with the best Internet tool to reach this market, but also helping to foster education to the partners we work with. We strive to create successful campaigns and at the same time help the schools by educating them about Internet advertising."[40]

You can visit Future Pages' Web site at **www.futurepages.com**.

Placing ads on interactive kiosks is one new way advertisers are finding useful to promote their products.

media mix
Combination of media to be used for a promotional campaign.

cost per contact
Cost of reaching one member of the target market.

reach
Number of target consumers exposed to a commercial at least once during a specific period, usually four weeks.

media mix, the combination of media to be used. Media mix decisions are typically based on cost per contact, reach, frequency, and target audience considerations.

Cost per contact is the cost of reaching one member of the target market. Naturally, as the size of the audience increases, so does the total cost. Cost per contact enables an advertiser to compare media vehicles such as television versus radio or magazine versus newspaper, or more specifically *Newsweek* versus *Time*. An advertiser debating whether to spend local advertising dollars for TV spots or radio spots could consider the cost per contact of each. The advertiser might then pick the vehicle with the lowest cost per contact to maximize advertising punch for the money spent.

Reach is the number of different target consumers who are exposed to a commercial at least once during a specific period, usually four weeks. The media plans for product introductions and attempts at increasing brand awareness usually emphasize reach. For example, an advertiser might try to reach 70 percent of the target audience during the first three months of the campaign. Because the typical ad is short lived and because often only a small portion of an ad may be perceived at one time, advertisers repeat their ads so consumers will remember the message. **Frequency** is the number of times an individual is exposed to a message. Average frequency is used by advertisers to measure the intensity of a specific medium's coverage. Exhibit 13.7 provides a glimpse at exposure and frequency rates for some of today's top brands.

exhibit 13.7

Exposure and Frequency of Top TV Advertisers*
Week of May 25–31, 1998

Advertised Brand	Household Exposures (in millions)**	Number of Times Ad Aired
Burger King	285.8	57
JCPenney	181.6	31
Pontiac Grand Am	173.3	25
Boston Market	166.1	27
Ford autos and trucks	162.5	21
Honda Accord	152.4	23
Nissan Altima	150.7	14
AT&T	143.4	22
Wendy's	137.0	26
Miller Lite	131.8	12

*Advertisers getting the most exposure during prime-time TV on ABC, CBS, NBC, Fox, UPN, and WB networks
**One household might be exposed to several ads each day.
SOURCES: "Nielsen's Top TV Advertisers," *USA Today*, 15 June 1998, p. 8B; Nielsen Media Research, Monitor Plus Service.

Women's Wire

Visit the Women's Wire Web site. Are there any ad placements on the site that you have seen recently on television or heard on the radio? Why do you think advertisers have chosen this site over or in conjunction with traditional advertising venues?
http://www.womenswire.com/

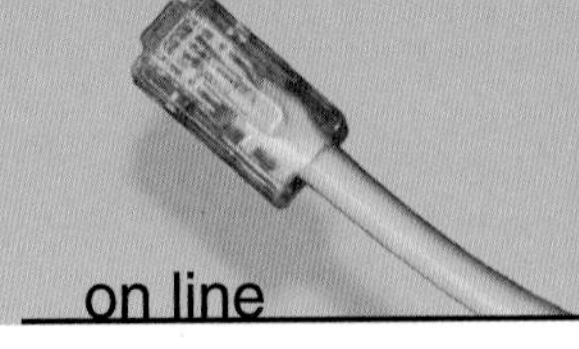

on line

Media selection is also a matter of matching the advertising medium with the product's target market. If marketers are trying to reach teenage females, they might select *Seventeen* magazine. If they are trying to reach consumers over fifty years old, they may choose *Modern Maturity* magazine. A medium's ability to reach a precisely defined market is its **audience selectivity**. Some media vehicles, like general newspapers and network television, appeal to a wide cross section of the population. Others—such as *Bride's, Popular Mechanics, Architectural Digest,* MTV, ESPN, and Christian radio stations—appeal to very specific groups. Viewer profiles for a sampling of popular cable networks are presented in Exhibit 13.8.

frequency
Number of times an individual is exposed to a given message during a specific period.

audience selectivity
Ability of an advertising medium to reach a precisely defined market.

media schedule
Designation of the media, the specific publications or programs, and the insertion dates of advertising.

continuous media schedule
Media scheduling strategy, used for products in the latter stages of the product life cycle, in which advertising is run steadily throughout the advertising period.

flighted media schedule
Media scheduling strategy in which ads are run heavily every other month or every two weeks, to achieve a greater impact with an increased frequency and reach at those times.

pulsing media schedule
Media scheduling strategy that uses continuous scheduling throughout the year coupled with a flighted schedule during the best sales periods.

Media Scheduling

After choosing the media for the advertising campaign, advertisers must schedule the ads. A **media schedule** designates the medium or media to be used (such as magazines, television, or radio), the specific vehicles (such as *People* magazine, "Friends" TV show, or Howard Stern's national radio program), and the insertion dates of the advertising.

There are three basic types of media schedules:

- Products in the latter stages of the product life cycle, which are advertised on a reminder basis, use a **continuous media schedule**. A continuous schedule allows the advertising to run steadily throughout the advertising period. Examples include Ivory soap, Coca-Cola, and Marlboro cigarettes.
- With a **flighted media schedule**, the advertiser may schedule the ads heavily every other month or every two weeks to achieve a greater impact with an increased frequency and reach at those times. Movie studios might schedule television advertising on Wednesday and Thursday nights, when moviegoers are deciding which films to see that weekend. A variation is the **pulsing media schedule**, which combines continuous scheduling with flighting. Continuous

exhibit 13.8

Selected Cable Television Network Viewer Profiles

Bravo Network	Popular with adults 25 to 54 with 4+ years of college and household incomes over $50,000
Cartoon Network	Delivers 20% of all kid viewing of children's programming; 88% national awareness with children age 6 to 11
Comedy Central	Appeals to adults 18 to 49 with household incomes over $75,000
Goodlife Television Network	Dedicated to the over-49 viewer, the fastest growing demographic
Home & Garden Television (HGTV)	Appeals strongly to men and women with incomes of $50,000 or more who own their own homes; most likely to be in professional or managerial position
Lifetime Network	Top cable network aimed at working women
MTV	Median viewer age of 22.2 years; reaches 22.3 million persons age 12 to 34 each week.

SOURCE: "1998 Cable Programming Guide," *Advertising Age*, 8 June 1998.

advertising is simply heavier during the best sale periods. A retail department store may advertise on a year-round basis but place more advertising during holiday sale periods such as Thanksgiving, Christmas, and back-to-school.

- Certain times of the year call for a **seasonal media schedule**. Products like Contac cold tablets and Coppertone suntan lotion, which are used more during certain times of the year, tend to follow a seasonal strategy. Advertising for champagne is concentrated during the weeks of Christmas and New Year's, whereas health clubs concentrate their advertising in January to take advantage of New Year's resolutions.

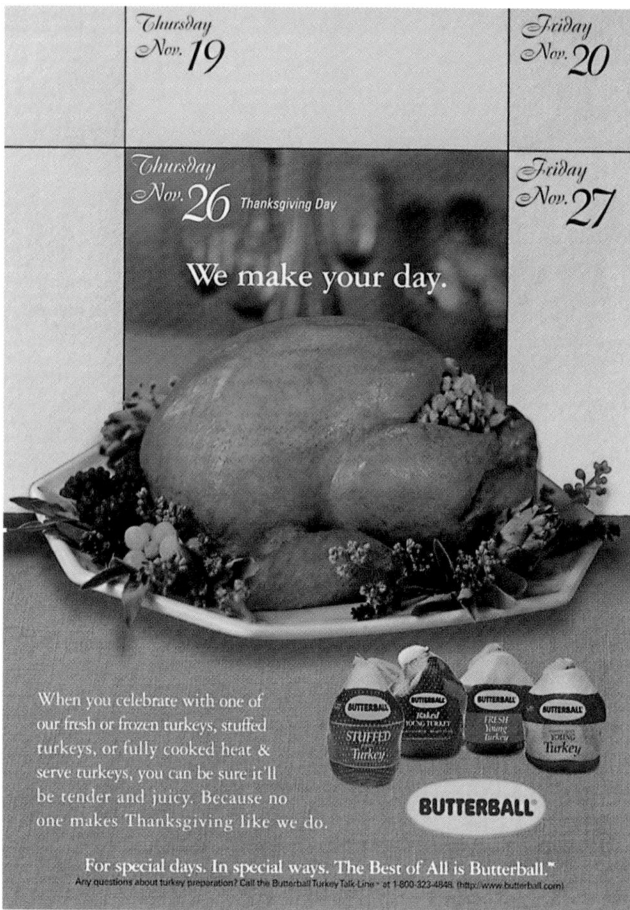

Thursday Nov. 19
Friday Nov. 20
Thursday Nov. 26 Thanksgiving Day
Friday Nov. 27
We make your day.
When you celebrate with one of our fresh or frozen turkeys, stuffed turkeys, or fully cooked heat & serve turkeys, you can be sure it'll be tender and juicy. Because no one makes Thanksgiving like we do.
BUTTERBALL
STUFFED Turkey
FRESH Young Turkey
Turkey
BUTTERBALL®
For special days. In special ways. The Best of All is Butterball.™
Any questions about turkey preparation? Call the Butterball Turkey Talk-Line at 1-800-323-4848. (http://www.butterball.com)

This ad for Butterball turkeys is an example of a seasonal advertising strategy. Besides Thanksgiving, what other times of year do you think Butterball would benefit from concentrated advertising? How could these be a part of an IMC? Courtesy The Butterball Turkey Company

Evaluate the Ad Campaign

Evaluating an advertising campaign can be the most demanding task facing advertisers. How do advertisers know whether the campaign led to an increase in sales or market share or elevated awareness of the product? Most advertising campaigns aim to create an image for the good or service instead of asking for action, so their real effect is unknown. So many variables shape the effectiveness of an ad that, in many cases, advertisers must guess whether their money has been well spent. Despite this gray area, marketers spend a considerable amount of time studying advertising effectiveness and its probable impact on sales, market share, or awareness.

Testing ad effectiveness can be done either before or after the campaign. Before a campaign is released, marketing managers use pretests to determine the best advertising appeal, layout, and media vehicle. After advertisers implement a campaign, they often conduct tests to measure its effectiveness. Several monitoring techniques can be used to determine whether the campaign has met its original goals. Even if a campaign has been highly successful, advertisers still typically do a postcampaign analysis. They assess how the campaign might have been more efficient and what factors contributed to its success.

Sales Promotion

seasonal media schedule
Media scheduling strategy that runs advertising only during times of the year when the product is most likely to be used.

In addition to using advertising, public relations, and personal selling, marketing managers can use sales promotion to increase the effectiveness of their promotional efforts. *Sales promotion* is marketing communication activities, other than advertising, personal selling, and public relations, in which a short-term incentive motivates consumers or members of the distribution channel to purchase a good or service immediately, either by lowering the price or by adding value.

Advertising offers the consumer a reason to buy; sales promotion offers an incentive to buy. Both are important, but sales promotion is usually cheaper than advertising and easier to measure. A major national TV advertising campaign may cost over $2 million to create, produce, and place. In contrast, a newspaper coupon campaign or promotional contest may cost only about half as much. It is hard to figure exactly how many people buy a product as a result of seeing a TV ad.

However, with sales promotion, marketers know the precise number of coupons redeemed or the number of contest entries.

Sales promotion is usually targeted toward either of two distinctly different markets. **Consumer sales promotion** is targeted to the ultimate consumer market. **Trade sales promotion** is directed to members of the marketing channel, such as wholesalers and retailers. Sales promotion has become an important element in a marketer's integrated marketing communications program. (See Chapter 10.) Sales promotion expenditures have been steadily increasing over the last several years as a result of increased competition, the ever-expanding array of available media choices, consumers and retailers demanding more deals from manufacturers, and the continued reliance on accountable and measurable marketing strategies. In addition, product and service marketers who have traditionally ignored sales promotion activities, such as power companies and restaurants, have discovered the marketing power of sales promotion. In fact, PROMO Magazine estimates that marketers spend some $20 billion a year on advertisements in which their sales promotions were either the star or co-star.[41]

consumer sales promotion
Sales promotion activities to the ultimate consumer.

trade sales promotion
Sales promotion activities targeted to a channel member, such as a wholesaler or retailer.

The Objectives of Sales Promotion

5
Define and state the objectives of sales promotion

Sales promotion usually works best in affecting behavior rather than attitudes. Immediate purchase is the goal of sales promotion, regardless of the form it takes. Therefore, it seems to make more sense when planning a sales promotion campaign to target customers according to their general behavior. For instance, is the consumer loyal to your product or to your competitor's? Does the consumer switch brands readily in favor of the best deal? Does the consumer buy only the least expensive product, no matter what? Does the consumer buy any products in your category at all?

The objectives of a promotion depend on the general behavior of target consumers. (See Exhibit 13.9.) For example, marketers who are targeting loyal users of their product actually don't want to change behavior. Instead, they need to reinforce existing behavior or increase product usage. An effective tool for strengthening brand loyalty is the *frequent buyer program* that rewards consumers for repeat purchases. Other types of promotions are more effective with customers prone to brand switching or with those who are loyal to a competitor's product. The cents-off coupon, free sample, or eye-catching display in a store will often entice shoppers to try a different brand. Consumers who do not use the product may be enticed to try it through the distribution of free samples.

Once marketers understand the dynamics occurring within their product category and have determined the particular consumers and consumer behaviors they want to influence, they can then go about selecting promotional tools to achieve these goals.

Tools for Consumer Sales Promotion

6
Discuss the most common forms of consumer sales promotion

Marketing managers must decide which consumer sales promotion devices to use in a specific campaign. The methods chosen must suit the objectives to ensure success of the overall promotion plan. Popular tools for consumer sales promotion are coupons and rebates, premiums, loyalty marketing programs, contests and sweepstakes, sampling, and point-of-purchase promotion.

Coupons and Rebates A **coupon** is a certificate that entitles consumers to an immediate price reduction when they buy the product. Coupons are a particularly good way to encourage product trial and repurchase. They are also likely to increase the amount of a product bought.

coupon
Certificate that entitles consumers to an immediate price reduction when they buy the product.

Coupon distribution has been steadily declining in recent years as packaged-goods marketers attempt to wean consumers off coupon clipping. Although approximately 268 billion coupons are distributed through freestanding newspaper inserts a year, only about 2 percent, or about 5 billion, are actually redeemed by

exhibit 13.9 | Types of Consumers and Sales Promotion Goals

Type of Buyer	Desired Results	Sales Promotion Examples
Loyal customers People who buy your product most or all of the time	Reinforce behavior, increase consumption, change purchase timing	• Loyalty marketing programs, such as frequent buyer cards or frequent shopper clubs • Bonus packs that give loyal consumers an incentive to stock up or premiums offered in return for proofs of purchase
Competitor's customers People who buy a competitor's product most or all of the time	Break loyalty, persuade to switch to your brand	• Sampling to introduce your product's superior qualities compared to their brand • Sweepstakes, contests, or premiums that create interest in the product
Brand switchers People who buy a variety of products in the category	Persuade to buy your brand more often	• Any promotion that lowers the price of the product, such as coupons, price-off packages, and bonus packs • Trade deals that help make the product more readily available than competing products
Price buyers People who consistently buy the least expensive brand	Appeal with low prices or supply added value that makes price less important	• Coupons, price-off packages, refunds, or trade deals that reduce the price of the brand to match that of the brand that would have been purchased

SOURCE: From *Sales Promotion Essentials*, 2nd Ed. by Don E. Schultz, William A. Robinson, and Lisa A. Petrison. Reprinted by permission of NTC Publishing Group, 4255 Touhy Ave., Lincolnwood, IL 60048.

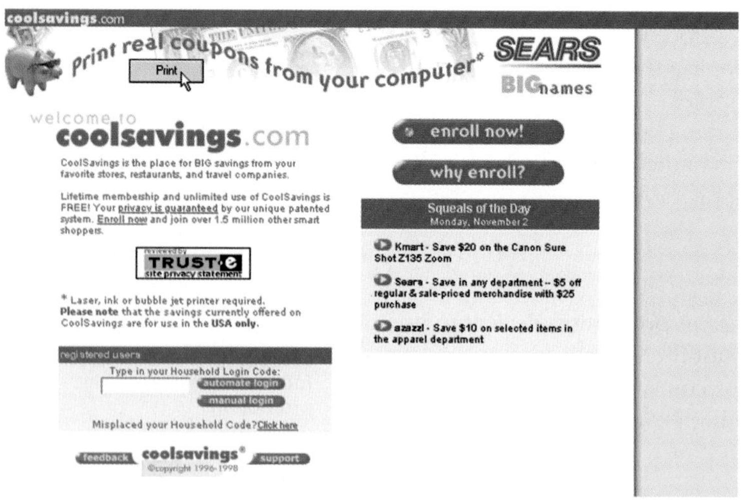

Faced with declining redemption of coupons, marketers are experimenting with new kinds of discounts. CoolSavings.com allows consumers to print their own coupons and gives companies using this service information on coupon users.
Courtesy CoolSavings.com, Inc.

consumers.[42] Part of the problem is that coupons are often wasted on consumers who have no interest in the product—for example, dog food coupons that reach the petless. Another problem is that most coupons expire before the consumer has the opportunity to use them. Additionally, coupons are more likely to encourage repeat purchases by regular users of a product than to encourage nonusers to try the brand.[43]

Because of their high cost and disappointing redemption rates, many marketers are reevaluating their use of coupons. Procter & Gamble, for example, has cut coupon distribution in half and shifted to a lower-price strategy. Similarly, Kraft has opted to distribute a single, all-purpose coupon good on any of its cereal brands. Other marketers are experimenting with on-line coupons over the Internet. Marketers such as JCPenney, Toys 'R' Us, H&R Block, and Boston Market that distribute coupons through CoolSavings.com, Inc. **(http://www.coolsavings.com)** have experienced redemption rates of 10 percent or more. In addition, marketers are provided with detailed anonymous information about how, where, and when consumers downloaded and used the coupons. Inter-

CoolSavings.com

Describe the special deals you can find advertised on CoolSavings.com. Are there any coupons that you would print and use? What seems to be the target market for this site? Are there any premiums currently being offered?

http://www.coolsavings.com/

net couponing can complement established promotional programs, reach more consumers, and help marketers gain valuable knowledge about their customers.[44]

Another bright spot for couponing is the trend toward in-store couponing, where coupons are most likely to affect customer buying decisions. Instant coupons on product packages, coupons distributed from on-shelf coupon-dispensing machines, and electronic coupons issued at the checkout counter are achieving much higher redemption rates. Redemption of instant coupons, for example, are about seventeen times that of traditional newspaper coupons, suggesting that consumers are making more in-store purchase decisions.[45]

rebate
Cash refund given for the purchase of a product during a specific period.

premium
Extra item offered to the consumer, usually in exchange for some proof of purchase of the promoted product.

loyalty marketing program
Promotional program designed to build long-term, mutually beneficial relationships between a company and its key customers.

frequent buyer program
Loyalty program in which loyal consumers are rewarded for making multiple purchases of a particular good or service.

Rebates are similar to coupons in that they offer the purchaser a price reduction; however, because the purchaser must mail in a rebate form and usually some proof of purchase, the reward is not as immediate. Traditionally used by food and cigarette manufacturers, rebates now appear on all types of products, from computers and software to film and baby seats. Consumers who purchased TurboTax 98 were recently offered a $10 rebate. Similarly, U.S. Robotics offered a $50 cash-back, mail-in rebate for several modem models.

Manufacturers prefer rebates for several reasons. Rebates also allow manufacturers to offer price cuts to consumers directly. Manufacturers have more control over rebate promotions because they can be rolled out and shut off quickly. Further, because buyers must fill out forms with their names, addresses, and other data, manufacturers use rebate programs to build customer databases. Perhaps the best reason of all to offer rebates is that although rebates are particularly good at enticing purchase, most consumers never bother to redeem them. Redemption rates for rebates run between 5 percent and 10 percent.[46]

Premiums A **premium** is an extra item offered to the consumer, usually in exchange for some proof that the promoted product has been purchased. Premiums reinforce the consumer's purchase decision, increase consumption, and persuade nonusers to switch brands. Premiums like telephones, tote bags, and umbrellas are available when consumers buy cosmetics, magazines, bank services, rental cars, and so on. Premiums can also include more product for the regular price, such as two-for-the-price-of-one bonus packs or packages that include more of the product. Kellogg's was hugely successful in its promotion of Pop Tarts that added two more pastries to the current six in a package without increasing the price. Kellogg's used the promotion to boost market share it had lost to private-label brands of pastries and new competitors.[47]

R.J. Milano, McDonald's assistant vice president for marketing, displays some of the 240 million Teenie Beanie Babies that the fast-food chain was selling in Spring 1998 for $1.59 with a food purchase. McDonald's was stung by criticism when they ran out of the stuffed critters in an earlier promotional campaign.
© Peter Barreras/AP Wide World Photos

Probably the best example of the use of premiums is the McDonald's Happy Meal in which children are rewarded with a small toy with their meal. The fast-food marketer's lucrative pact with Ty Inc., marketer of Beanie Babies, has made the annual Happy Meal and Teenie Beanie Babies combo a hot commodity. Demand was so high during the 1998 Teenie Beanie Babies promotion that many McDonald's outlets ran out of food items and the premiums lasted only days or, at best, two weeks in most stores.[48] McDonald's also routinely promotes Disney movies through Happy Meal premiums tied to films such as *101 Dalmations, Flubber,* and *Mulan.*

Loyalty Marketing Programs **Loyalty marketing programs**, or **frequent buyer programs**, reward loyal consumers for making multiple purchases. Popularized by the airline industry in the mid-80s through frequent flyer programs, loyalty marketing enables companies to strategically invest sales promotion dollars in activities designed to capture greater profits from customers already loyal to the product or company.[49] One study concluded that if a company retains an additional 5 percent of its customers each year, profits will increase by at least 25 percent. What's more, improving customer retention by a mere 2 percent can decrease costs by as much as 10 percent.[50]

The objective of loyalty marketing programs is to build long-term, mutually beneficial relationships between a company and its key customers. The Kidvantage program at Sears, for example, rewards parents spending $100 or more on their children's clothing with a 15 percent discount on their next purchase. Members of Kidvantage also can take advantage of Sears' wear-out warranty, which guarantees replacement of clothes that wear out before the child outgrows them.[51]

ON LINE

On-line versions of loyalty programs are also popping up. Computer users will soon be able to earn frequent flyer miles by surfing the Internet. Users will be awarded points for using the Web search engine Yahoo! to visit certain Web sites or buy from several retailers over the Internet. Consumers can then transfer their points into an airline frequent flyer account or a hotel frequent stay account.[52]

Contests and Sweepstakes Contests and sweepstakes are generally designed to create interest in the good or service, often to encourage brand switching. *Contests* are promotions in which participants use some skill or ability to compete for prizes. A consumer contest usually requires entrants to answer questions, complete sentences, or write a paragraph about the product and submit proof of purchase. Winning a *sweepstakes,* on the other hand, depends on chance or luck, and participation is free. Sweepstakes usually draw about ten times more entries than contests do.

Contests are a long-standing way to attract attention to a product. Guinness beer's essay contest received a response far greater than the company had anticipated and was more successful than any previous promotional campaign.
© John Welzenbach/The Stock Market

When setting up contests and sweepstakes, sales promotion managers must make certain that the award will appeal to the target market. Guinness Import Company recently sponsored its fifth annual essay contest that gives an actual Irish pub to the winner. The contest invites consumers to write a fifty-word essay on "Why Guinness Is My Perfect Pint."[53]

Sampling Consumers generally perceive a certain amount of risk in trying new products. Many are afraid of trying something they will not like (such as a new food item) or spending too much money and getting little reward. **Sampling** allows the customer to try a product risk-free. Recent research on sampling effectiveness indicates that among those consumers who had never before purchased the product, 71 percent indicated that the free sample would encourage them to try a product. Additionally, 67 percent said they have switched brands because they were satisfied with a free sample.[54]

sampling
Promotional program that allows the consumer the opportunity to try the product or service for free.

Sampling can be accomplished by directly mailing the sample to the customer, delivering the sample door to door, packaging the sample with another product, or demonstrating or sampling the product at a retail store. To help position Dunkin' Donuts as more than just a doughnut chain, the company gave away six million free doughnuts for one day to celebrate the retiring of its well-known Fred the Baker spokesman. The offer lured in new and lapsed customers to see

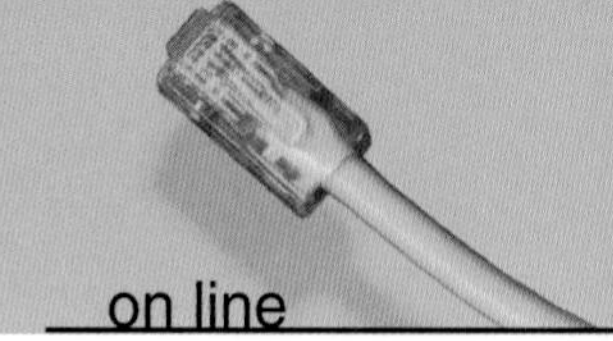

Starbucks

How does Starbucks use its Web site as a loyalty marketing program? Visit the site and see.
http://www.starbucks.com/

how the chain, with some thirty-three hundred U.S. outlets, has evolved from its doughnut roots to a place for bagels, pastries, and specialty coffee drinks.[55]

Sampling at special events is a popular, effective, and high-profile distribution method that permits marketers to piggyback onto fun-based consumer activities—including sporting events, college fests, fairs and festivals, beach events, and chili cook-offs. Pizza Hut's aggressive sampling promotion of its "totally new pizzas" gave away over one million of the reformulated pizzas at such high-profile events as the Kentucky Derby and the thirty-fifth anniversary of Seattle's Space Needle.[56]

Distributing samples to specific location types where consumers regularly meet for a common objective or interest, such as health clubs, churches or doctors' offices, is one of the most efficient methods of sampling. If someone visits a health club regularly, chances are he or she is a good prospect for a health-food product or vitamin supplement. Likewise, patients of doctors who specialize in diabetes management are excellent candidates for trial samples of sugar-free snacks, diagnostic kits, or other diabetes-related products. Additionally, the credibility of their being distributed at the health club or the doctor's office implies a powerful third-party endorsement.[57]

Point-of-Purchase Promotion **Point-of-purchase** promotion includes any promotional display set up at the retailer's location to build traffic, advertise the product, or induce impulse buying. Point-of-purchase promotions include shelf "talkers" (signs attached to store shelves), shelf extenders (attachments that extend shelves so products stand out), ads on grocery carts and bags, end-aisle and floor-stand displays, television monitors at supermarket checkout counters, in-store audio messages, and audiovisual displays. One big advantage of point-of-purchase promotion is that it offers manufacturers a captive audience in retail stores. Up to 70 percent of all purchase decisions are made in the store, according to research conducted by the Point-of-Purchase Advertising Institute, with 88 percent of food purchase decisions made in-store.[58] Therefore, point-of-purchase works better for impulse products—those products bought without prior decision by the consumer—than for planned purchases. Fifty-two percent of soft drink sales and 31 percent of chip and snack sales are attributable to in-store point-of-purchase promotions.[59]

point-of-purchase display
Promotional display set up at the retailer's location to build traffic, advertise the product, or induce impulse buying.

Tools for Trade Sales Promotion

7
List the most common forms of trade sales promotion

Whereas consumer promotions *pull* a product through the channel by creating demand, trade promotions *push* a product through the distribution channel. (See Chapter 10.) When selling to members of the distribution channel, manufacturers use many of the same sales promotion tools used in consumer promotions—such as sales contests, premiums, and point-of-purchase displays. Several tools, however, are unique to manufacturers and intermediaries:

- *Trade allowances:* A **trade allowance** is a price reduction offered by manufacturers to intermediaries such as wholesalers and retailers. The price reduction or rebate is given in exchange for doing something specific, such as allocating space for a new product or buying something during special periods. For example, a local dealer could receive a special discount for running its own promotion on GE telephones.
- *Push money:* Intermediaries receive **push money** as a bonus for pushing the manufacturer's brand through the distribution channel. Often the push money is directed toward a retailer's salespeople. Through its Retail Masters incentive program, cigarette marketer Philip Morris rewards participating retailers with cash payouts based on sales and display of Philip Morris cigarette brands. Retailers earn extra money by restricting displays of competing cigarette brands and offering a free Philip Morris cigarette to smokers of other brands to promote brand switching.[60]

trade allowance
Price reduction offered by manufacturers to intermediaries, such as wholesalers and retailers.

push money
Money offered to channel intermediaries to encourage them to "push" products—that is, to encourage other members of the channel to sell the products.

- *Training:* Sometimes a manufacturer will train an intermediary's personnel if the product is rather complex—as frequently occurs in the computer and telecommunication industries. For example, if a large department store purchases an NCR computerized cash register system, NCR may provide free training so the salespeople can learn how to use the new system.
- *Free merchandise:* Often a manufacturer offers retailers free merchandise in lieu of quantity discounts. For example, a breakfast cereal manufacturer may throw in one case of free cereal for every twenty cases ordered by the retailer. Occasionally, free merchandise is used as payment for trade allowances normally provided through other sales promotions. Instead of giving a retailer a price reduction for buying a certain quantity of merchandise, the manufacturer may throw in extra merchandise "free" (that is, at a cost that would equal the price reduction).
- *Store demonstrations:* Manufacturers can also arrange with retailers to perform an in-store demonstration. Food manufacturers often send representatives to grocery stores and supermarkets to let customers sample a product while shopping. Cosmetic companies also send their representatives to department stores to promote their beauty aids by performing facials and makeovers for customers.
- *Business meetings, conventions, and trade shows:* Trade association meetings, conferences, and conventions are an important aspect of sales promotion and a growing, multibillion-dollar market. At these shows, manufacturers, distributors, and other vendors have the chance to display their goods or describe their services to customers and potential customers. The cost per potential customer contacted at a show is estimated to be only 25 to 35 percent that of a personal sales call. Trade shows have been uniquely effective in introducing new products; they can establish products in the marketplace more quickly than can advertising, direct marketing, or sales calls. Companies participate in trade shows to attract and identify new prospects, serve current customers, introduce new products, enhance corporate image, test the market response to new products, enhance corporate morale, and gather competitive product information.

Trade promotions are popular among manufacturers for many reasons. Trade sales promotion tools help manufacturers gain new distributors for their products, obtain wholesaler and retailer support for consumer sales promotions, build or reduce dealer inventories, and improve trade relations. Car manufacturers annually sponsor dozens of auto shows for consumers. Many of the displays feature interactive computer stations where consumers enter vehicle specifications and get a printout of prices and local dealer names. In return, the local car dealers get the names of good prospects. The shows attract millions of consumers, providing dealers with increased store traffic as well as good leads.

Public Relations

8

Discuss the role of public relations in the promotional mix

Public relations is the element in the promotional mix that evaluates public attitudes, identifies issues that may elicit public concern, and executes programs to gain public understanding and acceptance. Like advertising and sales promotion, public relations is a vital link in a progressive company's marketing communication mix. Marketing managers plan solid public relations campaigns that fit into overall marketing plans and focus on targeted audiences. These campaigns strive to maintain a positive image of the corporation in the eyes of the public. Before launching public relations programs, managers evaluate public attitudes and company actions. Then they create programs to capitalize on the factors that enhance the firm's image and minimize the factors that could generate a negative image.

Many people associate public relations with publicity. *Publicity* is the effort to capture media attention—for example, through articles or editorials in publications or through human-interest stories on radio or television programs. Corporations usually initiate publicity through a press release that furthers their public relations plans. A company about to introduce a new product or open a new store may send press releases to the media in the hope that the story will be published or broadcast. Savvy publicity can often create overnight product sensations. Talk show host Rosie O'Donnell made *Sesame Street*'s Tickle Me Elmo doll the most sought after toy of the 1996 Christmas shopping season. Similarly, books picked to be in Oprah's Book Club become instant best-sellers, flying off the shelves of bookstores nationwide.

Donating products or services to worthy causes also creates favorable publicity. When the Iowa septuplets were born, consumer-products companies showered the babies and their parents with free goods. Gerber Products Company made an all-they-can-eat offer of baby and toddler food; Sony Electronics donated a camcorder to help the family capture the memories of the newborns; Toys 'R' Us outfitted the family with cribs, changing tables, car seats and strollers; Cadbury Schweppes PLC's Motts unit donated sixteen years' worth of apple sauce and juice; Procter & Gamble Company became the official diaper sponsor with a "lifetime" supply offer (about two years worth of diapers); and Maytag Corporation offered to design a new kitchen, complete with at least two of every appliance, in the new home being built to replace the family's modest two-bedroom dwelling.[61]

Public relations departments may perform any or all of the following functions:

- *Press relations:* placing positive, newsworthy information in the news media to attract attention to a product, a service, or a person associated with the firm or institution
- *Product publicity:* publicizing specific products or services
- *Corporate communication:* creating internal and external messages to promote a positive image of the firm or institution
- *Public affairs:* building and maintaining national or local community relations
- *Lobbying:* influencing legislators and government officials to promote or defeat legislation and regulation
- *Employee and investor relations:* maintaining positive relationships with employees, shareholders, and others in the financial community
- *Crisis management:* responding to unfavorable publicity or a negative event

Major Public Relations Tools

Several tools are commonly used by public relations professionals, including new product publicity, product placement, consumer education, event sponsorship, and issue sponsorship. A relatively new tool public relations professionals are using in increasing numbers is a Web site on the Internet. Although many of these tools require an active role on the part of the public relations professional, such as writing press releases and engaging in proactive media relations, many of these techniques create their own publicity.

New Product Publicity Publicity is instrumental in introducing new products and services. Publicity can help advertisers explain what's different about their new product by prompting free news stories or positive word of mouth about it. During the introductory period, an especially innovative new product often needs more exposure than conventional, paid advertising affords. Public relations professionals write press releases or develop videos in an effort to generate news about their new product. They also jockey for exposure of their product or service at major events, on popular television and news shows, or in the hands of influential people. Savvy game marketer id Software, Inc., maker of the popular computer games Doom and Quake, distributes early versions of its games free over the Internet, creating word-of-mouth excitement among its followers of young males that helps to sell follow-up sequels. The test version for Quake II was downloaded more than a million times. The game marketer further enticed followers by releasing manuals, game photos, and commentary from the game's programmers. As a result, Web sites dedicated to Quake play were abuzz with discussion of the new, soon-to-be-released version.[62]

Product Placement Marketers can also garner publicity by making sure their products appear at special events or in movies or television shows. For the 1997 Super Bowl in New Orleans between the New England Patriots and the Green Bay Packers, General Mills public relations employees brought two batches of Wheaties boxes—one bearing a photograph of the Patriots, the other of the Packers. When it became clear during the game that Green Bay would win, the employees distributed the Packers boxes to on-site television news crews. As a result, sportscasters displayed the Wheaties box on the Fox network as well as on CNN, ESPN, and countless local stations.[63]

Companies reap invaluable product exposure through product placement, usually at a fraction of the cost of paid-for advertising. Often, the fee for exposure is in merchandise. For example, The Gap outfitted thirty-five hundred traders, specialists, and clerks of the New York Stock Exchange in khaki pants and casual shirts for the exchange's first casual workday.[64] Exposure of controversial products like cigarettes and cigars, however, can invite unwanted criticism as you will see in the "Ethics in Marketing" box.

Consumer Education Some major firms believe that educated consumers are better, more loyal customers. Financial planning firms often sponsor free educational seminars on money management, retirement planning, and investing in the hope that the consumer will choose its organization for its future financial needs. Likewise, computer hardware and software firms, realizing that many consumers feel intimidated by new technology and recognizing the strong relationship between learning and purchasing patterns, sponsor computer seminars and free in-store demonstrations. In a prelaunch public relations push for its 1999 3-Series line, BMW of North America sponsored an instructional driving and educational tour in six major U.S. cities as a way to increase sales more cost efficiently than traditional advertising. The tour, called the Ultimate Driving Experience, targets prospective purchasers and current owners near the end of their leases. One event during the tour invites high school students and their parents to special weekend programs teaching driver safety.[65]

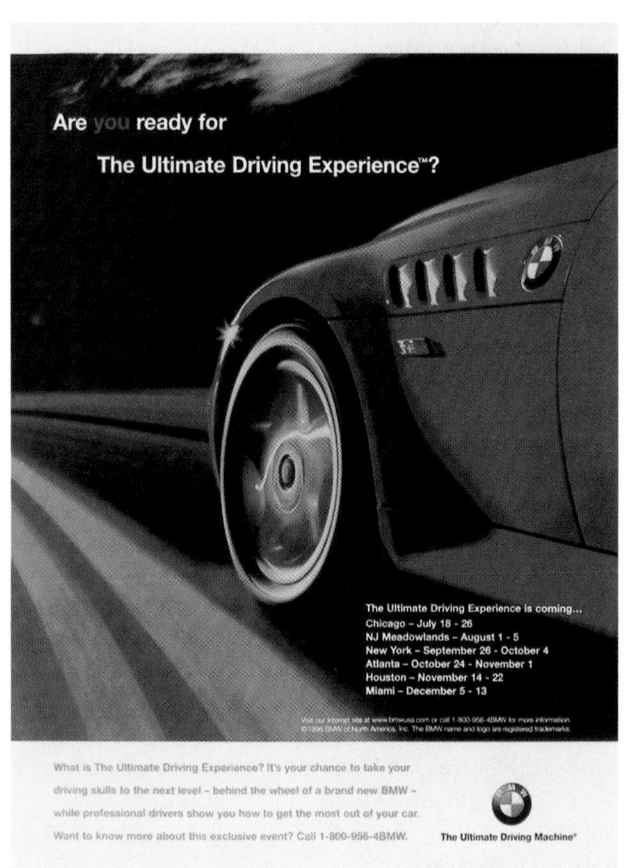

Consumer education can not only influence the buying decision but can result in better, more loyal customers. BMW's instructional driving tour is a way to show off its cars' capabilities to prospective purchasers and current owners without mounting expensive advertising campaigns.
Courtesy BMW of North America, Inc.

Event Sponsorship Public relations managers can sponsor events or community activities that are sufficiently newsworthy to achieve press coverage; at the same time, these events also reinforce brand identification. Sporting, music, and arts events remain the most popular choices of event sponsors, although many are now turning to more specialized events such as tie-ins with schools, charities, and other community service organizations. For example, Chrysler's Jeep division sponsors an annual Camp Jeep event in Vail, Colorado, where more than six thousand Jeep owners and their families convene for a three-day festival. Camp Jeep at-

ethics in marketing

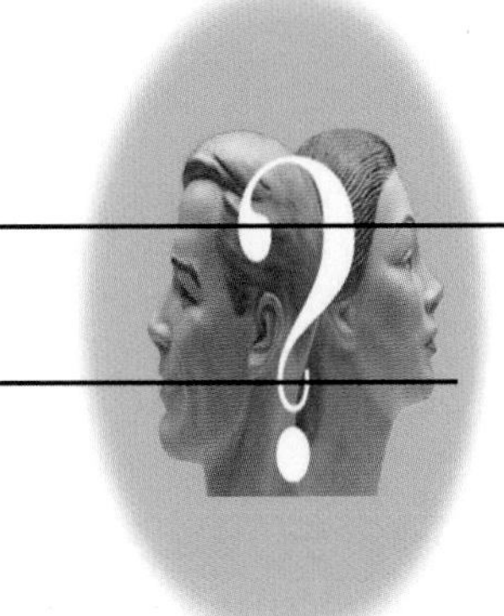

Cigars Become the Darling of Hollywood

Tobacco has long enjoyed a comfortable relationship with Hollywood. Since the 1930s, cigarettes have been found between the lips of sexy stars, such as Bette Davis, Humphrey Bogart, and Lauren Bacall. In Bogart's day, cigarettes became the ultimate accessory in movies with a little financial support from big tobacco. Later, when cigarette advertising was nudged off television, the pressure for product placement on the big screen intensified. One example comes from the leaked documents of tobacco company Brown and Williamson, which apparently paid Sylvester Stallone half a million dollars for brand placements in five of his movies.

Today, however, it's just as likely to see a cigar in a movie as a cigarette. Like their cigarette counterparts, cigar manufacturers routinely hire product-placement firms to get their products on the big screen. In the box office hit *Independence Day,* the pilot played by Will Smith couldn't save the world unless he had a cigar in his pocket. Arnold Schwarzenegger, Mr. Freeze in *Batman & Robin,* lights up a cigar in a big cloud of blue smoke. A cigar conveys status as it is placed in Tom Cruise's mouth in the hit *Jerry Maguire.* Actors lit cigars in 51 of 133 movies with a domestic box-office draw of at least $5 million in the most recent film survey by the American Lung Association. In 20th Century Fox's *Independence Day,* cigars appeared in twelve scenes, or once every 12.5 minutes.

How much marketing punch have cigars in the movies had on the cigar industry? Although a direct correlation can't be made, it should be noted that after a twenty-year decline, U.S. sales of cigars have jumped 53 percent to 5.2 billion cigars since 1993—proof that the stogie of old is no longer stodgy. Although other factors have certainly helped ignite the current cigar craze, Hollywood has definitely contributed to its "coolness." Although cigar smoking in and of itself is a choice consumers make, what alarms many is the increase in popularity of cigars with teenagers. A 1996 survey sponsored by the Centers for Disease Control and Prevention found that 27 percent of U.S. teenagers, or six million, have smoked at least one cigar.

Federal and state regulators, alarmed about booming sales of cigars and their sudden popularity among teenagers, are about to end the decades of leniency toward the cigar industry (most tobacco bills pending in Congress are silent on cigars). The Federal Trade Commission recently ordered five cigar makers to file advertising and marketing expenditures and told three of the five to report what they spend to have their cigars featured in movies. California's Department of Health Services recently used several hundred thousand dollars from the state's thirty-seven-cents-a-pack tobacco tax to combat movie and television smoking and smoking sponsorship of sports and community events.

The cigar industry, meanwhile, is voluntarily restricting the practice of putting cigars in celebrities' hands. The board of directors of the Cigar Association of America said it would "admonish" its members to stop paying Hollywood brokers for product placements in movies and television.[66]

Do you feel that product placement in movies and TV for controversial brands is unethical? Do you believe there should be laws governing this promotional practice?

tendees can participate in dozens of activities, including trail driving in their Jeeps, hiking, mountain biking, and white-water rafting. Attendees can also participate in roundtable discussions with Jeep engineers to help shape future Jeep models, and provide future car-buying plans so Jeep can follow up later with customers.[67]

Marketers can also create their own events tied around their product. Publicity surrounding IBM's highly publicized chess match between its Deep Blue supercomputer and Russian chess master Garry Kasparov reaped the equivalent of more than $100 million worth of favorable and free publicity. IBM's Internet site, which covered the competition live, drew one million viewers at the height of the match, making it one of the most highly trafficked events ever on the World Wide Web.[68]

Issue Sponsorship Corporations can build public awareness and loyalty by supporting their customers' favorite issues. Education, health care, and social programs get the largest share of corporate funding. Firms often donate a percentage of sales or profits to a worthy cause that their target market is likely to favor. For example, pantyhose maker Hanes supports national breast cancer organizations and prints instructions for breast self-examinations on packages of pantyhose.

"Green marketing" has also become an important way for companies to build awareness and loyalty by promoting a popular issue. Large numbers of consumers, mostly older, female and highly educated, profess a preference and are willing to pay more for products made by environmentally friendly companies.[69] By positioning their brands as ecologically sound, marketers can convey concern for the environment and society as a whole. Burger King and McDonald's no longer use styrofoam cartons to package their burgers in an effort to decrease waste in landfills. In a similar effort, Wal-Mart has opened environmentally friendly stores to appeal to consumers' desire to save the environment. The stores' air conditioning systems use a non-ozone-depleting refrigerant, rainwater is collected from parking lots and roofs for watering the landscape, skylights allow natural light into the store, cart corrals are made of recycled plastic, and parking lots are recycled asphalt.

ON LINE

Internet Web Sites Internet Web sites as public relations tools are a relatively new phenomenon in the marketing arena. Whereas many marketers initially used their Web sites as a way to advertise their products or services, public relations professionals now feel these sites are an excellent vehicle to post news releases on products, product enhancements, strategic relationships, and financial earnings. Corporate press releases, technical papers and articles, and product news help inform the press, customers, prospects, industry analysts, stockholders, and others of the firm's products and services and their applications. The Web site can also be an open forum for new product ideas and product improvements, and to obtain feedback on the Web site's usefulness to viewers. Additionally, a self-help desk at the Web site can also list the most common questions and answers to assist with customer support and satisfaction.[70]

Several companies are also experimenting with Internet chat rooms as a competitive advantage and a way to provide enhanced customer service. Merrill Lynch routinely sponsors moderated chat seminars hosted by expert employees. Recently, senior investment strategists at Merrill Lynch addressed international investing and members of its tax advisory group explored the implications of current tax legislation during a live chat event. Egghead, the software retailer, holds chat sessions Monday through Friday in its on-line store, offering customers instant advice about software and helping them with their purchases.[71]

Managing Unfavorable Publicity

Although the majority of marketers try to avoid unpleasant situations, crises do happen. Intel faced this reality after consumers became aware of an obscure flaw in its Pentium chip. In our free-press environment, publicity is not easily controlled, especially in a crisis. **Crisis management** is the coordinated effort to handle the effects of unfavorable publicity, ensuring fast and accurate communication in times of emergency.

crisis management
Coordinated effort to handle the effects of unfavorable publicity or of another unexpected, unfavorable event.

A good public relations staff is perhaps more important in bad times than in good. Critics chastised Trans World Airlines after its plane crash off Long Island, saying the airline was slow and uncooperative with family members wanting information about survivors, and calls from the media went unanswered. TWA's chief executive was also late in reassuring families and the public that his airline was doing all it could. All public relations professionals learned a valuable lesson from this blunder: Companies must have a communication policy firmly in hand before a disaster occurs, because timing is uncontrollable.

A good public relations and crisis management plan helped steer the Walt Disney Company out of a public relations mess after it was twice forced to postpone the maiden voyage of its new cruise ship, Disney Magic, due to production delays. Forty cruises originally scheduled to begin sailing in March 1998 were canceled, forcing approximately ninety-six thousand potential travelers to change their plans. Because travelers who booked early are Disney's most enthusiastic fans, the company had a virtual public relations nightmare. To begin fixing the damage, Disney overnighted apologies to disappointed travelers offering 50 percent discounts to those who had been inconvenienced twice, and 25 percent discounts to those bumped once. Disney also offered full refunds to those who didn't rebook and covered any lost commissions for travel agents.[72]

LOOKING BACK

As you finish reading this chapter, think back to the opening story about the advertising campaign for Mountain Dew. Pepsi-Cola's promotional team for Mountain Dew goes through the same creative steps as other large marketers—from determining what appeal to use to choosing the appropriate executional style. Great effort is also expended in deciding which medium will best reach the desired target markets. Pepsi-Cola takes into account such things as audience selectivity of the medium, cost per contact, frequency, and reach. Pepsi-Cola also complements its traditional media advertising with effective sales promotion and sponsorships that target teens.

Summary

1 Discuss the effect advertising has on market share, consumers, brand loyalty, and perception of product attributes. First, advertising helps marketers increase or maintain brand awareness and, subsequently, market share. Typically, more is spent to advertise new brands with a small market share than to advertise older brands. Brands with a large market share use advertising mainly to maintain their share of the market. Second, advertising affects consumers' daily lives as well as their purchases. Although advertising can seldom change strongly held consumer values, it may transform a consumer's negative attitude toward a product into a positive one. Third, when consumers are highly loyal to a brand, they may buy more of that brand when advertising is increased. Last, advertising can also change the importance of a brand's attributes to consumers. By emphasizing different brand attributes, advertisers can change their appeal in response to consumers' changing needs or try to achieve an advantage over competing brands.

2 Identify the major types of advertising. Advertising is any form of nonpersonal, paid communication in which the sponsor or company is identified. The two major types of advertising are institutional advertising and product advertising. Institutional advertising is not product oriented; rather, its purpose is to foster a positive company image among the general public, investment community, customers, and employees. Product advertising is designed mainly to promote goods and services, and it is classified into three main categories: pioneering, competitive, and comparative. A product's place in the product life cycle is a major determinant of the type of advertising used to promote it.

3 Describe the advertising campaign process. An advertising campaign is a series of related advertisements focusing on a common theme and common goals. The advertising campaign process consists of several important steps. Promotion managers first set specific campaign objectives. They then make creative decisions, often with the aid of an advertising agency, centered on developing advertising appeals. Once creative decisions have been made, media are evaluated and selected. Finally, the overall campaign is assessed through various forms of testing.

4 Describe media evaluation and selection techniques. Media evaluation and selection make up a crucial step in the advertising campaign process. Major types of advertising media include newspapers, magazines, radio, television, outdoor advertising such as billboards and bus panels, and the Internet and World Wide Web. Recent trends in advertising media include fax, video shopping carts, computer screen savers, and cinema and video advertising. Promotion managers choose the advertising media mix on the basis of the following variables: cost per contact, reach, frequency, and characteristics of the target market. After choosing the media mix, a media schedule designates when the advertisement will appear and the specific vehicles it will appear in.

5 Define and state the objectives of sales promotion. Sales promotion compromises those marketing communication activities, other than advertising, personal selling, and public relations, in which a short-term incentive motivates consumers or members of the distribution channel to purchase a good or service immediately, either by lowering the price or by adding value. The main objectives of sales promotion are to increase trial purchases, consumer inventories, and repeat purchases. Sales promotion is also used to encourage brand switching and to build brand loyalty. Sales promotion supports advertising activities.

6 Discuss the most common forms of consumer sales promotion. Consumer forms of sales promotion include coupons and rebates, premiums, loyalty marketing programs, contests and sweepstakes, sampling, and point-of-purchase displays. Coupons are certificates entitling consumers to an immediate price reduction when they purchase a product or service. Coupons are a particularly good way to encourage product trial and brand switching. Similar to coupons, rebates provide purchasers with a price reduction, although it is not immediate. To receive a rebate, consumers must generally mail in a rebate form with a proof of purchase. Premiums offer an extra item or incentive to the consumer for buying a product or service. Premiums reinforce the consumer's purchase decision, increase consumption, and persuade nonusers to switch brands. Rewarding loyal customers is the basis of loyalty marketing programs. Loyalty programs are extremely effective at building long-term, mutually beneficial relationships between a company and its key customers. Contests and sweepstakes are generally designed to create interest, often to encourage brand switching. Because consumers perceive risk in trying new products, sampling is an effective method for gaining new customers. Finally, point-of-purchase displays set up at the retailer's location build traffic, advertise the product, and induce impulse buying.

7 List the most common forms of trade sales promotion. Manufacturers use many of the same sales promotion tools used in consumer promotions, such as sales contests, premiums, and point-of-purchase displays. In addition, manufacturers and channel intermediaries use several unique promotional strategies: trade allowances, push money, training programs, free merchandise, store demonstrations, and meetings, conventions, and trade shows.

8 Discuss the role of public relations in the promotional mix. Public relations is a vital part of a firm's promotional mix. A company fosters good publicity to enhance its image and promote its products. Popular public relations tools include new product publicity, product placement, consumer education, event sponsorship, issue sponsorship, and Internet Web sites. An equally important aspect of public relations is managing unfavorable publicity in a way that is least damaging to a firm's image.

Discussion and Writing Questions

1. How can advertising, sales promotion, and publicity work together? Give an example.
2. Discuss the reasons why new brands with a smaller market share spend proportionately more on advertising and sales promotion than brands with a larger market share.
3. At what stage in a product's life cycle are pioneering, competitive, and comparative advertising most likely to occur? Give a current example of each type of advertising.

4. What is an advertising appeal? Give some examples of advertising appeals you have observed recently in the media.

5. What are the advantages of radio advertising? Why is radio expanding as an advertising medium?

6. WRITING You are the advertising manager of a sailing magazine, and one of your biggest potential advertisers has questioned your rates. Write the firm a letter explaining why you believe your audience selectivity is worth the extra expense for advertisers.

7. Discuss how different forms of sales promotion can erode or build brand loyalty. If a company's objective is to enhance customer loyalty to its products, what sales promotion techniques would be most appropriate?

8. WRITING As the new public relations director for a sportswear company, you have been asked to set public relations objectives for a new line of athletic shoes to be introduced to the teen market. Draft a memo outlining the objectives you propose for the shoe's introduction and your reasons for them.

9. WRITING Reports have just surfaced that your company, a fast-food chain, sold contaminated food products that have made several people seriously ill. As your company's public relations manager, devise a plan to handle the crisis.

10. Identify an appropriate media mix for the following products:
    a. chewing tobacco
    b. *People* magazine
    c. Weed-Eaters
    d. foot odor killers
    e. "drink responsibly" campaigns by beer brewers

11. WRITING Design a full-page magazine advertisement for a new brand of soft drink. The name of the new drink, as well as package design, is at the discretion of the student. On a separate sheet, specify the benefits stressed or appeals made in the advertisement.

12. TEAM Form a three-person team. Divide the responsibility for getting newspaper advertisements and menus for several local restaurants. While you are at the restaurants to obtain copies of their menus, observe the atmosphere and interview the manager to determine what he or she believes are the primary reasons people choose to dine with them. Pool your information and develop a table comparing the restaurants in terms of convenience of location, value for the money, food variety and quality, atmosphere, and so on. Rank the restaurants in terms of their appeal to college students. Explain the basis of your rankings. What other market segment would be attracted to the restaurants and why? Do the newspaper advertisements emphasize the most effective appeal for a particular restaurant? Explain.

13. ON LINE What associations and organizations are listed with the Black Information Network? How would you try to appeal to some of the diverse interests of these groups if you were an advertiser trying to reach these consumers?
    http://www.bin.com

14. ON LINE How might Nutrition Camp aid this corporation's public relations effort?
    http://www.kelloggs.com

Key Terms

advertising appeal 464
advertising campaign 463
advertising objective 463
advertising response function 460
advocacy advertising 462
audience selectivity 475
comparative advertising 462
competitive advertising 462
consumer sales promotion 477
continuous media schedule 475
cooperative advertising 469
cost per contact 474
coupon 477
crisis management 486
flighted media schedule 475
frequency 475
frequent buyer program 479
infomercial 471
institutional advertising 462
loyalty marketing program 479
media mix 474
media schedule 475
medium 464
pioneering advertising 462
point-of-purchase display 481
premium 479
product advertising 461
pulsing media schedule 475
push money 481
reach 474
rebate 479
sampling 480
seasonal media schedule 476
trade allowance 481
trade sales promotion 477
unique selling proposition 466

Application for Small Business

Quality of service is increasingly the basis for deciding where to do business. Customers are five times more likely to return to a particular business if they perceive that it is providing higher quality service than the competition.

The Student Copy Center is a local business competing with Kinko's and a couple of other national franchise copy centers. Its owner, Mack Bayles, just attended a Small Business Administration workshop on customer service. He learned that when people say they expect good customer service, they most often mean they want prompt and accurate service from friendly, knowledgeable, and courteous employees. The presenter also emphasized that all market segments, even the most price conscious, expect good customer service. Mack wants to use this knowledge to develop an effective advertising campaign.

Mack has no idea what his customers think about either his copy business or that of his competitors. He decides, therefore, to ask his customers to complete a brief survey while in his store. From his survey he learns that Student Copy Center is considered friendlier and more courteous than the major competitors but is rated lower on speed of service.

Questions

1. What should Mack do before developing his advertising campaign?
2. Should Mack use comparative ads?
3. What advertising appeal would be most effective for Mack? Why?

Review Quiz

1. Consumers are typically exposed to hundreds of ads each day. In just the television media alone, researchers estimate that the average person spends ______ hours per day watching TV.
   a. One
   b. Two
   c. Three
   d. Four
2. Which of the following is *not* one of the three basic types of advertising?
   a. Service advertising
   b. Product advertising
   c. Institutional advertising
   d. Advocacy advertising
3. Advertising that is intended to stimulate primary demand for a new product is called
   a. Advocacy advertising.
   b. Pioneering advertising
   c. Competitive advertising
   d. Comparative advertising
4. The goal of ______ advertising is to influence demand for a specific brand.
   a. Comparative
   b. Institutional
   c. Competitive
   d. Pioneering
5. The first step in any advertising campaign decision process must be to
   a. Determine campaign objectives
   b. Make creative decisions

c. Make media decisions
d. Evaluate the campaign

6. Which of the following types of media scheduling is based on advertisers scheduling ads heavily during certain periods and little or no advertising during other periods.
   a. Continuous
   b. Flighted
   c. Pulsing
   d. Seasonal
7. The primary objective of sales promotion is to influence
   a. Attitudes
   b. Behavior
   c. Beliefs
   d. Knowledge
8. That element of the promotional mix that is designed help gain public acceptance and understanding of issues important to the firm is known as
   a. Advertising
   b. Public relations
   c. Sales promotion
   d. Direct marketing
9. Beyond a certain level of spending for advertising, diminishing returns commonly set in for the advertiser.
   a. True
   b. False
10. A medium's ability to reach a precisely defined target market is its audience selectivity.
    a. True
    b. False
11. Trade sales promotion is targeted toward the ultimate consumer of a product.
    a. True
    b. False
12. A price reduction offered by manufacturers to intermediaries, such as retailers or wholesalers for allocating shelf space for a new product, is known as push money.
    a. True
    b. False
13. Describe the notion of cooperative advertising and identify which medium it is most commonly used in.

Check the Answer Key, which follows the Video Case, to see how well you understood the material.

VIDEO CASE

Red Roof Inns: Ads to Charm, Disarm, and Deliver

During the seventies and eighties, when economy lodging was far less competitive than it is today, billboards broadcasting "Sleep Cheap" grabbed the attention of road-weary business travelers and brought them to the nearest Red Roof Inn. In addition to saying "low cost," however, "Sleep Cheap" also said "low level," and occupancy rates at Red Roof Inns started to decline nationwide. Hired to reverse this image was the W. B. Doner advertising agency, whose philosophy was best articulated by its founder, Brod Doner: "Ads are created to charm, disarm, and deliver." For the Red Roof account, Brod wanted creativity that would persuade, motivate, and make something happen.

The Doner Agency realized that advertising copy cannot change consumers' deeply rooted values and attitudes, but it could succeed in transforming a person's negative attitude about Red Roof's economy lodging into a positive one. Advertising could affect the way consumers ranked Red Roof's primary attribute—prices lower than the competition for the same economy hotel room—and thus motivate them to try spending the night at a Red Roof Inn.

As part of a comprehensive promotion plan, an advertising campaign was set in motion to transmit the sales message to the target market. The Doner agency, in conjunction with Red Roof Inns executives, decided that the advertising campaign would target the business travelers on a limited expense account who most likely arrive late at night and leave early the next morning. The specific communication in the advertising campaign mirrored Red Roof's corporate objective to increase market share in the economy lodging market. The whole point of the advertising was to convey the idea that a hotel room doesn't have be expensive to be good. After all, "Why pay $70 when you can have the same good night's sleep for $30 less at Red Roof Inn?" the commercials asked.

The advertising campaign then moved into the creative and media decision phase. The Doner team stuck to its core philosophy: Although highly creative ads win accolades from peers in the advertising business, the bottom line is to sell products and services to the client. And the results have to be measurable. "Sleep Cheap" was replaced by "Hit the Roof," which was featured primarily in television spots. In addition to television, Doner's integrated marketing approach used radio, billboards, direct mail, print, and the Internet to drive home the same message of value.

The initial creative effort came alive in a television commercial centered around one simple concept—spending $70 for a night's stay in a hotel room is throwing money away. To make the concept visual, a business traveler stood at the top of Hoover Dam while a celebrity spokesperson literally threw the traveler's wallet from the dam into the raging waters below. Such an outrageous act provoked humor *and* underscored a well-known adage in advertising—sell the benefit. The message here was clear: What the consumer receives by staying at Red Roof Inns is money in his or her pocket. Put another way, a stay at Red Roof Inns keeps a customer from wasting hard-earned cash. Red Roof Inns was trying to differentiate itself on price, but more importantly on value.

Making claims of better value was not enough to universally boost business, so another TV spot was designed to increase occupancy rates at Red Roof during the slow period of January through March. The same celebrity, now well associated with Red Roof Inns, handed a telephone to a business customer and urged him to call and compare Red Roof's rates with those offered by other economy lodging chains like Hampton Inn. The competitors' rates were consistently $5 to $10 a night higher. The same tag line, "Hit the Roof," continued to reinforce the same unified message of value. Building on the success of prior campaigns, the Doner agency again selected humor as the creative style to execute the message. The commercial generated awareness by challenging viewers to call and compare rates. It sparked viewer interest in learning about room rates; it peaked viewer desire to save money; and, it is hoped, it resulted in a stay at Red Roof.

The Doner agency has handled the Red Roof Inns account for twelve years, and the advertising appeal has remained consistent the whole time. The appeal plays on the customer's desire for thrift, convenience, and a nice place to stay. Both the initial and subsequent ad campaigns produced measurable results. When the ad campaigns were evaluated, market share was shown to have increased despite heavy competition, and occupancy rates during slack periods had improved. Brod Doner's advertising mantra—ads that charm, disarm, and deliver—has certainly made today's business travelers "Hit the Roof."

Questions

1. Using Exhibit 13.2, describe the advertising campaign decision process for Red Roof Inns.
2. Why did the Doner Agency identify the benefits of Red Roof Inns in the TV commercial?
3. Describe the advertising appeal used in the campaign.
4. How does Red Roof's advertising campaign follow AIDA as depicted in Exhibit 12.5?

Bibliography

John DeCerchio, "Osmosis, Fiat Passed Doner Philosophy," *Advertising Age,* 3 March 1997, C6-7.

John McDonough, "W. B. Doner, 60th Anniversary," *Advertising Age,* 3 March 1997, C1-2.

Video by Learnet Inc.: A Case Study in Advertising Strategy: Red Roof Inn

Web site: **http://www.redroof.com**

Answer Key

1. *Answer:* d, p. 460

   Rationale: During each hour of network television, the average U.S. consumer is exposed to eighteen minutes of commercial advertising.

2. *Answer:* a, p. 461

   Rationale: Services are advertised in a fashion that is consistent with products. Therefore, a separate category does not exist for service advertising.

3. *Answer:* b, p. 462

   Rationale: Pioneering advertising is designed to generate awareness and create interest in new product offerings.

4. *Answer:* c, p. 462

   Rationale: Competitive advertising tends to rely more on emotional appeals and be less informative as it tries to encourage the target audience to consider a specific brand.

5. *Answer:* a, p. 463

   Rationale: Campaign objectives are set first to identify the specific communication tasks a campaign should accomplish for a specified target audience during a specified period of time.

6. *Answer:* b, p. 475

   Rationale: Flighted media schedules are used to achieve a greater impact with the audience during times that they are most likely to be making consumption preference decisions.

7. *Answer:* b, p. 477

   Rationale: Immediate purchase is the goal of sales promotion, regardless of the form it takes.

8. *Answer:* b, p. 482

   Rationale: Public relations is the element of the promotional mix that evaluates public attitudes, identifies issues that may elicit public concern, and executes programs to gain public acceptance and understanding.

9. *Answer:* a, pp. 459–460

   Rationale: This phenomenon is called the advertising response function and it suggests that advertisers must be careful to use advertising budgets wisely.

10. *Answer:* a, p. 475

    Rationale: Marketers look to a medium's audience selectivity when trying to reach a very specific group of customers with an advertising message.

11. *Answer:* b, p. 477

    Rationale: Trade sales promotion is directed at members of the distribution channel, such as wholesalers and retailers.

12. *Answer:* b, p. 481

    Rationale: This is known as a trade allowance. Push money is money that is used as a bonus to give to intermediaries for successfully pushing a manufacturer's brand through a distribution channel.

13. *Answer:* In cooperative advertising, the manufacturer and the retailer split the costs of advertising the manufacturer's brand. Used primarily in newspaper advertising, cooperative advertising encourages retailers to devote more effort to a manufacturer's lines.
    (p. 469)

CHAPTER

14

LEARNING OBJECTIVES

After studying this chapter, you should be able to

1. Understand how the Internet affects marketing
2. Describe various forms of Internet marketing
3. Discuss strategic considerations about Internet marketing
4. Discuss financial implications of Internet marketing
5. Explain how to incorporate Internet marketing into an overall marketing plan
6. Discuss several trends and the effects they may have on Internet marketing in the future

chapter 14 internet marketing

CHAPTER 14 INTERNET MARKETING

CHAPTER

15

LEARNING OBJECTIVES

After studying this chapter, you should be able to

1. Discuss the importance of pricing decisions to the economy and to the individual firm
2. List and explain a variety of pricing objectives
3. Explain the role of demand in price determination
4. Describe cost-oriented pricing strategies
5. Demonstrate how the product life cycle, competition, distribution and promotion strategies, the impact of the Internet, demands of large customers, and perceptions of quality can affect price
6. Describe the procedure for setting the right price
7. Identify the legal and ethical constraints on pricing decisions
8. Explain how discounts, geographic pricing, and other special pricing tactics can be used to fine-tune the base price

PRICING CONCEPTS

The full-page newspaper ads trumpeting the debut of **Priceline.com** showed *Star Trek* captain James T. Kirk (William Shatner) wearing such an intense expression that he seemed to be contemplating a Klingon attack rather than a new way to buy airline tickets. Or perhaps he was just trying to decide if this new Web site, which allows you to name your own airfare, is a good deal or a science fiction fantasy.

Here's how it works: The customer logs on to www.priceline.com—or calls 800-priceline—and types in when and where he wants to travel, what he wants to pay, and his credit card number. Priceline then sends this "bid" to the airlines. If a carrier accepts it, a ticket is issued within one hour (or one day for international flights) and the credit card charged.

The scheme, explains CEO Jay Walker, is based on the fact that major airlines fly with some 500,000 seats empty every day. For them, he says, "Priceline is a dream come true. When was the last time an airline had customers take out their credit card and say, 'Put me on any flight where you've got room'?"

Priceline has announced plans to start selling new cars, mortgages, insurance, and hotel rooms on the Internet—intent on boldly going where no online-ticketing service has gone before.[1]

The Priceline concept illustrates the notion of how demand and supply determine price. The consumer puts the price he or she is willing to pay (demand) into the system and the airlines decide if they want to issue the ticket at that price (supply). Will the Internet have a major impact on pricing? How does cost fit into the pricing equation? Can price influence the perceived quality of a product? How does competition affect price?

on line

Priceline

Find out more about how Priceline works by visiting its Web site. Would you be willing to book your next flight home this way? Which of Priceline's services would you be willing to try? Can you think of other markets Priceline can enter?

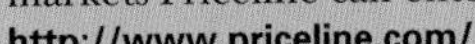

http://www.priceline.com/

The Importance of Price

1
Discuss the importance of pricing decisions to the economy and to the individual firm

Price means one thing to the consumer and something else to the seller. To the consumer, it is the cost of something. To the seller, price is revenue, the primary source of profits. In the broadest sense, price allocates resources in a free-market economy. With so many ways of looking at price, it's no wonder that marketing managers find the task of setting prices a challenge.

What Is Price?

price
That which is given up in an exchange to acquire a good or service.

Price is that which is given up in an exchange to acquire a good or service. Price is typically the money exchanged for the good or service. It may also be time lost while waiting to acquire the good or service. For example, many people waited all day at Southwest Airlines' ticket counters during the company's 25th anniversary sale. Even then, some people didn't get the deep-discounted tickets that they had been hoping for. Price might also include "lost dignity" for an individual who loses his or her job and must rely on charity to obtain food and clothing.

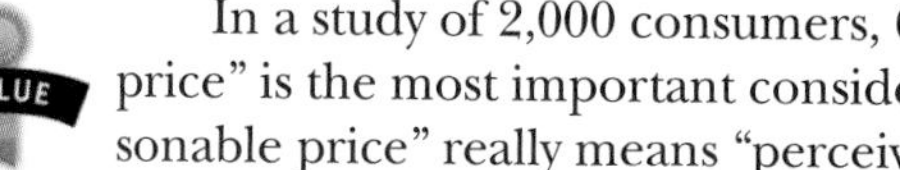

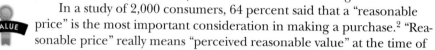

In a study of 2,000 consumers, 64 percent said that a "reasonable price" is the most important consideration in making a purchase.[2] "Reasonable price" really means "perceived reasonable value" at the time of the transaction. One of the authors of this textbook bought a fancy European-designed toaster for about $45. The toaster's wide mouth made it possible to toast a bagel, warm a muffin, and, with a special $15 attachment, make a grilled sandwich. The author felt that a toaster with all these features surely must be worth the total price of $60. But after three months of using the device, toast burned around the edges and raw in the middle lost its appeal. The disappointed buyer put the toaster in the attic. Why didn't he return it to the retailer? Because the boutique had gone out of business, and no other local retailer carried the brand. Also, there was no U.S. service center. Remember, the price paid is based on the satisfaction consumers *expect* to receive from a product and not necessarily the satisfaction they *actually* receive.

Price can relate to anything with perceived value, not just money. When goods and services are exchanged, the trade is called barter. For example, if you exchange this book for a chemistry book at the end of the term, you have engaged in barter. The price you paid for the chemistry book was this textbook.

revenue
The price charged to customers multiplied by the number of units sold.

profit
Revenue minus expenses.

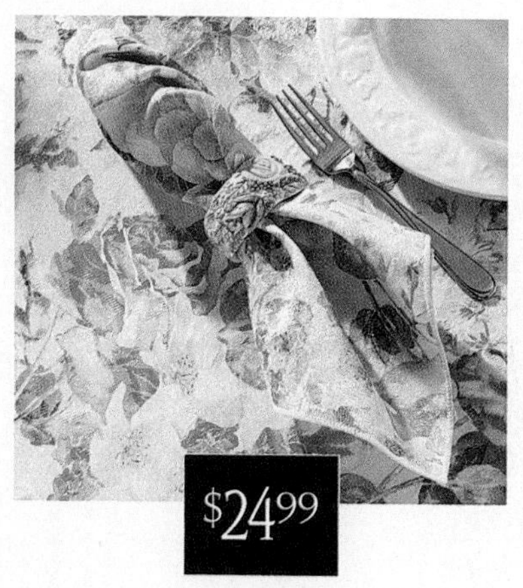

$24.99
Stop and smell the bargains.
These delightful floral-patterned table linens and accessories are a great way to celebrate spring. The 52x70" tablecloth shown is just $24.99. The bargains are in full bloom at Target.

Successful retailers like Target understand that "perceived reasonable value" is important to consumers.
Courtesy Target Stores

The Importance of Price to Marketing Managers

Prices are the key to revenues, which in turn are the key to profits for an organization. **Revenue** is the price charged to customers multiplied by the number of units sold. Revenue is what pays for all of a company's activities: production, finance, sales, distribution, and so on. What's left over (if anything) is **profit**. Managers usually strive to charge a price that will earn a fair profit.

To earn a profit, managers must choose a price that is not too high or too low, a price that equals the perceived value to target consumers. If a price is set too high in consumers' minds, the perceived value will be less than the cost, and sales opportunities will be lost. Many mainstream purchasers of cars, sporting goods, CDs, tools, wedding gowns, and computers are buying "used or pre-owned" items to get a better deal. Pricing a new product too high may give an incentive to some shoppers to go to a "pre-owned" or consignment retailer.[3]

Lost sales mean lost revenue. Conversely, if a price is too low, it may be perceived as a great value for the consumer, but the firm loses revenue it could have earned. Setting prices too low may not even attract as many buyers as managers might think. One study surveyed over 2,000 shoppers at national chains around the country and found that over 60 percent intended to buy full-price items only.[4] Retailers that place too much emphasis on discounts may not be able to meet the expectations of full-price customers.

Trying to set the right price is one of the marketing manager's most stressful and pressure-filled tasks, as trends in the consumer market attest:

- Confronting a flood of new products, potential buyers carefully evaluate the price of each one against the value of existing products.
- The increased availability of bargain-priced private and generic brands has put downward pressure on overall prices.
- Many firms are trying to maintain their market share by cutting prices. For example, Ford Taurus became the best-selling passenger car in America in 1992, after taking the lead from the Honda Accord. The Accord has been catching up with the Taurus by offering large discounts on an old, but popular, car. Ford is matching the discounts in an attempt to maintain its market share.[5]

ON LINE

In the organizational market, where customers include both governments and businesses, buyers are also becoming more price sensitive and better informed. In the consumer market, consumers are using the Internet to make wiser purchasing decisions. Computerized information systems enable the organizational buyer to compare price and performance with great ease and accuracy. Improved communication and the increased use of telemarketing and computer-aided selling have also opened up many markets to new competitors. Finally, competition in general is increasing, so some installations, accessories, and component parts are being marketed like indistinguishable commodities.

Pricing Objectives

To survive in today's highly competitive marketplace, companies need pricing objectives that are specific, attainable, and measurable. Realistic pricing goals then require periodic monitoring to determine the effectiveness of the company's strategy. For convenience, pricing objectives can be divided into three categories: profit oriented, sales oriented, and status quo.

Profit-Oriented Pricing Objectives

2
List and explain a variety of pricing objectives

Profit-oriented objectives include profit maximization, satisfactory profits, and target return on investment. A brief discussion of each of these objectives follows.

Profit Maximization. *Profit maximization* means setting prices so that total revenue is as large as possible relative to total costs. (A more theoretically precise definition and explanation of profit maximization appears later in the chapter.) Profit maximization does not always signify unreasonably high prices, however. Both price and profits depend on the type of competitive environment a firm faces, such as being in a monopoly position (being the only seller) or selling in a much more competitive situation. (See Chapter 2 for a description of the four types of competitive environments.) Also, remember that a firm cannot charge a price higher than the product's perceived value. Many firms do not have the accounting data they need for maximizing profits. It sounds simple to say that a company should keep producing and selling goods or services as long as revenues exceed costs. Yet it is often difficult to set up an accurate accounting system to determine the point of profit maximization.

ENTREPRENEUR

Satisfactory Profits. Satisfactory profits are a reasonable level of profits. Rather than maximizing profits, many organizations strive for profits that are satisfactory to the stockholders and management—in other words, a level of profits consistent with the level of risk an organization faces. In a high-risk industry, a satisfactory profit may be 35 percent. In a low-risk industry, it might be 7 percent. To maximize profits, a small-business owner might have to keep his or her store open seven days a week. But the owner might not want to work that hard and might be satisfied with less profit.

return on investment (ROI)
Net profit after taxes divided by total assets.

Target Return on Investment. The most common profit objective is target **return on investment (ROI)**, sometimes called the firm's return on total assets. ROI measures the overall effectiveness of management in generating profits with its available assets. The higher the firm's return on investment, the better off the firm is. Many companies—including Du Pont, General Motors, Navistar, Exxon, and Union Carbide—use target return on investment as their main pricing goal.

Return on investment is calculated as follows:

$$\text{Return on investment} = \frac{\text{Net profits after taxes}}{\text{Total assets}}$$

Assume that in 1999 Johnson Controls had assets of \$4.5 million, net profits of \$550,000, and a target ROI of 10 percent. This was the actual ROI:

$$\text{ROI} = \frac{550{,}000}{4{,}500{,}000}$$

$$= 12.2 \text{ percent}$$

As you can see, the ROI for Johnson Controls exceeded its target, which indicates that the company prospered in 1996.

Comparing the 12.2 percent ROI with the industry average provides a more meaningful picture, however. Any ROI needs to be evaluated in terms of the competitive environment, risks in the industry, and economic conditions. Generally speaking, firms seek ROIs in the 10 to 30 percent range. For example, General Electric seeks a 25 percent ROI, whereas Alcoa, Rubbermaid, and most major pharmaceutical companies strive for a 20 percent ROI. In some industries, however, such as the grocery industry, a return of under 5 percent is common and acceptable.

A company with a target ROI can predetermine its desired level of profitability. The marketing manager can use the standard, such as 10 percent ROI, to determine whether a particular price and marketing mix are feasible. In addition, however, the manager must weigh the risk of a given strategy even if the return is in the acceptable range.

Sales-Oriented Pricing Objectives

Sales-oriented pricing objectives are based either on market share or on dollar or unit sales. The effective marketing manager should be familiar with these pricing objectives.

market share
A company's product sales as a percentage of total sales for that industry.

Market Share **Market share** is a company's product sales as a percentage of total sales for that industry. Sales can be reported in dollars or in units of product. Many companies believe that maintaining or increasing market share is an indicator of the effectiveness of their marketing mix. Larger market shares have indeed often meant higher profits, thanks to greater economies of scale, market power, and ability to compensate top-quality management. Conventional wisdom also says that market share and return on investment are strongly related. For the most part they are; however, many companies with low market share survive and even

There Are No Ethics in Ethnic Pricing

Brendan McInerney, who lives in Frankfurt, Germany, could hardly believe his ears. His wife could fly to Osaka, Japan, for Christmas for 1,700 marks ($965) on Lufthansa, but he would have to pay 2,700 marks on the same flight. The reason: Mr. McInerney is American; his wife, Kyoko, is Japanese. "In America this is called racial discrimination," Mr. McInerney says, fuming, even after Lufthansa eventually offered him the same fare as his wife. "It's illegal. It's unfair."

It *is* illegal in Germany, and it is undoubtedly unfair. It goes on, however, fueled by increasing rivalry among carriers—and not only in Germany. Throughout Europe, lots of people are getting special deals on airline tickets and other items because of their passports—or those of their employers. Mr. McInerney works for a German bank, but according to his travel agent, he would automatically qualify for the same cut-rate fare as his wife if he worked for a Japanese bank.

Commonly called "ethnic pricing," the practice of giving discounts to people of certain nationalities has long been routine in developing countries such as India, China, and Russia. But in Europe, and especially in Germany, the practice is generally kept hush-hush because of the ethical and legal questions it raises.

Christian Hofer, an expert on air-traffic fares with the German Freight Agency, which is invested with the authority to approve special fares, says ethnic pricing such as that being offered by Lufthansa, Air France, and other carriers in Germany is against the law. "For all flights out of Germany," Mr. Hofer says, "there can't be any discrimination on the basis of nationality." Nevertheless, Mr. Hofer says he routinely hears about such deals being offered on the gray market and is essentially powerless to do anything about it. "We don't have the police powers to intervene as we'd like," he says.

The gray market comprises travel agencies specializing in long-distance, economy flights. Indeed, Lufthansa itself doesn't even advertise the special fares. Instead, it hammers them out in individual contracts with select travel offices that offer the special fares only on request. Thus, even in Germany ethnic pricing has largely remained a well-kept secret.

Not that Lufthansa denies its involvement with ethnic pricing. It says the practice is common in Germany and argues that it is only reacting to competition from the national carriers of Japan, South Korea, China, and Iran. "The others started it," says Dagmar Rotter, a Lufthansa spokeswoman. "We only offered it after the market forced us to do so."

For Mr. McInerney, the ethnic-pricing issue in Germany is academic. After being confronted with the absurdity of charging a husband and wife different prices, Lufthansa said it was changing its policy to include spouses traveling together, effective Jan. 1, and would make an exception for Mr. McInerney in advance. Best of all, Mr. McInerney says, is the frequent-flyer mileage: "I get Lufthansa miles." Otherwise, he says, he would have flown with All Nippon Airways to begin with.[6]

Do you think Lufthansa's response that it was "simply meeting competition" is sufficient justification for "ethnic pricing"? Does letting both spouses receive the ethnic fare solve the problem? Some airlines offer ethnic fares to their citizens when they are living abroad. The airlines say that this is the only way some workers can afford to go home to visit their families. How would you respond to this logic?

prosper. To succeed with a low market share, companies need to compete in industries with slow growth and few product changes—for instance, industrial component parts and supplies. Otherwise, they must vie in an industry that makes frequently bought items, such as consumer convenience goods.

Sales Maximization Rather than striving for market share, companies sometimes try to maximize sales. The objective of maximizing sales ignores profits, competition, and the marketing environment as long as sales are rising.

If a company is strapped for funds or faces an uncertain future, it may try to generate a maximum amount of cash in the short run. Management's task when using this objective is to calculate which price-quantity relationship generates the greatest cash revenue. Sales maximization can also be used effectively on a temporary basis to sell off excess inventory. It is not uncommon, for example, to find Christmas cards, ornaments, and so on discounted at 50 to 70 percent off retail

Kraft General Foods

Visit the Kraft pantry. Does Maxwell House emphasize taste in its Web advertising? If so, how?
http://www.kraftfoods.com/

on line

prices after the holiday season. In addition, management can use sales maximization for year-end sales to clear out old models before introducing the new ones.

Maximization of cash should never be a long-run objective, because cash maximization may mean little or no profitability. Without profits, a company cannot survive.

Status Quo Pricing Objectives

status quo pricing
Pricing objective that maintains existing prices or meets the competition's prices.

Status quo pricing seeks to maintain existing prices or to meet the competition's prices. This third category of pricing objectives has the major advantage of requiring little planning. It is essentially a passive policy.

Often, firms competing in an industry with an established price leader simply meet the competition's prices. These industries typically have fewer price wars than those with direct price competition. In other cases, managers regularly shop competitors' stores to ensure that their prices are comparable. Target's middle managers must visit competing Kmart stores weekly to compare prices and then make adjustments. In response to MCI and Sprint's claims that its long-distance service is overpriced, AT&T struck back with advertisements showing that its rates are esentially equal to competitors'. AT&T was attempting to convince target consumers that it follows a status quo pricing strategy.

The Demand Determinant of Price

3
Explain the role of demand in price determination

After marketing managers establish pricing goals, they must set specific prices to reach those goals. The price they set for each product depends mostly on two factors: the demand for the good or service and the cost to the seller for that good or service. When pricing goals are mainly sales oriented, demand considerations usually dominate. Other factors, such as distribution and promotion strategies, perceived quality, and stage of the product life cycle, can also influence price.

The Nature of Demand

demand
The quantity of a product that will be sold in the market at various prices for a specified period.

Demand is the quantity of a product that will be sold in the market at various prices for a specified period. The quantity of a product that people will buy depends on its price. The higher the price, the fewer goods or services consumers will demand. Conversely, the lower the price, the more goods or services they will demand.

supply
The quantity of a product that will be offered to the market by a supplier at various prices for a specified period.

Supply is the quantity of a product that will be offered to the market by a supplier or suppliers at various prices for a specified period. At higher prices, sellers will obtain more resources and produce more goods.

Elasticity of Demand

elasticity of demand
Consumers' responsiveness or sensitivity to changes in price.

elastic demand
Situation in which consumer demand is sensitive to changes in price.

inelastic demand
Situation in which an increase or a decrease in price will not significantly affect demand for the product.

To appreciate demand analysis, you should understand the concept of elasticity. **Elasticity of demand** refers to consumers' responsiveness or sensitivity to changes in price. **Elastic demand** occurs when consumers buy more or less of a product when the price changes. Conversely, **inelastic demand** means that an increase or a decrease in price will not significantly affect demand for the product.

Factors That Affect Elasticity Several factors affect elasticity of demand, including the following:

- *Availability of substitutes:* When many substitute products are available, the consumer can easily switch from one product to another, making demand elastic. The same is true in reverse: A ticket on the Concorde, which flies twice the ve-

Columbia House

How can Columbia House offer so many CDs or videos for one cent? Go to the Web site to see what kind of deals Columbia House is offering right now. Compare the introductory offers to the pricing for subsequent purchases. What conclusions can you draw about Columbia House's elasticity of demand for CDs based on the posted pricing for the initial sign-up and for subsequent purchases?
http://www.columbiahouse.com/

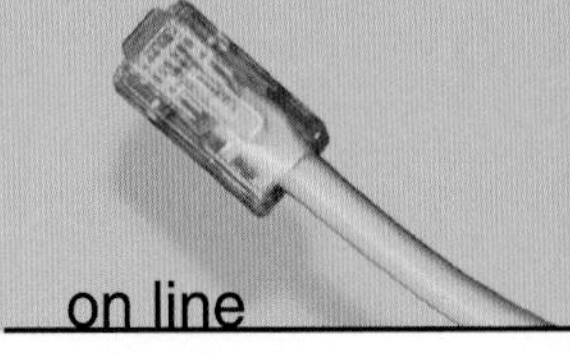

locity of a bullet, is $4,509 one way from New York to London. British Airways can charge this price and fill the seats because there is no substitute.

- *Price relative to purchasing power:* If a price is so low that it is an inconsequential part of an individual's budget, demand will be inelastic. For example, if the price of salt doubles, consumers will not stop putting salt on their eggs, because salt is cheap anyway.
- *Product durability:* Consumers often have the option of repairing durable products rather than replacing them, thus prolonging their useful life. For instance, if a person had planned to buy a new car and the prices suddenly began to rise, he or she might elect to fix the old car and drive it for another year. In other words, people are sensitive to the price increase, and demand is elastic.
- *A product's other uses:* The greater the number of different uses for a product, the more elastic demand tends to be. If a product has only one use, as may be true of a new medicine, the quantity purchased probably will not vary as price varies. A person will consume only the prescribed quantity, regardless of price. On the other hand, a product like steel has many possible applications. As its price falls, steel becomes more economically feasible in a wider variety of applications, thereby making demand relatively elastic.

Because steel has many possible applications, price changes have a great impact on demand. As its price falls, steel becomes a more economically feasible alternative, and so the demand is relatively elastic.
© Corbis/Adam Woolfitt

The Cost Determinant of Price

4

Describe cost-oriented pricing strategies

Sometimes companies minimize or ignore the importance of demand and decide to price their products largely or solely on the basis of costs. Prices determined strictly on the basis of costs may be too high for the target market, thereby reducing or eliminating sales. Or cost-based prices may be too low, causing the firm to earn a lower return than it should. However, costs should generally be part of any price determination, if only as a floor below which a good or service must not be priced in the long run.

Cost may seem simple, but it is actually a multifaceted concept, especially for producers of goods and services. **Variable costs** are those that deviate with changes in the level of output; an example of a variable cost is the cost of materials. In contrast, a **fixed cost** does not change as output is increased or decreased. Examples include rent and executives' salaries.

variable costs
Costs that vary with changes in the level of output.

fixed cost
Cost that does not change as output is increased or decreased.

Markup Pricing

Markup pricing, the most popular method used by wholesalers and retailers to establish a selling price, does not directly analyze the costs of production. Instead,

markup pricing
Cost of buying the product from the producer plus amounts for profit and for expenses not otherwise accounted for.

markup pricing is the cost of buying the product from the producer, plus amounts for profit and for expenses not otherwise accounted for. The total determines the selling price.

A retailer, for example, adds a certain percentage to the cost of the merchandise received to arrive at the retail price. An item that costs the retailer $1.80 and is sold for $2.20 carries a markup of 40¢, which is a markup of 22 percent of the cost (40¢ ÷ $1.80). Retailers tend to discuss markup in terms of its percentage of the retail price—in this example, 18 percent (40¢ ÷ $2.20). The difference between the retailer's cost and the selling price (40¢) is the gross margin, as Chapter 11 explained.

keystoning
Practice of marking up prices by 100 percent, or doubling the cost.

Markups are often based on experience. For example, many small retailers mark up merchandise 100 percent over cost. (In other words, they double the cost.) This tactic is called **keystoning**. Some other factors that influence markups are the merchandise's appeal to customers, past response to the markup (an implicit demand consideration), the item's promotional value, the seasonality of the good, its fashion appeal, the product's traditional selling price, and its competition. Most retailers avoid any set markup because of such considerations as promotional value and seasonality.

The biggest advantage of markup pricing is its simplicity. The primary disadvantage is that it ignores demand and may result in overpricing or underpricing the merchandise.

break-even analysis
Method of determining what sales volume must be reached before total revenue equals total costs.

Break-Even Pricing

Now let's take a closer look at the relationship between sales and cost. **Break-even analysis** determines what sales volume must be reached before the company breaks even (its total costs equal total revenue) and no profits are earned.

The typical break-even model assumes a given fixed cost and a constant average variable cost. Suppose that Universal Sportswear, a hypothetical firm, has fixed costs of $2,000 and that the cost of labor and materials for each unit produced is 50¢. Assume that it can sell up to 6,000 units of its product at $1 without having to lower its price.

Exhibit 15.1(a) illustrates Universal Sportswear's break-even point. As Exhibit 15.1(b) indicates, Universal Sportswear's total variable costs increase by 50¢ every time a new unit is produced, and total fixed costs remain constant at $2,000 regardless of the level of output. Therefore, 4,000 units of output give Universal Sportswear $2,000 in fixed costs and $2,000 in total variable costs (4,000 units × 50¢), or $4,000 in total costs.

Revenue is also $4,000 (4,000 units × $1), giving a new profit of zero dollars at the break-even point of 4,000 units. Notice that once the firm gets past the break-even point, the gap between total revenue and total cost gets wider and wider, because both functions are assumed to be linear.

The formula for calculating break-even quantities is simple:

$$\text{Break-even quantity} = \frac{\text{Total fixed costs}}{\text{Fixed cost contribution}}$$

Fixed cost contribution is the price minus the average variable cost. Average variable costs equal total variable costs divided by quantity of output. Therefore, for Universal Sportswear,

$$\text{Break-even quantity} = \frac{\$2{,}000}{(\$1.00 - 50¢)} = \frac{\$2{,}000}{50¢}$$
$$= 4{,}000 \text{ units}$$

The advantage of break-even analysis is that it provides a quick estimate of how much the firm must sell to break even and how much profit can be earned if a

exhibit 15.1

Costs, Revenues, and Break-Even for Universal Sportswear

(a) Break-even point

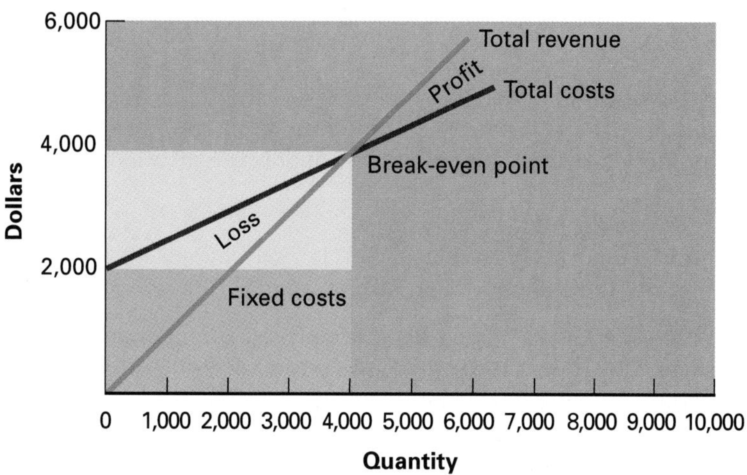

(b) Costs and revenues

Output	Total fixed costs	Average variable costs	Total variable costs	Average total costs	Average revenue (price)	Total revenue	Total costs	Profit or loss
500	$2,000	$0.50	$ 250	$4.50	$1.00	$ 500	$2,250	($1,750)
1,000	2,000	0.50	500	2.50	1.00	1,000	2,500	(1,500)
1,500	2,000	0.50	750	1.83	1.00	1,500	2,750	(1,250)
2,000	2,000	0.50	1,000	1.50	1.00	2,000	3,000	(1,000)
2,500	2,000	0.50	1,250	1.30	1.00	2,500	3,250	(750)
3,000	2,000	0.50	1,500	1.17	1.00	3,000	3,500	(500)
3,500	2,000	0.50	1,750	1.07	1.00	3,500	3,750	(250)
*4,000	2,000	0.50	2,000	1.00	1.00	4,000	4,000	(0)
4,500	2,000	0.50	2,250	.94	1.00	4,500	4,250	250
5,000	2,000	0.50	2,500	.90	1.00	5,000	4,500	500
5,500	2,000	0.50	2,750	.86	1.00	5,500	4,750	750
6,000	2,000	0.50	3,000	.83	1.00	6,000	5,000	1,000

*Break-even point

higher sales volume is obtained. If a firm is operating close to the break-even point, it may want to see what can be done to reduce costs or increase sales. Moreover, in a simple break-even analysis, it is not necessary to compute marginal costs and marginal revenues, because price and average cost per unit are assumed to be constant. Also, because accounting data for marginal cost and revenue are frequently unavailable, it is convenient not to have to depend on that information.

Break-even analysis is not without several important limitations. Sometimes it is hard to know whether a cost is fixed or variable. For example, if labor wins a tough guaranteed-employment contract, are the resulting expenses a fixed cost? Are middle-level executives' salaries fixed costs? More important than cost determination is the fact that simple break-even analysis ignores demand. For example, how does Universal Sportswear know it can sell 4,000 units at $1? Could it sell the same 4,000 units at $2 or even $5? Obviously, this information would profoundly affect the firm's pricing decisions.

Energy Marketplace

Visit the Energy Marketplace and choose a supplier. Are there other considerations besides price that influence your decision? What are they, and how important are they in your selection? Why?
http://www.energymarketplace.com/

on line

Other Determinants of Price

5

Demonstrate how the product life cycle, competition, distribution and promotion strategies, the impact of the Internet, demands of large customers, and perceptions of quality can affect price

Other factors besides demand and costs can influence price. For example, the stage of the product's life cycle, the competition, the product distribution strategy, the promotion strategy, and perceived quality can all affect pricing.

Stage in the Product Life Cycle

As a product moves through its life cycle (see Chapter 9), the demand for the product and the competitive conditions tend to change:

- *Introductory stage:* Management usually sets prices high during the introductory stage. One reason is that it hopes to recover its development costs quickly. In addition, demand originates in the core of the market (the customers whose needs ideally match the product's attributes) and thus is relatively inelastic. On the other hand, if the target market is highly price sensitive, management often finds it better to price the product at the market level or lower. For example, when Kraft General Foods brought out Country Time lemonade, it was priced like similar products in the highly competitive beverage market because the market was price sensitive.
- *Growth stage:* Prices generally begin to stabilize as the product enters the growth stage. There are several reasons. First, competitors have entered the market, increasing the available supply. Second, the product has begun to appeal to a broader market, often lower-income groups. Finally, economies of scale are lowering costs, and the savings can be passed on to the consumer in the form of lower prices.
- *Maturity stage:* Maturity usually brings further price decreases as competition increases and inefficient, high-cost firms are eliminated. Distribution channels become a significant cost factor, however, because of the need to offer wide product lines for highly segmented markets, extensive service requirements, and the sheer number of dealers necessary to absorb high-volume production. The manufacturers that remain in the market toward the end of the maturity stage typically offer similar prices. Usually only the most efficient remain, and they have comparable costs. At this stage, price increases are usually cost initiated, not demand initiated. Nor do price reductions in the late phase of maturity stimulate much demand. Because demand is limited and producers have similar cost structures, the remaining competitors will probably match price reductions.
- *Decline stage:* The final stage of the life cycle may see further price decreases as the few remaining competitors try to salvage the last vestiges of demand. When only one firm is left in the market, prices begin to stabilize. In fact, prices may eventually rise dramatically if the product survives and moves into the specialty good category, as horse-drawn carriages and vinyl records have.

The Competition

Competition varies during the product life cycle, of course, and so at times it may strongly affect pricing decisions. For example, although a firm may not have any competition at first, the high prices it charges may eventually induce another firm to enter the market.

Several companies have recently felt that the $300 billion used-car market was ripe for the used-car superstore. Peddling used cars, it turns out, is a more delicate task than selling televisions or refrigerators. "It's harder than we thought it would be," concedes W. Austin Ligon, president of CarMax Group, a used-car superstore chain controlled by electronics retailer Circuit City Stores, Inc.[7]

Levi Strauss & Company

What are the FAQs (frequently asked questions) for Levi's? How does Levi's address the price issue?
http://www.levi.com/

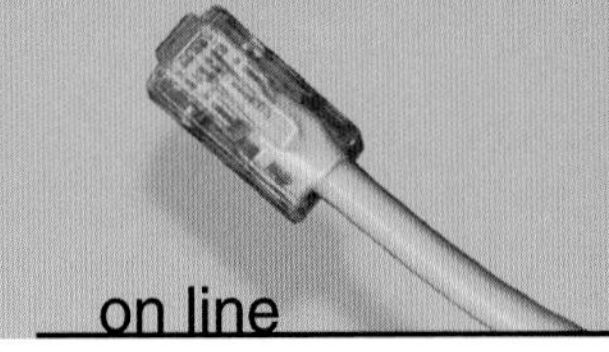

on line

Part of the problem is that used cars don't fit comfortably into retailing's "big box" model, which calls for vast quantities of high-quality merchandise at low prices. Not every customer wants a Ford Taurus. But filling the parking lot with more exotic makes and models has been a daunting task. And prepping used cars for resale is more expensive than they had expected.

Most damaging of all is an image for high prices. In an attempt to eliminate the mystery—and the haggling—the superstores have adopted fixed, or so-called transparent, pricing, in which all possible extra charges are shown up front. The fixed prices result in higher sticker prices at the superstores. This, in turn, has resulted in these companies not meeting their profit goals.

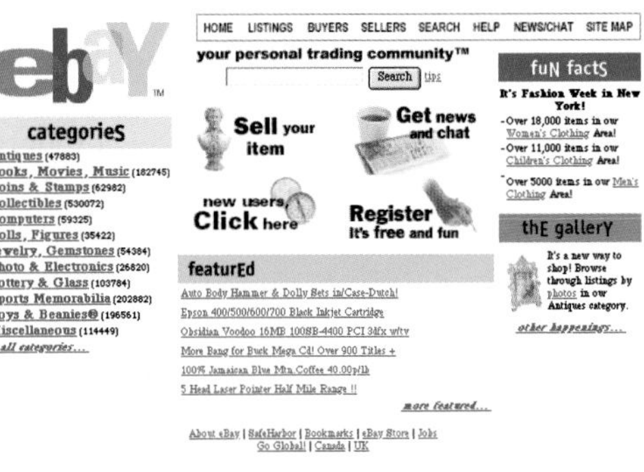

Shopping over the Internet is on the rise, and as part of that trend Internet auctions are becoming increasingly popular. At sites like ebay.com, consumers can purchase anything from computers to collectibles. How interested would you be in participating in an Internet auction, either as a buyer or a seller?
Courtesy eBay Inc.

Intense competition can sometimes lead to price wars. What leads companies into such self-defeating price wars? Often, they make the mistake of measuring their success by market share rather than by profitability. But something more is at play. Michael Marn, a partner at McKinsey who heads its pricing practice worldwide, says that price wars are often caused by companies misreading or misunderstanding competitors. Marn tells of one McKinsey client, a company that dominated the market for adhesive labels nationwide. After a small competitor built a tiny factory in southern Florida with no prospects for further expansion, the company reacted with a nationwide price cut of 15% to 20% and, says Marn, "gave away profitability for two years." Typically, concludes Marn, price wars are "overreactions to threats that either aren't there at all or are not as big as they seem."[8]

One company recently took action to avoid a calamitous price war by outsmarting its competition. A company (call it Acme) heard that its competitor was trying to steal some business by offering a low price to one of its best customers. Instead of immediately cutting its prices, Acme visited three of its competitor's best clients and said they figured the client was paying *x*, the same price that the competitor had quoted to Acme's own customer. Within days, Acme's competitor had retracted its low-price offer to its client. Presumably, the competitor had received calls from three angry clients asking for the same special deal.

Distribution Strategy

An effective distribution network can often overcome other minor flaws in the marketing mix. For example, although consumers may perceive a price as being slightly higher than normal, they may buy the product anyway if it is being sold at a convenient retail outlet.

Adequate distribution for a new product can often be attained by offering a larger-than-usual profit margin to distributors. A variation on this strategy is to give dealers a large trade allowance to help offset the costs of promotion and further stimulate demand at the retail level.

Promotion Strategy

Price is often used as a promotional tool to increase consumer interest. The weekly grocery section of the newspaper, for instance, advertises many products with special low prices. Pricing can be a tool for trade promotions as well. For example, Levi's Dockers (casual men's slacks) are very popular with white-collar men ages 25 to 45, and a growing and lucrative market. Sensing an opportunity, rival pantsmaker Bugle Boy began offering similar pants at cheaper wholesale prices, which gave retailers a bigger gross margin than they were getting with Dockers. Levi Strauss had to either lower prices or risk its $400 million annual Docker sales. Although Levi Strauss intended its cheapest Dockers to retail for $35, it started selling Dockers to retailers for $18 a pair. Retailers could then advertise Dockers at a very attractive retail price of $25.

ON LINE

The Impact of the Internet and Extranets

The Internet, corporate networks, and wireless setups are linking people, machines, and companies around the globe—and connecting sellers and buyers as never before. This is enabling buyers to quickly and easily compare products and prices, putting them in a better bargaining position. At the same time, the technology allows sellers to collect detailed data about customers' buying habits, preferences—even spending limits—so they can tailor their products and prices. This raises hopes of a more efficient marketplace.

Today, the first signs of this new fluid pricing can be found mostly on the Internet. Online auctions allow cybershoppers to bid on everything from collectibles to treadmills. Electronic exchanges, on the other hand, act as middlemen, representing a group of sellers of one type of product or service—say, long-distance service—that is matched with buyers.

extranet
A private electronic network that links a company with its suppliers and customers.

The pricing revolution, though, goes beyond the Net. Companies also are creating private networks, or **extranets**, that link them with their suppliers and customers. These systems make it possible to get a precise handle on inventory, costs, and demand at any given moment—and adjust prices instantly. In the past, there was a significant cost associated with changing prices, known as the "menu cost." For a company with a large product line, it could take months for price adjustments to filter down to distributors, retailers, and salespeople. Streamlined networks reduce menu cost and time to near zero.[9]

Two trailblazers in Net commerce are Southern California Gas Company and Priceline. Deregulation of the energy industry means that customers can shop for an energy supplier just like they would for a long-distance company. Southern California Gas saw this as an opportunity, and created the Energy Marketplace. This is a Web-based exchange that lets customers shop for the best gas prices. Small and midsize gas providers list their prices on the exchange. That lowers their marketing costs and gives them access to a broader market—putting them on equal footing with big energy suppliers. Customers—mostly businesses—save money by shopping for the best price, or locking in long-term deals when prices are low. And Southern California Gas, as a distributor, increases its volume of business and collects a subscription fee from gas providers that use the exchange.

Priceline lets anyone bid on the price of an airline ticket. It is already selling over a thousand tickets a day, as was discussed in detail in the opening vignette.[10]

Internet auctions are also growing. AucNet, for example, finds dealers and wholesalers currently buying and selling about 6,000 cars per month.[11] Auction sites are selling everything from electronics, old books, and furniture to samurai swords and real estate. Check out **ebay.com**, **onsale.com**, or **eworldauction.com** to get a feel for auction sites.

Demands of Large Customers

Large customers of manufacturers such as Wal-Mart, JCPenney, and other department stores often make specific pricing demands that the suppliers must agree to. Department stores are making greater-than-ever demands from their suppliers to cover the heavy discounts and markdowns on their own selling floors. They want suppliers to guarantee their stores' profit margins, and they insist on cash rebates if the guarantee isn't met. They are exacting fines for violations of ticketing, packing, and shipping rules. Cumulatively, the demands are nearly wiping out profits for all but the very biggest suppliers, according to fashion designers and garment makers.

Few stores ask for stiffer margin guarantees than does May's Lord & Taylor chain.[12] Makers of moderate-priced dresses say Lord & Taylor is the entry point for vendors hoping to do business with other May department store chains, like Hecht's and Foley's. May sets the profitability bar high, insisting on a guaranteed profit margin as high in some cases as 48%, according to Beau Baker, former chief executive officer of Beau David Inc., a small dress company.

It used to be that when a garment maker sold to a store, the two parties would agree on a retail price and at the end of the season the supplier would rebate some of the cost of markdowns. Discounts and markdowns were far rarer then than they are today: department stores could afford plenty of sales help to push products. But as stores cut labor costs, they came to rely on promotional markdowns and sales to move goods—with suppliers covering profit-margin shortfalls.

The Relationship of Price to Quality

Consumers tend to rely on a high price as a predictor of good quality when there is great uncertainty involved in the purchase decision. Reliance on price as an indicator of quality seems to exist for all products, but it reveals itself more strongly for some items than for others.[13] Among the products that benefit from this phenomenon are coffee, stockings, aspirin, salt, floor wax, shampoo, clothing, furniture, perfume, whiskey, and many services. If the consumer obtains additional information—for instance, about the brand or the store—then reliance on price as an indicator of quality decreases.[14] In the absence of other information, people typically assume that prices are higher because the products contain better materials, because they are made more carefully, or, in the case of professional services, because the provider has more expertise. In other words, consumers assume that "you get what you pay for." One study has shown that some people believe "you get what you pay for" much more strongly than others. That is, some consumers tend to rely much more heavily on price as a quality indicator than others do.[15] In general, consumers tend to be more accurate in their price-quality assessments for nondurable goods (such as ice cream, frozen pizza, or oven cleaner) than for durable goods (such as coffeemakers, gas grills, or 10-speed bikes).[16] Knowledgeable merchants take these consumer attitudes into account when devising their pricing strategies. **Prestige pricing** is charging a high price to help promote a high-quality image. A successful prestige-pricing strategy requires a retail price that is reasonably consistent with consumers' expectations. For example, no one goes shopping at a Gucci shop in New York and expects to pay $9.95 for a pair of loafers. In fact, demand would fall drastically at such a low price. Bayer aspirin would probably lose market share over the long run if it lowered its prices. A new mustard packaged in a crockery jar was not successful until its price was doubled.

prestige pricing
Charging a high price to help promote a high-quality image.

Consumers also expect private or store brands to be cheaper than national brands. However, if the price difference between a private brand and a nationally distributed manufacturer's brand is too great, consumers tend to believe that the private brand is inferior. On the other hand, if the savings aren't big enough, there is little incentive to buy the private brand. One study of scanner data found that if the price difference between the national brand and the private brand was less than 10 percent, people tended not to buy the private brand. If the price difference was greater than 20 percent, consumers perceived the private brand to be inferior.[17]

In sum, the most recent research has shown that a well-known brand name is used by people in many countries as their primary indicator of quality. If the product does not have this feature, then price, followed by the physical appearance of the item, is used to judge quality. After a well-known brand name, price, and physical appearance, the reputation of the retailer is used by consumers as an indicator of quality.[18]

Now that we understand the determinants of price, let's examine the process for setting a price.

How to Set a Price on a Product

Setting the right price on a product is a four-step process (see Exhibit 15.2):

1. Establish pricing goals.
2. Estimate demand, costs, and profits.

Describe the procedure for setting the right price

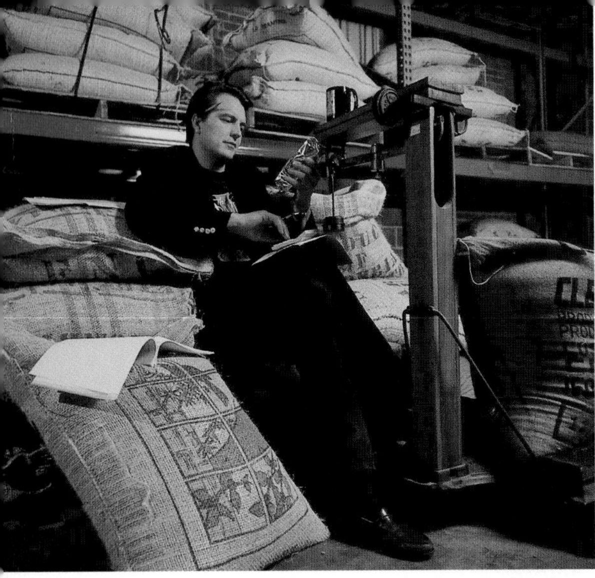

Although lower prices are generally more appealing to consumers, sometimes price increases are necessary; how a company communicates this change in pricing structure can be crucial to future success. After a recent price hike, coffee wholesaler Danny O'Neill explained the need for the increase to his customers and so lent credibility to his firm, the Roasterie, in Kansas City, Missouri.

3. Choose a price strategy to help determine a base price.
4. Fine tune the base price with pricing tactics.

The first three steps are discussed below; the fourth step is discussed later in the chapter.

Establish Pricing Goals

The first step in setting the right price is to establish pricing goals. Recall that pricing objectives fall into three categories: profit oriented, sales oriented, and status quo. These goals are derived from the firm's overall objectives.

A good understanding of the marketplace and of the consumer can sometimes tell a manager very quickly whether a goal is realistic. For example, if Firm A's objective is a 20 percent target return on investment (ROI) and its product development and implementation costs are $5 million, the market must be rather large or must support the price required to earn a 20 percent ROI. Assume that company B has a pricing objective that all new products must reach at least 15 percent market share within three years after their introduction. A thorough study of the environment may convince the marketing manager that the competition is too strong and the market share goal can't be met.

All pricing objectives have trade-offs that managers must weigh. A profit maximization objective may require a bigger initial investment than the firm can commit to or wants to commit to. Reaching the desired market share often means sacrificing short-term profit, because without careful management, long-

exhibit 15.2

Steps in Setting the Right Price on a Product

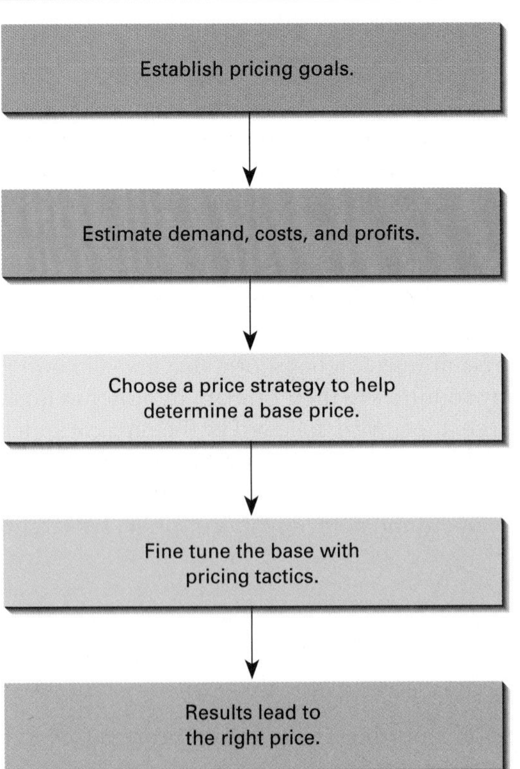
Establish pricing goals.
Estimate demand, costs, and profits.
Choose a price strategy to help determine a base price.
Fine tune the base with pricing tactics.
Results lead to the right price.

term profit goals may not be met. Meeting the competition is the easiest pricing goal to implement. Can managers, however, really afford to ignore demand and costs, the life cycle stage, and other considerations? When creating pricing objectives, managers must consider these trade-offs in light of the target customer and the environment.

Estimate Demand, Costs, and Profits

Earlier we explained that total revenue is a function of price and quantity demanded, and that quantity demanded depends on elasticity. After establishing pricing goals, managers should estimate total revenue at a variety of prices. Next, they should determine corresponding costs for each price. They are then ready to estimate how much profit, if any, and how much market share can be earned at each possible price. These data become the heart of the developing price policy. Managers can study the options in light of revenues, costs, and profits. This information, in turn, can help determine which price can best meet the firm's pricing goals.

Choose a Price Strategy

The basic, long-term pricing framework for a good or service should be a logical extension of the pricing objectives. The marketing manager's chosen **price strategy** defines the initial price and gives direction for price movements over the product life cycle.

price strategy
Basic long-term pricing framework, which establishes the initial price for a product and the intended direction for the price movements over the product life cycle.

The price strategy sets a competitive price in a specific market segment, based on a well-defined positioning strategy. For example, a car maker like Mercedes-Benz would set a base price at one of the six levels shown in Exhibit 15.3. The E-class models are in the premium range. Changing a price level from premium to super-premium may require a change in the product itself, the target customers served, the promotional strategy, or distribution channels. Thus, changing a price strategy can require dramatic alterations in the marketing mix. A carmaker cannot successfully compete in the super-premium category if the car looks and drives like an economy car.

A company's freedom in pricing a new product and devising a price strategy depends on the market conditions and the other elements of the marketing mix. For example, if a firm launches a new item resembling several others already on the market, its pricing freedom will be restricted. To succeed, the company will probably have to charge a price close to the average market price. In contrast, a firm that introduces a totally new product with no close substitutes will have considerable pricing freedom.

The three basic strategies for setting a price on a good or service are price skimming, penetration pricing, and status quo pricing. A discussion of each type follows.

Price Skimming Price skimming is sometimes called a "market-plus" approach to pricing because it denotes a high price relative to the prices of competing products. Radius Corporation produces unique oval-headed toothbrushes made of black neoprene that look like a scuba-diving accessory. Radius uses a skimming policy, pricing the toothbrushes at $9.95, compared to around $2.00 for a regular toothbrush.

The term **price skimming** is derived from the phrase "skimming the cream off the top." Companies often use this strategy for new products when the product is perceived by the target market as having unique advantages. For example, Caterpillar sets premium prices on its construction equipment to support and capture its high perceived value. Genzyme Corporation introduced Ceredase as the first effective treatment for Gaucher's disease. The pill allows patients to avoid years of painful physical deterioration and lead normal lives. A year's supply for one patient can exceed $300,000.

price skimming
Pricing policy whereby a firm charges a high introductory price, often coupled with heavy promotion.

Genentech, Incorporated

How does Genentech position and promote its products in light of the high prices often charged?
http://www.gene.com/

exhibit 15.3

Segmenting the Automobile Market by Price

Price range	Model		
Ultra-premium *(over $100,000)*	Lamborghini Rolls Royce	Lamborghini USA, Inc.	By permission of Rolls-Royce Motor Cars, Inc.
Super-premium *($60,000–$100,000)*	BMW 850Ci Porsche 928 GTS	BMW of North America, Inc.	Porsche Cars North America
Premium *($40,000–$60,000)*	Mercedes E-Class Lexus LS 400	Mercedes-Benz of North America, Inc.	Lexus, A Division of Toyota Motor Sales, USA, Inc.
Moderate *($15,000–$40,000)*	Buick Regal GS Mazda Miata	Buick Motor Division	Mazda Motor of America
Economy *($10,000–$15,000)*	Saturn SL1 Honda Civic	Saturn Corporation	Honda Motor Company, Ltd.
Basic *(under $10,000)*	Geo Metro Ford Aspire	Chevrolet Motor Division	Ford Motor Company

As a product progresses through its life cycle, the firm may lower its price to successfully reach larger market segments. Economists have described this type of pricing as "sliding down the demand curve." Not all companies slide down the curve. Genentech's TPA, a drug that clears blood clots, was still priced at $2,200 a dose four years after its introduction, despite competition from a much lower-priced competitor.

Price skimming works best when the market is willing to buy the product even though it carries an above-average price. If, for example, some purchasing agents feel that Caterpillar equipment is far superior to competitors' products, then Caterpillar can charge premium prices successfully. Firms can also effectively use price skimming when a product is well protected legally, when it represents a technological breakthrough, or when it has in some other way blocked entry to competitors. Managers may follow a skimming strategy when production cannot be expanded rapidly because of technological difficulties, shortages, or constraints imposed by the skill and time required to produce a product. As long as demand is greater than supply, skimming is an attainable strategy.

A successful skimming strategy enables management to recover its product development or "educational" costs quickly. (Often, consumers must be "taught" the advantages of a radically new item, such as high-definition TV.) Even if the market perceives an introductory price as too high, managers can easily correct the problem by lowering the price. Firms often feel it is better to test the market at a high price and then lower the price if sales are too slow. They are tacitly saying, "If there are any premium-price buyers in the market, let's reach them first and maximize our revenue per unit." Successful skimming strategies are not limited to products. Well-known athletes, entertainers, lawyers, and hairstylists are experts at price skimming. Naturally, a skimming strategy will encourage competitors to enter the market.

Penetration Pricing Penetration pricing is at the end of the spectrum, opposite skimming. **Penetration pricing** means charging a relatively low price for a product as a way to reach the mass market. The low price is designed to capture a large share of a substantial market, resulting in lower production costs. If a marketing manager has made obtaining a large market share the firm's pricing objective, penetration pricing is a logical choice.

penetration pricing
Pricing policy whereby a firm charges a relatively low price for a product initially as a way to reach the mass market.

Penetration pricing does mean lower profit per unit, however. Therefore, to reach the break-even point, it requires higher volume sales than would a skimming policy. If reaching a high volume of sales takes a long time, then the recovery of product development costs will also be slow. As you might expect, penetration pricing tends to discourage competition.

For some years now Fuji and Kodak have been battling it out in overseas film markets. But in the U.S. the picture was quite different. Kodak and Fuji treated that market like a cozy, mutually profitable duopoly. Both enjoyed large margins. Kodak controlled over 80% of the American film market, and distant No. 2 Fuji always priced its film just a little bit lower.

Then in 1997 Fuji began slashing prices by as much as 25%. Fuji's explanation is that Costco, one of its five largest distributors in the U.S., dropped Fuji for Kodak, and the company got stuck with 2.5 million rolls of film. Fuji sold the film at a steep discount to other distributors. When consumers saw that the familiar red, white, and green boxes were a dollar or two cheaper, they switched brands. In 1998 Fuji increased its share of the U.S. film market from 10% to nearly 16%, while Kodak's share took an unprecedented decline from 80% to just under 75%.

Penetration pricing can also be very effective in international marketing, as is described in the "Global Perspectives" box on page 514.

global perspectives

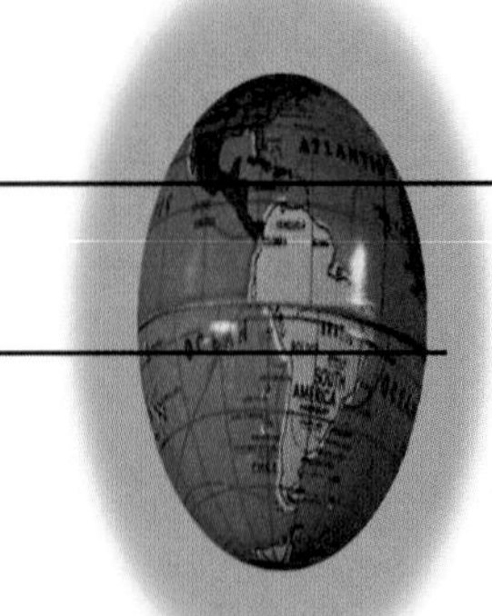

A French Retailer Uses Penetration Pricing to Enter Global Markets

Bargain-basement store Tati, which is to France what Kmart is to the U.S., has opened an outpost on New York's Fifth Avenue, down the street from Saks. But Saks it isn't. Tati is linoleum floors and fluorescent lights. It is women pawing through mounds of plastic raincoats, cheap underpants, and highly flammable, all-synthetic wedding dresses. Store displays? Here, it is bins piled high with clothes, school supplies, luggage, and other goods. "When I think that Tati is going to represent French fashion to New York, it makes my hair stand on end," says Eve Vilain, a French retail apparel consultant.

Tati may not represent what most people think of as French style, but it is big business, and it is going global. Besides the New York store, Tati has recently opened 18 other stores in countries ranging from the Ivory Coast, Lebanon, and Turkey to Germany, Belgium, and Switzerland.

The French have learned not to underestimate Mr. Ouaki. He has transformed a chain of grubby shops in depressed neighborhoods into a cultural phenomenon—a store so tacky that it has become chic. The mink-and-pearl set rummages through Tati's bins alongside the traditionally low-income clientele, and young hipsters have made toting Tati's pink-and-white-check shopping bags fashionable.

At 6 P.M. on a Tuesday evening, Tati's store in Paris's gritty Republique district teems with customers of all ages and social and ethnic backgrounds. Teflon pans, bulk candy, and women's underwear compete bazaar-style for shoppers' attention. Panty hose are selling briskly. At 32 cents apiece, "you can't afford not to buy them," says Cecile Delambre, a graphic designer, shoveling a dozen pairs into her basket.

Tati's latest venture is jewelry. The ugly duckling of French retailing has opened a Tati Gold shop near the Place Vendome, right next door to Cartier and Van Cleef & Arpels. The store is a hive of customers elbowing their way up to the counters and streaming out with purchases ranging from a heart pendant for $3.38 to a chunky $6,618 diamond ring. All but top-ticket purchases are packed in zip-locked baggies and carried off in Tati's plastic shopping bags.

The company, whose name is an anagram of Jules Ouaki's mother's name, Tita, remains very much a family company based on a somewhat unorthodox business theory. "We see ourselves more as clever traders than as seekers of market share," Mr. Ouaki says. The idea is to avoid middlemen and bargain prices down to rock-bottom by buying in massive quantities and paying cash. After that: produce maximum sales volume and rapid turnover by keeping margins low. The average purchase at Tati is less than $16; but with 25 million customers a year, that adds up.

Today, Mr. Ouaki's goal is internationalization. The world has long been coming to Tati—its main customers in France are immigrants. Now, he says, it is time for Tati to go to the world.[19]

Would you say that Mr. Ouaki is describing a penetration-pricing policy? What risks does the company face by using penetration pricing? Could the company have done as well by using a skimming policy?

Status Quo Pricing The third basic price strategy a firm may choose is status quo pricing, or meeting the competition. It means charging a price identical to or very close to the competition's price. JCPenney, for example, makes sure it is charging comparable prices by sending representatives to shop at Sears stores.

Although status quo pricing has the advantage of simplicity, its disadvantage is that the strategy may ignore demand or cost or both. But meeting the competition may be the safest route to long-term survival if the firm is comparatively small.

The Legality and Ethics of Price Strategy

7
Identify the legal and ethical constraints on pricing decisions

As we mentioned in Chapter 2, some pricing decisions are subject to government regulation. Before marketing managers establish any price strategy, they should know the laws that limit their decision making. Among the issues that fall into this category are unfair trade practices, price fixing, price discrimination, and predatory pricing.

Unfair Trade Practices

ETHICS

In over half the states, **unfair trade practice acts** put a floor under wholesale and retail prices. Selling below cost in these states is illegal. Wholesalers and retailers must usually take a certain minimum percentage markup on their combined merchandise cost and transportation cost. The most common markup figures are 6 percent at the retail level and 2 percent at the wholesale level. If a specific wholesaler or retailer can provide "conclusive proof" that operating costs are lower than the minimum required figure, lower prices may be allowed.

unfair trade practice acts
Laws that prohibit wholesalers and retailers from selling below cost.

The intent of unfair trade practice acts is to protect small local firms from giants like Wal-Mart and Target, which operate very efficiently on razor-thin profit margins. However, state enforcement of unfair trade practice laws has generally been lax, partly because low prices benefit local consumers.

Price Fixing

ETHICS

Price fixing is an agreement between two or more firms on the price they will charge for a product. For example, suppose two or more executives from competing firms meet to decide how much to charge for a product or to decide which of them will submit the lowest bid on a certain contract. Such practices are illegal under the Sherman Act and the Federal Trade Commission Act. Offenders have received fines and sometimes prison terms. Price fixing is one area where the law is quite clear, and the Justice Department's enforcement is vigorous.

price fixing
An agreement between two or more firms on the price they will charge for a product.

BayerAG, the huge German multinational corporation (makers of Bayer aspirin), recently agreed to pay $46 million to settle a price-fixing lawsuit accusing it of conspiring with Archer-Daniels-Midland (ADM) Company to fix citric acid prices. ADM has also pleaded guilty to one criminal charge of price fixing.[20]

Price Discrimination

ETHICS

The Robinson-Patman Act of 1936 prohibits any firm from selling to two or more different buyers, within a reasonably short time, commodities (not services) of like grade and quality at different prices where the result would be to substantially lessen competition. The act also makes it illegal for a seller to offer two buyers different supplementary services and for buyers to use their purchasing power to force sellers into granting discriminatory prices or services.

The Robinson-Patman Act provides three defenses for the seller charged with price discrimination (in each case the burden is on the defendant to prove the defense):

- *Cost:* A firm can charge different prices to different customers if the prices represent manufacturing or quantity discount savings.
- *Market conditions:* Price variations are justified if designed to meet fluid product or market conditions. Examples include the deterioration of perishable goods, the obsolescense of seasonal products, a distress sale under court order, and a legitimate going-out-of-business sale.
- *Competition:* A reduction in price may be necessary to stay even with the competition. Specifically, if a competitor undercuts the price quoted by a seller to a buyer, the law authorizes the seller to lower the price charged to the buyer for the product in question.

Predatory Pricing

ETHICS

Predatory pricing is the practice of charging a very low price for a product with the intent of driving competitors out of business or out of a market. Once competitors have been driven out, the firm raises its prices. This practice is illegal under the Sherman Act and the Federal Trade Commission Act. Proving

predatory pricing
The practice of charging a very low price for a product with the intent of driving competitors out of business or out of a market.

the use of the practice is difficult and expensive, however. A defendant must show that the predator—the destructive company—explicitly tried to ruin his or her business and that the predatory price was below the defendant's average cost.[21]

Tactics for Fine-Tuning the Base Price

8

Explain how discounts, geographic pricing, and other special pricing tactics can be used to fine-tune the base price

base price
The general price level at which the company expects to sell the good or service.

After managers understand both the legal and the marketing consequences of price strategies, they should set a **base price**, the general price level at which the company expects to sell the good or service. (Recall the car example in Exhibit 15.3.) The general price level is correlated with the pricing policy: above the market (price skimming), at the market (status quo pricing), or below the market (penetration pricing). The final step, then, is to fine-tune the base price.

Fine-tuning techniques are short-run approaches that do not change the general price level. They do, however, result in changes within a general price level. These pricing tactics allow the firm to adjust for competition in certain markets, meet ever-changing government regulations, take advantage of unique demand situations, and meet promotional and positioning goals. Fine-tuning pricing tactics include various sorts of discounts, geographic pricing, and special pricing tactics.

Discounts, Allowances, and Rebates

A base price can be lowered through the use of discounts and the related tactics of allowances and rebates. Managers use the various forms of discounts to encourage customers to do what they would not ordinarily do, such as paying cash rather than using credit, taking delivery out of season, or performing certain functions within a distribution channel. A summary of the most common tactics is as follows:

quantity discount
Price reduction offered to buyers buying in multiple units or above a specified dollar amount.

cumulative quantity discount
A deduction from list price that applies to the buyer's total purchases made during a specific period.

noncumulative quantity discount
A deduction from list price that applies to a single order rather than to the total volume of orders placed during a certain period.

cash discount
A price reduction offered to a consumer, an industrial user, or a marketing intermediary in return for prompt payment of a bill.

functional discount (trade discount)
Discount to wholesalers and retailers for performing channel functions.

seasonal discount
A price reduction for buying merchandise out of season.

promotional allowance (trade allowance)
Payment to a dealer for promoting the manufacturer's products.

- *Quantity discounts:* When buyers get a lower price for buying in multiple units or above a specified dollar amount, they are receiving a **quantity discount**. A **cumulative quantity discount** is a deduction from list price that applies to the buyer's total purchases made during a specific period; it is intended to encourage customer loyalty. In contrast, a **noncumulative quantity discount** is a deduction from list price that applies to a single order rather than to the total volume of orders placed during a certain period. It is intended to encourage orders in large quantities.
- *Cash discounts:* A **cash discount** is a price reduction offered to a consumer, an industrial user, or a marketing intermediary in return for prompt payment of a bill. Prompt payment saves the seller from carrying charges and billing expenses and allows the seller to avoid bad debt.
- *Functional discounts:* When distribution channel intermediaries, such as wholesalers or retailers, perform a service or function for the manufacturer, they must be compensated. This compensation, typically a percentage discount from the base price, is called a **functional discount** (or **trade discount**). Functional discounts vary greatly from channel to channel, depending on the tasks performed by the intermediary.
- *Seasonal discounts:* A **seasonal discount** is a price reduction for buying merchandise out of season. It shifts the storage function to the purchaser. Seasonal discounts also enable manufacturers to maintain a steady production schedule year-round.
- *Promotional allowances:* A **promotional allowance** (also known as a **trade allowance**) is a payment to a dealer for promoting the manufacturer's products. It is both a pricing tool and a promotional device. As a pricing tool, a promotional allowance is like a functional discount. If, for example, a retailer runs an ad for a manufacturer's product, the manufacturer may pay half the cost. If

Christmas Depot

What kind of discounts would you expect to find at a year-round Christmas store? Go to the on-line Christmas Depot and check some of the prices. Did you find any deals?
http://www.christmasdepot.com/

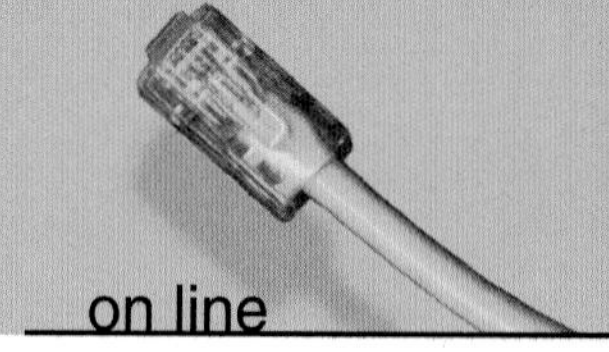

a retailer sets up a special display, the manufacturer may include a certain quantity of free goods in the retailer's next order.

- *Rebates:* A **rebate** is a cash refund given for the purchase of a product during a specific period. The advantage of a rebate over a simple price reduction for stimulating demand is that a rebate is a temporary inducement that can be taken away without altering the basic price structure. A manufacturer that uses a simple price reduction for a short time may meet resistance when trying to restore the price to its original, higher level.

rebate
Cash refund given for the purchase of a product during a specific period.

Value-Based Pricing

VALUE

Value-based pricing is a pricing strategy that has grown out of the quality movement. Instead of figuring prices based on costs or competitors' prices, it starts with the customer, considers the competition, and then determines the appropriate price. The basic assumption is that the firm is customer driven, seeking to understand the attributes customers want in the goods and services they buy and the value of that bundle of attributes to customers. Because very few firms operate in a pure monopoly, however, a marketer using value-based pricing must also determine the value to customers of competitive offerings. Customers evaluate the value of a product (not just its price) relative to the value of alternatives. In value-based pricing, therefore, the price of the product is set at a level that seems to the customer to be a good price compared with the prices of other options.

value-based pricing
The price is set at a level that seems to the customer to be a good price compared to the prices of other options.

An important type of value pricing is everyday low prices, which has evolved because of trade loading. **Trade loading** occurs when a manufacturer temporarily lowers the price to induce wholesalers and retailers to buy more goods than can be sold in a reasonable time. Say that Procter & Gamble offers Super Valu, an additional 30¢ off the normal price for a bottle of Prell. The Super Valu buyer jumps at the bargain and buys a three-month supply of Prell. Typically, Super Valu would pass along the discount to customers for about a month, but then return to the original price for the last two months, thereby reaping some extra profit.

trade loading
Practice of temporarily lowering the price to induce wholesalers and retailers to buy more goods than can be sold in a reasonable time.

An estimated $100 billion in grocery products, mostly nonperishables, sit at any one time on trucks and railcars or stacked inside distribution centers, caught in gridlock because of trade loading. This idle inventory is estimated to add about $20 billion a year to the nation's $400 billion grocery bill.[22]

However, it is estimated that such practices generate about 70 percent of wholesalers' profits and 40 percent of supermarkets' profits.[23] Wholesalers and retailers have understandably become addicted to trade-loading deals.

Unfortunately, trade loading ultimately costs consumers (and manufacturers) money. It "whipsaws" production and distribution and increases the manufacturer's costs. The largest U.S. packaged-goods manufacturer, Procter & Gamble, estimates that it has created over $1 billion worth of unproductive inventory which has sat in P&G's distribution pipeline.

P&G has decided to attack the trade-loading problem with **everyday low prices (EDLP),** the tactic of offering lower prices (often 10 to 25 percent lower) and maintaining those prices while eliminating functional discounts that result in trade loading. Instead of selling, say, a case of cake mix for $10.00 most of the time and then for $7.00 to load the trade, P&G will sell the case for $8.50 all the time. Since 1994, P&G has reduced its list prices by 12 to 24 percent on all of its U.S. brands.

everyday low prices (EDLP)
Price tactic of permanently reducing prices 10 to 25 percent below the traditional levels while eliminating trade discounts that create trade loading.

Geographic Pricing

Because many sellers ship their wares to a nationwide or even a worldwide market, the cost of freight can greatly affect the total cost of a product. Sellers may use several different geographic pricing tactics to moderate the impact of freight costs on distant customers. Following are the most common methods of geographic pricing:

FOB origin pricing
Price tactic that requires the buyer to absorb the freight costs from the shipping point ("free on board").

uniform delivered pricing
Price tactic in which the seller pays the actual freight charges and bills every purchaser an identical, flat freight charge.

zone pricing
Modification of uniform delivered pricing that divides the United States (or the total market) into segments or zones and charges a flat freight rate to all customers in a given zone.

freight absorption pricing
Price tactic in which the seller pays all or part of the actual freight charges and does not pass them on to the buyer.

basing-point pricing
Price tactic that charges freight from a given (basing) point, regardless of the city from which the goods are shipped.

- *FOB origin pricing:* **FOB origin pricing**, also called FOB factory or FOB shipping point pricing, is a price tactic that requires the buyer to absorb the freight costs from the shipping point. The farther buyers are from sellers, the more they pay, because transportation costs generally increase with the distance merchandise is shipped.
- *Uniform delivered pricing:* If the marketing manager wants total costs, including freight, to be equal for all purchasers of identical products, the firm will adopt uniform delivered pricing, or "postage stamp" pricing. With **uniform delivered pricing**, the seller pays the actual freight charges and bills every purchaser an identical, flat freight charge.
- *Zone pricing:* A marketing manager who wants to equalize total costs among buyers within large geographic areas—but not necessarily all of the seller's market area—may modify the base price with a zone-pricing tactic. **Zone pricing** is a modification of uniform delivered pricing. Rather than placing the entire United States (or its total market) under a uniform freight rate, the firm divides it into segments or zones and charges a flat freight rate to all customers in a given zone. The U.S. Postal Service's parcel post rate structure is probably the best-known zone-pricing system in the country.
- *Freight absorption pricing:* In **freight absorption pricing**, the seller pays all or part of the actual freight charges and does not pass them on to the buyer. The manager may use this tactic in intensely competitive areas or as a way to break into new market areas.
- *Basing-point pricing:* With **basing-point pricing**, the seller designates a location as a basing point and charges all buyers the freight cost from that point, regardless of the city from which the goods are shipped. Thanks to several adverse court rulings, basing-point pricing has waned in popularity. Freight fees charged when none were actually incurred, called *phantom freight,* have been declared illegal.

Special Pricing Tactics

Unlike geographic pricing, special pricing tactics are unique and defy neat categorization. Managers use these tactics for various reasons—for example, to stimulate demand for specific products, to increase store patronage, and to offer a wider variety of merchandise at a specific price point. Special pricing tactics include a single-price tactic, flexible pricing, professional services pricing, leader pricing, bait pricing, odd-even pricing, price bundling, and two-part pricing. A brief overview of each of these tactics follows, along with a manager's reasons for using that tactic or a combination of tactics to change the base price.

single-price tactic
Policy of offering all goods and services at the same price.

Single-Price Tactic A merchant using a **single-price tactic** offers all goods and services at the same price (or perhaps two or three prices). Retailers using this tactic include One Price Clothing Stores, Dre$$ to the Nine$, Your $10 Store, and Fashions $9.99. One Price Clothing Stores, for example, tend to be small—about 3,000 square feet. Their goal is to offer merchandise that would sell for at least $15 to $18 in other stores. The stores carry pants, shirts, blouses, sweaters, and shorts for juniors, misses, and large-sized women. The stores do not feature any seconds or irregular items, and everything is sold for $6.

Single-price selling removes price comparisons from the buyer's decision-making process. The consumer just looks for suitability and the highest perceived quality. The retailer enjoys the benefits of a simplified pricing system and minimal clerical errors. However, continually rising costs are a headache for retailers following this strategy. In times of inflation, they must frequently raise the selling price. The recession of the early 1990s resulted in the rapid growth of single-price chains.

flexible pricing (variable pricing)
Price tactic in which different customers pay different prices for essentially the same merchandise bought in equal quantities.

Flexible Pricing **Flexible pricing** (or **variable pricing**) means that different customers pay different prices for essentially the same merchandise bought in equal quantities. This tactic is often found in the sale of shopping goods, specialty

United Parcel Service

Go to UPS's Web site and do some quick cost comparison on sending the same package to a friend in town and to a friend out of state. Does the difference in cost surprise you? Do you think it is justified? Why or why not?

http://www.ups.com/

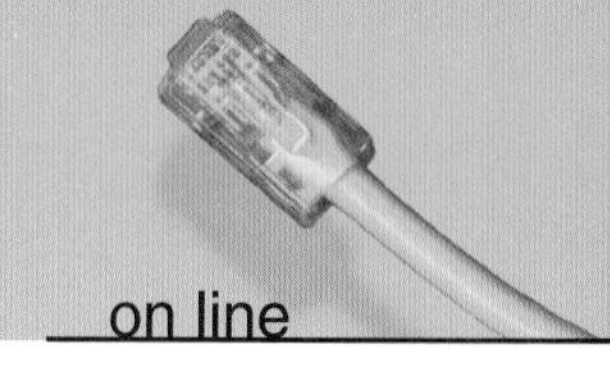

on line

merchandise, and most industrial goods except supply items. Car dealers, many appliance retailers, and manufacturers of industrial installations, accessories, and component parts commonly follow the practice. It allows the seller to adjust for competition by meeting another seller's price. Thus, a marketing manager with a status quo pricing objective might readily adopt the tactic. Flexible pricing also enables the seller to close a sale with price-conscious consumers. If buyers show promise of becoming large-volume shoppers, flexible pricing can be used to lure their business.

The obvious disadvantages of flexible pricing are the lack of consistent profit margins, the potential ill will of high-paying purchasers, the tendency for salespeople to automatically lower the price to make a sale, and the possibility of a price war among sellers. The disadvantages of flexible pricing have led the automobile industry to experiment with one price for all buyers. Ford started offering the Cougar at one price and has seen an 80 percent increase in sales. General Motors uses a one-price tactic for some of its models, including the Saturn and the Buick Regal.

Professional Services Pricing Professional services pricing is used by people with lengthy experience, training, and often certification by a licensing board—for example, lawyers, physicians, and family counselors. Professionals sometimes charge customers an hourly rate, but sometimes fees are based on the solution of a problem or performance of an act (such as an eye examination) rather than on the actual time involved. A surgeon may perform a heart operation and charge a flat fee of $10,000. The operation itself may require only four hours, resulting in a hefty $2,500 hourly rate. The physician justifies the fee because of the lengthy education and internship required to learn the complex procedures of a heart operation. Lawyers also sometimes use flat-rate pricing, such as $500 for completing a divorce and $50 for handling a traffic ticket.

Those who use professional services pricing have an ethical responsibility not to overcharge a customer. Because demand is sometimes highly inelastic, such as when a person requires heart surgery or a daily insulin shot to survive, there may be a temptation to charge "all the traffic will bear." Although drug companies are often criticized for their high prices, they claim that their charges are ethical. They say prices for new drugs need to be high to recover the research costs incurred in developing the drugs.

Leader Pricing **Leader pricing** (or **loss-leader pricing**) is an attempt by the marketing manager to attract customers by selling a product near or even below cost, hoping that shoppers will buy other items once they are in the store. This type of pricing appears weekly in the newspaper advertising of supermarkets, specialty stores, and department stores. Leader pricing is normally used on well-known items that consumers can easily recognize as bargains at the special price. The goal is not necessarily to sell large quantities of leader items, but to try to appeal to customers who might shop elsewhere.

leader pricing (loss-leader pricing)
Price tactic in which a product is sold near or even below cost in the hope that shoppers will buy other items once they are in the store.

ETHICS

Bait Pricing In contrast to leader pricing, which is a genuine attempt to give the consumer a reduced price, bait pricing is deceptive. **Bait pricing** tries to get the consumer into a store through false or misleading price advertising and then uses high-pressure selling to persuade the consumer to buy more expensive merchandise. You may have seen this ad or a similar one:

> REPOSSESSED . . . Singer slant-needle sewing machine . . . take over 8 payments of $5.10 per month . . . ABC Sewing Center

bait pricing
Price tactic that tries to get consumers into a store through false or misleading price advertising and then uses high-pressure selling to persuade consumers to buy more expensive merchandise.

This is bait. When a customer goes in to see the machine, a salesperson says that it has just been sold or else shows the prospective buyer a piece of junk no one would buy. Then the salesperson says, "But I've got a really good deal on this fine new model." This is the switch that may cause a susceptible consumer to walk out with a $400 machine. The Federal Trade Commission considers bait pricing a deceptive act and has banned its use in interstate commerce. Most states also ban bait pricing, but sometimes enforcement is lax.

odd-even pricing (psychological pricing)
Price tactic that uses odd-numbered prices to connote bargains and even-numbered prices to imply quality.

Odd-Even Pricing **Odd-even pricing** (or **psychological pricing**) means pricing at odd-numbered prices to connote a bargain and pricing at even-numbered prices to imply quality. For years, many retailers have used this tactic to price their products in odd numbers—for example, $99.95 or $49.95—in order to make consumers feel that they are paying a lower price for the product.

Some retailers favor odd-numbered prices because they believe that $9.99 sounds much less imposing to customers than $10.00. Other retailers believe that the use of an odd-numbered price signals to consumers that the price is at the lowest level possible, thereby encouraging them to buy more units. Neither theory has ever been conclusively proved, although one study found that consumers perceive odd-priced products as being on sale.[24]

Even-numbered pricing is sometimes used to denote quality. Examples include a fine perfume at $100 a bottle, a good watch at $500, or a mink coat at $3,000. The demand curve for such items would also be sawtoothed, except that the outside edges would represent even-numbered prices and, therefore, elastic demand.

price bundling
Marketing two or more products in a single package for a special price.

Price Bundling **Price bundling** is marketing two or more products in a single package for a special price. Examples include the sale of maintenance contracts with computer hardware and other office equipment, packages of stereo equipment, packages of options on cars, weekend hotel packages that include a room and several meals, and airline vacation packages. Microsoft now offers "suites" of software that bundle spreadsheets, word processing, graphics, electronic mail, Internet access, and groupware for networks of microcomputers. Price bundling can stimulate demand for the bundled items if the target market perceives the price as a good value.

Services like hotels and airlines sell a perishable commodity (hotel rooms and airline seats) with relatively constant fixed costs. Bundling can be an important income stream for these businesses because the variable cost—for instance, the cost of cleaning a hotel room or putting one more passenger on an airplane—tends to be low.[25] Therefore, most of the revenue can help cover fixed costs and generate profits.

The automobile industry has a different motive for bundling. People buy cars only every three to five years. Thus, selling options is a somewhat rare opportunity for the car dealer. Price bundling can help the dealer sell a maximum number of options.

unbundling
Reducing the bundle of services that comes with the basic product.

A related price tactic is **unbundling**, or reducing the bundle of services that comes with the basic product. Rather than raise the price of hotel rooms, some hotel chains have started charging registered guests for parking. To help hold the line on costs, some department stores require customers to pay for gift wrapping.

two-part pricing
Price tactic that charges two separate amounts to consume a single good or service.

Two-Part Pricing **Two-part pricing** means establishing two separate charges to consume a single good or service. Tennis clubs and health clubs, for example, charge a membership fee and a flat fee each time a person uses certain equipment or facilities. In other cases they charge a base rate for a certain level of usage, such as 10 racquetball games per month, and a surcharge for anything over that amount.

Consumers sometimes prefer two-part pricing because they are uncertain about the number and the types of activities they might use at places like an amusement park. Also, the people who use a service most often pay a higher total price. Two-part pricing can increase a seller's revenue by attracting consumers who would not pay a high fee even for unlimited use. For example, a health club might be able to sell only 100 memberships at $700 annually with unlimited use of facilities, for total revenue of $70,000. But perhaps it could sell 900 memberships at $200 with a guarantee of using the racquetball courts 10 times a month. Every usage over 10 would require the member to pay a $5 fee. Thus, membership revenue would provide a base of $180,000, with some additional usage fees coming in throughout the year.

LOOKING BACK

Look back at the beginning story on Priceline. There is no doubt that the Internet will have a major impact on pricing. Buyers will be able to quickly compare prices and products. Sellers will learn more about potential buyers and tailor their products accordingly. Extranets will lower costs and enable sellers to deliver better value to purchasers.

Summary

1 Discuss the importance of pricing decisions to the economy and to the individual firm. Pricing plays an integral role in the U.S. economy by allocating goods and services among consumers, governments, and businesses. Pricing is essential in business because it creates revenue, which is the basis of all business activity. In setting prices, marketing managers strive to find a level high enough to produce a satisfactory profit.

2 List and explain a variety of pricing objectives. Establishing realistic and measurable pricing objectives is a critical part of any firm's marketing strategy. Pricing objectives are commonly classified into three categories: profit oriented, sales oriented, and status quo. Profit-oriented pricing is based on profit maximization, a satisfactory level of profit, or a target return on investment. The goal of profit maximization is to generate as much revenue as possible in relation to cost. Often, a more practical approach than profit maximization is setting prices to produce profits that will satisfy management and stockholders. The most common profit-oriented strategy is pricing for a specific return on investment relative to a firm's assets. The second type of pricing objective is sales oriented, and it focuses on either maintaining a percentage share of the market or maximizing dollar or unit sales. The third type of pricing objective aims to maintain the status quo by matching competitors' prices.

3 Explain the role of demand in price determination. Demand is a key determinant of price. When establishing prices, a firm must first determine demand for its product. A typical demand schedule shows an inverse relationship between quantity demanded and price: that is, when price is lowered, sales increase; and when price is increased, the quantity demanded falls.

Marketing managers must also consider demand elasticity when setting prices. Elasticity of demand is the degree to which the quantity demanded fluctuates with changes in price. If consumers are sensitive to changes in price, demand is elastic. If they are insensitive to price changes, demand is inelastic. Thus, an increase in price will result in lower sales for an elastic product and little or no change in sales for an inelastic product.

4 Describe cost-oriented pricing strategies. The other major determinant of price is cost. Marketers use several cost-oriented pricing strategies. To cover their own expenses and obtain a profit, wholesalers and retailers commonly use markup pricing: They tack an extra amount onto the manufacturer's original price. Still another pricing strategy determines how much a firm must sell to break even and uses this amount as a reference point for adjusting price.

5 Demonstrate how the product life cycle, competition, distribution and promotion strategies, the impact of the Internet, demands of large customers, and perceptions of quality can affect price. The price of a product normally changes as it moves through its life cycle and as demand for the product and competitive conditions change. Management often sets a high price at the introductory stage, and the high price tends to attract competition. The competition usually drives prices down, because individual competitors lower prices to gain market share.

Adequate distribution for a new product can sometimes be obtained by offering a larger-than-profit margin to wholesalers and retailers. Price is also used as a promotional tool to attract customers. Special low prices often attract new customers and entice existing customers to buy more.

The Internet enables buyers to quickly and easily compare prices and products. This puts them in a better bargaining position. Internet auctions create a very efficient market for countless goods and services.

Large customers, like Wal-Mart, make strong pricing demands on suppliers. Retailers ask suppliers to cover heavy discounts made at the retail level. The retailers also want suppliers to guarantee their stores' profit margins. These demands are wiping out profits for many suppliers.

Perceptions of quality also can influence pricing strategies. A firm trying to project a prestigious image often charges a premium price for a product. Consumers tend to equate high prices with high quality.

6 Describe the procedure for setting the right price. Setting the right price on a product is a process with four major steps: (1) establishing pricing goals; (2) estimating demand, costs, and profits; (3) choosing a price policy to help determine a base price; and (4) fine-tuning the base price with pricing tactics.

A price strategy establishes a long-term pricing framework for a good or service. The three main types of price policies are price skimming, penetration pricing, and status quo pricing. A price-skimming policy charges a high introductory price, often followed by a gradual reduction. Penetration pricing offers a low introductory price to capture a large market share and attain economies of scale. Finally, status quo pricing strives to match competitors' prices.

7 Identify the legal and ethical constraints on pricing decisions. Government regulation helps monitor four major areas of pricing: unfair trade practices, price fixing, predatory pricing, and price discrimination. Enacted in many states, unfair trade practice acts protect small businesses from large firms that operate efficiently on extremely thin profit margins; the acts prohibit charging below-cost prices. The Sherman Act and the Federal Trade Commission Act prohibit both price fixing—an agreement on a particular price between two or more firms—and predatory pricing—undercutting competitors with extremely low prices to drive them out of business. Finally, the Robinson-Patman Act makes it illegal for firms to discriminate between two or more buyers in terms of price.

8 Explain how discounts, geographic pricing, and other special pricing tactics can be used to fine-tune the base price. Several techniques enable marketing managers to adjust prices within a general range in response to changes in competition, government regulation, consumer demand, and promotional and positioning goals. Techniques for fine-tuning a price can be divided into three main categories: discounts, allowances, and rebates; geographic pricing; and special pricing tactics.

The first type of tactic gives lower prices to those that pay promptly, order a large quantity, or perform some function for the manufacturer. Value-based pricing starts with the customer, considers the competition and costs, and then determines a price. Everyday low pricing, a form of value-based pricing, arose from trade loading. Trade loading is a manufacturer's temporary functional discount to induce wholesalers and retailers to buy more goods than can be sold in a reasonable length of time. Trade loading increases inventory expenses and channel expenses and lowers the manufacturer's profits. A tactic meant to overcome these problems is "everyday low pricing," or maintaining low prices over time while eliminating the discounts that result in trade loading. Other tactics in this category include seasonal discounts, promotion allowances, and rebates (cash refunds).

Geographic pricing tactics—such as FOB origin pricing, uniform delivered pricing, zone pricing, freight absorption pricing, and basing-point pricing—are ways of moderating the impact of shipping costs on distant customers.

A variety of special pricing tactics stimulate demand for certain products, increase store patronage, and offer more merchandise at specific prices.

Discussion and Writing Questions

1. Why is pricing so important to the marketing manager?
2. Explain the concepts of elastic and inelastic demand. Why should managers understand these concepts?
3. WRITING Your firm has based its past pricing strictly on cost. As the newly hired marketing manager, you believe this policy should change. Write the president a memo explaining your reasons.
4. Why is it important for managers to understand the concept of break-even points? Are there any drawbacks?
5. TEAM Divide the class into teams of five. Each team will be assigned a different grocery store from a different chain. (An independent is fine.) Appoint a group leader. The group leaders should meet as a group and pick 15 nationally branded grocery items. Each item should be specifically described as to brand name and size of the package. Each team will then proceed to its assigned store and collect price data on the 15 items. The team should also gather price data on 15 similar store brands and 15 generics, if possible.

   Each team should present its results to the class and discuss why there are price variations between stores, national brands, store brands, and generics.

   As a next step, go back to your assigned store and share the overall results with the store manager. Bring back the manager's comments and share them with the class.
6. How does the stage of a product's life cycle and the Internet affect price? Give some examples.
7. A manufacturer of office furniture decides to produce antique-style rolltop desks, but formatted for personal computers. The desks will have built-in surge protectors, a platform for raising or lowering the monitor, and a number of other features. The quality, solid-oak desks will be priced far below comparable products. The marketing manager says, "We'll charge a low price and plan on a high volume to reduce our risks." Comment.

Key Terms

bait pricing 519
base price 516
basing-point pricing 518
break-even analysis 504
cash discount 516
cumulative quantity discount 516
demand 502
elastic demand 502
elasticity of demand 502
everyday low prices (EDLP) 517
extranet 508
fixed cost 503
flexible pricing (variable pricing) 518
FOB origin pricing 518
freight absorption pricing 518
functional discount (trade discount) 516
inelastic demand 502
keystoning 504
leader pricing (loss-leader pricing) 519
market share 500
markup pricing 504
noncumulative quantity discount 516
odd-even pricing (psychological pricing) 520
penetration pricing 513
predatory pricing 515
prestige pricing 509
price 498
price bundling 520
price fixing 515
price skimming 511
price strategy 511
profit 498
promotional allowance (trade allowance) 516
quantity discount 516
rebate 517
return on investment (ROI) 500
revenue 498
seasonal discount 516
single-price tactic 518
status quo pricing 502
supply 502
trade loading 517
two-part pricing 520
unbundling 520
unfair trade practice acts 515
uniform delivered pricing 518
value-based pricing 517
variable costs 503
zone pricing 518

8. Janet Oliver, owner of a midpriced dress shop, notes, "My pricing objectives are simple: I just charge what my competitors charge. I'm happy because I'm making money." React to Janet's statement.
9. You are contemplating a price change for an established product sold by your firm. Write a memo analyzing the factors you need to consider in your decision.
10. Do you see everyday low prices as a strategy to offset trade loading? Why are many manufacturers resisting EDLP?
11. What is the difference between a price policy and a price tactic? Give an example.
12. ON LINE How should information on the Internet be priced? What are the pros and cons of the information-pricing models discussed at the following site?
http://www.sloan.mit.edu/15.967/group17/home.html
13. ON LINE If the Internet is accessible by people all over the world, how do marketers deal with consumers using different kinds of currency?
http://www.burmex.com/store/pricing.htm
14. ON LINE What pricing strategy does Microsoft seem to be using for the software offered via the following Web page?
http://www.microsoft.com/misdownload/
15. ON LINE What pricing advantages does the Auto Connection™ seem to offer compared to traditional auto dealers?
http://www.auto-connect.com

Application for Small Business

ENTREPRENEUR Midcontinent Perfume of Milwaukee, Wisconsin, is a small manufacturer that distributes a line of quality women's perfumes to intermediate and high-priced department and specialty stores. It has recently decided to add a new lower-priced line to its product mix in order to capture a slightly different segment of the market. The new product is called "Passion Flower."

A recent market test revealed the following estimated total demand for the product at the quoted prices.

Price	Quantity
$15.00	25,000 units
$20.00	20,000 units
$22.50	19,000 units
$25.00	11,000 units
$27.50	10,000 units

The accounting department figured that the average variable cost for the new perfume would be $13 per unit. Fixed costs are estimated at $40,000.

Questions

1. Assuming that the market research studies are accurate, what price should be charged for the perfume?
2. What kind of market research study could have been done to determine the demand schedule for the perfume? Assume that fixed costs are $140,000 rather than $40,000. Should the company have produced for the short run? For the long run?
3. Discuss the advantages and disadvantages of break-even analysis.
4. What is the break-even point for this perfume? Of what significance is that point?

Review Quiz

1. The price charged on a product multiplied by the number of units sold is
   a. Profit
   b. Cost of goods sold
   c. Gross margin
   d. Revenue
2. Which of the following pricing objectives requires the least planning and is considered a passive policy?
   a. Profit oriented
   b. Demand oriented
   c. Sales oriented
   d. Status quo
3. ______ occurs when total revenue increases in response to a decrease in price.
   a. Profit
   b. Unitary elasticity
   c. Inelastic demand
   d. Elastic demand
4. During which stage of the product life cycle do prices decline as competition intensifies and high-cost firms are eliminated?
   a. Introduction
   b. Growth
   c. Maturity
   d. Decline
5. When many substitute products are available for customers in the marketplace, demand for an individual product in that category tends to be elastic.
   a. True
   b. False
6. When a firm charges a high introductory price on a new product, frequently coupled with heavy promotion, it is practicing a ______ policy.
   a. Price-skimming
   b. Penetration-pricing
   c. Status quo
   d. Price-fixing
7. Which of the following is *not* a defense for price discrimination under the Robinson-Patman Act of 1936?
   a. The product is a commodity, not a specialty good.
   b. There are cost differences in dealing with different customers.
   c. Market conditions cause price variations to occur.
   d. Competitors have lowered prices.
8. ______ often causes distributors to overstock and eventually leaves products that may not be fresh on the shelves for consumers.
   a. Zone pricing
   b. Price lining
   c. Trade loading
   d. Delayed-quotation pricing
9. A pricing tactic used by marketers to attract customers to a store by selling products near or below cost is called
   a. Price bundling
   b. Bait pricing
   c. Leader pricing
   d. Everyday low pricing (EDLP)

10. The tactic of everyday low prices (EDLP) typically means permanently lower prices as an alternative to trade loading.
    a. True
    b. False

Check the Answer Key, which follows the Video Case, to see how well you understood the material.

VIDEO CASE

Toronto Blue Jays: Ballpark Pricing

The opening pitch of 1999 marked the start of the Toronto Blue Jays' twenty-third season in the American League for a 162-game schedule. In 1998, the Jays scored 88 wins against 74 losses and 1 tie, and brought in their first winning season since 1993. For home games, the Jays play in the world's most advanced retractable-roof stadium, with seating for 50,516. Called the Sky Dome, the ball club invested $5 million in the luxury stadium for preferred supplier status and a Sky Box.

With a winning record like this and a state-of-the-art ballpark, the Jays feel their tickets are a great value because of the satisfaction fans can expect to receive from the ball game. Their pricing structure is based on the perceived value of a game, for baseball-lovers—its entertainment and action—not just the money. Every season the Blue Jays have to balance two key economic factors when determining their ticket prices: the demand for seats by baseball fans and the skyrocketing costs of running a major league baseball club.

Despite this balancing act, the front office does not expect consumers to be really sensitive to fluctuations in price. This was particularly true of the 1999 season, when the fans were expected to turn out in great numbers in spite of rising ticket prices. This inelastic demand for Blue Jays tickets can be attributed in large part to the fact that the team played so well in 1998, but also to the fact that loyal Blue Jays fans could never stay away. They are simply willing to pay the price to support their team.

Another reason for the inelastic demand for Blue Jays tickets is that there is no locally available substitute. Sports fans can support any number of sports (baseball to tennis) or watch amateurs play; but for major league baseball in Toronto, the Blue Jays are the only game in town. The purchasing power of Torontonians is also an important factor in the inelastic demand for Blue Jays tickets. The Blue Jays' front office provides a wide range of ticket options (preferred or general seating, a season's subscription, or a single ticket), so that even if their prices were to increase, most residents in the Toronto area could still easily afford the same category of ticket, or a lower category ticket, and so would not miss a game.

For the Blue Jays, pricing strategies are not just a financial necessity, they are also a promotional tool used to increase fan attendance. At all Saturday home games and nonholiday weekday games, senior citizens and young people up to fourteen years old can purchase tickets (except the most expensive ones) for half price. Season ticket holders receive special benefits: the same seats for every game, guaranteed tickets for postseason games played at home, a complimentary Toronto Blue Jays media guide and calendar, and the convenience of entering the Sky Dome on game day without having to wait in line at the ticket window. Group ticket sales also receive special treatment: preferred seating; personal services from the group sales staff; and promotional posters, pocket schedules, and stickers. These perks help persuade large groups (five hundred or more) to use a game as a social event; a fund-raiser; or a way to promote a business, a social group, or a sports organization.

Ticket sales provide a large portion of the Blue Jays' revenue, but merchandising is also responsible for a significant percentage. A wide selection of Blue Jays souvenirs and gifts is sold at the ballpark, at Blue Jays

Bullpen Souvenir Stores, and at finer department stores across Canada. In addition to these retail outlets, free catalogs are available by calling a toll-free number, and the complete line of Jays merchandise is available online from a wholly owned Jays subsidiary. Caps, jerseys, and jackets, like those worn on the field by the players, and accessories, novelties, and collectibles are all available for sale.

The Blue Jays merchandising machine uses a prestige-pricing strategy; charging high prices helps promote the Jays' high-quality image. Although jackets range from $39.59 to $197.99 and jerseys range from $29.69 to $155.09, consumers are willing to pay a high price for official, authentic merchandise that has been approved by the Blue Jays and by Major League Baseball.

Inelastic ticket demand and the prestige pricing of merchandise are fueled by the success of the ball team. Because the Toronto Blue Jays are a winning team, their loyal fans are willing to pay the price to see them play ball.

Questions

1. What considerations are included in the Jays' ticket-pricing structure?
2. Why is demand for Blue Jays tickets inelastic?
3. How do the Jays use price as a promotional tool?
4. What pricing strategy is used for Blue Jays merchandise?

Bibliography

Toronto Blue Jays Web site: **http://www.bluejays.ca/**

Answer Key

1. *Answer:* d, p. 498

   Rationale: Revenue is the key to profits for the organization. It is calculated by multiplying the number of units sold by the price customers paid for the product.

2. *Answer:* d, p. 502

   Rationale: Status quo pricing objectives are based on maintaining existing prices or meeting the prices of competitors.

3. *Answer:* d, p. 502

   Rationale: Elasticity of demand is a concept that deals with consumers' sensitivity to price changes. Elastic demand means that total revenue increases when price decreases.

4. *Answer:* c, p. 506

   Rationale: Maturity usually brings price declines; later in the stage these declines are often not sufficient to stimulate additional demand.

5. *Answer:* a, p. 505

   Rationale: Availability of substitutes is a key factor that affects the elasticity of demand for any product.

6. *Answer:* a, p. 511

   Rationale: Companies often use this strategy when the product is perceived by the target market as having unique or superior product performance.

7. *Answer:* a, p. 515

   Rationale: The Robinson-Patman Act provides three defenses: cost, market conditions, and competition.

8. *Answer:* c, p. 517

   Rationale: Trade loading occurs as a result of a producer temporarily lowering prices to induce wholesalers and retailers to buy more goods than they can sell in a reasonable period of time.

9. *Answer:* c, p. 519

   Rationale: This tactic lowers prices to levels at or below cost to encourage customers to visit a store with hopes that the shoppers will buy other items once they are inside the store.

10. *Answer:* a, p. 517

    Rationale: EDLP usually means that the firm permanently lowers prices by 10 to 25 percent to avoid using functional or trade discounts that may vary from customer to customer.

still shaky?

Try making up a crossword puzzle for the key terms in this part. Writing the clues will help you remember the definitions and the context of each concept. Check your progress by using the *Grademaker Study Guide.*

marketing miscues

Advertising Abroad Can Create Headaches for Multinationals

Advertising in foreign countries often leads to embarrassing situations for U.S. multinational marketers. In a spot that ran briefly on Peruvian television, Africans are seen getting ready to devour some white tourists until they are appeased by Nabisco's Royal Pudding. Nabisco initially responded that although the commercial was "inconsistent" with company values, the Peruvian audience saw it as "a fantasy situation that was humorous in nature, and effectively communicated people's preference for Royal Desserts over all else."

After realizing that its explanation of local taste tests as justification for a racially insensitive ad was, to say the least, weak, Nabisco quickly moved to consolidate control of its international advertising under Foote, Cone & Belding in New York in an effort to keep ad campaigns more uniform. In a statement from Ann Smith, Nabisco's director of marketing and communications, the company wanted to "ensure that the quality of our ads meet the standards we set for our brands." The spot, she adds, was "a mistake."

In a separate but similar incident, a sketch on a popular Peruvian television show featured a Michael Jackson character complaining that his "son," played in black face and having a tail, looks "too black," prompting him to beg a doctor to bleach the boy's skin and cut off his tail. The show was sponsored by such major corporations as Chesebrough-Pond's, Procter & Gamble, PepsiCo, and Quaker Oats. To add to the insult, the characters of the popular show are featured in a commercial for Goodyear Tire & Rubber Co. shuffling around and stating that "Goodyear tires are as strong as a black man's lips." Goodyear quickly pulled the ad after its U.S. executives saw it and fired the Lima, Peru, agency that produced the tire ad. It also promptly issued an unsolicited apology to the NAACP even though the ad ran only in Peru for one week. Although the company determined it would be impractical to impose central review of all international advertising from its U.S. base, as Nabisco did, it stepped up sensitivity training for local managers and suppliers around the world.

Like a number of multinational companies, Nabisco and Goodyear were forced to address concerns about how to adapt sales pitches to foreign markets without violating domestic sensibilities. Such situations shed light not only on how far some ad agencies will go to create striking messages but also on how a lack of internal controls at agencies can cause problems. Because local units of international ad agencies aren't typically required to consult with parent companies when creating ads for domestic audiences, racially insensitive or otherwise controversial ads, such as those for Nabisco's Royal Pudding and Goodyear tires, sometimes slip through.

Questions:

1. What steps can a multinational company take, in addition to issuing ad guidelines, to ensure that embarrassing promotional situations like those discussed do not occur?
2. Assume that you are the international advertising manager for a large consumer products company. Write a brief list of ad standards pertaining to creative and media selection to which your foreign ad agencies would be required to adhere.

SOURCES: "1997: Ad Follies," *Advertising Age,* 22 December 1997, p. 14. "Tire Maker's Racist TV Ad Causes International Blowout," *Michigan Chronicle,* 22 December 1997, p. 6-A. Pichayaporn Utumporn, "Ad with Hitler Causes a Furor in Thailand," *Wall Street Journal,* 5 June 1998, p. B8. Leon E. Wynter, "Global Marketers Learn to Say No to Bad Ads," *Wall Street Journal,* 1 April 1998, p. B1.

critical thinking case

The Secret Appeal of Rebates

Rebates are booming—mainly because of a little-discussed marketers' secret: Most people never cash them in. The coupons are showing up on everything from computers and shredders to dishwashers and baby seats. OfficeMax Inc., an office-supply chain, sells 217 different products that carry them. The coupons do spur sales, but "the whole point behind rebates is to entice purchases and hope [consumers] don't remember to submit" their claims, says Charles Weil, president of Young America Inc. His company mails out thirty million rebate checks a year on behalf of companies like PepsiCo, Nestlé SA, and OfficeMax.

Rebates originated in the 1960s and boomed in the late 1980s and early 1990s when liquor bottles and cigarette cartons carried $1 and $2 mail-in rebates. However, those promotions, which sometimes required such exertions as soaking off labels to document purchases, soon lost their allure. At the same time, scamsters discovered they could submit dozens of rebate forms for every offer, which soured some marketers on the approach.

Now rebates are back. The Postal Service has cracked down on rebate fraud, and the money at stake is rising because computer and electronics makers have caught the bug.

Cox Direct Inc., a direct-marketing company based in Largo, Florida, says that 76 percent of surveyed packaged-goods companies use money-back offers. NCH NuWorld Marketing Ltd., the nation's biggest coupon processor, says the use of traditional cents-off coupons is down, but its mail-in rebate business is increasing, especially for higher-priced items. Young America says its business is growing 25 percent annually thanks to ever more complex rebate and premium programs.

Manufacturers like rebates because they let them offer price cuts to consumers directly. With a traditional price cut, retailers can keep the price on the shelf the same and pocket the difference. Rebates can also be rolled out and shut off quickly—that lets manufacturers fine-tune inventories or respond quickly to competitors without actually cutting prices. Because buyers fill out forms with names, addresses, and other data, rebates also set off a gusher of information about customers.

However, the best reason of all to offer rebates is that many consumers never bother to redeem them, allowing manufacturers to offer, in effect, phantom discounts. Many fliers prominently advertise low prices, noting in microscopic letters the requirement to send in for rebates. "That allows the retailer and manufacturer to advertise a very hot price when the costs aren't very high," says Wes Bray, a partner in Market Growth Resources Inc., a consulting firm. "Not many consumers redeem them—5% to 10% maximum."

Consumer advocates, meanwhile, hate rebates. "We feel companies should give a more honest reduction in the price," says Linda Colodner, executive director of the National Consumers League, a Washington, D.C., group. Her own son missed out on a $50 rebate offer for a cellular phone he gave her for Christmas because he failed to send in the proof of purchase in time to meet a December 31 deadline, she says.

Rebates can generate enormous ill will for companies that mishandle them. Bill Berdux, a California marketing executive, put up a "CompUSA Rebate Problems and Complaint" Web page criticizing the computer retailer after he failed to receive a $30 rebate for computer disks. After he posted an account of his experience, dozens of other frustrated customers sent him their sagas, which he also posted. "I got e-mail from all over the country. People are vengeful and nasty," he says. James Halpin, president of CompUSA, which is based in Dallas, says he isn't familiar with Mr. Berdux's situation, but says the company provides a toll-free number for complaints.

Kevin O'Leary, president of Learning Co., a Cambridge, Massachusetts-based maker of educational software, says the economics of rebates "are quite attractive" because the company pays out rebates to 8 percent to 10 percent of the customers eligible for its $10 offers, and 20 percent of the $20 offers. "Since we started, our market share has gone from 18% to 28%," Mr. O'Leary says.

Big $50 rebates have become commonplace in the modem industry. When manufacturers cut prices, they have to reimburse retailers for modems still on store shelves that were purchased at a higher wholesale price. "Rebates mean they don't have to do price protection," says Jennifer Glickman of ARS Research Inc., a Dallas market-research firm.

Rebates also offer research possibilities. Sharp Electronics Inc. offered a $500 rebate on its $4,695 projection TV. The company didn't want to just cut the price, fearing added sales wouldn't make up for the price cuts. When sales jumped beyond expectations, Sharp cut the list price to $3,995 permanently.

Some newer rebate programs are designed to build customer loyalty. OfficeMax, an office superstore chain based in Cleveland, recently introduced a service in which its customers fill out a single form to accompany their rebate receipts and proofs of purchase from the store each month. OfficeMax then mails the material to Young America, which sends back rebate checks. Michael Feuer, OfficeMax's chairman, says the plan is especially appealing to small businesses, which wouldn't bother with one-product rebates but can get back several hundred dollars a month.

Questions

1. "Rebates and discounts are really the same thing." Do you agree or disagree? Defend your position.
2. When should a company use a rebate rather than a discount?
3. Do you think that rebates are unethical? Why or why not?
4. How might rebates be useful to a company contemplating sliding down the demand curve?

Suggested Readings

"Carmakers May Be Flooding the Engine," *Business Week,* 21 May 1998, pp. 43–48.

Ed Foster, "Customers Whose Rebate Checks Aren't in the Mail Are Beginning to Fight Back," *Infoworld,* 9 February 1998, p. 62.

Kristen Kennedy, "Nintendo 64 Rebate May Jeopardize Pricing Strategy," *Computer Retail Week,* 22 June 1998, pp. 49–50.

SOURCE: William Bulkeley, "Rebates' Secret Appeal to Manufacturers: Few Consumers Actually Redeem Them," *Wall Street Journal,* 10 February 1998, pp. B1, B6.

critical thinking case

Amazon.com

Jeffrey Bezos believes the Internet store of the future should be able to guess what shoppers want before they know themselves. The founder and CEO of Amazon.com, the Internet's leading book and music store, is pioneering personalization on the Internet to make each visit to his on-line store one that is personal and tailor-made to each shopper's interests.

A Pioneer of Internet Retailing

Amazon.com, based in Seattle, opened its virtual doors in July 1995 with the mission of using the Internet to offer products that would educate, inform, and inspire people at a customer-friendly, easy-to-navigate Web site that would offer the broadest possible selection. Operating out of Bezos's basement, Amazon.com began selling books to Web surfers and paved the road for future Web merchants who would tap this new direct marketing channel.

Sales for 1997 grew to $147.8 million, an increase of 838 percent over 1996 sales of $15.7 million. At the same time, customer accounts grew from 180,000 to 1,510,000. Today, Amazon.com offers over three million book titles, CDs, audiobooks, DVDs, computer games, videos, and more. Some 4.5 million people in more than 160 countries around the world have bought from Amazon.com. The company now claims 85 percent of on-line book sales, making it the leading on-line shopping site. Sales for 1998 are expected to be four to five times 1997's level.

Personalization of the Web

Like their brick-and-mortar retailing counterparts, Web merchants must lure customers to their place of business, make it easy for them to buy products and services, and keep them coming back for more. As any good merchant knows, the key to securing repeat business is delivering custom-tailored products to shoppers. To do this, on-line businesses are implementing technologies that can make fairly accurate predictions about a person's preferences and furnish individually targeted Web pages that cater to his or her individual tastes and interests.

exhibit A — Amazon.com's Personalized Web Site

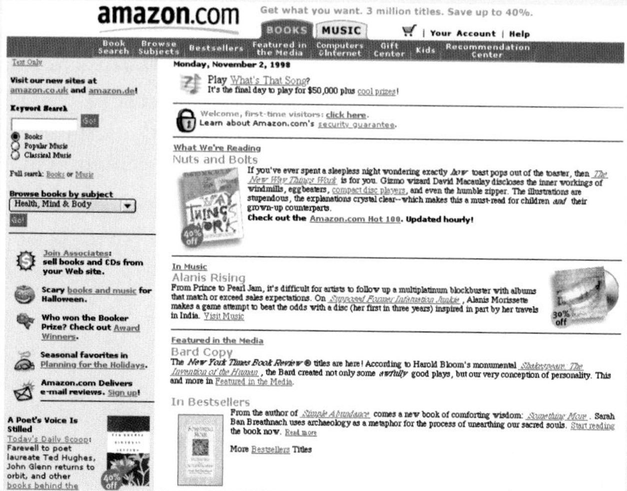

Through personalization, on-line merchants and other sites can communicate instantly with each one of their customers. Personalization also allows customers to talk back, so that they can demand unique products and customized services.

Web merchants are flocking to personalization for a number of reasons. First, customized Web sites can increase usage and repeat visits. Before launching a personalization service on its start page in 1998, Excite conducted in-house research and found that people who signed up for its personalized My Excite Channel returned five times more often than those without a personalized page. In addition, Web sites use personalization features to better utilize customer databases, deliver more targeted information and more expensive banner ads to users, and ultimately sell more merchandise online. Even at a cost of $50,000 to $3 million for the personalization software, along with computers to store the customer profiles, personalization generally pays for itself within a year.

The Personal Experience at Amazon.com

Amazon.com was one of the first Internet sites to use personalization software to customize pages for each registered customer, offering recommendations for books and music. Repeat visitors to Amazon.com are greeted by name, and recommendations are listed that are unique to each individual. If a customer buys bestsellers, for instance, a bestseller list might appear at the top of his home page.

Pumping out these recommendations is a computing process Amazon.com uses called *collaborative filtering*. Unlike mass-marketing tools, collaborative filtering doesn't

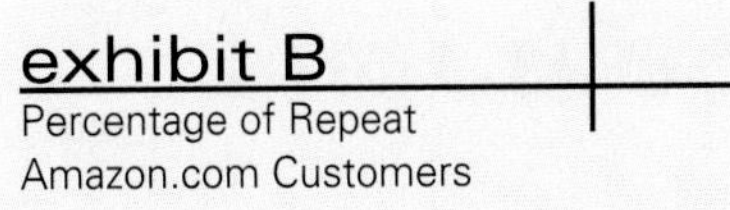

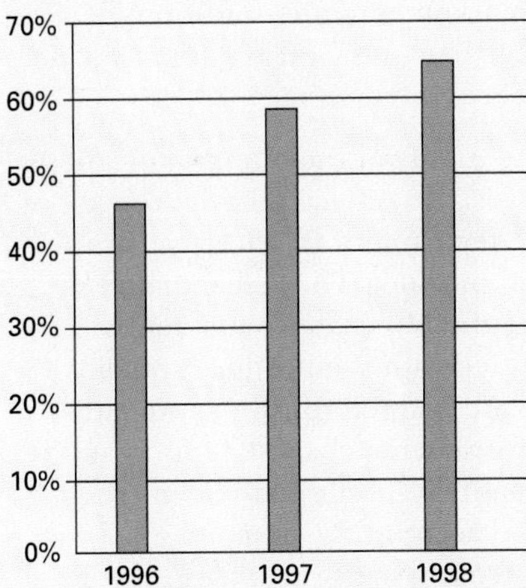

rely on demographic or psychographic profiles. Instead, collaborative filtering bases its predictions on the assumption that past action is the best indicator of future behavior. Specifically, it looks at each individual visitor's behavioral data, such as purchase history, stated preferences, search criteria, any ratings he may have given on another book, or clickstream—where a person goes on a site—to predict future behavior. This information is compared to that of other like-minded people who have a similar history and patterns to determine what books or music will likely interest them. The company also sends targeted e-mails, allegedly sent by Mr. Bezos, with recommendations. After purchasing a book, Amazon.com can remember the buyer's personal information so he can buy a book in the future with a single mouse click.

Personal recommendation software still has a long way to go. For instance, if a visitor at Amazon.com buys a gift for someone whose tastes are vastly different from hers, future recommendation lists may include selections that are way off the mark. Also, separate databases on customer habits aren't always matched up. Amazon.com, for instance, sometimes suggests books that the customer may have already bought there.

What Personalization Can Do for Amazon.com

Bezos sees personalization technology as the future of the Internet, a way to offer mass customization of products and a one-to-one marketing environment. A personalized Web experience is critical to Amazon's success. To keep coming back—or even to risk an on-line purchase for the first time—customers need to feel they're getting something no one else in the brick-and-mortar retail world can offer. By offering personalized recommendations that can change after every purchase and every visit, Amazon hopes to get people to keep coming back.

Bezos believes his customers will come back. Sixty-four percent of Amazon's sales in 1998 were from repeat customers, up from 58 percent in 1997 and 46 percent in 1996. He believes the Internet's retailing power lies in its ability to create a deeper relationship between merchants and customers, one that empowers customers and turns modern-day marketing upside down.

Bezos likens on-line retailing to the days before the Industrial Revolution ushered in mass production and mass merchandising. Back then clothes were custom-made and small-town merchants knew what their customers liked. The Internet, says Bezos, can bring the personal, one-to-one touch back to commerce, only this time on a mass scale. If electronic mass customization tools are implemented wisely, Bezos believes they can improve people's lives by helping them find things they would never otherwise have found.

Questions

1. Privacy advocates are skeptical about personalization tools, fearing they may expose personal information that might be harmful or embarrassing. Do you feel there should be government regulations on what types of information a Web marketer can collect about you? Why or why not?
2. Why is the Internet an ideal environment for one-to-one marketing?
3. Over 60 percent of Amazon.com's sales are from repeat customers. Why does personalization lead to loyal customers?
4. What advantages does a personalized Web site provide to customers? Do you believe you would be more likely to purchase products from a personalized Web site than from a traditional retail establishment? Why or why not?
5. Many people have predicted that the Internet will force many traditional brick-and-mortar retailers to close their doors. Do you think Web retailing may one day eclipse brick-and-mortar retailing? Why or why not?

References:

Amazon.com Web site: **http://www.amazon.com**

Amazon.com 1997 Annual Report

Dana Blankenhorn, "Let's Get Personal," *Advertising Age*, 26 October 1998, p. s22.

Robert D. Hof, Heather Green, and Linda Himelstein, "Now It's Your Web: The Net Is Moving Toward One-to-One Marketing—and That Will Change How All Companies Do Business," *Business Week*, 5 October 1998, p. 164.

Jennifer Lach, "Reading Your Mind, Reaching Your Wallet," *American Demographics*, November 1998, p. 39.

Noah Shachtman, "Get Personal—Business Sites Are Trying to Match Products and Services More Closely to Customers' Needs. Is It Working?" *InternetWeek*, 2 November 1998, p. 36.

Leslie Walker, "Looking Beyond Books; Amazon's Bezos Sees Personalization as Key to Cyber-Stores' Future," *The Washington Post*, 8 November 1998, p. H01.

Cross-Functional Connections Solutions

Questions:

1. Why are the company's pricing strategy and marketing communications of particular concern to research and development, manufacturing, finance, and accounting?

   Marketers have a tendency to refer to product quality in their communications with potential customers. This product quality is also reflected in the pricing of the product. However, it is not the marketing department that has its hands in the development and production of the actual product. The research and development and manufacturing groups provide the physical product marketing presents to customers. If a customer is dissatisfied with the product's quality, then it is typically the "hands-on" groups who are blamed for the low-quality product. It is rare to hear of the marketing group being chastised for creating demand for a high-quality product when in reality it should have been creating demand for a low-quality product! Finance and accounting are concerned about margins and profits for products. If marketing has priced a product low and/or spent large sums of money on marketing communications, a company's financial executives still expect to see profitable outcomes.

2. How has today's technology altered the role of information technologists?

   As computer scientists/mathematicians/engineers, information technologists have traditionally dealt solely with internal firm processes—e-mail systems, network capabilities, logistical systems, etc. Today, however, these same people are responsible for developing material that will often be a customer's first contact with a company. Information technologists are now working in the traditional realm of marketing communications—meaning that they must now study and understand customers' perceptions of the company and its product offerings. Additionally, information technologists must now work hand in hand with the company's marketing group—a group with what might be perceived to be a vastly different personality!

3. What are some of the benefits of networking functional departments, customers, and suppliers?

Very broadly, benefits include:

- *Facilitation of cross-functional communication:* All functional groups have access to the same information, at the same time.
- *Speed of transaction:* Customer orders can be sent electronically and simultaneously to all departments that will perform steps in processing the order, allowing all necessary groups to begin fulfilling necessary tasks to get the order out the door (e.g., accounting can begin checking the firm's credit records, production can check stock for adequate levels, shipping can begin preparing to get the product to the customer).
- *Immediate delivery of component parts, materials, etc.:* Suppliers become as aware of stock level as the customer and ship based on their reporting processes rather than waiting for the customer to place an order.

Suggested Readings:

George Foster and Mahendra Gupta, "Marketing, Cost Management and Management Accounting," *Journal of Management Accounting Research* (Fall 1994), pp. 43–77.

John A. Byrnes, "The Corporation of the Future," *Business Week,* 31 August 1998, pp. 102–106.

Marketing Planning Activities

Integrated Marketing Communications

The next part of the marketing mix to be described for the marketing plan is the promotion element, which covers areas such as advertising, public relations, sales promotion, personal selling, and Internet marketing. Be sure that your promotion plans match the needs and wants of the target market identified and described earlier and are compatible with the product, service, and distribution issues discussed in the previous sections.

JIAN®

1. Evaluate your firm's promotion objectives. Remember that promotions cannot be directly tied with sales because there are too many other factors (competition, environment, price, distribution, product, customer service, company reputation, and so on) that affect sales. State specific objectives that can be tied directly to the result of promotional activities—for example, number of people redeeming a coupon, share of audience during a commercial, percent attitude change before and after a telemarketing campaign, or number of people calling a toll-free information hotline.

Marketing*Builder* Exercises
- **Marketing Strategy** portion of **Marketing Communications** template
- **Marketing Budget** spreadsheet
- **Operating Budget** spreadsheet
- **Source Code Master List** spreadsheet
- **Agency Selection Matrix** spreadsheet

2. What is your chosen company's promotional message? Does this message inform, remind, persuade, or educate the target market?

Marketing*Builder* Exercise
- **Advertising and Promotion** portion of the **Marketing Communications** template

3. Investigate different media placement rates (such as for a school newspaper, local newspaper, national newspaper, local radio station, local TV station, general or specialty interest magazine, local billboard, transit advertising, or the Internet). You can either call local media or consult *Standard Rate and Data Services (SRDS)*. Which media should your firm use? Which media can your firm afford? When should media be used?

Marketing*Builder* Exercises
- **Advertising Schedule** template
- **Preliminary Media Schedule** portion of the **Marketing Communications** template

4. List the public relations activities that your chosen company should pursue. How should bad publicity be handled?

Marketing*Builder* Exercise
- **Public Relations** portion of the **Marketing Communications** template

5. Evaluate or create printed materials for your chosen company (such as data sheets, brochures, stationery, or rate cards). Does the literature sufficiently answer questions? Provide enough information for further contact? Effectively promote product features and customer service? Note a differential or competitive advantage.

Marketing*Builder* Exercises
- **Collateral Planning Matrix** spreadsheet
- **Direct Mail Analysis** spreadsheet
- **Sales Support Collateral Materials** section of the **Marketing Communications** template
- **Corporate Capabilities Brochure** section of the **Marketing Communications** template

6. What trade shows could your firm attend? Search the *Eventline* database for trade shows appropriate to your firm. Order media kits and explore the feasibility and costs of attending those trade shows.

Marketing*Builder* Exercises
- **Trade Show** portion of the **Marketing Communications** template
- **Trade Show Checklist** and **Schedule** template

7. What other sales promotion tools could your firm use? What are the costs? What is the impact on pricing of using these methods?
8. Identify and justify the best type (internal or external) and structure (product, customer, geographic, etc.) for your firm's sales force.

Marketing*Builder* Exercises
- **Current Selling Methods** portion of the **Sales Plan** template
- **Marketing Responsibilities** portion of the **Sales Plan** template
- **Sales Strategy** portion of the **Sales Plan** template
- **Sales Source Analysis** spreadsheet

9. How should your firm hire, motivate, and compensate its sales force?

Marketing*Builder* Exercise
- **Commission Sales Forecast & Tracker** spreadsheet

10. Design a sales approach for your company's sales force to use.

Marketing*Builder* Exercise
- **Next Steps** portion of the **Sales Plan** template

11. Explore the World Wide Web/Internet to research your company, its competition, and the industry in general. How is advertising and promotion being handled in this medium?

Technology-Driven Marketing

Technology will most likely play a key role in your marketing plan. Be sure to clearly identify the ways in which your company will leverage the capabilities of database technology and of the Internet in product, promotion, pricing, and distribution decisions.

1. Assume your company is or will be marketing its products and/or services over the Internet. How should your company enter this electronic marketplace? How will technology issues affect your firm?

Marketing*Builder* Exercises

- **Business Risk** portion of the **Market Analysis** template
- **Environmental Risk** portion of the **Market Analysis** template
- **Elements of Risk** table in the **Market Analysis** template

2. How will marketing over the Internet modify your target market segment(s)? Redefine the demographics, psychographics, geographics, economic factors, size, growth rate, trends, and any other applicable qualities of the target segment(s) you intend to reach through the Internet.

Marketing*Builder* Exercises

- **Market Segment** portion of the **Market Analysis** template
- **Customer Profile** portion of the **Market Analysis** template

3. What kinds of consumer or business product or service is your firm planning to market over the Internet? Identify ways that marketing over the Internet will change the basic design of your core product or service. How will modifications affect your costs? Identify any changes to your return policies that will need to be made to address new Internet customers.
4. Discuss the implications of adding the Internet as a channel to your already developed distribution network. How will this affect channel relationships? The final price offered to Internet customers? Any promotional efforts launched over the Internet?

Marketing*Builder* Exercises

- **Returns and Adjustments Policy** portion of the **Sales Plan** template
- **Distribution Channels** portion of the **Sales Plan** template
- **Product Launch Budget** portion of the **Marketing Budget** spreadsheet
- **Advertising Budget** portion of the **Marketing Budget** spreadsheet

5. Investigate the expansion of your marketing efforts to include a one-to-one database marketing program. How will you collect data? How will you use it? What effect will the creation of the database have on your diverse marketing methods (mailings, catalogs, e-mailings, coupon distribution, product sample distribution, and so on)?

Marketing*Builder* Exercises

- **Direct Mail** portion of the **Marketing Budget** spreadsheet
- **Direct Mail Analysis** spreadsheet
- **Source Code Master List** spreadsheet
- **Direct Response Mail, Direct Mail,** and **List Management** portions of the **Marketing Communications** template.

Pricing Decisions

The last part of the marketing mix to be described for the marketing plan is the price element. Be sure that

your pricing plans match the needs and wants of the target market identified and described earlier and that they are compatible with the product, service, distribution, and promotion issues discussed in the previous sections.

1. List possible pricing objectives for your chosen firm. How might adopting different pricing objectives change the behavior of the firm and its marketing plans?

Marketing*Builder* Exercises

- **Return on Investment** portion of the **Market Analysis** template
- **Break-Even Analysis** spreadsheet
- **Margin Structure** portion of the **Sales Plan** template

2. Pricing is an integral component of marketing strategy. Discuss how your firm's pricing can affect or be affected by competition, the economic environment, political regulations, product features, extra customer service, changes in distribution, or changes in promotion.

Marketing*Builder* Exercises

- **Pricing** portion of the **Sales Plan** template
- **Pricing** portion of the **Market Analysis** template

3. Is demand elastic or inelastic for your company's product or service? Why?
4. What are the costs that have to be covered in your chosen company?
5. What price policy should your firm use? Are there any legal implications of this choice?
6. List and describe the specific pricing tactics that your chosen company should use, including discounts, geographic pricing, and special prices.

APPENDIX

CAREERS IN MARKETING

One of the most important decisions in your life is deciding on your career. Not only will a career choice affect your income and lifestyle, but it also will have a major impact on your happiness and self-fulfillment. Probably the most difficult part of job hunting is deciding exactly what type of work you would like. Many students have had no working experience other than summer jobs, so they are not sure what career to pursue. Too often, college students and their parents rush toward occupational fields that seem to offer the highest monetary payoff or are currently "hot," instead of looking at the long run over a forty- to fifty-year working life.

In order to help you as you begin thinking about career goals and job hunting, our Web site contains an appendix titled "Careers in Marketing." Not only can it inform you about career opportunities in the marketing field, it also provides a wealth of information to help you at each stage of your job search:

- A self-assessment tool
- Career listings with compensation ranges
- Features-advantages-benefits model to help you determine job fit
- Resources for job prospecting
- How to write your résumé
- How to write a professional cover letter
- Self-preparedness test to determine readiness to interview
- Pre-interview checklist
- Tips to keep in mind while preparing for an interview
- More than seventy frequently asked job interview questions
- Questions to ask an interviewer
- How to conduct yourself during an interview
- How to handle objections raised by an interviewer
- Tips on following up after an interview
- How to write a letter accepting a job offer
- How to write a letter declining a job offer

Visit **http://lamb.swcollege.com** to find out how to market yourself to the marketing industry.

Getting Started

Getting started can be the toughest part of job hunting, especially if you are uncertain about what career you want to pursue. The careers appendix can help you in this initial stage with its self-assessment tool, career and compensation lists, features-advantages-benefits (FAB) matrix, and listing of resources for job prospecting.

A self-assessment tool can help you identify your personal needs, capabilities, characteristics, strengths, weaknesses, and desires. The on-line careers appendix includes a thirteen question assessment tool that can help you begin to analyze what is important to you in choosing the kind of work you will do and the kind of employer for whom you will work. There is also a complete listing of careers available in the marketing industry, with compensation figures for each. This information can help you determine what marketing fields interest you and meet your income needs. Using the FAB matrix, you can plot your abilities and skills against the employer's job requirements. Once you complete the model, you will have a better idea of what you have to sell a potential employer. If you have identified a career that suits you but are having trouble finding an employer that offers that particular career opportunity, the on-line careers appendix can help. It provides a list of resources that can be useful when prospecting for an employer. Information on where to locate and how to use the various resources is also included.

Are You Ready to Interview?

Once you have moved through the initial phase of your job search, the on-line careers appendix can still help you. It shows you how to write your résumé and cover letter so that you convey a positive and professional attitude. The information in the appendix can also help you determine how ready you are for a job interview. It provides you with a self-preparedness test, a pre-interview checklist, and a list of considerations to keep in mind when preparing for your interview.

Since interviewing can often be a source of nervousness and anxiety, the on-line careers appendix gives you tools you can use to feel calm and prepared during an interview. A list of over seventy frequently asked job interview questions is provided along with a list of questions for you to ask the interviewer. You can receive guidance on how to conduct yourself professionally during the interview and how to handle objections raised by the interviewer. You can also find tips on following up after the interview and on accepting or declining a job offer.

Go On-line!

Many of the basic concepts of marketing introduced in this book can be used to help you get the career you want by marketing yourself. This complete on-line appendix, "Careers in Marketing," is designed to help you do just that, so visit **http://lamb.swcollege.com** to begin learning how to successfully market yourself to prospective employers!

GLOSSARY

A

accessory equipment Goods, such as portable tools and office equipment, that are less expensive and shorter-lived than major equipment.
adaptive channel Alternative channel initiated when a firm identifies critical but rare customer requirements that they do not have the capability to fulfill.
adopter A consumer who was happy enough with his or her trial experience with a product to use it again.
advertising Impersonal, one-way mass communication about a product or organization that is paid for by a marketer.
advertising appeal Reason for a person to buy a product.
advertising campaign Series of related advertisements focusing on a common theme, slogan, and set of advertising appeals.
advertising objective Specific communication task a campaign should accomplish for a specified target audience during a specified period.
advertising response function Phenomenon in which spending for advertising and sales promotion increases sales or market share up to a certain level but then produces diminishing returns.
advocacy advertising Form of advertising in which an organization expresses its views on controversial issues or responds to media attacks.
agents and brokers Wholesaling intermediaries who facilitate the sale of a product from producer to end user by representing retailers, wholesalers, or manufacturers and who do not take title to the product.
AIDA concept Model that outlines the process for achieving promotional goals in terms of stages of consumer involvement with the message; the acronym stands for Attention, Interest, Desire, and Action.
applied research Attempts to develop new or improved products.
aspirational reference group Group that someone would like to join.
atmosphere The overall impression conveyed by a store's physical layout, decor, and surroundings.
attitude Learned tendency to respond consistently toward a given object.
audience selectivity Ability of an advertising medium to reach a precisely defined market.
audit Form of observation research that features people examining and verifying the sale of a product.
automatic vending The use of machines to offer goods for sale.

B

baby boomers People born between 1946 and 1964.
bait pricing Price tactic that tries to get consumers into a store through false or misleading price advertising and then uses high-pressure selling to persuade consumers to buy more expensive merchandise.
base price The general price level at which the company expects to sell the good or service.
basic research Pure research that aims to confirm an existing theory or to learn more about a concept or phenomenon.
basing-point pricing Price tactic that charges freight from a given (basing) point, regardless of the city from which the goods are shipped.
BehaviorScan Scanner-based research program that tracks the purchases of three thousand households through store scanners.
belief Organized pattern of knowledge that an individual holds as true about his or her world.
benefit segmentation The process of grouping customers into market segments according to the benefits they seek from the product.
brainstorming Getting a group to think of unlimited ways to vary a product or solve a problem.
brand A name, term, symbol, design, or combination thereof that identifies a seller's products and differentiates them from competitors' products.
brand equity The value of company and brand names.
brand loyalty A consistent preference for one brand over all others.
brand mark The elements of a brand that cannot be spoken.
brand name That part of a brand that can be spoken, including letters, words, and numbers.
break-even analysis Method of determining what sales volume must be reached before total revenue equals total costs.
business analysis The second stage of the screening process, at which time preliminary figures for demand, cost, sales, and profitability are calculated.
business marketing The marketing of goods and services to individuals and organizations for purposes other than personal consumption.
business product (industrial product) Product used to manufacture other goods or services, to facilitate an organization's operations, or to resell to other customers.

business services Expense items that do not become part of a final product.
buyer Department head who selects the merchandise for his or her department and may also be responsible for promotion and personnel.
buyer for export Intermediary in the global market that assumes all ownership risks and sells globally for its own account.
buying center All those persons who become involved in the purchase decision.

C

cannibalization Situation that occurs when sales of a new product cut into sales of a firm's existing products.
cash discount A price reduction offered to a consumer, an industrial user, or a marketing intermediary in return for prompt payment of a bill.
category killers Term often used to describe specialty discount stores because they so heavily dominate their narrow merchandise segment.
central-location telephone (CLT) facility A specially designed phone room used to conduct telephone interviewing.
chain stores Stores owned and operated as a group by a single organization.
channel Medium of communication—such as a voice, radio, or newspaper—for transmitting a message.
channel conflict Clash of goals and methods between distribution channel members.
channel control Situation that occurs when one marketing channel member intentionally affects another member's behavior.
channel leader (channel captain) Member of a marketing channel that exercises authority and power over the activities of other channel members.
channel members All parties in the marketing channel that negotiate with one another, buy and sell products, and facilitate the change of ownership between buyer and seller in the course of moving the product from the manufacturer into the hands of the final consumer.
channel partnering (channel cooperation) The joint effort of all channel members to create a supply chain that serves customers and creates a competitive advantage.
channel power Capacity of a particular marketing channel member to control or influence the behavior of other channel members.
closed-ended question Interview question that asks the respondent to make a selection from a limited list of responses.
cobranding Placing two or more brand names on a product or its package.
code of ethics A guideline to help marketing managers and other employees make better decisions.
cognitive dissonance Inner tension that a consumer experiences after recognizing an inconsistency between behavior and values or opinions.
cold calling Form of lead generation in which the salesperson approaches potential buyers without prior knowledge of the prospects' needs or financial status.
commercialization The decision to market a product.
communication Process by which we exchange or share meanings through a common set of symbols.
comparative advertising Form of advertising that compares two or more specifically named or shown competing brands on one or more specific attributes.
competitive advertising Form of advertising designed to influence demand for a specific brand.
component lifestyles Practice of choosing goods and services that meet one's diverse needs and interests rather than conforming to a single, traditional lifestyle.
component parts Either finished items ready for assembly or products that need very little processing before becoming part of some other product.
computer-assisted personal interviewing Interviewing method in which the interviewer reads the questions from a computer screen and enters the respondent's data directly into the computer.
computer-assisted self-interviewing Interviewing method in which a mall interviewer intercepts and directs willing respondents to a nearby computer where the respondent reads questions off the computer screen and directly keys his or her answers into the computer.
computer disk by mail survey Like a typical mail survey only the respondents receive and answer questions on a disk.
concentrated targeting strategy A strategy used to select one segment of a market or targeting marketing efforts.
concept test Test to evaluate a new product idea, usually before any prototype has been created.
consumer behavior Processes a consumer uses to make purchase decisions as well as to use and dispose of purchased goods or services; also includes factors that influence purchase decisions and the use of products.
consumer decision-making process Step-by-step process used by consumers when buying goods or services.
consumer product Product bought to satisfy an individual's personal wants.
Consumer Product Safety Commission (CPSC) Federal agency established to protect the health

and safety of consumers in and around their homes.

consumer sales promotion Sales promotion activities targeted to the ultimate consumer.

continuous media schedule Media scheduling strategy, used for products in the latter stages of the product life cycle, in which advertising is run steadily throughout the advertising period.

contract manufacturing Private label manufacturing by a foreign company.

convenience product A relatively inexpensive item that merits little shopping effort.

convenience sample A form of nonprobability sample using respondents who are convenient or readily accessible to the researcher, for example, employees, friends, or relatives.

convenience store A miniature supermarket, carrying only a limited line of high-turnover convenience goods.

cooperative advertising Arrangement in which the manufacturer and the retailer split the costs of advertising the manufacturer's brand.

corporate social responsibility Business's concern for society's welfare.

cost per contract Cost of reaching one member of the target market.

countertrade Form of trade in which all or part of the payment for goods or services is in the form of other goods or services.

coupon Certificate that entitles consumers to an immediate price reduction when they buy the product.

credence quality A characteristic that consumers may have difficulty assessing even after purchase because they do not have the necessary knowledge or experience.

crisis management Coordinated effort to handle the effects of unfavorable publicity or of another unexpected, unfavorable event.

cross-tabulation A method of analyzing data that lets the analyst look at the responses to one question in relation to the responses to one or more other questions.

culture Set of values, norms, attitudes, and other meaningful symbols that shape human behavior and the artifacts, or products, of that behavior as they are transmitted from one generation to the next.

cumulative quantity discount A deduction from list price that applies to the buyer's total purchases made during a specific period.

customer satisfaction The feeling that a product has met or exceeded the customer's expectations.

customer value The ratio of benefits to the sacrifice necessary to obtain those benefits.

D

database marketing The creation of a large computerized file of customers' and potential customers' profiles and purchase patterns.

decision support system (DSS) An interactive, flexible computerized information system that enables managers to obtain and manipulate information as they are making decisions.

decline stage A long-run drop in sales.

decoding Interpretation of the language and symbols sent by the source through a channel.

demand The quantity of a product that will be sold in the market at various prices for a specified period.

demographic segmentation Segmenting markets by age, gender, income, ethnic background, and family life cycle.

demography The study of people's vital statistics, such as their age, race and ethnicity, and location.

department store A store housing several departments under one roof.

derived demand The demand for business products.

development Stage in the product development process in which a prototype is developed and a marketing strategy is outlined.

differential advantage One or more unique aspects of an organization that cause target consumers to patronize that firm rather than competitors.

diffusion The process by which the adoption of an innovation spreads.

direct channel Distribution channel in which producers sell directly to consumers.

direct foreign investment Active ownership of a foreign company or of overseas manufacturing or marketing facilities.

direct marketing (direct-response marketing) Techniques used to get consumers to make a purchase from their home, office, or other nonretail setting.

direct retailing The selling of products door-to-door, office-to-office, or at home parties by representatives.

discount store A retailer that competes on the basis of low prices, high turnover, and high volume.

discrepancy of assortment Lack of all the items a customer needs to receive full satisfaction from a product or products.

discrepancy of quantity Difference between the amount of product produced and the amount a customer wants to buy.

distribution resource planning (DRP) Inventory control system that manages the replenishment of goods from the manufacturer to the final consumer.

drugstore A retail store that stocks pharmacy-related products and services as its main draw.

dual distribution (multiple distribution) Use of two or more channels to distribute the same product to target markets.
dumping The sale of an exported product at a price lower than that charged for the same or a like product in the "home" market of the exporter.

E

80/20 principle Principle that holds that 20 percent of all customers generate 80 percent of the demand.
elastic demand Situation in which consumer demand is sensitive to changes in price.
elasticity of demand Consumers' responsiveness or sensitivity to changes in price.
electronic data interchange (EDI) Information technology that replaces the paper documents that usually accompany business transactions, such as purchase orders and invoices, with electronic transmission of the needed information to reduce inventory levels, improve cash flow, streamline operations, and increase the speed and accuracy of information transmission.
electronic distribution Distribution technique that includes any kind of product or service that can be distributed electronically, whether over traditional forms such as fiber-optic cable or through satellite transmission of electronic signals.
empowerment Delegation of authority to solve customers' problems—usually by the first person that the customer notifies regarding a problem.
encoding Conversion of the sender's ideas and thoughts into a message, usually in the form of words or signs.
environmental management When a company implements strategies that attempt to shape the external environment within which it operates.
environmental scanning Collection and interpretation of information about forces, events, and relationships in the external environment that may affect the future of the organization or the implementation of the marketing plan.
ethics The standard of behavior by which conduct is judged.
evaluation Gauging the extent to which the marketing objectives have been achieved during the specified time period.
everyday low prices (EDLP) Price tactic of permanently reducing prices 10 to 25 percent below the traditional levels while eliminating trade discounts that create trade loading.
evoked set (consideration set) Group of brands, resulting from an information search, from which a buyer can choose.
exclusive distribution Form of distribution that establishes one or a few dealers within a given area.
experience quality A characteristic that can be assessed only after use.
experiment Method a researcher uses to gather primary data.
export agent Intermediary who acts like a manufacturer's agent for the exporter. The export agent lives in the foreign market.
export broker Intermediary who plays the traditional broker's role by bringing buyer and seller together.
exporting Selling domestically produced products to buyers in another country.
express warranty A written guarantee.
extensive decision making Most complex type of consumer decision making, used when buying an unfamiliar, expensive product or an infrequently bought item; requires use of several criteria for evaluating options and much time for seeking information.
external information search Process of seeking information in the outside environment.
extranet A private electronic network that links a company with its suppliers and customers.

F

factory outlet An off-price retailer that is owned and operated by a manufacturer.
family brand The marketing of several different products under the same brand name.
family life cycle (FLC) A series of stages determined by a combination of age, marital status, and the presence or absence of children.
Federal Trade Commission (FTC) Federal agency empowered to prevent persons or corporations from using unfair methods of competition in commerce.
feedback Receiver's response to a message.
field service firm A firm that specializes in interviewing respondents on a subcontracted basis.
fixed cost Cost that does not change as output is increased or decreased.
flexible pricing (variable pricing) Price tactic in which different customers pay different prices for essentially the same merchandise bought in equal quantities.
flighted media schedule Media scheduling strategy in which ads are run heavily every other month or every two weeks, to achieve a greater impact with an increased frequency and reach at those times.
FOB origin pricing Price tactic that requires the buyer to absorb the freight costs from the shipping point ("free on board").
focus group Seven to ten people who participate in a group discussion led by a moderator.
follow-up Final step of the selling process, in which the salesperson ensures that delivery schedules are

met, that the goods or services perform as promised, and that the buyers' employees are properly trained to use the products.

Food and Drug Administration (FDA) Federal agency charged with enforcing regulations against selling and distributing adulterated, misbranded, or hazardous food and drug products.

frame error Error that occurs when a sample drawn from a population differs from the target population.

franchise The right to operate a business or to sell a product.

franchisee Individual or business that is granted the right to sell another party's product.

franchiser Originator of a trade name, product, methods of operation, and so on, that grants operating rights to another party to sell its product.

freight absorption pricing Price tactic in which the seller pays all or part of the actual freight charges and does not pass them on to the buyer.

frequency Number of times an individual is exposed to a given message during a specific period.

frequent buyer program Loyalty program in which loyal consumers are rewarded for making multiple purchases of a particular good or service.

full-line discounter A retailer that offers consumers very limited service and carries a broad assortment of well-known, nationally branded "hard goods."

fully industrialized society The fifth stage of economic development, a society that is an exporter of manufactured products, many of which are based on advanced technology.

functional discount (trade discount) Discount to wholesalers and retailers for performing channel functions.

G

General Agreement on Tariffs and Trade (GATT) Agreement that provided loopholes that enabled countries to avoid trade-barrier reduction agreements.

Generation X People who are currently between the ages of 18 and 29.

generic product A no-frills, no-brand-name, low-cost product that is simply identified by its product category.

generic product name Name that identifies a product by class or type and that cannot be trademarked.

geodemographic segmentation Segmenting potential customers into neighborhood lifestyle categories.

geographic segmentation Segmenting markets by region of the country or world, market size, market density, or climate.

global marketing Marketing to target markets throughout the world.

global marketing standardization Production of uniform products that can be sold the same way all over the world.

global vision Recognizing and reacting to international marketing opportunities, being aware of threats from foreign competitors in all markets, and effectively using international distribution networks.

gross margin Amount of money the retailer makes as a percentage of sales after the cost of goods sold is subtracted.

group dynamics Interaction essential to the success of focus group research.

growth stage The second stage of the product life cycle when sales typically grow at an increasing rate, many competitors enter the market, large companies may start acquiring small pioneering firms, and profits are healthy.

H

heterogeneity Characteristic of services that makes them less standardized and uniform than goods.

horizontal conflict Channel conflict that occurs among channel members on the same level.

hypermarket Retail store that combines a supermarket and full-line discount store in a space ranging from 200,000 to 300,000 square feet.

I

ideal self-image The way an individual would like to be.

implementation The process that turns marketing plans into action assignments and ensures that these assignments are executed in a way that accomplishes the plans' objectives.

implied warranty An unwritten guarantee that the good or service is fit for the purpose for which it was sold.

in-bound telephone surveys A new trend in telephone interviewing in which an information packet is sent to consumers, who are then asked to call a toll-free, interactive voice-mail system and answer questions.

independent retailers Retailers owned by a single person or partnership and not operated as part of a larger retail institution.

individual branding Using different brand names for different products.

industrializing society The fourth stage of economic development when technology spreads from sectors of the economy that powered the takeoff to the rest of the nation.

inelastic demand Situation in which an increase or a decrease in price will not significantly affect demand for the product.

inflation A general rise in prices without a corresponding increase in wages, which results in decreased purchasing power.
infomercial Thirty-minute or longer advertisement that looks more like a TV talk show than a sales pitch.
informational labeling Labeling designed to help consumers make proper product selections and lower their cognitive dissonance after the purchase.
InfoScan A scanner-based sales-tracking service for the consumer packaged-goods industry.
innovation A product perceived as new by a potential adopter.
inseparability Characteristic of services that allows them to be produced and consumed simultaneously.
institutional advertising Form of advertising designed to enhance a company's image rather than promote a particular product.
intangibility Characteristic of services that cannot be touched, seen, tasted, heard, or felt in the same manner in which goods can be sensed.
integrated interviewing A new interviewing method in which a respondent is interviewed on the Internet.
integrated marketing communications (IMC) The method of carefully coordinating all promotional activities to produce a consistent, unified message that is customer focused.
intensive distribution Form of distribution aimed at having a product available in every outlet at which target customers might want to buy it.
internal information search Process of recalling past information stored in the memory.
Internet Worldwide telecommunications network allowing access to data, pictures, sound, and files throughout the world.
interpersonal communication Direct, face-to-face communication between two or more people.
introductory stage The full-scale launch of a new product into the marketplace.
inventory control system Method of developing and maintaining an adequate assortment of products to meet customer demand.
involvement Amount of time and effort a buyer invests in the search, evaluation, and decision processes of consumer behavior.

J

joint demand The demand for two or more items used together in a final product.
joint venture A venture in which a domestic firm buys part of a foreign company or joins with a foreign company to create a new entity.
just-in-time production (JIT) Redefining and simplifying manufacturing by reducing inventory levels and delivering raw materials just when they are needed on the production line.

K

keiretsu Japanese society of business, which takes one of two main forms: a bank-centered keiretsu, or a massive industrial combine centered around a bank; and a supply keiretsu, or a group of companies dominated by the major manufacturer they provide with supplies.
keystoning Practice of marking up prices by 100 percent, or doubling the cost.

L

leader pricing (loss-leader pricing) Price tactic in which a product is sold near or even below cost in the hope that shoppers will buy other items once they are in the store.
lead generation (prospecting) Identification of those firms and people most likely to buy the seller's offerings.
lead qualification Determination of a sales prospect's authority to buy and ability to pay for the good or service.
learning Process that creates changes in behavior, immediate or expected, through experience and practice.
licensing The legal process whereby a licensor agrees to let another firm use its manufacturing process, trademarks, patents, trade secrets, or other proprietary knowledge.
lifestyle Mode of living as identified by a person's activities, interests, and opinions.
limited decision making Type of decision making that requires a moderate amount of time for gathering information and deliberating about an unfamiliar brand in a familiar product category.
logistics The process of strategically managing the efficient flow and storage of raw materials, in-process inventory, and finished goods from point of origin to point of consumption.
logistics information system Information technology that integrates and links all of the logistics functions of the supply chain.
logistics service Interrelated activities performed by a member of the supply chain to ensure that the right product is in the right place at the right time.
loyalty marketing program Promotional program designed to build long-term, mutually beneficial relationships between a company and its key customers.

M

Maastricht Treaty Agreement among twelve countries of the European Community to pursue economic, monetary, and political union.
macrosegmentation Method of dividing business markets into segments based on general characteristics such as geographic location, customer type, customer size, and product use.
major equipment (installations) Capital goods such as large or expensive machines, mainframe computers, blast furnaces, generators, airplanes, and buildings.
mall intercept interview Survey research method that involves interviewing people in the common areas of shopping malls.
management decision problem Broad-based problem that requires marketing research in order for managers to take proper actions.
manufacturers' brand The brand name of a manufacturer.
market People or organizations with needs or wants and the ability and willingness to buy.
marketing The process of planning and executing the conception, pricing, promotion, and distribution of ideas, goods, and services to create exchanges that satisfy individual and organizational goals.
marketing channel (channel of distribution) Set of interdependent organizations that ease the transfer of ownership as products move from producer to business user or consumer.
marketing concept Idea that the social and economic justification for an organization's existence is the satisfaction of customer wants and needs while meeting organizational objectives.
marketing-controlled information source Product information source that originates with marketers promoting the product.
marketing intelligence Everyday information about developments in the marketing environment that managers use to prepare and adjust marketing plans.
marketing mix A unique blend of product, distribution, promotion, and pricing strategies designed to produce mutually satisfying exchanges with a target market.
marketing objective A statement of what is to be accomplished through marketing activities.
marketing research The process of planning, collecting, and analyzing data relevant to a marketing decision.
marketing research objective Specific information needed to solve a market research problem; the objective should provide insightful, decision-making information.
marketing research problem Determining what information is needed and how that information can be obtained efficiently and effectively.
marketing strategy The activity of selecting and describing one or more target markets and developing and maintaining a marketing mix that will produce mutually satisfying exchanges with target markets.
market opportunity analysis The description and estimation of the size and sales potential of market segments that are of interest to the firm and the assessment of key competitors in these market segments.
market orientation Philosophy that assumes that a sale does not depend on an aggressive sales force but rather on a customer's decision to purchase a product.
market segment A subgroup of people or organizations sharing one or more characteristics that cause them to have similar product needs.
market segmentation The process of dividing a market into meaningful, relatively similar, and identifiable segments or groups.
market share A company's product sales as a percentage of total sales for that industry.
markup pricing Cost of buying the product from the producer plus amounts for profit and for expenses not otherwise accounted for.
Maslow's hierarchy of needs Method of classifying human needs and motivations into five categories in ascending order of importance: physiological, safety, social, esteem, and self-actualization.
mass communication Communication to large audiences.
mass customization (build-to-order) Production method whereby products are not made until an order is placed by the customer; also a strategy that uses technology to deliver customized services on a mass basis, with products being made according to customer specifications.
mass merchandising Retailing strategy using moderate to low prices on large quantities of merchandise and lower service to stimulate high turnover of products.
master brand A brand so dominant in consumers' minds that they think of it immediately when a product category, use situation, product attribute, or customer benefit is mentioned.
materials-handling system Method of moving inventory into, within, and out of the warehouse.
materials requirement planning (MRP) Inventory control system that manages the replenishment of raw materials, supplies, and components from the supplier to the manufacturer.
maturity stage A period during which sales increase at a decreasing rate.

measurement error Error that occurs when there is a difference between the information desired by the researcher and the information provided by the measurement process.
media mix Combination of media to be used for a promotional campaign.
media schedule Designation of the media, the specific publications or programs, and the insertion dates of advertising.
medium Channel used to convey a message to a target market.
merchant wholesaler Institution that buys goods from manufacturers and resells them to businesses, government agencies, and other wholesalers or retailers and that receives and takes title to goods, stores them in its own warehouses, and later ships them.
Mercosur The largest new trade agreement, which includes Brazil, Argentina, Uruguay, and Paraguay.
microsegmentation The process of dividing business markets into segments based on the characteristics of decision-making units within a macrosegment.
modified rebuy Situation in which the purchaser wants some change in the original good or service.
morals The rules people develop as a result of cultural values and norms.
motive Driving force that causes a person to take action to satisfy specific needs.
multiculturalism A situation in which all major ethnic groups in an area—such as a city, county, or census tract—are roughly equally represented.
multinational corporation A company that is heavily engaged in international trade, beyond exporting and importing.
multiplier effect (accelerator principle) Phenomenon in which a small increase or decrease in consumer demand can produce a much larger change in demand for the facilities and equipment needed to make the consumer product.
multisegment targeting strategy A strategy that chooses two or more well-defined market segments and develops a distinct marketing mix for each.

N

need recognition Result of an imbalance between actual and desired states.
needs assessment Determination of the customer's specific needs and wants and the range of options a customer has for satisfying them.
negotiation Process of both the salesperson and the prospect offering special concessions in an attempt to arrive at a sales agreement.
networking Process of finding out about potential clients from friends, business contacts, coworkers, acquaintances, and fellow members in professional and civic organizations.
new buy A situation requiring the purchase of a product for the first time.
new product Product new to the world, the market, the producer, the seller, or some combination of these.
new-product strategy Linking the new-product development process with the objectives of the marketing department, the business unit, and the corporation.
niche One segment of a market.
noise Anything that interferes with, distorts, or slows down the transmission of information.
nonaspirational reference group Group with which an individual does not want to associate.
noncumulative quantity discount A deduction from list price that applies to a single order rather than to the total volume of orders placed during a certain period.
nonmarketing-controlled information source Product information source that is not associated with advertising or promotion.
nonprobability sample Any sample in which little or no attempt is made to get a representative cross section of the population.
nonstore retailing Shopping without visiting a store.
norm Value or attitude deemed acceptable by a group.
North American Free Trade Agreement (NAFTA) An agreement between Canada, the United States, and Mexico that created the world's largest free-trade zone.
North American Industry Classification System (NAICS) A detailed numbering system developed by the United States, Canada, and Mexico to classify North American business establishments by their main production processes.

O

observation research Research method that relies on three types of observation: people watching people, people watching activity, and machines watching people.
odd–even pricing (psychological pricing) Price tactic that uses odd-numbered prices to connote bargains and even-numbered prices to imply quality.
off-price retailer Retailer that sells at prices 25 percent or more below traditional department store prices because it pays cash for its stock and usually doesn't ask for return privileges.
open-ended question Interview question that encourages an answer phrased in the respondent's own words.

opinion leader Individual who influences the opinions of others.
optimizer Type of business customer that considers numerous suppliers, both familiar and unfamiliar, solicits bids, and studies all proposals carefully before selecting one.
order processing system System whereby orders are entered into the supply chain and filled.
outsourcing (contract logistics) Manufacturer's or supplier's use of an independent third party to manage an entire function of the logistics system, such as transportation, warehousing, or order processing.

P

penetration pricing Pricing policy whereby a firm charges a relatively low price for a product initially as a way to reach the mass market.
perception Process by which people select, organize, and interpret stimuli into a meaningful and coherent picture.
perceptual mapping A means of displaying or graphing, in two or more dimensions, the location of products, brands, or groups of products in customers' minds.
perishability Characteristic of services that prevents them from being stored, warehoused, or inventoried.
personality Way of organizing and grouping the consistencies of an individual's reactions to situations.
personalized economy Delivering goods and services at a good value on demand.
personal selling Planned presentation to one or more prospective buyers for the purpose of making a sale.
persuasive labeling Labeling that focuses on a promotional theme or logo with consumer information being secondary.
pioneering advertising Form of advertising designed to stimulate primary demand for a new product or product category.
planned obsolescence The practice of modifying products so those that have already been sold become obsolete before they actually need replacement.
point-of-purchase display Promotional display set up at the retailer's location to build traffic, advertise the product, or induce impulse buying.
position The place a product, brand, or group of products occupies in consumers' minds relative to competing offerings.
positioning Developing a specific marketing mix to influence potential customers' overall perception of a brand, product line, or organization in general.
poverty of time Lack of time to do anything but work, commute to work, handle family situations, do housework, shop, sleep, and eat.
preapproach A process that describes the "homework" that must be done by the salesperson before he or she contacts the prospect.
predatory pricing The practice of charging a very low price for a product with the intent of driving competitors out of business or out of a market.
preindustrial society A society in the second stage of economic development, involving economic and social change and the emergence of a middle class with an entrepreneurial spirit.
premium Extra item offered to the consumer, usually in exchange for some proof of purchase of the promoted product.
prestige pricing Charging a high price to help promote a high-quality image.
price That which is given up in an exchange to acquire a good or service.
price bundling Marketing two or more products in a single package for a special price.
price fixing An agreement between two or more firms on the price they will charge for a product.
price skimming Pricing policy whereby a firm charges a high introductory price, often coupled with heavy promotion.
price strategy Basic, long-term pricing framework, which establishes the initial price for a product and the intended direction for price movements over the product life cycle.
primary data Information collected for the first time; can be used for solving the particular problem under investigation.
primary membership group Reference group with which people interact regularly in an informal, face-to-face manner, such as family, friends, or fellow employees.
private brand A brand name owned by a wholesaler or a retailer.
private-label brands Brands that are designed and developed using the retailer's name.
probability sample A sample in which every element in the population has a known statistical likelihood of being selected.
processed materials Products used directly in manufacturing other products.
product Everything, both favorable and unfavorable, that a person receives in an exchange.
product advertising Form of advertising that touts the benefits of a specific good or service.
product category All brands that satisfy a particular type of need.
product development Marketing strategy that entails the creation of new products for present markets;

process of converting applications for new technologies into marketable products.
product differentiation A positioning strategy that some firms use to distinguish their products from those of competitors.
product item A specific version of a product that can be designated as a distinct offering among an organization's products.
production orientation A philosophy that focuses on the internal capabilities of the firm rather than on the desires and needs of the marketplace.
product life cycle A concept that provides a way to trace the stages of a product's acceptance, from its introduction (birth) to its decline (death).
product line A group of closely related product items.
product line depth The number of product items in a product line.
product line extension Adding additional products to an existing product line in order to compete more broadly in the industry.
product mix All products an organization sells.
product mix width The number of product lines an organization offers.
product modification Changing one or more of a product's characteristics.
product offering The mix of products offered to the consumer by the retailer, also called the product assortment or merchandise mix.
profit Revenue minus expenses.
promotion Communication by marketers that informs, persuades, and reminds potential buyers of a product in order to influence an opinion or elicit a response.
promotional allowance (trade allowance) Payment to a dealer for promoting the manufacturer's products.
promotional mix Combination of promotion tools—including advertising, public relations, personal selling, and sales promotion—used to reach the target market and fulfill the organization's overall goals.
promotional strategy Plan for the optimal use of the elements of promotion: advertising, public relations, personal selling, and sales promotion.
psychographic segmentation Market segmentation on the basis of personality, motives, lifestyles, and geodemographics.
publicity Public information about a company, good, or service appearing in the mass media as a news item.
public relations Marketing function that evaluates public attitudes, identifies areas within the organization that the public may be interested in, and executes a program of action to earn public understanding and acceptance.
pull strategy Marketing strategy that stimulates consumer demand to obtain product distribution.
pulsing media schedule Media scheduling strategy that uses continuous scheduling throughout the year coupled with a flighted schedule during the best sales periods.
push money Money offered to channel intermediaries to encourage them to "push" products—that is, to encourage other members of the channel to sell the products.
push strategy Marketing strategy that uses aggressive personal selling and trade advertising to convince a wholesaler or a retailer to carry and sell particular merchandise.
pyramid of corporate social responsibility Model that suggests corporate social responsibility is composed of economic, legal, ethical, and philanthropic responsibilites and that the firm's economic performance supports the entire structure.

Q

quantity discount Price reduction offered to buyers buying in multiple units or above a specified dollar amount.
quota Statement of the individual salesperson's sales objectives, usually based on sales volume alone but sometimes including key accounts (those with greatest potential), new accounts, and specific products.

R

random error Error that occurs because the selected sample is an imperfect representation of the overall population.
random sample Sample arranged in such a way that every element of the population has an equal chance of being selected as part of the sample.
raw materials Unprocessed extractive or agricultural products, such as mineral ore, lumber, wheat, corn, fruits, vegetables, and fish.
reach Number of target consumers exposed to a commercial at least once during a specific period, usually four weeks.
real self-image The way an individual actually perceives himself or herself.
rebate Cash refund given for the purchase of a product during a specific period.
receiver Person who decodes a message.
recession A period of economic activity when income, production, and employment tend to fall—all of which reduce demand for goods and services.
reciprocity A practice in which business purchasers choose to buy from their own customers.
recruited Internet sample Sample in which respondents are prerecruited and, after qualifying to participate, are sent a questionnaire by e-mail or directed to a secure Web site to fill out a questionnaire.

reference group Group in society that influences an individual's purchasing behavior.
referral Recommendation to a salesperson from a customer or business associate.
relationship marketing The name of a strategy that entails forging long-term partnerships with customers.
relationship selling (consultative selling) Sales practice of building, maintaining, and enhancing interactions with customers in order to develop long-term satisfaction through mutually beneficial partnerships.
repositioning Changing consumers' perceptions of a brand in relation to competing brands.
research design One that specifies which research questions must be answered, how and when the data will be gathered, and how the data will be analyzed.
retailer Channel intermediary that sells mainly to consumers.
retailing All the activities directly related to the sale of goods and services to the ultimate consumer for personal, nonbusiness use.
retailing mix Combination of the six Ps—product, place, promotion, price, personnel, and presentation—to sell goods and services to the ultimate consumer.
revenue The price charged to customers multiplied by the number of units sold.
routine response behavior Type of decision making exhibited by consumers buying frequently purchased, low-cost goods and services; requires little search and decision time.

S

sales orientation Idea that people will buy more goods and services if aggressive sales techniques are used and that high sales result in high profits.
sales presentation Face-to-face explanation of the sales proposal to a prospective buyer.
sales process (sales cycle) The set of steps a salesperson goes through in a particular organization to sell a particular product or service.
sales promotion Marketing activities—other than personal selling, advertising, and public relations—that stimulate consumer buying and dealer effectiveness.
sales proposal A formal written document or professional presentation that outlines how the salesperson's product or service will meet or exceed the prospect's needs.
sample A subset of a population.
sampling Promotional program that allows the consumer the opportunity to try the product or service for free.
sampling error Error that occurs when a sample somehow does not represent the target population.
satisfier Type of business customer that places an order with the first familiar supplier to satisfy product and delivery requirements.
scaled-response question A close-ended question designed to measure the intensity of a respondent's answer.
scanner-based research A system for gathering information from a single group of respondents by continuously monitoring the advertising, promotion, and pricing they are exposed to and the things they buy.
scrambled merchandising The tendency to offer a wide variety of nontraditional goods and services under one roof.
screened Internet sample Internet sample with quotas based on desired sample characteristics.
screening The first filter in the product development process that eliminates ideas that are inconsistent with the organization's new-product strategy or are obviously inappropriate for some other reason.
search quality A characteristic that can be easily assessed before purchase.
seasonal discount A price reduction for buying merchandise out of season.
seasonal media schedule Media scheduling strategy that runs advertising only during times of the year when the product is most likely to be used.
secondary data Data previously collected for any purpose other than the one at hand.
secondary membership group Reference group with which people associate less consistently and more formally than a primary membership group, such as a club, professional group, or religious group.
segmentation bases (variables) Characteristics of individuals, groups, or organizations.
selective distortion Process whereby a consumer changes or distorts information that conflicts with his or her feelings or beliefs.
selective distribution Form of distribution achieved by screening dealers to eliminate all but a few in any single area.
selective exposure Process whereby a consumer notices certain stimuli and ignores other stimuli.
selective retention Process whereby a consumer remembers only that information that supports his or her personal beliefs.
self-concept How a consumer perceives himself or herself in terms of attitudes, perceptions, beliefs, and self-evaluations.
sender Originator of the message in the communication process.
service The result of applying human or mechanical efforts to people or objects.

service mark Trademark for a service.
shopping product Product that requires comparison shopping, because it is usually more expensive than a convenience product and found in fewer stores.
simulated (laboratory) market testing Presentation of advertising and other promotion materials for several products, including a test product, to members of the product's target market.
single-price tactic Policy of offering all goods and services at the same price.
social class Group of people in a society who are considered nearly equal in status or community esteem, who regularly socialize among themselves both formally and informally, and who share behavioral norms.
socialization process Process by which cultural values and norms are passed down to children.
societal orientation The idea that an organization exists not only to satisfy customer wants and needs and to meet organizational objectives but also to preserve or enhance individuals' and society's long-term best interests.
spatial discrepancy Difference between the location of the producer and the location of widely scattered markets.
specialty discount store Retail store that offers a nearly complete selection of single-line merchandise and uses self-service, discount prices, high volume, and high turnover.
specialty product A particular item that consumers search extensively for and are very reluctant to accept substitutes for.
specialty store Retail store specializing in a given type of merchandise.
status quo pricing Pricing objective that maintains existing prices or meets the competition's prices.
stimulus Any unit of input affecting one or more of the five senses: sight, smell, taste, touch, hearing.
stimulus discrimination Learned ability to differentiate among stimuli.
stimulus generalization Form of learning that occurs when one response is extended to a second stimulus similar to the first.
stitching niches Strategy for multicultural marketing that combines ethnic, age, income, and lifestyle markets, on some common basis, to form a large market.
straight commission Method of compensation in which the salesperson is paid some percentage of sales.
straight rebuy Buying situation in which the purchaser reorders the same goods or services without looking for new information or investigating other suppliers.
straight salary Method of compensation in which the salesperson receives a salary regardless of sales productivity.
strategic alliance (strategic partnership) A cooperative agreement between business firms.
strategic channel alliance Cooperative agreement between business firms to use the other's already established distribution channel.
subculture Homogeneous group of people who share elements of the overall culture as well as unique elements of their own group.
supercenter Retail store that combines groceries and general merchandise goods with a wide range of services.
supermarket A large, departmentalized, self-service retailer that specializes in food and nonfood items.
supplies Consumable items that do not become part of the final product.
supply The quantity of a product that will be offered to the market by a supplier at various prices for a specified period.
supply chain The connected chain of all of the business entities, both internal and external to the company, that perform or support the logistics function.
supply chain management (integrated logistics) Management system that coordinates and integrates all of the activities performed by supply chain members from source to the point of consumption that results in enhanced customer and economic value.
supply chain team Entire group of individuals who orchestrate the movement of goods, services, and information from the source to the consumer.
survey research the most popular technique for gathering primary data in which a researcher interacts with people to obtain facts, opinions, and attitudes.

T

takeoff economy The third stage of economic development that involves a period of transition from a developing to a developed nation.
target market A group of people or organizations for which an organization designs, implements, and maintains a marketing mix intended to meet the needs of that group, resulting in mutually satisfying exchanges.
teamwork Collaborative efforts of people to accomplish common objectives.
telemarketing The use of the telephone to sell directly to consumers.
temporal discrepancy Difference between when a product is produced and when a customer is ready to buy it.

test marketing The limited introduction of a product and a marketing program to determine the reactions of potential customers in a market situation.
trade allowance Price reduction offered by manufacturers to intermediaries, such as wholesalers and retailers.
trade loading Practice of temporarily lowering the price to induce wholesalers and retailers to buy more goods than can be sold in a reasonable time.
trademark The exclusive right to use a brand or part of a brand.
trade sales promotion Sales promotion activities targeted to a channel member, such as a wholesaler or retailer.
traditional society A society in the earliest stages of economic development, largely agricultural, with a social structure and value system that provide little opportunity for upward mobility.
two-part pricing Price tactic that charges two separate amounts to consume a single good or service.

U

unbundling Reducing the bundle of services that comes with the basic product.
undifferentiated targeting strategy Marketing approach that views the market as one big market with no individual segments and thus requires a single marketing mix.
unfair trade practice acts Laws that prohibit wholesalers and retailers from selling below cost.
uniform delivered pricing Price tactic in which the seller pays the actual freight charges and bills every purchaser an identical, flat freight charge.
Uniform Reference Locator (URL) Similar to a street address in that it identifies a unique location on the Web.
unique selling proposition Desirable, exclusive, and believable advertising appeal selected as the theme for a campaign.
universal product codes (UPCs) Series of thick and thin vertical lines (bar codes), readable by computerized optical scanners, that represent numbers used to track products.
universe The population from which a sample will be drawn.
unrestricted Internet sample One in which anyone with a computer and modem can fill out the questionnaire.
unsought product A product unknown to the potential buyer or a known product that the buyer does not actively seek.
Uruguay Round An agreement to dramatically lower trade barriers worldwide.
usage-rate segmentation Dividing a market by the amount of product bought or consumed.

V

value Enduring belief that a specific mode of conduct is personally or socially preferable to another mode of conduct.
value-based pricing The price set at a level that seems to the customer to be a good price compared to the prices of other options.
variable costs Costs that vary with changes in the level of output.
vertical conflict Channel conflict that occurs between different levels in a marketing channel, most typically between the manufacturer and wholesaler or between the manufacturer and retailer.

W

want Recognition of an unfulfilled need and a product that will satisfy it.
warehouse membership clubs Limited-service merchant wholesalers that sell a limited selection of brand-name appliances, household items, and groceries on a cash-and-carry basis to members, usually small businesses and groups.
warranty Confirmation of the quality or performance of a good or service.
World Trade Organization (WTO) A new trade organization that replaces the old General Agreement on Trade and Tariffs (GATT).
World Wide Web (Web) Component of the Internet designed to simplify text and images.
WTO. *See* **World Trade Organization.**

Z

zone pricing Modification of uniform delivered pricing that divides the United States (or the total market) into segments or zones and charges a flat freight rate to all customers in a given zone.

ENDNOTES

CHAPTER 1

1. From "The Power of Reflection" by Michael Hammer and Steven A. Stanton, *Fortune*, November 24, 1997. © 1997 Time Inc. All rights reserved. Reprinted by permission.
2. Peter D. Bennett, *Dictionary of Marketing Terms*, 2d ed. (Chicago: American Marketing Association, 1995), p. 115.
3. Philip Kotler, *Marketing Management*, 9th ed. (Englewood Cliffs, NJ: Prentice-Hall, 1997), p. 11.
4. Stephen Baker, "A New Paint Job at PPG," *Business Week*, 13 November 1995, pp. 74, 78.
5. Graham J. Hooley, John A. Saunders, and Nigel Piercy, *Marketing Strategy & Competitive Positioning* (London: Prentice-Hall Europe, 1998), p. 6.
6. J. W. Marriott, Jr., and Kathi Ann Brown, *The Spirit to Serve: Marriott's Way* (New York: Harper Business, 1997), p. 5.
7. John A. Byrne, "Strategic Planning," *Business Week*, 26 August 1996, pp. 46–52.
8. Hammer and Stanton, p. 294.
9. David Cravens, Charles W. Lamb, Jr., and Victoria Crittenden, *Strategic Marketing Management Cases*, New York: McGraw-Hill, 1999), p. 81.
10. Sean Mehegan, "Sun Lotions Go Back into Frying Pan," *Brandweek*, 3 March 1997, p. 2.
11. "King Consumer," *Business Week*, 12 March 1990, p. 90.
12. Cyndee Miller, "Nordstrom Is Tops in Survey," *Marketing News*, 15 February 1993, p. 12.
13. From "Japanese Consumers Shun Local Catalogs to Buy American" by Mari Yamaguchi, *Marketing News*, December 2, 1996, p. 12. Reprinted by permission of the American Marketing Association.
14. Kevin J. Clancy and Robert S. Shulman, "Marketing—Ten Fatal Flaws," *The Retailing Issues Letter*, November 1995, p. 4.
15. Michael Treacy and Fred Wiersema, "How Market Leaders Keep Their Edge," *Fortune*, 6 February 1995, pp. 94–95.
16. Jonathan B. Levine, "Customer, Sell Thyself," *Fast Company*, June-July 1996, p. 148.
17. Roland T. Rust, Anthony J. Zahorik, and Timothy L. Keiningham, *Service Marketing* (New York: HarperCollins, 1996), p. 375.
18. Leonard L. Berry, "Relationship Marketing of Services," *Journal of the Academy of Marketing Science*, Fall 1995, pp. 236–245.
19. Berry, p. 241.
20. Leonard L. Berry and A. Parasuraman, *Marketing Services* (New York: Free Press, 1991), p. 49.
21. From "Main Street Revisited" by Becky Ebenkamp, *Brandweek*, April 7, 1997. © 1997 ASM Communications Inc. Used with permission from Brandweek.
22. Kotler, p. 22.
23. "The Checkoff," *Wall Street Journal*, 26 November 1996, p. A1.

CHAPTER 2

1. From "Sneaker Company Tags Out-of-Breath Baby Boomers" by Joseph Pereira, *Wall Street Journal*, January 16, 1998. Reprinted by permission of The Wall Street Journal, © 1998 Dow Jones & Company, Inc. All Rights Reserved Worldwide.
2. "Tracking Study Looks at Perceptions of Multimedia/Interactive Technologies," *Quirk's Marketing Research Review*, January 1996, pp. 27, 29.
3. From "The Emerging Culture" by Paul H. Ray, *American Demographics*, February 1997. Reprinted with permission from American Demographics magazine, © 1997 PRIMEDIA Intertec, Stamford, CT.
4. Leonard L. Berry, A. Parasuraman, and Valarie A. Zeithaml, "Improving Service Quality in America: Lessons Learned," *Academy of Management Executive* 8, No. 2, 1994, p. 36.
5. "No Place Like Home," *Wall Street Journal*, 16 June 1997, p. R4.
6. David Wolfe, "The Psychological Center of Gravity," *American Demographics*, April 1998, pp. 16–19.
7. "Latest Backlash Against Dual Earners Ignores Some Realities," *Wall Street Journal*, 14 May 1997, p. B1.
8. "Are Tech Buyers Different?" *Business Week*, 26 January 1998, pp. 64–68.
9. "Sorry, Boys—Donna Reed Is Still Dead," *American Demographics*, September 1995, pp. 13–14.
10. Gerry Myers, "Selling to Women," *American Demographics*, April 1996, pp. 36–42.
11. Ibid.
12. Ibid.
13. Melinda Beck, "Next Population Bulge Shows Its Might," *Wall Street Journal*, 3 February 1997, pp. B1, B6.
14. "Marketing to Generation X," *Advertising Age*, 6 February 1995, p. 27.
15. Susan Mitchell, "How to Talk to Young Adults," *American Demographics*, April 1993, pp. 50–54.
16. "Understanding Generation X," *Marketing Research*, Spring 1993, pp. 54–55.
17. "Xers Know They're a Target Market, and They Hate That," *Marketing News*, 6 December 1993, pp. 2, 15.
18. "Easy Pickup Line? Try Gen Xers," *Advertising Age*, 3 April 1995, pp. 5–22.
19. "Survey Sheds Light on Typical Boomer," *Marketing News*, 31 January 1994, p. 2.
20. Cheryl Russell, "The Master Trend," *American Demographics*, October 1993, pp. 28–37.
21. Russell, pp. 28–37.
22. "The Baby Boom at Mid-Decade," *American Demographics*, April 1995, pp. 40–45.
23. Russell, pp. 28–37.
24. Ruth Hamel, "Raging against Aging," *American Demographics*, March 1990, pp. 42–45.
25. "American Maturity," *American Demographics*, March 1993, pp. 31–42.
26. "Boomers Come of Old Age," *Marketing News*, 15 January 1996, pp. 1, 6.
27. "Mature Market Often Misunderstood," *Marketing News*, 28 August 1995, p. 28.
28. Michael Major, "Promoting to the Mature Market," *Promo*, November 1990, p. 7.
29. "Bond Stronger with Age," *Advertising Age*, 28 March 1994, pp. 5–6.
30. "Baby-Boomers May Seek Age-Friendly Stores," *Wall Street Journal*, 1 July 1992, p. B1.
31. Charles Schewe and Geoffrey Meredith, "Digging Deep to Delight the Mature Adult Customer," *Marketing Management*, Winter 1995, pp. 21–34.
32. "Americans on the Move," *American Demographics*, June 1990, pp. 46–48.
33. "The Hottest Metros," *American Demographics*, April 1995, pp. 4–5.
34. "The Most Populous Metros," *American Demographics*, June 1997, p. 17.
35. Willian Frey, "The New White Flight," *American Demographics*, April 1994, pp. 40–47.
36. "Influx of Immigrants Benefits American Economy Overall," *Fort Worth Star-Telegram*, 18 May 1997, p. A18.
37. "Work Slowdown," *American Demographics*, March 1996, pp. 4–7.
38. William Dunn, "The Move toward Ethnic Marketing," *Nation's Business*, July 1992, pp. 39–44; "The Numbers Bear Out Our Diversity," *Wall Street Journal*, 24 April 1994, p. B1.
39. Dunn, p. 40; "How to Sell Across Cultures," *American Demographics*, March 1994, pp. 56–58.
40. Jeffery O. Zbar, "With Right Touch, Marketers Can Hit Multiple Cultures," *Advertising Age*, 16 November 1998, p. 24.
41. Jon Berry, "An Empire of Niches," *Superbrands: A Special Supplement to Adweek's Marketing Week*, Fall 1991, pp. 17–22.
42. "The New Business Cycle," *Business Week*, 31 March 1997, pp. 58–60.
43. "Whodunnit To Inflation?" *Business Week*, 12 May 1997, pp. 36–37.
44. "The New Business Cycle," *Business Week*, 31 March 1997, pp. 58–68.
45. "America in the World: Still on Top, with No Challenger," *Fortune*, 9 June 1997, pp. 86–87.
46. "Driving Technology," *Wall Street Journal*, 16 June 1997, p. R4.
47. Motorola's Prospects Are Linked to New Technologies," *Wall Street Journal*, 11 April 1996, p. B4.

48. "What Price Science?" *Business Week,* 26 May 1997, pp. 166–170.
49. "Could America Afford the Transistor Today?" *Business Week,* 7 March 1994, pp. 80–84.
50. "Web Advertising Comes of Age," *Internet World,* 13 April 1998, p. 14.
51. From "The Myth of Email Privacy" by Eryn Brown. Reprinted from the February 3, 1997 issue of *Fortune* by special permission; copyright 1997. Time Inc.
52. "Frito-Lay Devours Snack-Food Business," *Wall Street Journal,* 27 October 1995, pp. B1, B4.
53. From "Beating the Odds" by Ronald Lieber, *Fortune,* March 31, 1997. © 1997 Time Inc. All rights reserved. Reprinted by permission.
54. From "France Rejects Coca-Cola's Purchase of Orangina" by Nikhil Deogun and Amy Barrett, *Wall Street Journal,* September 18, 1998. Reprinted by permission of The Wall Street Journal. © 1998 Dow Jones & Company, Inc. All Rights Reserved Worldwide.
55. Based on Edward Stevens, *Business Ethics* (New York: Paulist Press, 1979).
56. Anusorn Singhapakdi, Skott Vitell, and Kenneth Kraft, "Moral Intensity and Ethical Decisionmaking of Marketing Professionals," *Journal of Business Research* 36, March 1996, pp. 245–255; Ishmael Akaah and Edward Riordan, "Judgments of Marketing Professionals about Ethical Issues in Marketing Research: A Replication and Extension," *Journal of Marketing Research,* February 1989, pp. 112–120; see also Shelby Hunt, Lawrence Chonko, and James Wilcox, "Ethical Problems of Marketing Researchers," *Journal of Marketing Research,* August 1984, pp. 309–324; and Kenneth Andrews, "Ethics in Practice," *Harvard Business Review,* September–October 1989, pp. 99–104.
57. O.C. Ferrell, Debbie Thorne, and Linda Ferrell, "Legal Pressure for Ethical Compliance in Marketing," *Proceedings of the American Marketing Association,* Summer 1995, pp. 412–413.
58. This section adapted from Archie B. Carroll, "The Pyramid of Corporate Social Responsibility: Toward the Moral Management of Organizational Stakeholders," *Business Horizons,* July–August 1991, pp. 39–48; also see: Kirk Davidson, "Marketers Must Accept Greater Responsibilities," *Marketing News,* 2 February 1998, p. 6.
59. Stephanie N. Mehta, "Black Entrepreneurs Benefit from Social Responsibility," *Wall Street Journal,* 19 September 1995, p. B1
60. "Wrigley Ads to Focus on Minority Health," *Wall Street Journal,* 4 June 1997, p. B1.
61. Suzanne Alexander, "Life's Just a Bowl of Cherry Garcia for Ben & Jerry's," *Wall Street Journal,* 15 July 1992, p. B3.
62. Cara Appelbaum, "Jantzen to Pitch in for Clean Waters," *Adweek's Marketing Week,* 6 April 1992, p. 6.
63. Elyse Tanouye, "Drug Firms Start 'Compliance' Programs Reminding Patients to Take Their Pills," *Wall Street Journal,* 25 March 1992, pp. B1, B5.
64. Andrew Pollack, "Un-Writing a New Page in the Annals of Recycling," *New York Times,* 21 August 1993, p. 17.

CHAPTER 3

1. From "Plying Ex-Soviet Asia with Pepsi, Barbie and Barf" by Hugh Pope, *Wall Street Journal,* May 6, 1998. Reprinted by permission of The Wall Street Journal, © 1998 Dow Jones & Company, Inc. All Rights Reserved Worldwide.
2. Philip Siekman, "Brains Are Powering U.S. Exports," *Fortune,* 3 February 1997, pp. 70B–70L.
3. "Potato Chips—To Go Global—Or So Pepsi Bets," *Wall Street Journal,* 30 November 1995, pp. B1, B10.
4. "America in the World: Still on Top, with No Challenger," *Fortune,* 9 June 1997, p. 86.
5. "Riding High: Corporate America Now Has an Edge over Its Global Rivals," *Business Week,* 9 October 1995, pp. 134–146.
6. Paul Krugman, "Competitiveness: Does It Matter," *Fortune,* 7 March 1994, pp. 109–116; and "New Lift for the U.S. Export Boom," *Fortune,* 13 November 1995, pp. 73–75.
7. *Statistical Abstract of the United States* (Washington, DC: Government Printing Office, 1997), p. 871.
8. *The World Almanac* (Mahwah, NJ: World Almanac Books), 1997, p. 504.
9. "As U.S. Firms Gain on Rivals, the Dollar Raises Pesky Question," *Wall Street Journal,* 16 August 1996, pp. A1, A4.
10. "Current International Trade Position of the United States," *Business America,* March 1998, pp. 30–32.
11. Gene Koretz, "Awaiting the Export Surge," *Business Week,* 2 March 1998, p. 2.
12. Neil Jacoby, "The Multinational Corporation," *Center Magazine,* May 1970, p. 37.
13. "The Stateless Corporation," *Business Week,* 14 May 1990, pp. 98–105.
14. Theodore Levitt, "The Globalization of Markets," *Harvard Business Review,* May–June 1983, pp. 92–102.
15. Saeed Samiee and Kendall Roth, "The Influence of Global Marketing Standardization on Performance," *Journal of Marketing,* April 1992, pp. 1–17; also see Aviv Shoham, "Global Marketing Standardization," *Journal of Global Marketing,* September 1995, pp. 91–119.
16. "For Peruvians, Fizzy Yellow Drink Is the Real Thing," *International Herald Tribune,* 27 December, 1995, p. 3.
17. Eduardo Cue, "Sacrébleu! French Youth Prefer Coke," *U.S. News and World Report,* 9 March 1998, p. 38.
18. Ibid.
19. "Global Products Require Name-Finders," *Wall Street Journal,* 11 April 1996, p. B5.
20. "Don't Be an Ugly-American Manager," *Fortune,* 16 October 1995, p. 225.
21. From "Against the Grain: The Rice of India Sprouts in Texas" by Rehka Balu, *Wall Street Journal,* April 6, 1998. Reprinted by permission of The Wall Street Journal. © 1998 Dow Jones & Company, Inc. All Rights Reserved Worldwide.
22. "Portrait of the World," *Marketing News,* 28 August 1995, pp. 20–21.
23. "The Big Mac Index," *Parade,* 25 May 1996, p. 7.
24. "Kenya Set to Be the World's Largest Tea Exporter," *African Business,* November 1997, p. 46.
25. Zulia Hu and Mohsin Kahn, "Why Is China Growing So Fast?" *International Monetary Fund Staff Papers,* March 1997, pp. 103–131.
26. Kathy Chen, "Chinese Babies Are Coveted Customers," *Wall Street Journal,* 15 May 1998, pp. B1, B7.
27. Betsy McKay, "Out with the In-Laws, in with the MBAs: It's the New Russia," *Wall Street Journal,* 15 September 1997, pp. A1, A10.
28. "Profiting from India's Strong Middle Class," *Marketing News,* 7 October 1996, p. 6.
29. "Pop Radio in France Goes French," *International Herald Tribune,* 2 January 1996, p. 2.
30. Ibid.
31. "Ultimatum for the Avon Lady," *Business Week,* 11 May 1998, p. 33.
32. "CD Piracy Flourishes in China, and West Supplies the Equipment," *Wall Street Journal,* 24 April 1997, pp. A1, A12.
33. "This Is One the White House Can't Duck," *Business Week,* 8 April 1996, p. 52; also see Moshe Givon, Vijay Mahajan, and Eitan Muller, "Software Piracy: Estimation of Lost Sales and the Impact on Software Diffusion," *Journal of Marketing,* January 1995, pp. 29–37; Craig Smith, "CD Piracy Flourishes in China, and West Supplies Equipment," *Wall Street Journal,* 24 April 1997; and "Beijing's Backyard Industry," *International Herald Tribune,* 19 March 1998, p. 12.
34. Marie Anchordoguy, "A Brief History of Japan's Keiretsu," *Harvard Business Review,* July–August 1990, pp. 58–59.
35. Robert Cutts, "Capitalism in Japan: Cartels and Keiretsu," *Harvard Business Review,* July–August 1992, pp. 48–50.
36. "U.S. Sees Progress in Talks with Japan, but Seeks More Action on Trade Gap," *Wall Street Journal,* 31 July 1992, p. B2.
37. "Nogales, Arizona Throws a Post-NAFTA Party, but Locals Miss Out," *Wall Street Journal,* 21 March 1997, pp. A1, A6.
38. Karl Zinsmeister, "Swallowed Up at Work," *American Enterprise,* January 1996, pp. 16–19.
39. "How NAFTA Will Help America," *Fortune,* 19 April 1993, pp. 95–102.
40. "NAFTA: Where's That Giant Sucking Sound?" *Business Week,* 7 July 1997, p. 45; also see "United States: Deep in the Heart of NAFTA," *Economist,* 28 February 1998, pp. 55–57.

41. "Latin Nations, Unsure of U.S. Motives, Make Their Own Trade Pacts," *Wall Street Journal,* 9 January 1996, pp. A1, A4; also see Masaaki Kotabe and Maria Cecilia Coutinho de Arruda, "South America's Free Trade Gambit," *Marketing Management,* Spring 1998, pp. 39–46.
42. "Road to Unification," *Sky,* June 1993, pp. 32–41.
43. "Here Comes the Euro," *Business Week,* 27 April 1998, pp. 90–113; and "Euro Wins Wide Acceptance Before Milestone Summit," 30 April 1998, pp. A12–A14.
44. Tony Horwitz, "Europe's Borders Fade, and People and Goods Can Move More Freely," *Wall Street Journal,* 18 May 1993, pp. A1, A10. Reprinted by permission of The Wall Street Journal, © 1993 Dow Jones & Company, Inc. All Rights Reserved Worldwide.
45. "Can China Avert Crisis?" *Business Week,* 16 March 1998, pp. 44–49.
46. Rahul Jacob, "The Big Rise," *Fortune,* 30 May 1994, pp. 74–90.
47. "Plan Helps Exporters Fish Abroad from Docks at Home," *Wall Street Journal,* 5 March 1996, p. B2.
48. "The Trade Gap Won't Be All That Bad," *Business Week,* 30 March 1998, p. 24.
49. "AOL Launches New Assault in Europe By Building System of Local Alliances," *Wall Street Journal,* 27 February 1998, p. B11.
50. "Making Global Alliances Work," *Fortune,* 17 December 1990, pp. 121–123.
51. "P&G Squabbles with Vietnamese Partner," *Wall Street Journal,* 27 February 1998, p. A10.
52. "Federal Express, UPS Battle for a Foothold In Asia, " *Wall Street Journal,* 22 January 1997, pp. B1, B8.
53. "Old World, New Investment," *Business Week,* 7 October 1996, pp. 50–51.
54. From "Local Company Is Helping Business Go Global" by Lisa Werner Carr. This article appeared in the *Dallas Business Journal* on Dec. 26, 1997–Jan. 1, 1998. It has been reprinted with permission from the Dallas Business Journal. Any further reproduction in whole or part is strictly prohibited. Copyright 1997 by the Dallas Business Journal.
55. "TI Teams Up in Asia," *Dallas Morning News,* 4 February 1996, p. H1.
56. "Kodak Divides Up China in Order to Conquer It," *Ad Age International,* January 1998, pp. 20–23.
57. "Can TV Save the Planet," *American Demographics,* May 1996, pp. 43–47.
58. "In Global Drive, Nike Finds Its Brash Ways Don't Always Pay Off," *Wall Street Journal,* 5 May 1997, pp. A1, A10.
59. "Marketing Board Games Is No Trivial Pursuit," *Dallas Morning News,* 14 January 1996, pp. 1F, 4F.
60. "Europe's Unity Undoes a U.S. Exporter," *Wall Street Journal,* 1 April 1996, p. B1.
61. "For Coke in India, Thums Up Is the Real Thing," *Wall Street Journal,* 29 April 1998, pp. B1, B2.
62. "Pairing Bud with Sushi in South America," *Wall Street Journal,* 20 February 1997, pp. B1, B8.
63. "P&G's Joy Makes Unlikely Splash in Japan," *Wall Street Journal,* 10 December 1997, pp. B1, B8.
64. "Kiddi Just Fine in the U.K., but Here It's Binky," *Marketing News,* 28 August 1995, p. 8.
65. "Why Countertrade Is Hot," *Fortune,* 29 June 1992, p. 25; Nathaniel Gilbert, "The Case for Countertrade," *Across the Board,* May 1992, pp. 43–45.
66. "To All U.S. Managers Upset by Regulations: Try Germany or Japan," *Wall Street Journal,* 14 December 1995, p. A1.
67. From "Report from Tokyo" by Mary Haffenberg. *Marketing News,* May 25, 1998, pp. 2, 21. Reprinted by permission of the American Marketing Association.

CHAPTER 4

1. Corey Takahashi, "Midlife Crisis? Trucks, Vans Start to Lose Their Luster," *Wall Street Journal,* 14 August 1997, pp. B1, B9; Jean Halliday, "Euro Brands Head Station Wagon Surge: Luxury Carmakers Leading Charge As Sport-Ute, Minivan Alternative," *Advertising Age,* 8 June 1998, p. 50.
2. Nikhil Deogun, "Fat-Free Snacks Aren't Wowing Frito Customers," *Wall Street Journal,* 14 September 1998, pp. B1, B4; Rekha Balu, "Forget 'Fat-Free'; Now It's Foods Packed with Protein," *Wall Street Journal,* 17 September 1998, pp. B1, B4.
3. Douglas A. Blackmon, "Metamorphosis: Forget the Stereotype: America Is Becoming a Nation of Culture," *Wall Street Journal,* 17 September 1998, pp. A1, A8.
4. Joseph Pereira, "Going to Extremes: Board-Riding Youths Take Sneaker Maker on a Fast Ride Uphill," *Wall Street Journal,* 16 April 1998, pp. A1, A8; Barbara Martinez, "Kids' Pants Legs Get Wider and Wider," *Wall Street Journal,* 11 November 1997, pp. B1, B14.
5. Stacy Kravetz, "Surprise! A Home Builder (Finally) Surveys Buyers," *Wall Street Journal,* 11 February 1998, pp. B1, B12.
6. Norihiko Shirouzu, "P&G's Joy Makes an Unlikely Splash in Japan," *Wall Street Journal,* 10 December 1997, pp. B1, B2.
7. Nancy Ten Kate, "The Marketplace for Medicine," *American Demographics,* February 1998, p. 34.
8. Ibid.
9. Ibid.
10. D. S. Sundaram and Michael D. Richard, "Perceived Risk and the Information Acquisition Process of Computer Mail-Order Shoppers," in *1995 Southern Marketing Association Proceedings,* eds. Brian T. Engelland and Denise T. Smart (Houston: Southern Marketing Association), 1995, pp. 322–326.
11. Eric D. Bruce and Sam Fullerton, "Discount Pricing as a Mediator of the Consumer's Evoked Set," in *1995 Atlantic Marketing Association Proceedings,* eds. Donald L. Thompson and Cathy Owens Swift (Orlando: Atlantic Marketing Association), pp. 32–36.
12. F. Kelly Shruptrine, "Warranty Coverage: How Important in Purchasing an Automobile?" in *1995 Southern Marketing Association Proceedings,* eds. Brian T. Engelland and Denise T. Smart (Houston: Southern Marketing Association), 1995, pp. 300–303.
13. Greg Johnson, "Hoping Fixers Will Be Uppers: Big Firms See Profitable Market in Repair Services, *Los Angeles Times,* 2 October 1997, p. D-1.
14. Don Umphrey, "Consumer Costs: A Determinant of Upgrading or Downgrading of Cable Service," *Journalism Quarterly,* Winter 1991, pp. 698–708.
15. Robert L. Simison, "Infiniti Adopts New Sales Strategy to Polish Its Brand," *Wall Street Journal,* 10 June 1996, p. B1, B7.
16. Brandon Mitchener, "Mercedes Dealers Offer New Kind of Test Drive," *Wall Street Journal,* 26 March 1998, p. B8.
17. Michael J. McCarthy, "Kellogg Stirs Health Claims into Cereal Ads," *Wall Street Journal,* 4 June 1997, p. B7.
18. James R. Rosenfield, "Millennial Fever," *American Demographics,* December 1997, pp. 47–51; Joshua Harris Prager, "Millennium Madness Grips the Nation's Entrepreneurs," *Wall Street Journal,* 22 April 1998, pp. B1, B10; David Segal, "Companies Hope to Cash in on 'Official' Millennium Merchandise," *The Washington Post,* 19 July 1998, p. A01; David J. Morrow, "Cashing in on the Millennium: Forget Armageddon, Think Commercial Potential," *The New York Times,* 18 January 1997, p. 35; Center for Millennial Studies Web site at **www.mille.org**; Iron Horse Ranch & Vineyards Web site at **www.ironhorsevineyards.com.**
19. Bill Stoneman, "Beyond Rocking the Ages: An Interview with J. Walker Smith," *American Demographics,* May 1998, pp. 44–49.
20. Data obtained from The New Products Showcase & Learning Center, Ithaca, New York, Web site at **www.showlearn.com,** 1998.
21. David B. Wolfe, "The Psychological Center of Gravity," *American Demographics,* April 1998, pp. 16–19.
22. Jennifer Harrison, "Advertising Joins the Journey of the Soul," *American Demographics,* June 1997.
23. Diane Crispell, "Core Values," *American Demographics,* November 1996.
24. Jerry W. Thomas, "Finding Unspoken Reasons for Consumers' Choices," *Marketing News,* 8 June 1998, p. 10.
25. Carl Quintanilla, "Despite Setbacks, Whirlpool Pursues Overseas Markets," *Wall Street Journal,* 9 December 1997, p. B4.
26. Robert Levine, "The Pace of Life in 31 Countries," *American Demographics,* November 1997, pp. 20–29; John Robinson, Bart Landry, and Ronica Rooks, "Time and the Melting Pot," *American Demographics,* June 1998, pp. 18–24; John P. Robinson, Toon Van Der Horn, and Ryichi Kitamura,

"Less Work, More Play: Life's Good in Holland," *American Demographics,* September 1993; Robert Levine, "Re-Learning to Tell Time," *American Demographics,* January 1998, pp. 20–25.
27. John W. Schouten and James H. McAlexander, "Subcultures of Consumption: An Ethnography of the New Bikers," *Journal of Consumer Research,* June 1995, pp. 43–61.
28. Ann Marie Kerwin, "Time's 'People en Espanol' to Boost Frequency in '98," *Advertising Age,* 30 June 1997, p. 12; James B. Arndorfer, "Brewers Fight for Hispanic Market," *Advertising Age,* 8 June 1998, p. 40.
29. James B. Arndorfer, "Bank of America Campaign Aims for Asian-Americans," *Advertising Age,* 9 June 1997, p. 6.
30. Rebecca Piirto Heath, "Life on Easy Street," *American Demographics,* April 1997.
31. Elia Kacapyr, "Are You Middle Class?" *American Demographics,* October 1996.
32. Rebecca Piirto Heath, "The New Working Class," *American Demographics,* January 1998, pp. 51–55.
33. Heath, "Life on Easy Street."
34. Michael J. Weiss, "A Tale of Two Cheeses," *American Demographics,* February 1998, pp. 16–17.
35. Grahame R. Dowling and Richard Staelin, "A Model of Perceived Risk and Intended Risk-Handling Activity," *Journal of Consumer Research,* June 1994, pp. 119–134.
36. Chip Walker, "Word of Mouth," *American Demographics,* July 1995, pp. 38–44.
37. Norihiko Shirouzu, "Japan's High-School Girls Excel in Art of Setting Trends," *Wall Street Journal,* 24 April 1998, pp. B1, B6.
38. Ibid.
39. Nina Munk, "Peddling Cool: How Teens Buy," *Fortune,* 13 April 1998, pp. 28–30.
40. Laura Johannes, "Kodak Looks for Another Moment with Film for Pros," *Wall Street Journal,* 13 March 1998, pp. B1, B6.
41. Stephen E. Frank, "Tiger Woods Plugs American Express," *Wall Street Journal,* 20 May 1997, pp. B1, B14.
42. "Chrysler, Johnson & Johnson Are New Product Marketers of the Year," *Marketing News,* 8 May 1995, pp. E2, E11.
43. James U. McNeal, "Tapping the Three Kids' Markets," *American Demographics,* April 1998, pp. 37–41.
44. Matthew Klein, "He Shops, She Shops," *American Demographics,* March 1998, pp. 34–35.
45. Diane Crispell, "Fruit of the Boom," *Marketing Tools,* April 1998.
46. Marcia Mogelonsky, "The Breakfast of Everyone," *American Demographics,* February 1998, p. 36.
47. Nancy Ten Kate, "Two Careers, One Marriage," *American Demographics,* April 1998, p. 28.
48. Dana Milbank, "More Dads Raise Families Without Mom," *Wall Street Journal,* 3 October 1997, pp. B1, B2.
49. Maxine Wilkie, "Names That Smell," *American Demographics,* August 1995, pp. 48–49.
50. Yumiko Ono, "Victoria's Secret Launches Cosmetics Line," *Wall Street Journal,* 14 September 1998, p. B6.
51. Nora J. Rifon and Molly Catherine Ziske, "Using Weight Loss Products: The Roles of Involvement, Self-Efficacy and Body Image," in *1995 AMA Educators' Proceedings,* eds. Barbara B. Stern and George M. Zinkhan (Chicago: American Marketing Association, 1995), pp. 90–98.
52. Pat Sloan and Jack Neff, "With Aging Boomers in Mind, P&G, Den-Mat Plan Launches," *Advertising Age,* 13 April 1998, pp. 3, 38.
53. Rebecca Piirto Heath, "Different by Design," *Marketing Tools,* October 1997.
54. William D. Wells and David Prensky, *Consumer Behavior* (New York: John Wiley & Sons, Inc., 1996), p. 46.
55. Robert M. McMath, "What's in a Name?" *American Demographics,* December 1996.
56. Joshua Rosenbaum, "Guitar Maker Looks for a New Key," *Wall Street Journal,* 11 February 1998, pp. B1, B5.
57. Gene Koprowski, "The Name Game," *Marketing Tools,* September 1996.
58. Benjamin A. Holden, "Utilities Pick New, Nonutilitarian Names," *Wall Street Journal,* 7 April 1997, pp. B1, B14.
59. Elizabeth J. Wilson, "Using the Dollarmetric Scale to Establish the Just Meaningful Difference in Price," in *1987 AMA Educators' Proceedings,* ed. Susan Douglas et al. (Chicago: American Marketing Association, 1987), p. 107.
60. Sunil Gupta and Lee G. Cooper, "The Discounting of Discounts and Promotion Thresholds," *Journal of Consumer Research,* December 1992, pp. 401–411.
61. Mark Stiving and Russell S. Winer, "An Empirical Analysis of Price Endings with Scanner Data," *Journal of Consumer Research,* June 1997, pp. 57–67; also see Robert M. Schindler and Patrick N. Kirby, "Patterns of Rightmost Digits Used in Advertised Price: Implications for Nine-Ending Effects," *Journal of Consumer Research,* September 1997, pp. 192–201.
62. Stacy Kravetz, "Dry Cleaners' New Wrinkle: Going Green," *Wall Street Journal,* 3 June 1998, pp. B1, B2.
63. Tara Parker-Pope, "Health Activists Light Into Cigars' Glamorous Image," *Wall Street Journal,* 8 July 1997, pp. B1, B8; Sally Goll Beatty and Bruce Ingersoll, "Drug Marketers Try New Tactic: Spreading Fear," *Wall Street Journal,* 12 June 1997, pp. B1, B6; Cynthia Crossen, "Fright by the Numbers: Alarming Disease Data Are Frequently Flawed," *Wall Street Journal,* 11 April 1996, pp. B1, B5.
64. Maria Mallory and Kevin Whitelaw, "The Power Brands," *U.S. News & World Report,* May 13, 1996, p. 58.
65. "Asian Culture and the Global Consumer," *Financial Times,* 21 September 1998, p. 1.
66. Yumiko Ono, "Tiffany Glitters, Even in Gloomy Japan," *Wall Street Journal,* 21 July 1998, pp. B1, B18.
67. Gene Del Vecchio, "Keeping It Timeless, Trendy: From Barbie to Pez, 'Ever-Cool' Kids Brands Meet Both Needs," *Advertising Age,* 23 March 1998, p. 24.
68. Kate Fitzgerald, "The Marketing 100: Starbucks Ice Cream Shari Fujii," *Advertising Age,* 29 June 1998, p. s39.
69. Steven Lipin, Brian Coleman, and Jeremy Mark, "Pick a Card: Visa, American Express, and MasterCard Vie in Overseas Strategies," *Wall Street Journal,* 15 February 1994, pp. A1, A5.
70. Judann Pollack, "Egg Board Budgets $11 Mil for '98 Ads to Combat Cereal," *Advertising Age,* 25 May 1998, p. 10.
71. Tara Parker-Pope, "P&G Dresses Up Olestra in Farm Images," *Wall Street Journal,* 11 February 1998, p. B6.
72. Stephen E. Frank, "Got a Bank? Industry Launches TV Ads," *Wall Street Journal,* 23 September 1997, p. B8.
73. Gregory L. White, "Jeep's Challenge: Stay Rugged but Add Room for Golf Clubs," *Wall Street Journal,* 26 August 1998, pp. B1, B4.
74. Jack Neff, "James River Puts Muscle Behind Dixie Paper Brand," *Advertising Age,* 16 June 1997, p. 22.
75. Jean Halliday and Laura Petrecca, "Volvo Effort Extends Image Positioning," *Advertising Age,* 30 March 1998, p. 9; William J. Holstein, "Volvo Can't Play Safe: To Survive, the Swedish Auto Maker Needs to Be Fun, Too," *U.S. News & World Report,* 27 July 1998, pp. 40–41.
76. Ernest Beck and Rekha Balu, "Europe Is Deaf to Snap! Crackle! Pop!" *Wall Street Journal,* 22 June 1998, pp. B1, B2.

CHAPTER 5

1. From "Alliances" by Jerry Bowles, *Fortune,* November 24, 1997. Reprinted by permission.
2. *Technology Forecast* (Menlo Park, California: Price Waterhouse, 1997), p. 1.
3. Kenneth Leung, "Keep This in Mind About Internet Marketing," *Marketing News,* 23 June 1997, p. 7.
4. "Big, Boring, Booming," *The Economist,* 19 May 1997, on-line.
5. "In Search of a Perfect Market," *The Economist,* 19 May 1997, on-line.
6. Ibid.
7. David L. Wilson, "Business-to-Business Commerce Going Strong on the Internet," *Tarrant Business,* 17 November 1997, p. 23.
8. "In Search of a Perfect Market," on-line.
9. Ibid.
10. Tim Smart, "E-Sourcing: A Cheaper Way of Doing Business," *Business Week,* 5 August 1996, pp. 82–83.
11. Alan M. Patterson, "Customers Can Be Partners," *Marketing News,* 9 September 1996, p. 10.
12. Ira Sager, "How IBM Became a Growth Company Again," *Business Week,* 9 December 1996, pp. 155–156.

13. "The Science of Alliance," *The Economist,* 4 April 1998, p. 69.
14. "The Science of Alliance," p. 69.
15. David Woodruff, "VW's Factory of the Future," *Business Week,* 7 October 1996, p. 52.
16. Michael D. Hutt and Thomas W. Speh, *Business Marketing,* 5th ed. (Fort Worth, TX: Dryden, 1998), p. 121.
17. Adapted from Robert L. Rose, "For Whirlpool, Asia Is the New Frontier," *Wall Street Journal,* 25 April 1996, pp. B1, B4.
18. Frank G. Bingham, Jr., and Barney T. Raffield, III, *Business Marketing Management* (Cincinnati, OH: South-Western College Publishing, 1995), pp. 18–19.
19. Hutt and Speh, pp. 139–141.
20. Justin Martin, "Are You As Good As You Think You Are?" *Fortune,* 30 September 1996, p. 143.
21. Jonah Gitlitz, "Direct Marketing in the B-to-B Future," *Business Marketing,* July/August 1996, pp. A2, A5.
22. Sager, pp. 154–162.
23. Robert W. Haas, *Business Marketing,* 6th ed. (Cincinnati, OH: South-Western College Publishing, 1995), p. 190.
24. Harris Gordon, "B-to-B Marketing in the Interactive Age," *Business Marketing,* July/August 1996, p. A2.
25. Amy Cortese, "Here Comes the Intranet," *Business Week,* 26 February 1996, p. 76.

CHAPTER 6

1. Sandra Baker, "A Uniform Approach to Expansion," *Fort Worth Star-Telegram*, Tarrant Business, June 15, 1998. Reprinted by permission of Fort Worth Star Telegram.
2. Faye Rice, "Making Generational Marketing Come of Age," *Fortune,* 26 June 1995, pp. 110–114.
3. "IBM, 15 Banks Introduce Online Service Company," *Arlington Star Telegram,* 10 September 1996, p. C4.
4. J. Alex Tarquinio, "King of Grits Alters Menu to Reflect Northern Tastes," *Wall Street Journal,* 22 September 1997, p. B1.
5. Steve Gelsi, "Driving Minivan Sales in Ecotopia," *Brandweek,* 17 June 1996, pp. 22–28.
6. David Leonhardt, "Hey Kid, Buy This," *Business Week,* 30 June 1997, pp. 86–88.
7. Ellen Graham, "When Terrible Two's Become Terrible Teens," *Wall Street Journal,* 5 February 1997, p. B1.
8. Emily Nelson, "Kodak Focuses on Putting Kids Behind Instead of Just in Front of a Camera," *Wall Street Journal,* 6 May 1997, p. B8.
9. The Associated Press, "Little Girls, Big Bucks," *Marketing News* 32 No. 7, 30 March 1998, p. 1.
10. From "Europe Is Deaf to Snap! Crackle! Pop!" by Ernest Beck and Rehka Balu, *Wall Street Journal,* June 22, 1998. Reprinted by permission of The Wall Street Journal, © 1998 Dow Jones & Company, Inc. All Rights Reserved Worldwide.
11. Faye Rice, "Making Generational Marketing Come of Age," *Fortune,* 26 June 1995, pp. 110–114.
12. "How Spending Changes During Middle Age," *Wall Street Journal,* 14 January 1992, p. B1.
13. Pam Weisz, "The New Boom Is Colored Gray," *Brandweek,* 22 January 1996, pp. 28–29.
14. Gaile Robinson, "User-Friendly Products Target 50-Plus Set," *Fort Worth Star-Telegram,* 2 December 1997, pp. E1–2
15. "Marketers Reveal Industry Dos and Don'ts; Say Capitalize on Relationship Building," *Selling to Seniors,* November 1997, No. 97-11, pp. 1–2.
16. Marc Spiegler, "Betting on Web Sports," *American Demographics,* May 1996, p. 24.
17. Mark Maremont, "Gillette's New Strategy Is to Sharpen Pitch to Women," *Wall Street Journal,* 11 May 1998, p. B1; Tara Parker-Pope, "Minoxidil Tries to Grow Women's Market," *Wall Street Journal,* 27 January 1997, p. B1.
18. Margaret Littman, "Women Fans Have Gridiron Pros Grinning," *Marketing News,* Vol. 32 No. 3, 2 February 1998, p.1.
19. Anne Faircloth, "Value Retailers Go Dollar for Dollar," *Fortune,* 6 July 1998, pp. 164–166.
20. Louise Lee, "Discounter Wal-Mart Is Catering to Affluent to Maintain Growth," *Wall Street Journal,* 7 February 1996, pp. 1, 6.
21. Maricris G. Briones, "Coors Turns Up the Heat; Ethnic Drinkers More Key to Summer Sales," *Marketing News,* Vol. 32 No. 13, 22 June 1998, pp. 1, 15.
22. Ibid.
23. Ibid.
24. Mark Maremont, "Close vs. Safe: Rivals Prepare to Market New Razors," *Wall Street Journal,* 29 September 1997, pp. B1, B8.
25. "The Largest Minority," *American Demographics,* February 1993, p. 59; "Profile: Hispanics," *Advertising Age,* 3 April 1995, p. S-18.
26. Briones, pp. 1, 15.
27. Becky Ebenkamp and Gerry Khermouch, "Why Major Marketers Are Latin Lovers," *Brandweek,* 5 August 1996, pp. 20–24.
28. Ibid.
29. Advertising in Hispanic Media Rises Sharply," *Marketing News,* 18 January 1993, p. 9.
30. Sydney Roslow and J. A. F. Nicholls, "Hispanic Mall Customers Outshop Non-Hispanics," *Marketing News,* 6 May 1996, p. 14.
31. Adapted from William O'Hare, "A New Look at Asian Americans," *American Demographics,* October 1990, pp. 26–31. Reprinted with permission © *American Demographics,* October 1990.
32. "Asian Ads Shuffled Behind Curtain," *Advertising Age,* 3 April 1995, p. S-26.
33. "Wrigley Ads to Focus on Minority Health," *Wall Street Journal,"* 4 June 1997, p. 1.
34. Alex Taylor III, "Porsche Slices Up Its Buyers," *Fortune,* 16 January 1995, p. 24.
35. Karen Benezra, "The Fragging of the American Mind," *Superbrands,* 15 June 1998, pp. S12–S19.
36. "Target TV Ads," *Marketing News,* Vol. 32 No. 5, 2 March 1998, p. 1.
37. Sally Beatty, "Drug Companies Are Minding Your Business: *Reader's Digest* Targets Patients By Their Ailments," *Wall Street Journal,* pp. B1, B3.
38. Laurie Freeman, "Marketing the Market: Savvy Grocers Reach Out to Their Super Customers," *Marketing News,* Vol. 32 No. 5, 2 March 1998, pp. 1, 14.
39. Stan Rapp and Thomas Collins, *The New Maxi Marketing,* excerpted in *Success,* April 1996, pp. 39–45.
40. Nicole Harris, "Home Depot: Beyond Do-It-Yourselfers," *Business Week,* 30 June 1997, pp. 86–88.
41. Much of the material in this section is based on Michael D. Hurt and Thomas W. Speh, *Business Marketing Management,* 6th ed. (Hinsdale, IL: Dryden Press, 1998), pp. 176–181.
42. Kelly Shermach, "Niche Malls: Innovation for an Industry in Decline," *Marketing News,* 26 February 1996, pp. 1–2.
43. Michelle Wirth Fellman, "Destination: Culture," *Marketing News,* Vol. 32 No. 14, 6 July 1998, pp. 1, 15.
44. From "Businesses Gain a Foothold Through Niche Marketing" by Jeff Rubin, *Wall Street Journal,* June 25, 1998. Reprinted by permission of The Wall Street Journal, © 1998 Dow Jones & Company, Inc. All Rights Reserved Worldwide.
45. Susan Chandler, "Kids' Wear Is Not Child's Play," *Business Week,* 19 June 1995, p. 118.
46. "J.C. Penney Launches Diahann Carroll Line," *Wall Street Journal,* 2 July 1997, p. B1.
47. Melcher, "Coors Targets the Growing Hispanic Market," *Marketing News,* 17 February 1997, p. 15.
48. Leon Jaroff, "Fire in the Belly, Money in the Bank," *Time,* 6 November 1995, pp. 56–58.
49. Tim Triplett, "Consumers Show Little Taste for Clear Beverages," *Marketing News,* 23 May 1994, pp. 1, 11.
50. Steve Gelsi, "GMC Moves Further into Luxury Tier," *Brandweek,* 15 April 1997, p. 4.
51. These examples were provided by David W. Cravens, Texas Christian University.
52. Steve Gelsi, "Staying True to the Sole," *Brandweek,* 8 April 1996, pp. 24, 26.
53. Elaine Underwood, "Sea Change," *Brandweek,* 22 April 1996, pp. 33–36.
54. Kathryn Hopper, "Polished and Profitable," *Fort Worth Star-Telegram,* 22 March 1996, pp. B1, 3.
55. Louise Kramer, "Mountain Dew Stays True to Its Brand Positioning," *Advertising Age,* 18 May 1998, p. 26.
56. Vanessa O'Connell, "What's Tasteless but Very Expensive?," *Wall Street Journal,* 12 May 1998, pp. B1, 8.

57. Cliff Edwards, "Florsheim Tries for Good Fit with Young Crowd," *Marketing News,* 20 January 1997, p. 6.
58. Ellen Rooney Martin, "Midas Breaks $25M Makeover Effort," *Brandweek,* 11 March 1996, p. 8.

CHAPTER 7

1. From "What Makes Women Click?" by Bernadette Tracy, *IAB Online Advertising Guide,* Spring 1998. Reprinted by permission of Bernadette Tracy, President, Netsmart-Research.com.
2. "Keebler Learns to Pay Attention to Research Right from the Start," *Marketing News,* 11 March 1996, p. 10.
3. "Why Some Customers Are More Equal Than Others," *Fortune,* 19 September 1994, pp. 215–224.
4. Ibid.
5. "Major U.S. Companies Expand Efforts to Sell to Consumers Abroad," *Wall Street Journal,* 13 June 1996, pp. A1, A6.
6. "Hey Kid, Buy This," *Business Week,* 30 June 1997, pp. 63–66.
7. Andrew Bean and Michael Roszkowski, "The Long and Short of It," *Marketing Research,* Winter 1995, pp. 21–26.
8. John Vidmar, "Just Another Metamorphosis," *Marketing Research,* Spring 1996, pp. 16–18; Sharon Munger, "Premium Medium," *Marketing Research,* Spring 1996, pp. 10–12; and William Nicholls, "Highest Response," *Marketing Research,* Spring 1996, pp. 5–8.
9. "New Product Survey Uses Voice Mail," *Dallas Morning News,* 14 October 1995, p. 2F.
10. Trish Shukers, "Integrated Interviewing," *Marketing Research,* Spring 1996, pp. 20–21.
11. James Watt, "Using the Internet for Quantitative Survey Research," *Quirk's Marketing Research Review,* June/July 1997, pp. 18–19, 67–71.
12. Quote from Cyber Dialogue Web site, **http://www.cyberdialogue.com/NewPages/PS/PSFrame.html**, April 16, 1997.
13. Sharon Weissbach, "Internet Research: Still a Few Hurdles to Clear," *Quirk's Marketing Research Review,* June/July 1997, pp. 22–26.
14. Ibid.
15. James Watt, "Using the Internet for Quantitative Survey Research," *Quirk's Marketing Research Review,* June/July 1997, p. 67.
16. Bill Eaton, "Internet Surveys: Does WWW Stand for 'Why Waste the Work?'" *Quirk's Marketing Research Review,* June/July 1997, pp. 28–30; also see: Robert Peterson, Sridhar Balasubramanian, and Bart Bronnenberg, "Exploring the Implications of the Internet for Consumer Marketing," *Journal of the Academy of Marketing Science,* Fall 1977, pp. 329–346.
17. This section is adapted from James Watt, "Using the Internet for Quantitative Survey Research," *Quirk's Marketing Research Review,* June/July 1997, pp. 67–71.
18. See: Donna Guido, "Constructing an Effective Mystery Shopping Program," *Quirk's Marketing Research Review,* January 1985, pp. 12–13, 48–49.
19. "Do Not Adjust Your Set," *American Demographics,* March 1993, p. 6; "Nielsen Rival to Unveil New Peoplemeter," *Wall Street Journal,* 4 December 1992, p. B8.
20. "TVB, Nielsen Examining TV Sweeps Alternatives," *Advertising Age,* 12 May 1997, pp. 10, 87; also see: "TV Execs to Nielsen: Get Smart," *American Demographics,* October 1997, pp. 10–15.
21. From "Familiar Refrain: Consultant's Advice on Diversity Was Anything But Diverse" by Douglas A. Blackmon, *Wall Street Journal,* March 11, 1997. Reprinted by permission of The Wall Street Journal, © 1997 Dow Jones & Company, Inc. All Rights Reserved Worldwide.

CHAPTER 8

1. From "Taking Off the McWraps" by Karen Benezra and Stephanie Thompson, *Brandweek,* May 21, 1998. © 1998 ASM Communications, Inc. Used with permission from BRANDWEEK.
2. Shannon Dortch, "Metros at Your Service," *American Demographics,* May 1996, pp. 4–5.
3. Ronald Henkoff, "Service Is Everybody's Business," *Fortune,* 27 June 1994, pp. 48–49. © 1994 Time Inc. All rights reserved.
4. "The Manufacturing Myth," *Economist,* 19 March 1994.
5. Gail Gaboda, "Filling Up a Niche," *Marketing News,* 27 October 1997, p. 2.
6. Lynn Beresford, "Visual Aid," *Entrepreneur,* March 1996, p. 38.
7. David Kirkpatrick, "Old PC Dogs Try New Tricks," *Fortune,* 6 July 1998, pp. 186–188.
8. Yumiko Ono, "Limited Tips Hand in Lauder Raid," *Wall Street Journal,* 23 June 1998, pp. B1, B6.
9. Chris Roush, "At Times, They're Positively Glowing," *Business Week,* 12 July 1993, p. 141.
10. Matt Murray, "Kodak Considers Selling Discount Film to Compete with Private-Label Brands," *Wall Street Journal,* 4 June 1997, p. B3.
11. Gerry Khermouch, "Woodbridge Aims Higher," *Brandweek,* 16 February 1998, p. 14.
12. Stephanie Thompson, "Hostess Promises Great Taste Plus Nutrition with New Cereal Bar Line," *Brandweek,* 9 March 1998, p. 44.
13. Stephanie Thompson, "No-Mess Packs Aimed at Steak Sauce," *Brandweek,* 24 August 1998, p. 6.
14. Stephanie Thompson, "Choice Soup Intros Gloss Up Brand," *Brandweek,* 30 June 1997, p. 3.
15. Noreen O'Leary, "The Old Bunny Trick," *Brandweek,* 18 March 1996, pp. 26–30.
16. Brandon Mitchener, "Mercedes Adds Down-Market Niche Cars," *Wall Street Journal,* 21 February 1996, p. A10.
17. Sean Mehegan, "Would She Buy Dandruff Shampoo?" *Brandweek,* 26 January 1998, p. 6.
18. "Make it Simple," *Business Week,* 9 September 1996, p. 96.
19. Ibid.
20. Jonathan Welsh, "Black & Decker to Shed Some Lines and Focus on Tools," *Wall Street Journal,* 28 January 1998, p. B7.
21. "Teens Name Coolest Brands," *Marketing News,* 12 February 1996, p. 6.
22. Peter H. Farquhar et al., "Strategies for Leveraging Master Brands," *Marketing Research,* September 1992, pp. 32–43.
23. Diane Crispell and Kathleen Brandenburg, "What's in a Brand?" *American Demographics,* May 1993, pp. 26–32.
24. From "The Name Game Heats Up" by Steve Rivkin, *Marketing News,* April 22, 1996, p. 8. Reprinted by permission of the American Marketing Association.
25. Bernhard Warner, "Digitizing Dinner," *Brandweek,* 16 February 1998, p. 38.
26. From "Brand Name Diamonds: a Cut Above?" by Rodney Ho, *Wall Street Journal,* June 1, 1998. Reprinted by permission of The Wall Street Journal, © 1998 Dow Jones & Company, Inc. All Rights Reserved Worldwide.
27. Sandra Baker, "Savvy Shoppers," *Fort Worth Star-Telegram,* 31 March 1996, p. D1.
28. Chad Rubel, "Price, Quality Important for Private Label Goods," *Marketing News,* 2 January 1995, p. 24.
29. "Kmart Accelerates Private Label Push," *Brandweek,* 29 January 1996, p. 6.
30. Ellen Neuborne and Stephanie Anderson Forest, "Look Who's Picking Levi's Pocket," *Business Week,* 8 September 1997, pp. 68, 72.
31. Bruce Orwall, "Multiplying Hotel Brands Puzzle Travelers," *Wall Street Journal,* 17 April 1996, p. B1.
32. Stephanie Thompson, "Brand Buddies," *Brandweek,* 23 February 1998, pp. 23–30.
33. Kelly Shermach, "Cobranded Credit Cards Inspire Consumer Loyalty," *Marketing News,* 9 September 1996, p. 12.
34. Karen Benezra, "New Tabasco Product a Chip Shot for Frito," *Brandweek,* 22 April 1996, p. 8.
35. Stephanie Thompson, "The O's Have It," *Brandweek,* 30 March 1998, p. 1.
36. "Cobranding Just Starting in Europe," *Marketing News,* 13 February 1995, p. 5.
37. David D. Kirkpatrick, "No T-shirts! Landmark Buildings Trademark Images," *Wall Street Journal,* 10 June 1998, pp. B1, B12.
38. From "'Ti-Gear': Owning Up to a Name" by Michelle Wirth Fellman, *Marketing News,* October 26, 1998, p. 2. Reprinted by permission of the American Marketing Association.
39. Maxine Lans Retsky, "You Can Make Your Mark with Your Signature," *Marketing News,* 23 September 1996, p. 13.
40. Steven C. Bahls and Jane Easter Bahls, "Fighting Fakes," *Entrepreneur,* February 1996, pp. 73–76.

41. Michael Rapoport, "Clash of Symbols: DKNY Sues DNKY Over Trademark," *Wall Street Journal,* 26 August 1996, p. A7B.
42. Lisa Brownlee, "Polo Magazine Angers Polo Ralph Lauren," *Wall Street Journal,* 21 October 1997, p. B10.
43. Michael J. McCarthy, "Fake King Cobras Tee Off the Makers of High-End Clubs," *Wall Street Journal,* 11 February 1997, pp. A1, A17.
44. Maxine Lans Retsky, "Who Needs the New Community Trademark?" *Marketing News,* 3 June 1996, p. 11.
45. Betsy Spethmann, "Getting Fresh," *Brandweek,* 20 May 1996, pp. 44–47.
46. Stephanie Thompson, "Welch's Redesigns Entire Line for More Unified Shelf Presence," *Brandweek,* 28 April 1997, p. 6.
47. Tammy Reiss, "Hey, It's Green—It Must Be Healthy," *Business Week,* 13 July 1998, p. 6.
48. Raju Narisetti, "Plotting to Get Tissues into Living Rooms, *Wall Street Journal,* 3 May 1996, pp. B1, B12.
49. Stephanie Thompson. "C&H Pours Forth Innovation in Sugar," *Brandweek,* 23 March 1998, p. 14. Reprinted with permission.
50. "Just Enough Packaging," *Wall Street Journal,* 7 September 1995, p. A1.
51. "A Biodegradable Plastic Gains Notice," *Wall Street Journal,* 4 February 1993, p. A1; Robert McMath, "It's All in the Trigger," *Adweek's Marketing Week,* 6 January 1992, pp. 25–28.
52. Pam Weisz, "Price Tools for Pfixer-Uppers," *Brandweek,* 18 April 1994, p. 8.
53. Beverly Bundy, "What's in It for You?" *Fort Worth Star-Telegram,* 4 May 1994, p. D1.

CHAPTER 9

1. Ben Dobbin, "Breakthrough Photo System Is Off to Slow Start," *Marketing News,* 12 May 1997, p. 5.
2. Laura Johannes, "For New Film, a Brighter Picture," *Wall Street Journal,* 5 May 1998, p. B1.
3. Johannes, p. B11.
4. Brian O'Reilly, "The Secrets of America's Most Admired Corporations: New Ideas, New Products," *Fortune,* 3 March 1997, p. 60.
5. Fellman, p. E2.
6. Howard Rudnitsky, "One Hundred Sixty Companies for the Price of One," *Forbes,* 26 February 1996, p. 57; William C. Symonds, "Gillette's Edge," *Business Week,* 19 January 1998, p. 71.
7. Richard Gibson, "A Cereal Maker's Quest for the Next Grape Nuts," *Wall Street Journal,* 23 January 1997, p. B1.
8. Sandra Baker, "Made for Walking," *Fort Worth Star-Telegram,* 28 June 1997, pp. C1, C3.
9. Sam Bradley, "Hallmark Enters $20B Pet Category," *Brandweek,* 1 January 1996, p. 4.
10. "Never Say 'Old and Lousy'," *Fortune,* 13 October 1997, p. 40.
11. "New But Not Necessarily Improved," *Wall Street Journal,* 15 January 1997, p. A1.
12. Stephanie Thompson, "Quaker Puts $15M into Indulgence-Oriented Rice Cake Makeover," *Brandweek,* 2 March 1998, p. 6.
13. Brendan I. Koerner, "A New Breed of Smokes," *U.S. News & World Report,* 21 April 1997, p. 8. Reprinted with permission of U.S. News & World Report © 1997. All Rights Reserved Worldwide.
14. Stephen H. Wilstrom, "A Fax That Does It All," *Brandweek,* 25 May 1998, p. 18.
15. *New Product Management in the 1980s* (New York: Booz, Allen and Hamilton, 1982), p. 3.
16. "Search and Employ," *Forbes,* 3 June 1996, p. 88.
17. "New Products," *Fort Worth Star-Telegram,* 11 May 1997, p. E1.
18. Norhiko Shirouzu, "For Coca-Cola in Japan, Things Go Better with Milk," *Wall Street Journal,* 20 January 1997, p. B1.
19. Shirouzu, p. B1.
20. David W. Cravens, *Strategic Marketing,* 5th ed. (Homewood, IL: IRWIN/McGraw-Hill, 1997), p. 255.
21. Mark Maremont, "How Gillette Brought Its MACH3 to Market," *Wall Street Journal,* 15 April 1998, p. B1.
22. Maremont, p. B1.
23. Tom Lynch, "Internet: A Strategic Product Introduction Tool," *Marketing News,* 22 April 1996, p. 15.
24. Linda Grant, "Gillette Knows Shaving—and How to Turn Out," *Fortune,* 14 October 1996, on-line.
25. Roy Rivenburg, "A Close Shave Is Good News in the Gillette Laboratory," *Fort Worth Star-Telegram,* 29 June 1996, Sec. E, p. 6.
26. "Procter & Gamble Co. to Test a New Spray for Removing Odors," *Wall Street Journal,* 8 May 1996, p. A5.
27. Karen Benezra, "Contour Can Sales Drop," *Brandweek,* 19 May 1997, p. 2.
28. Maremont, p. B1.
29. Lynch, p. 15.
30. "Is the Cassette Doomed?", *Fortune,* 27 October 1997, p. 74.
31. Ibid.

CHAPTER 10

1. Daniel Lyons, "Games Dealers Play," *Forbes,* 19 October 1998, pp. 132–134; Andrew Serwer, "Michael Dell Rocks," *Fortune,* 11 May 1998, p. 58; David E. Kalish, "Dell Computer Outsmarts IBM, Compaq," *AP Online,* 19 August 1998; Raju Narisetti, "IBM Plans to Sell Some Gear Directly to Fight Its Rivals," *Wall Street Journal,* 5 June 1998, p. B6; Evan Ramstad, "PC Playing Field Tilts in Favor of Dell," *Wall Street Journal,* 21 May 1998, p. B8; "Dell Selling PCs in China Through Its Internet Store," *The New Straits Times,* 25 August 1998, p. 22.
2. "Dell Seizes No. 1 Market Position in U.S. Corporate Desktop PC Sales," 10 September 1997, Dell Computer Corporation press release, **www.dell.com**.
3. Evan Ramstad, "Gateway Unit to Bolster Ties to PC Dealers," *Wall Street Journal,* 20 April 1998, p. B2.
4. Louise Lee, "School's Back, and So Are the Marketers," *Wall Street Journal,* 15 September 1997, pp. B1, B6.
5. Richard Gibson, "Attention, Wal-Mart Shoppers: You Want Fries with That?" *Wall Street Journal,* 25 July 1997, p. B6.
6. John Heinzl, "Internet Becomes World's Biggest Car Lot," *The Globe and Mail,* 23 September 1998, p. B25; Phil Scott, "Modem Up, Move 'Em Out," *Sydney Morning Herald,* 1 August 1997, p. 6; Gina Fann, "Consumers Hop on the Internet to Price and Research Vehicles," *Knight-Ridder Tribune Business News,* 2 February 1998; Rebecca Blumenstein, "Haggling in Cyberspace Transforms Car Sales," *Wall Street Journal,* 30 December 1997, p. B1; "Change Is Fast, But Most Dealers Are Adapting," *Automotive News,* 9 February 1998, p. 12; Gregory L. White, "General Motors to Take Nationwide Test Drive on Web," *Wall Street Journal,* 28 September 1998, p. B4; Auto-By-Tel Web site at **www.autobytel.com**.
7. James A. Narus and James C. Anderson, "Rethinking Distribution," *Harvard Business Review,* July/August 1996, pp. 112–120.
8. Vanessa O'Connell, "Starbucks, Kraft to Announce Pact for Selling Coffee," *Wall Street Journal,* 28 September 1998, p. B4.
9. "Fujitsu, Oracle Form Strategic Alliance in Asia," *Reuters,* 21 August 1997.
10. William M. Bulkeley and Joseph Pereira, "Toy Stores Spur Buying Frenzies with Exclusives," *Wall Street Journal,* 2 December 1997, pp. B1, B10.
11. G. Bruce Knecht, "Rack or Ruin: How Magazines Arrive on Shelves, and Why Some Soon May Not," *Wall Street Journal,* 26 February 1998, pp. A1, A6.
12. William M. Bulkeley and John R. Wilke, "Toys Loses a Warehouse-Club Ruling with Broad Marketing Implications," *Wall Street Journal,* 1 October 1997, p. B10.
13. Laura Bird and Wendy Bounds, "Stores' Demands Squeeze Apparel Companies," *Wall Street Journal,* 15 July 1997, pp. B1, B3.
14. G. Bruce Knecht, "Independent Bookstores Are Suing Borders Group and Barnes & Noble," *Wall Street Journal,* 19 March 1998, p. B10.
15. Stephanie N. Mehta, "Cellular Carriers Bypass Dealers, Creating Static," *Wall Street Journal,* 9 March 1998, pp. B1, B10.
16. Mary J. Cronin, "The Travel Agents' Dilemma," *Fortune,* 11 May 1998, pp. 163–164.
17. David Frederick Ross, *Competing Through Supply Chain Management: Creating Market-Winning Strategies Through Supply Chain Partnerships* (New York: Chapman & Hall, 1998), pp. 60–61.
18. "Retailing: General," *Standard & Poor's Industry Surveys,* Volume 166, Number 6, Section 1, 5 February 1998, p. 21.
19. Francis J. Quinn, "Supply-Chain Management Report: What's the Buzz?" *Logistics Management,* February 1997.
20. Ross, *Competing Through Supply Chain Management,* pp. 9–12.

21. Quinn, "Supply-Chain Management Report: What's the Buzz?"
22. Ross, *Competing Through Supply Chain Management,* pp. 9–12.
23. Ibid.
24. This section based on John L. Kent, Jr. and Daniel J. Flint, "Perspectives on the Evolution of Logistics Thought," *Journal of Business Logistics,* Volume 18, Number 2 (1997), p. 15 and Francis J. Quinn, "What's the Buzz?" *Logistics Management & Distribution Report,* 1 February 1997.
25. Benefits based on Francis J. Quinn, "The Payoff! Benefits of Improving Supply Chain Management," *Logistics Management,* December 1997, p. 37.
26. Theodore P. Stank, Patricia J. Daugherty and Alexander E. Ellinger, "Pulling Customers Closer Through Logistics Service," *Business Horizons,* September 1998, p. 74.
27. Ibid. p. 74.
28. James Aaron Cooke, "Warehousing: Great Expectations," 1998 Annual Report, *Logistics Management & Distribution Report,* July 1998.
29. "KPMG: Customer Service Increasingly Important in Supply Chain Management," M2 *PRESSWIRE,* 28 September 1998.
30. Quinn, "Supply-Chain Management Report: What's the Buzz?"
31. Francis Quinn, "Team Up for Supply-Chain Success," *Logistics Management,* October 1997, p. 39.
32. Toby B. Gooley, "On the Front Lines," *Logistics Management,* June 1997, p. 39.
33. Gooley, "On the Front Lines," p. 39.
34. Susan Avery, "Purchasing Forges New Supplier Relationships," *Purchasing,* 5 June 1998.
35. Erick Schonfeld, "The Customized, Digitized, Have-It-Your-Way Economy," *Fortune,* 28 September 1998, pp. 114–124.
36. Evan Ramstad, "PC Playing Field Tilts in Favor of Dell," *Wall Street Journal,* 21 May 1998, p. B8; Andrew Serwer, "Michael Dell Turns the PC World Inside Out," *Fortune,* 8 September 1997; Evan Ramstad, "Dell Takes Another Shot at Booming Home-PC Market," *Wall Street Journal,* 16 December 1997, p. B4.
37. Robert Keehn, "Transforming the Grocery Industry," *Meeting the Challenge of Global Logistics,* Report Number 1207-98-CR (New York: The Conference Board, Inc., 1998), pp. 25– 27.
38. Ross, *Competing Through Supply Chain Management,* p. 232.
39. Ken Cottrill, "Reforging the Supply Chain," *Journal of Business Strategy,* 19 November 1997.
40. William Pesek, Jr., "Inventory Control Stabilizes Economy: Better Management Helps Companies Avoid Missteps," *Wall Street Journal,* 29 August 1997, p. B8B.
41. Scott Woolley, "Replacing Inventory with Information," *Forbes,* 24 March 1997, p. 54.
42. Anna Wilde Mathews, "Cargo in Ships Offers Clues to What Will Go Under Tree," *Wall Street Journal,* 6 August 1997, p. B1.
43. Evan Ramstad, "Dell Takes Another Shot at Booming Home-PC Market," *Wall Street Journal,* 16 December 1996, p. B4.
44. Anna Wilde Mathews, "New Gadgets Trace Truckers' Every Move," *Wall Street Journal,* 14 July 1997, pp. B1, B10.
45. Douglas A. Blackmon, "Shippers Pitch Power of Gizmos, Gadgets," *Wall Street Journal,* 2 June 1997, pp. B1, B4.
46. Paul Gettings, "Top Three Trends in Logistics Today," *Industrial Distribution,* November 1997, p. S17.
47. Helen Atkinson, "Use of 3rd-Party Logistics Rising," *Journal of Commerce,* 13 October 1998, p. 16A.
48. Eryn Brown, "Costs Too High? Bring In the Logistics Experts," *Fortune,* 10 November 1997.
49. Ibid.
50. Raju Narisetti, "How IBM Turned Around Its Ailing PC Division," *Wall Street Journal,* 12 March 1998, pp. B1, B6.
51. Anna Wilde Mathews, "Logistics Firms Flourish amid Trend in Outsourcing," *Wall Street Journal,* 2 June 1998, p. B4.
52. Richard Gibson, "Merchants Mull the Long and the Short of Lines," *Wall Street Journal,* 3 September 1998, pp. B1, B4.
53. Matt Murray, "On the Road with a Rolling Bank Branch," *Wall Street Journal,* 6 November 1997, pp. B1, B13.
54. Kate Fitzgerald, "KeyCorp Invests $100 Mil to Expand, Build Brand," *Advertising Age,* 28 April 1997, p. 20.
55. Lisa Miller, "Airlines Land in Travel Agents' Territory," *Wall Street Journal,* 24 September 1997, pp. B1, B18.
56. Melinda Jensen Ligos, "Direct Sales: The Secret to Success in Japan," *Sales & Marketing Management,* February 1997, p. 14.
57. Cindy Kano and Alex Taylor III, "The Cult of the Astro Van," *Fortune,* 18 August 1997.
58. G. Bruce Knecht, "Pedaling Success: Bertelsmann Breaks Through a Great Wall with Its Book Clubs," *Wall Street Journal,* 18 September 1998, pp. A1, A6.
59. Greg Steinmetz and Tara Parker-Pope, "All Over the Map," *Wall Street Journal,* 26 September 1996, pp. R4, R6.
60. Mara Lemos, "There's Awful Lot for Coffee in Brazil: As Its Price Climbs, Thieves Get Bolder," *Wall Street Journal,* 22 September 1997, p. B18E.

CHAPTER 11

1. Nina Munk, "Gap Gets It," *Fortune,* 3 August 1998, pp. 68–82; Leslie Kaufman, "Downscale Moves Up," *Newsweek,* 27 July 1998, p. 32; Valerie Seckler, "Gap's Millard Drexler Outlines Plan to Get Even More Business," *WWD,* 14 September 1998, p. 1; Robert Berner, "Gap Dresses Up Its Results with Casual Men's Clothing: In Fashion Turnaround, T-Shirts and Khakis Become a Hit with Male Shoppers," *Wall Street Journal,* 11 June 1998, p. B4.
2. Karen J. Sack, "Retailing: General," *Standard & Poor's Industry Surveys,* Volume 166, Number 6, Section 1, 5 February 1998, p. 5.
3. Hilary Stout, "Tiny Toy Stores Scramble for Ways to Lure Customers," *Wall Street Journal,* 9 December 1997, p. B2.
4. Laura Bird, "Woolworth Is Hoping to Score in Sportswear," *Wall Street Journal,* 12 March 1997, pp. B1, B6.
5. Maureen C. Carini, "Retailing: Supermarkets and Drugstores," *Standard & Poor's Industry Surveys,* Volume 166, Number 14, Section 1, 2 April 1998, pp. 12–13.
6. Calmetta Y. Coleman, "Selling Jewelry, Dolls and TVs Next to Corn Flakes," *Wall Street Journal,* 19 November 1997, pp. B1, B2.
7. Carini, "Retailing: Supermarkets and Drugstores," p. 13.
8. Calmetta Y. Coleman, "Albertson's Leaves Industry Trends in the Checkout Line," *Wall Street Journal,* 6 August 1997, p. B4.
9. Carini, "Retailing: Supermarkets and Drugstores," p. 14.
10. "Wal-Mart Names New Retailing Concept: The Wal-Mart Neighborhood Market," Wal-Mart press release, 10 July 1998, **http://www.wal-mart.com**.
11. Carini, "Retailing: Supermarkets and Drugstores," p. 12.
12. Wal-Mart Data Sheet, 28 August 1998, **http://www.wal-mart.com**; "Wal-Mart Enters Korea, Continues Asia Expansion," Wal-Mart press release, 10 July 1998, **http:/www.wal-mart.com**; Robert O'Connor, "Target Europe: Wal-Mart Set Up a Beachhead in Germany," *Chain Store Age,* March 1998, pp. 55–60.
13. General Merchandise Updates, *Chain Store Age,* August 1997, **http://www.chainstoreage.com**.
14. Carini, "Retailing: Supermarkets and Drugstores," p. 15.
15. Anne Faircloth, "Value Retailers Go Dollar for Dollar," *Fortune,* 6 July 1998, pp. 164–166.
16. "Toys 'R' Us Introduces Its First Mail-Order Catalog," Toys 'R' Us press release, 27 October 1998, **http://www.toysrus.com**.
17. Toys 'R' Us Web site at **http://www.toysrus.com**.
18. Robert J. Izmirlian, "Retailing: Specialty," *Standard & Poor's Industry Surveys,* Volume 166, Number 4, Section 2, 22 January 1998, pp. 14–15.
19. Carini, "Retailing: Supermarkets and Drugstores," p. 15.
20. "Outlet Malls: Do They Deliver the Goods?" *Consumer Reports,* August 1998, pp. 20–25.
21. "The Evolution of Outlets: From Simple to Showy," *Consumer Reports,* August 1998, pp. 24–25.
22. "Developers Bring Value Closer to Shoppers," *Chain Store Age,* September 1998, pp. 168–170.
23. Karen J. Sack, "Restaurants," *Standard & Poor's Industry Surveys,* Volume 166, Number 23, Section 1, 4 June 1998, pp. 4, 7–8.
24. Sack, "Restaurants," p. 8.
25. Sack, "Restaurants," p. 11.

26. Ann Carrns, "Fill It Up and a Cheeseburger, Please: Gas Stations, Fast-Food Outlets Sharing Prime Space," *Wall Street Journal,* 15 October 1997, p. B18.
27. Eatzi's Market & Bakery Web site at **http://www.eatzis.com**.
28. Paul Schlossberg, "How Vending Turns Off Consumers; What Can Be Done," *Automatic Merchandiser,* September 1997, p. 72.
29. Lorrie Grant, "Vending Machines Offer Movie T-Shirts," *USA Today,* 3 April 1998, p. 6B.
30. Lore Postman, "N.C.-Based Canteen to Sell Brand-Name Burgers in Vending Machines," *KRTBN Knight-Ridder Tribune Business News: The Charlotte (N.C.) Observer,* 18 June 1998; Kip Wollenberg, "Vending Machines Get Name Brands," *AP On-line,* 20 October 1998.
31. Wendy Bounds, "For Fashion Action, Look in Suburban Living Rooms," *Wall Street Journal,* 24 November 1997, pp. B1, B4.
32. "Avon Planning 100 Retail Kiosks by Mid-1999," Retail News Updates, *Chain Store Age,* 23 October 1998, **www.chainstoreage.com**.
33. Yumiko Ono, "On a Mission: Amway Grows Abroad, Sending 'Ambassadors' to Spread the Word," *Wall Street Journal,* 14 May 1997.
34. Nigel Powell, "PC Salesmen Go Door to Door," *Times of London,* 16 July 1997, p. 6; "Reaching Out to Small-Town USA: Move Over Amway, PC Sales Firm Hand Technologies Adds Hi-Tech Touch," *South China Morning Post,* 12 May 1998, p. 8; Barbara Carton, "PCs Replace Lettuce Tubs at Sales Parties," *Wall Street Journal,* 26 March 1997, p. B1; "Hand Technologies: Background Information," *M2 Presswire,* 2 May 1997; Chad Kaydo, "Are PCs Like Tupperware?" *Sales & Marketing Management,* June 1998, p. 20.
35. Calmetta Y. Coleman, "Mail Order Is Turning into Male Order," *Wall Street Journal,* 25 March 1996, p. B9A.
36. Neal Templin, "Veteran PC Customers Spur Mail-Order Boom," *Wall Street Journal,* 17 July 1996, pp. B1, B5.
37. Judann Pollack, "Food Marketers Develop Taste for Selling on QVC," *Advertising Age,* 2 June 1997, p. 20.
38. Alice Z. Cuneo, "The Gap Readies Electronic Commerce Plan for Web Site," *Advertising Age,* 23 June 1997, p. 18.
39. Michael Krantz, "Click Till You Drop: The Internet Has Become a Shopper's Paradise, Stocked with Everything from Wine to Cars. Business Will Never Be the Same," *Time,* 20 July 1998, p. 34.
40. "Sticking to the Web," *Chain Store Age,* June 1998, pp. 153–155.
41. Jared Sandberg, "On-Line Shopping Shows Signs of Life, But Still No Mass Appeal, Survey Says," *Wall Street Journal,* 12 March 1998, p. B8.
42. Thomas E. Weber, "IBM's Electronic Mall to Close Up Shop," *Wall Street Journal,* 10 June 1997, pp. B1, B5.
43. "A Good Egg?" *Chain Store Age,* June 1998, pp. 61–62.
44. Richard Gibson, "Still-Golden Arches: McDonald's Problems in Kitchen Don't Dim the Lure of Franchises," *Wall Street Journal,* 3 June 1998, pp. A1, A6.
45. Therese Thilgen, "Corporate Clout Replaces 'Small is Beautiful'," special advertising section for the International Franchise Expo in the *Wall Street Journal,* 27 March 1997, pp. B14, B16; S. J. Kelly, "Is Your Future in Franchising? Assess the Opportunity and Risk," *Los Angeles Times,* 3 June 1998, p. D-7.
46. Gibson, "Still-Golden Arches," p. A6.
47. Thilgen, "Corporate Clout Replaces 'Small Is Beautiful'," p. B16.
48. Emily Nelson and Alejandro Bodipo-Memba, "Gadzooks! Claire's Stores Moves in on a Rival," *Wall Street Journal,* 17 September 1998, pp. B1, B4.
49. Dan Hanover, "Windows of Opportunity," *Chain Store Age,* August 1998, pp. 51–54.
50. "Brooks Brothers Moves Beyond the Gray Flannel Suit," *New York Times,* 19 September 1997.
51. "Sears to Carry Line of Clothing Designed by Benetton Group," *Wall Street Journal,* 6 October 1998, p. B4.
52. "An Exclusive Club," *Chain Store Age,* October 1998.
53. Sack, "Retailing: General," p. 19.
54. Robert Berner, "Safeway's Resurgence Is Built on Attention to Detail," *Wall Street Journal,* 2 October 1998, p. B4.
55. Raju Narisetti, "Joint Marketing with Retailers Spreads," *Wall Street Journal,* 24 October 1996, p. B6.
56. Sack, "Retailing: General," p. 13–14.
57. Rekha Balu, "Rural Kids Like Hip Clothes, Too, Hot Chain Discovers," *Wall Street Journal,* 15 January 1998, pp. B1, B10.
58. William M. Bulkeley, "Office-Supply Superstores Find Bounty in the Boonies," *Wall Street Journal,* 1 September 1998, pp. B1, B4.
59. "Updated Site-Selection Guide Covers All Bases," *Chain Store Age,* October 1998.
60. Joanne Gordon, "Saks Appeal: The Upscale Retailer's Main Street Stores Prove Size Doesn't Always Matter," *Chain Store Age,* May 1998, pp. 84–90.
61. Bill Levine, "The Store Stands Alone: For Some Retailers, Freestanding Sites Look Good from All Angles," *Chain Store Age,* April 1998, pp. 107–108.
62. "Chains in Streetfight for Prime Corners," *Chain Store Age,* October 1998.
63. "Growing Season: Iowa's Eastern Hub Gets Superregional Center," *Chain Store Age,* September 1998, pp. 159–160.
64. Mitchell Pacelle, "The Aging Shopping Mall Must Either Adapt or Die," *Wall Street Journal,* 16 April 1996, pp. B1, B13.
65. Faircloth, "Value Retailers Go Dollar for Dollar," p. 166.
66. "Specialty Stores Dress Up with Fixtures," *Chain Store Age,* January 1998, pp. 86–87.
67. Ronald Paul Hill, David L. Ramp, and Linda Silver, "The Rent-to-Own Industry and Pricing Disclosure Tactics," *Journal of Public Policy & Marketing,* Spring 1998, p. 3; Kathy M. Kristof, "Rent Now, Pay Forever: Consumers Would Be Wise to Consider Other Options Before Entering Into a Rent-to-Own Contract," *Chicago Tribune,* 15 September 1998, p. 7; Pamela C. Turfa, "Pennsylvania Customers to Share Settlement with Rent-to-Own Chain," *KRTBN Knight-Ridder Tribune Business News,* 6 May 1998; Scott Carlson, "Judge Awards Rent-a-Center Customers $30 Million in Class-Action Suit," *KRTBN Knight-Ridder Tribune Business News,* 16 April 1998; "Rent-to-Own Stores Gouge Consumers, Group Charges," *Los Angeles Sentinel,* 2 July 1997, p. A4; "Consumer Protection: Reforming the 'RTO' Rip-Off," *Consumer Reports,* August 1995.
68. "Data Mining Is More Than Beer and Diapers," *Chain Store Age,* June 1998, pp. 64–68.
69. Emily Nelson, "Why Wal-Mart Sings, 'Yes, We Have Bananas!'," *Wall Street Journal,* 6 October 1998, pp. B1, B4.
70. Benjamin Todd, "Super Kmart Strives for Inner Peace," *Chain Store Age,* January 1998, p. 68.
71. Diane Welland, "Rhythm and Chews," *Cooking Light,* January/February 1997, p. 22.
72. Kate Murphy, "A Sales Pitch Right Under Your Nose," *New York Times,* 13 September 1998, p. 8.
73. "Playful Touches Dress Up the Box," *Chain Store Age,* June 1998, pp. 110–111.
74. "Repeat Business," *Chain Store Age,* October 1998.
75. Karen J. Sack, "Mergers, Rivalry, and Price Sensitivity Will Continue," *Standard & Poor's Industry Surveys,* 9 May 1996, pp. R75–R78.
76. "Global Retailing '97," Ernst & Young special report for *Chain Store Age,* December 1997, p. 4.
77. "Global Retailing '97," pp. 14–18.
78. "Global Retailing '97," p. 18.
79. Norihiko Shirouzu, "Japan's Staid Coffee Bars Wake Up and Smell Starbucks," *Wall Street Journal,* 25 July 1996, pp. B1, B8; Martin Wolk, "Starbucks to Enter S. Korea in Pacific Plan," *Reuters News Service,* 1 October 1997; Seth Sutel, "Japan Wakes Up and Smells the Latte—Starbucks Is Here," *The San Diego Daily Transcript,* Internet address: **/96wireheadlines/08_96/DN96_08_02/DN96_08_02_fa.html**, 2 August 1996.
80. "Sound Win for Virgin," *Chain Store Age,* February 1998, pp. 2RSOY–3RSOY.
81. Sack, "Retailing: General," p. 1.
82. Izmirlian, "Retailing: Specialty," p. 3.
83. Ibid.
84. Calmetta Y. Coleman, "Supermarkets Build Sales by Beguiling Shoppers' Kids," *Wall Street Journal,* 19 January 1998, pp. B1, B5.
85. Calmetta Y. Coleman, "Grocery List: Peas, Veal, Throat Culture," *Wall Street Journal,* 20 May 1998, pp. B1, B26.
86. Ahmed Taher, Thomas W. Leigh, and Warren A. French, "The Retail Patronage Experience and Customer Affection," *The Cutting Edge IV, Proceedings of the 1995*

Symposium on Patronage Behavior and Retail Strategy, Ed. William R. Darden, American Marketing Association, May 1995, pp. 35–51.
87. Alice Z. Cuneo, "Gap Puts Delivery on Menu for Summer," *Advertising Age,* 15 June 1998, p. 8.
88. This section based on "Customer Management," State of the Industry special report, *Chain Store Age,* August 1998, pp. 20A–23A.
89. "Camelot Reigns," *Chain Store Age,* October 1998.

CHAPTER 12

1. PepsiCo 1997 Annual Report; "Top 200 Brands: January–June 1997," *Advertising Age,* 3 November 1997, p 48; "Pepsi's Supermarket Squeeze," *Brandweek,* 1 June 1998, p. 1; "A-B Buddies Up with Frito for Fall Promo," *Brandweek,* 6 July 1998, p. 12; Kirk Laughlin, "Bowled Away," *Food & Beverage Marketing,* January 1998, p. 6; Greg Johnson, "Chips Are Down in Marketing Olestra Food: Critics Say the Fat-Free Additive Poses Health Risks," *Los Angeles Times,* 10 March 1998, p. A-1; Judann Pollack, "Frito Claims Success, but Sales Slow for Wow! Chips," *Advertising Age,* 20 July 1998, pp. 1, 30; Sarah Lorge, "Top of the Charts: No. 3 Frito-Lay," *Sales & Marketing Management,* July 1998, p. 38; Frito-Lay press releases, **www.fritolay.com**.
2. Frank G Bingham, Jr., Charles J. Quigley, Jr., and Elaine M. Notarantonio, "The Use of Communication Style in a Buyer–Seller Dyad: Improving Buyer–Seller Relationships," *Proceedings: Association of Marketing Theory and Practice,* 1996 Annual Meeting, Hilton Head, South Carolina, March 1996, pp. 188–195.
3. Bingham, Quigley, and Notarantonio, pp. 188–195.
4. Jean Halliday, "Cougar Gets $70 Mil Intro Effort,"*Advertising Age,* 4 May 1998, p. 16.
5. Rekha Balu, "Ingredients for Holiday Sales: Red Dye, Green Sprinkles," *Wall Street Journal,* 15 December 1997, pp. B1, B10.
6. Jeanne Whalen, "Pizza Hut Uses Events to Help Give Away 1 Mil New Pies," *Advertising Age,* 9 June 1997
7. Scott McCartney, "Southwest Airlines Lands Plenty of Florida Passengers," *Wall Street Journal,* 11 November 1997, p. B4.
8. Kevin Helliker, "A New Mix: Old-Fashioned PR Gives General Mills Advertising Bargains," *Wall Street Journal,* 20 March 1997, pp. A1, A6.
9. Philip J Kitchen, "Marketing Communications Renaissance," *International Journal of Advertising,* 12 (1993), pp. 367–386.
10. Kitchen, p 372.
11. See Don E. Schultz, Stanley I. Tannenbaum, and Robert F. Lauterborn, *Integrated Marketing Communications* (Lincolnwood, IL: NTC Business Books), 1993.
12. Jeff Jensen, "'Godzilla' Effort Looms Over '98 Movie Marketing," *Advertising Age,* 4 May 1998, p 12; Jeff Jensen, "Monster-Size Outdoor Ads Presage Arrival of 'Godzilla,'" *Advertising Age,* 6 April 1998, p. 3.
13. AIDA concept based on the classic research of E. K. Strong, Jr., as theorized in *The Psychology of Selling and Advertising* (New York: McGraw-Hill, 1925) and "Theories of Selling," *Journal of Applied Psychology,* 9 (1925), pp. 75–86.
14. Thomas E Barry and Daniel J. Howard, "A Review and Critique of the Hierarchy of Effects in Advertising," *International Journal of Advertising,* 9 (1990), pp. 121–135.
15. Kim Cleland, "The Marketing 100: Colgate Total, Jack Haber," *Advertising Age,* 29 June 1998, p. s44.
16. Elyse Tanouye, "Drug Ads Spur Patients to Demand More Prescriptions," *Wall Street Journal,* 22 December 1997, p B1; Patricia Braus, "Selling Drugs," *American Demographics,* January 1998, pp. 26–29; Michael Wilke, "Prescription for Profit," *Advertising Age,* 16 March 1998, pp. s1, s-26; Robert Langreth and Andrea Petersen, "A Stampede Is on for Impotence Pill," *Wall Street Journal,* 20 April 1998, pp. B1, B6; Ira Teinowitz, "New TV Guidelines Bring Wishes for Further Changes," *Advertising Age,* 16 March 1998, p. s10; also see David Stipp and Robert Whitaker, "The Selling of Impotence," *Fortune,* 16 March 1998, pp. 115–124.
17. Bingham, Quigley, and Notarantonio, pp. 188–195.
18. Marvin A. Jolson, "Broadening the Scope of Relationship Selling," *Journal of Personal Selling & Sales Management,* Fall 1997, p. 75; also see Donald W. Jackson, Jr., "Relationship Selling: The Personalization of Relationship Marketing," *Asia-Australia Marketing Journal,* August 1994, pp. 45–54.
19. Bingham, Quigley, and Notarantonio, pp. 188–195.
20. Geoffrey Brewer, "The Customer Stops Here," *Sales & Marketing Management,* March 1998, pp. 30–36.
21. James Champy, "Taking Sales to New Heights," *Sales & Marketing Management,* July 1998, p. 26.
22. Sarah Lorge, "Online Bidding Keeps Suppliers in Line," *Sales & Marketing Management,* August 1998, p. 16; Gregory Dalton, "Web Services Help Buyers Get Right Price—Online Bidding Being Used for Mortgages and Airline Tickets," *Information Week,* 27 April 1998, p. 26; "UTC Uses Net-Based Auction to Help Craft Optimal Supply Base," *Purchasing,* 18 June 1998, p. s4; Claudia Coates, "Online Auction: Ding! The Price of Widgets Just Went Down," *The Associated Press,* 11 March 1998; Clinton Wilder, "What's Your Bid?—FreeMarkets' Real-Time Online Bidding Technology Lets Clients Drive Down Costs and Improve Product Value," *Information Week,* 10 November 1997, p. 54.
23. Erika Rasmusson, "How to Manage Long-Term Leads," *Sales & Marketing Management,* January 1998, p. 77.
24. Roger Brooksbank, "The New Model of Personal Selling: Micromarketing," *Journal of Personal Selling & Sales Management,* Spring 1995, pp. 61–66; Donald W. Jackson, Jr., "Relationship Selling: The Personalization of Relationship Marketing," *Asia-Australia Marketing Journal,* August 1994, pp. 45–54.
25. "By the Numbers: How Web Sites Are Used," *Sales & Marketing Management,* February 1998, p. 20; Direct Marketing Association.
26. Sarah Lorge, "The Best Way to Prospect," *Sales & Marketing Management,* January 1998, p. 80; Tricia Campbell, "What's a Referral Worth to You?" *Sales & Marketing Management,* September 1997, p. 103.
27. Lorge, "The Best Way to Prospect," p. 80.
28. Michele Marchetti, "Is Cold Calling Worth It?" *Sales & Marketing Management,* August 1997, p. 103.
29. "Leads Are a Terrible Thing to Waste," *Sales & Marketing Management,* August 1997, p. 108; Center for Strategic Communication.
30. Marvin A. Jolson and Thomas R. Wotruba, "Selling and Sales Management in Action: Prospecting: A New Look at This Old Challenge," *Journal of Personal Selling & Sales Management,* Fall 1992, pp. 59–66.
31. Robyn Griggs, "Give Us Leads! Give Us Leads!" *Sales & Marketing Management,* July 1997, pp. 67–72.
32. Robyn Griggs, "Qualifying Leads Online," *Sales & Marketing Management,* July 1997, p. 68.
33. Jolson, "Broadening the Scope of Relationship Selling," p. 75.
34. Adapted from Bob Kimball, *Successful Selling,* Chicago: American Marketing Association, 1994.
35. "Five Steps to Wrapping Up a Sales Call," *Sales & Marketing Management,* January 1998, p. 84.
36. Jolson, "Broadening the Scope of Relationship Selling," p. 75.
37. Geoffrey Brewer, "Dell's 'Expert' Advice for Customers," *Sales & Marketing Management,* April 1997, p. 77.
38. "How to Sound Like a Pro," *Sales & Marketing Management,* October 1997, p. 136, from *50 More Ways to Sell Smarter,* by Jim Meisenheimer; "Delivering a Great Presentation," *Sales & Marketing Management,* July 1998, p. 80.
39. Colleen Cooper, "Overcoming Last-Minute Objections," *Sales & Marketing Management,* March 1997, p. 32; Sarah Lorge, "How to Close the Deal," *Sales & Marketing Management,* April 1998, p. 84.
40. Cooper, "Overcoming Last-Minute Objections," p. 32.
41. Michele Marchetti, "Hey Buddy, Can You Spare $113.25?" *Sales & Marketing Management,* August 1997, pp. 69–77.
42. Sarah Lorge, "The Best Way to Negotiate," *Sales & Marketing Management,* March 1998, p. 92.
43. "Can Your Reps Sell Overseas?" *Sales & Marketing Management,* February 1998, p. 110.

44. Andy Cohen, "Global Dos and Don'ts," *Sales & Marketing Management,* June 1996, p. 72; Esmond D. Smith, Jr., and Cuong Pham, "Doing Business in Vietnam: A Cultural Guide," *Business Horizons,* May–June 1996, pp. 47–51; "Five Tips for International Handshaking," *Sales & Marketing Management,* July 1997, p. 90, from Dorothea Johnson, director of The Protocol School of Washington; Tricia Campbell, "What to Give Overseas," *Sales & Marketing Management,* September 1997, p. 85; "Negotiating: Getting to Yes, Chinese-Style," *Sales & Marketing Management,* July 1996, pp. 44–45; Michelle Marchetti, "Selling in China? Go Slowly," *Sales & Marketing Management,* January 1997, pp. 35–36; Sergey Frank, "Global Negotiating: Vive Les Différences!" *Sales & Marketing Management,* May 1992, pp. 64–69.
45. "It's No Secret: Why Dell Gives Customers Insider Access to Prices and Products," *Sales & Marketing Management,* May 1998, p. 93.
46. Geoffrey Brewer, "America's Best Sales Forces: No. 5 Hewlett-Packard," *Sales & Marketing Management,* October 1997, p. 58.
47. Arun Sharma, "Customer Satisfaction–Based Incentive Systems: Some Managerial and Saleperson Considerations," *Journal of Personal Selling & Sales Management,* April 1997, p. 61.
48. Andy Cohen, "America's Best Sales Forces: No. 4 General Electric," *Sales & Marketing Management,* October 1997, p. 57.
49. Vincent Alonzo, "Getting the Best Out of 'Em," *Sales & Marketing Management,* October 1997, pp. 34–38; "More Incentives on the Way," *Sales & Marketing Management,* December 1997, p. 96.

CHAPTER 13

1. Louise Kramer, "Mountain Dew Stays True to Its Brand Positioning," *Advertising Age,* 18 May 1998, p. 26; Dottie Enrico, "Mountain Dew's Hip Ads Refresh Viewers," *USA Today,* 18 May 1998, p. 4B; "Mountain Dew Posts Top Growth Rate," *Advertising Age,* 13 February 1998; Louise Kramer, "Coca-Cola Backing Surge with Promo Offering Trips," *Advertising Age,* 13 April 1998, p. 38; Bruce Orr, "Dew Gets Personal: Brand-Building with Beepers," *Marketing News,* 6 July 1998, p. 13; "Haven't Done That," *Advertising Age,* 14 May 1996; Louise Kramer, "Coca-Cola's Surge, Cherry Coke Plot New Promos," *Advertising Age,* 22 December 1997; Pepsi's Web site at **www.pepsi.com**.
2. "National Ad Spending by Media," *Advertising Age,* 28 September 1998, p. s50.
3. US. Department of Commerce, Bureau of the Census, *Statistical Abstract of the United States* (Washington, DC: Government Printing Office, September 1995), p. 416.
4. "1998 Advertising-to-Sales Ratios for the 200 Largest Ad Spending Industries," *Advertising Age,* 29 June 1998, p. 22.
5. "Time Spent with Media," *Standard & Poor's Industry Surveys,* 14 March 1996, p. M1; "Radio & TV Broadcasting: Commercials Clog the Airways," *Standard & Poor's Industry Surveys,* 12 May 1994, p. M35.
6. Amitava Chattaopadhyay and Kunal Basu, "Humor in Advertising: The Moderating Role of Prior Brand Evaluation," *Journal of Marketing Research,* November 1990, pp. 466–476.
7. Rajiv Grover and V. Srinivasan, "Evaluating the Multiple Effects of Retail Promotions on Brand Loyalty and Brand Switching Segments," *Journal of Marketing Research,* February 1992, pp. 76–89; see also S. P. Raj, "The Effects of Advertising on High and Low Loyalty Consumer Segments," *Journal of Consumer Research,* June 1982, pp. 77–89.
8. Jean Halliday, "Ford Corporate Ads Push 'A Relationship of Trust'," *Advertising Age,* 4 May 1998, p. 3.
9. Michael Burgoon, Michael Pfau, and Thomas S. Birk, "An Inoculation Theory Explanation for the Effects of Corporate Issue/Advocacy Advertising Campaigns, *Communication Research,* August 1995, p. 485(21).
10. Richard B Schmitt, "Can Corporate Advertising Sway Juries?" *Wall Street Journal,* 3 March 1997, pp. B1, B3.
11. Mark Maremont, "How Gillette Brought Its MACH3 to Market," Wall Street Journal, 15 April 1998, pp. B1, B10; Sharon T. Klahr, "Gillette Puts $300 Mil Behind Its MACH3 Shaver," *Advertising Age,* 20 April 1998, p. 6.
12. Louise Kramer, "As Sales Flatten, Top Pizza Chains Turn Up the Heat," *Advertising Age,* 23 February 1998, p. 4.
13. Bruce Ingersoll, "Government Tells Gerber to Put a Lid on Some of Its Ad Claims," *Wall Street Journal,* 13 March 1997, p. B15.
14. Martin DuBois and Tara Parker-Pope, "Philip Morris Campaign Stirs Uproar in Europe," *Wall Street Journal,* 1 July 1996, pp. B1, B5; "French Block Philip Morris Ad," *New York Times,* 26 June 1996, p. C5.
15. Maremont, "How Gillette Brought Its MACH3 to Market," pp. B1, B10; Klahr, "Gillette Puts $300 Mil Behind Its Mach3 Shaver," p. 6.
16. Mark Maremont, "Close vs Safe: Rivals Prepare to Market New Razors," *Wall Street Journal,* 29 September 1997, pp. B1, B6.
17. Klahr, "Gillette Puts $300 Mil Behind Its Mach3 Shaver," p. 6.
18. James B Arndorfer, "Miller Restages High Life Brand with Nod to Past," *Advertising Age,* 18 May 1998, p. 27.
19. Michael J McCarthy, "StarKist Still Has Charlie to Kick Around," *Wall Street Journal,* 17 November 1997.
20. Marc G. Weinberger, Harlan Spotts, Leland Campbell, and Amy L. Parsons, "The Use and Effect of Humor in Different Advertising Media," *Journal of Advertising Research,* May–June 1995, pp. 44–56.
21. Noreen O'Leary, "New Life on Mars," *Brandweek,* 6 May 1996, p. 44(3).
22. Roger Thurow, "Shtick Ball: In Global Drive, Nike Finds Its Brash Ways Don't Always Pay Off," *Wall Street Journal,* 5 May 1997, pp. A1, A10.
23. Johnny K. Johansson, "The Sense of 'Nonsense': Japanese TV Advertising," *Journal of Advertising,* March 1994, pp. 17–26.
24. "National Ad Spending by Media," *Advertising Age,* 28 September 1998, p. s50.
25. Audrey Snee, "Kodak Divides Up China in Order to Conquer It," *Ad Age International,* January 1998, p. 20; Juliana Koranteng, "Reebok Finds Its Second Wind as It Pursues Global Presence," *Ad Age International,* January 1998, p. 18; James Caporimo, "Worldwide Advertising Has Benefits, but One Size Doesn't Always Fit All," *Brandweek,* 17 July 1995, p. 16; Ali Kanso, "International Advertising Strategies: Global Commitment to Local Vision," *Journal of Advertising Research,* January–February 1992, pp. 10–14; Wayne M. McCullough, "Global Advertising Which Acts Locally: The IBM Subtitles Campaign," *Journal of Advertising Research,* May–June 1996, pp. 11–15; Martin S. Roth, "Effects of Global Market Conditions on Brand Image Customization and Brand Performance," *Journal of Advertising,* Winter 1995, p. 55(21). Also see Carolyn A. Lin, "Cultural Differences in Message Strategies: A Comparison Between American and Japanese Television Commercials," *Journal of Advertising Research,* July–August, 1993, pp. 40–47; Fred Zandpour et al., "Global Reach and Local Touch: Achieving Cultural Fitness in TV Advertising," *Journal of Advertising Research,* September–October, 1994, pp. 35–63.
26. "Radio: No Longer an Advertising Afterthought," *Standard & Poor's Industry Surveys,* 20 July 1995, p. M36; Rebecca Piirto, "Why Radio Thrives," *American Demographics,* May 1994, pp. 40–46.
27. Joe Mandese "Cable TV," *Advertising Age,* 13 April 1998, p. s1.
28. Rekha Balu, "Heinz Ketchup Readies Super Bowl Blitz," *Wall Street Journal,* 5 January 1998, p. B6; Chuck Ross, "Super Sein-off," *Advertising Age,* 11 May 1998, pp. 1, 62.
29. Kim Cleland, "Arthritis Foundation Turns to Infomercial," *Advertising Age,* 9 June 1997, p. 14.
30. Rhonda L Rundle, "Outdoor Plans Billboard-Sized Purchase," *Wall Street Journal,* 11 July 1996, p. B6; Cyndee Miller, "Outdoor Gets a Makeover," *Marketing News,* 10 April 1995, pp. 1, 26.
31. Sally Goll Beatty, "Billboard Firms Ease into Smokeless Era," *Wall Street Journal,* 30 October 1997, p. B6.
32. Kate Maddox, "Internet Ad Sales Approach $1 Billion," *Advertising Age,* 6 April 1998, pp. 1, 1AB.
33. Kate Maddox, "ANA Study Finds Marketers Triple 'Net Ad Budgets," *Advertising Age,* 11 May 1998, p. 63.
34. "Year in Review: Interactive/Web Becomes a Viable Channel," *Advertising Age,* 22 December 1997, pp. 21–22.

35. Sally Goll Beatty, "Internet Ad Proponents Try a New Tack," *Wall Street Journal,* 25 September 1997, p. B8.
36. Pierre Berthon, Leyland F. Pitt, and Richard T. Watson, "The World Wide Web as an Advertising Medium: Toward an Understanding of Conversion Efficiency," *Journal of Advertising Research,* January/ February 1996, pp. 43–54.
37. Cybergold Web site at **www.cybergold.com**.
38. Laurie Freeman, "Internet Visitors' Traffic Jam Makes Buyers Web Wary," *Advertising Age,* 22 July 1996, pp. S14–15.
39. Jeff Jensen, "Disney, Gillette Sign for Adsticks," *Advertising Age,* 8 June 1998, p. 48.
40. Telephone interview with Lance Stendal and Tom Borgerding of Future Pages, 16 July 1998; Patricia Riedman, "College Web Ad Networks Compete for Marketers," *Advertising Age,* 20 April 1998, p. 34; "Future Pages Introduces New and Innovative Ways to Reach the 18–24 Market," *PR Newswire,* 21 April 1998; Future Pages' Web site at **www.futurepages.com**.
41. "The 1997 Annual Report of the Promotion Industry," *PROMO Magazine.*
42. Raju Narisetti, "Many Companies Are Starting to Wean Shoppers off Coupons," *Wall Street Journal,* 22 January 1997, p. B1.
43. Laura Reina, " Manufacturers Still Believe in Coupons," *Editor & Publisher,* 28 October 1995, p. 24; Betsy Spethmann, "Coupons Shed Low-Tech Image; Sophisticated Tracking Yields Valuable Consumer Profile," *Brandweek,* 24 October 1994, p. 30(2); and Scott Hume, "Coupons: Are They Too Popular?" *Advertising Age,* 15 February 1993, p. 32.
44. Kate Fitzgerald, "Coupons Expand on Web," *Advertising Age,* 31 March 1997, p. 24; "Internet Coupons Driving Store Traffic," *Chain Store Age,* September 1997, **www.chainstoreage.com**.
45. Kate Fitzgerald, "Instant-Reward Coupons Show Rebound," *Advertising Age,* 12 May 1997, p. 20.
46. William M Bulkeley, "Rebates' Secret Appeal to Manufacturers: Few Consumers Actually Redeem Them," *Wall Street Journal,* 10 February 1998, pp. B1, B2.
47. Judann Pollack, "Pop Tarts Packs More Pastry for Same Price," *Advertising Age,* 5 August 1996, p. 6.
48. Richard Gibson, "At McDonald's, a Case of Mass Beaniemania," *Wall Street Journal,* 5 June 1998, pp. B1, B8.
49. Mark Lacek, "Loyalty Marketing No Ad Budget Threat," *Advertising Age,* 23 October 1995, p. 20.
50. Ginger Conlon, "True Romance," *Sales & Marketing Management,* May 1996, pp. 85–90.
51. Alice Z Cuneo, "Sears Breaks New Ad Theme for Back-to-School Effort," *Advertising Age,* 21 July 1997, p. 9.
52. Keith L. Alexander, "Net Surfers Rack Up Travel Miles," *USA Today,* 29 September 1997, p. 1B.
53. Kate Fitzgerald, "Guinness Looks to Its Past to Freshen 5th Pub Giveaway," *Advertising Age,* 30 March 1998, p. 46.
54. "Samples Have Ample Impact," *Sales & Marketing Management,* September 1997, p. 108.
55. Louise Kramer, "The Marketing 100: Dunkin' Donuts Eddie Binder," *Advertising Age,* 29 June 1998, p. s30.
56. Jeanne Whalen, "A Feast of Free Food," *Advertising Age,* 9 June 1997, p. 22.
57. Kate Fitzgerald, "Venue Sampling Hot," *Advertising Age,* 12 August 1996, p. 19.
58. Matthew Martinez and Mercedes M. Cardona, "Study Shows POP Gaining Ground as Medium," *Advertising Age,* 24 November 1997, p. 43.
59. Rebecca Piirto Heath, "Pop Art," *Marketing Tools,* April 1997.
60. Yumiko Ono, "For Philip Morris, Every Store Is a Battlefield," *Wall Street Journal,* 29 June 1998, pp. B1, B6.
61. Tara Parker-Pope, "The Magnificent Seven: Marketers Fete Bare Bottoms, Open Mouths," *Wall Street Journal,* 21 November 1997, p. B1.
62. Dean Takahashi and Evan Ramstad, "Quake Sequel Beefs Up Blood and Guts," *Wall Street Journal,* 9 December 1997, pp. B1, B16.
63. Kevin Helliker, "A New Mix: Old-Fashioned PR Gives General Mills Advertising Bargains," *Wall Street Journal,* 20 March 1997, pp. A1, A6.
64. Robert Berner, "Thanks to the Gap, Stock Exchange Lets Suits Cut Loose for One Day Only," *Wall Street Journal,* 26 September 1997, p. B10A.
65. Jean Halliday, "BMW Driver Tour Hypes New 3-Series," *Advertising Age,* 8 June 1998, p. 8.
66. "Smoke Dreams: NPR's Brooke Gladstone Reports on the Long Cinematic History of Cigarettes," *National Public Radio: Morning Edition,* 1 July 1997; Bruce Ingersoll, "US. Regulators to Raise a Stink about Cigars," *Wall Street Journal,* 9 February 1998, pp. B1, B4; Alec Klein, "Advertising & Marketing: Igniting Cigar Puffery," *Los Angeles Times,* 12 February 1998, p. D-4; Jennifer Kerr, "California's Targeting Cigar-Smoking among Youths, in the Movies," *Chicago Tribune,* 25 March 1998, p. 2; Suein L. Hwang and John Lippman, "Hollywood to Antismoking Activists: Butt Out," *Wall Street Journal,* 17 March 1998, pp. B1, B10.
67. Kate Fitzgerald, "Events Entice Car Buyers to Kick Tires, Smell Interior," *Advertising Age,* 6 April 1998, p. s8.
68. Bart Ziegler, "Checkmate! Deep Blue Is IBM Publicity Coup," *Wall Street Journal,* 9 May 1997, p. B1, B4.
69. James A. Roberts, "Green Consumers in the 1990s: Profile and Implications for Advertising," *Journal of Business Research 36* (1996), pp. 217–231.
70. G. A. Marken, "Getting the Most from Your Presence in Cyberspace," *Public Relations Quarterly,* Fall 1995, p. 36(2).
71. Lisa Bransten, "Companies Are Talking Up Chat Rooms; More Companies See Them as Way to Improve Service," *Wall Street Journal,* 15 December 1997, p. B5B.
72. Bruce Orwall and Nancy Keates, "Disney Ship's Maiden Voyage Delayed Again," *Wall Street Journal,* 19 February 1998, pp. B1, B8.

CHAPTER 14

Notes appear with the chapter on-line.

CHAPTER 15

1. Stephen Whitlock, "Going, going . . . Not going," *Conde Nast Traveler* (July 1998), p. 46.
2. "Cost-conscious Shoppers Seek Secondhand," *USA Today,* 14 March 1996, p. B1.
3. "Retailers Are Giving Profits Away," *American Demographics,* June 1994, p. 14.
4. "How IBM Turned Around Its Ailing PC Division," *Wall Street Journal* (March 12, 1998), pp. B1, B4.
5. "Unsold Seats Sully Concord's Snooty Image," *Wall Street Journal* (23 February 1996), p. B1; also see: "The Power to Raise Prices," *Business Week* (May 4, 1998), pp. 38–39.
6. Brandon Michener, "Ethnic Pricing Means Unfair Airfares," *Wall Street Journal* (December 5, 1997), pp. B1, B14.
7. "Used Cars Are a Tough Sell for Automobile Superstores," *Wall Street Journal* (March 31, 1998), pp. B1, B8.
8. David Henderson, "What Are Price Wars Good For? Absolutely Nothing," *Fortune* (May 12, 1997), p. 156.
9. "Good-bye to Fixed Pricing?" *Business Week* (May 4, 1998), pp. 71–84.
10. "Fixed Prices: Thing of the Past?" *Internet World* (June 1, 1998), p. 54.
11. "Web Offers Biggest Prize in Product Pricing Game," *Marketing News* (July 6, 1998), p. 8.
12. "Stores' Demands Squeeze Apparel Companies," *Wall Street Journal* (July 15, 1997), pp. B1, B12.
13. Praveen Kopalle and Donald Lehmann, "The Effects of Advertised and Observed Quality on Expectations About New Product Quality," *Journal of Marketing Research,* August 1995, pp. 280–290; Akshay Rao and Kent Monroe, "The Effect of Price, Brand Name, and Store Name on Buyers' Perceptions of Product Quality: An Integrative Review," *Journal of Marketing Research,* August 1989, pp. 351–357; Gerard Tellis and Gary Gaeth, "Best Value, Price-Seeking, and Price Aversion: The Impact of Information and Learning on Consumer Choices," *Journal of Marketing,* April 1990, pp. 34–35.
14. William Dodds, Kent Monroe, and Dhruv Grewal, "Effects of Price, Brand, and Store Information on Buyers' Product Evaluations," *Journal of Marketing Research,* August 1991, pp. 307–319; see also Akshay Rao and Wanda Sieben, "The Effect of Prior Knowledge on Price Acceptability and the Type of Information Examined," *Journal of*

Consumer Research, September 1992, pp. 256–270; Ajay Kalra and Ronald Goldman, "The Impact of Advertising Positioning Strategies on Consumer Price Sensitivity," *Journal of Marketing Research* (May 1998), pp. 210–224.

15. Phillip Parker, "Sweet Lemons: Illusory Quality, Self-Deceivers, Advertising, and Price," *Journal of Marketing Research*, August 1995), pp. 291–307; Michael Etgar and Naresh Malhotra, "Determinants of Price Dependency: Personal and Perceptual Factors," *Journal of Consumer Research*, September 1981, pp. 217–222; Jeen-Su Lim and Richard Olshavsky, "Impacts of Consumers' Familiarity and Product Class on Price-Quality Inference and Product Evaluations," *Quarterly Journal of Business and Economics*, Summer 1988, pp. 130–141.

16. Donald Lichtenstein and Scott Burton, "The Relationship between Perceived and Objective Price-Quality," *Journal of Marketing Research*, November 1989, pp. 429–443.

17. "Store-Brand Pricing Has to be Just Right," *Wall Street Journal* (14 February 1992), p. B1; see also George Cressman, Jr., "Snatching Defeat From the Jaws of Victory," *Marketing Management* (Summer 1997), pp. 9–19.

18. Dawar Niraj and Phillip Parker, "Marketing Universals: Consumers' Use of Brand Name, Price, Physical Appearance, and Retailer Reputation as Signals of Product Quality," *Journal of Marketing*, April 1994, pp. 81–95.

19. Amy Barrett, "French Discounter Takes Cheap Chic World-Wide," *Wall Street Journal* (27 May 1998), pp. B1, B8.

20. "Bayer's U.S. Unit Has Agreed to Pay $46 Million to Settle Price-Fixing Suit," *Wall Street Journal* (10 December 1996), p. B12.

21. For an excellent article on predatory pricing, see: "Joseph P. Guiltinan and Gregory T. Gundlack, "Aggressive and predatory Pricing: A Framework for Analysis," *Journal of Marketing* (July 1966), pp. 87–102.

22. "Eliminated Discounts on P&G Goods Annoy Many Who Sell Them," *Wall Street Journal* (11 August 1992), pp. A1, A6.

23. "Ed Artzt's Elbow Grease Has P&G Shining," *Business Week* (10 October 1994), pp. 84–86. For an excellent study on EDLP and its impact on retailers and manufacturers, see Stephen J. Hoch, Xavier Dreze, and Mary E. Purk, "EDLP, Hi-Low, and Margin Arithmetic, *Journal of Marketing*, October 1994, pp. 16–27.

24. Charles Quigley and Elaine Notarantonio, "An Exploratory Investigation of Perceptions of Odd and Even Pricing," in *Developments in Marketing Science*, ed. Victoria Crittenden (Miami: Academy of Marketing Science, 1992), pp. 306–309.

25. Francis Mulhern and Robert Leone, "Implicit Price Bundling of Retail Products: a Multiproduct Approach to Maximizing Store Profitability," *Journal of Marketing*, October 1991, pp. 63–76; Dorothy Paun, "Product Bundling: A Normative Model Based on an Orientation Perspective," in *Developments in Marketing Science*, ed. Victoria Crittenden (Miami: Academy of Marketing Science, 1992), pp. 301–305; Manjit Yadav and Kent Monroe, "How Buyers Perceive Savings in a Bundle Price: An Examination of a Bundle's Transaction Value," *Journal of Marketing Research*, August 1993, pp. 350–358; R. Venkatesh and Vijay Mahajan, "A Probabilistic Approach to Pricing a Bundle of Services," *Journal of Marketing Research*, November 1993, pp. 509–521; and Asim Ansari, S. Siddarth, and Charles Weinberg, "Pricing a Bundle of Products or Services: The Case of Nonprofits," *Journal of Marketing Research*, February 1996, pp. 86–93.

COMPANY AND ORGANIZATION INDEX

A

B

C

D

E

F

G

H

I

J

K

SUBJECT INDEX

A

B

C

D

H

I

J

K

L

M

N

O

P

Q

R

S

T

U

V

W

Z

INTERNET INDEX

ABC	http://www.abc.com/
A.C. Nielsen Company, Inc.	http://www.acnielsen.com/
Alta Vista	http://www.altavista.digital.com/
	http://www.alta-vista.com/
Amazon.com	http://www.amazon.com/
American Demographics/Marketing Tools	http://www.marketingtools.com/
American Marketing Association	http://www.ama.org/
Apple Computer	http://www.apple.com/
Archer Daniels Midland	http://www.admworld.com/
Arts and Entertainment Television Network	http://www.sande.com/
	http://www.historychannel.com/
	http://www.biography.com/
	http://www.historytravel.com/
	http://www.mysteries.com/
Asia Manufacturing Online	http://www.asia-mfg.com/
Auchan	http://www.auchan.com/
Auto-by-Tel	http://www.autobytel.com/
Auto Connection	http://www.auto-connect.com/
Baby Jogger Company	http://www.babyjogger.com/
Bally Total Fitness	http://www.ballyfitness.com/
Barnes & Noble	http://www.barnesandnoble.com/
Ben & Jerry's	http://www.benjerry.com/
Berkeley Roundtable on Internation Economy	http://server.berkeley.edu/BRIE
BLS Consumer Expenditure Surveys	http://stats.gls.gov/esxprod.htm
Bluefly.com	http://www.bluefly.com/
Boyne USA	http://www.boyne.com/
Brand Marketing International	http://www.bmiltd.com/
Bureau of Economic Analysis	http://www.bea.doc.gov
Bureau of Labor Statistics	http://www.stats.bls.gov
Bureau of Transportation Statistics	http://www.stats.bts.gov
Burger King	http://www.burgerking.com/
Burke, Inc.	http://www.burke.com
Burton Snowboards	http://www.burton.com/
BusinessWire	http://www.businesswire.com/
CAMI Automotive	http://www.cami.ca/
CarPoint	http://carpoint.msn.com/
Census and Demographic Information	http://www.clark.net
Center for Science in the Public Interest	http://www.cspinet.org/
Christmas Depot	http://www.christmasdepot.com/
Cincinnati Milacron	http://www.milacron.com/
Coca-Cola Company	http://www.cocacola.com/
Colgate-Palmolive	http://www.colgate.com/
Columbia House	http://www.columbiahouse.com/
CommerceNet/Nielsen Internet Demographics Study	http://www.nielsenmedia.com
CoolSavings.com, Inc.	http://www.coolsavings.com/
Cyber Dialogue	http://www.cyberdialogue.com
Database America	http://www.databaseamerica.com/
DejaNews	http://www.dejanews.com/
Dell Computer	http://www.dell.com/
Delta Airlines	http://www.tdelta-air.com/
Dickies	http://www.dickies.com/
Disney	http://www.disney.com/
Eastman Kodak	http://www.kodak.com/
Eatzi's Market & Bakery	http://www.eatzis.com/
ebay.com	http://www.ebay.com
Economic Research Service, Department of Agriculture	http://www.econ.ag.gov
Egghead Computer	http://www.egghead.com/
Encyclopaedia Britannica	http://www.britannica.com/
Energy Marketplace	http://www.energymarketplace.com/
Equifax National Decision Systems	http://www.ends.com/
eworldauction.com	http://www.eworldauction.com
Excite	http://www.excite.com/
EXE Technologies	http://www.exe.com/
Export Hotline	http://www.exporthotline.com
Export-Import Bank of the United States	http://www.exim.gov
Federal Express	http://www.fedex.com
Federal Trade Commission (FTC)	http://www.ftc.gov/index.html
Find/SVP	http://www.findsvp.com/
Food and Drug Administration	http://www.fda.gov/hometext.html
Foot Locker	http://www.footlocker.com/
Fox Network	http://www.fox.com/
Fragrance Net	http://www.fragrance.com/

Frito-Lay	http://www.fritolay.com/
Fuji	http://www.fujifilm.net/
Future Pages College Network	http://www.futurepages.com/
The Gap	http://www.gap.com/onlinestore/gap/
Gateway	http://www.gateway.com/
Gatorade	http://gatorade.com/
GE Information Systems	http://www.geis.com/
Genentech, Incorporated	http://www.gene.com/
Geographic Data Technology	http://www.geographic.com/
Georgia Institute of Technology	http://www.cc.gatech.edu/gvu/user_surveys
Gillette	http://www.gillette.com/
Godiva chocolates	http://www.godiva.com/
Grand Circle Travel	http://www.gct.com/
Grateful Dead	http://www.dead.net
Greenfield On-line	http://www.greenfieldonline.com/
Harley Davidson	http://www.harley-davidson.com/
Hasbro, Monopoly	http://www.monopoly.com/
Healthy Choice	http://www.healthychoice.com/
Hewlett-Packard	http://www.hp.com/abouthp/environment/
Hilton	http://www.hilton.com/
Home Depot	http://www.homedepot.com
HotBot	http://www.hotbot.com/
IBM	http://www.ibm.com/
Infoseek	http://www.infoseek.com/
Intellectual Property Owners Association	http://www.ipo.org/
Internal Revenue Service, Statistics of Income	http://www.irs.ustreas.gov/basic/tax_stats/index.html
International Franchise Association	http://www.franchise.org/
International Sony Music Webs	http://www.sonymusic.be/
Internet Business Library	http://www.bschool.ukans.edu.com/intbuslib/virtual.htm
Internet Public Library	http://www.ipl.org/
Infoseek	http://www.infoseek.com/
i2 Technologies	http://www.i2.com/
Japan Information Network	http://www.jin.jcic.or.jp/statistics
Keebler	http://www.keebler.com
Kellogg's	http://www.kellogs.com/
	http://www.kellogs.co.uk/
	http://www.kellogs.co.kr/
	http://www.kellogs.ca/
	http://www.kellogs.de/
Koblas Currency Converter	http://www.bin.gnn.com/gci-bin/gnn/
Kraft General Foods	http://www.kraftfoods.com/
Kroger Company	http://www.kroger.com/
Labelle Managment	http://www.labellemgt.com/
Levi Strauss & Co.	http://www.levi.com/
Lillian Vernon	http://www.lillianvernon.com/
L.L. Bean	http://www.llbean.com/
Loctite Corporation	http://www.loctite.com/
Lycos	http://www.lycos.com/
Magellan	http://www.mckinley.com/
Malls of Canada International	http://www.canadamalls.com/
Marketing	http://lamb.swcollege.com/
Mary Kay Cosmetics	http://www.marykay.com/
Mattel	http://www.mattelscrabble.com/
Maupintour	http://www.maupintour.com/
McDonald's	http://www.mcdonald's.com/
Mead Johnson Nutritionals	http://www.meadjohnson.ca/
Menlo Logistics	http://www.menlolog.com/
Metacrawler	http://www.metacrawler.com/
MexPlaza	http://www.mexplaza.udg.mx
Microsoft	http://www.microsoft.com/
M&M/Mars	http:www.m-ms.com/millennium/
Moody's Investors Services	http://www.moodys.com/
Multilingual International Business Directory	http://www.m-link.com/menu.html
Nabisco	http://www.nabisco.com/
National Managment Services	http://www.dallas.net
National Pork Producers Council	http://www.nppc.org
NetSmart	http://www.netsmart-research.com/main-sum.html
New Balance	http://www.newbalanceus.com/
New York Times	http://www.nytimes.com/
Nike	http://www.nike.com/
NWDP.COM	http://www.netcasino.com
onsale.com	http://www.onsale.com
Oneida Limited	http://www.oneida.com/
Open Market	http://www.openmarket.com/

Oprah Winfrey	http://www.oprah.com/
Outpost	http://www.outpost.com/
Owens-Corning	http://www.ownes-corning.com/
Pacific Region Forum on Business and Management Communication	gopher://hoshi.cic.sfu.ca/11/dlam/business/forum
Pcensus for Windows	http://www.tetrad.com
PepsiCo	http://www.pepsico.com/
Pizza Hut	http://www.pizzahut.com/
Population Reference Bureau	http://www.prb.org/prb/media.html
Priceline.com	http://www.priceline.com/
Procter & Gamble	http://www.pg.com/
Quaker Oatmeal	http://www.quakeroatmeal.com/
Research Foundation for Science, Technology, and Ecology	http://www.indiaserver.com/betas/vhisva
Rossignol	http://www.rossignol.com/
Rubbermaid	http://www.rubbermaid.com/
Russian and East European Studies Business and Economic Resources	http://www.pitt.edu/~cjp/rsecon.html
SavvySearch	http://www.cs.colostat.edu/~dreiling/smarktform.htm.
Sears Roebuck	http://www.sears.com/
Senco Products, Inc.	http://www.senco.com
Social Security Administration, Office of Research and Statistics	http://www.ssa.gov/statistics/ors_home.html
Southwest Airlines	http://www.iflyswa.com/
Starbucks	http://www.starbucks.com/
Star-Kist Foods	http://www.starkist.com/
Stat-USA	http://www.stat-usa.gov
Strategic Mapping	http://www.stratmap.com/
3Com	http://www.pam.com/home.html
Too Faced Cosmetics	http://www.toofaced.com/
Toronto Blue Jays	http//www/bluejays.com
Toyota	http://www.toyota.com/
Toys 'R' Us	http://www.toysrus.com
Trade Point Internet Incubator	http://www.wnicc.org/untpdc/training/ http://www.unicc.org/untpdc/eto/abouteto.html
Tylenol	http://www.tylenol.com/
United Parcel Service (UPS)	http://www.ups.com/
University of British Columbia Department of Applied Ethics	http://www.ethics.ubc.ca/
Upjohn	http://www.upjohn.com/
USA Data	http://www.usadata.com/
US Airways	http://www.usair.com/
USA Today	http://www.usatoday.com/
U.S. Census Bureau	http://www.census.org
U.S. Council for International Business	http://www.uscib.org
U.S. Department of Education	http://www.ed.gov
U.S. Demography	http://www.infoserver.ciesin.org
U.S. International Trade Administration	http://www.ita.doc.gov/
U.S. Small Business Administration	http://www.sbaonline.sba.gov/OIT
Vermont Teddy Bear Co.	http://www.vtbear.com/
Virtual Business Plaza (Czech Republic)	http://www.inet.cz
Virtual Vineyards	http://www.virtualvin.com/
Volvo	http://www.volvocars.com/
Wal-Mart	http://www.wal-mart.com/
Wendy's	http://www.wendys.com/the...ads/ads...frame.html
Women's Wire	http://www.womenswire.com/
Worldbank	http://www.worldbank.org/
World Factbook	http://www.odci.gov/cia/publications
World Gym	http://www.worldgym.com/
World Index of Chambers of Commerce & Industry	http://www1.usa1.com/
World Wide Web Virtual Library	http://www.w3.org/vl
Wrigley's	http://www.wrigley.com/
Xerox	http://www.xerox.com/
Yahoo!	http://www.yahoo.com/
Yahoo Index to Countries & Regions	http://www.yahoo.com/Regional/Countries/
Yankelovich Partners	http://www.yankelovich.com/